Shakespeare's
Romances and Poems

Shakespeare's Romances and Poems

Edited by

David Bevington

The University of Chicago

PEARSON
Longman

New York   San Francisco   Boston
London   Toronto   Sydney   Tokyo   Singapore   Madrid
Mexico City   Munich   Paris   Cape Town   Hong Kong   Montreal

Managing Editor: Erika Berg
Development Editor: Michael Greer
Executive Marketing Manager: Ann Stypuloski
Project Coordination and Electronic Page Makeup: Electronic Publishing Services Inc., NYC
Cover Designer/Manager: Wendy Ann Fredericks
Cover Art: *The Winter's Tale* by William Shakespeare with Elizabeth Hartley as Hermione; Kauffman, Angelica, 1741–1807, Swiss; The Art Archive/Garrick Club.
Manufacturing Buyer: Lucy Hebard
Printer and Binder: Hamilton Printing Co.
Cover Printer: Lehigh Press, Inc.

About the cover:
The Winter's Tale by William Shakespeare with Elizabeth Harley as Hermione, by Swiss neoclassical painter Angelica Kauffman (1741–1807). In the play's final scene (5.3), the actress portraying Hermione must stand perfectly motionless on stage as though she is a statue, until the moment comes for her to "Be stone no more" and come down off her pedestal.

The Library of Congress has cataloged the single volume, hardcover edition as follows:
Shakespeare, William, 1564–1616.
    [Works. 2003]
    The complete works of Shakespeare / edited by David Bevington.—5th ed.
        p. cm.
    Includes bibliographical references and index.
    ISBN 0-321-09333-X
    I. Bevington, David M. II. Title.
PR2754.B4 2003
822.3'3—dc21   2003045975

Please visit us at http://www.ablongman.com

ISBN 0-321-36625-5

1 2 3 4 5 6 7 8 9 10—HT—09 08 07 06

CONTENTS

Preface   vi

PREFACE

I have had the extraordinary privilege of editing and reediting *The Complete Works of Shakespeare* throughout my career as teacher and scholar, beginning in the early 1970s. The work is now in its fifth edition. Each new edition has, I hope, made advances in thoroughness and accuracy. Now seems a good time to publish that edition in four separate volumes. Shakespeare was such a prolific writer that the single-volume edition is heavy and hard to carry around. At the same time, his work can be conveniently and logically divided into four volumes of more or less equal size: the comedies, the English history plays, the tragedies, and the late romances combined with the poems and sonnets. These units can lend themselves well to classroom use or to general reading: sometimes courses in Shakespeare focus during one term on the comedies and histories, and during another on the tragedies and late romances, whereas more general courses in literary study and appreciation may sometimes choose to study the sonnets, or a few particular plays.

My hope is that this four-volume edition, with each volume separately available, can offer to students and general readers an unusually flexible and accessible anthology for study, for pleasure, and for continued reference.

KEY FEATURES OF THE FOUR-VOLUME PORTABLE EDITION

- **Flexible arrangement in volumes of convenient size,** grouped according to genres of comedy, history, tragedy, and romances and poems.

- **Thoroughly revised and updated notes and glosses** provide contemporary readers the support they need to understand Elizabethan language and idioms in accessible and clear modern language, line by line.
- **A richly illustrated general introduction** provides readers with the historical and cultural background required to understand Shakespeare's works in context.
- **Significantly revised introductory essays on each of the plays and poems** offer new insight into major themes, cultural issues, and critical conflicts.
- **Updated appendices** include the most recent information on sources, textual choices, performance history, dating of the works, and bibliographic resources.

From the start of my editing career I have aimed at explaining difficult passages, not just single words, keeping in mind the questions that readers might ask as to possible meanings. In undertaking the latest revision I was astonished to discover how extensively I have wanted to rewrite the commentary notes. The present edition incorporates many such changes. Some notes I had written seemed to me just plain wrong; many others seemed to me in need of greater clarity and accessibility. I have been both abashed to see how much improvement was necessary and grateful to be able to profit from my own experience with these texts in the classroom.

Issues of post-colonialism, gender relations, ethnic conflict, attitudes toward war and politics, ambiguities of language, the canon, dating, multiple authorship, and textual revision have been on the march since the early 1980s especially. These are heady times in which to attempt to practice literary criticism. Introductory essays need to be open to recent as well as more traditional critical approaches; they should open up issues for examination rather than offer pronouncements. I have listened carefully to reviewers who have occasionally found my introductions to earlier editions too confident of my own reading of the plays and poems. I have attempted to make an important correction in this matter, especially by adding some examples of production history and recent criticism that offer radically different readings of the dramatic texts. A teaching text should ask questions and offer the reader alternative possibilities. Discussion of recent film and stage history can enhance our appreciation of the plays in performance while at the same time enriching possibilities of interpretation.

This edition differs from other currently available editions of the *Complete Works* in being presented from the viewpoint of a single editor. That is at once its strength and no doubt its weakness. The viewpoint is, I would venture to say, a moderate and inclusive one, deeply interested in new critical approaches while also attuned to the kinds of responses that Shakespeare has evoked in past generations. I like the fact that this edition began in the Middle West, in Chicago, and that it serves a host of colleges and universities many of which are also in the great heartland of America. This edition attempts to be middle American, intended for a broad spectrum of educational uses and for private enjoyment as well.

I hope that the potential hubris of a single editorship is significantly ameliorated by the way in which this edition, like its predecessors, has made extensive use of editorial consultants. Each consultant was asked to respond to a particular play or work, including the notes and commentary. Many of the responses have been extraordinary and have sharpened issues I could never have addressed sufficiently on my own. The consultants, listed in the front of the book, are experts not only in Shakespeare studies but in the particular work I asked them to consider. I am deeply grateful for their help. Lois Potter, originally asked to serve as a consultant on performance history, presented so many suggestions that Longman and I asked her to write a new essay on the subject.

A BRIEF GUIDE TO THE EDITORIAL PRACTICES AND STYLE USED IN THIS EDITION

The running title at the top of each page of text gives the Through Line Numbers (TLN) of each play based on the *Norton First Folio of Shakespeare*. That facsimile of the original provides line numberings throughout, one number for each line of type. The advantage of this system is that it is universal, applying to all editions whether new or old. Such editions vary in line numbering depending on how the text is divided into scenes and how prose is numbered in columns of varying width. Because the TLN system is truly universal it is often used by textual scholars.

Line numbers in the text indicate that a gloss is to be found at the foot of the column for some word or phrase in the line in question.

Stage directions in square brackets are editorially added. Those without brackets, or in parentheses, are from the original Folio or Quarto text. The same is true of the numberings of acts and scenes.

The notes indicate the place of each scene. These indications should not be read as meaning that the stage needs to "look" like a particular street or house or room. Shakespeare's plays were acted essentially without scenery, as is often the case today. The indications of place are meant solely to give the reader information on the imagined location, as those locations can shift quite rapidly.

When the scansion of verse requires that vowels are to receive a syllable they would not normally receive, the vowel in question is marked with an accent grave. Thus, "lovèd" is to be pronounced in two syllables, "lov-ed." When the word has no such accented vowel it should receive the normal pronunciation. These markings normally correspond with a similar system in the original Folio and Quarto texts, although in those texts "loved" is normally bisyllabic, whereas "lov'd" is monosyllabic.

In the commentary notes, capitalization and end punctuation of each note is determined by how the paraphrase in the note fits into the Shakespearean text it represents. If the phrase being glossed begins a sentence, the note will begin with a capital letter, and correspondingly with end punctuation. The idea here is to make the paraphrase as smoothly compatible with the text as possible.

Any reader interested in further discussion on modernizing of spelling is invited to consult the Preface of the fourth updated edition.

ACKNOWLEDGMENTS

I am grateful to the reviewers who made numerous suggestions for improvements in this new edition. For their detailed and thoughtful suggestions, I would like to thank the following: Nick Barker, Covenant College, Lookout Mountain, Georgia; Celia A. Easton, SUNY Geneseo; Peter Greenfield, University of Puget Sound; Glenn Hopp, Howard Payne University; George Justice, Louisiana State University; Joseph Tate, University of Washington; Ann Tippett, Monroe Community College; Lewis Walker, University of North Carolina, Wilmington; Robert F. Wilson Jr., University of Missouri, Kansas City; and David Wilson-Okamura, East Carolina University.

A number of faculty were generous enough to respond to a survey we conducted to learn more about the undergraduate Shakespeare course market today. Thanks to the following for providing guidance and information: Mark Aune, North Dakota State University; Douglas A. Brooks, Texas A & M University; Robert Cirasa, Kean University; Bill Dynes, University of Indianapolis; Lisa Freinkel, University of Oregon; John Hagge, Iowa State University; Ritchie D. Kendall, University of North Carolina, Chapel Hill; Robert Levine, Boston University; Allen Michie, Iowa State University; Neil Nakadate, Iowa State University; Bonnie Nelson, Kansas State University; Robert O'Brien, California State University, Chico; Arlene Okerlund, San Jose State University; George Rowe, University of Oregon; Lisa S. Starks, University of South Florida; and Nathaniel Wallace, South Carolina State University.

I want to acknowledge a special debt of gratitude to the editorial advisory board members, who provided detailed suggestions on the plays, commentaries, notes, and appendixes. The names of our editorial consultants are listed facing the title page.

Lois Potter of the University of Delaware went far beyond the call of duty by completely rewriting Appendix 3 on Shakespeare in Performance. That her work was done under intense deadline pressure makes the achievement of her wonderful and learned essay all the more impressive.

SUPPLEMENTS

The following supplements are available free when ordered with this text. Please consult your local Longman representative if you would like to set up a value pack.

Evaluating a Performance, **by Mike Greenwald,** informs students about stage and theatrical performance and helps them to become more critical viewers of dramatic productions (ISBN 0-321-09541-3).

Screening Shakespeare: Using Film to Understand the Plays, **by Michael Greer,** is a brief, practical guide to select feature films of the most commonly taught plays (ISBN 0-321-19479-9).

Shakespeare: Script, Stage, Screen, **by David Bevington, Anne Marie Welsh, and Michael L. Greenwald,** is an edition designed for the teaching of Shakespeare plays most usefully studied in these contexts, with extensive discussions and commentary on stage and screen adaptations (ISBN 0-321-19813-1).

I would be most grateful if you would bring to my attention any errors you find. Such errors can be corrected in a subsequent printing. My e-mail address is bevi@uchicago.edu.

David Bevington

GENERAL INTRODUCTION

THE ROMANCES AND POEMS

When Shakespeare's plays were first published in a one-volume complete edition in the so-called First Folio of 1623, seven years after his death, they were grouped by the editors into three categories: comedies, histories, and tragedies. This classification did not recognize a separate category for the so-called late romances or tragicomedies. Instead, two of these plays—*The Winter's Tale* and *The Tempest*—were grouped with the fourteen comedies. *Cymbeline* was printed at the end of the volume, as one of the tragedies. *Pericles* was left out entirely, seemingly because the editors did not regard it as entirely or predominantly by Shakespeare. *The Two Noble Kinsmen* was similarly omitted, probably for the same reason; it seems to have been written collaboratively by Shakespeare and John Fletcher. (See Play Introduction.) The late romances, then, are an anomalous group.

The idea of differentiating the late romances from earlier romantic comedies did not materialize until the late nineteenth century, after scholarship had managed to determine an approximate chronology for Shakespeare's work. Once that chronology was established, a pattern was perceived. Edward Dowden's influential *Shakspere: A Critical Study of His Mind and Art,* 1875, proposed four periods of creativity in Shakespeare's life work: an apprenticeship of experimental imitation in the late 1580s and early 1590s, a flowering of success in the writing especially of romantic comedies and history plays in the later 1590s, a period of soul-searching and disillu-

sionment that produced the great tragedies in the early years of the seventeenth century, and then finally a movement out of the depths and onto the heights toward serenity and resignation as Shakespeare approached his retirement from the theater in 1611 or thereabouts. The pattern lends itself to a romanticized view of the author's purported struggles with the meaning of life that needs to be viewed with some caution, but by and large the outline has held.

This scheme proposes a crucial role for the late romances as a kind of recovery from the shock of tragic disillusionment in plays like *Hamlet, Othello, King Lear,* and *Macbeth.* Having dramatized nightmarish visions of murderous ambition, sibling rivalries, philosophical despair, sexual jealousy, midlife crisis, misanthropy, fear of aging, and the terrors of being forgotten or rejected by one's offspring, Shakespeare seems to have returned to the genre of romantic comedy for the consoling vision of a world in which humanity is eventually saved from its own worst self-destroying instincts by some sort of benign providential force. Whether that force is divine, or more simply the world of dramatic art in which the artist finds ultimate happiness through the medium in which he works, is uncertain, but the consolations are in any case restorative.

Shakespeare's earlier romantic comedies are also invested with a sense of comic providence that yields a rich reward of forgiveness and reunion. Such a restorative idea is achieved only in the face of much human cruelty and misunderstanding, as in *The Merchant of Venice,* or *As You Like It,* or a problem play like *Measure for Measure.* The difference between the earlier romantic comedies and the late romances is thus one of degree only, with large areas of overlapping concerns. Yet many readers and directors and actors have perceived a difference in degree, as though to recognize that the dark shadow of Shakespeare's tragic vision has intervened. The late romances seem to come from a mind that is older, wiser, and sadder, albeit seeking a restorative vision that can help make sense out of life's sometimes appalling misfortunes.

That restorative vision takes the form of family reunion in Shakespeare's late romances. All four plays dwell intently on the family that is divided and then reconnected: on fathers and daughters, on lost sons that sometimes are recovered and sometimes not, on wives that are abandoned and then eventually recovered or not recovered. The circumstances of Shakespeare's own life take on a potential relevance: his hastily arranged marriage in 1582 at the young age of eighteen to a woman eight years his senior, the birth of their first daughter (Susanna) some six months after the marriage, the birth of twins (Judith and Hamnet) in 1585, Shakespeare's moving to London without his family for the entire span of his professional life in the theater, the death of Hamnet at the age of eleven in 1596, the lack of any more births to Shakespeare and his wife Ann, the retirement to Stratford-upon-Avon some time evidently around 1611, the last will and testament in 1616 in which the only mention of Ann is as the recipient of the family's "second best bed." What was that retirement like? What were Shakespeare's relations with his two daughters and the men they married, Dr. John Hall to Susannah in 1607 and Thomas Quiney to Judith in 1616? We know nothing as biographic fact. We do however have the late romances, and their continuing fascination with the family as though Shakespeare used his dramatic art to meditate upon and fantasize about a recurring family constellation with intriguing hypothetical relevance to his own thoughts about retirement.

Among the many adventures of the protagonist in *Pericles* is his marriage to Thaisa, the daughter of King Simonides, and her giving birth to a daughter, Marina, during a sea voyage. A terrible storm at sea at this critical venture prompts the sailors to insist that Pericles throw overboard his wife, as she appears to have died in childbirth, and because the storm reputedly will not calm itself until her body is committed to the deep. He does so with intense reluctance. She washes ashore in her coffin and is magically restored to life by a learned man who then places her as a priestess in the Temple of Diana. Much later, when Pericles has been restored to his daughter after her many years of adventure and hairbreadth escapes, the two of them are directed by a vision to go the Temple of Diana, where they find the mother and wife. The family is thus finally happily reconstituted in this romance. Pericles is thus cured of the disabling melancholy that left him virtually incapable of action or human relationship. Was that melancholy the result of a sense of guilt for having abandoned his wife, however necessarily? The play does not answer this question, but it does prompt us to wonder why Shakespeare chose to dramatize this particular tale.

In *Cymbeline*, an aging king of that name in pre-Christian Britain enters into a disastrous marriage after the death of his first wife and then makes things much worse by exiling his only daughter, Imogen, for her refusal to marry the new queen's repulsive son, Cloten, and Imogen's insistence on marrying the man of her choice against her father's wishes. After long separation and estrangement from her husband, who has been misled into thinking her unchaste, Imogen is eventually aided by two young men in the mountains of Wales who turn out to be her own long-lost brothers. All are finally reconciled with the King, whose wicked consort reveals in a deathbed confession that she has plotted the death of her royal husband. In this story, then, sons and daughter are restored to the erring protagonist; being now forgiven for his potentially tragic mistakes, he agrees happily to his daughter's marriage and rejoices in the recovery of his male heirs. The mother is scapegoated into a wicked stepmother whose deserved and miserable death leaves in its wake an otherwise reunited and happy family. The sons who were supposed dead are in fact alive.

The Winter's Tale is perhaps the most suggestive of an autobiographical fantasy about retirement and reconciliation. Leontes, King of Sicilia, conceives an insane jealousy for his wife, Hermione, whose nine-months' pregnancy seems to Leontes uncomfortably related to the fact that his best friend, Polixenes of Bohemia, has been visiting the court of Sicilia for that same period of time. The King insists on putting his queen on trial for adultery, against the unanimous advice of his counselors, who are sure that the charge is utterly groundless. Hermione appears to die as a result of the immense strain of the trial, and so does the young son she bore to Leontes named Mamillius. The daughter who is born at this critical juncture, Perdita, is ordered executed by the insanely jealous Leontes, until the King relents and agrees that the child be abandoned on some distant shore. This cruel sentence is carried out on the coast of Bohemia, whereupon Perdita is found and raised by shepherds. When King Polixenes's son Florizel falls in love some sixteen years later with the seeming shepherdess, and has to cope with his father's stern disapproval of such an uneven match, the elopement of the young couple by means of a sea voyage takes them to Sicilia and to the court of Leontes, where father and daughter are happily reunited. But what of the mother? It turns out that Hermione did not in fact die, though we as audience have been misled into believing that she did; instead, she has been sequestered by a woman of the court, Paulina, who insists that King Leontes cannot enjoy happiness ever again until that which has lost has been found. Because the finding of

Perdita fulfills the terms of this oracular statement, Paulina now reveals to Leontes and Perdita a statue of Hermione. The statue comes to life as if by magic, and is reunited with a grateful king who finds her beautiful still, even though she has aged during the long interval of separation. King Leontes, whose self-castigation throughout these years has been commensurate with the vastness of his guilt, perceives that he has been forgiven and restored to happiness. The son Mamillius is indeed dead (as was Hamnet), but the rest of the family is together once again. We are left to wonder whether this story has some bearing, as a fiction, a fantasy, on the circumstances of Shakespeare's retiring to Stratford-upon-Avon and to a wife he had, in a sense, long abandoned, even if he had continued to support his family while he lived in London.

The last chapter of this continuing fantasy about the family constellation is *The Tempest*, in which Duke Prospero of Milan is exiled with his three-year-old daughter, Miranda, to a desert island somewhere in the Mediterranean (but with many suggestions also of the Bermudas across the Atlantic Ocean). For twelve years they have lived together with no other company than a strange islander, Caliban, who, when he came of age sexually, has attempted to rape Miranda and is accordingly forced to become their slave. Now that Miranda is fifteen, Prospero engenders a fearful storm and shipwreck that brings to the shore of his island the brother (Antonio) who ousted him from the dukedom of Milan, the King of Naples (Alonso) who assisted in that coup d'état, Alonso's brother Sebastian, a genial old counselor named Gonzalo, and some other Italians. In a separate part of the island, Prospero and his airy spirit Ariel arrange matters so that a drunken butler (Stephano) and a jester (Trinculo) wash ashore and discover the islander, Caliban, with whom they unsuccessfully plot to assassinate Prospero. In still another location, Alonso's son Ferdinand is brought ashore in such a way that he immediately encounters and falls in love with Miranda, and she with him. Prospero oversees all this, including the growing attraction of the young lovers; he makes plain to us as audience that he approves of the match, even though for a time he plays the role of the angry father because a love story needs some sort of complication to make the final resolution more endearing and precious. Prospero thus does successfully what Cymbeline and Leontes (and also King Lear) have failed at: he presides over the marriage of his daughter, accepting that she must now have her own happy married life, while he grows older. The son-in-law, Ferdinand, is the perfect match, not simply because he and Miranda are in love, and not just because their marriage will reunite politically Milan and Naples after so many years of disharmony and machination. The marriage is also a triumph for Prospero because he has arranged it, and because the son-in-law is admiringly fond of his new father-in-law. Ferdinand thus replaces the lost son. He was feared drowned, but he is in fact alive. Similarly, Prospero has brought his enemies to a realization of the enormity of their crimes. Sensing that it is time for him to return to Italy and to his dukedom, he also announces his intention to turn affairs over to his children while he grows old, gives up his magic, and meditates on the approach of death. In this sense, *The Tempest* reads as a retirement play, and is often interpreted as such: retirement from the theater, from the practice of art, from ownership of a daughter, and from life itself. Not without a struggle, Prospero achieves all that his predecessors in the late plays have achieved only fitfully and belatedly.

The poems tell another story. Shakespeare appears to have been serious about writing nondramatic poetry, especially when he was young and starting his career in London. Two substantial poems by him were published in book form by Richard Field, the Stratford-born son of an associate of Shakespeare's father: *Venus and Adonis* in 1593 and *The Rape of Lucrece* in 1594. The first is an amatory poem in the popular vein of mildly erotic mythological verse; it tells in sensuous and witty detail of the attempts of the goddess Venus to seduce a young man whose equally strong inclination is to eschew sex in favor of the manly sport of hunting. The second is a more tragic and lugubrious meditation on the rape of Lucrece, or Lucretia, wife of the Roman Collatine, by Tarquin the Proud. The rape itself, told in melodramatic terms, is anticipated by a psychological study of Tarquin's guilt-ridden thoughts, and is then followed by Lucrece's unhappy reflections on her fate as she prepares to inform her husband of the tragic event and then to take her own life, lest her existence cast a continuing blight on her husband's honorable reputation. These two poems were dedicated to young Henry Wriothesley, third Earl of Southampton. The dedication letter to the second publication is especially effusive. Quite possibly, Shakespeare was hoping for a continuing patronage that would have enabled him to write poetry. He may have found the opportunity to write these poems in a time when virulent outbreaks of the plague forced the closing of the theaters, thereby giving Shakespeare some leisure time. An unauthenticated but plausible story speculates that Southampton did give Shakespeare the considerable stake of money that we would have needed as the price of becoming one of the actor-sharers in the Lord Chamberlain's men, when they formed in 1594. If so, the profit that Shakespeare realized from writing and dedicating these two poems to Southampton was a major event in his professional life, for the Lord Chamberlain's men went quickly on their way to becoming London's most successful acting company.

An often-repeated tradition also speculates that Southampton is the young man who whom Shakespeare's sonnets are addressed. This hypothesis too is plausible enough. Southampton was young and almost girlishly handsome; his family was anxious that he marry and produce an heir. That theme of marriage and the siring of progeny is the burden of many of the early sonnets in this famous sequence of poems. The sonnets go on to other themes, not always happy. The speaker-poet is deeply attached to the young man to whom he writes, but is also unhappily aware of his own unworthiness in seeking the affection of one who is so desired by others. At times the loving relationship is a source of immeasurable comfort to the speaker-poet; at other times the speaker finds physical absence unbearable, or, worse still, experiences the jealous pangs of seeing the young man turn to other friends and to other poets. When, toward the end of the sonnet sequence, the friend becomes the lover of the "dark lady" whom the poet has courted as his own mistress, the pain of jealousy is unbearable. The poet is deeply ashamed of and distressed by his own physical desires.

Whether these 154 sonnets are in the order that Shakespeare intended is hard to tell, because he seems not to have been involved in the printing of the sequence in 1609. Nor can we be at all sure that they narrate a story that bears on Shakespeare's own life experience. He was, after all, supremely skillful in dramatizing many things

BY PERMISSION OF THE FOLGER SHAKESPEARE LIBRARY

The plowman

"Enclosure" was a problem throughout the sixteenth century in England. Crop lands were converted into pasturage. The livelihood of the plowman was threatened by the pasturing of sheep and the growing production of wool.

that cannot be understood as autobiographical: civil war, great battles against the French, the killing of kings or wives, and much more. Even so, the tendency in criticism today is to suppose that the sonnets do tell us something about their author. Part of their fascination arises from the fact that we have so little hard biographical information about this greatest of English dramatists.

Shakespeare is sometimes credited with a few other poems and plays, but they are either so minor or so questionable as to authorship that most are not included here. A poetic miscellany published in 1599 as *The Passionate Pilgrim* contains five poems certainly by Shakespeare, but they also appear elsewhere. The poem entitled "A Funeral Elegy for Master William Peter" has now been shown to be the work of John Ford. Another poem that begins "Shall I die? Shall I fly" has been claimed for Shakespeare on grounds of word patterns, but the claim is much disputed and the poem is generally regarded as a minor effort at best. A more serious claim can be made for "The Phoenix and Turtle," published in a collection of poems called *Love's Martyr: Or, Rosalins Complaint* in 1601, and "A Lover's Complaint," published with the Sonnets, and they are included here. Equally serious is the candidacy for Shakespearean authorship of two brief passages from the play *Sir Thomas More*, but this material is omitted here because of its fragmentary and uncertain character. An anonymous play, *Edward III*, is sometimes attributed to Shakespeare in part, but that attribution is much disputed.

LIFE IN SHAKESPEARE'S ENGLAND

England during Shakespeare's lifetime (1564–1616) was a proud nation with a strong sense of national identity, but it was also a small nation by modern standards. Probably not more than five million people lived in the whole of England, considerably fewer than now live in London. England's territories in France were no longer extensive, as they had been during the fourteenth century and earlier; in fact, by the end of Queen Elizabeth's reign (1558–1603), England had virtually retired from the territories she had previously controlled on the Continent, especially in France. Wales was a conquered principality. England's overseas empire in America had scarcely begun, with the Virginia settlement established in the 1580s. Scotland was not yet a part of Great Britain; union with Scotland would not take place until 1707, despite the fact that King James VI of Scotland assumed the English throne in 1603 as James I of England. Ireland, although declared a kingdom under English rule in 1541, was more a source of trouble than of economic strength. The last years of Elizabeth's reign, especially from

1597 to 1601, were plagued by the rebellion of the Irish under Hugh O'Neill, Earl of Tyrone. Thus, England of the sixteenth and early seventeenth centuries was both small and isolated.

THE SOCIAL AND ECONOMIC BACKGROUND

By and large, England was a rural land. Much of the kingdom was still wooded, though timber was being used increasingly in manufacturing and shipbuilding. The area of the Midlands, today heavily industrialized, was at that time still a region of great trees, green fields, and clear streams. England's chief means of livelihood was agriculture. This part of the economy was generally in a bad way, however, and people who lived off the land did not share in the prosperity of many Londoners. A problem throughout the sixteenth century was that of "enclosure": the conversion by rich landowners of croplands into pasturage. Farmers and peasants complained bitterly that they were being dispossessed and starved for the benefit of livestock. Rural uprisings and food riots were common, to the dismay of the authorities. Some Oxfordshire peasants arose in 1596, threatening to massacre the gentry and march on London; other riots had occurred in 1586 and 1591. There were thirteen riots in Kent alone during Elizabeth's reign. Unrest continued into the reign of James I, notably the Midlands' rising of 1607. Although the government did what it could to inhibit enclosure, the economic forces at work were too massive and too inadequately understood to be curbed by governmental fiat. The absence of effective bureaucracies or agencies of coercion compounded the difficulty of governmental control. Pasture used large areas with greater efficiency than crop farming, and required far less labor. The wool produced by the pasturing of sheep was needed in ever increasing amounts for the manufacture of cloth.

The wool industry also experienced occasional economic difficulties, to be sure; overexpansion in the early years of the sixteenth century created a glutted market that collapsed disastrously in 1551, producing widespread unemployment. Despite such fluctuations and reversals, however, the wool industry at least provided handsome profits for some landowners and middlemen. Mining and manufacture in coal, iron, tin, copper, and lead, although insignificant by modern standards, also were expanding at a significant rate. Trading companies exploited the rich new resources of the Americas, as well as of eastern Europe and the Orient. Queen Elizabeth aided economic development by keeping England out of war with her continental enemies as long as possible, despite provocations from those powers and despite the eagerness of some of her advisers to retaliate.

Certainly England's economic condition was better than the economic condition of the rest of the Continent; an Italian called England "the land of comforts." Yet although some prosperity did exist, it was not evenly distributed. Especially during Shakespeare's first years in London, in the late 1580s and the 1590s, the gap between rich and poor grew more and more extreme. Elizabeth's efforts at peacemaking were no longer able to prevent years of war with the Catholic powers of the Continent. Taxation grew heavier, and inflation proceeded at an

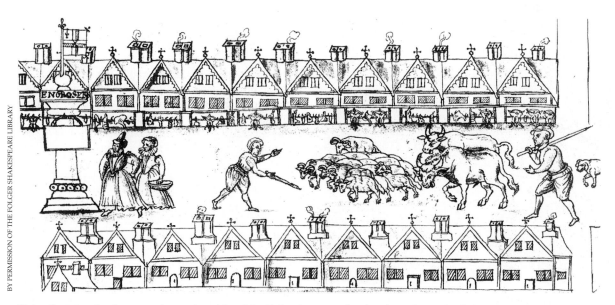

Sixteenth-century London was a city teeming with activity. Pedestrians were often forced to make way for the livestock being driven through the streets.

unusually rapid rate during this period. A succession of bad harvests compounded the miseries of those who dwelled on the land. When the hostilities on the Continent ceased for a time in about 1597, a wave of returning veterans added to unemployment and crime. The rising prosperity experienced by Shakespeare and other fortunate Londoners was undeniably real, but it was not universal. Nowhere was the contrast between rich and poor more visible than in London.

London

Sixteenth-century London was at once more attractive and less attractive than twenty-first-century London. It was full of trees and gardens; meadows and cultivated lands reached in some places to its very walls. Today we can perhaps imagine the way in which it bordered clear streams and green fields when we approach from a distance some noncommercial provincial city such as Lincoln, York, or

Hereford. Partly surrounded by its ancient wall, London was by no means a large metropolis. With 190,000 to 200,000 inhabitants in the city proper and its suburbs, it was nonetheless the largest city of Europe, and its dominance among English cities was even more striking; in 1543–1544, London paid thirty times the subsidy of Norwich, then the second-largest city in the kingdom (15,000 inhabitants). Although London's population had expanded into the surrounding area in all directions, the city proper stretched along the north bank of the Thames River from the old Tower of London on the east to St. Paul's Cathedral and the Fleet Ditch on the west—a distance of little more than a mile. Visitors approaching London from the south bank of the Thames (the Bankside) and crossing London Bridge could see virtually all of this exciting city lying before them. London Bridge itself was one of the major attractions of the city, lined with shops and richly decorated on occasion for the triumphal entry of a king or queen.

Yet London had its grim and ugly side as well. On London Bridge could sometimes be seen the heads of executed traitors. The city's houses were generally small and crowded; its streets were often narrow and filthy. In the absence of sewers, open ditches in the streets served to collect and carry off refuse. Frequent epidemics of the

This detail from a 1572 map of London shows closely packed buildings intersected with throroughfares, with gardens and open spaces on the outskirts.

London Bridge, lined with shops, houses, and severed heads on poles, provided a colorful route for those traveling between the north and south banks of the Thames. A number of Elizabethan theaters, including the Globe, were located on the south bank.

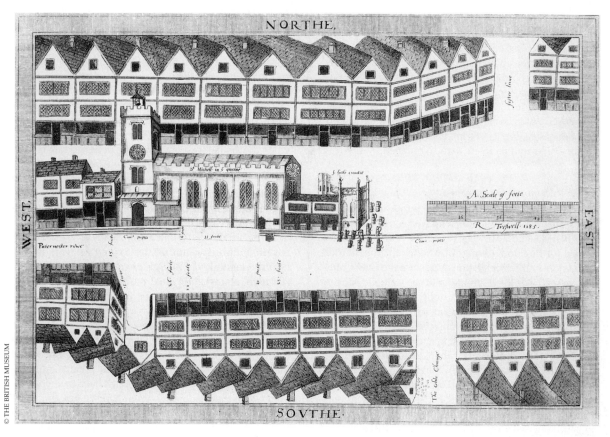

The taverns of Cheapside in London were popular and occasionally rowdy.

bubonic plague were the inevitable result of unsanitary conditions and medical ignorance. Lighting of the streets at night was generally nonexistent, and the constabulary was notoriously unreliable. Shakespeare gives us unforgettable satires of night watchmen and bumbling police officials in *Much Ado About Nothing* (Dogberry and the night watch) and *Measure for Measure* (Constable Elbow). Prostitution thrived in the suburbs, conveniently located, although beyond the reach of the London authorities. Again, we are indebted to Shakespeare for a memorable portrayal in *Measure for Measure* of just such a demimonde (Mistress Overdone the bawd, Pompey her pimp, and various customers). Houses of prostitution were often found in the vicinity of the public theaters, since the theaters also took advantage of suburban locations to escape the stringent regulations imposed by London's Lord Mayor and Council of Aldermen. The famous Globe Theatre, for example, was on the south bank of the Thames, a short distance west of London Bridge. Another theatrical building (called simply "The Theatre"), used earlier by Shakespeare and the Lord Chamberlain's players, was located in Finsbury Fields, a short distance across Moorfields from London's northeast corner. The suburbs

also housed various con games and illegal operations, some of them brilliantly illustrated (and no doubt exaggerated) in Ben Jonson's *The Alchemist* (1610).

Roughly half of London's total population, perhaps 100,000 people, lived within its walls, and as many more in the suburbs. The royal palace of Whitehall, Westminster Abbey (then known as the Abbey Church of St. Peter), the Parliament House, and Westminster Hall were well outside London, two miles or so to the west on the Thames River. They remain today in the same location, in Westminster, although the metropolis of London has long since surrounded these official buildings.

Travel

Travel was still extremely painful and slow because of the poor condition of the roads. Highway robbers were a constant threat. (The celebrated highway robbery in Shakespeare's *1 Henry IV* takes place at Gads Hill, on the main road between London and Canterbury.) English inns seem to have been good, however, and certainly much better than the inns of the Continent. Travel on horseback was the most common method of transportation, and probably the most comfortable, since coach building was a new and imperfect art. Coaches of state, some of which we see in prints and pictures of the era, were lumbering affairs, no doubt handsome enough in processions, but springless, unwieldly, and hard to pull. Carts and wagons were used for carrying merchandise, but packsaddles were safer and quicker. Under such difficulties, no metropolitan area such as London could possibly have thrived in the interior. London depended for its commercial greatness upon the Thames River and its access to the North Sea.

Commerce

When Elizabeth came to the English throne in 1558, England's chief foreign trade was with Antwerp, Bruges, and other Belgian cities. Antwerp was an especially important market for England's export of wool cloth. This market was seriously threatened, however, since the Low Countries were under the domination of the Catholic King of Spain, Philip II. When Philip undertook to punish his Protestant subjects in the Low Countries for their religious heresy, many of Elizabeth's counselors and subjects urged her to come to the defense of England's Protestant neighbors and trading allies. Elizabeth held back. Philip's armies attacked Antwerp in 1576 and again in 1585, putting an end to the commercial ascendancy of that great northern European metropolis. Perhaps as many as one-third of Antwerp's merchants and artisans settled in London, bringing with them their expert knowledge of commerce and manufacture. The influx of so many skilled workers and merchants into London produced problems of unemployment and overcrowding but contributed nevertheless to London's emergence as a leading port of trade.

English ships assumed a dominant position in Mediterranean trade, formerly carried on mainly by the Venetians. In the Baltic Sea, England competed successfully in trade that had previously been controlled by the Hanseatic League. Bristol thrived on commerce with Ireland and subsequently on trade with the Western Hemisphere. Boston and Hull increased their business with Scandinavian ports. The Russia Company was founded in 1555; the Levant Company became the famous East India Company in 1600; and the Virginia Company opened up trade with the New World in the Western Hemisphere. Fisheries were developed in the North Sea, in the waters north of Ireland, and off the banks of Newfoundland. Elizabeth and her ministers encouraged this commercial expansion.

The Poor Laws and Apprenticeship

Despite the new prosperity experienced by many Elizabethans, especially in London, unemployment remained a serious problem. The suppresssion of the monasteries in 1536–1539, as part of Henry VIII's reformation of the Catholic Church, had dispossessed a large class of persons who were not easily reemployed. Other causes of unemployment, such as the periodic collapse of the wool trade, dispossession of farm workers by enclosure of land, the sudden influx of skilled artisans from Antwerp, and the return of army veterans, have already been mentioned. Elizabethan parliaments attempted to cope with the problem of unemployment but did so in ways that seem unduly harsh today. Several laws were passed between 1531, when the distinction between those poor needing charity and those unwilling to work first became law, and 1597–1598. The harshest of the laws was that of 1547, providing that vagabonds be branded and enslaved for two years; escape was punishable by death or life enslavement. This act was repealed in 1549, but subsequent acts of 1572 and 1576 designated ten classes of vagrants and required municipal authorities to provide work for the healthy unemployed of each town or parish. This localization of responsibility laid the basis for what has been known historically as the "poor rate" (a local tax levied for the support of the poor) and for that sinister institution, the workhouse. The provisions of this act remained in force for centuries. The most comprehensive laws were those of the Parliament of 1597–1598, which repeated many provisions of earlier acts and added harsh, punitive penalties intended to send vagabonds back to the parishes in which they had been born or had last worked. After 1597, no begging was permitted; the poor were supposed to be provided for by the "poor rate" already established.

Regulations for apprentices were no less strict. An act of Parliament of 1563, known as the Statute of Artificers, gave the craft trades of England—still organized as medieval guilds—virtually complete authority over the young persons apprenticed to a trade. The law severely

Although some Elizabethans rose to great wealth, poverty and unemployment were widespread.

limited access to apprenticeship to sons of families with estates worth at least forty shillings of income. Apprenticeship usually began between the ages of fourteen and seventeen, and lasted for a period of not less than seven years. During this time, the young worker lived with the family of the employer. Without such an extensive apprenticeship, entry into the skilled crafts was virtually impossible. Apprenticeships were not open, however, in all guilds, and the law courts subsequently ruled that apprenticeship rules did not apply to crafts developed after 1563, so that exceptions did exist. All able-bodied workers not bound to crafts were supposed to work in agriculture. Acting companies, such as the company Shakespeare joined, were not technically organized as guilds, though the boys who played women's parts were in some cases at least bound by the terms of apprenticeship; a number of the adult actors belonged to one London guild or another and could use that status to apprentice boys. We do not know whether Shakespeare actually served such an indenture before becoming a full member of his acting company.

Social Change

The opportunities for rapid economic advance in Elizabethan England, though limited almost entirely to those who were already prosperous, did produce social change and a quality of restlessness in English society. "New men" at court were an increasing phenomenon under the Tudor monarchs, especially Henry VII and Henry VIII, who tended to rely on loyal counselors of humble origin rather than on the once-too-powerful nobility. Cardinal Wolsey, for example, rose from obscurity to become the most mighty subject of Henry VIII's realm, with a newly built residence (Hampton Court) rivaling the splendor of the King's own palaces. He was detested as an upstart by old aristocrats, such as the Duke of Norfolk, and his sudden fall was as spectacular as had been his rise to power. The Earl of Leicester, Queen Elizabeth's first favorite, was a descendant of the Edmund Dudley who had risen from unpretentious beginnings to great eminence under Henry VII, Queen Elizabeth's grandfather. Although Queen Elizabeth did not contribute substantially to the new aristocracy—she created only three peers from 1573 onward—new and influential families were numerous throughout the century. Conversely, the ancient families discovered that they were no longer entrusted with positions of highest authority. To be sure, the aristocracy remained at the apex of England's social structure. New aspirants to power emulated the aristocracy by purchasing land and building splendid residences, rather than defining themselves as a rich new "middle class." Bourgeois status was something the new men put behind them as quickly as they could. Moreover, social mobility could work in both directions: upward and downward. Many men were quickly ruined by the costly and competitive business of seeking favor at the Tudor court. The poor, in a vast majority, enjoyed virtually no rights at all. Nonetheless, the Elizabethan era was one of greater opportunity for rapid social and economic advancement among persons of wealth than England had heretofore known.

Increased economic contacts with the outside world inevitably led to the importation of new styles of living. Such new fashions, together with the rapid changes now possible in social position, produced a reaction of dismay from those who feared the destruction of traditional English values. Attitudes toward Italy veered erratically between condemnation and admiration: on the one hand, Italy was the home of the Catholic Church and originator of many supposedly decadent fashions, whereas, on the other hand, Italy was the cradle of humanism and the country famed for Venice's experiment in republican government. To many conservative Englishmen, the word *Italianate* connoted a whole range of villainous practices, including diabolical methods of torture and revenge: poisoned books of devotion that would kill the unsuspecting victims who kissed them, ingeniously contrived chairs that would close upon the person who sat in them, and the like. The revenge plays of Shakespeare's contemporaries, such as *Antonio's Revenge* by John Marston, *The Revenger's Tragedy* probably by Thomas Middleton, and *The White Devil* by John Webster, offer spectacular caricatures of the so-called Italianate style in murder. The name of Italy was also associated with licentiousness, immorality, and outlandish fashions in clothes. France, too, was accused of encouraging such extravagances in dress as ornamented headdresses, stiffly pleated ruffs, padded doublets, puffed or double sleeves, and richly decorated hose. Rapid changes in fashion added to the costliness of being up to date and thereby increased the outcry against vanity in dress. Fencing, dicing, the use of cosmetics, the smoking of tobacco, the drinking of imported wines, and almost every vice known to humanity were attributed by angry moralists to the corrupting influence from abroad.

Not all Englishmen deplored continental fashion, of course. Persons of advanced taste saw the importation of European styles as a culturally liberating process. Fashion thus became a subject of debate between moral traditionalists and those who welcomed the new styles. The controversy was a bitter one, with religious overtones, in which the reformers' angry accusations became increasingly extreme. This attack on changing fashion was, in fact, an integral part of the Puritan movement. It therefore stressed the sinfulness, not only of extravagance in clothing, but also of the costliness in building great houses and other such worldly pursuits. Those whose sympathies were Puritan became more and more disaffected with the cultural values represented by the court, and thus English society drifted further and further toward irreconcilable conflict.

This brothel scene, featuring gambling or dicing, illustrates some of the vices that were attributed to the corrupting influence from abroad.

Shakespeare's personal views on this controversy are hard to determine and do not bear importantly on his achievement as an artist. Generally, however, we can observe that his many references to changes in fashion cater neither to the avant-garde nor to reactionary traditionalists. Shakespeare's audience was, after all, a broadly national one. It included many well-informed Londoners who viewed "Italianate" fashion neither with enthusiasm nor with alarm, but with satiric laughter. Such spectators would certainly have seen the point, for example, in Mercutio's witty diatribe at the expense of the new French style in fencing. The object of his scorn is Tybalt, who, according to Mercutio, "fights as you sing prick song" and fancies himself to be "the very butcher of a silk button." "Is not this a lamentable thing," asks Mercutio rhetorically, "that we should be thus afflicted with these strange flies, these fashionmongers, these pardon-me's, who stand so much on the new form that they cannot sit at ease on the old bench?" (*Romeo and Juliet*, 2.4.20–35). In a similar vein, Shakespeare's audience would have appreciated the joking in *The Merchant of Venice* about England's servile imitation of continental styles in clothes. "What say you, then, to Falconbridge, the young baron of England?" asks Nerissa of her mistress Portia concerning one of Portia's many suitors. Portia replies, "How oddly he is suited! I think he bought his doublet in Italy, his round hose in France, his bonnet in Germany, and his behavior everywhere" (1.2.64–74). Court butterflies in Shakespeare's plays who bow and scrape and fondle their plumed headgear, like Le Beau in *As You Like It* and Osric in *Hamlet*, are the objects of ridicule. Hotspur in *1 Henry IV*, proud northern aristocrat that he is, has nothing but contempt for an effeminate courtier, "perfumèd like a milliner," who has come from King Henry to discuss the question of prisoners (1.3.36). Throughout Shakespeare's plays, the use of cosmetics generally has the negative connotation of artificial beauty used to conceal inward corruption, as in Claudius's reference to "the harlot's cheek, beautied with plast'ring art" (*Hamlet*, 3.1.52). Yet Shakespeare's treatment of newness in fashion is never shrill in tone. Nor does he fail in his dramas to give an honorable place to the ceremonial use of wealth and splendid costuming. His plays thus avoid both extremes in the controversy over changing fashions, though they give plentiful evidence as to the liveliness and currency of the topic.

Shakespeare also reflects a contemporary interest in the problem of usury, especially in *The Merchant of Venice*. Although usury was becoming more and more of a necessity, emotional attitudes toward it changed only slowly. The traditional moral view condemned usury as forbidden by Christian teaching; on the other hand, European governments of the sixteenth century found themselves increasingly obliged to borrow large sums of money. The laws against usury were alternatively relaxed and enforced, according to the economic exigencies of the moment. Shakespeare's plays capture the Elizabethan ambivalence of attitude toward this feared but necessary practice (see Introduction to *The Merchant of Venice*). Similarly, most Englishmen had contradictory attitudes toward what we today would call the law of supply and demand in the marketplace. Conservative moralists complained bitterly when merchants exploited the scarcity of some commodity by forcing up prices; the practice was denounced as excessive profit taking and declared to be sinful, like usury. In economic policy, then, as in matters of changing fashion or increased social mobility, many Englishmen were ambivalent about the perennial conflict between the old order and the new.

Elizabethan Houses

Those fortunate Englishmen who grew wealthy in the reign of Elizabeth took special pleasure in building

THE NATIONAL TRUST PHOTOGRAPHIC LIBRARY. PHOTO BY GEOFF MORGAN

Tudor mansions were often splendid, with impressive gardens and terraces. Shown here is Little Moreton Hall, in Cheshire, built in 1559.

themselves fine new houses with furnishings to match. Chimneys were increasingly common, so that smoke no longer had to escape through a hole in the roof. Pewter, or even silver dishes, took the place of the wooden spoon and trencher. Beds, and even pillows, became common. Carpets were replacing rushes as covering for the floors; wainscoting, tapestries or hangings, and pictures appeared on the walls; and glass began to be used extensively for windows.

Despite the warnings of those moralists who preached against the vanity of worldly acquisition, domestic comfort made considerable progress in Elizabethan England. Many splendid Tudor mansions stand today, testifying to the important social changes that had taken place between the strife-torn fifteenth century and the era of relative peace under Elizabeth. The battlement, the moat, the fortified gate, and the narrow window used for archery or firearms generally disappeared in favor of handsome gardens and terraces. At the lower end of the social scale, the agricultural laborers who constituted the great mass of the English population were generally poor, malnourished, and uneducated, but they seem to have enjoyed greater physical security than did their ancestors

in the fifteenth century, and no longer needed to bring their cows, pigs, and poultry into their dwellings at night in order to protect them from thieves. City houses, of which many exist today, were often large and imposing structures, three or four stories in height, and framed usually of strong oak with the walls filled in with brick and plaster. Although the frontage on the streets of London was usually narrow, many houses had trees and handsome gardens at the rear. Of course London also had its plentiful share of tenements for the urban poor.

With the finer houses owned by the fortunate elite came features of privacy that had been virtually unknown to previous generations. Life in the household of a medieval lord had generally focused on the great hall, which could serve variously as the kitchen, dining hall, and sitting room for the entire family and its retainers. The men drank in the hall in the evenings and slept there at night. The new dwellings of prosperous Elizabethans, on the other hand, featured private chambers into which the family and the chief guests could retire.

The Elizabethans built well. Not only do we still admire their houses, but also we can see from their oriel windows and stained glass, their broad staircases, their jewels, and their costumes that they treasured the new beauty of their lives made possible by the culture of the Renaissance. Although the graphic and plastic arts did not thrive in England to the same extent as in Italy, France, and the Low Countries, England made lasting achievements in architecture, as well as in music, drama, and all forms of literature.

THE POLITICAL AND RELIGIOUS BACKGROUND

England under the Tudors suffered from almost unceasing religious conflict. The battle over religion affected every aspect of life and none more so than politics. At the very beginning of the Tudor reign, to be sure, England's problem was not religious but dynastic. Henry VII, the first of the Tudor kings, brought an end to the devastating civil wars of the fifteenth century with his overthrow of Richard III at the battle of Bosworth Field in 1485. The civil wars thus ended were the so-called Wars of the Roses, between the Lancastrian House of Henry VI (symbolized by the red rose) and the Yorkist House of Edward IV (symbolized by the white rose). Shakespeare chose these eventful struggles as the subject for his first series of English history plays, from *Henry VI* in three parts to *Richard III*. The House of Lancaster drew its title from John of Gaunt, Duke of Lancaster, father of Henry IV and great-grandfather of Henry VI; the House of York drew its title from Edmund Langley, Duke of York, great-grandfather of Edward IV and Richard III. Because John of Gaunt and Edmund Langley had been brothers, virtually all the noble contestants in this War of the Roses were cousins of one another, caught in a remorseless dynastic struggle for control of the English crown. Many of them lost their lives in the fighting. By 1485, England was exhausted from civil conflict. Although Henry VII's own dynastic claim to the throne was weak, he managed to suppress factional opposition and to give England the respite from war so desperately needed. His son, Henry VIII, inherited a throne in 1509 that was more secure than it had been in nearly a century.

On Sundays crowds gathered to listen to the sermon at St. Paul's Cathedral, the subject of this anonymous painting dated 1616.

Henry VIII's notorious marital difficulties, however, soon brought an end to dynastic security and civil accord. Moreover, religious conflict within the Catholic Church was growing to the extent that a break with Rome appeared inevitable. Henry's marriage troubles precipitated that momentous event. Because he divorced his first wife, Katharine of Aragon, in 1530 without the consent of Rome, he was excommunicated by the pope. His response in 1534 was to have himself proclaimed "Protector and only Supreme Head of the Church and Clergy of England." This decisive act signaled the beginning of the Reformation in England, not many years after Martin Luther's momentous break with the papacy in 1517 and the consequent beginning of Lutheran Protestantism on the Continent. In England, Henry's act of defiance split the Church and the nation. Many persons chose Sir Thomas More's path of martyrdom rather than submit to Henry's new title as supreme head of the English church. Henry's later years did witness a period of retrenchment in religion, after the downfall of Thomas Cromwell in 1540, and indeed Henry's break with Rome had had its origin in political and marital strife as well as in matters of dogma and liturgy. Nevertheless, the establishment of an English church was now an accomplished fact. The accession of Henry's ten-year-old son Edward VI in 1547 gave reformers an opportunity to bring about rapid changes in English Protestantism. Archbishop Cranmer's forty-two articles of religion (1551) and his prayer book laid the basis for the Anglican Church of the sixteenth century.

The death of the sickly Edward VI in 1553 brought with it an intense crisis in religious politics and a temporary reversal of England's religious orientation. The Duke of Northumberland, Protector and virtual ruler of England in Edward's last years, attempted to secure a Protestant succession and his own power by marrying his son to Lady Jane Grey, a granddaughter of Henry VII, whom Edward had named heir to the throne, but the proclamation of Lady Jane as Queen ended in failure. She was executed, as were her husband and father-in-law. For five years, England returned to Catholicism under the rule of Edward's elder sister Mary, daughter of the Catholic Queen Katharine of Aragon. The crisis accompanying such changes of government during this midcentury period was greatly exacerbated by the fact that all three of Henry VIII's living children were considered illegitimate by one faction or another of the English people. In Protestant eyes, Mary was the daughter of the divorced Queen Katharine, whose marriage to Henry had never been valid because she had previously been the spouse of Henry VIII's older brother Arthur. This Arthur had died at a young age, in 1502, shortly after his state marriage to the Spanish princess. If, as the Protestants insisted, Arthur had consummated the marriage, then Katharine's subsequent union with her deceased husband's brother was invalid, and Henry was free, instead, to marry Anne Boleyn—the mother-to-be of Elizabeth. In Catholic eyes, however, both Elizabeth and her brother Edward VI (son of Jane Seymour, Henry VIII's third wife) were the bastard issue of Henry's bigamous marriages; Henry's one and only true marriage in the Catholic faith was that to Katharine of Aragon. Edward and Elizabeth were regarded by many Catholics, at home and abroad, not only as illegitimate children, but also as illegitimate rulers, to be disobeyed and even overthrown by force. Thus, dynastic and marital conflicts became matters of grave political consequence.

Because of these struggles, Elizabeth's accession to the throne in 1558 remained an uncertainty until the last moment. Once she actually became ruler, England returned once more to the Protestant faith. Even then, tact and moderation were required to prevent open religious war. Elizabeth's genius at compromise prompted her to seek a middle position for her church, one that combined an episcopal form of church government (owing no allegiance to the pope) with an essentially traditional form of liturgy and dogma. As much as was practicable, she left matters up to individual conscience; she drew the line, however, where matters of conscience tended to "exceed their bounds and grow to be matter of faction." In practice, this meant that she did not tolerate avowed Catholics on the religious right or Protestant sects who denied the doctrine of the Trinity on the religious left. The foundation for this so-called Elizabethan compromise was the thirty-nine articles, adopted in 1563 and based in many respects upon Cranmer's forty-two articles of 1551. The compromise did not please everyone, of course, but it did achieve a remarkable degree of consensus during Elizabeth's long reign.

Queen Elizabeth and Tudor Absolutism

Elizabeth had to cope with a religiously divided nation and with extremists of both the right and the left who wished her downfall. She was a woman, in an age openly skeptical of women's ability or right to rule. Her success in dealing with such formidable odds was in large measure the result of her personal style as a monarch. Her combination of imperious will and femininity and her brilliant handling of her many contending male admirers have become legendary. She remained unmarried throughout her life, in part, at least, because marriage would have upset the delicate balance she maintained among rival groups, both foreign and domestic. Marriage would have committed her irretrievably to either one foreign nation or to one constituency at home. She chose instead to bestow her favor on certain courtiers, notably Robert Dudley (whom she elevated to be the Earl of Leicester) and, after Leicester's death in 1588, Robert

The Knights of the Garter belonged to the highest order of knighthood; many were influential courtiers and favorites of Queen Elizabeth. A masterful politician, Elizabeth remained unmarried throughout her life. A marriage would have upset the political balance and would have committed her to one foreign nation or to one constituency at home.

Devereux, second Earl of Essex. Her relationship with these men, despite her partiality to them, was marked by her outbursts of tempestuous jealousy. In addition, she relied on the staid counsel of her hard-working ministers: Lord Burghley, Sir Francis Walsingham, Burghley's son Robert Cecil, and a few others.

In her personal style as monarch, Elizabeth availed herself of the theory of absolute supremacy. Under all the Tudors, England was nominally at least an absolute monarchy in an age when many of England's greatest rivals—France, Spain, the Holy Roman Empire—were also under absolutist rule. "Absolutism" meant that the monarch served for life, could not legally be removed from office, and was normally succeeded by his eldest son—all of this bolstered by claims of divine sanction, though the claims were frequently contested. The rise of absolutism throughout Renaissance Europe was the result of an increase of centralized national power and a corresponding decrease in autonomous baronial influence. Henry VII's strong assertion of his royal authority at the expense of the feudal lords corresponded roughly in time with the ascendancy of Francis I of France (1515) and Charles V of the Holy Roman Empire (1519). Yet England had long enjoyed a tradition of rule by consensus. When Elizabeth came to the throne, England was already

in some ways a "limited" monarchy. Parliament, and especially the members of the House of Commons, claimed prerogatives of their own and were steadily gaining in both experience and power. In the mid-1560s, for example, the Commons made repeated attempts to use parliamentary tax-levying authority as a means of obliging Elizabeth to name a Protestant successor to the throne. The attempt, despite its failure to achieve its immediate goal, was significant; the Commons had shown that they were a force to be reckoned with. Even though Elizabeth made skillful rhetorical use of the theory of absolutism, portraying herself as God's appointed deputy on earth, her idea of absolutism should not be confused with despotism. To be sure, Elizabeth learned to avoid parliamentary interference in her affairs whenever possible; there were only thirteen sessions of Parliament in her forty-five years of rule. Still, Parliament claimed the right to establish law and to levy taxes on which the monarchy had to depend. Elizabeth needed all her considerable diplomatic skills in dealing with her parliaments and with the English people, who were self-reliant and proud of their reputation for independence. Elizabeth had more direct authority over her Privy Council, since she could appoint its members herself, yet even here she consulted faithfully with them on virtually everything she did. Nor

were her closest advisers reluctant to offer her advice. Many vocal leaders in her government, including Walsingham and Leicester, urged the Queen during the 1570s and 1580s to undertake a more active military role on the Continent against the Catholic powers. So did her later favorite, the Earl of Essex. With remarkable tact, she managed to retain the loyalty of her militant and sometimes exasperated counselors, and yet to keep England out of war with Spain until that country actually launched an invasion attempt in 1588 (the Great Armada).

Catholic Opposition

During her early years, Elizabeth sought through her religious compromise to ease the divisions of her kingdom and attempted to placate her enemies abroad (notably Philip of Spain) rather than involve England in a costly war. For about twelve years, while England's economy gained much-needed strength, this policy of temporizing succeeded. Yet Elizabeth's more extreme Catholic opponents at home and abroad could never be reconciled to the daughter of that Protestant "whore," Anne Boleyn. England's period of relative accommodation came to an end in 1569 and 1570, with Catholic uprisings in the north and with papal excommunication of the English Queen.

As a declared heretic, Elizabeth's very life was in danger; her Catholic subjects were encouraged by Rome to disobey her and to seek means for her violent overthrow.

Conspirators did, in fact, make attempts on the Queen's life, notably in the so-called Babington conspiracy of 1586, named for one of the chief participants. This plot, brought to light by Secretary of State Walsingham, sought to place Mary, Queen of Scots on the English throne in Elizabeth's stead. Mary was Elizabeth's kinswoman; Mary's grandmother, sister to Henry VIII, had been married to James IV of Scotland. So long as Elizabeth remained childless, Mary was a prominent heir to the English throne. Catholics pinned their hopes on her succession, by force if necessary; Protestant leaders urged Elizabeth to marry and give birth to a Protestant heir or at least to name a Protestant successor. Mary had abdicated the Scottish throne in 1567 after the sensational murder of her Catholic counselor David Rizzio, the murder of Mary's husband, the Earl of Darnley (in which Mary was widely suspected to have taken part), and her subsequent marriage to Darnley's slayer, the Earl of Bothwell. Taking refuge in England, Mary remained a political prisoner and the inevitable focus of Catholic plotting against Elizabeth for approximately two decades. She, in fact, assented in writing to Babington's plot

Along with the defeat of the Spanish Armada in 1588, the 1587 beheading of Mary, Queen of Scots, shown holding a crucifix and surrounded by official witnesses in this contemporary illustration, virtually ended any serious Catholic challenge to Elizabeth's throne.

against Elizabeth. All that long while Elizabeth resisted demands from her Protestant advisers that she execute her kinswoman and thereby end a constant threat to the throne; Elizabeth was reluctant to kill a fellow monarch and agreed fully with Mary's son James that "anointing by God cannot be defiled by man." Nonetheless, Mary's clear involvement in the Babington conspiracy led to the so-called Bond of Association, in which thousands of Englishmen pledged to prevent the succession of any person plotting Elizabeth's death, and then at last to Mary's execution in 1587. By that time, Spain was mounting an invasion against England, the Great Armada of 1588, and Elizabeth's temporizing tactics were no longer feasible. The long years of peace had done their work, however, and England was considerably stronger and more resolute than thirty years before. With Elizabeth's tacit approval, Sir Francis Drake and other naval commanders carried the fighting to Spain's very shore and to her American colonies. The war with Spain continued from 1588 until about 1597.

Elizabeth's great compromise dealt not only with the political dangers of opposition but also with the more central theological issues. England was sorely divided, as was much of Europe, on such matters as whether Christ's body was transubstantially present in the Mass, as Catholic faith maintained; whether good works were effi-

cacious in salvation or whether people could be saved by God's grace alone, as the Reformers insisted; whether a portion of humankind was predeterminately damned, as the Calvinists believed; and the like. During the turbulent years of the Reformation, many people died for their faith. In general, the Elizabethan compromise insisted on allegiance to the English throne, church, and ecclesiastical hierarchy but allowed some latitude in matters of faith. The degree of elaboration in vestments and ritual was also an explosive issue on which the English church attempted to steer a central and pragmatic course, although conflicts inevitably arose within the church itself.

Protestant Opposition

The threat from the Protestant left was no less worrisome than that from the Catholic right. Protestant reformers had experienced their first taste of power at the time of Henry VIII's break with Rome in 1534. Under Thomas Cromwell, Cardinal Wolsey's successor as the King's chief minister, the monasteries were suppressed and William Tyndale's English Bible was authorized. The execution of Cromwell introduced a period of conservative retrenchment, but the accession of Edward VI in 1547 brought reform once more into prominence. Thereafter, Mary's Catholic reign drove most of the reformers into exile on the Continent. When they returned after 1558, many had been made more radical by their continental experience.

To be sure, reform covered a wide spectrum, from moderation to radicalism. Some preferred to work within the existing hierarchical structure of church and state, whereas others were religious separatists. Only the more radical groups, such as the Brownists and Anabaptists, endorsed ideas of equality and communal living. The abusive epithet "Puritan," applied indiscriminately to all reformers, tended to obscure the wide range of difference in the reform movement. The reformers were, to some extent, united by a dislike for formal ritual and ecclesiastical garments, by a preference for a simple and pious manner of living, and by a belief in the literal word of the Bible rather than the traditional teachings of the church fathers. They stressed personal responsibility in religion and were Calvinist in their emphasis on human depravity and the need for grace through election. Yet at first only the more radical were involved in a movement to separate entirely from the established English church.

The radicals on the religious left, even if they represented at first only a minority of the reformers, posed a serious threat to Elizabeth's government. Their program bore an ironic resemblance to that of the Catholic opposition on the religious right. In their theoretical writings, the extreme reformers justified overthrow of what they considered to be tyrannical rule, just as Catholic spokesmen had absolved Elizabeth's subjects of obedience to her on the grounds that she was illegitimate. Both extremes appealed to disobedience in the name of a higher religious law, as enunciated in Romans 13:1–2: "For there is no power but of God." Among the reforming theoreticians was John Ponet, whose *Short Treatise of Politic Power* (1556) argued that a monarch is subject to a social contract and must rule according to laws that are equally subscribed to by Parliament, the clergy, and the people.

The Doctrine of Passive Obedience

Elizabeth's government countered such assaults on its authority, from both the right and the left, with many arguments, of which perhaps the most central was that of passive obedience. This doctrine condemned rebellion under virtually all circumstances. Its basic assumption was that the king or queen is God's appointed deputy on earth. To depose such a monarch must therefore be an act of disobedience against God's will. Since God is all-wise and all-powerful, his placing of an evil ruler in power must proceed from some divine intention, such as the punishment of a wayward people. Rebellion against God's "scourge" merely displays further disobedience to God's will. A people suffering under a tyrant must wait patiently for God to remove the burden, which he will surely do when the proper time arrives.

This doctrine was included in the official book of homilies of the Church of England and was read from the pulpit at regular intervals. The best-known such homily, entitled *Against Disobedience and Willful Rebellion,* had been preceded by such tracts as William Tyndale's *Obedience of a Christian Man* (1528); a book of homilies, published in 1547, including an "Exhortation Concerning Good Order and Obedience"; Thomas Cranmer's *Notes for a Sermon on the Rebellion of 1549;* and Hugh Latimer's *Sermon on the Lord's Prayer* (1552). Shakespeare heard such homilies often, and he expresses their ideas through several of his characters, such as John of Gaunt and the Bishop of Carlisle in *Richard II* (1.2.37–41, 4.1.115–50). This is not to say that he endorses such ideas, for he sets them in dramatic opposition to other and more heterodox concepts. We can say, nevertheless, that Shakespeare's audience would have recognized in Gaunt's speeches a clear expression of a familiar and officially correct position.

The Political Ideas of Machiavelli

The orthodoxies of the Elizabethan establishment were under attack, not only from the Catholic right and the Protestant left, but also from a new and revolutionary point of view that set aside all criteria of religious morality. Tudor defense of order was based, as we have seen, on the assumption that the monarch rules in accord with a divine plan, a higher Law of Nature to which every just ruler is attuned. Political morality must be at one with religious morality. Catholic and Protestant critiques of the Tudor establishment made similar assumptions, even though they appealed to revolution in the name of that religious morality. To Niccolò Machiavelli, on the other hand, politics was a manipulative science best governed by the dictates of social expediency. His philosophy did not, as many accusingly charged, lead necessarily to the cynical promotion of mere self-interest. Nevertheless, he did argue, in his *Discourses* and *The Prince,* that survival and political stability are the first obligations of any ruler. Machiavelli regarded religion as a tool of the enlightened ruler rather than as a morally absolute guide. He extolled in his ideal leader the quality of *virtù*—a mixture of cunning and forcefulness. He saw history as a subject offering practical lessons in the kind of pragmatic statecraft he proposed.

Machiavelli was a hated name in England, and most of his works were never available in an English printed edition during Shakespeare's lifetime. (The *Florentine History* was translated in 1595; *The Prince* was not translated until 1640.) Nevertheless, his writings were available in Italian, French, and Latin editions, and in manuscript English translations. His ideas certainly had a profound impact on the England of the 1590s. Marlowe caricatures the Italian writer in his *The Jew of Malta,* but he clearly was fascinated by what Machiavelli had to say. Shakespeare, too, reveals a complex awareness. However much he may lampoon the Machiavellian type of conscienceless villain in *Richard III*, he shows us more plausible pragmatists in *Richard II* and *1 Henry IV*. Conservative theories of the divine right of kings are set in debate with the more heterodox ambitions of Henry Bolingbroke (who then adopts the most orthodox of political vocabularies once he is king). Bolingbroke is not a very attractive figure, but he does succeed politically where Richard has failed.

Shakespeare thus reveals himself as less a defender of the established order than as a great dramatist able to give sympathetic expression to the aspirations of all sides in a tense political struggle. His history plays have been variously interpreted either as defenses of monarchy or as subtle pleas for rebellion, but the consensus today is that the plays use political conflict as a way of probing the motivations of social behavior. To be sure, the plays do stress the painful consequences of disorder and present, on the whole, an admiring view of monarchy (especially in *Henry V*), despite the manifest limitations of that institution. Certainly, we can sense that Shakespeare's history plays were written for a generation of Englishmen who had experienced political crisis and who could perceive issues of statecraft in Shakespeare's plays that were relevant to England's struggles in the 1580s and the 1590s. The play of *King John*, for example, deals with a king whose uncertain claim to the throne is challenged by France and the papacy in the name of John's nephew, Arthur; Elizabeth faced a similar situation in her dilemma over her kinswoman, Mary, Queen of Scots. Elizabeth also bitterly acknowledged the cogency of a popular analogy comparing her reign with that of King Richard II, and, when Shakespeare's play about Bolingbroke's overthrow of Richard was apparently revived for political purposes shortly before the Earl of Essex's abortive rebellion against Elizabeth in 1601, Shakespeare's acting company had some explaining to do to the authorities (see Introduction to *Richard II*). Nevertheless, Shakespeare's attitudes toward the issues of his own day are ultimately unknowable and unimportant, since his main concern seems to have been with the dramatization of political conflict rather than with the urging of a polemical position.

Shakespeare on Religion

Our impressions of Shakespeare's personal sympathies in religion are similarly obscured by his refusal to use his art for polemical purposes. To be sure, members of his mother's family in Warwickshire seem to have remained loyal to Catholicism, and his father John Shakespeare may conceivably have undergone financial and other difficulties in Stratford for reasons of faith. (See "Shakespeare's Family" below, in the section on Shakespeare's Life and Work.) Certainly Shakespeare himself displays a familiarity with some Catholic practices and theology,

as when the Ghost of Hamlet's father speaks of being "Unhousled, disappointed, unaneled" (i.e., not having received last rites) at the time of his murder (*Hamlet*, 1.5.78). Nonetheless, we see in his plays a spectrum of religious attitudes portrayed with an extraordinary range of insight. In matters of doctrine, his characters are at various times acquainted with Catholic theology or with the controversy concerning salvation by faith or good works (see *Measure for Measure*, 1.2.24–5), and yet a consistent polemical bias is absent. Some Catholic prelates are schemers, like Pandulph in *King John*. Ordinarily, however, Shakespeare's satirical digs at ecclesiastical pomposity and hypocrisy have little to do with the Catholic question. Cardinal Beaufort in *1 Henry VI* is a political maneuverer, but so are many of his secular rivals. Cardinal Wolsey in *Henry VIII* is motivated by personal ambition, rather than by any sinister conspiracy of the international church. Many of Shakespeare's nominally Catholic clerics, such as Friar Laurence in *Romeo and Juliet* or Friar Francis in *Much Ado About Nothing*, are gentle and well-intentioned people, even if occasionally bumbling. We can certainly say that Shakespeare consistently avoids the chauvinistic anti-Catholic baiting so often found in the plays of his contemporaries.

The same avoidance of extremes can be seen in his portrayal of Protestant reformers, though the instances in this case are few. Malvolio in *Twelfth Night* is fleetingly compared with a "puritan" (2.3.139–46), although Shakespeare insists that no extensive analogy can be made. Angelo in *Measure for Measure* is sometimes thought to be a critical portrait of the Puritan temperament. Even if this were so, Shakespeare's satire is extremely indirect compared with the lampoons written by his contemporaries Ben Jonson and Thomas Dekker.

Stuart Absolutism

Queen Elizabeth's successor, James I of the Scottish house of Stuarts, reigned from 1603 to 1625. Even more than Elizabeth, he was a strong believer in the divinely appointed authority of kings; whereas she had insisted on divine sanction, James and his successor Charles called it a divine right. Although James succeeded easily to the throne in 1603, since he was Protestant with a legitimate claim of descent from Henry VIII, the English people did not take to this foreigner from the north. James was eccentric in his personal habits, and the English were always inclined to be suspicious of the Scots in any case. As a result, James was less successful in dealing with the heterogeneous and antagonistic forces that Elizabeth had kept in precarious balance. At the Hampton Court Conference of 1604, relations quickly broke down between James and the Puritan wing of the church, so that even its more moderate adherents joined forces with the separatists. James had similar difficulties with an increasingly radical group in the House of Commons. In the widening rift between the absolutists and those who defended the supremacy of Parliament, James's court moved toward the right. Catholic sympathies at court became common. Civil war was still a long way off and by no means inevitable; the beheading of King Charles I (James's son) would not occur until 1649. Still, throughout James's reign, the estrangement between the right and the left was becoming more and more uncomfortable. The infamous Gunpowder Plot of 1605, in which Guy Fawkes and other Catholic conspirators were accused of having plotted to blow up the houses of Parliament, raised hysteria to a new intensity. Penal laws against papists were harshly enforced. The Parliament of 1614 included in its membership John Pym, Thomas Wentworth, and John Eliot—men who were to become turbulent spokesmen against taxes imposed without parliamentary grant, imprisonment without the stating of specific criminal charges, and other purported abuses of royal power. The polarization of English society naturally affected the London theaters. Popular London audiences (generally sympathetic with religious reform) eventually grew disaffected with the stage, while even the popular acting companies came under the increasing domination of the court. Shakespeare's late plays reflect the increasing influence of a courtly audience.

THE INTELLECTUAL BACKGROUND

Renaissance Cosmology

In learning, as in politics and religion, Shakespeare's England was a time of conflict and excitement. Medieval ideas of a hierarchical and ordered creation were under attack but were still widely prevalent, and were used to justify a hierarchical order in society itself. According to the so-called Ptolemaic system of the universe, formulated by Ptolemy of Alexandria in the second century A.D., the earth stood at the center of creation. Around it moved, in nine concentric spheres, the heavenly bodies of the visible universe, in order as follows (from the earth outward): the moon, Mercury, Venus, the sun, Mars, Jupiter, Saturn, the fixed stars on a single plane, and lastly the *primum mobile*, imparting motion to the whole system. (See the accompanying illustration.) Some commentators proposed alternate arrangements or speculated as to the existence of one or two additional spheres, in particular a "crystalline sphere" between the fixed stars and the *primum mobile*. These additional spheres were needed to cope with matters not adequately explained in Ptolemaic astronomy, such as the precession of the equinoxes. More troublesomely, the seemingly erratic retrograde motion of the planets—that is, the refusal of Mars and other planets to move around the earth in steady orbit—

called forth increasingly ingenious theories, such as Tycho Brahe's scheme of epicycles. Still, the conservative appeal of the earth-centered cosmos remained very strong. How could one suppose that the earth was not at the center of the universe?

The *primum mobile* was thought to turn the entire universe around the earth once every twenty-four hours. Simultaneously, the individual heavenly bodies moved more slowly around the earth on their individual spheres, constantly changing position with respect to the fixed stars. The moon, being the only heavenly body that seemed subject to change in its monthly waxing and waning, was thought to represent the boundary between the unchanging universe and the incessantly changing world. Beneath the moon, in the "sublunary" sphere, all creation was subject to death as a result of Adam's fall from grace; beyond the moon lay perfection. Hell was imagined to exist deep within the earth, as in Dante's *Inferno,* or else outside the *primum mobile* and far below the created universe in the realm of chaos, as in Milton's *Paradise Lost.*

Heaven or the Empyrean stood, according to most Ptolemaic systems, at the top of the universe. Between heaven and earth dwelled the nine angelic orders, each associated with one of the nine concentric spheres. According to a work attributed to Dionysius the Areopagite, *On the Heavenly Hierarchy* (fifth century A.D.), the nine angelic orders consisted of three hierarchies. Closest to God were the contemplative orders of Seraphim, Cherubim, and Thrones; next, the intermediate orders of Dominions, Powers, and Virtues; and finally the active orders of Principalities, Archangels, and Angels. These last served as God's messengers and intervened from time to time in the affairs of mortals. Ordered life among humans, although manifestly imperfect when compared with the eternal bliss of the angelic orders, still modeled itself on that platonic idea of perfect harmony. Thus the state, the church, and the family all resembled one another because they resembled (however distantly) the kingdom of God. Richard Hooker, in his *Of the Laws of Ecclesiastical Polity* (1594–1597), defends the established Church of England in terms that emanate from a comparable idea of a divine, creative, and ordering law of nature "Whose seat is the bosom of God, whose voice the harmony of the world."

The devils of hell were fallen angels, with Satan as their leader. Such evil spirits might assume any number of shapes, such as demons, goblins, wizards, or witches. Believers in evil spirits generally made no distinction between orthodox Christian explanations of evil and the more primitive folklore of witchcraft. Belief in witchcraft was widespread indeed; King James I took the matter very seriously. So did Reginald Scot's *The Discovery of Witchcraft* (1584), though its author also attempted to confute what he regarded as ignorant superstition and

Ptolemy's earth-centered system of the universe (top) was challenged by the sun-centered system of Copernicus (bottom) with the publishing of De revolutionibus orbium coelestium *in 1543. Shakespeare, like other major poets of the English Renaissance, poetically represents the universe in cosmic terms as described by Ptolemy, but also reflects uncertainties generated by the new cosmology.*

charlatanism. Throughout Shakespeare's lifetime, belief and skepticism about such matters existed side by side.

A similar ambiguity pertained to belief in the Ptolemaic universe itself. All major poets of the Renaissance, including Shakespeare, Spenser, and Milton (who completed *Paradise Lost* after 1660), represented the universe in cosmic terms essentially as described by Ptolemy. Yet Nicolaus Copernicus's revolutionary theory of a sun-centered solar system (*De revolutionibus orbium coelestium,* published on the Continent in 1543) and the discovery of a new star in Cassiopeia in 1572 stimulated much new thought. Galileo Galilei, born in the same year as Shakespeare (1564), published in 1610 the results of his telescopic examinations of the moon, thereby further confirming Copernicus's hypothesis. Although the news of Galileo's astounding discovery came too late to affect any but the latest of Shakespeare's plays, a sense of excitement and dislocation was apparent throughout most of the years of his writing career. Thomas Nashe, in 1595, referred familiarly to Copernicus as the author "who held that the sun remains immobile in the center of the world, and that the earth is moved about the sun" (Nashe, *Works,* ed. R. B. McKerrow, 1904–1910, 3.94). John Donne lamented in 1611–1612 that the "new philosophy" (i.e., the new science) "calls all in doubt." Skeptical uncertainty about the cosmos was on the rise. The poetic affirmations in Renaissance art of traditional ideas of the cosmos can best be understood as a response to uncertainty—a statement of faith in an age of increasing skepticism.

Alchemy and Medicine

In all areas of Renaissance learning, the new and the old science were juxtaposed. Alchemy, for example, made important contributions to learning, despite its superstitious character. Its chief goal was the transformation of base metals into gold, on the assumption that all metals were ranked on a hierarchical scale and could be raised from lower to higher positions on that scale by means of certain alchemical techniques. Other aims of alchemy included the discovery of a universal cure for diseases and of a means for preserving life indefinitely. Such aims encouraged quackery and prompted various exposés, such as Chaucer's "The Canon's Yeoman's Tale" (late fourteenth century) and Jonson's *The Alchemist* (1610). Yet many of the procedures used in alchemy were essentially chemical procedures, and the science of chemistry received a valuable impetus from constant experimentation. Queen Elizabeth was seriously interested in alchemy throughout her life.

In physics, medicine, and psychology, as well, older concepts vied with new. Traditional learning apportioned all physical matter into four elements: earth, air, fire, and water. Each of these was thought to be a different combination of the four "qualities" of the universe: hot, cold,

Alchemists employed relatively sophisticated equipment in their futile search for the "philosopher's stone," a reputed substance supposed to possess the property of changing other metals into gold and silver.

hand (*Othello,* 3.4.39); those of age were "a moist eye, a dry hand, a yellow cheek, a white beard, a decreasing leg, an increasing belly" (*2 Henry IV,* 1.2.179–81). A common remedy for illness was to let blood and thereby purge the body of unwanted humors.

The name traditionally associated with such theories was that of Galen, the most celebrated of ancient writers on medicine (c. 130 A.D.). A more revolutionary name was that of Paracelsus, a famous German physician (c. 1493–1541) who attacked the traditional medical learning of his time and urged a more unfettered pragmatic research into pharmacy and medicine. Such experimentalism bore fruit in the anatomical research of Vesalius (1514–1564) and in William Harvey's investigations of the circulation of the blood (c. 1616). Nevertheless, the practice of medicine in Renaissance times remained under the influence of the "humors" theory until quite late, and its ideas are found throughout Shakespeare's writings.

moist, and dry. Earth combined cold and dry; air, hot and moist; fire, hot and dry; and water, cold and moist. Earth and water were the baser or lower elements, confined to the physical world; fire and air were aspiring elements, tending upward. Humans, as a microcosm of the larger universe, contained in themselves the four elements. The individual's temperament, or "humor" or "complexion," depended on which "humor" predominated in that person. The four humors in humans corresponded to the four elements of physical matter. The blood was hot and moist, like air; yellow bile or choler was hot and dry, like fire; phlegm was cold and moist, like water; and black bile was cold and dry, like earth. A predominance of blood in an individual created a sanguine or cheerful temperament (or humor), yellow bile produced a choleric or irascible temperament, phlegm produced a phlegmatic or stolid temperament, and black bile produced a melancholic temperament. Diet could affect the balance among these humors, since an excess of a particular food would stimulate overproduction of one humor. The stomach and the liver, which converted food into humors, were regarded as the seat of human passions. The spleen was thought to be the seat of laughter, sudden impulse, or caprice, and also melancholy. (Hotspur, in *1 Henry IV,* is said to be "governed by a spleen," 5.2.19.) Strong emotional reactions could be explained in terms of the physiology of the humors: in anger, the blood rushed to the head and thereby produced a flush of red color and staring eyes; in fear, the blood migrated to the heart and thus left the face and liver pale, and so on. Sighs supposedly cost the heart a drop of blood, while wine could refortify it (as Falstaff insists in *2 Henry IV,* 4.3.90–123). The signs of youth were warmth and moisture, as in Desdemona's "hot and moist"

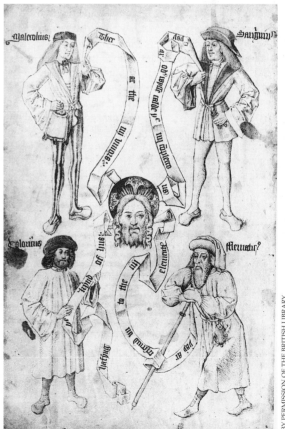

The four humors of black bile, blood, yellow bile or choler, and phlegm, as shown in this illustration from an illuminated manuscript, were believed to govern the human personality by producing a disposition toward melancholic, sanguine, choleric, or phlegmatic temperaments.

Learning

In learning generally, and in theories of education, new ideas conflicted with old. The curriculum of schools and colleges in the Renaissance was inherited largely from the Middle Ages and displayed many traditional characteristics. The curriculum consisted of the seven Liberal Arts: a lower division, called the trivium, comprised of grammar, rhetoric, and logic; and an upper division, called the quadrivium, comprised of arithmetic, geometry, astronomy, and music. In addition, there were the philosophical studies associated chiefly with Aristotle: natural philosophy, ethics, and metaphysics.

Aristotle's name had a towering influence in medieval times and remained important to the Renaissance as well. Even among his Renaissance admirers, however, Aristotle proved more compelling in practical matters than in the abstract scholastic reasoning associated with his name in the Middle Ages. The Italian Aristotelians whose work made its way into England were interested primarily in the science of human behavior. Aristotelian ethics was for them a practical subject, telling people how to live usefully and well and how to govern themselves politically. Rhetoric was the science of persuasion, enabling people to use eloquence for socially useful goals. Poetry was a kind of rhetoric, a language of persuasion which dramatists, too, might use for morally pragmatic ends.

At the same time, new thinkers were daring to attack Aristotle by name as a symbol of traditional medieval thought. The attack was not always fair to Aristotle himself, whose work had been bent to the *a priori* purposes of much medieval scholasticism. Nevertheless, his name had assumed such symbolic importance that he had to be confronted directly. The Huguenot logician Petrus Ramus (1515–1572), defiantly proclaiming that "everything that Aristotle taught is false," argued for rules of logic as derived from observation. He urged, for example, that his students learn about rhetoric from observing in detail Cicero's effect on his listeners, rather than by the rote practice of syllogism. Actually, Ramus's thought was less revolutionary in its concepts of logic than in the tremendous ferment of opinion caused by his iconoclastic teaching.

A basic issue at stake in the anti-Aristotelian movement was that of traditional authority versus independent observation. How do people best acquire true knowledge—through the teachings of their predecessors or through their own discovery? The issue had profound implications for religious truth as well: should individuals heed the collective wisdom of the earthly church or read the Bible with their individual perceptions as their guide? Is "reason" an accretive wisdom handed down by authority or a quality of the individual soul? Obviously, a middle ground exists between the two extremes, and no new thinker of the Renaissance professed to abandon entirely the use of ancient author-

ity. For men like Henricus Agrippa (1486–1535) and Sir Francis Bacon (1561–1626), however, scholastic tradition had exerted its oppressive influence far too long. Authority needed to be examined critically and scientifically. Bacon, in his *The Advancement of Learning* (1605), fought against the blind acceptance of ancient wisdom and argued that "knowledge derived from Aristotle, and exempted from liberty of examination, will not rise again higher than the knowledge of Aristotle." Sir Walter Ralegh and others joined in the excited new search for what human "reason" could discover when set free from scholastic restraint. Such belief in the perfectibility of human reason owed some of its inspiration to Italian Neoplatonic humanists like Giovanni Pico della Mirandola (1463–1494), who, in his *Oration on the Dignity of Man*, celebrated a human race "constrained by no limits" in accordance with the potential of its own free will. The new learning did not seem to trouble these men in their religious faith, although a tension between scientific observation and faith in miracles was to become plentifully evident in the seventeenth century.

The Nature of Humankind

Medieval thought generally assigned to humankind a uniquely superior place in the order of creation on earth. That assumption of superiority rested on biblical and patristic teachings about the hierarchy of creation, in which humanity stood at the apex of physical creation nearest God and the angels. Humankind was thus supreme on earth in the so-called chain of being. Human reason, though subject to error because of sinfulness, enabled humans to aspire toward divinity. Humans were, in the view of medieval philosophers, the great amphibians, as well as the microcosm of the universe, part bestial and part immortal, doomed by Adam's fall to misery and death in this life but promised eternal salvation through Christ's atonement. Right reason, properly employed, could lead to the truths of revealed Christianity and thus give humankind a glimpse of the heavenly perfection one day to be ours. Renaissance Neoplatonism, as expounded, for example, in the writings of Marsilio Ficino, Pico della Mirandola, and Baldassare Castiglione (in *The Courtier*, translated by Sir Thomas Hoby in 1561), offered humanity a vision of a platonic ladder, extending from the perception of physical beauty to contemplation of the platonic idea of beauty and finally to the experiencing of God's transcendent love.

Protestant thought of the Renaissance did not wholly disagree with this formulation, but it did place a major new emphasis on human reprobation. The idea was not new, for Saint Augustine (354–430) had insisted on human depravity and our total dependence on God's inscrutable grace, but, in the years of the Reformation, this theology took on a new urgency. Martin Luther

(1483–1540), by rejecting veneration of the Virgin Mary and the saints, and by taking away the sacraments of confession and penance, by which individual Christians could seek the institutional comforts of the Catholic Church, exposed the individual sinner to agonies of conscience that could result in a sense of alienation and loss. The rewards were great for those who found new faith in God's infinite goodness, but the hazards of predestinate damnation were fearsome to those who were less sure of their spiritual welfare. Luther's God was inscrutable, majestic, and infallible. Luther's God decreed salvation for the elect and damnation for all others, and His will could not be challenged or questioned. The individual was to blame for sin, even though God hardened the hearts of the reprobate. John Calvin (1509–1564) placed even greater stress on predestinate good and evil and insisted that the grace of salvation was founded on God's freely given mercy that humans could not possibly deserve. Salvation was God's to give or withhold as He wished; humans might not repine that in His incomprehensible wisdom God has "barred the door of life to those whom He has given over to damnation." Faced with such

a view of human spiritual destiny, the individual Christian's lot was one of potential tragedy. The human soul was a battleground of good and evil.

Michel de Montaigne (1533–1592), Shakespeare's great French contemporary, provided a very different and heterodox way of thinking about human imperfection. In his "Apology for Raymond Sebond" and other of his essays, Montaigne questioned the assumption of humanity's superiority to the animal kingdom, and in doing so gave Shakespeare a fundamentally different way to consider the nature of humankind—a way that reflects itself, for example, in Hamlet's observations on humans as "quintessence of dust." Montaigne stressed humans' arrogance, vanity, and frailty. He was unconvinced of humanity's purported moral superiority to the animals and argued that animals are no less endowed with a soul. Montaigne undermined, in other words, the hierarchy in which the human race was the unquestioned master of the physical world, just as Copernican science overturned the earth-centered cosmos and Machiavelli's political system dismissed as an improbable fiction the divinely constituted hierarchy of the state. Montaigne's very choice of

This guide, graphically setting forth the ideals to which every English gentlewoman and gentleman should aspire, illustrates the Renaissance concept that outward deportment and accomplishments should correctly and invariably mirror a person's inner nature.

the essay as his favorite literary form bespeaks his commitment to attempts and explorations, rather than to definite solutions; etymologically, the very word "essay" signifies an exploration or inquiry. Montaigne was not alone in his skepticism about human nature; his ideas had much in common with Bernardino Telesio's *De Rerum Natura* and with the writings of the Italian Giordano Bruno. Montaigne was followed in the seventeenth century by that overpowering iconoclast, Thomas Hobbes, who extended the concept of mechanical laws governing human society and human psychology. Hobbes postdates Shakespeare, to be sure, but one has only to consider Iago's philosophy of the assertive individual will (in *Othello*) or Edmund's contempt for his father Gloucester's astrological pieties (in *King Lear*) to see the enormous impact on Shakespeare of the new heterodoxies of his age. Shakespeare makes us aware that skeptical thought can be used by dangerous men like Iago, Edmund, and Richard III to promote their own villainies in a world no longer held together by the certitudes of traditional faith, but he also shows us the gullibility of some traditionalists and the abuses of power that can be perpetrated in the name of ancient and divine privilege by a king like Richard II. Above all, Shakespeare delights in the play of mind among competing ideas, inviting us to wonder, for example, if Caliban in *The Tempest* is not invested with natural qualities that Prospero, his Christian colonizer, does not sufficiently understand, and whether some of the other supposedly civilized Europeans who come to Caliban's island do not have a great deal to learn from its uncivilized beauty.

LONDON THEATERS AND DRAMATIC COMPANIES

Throughout Shakespeare's life, the propriety of acting any plays at all was a matter of bitter controversy. Indeed, when one considers the power and earnestness of the opposition, one is surprised that such a wealth of dramatic excellence could come into being and that Shakespeare's plays should reflect so little the anger and hostility generated by this continuing conflict.

Religious and Moral Opposition to the Theater

From the 1570s onward, and even earlier, the city fathers of London revealed an ever-increasing distrust of the public performance of plays. They fretted about the dangers of plague and of riotous assembly. They objected to the fact that apprentices idly wasted their time instead of working in their shops. And always the municipal authorities suspected immorality. Thus, by an order of the Common Council of London, dated December 6, 1574, the players were put under severe restrictions.

The order cites the reasons. The players, it was charged, had been acting in the innyards of the city, which in consequence were haunted by great multitudes of people, especially youths. These gatherings had been the occasions of frays and quarrels, "evil practices of incontinency in great inns"; the players published "uncomely and unshamefast speeches and doings," withdrew the Queen's subjects from divine service on Sundays and holidays, wasted the money of "poor and fond persons," gave opportunity to pick pockets, uttered "busy and seditious matters," and injured and maimed people by the falling of their scaffolds and by weapons and powder used in plays. The order goes on to state the Common Council's fear that if the plays, which had been forbidden on account of the plague, should be resumed, God's wrath would manifest itself by an increase of the infection. Therefore, no innkeeper, tavernkeeper, or other person might cause or suffer to be openly played "any play, interlude, comedy, tragedy, matter, or show" which had not been first licensed by the mayor and the Court of Aldermen.

The mayor and aldermen did not always state their case plainly, because Queen Elizabeth was a patron of the players, and because the players had friends and patrons in the Privy Council and among the nobility; sometimes, however, they did so quite boldly. One sees the case against plays stated syllogistically in the following words of Thomas White, a preacher at Paul's Cross in 1577:

Look but upon the common plays of London, and see the multitude that flocketh to them and followeth them! Behold the sumptuous theater houses, a continual monument of London prodigality and folly! But I understand they are now forbidden because of the plague. I like the policy well if it hold still, for a disease is but botched and patched up that is not cured in the cause, and the cause of plagues is sin, if you look to it well, and the cause of sin are plays. Therefore the cause of plagues are plays. (From *A Sermon preached at Paul's Cross . . . in the Time of the Plague,* 1578.)

Moved, no doubt, by the prohibition of the Common Council, James Burbage, with a company of actors under the patronage of the Earl of Leicester, leased a site in Shoreditch, a London suburb in Middlesex, beyond the immediate jurisdiction of the official enemies in the Common Council, whose authority extended only to the city limits. By 1576, he had completed the Theatre. Perhaps he called it "the Theatre" because it had no competitor (other than the Red Lion, established in 1567 and used seemingly as a playing place for feasts and festival days in the performance style of Corpus Christi and saints' plays). Burbage erected what may have been England's first permanent commercial theatrical building. In general, the building combined features of the innyard and the animal-baiting house, having a central and probably paved courtyard open to the sky (like an innyard) and sur-

The George Inn of Southwark, England, London's only surviving galleried inn, was destroyed by fire in 1676 but rebuilt the following year with two galleries instead of the original three. Despite these changes, the George Inn gives us the best picture we have of the kind of space in which traveling companies could mount their plays on bare platform stages.

rounding galleries on all sides (like an animal-baiting house). Burbage erected a stage at one side of the circular arena and put dressing rooms behind it to form the "tiring house" or backstage area for the actors; the facade of this "tiring house" served as a visible backdrop to the stage itself. Burbage's Theatre became the model for other public playhouses, such as the Curtain, the Swan, and the Globe, which were constructed later.

By building his playhouse in Shoreditch, Burbage gained immunity from the London authorities. The city fathers could not suppress plays or control them with perfect success if they were performed in Middlesex, or in the "liberty" of Blackfriars and similar districts exempted by charters from London's civic authority (see "London's Private Theaters," below), or (in the case of later playhouses) on the Bankside across the Thames in Surrey. In order to get at them in these suburban regions, the city authorities had to petition the Queen's Privy Council to give orders to the magistrates and officers of the law in these counties. The Queen's Privy Council, although always on the most polite terms with the Lord Mayor and

his brethren of the city and always open to the argument that the assemblage of crowds caused the spread of the plague, was to a much less degree in sympathy with the moral scruples of the city. Current arguments for the plays, derived from the works of scholars, poets, and playwrights, were numerous and often heard: namely, that classical antiquity gave precedent for dramatic spectacles; that by drawing a true picture of both the bad and the good in life, plays enabled people to choose the good; that people should have wholesome amusement; and that plays provided livelihood for loyal subjects of the Queen.

Of these arguments, to be sure, the Privy Council made little use, resting the case for plays instead on what was, no doubt, an unanswerable argument: that since the players were to appear before Her Majesty, especially during the Christmas/Shrovetide period, the players needed practice in order to prepare themselves to please the royal taste. A good deal of politic fencing ensued, and, so far as orders, complaints, and denunciations were concerned, the reforming opposition had much the better of it. The preachers thundered against plays. Pamphleteers denounced all matters pertaining to the stage: Stephen Gosson in *The School of Abuse, Containing a Pleasant Invective Against Poets, Pipers, Players, Jesters and Suchlike Caterpillars of a Commonwealth* (1579) and other works; Philip Stubbes in *The Anatomy of Abuses* (1583); and finally and most furiously of all, William Prynne in *Histrio-Mastix: The Players' Scourge or Actor's Tragedy* (1633). Gosson spoke of plays as "the inventions of the devil, the offerings of idolatry, the pomp of worldlings, the blossoms of vanity, the root of apostacy, food of iniquity, riot and adultery." "Detest them," he warned. "Players are masters of vice, teachers of wantonness, spurs to impurity, the sons of idleness."

At first, such diatribes represented an extreme reforming opinion obviously not shared by a majority of London viewers. They kept coming to plays, and the flourishing public theaters attracted the talents of the age's leading dramatists. An ominous note of polarization was sounded, however, early in the reign of James I (1603–1625) when the rift between the Puritans and the court broke into open antagonism. After about 1604, when James alienated the Puritans at the Hampton Court Conference, the split between popular audiences and the best drama of the age became increasingly evident. Shakespeare's company, now the King's men, gravitated, whether through choice or necessity, toward the precinct of the court. Although the public theater, with its capacity for large audiences, continued to serve as a lively center of theatrical activity, Puritan opposition to the stage gathered momentum. Many dramatists, in turn, grew more satirical of London customs and more attuned to courtly tastes. Eventually, Puritan hostility to the theater was at least part of the motive behind Parliament's order to close the theaters in 1642.

The Public Theaters

A year or more after Burbage built the Theatre in 1576, the Curtain was put up near it by Philip Henslowe, or possibly by Henry Laneman, or Lanman. About ten years later, Philip Henslowe built the Rose, the first playhouse on the Bankside (the southern bank of the Thames River). In 1599, James Burbage's sons Richard and Cuthbert dismantled the Theatre because of trouble about the lease of the land and rebuilt it as the Globe on the Bankside. This Globe playhouse burned on June 29, 1613, from the discharge of cannon backstage during a performance of *All Is True*, a play thought to be identical with Shakespeare's *Henry VIII*. The Globe was rebuilt, probably in its original polygonal form, that is, essentially round with a large number of sides. In 1600, Henslowe built the Fortune as a theater for the Lord Admiral's men, who were chief rivals to the Lord Chamberlain's men. The companies were differently organized, in that the Lord Chamberlain's men were joint sharers in their own enterprise and owners of their own theatrical building, whereas Henslowe owned the Fortune (and the Rose before it) and

served as landlord to the Admiral's men—no doubt profiting handsomely from their activities.

Various records of these theatrical buildings have survived. One such record is the Fortune contract, preserved at Dulwich College among other invaluable papers of Philip Henslowe, theatrical entrepreneur and father-in-law of the famous Edward Alleyn of the Lord Admiral's men. The contract for building the Fortune was let to the same contractor who had built the new Globe, and, since the specifications required that the Fortune should be like the Globe in all its main features, except that it was to be square instead of polygonal, we may gain from these specifications an idea of the Globe. A second documentary record is a drawing of the Swan, a Bankside theater, accompanying a description of the playhouse by Johannes De Witt, who visited London in 1596. The drawing, which was discovered in the University Library at Utrecht, is the work of one Van Buchell and may be based on drawings by De Witt himself. Besides the Fortune contract and the Swan drawing, we have two or three little pictures of the Elizabethan public stage on the title pages of published plays, the most important being that on the title page of William Alabaster's *Roxana* (1632). Just recently, in 1989, the discovery and excavation of the foundations of the Rose playhouse and partial excavation of the Globe playhouse foundations in Southwark, together with the construction of a modern replica of the Globe playhouse near the site of these two theaters, have added invaluable archeological information about the dimensions of that acting arena.

The London Public Stage

From these documents and pictures and from scattered references to the theaters, as well as from extended studies of stage directions and scenic conditions in plays themselves, we have a fairly clear idea of the public stage in London. Its features are these: a pit about seventy feet in diameter, usually circular and open to the sky; surrounding this, galleries in three tiers, containing the most expensive seats; and a rectangular stage, about forty-three by twenty-seven feet, wider than it was deep, raised about five and one-half feet above the surface of the yard, sometimes built on trestles so that it could be removed if the house was also customarily used for bearbaiting and bullbaiting. The flat, open stage usually contained one trapdoor. Part of the stage was afforded some protection from the weather by a brightly decorated wooden roof supported by posts, constituting the "heavens." Above this roof was a "hut," perhaps containing suspension gear for ascents and descents. (The Rose appears originally to have been generally smaller than what is described here, with a stage that tapered toward the front to a width of only twenty-five feet or so. The building was somewhat expanded in 1592 but was

BY PERMISSION OF THE FOLGER SHAKESPEARE LIBRARY

This drawing of an Elizabethan public stage appeared on the title page of the published version of William Alabaster's play Roxana *(1632).*

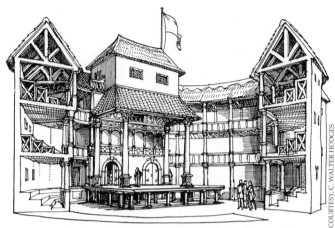

This diagram of the Swan Theatre (left) by Van Buchell (c. 1596), based on the observations of Johannes De Witt, shows features of the public playhouse shared by James Burbage's Theatre and the Globe. A modern sketch of the Swan Theatre (right) shows the open, encircling roof and a full view of the tiring house. Like the Globe and other open theaters, the design of the Swan seems to resemble the Elizabethan innyard with an added stage.

still small compared with other theaters. The original building shows no certain evidence of a roof over the stage supported by pillars, but the later building appears to have had roof pillars at the front of the stage.)

At the back of the stage was a partition wall, the "tiring-house facade," with at least two doors in it connecting the stage with the actors' dressing rooms or "tiring house." In the Rose, the tiring-house facade seems to have curved with the polygonal shape of the theater building, but in the DeWitt drawing the Swan facade looks perfectly straight across. Some theaters appear to have had no more than two doors, left and right, as shown in the Swan drawing; other theaters may have had a third door in the center. The arrangement of the Globe playhouse in this important matter cannot be finally determined, although some particular scenes from Shakespeare's plays seem to demand a third door. In any case, the so-called inner stage, long supposed to have stood at the rear of the Elizabeth stage, almost certainly did not exist. A more modest "discovery space" could be provided at one of the curtained doors when needed, as for example in *The Tempest* when Ferdinand and Miranda are suddenly "discovered" at their game of chess by Prospero. Such scenes never called for extensive action within the discovery space, however, and, indeed, the number of

such discoveries in Elizabethan plays is very few. Well-to-do spectators who may have been seated in the gallery above the rear of the stage could not see into the discovery space. Accordingly, it was used sparingly and only for brief visual effects. Otherwise, the actors performed virtually all their scenes on the open stage. Sometimes curtains were hung over the tiring-house facade between the doors to facilitate scenes of concealment, as when Polonius and Claudius eavesdrop on Hamlet and Ophelia.

An upper station was sometimes used as an acting space, but not nearly so often as was once supposed. The gallery seats above the stage, sometimes known as the "Lord's room," were normally sold to well-to-do spectators. (We can see such spectators in the Swan drawing and in Alabaster's *Roxana*.) Occasionally, these box seats could be used by the actors, as when Juliet appears at her window (it is never called a balcony). In military sequences, as in the *Henry VI* plays, the tiring-house facade could represent the walls of a besieged city, with the city's defenders appearing "on the walls" (i.e., in the gallery above the stage) in order to parley with the besieging enemy standing below on the main stage. Such scenes were relatively infrequent, however, and usually required only a small number of persons to be aloft. A music room, when needed, could be located in one of the gallery boxes

Elizabethan dancers, shown above, perform on a stage below a gallery of musicians. Imported stage designs from Italy made more use of perspective scenery than did the commercial theaters.

over the stage, but public theaters did not emulate the private stages with music rooms and music between the acts until some time around 1609.

The use of scenery was almost wholly unknown on the Elizabethan public stage, although we do find occasional hints of the use of labels to designate a certain door or area as a fixed location (as, perhaps, in *The Comedy of Errors*). For the most part, the scene was unlimited and the concept of space was fluid. No proscenium arch or curtain stood between the actors and the audience, and so the action could not be easily interrupted. Only belatedly did the public companies adopt the private-theater practice of entr'acte music, as we have seen. Most popular Elizabethan plays were written to be performed nonstop. Five-act structure had little currency, especially at first, and the occasional act divisions in the published versions of Shakespeare's plays may be nonauthorial. Acting tempo was brisk. The Prologue of *Romeo and Juliet* speaks of "the two hours' traffic of our stage." Plays were performed in the afternoons and had to be completed by

dark in order to allow the audience to return safely to London. During the winter season, playing time was severely restricted. Outbreaks of plague often occasioned the closing of the theaters, especially in warm weather.

A capacity audience for the popular theaters came to about 2,000 to 3,000 persons. (The recently excavated Rose playhouse foundations suggest an audience there of around 2,000.) For the most part, the audience was affluent, consisting chiefly of the gentry and of London's substantial mercantile citizenry who paid two to three pence or more for gallery seats or the "Lord's room," but the ample pit or yard also provided room for small shopkeepers and artisans who stood for a penny. The spectators were lively, demanding, and intelligent. Although Shakespeare does allow Hamlet to refer disparagingly on one occasion to the "groundlings" who "for the most part are capable of nothing but inexplicable dumbshows and noise" (*Hamlet*, 3.2.11–12), Shakespeare appealed to the keenest understanding of his whole audience, thereby achieving a breadth of vision seldom found in continental courtly drama of the same period. The vitality and financial success of the Elizabethan public theater is without parallel in English history. The city of London itself, in 1600 or so, had only about 100,000 inhabitants, yet throughout Shakespeare's career several companies were competing simultaneously for this audience and constantly producing new plays. Most new plays ran for only a few performances, so that the acting companies were always in rehearsal with new shows. The actors needed phenomenal memories and a gift of improvisation as well. Their acting seems to have been of a high caliber, despite the speed with which they worked. Among other things, many of them were expert fencers and singers.

The London public stage inherited many of its practices from native and medieval traditions. The fluid, open stage, with spectators on four sides, recalled the arena staging of many early Corpus Christi cycles, saints' plays, and morality plays. The adult professional companies were, as we have seen, descended from the itinerant troupes that had acted their plays throughout England in guildhalls, private residences, monastic houses and schools, and perhaps occasionally outdoors on booth stages (though the evidence for this last possible venue is scarce). The Elizabethan tiring-house facade and platform stage may have owed much to the kinds of theatrical space that touring actors had known, and perhaps to the arrangement of a booth stage and a trestle platform set up against one wall of an innyard where the guests of the inn could enjoy a performance, along with standing spectators in the yard. When the itinerant actors had set up their plays in noblemen's banqueting halls or at court, at any rate, they encountered another space that had an important influence on their concept of a theater: the Tudor hall. We must next examine the significance of this indoor theatrical setting.

The Tudor Hall

The Tudor banqueting hall played a major part in the staging of much early Tudor drama. Medwall's *Fulgens and Lucrece*, one of the earliest such plays, was written to be performed during the intervals of a state banquet. The patrician guests were seated at tables, while servingmen bustled to and fro or stood crowded together at the doors in the hall "screen." This screen or partition traversed the lower end of the rectangular hall, providing a passageway to the kitchens and to the outside. Its doors—often two, sometimes three—were normally curtained to prevent drafts. This arrangement of the doors bears an interesting resemblance to that of many playhouses in late Elizabethan England, both public and private. Moreover, hall screens and passageways were normally surmounted by a gallery, where musicians could play—an architectural feature markedly resembling the upper galleries of late Elizabethan theaters. Could the Tudor hall screen provide a natural facade for dramatic action? Perhaps it did, although records from Shakespeare's era only rarely document an actual performance in front of the screen, whereas performances were common at the upper end of the hall in front of the dais or in the midst of the hall, where the persons of highest social rank sitting on the dais would have had the best view. The actors of *Fulgens and Lucrece* clearly made use of the doorways in the hall screen, sometimes joking with the servingmen as the actors pushed their way into the hall, but they probably acted in the center, among the spectators' tables. John Heywood's *Play of the Weather* calls for a similar *mise en scène*. Although this ready-made "stage" sufficed for most Tudor plays, the actors sometimes provided additional stage structures; *Weather,* for example, calls for a throne room into which Jupiter can retire without leaving the hall. Similar structures could represent a shop, an orchard, a mountain, or what have you.

Guild and town halls, where players on tour performed before the mayor and council (and sometimes a wider public), provided a similar physical environment except that we cannot be sure that such spaces had galleries in the sixteenth century. Since the gallery is not necessary for many Tudor plays, the players may well have gained experience in halls of this kind that influenced their techniques of staging once they had gravitated to London.

Although both medieval and continental drama offered traditions of multiple staging, in which a series of simultaneously visible and adjacent structures would represent as fixed locations all the playing areas needed for the performance of a play, Tudor indoor staging seems to have made less use of this method than was once supposed. Nor did the various indoor theaters of Tudor England make extensive use of neoclassical staging from Italy, with its street scene in perspective created by means of lath-and-canvas stage "houses." Italian scenery of this sort came into use sooner in the court masque than in regular drama. Nevertheless, we do find in the Tudor indoor theater a neoclassical tendency toward a fixed locale, in preference to the unlimited open stage. *Gammer Gurton's Needle*, for example, acted probably in a university hall, seems to have used one stage structure, or possibly one

The Tudor banqueting hall provided a place to "stage" much early Tudor drama. The actors performed on the floor among the tables of the guests. The Middle Temple Hall, shown here, later served as the location for a performance of Shakespeare's Twelfth Night *on February 2, 1602. The Middle Temple is one of the Inns of Court, where young men studied law and occasionally relaxed by staging dramatic entertainments.*

door, to represent Gammer's house throughout the action, and another to represent Dame Chat's house. Shakespeare may have been influenced by this kind of fixed-locale staging in *The Comedy of Errors*. (Alan Nelson's *Early Cambridge Theaters*, 1994, is an important resource for school staging.)

The Private Stage

Despite such influences on the public stage, the most significant contribution of the Tudor hall and its hall screen was to the so-called private stage of the late Elizabethan period—"private" in the sense of being intended for a more select and courtly audience than that which frequented the "public" theaters. In the 1570s, choir boys began performing professionally to courtly and intellectual audiences in London. The choir boys had long performed plays for the royal and noble households to which they were attached, but in the 1570s they were, in effect, organized into professional acting companies. Sebastian Westcote and the Children of Paul's may have originated this enterprise. Their theater was apparently some indoor hall in the vicinity of St. Paul's in London, outfitted much like the typical domestic Tudor hall to which the boys had grown accustomed. Comparable indoor "private" theaters soon followed at Blackfriars and Whitefriars.

At some point, a low stage was constructed in front of the hall screen, and seats were provided for all the spectators. Many of these seats were in the "pit," or what we would call the "orchestra," facing toward the stage at one end of the rectangular room. Other seats were in galleries along both sides of the room; these were quite elaborate

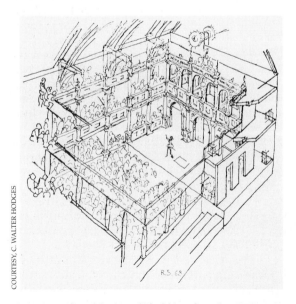

COURTESY, C. WALTER HODGES

A reconstruction of the Second Blackfriars, featuring a rectangular stage, a tiring house with three doors, and a gallery.

in the so-called Second Blackfriars of 1596 and provided two or three tiers of seats. Elegant box seats stood at either side of the stage itself. The Second Blackfriars had a permanently built tiring house to the rear of the stage, with probably three doors. Above it was a gallery used variously as a lord's room, a music room, and an upper station for occasional acting.

The private theater flourished during the 1580s and again after 1598–1599, having been closed down during most of the 1590s because of its satirical activities. Although it was a commercial theater, it was "private" in its clientele, because its high price of admission (sixpence) excluded those who could stand in the yards of the "public" theaters for a penny (roughly the equivalent of an hour's wage for a skilled worker). Plays written for the more select audiences of the "private" theaters tended to be more satirical and oriented to courtly values than those written for the "public" theaters, although the distinction is by no means absolute.

London Private Theaters

The important private theaters of Shakespeare's London were two in the precinct, or "liberty," of Blackfriars, an early one in Whitefriars about which little is known, a later one there, and a theater at Paul's, the exact location and nature of which is not known. In the thirteenth century, the mother house of the Dominican friars, or Blackfriars, was established on the sloping ground between St. Paul's Cathedral and the river. It was a sizable institution, ultimately covering about five acres of ground. It stood on the very border of the city and, after the custom of the time, was made a liberty; that is to say, it had its own local government and was removed from the immediate jurisdiction of the city of London. After the suppression of the friary and the confiscation of its lands, the jealousy existing between the Privy Council, representing the crown, and the mayor and aldermen, representing the city and probably also the rights of property holders, prevented the district of the Blackfriars from losing its political independence of the municipality. It was still a liberty and therefore attractive to players and other persons wishing to avoid the London authorities. At the same time, aristocrats residing in the area required protection, and the crown had certain rights still in its control.

From 1576 to 1584, the Children of the Queen's Chapel, one of the two most important companies of boy actors, had used a hall in the precinct of Blackfriars in which to act their plays. Here were acted at least some of John Lyly's plays. In 1596, James Burbage purchased property in this precinct and seems to have spent a good deal of money in its adaptation for use as an indoor theater (the so-called Second Blackfriars). He probably appreciated its advantages over Cripplegate or the Bankside of greater proximity to London and of protection against the elements, particularly for use in winter. But the aristocratic residents of the Blackfriars by petition to the Privy Council prevented him from making use of his theater. Plays within the city proper had only recently been finally and successfully prohibited, and the petitioners no doubt objected to their intrusion into Blackfriars on the grounds that the plays and their crowds were a nuisance.

Burbage's new indoor theater may have lain idle from the time of its preparation until 1600; but, in any case, in that year it became the scene of many plays. It was let by lease for the use of the Children of the Chapel, who in 1604 became the Children of the Queen's Revels. Their theater managers brought into their service a number of new dramatists—Ben Jonson, John Marston, George Chapman, and later John Webster. The vogue of the plays acted by the Children of the Chapel was so great as to damage the patronage of the established companies and to compel them to go on the road. Out of this rivalry between the children and the adult actors arose that open competition alluded to in *Hamlet* (2.2.328–362) and sometimes referred to today as the "War of the Theaters." The skirmishes were relatively brief, arising in part from a clash of personalities among Jonson, Marston, and Thomas Dekker, but the debate between public and private acting companies was significant as an indication of whether London drama would continue to play to large popular audiences or would increasingly turn to a more courtly clientele. In 1608, the Burbage interests secured the evacuation of the lease, so that the theater in Blackfriars became the winter playhouse of Shakespeare's company from that time forward.

System of Patronage

In 1572, common players of interludes, along with minstrels, bearwards, and fencers, were included within the hard terms of the act for the punishment of vagabonds, provided that such common players were not enrolled as the servants of a baron of the realm or of some honorable person of greater degree. The result was a system of patronage of theatrical companies in Elizabethan and Jacobean times, according to which players became the "servants" of some nobleman or of some member of the royal family.

By the time Shakespeare came to London in the late 1580s, many of these companies were already in existence, some of which long antedated the passage of the act of 1572. Provincial records of the visits of players, to be sure, sometimes failed to distinguish actors from acrobats or other public performers who were similarly organized. Nonetheless, we have evidence that various companies of players performed in London and elsewhere in the late 1580s under the patronage of the Queen, the Earl of Worcester, the Earl of Leicester, the Earl of Oxford, the Earl of Sussex, the Lord Admiral, and

Charles, Lord Howard of Effingham. These companies were eventually much reduced in number; usually only three adult companies acted at any given time in London during Shakespeare's prime. In addition, the children's companies, privately controlled, acted intermittently but at times very successfully. The most important of these were the Children of the Chapel and Queen's Revels and the Children of Paul's, but there were also boy players of Windsor, Eton College, the Merchant Taylors, Westminster, and other schools.

Shakespeare and the London Theatrical Companies

We know that by 1592 Shakespeare had arrived in London and had achieved sufficient notice as a young playwright to arouse the resentment of a rival dramatist, Robert Greene. In that year, shortly before he died, Greene—or possibly his editor after Greene's death—lashed out at an "upstart crow, beautified with our feathers," who had had the audacity to fancy himself "the only Shake-scene in a country" (*Groats-worth of Wit*). This petulant outburst was plainly directed at Shakespeare, since Greene included in his remarks a parody of some lines from *3 Henry VI*. As a university man and an established dramatist, Greene seems to have resented the intrusion into his profession of a mere player who was not university trained. This "upstart crow" was achieving a very real success on the London stage. Shakespeare had probably already written *The Comedy of Errors*, *Love's Labor's Lost*, *The Two Gentlemen of Verona*, the *Henry VI* plays, and *Titus Andronicus*, and perhaps also *Richard III* and *The Taming of the Shrew*.

For which acting company or companies had he written these plays, however? By 1594, we know that Shakespeare was an established member of the Lord Chamberlain's company, important enough, in fact, to have been named, along with Will Kempe and Richard Burbage, as payee for court performances on December 26 and 28 of 1594. But when had he joined the Chamberlain's men, and for whom had he written and acted previously? These are the problems of the so-called dark years, during which Shakespeare came to London (perhaps around 1587) and got started on his career.

One prestigious acting company he could have joined was the Earl of Leicester's company, led by James Burbage, father of Shakespeare's later colleague, Richard Burbage. Leicester was a favorite minister of Queen Elizabeth until his death in 1588, and his company of actors received from the Queen in 1574 an extraordinary patent to perform plays anywhere in England, despite all local prohibitions, provided that the plays were approved beforehand by the master of the Queen's Revels. Since an act of 1572 had outlawed all unlicensed troupes, Leicester's men and similar companies attached to important noblemen were given a virtual monopoly over public acting. In 1576, Burbage built the Theatre for his company in the northeast suburbs of

Clowns were enormously popular on the Elizabethan stage. Of the many Elizabethan clowns whose names are known to us, Richard Tarlton is one of the most famous. (Will Kempe, in Shakespeare's company, the Lord Chamberlain's men, is another; see pp. lxviii-lxix.) Tarlton is shown here inside an elaborate letter T, dancing a jig with his pipe and tabor. Such jigs were often used at the conclusion of a play.

London. This group also toured the provinces: Leicester's company visited Stratford-upon-Avon in 1587. Conceivably, Shakespeare served an apprenticeship in this company, though no evidence exists to prove a connection. Leicester's company had lost some of its prominence in 1583, when several of its best men joined the newly formed Queen's men, with Richard Tarlton as its most famous actor. The remaining members of Leicester's company disbanded in 1588 upon the death of the Earl, and many of its principal actors ultimately became part of Lord Strange's company. These probably included George Bryan, Will Kempe, and Thomas Pope, all of whom subsequently went on to become Lord Chamberlain's men.

Lord Strange's (The Earl of Derby's) Men

The Queen's men gained an extraordinary prominence in the 1580s, as Scott McMillin and Sally-Beth MacLean have shown in the *Queen's Men and Their Plays* (1998). This acting group was assembled under royal sponsorship as an instrument of furthering the Protestant Reformation through its performances of plays, and did so with notable success, although it then declined rapidly in the early 1590s chiefly because as a touring company it was unprepared to compete with the new companies that learned how to succeed in the metropolis by staging a wide vari-

ety of plays in a fixed London theater. Prominent among the acting companies to which Shakespeare could have belonged when he came to London, probably in the late 1580s, were Lord Strange's men, the Lord Admiral's men, the Earl of Pembroke's men, and the Earl of Sussex's men. Scholars have long speculated that Shakespeare may have joined the company of Ferdinando Stanley, Lord Strange (who in 1593 became the Earl of Derby). The names of George Bryan, Will Kempe, and Thomas Pope appear on a roster of Strange's company in 1593, along with those of John Heminges and Augustine Phillips. All of these men later became part of the Lord Chamberlain's company, most of them when it was first formed in 1594. Shakespeare's name does not appear on the 1593 Lord Strange's list (which was a license for touring in the provinces), but he may possibly have stayed in London to attend to his writing while the company toured. Certainly, an important number of his later associates belonged to this group.

During the years from 1590 to 1594, some of Lord Strange's men appear to have joined forces on occasion with Edward Alleyn and others of the Admiral's men. This impressive combination of talents enjoyed a successful season in 1591–1592, with six performances at court. Alleyn's father-in-law, Philip Henslowe, recorded in his *Diary* the performances of the combined players in early 1592, probably at the Rose Theatre. Their repertory included a *Harey the vj* and a *Titus & Vespacia*. The latter play is, however, no longer thought to have any connection with Shakespeare's *Titus Andronicus*; and the *Harey the vj* may or may not have been Shakespeare's, since *3 Henry VI* was (according to its 1595 title page) acted by Pembroke's men, rather than Lord Strange's men. If Shakespeare was a member of the Strange-Admiral's combination in 1591–1592, we are at a loss to explain why Henslowe's 1592 list records so many performances of plays by Marlowe, Greene, Kyd, and others, but none that are certainly by Shakespeare. On the other hand, the *Harey the vj* may be his, and the title page of the 1594 Quarto of *Titus Andronicus* does list the Earl of Derby's men as performers of the play, in addition to the Earl of Pembroke's and the Earl of Sussex's men. (Lord Strange's men became officially known as the Earl of Derby's men when Lord Strange was made an earl in September 1593.) At any rate, the company disbanded when the Earl died in April 1594, leaving them without a patron. The connection with the Admiral's men was discontinued, with Alleyn returning to the Admiral's men and the rest of the group forming a new company under the patronage of Henry Carey, first Lord Hunsdon, the Lord Chamberlain.

The Earl of Pembroke's Men

The other company to which Shakespeare is most likely to have belonged prior to 1594 is the Earl of Pembroke's company. This group came to grief in 1593–1594, evidently as a result of virulent outbursts of the plague, which had kept the theaters closed during most of 1592 and 1593. Pembroke's men were forced to tour the provinces and then to sell a number of their best plays to the booksellers. Henslowe wrote to Alleyn in September 1593 of the extreme financial plight of Pembroke's company: "As for my lord of Pembroke's [men], which you desire to know where they be, they are all at home and has been this five or six weeks, for they cannot save their charges [expenses] with travel, as I hear, and were fain to pawn their parell [apparel] for their charge." Soon thereafter this company disbanded.

Pembroke's men were associated with a significant number of Shakespeare's early plays. Among the playbooks they evidently sold in 1593–1594 were *The Taming of a Shrew* and *The True Tragedy of Richard Duke of York.* The first of these was published in 1594 with the assertion that it had been "sundry times acted by the Right Honorable the Earle of Pembroke his Servants." Although the text of this quarto is not Shakespeare's play as we know it but, instead, an anonymous version, most scholars now feel certain that it was an imitation of Shakespeare's play and that the work performed by Pembroke's men was, in fact, Shakespeare's. The same conclusion pertains to a performance in 1594 of "*the Tamynge of a Shrowe*" at Newington Butts, a playhouse south of London Bridge. Henslowe's *Diary* informs us that the actors on this occasion were either the Lord Chamberlain's or the Lord Admiral's men. The probability, then, is that Shakespeare's *The Taming of the Shrew* passed from Pembroke's men to the Chamberlain's men when Pembroke's company collapsed in 1593–1594.

The True Tragedy of Richard Duke of York, published in 1595, was a seemingly unauthorized quarto of Shakespeare's *3 Henry VI.* Its title page declared that it had been "sundry times acted by the Right Honorable the Earl of Pembroke his Servants." Probably they acted *2 Henry VI*

as well, to which part three was a sequel. In addition, the 1594 Quarto of *Titus Andronicus* mentions on its title page the Earl of Pembroke's servants, although the Earl of Derby's and the Earl of Sussex's men are named there as well. Thus, Pembroke's men performed as many as four of Shakespeare's early plays—more than we can assign to any other known company. Nevertheless, their claim to Shakespeare remains uncertain. We simply do not know who acted several of Shakespeare's earliest plays, such as *The Comedy of Errors, Love's Labor's Lost*, and *The Two Gentlemen of Verona.* Lord Strange's (Derby's) men, as we have seen, did act something called *Harey the vj* and are named on the 1594 title page of *Titus Andronicus.* Sussex's men may conceivably have owned for a time some early Shakespearean plays that later went to the Lord Chamberlain's men, such as *Titus Andronicus.* The Queen's men, although associated with no known Shakespeare play, other than the old *King Lear* (acted jointly with Sussex's men in 1593), were a leading company during the years in question. All we can say for sure is that the difficulties of 1592–1593 with the plague and the death of the Earl of Derby in 1594 led to a major reshuffling of the London acting companies. From this reshuffling emerged in 1594 the Lord Chamberlain's company, with Shakespeare and Richard Burbage (whose earlier history is also difficult to trace) as two of its earliest and most prominent members.

SHAKESPEARE'S LIFE AND WORK

THE EARLY YEARS, 1564–C. 1594

Stratford-upon-Avon

About Shakespeare's place of birth, Stratford-upon-Avon, there is no doubt. He spent his childhood there and returned periodically throughout his life. During most or

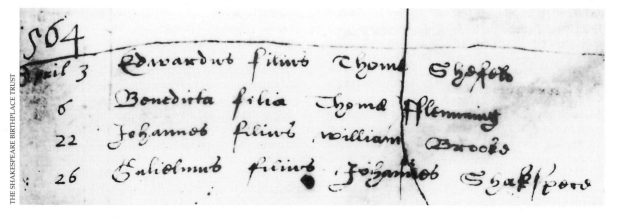

The earliest written reference to William Shakespeare is this record of his christening in the register of Holy Trinity Church at Stratford, April 26, 1564. The entry reads, "Gulielmus filius Johannes Shakspere."

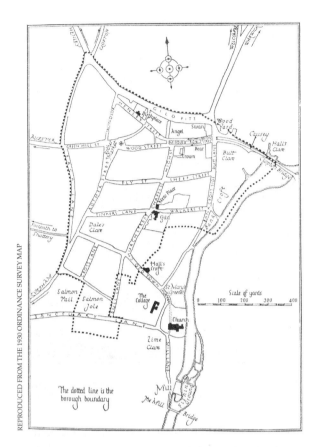

REPRODUCED FROM THE 1930 ORDINANCE SURVEY MAP

The town of Stratford-upon-Avon as Shakespeare knew it. The house in which he is considered to have been born is on Henley Street; the larger house he purchased in 1597, New Place, is on Chapel Street.

all of his long professional career in London, his wife and children lived in Stratford. He acquired property and took some interest in local affairs. He retired to Stratford and chose to be buried there. Its Warwickshire surroundings lived in his poetic imagination.

The Stratford of Shakespeare's day was a "handsome small market town" (as described by William Camden) of perhaps 1,500 inhabitants, with fairly broad streets and half-timbered houses roofed with thatch. It could boast of a long history and an attractive setting on the river Avon. A bridge of fourteen arches, built in 1496 by Sir Hugh Clopton, Lord Mayor of London, spanned the river. Beside the Avon stood Trinity Church, built on the site of a Saxon monastery. The chapel of the Guild of the Holy Trinity, dating from the thirteenth century, and an old King Edward VI grammar school were buildings of note. Stratford had maintained a grammar school at least since 1424 and probably long before that. It was a town without the domination of clergy, aristocracy, or great wealth. It lay in a rich agricultural region, in the county of Warwickshire. To the north of Stratford lay the Forest of Arden.

Shakespeare's Family

The family that bore the name of Shakespeare was well distributed throughout England, but was especially numerous in Warwickshire. A name "Saqueepee," in various spellings, is found in Normandy at an early date. It means, according to J. Q. Adams, "to draw out the sword quickly." That name, in the form "Sakspee," with many variants, is found in England; also the name "Saksper," varying gradually to the form "Shakespeare." It may have been wrought into that form by the obvious military meaning of "one who shakes the spear."

Our first substantial records of the family begin with Richard Shakespeare, who was, in all probability, Shakespeare's grandfather, a farmer living in the village of Snitterfield four miles from Stratford. He was a tenant on the property of Robert Arden of Wilmcote, a wealthy man with the social status of gentleman. Richard Shakespeare died about 1561, possessed of an estate valued at the very respectable sum of thirty-eight pounds and seventeen shillings.

His son John made a great step forward in the world by his marriage with Mary Arden, daughter of his father's landlord. John Shakespeare had some property of his own and through his wife acquired a good deal more. He moved from Snitterfield to Stratford at some date before 1552. He rose to great local importance in Stratford and bought several houses, among which was the one on Henley Street traditionally identified as Shakespeare's birthplace. William Shakespeare was born in 1564 and was baptized on April 26. The exact date of his birth is not known, but traditionally we celebrate it on April 23, the feast day of St. George, England's patron saint. (The date is at least plausible in view of the practice of baptizing infants shortly after birth.) The house in which Shakespeare was probably born, though almost entirely rebuilt and changed in various and unknown ways during the years that have intervened since Shakespeare's birth, still stands. It is of considerable size, having four rooms on the ground floor, and must, therefore, have been an important business house in the Stratford of those days. John Shakespeare's occupation seems to have been that of a tanner and glover; that is, he cured skins, made gloves and some other leather goods, and sold them in his shop. He was also a dealer in wool, grain, malt, and other farm produce.

The long story, beginning in 1552, of John Shakespeare's success and misfortunes in Stratford is attested to by many borough records. He held various city offices. He was ale taster (inspector of bread and malt), burgess (petty constable), affeeror (assessor of fines), city chamberlain (treasurer), alderman, and high bailiff of the town—the highest municipal office in Stratford. At some time around 1576, he applied to the Herald's office for the right to bear arms and style himself a gentleman. This petition was later to be renewed and successfully carried through to

This house on Henley Street in Stratford is considered to have been the birthplace of Shakespeare. Its considerable size shows what must have been an important house of business. Shakespeare's father dealt chiefly in leather goods, though he also traded in wool, grain, and other farm produce.

completion by his famous son. In 1577 or 1578, however, when William was as yet only thirteen or fourteen years old, John Shakespeare's fortunes began a sudden and mysterious decline. He absented himself from council meetings. He had to mortgage his wife's property and showed other signs of being in financial difficulty. He became involved in serious litigation and was assessed heavy fines. Although he kept his position on the corporation council until 1586 or 1587, he was finally replaced as alderman because of his failure to attend. Conceivably, John Shakespeare's sudden difficulties were the result of persecution for his Catholic faith, since John's wife's family had remained loyal to Catholicism, and the old faith was being attacked with new vigor in the Warwickshire region in 1577 and afterwards. This hypothesis is unsubstantial, however, especially in view of the fact that some Catholics and Puritans seemed to have held posts of trust and to have remained prosperous in Stratford during this period. In the last analysis, we have little evidence as to John Shakespeare's religious faith or as to the reasons for his sudden reversal of fortune.

The family of Shakespeare's mother could trace its ancestry back to the time of William the Conqueror, and Shakespeare's father, in spite of his troubles, was a citizen of importance. John Shakespeare made his mark, instead of writing his name, but so did other men of the time who we know could read and write. His offices, particularly that of

chamberlain, and the various public functions he discharged indicate that he must have had some education.

Shakespeare in School

Nicholas Rowe, who published in 1709 the first extensive biographical account of Shakespeare, reports the tradition that Shakespeare studied "for some time at a Free-School." Although the list of students who actually attended the King's New School at Stratford-upon-Avon in the late sixteenth century has not survived, we cannot doubt that Rowe is reporting accurately. Shakespeare's father, as a leading citizen of Stratford, would scarcely have spurned the benefits of one of Stratford's most prized institutions. The town had had a free school since the thirteenth century, at first under the auspices of the Church. During the reign of King Edward VI (1547–1553), the Church lands were expropriated by the crown and the town of Stratford was granted a corporate charter. At this time, the school was reorganized as the King's New School, named in honor of the reigning monarch. It prospered. Its teachers, or "masters," regularly held degrees from Oxford during Shakespeare's childhood and received salaries that were superior to those of most comparable schools.

Much has been learned about the curriculum of such a school. A child would first learn the rudiments of read-

The interior of the Stratford grammar school: a late and not very reliable tradition claims that Shakespeare's desk was third from the front on the left-hand side.

ing and writing English by spending two or three years in a "petty" or elementary school. The child learned to read from a "hornbook," a single sheet of paper mounted on a board and protected by a thin transparent layer of horn, on which was usually printed the alphabet in small and capital letters and the Lord's Prayer. The child would also practice an ABC book with catechism. When the child had demonstrated the ability to read satisfactorily, the child was admitted, at about the age of seven, to the grammar school proper. Here the day was a rigorous one, usually extending from 6 A.M. in the summer or 7 A.M. in the winter until 5 P.M. Intervals for food or brief recreation came at midmorning, noon, and midafternoon. Holidays occurred at Christmas, Easter, and Whitsuntide (usually late May and June), comprising perhaps forty days in all through the year. Discipline was strict, and physical punishment was common.

Latin formed the basis of the grammar school curriculum. The scholars studied grammar, read ancient writers, recited, and learned to write in Latin. A standard text was the *Grammatica Latina* by William Lilly or Lyly,

grandfather of the later Elizabethan dramatist John Lyly. The scholars also became familiar with the *Disticha de Moribus* (moral proverbs) attributed to Cato, *Aesop's Fables*, the *Eclogues* of Baptista Spagnuoli Mantuanus or Mantuan (alluded to in *Love's Labor's Lost*), the *Eclogues* and *Aeneid* of Virgil, the comedies of Plautus or Terence (sometimes performed in Latin by the children), Ovid's *Metamorphoses* and other of his works, and possibly some Horace and Seneca.

Shakespeare plentifully reveals in his dramatic writings an awareness of many of these authors, especially Plautus (in *The Comedy of Errors*), Ovid (in *A Midsummer Night's Dream* and elsewhere), and Seneca (in *Titus Andronicus*). Although he often consulted translations of these authors, he seems to have known the originals as well. He had, in Ben Jonson's learned estimation, "small Latin and less Greek"; the tone is condescending, but the statement does concede that Shakespeare had some of both. He would have acquired some Greek in the last years of his grammar schooling. By twentieth-century standards, Shakespeare had a fairly comprehensive amount of training in the ancient classics, certainly enough to account for the general, if unscholarly, references we find in the plays.

Shakespeare's Marriage

When Shakespeare was eighteen years old, he married Anne Hathaway, a woman eight years his senior. (The inscription on her grave states that she was sixty-seven when she died in August 1623.) The bishop's register of Worcester, the central city of the diocese, shows for November 27, 1582, the issue of a bishop's license for the marriage of William Shakespeare and Anne "Whately"; the bond of sureties issued next day refers to her as "Hathaway." She has been identified with all reasonable probability as Agnes (or Anne) Hathaway, daughter of the then recently deceased Richard Hathaway of the hamlet of Shottery, a short distance from Stratford.

The obtaining of a license was not normally required for a marriage. William Shakespeare and Anne Hathaway seem to have applied for a license on this occasion because they wished to be married after only one reading of the banns rather than the usual three. (The reading of the banns, or announcement in church of a forthcoming marriage, usually on three successive Sundays, enabled any party to object to the marriage if he or she knew of any legal impediment.) Since the reading of all banns was suspended for long periods during Advent (before Christmas) and Lent (before Easter), a couple intending to marry shortly before Christmas might have had to wait until April before the banns could be read thrice. Accordingly, the bishop not uncommonly granted a license permitting couples to marry during the winter season with only one reading of the banns. To obtain such a license, two friends of the bride's family had to sign a bond obligating themselves to pay the bishop up to forty pounds, should any impediment to the marriage result in a legal action against the bishop for having issued the license.

The actual record of the marriage in a parish register has not survived, but presumably the couple were married shortly after obtaining the license. They may have been married in Temple Grafton, where Anne had relatives. The couple took up residence in Stratford. Anne was already pregnant at the time of the marriage, for she gave birth to a daughter, Susanna, on May 26, 1583. The birth of a child six months after the wedding may explain the need for haste the previous November. These circumstances, and Anne's considerable seniority in age to William, have given rise to much speculation about matters that can never be satisfactorily resolved. We do know that a formal betrothal in the presence of witnesses could legally validate a binding relationship, enabling a couple to consummate their love without social stigma. We know also that Shakespeare dramatized the issue of pre-

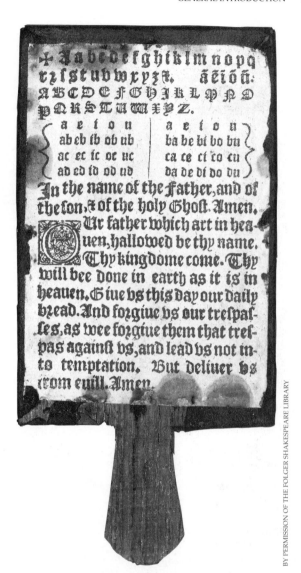

The hornbook pictured here—showing the alphabet and the Lord's Prayer—was part of a child's education in Shakespeare's time.

marital contract and pregnancy in *Measure for Measure*. Whether Shakespeare entered into such a formal relationship with Anne is, however, undiscoverable.

On February 2, 1585, Shakespeare's only other children, the twins Hamnet and Judith, were baptized in Stratford Church. The twins seem to have been named after Shakespeare's friends and neighbors, Hamnet Sadler, a baker, and his wife, Judith.

The Seven "Dark" Years

From 1585, the year in which his twins were baptized, until 1592, when he was first referred to as an actor

A schoolroom in Tudor England.

and dramatist of growing importance in London, Shakespeare's activities are wholly unknown. Presumably, at some time during this period he made his way to London and entered its theatrical world, but otherwise we can only record traditions and guesses as to what he did between the ages of 21 and 28.

One of the oldest and most intriguing suggestions comes from John Aubrey, who, in collecting information

The substantial farmhouse owned by the Hathaways of Shottery, originally known as "Hewland" but now almost universally famous as Anne Hathaway's Cottage.

in the late seventeenth century about actors and drama-tists for his "Minutes of Lives," sought the help of one William Beeston. John Dryden believed Beeston to be "the chronicle of the stage," and Aubrey seems also to have had a high opinion of Beeston's theatrical knowl-edge. In his manuscript, Aubrey made a note to himself: "W. Shakespeare—quaere [i.e., inquire of] Mr. Beeston, who knows most of him." Aubrey then cites Beeston as his authority for this tradition about Shakespeare:

Though, as Ben Jonson says of him, that he had but little Latin and less Greek, he understood Latin pretty well, for he had been in his younger years a schoolmaster in the country.

Beeston had been a theatrical manager all his life. He was the son of the actor Christopher Beeston, who had been a member of Shakespeare's company, probably from 1596 until 1602, and who therefore had occasion to know Shakespeare well.

Shakespeare's own grammar school education would not have qualified him to be the master of a school, but he could have served as "usher" or assistant to the mas-ter. The idea that Shakespeare may have taught in this way is not unattractive. Although, as we have seen, he had some acquaintance with Plautus, Ovid, and other classical writers through his own grammar school read-ing, a stint as schoolmaster would have made these authors more familiar and readily accessible to him when he began writing his plays and nondramatic poems. His earliest works—*The Comedy of Errors, Love's Labor's Lost, Titus Andronicus, Venus and Adonis, The Rape of Lucrece*—show most steadily and directly the effect of his classical reading. Schoolteaching experience might have encour-aged his ambitions to be a writer, like Marlowe or Greene, who went to London not to be actors but to try their hands at poetry and playwriting. All in all, however, it seems more probable that Shakespeare became a young actor rather than a schoolteacher.

Another tradition about the years from 1585 to 1592 asserts that Shakespeare served part of an apprenticeship in Stratford. This suggestion comes to us from one John Dowdall, who, traveling through Warwickshire in 1693, heard the story from an old parish clerk who was show-ing him around the town of Stratford. According to this parish clerk, Shakespeare had been bound as apprentice to a butcher but ran away from his master to London where he was received into a playhouse as "servitor." John Aubrey records a similar tradition: "When he [Shakespeare] was a boy he exercised his father's trade." Aubrey believed this trade to have been that of a butch-er. Moreover, says Aubrey, "When he killed a calf, he would do it in a high style, and make a speech." No other evidence confirms, however, that Shakespeare was a run-away apprentice. The allusion to "killing a calf" may, instead, refer to an ancient rural amusement in which the slaughter of a calf was staged behind a curtain for the entertainment of visitors at county fairs. Conceivably, Shakespeare's participation in such a game during his youth may have given rise to the tradition that he had been a butcher's apprentice.

Another legend, that of Shakespeare's deer stealing, has enjoyed wide currency. We are indebted for this story to the Reverend Richard Davies, who, some time between 1688 and 1709, jotted down some gossipy inter-polations in the manuscripts of the Reverend William Fulman. (Fulman himself was an antiquarian who had collected a number of notes about Shakespeare and Strat-ford.) According to Davies, Shakespeare was "much given to all unluckiness in stealing venison and rabbits, particularly from Sir ——— Lucy, who had him oft whipped and sometimes imprisoned and at last made him fly his native country, to his great advancement." This tradition has led to speculation by Nicholas Rowe that Justice Shallow of *2 Henry IV* and *The Merry Wives of Windsor* is a satirical portrait of Sir Thomas Lucy of Charlecote Hall and that Shakespeare even composed an irreverent ballad about Lucy that added to the urgency of Shakespeare's departure for London. In fact, howev-er, there is no compelling reason to believe that Shallow is based on Lucy, on Justice William Gardiner of Surrey (as Leslie Hotson insists), or on any live Elizabethan. We don't know that Shakespeare ever drew contemporary portraits in his plays, as is sometimes alleged; is Polonius in *Hamlet* Lord Burghley, for example, or is he Shake-speare's original portrait of a minister of state who is also a busybody? Nor do we know if the deer-slaying inci-dent took place at all. It makes interesting fiction but unreliable biography.

Shakespeare's Arrival in London

Because of the total absence of reliable information con-cerning the seven years from 1585 to 1592, we do not know how Shakespeare got his start in the theatrical world. He may have joined one of the touring companies that came to Stratford and then accompanied the players to London. Edmund Malone offered the unsupported statement (in 1780) that Shakespeare's "first office in the theater was that of prompter's attendant." Presumably, a young man from the country would have had to begin at the bottom. Shakespeare's later work certainly reveals an intimate and practical acquaintance with technical mat-ters of stagecraft. In any case, his rise to eminence as an actor and a writer seems to have been rapid. He was for-tunate also in having at least one prosperous acquain-tance in London, Richard Field, formerly of Stratford and the son of an associate of Shakespeare's father. Field was a printer, and in 1593 and 1594 he published two hand-some editions of Shakespeare's first serious poems, *Venus and Adonis* and *The Rape of Lucrece*.

"The Only Shake-scene in a Country"

The first allusion to Shakespeare after his Stratford days is a vitriolic attack on him. It occurs in *Greene's Groatsworth of Wit Bought with a Million of Repentance,* written by Robert Greene during the last months of his wretched existence (he died in poverty in September 1592). A famous passage in this work lashes out at the actors of the public theaters for having deserted Greene and for bestowing their favor instead on a certain upstart dramatist. The passage warns three fellow dramatists and University Wits, Christopher Marlowe, Thomas Nashe, and George Peele, to abandon the writing of plays before they fall prey to a similar ingratitude. The diatribe runs as follows:

> . . . Base minded men all three of you, if by my misery you be not warned. For unto none of you (like me) sought those burs to cleave—those puppets, I mean, that spake from our mouths, those antics garnished in our colors. Is it not strange that I, to whom they all have been beholding, is it not like that you, to whom they all have been beholding, shall (were ye in that case as I am now) be both at once of them forsaken? Yes, trust them not. For there is an upstart crow, beautified with our feathers, that with his "Tiger's heart wrapped in a player's hide" supposes he is as well able to bombast out a blank verse as the best of you, and, being an absolute *Johannes Factotum,* is in his own conceit the only Shake-scene in a country.

The "burs" here referred to are the actors who have forsaken Greene in his poverty for the rival playwright "Shake-scene"—an obvious hit at Shakespeare. The sneer at a *"Johannes Factotum"* suggests another dig at Shakespeare for being a jack-of-all-trades—actor, playwright, poet, and theatrical handyman in the directing and producing of plays. The most unmistakable reference to Shakespeare, however, is to be found in the burlesque line, "Tiger's heart wrapped in a player's hide," modeled after "Oh, tiger's heart wrapped in a woman's hide!" from *3 Henry VI* (1.4.137). Shakespeare's success as a dramatist had led to an envious outburst from an older, disappointed rival. (Did Shakespeare possibly have this attack in mind some years later when he has Polonius object, in *Hamlet,* 2.2.111–12, "'beautified' is a vile phrase"?)

Soon after Greene's death, Henry Chettle, who had seen the manuscript through the press (and who today some believe to have written the attack himself), issued an apology in his *Kind-Heart's Dream* that may refer to Shakespeare. The apology begins with a disclaimer of all personal responsibility for the incident and with Chettle's insistence that he has neither known nor wishes to know Marlowe (whom Greene's pamphlet had accused of atheism). Toward another unidentified playwright, on the other hand, Chettle expresses genuine concern and regret that Chettle had not done more to soften the acerbity of Greene's vitriol:

> The other, whom at that time I did not so much spare as since I wish I had, for that, as I have moderated the heat of living writers and might have used my own discretion (especially in such a case, the author being dead), that I did not I am as sorry as if the original fault had been my fault; because myself have seen his demeanor no less civil than he excellent in the quality he professes. Besides, divers of worship have reported his uprightness of dealing, which argues his honesty and his facetious grace in writing that approves his art.

If the unnamed person here is to be understood as Shakespeare, it represents him in a most attractive light. Chettle freely admits to having been impressed by this person's civility. He praises the dramatist as "excellent in the quality he professes," that is, excellent as an actor. Chettle notes with approval that the man he is describing enjoys the favor of certain persons of importance, some of whom have borne witness to his uprightness in dealing. *Greene's Groatsworth of Wit,* then, with its rancorous attack on Shakespeare, has paradoxically led to the plausible inference (though not certain in its identification) that in 1592 Shakespeare was regarded as a man of pleasant demeanor, honest reputation, and acknowledged skill as an actor and writer.

Dramatic Apprenticeship

By the end of the year 1594, when after the long plague the theatrical companies were again permitted to act before London audiences, we find Shakespeare as a member of the Lord Chamberlain's company. Probably he had already written *The Comedy of Errors, Love's Labor's Lost, The Two Gentlemen of Verona,* the *Henry VI* plays, and *Titus Andronicus.* (*A Love's Labor's Won,* mentioned by Francis Meres in 1598, is possibly either a lost play or an alternate title for one of the extant comedies.) He may also have completed *The Taming of the Shrew, A Midsummer Night's Dream, Richard III, King John,* and *Romeo and Juliet.* Although some scholars still question his authorship in part or all of *Titus* and the *Henry VI* plays, no one questions that they are from the period around 1590.

Shakespeare's early development is hard to follow because of difficulties in exact dating of the early plays and because some of the texts (such as *Love's Labor's Lost*) may have been later revised. As a learner making rapid progress in the skill of his art, Shakespeare was also subjected to outside influences that can only partly be determined. Among these influences, we may be sure, were the plays of his contemporary dramatists. If we could define these influences and form an idea of the kinds of plays acceptable on the stage during Shakespeare's early period, we could better understand the milieu in which he began his work.

Fortunately, we know a fair amount concerning the dramatic repertory in London during Shakespeare's early years. Henslowe's *Diary,* for example, records the daily performances of plays by the Lord Strange's men, in conjunction with the Admiral's men, from February 19, 1592 to June 22, 1592. Many of their plays unfortunately are lost, but enough of them are preserved to indicate the sorts of drama then in vogue. The Strange-Admiral's repertory included Christopher Marlowe's *The Jew of Malta*, Robert Greene's *Orlando Furioso* and *Friar Bacon and Friar Bungay*, Robert Greene and Thomas Lodge's *A Looking Glass for London and England*, Thomas Kyd's *The Spanish Tragedy*, the anonymous *A Knack to Know a Knave*, and possibly George Peele's *The Battle of Alcazar*, and Shakespeare's *1 Henry VI*. We find, in other words, a tragedy with a villain as hero, a romantic comedy masquerading as a heroic play, a love comedy featuring a lot of magic, a biblical moral, England's first great revenge tragedy, a popular satiric comedy aimed at dissolute courtiers and usurers, a history play about Portugal's African empire, and an English history play. The titles of other works now lost suggest a similar amalgam of widely differing genres.

Comparatively few plays may have been written during the period when plays were forbidden because of the long plague of 1592–1594. When the Lord Chamberlain's men and the Lord Admiral's men acted under Henslowe's management at the suburban theater of Newington Butts from June 3–13, 1594, their repertories seem to have consisted largely of old plays. In this brief period, they are thought to have acted *Titus Andronicus*, *Hamlet* (the pre-Shakespearean version), *The Taming of a Shrew* (quite possibly Shakespeare's version), *The Jew of Malta*, a lost play called *Hester and Ahasuerus*, and others.

The Lord Admiral's men probably moved soon afterwards in 1594 to the Rose on the Bankside, across the river Thames from the city of London, where they continued to play under Henslowe's management until 1603. During the years 1594–1597, Henslowe kept in his *Diary* a careful record of their plays and of the sums of money taken in. This circumstance enables us to know a great deal more about the repertory of Shakespeare's rival company than we can ever know about his own. When the Lord Admiral's men began again in 1594, they had five of Marlowe's plays. They seem also to have had Peele's *Edward I*, Kyd's *The Spanish Tragedy*, and a Henry V play. They may also have had plays by both Greene and Peele (Henslowe's chaotic spelling makes it hard to determine), although some of the principal dramas of these two authors had probably ceased to be acted.

We do not know as much about the repertory of the Lord Chamberlain's company as we do about that of the Lord Admiral's men. We know enough, however, to be sure that in 1594 both companies were acting the same sorts of plays that had been on the boards in 1592. We have, therefore, grounds for assuming that, in spite of the loss of many plays (some of which may have been important), the chief contemporary influences upon Shakespeare during his early period were those of Marlowe, Greene, Peele, and Kyd. As an actor possibly in Lord Strange's company or the Earl of Pembroke's company, he would have been familiar with their plays.

Shakespeare learned also from Lyly, though perhaps more from reading Lyly's plays than from actually seeing or performing in them. The boy actors for whom Lyly wrote were forced by the authorities to suspend acting in about 1591 because of their tendency toward controversial satire, and a number of Lyly's plays were printed at that time. As a theatrical figure, therefore, Lyly belonged really to the previous decade.

The Early Plays

Although Shakespeare's genius manifests itself in his early work, his indebtedness to contemporary dramatists and to classical writers is also more plainly evident than in his later writings. His first tragedy, *Titus Andronicus* (c. 1589–1592), is more laden with quotations and classical references than any other tragedy he wrote. Its genre owes much to the revenge play that had been made so popular by Thomas Kyd. Like Kyd, Shakespeare turns to Seneca but also reveals on stage a considerable amount of sensational violence in a manner that is distinctly not classical. For his first villain, Aaron the Moor, Shakespeare borrows some motifs from the morality play and its gleefully sinister tempter, the Vice. Shakespeare may also have had in mind the boastful antics of Marlowe's Vicelike Barabas, in *The Jew of Malta*. Certainly, Shakespeare reveals an extensive debt in his early works to Ovid and to the vogue of Ovidian narrative poetry in the early 1590s, as, for example, in his repeated allusions to the story of Philomela and Tereus (in *Titus Andronicus*) and in his Ovidian poems, *Venus and Adonis* and *The Rape of Lucrece* (1593, 1594).

Shakespeare was still questing for a suitable mode in tragedy and was discovering that the English drama of the 1590s offered no single, clear model. His only other early tragedy, *Romeo and Juliet* (c. 1594–1596), proved to be as different a tragedy from *Titus Andronicus* as could be imagined. Revenge is still prominent in *Romeo and Juliet* but is ultimately far less compelling a theme than the brevity of love and the sacrifice the lovers make of themselves to one another. Shakespeare's source is not the revenge drama of Seneca or Kyd, but a romantic love narrative derived from the fiction of Renaissance Italy. Elements of comedy so predominate in the play's first half that one senses a closer affinity to *A Midsummer Night's Dream* than to *The Spanish Tragedy*.

Shakespeare discovered his true bent more quickly in comedy than in tragedy. Again, however, he experimented with a wide range of models and genres. *The Comedy of Errors* (c. 1589–1594) brings together elements of two plots from the Latin drama of Plautus. The character types

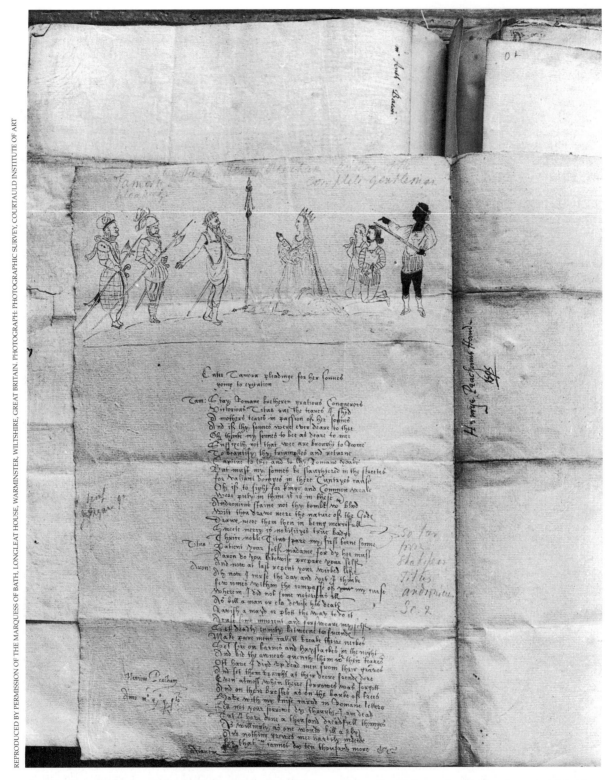

A contemporary illustration of Titus Andronicus, *the earliest of Shakespeare's tragedies. Shakespeare's early plays demonstrated that he was more than a slavish imitator of predecessors such as Kyd and Marlowe.*

THE GREAT POND AT ELVETHAM
arranged for the Second Day's Entertainment.

A. Her Majestie's presence seate and traine.   B. Nereus and his followers.   C. The pinnace of Neæra and her musicke.   D. The Ship-ile.
E. A boate with musicke, attending on the pinnace of Neæra.   F. The Fort-mount.   G. The Snaile-mount.   H. The Roome of Estate.
I. Her Majestie's Court.   K. Her Majestie's Wardrop.   L. The place whence Silvanus and his companie issued.

An entertainment presented by the Earl of Hertford to Queen Elizabeth during her visit to Elvetham in 1591 is seemingly referred to by Shakespeare in A Midsummer Night's Dream, *2.1.157–64. The scene shows an elaborate water pageant in honor of the Queen, who appears enthroned at the left of the picture.*

and situations are partly derivative, but Shakespeare still reveals an impressive skill in plot construction. *Love's Labor's Lost* (c. 1588–1597) is Shakespeare's most Lylyan early comedy, with its witty debates and its amicable, if brittle, war between the sexes. The play also features an array of humorous characters, including a clownish bumpkin, a country slut, a fantastic courtier, a pedant, a country curate, and the like, whose mannerisms and wordplay add to the rich feast of language in a play that centers its attention on proper and improper styles. *The Two Gentlemen of Verona* (c. 1590–1594) and *The Taming of the Shrew* (c. 1590–1593) are derived from Italianate romantic fiction and comedy. In both, Shakespeare skillfully combines simultaneous plots that offer contrasting views on love and friendship. (*The Taming of the Shrew* makes effective use of a "frame" plot involving a group of characters who serve as

audience for the rest of the play.) *A Midsummer Night's Dream* (c. 1595), with its four brilliantly interwoven actions involving court figures, lovers, fairies, and Athenian tradesmen, shows us Shakespeare already at the height of his powers in play construction, even though the comic emphasis on love's irrationality in this play is still in keeping with Shakespeare's early style. The early comedies do not ignore conflict and danger, as we see in the threatened execution of Egeon in *The Comedy of Errors* and the failure of courtships in *Love's Labor's Lost*, but these plays do not as yet fully explore the social dilemmas of *The Merchant of Venice*, the narrowly averted catastrophe of *Much Ado About Nothing*, or the melancholy vein of *As You Like It* and *Twelfth Night*. On stage, early comedies such as *The Comedy of Errors* and *The Taming of the Shrew* are as hilariously funny as anything Shakespeare ever wrote.

Shakespeare's early history plays show a marked affinity with those of Marlowe, Peele, and Greene. Yet today Shakespeare is given more credit for pioneering in the genre of the English history play than he once was. If all the *Henry VI* plays (c. 1589–1592) are basically his, as scholars now often allow, he had more imitators in this genre than predecessors. He scored a huge early success with the heroic character of Lord Talbot in *1 Henry VI*, and by the time Richard Duke of Gloucester had emerged from the *Henry VI* plays to become King Richard III, Shakespeare's fame as a dramatist was assured. He had, of course, learned much from Marlowe's "mighty line" in *Tamburlaine* (1587–1588) and perhaps from Peele's *The Battle of Alcazar* (1588–1589). The anonymous *Famous Victories of Henry V* (1583–1588) must have preceded and influenced his work. Even so, Shakespeare had done much more than simply "beautify" himself with the "feathers" of earlier dramatists, as Greene (or Chettle) enviously charged. Even in his earliest work, Shakespeare already displayed an extraordinary ability to transcend the models from which he learned.

SHAKESPEARE IN THE THEATER, C. 1594–1601

By the year 1594, Shakespeare had already achieved a considerable reputation as a poet and dramatist. We should not be surprised that many of his contemporaries thought of his nondramatic writing as his most significant literary achievement. Throughout his lifetime, in fact, his contemporary fame rested, to a remarkable degree, on his nondramatic poems, *Venus and Adonis*, *The Rape of Lucrece*, and the *Sonnets* (which were circulated in manuscript prior to their unauthorized publication in 1609). One of the earliest tributes suggesting the importance of the poems is found in an anonymous commendatory verse prefixed to Henry Willobie's *Willobie His Avisa* (1594). It summarizes the plot and theme of *The Rape of Lucrece*:

> Though *Collatine* have dearly bought,
> To high renown, a lasting life,
> And found—that most in vain have sought—
> To have a fair and constant wife,
>   Yet Tarquin plucked his glittering grape,
>   And Shakespeare paints poor Lucrece' rape.

Richard Barnfield, in his *Poems in Divers Humors* (1598), praised the "honey-flowing vein" of Shakespeare's *Venus and Adonis* and *The Rape of Lucrece*.

Yet Shakespeare's plays were also highly regarded by his contemporaries, even if those plays were accorded a literary status below that given to the narrative and lyrical poems. Francis Meres insisted, in 1598, that Shakespeare deserved to be compared not only with Ovid for his verse but also with Plautus and Seneca for his comedies and tragedies:

As the soul of Euphorbus was thought to live in Pythagoras, so the sweet, witty soul of Ovid lives in mellifluous and honey-tongued Shakespeare: witness his *Venus and Adonis*, his *Lucrece*, his sugared sonnets among his private friends, etc.

As Plautus and Seneca are accounted the best for comedy and tragedy among the Latins, so Shakespeare among the English is the most excellent in both kinds for the stage: for comedy, witness his *Gentlemen of Verona*, his *Errors*, his *Love's Labor's Lost*, his *Love's Labor's Won*, his *Midsummer Night's Dream*, and his *Merchant of Venice*; for tragedy, his *Richard the II*, *Richard the III*, *Henry the IV*, *King John*, *Titus Andronicus*, and his *Romeo and Juliet*.

Comedy and tragedy were, after all, literary forms sanctioned by classical precept. By calling some of Shakespeare's English history plays "tragedies," Meres endowed them with the respectability of an ancient literary tradition, recognizing, too, that many of Shakespeare's historical plays culminate in the death of an English king.

John Weever, too, in his epigram *Ad Gulielmum Shakespeare* in *Epigrams in the Oldest Cut and Newest Fashion* (1599), mentioned not only the ever-popular narrative poems but also *Romeo and Juliet* and a history play about one of the Richards:

> Honey-tongued Shakespeare! When I saw thine issue,
> I swore Apollo got them and none other:
> Their rosy-tainted features clothed in tissue,
> Some heaven-born goddess said to be their mother;
> Rose-cheeked Adonis, with his amber tresses,
> Fair fire-hot Venus, charming him to love her;
> Chaste Lucretia virgin-like her dresses,
> Proud lust-stung Tarquin seeking still to prove her;
> *Romeo, Richard*—more whose names I know not.
> Their sugared tongues and power-attractive beauty
> Say they are saints, although that saints they show not,
> For thousands vows to them subjective duty;
> They burn in love thy children. Shakespeare het them.
> Go, woo thy muse more nymphish brood beget them.

Even Gabriel Harvey, an esteemed classical scholar and friend of Edmund Spenser, considered Shakespeare's play *Hamlet* to be worthy of no less praise than the best of the Ovidian poems. Harvey's comments are to be found in a marginal note to a copy of Speght's *Chaucer*, written down some time between 1598 and 1601:

The younger sort takes much delight in Shakespeare's *Venus and Adonis*, but his *Lucrece* and his tragedy of *Hamlet, Prince of Denmark* have it in them to please the wiser sort.

Shakespeare's growing fame was even such that his dramatic characters began to enter into the intellectual life of the time. The name of Falstaff became a byword almost as soon as he made his appearance on the stage. The references were not always friendly. A play written to be performed by the rival Admiral's company in answer to *1 Henry IV*, called *Sir John Oldcastle* (1599), took Falstaff to

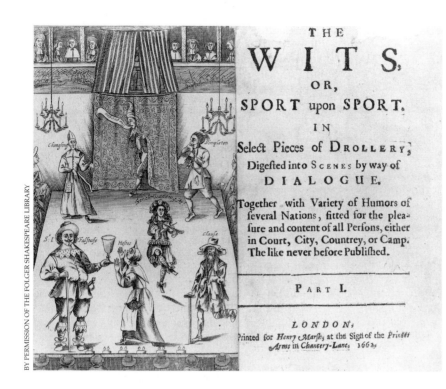

BY PERMISSION OF THE FOLGER SHAKESPEARE LIBRARY

Falstaff and Mistress Quickly are shown here in a composite theatrical illustration of about 1662. The engraving, used as the frontispiece to Francis Kirkman's The Wits, or Sport upon Sport, *also shows other theatrical types. Visible are candelabras and footlights for stage lighting and a curtained area used perhaps for "discoveries." Spectators are visible in the gallery above, as they are also in the De Witt drawing of the Swan Theatre on p. xlvi and in Alabaster's* Roxana *on p. xlv.*

task for being a "pampered glutton" and an "aged counsellor to youthful sin." Evidently, the authors of this attack were offended by the fact that Falstaff had been named "Oldcastle" in an early version of *1 Henry IV*, thereby dishonoring the name of one whom many Puritans regarded as a martyr to their cause (see the Introduction to *1 Henry IV*). Generally, however, the references during this period to Falstaff and his cronies were fond. In a letter to a friend in London, for example, Sir Charles Percy fretted jocosely that his prolonged stay in the country among his rustic neighbors might cause him to "be taken for Justice Silence or Justice Shallow" (1600). In another letter, from the Countess of Southampton to her husband (written seemingly in 1599), Falstaff's name had become so familiar that it was used apparently as a privately understood substitute for the name of some real person in an item of court gossip:

All the news I can send you, that I think will make you merry, is that I read in a letter from London that Sir John Falstaff is by his Mistress Dame Pintpot made father of a godly miller's thumb, a boy that's all head and very little body; but this is a secret.

Shakespeare's immense popularity as a dramatist was bound to invite some resentment. One irreverent reaction is found in the so-called *Parnassus* trilogy (1598–1603). The three plays in this series consist of *The Pilgrimage to Parnassus* and *The Return from Parnassus*, in two parts, all of which were acted by the students of St. John's College, Cambridge.

These *Parnassus* plays take a mordantly satirical view of English life around 1600, from the point of view of university graduates attempting to find gainful employment. The graduates discover, to their vocal dismay, that they must seek the patronage of fashion-mongering courtiers, complacent justices of the peace, professional acting companies who offer them pitifully small wages, and the like. One especially foolish patron, to whom the witty Ingenioso applies for a position, is a poetaster named Gullio. This courtly fop aspires to be a fashionable poet himself, and agrees to hire Ingenioso if the latter will help him with his verse writing. In fact, however, as Ingenioso scornfully observes in a series of asides, Gullio's verses are "nothing but pure Shakespeare and shreds of poetry that he hath gathered at the theaters." Most of all, Gullio loves to plagiarize from *Venus and Adonis* and *Romeo and Juliet*. With unparalleled presumption, he actually requests Ingenioso to compose poems "in two or three divers veins, in Chaucer's, Gower's and Spenser's and Mr. Shakespeare's," which Gullio will then pass off as his own inspiration. When Ingenioso does so extempore, producing, among other things, a fine parody of *Venus and Adonis*, Gullio is as delighted as a child. Although he admires Spenser, Chaucer, and Gower, Gullio confesses that Shakespeare is his favorite; he longs to hang Shakespeare's portrait "in my study at the court" and vows he will sleep with *Venus and Adonis* under his pillow (*The Return from Parnassus*, Part I, 1009–1217). Later on (lines 1875–1880), some university graduates trying out as actors

Henry Fuseli's nineteenth-century interpretation of Falstaff shows him in the tavern in Eastcheap with Doll Tearsheet on his lap while Prince Hal and Poins, disguised as tapsters, enter from behind. Falstaff is perhaps saying, "Peace, good Doll, do not speak like a death's-head" (2 Henry IV, 2.4.232–3).

in Shakespeare's company are requested to recite a few famous lines from the beginning of *Richard III*—lines that, in the satirical context of this play, sound both stereotyped and bombastic. Shakespeare's fame made him an easy target for university "wits" who regarded the theater of London as lowbrow. Still, the portrait throughout is more satirical of those who plagiarize and idolize Shakespeare than of the dramatist's own work. In their backhanded tribute, the *Parnassus* authors make plain that Shakespeare was a household name even at the universities.

Shakespeare's Career and Private Life

During the years from 1594 to 1601, Shakespeare seems to have prospered as an actor and writer for the Lord Chamberlain's men. Whether he had previously belonged to Lord Strange's company or to the Earl of Pembroke's company, or possibly to some other group, is uncertain, but we know that he took part in 1594 in the general reorganization of the companies, out of which emerged the Lord Chamberlain's company. In 1595, his name appeared, for the first time, in the accounts of the

Treasurer of the Royal Chamber as a member of the Chamberlain's company of players, which had presented two comedies before Queen Elizabeth at Greenwich in the Christmas season of 1594. This company usually performed at the Theatre, northeast of London, from 1594 until 1599, when they moved to the Globe playhouse south of the Thames. They seem to have been the victors in the intense economic rivalry between themselves and the Lord Admiral's company at the Rose playhouse under Philip Henslowe's management. Fortunately for all the adult companies, the boys' private theatrical companies were shut down during most of the 1590s. Shakespeare's company enjoyed a phenomenal success, and in short time it became the most successful theatrical organization in England.

The nucleus of the Chamberlain's company in 1594 was the family of Burbage. James Burbage, the father, was owner of the Theatre, Cuthbert Burbage was a manager, and Richard Burbage became the principal actor of the troupe. Together the Burbages owned five "shares" in the company, entitling them to half the profits. Shakespeare and four other principal actors—John Heminges, Thomas Pope, Augustine Phillips, and Will Kempe—owned one share each. Not only was Shakespeare a full sharing actor, but also he was the principal playwright of the company. He was named as a chief actor in the 1616 edition of Ben Jonson's *Every Man in His Humor*, performed by the Chamberlain's company in 1598. Later tradition reports, with questionable reliability, that Shakespeare specialized in "kingly parts" or in the roles of older men, such as Adam in *As You Like It* and the Ghost in *Hamlet*. Shakespeare was more celebrated as a playwright than as an actor, and his acting responsibilities may well have diminished as his writing reputation grew. The last occasion on which he is known to have acted was in Jonson's *Sejanus* in 1603.

His prosperity appears in the first record of his residence in London. The tax returns, or Subsidy Rolls, of a parliamentary subsidy granted to Queen Elizabeth for the

First among the actors in Shakespeare's company was Richard Burbage (1567–1619). He played Hamlet, Othello, King Lear, and presumably other major roles including Macbeth, Antony, Coriolanus, and Prospero.

year 1596 show that Shakespeare was a resident in the parish of St. Helen's, Bishopsgate, near the Theatre, and was assessed at the respectable sum of five pounds. By the next year, Shakespeare had evidently moved to Southwark, near the Bear Garden, for the returns from Bishopsgate show his taxes delinquent. He was later located and the taxes paid.

In 1596, Shakespeare suffered a serious personal loss: the death of his only son Hamnet, at the age of eleven. Hamnet was buried at Stratford in August.

Shakespeare acquired property in Stratford during these years, as well as in London. In 1597 he purchased New Place, a house of importance and one of the two largest in the town. Shakespeare's family entered the house as residents shortly after the purchase and continued to live there until long after Shakespeare's death. The last of his family, his granddaughter, Lady Bernard, died in 1670, and New Place was sold.

Shakespeare was also interested in the purchase of land at Shottery in 1598. He was listed among the chief holders of corn and malt in Stratford that same year and sold a load of stone to the Stratford corporation in 1599.

No less suggestive of Shakespeare's rapid rise in the world is his acquisition of the right to bear arms, or, in other words, his establishment in the rank and title of gentleman. The Herald's College in London preserves two drafts of a grant of arms to Shakespeare's father, devised by one William Dethick and dated October 20, 1596. Although we may certainly believe that the application was put forward by William Shakespeare, John Shakespeare was still living, and the grant was drawn up in the father's name. The device for Shakespeare's coat of arms makes a somewhat easy use of the meaning of his name:

Gold on a bend sables, a spear of the first steeled argent. And for his crest of cognizance a falcon, his wings displayed argent, standing on a wreath of his colors, supporting a spear, gold steeled as aforesaid, set upon a helmet with mantles and tassels, as hath been accustomed and doth more plainly appear depicted on this margent.

According to one of the documents in the grant, John Shakespeare, at the height of his prosperity as a Stratford burgher, had applied twenty years before to the Herald's College for authority to bear arms. The family may not have been able to meet the expense of seeing the application through, however, until William Shakespeare had made his fortune. The grant of heraldic honors to John Shakespeare was confirmed in 1599.

A lawsuit during this period gives us a rather baffling glimpse into Shakespeare's life in the theater. From a writ discovered by Leslie Hotson (*Shakespeare Versus Shallow*, 1931) in the records of the Court of the Queen's Bench, Michaelmas term 1596, we learn that a person named William Wayte sought "for fear of death" to have William Shakespeare, Francis Langley, and two unknown women bound over to keep the peace. Earlier in the same term, moreover, Francis Langley had sworn out a similar writ against this same William Wayte and his stepfather William Gardiner, a justice of the peace in Surrey. Langley was owner of the Swan playhouse on the bankside, near the later-built Globe. His quarrel with Gardiner and Wayte appears to have jeopardized all the acting companies that

This recreation of what New Place purportedly looked like during Shakespeare's ownership suggests that it must have indeed been an imposing structure. It was warmed by ten fireplaces and had surrounding grounds that included two gardens and two barns.

performed plays south of the Thames, for William Gardiner's jurisdiction included the Bankside theater district. Gardiner and Wayte vengefully tried to drive the theaters out of the area. Possibly Shakespeare's company acted occasionally at the Swan in 1596. Hotson speculates that Shakespeare retaliated by immortalizing Gardiner and Wayte as Shallow and Slender in *The Merry Wives of Windsor*. The date of 1596 is too early for that play, and we do not know that Shakespeare drew contemporary portraits in his drama, but we can wonder if lawsuits of this sort gave him no very high opinion of the law's delay and the insolence of office.

During this period Shakespeare's plays began to appear occasionally in print. His name was becoming such a drawing card that it appeared on the title pages of the Second and Third Quartos of *Richard II* (1598), the Second Quarto of *Richard III* (1598), *Love's Labor's Lost* (1598), and the Second Quarto of *1 Henry IV* (1599).

In 1599, the printer William Jaggard sought to capitalize unscrupulously on Shakespeare's growing reputation by bringing out a slender volume of twenty or twenty-one poems called *The Passionate Pilgrim*, attributed to Shakespeare. In fact, only five of the poems were assuredly his, and none of them was newly composed for the occasion. Three came from *Love's Labor's Lost* (published in 1598) and two from Shakespeare's as yet unpublished sonnet sequence.

Contemporary Drama

Shakespeare was without doubt the leading dramatist of the period from 1594 to 1601, not only in our view, but also in that of his contemporaries. The earlier group of dramatists from whom he had learned so much—Lyly, Greene, Marlowe, Peele, Kyd, Nashe—were either dead or no longer writing plays. The group of dramatists who were to rival him in the 1600s and eventually surpass him in contemporary popularity had not yet become well known.

Ben Jonson's early career is obscure. He may have written an early version of his *A Tale of a Tub* in 1596 and *The Case Is Altered* in 1597, though both were later revised. Unquestionably, his first major play was *Every Man in His Humor* (1598), in which Shakespeare acted. This comedy did much to establish the new vogue of comedy of humors, a realistic and satirical kind of drama featuring "humors" characters whose personalities are dominated by some exaggerated trait. We are invited to laugh at the country simpleton, the jealous husband, the overly careful father, the cowardly braggart soldier, the poetaster, and the like. Shakespeare responded to the vogue of humors comedy in his *Henry IV* plays and *The Merry Wives*. Jonson followed his great success with *Every Man Out of His Humor* (1599), an even more biting vision of human folly. George Chapman also deserves important credit for the establish-

ment of humors comedy, with his *The Blind Beggar of Alexandria* (1596) and *An Humorous Day's Mirth* (1597).

Despite the emergence of humors comedy, however, with its important anticipations of Jacobean and even Restoration comedy of manners, the prevailing comedy to be seen on the London stage between 1595 and 1601 was romantic comedy. William Haughton wrote *Englishmen for My Money* in 1598. Thomas Dekker's *Old Fortunatus*, the dramatization of a German folktale, appeared in 1599. Dekker's *The Shoemaker's Holiday* (1599), despite its seemingly realistic touches of life among the apprentices of London, is a thoroughly romanticized saga of rags to riches. A young aristocrat disguises himself as a shoemaker to woo a mayor's daughter; love conquers social rank, and the King himself sentimentally blesses the union. Thomas Heywood wrote heroical romances and comedies, perhaps including *Godfrey of Boulogne* (1594), although most of his early works have disappeared. The boys' private theaters were closed during most of the 1590s, until 1598–1599, and thus the child actors could not perform the satirical comedies at which they were so adept.

Patriotic history drama also continued to flourish on the public stage during those years when Shakespeare wrote his best history plays. Heywood wrote the two parts of *Edward IV* between 1592 and 1599. The anonymous *Edward III* appeared in 1595 or earlier, enough in the vein of Shakespeare's histories that it is sometimes attributed (albeit on uncertain and impressionistic grounds) to him. *Sir Thomas More,* by Munday, Dekker, Chettle, and perhaps Heywood, was written sometime in the later 1590s and very probably revised by Shakespeare himself. Chettle and Munday wrote a trilogy of plays about *Robert, Earl of Huntingdon,* or Robin Hood (1598–1599), on themes that remind us of Shakespeare's *As You Like It*. These plays were performed by the Admiral's men, who also produced the two parts of *Sir John Oldcastle* (1599–1600) by Drayton, Hathway, Munday, and others, in rivalry with Shakespeare's *Henry IV* plays.

Shakespeare's Work

Shakespeare thus wrote his greatest history plays for an audience that knew the genre well. The history play had first become popular just at the start of Shakespeare's career, during the patriotic aftermath of the defeat of the Spanish Armada (1588). Shakespeare himself did much to establish the genre. He wrote first his four-play series dealing with the Lancastrian wars of the fifteenth century, and then went backwards in historical time to King John's reign and to the famous reigns of Henry IV and Henry V.

His romantic comedies were also written for audiences that knew what to expect from the genre. From the comedies of Greene, Peele, Munday, and the rest, as well as Shakespeare himself, Elizabethan audiences were thoroughly familiar with such conventions as fairy charms, improbable adventures in forests, heroines disguised as young men, shipwrecks, love overcoming differences in social rank, and the like. Yet the conventions also demanded more than mere horseplay or foolish antics. Plays of this sort customarily affirmed "wholesome" moral values and appealed to generosity and decency. They were written, like the history plays, for a socially diversified, though generally intelligent and well-to-do, audience.

Several critical terms have been used to suggest the special quality of Shakespeare's comedies during this period of the later 1590s. "Romantic comedy" implies first of all a story in which the main action is about love, but it can also imply elements of the improbable and the miraculous. (The difference between the "romantic comedies" of the later 1590s and the "romances" of Shakespeare's last years, 1606–1613, is that, in part at least, romantic comedy seeks to "make wonder familiar," whereas the romances seek to make the familiar wonderful.) "Philosophical comedy" emphasizes the moral and sometimes Christian idealism underlying many of these comedies of the 1590s: the quest for deep and honest understanding between men and women in *Much Ado About Nothing,* the awareness of an eternal and spiritual dimension to love in *The Merchant of Venice,* and the theme of love as a mysterious force able to regenerate a corrupted social world from which it has been banished in *As You Like It*. "Love-game comedy" pays particular attention to the witty battle of the sexes that we find in several of these plays. "Festive comedy" urges the celebratory nature of comedy, especially in *Twelfth Night* and the *Henry IV* plays, in which Saturnalian revelry must contend against grim and disapproving forces of sobriety. "Comedy of forgiveness," although applicable to only a limited number of plays of this period (especially *Much Ado*), stresses the unexpected second chance that the world of comedy extends to even the most undeserving of heroes; Claudio is forgiven his ill treatment of Hero, although the play's villain, Don John, is not.

SHAKESPEARE IN THE THEATER, C.1601–1608

When the Globe, the most famous of the London public playhouses, was built in 1599, one-half interest in the property was assigned to the Burbage family, especially to the brothers Cuthbert and Richard Burbage. The other half was divided among five actor-sharers: Shakespeare, Will Kempe, Thomas Pope, Augustine Phillips, and John Heminges. Kempe left the company, however, in 1599 and subsequently became a member of the Earl of Worcester's men. His place as leading comic actor was taken by Robert Armin, an experienced man of the theater and occasional author, whose comic specialty was the role of the wise fool. We can observe in Shakespeare's plays the effects of Kempe's departure and of Armin's arrival. Kempe had apparently specialized in clownish and rustic parts, such as those of Dogberry in *Much Ado,* Lancelot Gobbo in *The Merchant of Venice,* and Bottom in *A Midsummer Night's Dream*. (We know that he played Dogberry because his name appears in the early Quarto, derived from the play manuscript; similar evidence links his name to the role of Peter in *Romeo and Juliet*.) For Armin, on the other hand, Shakespeare evidently created such roles as Touchstone in *As You Like It,* Feste in *Twelfth Night,* Lavatch in *All's Well That Ends Well,* and the Fool in *King Lear*.

Other shifts in personnel can sometimes be traced in Shakespeare's plays, especially changes in the number and ability of the boy actors (whose voices would suddenly start to crack at puberty). Shakespeare makes an amusing point about the relative size of two boy actors, for example, in *A Midsummer Night's Dream* and in *As You*

Among the members of Shakespeare's acting company were John Lowin, William Sly, and Nathaniel Field.

Will Kempe (above), for whom Shakespeare created several clownish roles, was a member of the Lord Chamberlain's men and a noted Elizabethan comic. Kempe left the company in 1599 and was replaced by Robert Armin (right), an accomplished actor who specialized in fool's roles.

Like It; this option may have been available to him only at certain times. On the other hand, not all changes in the company roster can be related meaningfully to Shakespeare's dramatic development. Augustine Phillips, who died in 1605, was a full actor-sharer of long standing in the company, but his "type" of role was probably not sharply differentiated from that of several of his associates. Shakespeare's plays, after all, involve many important supporting roles, and versatility in the undertaking of such parts must have been more common than specialization. (Phillips is remembered also for his last will and testament: he left a bequest of "a thirty shillings piece in gold" to "my fellow, William Shakespeare," and similar bequests to other members of the troupe.)

With the reopening of the boys' acting companies in 1598–1599, a serious economic rivalry sprang up between them and the adult companies. The Children of the Chapel Royal occupied the theater in Blackfriars, and the Children of Paul's probably acted in their own singing school in St. Paul's churchyard. Their plays exploited a new vogue for satire. The satiric laughter was often directed at the city of London and its bourgeois inhabitants: socially ambitious tradesmen's wives, Puritan zealots, and the like. Other favorite targets included parvenu knights at court, would-be poets, and hysterical governmental officials. The price of admission at the private theaters was considerably higher than at the Globe or Rose, so the clientele tended to be more fashionable. Sophisticated authors like Ben Jonson, George Chapman, and John Marston tended to find writing for the boy actors more rewarding literarily than writing for the adult players.

One manifestation of the rivalry between public and private theaters was the so-called War of the Theaters, or Poetomachia. In part, this was a personal quarrel between Jonson on one side and Marston and Thomas Dekker on the other. Underlying this quarrel, however, was a serious hostility between a public theater and one that catered more to the elite. Dekker, with Marston's encouragement, attacked Jonson as a literary dictator and snob—one who subverted public decency. Jonson replied with a fervent defense of the artist's right to criticize everything that the artist sees wrong. The major plays in the exchange (1600–1601) were Jonson's *Cynthia's Revels*, Dekker and Marston's *Satiromastix*, and Jonson's *The Poetaster*.

Shakespeare allows Hamlet to comment on the theatrical rivalry (2.2.330–62), with seeming regret for the fact that the boys have been overly successful and that many adult troupes have been obliged to tour the provinces. Most of all, though, Hamlet's remarks deplore the needless bitterness on both sides. The tone of kindly remonstrance makes it seem unlikely that Shakespeare took an active part in the fracas. To be sure, in the Cambridge play *2 Return from Parnassus* (1601–1603), the character called Will Kempe does assert that his fellow actor, Shakespeare, had put down the famous Ben Jonson:

Why, here's our fellow Shakespeare puts them all down, ay, and Ben Jonson, too. O, that Ben Jonson is a pestilent fellow! And he brought up Horace giving the poets a pill, but our fellow Shakespeare hath given him a purge that made him bewray his credit (lines 1809–1813).

Nevertheless, no play exists in which Shakespeare did put down Jonson, and the reference may be instead to *Satiromastix,* which was performed by Shakespeare's company. Or perhaps "put down" means simply "surpassed." In fact, Shakespeare and Jonson remained on cordial terms, despite their differences in artistic outlook.

Upon the death of Queen Elizabeth in 1603 and the accession to the throne of King James I, Shakespeare's company added an important new success to their already great prosperity. According to a document of instruction from King James to his Keeper of the Privy Seal, dated May 19, 1603, and endorsed as "The Players' Privilege," the acting company that had formerly been the Lord Chamberlain's men now became the King's company. The document names Shakespeare, Richard Burbage, Augustine Phillips, John Heminges, Henry Condell, Will Sly, Robert Armin, Richard Cowley, and Lawrence Fletcher—the last, an actor who had played before the King and the Scottish court in 1599 and 1601. These players are accorded the usual privileges of exercising their art anywhere within the kingdom and are henceforth to be known as the King's company. The principal members of the troupe also were appointed to the honorary rank of Grooms of the Royal Chamber. We therefore find them duly recorded in the Accounts of the Master of the Wardrobe on March 15, 1604, as recipients of the customary grants of red cloth, so that they, dressed in the royal livery, might take part in the approaching coronation procession of King James. The same men are mentioned in these grants as in the Players' Privilege. Shakespeare's name stands second in the former document and first in the latter. In a somewhat similar manner, the King's players, as Grooms of the Royal Chamber, were called in attendance on the Spanish ambassador at Somerset House in August 1604.

The Revels Accounts of performances at court during the winter season of 1604–1605 contain an unusually full entry, listing several of Shakespeare's plays. The list includes *Othello, The Merry Wives of Windsor, Measure for Measure,* "The play of Errors," *Love's Labor's Lost, Henry V,* and *The Merchant of Venice.* The last play was "again commanded by the King's majesty," and so was performed a second time. This list also sporadically notes the names of "the poets which made the plays," ascribing three of these works to "Shaxberd." (Probably the final *d* is an error for *e,* since the two characters are easily confused in Elizabethan handwriting; the word represents "Shaxbere" or "Shaxpere.") The entire entry was once called into question as a possible forgery but is now generally regarded as authentic.

A number of records during this period show us glimpses of Shakespeare as a man of property. On May 1, 1602, John and William Combe conveyed to Shakespeare one hundred and seven acres of arable land, plus twenty acres of pasture in the parish of Old Stratford, for the siz-

able payment of three hundred and twenty pounds. The deed was delivered to Shakespeare's brother Gilbert and not to the poet, who was probably at that time occupied in London. On September 28 of the same year, Shakespeare acquired the title to "one cottage and one garden by estimation a quarter of an acre," located opposite his home (New Place) in Stratford.

Shakespeare made still other real-estate investments in his home town. In 1605 he purchased an interest in the tithes of Stratford and adjacent villages from one Ralph Hubaud for the considerable sum of four hundred and forty pounds. The purchasing of tithes was a common financial transaction in Shakespeare's time, though unknown today. Tithes were originally intended for the support of the Church but had, in many cases, become privately owned and hence negotiable. The owners of tithes paid a fixed rental sum for the right to collect as many of these taxes as they could, up to the total amount due under the law. Shakespeare seems, on this occasion in 1605, to have bought from Ralph Hubaud a one-half interest, or "moiety," in certain tithes of Stratford and vicinity. Later, probably in 1609, Shakespeare was one of those who brought a bill of complaint before the Lord Chancellor, requesting that certain other titheholders be required to come into the High Court of Chancery and make answer to the complaints alleged, namely, that they had not paid their proportional part of an annual rental of twenty-seven pounds, thirteen shillings, and four pence on the whole property in the tithes to one Henry Barker. This Barker had the theoretical right to foreclose on the entire property if any one of the forty-two titheholders failed to contribute his share of the annual fee. The suit was, in effect, a friendly one, designed to ensure that all those who were supposed to contribute did so on an equitable and businesslike basis.

We learn from the Stratford Registers of baptism, marriage, and burial of the changes in Shakespeare's family during this period. His father died in 1601, his brother Edmund in 1607, and his mother in 1608. On June 5, 1607, his daughter Susanna was married to Dr. John Hall in Holy Trinity Church, Stratford. Their first child, and Shakespeare's first grandchild, Elizabeth, was christened in the same church on February 21, 1608.

Shakespeare's Reputation, 1601–1608

Allusions to Shakespeare are frequent during this period of his life. One amusing reference is not literary but professes to tell about Shakespeare's prowess as a lover and rival of his good friend and theatrical colleague, Richard Burbage. Perhaps the joke was just a good bawdy story and should not be taken too seriously, but it is nonetheless one of the few anecdotes that date from Shakespeare's lifetime. Our informant is John Manningham, a young law student, who notes in his commonplace book in 1602 the following:

13 March 1601 [1602] . . . Upon a time, when Burbage played Richard III there was a citizen grew so far in liking with him that, before she went to the play, she appointed him to come that night unto her by the name of Richard the Third. Shakespeare, overhearing their conclusion, went before, and was entertained and at his game ere Burbage came. Then message being brought that Richard the Third was at the door, Shakespeare caused return to be made that William the Conqueror was before Richard the Third. Shakespeare's name William.

Other allusions of the time are more literary. Shakespeare's greatness is, by this time, taken for granted. Anthony Scoloker, for example, in his epistle prefatory to *Diaphantus, or the Passions of Love* (1604), attempts to describe an excellent literary work in this way:

It should be like the never-too-well read Arcadia . . . or to come home to the vulgar's element, like friendly Shakespeare's tragedies, where the comedian rides, when the tragedian stands on tip-toe. Faith, it should please all, like Prince Hamlet.

The antiquarian William Camden includes Shakespeare's name among his list of England's greatest writers in his *Remains of a Greater Work Concerning Britain* (1605):

These may suffice for some poetical descriptions of our ancient poets. If I would come to our time, what a world could I present to you out of Sir Philip Sidney, Edmund Spenser, Samuel Daniel, Hugh Holland, Ben Jonson, Thomas Campion, Michael Drayton, George Chapman, John Marston, William Shakespeare, and other most pregnant wits of these our times, whom succeeding ages may justly admire.

An attempt to use one of Shakespeare's plays for political purposes had some potentially serious repercussions. Two days before the abortive rebellion of the Earl of Essex on February 7, 1601, Shakespeare's company was commissioned to perform a well-known play in its repertory about King Richard II. This play must almost surely have been Shakespeare's. Evidently, the purpose of this extraordinary performance was to awaken public sympathy for Essex by suggesting that Queen Elizabeth was another Richard II, surrounded by corrupt favorites and deaf to the pleas of her subjects. Essex's avowed intention was to remove from positions of influence those men whom he considered his political enemies. Fortunately, Shakespeare's company was later exonerated of any blame in the affair (see the Introduction to *Richard II*).

Perhaps no other allusion to Shakespeare during this period can suggest so well as the following quotation the extent to which Shakespeare's plays had become familiar to English citizens everywhere. The quotation is taken from the notes of a certain Captain Keeling, commander

of the East India Company's ship *Dragon*, off Sierra Leone, in the years 1607 and 1608:

1607, Sept. 5. I sent the interpreter, according to his desire, aboard the *Hector*, where he broke fast, and after came aboard me, where we gave the tragedy of *Hamlet*.

30. Captain Hawkins dined with me, where my companions acted *King Richard the Second*.

[March 31.] I invited Captain Hawkins to a fish dinner and had *Hamlet* acted aboard me, which I permit to keep my people from idleness and unlawful games or sleep.

Other Drama of the Period

Even without Shakespeare, the early Jacobean drama in England would rank as one of the most creative periods in the history of all theater. (The word *Jacobean* is derived from *Jacobus*, the Latin form of the name of King James I.) Shakespeare's earlier contemporaries—Lyly, Greene, Marlowe, Peele, Kyd—were dead or silent, but another generation of playwrights was at hand. George Chapman, John Marston, and Ben Jonson all began writing plays shortly before 1600. So did Thomas Dekker and Thomas Heywood, whose dramatic output, often in collaboration, would prove to be considerable. Francis Beaumont, John Fletcher, Cyril Tourneur, and Thomas Middleton emerged into prominence in about 1606 or 1607. John Webster collaborated with Dekker and others in such plays as *Westward Ho* and *Sir Thomas Wyatt* around 1604, although he did not write his great tragedies until 1609–1614. Lesser talents, such as Henry Chettle, Anthony Munday, Henry Porter, John Day, and William Haughton, continued to pour forth an abundant supply of workmanlike plays. As Shakespeare's career developed, therefore, he enjoyed the fellowship and, no doubt, the rivalry of a remarkably gifted and diverse group of practicing dramatists.

Early Jacobean drama is, on the whole, characteristically different from the late Elizabethan drama that had preceded it. Other dramatists besides Shakespeare mirror his shift of focus from romantic comedies and patriotic histories to "problem" plays and tragedies. The boys' companies, reopening in 1598–1599 after virtually a decade of silence, did much to set the new tone. They avoided almost entirely the English history play, with its muscularly heroic style, so unsuited for the acting capabilities of boys. Besides, sophisticated audiences were sated with jingoistic fare, and even in the public theaters the genre had pretty well run its course. The fashion of the moment turned instead to revenge tragedy and satiric comedy.

The Jacobean revenge play owed much of its original inspiration to Thomas Kyd's *The Spanish Tragedy* (c. 1587), with its influential conventions: the intervention of supernatural forces, the feigned madness of the avenger, his difficulty in ascertaining the true facts of the murder, his morbid awareness of the conflict between human injustice and divine justice, his devising of a play within the play, and his invention of ingenious methods of slaughter in the play's gory ending. Kyd may also have written an early version of *Hamlet* featuring similar motifs. Shakespeare confronted cosmic issues of justice and human depravity in his revenge tragedy, *Hamlet* (c. 1599–1601), as indeed Kyd had done, but most followers of Kyd preferred to revel in the sensationalism of the genre. Some private-theater dramatists, such as Marston, subjected the conventions of the genre to caricature. Marston's revenge plays, written chiefly for Paul's boys and (after 1604) for the Children of the Queen's Revels, include *Antonio's Revenge* (1599–1601) and *The Malcontent* (1600–1604). These dramas are marked by flamboyantly overstated cynicism and are, in many ways, as close to satire as they are to tragedy. Marston had, in fact, made his first reputation as a nondramatic satirist, with *The Metamorphosis of Pygmalion's Image* and *The Scourge of Villainy* in 1598. His plays represent a continuation in dramatic form of the techniques of the Roman satirist. The typical Marstonian avenger, such as Malevole in *The Malcontent*, is an exaggeratedly unattractive authorial spokesman, pouring forth venomous hatred upon the loathsome and degenerate court in which he finds himself.

Similar in their exaggerated pursuit of the grotesque and the morbid are Cyril Tourneur's *The Atheist's Tragedy* (1607–1611) and a play formerly attributed to Tourneur but probably by Thomas Middleton, *The Revenger's Tragedy* (1606–1607). These plays are brilliant in the plotting of impossible situations and in the invention of cunning Italianate forms of torture and murder. Any sympathetic identification with the characters of these plays is sacrificed in the interests of technical virtuosity. As a result, the plays are more ironic than cathartic in their effect; we are overwhelmed by life's dark absurdities rather than ennobled by a vision of humanity's tragic grandeur. *The Tragedy of Hoffman, or A Revenge for a Father* by Henry Chettle (Admiral's men, 1602) is similarly grotesque and lacking in sympathy for its revenger hero. To be sure, George Chapman's *Bussy D'Ambois* (1600–1604) and its sequel, *The Revenge of Bussy D'Ambois* (1607–1612), are thoughtful plays about human aspiration, in the vein of Marlowe's *Tamburlaine*, but even these plays employ a good deal of Senecan bloody melodrama.

The revenge play enjoyed a great popularity on the public stage and (in a caricatured form) on the private stage. The public theater did, however, cater also to its Puritan-leaning audiences with more pious and moral tragedy. *Arden of Feversham* (c. 1591) is a good early example of what has come to be called domestic or homiletic tragedy. In the studiously plain style of a broadside ballad, it sets forth the facts of an actual murder that had occurred in 1551 and had been reported in Holinshed's *Chronicles*. The play interprets those events earnestly and providen-

tially. The most famous play in the genre of domestic tragedy is Thomas Heywood's *A Woman Killed with Kindness* (1603). It tells, not of a murder, but of an adultery, for which the goodhearted but offending wife must be perpetually banished by her grieving husband. The play succeeds in elevating the private sorrows of its ordinary characters to tragic stature. The moral stances appear to be unambiguous: adultery is a heinous offense but can be transcended by Christian forgiveness; dueling is evil. Still, a mix of sympathies is perhaps reflective of shifting public attitudes toward the role of women in marriage. Other plays in the vein of domestic tragedy include *A Yorkshire Tragedy* (1605–1608), *The Miseries of Enforced Marriage* (1605–1606), and *Two Lamentable Tragedies* (c. 1594–1598).

In comedy, the greatest writer of the period besides Shakespeare was Ben Jonson. His predilection was toward the private theater, though he continued to write occasionally for the public stage as well. To an ever-increasing extent, he fixed his satirical gaze on those values and institutions which Thomas Heywood cherished: the city of London, its bourgeois citizens, its traditional approach to morality, and its religious zeal. *Every Man Out of His Humor* (1599), written for the Chamberlain's men, features a foolish uxorious citizen, his socially aspiring wife, and her fashionmongering lover—humors types that were to appear again and again in the genre of satirical comedy known as "city comedy." (See Brian Gibbons, *Jacobean City Comedy*, 1968.) *Volpone* (1605–1606), though technically not a London city comedy, since it purportedly takes place in Venice, castigates greed among lawyers, businessmen, and other professional types. *The Alchemist* (1610) ridicules the affectations of petty shopkeepers, lawyers' clerks, Puritan divines, and others. *Bartholomew Fair* (1614) and *The Alchemist* give us Jonson's most memorable indictment of the Puritans.

Numerous other writers contributed to humors comedy and city comedy. George Chapman probably deserves more credit than he usually receives for having helped determine the shape of humors comedy in his *The Blind Beggar of Alexandria* (1596), *An Humorous Day's Mirth* (1597), *All Fools* (1599–1604), *May-Day* (1601–1609), *The Gentleman Usher* (1602–1604), and others. Francis Beaumont, assisted perhaps by John Fletcher, ridicules London grocers and apprentices for their naive tastes in romantic chivalry in *The Knight of the Burning Pestle* (1607–1610). Some satire in this vein, to be sure, is reasonably good-humored. *Eastward Ho* (1605), by Chapman, Jonson, and Marston, is genially sympathetic toward the lifestyle of the small shopkeeper, even though the play contains a good deal of satire directed at social climbing and sharp business practices. Thomas Dekker's collaboration with Thomas Middleton on *The Honest Whore* (Part I, 1604) gives us an amused and yet warm portrayal of a linen draper who succeeds in business by insisting that the customer is always right. Dekker often shows a wry but generous appreciation of bourgeois ethics, as in *The Shoemaker's Holiday* (1599). Yet even he turns against the Puritans in *If This Be Not a Good Play, the Devil Is in It* (1611–1612).

Marston shows his talent for city comedy in *The Dutch Courtesan* (1603–1605). Perhaps the most ingratiating and truly funny of the writers of city comedy, however, is Middleton. His *A Trick to Catch the Old One* (1604–1607) illustrates the tendency of Jacobean comedy to move away both from Shakespeare's romantic vein and Jonson's morally satirical vein toward a more lighthearted comedy of manners, anticipating the style of Restoration comedy. One of Middleton's most hilarious and philosophically unpretentious plays, though plotted with great ingenuity of situation, is *A Mad World, My Masters* (1604–1607). *Michaelmas Term*, written about the same time, exposes the sharp practices of usurers and lawyers. All these Middleton plays were written for Paul's boys.

Romantic comedy, though overshadowed by humors and city comedy during the 1600s, still held forth at the public theaters. A leading exponent was Thomas Heywood, in such plays as *The Fair Maid of the West,* or *A Girl Worth Gold* (1597–1610). Heywood also wrote English history plays designed to prove the sturdiness and historical importance of the London citizenry he so loved, as in *Edward IV* (1597–1599), *The Four Prentices of London* (c. 1600), and *If You Know Not Me You Know Nobody* (1605). Classical tragedy also continued to be written, despite the vogue of revenge tragedy. Ben Jonson rather dogmatically illustrated his classical theories of tragedy in *Sejanus* (1603) and *Catiline* (1611). Samuel Daniel wrote *Philotas* in 1604 and a revision of his *Cleopatra* in 1607. Heywood's

The Rape of Lucrece appeared in 1606–1608. These are not, however, the immortal tragedies for which the Jacobean period is remembered.

Shakespeare's Work, 1601–1608

Shakespeare's plays of this period are characteristically Jacobean in their fascination with the dark complexities of sexual jealousy, betrayal, revenge, and social conflict. The comedies are few in number and lack the joyous affirmation we associate with *Twelfth Night* and earlier plays. *Measure for Measure*, for example, is not about young men and women happily in love, but about premarital sex and the insoluble problems that arise when vice-prone men attempt to legislate morality for their fellow mortals. Angelo, self-hating and out of emotional control, is a tragic hero providentially rescued from his own worst self. The Duke and Isabella must use ethically dubious means—the bed trick—to effect their virtuous aims. Comedy in the play deals darkly in terms of prostitution, slander, and police inefficiency.

All's Well That Ends Well, though less grim than *Measure for Measure* in its confrontation of human degeneracy, does apply a similar bed trick as its central plot device. Just as important, the obstacles to love are internal and psychological, rather than external; that is, the happy union of Bertram and Helena is delayed, not by parental objections or by accident (as in *Romeo and Juliet* and *A Midsummer Night's Dream*), but by Bertram's unreadiness for the demands of a mature marital relationship. *Troilus and Cressida* is a play in which love is paralyzed by a combination of external and internal forces. Troilus must hand Cressida over to the Greeks because

Raphael Holinshed's Chronicles of England, Scotland, and Ireland, *which was published (1577, 2nd edition in 1587) before Shakespeare's career began, served as principal historic source for many plays, including* Macbeth, King Lear, *and* Cymbeline, *as well as the history plays. Here, in a woodcut from the* Chronicles, *Macbeth and Banquo are shown encountering the three weird sisters.*

his code of honor bids him put his country's cause before his own, and yet that code of "honor" is based on Paris's rape of Helen. Cressida simply gives herself up to Diomedes, knowing she is not strong enough to stand alone in a moral wilderness. The combatants in the greatest war in all history turn out to be petty bickerers who play nasty games on one another and sulk when their reputations are impugned. The cause for which both sides fight is squalid and senseless.

In *Hamlet*, Shakespeare explores similar dilemmas posed by human carnality. Women, in Hamlet's misogynistic angst, are too often frail; men are too often importunate and brutal. How is a thoughtful person to justify his or her own existence? Should one struggle actively against injustice and personal wrong? How can one know what is really true or foresee the complex results of action? How, in *Othello*, can the protagonist resist temptation and inner weakness, prompting him to destroy the very thing on which his happiness depends? Is Macbeth tempted to sin by the weird sisters and his wife, or is the choice to murder Duncan ultimately his? To what extent is humanity responsible for its tragic fate? Most of all, in *King Lear*, are the heavens themselves indifferent to human bestiality? Must Cordelia die? Yet, despite these overwhelmingly pessimistic questions, and the tragic consequences they imply for all human life, Shakespeare's "great" tragedies affirm at least the nobility of humanity's striving to know itself, and the redeeming fact that human goodness does exist (in Desdemona, Duncan, Cordelia), even if those who practice goodness are often slaughtered.

The Roman or classical tragedies are something apart from the "great" tragedies. They are more ironic in tone, more dispiriting, though they, too, affirm an essential nobility in humanity. Brutus misguidedly leads a revolution against Caesar but dies loyal to his great principles. Timon of Athens proves the appalling ingratitude of his fellow creature and resolutely cuts himself off from all human contact. Coriolanus proclaims himself an enemy of the Roman people and seeks to destroy them for their ingratitude, though he is compromised and destroyed at last by his promptings of human feeling. Antony, too, is pulled apart by an irreconcilable conflict. Yet, in this play at least, Shakespeare achieves, partly through the greatness of Cleopatra, a triumph over defeat that seems to offer a new resolution of humanity's tragic dilemma.

THE LATE YEARS: 1608–1616

In the summer of 1608, Shakespeare's acting company signed a twenty-one-year lease for the use of the Blackfriars playhouse, an indoor and rather intimate, artificially lighted theater inside the city of London, close to the site of St. Paul's cathedral. A private theater had existed on this spot since 1576, when the Children of the

Chapel and then Paul's boys began acting their courtly plays for paying spectators in a building that had once belonged to the Dominicans, or Black Friars. James Burbage had begun construction in 1596 of the so-called Second Blackfriars theater in the same building. Although James encountered opposition from the residents of the area and died before he could complete the work, James's son Richard did succeed in opening the new theater in 1600. At first, he leased it (for twenty-one years) to a children's company, but when that company was suppressed in 1608 for offending the French ambassador in a play by George Chapman, Burbage seized the opportunity to take back the unexpired lease and to set up Blackfriars as the winter playhouse for his adult company, the King's men. By this time, the adult troupes could plainly see that they needed to cater more directly to courtly audiences than they once had done. Their popular audiences were becoming increasingly disenchanted with the drama. Puritan fulminations against the stage gained in effect, especially when many playwrights refused to disguise their satirical hostility toward Puritans and the London bourgeoisie.

Several of Shakespeare's late plays may have been acted both at the Globe and at Blackfriars. The plays he wrote after 1608–1609—*Cymbeline, The Winter's Tale*, and *The Tempest*—all show the distinct influence of the dramaturgy of the private theaters. Also, we know that an increasing number of Shakespeare's plays were acted at the court of King James. *Othello, King Lear*, and *The Tempest* are named in court revels accounts, and *Macbeth* dramatizes Scottish history with a seemingly explicit reference to King James as the descendant of Banquo who bears the "twofold balls and treble scepters" (4.1.121); James had received a double coronation as King of England and Scotland, and took seriously his assumed title as King of Great Britain, France, and Ireland. On the other hand, Shakespeare's plays certainly continued to be acted at the Globe to the very end of his career. The 1609 Quarto of *Pericles* advertises that it was acted "by his Majesty's Servants, at the Globe on the Bankside." The 1608 Quarto of *King Lear* mentions a performance at court and assigns the play to "his Majesty's servants playing usually at the Globe on the Bankside." Simon Forman saw *Macbeth, Cymbeline*, and *The Winter's Tale* at the Globe. Finally, a performance of *Henry VIII* on June 29, 1613, resulted in the burning of the Globe to the ground, though afterwards it soon was rebuilt.

Shakespeare's last plays, written with a view to Blackfriars and the court, as well as to the Globe, are now usually called "romances" or "tragicomedies," or sometimes both. Although they were not known by these terms in Shakespeare's day—they were grouped with the comedies in the First Folio of 1623, except for *Cymbeline*, which was placed among the tragedies—the very ambiguity about the genre in this arrangement is suggestive of an uncertainty

COURTESY, GUILDHALL LIBRARY, CORPORATION OF LONDON

This section of Wenceslaus Hollar's "Long View" of London dates from 1647, some years after Shakespeare's death, but gives nonetheless a fine view of two theater buildings on the south bank of the Thames River, across from the city. The two labels of "The Globe" and "Beere bayting" should in fact be reversed; the Globe (rebuilt in 1613) appears to the left and below the bearbaiting arena.

as to whether they were seen as predominantly comic or tragic. The term "romance" suggests a return to the kind of story Robert Greene had derived from Greek romance: tales of adventure, long separation, and tearful reunion, involving shipwreck, capture by pirates, riddling prophecies, children set adrift in boats or abandoned on foreign shores, the illusion of death and subsequent restoration to life, the revelation of the identity of long-lost children by birthmarks, and the like. The term "tragicomedy" suggests a play in which the protagonist commits a seemingly fatal error or crime, or (as in *Pericles*) suffers an extraordinarily adverse fortune to test his patience; in either event, he must experience agonies of contrition and bereavement until he is providentially delivered from his tribulations. The tone is deeply melancholic and resigned, although suffused also with a sense of gratitude for the harmonies that are mysteriously restored.

The appropriateness of such plays to the elegant atmosphere of Blackfriars and the court is subtle but real. Although one might suppose at first that old-fashioned naiveté would seem out of place in a sophisticated milieu,

the naiveté is only superficial. Tragicomedy and pastoral romance were, in the period from 1606 to 1610, beginning to enjoy a fashionable courtly revival. The leading practitioners of the new genre were Beaumont and Fletcher, though Shakespeare made a highly significant contribution. Perhaps sophisticated audiences responded to pastoral and romantic drama as the nostalgic evocation of an idealized past, a chivalric "golden world" fleetingly recovered through an artistic journey back to naiveté and innocence. The evocation of such a world demands the kind of studied but informal artifice we find in many tragicomic plays of the period: the elaborate masques and allegorical shows, the descents of enthroned gods from the heavens (as in *Cymbeline*), the use of quaint Chorus figures like Old Gower or Time (in *Pericles* and *The Winter's Tale*), and the quasi-operatic blend of music and spectacle. At their best, such plays powerfully compel belief in the artistic world thus artificially created. The very improbability of the story becomes, paradoxically, part of the means by which an audience must "awake its faith" in a mysterious truth.

Shakespeare did not merely ape the new fashion in tragicomedy and romance. In fact, he may have done much to establish it. His *Pericles*, written seemingly in about 1606–1608 for the public stage before Shakespeare's company acquired Blackfriars, anticipated many important features, not only of Shakespeare's own later romances, but also of Beaumont and Fletcher's *The Maid's Tragedy* and *Philaster* (c. 1608–1611). Still, Shakespeare was on the verge of retirement, and the future belonged to Beaumont and Fletcher. Gradually, Shakespeare disengaged himself, spending more and more time in Stratford. His last-known stint as an actor was in Jonson's *Sejanus* in 1603. Some time in 1611 or 1612, he probably gave up his lodgings in London, though he still may have returned for such occasions as the opening performance of *Henry VIII* in 1613. He continued to be one of the proprietors of the newly rebuilt Globe, but his involvement in its day-to-day operations dwindled.

Shakespeare's Reputation, 1608–1616

Shakespeare's reputation among his contemporaries was undiminished in his late years, even though Beaumont and Fletcher were the new rage at the Globe and Blackfriars. Among those who apostrophized Shakespeare was John Davies of Hereford in *The Scourge of Folly* (entered in the Stationers' Register in 1610):

To our English Terence, Mr. Will Shakespeare.

Some say, good Will, which I, in sport, do sing:
Hadst thou not played some kingly parts in sport,
Thou hadst been a companion for a king,
And been a king among the meaner sort.
Some others rail. But, rail as they think fit,
Thou hast no railing, but a reigning, wit.

And honesty thou sow'st, which they do reap,
So to increase their stock which they do keep.

The following sonnet is from *Run and a Great Cast* (1614) by Thomas Freeman:

To Master W. Shakespeare.

Shakespeare, that nimble Mercury thy brain
Lulls many hundred Argus-eyes asleep,
So fit, for all thou fashionest thy vein,
At th' horse-foot fountain thou hast drunk full deep.
Virtue's or vice's theme to thee all one is.
Who loves chaste life, there's *Lucrece* for a teacher;
Who list read lust, there's *Venus and Adonis,*
True model of a most lascivious lecher.
Besides, in plays thy wit winds like Meander,
Whence needy new composers borrow more
Than Terence doth from Plautus or Menander.
But to praise thee aright, I want thy store.
   Then let thine own works thine own worth upraise,
   And help t' adorn thee with deservèd bays.

Ben Jonson took a more critical view, though he also admired Shakespeare greatly. In the Induction to his *Bartholomew Fair* (1631 edition), Jonson compared the imaginary world he presented in his play with the more improbable fantasies of romantic drama:

If there be never a servant-monster i' the fair, who can help it? He [the author, Jonson] says; nor a nest of antics? He is loath to make Nature afraid in his plays, like those that beget tales, Tempests, and suchlike drolleries to mix his head with other men's heels.

From this, one judges that Jonson had in mind not only *The Tempest* but also Shakespeare's other late romances. He similarly protested in the Prologue to his 1616 edition of *Every Man in His Humor* that his own playwriting was free of the usual romantic claptrap:

Where neither Chrous wafts you o'er the seas,
Nor creaking throne comes down the boys to please,
Nor nimble squib is seen to make afeard
The gentlewomen, nor rolled bullet heard
To say it thunders, nor tempestuous drum
Rumbles to tell you when the storm doth come.

Still, Shakespeare's reputation was assured. John Webster paid due homage, in his note To the Reader accompanying *The White Devil* (1612), to "the right happy and copious industry of M. *Shakespeare,* M. *Dekker,* & M. *Heywood,*" along with Chapman, Jonson, Beaumont, and Fletcher.

Records of the Late Years

Shakespeare's last recorded investment in real estate was the purchase of a house in Blackfriars, London, in 1613. There is no indication he lived there, for he had retired to Stratford. He did not pay the full purchase price of one hundred and forty pounds, and the mortgage deed executed for the unpaid balance furnishes one of the six unquestioned examples of his signature.

John Combe, a wealthy bachelor of Stratford and Shakespeare's friend, left him a legacy of five pounds in his will at the time of Combe's death in 1613. At about the same time, John's kinsman William Combe began a controversial attempt to enclose Welcombe Common, that is, to convert narrow strips of arable land to pasture. Presumably, Combe was interested in a more efficient means of using the land. Enclosure was, however, an explosive issue, since many people feared they would lose the right to farm the land and would be evicted to make room for cattle and sheep. Combe attempted to guarantee Shakespeare and other titheholders that they would lose no money. He offered similar assurances to the Stratford Council, but the townspeople were adamantly opposed. Shakespeare was consulted by letter as a leading titheholder. The letter is lost, but, presumably, it set forth the Council's reasons for objecting to enclosure. Shakespeare's views on the controversy remain unknown. Eventually, the case went to the Privy Council, where Combe was ordered to restore the land to its original use.

One of the most interesting documents from these years consists of the records of a lawsuit entered into in 1612 by Stephen Belott against his father-in-law, Christopher Mountjoy, a Huguenot maker of women's ornamental headdresses who resided on Silver Street, St. Olave's parish, London. Belott sought to secure the payment of a dower promised him at the time of his marriage to Mountjoy's daughter. In this suit, Shakespeare was summoned as a witness and made deposition on five interrogatories. From this document we learn that Shakespeare was a lodger in Mountjoy's house at the time of the marriage in 1604 and probably for some time before that, since he states in his testimony that he had known Mountjoy for more than ten years. Shakespeare admitted that, at the solicitation of Mountjoy's wife, he had acted as an intermediary in the arrangement of the marriage between Belott and Mountjoy's daughter. Shakespeare declared himself unable, however, to recall the exact amount of the portion or the date on which it was to have been paid. Shakespeare's signature to his deposition is authentic and one of the best samples of his handwriting that we have.

In January of 1615 or 1616, Shakespeare drew up his last will and testament with the assistance of his lawyer Francis Collins, who had aided him earlier in some of his transactions in real estate. On March 25, 1616, Shakespeare revised his will in order to provide for the marriage of his daughter Judith and Thomas Quiney in that same year. Shakespeare's three quavering signatures, one on each page of this document, suggest that he was in failing health. The cause of his death on April 23 is not known. An intriguing bit of Stratford gossip is reported by John Ward, vicar of Holy Trinity in Stratford from 1662 to 1689, in his diary: "Shakespeare, Drayton, and Ben Jonson had a merry meeting, and it seems drank too hard, for Shakespeare died of a fever there contracted." The report comes fifty years after Shakespeare's death, however, and is hardly an expert medical opinion.

The will disposes of all the property of which Shakespeare is known to have died possessing, the greater share of it going to his daughter Susanna. His recently married daughter Judith received a dowry, a provision for any children that might be born of her marriage, and other gifts. Ten pounds went to the poor of Stratford; Shakespeare's sword went to Mr. Thomas Combe; twenty-six shillings and eight pence apiece went to Shakespeare's fellow actors Heminges, Burbage, and Condell to buy them mourning rings; and other small bequests went to various other friends and relatives.

An interlineation contains the bequest of Shakespeare's "second best bed with the furniture," that is, the hangings, to his wife. Anne's name appears nowhere else in the will. Some scholars, beginning with Edmund Malone, have taken this reference as proof of an unhappy marriage, confirming earlier indications, such as the hasty

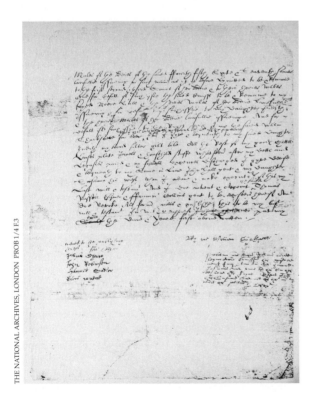

As with so many other things in his life, the curious terms of Shakespeare's will have led to endless and provocative conjecture.

wedding to a woman who was William's senior by eight years and his prolonged residence in London for twenty years or more seemingly without his family. The evidence is inconclusive, however. Shakespeare certainly supported his family handsomely, acquired much property in Stratford, and retired there when he might have remained still in London. Although he showed no great solicitude for Anne's well-being in the will, her rights were protected by law; a third of her husband's estate went to her without having to be mentioned in the will. New Place was to be the home of Shakespeare's favorite daughter Susanna, wife of the distinguished Dr. John Hall. Anne Shakespeare would make her home with her daughter and, with her dower rights secured by law, would be quite as wealthy as she would need to be.

The date of Shakespeare's death (April 23, 1616) and his age (his fifty-third year) are inscribed on his monument. This elaborate structure, still standing in the chancel of Trinity Church, Stratford, was erected some time before 1623 by the London stonecutting firm of Gheerart Janssen and his sons. Janssen's shop was in Southwark, near the Globe, and may have been familiar to the actors. The bust of Shakespeare is a conventional sort of statuary for its time. Still, it is one of the only two contemporary likenesses we have. The other is the Droeshout engraving of Shakespeare in the Folio of 1623.

The epitaph on the monument reads as follows:

Iudicio Phylium, genio Socratem, arte Maronem;
Terra tegit, populus maeret, Olympus habet.
Stay passenger. Why goest thou by so fast?
Read, if thou canst, whom envious Death hath placed
Within this monument: Shakespeare, with whom
Quick Nature died, whose name doth deck this tomb
Far more than cost, sith all that he hath writ
Leaves living art but page to serve his wit.
Obiit anno domini 1616,
Aetatis 53, die 23 April.

These lines, of which the beginning Latin couplet compares Shakespeare with Nestor (King of Pylos) for wise judgment, Socrates for genius, and Virgil (Maro) for poetic art, and avers that the earth covers him, people grieve for him, and Mount Olympus (that is, heaven) has him, indicate the high reputation he enjoyed at the time of his death. More widely known, perhaps, are the four lines inscribed over Shakespeare's grave near the north wall of the chancel. A local tradition assigns them to Shakespeare himself and implies that he wrote them "to suit the capacity of clerks and sextons," whom he wished apparently to frighten out of the idea of opening the grave to make room for a new occupant:

Good friend, for Jesus' sake forbear
To dig the dust enclosèd here.
Blest be the man that spares these stones,
And curst be he that moves my bones.

Martin Droeshout's engraving on the title page of the First Folio is one of only two authentic likenesses of Shakespeare in existence.

Whether Shakespeare actually wrote these lines cannot, however, be determined.

Other Dramatists

The most significant new development in the drama of the period from about 1608 to 1616, apart from Shakespeare's new interest in romance and tragicomedy, was the emergence of the famous literary partners Francis Beaumont and John Fletcher. Beaumont, the son of a distinguished lawyer, studied for a while at Oxford and then at the Inner Temple before drifting into a literary career. In 1613, he married an heiress and retired almost completely from the theater. John Fletcher was the son of Richard Fletcher, Queen Elizabeth's chaplain and later Bishop of London. The young man probably studied at Cambridge. The father died in 1596 heavily in debt, leaving the young Fletcher to support a family of eight children. Fletcher became a professional writer, earning his living as chief dramatist for the King's men. He was Shakespeare's successor. Fletcher's cousins, Giles and Phineas Fletcher,

gained some reputation as poets. Beaumont and Fletcher, who were close friends, regarded themselves also as poets and as members of the "tribe of Ben"—the disciples of the great Ben Jonson who often gathered together at the Mermaid Tavern for an evening of witty literary conversation.

> What things have we seen
> Done at the Mermaid! heard words that have been
> So nimble, and so full of subtle flame,
> As if that every one from whence they came
> Had meant to put his whole wit in a jest,
> And had resolved to live a fool the rest
> Of his dull life!

(Master Francis Beaumont's Letter to Ben Jonson)

Beaumont and Fletcher actually collaborated on only about seven plays: *The Woman Hater,* a comedy (1606); *The Maid's Tragedy*, a tragedy (1608–1611); *Philaster,* a tragicomedy (1608–1610); *Cupid's Revenge,* a tragedy (c. 1607–1612); *The Coxcomb,* a comedy (1608–1610); *A King and No King,* a tragicomedy (1611); *The Scornful Lady,* a tragicomedy (1613–1616); and perhaps one or two others. They may have collaborated on *The Knight of the Burning Pestle* (c. 1607–1610), though it was chiefly Beaumont's. Beaumont also wrote *Mask of the Inner Temple and Gray's Inn* (1613). Fletcher unassisted wrote *The Faithful Shepherdess* (1608–1609), *The Night Walker* (c. 1611), *Bonduca* (1611–1614), *Valentinian* (1610–1614), and others. He also collaborated with several other writers, including Massinger, Middleton, Field, and Rowley. Importantly, he seems to have collaborated with Shakespeare on *The Two Noble Kinsmen* (1613–1616) and, probably, on *Henry VIII.* Eventually, most of these various dramatic enterprises were gathered together in 1647 as the works of Beaumont and Fletcher. They have remained known as such ever since, partly because the original collaboration of these two men did so much to set a new style in coterie drama.

The plays they wrote together, such as *The Maid's Tragedy* and *Philaster,* offer an interesting comparison with Shakespeare's contemporary writing in a similar genre. Beaumont and Fletcher often employ exotic settings, like Rhodes or Sicily. In such an environment, refined aristocratic characters are caught in dynastic struggles or in a rarified conflict between love and honor. They must cope with stereotyped villains, such as tyrants or shamelessly lustful courtiers. The sentiments are lofty, the rhetoric is mannered; elaborately contrived situations are offered with no pretense of verisimilitude. The characters live according to lofty chivalric codes and despise ill breeding above all else. In the plotting of the tragicomic reversal, the audience is sometimes deliberately deceived into believing something that is not true, so that the sudden happy outcome arrives as a theatrically contrived surprise. Disguising and masking are common motifs. The audience is deliberately made aware throughout of the play's theatrical artifice, statuesque scene building, and titillating sensationalism.

Although Shakespeare wrote no tragedies after *Coriolanus,* great tragedy did continue to appear on the Jacobean stage. John Webster wrote his two most splendid plays, *The White Devil* and *The Duchess of Malfi,* between 1609 and 1614. Both contain elements of the still-popular revenge tradition. They also manage to achieve a vision of triumphant human dignity in defeat that merits comparison with Shakespeare's greatest tragic achievement. Still to come were *The Changeling* (1622) by Thomas Middleton and William Rowley, *Women Beware Women* (c. 1620–1627) by Middleton, *'Tis Pity She's a Whore* (1629?–1633) by John Ford, and others. Although these tragedies are more concerned with the grotesque than are Shakespeare's great tragedies, and more obsessed with abnormal human psychology (incest, werewolfism, and the like), they are nonetheless sublime achievements in art. The genius of the age for tragedy did not die with Shakespeare. During Shakespeare's last years, George Chapman was also writing his best tragedies, including *Charles Duke of Byron* in 1608, *The Revenge of Bussy D'Ambois* in about 1610, and *Chabot, Admiral of France* between 1611 and 1622. Ben Jonson's *Catiline His Conspiracy,* a classical tragedy, appeared in 1611; Marston's *The Insatiate Countess,* in about 1610.

The Anti-Stratfordian Movement

What we know of Shakespeare's life is really quite considerable. The information we have is just the kind one would expect. It hangs together and refers to one man and one career. Though lacking in the personal details we should like to have, it is both adequate and plausible. Yet the past hundred years or so have seen the growth of a tendency to doubt Shakespeare's authorship of the plays and poems ascribed to him. The phenomenon is sometimes called the "anti-Stratfordian" movement, since its attack is leveled at the literary credentials of the man who was born in Stratford and later became an actor in London. Although based on no reliable evidence, the movement has persisted long enough to become a kind of myth. It also has the appeal of a mystery thriller: who really wrote Shakespeare's plays? A brief account must be made here of the origins of the anti-Stratfordian movement.

Beginning in the late eighteenth century, and especially in the mid nineteenth century, a few admirers of Shakespeare began to be troubled by the scantiness of information about England's greatest author. As we have already seen, good reasons exist for the scarcity: the great London fire of 1666 that destroyed many records, the relatively low social esteem accorded to popular dramatists during the Elizabethan period, and the like. Also, we do actually know more about Shakespeare than about most of his contemporaries in the theater, despite the difficulties imposed by the passage of time. Still, some nineteenth-century readers saw only that they knew far less about Shakespeare than about many authors of more recent date.

Moreover, the impressions of the man did not seem to square with his unparalleled literary greatness. William Shakespeare had been brought up in a small country town; were his parents cultured folk or even literate? No record of his schooling has been preserved; was Shakespeare himself able to read and write, much less write immortal plays and poems? The anti-Stratfordians did not deny the existence of a man called Shakespeare from Stratford-upon-Avon, but they found it incredible that such a person should be connected with the works ascribed to him. Mark Twain, himself an anti-Stratfordian, was fond of joking that the plays were not by Shakespeare but by another person of the same name. Beneath the humor in this remark lies a deep-seated mistrust: how could a country boy have written so knowledgeably and eloquently about the lives of kings and queens? Where could such a person have learned so much about the law, about medicine, about the art of war, about heraldry? The puzzle seemed a genuine one, even though no one until the late eighteenth century had thought to question Shakespeare's authorship of the plays—least of all his colleagues and friends, such as Ben Jonson, who admitted that Shakespeare's classical learning was "small" but insisted that Shakespeare was an incomparable genius.

The first candidate put forward in the anti-Stratfordian cause as the "real" author of the plays was Sir Francis Bacon, a reputable Elizabethan writer with connections at court and considerable cultural attainments. Yet the ascription of the plays to Bacon was based on no documentary evidence. It relied, instead, on the essentially snobbish argument that Bacon was better born and purportedly better educated than Shakespeare—an argument that appealed strongly to the nineteenth century in which a university education was becoming more and more a distinctive mark of the cultivated person. The assertion of Bacon's authorship was also based on a conspiratorial theory of history; that is, its believers had to assume the existence of a mammoth conspiracy in Elizabethan times in which Shakespeare would allow his name to be used by Bacon as a *nom de plume* and in which Shakespeare's friends, such as Ben Jonson, would take part. (Jonson knew Shakespeare too well, after all, to have been duped for a period of almost twenty years.) The motive for such an arrangement, presumably, was that Bacon did not deign to lend his dignified name to the writing of popular plays (since they were considered subliterary) and so chose a common actor named Shakespeare to serve as his alter ego. This theory of an elaborate hoax involving England's greatest literary giant has proved powerfully attractive to modern writers like Mark Twain who have sometimes referred to themselves as rebels against the cultural "Establishment" of their own times.

The claim that Bacon wrote Shakespeare's works was soon challenged in the name of other prominent Elizabethans: the Earl of Oxford, the Earl of Southampton, Anthony Bacon, the Earl of Rutland, the Earl of Devonshire, Christopher Marlowe, and others. Since documentary claims as to Bacon's authorship of the Shakespearen canon were nonexistent, other Elizabethans could be proposed to fill his role just as satisfactorily as Bacon himself. The anti-Stratfordian movement gained momentum and came to include several prominent persons, including Delia Bacon and Sigmund Freud, as well as Mark Twain. One of the appeals of the anti-Stratfordian movement in recent years has proved to be a kind of amateur sleuthing or scholarship, carried on by professional lawyers, doctors, and the like, who have explored Shakespeare's interest in law and medicine as a hobby and have convinced themselves that Shakespeare's wisdom in these subjects entitles him to claim a better birth than that of a glover's son from Stratford. Ingenious efforts at "deciphering" hidden meanings in the works have been adduced to prove one authorship claim or another. The academic "Establishments" of modern universities have been accused of perpetuating Shakespeare's name out of mere vested self-interest: Shakespeare scholarship is an industry, and its busy workers need to preserve their source of income.

We must ask in all seriousness, however, whether such assertions are not offering answers to nonexistent questions. Responsible scholarship has admirably dispelled the seeming mystery of Shakespeare's humble beginnings. T. W. Baldwin, for example, in *William Shakespeare's Petty School* (1943) and *William Shakspere's Small Latine and Lesse Greeke* (1944), has shown just what sort of classical training Shakespeare almost surely received in the free grammar school of Stratford. It is precisely the sort of training that would have enabled him to use classical authors as he does, with the familiarity of one who likes to read. His Latin and Greek were passable but not strong; he often consulted modern translations, as well as classical originals. Just as importantly, Shakespeare's social background was, in fact, typical of many of the greatest writers of the English Renaissance. He earned his living by his writing, and thus had one of the strongest of motives for success. So did his contemporaries Marlowe (who came from a shoemaker's family) and Jonson (whose stepfather was a brickmason). Greene, Peele, Nashe, and many others sold plays and other writings for a livelihood. Although a few wellborn persons, such as Bacon and Sir Philip Sidney, also made exceptional contributions to literature, and although a number of courtiers emulated Henry VIII and Elizabeth as gifted amateurs in the arts, the court was not the direct or major source of England's literary greatness. Most courtiers were not, like Shakespeare, professional writers. A man like Bacon lacked Shakespeare's connection with a commercial acting company. Surely the theater was a more relevant "university" for Shakespeare than Oxford or Cambridge, where most of his studies would have been in ancient languages and in divinity.

SHAKESPEARE'S LANGUAGE: HIS DEVELOPMENT AS POET AND DRAMATIST

LANGUAGE AND ARTISTIC DEVELOPMENT

One indication of Shakespeare's greatness is his extraordinary development. As he worked through his writing career of more than twenty years, he constantly explored new themes, perfected genres and moved on to new ones, and saw ever more deeply into the human condition. Many of the works that have made him immortal were not written until he was nearly forty years old or more. The study of his development is, in itself, an interesting and complex subject. It is one that requires an accurate dating of his plays and poems.

The First Folio, published in 1623 as the first "complete edition" of Shakespeare's plays in the large and handsome folio format for which the printed sheet was folded only once, gives no help in determining the order of composition of Shakespeare's plays. They are arranged in three groups—comedies, histories, and tragedies—without regard for dates of composition. The first comedy in the Folio is *The Tempest*, known to be one of Shakespeare's latest plays; the second is *The Two Gentlemen of Verona*, one of the earliest. The histories are arranged in order of the English kings whose reigns they treat, although Shakespeare clearly did not write them in that order. The tragedies show no discernible arrangement by date. Information about dating can partially be recovered from the fact that eighteen of the thirty-six plays in the First Folio had previously been published in single quarto volumes at various times, with dates on their title pages. *Pericles*, which was not included in the First Folio, appeared in quarto format in 1609. (The quarto format required that the printed sheet be folded twice, resulting in a smaller page than that of a folio volume.) All the quarto editions, except *Romeo and Juliet* and *Love's Labor's Lost*, were entered in the Register of the Stationers' Company of London; two other plays, *As You Like It* (entered in the Stationers' Register in 1600) and *Antony and Cleopatra* (S.R. 1608), although not printed in quarto, were entered in the Stationers' Register possibly in order to forestall publication by printers who had no right to them. The date of entry of a play in the register indicates that, at least by that time, the play was in existence. The quarto editions also have certain information on their title pages regarding date, author, and publisher, and sometimes tell what theatrical company acted

A CATALOGVE

of the ſeuerall Comedies, Hiſtories, and Tragedies contained in this Volume.

John Heminges and Henry Condell, Shakespeare's fellow actors, gathered contents for the First Folio, published in 1623. They collected thirty-six plays in the volume, omitting Pericles *and* The Two Noble Kinsmen. Troilus and Cressida *is included in most copies of the First Folio but is not listed here in the contents.*

the play. Other kinds of external evidence of date include references to Shakespeare's plays in diaries, journals, or accounts of the period, and quotations from his plays in the literary works of Elizabethan and Jacobean writers. Allusions in Shakespeare's plays themselves to contemporary events, although difficult to prove beyond dispute, can sometimes be helpful. See Appendix 1, at the end of this volume, for a detailed discussion on "Canon, Dates, and Early Texts" of each of Shakespeare's plays.

Once Shakespeare's plays have been arranged in approximate chronological order on the basis of the kinds of external evidence already described, we can perceive that his style underwent a continuous development from his earliest work to the end of his career as a dramatist. Matters of style are not easy to talk about precisely, and we can hardly expect to be able to date a particular passage as having been written in 1604, say, as distinguished from 1602. Overall, on the other hand, the early and late Shakespeare are strikingly distinguishable. Take, for example, the following two passages. One is from the Duke of Clarence's description of his dream in *Richard III* (1.4.21–33), written in about 1591–1594, near the start of Shakespeare's career:

> Oh, Lord, methought what pain it was to drown!
> What dreadful noise of waters in my ears!
> What sights of ugly death within my eyes!
> Methoughts I saw a thousand fearful wracks;
> Ten thousand men that fishes gnawed upon;
> Wedges of gold, great anchors, heaps of pearl,
> Inestimable stones, unvalued jewels,
> All scattered in the bottom of the sea.
> Some lay in dead men's skulls, and in the holes
> Where eyes did once inhabit there were crept,
> As 'twere in scorn of eyes, reflecting gems,
> That wooed the slimy bottom of the deep
> And mocked the dead bones that lay scattered by.

The second is Prospero's description of his magic in *The Tempest* (5.1.33–50), from about 1610–1611 when Shakespeare was on the verge of retirement:

> Ye elves of hills, brooks, standing lakes, and groves,
> And ye that on the sands with printless foot
> Do chase the ebbing Neptune, and do fly him
> When he comes back; you demi-puppets that
> By moonshine do the green sour ringlets make,
> Whereof the ewe not bites; and you whose pastime
> Is to make midnight mushrooms, that rejoice
> To hear the solemn curfew; by whose aid,
> Weak masters though ye be, I have bedimmed
> The noontide sun, called forth the mutinous winds,
> And twixt the green sea and the azured vault
> Set roaring war; to the dread rattling thunder
> Have I given fire, and rifted Jove's stout oak
> With his own bolt; the strong-based promontory
> Have I made shake, and by the spurs plucked up
> The pine and cedar; graves at my command

> Have waked their sleepers, oped, and let 'em forth
> By my so potent art.

These two passages have been chosen for comparison, in part because they are both set speeches in blank verse, rich in formal characteristics. Put side by side, they reveal a stylistic shift that we can observe in other less formal poetry and even in prose. The shift is away from rhetorical balance toward a freedom from verse restraint, a deliberate syncopation of blank verse rhythms, and a complication of syntax.

Completely regular blank verse, invariably consisting of ten syllables to each unrhymed line, with an accent falling on every other syllable, soon becomes monotonous. The iambic pattern can, however, be varied by a number of subtle changes. Extra syllables, accented and unaccented, can be added to the line, or a line may occasionally be short by one or more syllables. The regular alternation of accented and unaccented syllables, producing the effect of five iambic "feet" in each line (each foot consisting of an accented and an unaccented syllable), can be interrupted by the occasional inversion of a foot. Pauses, or caesuras, may occur at several points in the line. Most importantly, the line can be "endstopped"—with a strong pause at the end of the line—or "run on" without interruption into the next line. Variations of this sort can transform blank verse from a formal and rhetorical vehicle into one that is highly conversational and supple.

Shakespeare increasingly abandons formal endstopped verse for a fluid and more conversational style. In the preceding two passages, the first introduces a grammatical stop at the end of every line, except the ninth, whereas the second passage tends to run on past the end of the line; it does so in all but the fifth and tenth lines. Similarly, the passage from *The Tempest* is more apt to introduce a grammatical pause in the middle of a verse line, whereas the passage from *Richard III* stops between clauses in midline only in line 9. Shakespeare's later style is freer in its use of so-called feminine ends at the ends of lines, that is, endings with an unstressed syllable added on to the final stress of the iambic pattern; "fly him," "pastime," and "thunder" are good examples of this. A corollary of Shakespeare's increased use of feminine line endings and nonstopped blank verse is that the lines of his later verse are more apt to end in conjunctions, prepositions, auxiliary verbs, possessive pronouns, and other lightly stressed words. The *Richard III* passage generally ends in strong verbs and nouns, such as "drown," "ears," "eyes," and so on, whereas the *Tempest* passage makes use of "that," "up," and "forth."

Stylistic traits such as these can be quantified to demonstrate a fairly steady course of progression from the early to later plays. Early plays have low percentages of run-on lines in relation to the total number of lines: *1*

Henry VI has 10.4 percent, *2 Henry VI* 11.4 percent, *3 Henry VI* 9.5 percent, *The Comedy of Errors* 12.9 percent, and *The Two Gentlement of Verona* 12.4 percent, whereas *Cymbeline* has 46.0 percent, *The Winter's Tale* 37.5 percent, *The Tempest* 41.5 percent, and *Henry VIII* 46.3 percent. Feminine or "double" endings run from a total of 9 in *Love's Labor's Lost* and 29 in *A Midsummer Night's Dream* to 708 in *Coriolanus*, 726 in *Cymbeline*, and 1,195 in *Henry VIII*. The actual number of light or weak endings increases from none in *The Comedy of Errors* and *The Two Gentlemen of Verona* to 104 in *Coriolanus*, 130 in *Cymbeline*, and 100 in *The Tempest*.

Other stylistic characteristics, though not discernible in the two examples from *Richard III* and *The Tempest*, spell out a similar development toward flexibility. For example, Shakespeare increasingly divides a verse line between two or more speakers. *The Comedy of Errors* and *1 Henry VI* do so hardly at all, whereas in *Cymbeline* the figures rise to a remarkable 85 percent of all instances in which one speaker stops speaking and another begins; *The Winter's Tale* does so in 87.6 percent of such instances, and *The Tempest*, in 84.5 percent.

Shakespeare's use of prose in his plays depends, to a significant extent, on genre, especially in his early work. At the start of his career, Shakespeare seldom uses prose, except in the speeches of clowns, servants, and rustics, whereas blank verse is his common vehicle of expression in speeches of heightened oratory or dramatic seriousness. *1 Henry VI* and *3 Henry VI*, *King John*, and *Richard II* are essentially written throughout in verse—usually blank verse. Prose is more common in the early comedies because of the presence of the Dromios, Christopher Sly, and Bottom the Weaver, but the love scenes are generally in verse. Poetry is important to the lyric plays of the mid-1590s, such as *The Merchant of Venice, A Midsummer Night's Dream,* and *Romeo and Juliet*. Prose assumes a major function, on the other hand, in plays of comic wit in the later 1590s, including *1 Henry IV* (45 percent), *2 Henry IV* (54 percent), *Much Ado About Nothing* (74 percent), and *The Merry Wives of Windsor* (81 percent), and here we see that comedy is used not for wisecracking servants so much as for Falstaff, Beatrice, and Benedick. Thereafter, prose is essential to Shakespeare's comic world. It also takes on a major function in *Hamlet* (31 percent), as, for instance, when Hamlet converses with his onetime friends Rosencrantz and Guildenstern, when he plagues Polonius with his satirical wit, or when he philosophizes with Horatio, though verse is, of course, appropriate for the soliloquies and the moments of confrontation with Claudius. In the other great tragedies as well, prose has become for Shakespeare an instrument of limitless flexibility. Although the mixture of prose and blank verse is thus hard to quantify in any steady progression of percentages, the pattern of increased versatility is undeniable. Many of the late plays make less use of prose because of

their choice of subject, but all excel in prose comic scenes for Autolycus, Caliban, and many others.

In his use of rhyme, as well, Shakespeare's practice changes from the early to late plays. Early plays and those of the lyric period, such as *A Midsummer Night's Dream* and *Romeo and Juliet*, use a great deal of rhyme, whereas late plays, such as *The Tempest*, use practically none. The commonest form of rhyme is the iambic pentameter measure rhymed in couplet, as when Phoebe, quoting Marlowe's *Hero and Leander,* says in *As You Like It* (3.5.81–2):

> Dead shepherd, now I find thy saw of might,
> "Who ever loved that loved not at first sight?"

Shakespeare does not limit his use of rhyme to the couplet, however. *Romeo and Juliet* and *Love's Labor's Lost* each contains a number of complete sonnets, as well as rhymed sequences made up of a quatrain followed by a couplet, and a good deal of alternate rhyme. Doggerel lines of verse appear in some of the early plays.

One quite formal use of the rhymed couplet does not conform to the statistical pattern that we observe generally in the use of rhyme. Because the Elizabethan theater lacked a front curtain to mark a pause between scenes in a play, Elizabethan dramatists often gave emphasis to a scene ending by means of a rhymed couplet. Possibly the device served also as a cue to those actors backstage who were waiting to begin the next scene. At any rate, the use of scene-ending couplets is common in some plays that otherwise make little use of rhyme. For example, Act 1, scene 5 of *Hamlet* virtually ends with the following concluding statement by the protagonist:

> The time is out of joint. O cursèd spite,
> That ever I was born to set it right!

Apart from this convention, however, use of rhyme in Shakespeare is normally indicative of early style. His lovers in the early plays often speak in rhyme; later, they tend to use prose.

Impossible to quantify, but no less significant in any study of the evolution of Shakespeare's art, is his use of imagery. Images are key to his poetic imagination, and, in part, they can be appreciated out of chronological context, because Shakespeare's mind dwells incessantly on certain image clusters: the family as a metaphor for the state, the garden as an image of social order and disorder, images of medicine and healing applied to the ills of the individual and the commonwealth, images of sexual desire and activity, images of hunting and of other sports, biblical images (Eden, Cain and Abel, Christ's ministry, his Passion, the Last Judgment, etc.), mythological allusions (Danae, Actaeon, Phaethon, Noah, Niobe), and many others. Patterns of imagery have been well studied by Caroline Spurgeon in her *Shakespeare's Imagery and What It Tells Us* (1935), Maurice Charney in *The Function of Imagery in the Drama* (1961), and others. In addition, we can see throughout Shakespeare's career the evolution of an imagistic style, as convincingly demonstrated by Wolfgang Clemen in *The Development of Shakespeare's Imagery* (1951). The early Shakespeare uses figures of speech for decoration and amplification, and learns only gradually to integrate these figures into a presentation of theme, subject, and individual character. In Shakespeare's later work, simile is often transformed into metaphor and assumes an organic function in relation to the entire play. By the end of his career, virtually every aspect of his style has been transformed from one of formal and rhetorical regularity to one of vast flexibility and range.

SHAKESPEARE'S ENGLISH

Pronunciation

How would Shakespeare's plays have sounded to our ears? The distance between Shakespearean and modern English is clearly not as great as in the case of Chaucer, and yet significant differences remain. Spoken English, especially in the pronunciation of vowel sounds, has undergone many striking changes since the early seventeenth century. We can assume that however much Shakespeare's own speech may have been colored by his Warwickshire boyhood, his acting company as a whole was most heavily influenced by London dialect. This form of English had become notably more dominant than in Chaucer's day, though it also included an admixture of northern, eastern, and southern forms because of the cosmopolitan character of the city. Shakespeare often pokes fun at regional dialects in his plays, especially at Welsh, Scottish, and Irish, and at the accents of Frenchmen or other foreigners attempting to speak English (see, for example, *Henry V* and *The Merry Wives of Windsor*).

Reconstructing how early modern English would have sounded is, to be sure, not always easy, since dialect did vary substantially from region to region, and since the ascertaining of pronunciations is often based on rhymes when we cannot be sure how either word in a rhyming pair was pronounced and cannot safely assume that rhymes were exact. Nevertheless, here, in summary form, are some approximate suggestions for pronouncing words in Shakespeare that are not similarly pronounced today. These examples can be applied to similar words: for example, *way* and *say* have the same vowel sound as *day*; *night*, the same vowel sound as *wide*.

folk (sound the *l*)
gnaw (sound the *g*)
knife (sound the *k*; *i* as in *wide*, below)
brush (rhymes with *push*; *r* somewhat trilled)

dull (rhymes with *pull*)
seam (pronounced *same*, with open *a*)
old (pronounced *auld*)
now (pronounced *noo*)
house (pronounced *hoos*)
soul (pronounced *saul*)
know (pronounced *knaw*, with sounded *k*)
own (pronounced *awn*)
tune (pronounced *tiwn*)
rule (pronounced *riwl*; *r* somewhat trilled)
day (pronounced *die*)
time (pronounced *toime*)
wide (pronounced *woide*)
join (rhymes with *line*)
creeping (pronounced *craypin*, with open *a*)
dissention (in four syllables, without *sh* sound)
persuasion (in four syllables, without *zh* sound)

A matter of more practical importance than phonetic changes is that of differences in Shakespeare's English and ours in the accentuation of syllables. Many cases of variable stress can be found in which he seems to have been at liberty to accent the word in two different ways; in other cases, words were customarily accented on a different syllable from that in current speech. For example, the following accentuations are either usual or frequent: *aspect´, charac´ter, com´mendable, com´plete, con´cealed, con´fessor, consort´* (as a noun), *contract´* (noun), *de´testable, dis´tinct, envy´, for´lorn, hu´mane, instinct´, ob´scure, persev´er, pi´oner, ple´beians, portents´, pur´sue, record´* (noun), *reven´ue, se´cure, sinis´ter, welcome´.*

Not only are *-tion* and *-sion* regularly pronounced as two syllables, but the same situation causes other words in which *e* or *i* stand before vowels to be uttered in Shakespeare's language with one more syllable than in ours; for example, *oce-an, courti-er, marri-age.* We may even have *cre-ature, tre-asure,* and *venge-ance.* Nasals and liquids are frequently pronounced as if an extra vowel were introduced between them and a preceding letter. Accordingly, we have *wrest(e)ler, Eng(e)land, assemb(e)ly,* and *ent(e)rance,* as well as *de-ar, you(e)r,* and *mo-re.* Final *-er* often has a greater syllabic importance than it has in later poetry. Final *-(e)s* in the genitive singular and the plural of nouns not ending in an *-s* sound may constitute a separate syllable; for example, "To show his teeth as white as whale's bone" (*Love's Labor's Lost,* 5.2.333).

The study of metrics is fraught with peril. Knowledge of syllabification can often be circular in that it has to assume a kind of metrical regularity in the line of a verse. Even so, in scanning of Shakespeare's verse it helps to ascertain as accurately as we can how many syllables he intended a given word to have. As compared to modern-day English, a Shakespearean word may have (1) an additional syllable, or (2) one fewer syllables, or (3) two adjoining syllables in adjoining words that coalesce or elide. Spelling may not always indicate these differences to a modern reader.

1. The following lines give us extra-syllable words in *moon's, juggler, entrance*, and *complexion*:

> I do wander everywhere,
> Swifter than the moon's sphere.
> (A Midsummer Night's Dream, 2.1.6–7)

> O me! You juggler! You cankerblossom!
> (A Midsummer Night's Dream, 3.2.282)

> After the prompter, for our entrance.
> (Romeo and Juliet, 1.4.8)

> Mislike me not for my complexion.
> (The Merchant of Venice, 2.1.1)

Similarly, the words *captain, monstrous, esperance, this* (*this is*), *George* (*Richard III*, 5.5.9), *valiant, villain*, and *jealous* sometimes have extra syllables in pronunciation.

2. In the following line, *marry* is elided into one syllable:

> Good mother, do not *marry* me to yond fool.
> (The Merry Wives of Windsor, 3.4.83)

Similarly, the words *lineal, journeying, carrion, celestial, herald, royal, malice, absolute, perjury, madame, needle, taken, heaven, spirit, devil, gentleman, unpeople, forward, gather, innocent, violet, Africa, eagle, listen*, and *venomous* have usually one fewer syllables than in current English.

3. The following examples are of elision between the syllables of adjoining words:

> Why should I joy in *an abortive* birth?
> (Love's Labor's Lost, 1.1.104)

> The *lover, all* as frantic,
> (A Midsummer Night's Dream, 5.1.10)

> Romans, *do me* right.
> (Titus Andronicus, 1.1.204)

Differences in accentuation and lengthening or shortening of words thus have great importance in the reading and scanning of Shakespeare's verse. Shortening of words by elision or by slurring is common in Shakespeare, but at least in this matter modern practice forms a good guide. Syllables ending in vowels are not infrequently elided before words beginning with a vowel, as in "How cáme / we ashóre" (*The Tempest*, 1.2.159) and "too hárd / a knót / for mé / t' untie" (*Twelfth Night*, 2.2.41). Syncopation, or the omission of a syllable, often occurs in words with *r*, as in "I wár-rant / it wíll" (*Hamlet*, 1.2.248); and in final *-er, -el*, and *-le*, as in "Trável you / farre ón" (*The Taming of the Shrew*, 4.2.74). The following words and other similar ones may be treated as monosyllabic in Shakespeare's verse: *whether, ever, hither, other, father, evil, having*. Almost any unaccented syllable of a polysyllabic word (especially if it contains an *i*) may be softened and ignored. This syncopation is frequent in polysyllabic words and proper names: "Thoughts spécu / latíve" (*Macbeth*, 5.4.19) and "Did sláy / this Fórtinbras; / who by / a seáled /compáct" (*Hamlet*, 1.1.90). Other occasions for slurring, as listed by Abbott in his *Shakespearian Grammar*, are light vowels preceded by heavy vowels, as in *power, dying*, and so on; plurals and possessives of nouns ending in an *s* sound, as in *empress'* and *Mars'*; final *-ed* following *d* or *t*, as in "you háve / exceéded / all prómise" (*As You Like It*, 1.2.234); and the *-est* of superlatives (pronounced *-st*) after dentals and liquids, as "the stérn'st / good-níght" (*Macbeth*, 2.2.4) and "thy éldest / son's són" (*King John*, 2.1.177).

Grammar and Rhetoric

Shakespeare's grammar presents but few differences in forms from the grammar of current modern English. The *-eth* ending in the third person singular of the present tense, indicative mood, was very commonly used, especially in serious prose. Shakespeare frequently uses this older form, especially *hath, doth*, and *saith*, but seems to prefer the form in *-s* or *-es*. In a few cases, he also seems to use the old northern plural in *-s* or *-es* in the third person of the present indicative, as " . . . at those springs, / On chaliced flowers that *lies*" (*Cymbeline*, 2.3.22–3). He does not always agree with modern usage in the forms of the past tenses and the perfect participles of the verbs that he employs. He retains some lost forms of the strong verbs, sometimes ignores distinctions we make between the past tense and the perfect participle, and treats some verbs as weak (or regular) which are now strong (or irregular). For example, he uses *arose* for *arisen, swam* for *swum, foughten* for *fought, gave* for *given, took* for *taken, sprung* for *sprang, writ* for *wrote, blowed* for *blew, weaved* for *wove*, and *shaked* for *shaken*. Forms like *degenerate* for *degenerated* and *exhaust* for *exhausted* are especially common. A few instances are to be found of the archaic *y-* with the past participle, as in *yclad*. For the possessive case of the neuter personal pronoun *it*, Shakespeare normally uses the regular form at that time, *his*; but he also uses the possessive form *it*, and in his plays first published in the First Folio in 1623 we find several occurrences of the new form *its*. Shakespeare uses the old form *moe*, as well as *more*, and *enow* as the plural of *enough*, though these forms have been modernized in this edition because they are used so inconsistently. He uses *near* and *next* along with *nearer* and *nearest*, as the comparative and superlative of *nigh*. These are the most obvious of the formal differences between Shakespeare's grammar and our own.

The functional differences are more considerable. Elizabethan language exercised an extraordinary freedom, even for English, in the use of one part of speech for another. Shakespeare uses verbs, adjectives, adverbs, and pronouns as nouns. He makes verbs out of nouns and adjectives and, of course, uses nouns as adjectives, for this is a distinguishing characteristic of English speech, but he also uses adverbs, verbs, and prepositional phrases as adjectives, as in "Looks he as freshly as he did . . . ?" (*As You Like It*, 3.2.227). Almost any adjective may be freely used as an adverb, as in "And in my house you shall be friendly lodged" (*The Taming of the Shrew*, 4.2.109). He makes active words—both adjectives and verbs—discharge a passive function, as in "the sightless [invisible] couriers of the air" (*Macbeth*, 1.7.23) and "this aspect of mine / Hath feared the valiant," that is, caused the valiant to be afraid (*The Merchant of Venice*, 2.1.8–9). He makes wider use of the infinitive as a verbal noun or as a gerundive participle than do we: "This to be true / I do engage my life" (*As You Like It*, 5.4.164–5), "My operant powers their functions leave to do" (*Hamlet*, 3.2.172), "Nor do I now make moan to be abridged" (*The Merchant of Venice*, 1.1.126), and "You might have saved me my pains, to have taken [by having taken] it away yourself" (*Twelfth Night*, 2.2.5–7). The functions of prepositions in Elizabethan English were so various that one can only refer the student to the notes to the text or to a dictionary.

In certain other features, however, as, for example, in the use of modal auxiliaries, Shakespeare's language is as restricted and conventional as ours is at formal levels, or even more so. *Shall* is regularly used in Shakespeare to express something inevitable in future time and is, therefore, the usual future tense for all persons. *Will*, which originally expressed intention, determination, or willingness, was, to be sure, beginning to encroach on *shall* for the expression of futurity in the second and third persons, but its use usually still retains in Shakespeare a consciousness of its original meaning. *Should* and *would* had their original senses of obligation and volition, respectively, and had other peculiarities, then as now, of considerable difficulty. The subjunctive mood was vital to Shakespeare as a means of expressing condition, doubt, concession, command, wish, or desire, and, in dependent clauses, indefiniteness, purpose, or sometimes simple futurity. Note the following examples:

But if my father *had* not scanted me . . .
Yourself, renownèd prince, then *stood* as fair.
(*The Merchant of Venice*, 2.1.17, 20)

Live a thousand years,
I *shall* not find myself so apt to die.
(*Julius Caesar*, 3.1.161–2)

Lest your retirement do *amaze* your friends.
(*1 Henry IV*, 5.4.6)

'Twere best he speak no harm of Brutus here.
(*Julius Caesar*, 3.2.70)

Melt Egypt into Nile, and kindly creatures
Turn all to serpents!
(*Antony and Cleopatra*, 2.5.79–80)

Yet were it true
To say this boy *were* like me.
(*The Winter's Tale*, 1.2.134–5)

And may direct his course as *please* himself.
(*Richard III*, 2.2.129)

Some other features of Shakespeare's grammar are as follows: he often omits the relative pronoun; he often uses the nominative case of the pronoun for the accusative case, and vice versa; he uses *him*, *her*, *me*, and *them* as true reflexives to mean *himself*, *herself*, *myself*, and *themselves*; he employs double negatives and double comparatives and superlatives; he shows a consciousness in the use of *thee* and *thou* of their application to intimates and inferiors and of their insulting quality when addressed to strangers (e.g., "If thou 'thou'-est him some thrice, it shall not be amiss," *Twelfth Night*, 3.2.43–4); he employs *which* to refer to both persons and things; and he does not discriminate closely between *ye*, nominative, and *you*, objective. He makes frequent use of the dative constructions, that is, the objective forms of the pronouns, *me*, *thee*, *you*, *him*, *her*, and so on, without prepositions where the meaning is "by me," "for me," "with me," "to me," "of me," and the like. For example:

I am appointed *him* [by him] to murder you.
(*The Winter's Tale*, 1.2.411)

She looks *us* [to us] like
A thing made more of malice than of duty.
(*Cymbeline*, 3.5.32–3)

One prominent feature of Shakespeare's grammar is his use of the ethical dative, a construction in which the pronoun is generally used to indicate the person interested in the statement. In *King John* (3.4.146), the phrase "John lays you plots," means something like "John lays plots which you may profit by." In the following, *me* means "to my detriment" or "to my disadvantage":

See how this river comes *me* cranking in
And cuts *me* from the best of all my land
A huge half-moon.
(*1 Henry IV*, 3.1.95–7)

"Whip *me* such honest knaves" (*Othello*, 1.1.51) means "In my judgment such knaves should be whipped." In Quickly's description of Mistress Page, the dative *you* is equivalent to "mark you," "take notice":

. . . a civil modest wife, and one, I tell you, that will not
miss *you* morning nor evening prayer, as any is in Windsor.
(*The Merry Wives of Windsor*, 2.2.92–4)

At times, however, the ethical dative is idiomatic and virtually without equivalent meaning in modern English; the sense of the passage is best obtained by omitting the pronoun.

Shakespeare, like other Renaissance poets, makes extensive use of the forms and figures of rhetoric. He is fond, for example, of using the abstract for the concrete, as in the words addressed by Surrey to Cardinal Wolsey: "Thou scarlet sin" (*Henry VIII*, 3.2.255). Transpositions are numerous, as are inversions, ellipses, and broken or confused constructions, as in the following examples:

That thing you speak of,
I took it for a man. (*Absolute construction.*)
(*King Lear*, 4.6.77–8)

Souls and bodies hath he divorced three. (*Transposition of adjective.*)
(*Twelfth Night*, 3.4.238–9)

A happy gentleman in blood and lineaments. (*Transposition of adjectival phrase.*)
(*Richard II*, 3.1.9)

Your state of fortune and your due of birth. (*Transposition of pronoun.*)
(*Richard III*, 3.7.120)

She calls me proud, and [says] that she could not love me. (*Ellipsis.*)
(*As You Like It*, 4.3.17)

Returning were as tedious as [to] go o'er. (*Ellipsis.*)
(*Macbeth*, 3.4.139)

They call him Doricles, and boasts himself
To have a worthy feeding. (*Ellipsis of nominative.*)
(*The Winter's Tale*, 4.4.168–9)

Of all men else I have avoided thee. (*Confusion of two constructions.*)
(*Macbeth*, 5.8.4)

The venom of such looks, we fairly hope,
Have lost their quality. (*Confusion of number arising from proximity.*)
(*Henry V*, 5.2.18–19)

Rather proclaim it, Westmorland, through my host
That he which hath no stomach to this fight,
Let him depart. (*Construction changed by change of thought.*)
(*Henry V*, 4.3.34–6)

For always I am Caesar. (*Inversion of adverb.*)
(*Julius Caesar*, 1.2.212)

Shakespeare often uses rhetorical figures for symmetrical effects, especially in the early, ornamental style of *Richard III* and the nondramatic poems. Following are definitions of some of the most popular figures he uses, with illustrations from *Venus and Adonis*:

1. *Parison*. The symmetrical repetition of words in grammatically parallel phrases: "How love makes young men thrall, and old men dote" (line 837).

2. *Isocolon*. The symmetrical repetition of sounds and words in phrases of equal length, as in the previous example, and in this: "Or as the wolf doth grin before he barketh, / Or as the berry breaks before it staineth" (lines 459–60). Parison and isocolon are frequently combined.

3. *Anaphora*. The symmetrical repetition of a word at the beginning of a sequence of clauses or sentences, often at the beginning of lines. Anaphora is frequently combined with parison and isocolon, as in the second example already given, and in this: " 'Give me my hand,' saith he. 'Why dost thou feel it?' / 'Give me my heart,' saith she, 'and thou shalt have it' " (lines 373–4).

4. *Antimetabole*. The symmetrical repetition of words in inverted order: "She clepes him king of graves and grave for kings" (line 995).

5. *Anadiplosis*. The beginning of a phrase with the final words of the previous phrase: "O, thou didst kill me; kill me once again!" (line 499).

6. *Epanalepsis*. The symmetrical repetition of a word or words at the beginning and ending of a line: "He sees his love, and nothing else he sees" (line 287).

7. *Ploce*. The insistent repetition of a word within the same line or phrase: "Then why not lips on lips, since eyes in eyes?" (line 120).

8. *Epizeuxis*. An intensified form of ploce, repeating the word without another intervening word: " 'Ay me!' she cries, and twenty times, 'Woe, woe!' / And twenty echoes twenty times cry so" (lines 833–4).

9. *Antanaclasis*. The shifting of a repeated word from one meaning to another: "My love to love is love but to disgrace it," or " 'Where did I leave?' 'No matter where,' quoth he, / 'Leave me' " (lines 412, 715–6).

For other figures and illustrations, see Sister Miriam Joseph, *Shakespeare's Use of the Arts of Language* (1947) and Brian Vickers, "Shakespeare's Use of Rhetoric," in *A New Companion to Shakespeare Studies*, edited by Kenneth Muir and S. Schoenbaum (1971).

Vocabulary

Renaissance English was hospitable to foreign importation. Many words taken directly from Latin became a permanent part of the language, serving to enrich its power to express thought and its rhythmical capabilities; others were ultimately discarded. The principal borrowings were in the realm of learning and culture. Such words usually retained a vital sense of their original Latin meaning. Sometimes such words have not replaced native words of the same meaning, so that we have such pairs of synonyms as *acknowledge* and *confess*, just as Shakespeare had *wonder* and *admiration*. Because of this Latin heritage, even a slight knowledge of Latin is a great advantage in the correct understanding of Elizabethan writers, since many Latin borrowings have taken on since the sixteenth century a different shade of meaning from that in which they were borrowed. The Latin sense of *aggravate* ("to add weight to") still struggles for recognition; but *apparent* no longer means primarily "visible to sight," and *intention* does not convey the idea of "intentness." The *Oxford English Dictionary* (*OED*) provides a wealth of information about derivations and changes in meaning.

Latin words were often taken over in their Latin forms, as *objectum* and *subjectum*, *statua* and *aristocratia*, and later were made to conform to English spelling and stress, though a few, such as *decorum*, still have a Latin form. French continued to be drawn upon and sometimes caused a new Latin borrowing to be adopted in a French form, just as, on the other hand, such words as *adventure* were supplied with a *d* to make them conform to Latin spelling. This principle is illustrated in the pedantry of Holofernes when he objects (*Love's Labor's Lost*, 5.1.20) to "det" as the pronunciation of "debt." Spanish, Italian, and Dutch also supplied many terms. Spanish gave words having to do with commerce, religion, and the New World, such as *mosquito, alligator, ambuscado,* and *grandee*. From Italian came terms of art, learning, and dueling: *bandetto, portico, canto, stoccato*. The Dutch contributed many nautical and oriental words.

These foreign borrowings were a part of what might be called the linguistic ambition of the age, a desire for forcible expression. Language was in a plastic state, so that it had an unparalleled freedom in both vocabulary and form. With this freedom, to be sure, came some confusion, since the Elizabethan era saw few efforts at grammatical precision. Such efforts were later to be made by the age of Dryden and the Royal Society, and by learned men ever since, prompted by an awareness that English was too vague and irregular for use as a means of scientific expression. Still, we readily perceive that English profited from its Renaissance expansion and its subsequent absorption with Shakespeare and the English Bible. It gained, for example, an increased facility in making compounds. Shakespeare, with his *cloud-capped towers* and his *home-keeping wits*, was a genius at this. Also from Shakespeare's time came the English adaptability in the use of prefixes, such as *dis-, re-,* and *en-,* and of suffixes, such as *-ful, -less, -ness,* and *-hood*.

SHAKESPEARE CRITICISM

In his own time, Shakespeare achieved a reputation for immortal greatness that is astonishing when we consider the low regard in which playwrights were then generally held. Francis Meres compared him to Ovid, Plautus, and Seneca, and proclaimed Shakespeare to be England's most excellent writer in both comedy and tragedy. John Weever spoke of "honey-tongued Shakespeare." The number of such praising allusions is high. Even Ben Jonson, a learned writer strongly influenced by the classical tradition, lauded Shakespeare as "a monument without a tomb," England's best poet, exceeding Chaucer, Spenser, Beaumont, Kyd, and Marlowe. In tragedy, Jonson compared Shakespeare with Aeschylus, Euripides, and Sophocles; in comedy, he insisted Shakespeare had no rival even in "insolent Greece or haughty Rome." This tribute appeared in Jonson's commendatory poem written for the Shakespeare First Folio of 1623.

To be sure, Jonson had more critical things to say about Shakespeare. Even in the Folio commendatory poem, Jonson could not resist a dig at Shakespeare's "small Latin, and less Greek." To William Drummond of Hawthornden, he objected that Shakespeare "wanted art" because in a play (*The Winter's Tale*) he "brought in a number of men saying they had suffered shipwreck in Bohemia, where there is no sea near by some hundred miles." In *Timber,* or *Discoveries*, Jonson chided Shakespeare for his unrestrained facility in writing. "The players have often mentioned it as an honor to Shakespeare, that in his writing, whatsoever he penned he never blotted out [a] line. My answer hath been, would he had blotted a thousand." In a preface to his own play, *Every Man in His Humor* (1616 edition), Jonson satirized English history plays (such as Shakespeare's) that "with three rusty swords, / And help of some few foot-and-half-foot words, / Fight over York and Lancaster's long jars, / And in the tiring-house bring wounds to scars." He also jeered at plays lacking unity of time in which children grow to the age of sixty or older and at nonsensical romantic plays featuring fireworks, thunder, and a chorus that "wafts you o'er the seas."

These criticisms are all of a piece. As a classicist himself, Jonson held in high regard the classical unities. He deplored much English popular drama, including some of Shakespeare's plays, for their undisciplined mixture of comedy and tragedy. Measured against his cherished ideals of classical decorum and refinement of language, Shakespeare's histories and the late romances—*Pericles, Cymbeline, The Winter's Tale,* and *The Tempest*—seemed irritatingly naive and loose-jointed. Yet Jonson knew that Shakespeare had an incomparable genius, superior even to his own. Jonson's affection and respect for Shakespeare seem to have been quite unforced. In the midst of his critical remarks in *Timber,* he freely conceded that "I loved the man, and do honor his memory (on this side idolatry) as much as any. He was indeed honest, and of an open and free nature, had an excellent fantasy, brave notions, and gentle expressions."

The Age of Dryden and Pope

Jonson's attitude toward Shakespeare lived on into the Restoration period of the late seventeenth century. A commonplace of that age held it proper to "admire" Ben Jonson but to "love" Shakespeare. Jonson was the more correct poet, the better model for imitation. Shakespeare often had to be rewritten according to the sophisticated tastes of the Restoration (see Appendix 3 for an account of Restoration stage adaptations of Shakespeare), but he was also regarded as a natural genius. Dryden reflected this view in his *Essay of Dramatic Poesy* (1668) and his *Essay on the Dramatic Poetry of the Last Age* (1672). Dryden condemned *The Winter's Tale, Pericles,* and several other late romances for "the lameness of their plots" and for their "ridiculous incoherent story" which is usually "grounded on impossibilities." Not only Shakespeare, he charged, but several of his contemporaries "neither understood correct plotting nor that which they call *the decorum of the stage.*" Had Shakespeare lived in the Restoration, Dryden believed, he would doubtless have written "more correctly" under the influence of a language that had become more "courtly" and a wit that had grown more "refined." Shakespeare, he thought, had limitless "fancy" but sometimes lacked "judgment." Dryden regretted that Shakespeare had been forced to write in "ignorant" times and for audiences who "knew no better." Like Jonson, nevertheless, Dryden had the magnanimity to perceive that Shakespeare transcended his limitations. Shakespeare, said Dryden, was "the man who of all modern and perhaps ancient poets had the largest and most comprehensive soul." From a classical writer, this was high praise indeed.

Alexander Pope's edition of Shakespeare (1725) was based upon a similar estimate of Shakespeare as an untutored genius. Pope freely "improved" Shakespeare's language, rewriting lines and excising those parts he considered vulgar, in order to rescue Shakespeare from the barbaric circumstances of his Elizabethan milieu. Other critics of the Restoration and early eighteenth century who stressed Shakespeare's "natural" genius and imaginative powers were John Dennis, Joseph Addison, and the editors Nicholas Rowe and Lewis Theobald.

The Age of Johnson

Shakespeare was not without his detractors during the late seventeenth and early eighteenth centuries; after all,

classical criticism tended to distrust imagination and fancy. Notable among the harsher critics of the Restoration period was Thomas Rymer, whose *Short View of Tragedy* (1692) included a famous attack on *Othello* for making too much out of Desdemona's handkerchief. In the eighteenth century, Voltaire spoke out sharply against Shakespeare's violation of the classical unities, though Voltaire also had some admiring things to say.

The most considered answer to such criticism in the later eighteenth century was that of Dr. Samuel Johnson, in his edition of Shakespeare's plays and its great preface (1765). Shakespeare, said Johnson, is the poet of nature who "holds up to his readers a faithful mirror of manners and of life. His characters are not modified by the customs of particular places, unpracticed by the rest of the world. . . . In the writings of other poets a character is too often an individual; in those of Shakespeare it is commonly a species." Johnson's attitudes were essentially classical in that he praised Shakespeare for being universal, for having provided a "just representation of general nature," and for having stood the test of time. Yet Johnson also magnanimously praised Shakespeare for having transcended the classical rules. Johnson triumphantly vindicated the mixture of comedy and tragedy in Shakespeare's plays and the supposed indecorum of his characters.

Of course, Johnson did not praise everything he saw. He objected to Shakespeare's loose construction of plot, careless huddling together of the ends of his plays, licentious humor, and, above all, the punning wordplay. He deplored Shakespeare's failure to satisfy the demands of poetic justice, especially in *King Lear,* and he regretted that Shakespeare seemed more anxious to please than to instruct. Still, Johnson did much to free Shakespeare from the constraint of an overly restrictive classical approach to criticism.

The Age of Coleridge

With the beginning of the Romantic period, in England and on the Continent, Shakespeare criticism increasingly turned away from classical precept in favor of a more spontaneous and enthusiastic approach to Shakespeare's creative genius. The new Shakespeare became indeed a rallying cry for those who now deplored such "regular" dramatic poets as Racine and Corneille. Shakespeare became a seer, a bard with mystic powers of insight into the human condition. Goethe, in *Wilhelm Meister* (1796), conceived of Hamlet as the archetypal "Romantic" poet: melancholic, delicate, and unable to act.

Critical trends in England moved toward similar conclusions. Maurice Morgann, in his *Essay on the Dramatic Character of Sir John Falstaff* (1777), glorified Falstaff into a rare individual of courage, dignity, and—yes—honor. To do so, Morgann had to suppress much evidence as to Falstaff's overall function in the *Henry IV* plays. Dramatic structure, in fact, did not interest him; his passion was "character," and his study of Falstaff reflected a new Romantic preoccupation with character analysis. Like other character critics who followed him, Morgann tended to move away from the play itself and into a world where the dramatic personage being considered might lead an independent existence. What would it have been like to know Falstaff as a real person? How would he have behaved on occasions other than those reported by Shakespeare? Such questions fascinated Morgann and others because they led into grand speculations about human psychology and philosophy. Shakespeare's incomparably penetrating insights into character prompted further investigations of the human psyche.

Other late eighteenth-century works devoted to the study of character included Lord Kames's *Elements of Criticism* (1762), Thomas Whately's *Remarks on Some of the Characters of Shakespeare* (1785), William Richardson's *Philosophical Analysis and Illustration of Some of Shakespeare's Remarkable Characters* (1774), and William Jackson's *Thirty Letters on Various Subjects* (1782). Morgann spoke for this school of critics when he insisted, "It may be fit to consider them [Shakespeare's characters] rather as historic than dramatic beings; and, when occasion requires, to account for their conduct from the whole of character, from general principles, from latent motives, and from policies not avowed."

Samuel Taylor Coleridge, the greatest of the English Romantic critics, was profoundly influenced by character criticism, both English and continental. He himself made important contributions to the study of character. His conception of Hamlet, derived in part from Goethe and Hegel, as one who "vacillates from sensibility, and procrastinates from thought, and loses the power of action in the energy of resolve," was to dominate nineteenth-century interpretations of Hamlet. His insight into Iago's evil nature—"the motive-hunting of a motiveless malignity"— was also influential.

Nevertheless, Coleridge did not succumb to the temptation, as did so many character critics, of ignoring the unity of an entire play. Quite to the contrary, he affirmed in Shakespeare an "organic form" or "innate" sense of shape, developed from within, that gave new meaning to Shakespeare's fusion of comedy and tragedy, his seeming anachronisms, his improbable fictions, and his supposedly rambling plots. Coleridge heaped scorn on the eighteenth-century idea of Shakespeare as a "natural" but untaught genius. He praised Shakespeare not for having mirrored life, as Dr. Johnson had said, but for having created an imaginative world attuned to its own internal harmonies. He saw Shakespeare as an inspired but deliberate artist who fitted together the parts of his imaginative world with consummate skill. "The judgment of Shakespeare is commensurate with his genius."

In all this, Coleridge was remarkably close to his German contemporary and rival, August Wilhelm Schlegel, who insisted that Shakespeare was "a profound artist, and not a blind and wildly luxuriant genius." In Shakespeare's plays, said Schlegel, "The fancy lays claim to be considered as an independent mental power governed according to its own laws." Between them, Coleridge and Schlegel utterly inverted the critical values of the previous age, substituting "sublimity" and "imagination" for universality and trueness to nature.

Other Romantic critics included William Hazlitt (*Characters of Shakespear's Plays*, 1817), Charles Lamb (*On the Tragedies of Shakespeare*, 1811), and Thomas De Quincey (*On the Knocking at the Gate in Macbeth*, 1823). Hazlitt reveals a political liberalism characteristic of a number of Romantic writers in his skeptical view of Henry V's absolutism and his imperialist war against the French. John Keats has some penetrating things to say in his letters about Shakespeare's "negative capability," or his ability to see into characters' lives with an extraordinary self-effacing sympathy. As a whole, the Romantics were enthusiasts of Shakespeare, and sometimes even idolaters. Yet they consistently refused to recognize him as a man of the theater. Lamb wrote, "It may seem a paradox, but I cannot help being of opinion that the plays of Shakespeare are less calculated for performance on a stage than those of almost any other dramatist whatever." Hazlitt similarly observed: "We do not like to see our author's plays acted, and least of all, *Hamlet*. There is no play that suffers so much in being transferred to the stage." These hostile attitudes toward the theater reflected, in part, the condition of the stage in nineteenth-century England. In part, however, these attitudes were the inevitable result of character criticism, or what Lamb called the desire "to know the internal workings and movements of a great mind, of an Othello or a Hamlet for instance, the *when* and the *why* and the *how far* they should be moved." This fascination with character swept everything before it during the Romantic period.

A. C. Bradley and the Turn of the Century

The tendency of nineteenth-century criticism, then, was to exalt Shakespeare as a poet and a philosopher rather than as a playwright, and as a creator of immortal characters whose "lives" might be studied as though existing independent of a dramatic text. Not infrequently, this critical approach led to a biographical interpretation of Shakespeare through his plays, on the assumption that what he wrote was his own spiritual autobiography and a key to his own fascinating character. Perhaps the most famous critical study in this line was Edward Dowden's *Shakspere: A Critical Study of His Mind and Art* (1875), in which he traced a progression from Shakespeare's early exuberance and passionate involvement through brooding pessimism to a final philosophical calm.

At the same time, the nineteenth century also saw the rise of a more factual and methodological scholarship, especially in the German universities. Dowden, in fact, reflected this trend as well, for one of the achievements of philological study was to establish with some accuracy the dating of Shakespeare's plays and thus make possible an analysis of his artistic development. Hermann Ulrici's *Über Shakespeares dramatische Kunst* (1839) and Gottfried Gervinus's edition of 1849 were among the earliest studies to interest themselves in Shakespeare's chronological development.

The critic who best summed up the achievement of nineteenth-century Shakespeare criticism was A. C. Bradley, in his *Shakespearean Tragedy* (1904) and other studies. *Shakespearean Tragedy* dealt with the four "great" tragedies: *Hamlet, Othello, King Lear,* and *Macbeth.* Bradley revealed his Romantic tendencies in his focus on psychological analysis of character, but he also brought to his work a scholarly awareness of the text that had been missing in some earlier character critics. His work continues to have considerable influence today, despite modern tendencies to rebel against nineteenth-century idealism. To Bradley, Shakespeare's tragic world was ultimately explicable and profoundly moral. Despite the overwhelming impression of tragic waste in *King Lear,* he argued, we as audience experience a sense of compensation and completion that implies an ultimate pattern in human life. "Good, in the widest sense, seems thus to be the principle of life and health in the world; evil, at least in these worst forms, to be a poison. The world reacts against it violently, and, in the struggle to expel it, is driven to devastate itself." Humanity must suffer because of its fatal tendency to pursue some extreme passion, but humanity learns through suffering about itself and the nature of its world. We as audience are reconciled to our existence through purgative release; we smile through our tears. Cordelia is wantonly destroyed, but the fact of her transcendent goodness is eternal. Although in one sense she fails, said Bradley, she is "in another sense superior to the world in which [she] appears; is, in some way which we do not seek to define, untouched by the doom that overtakes [her]; and is rather set free from life than deprived of it."

Historical Criticism

The first major twentieth-century reaction against character criticism was that of the so-called historical critics. (On the later critical movement known as the New Historicism, see below, following "Jan Kott and the Theater of the Absurd.") These critics insisted on a more hardheaded and skeptical appraisal of Shakespeare through better understanding of his historical milieu: his theater, his audience, and his political and social environment. In good part, this movement was the result of a new professionalism of Shakespearean studies in the twentieth century. Whereas earlier critics—Dryden, Pope, Johnson, and Coleridge—had generally been literary amateurs in the best sense, early twentieth-century criticism became increasingly the province of those who taught in universities. Historical research became a professional activity. Bradley himself was Professor of English Literature at Liverpool and Oxford, and did much to legitimize the incorporation of Shakespeare into the humanities curriculum. German scholarship produced the first regular periodical devoted to Shakespeare studies, *Shakespeare-Jahrbuch,* to be followed in due course in England and America by *Shakespeare Survey* (beginning in 1948), *Shakespeare Quarterly* (1950), and *Shakespeare Studies* (1965).

From the start, historical criticism took a new look at Shakespeare as a man of the theater. Sir Walter Raleigh (Professor of English Literature at Oxford, not to be confused with his Elizabethan namesake) rejected the Romantic absorption in psychology and turned his attention instead to the artistic methods by which plays affect theater-going spectators. The poet Robert Bridges insisted that Shakespeare had often sacrificed consistency and logic for primitive theatrical effects designed to please his vulgar audience. Bridges's objections were often based on serious lack of information about Shakespeare's stage, but they had a healthy iconoclastic effect nonetheless on the scholarship of his time. In Germany, Levin Schücking pursued a similar line of reasoning in his *Character Problems in Shakespeare's Plays* (1917, translated into English in 1922). Schücking argued that Shakespeare had disregarded coherent structure and had striven instead for vivid dramatic effect ("episodic intensification") in his particular scenes. Schücking's *The Meaning of Hamlet* (1937) explained the strange contradictions of that play as resulting from primitive and brutal Germanic source materials which Shakespeare had not fully assimilated.

A keynote for historical critics of the early twentieth century was the concept of artifice or convention in the construction of a play. Perhaps the leading spokesman for this approach was E. E. Stoll, a student of G. L. Kittredge of Harvard University, himself a leading force in historical scholarship in America. Stoll vigorously insisted, in such works as *Othello: An Historical and Comparative Study* (1915), *Hamlet: An Historical and Comparative Study* (1919), and *Art and Artifice in Shakespeare* (1933), that a critic must never be sidetracked by moral, psychological, or biographical interpretations. A play, he argued, is an artifice arising out of its historical milieu. Its conventions are implicit agreements between playwright and spectator. They alter with time, and a modern reader who is ignorant of Elizabethan conventions is all too apt to be misled by his own post-Romantic preconceptions. For example, a calumniator like Iago in *Othello* is conventionally supposed to be believed by the other characters on stage. We do not need to speculate about the "realities" of Othello's being duped, and, in fact, we are likely to be led astray by such Romantic speculations. Stoll went so far as to affirm, in fact, that Shakespearean drama intentionally distorts reality through its theatrical conventions in order to fulfill its own existence as artifice. *Hamlet* is not a play about delay but a revenge story of a certain length, containing many conventional revenge motifs, such as the ghost and the "mousetrap" scheme used to test the villain, and deriving many of its circumstances from Shakespeare's sources; delay is a conventional device needed to continue the story to its conclusion.

Stoll's zeal led to excessive claims for historical criticism, as one might expect in the early years of a pioneering movement. At its extreme, historical criticism came close to implying that Shakespeare was a mere product of his environment. Indeed, the movement owed many of its evolutionist assumptions to the supposedly scientific "social Darwinism" of Thomas Huxley and other late nineteenth-century social philosophers. In more recent years, however, the crusading spirit has given way to a more moderate historical criticism that continues to be an important part of Shakespearean scholarship.

Alfred Harbage, for example, in *As They Liked It* (1947) and *Shakespeare and the Rival Traditions* (1952), has analyzed the audience for which Shakespeare wrote and the rivalry between popular and elite theaters in the London of his day. Harbage sees Shakespeare as a popular dramatist writing for a highly intelligent, enthusiastic, and socially diversified audience. More recently, in *The Privileged Playgoers of Shakespeare's London, 1576–1642* (1981), Ann Jennalie Cook has qualified Harbage's view, arguing that Shakespeare's audience was, for the most part, affluent and well connected. G. E. Bentley has amassed an invaluable storehouse of information about *The Jacobean and Caroline Stage* (1941–1968), just as E. K. Chambers earlier had collected documents and data on *The Elizabethan Stage* (1923). Other studies by these historical scholars include Chambers's *William Shakespeare: A Study of Facts and Problems* (1930), and Bentley's *Shakespeare and His Theatre* (1964) and *The Profession of Dramatist in Shakespeare's Time* (1971). T. W. Baldwin exemplifies the historical scholar who, like Stoll, claims too much for the method; nevertheless, much information on Shakespeare's schooling, reading, and professional theatrical life is available in such works as *William Shakspere's Small Latine and Lesse Greeke* (1944) and *The Organization and Personnel of the Shakespearean Company* (1927). Hardin Craig uses historical method in *An Interpretation of Shakespeare* (1948).

Historical criticism has contributed greatly to our knowledge of the staging of Shakespeare's plays. George Pierce Baker, in *The Development of Shakespeare as a Dramatist* (1907), continued the line of investigation begun by Walter Raleigh. Harley Granville-Barker brought to his *Prefaces to Shakespeare* (1930, 1946) a wealth of professional theatrical experience of his own. Ever since his time, the new theatrical method of interpreting Shakespeare has been based to an ever increasing extent on a genuine revival of interest in Shakespearean production. John Dover Wilson shows an awareness of the stage in *What Happens in Hamlet* (1935) and *The Fortunes of Falstaff* (1943). At its best, as in John Russell Brown's *Shakespeare's Plays in Performance* (1966), in John Styan's *Shakespeare's Stagecraft* (1967), in Michael Goldman's *Shakespeare and the Energies of Drama* (1972), and in Alan Dessen's *Elizabethan Drama and the Viewer's Eye* (1977) and his *Recovering Shakespeare's Theatrical Vocabulary* (1995), this critical method reveals many insights into the text that are hard to obtain without an awareness of theatrical technique.

Supporting this theatrical criticism, historical research has learned a great deal about the physical nature of Shakespeare's stage. J. C. Adams's well-known model of the Globe Playhouse, as presented in Irwin Smith's *Shakespeare's Globe Playhouse: A Modern Reconstruction* (1956), is now generally discredited in favor of a simpler building, as reconstructed by C. Walter Hodges (*The Globe Restored*, 1953, 2nd edition, 1968), Bernard Beckerman (*Shakespeare at the Globe*, 1962, 2nd edition, 1967), Richard Hosley ("The Playhouses and the Stage" in *A New Companion to Shakespeare Studies*, edited by K. Muir and S. Schoenbaum, 1971, and several other good essays), T. J. King (*Shakespearean Staging*, 1599–1642, 1971), and others. Information on the private theaters, such as the Blackfriars, where Shakespeare's plays were also performed, appears in William Armstrong, *The Elizabethan Private Theatres* (1958); Richard Hosley, "A Reconstruction of the Second Blackfriars" (*The Elizabethan Theatre*, 1969); Glynne Wickham, *Early English Stages* (1959–1972); and others. For further information on innyard theaters and on courtly or private theaters, see the contributions of Herbert Berry, D. F. Rowan, W. Reavley Gair, and others cited in the bibliography at the end of this volume.

A related pursuit of historical criticism has been the better understanding of Shakespeare through his dramatic predecessors and contemporaries. Willard Farnham, in *The Medieval Heritage of Elizabethan Tragedy* (1936), traces the evolution of native English tragedy through the morality plays of the early Tudor period. J. M. R. Margeson's *The Origins of English Tragedy* (1967) broadens the pattern to include still other sources for Elizabethan ideas on dramatic tragedy. Bernard Spivack, in *Shakespeare and the Allegory of Evil* (1958), sees Iago, Edmund, Richard III, and other boasting villains in Shakespeare as descendants of the morality Vice. In *Shakespeare and the Idea of the Play* (1962), Anne Righter (Barton) traces the device of the play-within-the-play and the metaphor of the world as a stage back to medieval and classical ideas of dramatic illusion. Irving Ribner's *The English History Play in the Age of Shakespeare* (1959, revised 1965) examines Shakespeare's plays on English history in the context of the popular Elizabethan genre to which they belonged. Robert Weimann's *Shakespeare and the Popular Tradition in the Theatre* (translated from the German in 1978) is a Marxist study in the social dimension of dramatic form and function. Many other studies of this sort could be cited, including Glynne Wickham's *Shakespeare's Dramatic Heritage* (1969), Oscar J. Campbell's *Shakespeare's Satire* (1943), M. C. Bradbrook's *Themes and Conventions of Elizabethan Tragedy* (1935), and S. L. Bethell's *Shakespeare and the Popular Dramatic Tradition* (1944).

Another important concern of historical criticism has been the relationship between Shakespeare and the ideas of his age—cosmological, philosophical, and political. Among the first scholars to study Elizabethan cosmology were Hardin Craig in *The Enchanted Glass* (1936) and A. O. Lovejoy in *The Great Chain of Being* (1936). As their successor, E. M. W. Tillyard provided in *The Elizabethan World Picture* (1943) a definitive view of the conservative and hierarchical values that Elizabethans were supposed to have espoused. In *Shakespeare's History Plays* (1944), Tillyard extended his essentially conservative view of Shakespeare's philosophical outlook to the histories, arguing that they embody a "Tudor myth" and thereby lend support to the Tudor state. Increasingly, however, critics have disputed the extent to which Shakespeare in fact endorsed the "establishment" values of the Elizabethan world picture. Theodore Spencer, in *Shakespeare and the Nature of Man* (1942), discusses the impact on Shakespeare of radical new thinkers like Machiavelli, Montaigne, and Copernicus. In political matters, Henry A. Kelly's *Divine Providence in the England of Shakespeare's Histories* (1970) has challenged the existence of a single "Tudor myth" and has argued that Shakespeare's history plays reflect contrasting political philosophies set dramatically in conflict with one another. M. M. Reese's *The Cease of Majesty* (1961) also offers a graceful corrective to Tillyard's lucid but occasionally one-sided interpretations. Revisions in this direction continue in the work of the so-called new historicists and cultural materialists, to be discussed below.

Historical criticism has also yielded many profitable specialized studies, in which Shakespeare is illuminated by a better understanding of various sciences of his day. Lily Bess Campbell approaches Shakespearean tragedy through Renaissance psychology in *Shakespeare's Tragic Heroes: Slaves of Passion* (1930). Paul Jorgensen uses Elizabethan documents on the arts of war and generalship in his study *Shakespeare's Military World* (1956). Many similar studies examine Shakespeare in relation to law, medicine, and other professions.

"New" Criticism

As we have seen, historical criticism is still an important part of Shakespeare criticism; for better or worse, it is the stuff of some research-oriented universities and their Ph.D. programs. Since its beginning, however, historical criticism has had to face a critical reaction, generated, in part, by its own utilitarian and fact-gathering tendencies. The suggestions urged by Stoll and others that Shakespeare was the product of his cultural and theatrical environment tended to obscure his achievement as a poet. Amassing of information about Shakespeare's reading or his theatrical company often seemed to inhibit the scholar from responding to the power of words and images.

Such at any rate was the rallying cry of the *Scrutiny* group in England, centered on F. R. Leavis, L. C. Knights, and Derek Traversi, and the "new" critics in America, such as Cleanth Brooks. The new critics demanded close attention to the poetry without the encumbrance of historical research. Especially at first, the new critics were openly hostile to any criticism distracting readers from the text. The satirical force of the movement can perhaps best be savored in L. C. Knights's "How Many Children Had Lady Macbeth?" (1933), prompted by the learned appendices in Bradley's *Shakespearean Tragedy*: "When was the murder of Duncan first plotted? Did Lady Macbeth really faint? Duration of the action in *Macbeth*. Macbeth's age. 'He has no children.'"

In part, the new critical movement was (and still is) a pedagogical movement, a protest against the potential dryness of historical footnoting and an insistence that classroom study of Shakespeare ought to focus on a response to his language. Cleanth Brooks's "The Naked Babe and the Cloak of Manliness" (in *The Well Wrought Urn*, 1947) offers to the teacher a model of close reading that focuses on imagery and yet attempts to see a whole vision of the play through its language. G. Wilson Knight concentrates on imagery and verbal texture, sometimes to the exclusion of the play as a whole, in his *The Wheel of Fire* (1930), *The Imperial Theme* (1931), *The Shakespearian Tempest* (1932), *The Crown of Life* (1947), and others. William Empson is best known for his *Seven Types of Ambiguity* (1930) and *Some Versions of Pastoral* (1935). Derek Traversi's works include *An Approach to Shakespeare* (1938), *Shakespeare: The Last Phase* (1954), *Shakespeare: From Richard II to Henry V* (1957), and *Shakespeare: The Roman Plays* (1963). Perhaps the greatest critic of this school has been L. C. Knights, whose books include *Explorations* (1946), *Some Shakespearean Themes* (1959), *An Approach to Hamlet* (1960), and *Further Explorations* (1965). T. S. Eliot's perceptive and controversial observations have also had an important influence on critics of this school. Other studies making good use of the new critical method include Robert Heilman's *This Great Stage* (1948) and *Magic in the Web* (1956). Many of these critics are concerned not only with language but also with the larger moral and structural implications of Shakespeare's plays as discovered through a sensitive reading of the text.

More specialized studies of Shakespearean imagery and language include Caroline Spurgeon's *Shakespeare's Imagery and What It Tells Us* (1935). Its classifications are now recognized to be overly statistical and restricted in definition, but the work has nonetheless prompted valuable further study. Among later works are Sister Miriam Joseph's *Shakespeare's Use of the Arts of Language* (1947, partly reprinted in *Rhetoric in Shakespeare's Time*, 1962), Wolfgang Clemen's *The Development of Shakespeare's Imagery* (1951), and M. M. Mahood's *Shakespeare's Wordplay* (1957). The study of prose has not received as much attention as that of poetry, although Brian Vickers's *The Artistry of Shakespeare's Prose* (1968) and Milton Crane's *Shakespeare's Prose* (1951) make significant contributions. See also Edward Armstrong's *Shakespeare's Imagination* (1963) and Kirby Farrell's *Shakespeare's Creation: The Language of Magic and Play* (1975).

A more recent development in studies of Shakespeare's imagery has led to the examination of visual images in the theater as part of Shakespeare's art. Reginald Foakes ("Suggestions for a New Approach to Shakespeare's Imagery," *Shakespeare Survey*, 5, 1952, 81–92) and Maurice Charney (*Shakespeare's Roman Plays: The Function of Imagery in the Drama*, 1961) were among the first to notice that Caroline Spurgeon and other "new" critics usually excluded stage picture in their focus on verbal image patterns. Yet Shakespeare's extensive involvement with the practicalities of theatrical production might well lead one to suspect that he arranges his stage with care and that the plays are full of hints as to how he communicates through visual means. Costume, properties, the theater building, the blocking of actors in visual patterns onstage, expression, movement—all of these contribute to the play's artistic whole. Francis Fergusson analyzes the way in which the Elizabethan theatrical building provides *Hamlet* with an eloquently expressive idea of order and hierarchy, against which are ironically juxtaposed Claudius's acts of killing a king and marrying his widow (*The Idea of a Theater*, 1949). Other studies of stage imagery include Ann Pasternak Slater's *Shakespeare the Director* (1982) and David Bevington's *Action Is Eloquence: Shakespeare's Language of Gesture* (1984).

Another call for expansion of the occasionally narrow limits of "new" criticism comes from the so-called Chicago school of criticism, centered on R. S. Crane, Richard McKeon, Elder Olson, Bernard Weinberg, and others, who, in the 1950s and 1960s, espoused a formal or structural approach to criticism, using Aristotle as its point of departure. Crane was reacting to the new critics who, in his view, restricted the kinds of answers they could obtain by limiting themselves to one methodology. Critics hostile to the Chicago school have responded, to be sure, that Crane's own approach tends to produce its own dogmatism. Formalist analyses of Shakespeare plays are to be found, for example, in the work of W. R. Keast, Wayne Booth, and Norman Maclean; see *Critics and Criticism*, edited by R. S. Crane (1952) and the bibliography at the back of this book.

Psychological Criticism

In a sense, Freudian and other psychological criticism continues the "character" criticism of the nineteenth century. Freudian critics sometimes follow a character into a world outside the text, analyzing Hamlet (for instance) as though he were a real person whose childhood traumas can be inferred from the symptoms he displays. The most famous work in this vein is *Hamlet and Oedipus* (1910, revised 1949), by Freud's disciple, Ernest Jones. According to Jones, Hamlet's delay is caused by an oedipal trauma. Hamlet's uncle, Claudius, has done exactly what Hamlet himself incestuously and subconsciously wished to do: kill his father and marry his mother. Because he cannot articulate these forbidden impulses to himself, Hamlet is paralyzed into inactivity. Jones's critical analysis thus assumes, as did such Romantic critics as Coleridge, that the central problem of *Hamlet* is one of character and motivation: why does Hamlet delay? (Many modern critics would deny that this is a problem or would insist, at least, that by setting such a problem, Jones has limited the number of possible answers. Avi Erlich proposes an entirely different psychological reading of the play in *Hamlet's Absent Father*, 1972.) Psychological criticism sometimes also reveals its affinities with nineteenth-century character criticism in its attempt to analyze Shakespeare's personality through his plays, as though the works constituted a spiritual autobiography. The terminology of psychological criticism is suspect to some readers because it is at least superficially anachronistic when dealing with a Renaissance writer. The terminology is also sometimes overburdened with technical jargon.

Nonetheless, psychological criticism has afforded many insights into Shakespeare not readily available through other modes of perception. Jones's book makes clear the intensity of Hamlet's revulsion toward women as a result of his mother's inconstancy. At a mythic level, Hamlet's story certainly resembles that of Oedipus, and Freudian criticism is often at its best when it shows us this universal aspect of the human psyche. Freudian terminology need not be anachronistic when it deals with timeless truths. Psychological criticism can reveal to us Shakespeare's preoccupation with certain types of women in his plays, such as the domineering and threatening masculine type (Joan of Arc, Margaret of Anjou) or, conversely, the long-suffering and patient heroine (Helena in *All's Well*, Hermione in *The Winter's Tale*). Psychological criticism is perhaps most useful in studying family relationships in Shakespeare. It also has much to say about the psychic or sexual connotations of symbols. Influential books include Norman O. Brown's *Life Against Death: The Psychoanalytical Meaning of History* (1959) and Norman Holland's *Psychoanalysis and Shakespeare* (1966) and *The Shakespearean Imagination* (1964).

Richard Wheeler's *Turn and Counter-Turn: Shakespeare's Development and the Problem Comedies* (1981) applies psychoanalytic method to a study of Shakespeare's development, in which, as Wheeler sees it, the sonnets and the problem plays are pivotal as Shakespeare turns from the safely contained worlds of romantic comedy (with non-threatening heroines) and the English history play (in which women are generally denied anything more than a marginal role in state affairs) to the tragedies, in which sexual conflict is shown in all its potentially terrifying destructiveness. Wheeler's completion of C. L. Barber's *The Whole Journey: Shakespeare's Power of Development* (1986) continues the study of Shakespeare's development in the late plays. The dichotomies of gender and genre urged in these studies and continued by Linda Bamber (*Comic Women, Tragic Men: A Study of Gender and Genre in Shakespeare,* 1982), among others, have been challenged by Jonathan Goldberg in his essay, "Shakespearean Inscriptions: The Voicing of Power," in *Shakespeare and the Question of Theory* (edited by Patricia Parker and Geoffrey Hartman, 1985). A collection of essays under the editorship of Murray Schwartz and Coppélia Kahn, *Representing Shakespeare* (1980), affords a sample of work by Janet Adelman, David Willbern, Meredith Skura, David Sundelson, Madelon Gohlke Sprengnether, Joel Fineman, and others.

Much psychoanalytic criticism of the 1980s has sought to displace Freud's emphasis upon the relation of son and father in the oedipal triangle in favor of attention to the mother and child preoedipal relation; a model here is the work of Karen Horney (e.g., *Neurosis and Human Growth: The Struggle Toward Self-Realization,* 1950). Jacques Lacan (*Écrits,* translated by Alan Sheridan, 1977) and Erik Erikson (*Childhood and Selfhood,* 1978) are also prominent theorists in the post-Freudian era. Despite such changes, the psychoanalytic critic still attempts to discover in the language of the play the means by which he or she can reconstruct an early stage in the development of one or more of the dramatic characters.

Mythological Criticism

Related to psychological criticism is the search for archetypal myth in literature, as an expression of the "collective unconscious" of the human race. Behind such an approach lie the anthropological and psychological assumptions of Jung and his followers. One of the earliest studies of this sort was Gilbert Murray's *Hamlet and Orestes* (1914), analyzing the archetype of revenge for a murdered father. Clearly this custom goes far back into tribal prehistory and emerges in varying but interrelated forms in many different societies. This anthropological universality enables us to look at Hamlet as the heightened manifestation of an incredibly basic story. *Hamlet* gives shape to urgings that are a part of our innermost

social being. The struggle between the civilized and the primitive goes on in us as in the play *Hamlet.*

The vast interdisciplinary character of mythological criticism leaves it vulnerable to charges of speculativeness and glib theorizing. At its best, however, mythological criticism can illuminate the nature of our responses as audience to a work of art. Northrop Frye argues, in *A Natural Perspective* (1965), that we respond to mythic patterns by imagining ourselves participating in them communally. The Greek drama emerged, after all, from Dionysiac ritual. All drama celebrates in one form or another the primal myths of vegetation, from the death of the year to the renewal or resurrection of life. In his most influential book, *Anatomy of Criticism* (1957), Frye argues that mythic criticism presents a universal scheme for the investigation of all literature, or all art, since art is itself the ordering of our most primal stirrings. Frye sees in drama (as in other literature) a fourfold correspondence to the cyclical pattern of the year: comedy is associated with spring, romance with summer, tragedy with autumn, and satire with winter. Historically, civilization moves through a recurrent cycle from newness to decadence and decay; this cycle expresses itself culturally in a progression from epic and romance to tragedy, to social realism, and, finally, to irony and satire before the cycle renews itself. Thus, according to Frye, the genres of dramatic literature (and of other literary forms as well) have an absolute and timeless relationship to myth and cultural history. That is why we as audience respond so deeply to form and meaning as contained in genre. C. L. Barber, in *Shakespeare's Festive Comedy* (1959), makes a similar argument: our enjoyment of comedy arises from our intuitive appreciation of such "primitive" social customs as Saturnalian revels, May games, and fertility rites. John Holloway offers an anthropological study of Shakespeare's tragedies in *The Story of the Night* (1961).

Frye's critical system has not been without its detractors. For example, Frederick Crews (*Psychoanalysis and Literary Process,* 1970) argues that Frye's system is too self-contained in its ivory tower and too much an abstract artifact of the critical mind to be "relevant" to the social purposes of art. Nevertheless, Frye continues to be one of the most influential critics of the late twentieth century.

Typological Criticism

Another controversy of the later twentieth century has to do with the Christian interpretation of Shakespeare. Do the images and allusions of Shakespeare's plays show him to be deeply immersed in a Christian culture inherited from the Middle Ages? Does he reveal a typological cast of mind, so common in medieval literature, whereby a story can suggest through analogy a universal religious archetype? For example, does the mysterious Duke in *Measure for Measure* suggest to us a God figure, hovering unseen throughout the play to test human will and then to present humanity with an omniscient but merciful judgment? Is the wanton slaughter of the good Cordelia in *King Lear* reminiscent of the Passion of Christ? Can Portia in *The Merchant of Venice* be seen as an angelic figure descending from Belmont into the fallen human world of Venice? Often the operative question we must ask is: "How far should such analogy be pursued?" Richard II unquestionably likens himself to Christ betrayed by the disciples, and at times the play evokes images of Adam banished from Paradise, but do these allusions coalesce into a sustained analogy?

Among the most enthusiastic searchers after Christian meaning are J. A. Bryant, in *Hippolyta's View* (1961); Roy Battenhouse, in *Shakespearean Tragedy: Its Art and Christian Premises* (1969); and R. Chris Hassel, in *Renaissance Drama and the English Church* (1979) and *Faith and Folly in Shakespeare: Romantic Comedies* (1980). Their efforts have encountered stern opposition, however. One notable dissenter is Roland M. Frye, whose *Shakespeare and Christian Doctrine* (1963) argues that Shakespeare cannot be shown to have known much Renaissance theology and that, in any case, his plays are concerned with human drama rather than with otherworldly questions of damnation or salvation. Frye's argument stresses the incompatibility of Christianity and tragedy, as do also D. G. James's *The Dream of Learning* (1951) and Clifford Leech's *Shakespeare's Tragedies and Other Studies in Seventeenth-Century Drama* (1950). Virgil Whitaker's *The Mirror Up to Nature* (1965) sees religion as an essential element in Shakespeare's plays but argues that Shakespeare uses the religious knowledge of his audience as a shortcut to characterization and meaning, rather than as an ideological weapon. The controversy will doubtless long continue, even though the typological critics have had to assume a defensive posture.

Jan Kott and the Theater of the Absurd

At an opposite extreme from the Christian idealism of most typological critics is the iconoclasm of those who have been disillusioned by recent events in history. One who brilliantly epitomizes political disillusionment in the aftermath of World War II, especially in Eastern Europe, is Jan Kott. The evocative debunking of romantic idealism set forth in his *Shakespeare Our Contemporary* (1964, translated from the Polish) has enjoyed enormous influence since the 1960s, especially in the theater. Kott sees Shakespeare as a dramatist of the absurd and the grotesque. In this view, Shakespearean plays are often close to "black" comedy or comedy of the absurd, as defined by Antonin Artaud (*The Theatre and Its Double*, 1958) and Jerzy Grotowski (*Towards a Poor Theatre*, 1968). Indeed, Kott has inspired productions that expose traditional values to skepticism and ridicule. Portia and Bassanio in *The Merchant of Venice* become scheming adven-

turers; Henry V becomes a priggish warmonger. History is for Kott a nightmare associated with his country's experience in World War II, and Shakespeare's modernity can be seen in his sardonic portrayal of political opportunism and violence. Even *A Midsummer Night's Dream* is a play of disturbingly erotic brutality, Kott argues. Here is an interpretation of Shakespeare that was bound to have an enormous appeal in a world confronted by the assassinations of the Kennedys and Martin Luther King, Jr.; by incessant war in the Middle East, Southeast Asia, and much of the third world; by the threat of nuclear annihilation and ecological disaster; and by political leadership generally perceived as interested only in the public-relations techniques of self-preservation. An essentially ironic view of politics and, more broadly, of human nature has informed a good deal of criticism since Kott's day and has led to the dethronement of E. M. W. Tillyard and his essentially positive view of English patriotism and heroism in the history plays.

New Historicism and Cultural Materialism

A more recent way of investigating Shakespeare through the demystifying perspective of modern experience—the so-called new historicism— has focused on the themes of political self-fashioning and role playing in terms of power and subversion. This critical school has paid close attention to historians and cultural anthropologists like Lawrence Stone (*The Crisis of the Aristocracy, 1558–1641*, 1965) and Clifford Geertz (*Negara: The Theatre State in Nineteenth-Century Bali*, 1980), who explore new ways of looking at the relationship between historical change and the myths generated to bring it about or to retain power. Geertz analyzes the way in which the ceremonies and myths of political rule can, in effect, become a self-fulfilling reality; kings and other leaders, acting out their roles in ceremonials designed to encapsulate the myth of their greatness and divine origin, essentially become what they have created in their impersonations of power. Such a view of political authority is an inherently skeptical one, seeing government as a process of manipulating illusions. When Shakespeare's English history plays—or indeed any plays dealing with conflicts of authority—are analyzed in these terms, subversion and containment become important issues. Do the plays of Shakespeare and other Renaissance dramatists celebrate the power of the Tudor monarchs, or do they question and undermine assumptions of hierarchy? Did Elizabethan drama serve to increase skepticism and pressure for change, or was it, conversely, a way of easing that pressure so that the power structure could remain in force?

The "new historicism" is a name applied to a kind of literary criticism practiced in America, prominently by Stephen Greenblatt. Especially influential have been his *Renaissance Self-Fashioning* (1980), *Shakespearean Negotiations*

(1988), and his editing of the journal *Representations*. Those who pursue similar concerns, including Louis Montrose, Stephen Orgel, Richard Helgerson, Don E. Wayne, Frank Whigham, Richard Strier, Jonathan Goldberg, David Scott Kastan, and Steven Mullaney, share Greenblatt's goals to a greater or lesser extent and think of themselves only with important reservations as "new historicists"; the term is misleadingly categorical, and Greenblatt, among others, is eager to enlarge the parameters of the method rather than to allow it to harden into an orthodoxy. (Greenblatt, in fact, prefers the term "poetics of culture" to "new historicism," even though the latter phrase remains better known.) Still, these critics do generally share a number of common concerns. Among the ways in which new historicists seek to separate themselves from earlier historical critics is by denying that the work of art is a unified and self-contained product of an independent creator in masterful control of the meaning of the work. Instead, the new historicists represent the work as shot through with the multiple and contradictory discourses of its time. New historicists also deny the notion that art merely "reflects" its historical milieu; instead, they argue that art is caught up in, and contributes to, the social practices of its time. Although the boundary between new and old historical criticism is often hard to draw, in general the new historicists are apt to be skeptical of the accepted canon of literary texts and are drawn to a markedly politicized reading of Renaissance plays. One finds everywhere in the new historicism a deep ambivalence toward political authority.

Mikhail Bakhtin's provocative ideas on carnival (*L'Oeuvre de François Rabelais et la Culture Populaire du Moyen Age*, 1970) have had an important influence in new historical circles, as reflected, for example, in the work of Michael Bristol (*Carnival and Theatre: Plebeian Culture and the Structure of Authority in Renaissance England*, 1985), Peter Stallybrass, Gail Paster, and others. Like new historicism, this critical approach looks at so-called high cultural entertainment, including Shakespeare, in relation to the practices of popular culture, thereby breaking down the distinction between "high" and "popular." Literary and nonliterary texts are subjected to the same kind of serious scrutiny. Popular origins of the theater receive new attention, as in Robert Weimann's *Shakespeare and the Popular Tradition in the Theater: Studies in the Social Dimension of Dramatic Form and Function* (published in German in 1967 and in English translation in 1978).

Cultural materialism, in Britain, takes an analogous approach to the dethroning of canonical texts and the emphasis on art as deeply implicated in the social practices of its time but differs from American new historicism on the issue of change. New historicism is sometimes criticized for its lack of a model for change and for its reluctant belief, instead (in Greenblatt's formulation especially), that all attempts at subversion through art are destined to be contained by power structures in society; art permits the expression of heterodox points of view, but only as a way of letting off steam, as it were, and thereby easing the pressures for actual radical change. British cultural materialism, in contrast, is more avowedly committed not only to radical political interpretation but also to rapid political change, partly in response to what are perceived to be more deeply rooted class differences than are found in America. Jonathan Dollimore's *Radical Tragedy* (1984) and *Political Shakespeare* (1985), edited by Dollimore and Alan Sinfield, enlist the dramatist on the side of class struggle. So do *Alternative Shakespeares*, edited by John Drakakis (1985), and Terry Eagleton's *Shakespeare and Society* (1967) and *William Shakespeare* (1986). Raymond Williams, not himself a Shakespearean critic, is an acknowledged godfather of the movement.

Feminist Criticism

Feminist criticism is such an important and diverse field that it has necessarily and productively reached into a number of related disciplines, such as cultural anthropology and its wealth of information about family structures. In his *The Elementary Structures of Kinship* (1949, translated 1969) and other books, Claude Lévi-Strauss analyzes the way in which men, as fathers and as husbands, control the transfer of women from one family to another in an "exogamous" marital system designed to strengthen commercial and other ties among men. Recent feminist criticism has had a lot to say about patriarchal structures in the plays and poems of Shakespeare, some of it building upon Lévi-Strauss's analysis of patriarchy; see, for example, Karen Newman, "Portia's Ring: Unruly Women and Structures of Exchange in *The Merchant of Venice*," *Shakespeare Quarterly*, 38 (1987), 10–33, and Lynda Boose, "The Father and the Bride in Shakespeare," *PMLA*, 97 (1982), 325–47. Coppélia Kahn has examined the ideology of rape in *The Rape of Lucrece*, showing how the raped woman is devalued by the shame that attaches to her husband, even though she is innocent (*Shakespeare Studies*, 9, 1976, 45–72).

Another important source of insight for feminist criticism is the anthropological work on rites of passage by Arnold Van Gennep (*The Rites of Passage*, translated by M. B. Vizedom and G. L. Caffee, 1960) and Victor Turner (*The Ritual Process*, 1969), among others. The focus here is on the dangers of transition at times of birth, puberty, marriage, death, and other turning points of human life. Feminist criticism, in dealing with such crises of transition, concerns itself not only with women's roles but also, more broadly, with gender relations, with family structures, and with the problems that males encounter in their quest for mature sexual identity. Coppélia Kahn's *Man's Estate; Masculine Identity in Shakespeare* (1981) looks particularly at the difficulty of the male in confronting the hazards of maturity. Robert Watson's *Shakespeare and the Hazards of Ambition* (1984) also looks at the male in the political context of career and self-fashioning. Marjorie Garber's *Coming of Age in Shakespeare* (1981) takes a broad look at maturation.

As these titles suggest, the models are often psychological, as well as anthropological. One focus of feminist criticism is the role of women in love and marriage. Feminist critics disagree among themselves as to whether the portrait painted by Shakespeare and other Elizabethan dramatists is a hopeful one, as argued, for example, by Juliet Dusinberre in *Shakespeare and the Nature of Women* (1975, 1996), or repressive, as argued by Lisa Jardine in *Still Harping on Daughters: Women and Drama in the Age of Shakespeare* (1983). Recent historians add an important perspective, especially Lawrence Stone in his *The Family, Sex, and Marriage in England, 1500–1800* (1977). Did the Protestant emphasis on marriage as a morally elevated and reciprocal relationship have the paradoxical effect of arousing in men an increased hostility and wariness toward women and a resulting increase in repression and violence? Or, as David Underdown suggests, should we look to economic explanations of hostility and wariness toward women in the Renaissance? His studies indicate that repression of women is greatest in regions of the country where their place in the economy offers the possibility of their having some control over family finances. (See *Revel, Riot, and Rebellion: Popular Culture in England, 1603–1660,* 1985, pp. 73–105, especially p. 99.)

Certainly, recent criticism has paid a lot of attention to male anxieties about women in Shakespeare's plays, as various male protagonists resolve to teach women a lesson (*The Taming of the Shrew*), succumb to dark fantasies of female unfaithfulness (*Much Ado About Nothing, Othello*), or are overwhelmed by misogynistic revulsion (*Hamlet, King Lear*). It is as though Shakespeare, in his plays and poems, works through the problems that men experience throughout their lives in their relationships with women, from the insecurities of courtship to the desire for possession and control in marriage, and from jealous fears of betrayal to the longing for escape into middle-age sexual adventure (as in *Antony and Cleopatra*). The late plays show us the preoccupation of the aging male with the marriages of his daughters (another form of betrayal) and with the approach of death.

Recently, feminist criticism has begun to increase its historical consciousness. Critics such as Gail Paster, Jean Howard, Phyllis Rackin, Dympna Callaghan, Lorraine Helms, Jyotsna Singh, Alison Findlay, Lisa Jardine, and Karen Newman focus on the construction of gender in early modern England in terms of social and material conditions, abandoning the nonhistorical psychological model of earlier feminist criticism. See the bibliography at the end of this book for feminist studies by these and other feminist critics, including Catherine Belsey, Carol Neely,

Peter Erickson, Meredith Skura, Marianne Novy, Margo Hendricks, Kim Hall, Philippa Berry, Frances Dolan, Mary Beth Rose, Valerie Traub, Susan Zimmerman, Lynda Boose, and Ania Loomba. Gender studies concerned with issues of same-sex relationships have made important contributions in recent years, in the work of Bruce Smith, Laurie Shannon, Jonathan Goldberg, Stephen Orgel, Leonard Barkan, Mario DiGangi, and others.

Poststructuralism and Deconstruction

A major influence today in Shakespeare criticism, as in virtually all literary criticism of recent date, is the school of analysis known as poststructuralism or deconstruction; the terms, though not identical, significantly overlap. This school derives its inspiration originally from the work of certain French philosophers and critics, chief among whom are Ferdinand de Saussure, a specialist in linguistics, Michel Foucault, a historian of systems of discourse, and Jacques Derrida, perhaps the most highly visible exponent and practitioner of deconstruction. The ideas of these men were first introduced into American literary criticism by scholars at Yale such as Geoffrey Hartman, J. Hillis Miller, and Paul de Man. The ideas are controversial and difficult.

Poststructuralism and deconstruction begin with an insistence that language is a system of difference—one in which the signifiers (such as words and gestures) are essentially arbitrary to the extent that "meaning" and "authorial intention" are virtually impossible to fix precisely; that is, language enjoys a potentially infinite subjectivity. To an extent, this approach to the subjectivity of meaning in a work of art resembles "new" criticism in its mistrust of "message" in literature, but the new method goes further. It resists all attempts at paraphrase, for example, insisting that the words of a text cannot be translated into other words without altering something vital; indeed, there is no way of knowing if an author's words will strike any two readers or listeners in the same way. The very concept of an author has been challenged by Michel Foucault ("What Is an Author?" in *Language, Counter-Memory, Practice,* edited by Donald F. Bouchard, 1977). Deconstruction proclaims that there is no single identifiable author in the traditional sense; instead of a single text, we have a potentially infinite number of texts.

Both the theory and practice of deconstruction remain highly controversial. Although poststructuralism and deconstruction owe a debt to the general philosophical theory of signs and symbols known as semiotics, in which the function of linguistic signs is perceived to be artificially constructed, the new method also calls into question the very distinctions on which the discipline of semiotics is based. Derrida builds upon the work of Saussure and yet goes well beyond him in an insistence that words (signifiers) be left in play rather than attached to their alleged meaning (signifieds). Frank Lentricchia

(*After the New Criticism*, 1980) takes the Yale school critics to task for interpreting Derrida in too formalist and apolitical a sense. Despite disagreements among theorists, nevertheless, the approach has deeply influenced Shakespeare criticism as a whole by urging critics to consider the suppleness with which signifiers (words) in the Shakespearean text are converted by listeners and readers into some approximation of meaning.

The ramifications of poststructuralism and deconstruction are increasingly felt in other forms of criticism, even those at least nominally at odds with poststructuralist assumptions. Some radical textual critics, for example, are fascinated by the unsettling prospects of the deconstructed text. What does one edit and how does one go about editing when words are to be left in play, to the infinite regress of meaning? The problems are acutely examined in a collection of essays called *The Division of the Kingdom*, edited by Gary Taylor and Michael Warren, on the two early and divergent texts of *King Lear* (1983). The method of linguistic analysis known as "speech-act theory," developed by the philosopher J. L. Austin as a way of exploring how we perform certain linguistic acts when we swear oaths or make asseverations and the like, is sharply at variance with deconstruction in its premises about a correlation between speech and intended meaning, and yet it, too, can help us understand the instability of spoken or written language in Shakespeare. Joseph Porter's *The Drama of Speech Acts* (1979), for example, looks at ways in which Shakespeare's characters in the plays about Henry IV and Henry V reveal, through their language of oath making and oath breaking, asseveration, and the like, their linguistic adaptability or lack of adaptability to historical change. Richard II resists historical change in the very way he speaks; Prince Hal embraces it. A third related field of analysis that is interested in the instability of meaning in Shakespeare's texts is metadramatic criticism, where the focus is on ways in which dramatic texts essentially talk about the drama itself, about artistic expression, and about the artist's quest for immortality in art. James Calderwood's *Shakespearean Metadrama* (1971) is an influential example.

At its extreme, then, deconstructive criticism comes close to undermining all kinds of "meaningfulness" in artistic utterance and to being thus at war with other methods of interpretation. Still, deconstruction continues to remain influential, because it also usefully challenges complacent formulations of meaning and because it promotes such a subtle view of linguistic complexity.

At its best, late twentieth-century criticism transcends the splintering effect of a heterogeneous critical tradition to achieve a synthesis that is at once unified and multiform in its vision. The pluralistic approach aims at overall balance and a reinforcement of one critical approach through the methodology of another. Many of the works already cited in this introduction refuse to be constricted by methodological boundaries. The best historical criticism makes use of close explication of the text where appropriate; image patterns can certainly reinforce mythological patterns; typological interpretation, when sensibly applied, serves the cause of image study. Some fine books are so eclectic in their method that one hesitates to apply the label of any one critical school. Among such works are Maynard Mack's *King Lear in Our Time* (1965), David Young's *Something of Great Constancy: The Art of A Midsummer Night's Dream* (1966), R. G. Hunter's *Shakespeare and the Comedy of Forgiveness* (1965), Janet Adelman's *The Common Liar: An Essay on "Antony and Cleopatra"* (1973), Stanley Cavell's "The Avoidance of Love: A Reading of King Lear," in *Must We Mean What We Say?* (1969, reprinted in *Disowning Knowledge in Six Plays of Shakespeare*, 1987), and Paul Jorgensen's *Our Naked Frailties: Sensational Art and Meaning in Macbeth* (1971).

Into the Twenty-First Century

The sense of where we are in the twenty-first century in Shakespeare criticism reflects the uncertainties and guardedly hopeful expectations of the academic profession as a whole. The period of the 1970s and 1980s, described previously, was one of extraordinary ferment, brought on by a host of developments: the Vietnam War and its aftermath, the assassinations of the Kennedys and Martin Luther King, the impact of French linguistic and philosophical thought on American intellectual writing, the frustrations of many academics with Reaganomics and their consequent fascination with British Marxism, emerging demands on behalf of minorities and women, a revolution in social and sexual mores accompanied by a backlash in the name of "family values," conflict over American foreign policy in the Middle East (Israel, Iraq), and much more. The result was what must be regarded as a genuine revolution in methods of critical analysis and reading. The literary text became multivalent, ambiguous, deconstructed, dethroned as a unique artifact, and was seen, instead, as a product of and contributing to its social and intellectual environment. The author became a construction of criticism and of a new kind of literary history.

Shakespeare studies have taken a lead in all of this new exploration. Although one of the postmodern demands has been for a recanonizing of literature in favor of newer literature, works by women and minorities, and works from countries other than Britain and the United States instead of the traditional canon of dead white European males, Shakespeare not only has survived this recanonization but also has become more prominent than ever. Other Renaissance writers such as Ben Jonson, John Webster, Thomas Dekker, Thomas Nashe, John Lyly, Edmund Spenser, and even Christopher Marlowe, John Milton, and John Donne have been the victims of declining enrollments in classes generally, but Shakespeare triumphs. Why?

One compelling answer is that Shakespeare is simply indispensable to postmodern critical inquiry. His texts are so extraordinarily responsive that new questions put to them—about the changing role of women, about cynicism in the political process, about the protean near-indeterminacy of meaning in language—evoke insights that are hard to duplicate in other literary texts. Shakespeare does not seem out of date. The very impulse of so much recent criticism to claim Shakespeare as "our contemporary," attuned to our own skepticisms and disillusionment and even despair (as in the writings of Jan Kott, for example), attests to his unparalleled engagement with the issues about which we care so deeply. Even those who argue that Shakespeare exhibits the male hang-ups of a patriarchal society and that he is a social snob who glorifies aristocracy and warfare do not see Shakespeare as a writer who is out of touch with the values of our contemporary society but, rather, as one who gives eloquent testimonial to structures that were alive in our cultural past and with which we sense a continuum today even if outward circumstances have changed. The best scholarship does not condemn Shakespeare for believing in kingship or for sometimes showing men as victorious in the battle of the sexes; instead, that criticism is interested in the whole process of the literary text's participation in the creation of culture. Even when recent scholarship is concerned with examining class and gender issues to clarify some of the systematic oppressiveness of early modern culture, it does so generally in an attempt to negotiate the relationship of the present to the past, rather than assuming a superiority in our modern world's approaches to issues of class, gender, and ethnicity.

To be sure, a number of Shakespeare's plays are in trouble today because they make us uncomfortable about these issues. *The Merchant of Venice* is, in the eyes of many, almost unproduceable, because the anti-Semitic emotions it explores are so distasteful. It is less often assigned now in classrooms than it once was, even though, when it is taught or produced onstage, it can lead to extraordinarily searching discussions of painful but real issues. The same is true of *The Taming of the Shrew,* which is being taken from the shelves of more than a few libraries because of its apparent flaunting of sexist behavior toward women. *Othello* offends some readers and viewers because of its racist language and, in the view of some, racial stereotypes. Yet, the power of Shakespeare's language continues to exert its spell despite, and in part because of, these troubling conflicts over the role of dramatic art in modern society.

The world of Shakespeare criticism today, after two decades or so of revolution, is seemingly one of consoli-

dation. At a March 1995 meeting of the Shakespeare Association of America in Chicago, many conferees wondered: Where is the profession going? What are the hot new issues? Who are the new critics that no one wants to miss? And, in fact, there seemed to be little dramatic excitement of this sort, little agreement as to any discernible new trend. To some, this is frustrating. Where does one turn for real creativity after a thoroughgoing revolution such as we have experienced?

To others, a time of stocktaking is potentially healthy. There seems to be relatively little interest in turning the clock back; postmodernism and indeterminacy have changed the critical landscape for better and for worse. Now that this new landscape begins to seem familiar, however, new members of the profession seem less anxious to resolve their own identity crises in terms of affiliating with some critical school or other. The critical challenges are there, not so stridently new as they were ten years ago, and adaptable to various uses.

The result is increasing variety in the kinds of critical work being done. Some of it is recognizably traditional, dealing with stage history and conditions of performance during Shakespeare's lifetime, as, for example, in T. J. King, *Casting Shakespeare's Plays: London Actors and Their Roles* (1992); William Ingram, *The Business of Playing: The Beginnings of the Adult Professional Theater in Elizabethan London* (1992); David Bradley, *From Text to Performance in the Elizabethan Theatre: Preparing the Play for the Stage* (1992); David Mann, *The Elizabethan Player: Contemporary Stage Representation* (1991); John H. Astington, ed., *The Development of Shakespeare's Theater* (1992); Andrew Gurr, *Playgoing in Shakespeare's London* (1987, 2nd edition, 1996) and *The Shakespearian Playing Companies* (1996); and Roslyn Lander Knutson, *The Repertory of Shakespeare's Company, 1594–1613* (1991). Background and historical studies of the conditions that helped produce Shakespeare's theater can sometimes be informatively revisionist in the sense of toppling cherished older notions without at the same time being postmodern in approach. Examples here might include Richard Dutton, *Mastering the Revels: The Regulation and Censorship of English Renaissance Drama* (1991); Scott McMillin and Sally-Beth MacLean, *The Queen's Men and Their Plays* (1998); and Leeds Barroll, *Politics, Plague, and Shakespeare's Theater: The Stuart Years* (1991).

Other studies are more openly revisionist in a postmodern vein, sometimes in dealing with hypotheses about bibliography and textual studies, as in Margreta de Grazia, *Shakespeare Verbatim: The Reproduction of Authenticity and the 1790 Apparatus* (1991) and Grace Ioppolo, *Revising Shakespeare* (1991). The New Folger Library Shakespeare, edited by Barbara Mowat and Paul Werstine (1992—), gives a more measured approach. The Arden Shakespeare is currently bringing out new critical editions of all the plays in individual volumes (Arden 3), as are the New Cambridge Shakespeare and the Oxford Shakespeare. Occasionally a conservative counterblast is heard, as in Brian Vickers's entertaining, learned, and feisty polemic, *Appropriating Shakespeare: Contemporary Critical Quarrels* (1993). A forum of essays edited by Ivo Kamps, called *Shakespeare Left and Right*, gives us a chance to weigh arguments from various sides.

What the contemporary critical scene does best is to free critics to be who they are and to write without paying dues to any particular affiliation. The results are refreshingly diverse. Among the books that show this spread of critical approaches are Karen Newman, *Fashioning Femininity and the English Renaissance Drama* (1991); Bruce R. Smith, *Homosexual Desire in Shakespeare's England* (1991); Janet Adelman, *Suffocating Mothers: Fantasies of Maternal Origin in Shakespeare's Plays, "Hamlet" to "The Tempest"* (1992); Alan Sinfield, *Faultlines: Cultural Materialism and the Politics of Dissident Reading* (1992); Valerie Traub, *Desire and Anxiety: Circulations of Sexuality in Shakespearean Drama* (1992); Richard Burt, *Licensed by Authority: Ben Jonson and the Discourses of Censorship* (1993); Linda Charnes, *Notorious Identity: Materializing the Subject in Shakespeare* (1993); Lars Engle, *Shakespearean Pragmatism: Market of His*

Time (1993); Gail Kern Paster, *The Body Embarrassed: Drama and the Disciplines of Shame in Early Modern England* (1993); Meredith Anne Skura, *Shakespeare the Actor and the Purposes of Playing* (1993); Frances E. Dolan, *Dangerous Familiars: Representations of Domestic Crime in England, 1550–1700* (1994); Kim F. Hall, *Things of Darkness: Economies of Race and Gender in Early Modern England* (1994); Jean Howard, *The Stage and Social Struggle in Early Modern England* (1994); Robert Watson, *The Rest Is Silence: Death as Annihilation in the English Renaissance* (1994); Katharine Eisaman Maus, *Inwardness and Theatre in the English Renaissance Drama* (1995); Louis Montrose, *The Purpose of Playing: Shakespeare and the Cultural Politics of the Elizabethan Theatre* (1996); Patricia Parker, *Shakespeare from the Margins: Language, Culture, Context* (1996); Jean E. Howard and Phyllis Rackin, *Engendering a Nation: A Feminist Account of Shakespeare's English Histories* (1997); Anthony B. Dawson and Paul Yachnin, *The Culture of Playgoing in Shakespeare's England* (2001); David Scott Kastan, *Shakespeare and the Book* (2001); Mary Beth Rose, *Gender and Heroism in Early Modern English Literature* (2002); and Stephen Orgel, *The Authentic Shakespeare* (2002). For other suggestions, see recent entries in the bibliography at the back of this volume.

The Romances

Pericles   *The Tempest*

Cymbeline   *The Two Noble Kinsmen*

The Winter's Tale

Pericles

Pericles is a deceptively simple play. Although it was popular in its own time and in recent years has proved to be successful and deeply moving onstage, the play may seem naive and trivial on the printed page. Its apparent lack of "depth" seems especially striking when we compare it with its contemporaries, *King Lear, Macbeth, Timon of Athens*, and *Antony and Cleopatra*. It purports to be the work of a medieval poet, John Gower, who, as presenter, or chorus, apologizes to his sophisticated Jacobean audience ("born in these latter times / When wit's more ripe") for the "lame feet of my rhyme" and the quaintness of his ditty (1.0.11–12; 4.0.48). The narrative offers a series of sea voyages, separations, hairbreadth escapes, and reunions. Thrilling circumstances abound: Pericles fleeing the wrath of Antiochus; his wife, Thaisa, giving birth to their daughter, Marina, on board ship in the midst of a gigantic storm; and Marina later being rescued by pirates from a would-be murderer only to be sold by her new captors to a house of prostitution. Time leaps forward from Pericles's own youth to that of his daughter. The action takes place in remote lands, shifting constantly back and forth among six eastern Mediterranean localities: Antioch, Tyre, Tarsus, Pentapolis, Ephesus, and Mytilene. Conventional devices of plot include the expounding of riddles, the discovery of incest at court, the exposure of infants to the hostile elements, the miraculous restoration of life after seeming death, the appearance of the gods in a vision, and recognition of long-lost loved ones by means of signs or tokens.

These are the attributes of popular romance, a distinctly old-fashioned genre in 1606–1608 when *Pericles* was apparently written. Robert Greene had composed prose romances of this sort in the 1580s and early 1590s, including *Pandosto*, Shakespeare's source for *The Winter's Tale*. Sir Philip Sidney's *Arcadia* had endowed romance with noble eloquence and literary fashionableness, but that, too, was in the late 1580s. (The name Pericles may

well owe something to the *Arcadia's* Pyrocles, though Shakespeare may also have been attracted to the Pericles of fifth-century Athens and to the mellifluous quality of the name.) One source for *Pericles* itself, a prose history of Apollonius of Tyre by Laurence Twine, was registered for publication in 1576, although no edition exists before that of 1594 or 1595. Earlier accounts of Apollonius (as the hero was originally named), going back to Greek romance, include a ninth-century *Historia Apollonii Regis Tyri*, Godfrey of Viterbo's *Pantheon* (c. 1186), John Gower's *Confessio Amantis* (c. 1383–1393), and the *Gesta Romanorum*. Why did Shakespeare's company refurbish such an outmoded romantic story in 1606–1608?

The puzzle is aggravated by questions of authorship and textual reliability. The editors of the First Folio did not include *Pericles* in the canon of Shakespeare's plays. Perhaps they experienced copyright difficulties or could not lay their hands on the playbook, but it is also possible they either suspected or knew that Shakespeare was not the sole author. Printed editions were available to them: the First Quarto of 1609 and the subsequent quartos of 1609, 1611, and 1619, each based on the preceding edition. The First Quarto was, however, a bad text with occasional glaring contradictions. In 1.2, for example, Pericles's lords wish him a safe journey when no one has yet spoken of his departure, and Helicanus rebukes these same lords for flattery even though they have not said anything remotely sycophantic. Other scenes present similar difficulties, especially in the first two acts. The characters do not always seem consistent: Cleon is condemned in Act 5 for having tried to murder Marina, even though our earlier impression of him is of a man who is genuinely horrified at his wife's villainy. He weakly bends to the will of Dionyza but is no murderer. Such inconsistencies and errors, and the naiveté of the whole, have generally led to three hypotheses: that Shakespeare worked with a collaborator such as Thomas Heywood or George Wilkins, that he revised an older play and left the first two acts pretty much as they were, or that he wrote the entire play, which was then "pirated" by two unemployed actors whose portions differed markedly in accuracy.

To complicate matters still further, a prose version of the story called *The Painful Adventures of Pericles* by George Wilkins appeared in 1608, purporting to be "the true History of the Play of Pericles," that is, to be a prose account of a dramatic performance. This redaction is indeed close at times to the play we have, but at other times it departs widely. The departures of the later work are sometimes explained with the hypothesis that Wilkins based his account on an older play, to which Wilkins might have contributed himself; another and more current opinion favors the notion that Wilkins took what he needed from the play we have, borrowing also from Twine's prose version or from his own imagination. Apparently, then, *Pericles* was such a popular stage success that it inspired Wilkins's *Painful Adventures* in 1608, a new reprint in 1607 of Twine's *Pattern of Painful Adventures* on which the play itself had been partly based, and a botched surreptitious quarto edition of the play in 1609. Shakespeare's sole authorship must remain in doubt, although the incongruities, especially in the first two acts, are sometimes explained as the result of faulty memorial reporting and compositorial error. Onstage, to be sure, even the first two acts make fine dramatic sense, establishing motifs and situations that are essential to the rest of the play, so that the overall impression in the theater is of cohesion.

The naiveté of *Pericles* is probably deliberate. Its romantic motifs continue on into that group of plays known generally as the late romances: *Cymbeline* (c. 1608–1610), *The Winter's Tale* (c. 1609–1611), and *The Tempest* (c. 1610–1611). Nor are these motifs entirely new in *Pericles:* the "problem" comedies *All's Well That Ends Well* and *Measure for Measure* use a tragicomic structure in which miraculous cures or providential interventions triumph over the semblance of death. *Pericles* occupies an integral place, then, in the development of Shakespearean comedy during the period of his great tragedies. To that development, it offers a new emphasis on the simplicity of folk legend. Of the four late romances, *Pericles*, the earliest, is also the nearest in tone to the romances of the 1580s. The play seems to have constituted a revival of that old genre and was so immensely popular that it did much to establish the vogue of tragicomedy exploited by Beaumont and Fletcher.

The Chorus, old Gower, gives to the episodic materials of the play a unified point of view. He speaks with the authority of one who has told the story before, even though his *Confessio Amantis* (c. 1383–1393) was probably not Shakespeare's immediate source. Gower adopts a kind of Chaucerian persona, appealing to "what mine authors say" (1.0.20) and apologizing for his rude simplicity. Like the Chorus of *Henry V*, he repeatedly urges his auditors to transcend the limitations of his naive art, using the power of imagination to bridge gaps in time and to suppose the stage a storm-tossed ship or the city of Antioch. His appearances divide the action into seven episodic segments, surely a more authentic structure than the five "acts" conventionally employed by later editions. He offers moral appraisals of his various characters, often before we have had a chance to see them, contrasting the good with the bad. Most important, he presides as a sort of benign deity over the changing fortunes of his characters, assuring us that as narrator he will not allow the virtuous to come to grief or the wicked to escape punishment. He thus paces our expectations and provides a comic reassurance appropriate to romance. He promises to "show you those in trouble's reign, / Losing a mite, a mountain gain." To the virtuous, he will ultimately give his "benison." Under his direction, the vacillations of fortune take on a predictable rhythm, whereby the rewards of virtuous conduct may be delayed but cannot eventually fail. Pericles, he tells us, will suffer adversity "Till fortune, tired with doing bad, / Threw him ashore, to give him glad" (2.0.7–38). This pattern is repeated several times.

The characters often remind us of characters from a fairy story, outwardly stereotyped and one-dimensional, divided for the most part into contrasting types of villainy and virtue, and yet suggesting beneath their conventional surfaces the conflicts in family relationships that are essential to the fairy story. Incest is a recurrent motif, from its most blunt and evil manifestation in the court of Antiochus to more subtle inversions and variations in the relationships of Simonides and his daughter Thaisa, and, most centrally, of Pericles and his daughter Marina. The interest in fathers and daughters, and in the difficulties fathers have in coming to terms with their daughters' marrying other younger men, continues to fascinate Shakespeare from *Othello* and *King Lear* into all of his late romances. The mystery of incest is posed in terms of a riddle at the start of *Pericles*, and the moving dramatic conclusion in which the hero is reunited at last with his daughter seems to represent at some level a resolution of conflict between father and daughter. Pericles and Marina have "found" each other and themselves, literally in the narrative sense and also in some deeper psychic and spiritual way.

The characters expressing this and other conflicts are repeatedly paired opposite to one another as contrasting foils, illustrating a type of human depravity and its ideal opposite. One such contrast is that of tyranny and true monarchy. For example, both Antiochus and Simonides seem to welcome the various suitors who flock to their courts, seeking the hand in marriage of the two kings' daughters. Antiochus does so deceitfully, however, since he is his daughter's incestuous lover. Pericles learns in Antioch the danger of perceiving too much about the private affairs of a suspicious and vengeful tyrant. Simonides is, on the other hand, a true prince, beloved by even the simplest of his subjects, generous, lacking in envy, courteous to strangers, and more impressed with inner substance than with outward show. He approves of Pericles as a son-in-law, though (like Prospero in *The Tempest*) he imposes artificial restraints on the lovers to make their eventual triumph of love seem all the more sweet. Antiochus and his daughter are eventually shriveled up by a fire from heaven, whereas Simonides and Thaisa earn the just rewards of gracious hospitality. Another opposing pair of characters, Thaliard and Helicanus, are conventionally typed as false and true courtiers. Thaliard, ordered by Antiochus to murder Pericles, is evasive and self-serving; Helicanus, when offered the opportunity to supplant Pericles as ruler of Tyre, loyally awaits his master's return.

Pericles is apparently conceived in these same conventional terms as a prince of chivalry, young, brave, admirable both as a romantic wooer and as a resolute adventurer. His visit to the city of Tarsus, which has recently been toppled from wealth to poverty, shows him practicing the generosity that befits his lofty rank and innately noble qualities. Even when fortune strips him of his finery, his princely bearing is evident to discerning observers like King Simonides and Thaisa. Pericles thus differs outwardly from the flawed tragicomic protagonists more often found in the late romances, such as Posthumus in *Cymbeline* and Leontes in *The Winter's Tale*, who bring grief upon themselves and must suffer agonizing contrition before gaining an unexpected second chance. Pericles seems to be virtually without fault, a hero of romance rather than of tragedy. His soliloquies and eloquent speeches are not darkly introspective and psychological, like Leontes's. Although he grieves in sackcloth and ashes, he does so for undeserved misfortune rather than for his own follies. The play accordingly has little to say about humanity's perverse instinct for self-destruction. Yet critics have been unable to agree as to whether Pericles is simply a good man buffeted by misfortune or a man somehow perplexed by inner conflict. Are there unresolved wishes in his relationships to Thaisa and Marina that link him to the manifestly flawed protagonists of *Cymbeline* and *The Winter's Tale*, and, more explicitly, to Antiochus and his daughter in this play? What is it that causes his excessive despair in his grief and his withdrawal into absolute silence? On the surface, his story is one of undeserved misfortune, leading at last to happy reunion and an end of his trials. He learns a more affirmative and patient response from his courageous daughter Marina, whereupon his trials have run their necessary course. Even his learning such a lesson is of less importance than the sublime sense of mystery and joy that accompanies his reunion with Marina.

In several ways, Marina is a typical heroine of Shakespeare's late romances. Her name, like that of Perdita in *The Winter's Tale*, signifies loss and recovery. Marina is the gift of the sea, that mysterious power of fortune in *Pericles* that takes with one hand even while it gives with the other. Just as the sea tosses Pericles on the coast of Pentapolis and then returns to him the suit of armor in which he will joust for the love of fair Thaisa, so in another storm at sea Thaisa apparently dies giving birth to Marina. The child is a "fresh new seafarer" on the troubled voyage of life (3.1.41). The sea parts her from her mother and father and leads to the misunderstandings whereby Marina is supposed dead, but the sea also eventually deposits Pericles on the coast of Mytilene, where he finds his long-lost daughter. Like Perdita, Marina is associated with flowers and with Tellus, a divinity of the earth. The inscription on her monument, when she is thought dead, speaks of elemental strife between the sea and the shore caused by her death, in which the angry sea gods "Make raging battery upon shores of flint" (4.4.39–43). She is a princess from folk legend, like Snow White or like Imogen in *Cymbeline*, who must flee the envious wrath of a witchlike stepmother and queen. Her true mother, Thaisa, another princess in a folktale, is washed ashore in a treasure-filled chest, smelling sweetly and betokening some miraculous change of fortune.

Most important, Marina is one who can preach conversion to the sinful and cure distempered souls. She recovers her husband-to-be, Lysimachus, from the brothels of Mytilene, and even converts pimps and prostitutes by her innocent faith. As one with a strange power to bring new life to dead hope, she resembles a number of mysterious artist-figures and magicians in the late romances (or, earlier, in *All's Well That Ends Well*). One such is Cerimon, who restores life to Thaisa. Like him, or like Paulina in *The Winter's Tale*, whose devices are "lawful" though seemingly magical, Marina offers cures that can be rationally explained and yet appear to be miraculous. To Pericles, her ministrations seem "the rarest dream that e'er dull sleep / Did mock sad fools withal" (5.1.166–7). Yet what she has taught him, by her own example, is simple patience; she has suffered even more than he but nevertheless knows how to endure, how to "look / Like Patience gazing on kings' graves and smiling / Extremity out of act" (lines 140–2). Marina has the power to renew her father and restore him to life, perhaps because she represents the way in which the sexuality of women can be legitimated: she dwells for a time in a house of prostitution and is eminently desirable to men, and yet at the same time is so pure that she can teach men the way to control their own libidinousness. She is thus whore and saint in one person, able to refute the low premise about the carnality of the human condition that Pericles elsewhere finds so threatening. In his recovery of Marina and in his glad disposing of her as the bride of Lysimachus, Pericles at last comes to terms with the incestuous bond between father and daughter that had posed itself so menacingly for him in the court of King Antiochus.

Through Marina's ministrations, Pericles is reunited with his wife as well. Here, too, the narrative suggests a successful resolution of guilt after long years of inner conflict. Pericles is obliged to throw his wife's body overboard in a storm after she has died in childbirth. The fault is not his, since the sailors insist that the storm cannot be abated until the ship is cleared of the dead (3.1.47–9), but the emotional burden of loss is incalculable. Thaisa's miraculous recovery makes possible an eventual reunion that coincides with the rediscovery of the daughter. Viewed in these terms, the tale is one in which a husband finds it possible to love again a wife he lost and in a sense abandoned long ago. As in *The Winter's Tale*, where King Leontes causes the death of his queen at the time of her childbearing and then regains her after years of penance, the husband learns again, late in life, to cherish a long-lost wife who has aged and whom he is now able to love in spite of that aging. In *Pericles*, the husband's guilt is not manifest, nor is his wife's sexuality an open threat to him in her youthful childbearing vitality, and yet the narrative itself of separation and reunion resembles a slow and difficult coming to terms with the emotional demands of marriage. Perhaps it is significant in some way that Shakespeare lived apart from his family most of his working life and that when he wrote his late romances he was about to retire from London to Stratford.

Whatever the psychological dimension of the story of Pericles, his daughter, and his wife, old Gower as Chorus searches for meaning in simpler, pious terms. Gower wishes us to understand finally why Providence has allowed so much misfortune to afflict the virtuous: only by such testing can humanity learn to conquer time and death. Time will always remain "the king of men;/He's both their parent and he is their grave, / And gives them

what he will, not what they crave" (2.3.47–9). Nevertheless, Providence can turn the accidents of time and fortune to good purpose for those who are Joblike in their patient faith. Even pirates unknowingly take part in a divine plan, rescuing Marina from the clutches of the evil Dionyza. As Gower puts it, those who are "assailed with fortune fierce and keen" are also "Led on by heaven, and crowned with joy at last" (5.3.90–2). To Pericles, such a delayed reward is ample compensation for his sorrows, almost indeed an unbearable joy. "No more, you gods!" he movingly pleads. "Your present kindness / Makes my past miseries sports" (lines 41–2).

After centuries of neglect, other than in an occasional much-transmuted alteration, *Pericles* has come into its own in recent decades on stage. The tendency of late is to emphasize the play's fairy-tale-like and paradoxical elements in such a way as to call attention to the contrivances of theatrical illusion. Terry Hands, at Stratford-upon-Avon in 1969, employed a bare stage to emphasize the fluidity of movement and need for the audience's complicity in the creation of theatrical illusion; Gower (Emrys James) was a Welsh bard, and the parts of Thaisa and Marina were doubled by Susan Fleetwood—not without some contrivance at the end, when the two are onstage together. Toby Robertson chose a Brechtian modern-dress decor in order to emphasize the corruption of the brothel scenes (1973, the Roundhouse Theatre, London). Gower has taken on a number of modern guises, including that of a calypso singer (Edric Connor) in Tony Richardson's 1958 production at Stratford-upon-Avon, a blues gospel singer (Renee Rogers) in Richard Ouzounian's fine production at Stratford, Canada, in 1986, and a singing bus driver in Barbara Gaines's production for the Chicago Shakespeare Theatre in 1998. The play lends itself to oriental opulence and romance-like variety of setting. Its continued success in the theater is an effective antidote to the problems of textual uncertainty that afflict the play on the printed page.

Pericles

[*Dramatis Personae*

GOWER, *as Presenter or Chorus*

ANTIOCHUS, *King of Antioch*
DAUGHTER *of Antiochus*
THALIARD, *a lord of Antioch*
MESSENGER *to Antiochus*

PERICLES, *Prince of Tyre*
THAISA, *his wife, daughter of Simonides*
MARINA, *their daughter*
HELICANUS, ⎱
ESCANES, ⎰ *two lords of Tyre*
Three other LORDS *of Tyre*

CLEON, *Governor of Tarsus*
DIONYZA, *his wife*
LEONINE, *a murderer*
A LORD *of Tarsus*

SIMONIDES, *King of Pentapolis*
Three FISHERMEN *of Pentapolis*
Five KNIGHTS *who compete for Thaisa's hand*
Three LORDS *of Pentapolis*
A MARSHAL

LYCHORIDA, *Marina's nurse*

MASTER *of a ship*
A SAILOR *of the ship*

CERIMON, *a lord of Ephesus*
PHILEMON, *his servant*
Two GENTLEMEN *of Ephesus*
Two SERVANTS *of Ephesus*

Three PIRATES

LYSIMACHUS, *Governor of Mytilene*
PANDER, ⎱
BAWD, *his wife,* ⎰ *three bawds, or dealers*
BOLT, *their man,* ⎰ *in prostitution*
Two GENTLEMEN *of Mytilene*

SAILOR *of Tyre*
SAILOR *of Mytilene*
GENTLEMAN *of Tyre*
LORD *of Mytilene*

DIANA, *goddess of chastity*

*Lords, Ladies, Gentlemen, Attendants, Servants,
Messengers, young Ladies accompanying Marina,
Vestal Virgins, inhabitants of Ephesus*

SCENE: *In various eastern Mediterranean countries*]

1. Chorus

*Enter Gower [before the palace of Antioch, on the
walls of which can be seen a row of impaled heads].*

GOWER
> To sing a song that old was sung,   1
> From ashes ancient Gower is come,   2
> Assuming man's infirmities   3
> To glad your ear and please your eyes.
> It hath been sung at festivals,
> On ember eves and holy-ales;   6
> And lords and ladies in their lives
> Have read it for restoratives.   8
> The purchase is to make men glorious,   9

1.0. (Gower is seen to be standing before the palace of Antioch,
where scene 1 will take place.)
1 old of old   **2 ancient Gower** the fourteenth-century poet John
Gower, who related the adventures of Apollonius of Tyre (of which
Pericles is a version) in his *Confessio Amantis*

3 Assuming man's infirmities taking on a mortal body   **6 ember
eves** evenings before the ember days—the periodic fast days which
coincide with the four changes of the seasons.   **holy-ales** i.e., church
ales or festivals   **8 for restoratives** for its nourishing or healing properties.   **9 purchase** gain, benefit.   **glorious** renowned

Et bonum quo antiquius, eo melius.   10
If you, born in these latter times
When wit's more ripe, accept my rhymes,   12
And that to hear an old man sing   13
May to your wishes pleasure bring,
I life would wish, and that I might
Waste it for you, like taper light.   16
This Antioch, then. Antiochus the Great   17
Built up this city for his chiefest seat,
The fairest in all Syria—
I tell you what mine authors say.   20
This king unto him took a peer,   21
Who died and left a female heir,
So buxom, blithe, and full of face   23
As heaven had lent her all his grace;   24
With whom the father liking took   25
And her to incest did provoke.
Bad child, worse father, to entice his own
To evil should be done by none!   28
But custom what they did begin   29
Was with long use account'd no sin.
The beauty of this sinful dame
Made many princes thither frame   32
To seek her as a bedfellow,
In marriage pleasures playfellow;
Which to prevent he made a law,
To keep her still, and men in awe,   36
That whoso asked her for his wife,
His riddle told not, lost his life.   38
So for her many a wight did die,   39
As yon grim looks do testify.
            [*He points to the heads of the unsuccessful
                   suitors, displayed on the walls.*]
What now ensues, to the judgment of your eye
I give my cause, who best can justify.   *Exit.* 42

❖

[1.1]

Enter Antiochus, Prince Pericles, and followers.

ANTIOCHUS
Young Prince of Tyre, you have at large received   1
The danger of the task you undertake.
PERICLES
I have, Antiochus, and with a soul
Emboldened with the glory of her praise
Think death no hazard in this enterprise.

ANTIOCHUS   Music!
Bring in our daughter, clothèd like a bride
For th'embracements even of Jove himself,
At whose conception, till Lucina reigned,   9
Nature this dowry gave: to glad her presence,   10
The senate house of planets all did sit   11
To knit in her their best perfections.   12

        [*Music.*] *Enter Antiochus's Daughter.*

PERICLES
See where she comes, appareled like the spring,
Graces her subjects, and her thoughts the king   14
Of every virtue gives renown to men!   15
Her face the book of praises, where is read   16
Nothing but curious pleasures, as from thence   17
Sorrow were ever razed, and testy wrath   18
Could never be her mild companion.   19
You gods that made me man, and sway in love,   20
That have inflamed desire in my breast
To taste the fruit of yon celestial tree
Or die in the adventure, be my helps,
As I am son and servant to your will,
To compass such a boundless happiness!   25
ANTIOCHUS   Prince Pericles—
PERICLES
That would be son to great Antiochus.
ANTIOCHUS
Before thee stands this fair Hesperides,   28
With golden fruit, but dangerous to be touched,
For deathlike dragons here affright thee hard.   30
Her face, like heaven, enticeth thee to view
Her countless glory, which desert must gain;   32
And which, without desert, because thine eye   33
Presumes to reach, all the whole heap must die.   34
Yon sometimes famous princes, like thyself,   35
               [*pointing to the heads on the walls*]
Drawn by report, advent'rous by desire,
Tell thee with speechless tongues and semblance pale   37
That without covering, save yon field of stars,
Here they stand martyrs slain in Cupid's wars,
And with dead cheeks advise thee to desist
For going on death's net, whom none resist.   41

10 *Et . . . melius* a good thing is better for being older. (Latin.)
12 **wit's more ripe** wisdom is more seasoned   13 **And that** i.e., and if
16 **Waste** spend.   **like taper light** i.e., like a candle that consumes
itself in giving illumination.   17 **This** i.e., This is   20 **authors** authorities   21 **peer** consort   23 **buxom** cheerful, lively.   **full of face** beautiful and round of face   24 **As** as if.   **his** its   25 **liking** a lustful
desire   28 **should** that should   29 **custom** continued practice (of)
32 **frame** direct their steps   36 **still** always, forever.   **and men** and to
keep men   38 **His riddle told not** if he left his (Antiochus's) riddle
unsolved   39 **wight** person   42 **I . . . justify** I submit my case, my
story, to you who can best adjudge its truthful value.
1.1. Location: Antioch. The palace, as before.
1 **at large received** heard in detail

9 **At . . . reigned** during whose gestation period between conception
and birth. (Lucina was the Roman goddess of childbirth in her capacity as goddess of light.)   **10–12 Nature . . . perfections** i.e., Nature
bestowed on her, to make her presence gladsome, a favorable aspect
of all the planets so that all perfect qualities would be combined in
her.   **14 Graces her subjects** with graces for her subjects. (She commands every graceful quality and virtue known to humanity.)
15 **gives** that gives   16 **book of praises** collection of praiseworthy
qualities   17 **curious** exquisite.   **as** as if   18 **ever razed** forever
scraped away or erased   19 **her mild companion** companion of her
mildness.   20 **sway** rule   25 **compass** encompass   28 **Hesperides**
(Correctly speaking, the nymphs who guarded Juno's golden fruit in
the garden of Hesperus. Here the name applies to the Princess,
beyond price but dangerous to seek.)   30 **deathlike dragons**
(Alludes to the dragon that guarded the garden of the Hesperides.)
32 **countless glory** innumerable beauties   33–4 **And . . . die** and if
you presume to aspire to her beauty without deserving, you (literally,
your entire body) will die.   35 **sometimes** once, formerly   37 **semblance** outward aspect   41 **For going on** from entering

PERICLES
Antiochus, I thank thee, who hath taught
My frail mortality to know itself,
And by those fearful objects to prepare
This body, like to them, to what I must;   45
For death remembered should be like a mirror,   46
Who tells us life's but breath, to trust it error.
I'll make my will then, and, as sick men do,
Who know the world, see heaven, but, feeling woe,   49
Grip not at earthly joys as erst they did,   50
So I bequeath a happy peace to you
And all good men, as every prince should do;
My riches to the earth from whence they came,
[_To the Princess_] But my unspotted fire of love to you.
Thus ready for the way of life or death,
I wait the sharpest blow, Antiochus.
ANTIOCHUS
Scorning advice, read the conclusion, then;   57
Which read and not expounded, 'tis decreed,
As these before thee, thou thyself shalt bleed.
DAUGHTER
Of all 'sayed yet, mayst thou prove prosperous!   60
Of all 'sayed yet, I wish thee happiness!   61
PERICLES
Like a bold champion, I assume the lists,   62
Nor ask advice of any other thought
But faithfulness and courage.   [_He reads_] _the riddle._
I am no viper, yet I feed   65
On mother's flesh which did me breed.   66
I sought a husband, in which labor
I found that kindness in a father.   68
He's father, son, and husband mild;
I mother, wife, and yet his child.
How they may be, and yet in two,   71
As you will live, resolve it you.
[_Aside_] Sharp physic is the last! But, O you powers   73
That gives heaven countless eyes to view men's acts,   74
Why cloud they not their sights perpetually   75
If this be true which makes me pale to read it?
Fair glass of light, I loved you, and could still,   77
Were not this glorious casket stored with ill.
But I must tell you now my thoughts revolt,
For he's no man on whom perfections wait   80
That, knowing sin within, will touch the gate.   81
You are a fair viol, and your sense the strings   82
Who, fingered to make man his lawful music,

Would draw heaven down and all the gods to
    hearken,
But, being played upon before your time,   85
Hell only danceth at so harsh a chime.   86
Good sooth, I care not for you.   87
ANTIOCHUS
Prince Pericles, touch not, upon thy life,   88
For that's an article within our law
As dangerous as the rest. Your time's expired.
Either expound now, or receive your sentence.
PERICLES   Great King,
Few love to hear the sins they love to act;
'Twould braid yourself too near for me to tell it.   94
Who has a book of all that monarchs do,   95
He's more secure to keep it shut than shown.
For vice repeated is like the wand'ring wind,   97
Blows dust in others' eyes to spread itself;   98
And yet the end of all is bought thus dear,   99
The breath is gone, and the sore eyes see clear   100
To stop the air would hurt them. The blind mole
    casts   101
Copped hills towards heaven to tell the earth is
    thronged   102
By man's oppression, and the poor worm doth die
    for 't.   103
Kings are earth's gods; in vice their law's their will;
And if Jove stray, who dares say Jove doth ill?
It is enough you know; and it is fit,   106
What being more known grows worse, to smother it.   107
All love the womb that their first being bred;
Then give my tongue like leave to love my head.   109
ANTIOCHUS [_aside_]
Heaven, that I had thy head! He has found the
    meaning.
But I will gloze with him.—Young Prince of Tyre,   111
Though by the tenor of our strict edict,
Your exposition misinterpreting,   113
We might proceed to cancel of your days,   114
Yet hope, succeeding from so fair a tree   115
As your fair self, doth tune us otherwise.   116
Forty days longer we do respite you,

---

85 before your time i.e., before marriage   **86 only** alone   **87 Good sooth** In truth   **88 touch not** (Antiochus evidently believes Pericles is about to touch the Princess's hand or some such forbidden thing.)   **94 braid . . . near** upbraid you too directly   **95 Who** He who   **97 repeated** proclaimed   **98–101 Blows . . . hurt them** which, in seeking to disseminate its report of vice, manages only to blow dust in people's eyes, the result being costly to the one attempting to tell the truth; his breath is spent in vain, whereas the offenders can see clearly enough, despite the irritation, how to prevent the talk from hurting them.   **101–3 The blind . . . for 't** (Pericles's example is of a lowly creature like the worm who dares to sound a warning against incest and tyranny only to suffer for the attempt, while spiritually blind figures of authority, like the mole, insolently build up peaked [_copped_] monuments, thereby demonstrating how the earth is beset [_thronged_] with such oppressive uses of power.)   **106 you know** i.e., that you know that I know your riddle   **107 What . . . it** to cover up a deed that is only worsened by revelation.   **109 like leave** similar permission   **111 gloze** talk smoothly and speciously   **113 Your . . . misinterpreting** since your exposition interprets wrongly   **114 to cancel . . . days** to end your life   **115 Yet . . . tree** yet hope (or fear) of your answering correctly, issuing from so fair a royal stock   **116 doth . . . otherwise** alters my intention. (_Us_ is the royal "we.")

---

45 must must someday be   **46 remembered** called to mind   **49 Who . . . woe** i.e., who, weary of this world's miseries and seeing the imminence of heavenly bliss   **50 Grip** clutch.   **erst** formerly   **57 conclusion** problem, riddle   **60 'sayed** who have assayed, attempted. (Also in line 61.)   **62 assume the lists** i.e., undertake the combat, enter the tournament ground   **65–6 I am . . . breed** (Vipers at birth were thought to gnaw their way through their mother's sides, thus killing the mother.)   **68 kindness** (1) affection (2) kinship   **71 two** i.e., two people   **73 Sharp . . . last!** i.e., This last condition—to stake my life on solving this riddle—is bitter medicine!   **powers** celestial beings who control destiny   **74 eyes** i.e., the stars   **75 Why . . . perpetually** i.e., why do the gods not forever turn their gaze aside in dismay   **77 glass of light** beautiful (but deceptive) glass vessel   **80–1 For . . . gate** i.e., the man who will meddle with incest is not one on whom virtues attend.   **82 sense** senses

If by which time our secret be undone,   118
This mercy shows we'll joy in such a son.
And until then your entertain shall be   120
As doth befit our honor and your worth.   121
           [Exeunt.] Manet Pericles solus.

PERICLES
How courtesy would seem to cover sin,   122
When what is done is like an hypocrite,
The which is good in nothing but in sight!   124
If it be true that I interpret false,   125
Then were it certain you were not so bad
As with foul incest to abuse your soul,
Where now you're both a father and a son   128
By your untimely claspings with your child,
Which pleasures fits a husband, not a father,
And she an eater of her mother's flesh
By the defiling of her parents' bed;
And both like serpents are, who, though they feed
On sweetest flowers, yet they poison breed.
Antioch, farewell, for wisdom sees those men   135
Blush not in actions blacker than the night
Will 'schew no course to keep them from the light.   137
One sin, I know, another doth provoke;
Murder's as near to lust as flame to smoke.   139
Poison and treason are the hands of sin,
Ay, and the targets, to put off the shame.   141
Then, lest my life be cropped to keep you clear,   142
By flight I'll shun the danger which I fear.   *Exit.*

      Enter Antiochus.

ANTIOCHUS   He hath found the meaning,
For which we mean to have his head.
He must not live to trumpet forth my infamy,
Nor tell the world Antiochus doth sin
In such a loathèd manner;
And therefore instantly this prince must die,
For by his fall my honor must keep high.
[Calling] Who attends us there?

      Enter Thaliard.

THALIARD   Doth Your Highness call?
ANTIOCHUS
Thaliard, you are of our chamber, Thaliard,   153
And our mind partakes her private actions   154
To your secrecy; and for your faithfulness
We will advance you, Thaliard. Behold.
           [He gives poison and money.]
Here's poison and here's gold. We hate the Prince
Of Tyre, and thou must kill him. It fits thee not
To ask the reason why: because we bid it.

Say, is it done?
THALIARD   My lord, 'tis done.
ANTIOCHUS   Enough.

      Enter a Messenger.

Let your breath cool yourself, telling your haste.   161
MESSENGER   My lord, Prince Pericles is fled.   *[Exit.]*
ANTIOCHUS *[to Thaliard]*   As thou wilt live, fly after,
and like an arrow shot from a well-experienced archer
hits the mark his eye doth level at, so thou never re-   165
turn unless thou say Prince Pericles is dead.
THALIARD   My lord, if I can get him within my pistol's
length, I'll make him sure enough. So farewell to Your   168
Highness.
ANTIOCHUS   Thaliard, adieu!   *[Exit Thaliard.]*
             Till Pericles be dead,
My heart can lend no succor to my head.   *[Exit.]*   171

[1.2]

      Enter Pericles with his Lords.

PERICLES
Let none disturb us.   *[The Lords stay at the door.]*
           Why should this change of thoughts,   1
The sad companion, dull-eyed melancholy,
Be my so used a guest as not an hour   3
In the day's glorious walk or peaceful night,   4
The tomb where grief should sleep, can breed me
    quiet?
Here pleasures court mine eyes, and mine eyes shun
    them,
And danger, which I feared, is at Antioch,
Whose arm seems far too short to hit me here.
Yet neither pleasure's art can joy my spirits,
Nor yet the other's distance comfort me.
Then it is thus: the passions of the mind,   11
That have their first conception by misdread,   12
Have after-nourishment and life by care;   13
And what was first but fear what might be done   14
Grows elder now, and cares it be not done.   15
And so with me: the great Antiochus,
'Gainst whom I am too little to contend,
Since he's so great can make his will his act,   18
Will think me speaking, though I swear to silence;
Nor boots it me to say I honor him,   20
If he suspect I may dishonor him.
And what may make him blush in being known,   22
He'll stop the course by which it might be known.

---

118 undone unraveled, solved   **120 entertain** entertainment, reception   **121.1 *Manet*** He remains onstage.   *solus* alone.   **122 would seem** speciously endeavors   **124 sight** appearance.   **125 If . . . false** If I were mistaken (which I am not)   **128 Where** whereas   **135 sees those men** sees that those men who   **137 'schew** eschew. (Or "shew," the Quarto reading, could mean "show, reveal.")   **keep . . . light** i.e., keep their guilty actions hidden.   **139 Murder's . . . lust** (A sententious truism of the time.)   **141 targets** shields.   **put off** deflect   **142 cropped** harvested, cut down.   **clear** free from accusation   **153 of our chamber** my chamberlain   **154 partakes** imparts

161 Let . . . haste Cool your hot haste by breathing or panting out your report.   **165 level** aim   **168 length** range.   **sure** harmless (i.e., dead)   **171 My . . . head** i.e., my anxieties cannot calm my fears.   **1.2. Location:** Tyre. The palace.   **1 us** i.e., me.   **change of thoughts** altered disposition of mind   **3 Be . . . guest as** be so familiar a guest with me that   **4 walk** i.e., traversing of the sun   **11–15 the passions . . . not done** passions such as fear, that originate in apprehension of some evil, are kept alive by anxiety; and what at first was simple apprehension gives way in time to an anxious care to prevent from happening what at first had seemed only a worrisome possibility.   **18 so great can** so powerful that he can   **20 boots** avails   **22 known** publicly revealed

With hostile forces he'll o'erspread the land,
And with th'ostent of war will look so huge   25
Amazement shall drive courage from the state,   26
Our men be vanquished ere they do resist,
And subjects punished that ne'er thought offense;
Which care of them, not pity of myself—
Who am no more but as the tops of trees
Which fence the roots they grow by, and defend
    them—   31
Makes both my body pine and soul to languish,
And punish that before that he would punish.   33

Enter [Helicanus and] all the Lords to Pericles.

FIRST LORD
Joy and all comfort in your sacred breast!
SECOND LORD
And keep your mind, till you return to us,   35
Peaceful and comfortable!
HELICANUS
Peace, peace, and give experience tongue.   37
They do abuse the King that flatter him.
For flattery is the bellows blows up sin;   39
The thing the which is flattered, but a spark   40
To which that blast gives heat and stronger glowing; 41
Whereas reproof, obedient and in order,
Fits kings as they are men, for they may err.
When Signor Sooth here does proclaim peace,   44
He flatters you, makes war upon your life.
Prince, pardon me, or strike me, if you please;
I cannot be much lower than my knees.   [*He kneels.*]
PERICLES
All leave us else; but let your cares o'erlook   48
What shipping and what lading's in our haven,   49
And then return to us.   [*Exeunt Lords.*]
                    Helicanus,
Thou hast moved us. What see'st thou in our looks?   51
HELICANUS   An angry brow, dread lord.
PERICLES
If there be such a dart in princes' frowns,
How durst thy tongue move anger to our face?
HELICANUS
How dares the plants look up to heaven,
From whence they have their nourishment?

PERICLES
Thou knowest I have power to take thy life from thee.
HELICANUS   I have ground the ax myself;
Do you but strike the blow.
PERICLES
Rise, prithee, rise. [*He rises.*] Sit down. Thou art no
    flatterer,
I thank thee for't, and heaven forbid
That kings should let their ears hear their faults hid!   62
Fit counselor and servant for a prince,
Who by thy wisdom makes a prince thy servant,
What wouldst thou have me do?
HELICANUS   To bear with patience such griefs
As you yourself do lay upon yourself.
PERICLES
Thou speak'st like a physician, Helicanus,
That ministers a potion unto me
That thou wouldst tremble to receive thyself.
Attend me, then: I went to Antioch,   71
Where, as thou know'st, against the face of death
I sought the purchase of a glorious beauty   73
From whence an issue I might propagate,   74
Are arms to princes and bring joys to subjects.   75
Her face was to mine eye beyond all wonder;
The rest—hark in thine ear—as black as incest,
Which by my knowledge found, the sinful father
Seemed not to strike, but smooth. But thou know'st
    this,   79
'Tis time to fear when tyrants seem to kiss.
Which fear so grew in me, I hither fled
Under the covering of a careful night,   82
Who seemed my good protector, and, being here,
Bethought me what was past, what might succeed.   84
I knew him tyrannous, and tyrants' fears
Decrease not, but grow faster than the years;
And should he doubt—as doubt no doubt he doth—   87
That I should open to the list'ning air   88
How many worthy princes' bloods were shed
To keep his bed of blackness unlaid ope,   90
To lop that doubt he'll fill this land with arms   91
And make pretense of wrong that I have done him;
When all for mine—if I may call't—offense   93
Must feel war's blow, who spares not innocence;   94
Which love to all, of which thyself art one,   95
Who now reprov'st me for't—   96
HELICANUS   Alas, sir!
PERICLES
Drew sleep out of mine eyes, blood from my cheeks,
Musings into my mind, with thousand doubts
How I might stop this tempest ere it came;

---

25 th'ostent the display   **26 Amazement** fear, terror   **31 fence** shield, shelter. (As a virtuous prince, Pericles sees his exalted role at the top of the hierarchy, like a treetop, as one of defending the common people, who are lowly and earthbound like the tree's roots but are also its center of life and source of sustenance.)   **33 And . . . would punish** and punishes me beforehand (through fear) whom he (Antiochus) wishes to punish.   **35 till you return to us** (Here, the lords of Tyre appear to know of Pericles's departure. In the next scene, we find that he left *unlicensed of their loves,* i.e., without their knowledge. The prose narratives that recount the same story state that his departure was accomplished secretly. This is one of the several inconsistencies of this rather garbled text.)   **37 give . . . tongue** listen to the voice of experience.   **39 blows up** that inflames, heats   **40 the which** which   **41 blast** i.e., flattering speech. (In Wilkins's *Painful Adventures,* this scene is more clearly presented: Helicanus upbraids Pericles for his bad humor and then justifies such plain talk as preferable to flattery.)   **44 When Signor Sooth** When Sir Flattery. (Though, puzzlingly, no one in this scene has, in fact, flattered Pericles; see the note for line 41.)   **48 else** i.e., except Helicanus.   **cares o'erlook** watchfulness supervise   **49 lading's** cargo is   **51 moved** angered

62 hear . . . hid listen to flattery that glosses over their faults.   **71 Attend** Listen to   **73 purchase** acquisition   **74–5 From . . . princes** upon whose body I might beget an heir, such as are the props and supports of princes   **79 Seemed** pretended.   **smooth** gloss over, conciliate.   **82 careful** protecting   **84 succeed** follow.   **87 And should . . . doth** and should he fear—as no doubt he does fear—   **88 open** reveal   **90 unlaid ope** unrevealed   **91 lop that doubt** cut off that fear   **93–4 When . . . innocence** in which event, all my subjects will, because of my offense (if I may call it that), be subjected to the blows of war that spare not the innocent   **95 Which . . . one** which love for all my subjects, of whom you are one   **96 now** just now

And finding little comfort to relieve them,
I thought it princely charity to grieve for them.
HELICANUS
Well, my lord, since you have given me leave to speak,
Freely will I speak. Antiochus you fear,
And justly too, I think, you fear the tyrant,
Who either by public war or private treason
Will take away your life.
Therefore, my lord, go travel for a while,
Till that his rage and anger be forgot,
Or till the Destinies do cut his thread of life.
Your rule direct to any; if to me,   111
Day serves not light more faithful than I'll be.
PERICLES   I do not doubt thy faith;
But should he wrong my liberties in my absence?   114
HELICANUS
We'll mingle our bloods together in the earth,   115
From whence we had our being and our birth.
PERICLES
Tyre, I now look from thee, then, and to Tarsus
Intend my travel, where I'll hear from thee,   118
And by whose letters I'll dispose myself.
The care I had and have of subjects' good
On thee I lay, whose wisdom's strength can bear it.
I'll take thy word for faith, not ask thine oath.
Who shuns not to break one will sure crack both.   123
But in our orbs we'll live so round and safe   124
That time of both this truth shall ne'er convince: 125
Thou showed'st a subject's shine, I a true prince'.   126
                                            Exeunt.

❖

[1.3]

Enter Thaliard solus.

THALIARD   So, this is Tyre, and this the court. Here
must I kill King Pericles; and if I do it not, I am sure to
be hanged at home. 'Tis dangerous. Well, I perceive he   3
was a wise fellow and had good discretion that, being
bid to ask what he would of the King, desired he might
know none of his secrets. Now do I see he had some   6
reason for't; for if a king bid a man be a villain, he's
bound by the indenture of his oath to be one. Husht!   8
Here comes the lords of Tyre.

*Enter Helicanus [and] Escanes, with other
Lords [of Tyre. Thaliard stands aside.]*

HELICANUS
You shall not need, my fellow peers of Tyre,
Further to question me of your king's departure.
His sealed commission left in trust with me   12
Does speak sufficiently he's gone to travel.
THALIARD [*aside*]   How? The King gone?
HELICANUS
If further yet you will be satisfied
Why, as it were, unlicensed of your loves   16
He would depart, I'll give some light unto you.
Being at Antioch—
THALIARD [*aside*]   What from Antioch?
HELICANUS
Royal Antiochus—on what cause I know not—
Took some displeasure at him, at least he judged so;
And doubting lest he had erred or sinned,   21
To show his sorrow, he'd correct himself;   22
So puts himself unto the shipman's toil,   23
With whom each minute threatens life or death.
THALIARD [*aside*]   Well, I perceive
I shall not be hanged now, although I would;   26
But since he's gone, the King's ears it must please
He scaped the land, to perish at the seas.
I'll present myself.—Peace to the lords of Tyre!
HELICANUS
Lord Thaliard from Antiochus is welcome.
THALIARD   From him I come
With message unto princely Pericles;
But since my landing I have understood
Your lord has betaken himself to unknown travels;
Now message must return from whence it came.   35
HELICANUS
We have no reason to desire it,   36
Commended to our master, not to us.   37
Yet ere you shall depart, this we desire,
As friends to Antioch, we may feast in Tyre.
                                            Exeunt.

❖

[1.4]

*Enter Cleon, the Governor of Tarsus, with
[Dionyza] his wife, and others.*

CLEON
My Dionyza, shall we rest us here
And, by relating tales of others' griefs,
See if 'twill teach us to forget our own?
DIONYZA
That were to blow at fire in hope to quench it,
For who digs hills because they do aspire   5

---

111 direct delegate   **114 should he** what if he (Antiochus) should.
liberties royal rights and prerogatives, and those of my subjects
115 mingle . . . earth i.e., die fighting him   **118 Intend** direct, purpose   **123 Who** He who   **124 orbs** orbits, spheres.   **round** with pro-
bity. (But punning on the idea of circularity in *round*. A line appears
to be lost here, rhyming with *safe*.)   **125 time . . . convince** time will
never confute this truth regarding us two   **126 shine** brightness,
honor (as of true gold).   **prince'** prince's.
1.3. Location: Tyre. The palace.
3–6 he . . . secrets (So the poet Philippides asked of Lysimachus; mentioned by Plutarch and Barnabe Riche.)   **8 indenture** terms by which
a servant is bound to his master

12 sealed bearing the royal seal   **16 unlicensed . . . loves** without your
loving assent. (Compare with the note for 1.2.35.)   **21 doubting lest**
fearing that   **22 he'd correct himself** he wished to impose a penalty
on himself   **23 toil** travail, hence dangers   **26 although I would**
even if I wished to be   **35 message** my message   **36 desire it** i.e., wish
to know the message's contents   **37 Commended** directed as it is
1.4. Location: Tarsus. The Governor's house.
5 who digs whoever digs up, removes.   **aspire** mount up

Throws down one mountain to cast up a higher.
Oh, my distressed lord, even such our griefs are;
Here they are but felt, and seen with mischief's eyes,   8
But like to groves, being topped, they higher rise.   9
CLEON   Oh, Dionyza,
Who wanteth food and will not say he wants it,   11
Or can conceal his hunger till he famish?   12
Our tongues and sorrows do sound deep our woes   13
Into the air; our eyes do weep till lungs
Fetch breath that may proclaim them louder, that,   15
If heaven slumber while their creatures want,   16
They may awake their helps to comfort them.   17
I'll then discourse our woes, felt several years,
And, wanting breath to speak, help me with tears.   19
DIONYZA   I'll do my best, sir.
CLEON
This Tarsus, o'er which I have the government,   21
A city on whom Plenty held full hand,   22
For Riches strewed herself even in her streets;   23
Whose towers bore heads so high they kissed the
   clouds,
And strangers ne'er beheld but wondered at;
Whose men and dames so jetted and adorned,   26
Like one another's glass to trim them by;   27
Their tables were stored full, to glad the sight,
And not so much to feed on as delight;
All poverty was scorned, and pride so great,
The name of help grew odious to repeat.   31
DIONYZA   Oh, 'tis too true.
CLEON
But see what heaven can do by this our change: 33
These mouths who but of late earth, sea, and air
Were all too little to content and please,
Although they gave their creatures in abundance,
As houses are defiled for want of use,   37
They are now starved for want of exercise.
Those palates who, not yet two summers younger,
Must have inventions to delight the taste,   40
Would now be glad of bread and beg for it.
Those mothers who, to nuzzle up their babes,   42
Thought naught too curious, are ready now   43
To eat those little darlings whom they loved.
So sharp are hunger's teeth that man and wife

8–9 Here . . . rise our misfortunes seem bad enough when we mutely
behold them with the eyes of calamity, but will only grow worse if we
talk about them, like trees that, being cut off at the top, merely sprout
new growth.   11 wanteth lacks   12 famish starve to death.
13 sound deep sound forth solemnly. (With suggestion of plumbing
unfathomable depths.)   15 them our woes   16–17 while . . . them
while living beings are in need, our tears and prayers may awaken
the help of the heavens to provide comfort.   19 wanting i.e., when I
lack.   help me i.e., you help me   21 This Tarsus This is Tarsus
22 on whom . . . hand over which Plenty poured her gifts generously
23 Riches (A singular concept, probably derived from the French
richesse, equivalent to "plenty"; the image is that of the cornucopia
being held aloft over the city.)   26 jetted and
adorned strutted and adorned themselves   27 glass . . . by mirror by
which to adorn themselves, or, to mirror each other's finery   31 The
name . . . repeat i.e., that it became odious even to mention the very
possibility of asking for help.   33 see . . . change see by our change in
fortune what heaven can do   37 for want through lack   40 Must
have inventions insisted on novelties   42 nuzzle up nurture
43 naught too curious nothing too choice (for their babes)

Draw lots who first shall die to lengthen life.   46
Here stands a lord and there a lady weeping;
Here many sink, yet those which see them fall
Have scarce strength left to give them burial.
Is not this true?
DIONYZA
Our cheeks and hollow eyes do witness it.
CLEON
Oh, let those cities that of Plenty's cup
And her prosperities so largely taste,
With their superfluous riots, hear these tears!   54
The misery of Tarsus may be theirs.

Enter a Lord.

LORD   Where's the Lord Governor?
CLEON   Here.
Speak out thy sorrows which thou bring'st in haste,
For comfort is too far for us to expect.
LORD
We have descried, upon our neighboring shore,
A portly sail of ships make hitherward.   61
CLEON   I thought as much.
One sorrow never comes but brings an heir
That may succeed as his inheritor,
And so in ours. Some neighboring nation,
Taking advantage of our misery,
Hath stuffed these hollow vessels with their power   67
To beat us down, the which are down already,
And make a conquest of unhappy men,
Whereas no glory's got to overcome.   70
LORD
That's the least fear, for by the semblance   71
Of their white flags displayed they bring us peace,
And come to us as favorers, not as foes.
CLEON
Thou speak'st like him 's untutored to repeat: 74
Who makes the fairest show means most deceit.   75
But bring they what they will and what they can,
What need we fear?
Our ground's the lowest, and we are halfway there.   78
Go tell their general we attend him here,
To know for what he comes and whence he comes
And what he craves.
LORD   I go, my lord.   [*Exit.*]
CLEON
Welcome is peace, if he on peace consist;   83
If wars, we are unable to resist.

Enter Pericles with attendants.

PERICLES
Lord Governor, for so we hear you are,

46 lengthen life i.e., provide food for the other to cannibalize.
54 superfluous riots prodigal living.   tears i.e., sounds of weeping.
61 A portly . . . hitherward a stately fleet of ships sails toward us.
67 power force of armed men   70 Whereas . . . overcome whereby no
glory is gained by the conqueror.   71 the least fear i.e., something
not to be feared in the least   74 him 's . . . repeat one who has never
been taught to recite (the following maxim) and is therefore unaware
of its truth   75 Who He who   78 Our . . . lowest i.e., One who's
already down on the ground can fall no lower. (Proverbial.)   83 on
peace consist is resolved on peace.

Let not our ships and number of our men
Be like a beacon fired t'amaze your eyes.   87
We have heard your miseries as far as Tyre
And seen the desolation of your streets;
Nor come we to add sorrow to your tears,
But to relieve them of their heavy load;
And these our ships, you happily may think   92
Are like the Trojan horse was stuffed within   93
With bloody veins expecting overthrow,   94
Are stored with corn to make your needy bread   95
And give them life whom hunger starved half dead.

ALL [*kneeling*]   The gods of Greece protect you!
And we'll pray for you.

PERICLES   Arise, I pray you, rise.
We do not look for reverence but for love,
And harborage for ourself, our ships, and men.

CLEON [*rising*]
The which when any shall not gratify,   102
Or pay you with unthankfulness in thought,
Be it our wives, our children, or ourselves,
The curse of heaven and men succeed their evils!   105
Till when—the which I hope shall ne'er be seen—
Your Grace is welcome to our town and us.

PERICLES
Which welcome we'll accept, feast here awhile,
Until our stars that frown lend us a smile.   *Exeunt.*

❖

[2. Chorus]

Enter Gower.

GOWER
Here have you seen a mighty king
His child, iwis, to incest bring;   2
A better prince and benign lord,   3
That will prove awful both in deed and word.   4
Be quiet then, as men should be,
Till he hath passed necessity.   6
I'll show you those in trouble's reign,   7
Losing a mite, a mountain gain.
The good in conversation,   9
To whom I give my benison,   10
Is still at Tarsus, where each man
Thinks all is writ he speken can;   12
And, to remember what he does,   13
Build his statue to make him glorious.

But tidings to the contrary   15
Are brought your eyes. What need speak I?

Dumb Show.

Enter at one door Pericles talking with Cleon, all the train with them. Enter at another door a Gentleman, with a letter to Pericles; Pericles shows the letter to Cleon; Pericles gives the Messenger a reward, and knights him. Exit Pericles at one door, and Cleon at another.

Good Helicane, that stayed at home—
Not to eat honey like a drone   18
From others' labors, for though he strive   19
To killen bad, keep good alive,   20
And to fulfill his prince' desire—   21
Sends word of all that haps in Tyre:
How Thaliard came full bent with sin   23
And hid intent to murder him,   24
And that in Tarsus was not best
Longer for him to make his rest.
He, doing so, put forth to seas,   27
Where when men been there's seldom ease;   28
For now the wind begins to blow;
Thunder above and deeps below
Makes such unquiet that the ship
Should house him safe is wrecked and split,   32
And he, good prince, having all lost,
By waves from coast to coast is tossed.
All perishen of man, of pelf,   35
Ne aught escapend but himself;   36
Till fortune, tired with doing bad,
Threw him ashore, to give him glad.   38
And here he comes. What shall be next,
Pardon old Gower—this 'longs the text.   [*Exit.*] 40

❖

[2.1]

Enter Pericles, wet.

PERICLES
Yet cease your ire, you angry stars of heaven!
Wind, rain, and thunder, remember earthly man   2
Is but a substance that must yield to you,
And I, as fits my nature, do obey you.
Alas, the seas hath cast me on the rocks,
Washed me from shore to shore, and left me breath
Nothing to think on but ensuing death.
Let it suffice the greatness of your powers
To have bereft a prince of all his fortunes,
And, having thrown him from your wat'ry grave,

---

87 **t'amaze** to terrify   92 **you happily** which you perchance   93 **was** which was   94 **bloody veins** i.e., bloodthirsty Greek warriors. **expecting overthrow** i.e., in anticipation of the overthrow of Troy. (Or the phrase perhaps modifies *you* in line 92.)   95 **corn** grain.   **your needy bread** desperately needed bread, or, bread for your needy people   102 **gratify** show gratitude for or toward   105 **succeed** follow as a consequence of
2.0.
2 **iwis** certainly   3 **A better prince** i.e., and you have also seen a better prince, Pericles   4 **awful** deserving of awe, respect   6 **necessity** those hardships imposed by fate.   7 **those** i.e., those who   9 **The good in conversation** The good man (Pericles) in matters of conduct   10 **benison** blessing   12 **writ** holy writ.   **he speken can** that he (Pericles) speaks. (A deliberately medieval expression, as also in *killen, been, perishen,* and *Ne aught escapend,* lines 20, 28, 35, and 36.)
13 **remember** commemorate

15 **to the contrary** adverse   18–21 **Not . . . desire** (Helicanus strives to punish evildoers and reward the virtuous, much as a good bee refuses to be a drone, choosing instead to labor in the interests of the hive's ruler.)   23 **bent with** intent upon   24 **hid** hidden   27 **so** i.e., as advised   28 **been** are   32 **Should** that should   35 **pelf** goods, property   36 **Ne aught escapend** nothing escaping   38 **glad** gladness.
40 **'longs the text** belongs to the text of the play proper. (Or Gower may be saying that his speech is already long enough or too long.)
2.1. Location: Pentapolis. The seaside.
2 **remember** remember that

Here to have death in peace is all he'll crave.

Enter three Fishermen.

FIRST FISHERMAN   What, ho, Pilch!   12
SECOND FISHERMAN   Ha, come and bring away the nets!   13
FIRST FISHERMAN   What, Patchbreech, I say!   14
THIRD FISHERMAN   What say you, master?
FIRST FISHERMAN   Look how thou stirr'st now! Come   16
away, or I'll fetch th' with a wanion.   17
THIRD FISHERMAN   Faith, master, I am thinking of the
poor men that were cast away before us even now.   19
FIRST FISHERMAN   Alas, poor souls, it grieved my heart
to hear what pitiful cries they made to us to help them,
when, welladay, we could scarce help ourselves.   22
THIRD FISHERMAN   Nay, master, said not I as much
when I saw the porpoise how he bounced and tum-   24
bled? They say they're half fish, half flesh. A plague
on them, they ne'er come but I look to be washed.   26
Master, I marvel how the fishes live in the sea.
FIRST FISHERMAN   Why, as men do aland: the great   28
ones eat up the little ones. I can compare our rich mi-
sers to nothing so fitly as to a whale: 'a plays and tum- 30
bles, driving the poor fry before him, and at last devours them all at a mouthful. Such whales have I heard   32
on o' th' land, who never leave gaping till they swal-   33
lowed the whole parish, church, steeple, bells, and all.
PERICLES [*aside*]   A pretty moral.
THIRD FISHERMAN   But, master, if I had been the sexton,
I would have been that day in the belfry.
SECOND FISHERMAN   Why, man?
THIRD FISHERMAN   Because he should have swallowed
me too, and when I had been in his belly I would
have kept such a jangling of the bells that he should
never have left till he cast bells, steeple, church, and   42
parish up again. But if the good King Simonides were
of my mind—
PERICLES [*aside*]   Simonides?
THIRD FISHERMAN   We would purge the land of these
drones that rob the bee of her honey.
PERICLES [*aside*]
How from the finny subject of the sea   48
These fishers tell the infirmities of men,
And from their wat'ry empire recollect   50
All that may men approve or men detect!—   51
Peace be at your labor, honest fishermen.   52
SECOND FISHERMAN   "Honest," good fellow? What's that?   53
If it be a day fits you, search out of the calendar, and   54
nobody look after it.   55

PERICLES
May see the sea hath cast upon your coast—   56
SECOND FISHERMAN   What a drunken knave was the
sea to cast thee in our way!   58
PERICLES
A man whom both the waters and the wind,
In that vast tennis court, hath made the ball
For them to play upon, entreats you pity him.
He asks of you that never used to beg.   62
FIRST FISHERMAN   No, friend, cannot you beg? Here's
them in our country of Greece gets more with begging
than we can do with working.
SECOND FISHERMAN   Canst thou catch any fishes, then?
PERICLES   I never practiced it.
SECOND FISHERMAN   Nay, then, thou wilt starve, sure,
for here's nothing to be got nowadays unless thou
canst fish for't.   70
PERICLES
What I have been I have forgot to know,
But what I am, want teaches me to think on:
A man thronged up with cold. My veins are chill,   73
And have no more of life than may suffice
To give my tongue that heat to ask your help—
Which if you shall refuse, when I am dead,
For that I am a man, pray you see me buried.   77
FIRST FISHERMAN   Die, quotha? Now gods forbid't, an I   78
have a gown here! Come, put it on, keep thee warm.
[*He gives a garment; Pericles puts it on.*] Now, afore me, a 80
handsome fellow! Come, thou shalt go home, and
we'll have flesh for holidays, fish for fasting days, and
moreo'er puddings and flapjacks, and thou shalt be   83
welcome.
PERICLES   I thank you, sir.
SECOND FISHERMAN   Hark you, my friend. You said
you could not beg?
PERICLES   I did but crave.   88
SECOND FISHERMAN   But crave? Then I'll turn craver
too, and so I shall scape whipping.   90
PERICLES   Why, are your beggars whipped, then?
SECOND FISHERMAN   Oh, not all, my friend, not all; for if
all your beggars were whipped, I would wish no better
office than to be beadle. But, master, I'll go draw up   94
the net.   [*Exit with Third Fisherman.*]
PERICLES [*aside*]
How well this honest mirth becomes their labor!   96
FIRST FISHERMAN   Hark you, sir, do you know where
ye are?
PERICLES   Not well.
FIRST FISHERMAN   Why, I'll tell you. This is called
Pentapolis, and our king the good Simonides.

---

12 Pilch (A name derived from what he wears, a leather garment.)
13 bring away bring along   **14 Patchbreech** (Comically named for his patched breeches.)   **16 Look . . . now!** i.e., Get a move on!   **17 I'll . . . wanion** I'll deal you a blow, a vengeance take you!   **19 before us** before our eyes   **22 welladay** alas   **24 porpoise** (Porpoises were popularly supposed to be prognosticators of storms.)   **26 washed** wetted by a storm.   **28 aland** on the land   **30 'a** he   **32–3 heard on** heard of   **42 cast** vomited   **48 subject** i.e., residents, citizens   **50 recollect** gather up   **51 may . . . detect** may commend men or expose them.   **52–5 Peace . . . after it** (Most commentators think something has been lost here, perhaps a line in which Pericles bids the fishermen good day; if so, the Second Fisherman's reply could mean, "if the day fits your wretched condition, scratch it out of the calendar and let no one miss it.")

56 May You may   **58 cast** (Punning on *vomit*, as suggested by *drunken*; see line 42.)   **62 used** made it a practice   **70 fish for't** i.e., angle for it, look out for one's own interests.   **73 thronged up** overwhelmed   **77 For that** because   **78 quotha** says he.   **an** if, so long as   **80 afore me** (A mild oath.)   **83 puddings** sausages   **88 crave** request.   **90 scape whipping** i.e., escape the punishment for begging (as required by Elizabethan law. The Second Fisherman jokes that *crave* is only a polite term for *beg*.)   **94 beadle** parish official responsible for administering corporal punishment (who would be busy and well paid if all those who beg under the pretext of seeking favor at court were to be whipped as beggars)   **96 becomes** suits

PERICLES   "The good Simonides" do you call him?

FIRST FISHERMAN   Ay, sir, and he deserves so to be called for his peaceable reign and good government.

PERICLES   He is a happy king, since he gains from his subjects the name of "good" by his government. How far is his court distant from this shore?

FIRST FISHERMAN   Marry, sir, half a day's journey. And 108 I'll tell you, he hath a fair daughter, and tomorrow is her birthday; and there are princes and knights come from all parts of the world to joust and tourney for her 111 love.

PERICLES   Were my fortunes equal to my desires, I could wish to make one there.   114

FIRST FISHERMAN   Oh, sir, things must be as they may; and what a man cannot get, he may lawfully deal for 116 his wife's soul.   117

Enter the two [other] Fishermen, drawing up a net.

SECOND FISHERMAN   Help, master, help! Here's a fish hangs in the net like a poor man's right in the law; 'twill hardly come out. Ha! Bots on 't, 'tis come at last, 120 and 'tis turned to a rusty armor.
                                    [He hauls in Pericles's armor.]

PERICLES
An armor, friends? I pray you, let me see it.
Thanks, Fortune, yet that after all thy crosses   123
Thou givest me somewhat to repair myself;
And though it was mine own, part of my heritage
Which my dead father did bequeath to me
With this strict charge, even as he left his life:
"Keep it, my Pericles; it hath been a shield
Twixt me and death," and pointed to this brace;   129
"For that it saved me, keep it. In like necessity—   130
The which the gods protect thee from!—may't defend thee."
It kept where I kept, I so dearly loved it,   132
Till the rough seas, that spares not any man,
Took it in rage, though calmed have given 't again.
I thank thee for 't. My shipwreck now's no ill,
Since I have here my father gave in his will.   136

FIRST FISHERMAN   What mean you, sir?

PERICLES
To beg of you, kind friends, this coat of worth,   138
For it was sometime target to a king;   139
I know it by this mark. He loved me dearly,
And for his sake I wish the having of it,
And that you'd guide me to your sovereign's court,
Where with it I may appear a gentleman.
And if that ever my low fortune's better,

I'll pay your bounties; till then rest your debtor.   145

FIRST FISHERMAN   Why, wilt thou tourney for the lady?

PERICLES
I'll show the virtue I have borne in arms.   147

FIRST FISHERMAN   Why, d' ye take it, and the gods give thee good on 't!   *[Pericles puts it on.]* 149

SECOND FISHERMAN   Ay, but hark you, my friend, 'twas we that made up this garment through the rough seams of the waters. There are certain condolements, 152 certain vails. I hope, sir, if you thrive, you'll remember 153 from whence you had them.   154

PERICLES   Believe 't, I will.
By your furtherance I am clothed in steel,
And spite of all the rapture of the sea   157
This jewel holds his building on my arm.   158
Unto thy value I will mount myself   159
Upon a courser, whose delightful steps   160
Shall make the gazer joy to see him tread.
Only, my friend, I yet am unprovided
Of a pair of bases.   163

SECOND FISHERMAN   We'll sure provide. Thou shalt have my best gown to make thee a pair; and I'll bring thee to the court myself.

PERICLES
Then honor be but equal to my will,
This day I'll rise, or else add ill to ill.   *[Exeunt.]*

❖

[2.2]

Enter [King] Simonides, with attendance, and Thaisa, [and take their places].

SIMONIDES
Are the knights ready to begin the triumph?   1

FIRST LORD   They are, my liege,
And stay your coming to present themselves.   3

SIMONIDES
Return them we are ready; and our daughter,   4
In honor of whose birth these triumphs are,
Sits here like Beauty's child, whom Nature gat   6
For men to see and, seeing, wonder at.   *[Exit one.]*

THAISA
It pleaseth you, my royal father, to express
My commendations great, whose merit's less.

---

108 Marry (A mild oath, originally "by the Virgin Mary.")   **111 tour-ney** take part in a tournament   **114 make one** be among those **116–17 what ... soul** (A difficult line. Perhaps the Fisherman jokes that if a man cannot prosper any other way, he could prostitute his wife, at the expense of her—and his—soul.)   **120 'twill ... out** it will hardly ever be disentangled, set to rights.   **Bots on't** i.e., Plague take it. (*Bots* is a disease of horses.)   **123 crosses** thwartings, misfortunes **129 brace** mailed arm protector   **130 For that** because.   **like** similar **132 kept** lodged   **136 my father** what my father   **138 coat** i.e., armor, coat of mail   **139 target** shield, i.e., protector

145 pay your bounties repay your generosity.   **rest** I will remain **147 virtue** bravery, knightly qualities   **149 on't** of it, from it. **152 seams** (The metaphor is from tailoring, as if the waves of the sea were seams.)   **condolements** (Probably confused with "dole," portion or share, or with "emoluments." The Fisherman hopes for a gratuity.) **153 vails** (1) perquisites, tips (2) tailors' remnants of cloth.   **154 them** the pieces of armor.   **157 rapture** plundering   **158 This ... arm** i.e., this armor is my strength and my defense.   **159 Unto thy value** In keeping with the worthiness of you, my armor   **160 courser** spirited horse   **163 bases** pleated skirts attached to the doublet and reaching from the waist to the knee, worn under the armor by a mounted knight.
2.2. Location: Pentapolis. A public way leading to the lists. A pavilion by the side of it for the reception of the King, Princess, Lords, etc.
1 triumph tournament, festive spectacle.   **3 stay** await   **4 Return** Reply to   **6 gat** begot

SIMONIDES
It's fit it should be so, for princes are   10
A model which heaven makes like to itself.
As jewels lose their glory if neglected,
So princes their renowns if not respected.
'Tis now your honor, daughter, to entertain   14
The labor of each knight in his device.   15
THAISA
Which, to preserve mine honor, I'll perform.

The First Knight passes by [and his Squire presents
his shield to the Princess].

SIMONIDES
Who is the first that doth prefer himself?   17
THAISA
A knight of Sparta, my renownèd father,
And the device he bears upon his shield
Is a black Ethiop reaching at the sun;
The word, *Lux tua vita mihi.*   21
SIMONIDES
He loves you well that holds his life of you.
                          The Second Knight [passes by].
Who is the second that presents himself?
THAISA
A prince of Macedon, my royal father,
And the device he bears upon his shield
Is an armed knight that's conquered by a lady;
The motto thus, in Spanish, *Piùe per dolcezza che per*
     forza.   *Third Knight [passes by].*   27
SIMONIDES
And what's the third?
THAISA   The third of Antioch,
And his device, a wreath of chivalry;   29
The word, *Me pompae provexit apex.*   30
                         Fourth Knight [passes by].
SIMONIDES   What is the fourth?
THAISA
A burning torch that's turnèd upside down;
The word, *Quod me alit, me extinguit.*   33
SIMONIDES
Which shows that beauty hath his power and will,   34
Which can as well inflame as it can kill.
                              Fifth Knight [passes by].
THAISA
The fifth, an hand environèd with clouds,
Holding out gold that's by the touchstone tried;   37
The motto thus, *Sic spectanda fides.*   38
                    Sixth Knight, [Pericles, passes by;
                    he himself presents his device to Thaisa].
SIMONIDES   And what's

The sixth and last, the which the knight himself
With such a graceful courtesy delivered?
THAISA
He seems to be a stranger; but his present is   42
A withered branch, that's only green at top;
The motto, *In hac spe vivo.*   44
SIMONIDES   A pretty moral;
From the dejected state wherein he is,
He hopes by you his fortunes yet may flourish.
FIRST LORD
He had need mean better than his outward show   48
Can any way speak in his just commend,   49
For by his rusty outside he appears
To have practiced more the whipstock than the lance.   51
SECOND LORD
He well may be a stranger, for he comes
To an honored triumph strangely furnished.   53
THIRD LORD
And on set purpose let his armor rust
Until this day, to scour it in the dust.   55
SIMONIDES
Opinion's but a fool, that makes us scan   56
The outward habit by the inward man.   57
But stay, the knights are coming.
We will withdraw into the gallery.   [*Exeunt.*]   59
                    Great shouts [within], and all cry
                    "The mean knight!"

❖

[2.3]

[A banquet prepared.] Enter the King [Simonides,
Thaisa, Marshal, Ladies, Lords, attendants], and
Knights from tilting, [in armor].

SIMONIDES   Knights,
To say you're welcome were superfluous.
To place upon the volume of your deeds,
As in a title page, your worth in arms
Were more than you expect or more than's fit,
Since every worth in show commends itself.   6
Prepare for mirth, for mirth becomes a feast.   7
You are princes and my guests.
THAISA [*to Pericles*]   But you my knight and guest,   9
To whom this wreath of victory I give,
And crown you king of this day's happiness.
                    [*She crowns Pericles with a wreath.*]

---

10 **princes** royalty of either sex   14 **honor** i.e., honorable duty.
entertain receive, review   15 **device** emblem with motto on the
knights' shields.   17 **prefer** present   21 **word** motto.   *Lux . . . mihi*
Your light is my life. (Latin; also at lines 30, 33, 38, 44.)   27 *Piùe . . .*
forza More by gentleness than by force. (Italian, not Spanish.)
29 **wreath of chivalry** twisted band joining the crest to the knight's
helmet   30 *Me . . . apex* The highest summit of honor has led me on.
33 *Quod . . . extinguit* The person who feeds my flame puts out my
light.   34 **his** its   37 **touchstone** black quartz, used to test gold for
purity   38 *Sic spectanda fides* Thus is faith to be tried.

42 **present** presented device   44 *In . . . vivo* In this hope I live.
48–9 **He . . . commend** He'd certainly better have some nobler meaning, more than his present wretched outward appearance can in any
way speak to commend him.   51 **whipstock** handle of a whip (which
he would use to drive workhorses)   53 **strangely** (The witticism
plays on *strangely,* "oddly," and *stranger,* "a visitor from a foreign
land.")   55 **scour** (The joke is that he will polish his rusty armor by
falling off his horse in the dust.)   56 **Opinion** Judgment of a person's
worth in terms of mere reputation   56–7 **Opinion's . . . man** i.e., Only
a fool belives that one can judge a person's inner qualities by outward
appearance.   59.2 **mean** humble, undistinguished in appearance
2.3. Location: Pentapolis. The palace.
6 **in show** by being revealed through deeds   7 **becomes** suits   9 **you**
you are

PERICLES
'Tis more by fortune, lady, than by merit.

SIMONIDES
Call it by what you will, the day is yours,
And here, I hope, is none that envies it.
In framing an artist, art hath thus decreed: 15
To make some good but others to exceed;
And you are her labored scholar.—Come, queen o'th'
    feast—   17
For, daughter, so you are—here take your place.
[*To the Marshal*] Marshal, the rest, as they deserve their
    grace.   19

KNIGHTS
We are honored much by good Simonides.
                                    [*They take their places.*]

SIMONIDES
Your presence glads our days. Honor we love,
For who hates honor hates the gods above.   22

MARSHAL [*to Pericles*]   Sir, yonder is your place.

PERICLES   Some other is more fit.

FIRST KNIGHT
Contend not, sir, for we are gentlemen   25
Have neither in our hearts nor outward eyes   26
Envies the great, nor shall the low despise.   27

PERICLES   You are right courteous knights.

SIMONIDES   Sit, sir, sit.   [*They sit.*]
[*Aside*] By Jove, I wonder, that is king of thoughts, 30
These cates resist me, he not thought upon.   31

THAISA [*aside*]
By Juno, that is queen of marriage,
All viands that I eat do seem unsavory,
Wishing him my meat. [*To Simonides*] Sure he's a
    gallant gentleman.

SIMONIDES [*to Thaisa*]
He's but a country gentleman.
He's done no more than other knights have done;
He's broken a staff or so. So let it pass.   37

THAISA [*aside*]
To me he seems like diamond to glass.   38

PERICLES [*aside*]
Yon king's to me like to my father's picture,
Which tells me in that glory once he was—   40
Had princes sit like stars about his throne,
And he the sun for them to reverence.
None that beheld him but, like lesser lights,
Did vail their crowns to his supremacy;   44
Where now his son's like a glowworm in the night,   45
The which hath fire in darkness, none in light.   46

Whereby I see that Time's the king of men;
He's both their parent and he is their grave,
And gives them what he will, not what they crave.

SIMONIDES   What, are you merry, knights?

KNIGHTS
Who can be other in this royal presence?

SIMONIDES
Here, with a cup that's stored unto the brim—
As you do love, fill to your mistress' lips—   53
We drink this health to you.   [*He drinks a toast.*]

KNIGHTS   We thank Your Grace.

SIMONIDES   Yet pause awhile.
Yon knight doth sit too melancholy,
As if the entertainment in our court
Had not a show might countervail his worth.   58
Note it not you, Thaisa?

THAISA   What is't to me, my father?

SIMONIDES
Oh, attend, my daughter. Princes in this
Should live like gods above, who freely give
To everyone that come to honor them;
And princes not doing so are like to gnats,
Which make a sound but, killed, are wondered at.   65
Therefore to make his entrance more sweet,
Here, say we drink this standing-bowl of wine to him.   67
                                    [*He drinks a toast.*]

THAISA
Alas, my father, it befits not me
Unto a stranger knight to be so bold.
He may my proffer take for an offense,
Since men take women's gifts for impudence.

SIMONIDES   How?
Do as I bid you, or you'll move me else.   73

THAISA [*aside*]
Now, by the gods, he could not please me better.

SIMONIDES
And furthermore tell him we desire to know of him
Of whence he is, his name and parentage.

THAISA [*going to Pericles*]
The King my father, sir, has drunk to you—

PERICLES   I thank him.

THAISA
Wishing it so much blood unto your life.   79

PERICLES
I thank both him and you, and pledge him freely.   80

THAISA
And further, he desires to know of you
Of whence you are, your name and parentage.

PERICLES
A gentleman of Tyre, my name Pericles,
My education been in arts and arms;   84
Who, looking for adventures in the world,
Was by the rough seas reft of ships and men,   86

---

15 **framing** making   17 **her labored scholar** the one on whom art has
bestowed the most pains.   19 **the rest** i.e., place the rest of the company. **grace** favor.   22 **who** one who   25–7 **for . . . despite** for we
are gentlemen who have nothing in our hearts or outward-seeing
eyes that envies the great or shall despise those of low birth.
30–1 **By Jove . . . upon** By Jove, who rules over human thoughts, I
marvel that these delicacies do not seem appealing to me, since I
would rather be thinking about him (Pericles).   37 **broken a staff**
(Shattering the lance became the aim in sixteenth-century tilting
matches.)   38 **to** compared with   40 **Which . . . was** a picture that
recalls to me my father's former glory   44 **vail** lower, remove submis-
sively   45–6 **Where . . . light** i.e., whereas I, my kingly father's son, am
a pale light by comparison, one best seen at night like a glowworm.

53 **fill . . . lips** i.e., drink a full cup to your mistress   58 **might countervail** that could equal   65 **are wondered at** i.e., cause amazement
at the loud noise such small insects could make while living.
67 **standing-bowl** drinking vessel that stands on feet or on stem and
base   73 **move me else** anger me otherwise.   79 **Wishing . . . life**
(Wine was thought to replenish the blood.)   80 **pledge him** drink his
health (in a return toast)   84 **been . . . arms** has been in humane
learning and the arts of warfare   86 **reft** bereft

And after shipwreck driven upon this shore.
THAISA [*returning to the King*]
    He thanks Your Grace; names himself Pericles,
    A gentleman of Tyre,
    Who only by misfortune of the seas,
    Bereft of ships and men, cast on this shore.   91
SIMONIDES
    Now, by the gods, I pity his misfortune
    And will awake him from his melancholy.—
    Come, gentlemen, we sit too long on trifles
    And waste the time which looks for other revels.
    Even in your armors, as you are addressed,   96
    Will well become a soldier's dance.   97
    I will not have excuse with saying this: 98
    Loud music is too harsh for ladies' heads,   99
    Since they love men in arms as well as beds.   100
                                           They dance.
    So this was well asked, 'twas so well performed.   101
    Come, sir,   [*presenting Thaisa to Pericles*]
    Here's a lady that wants breathing too.   103
    And I have heard you knights of Tyre
    Are excellent in making ladies trip,   105
    And that their measures are as excellent.   106
PERICLES
    In those that practice them they are, my lord.
SIMONIDES
    Oh, that's as much as you would be denied   108
    Of your fair courtesy.   *They dance.*
                    Unclasp, unclasp!   109
    Thanks, gentlemen, to all; all have done well,
        [*To Pericles*] But you the best.—Pages and lights, to
        conduct
    These knights unto their several lodgings!
        [*To Pericles*] Yours, sir,   112
    We have given order to be next our own.
PERICLES   I am at Your Grace's pleasure.
SIMONIDES
    Princes, it is too late to talk of love,
    And that's the mark I know you level at.   116
    Therefore each one betake him to his rest.
    Tomorrow all for speeding do their best.   [*Exeunt.*] 118

❖

91 **cast** was cast   96 **addressed** accoutered   97 **Will** you will
98–100 **I will . . . beds** I won't allow any of you to beg off by saying
that the clanging of armor on the dance floor is too loud for the
ladies, since they love men as soldiers no less than as bed-partners.
(With a pun on "men in armor" and "men in ladies' arms.")
100.1 **They dance** (Dancing in armor gave courtly dancers opportunity to display strength and swordsmanship.)   101 **So . . . performed**
As I did well to suggest that you dance, so you have done it well.
103 **breathing** exercise   105 **trip** dance lightly. (With a suggestion of
"go astray.")   106 **measures** stately, formal dances. (With suggestion
of "stratagems in wooing.")   108–9 **that's . . . courtesy** i.e., that's as
much as to say you wish to claim inexperience in courtly ways as
your reason for asking not to dance with Thaisa (but I won't let you
get away with your denial).   **Unclasp** either (1) Time for you to stop
dancing, or (2) Remove your armor so that you can dance in more
courtly fashion.   112 **several** various   116 **level** aim   118 **speeding**
succeeding (as wooers)

[2.4]

Enter Helicanus and Escanes.

HELICANUS   No, Escanes, know this of me,
    Antiochus from incest lived not free;
    For which, the most high gods not minding longer   3
    To withhold the vengeance that they had in store
    Due to this heinous capital offense,
    Even in the height and pride of all his glory,
    When he was seated in a chariot of
    An inestimable value, and his daughter with him,
    A fire from heaven came and shriveled up
    Those bodies even to loathing; for they so stunk
    That all those eyes adored them ere their fall   11
    Scorn now their hand should give them burial.
ESCANES
    'Twas very strange.
HELICANUS   And yet but justice, for though
    This king were great, his greatness was no guard
    To bar heaven's shaft, but sin had his reward.   15
ESCANES   'Tis very true.

                Enter two or three Lords.

FIRST LORD
    See, not a man in private conference
    Or council has respect with him but he.   18
SECOND LORD
    It shall no longer grieve without reproof.   19
THIRD LORD
    And curst be he that will not second it.
FIRST LORD
    Follow me, then.—Lord Helicane, a word.
HELICANUS
    With me? And welcome. Happy day, my lords.
FIRST LORD
    Know that our griefs are risen to the top,   23
    And now at length they overflow their banks.
HELICANUS
    Your griefs? For what? Wrong not your prince you
        love.
FIRST LORD
    Wrong not yourself, then, noble Helicane;
    But if the Prince do live, let us salute him,
    Or know what ground's made happy by his breath.   28
    If in the world he live, we'll seek him out;
    If in his grave he rest, we'll find him there,
    And be resolved he lives to govern us,   31
    Or dead, give 's cause to mourn his funeral
    And leave us to our free election.
SECOND LORD
    Whose death's indeed the strongest in our censure;   34
    And knowing this kingdom is without a head—
    Like goodly buildings left without a roof   36

2.4. Location: Tyre. The Governor's house.
3 **minding** intending   11 **adored** that adored   15 **shaft** bolt, arrow.
his its   18 **respect** influence.   **he** i.e., Escanes.   19 **grieve without
reproof** cause grievance without (our) protest.   23 **griefs** grievances.
(Also in line 25.)   28 **ground** i.e., country.   **breath** i.e., presence.
31 **resolved** satisfied, assured   34 **Whose . . . censure** And indeed his
death is the likeliest probability in our judgment   36 **Like** as

Soon fall to ruin—your noble self,
That best know how to rule and how to reign,
We thus submit unto, our sovereign.
ALL   Live, noble Helicane!
HELICANUS
Try honor's cause; forbear your suffrages.   41
If that you love Prince Pericles, forbear.   42
Take I your wish, I leap into the seas,   43
Where's hourly trouble for a minute's ease.
A twelvemonth longer let me entreat you
To forbear the absence of your king,   46
If in which time expired he not return,
I shall with agèd patience bear your yoke.
But if I cannot win you to this love,   49
Go search like nobles, like noble subjects,
And in your search spend your adventurous worth;   51
Whom if you find, and win unto return,   52
You shall like diamonds sit about his crown.
FIRST LORD
To wisdom he's a fool that will not yield;
And since Lord Helicane enjoineth us,
We with our travels will endeavor.   56
HELICANUS
Then you love us, we you, and we'll clasp hands.
When peers thus knit, a kingdom ever stands.
                                            [*Exeunt.*]

[2.5]

*Enter the King [Simonides] reading of a letter, at
one door; the Knights meet him.*

FIRST KNIGHT
Good morrow to the good Simonides.
SIMONIDES
Knights, from my daughter this I let you know,
That for this twelvemonth she'll not undertake
A married life.
Her reason to herself is only known,
Which from her by no means can I get.
SECOND KNIGHT
May we not get access to her, my lord?
SIMONIDES
Faith, by no means. She hath so strictly tied
Her to her chamber that 'tis impossible.
One twelve moons more she'll wear Diana's livery.   10
This by the eye of Cynthia hath she vowed,   11
And on her virgin honor will not break it.

---

41 **Try ... suffrages** i.e., Follow the honorable course; refrain from
choosing me in your *free election* (line 33).   **42 If that** If   **43 Take ...
wish** If I should act on your wish   **46 forbear** put up with   **49 love**
act of loyal devotion   **51 spend ... worth** use up your noble adventurous spirits   **52 Whom ... return** i.e., and if you find Pericles during this year of probation and persuade him to return   **56 endeavor**
i.e., try to find him.
2.5. Location: Pentapolis. The palace.
10 wear Diana's livery continue to serve Diana, goddess of chastity.
11 Cynthia the moon goddess, equated with Diana

THIRD KNIGHT
Loath to bid farewell, we take our leaves.
                                       [*Exeunt Knights.*]
SIMONIDES   So,
They are well dispatched. Now to my daughter's
   letter.
She tells me here she'll wed the stranger knight,
Or never more to view nor day nor light.   17
'Tis well, mistress. Your choice agrees with mine;
I like that well. Nay, how absolute she's in 't,   19
Not minding whether I dislike or no!
Well, I do commend her choice
And will no longer have it be delayed.
Soft, here he comes. I must dissemble it.

           Enter Pericles.

PERICLES
All fortune to the good Simonides!
SIMONIDES
To you as much! Sir, I am beholding to you   25
For your sweet music this last night. I do
Protest my ears were never better fed
With such delightful pleasing harmony.
PERICLES
It is Your Grace's pleasure to commend,
Not my desert.
SIMONIDES   Sir, you are music's master.
PERICLES
The worst of all her scholars, my good lord.
SIMONIDES   Let me ask you one thing:
What do you think of my daughter, sir?
PERICLES   A most virtuous princess.
SIMONIDES   And she is fair too, is she not?
PERICLES
As a fair day in summer, wondrous fair.
SIMONIDES
Sir, my daughter thinks very well of you,
Ay, so well that you must be her master,
And she will be your scholar. Therefore look to it.
PERICLES
I am unworthy for her schoolmaster.
SIMONIDES
She thinks not so. Peruse this writing else.   41
                                       [*He gives a letter.*]
PERICLES [*aside*]   What's here?
A letter, that she loves the knight of Tyre!
'Tis the King's subtlety to have my life.—   44
Oh, seek not to entrap me, gracious lord,
A stranger and distressèd gentleman,
That never aimed so high to love your daughter,   47
But bent all offices to honor her.   48
SIMONIDES
Thou hast bewitched my daughter, and thou art
A villain.
PERICLES   By the gods, I have not!

---

17 **nor day nor** either day or. (A double negative.)   **19 absolute**
unconditional, positive   **25 beholding** beholden   **41 else** i.e., if you
don't believe me.   **44 subtlety** trick   **47 to** as to   **48 bent all offices**
devoted all my service

Never did thought of mine levy offense,   52
Nor never did my actions yet commence
A deed might gain her love or your displeasure.   54

SIMONIDES
Traitor, thou liest!

PERICLES   Traitor?

SIMONIDES   Ay, traitor.

PERICLES
Even in his throat—unless it be the King—   56
That calls me traitor, I return the lie.   57

SIMONIDES [aside]
Now, by the gods, I do applaud his courage.

PERICLES
My actions are as noble as my thoughts,
That never relished of a base descent.   60
I came unto your court for honor's cause,
And not to be a rebel to her state;   62
And he that otherwise accounts of me,
This sword shall prove he's honor's enemy.

SIMONIDES   No?
Here comes my daughter. She can witness it.

              Enter Thaisa.

PERICLES [to Thaisa]
Then, as you are as virtuous as fair,
Resolve your angry father if my tongue   68
Did e'er solicit, or my hand subscribe
To any syllable that made love to you.

THAISA
Why, sir, say if you had, who takes offense
At that would make me glad?   72

SIMONIDES
Yea, mistress, are you so peremptory?   73
(Aside) I am glad on't with all my heart.—
[To her] I'll tame you; I'll bring you in subjection!
Will you, not having my consent,
Bestow your love and your affections
Upon a stranger? (Aside) Who, for aught I know,
May be, nor can I think the contrary,
As great in blood as I myself.—
Therefore hear you, mistress: either frame   81
Your will to mine—and you, sir, hear you—
Either be ruled by me, or I'll make you—
Man and wife.
Nay, come, your hands and lips must seal it too.
And being joined, I'll thus your hopes destroy;
And for further grief—God give you joy!
What, are you both pleased?

THAISA   Yes, if you love me, sir.

PERICLES
Even as my life my blood that fosters it.   90

SIMONIDES   What, are you both agreed?

BOTH   Yes, if't please Your Majesty.

SIMONIDES
It pleaseth me so well that I will see you wed,
And then, with what haste you can, get you to bed.
                                                        Exeunt.

[3. Chorus]

          Enter Gower.

GOWER
Now sleep yslakèd hath the rout;   1
No din but snores the house about,
Made louder by the o'erfed breast
Of this most pompous marriage feast.   4
The cat, with eyne of burning coal,   5
Now couches 'fore the mouse's hole,
And crickets sing at the oven's mouth,
Are the blither for their drouth.   8
Hymen hath brought the bride to bed,   9
Where, by the loss of maidenhead,
A babe is molded. Be attent,   11
And time that is so briefly spent   12
With your fine fancies quaintly eche.   13
What's dumb in show I'll plain with speech.   14

              [Dumb Show.]

Enter Pericles and Simonides, at one door, with
attendants. A Messenger meets them, kneels, and
gives Pericles a letter. Pericles shows it Simonides;
the Lords kneel to him [Pericles]. Then enter
Thaisa with child, with Lychorida, a nurse. The
King shows her [Thaisa] the letter; she rejoices. She
and Pericles take leave of her father, and depart [with
Lychorida and their attendants. Then exeunt
Simonides and the rest.]

By many a dern and painful perch   15
Of Pericles the careful search,
By the four opposing coigns   17
Which the world together joins,
Is made with all due diligence
That horse and sail and high expense
Can stead the quest. At last from Tyre,   21
Fame answering the most strange inquire,   22
To th' court of King Simonides
Are letters brought, the tenor these:
Antiochus and his daughter dead,
The men of Tyrus on the head
Of Helicanus would set on
The crown of Tyre, but he will none.
The mutiny he there hastes t'appease;

---

52 **levy** i.e., level, aim at; or undertake   54 **might** that might
56–7 **Even . . . lie** i.e., to any man except you as king I would give the
lie in the throat, the deepest kind of insult and challenge to a duel.
60 **relished of** showed any trace of   62 **her** i.e., honor's   68 **Resolve**
satisfy, explain to   72 **that** that which   73 **peremptory** willfully
determined.   81 **frame** accommodate, shape   90 **my life** i.e., my
life loves

3.0.
1 **yslakèd . . . rout** has laid to rest the whole assembly   4 **pompous**
ceremonial, splendid   5 **eyne** eyes   8 **Are . . . drouth** (and) are the
happier for their dryness.   9 **Hymen** god of marriage   11 **attent**
attentive   12–13 **And time . . . eche** and use your fine imaginations to
eke or stretch out the time that I can describe here only briefly.
14 **plain** make plain   15 **By many . . . perch** By many a dreary and
laborious measure of distance, many a weary mile   17 **opposing
coigns** opposite corners, compass points   21 **stead** assist   22 **Fame . . .
inquire** rumor answering inquiry into the most remote areas

Says to 'em, if King Pericles
Come not home in twice six moons,
He, obedient to their dooms,   32
Will take the crown. The sum of this,
Brought hither to Pentapolis,
Y-ravishèd the regions round,   35
And everyone with claps can sound,   36
"Our heir apparent is a king!
Who dreamt, who thought of such a thing?"
Brief, he must hence depart to Tyre.   39
His queen, with child, makes her desire—
Which who shall cross?—along to go.   41
Omit we all their dole and woe.   42
Lychorida, her nurse, she takes,
And so to sea. Their vessel shakes
On Neptune's billow; half the flood   45
Hath their keel cut. But Fortune's mood   46
Varies again; the grizzled North   47
Disgorges such a tempest forth
That, as a duck for life that dives,
So up and down the poor ship drives.
The lady shrieks, and well-a-near   51
Does fall in travail with her fear;   52
And what ensues in this fell storm   53
Shall for itself itself perform;
I nill relate; action may   55
Conveniently the rest convey,
Which might not what by me is told.   57
In your imagination hold   58
This stage the ship, upon whose deck
The sea-tossed Pericles appears to speak.   [*Exit.*] 60

❧

[3.1]

Enter Pericles, a-shipboard.

PERICLES
Thou god of this great vast, rebuke these surges,   1
Which wash both heaven and hell! And thou that hast   2
Upon the winds command, bind them in brass,
Having called them from the deep! Oh, still
Thy deaf'ning, dreadful thunders; gently quench   5
Thy nimble, sulfurous flashes! [*Calling*] Oh, how,
     Lychorida,
How does my queen?—Thou stormest venomously;
Wilt thou spit all thyself? The seaman's whistle   8

Is as a whisper in the ears of death,   9
Unheard. [*Calling*] Lychorida!—Lucina, O   10
Divinest patroness and midwife gentle
To those that cry by night, convey thy deity
Aboard our dancing boat; make swift the pangs
Of my queen's travails!

          Enter Lychorida [with an infant].

                    Now, Lychorida!
LYCHORIDA
Here is a thing too young for such a place,
Who, if it had conceit, would die, as I   16
Am like to do. Take in your arms this piece   17
Of your dead queen.
PERICLES   How? How, Lychorida?
LYCHORIDA
Patience, good sir. Do not assist the storm.   19
Here's all that is left living of your queen,
A little daughter. For the sake of it,
Be manly and take comfort.   [*She gives him the child.*]
PERICLES   O you gods!
Why do you make us love your goodly gifts
And snatch them straight away? We here below
Recall not what we give, and therein may   25
Use honor with you.
LYCHORIDA   Patience, good sir,   26
Even for this charge.
PERICLES [*to the babe*]   Now, mild may be thy life!   27
For a more blustrous birth had never babe.
Quiet and gentle thy conditions! For   29
Thou art the rudeliest welcome to this world   30
That ever was prince's child. Happy what follows!   31
Thou hast as chiding a nativity   32
As fire, air, water, earth, and heaven can make
To herald thee from the womb. Poor inch of nature!   34
Even at the first thy loss is more than can   35
Thy portage quit, with all thou canst find here.   36
Now the good gods throw their best eyes upon't!   37

          Enter two Sailors, [one the ship's Master].

MASTER   What courage, sir? God save you!
PERICLES
Courage enough. I do not fear the flaw;   39
It hath done to me the worst. Yet for the love
Of this poor infant, this fresh new seafarer,
I would it would be quiet.

9–10 Is . . . Unheard is no more audible than a whisper in the ears of a
dead person.   **10 Lucina** goddess of childbirth (as in 1.1.9)   **16 conceit** understanding (of its precarious position)   **17 like** likely
19 assist i.e., with your sighs and tears   **25 Recall** take back.
therein in that respect   **26 Use . . . you** i.e., challenge our right to be
treated by you in like honorable fashion.   **27 for this charge** for the
sake of this infant, this responsibility.   **29 Quiet . . . conditions!** May
the conditions of your life be quiet and gentle!   **30 the rudeliest welcome** the most rudely welcomed   **31 Happy what follows!** May
what is to come be happy for you!   **32 chiding** clamorous   **34 Poor
. . . nature!** i.e., Poor tiny babe! (This half-line is from Wilkins's
Painful Adventures.)   **35–6 Even . . . here** Your loss at birth (of your
mother) exceeds anything that your life can offer by way of compensation. (*Portage* is the cargo that one has aboard at the start of a voyage, i.e., one's natural endowments; *quit* means "requite.")   **37 best
eyes** most auspicious looks   **39 flaw** gust, squall

---

32 dooms judgments   **35 Y-ravishèd** delighted   **36 can sound** began
to proclaim   **39 Brief** In short   **41 cross** thwart, deny   **42 dole** sorrow (of leave-taking)   **45 On Neptune's billow** on the foaming
ocean   **45–6 half . . . cut** i.e., their vessel has completed half the voyage.   **47 grizzled** gray, grizzly.   **North** north wind   **51 well-a-near**
alas   **52 travail** labor   **53 fell** fierce   **55 nill** will not   **57 Which . . .
told** which action could not dramatize easily the story I've just told.
58 hold suppose   **60 appears to speak** appears and speaks.
3.1. Location: A ship at sea.
1 Thou god i.e., Neptune.   **vast** expanse (of sea)   **2 thou** i.e., Aeolus,
god of the winds   **5 Thy** i.e., Jupiter, god of thunder's   **8 Wilt . . .
thyself?** Are you going to spit all of yourself at us? (Said to the storm.)

MASTER [*calling*]   Slack the bowlines there!—Thou wilt not,   43
wilt thou? Blow, and split thyself.   44
SAILOR   But sea room, an the brine and cloudy billow   45
kiss the moon, I care not.
MASTER   Sir, your queen must overboard. The sea
works high, the wind is loud, and will not lie till the   48
ship be cleared of the dead.
PERICLES   That's your superstition.
MASTER   Pardon us, sir. With us at sea it hath been still   51
observed, and we are strong in custom. Therefore
briefly yield 'er, for she must overboard straight.   53
PERICLES   As you think meet. Most wretched queen!
LYCHORIDA   Here she lies, sir.   55
PERICLES
  A terrible childbed hast thou had, my dear;
  No light, no fire. Th'unfriendly elements
  Forgot thee utterly, nor have I time
  To give thee hallowed to thy grave, but straight
  Must cast thee, scarcely coffined, in the ooze;   60
  Where, for a monument upon thy bones,   61
  And aye-remaining lamps, the belching whale   62
  And humming water must o'erwhelm thy corpse,
  Lying with simple shells. Oh, Lychorida,
  Bid Nestor bring me spices, ink and paper,   65
  My casket and my jewels; and bid Nicander
  Bring me the satin coffin. Lay the babe   67
  Upon the pillow. Hie thee, whiles I say   68
  A priestly farewell to her. Suddenly, woman.   69
                        [*Exit Lychorida.*]
SAILOR   Sir, we have a chest beneath the hatches,
caulked and bitumed ready.   71
PERICLES
  I thank thee. Mariner, say what coast is this?
MASTER   We are near Tarsus.
PERICLES   Thither, gentle mariner,
  Alter thy course for Tyre. When canst thou reach it?   75
MASTER   By break of day, if the wind cease.
PERICLES   Oh, make for Tarsus!
  There will I visit Cleon, for the babe
  Cannot hold out to Tyrus. There I'll leave it
  At careful nursing. Go thy ways, good mariner.   80
  I'll bring the body presently.   *Exeunt.*   81

❖

43–4 Thou wilt . . . thyself (Addressed to the storm.)   **45 But sea room**
So long as we have room enough to maneuver without being driven on
the rocks.   **an** even if.   **cloudy billow** waves breaking into misty
spray, high as the clouds   **48 lie** subside   **51 still** always   **53 briefly**
quickly.   **straight** straightway. (Also in line 59.)   **55 Here she lies**
(Perhaps Lychorida reveals Thaisa's body by drawing the curtains of a
"discovery space" rearstage, or possibly the sailors have brought the
Queen's body onstage, but it may be that Pericles apostrophizes her in
her absence in lines 56–64. Line 55 could mean, "Here is what is left of
the Queen; here is her daughter.")   **60 ooze** muddy ocean bed   **61 for**
in place of   **62 aye-remaining** ever burning.   **belching** blowing,
spouting   **65 Nestor** (A servant who remains silent. So too with
Nicander in line 66.)   **67 coffin** coffer.   **68 Hie thee** Hasten   **69 Suddenly** Quickly   **69.1 Exit Lychorida** (Probably she takes the babe with
her.)   **71 bitumed** caulked with pitch   **75 Alter . . . Tyre** change your
course, which has been for Tyre.   **80 Go thy ways** i.e., About it
81 presently immediately.   **s.d. *Exeunt*** (If Thaisa's body was brought
onstage before line 55, it must presumably be carried off now.)

[3.2]

*Enter Lord Cerimon, with a Servant [and one or
more other persons who have suffered from the
storm].*

CERIMON   Philemon, ho!

  Enter Philemon.

PHILEMON   Doth my lord call?
CERIMON
  Get fire and meat for these poor men.   3
                    [*Exit Philemon.*]
  'T has been a turbulent and stormy night.
SERVANT
  I have been in many, but such a night as this
  Till now I ne'er endured.
CERIMON [*to a Servant*]
  Your master will be dead ere you return;   7
  There's nothing can be ministered to nature   8
  That can recover him. [*To another*] Give this to the
    pothecary,   9
  And tell me how it works.   [*Exeunt all but Cerimon.*]

  Enter two Gentlemen.

FIRST GENTLEMAN   Good morrow.
SECOND GENTLEMAN   Good morrow to Your Lordship.
CERIMON
  Gentlemen, why do you stir so early?
FIRST GENTLEMAN   Sir,
  Our lodgings , standing bleak upon the sea,   15
  Shook as the earth did quake;   16
  The very principals did seem to rend   17
  And all to topple. Pure surprise and fear   18
  Made me to quit the house.
SECOND GENTLEMAN
  That is the cause we trouble you so early;
  'Tis not our husbandry.   21
CERIMON   Oh, you say well.
FIRST GENTLEMAN
  But I much marvel that Your Lordship, having
  Rich tire about you, should at these early hours   24
  Shake off the golden slumber of repose.
  'Tis most strange
  Nature should be so conversant with pain,   27
  Being thereto not compelled.
CERIMON   I hold it ever   28
  Virtue and cunning were endowments greater   29
  Than nobleness and riches. Careless heirs
  May the two latter darken and expend,   31

3.2. Location: Ephesus. Cerimon's house.
3 meat food   **7 Your master** i.e., One of those who have suffered in
the storm and have been brought to Cerimon for help   **8 can . . .
nature** that can be administered in aid of nature   **9 recover** restore.
pothecary druggist   **15 bleak upon** exposed to   **16 as** as if   **17 principals** main timbers of houses.   **rend** come apart   **18 all to topple**
(or "to-topple") topple completely.   **Pure** Sheer   **21 husbandry**
industrious habits, zeal for rising early.   **24 tire** accoutrement, furnishings   **27 pain** toil   **28 hold it ever** have always believed that
29 cunning knowledge, skill   **31 May . . . expend** may sully the gloss
of nobility and squander riches

But immortality attends the former,
Making a man a god. 'Tis known I ever
Have studied physic, through which secret art, 34
By turning o'er authorities, I have, 35
Together with my practice, made familiar
To me and to my aid the blest infusions 37
That dwells in vegetives, in metals, stones; 38
And can speak of the disturbances
That nature works, and of her cures; which doth give me
A more content in course of true delight 41
Than to be thirsty after tottering honor, 42
Or tie my pleasure up in silken bags 43
To please the fool and death. 44

SECOND GENTLEMAN
Your Honor has through Ephesus poured forth 45
Your charity, and hundreds call themselves
Your creatures, who by you have been restored; 47
And not your knowledge, your personal pain, but even 48
Your purse, still open, hath built Lord Cerimon 49
Such strong renown as time shall never— 50

Enter two or three [Servants] with a chest.

FIRST SERVANT
So, lift there.

CERIMON   What's that?

FIRST SERVANT   Sir, even now
Did the sea toss up upon our shore this chest.
'Tis of some wreck.

CERIMON   Set 't down. Let's look upon 't.

SECOND GENTLEMAN
'Tis like a coffin, sir.

CERIMON   Whate'er it be,
'Tis wondrous heavy. Wrench it open straight.
If the sea's stomach be o'ercharged with gold,
'Tis a good constraint of fortune it belches upon us. 57

SECOND GENTLEMAN
'Tis so, my lord.

CERIMON   How close 'tis caulked and bitumed! 58
Did the sea cast it up?

FIRST SERVANT
I never saw so huge a billow, sir,
As tossed it upon shore.

CERIMON   Wrench it open.
Soft! It smells most sweetly in my sense. 62

SECOND GENTLEMAN   A delicate odor.

CERIMON
As ever hit my nostril. So, up with it.

[They open the chest.]
O you most potent gods! What's here? A corpse?

SECOND GENTLEMAN   Most strange!

CERIMON
Shrouded in cloth of state, balmed and entreasured 67
With full bags of spices! A passport too! 68
Apollo, perfect me in the characters! 69

[He reads from a scroll.]
"Here I give to understand,
If e'er this coffin drives aland,
I, King Pericles, have lost
This queen, worth all our mundane cost. 73
Who finds her, give her burying; 74
She was the daughter of a king.
Besides this treasure for a fee,
The gods requite his charity!" 77
If thou livest, Pericles, thou hast a heart
That even cracks for woe! This chanced tonight. 79

SECOND GENTLEMAN
Most likely, sir.

CERIMON   Nay, certainly tonight,
For look how fresh she looks. They were too rough 81
That threw her in the sea. Make a fire within.
Fetch hither all my boxes in my closet.

[Exit a Servant.]
Death may usurp on nature many hours,
And yet the fire of life kindle again
The o'erpressed spirits. I heard of an Egyptian
That had nine hours lain dead,
Who was by good appliance recovered.

Enter one with [boxes,] napkins, and fire.

Well said, well said! The fire and cloths. 89
The rough and woeful music that we have, 90
Cause it to sound, beseech you.
The vial once more. How thou stirr'st, thou block! 92
The music there! [Music.] I pray you, give her air.
Gentlemen, this queen will live. Nature awakes;
A warmth breathes out of her. She hath not been
Entranced above five hours. See how she 'gins 96
To blow into life's flower again!

FIRST GENTLEMAN   The heavens, 97
Through you, increase our wonder and sets up
Your fame forever.

CERIMON   She is alive! Behold,
Her eyelids, cases to those heavenly jewels
Which Pericles hath lost, begin to part

---

34 physic medicine **35–7 By . . . infusions** by turning the pages of learned texts, together with practical experiments, I have familiarized myself with and made available to my art the sacred medicinal properties **38 vegetives** herbs, plants **41 more** greater. **course** pursuit **42 tottering honor** wavering, unstable reputation **43 tie . . . bags** confine my pleasures to the hoarding of silken moneybags **44 the fool** anyone who is fool enough to trust in wealth. **death** (since all wealth ends in death). **45 through** throughout **47 Your creatures** i.e., people dependent for their very lives on your restoratives **48 not** not only. **pain** labor **49 still** always **50.1 *two or three*** (One of these may well be Philemon or at least the same actor; also at line 88.1). **57 'Tis . . . us** it's a lucky thing that it disgorges this chest upon our shore. **58 close** tightly. **bitumed** (See 3.1.71.) **62 Soft!** Gently, wait a minute!

67 cloth of state fabric fit for royalty; literally, a canopy for a chair of state. **balmed** anointed. **entreasured** laid up like valuables in a treasury **68 passport** document identifying the bearer **69 Apollo** god of eloquence and of medicine. **perfect . . . characters** enable me to read the writing. **73 mundane cost** worldly wealth. **74 Who** Whoever **77 his** the finder's **79 chanced tonight** happened last night. **81 rough** i.e., hasty **89 Well said** Well done **90 rough and woeful** i.e., discordant in such a way as to stimulate and awaken **92 vial** (The Quarto text reads "Violl," appropriate perhaps to the music just ordered, but it could mean a *vial* of medicine.) **How thou stirr'st** i.e., How slow you are. **block** blockhead. **96 Entranced** unconscious **97 blow** bloom

Their fringes of bright gold. The diamonds
Of a most praisèd water doth appear,   103
To make the world twice rich.—Live, and make
Us weep to hear your fate, fair creature,
Rare as you seem to be.   *She moves.*
THAISA   O dear Diana,   106
Where am I? Where's my lord? What world is this?
SECOND GENTLEMAN   Is not this strange?
FIRST GENTLEMAN   Most rare.
CERIMON   Hush, my gentle neighbors!
Lend me your hands. To the next chamber bear her.
Get linen. Now this matter must be looked to,   112
For her relapse is mortal. Come, come!   113
And Aesculapius guide us!   114
                     They carry her away. Exeunt omnes.

❧

[3.3]

Enter Pericles at Tarsus, with Cleon and Dionyza
[and Lychorida with Marina in her arms].

PERICLES
Most honored Cleon, I must needs be gone.
My twelve months are expired, and Tyrus stands   2
In a litigious peace. You and your lady   3
Take from my heart all thankfulness! The gods   4
Make up the rest upon you!   5
CLEON
Your shakes of fortune, though they haunt you
    mortally,   6
Yet glance full wonderingly on us.   7
DIONYZA
Oh, your sweet queen! That the strict fates had pleased
You had brought her hither, to have blessed mine eyes
    with her!
PERICLES
We cannot but obey the powers above us.
Could I rage and roar as doth the sea
She lies in, yet the end must be as 'tis.
My gentle babe Marina,
Whom, for she was born at sea, I have named so,   14
Here I charge your charity withal,   15
Leaving her the infant of your care,
Beseeching you to give her princely training,
That she may be mannered as she is born.   18
CLEON   Fear not, my lord, but think
Your Grace, that fed my country with your corn,
For which the people's prayers still fall upon you,

Must in your child be thought on. If neglection   22
Should therein make me vile, the common body,   23
By you relieved, would force me to my duty.
But if to that my nature need a spur,   25
The gods revenge it upon me and mine
To the end of generation!
PERICLES   I believe you.   27
Your honor and your goodness teach me to't   28
Without your vows. Till she be married, madam,
By bright Diana, whom we honor, all
Unscissored shall this hair of mine remain,
Though I show ill in't. So I take my leave.   32
Good madam, make me blessèd in your care   33
In bringing up my child.
DIONYZA   I have one myself,
Who shall not be more dear to my respect   35
Than yours, my lord.
PERICLES   Madam, my thanks and prayers.
CLEON
We'll bring Your Grace e'en to the edge o'th' shore,
Then give you up to the masked Neptune and   38
The gentlest winds of heaven.
PERICLES
I will embrace your offer.—Come, dearest madam.—
Oh, no tears, Lychorida, no tears.
Look to your little mistress, on whose grace   42
You may depend hereafter.—Come, my lord.
                                          [Exeunt.]

❧

[3.4]

Enter Cerimon and Thaisa.

CERIMON
Madam, this letter and some certain jewels
Lay with you in your coffer, which are
At your command. Know you the character?   3
                        [He shows her the letter.]
THAISA
It is my lord's. That I was shipped at sea
I well remember, even on my eaning time;   5
But whether there delivered, by the holy gods,   6
I cannot rightly say. But since King Pericles,
My wedded lord, I ne'er shall see again,
A vestal livery will I take me to,   9
And never more have joy.
CERIMON
Madam, if this you purpose as ye speak,

---

103 **water** luster and clearness. (Used about precious stones.)
106 **Rare** of rare beauty and excellence   112 **Now** Right now   113 **is
mortal** would be fatal.   114 **Aesculapius** god of healing
3.3. Location: Tarsus. Cleon's (the Governor's) house.
2 **twelve months** (Pericles was given a year to return to Tyre; see
3.0.30–3.)   3 **litigious** disturbed by disputes (especially legal)   4 **Take**
receive   4–5 **The gods . . . you!** May the gods requite your goodness
as fully as it deserves (of which my gratitude can supply only part)!
6–7 **Your . . . on us** Your violent shocks of fortune, though they prey
upon you with deadly intent, fill us, too, with amazement and sor-
row.   14 **for** since   15 **charge** burden.   **withal** with   18 **mannered . . .
born** taught manners and graces to accord with her high birth.

22 **Must . . . on** must be recompensed by our kind treatment of
Marina.   **neglection** neglect   23 **common body** common people
25 **But . . . spur** But if my own nature needed to be prodded to do
what the commoners will insist on in any case   27 **of generation** of
my line of descent or of the human race.   28 **to't** to do so   32 **show
ill** look unattractive. (The Quarto's "shew will" could mean "display
willfulness.")   33 **blessèd in your care** fortunate in having the care
you provide   35 **to my respect** in my regard   38 **masked** i.e., deceiv-
ingly calm   42 **grace** favor
3.4. Location: Ephesus. Cerimon's house.
3 **character** handwriting.   5 **eaning time** time of delivery
6 **whether there delivered** whether I gave birth there   9 **A vestal livery** garments of chastity, nun's habit

Diana's temple is not distant far,
Where you may abide till your date expire.   13
Moreover, if you please, a niece of mine
Shall there attend you.

THAISA
My recompense is thanks, that's all;
Yet my good will is great, though the gift small.

Exeunt.

❧

[4. Chorus]

Enter Gower.

GOWER
Imagine Pericles arrived at Tyre,
Welcomed and settled to his own desire.   2
His woeful queen we leave at Ephesus,
Unto Diana there 's a votaress.   4
Now to Marina bend your mind,
Whom our fast-growing scene must find
At Tarsus, and by Cleon trained
In music, letters, who hath gained
Of education all the grace,
Which makes high both the art and place   10
Of general wonder. But, alack,   11
That monster Envy, oft the wrack   12
Of earnèd praise, Marina's life
Seeks to take off by treason's knife.   14
And in this kind hath our Cleon   15
One daughter, and a wench full grown,
Even ripe for marriage rite. This maid
Hight Philoten, and it is said   18
For certain in our story, she
Would ever with Marina be.
Be't when she weaved the sleided silk   21
With fingers long, small, white as milk;   22
Or when she would with sharp needle wound
The cambric, which she made more sound   24
By hurting it; or when to th' lute
She sung, and made the night bird mute,   26
That still records with moan; or when   27
She would with rich and constant pen   28
Vail to her mistress Dian; still   29
This Philoten contends in skill
With absolute Marina. So   31
With the dove of Paphos might the crow
Vie feathers white. Marina gets   33

All praises, which are paid as debts,   34
And not as given. This so darks   35
In Philoten all graceful marks
That Cleon's wife, with envy rare,   37
A present murder does prepare   38
For good Marina, that her daughter
Might stand peerless by this slaughter.   40
The sooner her vile thoughts to stead,   41
Lychorida, our nurse, is dead;
And cursèd Dionyza hath
The pregnant instrument of wrath   44
Prest for this blow. The unborn event   45
I do commend to your content;   46
Only I carry wingèd Time
Post on the lame feet of my rhyme,   48
Which never could I so convey
Unless your thoughts went on my way.
Dionyza does appear,
With Leonine, a murderer.   *Exit.*

❧

[4.1]

Enter Dionyza with Leonine.

DIONYZA
Thy oath remember. Thou hast sworn to do't.
'Tis but a blow, which never shall be known.
Thou canst not do a thing in the world so soon
To yield thee so much profit. Let not conscience,   4
Which is but cold, inflaming love i'thy bosom,   5
Inflame too nicely; nor let pity, which   6
Even women have cast off, melt thee, but be   7
A soldier to thy purpose.
LEONINE   I will do't;
But yet she is a goodly creature.
DIONYZA
The fitter, then, the gods should have her.
Here she comes, weeping for her only nurse's death. 11
Thou art resolved?
LEONINE   I am resolved.

Enter Marina, with a basket of flowers.

MARINA
No, I will rob Tellus of her weed   14
To strew thy green with flowers. The yellows, blues, 15
The purple violets, and marigolds
Shall as a carpet hang upon thy grave
While summer days doth last. Ay me, poor maid,
Born in a tempest when my mother died,

---

13 date term of life
4.0.
2 to in accordance with   **4 there 's** there as, or there (she) is
10–11 Which . . . wonder which raises to an exalted level both her art
(in music and literature) and the general wonderment it occasions.
12 wrack ruin, destruction   **14 treason's** treachery's   **15 kind** manner   **18 Hight** was called   **21 sleided** divided into filaments for
embroidery   **22 small** slender   **24 cambric** a fine white linen.   **more
sound** more whole, with its embroidery   **26 night bird** nightingale
with its sad song (*moan*, line 27)   **27 still records with moan** incessantly tells her story in plaintive song   **28 constant** fixedly loyal.
pen (Used in writing hymns of praise.)   **29 Vail** do homage
31 absolute free from any imperfection   **31–3 So . . . white** With
equal ill success might the crow attempt to outdo the white plumage
of Venus's doves. (*Paphos* is a city in Cyprus sacred to Venus.)

34 as debts as owed to her   **35 given** i.e., gratuitous gifts, compli-
ments.   **darks** darkens, obscures   **37 rare** keen   **38 present** immediate   **40 by** by means of   **41 stead** assist   **44 pregnant** willing, ready
45 Prest prepared.   **event** outcome   **46 content** pleasure (in watching)   **48 Post** swiftly
4.1. Location: Tarsus. An open place near the seashore.
4–6 Let . . . nicely Do not let conscience, thus far unawakened,
inflame your heart with love of goodness and scruples. (*Too nicely*
means "overscrupulously.")   **6–7 which . . . off** i.e., which even some
women, such as I, have cast off   **11 only nurse's** i.e., Lychorida's.
(*Only* means "one and only.")   **14 Tellus** goddess of the earth.
weed garment (here, flowers)   **15 green** i.e., grass-covered grave

This world to me is a lasting storm
Whirring me from my friends.   21
DIONYZA
How now, Marina? Why do you keep alone?   22
How chance my daughter is not with you?   23
Do not consume your blood with sorrowing;   24
Have you a nurse of me. Lord, how your favor's   25
Changed with this unprofitable woe!
Come, give me your flowers. On the sea margent   27
Walk with Leonine; the air is quick there,   28
And it pierces and sharpens the stomach.   29
Come, Leonine, take her by the arm, walk with her.
MARINA   No, I pray you,
I'll not bereave you of your servant.
DIONYZA   Come, come,
I love the King your father and yourself
With more than foreign heart. We every day   35
Expect him here. When he shall come and find
Our paragon to all reports thus blasted,   37
He will repent the breadth of his great voyage,
Blame both my lord and me that we have taken
No care to your best courses. Go, I pray you,   40
Walk, and be cheerful once again. Reserve   41
That excellent complexion which did steal
The eyes of young and old. Care not for me;   43
I can go home alone.
MARINA   Well, I will go,
But yet I have no desire to it.
DIONYZA
Come, come, I know 'tis good for you.—
Walk half an hour, Leonine, at the least.
Remember what I have said.
LEONINE   I warrant you, madam.   48
DIONYZA
I'll leave you, my sweet lady, for a while.
Pray walk softly; do not heat your blood.   50
What, I must have a care of you.
MARINA   My thanks, sweet madam.   [Exit Dionyza.]
Is this wind westerly that blows?
LEONINE   Southwest.
MARINA
When I was born, the wind was north.
LEONINE   Was't so?
MARINA
My father, as Nurse says, did never fear,
But cried "Good seamen!" to the sailors,
Galling his kingly hands, haling ropes,   57
And, clasping to the mast, endured a sea
That almost burst the deck.
LEONINE   When was this?

MARINA   When I was born.
Never was waves nor wind more violent;
And from the ladder-tackle washes off   63
A canvas-climber. "Ha!" says one, "wolt out?"   64
And with a dropping industry they skip   65
From stem to stern. The boatswain whistles, and
The master calls and trebles their confusion.
LEONINE   Come, say your prayers.
MARINA   What mean you?
LEONINE
If you require a little space for prayer,
I grant it. Pray, but be not tedious, for   71
The gods are quick of ear, and I am sworn
To do my work with haste.
MARINA   Why will you kill me?
LEONINE   To satisfy my lady.
MARINA   Why would she have me killed?
Now, as I can remember, by my troth,   77
I never did her hurt in all my life.
I never spake bad word nor did ill turn
To any living creature. Believe me, la,
I never killed a mouse nor hurt a fly.
I trod upon a worm against my will,
But I wept for 't. How have I offended,
Wherein my death might yield her any profit,
Or my life imply her any danger?
LEONINE   My commission
Is not to reason of the deed, but do't.
MARINA
You will not do't for all the world, I hope.
You are well favored, and your looks foreshow   89
You have a gentle heart. I saw you lately,
When you caught hurt in parting two that fought;   91
Good sooth, it showed well in you. Do so now.   92
Your lady seeks my life; come you between
And save poor me, the weaker.
LEONINE   I am sworn,
And will dispatch.   [He seizes her.]

Enter Pirates.

FIRST PIRATE   Hold, villain!   [Leonine runs away.]
SECOND PIRATE   A prize, a prize!
THIRD PIRATE   Half-part, mates, half-part. Come, let's   98
have her aboard suddenly.   99
                          Exeunt [Pirates with Marina].

Enter Leonine.

LEONINE
These roguing thieves serve the great pirate Valdes,   100
And they have seized Marina. Let her go.
There's no hope she will return. I'll swear she's dead
And thrown into the sea. But I'll see further;

21 **Whirring** whirling, blowing   22 **keep** remain   23 **How chance**
How does it happen that   24 **with sorrowing** i.e., with sighs, thought
to cost the heart its blood   25 **Have . . . me** i.e., Take me as your
nurse.   **favor's** face is, appearance is   27 **margent** margin, shore
28 **quick** fresh, invigorating   29 **stomach** appetite.   35 **more . . .**
heart i.e., as though we were related by blood.   37 **Our . . . blasted**
the person whom all regard as a paragon of beauty thus withered
40 **courses** interests.   41 **Reserve** Preserve, maintain   43 **Care not**
for me Don't concern yourself about me   48 **warrant** promise
50 **softly** gently, slowly   57 **Galling** chafing, blistering.   **haling**
hauling on

63 **ladder-tackle** rope ladder in the ship's rigging   64 **"wolt out?"** so
you want to get out? (Addressed perhaps as a cruel jest to the *canvas-*
climber or sailor in the rigging who is washed overboard.)   65 **with**
. . . industry dripping wet as they labor   71 **tedious** long-winded
77 **as** as far as   89 **well favored** pleasant-looking.   **foreshow** proclaim   91 **caught hurt** received an injury   92 **Good sooth** (A mild
oath.)   98 **Half-part** Let's share   99 **suddenly** immediately.
100 **roguing** roving about like rogues

Perhaps they will but please themselves upon her,   104
Not carry her aboard. If she remain,
Whom they have ravished must by me be slain. *Exit.*

❖

[4.2]

Enter the three bawds [Pander, Bawd, and Bolt].

PANDER   Bolt!

BOLT   Sir?

PANDER   Search the market narrowly. Mytilene is full of   3
gallants. We lost too much money this mart by being   4
too wenchless.

BAWD   We were never so much out of creatures. We   6
have but poor three, and they can do no more than
they can do; and they with continual action are even
as good as rotten.   9

PANDER   Therefore let's have fresh ones, whate'er we
pay for them. If there be not a conscience to be used in   11
every trade, we shall never prosper.

BAWD   Thou say'st true. 'Tis not our bringing up of poor   13
bastards—as, I think, I have brought up some   14
eleven—

BOLT   Ay, to eleven, and brought them down again.   16
But shall I search the market?

BAWD   What else, man? The stuff we have, a strong   18
wind will blow it to pieces, they are so pitifully
sodden.   20

PANDER   Thou sayest true. There's two unwholesome,   21
o' conscience. The poor Transylvanian is dead that lay   22
with the little baggage.   23

BOLT   Ay, she quickly pooped him. She made him   24
roast meat for worms. But I'll go search the market.   25
Exit.

PANDER   Three or four thousand chequins were as   26
pretty a proportion to live quietly, and so give over.   27

BAWD   Why to give over, I pray you? Is it a shame to get   28
when we are old?

PANDER   Oh, our credit comes not in like the commodity,   30
nor the commodity wages not with the danger. There-   31
fore, if in our youths we could pick up some pretty

estate, 'twere not amiss to keep our door hatched. Be-   33
sides, the sore terms we stand upon with the gods will
be strong with us for giving o'er.   35

BAWD   Come, other sorts offend as well as we.   36

PANDER   As well as we? Ay, and better too; we offend   37
worse. Neither is our profession any trade; it's no   38
calling. But here comes Bolt.   39

Enter Bolt with the Pirates and Marina.

BOLT   Come your ways, my masters. You say she's a   40
virgin?

FIRST PIRATE   Oh, sir, we doubt it not.

BOLT   Master, I have gone through for this piece you   43
see. If you like her, so; if not, I have lost my earnest.   44

BAWD   Bolt, has she any qualities?

BOLT   She has a good face, speaks well, and has excellent good clothes. There's no farther necessity of qualities can make her be refused.   48

BAWD   What's her price, Bolt?

BOLT   I cannot be bated one doit of a thousand pieces.   50

PANDER   Well, follow me, my masters; you shall have
your money presently. Wife, take her in. Instruct her   52
what she has to do, that she may not be raw in her   53
entertainment.   *[Exeunt Pander and Pirates.]*   54

BAWD   Bolt, take you the marks of her, the color of her
hair, complexion, height, her age, with warrant of her
virginity, and cry, "He that will give most shall have
her first." Such a maidenhead were no cheap thing, if
men were as they have been. Get this done as I
command you.

BOLT   Performance shall follow.   *Exit.*

MARINA
Alack that Leonine was so slack, so slow!
He should have struck, not spoke; or that these pirates,
Not enough barbarous, had not o'erboard thrown me
For to seek my mother!

BAWD   Why lament you, pretty one?

MARINA   That I am pretty.

BAWD   Come, the gods have done their part in you.

MARINA   I accuse them not.

BAWD   You are light into my hands, where you are like   70
to live.   71

---

104 please . . . her take their sexual pleasure with her
4.2. Location: Mytilene, on the island of Lesbos. A brothel.
0.1 *bawds* (Used for either sex to mean dealers in prostitution.) ***Bolt***
(The name phallically suggests a shaft, projectile, or arrow.) **3 narrowly** carefully. **4 this mart** at the last market time **6 creatures** i.e.,
prostitutes. **9 rotten** i.e., with venereal disease. **11 If . . . used** i.e., If
one does not conscientiously offer good quality **13–14 'Tis . . . bastards** i.e., Raising bastard children doesn't bring us enough wealth.
(As Bolt points out, the children are raised only to be introduced into
prostitution.) **16 to eleven** to the age of eleven. **brought . . . again**
i.e., lowered them into debauchery. (With a pun on going to bed with
customers.) **18 stuff** goods **20 sodden** boiled (by being treated in
the sweating tub for venereal disease). **21 unwholesome** who are
diseased **22 o 'conscience** i.e., I must admit. **Transylvanian** a customer from Transylvania (in modern Romania and Hungary)
23 baggage whore. **24 pooped him** i.e., did for him, by infecting
him with venereal disease **24–5 She . . . worms** She made a corpse
of him, a feast for worms. **26 chequins** gold coins **26–7 were . . .
over** would be a fine portion to live on quietly in retirement. **28 get**
earn money **30–1 our . . . danger** i.e., our reputation does not keep
pace with our profit, and such profits as we make aren't worth the
risk (of dealing in whores, disease, etc.).

33 estate savings for a rainy day. **'twere . . . hatched** it wouldn't be a
bad idea to close our door to business. (*Hatched* doors, common in
brothels, were divided at the middle so that business could be conducted through the upper door.) **35 strong** strong inducement
36 sorts kinds of people. **as well as we** in addition to ourselves.
37–8 Ay . . . worse (The Pander plays with the meanings of *better* and
worse: we bawds and panders may offend *worse* in the sense of profiting from degrading sexual activity, whereas the better-born, no less
sinful, may be said to offend *better* because of their higher social
standing.) **38–9 it's no calling** i.e., it is not a recognized and ostensi-
bly legitimate vocation (even if it is, as the saying goes, the oldest of
the professions). **40 Come . . . masters** Come along, my good fellows. **43 I . . . piece** I have made the best deal I could for this piece
of flesh **44 so** well and good. **earnest** earnest money, deposit.
48 can i.e., the lack of which can **50 I . . . pieces** i.e., They won't settle for anything less than a thousand gold coins (each worth about a
pound). **52 presently** immediately. **53 raw** inexperienced
54 entertainment servicing of customers. **70 are light** have chanced
to light. (With a pun on becoming a *light* or immoral woman.) **like**
likely **71 live** remain.

MARINA   The more my fault,   72
To scape his hands where I was like to die.

BAWD   Ay, and you shall live in pleasure.

MARINA   No.

BAWD   Yes, indeed shall you, and taste gentlemen of all
fashions. You shall fare well; you shall have the dif-   77
ference of all complexions. What do you stop your ears?   78

MARINA   Are you a woman?

BAWD   What would you have me be, an I be not a   80
woman?

MARINA   An honest woman, or not a woman.   82

BAWD   Marry, whip the gosling! I think I shall have   83
something to do with you. Come, you're a young fool-   84
ish sapling and must be bowed as I would have you.

MARINA   The gods defend me!

BAWD   If it please the gods to defend you by men, then   87
men must comfort you, men must feed you, men must
stir you up. Bolt's returned.

[*Enter Bolt.*]

Now, sir, hast thou cried her through the market?   90

BOLT   I have cried her almost to the number of her   91
hairs; I have drawn her picture with my voice.   92

BAWD   And, I prithee, tell me how dost thou find the
inclination of the people, especially of the younger
sort?

BOLT   Faith, they listened to me as they would have
hearkened to their father's testament. There was a   97
Spaniard's mouth watered an he went to bed to her   98
very description.

BAWD   We shall have him here tomorrow with his best
ruff on.   101

BOLT   Tonight, tonight. But, mistress, do you know
the French knight that cowers i'th' hams?   103

BAWD   Who, Monsieur Verolles?   104

BOLT   Ay, he. He offered to cut a caper at the procla-   105
mation, but he made a groan at it, and swore he
would see her tomorrow.

BAWD   Well, well, as for him, he brought his disease   108
hither; here he does but repair it. I know he will come   109
in our shadow, to scatter his crowns in the sun.   110

BOLT   Well, if we had of every nation a traveler, we
should lodge them with this sign.   112

BAWD   [*to Marina*]   Pray you, come hither awhile. You
have fortunes coming upon you. Mark me: you must
seem to do that fearfully which you commit willingly,
despise profit where you have most gain. To weep   116
that you live as ye do makes pity in your lovers; seldom but that pity begets you a good opinion, and that
opinion a mere profit.   119

MARINA   I understand you not.

BOLT   Oh, take her home, mistress, take her home!   121
These blushes of hers must be quenched with some
present practice.

BAWD   Thou sayest true, i'faith, so they must, for your   124
bride goes to that with shame which is her way to go   125
with warrant.   126

BOLT   Faith, some do and some do not. But, mistress,
if I have bargained for the joint—   128

BAWD   Thou mayst cut a morsel off the spit.   129

BOLT   I may so.

BAWD   Who should deny it?—Come, young one, I like
the manner of your garments well.

BOLT   Ay, by my faith, they shall not be changed   133
yet.   134

BAWD   Bolt, spend thou that in the town. [*She gives
money.*] Report what a sojourner we have; you'll lose
nothing by custom. When nature framed this piece,   137
she meant thee a good turn; therefore say what a para-   138
gon she is, and thou hast the harvest out of thine own
report.

BOLT   I warrant you, mistress, thunder shall not so
awake the beds of eels as my giving out her beauty   142
stirs up the lewdly inclined. I'll bring home some
tonight.   [*Exit.*]

BAWD   Come your ways. Follow me.   145

MARINA
If fires be hot, knives sharp, or waters deep,
Untied I still my virgin knot will keep.
Diana aid my purpose!   148

BAWD   What have we to do with Diana? Pray you, will
you go with us?   *Exeunt.*

❖

[4.3]

Enter Cleon and Dionyza.

DIONYZA
Why, are you foolish? Can it be undone?

---

72 **fault** misfortune   77–8 **difference . . . complexions** variety of men
of all races and temperaments.   78 **What** Why   80 **an** if   82 **honest**
chaste   83 **whip the gosling!** i.e., the devil take this goose of a young
whore!   84 **something to do** i.e., my hands full   87 **by men** by way
of men   90 **cried** proclaimed, advertised   91–2 **almost . . . hairs**
almost to the point of numbering the hairs of her head   97 **testament**
will.   98 **an** as if   101 **ruff** (The large starched collars worn by Spanish gentlemen were a matter of jest to the English.)   103 **cowers i'th'
hams** i.e., crouches, showing a weakness typical of venereal disease.
104 **Verolles** (From the French *vérole*, "pox," "syphilis.")   105 **offered**
tried, made as if to.   **cut a caper** leap up and click his heels together
108–9 **brought . . . hither** was already diseased when he came.
(Syphilis was popularly known in England as "the French disease.")
109 **repair** (1) return with (2) mend, renew   110 **in our shadow** i.e.,
under our roof.   **crowns in the sun** i.e., gold coins, known as
"crowns of the sun," with perhaps the suggestion of squandering
gold on bright beauty. (A French crown also plays on the idea of a
bald head resulting from venereal disease.)   112 **lodge . . . sign** i.e.,
attract them to lodge here by means of Marina's picture, metaphorically hung out as though it were a shop sign.

116 **despise** and must seem to despise   119 **mere** utter, absolute
121 **take her home** talk plainly, i.e., be direct with her, or, take her inside
124–5 **your bride** even your ordinary bride   125 **that** i.e., first sex
126 **with warrant** with lawful sanction.   128 **joint** roast of meat
129 **off the spit** while it is still roasting on the spit, before it is served up
to customers. (Bolt is bargaining for the right to take Marina's chastity.)
133–4 **they shall . . . yet** (Marina's clothes proclaim her to be a wellborn
virgin; she does not wear a prostitute's distinctive dress.)   137 **by custom** by increasing our trade (since you'll get a commission).   **piece** (1)
masterpiece (2) piece of woman's flesh, as in line 43   138 **a good turn**
(1) a favor (2) an occasion for sex, a *piece* in the sexual sense   142 **beds
of eels** (Seager, *Natural History*, p. 98, quotes *Hortus Sanitatus*: the eel "is
disturbed by the sound of thunder." Used here with possible bawdy
connotation; eels are often associated with the penis.)   145 **Come your
ways** Come along.   148 **Diana** goddess of chastity, as in 2.5.10
4.3. Location: Tarsus. Cleon's (the Governor's) house.

CLEON
　Oh, Dionyza, such a piece of slaughter
　The sun and moon ne'er looked upon!
DIONYZA
　I think you'll turn a child again.
CLEON
　Were I chief lord of all this spacious world,
　I'd give it to undo the deed. A lady   6
　Much less in blood than virtue, yet a princess   7
　To equal any single crown o'th'earth
　I'th' justice of compare! O villain Leonine!   9
　Whom thou hast poisoned too.
　If thou hadst drunk to him, 't had been a kindness   11
　Becoming well thy fact. What canst thou say   12
　When noble Pericles shall demand his child?
DIONYZA
　That she is dead. Nurses are not the Fates;
　To foster is not ever to preserve.   15
　She died at night; I'll say so. Who can cross it,   16
　Unless you play the impious innocent   17
　And, for an honest attribute, cry out,   18
　"She died by foul play"?
CLEON   Oh, go to. Well, well,   19
　Of all the faults beneath the heavens, the gods
　Do like this worst.
DIONYZA   Be one of those that thinks
　The petty wrens of Tarsus will fly hence
　And open this to Pericles. I do shame   23
　To think of what a noble strain you are,
　And of how coward a spirit.
CLEON   To such proceeding   25
　Whoever but his approbation added,   26
　Though not his prime consent, he did not flow   27
　From honorable courses.
DIONYZA   Be it so, then.   28
　Yet none does know but you how she came dead,
　Nor none can know, Leonine being gone.
　She did distain my child and stood between   31
　Her and her fortunes. None would look on her,
　But cast their gazes on Marina's face,
　Whilst ours was blurted at and held a malkin   34
　Not worth the time of day. It pierced me through;
　And though you call my course unnatural,   36
　You not your child well loving, yet I find   37
　It greets me as an enterprise of kindness   38

　Performed to your sole daughter.
CLEON   Heavens forgive it!
DIONYZA   And as for Pericles,
　What should he say? We wept after her hearse,
　And yet we mourn. Her monument   43
　Is almost finished, and her epitaphs
　In glitt'ring golden characters express
　A general praise to her and care in us
　At whose expense 'tis done.
CLEON   Thou art like the harpy,   47
　Which, to betray, dost, with thine angel's face,
　Seize with thine eagle's talons.
DIONYZA
　You're like one that superstitiously   50
　Do swear to th' gods that winter kills the flies.   51
　But yet I know you'll do as I advise.   [Exeunt.]

❧

[4.4]

[Enter Gower, before the monument of Marina at
Tarsus.]

GOWER
　Thus time we waste and long leagues make short,   1
　Sail seas in cockles, have and wish but for't,   2
　Making to take your imagination   3
　From bourn to bourn, region to region.   4
　By you being pardoned, we commit no crime
　To use one language in each several clime   6
　Where our scenes seem to live. I do beseech you
　To learn of me, who stand i'th' gaps to teach you,   8
　The stages of our story. Pericles
　Is now again thwarting the wayward seas,   10
　Attended on by many a lord and knight,
　To see his daughter, all his life's delight.
　Old Helicanus goes along. Behind
　Is left to govern, if you bear in mind,
　Old Escanes, whom Helicanus late   15
　Advanced in time to great and high estate.
　Well-sailing ships and bounteous winds have brought
　This King to Tarsus—think his pilot thought;   18
　So with his steerage shall your thoughts grow on—   19
　To fetch his daughter home, who first is gone.   20

---

6 **lady** i.e., Marina   7 **Much . . . virtue** i.e., noble in birth but even more so in virtue   9 **I'th' . . . compare** if justly compared.   **11 drunk to him** i.e., drunk poison yourself while giving him poison   **12 Becoming . . . fact** well suited to the horror of your crime.   **15 To . . . preserve** i.e., one can foster life, but one cannot preserve it forever; that is in the hands of the Fates.   **16 cross** contradict   **17 play . . . innocent** impiously play the innocent. (*Impious* suggests "undutiful to me, your wife.")   **18 for** to gain   **attribute** reputation   **19 go to** (A term of reproach or anger.)   **23 open** reveal. (In ancient times, birds were thought to reveal murders.)   **25–8 To . . . courses** Anyone who would merely assent to such a proceeding, let alone conspiring in the first place, would betray his dishonorable origins.   **31 distain** tarnish by comparison   **34 blurted at** scorned (by means of a derisive noise made with the lips).   **malkin** slut   **36–8 And though . . . kindness** and though you, who do not know how to love your daughter properly, call my course unnatural, my deed strikes me as an enterprise of natural affection

43 yet still   **47 harpy** monstrous bird with the face and torso of a woman   **50–1 You're . . . flies** i.e., You are one of those bleeding hearts who protest against the harsh necessity of death; you'd appeal to the gods to take pity on flies that die in the wintertime.
4.4. Location: Tarsus.
0.1 the monument of Marina (Perhaps Gower reveals this monument by drawing a curtain hung before the "discovery space" here, or perhaps Cleon draws back the curtain at line 22.1)   **1 waste** i.e., pass quickly over   **2 cockles** scallop shells, or, small boats. (Supernatural creatures sometimes sail in this fashion. Gower is alluding to the imaginary crossing of the seas between scenes of the play.)   **have . . . for't** have something if we but wish it   **3 Making** proceeding   **4 bourn** frontier   **6 several clime** different region   **8 stand i'th' gaps** bridge the gaps (of time and space between scenes)   **10 thwarting** crossing.   **wayward** unruly, hostile   **18 think . . . thought** imagine that he is being piloted by our swift thoughts as we accompany him   **19 with his steerage** with Thought as pilot steering our thoughts.   **grow on** proceed   **20 first** already

Like motes and shadows see them move awhile;   21
Your ears unto your eyes I'll reconcile.   22

[*Dumb Show.*]

*Enter Pericles at one door with all his train, Cleon
and Dionyza at the other. Cleon shows Pericles the
tomb, whereat Pericles makes lamentation, puts on
sackcloth, and in a mighty passion departs.* [*Then
exeunt Cleon and Dionyza.*]

See how belief may suffer by foul show!   23
This borrowed passion stands for true-owed woe;   24
And Pericles, in sorrow all devoured,
With sighs shot through and biggest tears o'er-
    showered,
Leaves Tarsus and again embarks. He swears
Never to wash his face nor cut his hairs;
He puts on sackcloth, and to sea. He bears   29
A tempest, which his mortal vessel tears,   30
And yet he rides it out. Now please you wit   31
The epitaph is for Marina writ   32
By wicked Dionyza.

[*He reads the inscription on Marina's monument.*]

"The fairest, sweetest, and best lies here,
Who withered in her spring of year.
She was of Tyrus the King's daughter,
On whom foul death hath made this slaughter.
Marina was she called, and at her birth,
Thetis, being proud, swallowed some part o'th'earth.   39
Therefore the earth, fearing to be o'erflowed,
Hath Thetis' birth-child on the heavens bestowed;
Wherefore she does, and swears she'll never stint,   42
Make raging battery upon shores of flint."   43
No visor does become black villainy
So well as soft and tender flattery.
Let Pericles believe his daughter's dead
And bear his courses to be orderèd   47
By Lady Fortune, while our scene must play   48
His daughter's woe and heavy welladay   49
In her unholy service. Patience, then,   50
And think you now are all in Mytilene.   *Exit.*

[4.5]

Enter [*from the brothel*] *two Gentlemen.*

FIRST GENTLEMAN   Did you ever hear the like?
SECOND GENTLEMAN   No, nor never shall do in such a
    place as this, she being once gone.
FIRST GENTLEMAN   But to have divinity preached there!
    Did you ever dream of such a thing?
SECOND GENTLEMAN   No, no. Come, I am for no more
    bawdy houses. Shall 's go hear the vestals sing?   7
FIRST GENTLEMAN   I'll do anything now that is virtuous,
    but I am out of the road of rutting forever.   *Exeunt.*   9

[4.6]

Enter three bawds [*Pander, Bawd, and Bolt*].

PANDER   Well, I had rather than twice the worth of her
    she had ne'er come here.
BAWD   Fie, fie upon her! She's able to freeze the god
    Priapus and undo a whole generation. We must ei-   4
    ther get her ravished or be rid of her. When she
    should do for clients her fitment and do me the kind-   6
    ness of our profession, she has me her quirks, her rea-
    sons, her master reasons, her prayers, her knees, that
    she would make a puritan of the devil if he should
    cheapen a kiss of her.   10
BOLT   Faith, I must ravish her, or she'll disfurnish us   11
    of all our cavalleria and make our swearers priests.   12
PANDER   Now, the pox upon her greensickness for me!   13
BAWD   Faith, there's no way to be rid on't but by the   14
    way to the pox. Here comes the Lord Lysimachus dis-   15
    guised.
BOLT   We should have both lord and loon, if the pee-   17
    vish baggage would but give way to customers.   18

Enter Lysimachus.

LYSIMACHUS   How now? How a dozen of virginities?   19
BAWD   Now, the gods to-bless Your Honor!   20
BOLT   I am glad to see Your Honor in good health.
LYSIMACHUS   You may so; 'tis the better for you that
    your resorters stand upon sound legs. How now?   23
    Wholesome iniquity have you, that a man may deal   24
    withal and defy the surgeon?   25

---

21 **motes** specks in a beam of light.   **shadows** (With a suggestion of
the ever-changing images created by actors.)   22.5 *passion* grief
23 **suffer by foul show** be abused by dissembling.   24 **This . . . woe**
This feigned lamentation (of Cleon and Dionyza) usurps the place
that should be occupied by genuine woe   29 **He bears** i.e., He bears
within him   30 **his mortal vessel tears** afflicts with anguish his
human body, racks his frame   31 **wit** know   32 **is** that is   39 **Thetis**
a sea nymph, often confused (as here) with Tethys, a Titaness and
consort of Oceanus.   **swallowed . . . earth** (The fanciful image is that
of the oceans rejoicing over Marina's birth at sea with such destructive flood tides that the earth resolves to be rid of Marina by sending
her to heaven; it is in angry reprisal that the sea continues to beat
against the shore.)   42 **she** i.e., Thetis.   **stint** cease   43 **Make . . .**
flint continuously beat upon rocky shores.   47–8 **bear . . . Fortune**
direct his passage as Fortune orders   49 **welladay** grief, lamentation
50 **In her unholy service** i.e., in the brothel.

4.5. Location: Mytilene. The brothel.
7 **Shall 's** Shall we.   **vestals** virgins consecrated to tend the sacred
altar   9 **rutting** sexual indulgence
4.6. Location: The brothel, as before.
4 **Priapus** god of fertility and lechery.   **undo . . . generation** (1) prevent the engendering of the next generation (2) prevent the pleasures
of the present generation.   6 **fitment** sexual duty.   **do me** do. (*Me* is
an emphatic marker; see also *has me* in the next line.)   10 **cheapen**
bargain for   11 **disfurnish** deprive   12 **cavalleria** cavaliers.
swearers profane swaggerers   13 **the pox . . . me!** i.e., a curse upon
her moody obstinacy and squeamishness (literally, an anemia suffered by young women), as far as I'm concerned!   14 **on't** of it, of this
difficulty   15 **pox** syphilis. (Playing on *pox* as a familiar curse in line
13.)   17 **loon** low fellow, person of low birth   17–18 **peevish bag-**
gage stubborn hussy   19 **How a** What price for   20 **to-bless** bless
completely   23 **your resorters** those who resort to your place, customers   24 **Wholesome iniquity** Healthy prostitutes   25 **withal**
with.   **surgeon** barber-surgeon (to treat syphilis).

BAWD   We have here one, sir, if she would—but there never came her like in Mytilene.

LYSIMACHUS   If she'd do the deeds of darkness, thou wouldst say.

BAWD   Your Honor knows what 'tis to say well enough.   30

LYSIMACHUS   Well, call forth, call forth.   [*Exit Pander.*]

BOLT   For flesh and blood, sir, white and red, you shall see a rose; and she were a rose indeed, if she had but—   34

LYSIMACHUS   What, prithee?

BOLT   Oh, sir, I can be modest.

LYSIMACHUS   That dignifies the renown of a bawd no   37
less than it gives a good report to a number to be   38
chaste.   39

[*Enter Pander with Marina.*]

BAWD   Here comes that which grows to the stalk; never plucked yet, I can assure you. Is she not a fair creature?

LYSIMACHUS   Faith, she would serve after a long voyage   43
at sea. Well, there's for you. [*He gives money.*] Leave us.   44

BAWD   I beseech Your Honor, give me leave a word, and   45
I'll have done presently.   46

LYSIMACHUS   I beseech you, do.

BAWD   [*aside to Marina*]   First, I would have you note this is an honorable man.

MARINA   I desire to find him so, that I may worthily   50
note him.   51

BAWD   Next, he's the Governor of this country, and a man whom I am bound to.   53

MARINA   If he govern the country, you are bound to   54
him indeed, but how honorable he is in that, I know not.

BAWD   Pray you, without any more virginal fencing, will you use him kindly? He will line your apron with gold.

MARINA   What he will do graciously, I will thankfully receive.

LYSIMACHUS   Ha' you done?

BAWD   My lord, she's not paced yet. You must take   63
some pains to work her to your manage.—Come, we   64
will leave His Honor and her together. Go thy ways.

[*Exeunt Bawd, Pander, and Bolt.*]

LYSIMACHUS   Now, pretty one, how long have you been at this trade?

MARINA   What trade, sir?

LYSIMACHUS   Why, I cannot name 't but I shall offend.   69

MARINA   I cannot be offended with my trade. Please you to name it.

LYSIMACHUS   How long have you been of this profession?

MARINA   E'er since I can remember.

LYSIMACHUS   Did you go to't so young? Were you a   75
gamester at five, or at seven?   76

MARINA   Earlier too, sir, if now I be one.

LYSIMACHUS   Why, the house you dwell in proclaims you to be a creature of sale.

MARINA   Do you know this house to be a place of such   80
resort, and will come into't? I hear say you're of hon-   81
orable parts and are the governor of this place.   82

LYSIMACHUS   Why, hath your principal made known unto you who I am?

MARINA   Who is my principal?

LYSIMACHUS   Why, your herbwoman, she that sets seeds and roots of shame and iniquity. Oh, you have heard something of my power, and so stand aloof for more serious wooing. But I protest to thee, pretty one, my authority shall not see thee, or else look friendly   90
upon thee. Come, bring me to some private place. Come, come.

MARINA
If you were born to honor, show it now;
If put upon you, make the judgment good   94
That thought you worthy of it.

LYSIMACHUS
How's this? How's this? Some more. Be sage.

MARINA   For me,
That am a maid, though most ungentle fortune
Have placed me in this sty, where, since I came,
Diseases have been sold dearer than physic—   99
That the gods
Would set me free from this unhallowed place,
Though they did change me to the meanest bird   102
That flies i'th' purer air!

LYSIMACHUS   I did not think
Thou couldst have spoke so well, ne'er dreamt thou couldst.
Had I brought hither a corrupted mind,
Thy speech had altered it. Hold, here's gold for thee.   106
Persevere in that clear way thou goest,   107
And the gods strengthen thee!   [*He gives gold.*]

MARINA   The good gods preserve you!

LYSIMACHUS   For me, be you thoughten   110
That I came with no ill intent, for to me
The very doors and windows savor vilely.
Fare thee well. Thou art a piece of virtue, and
I doubt not but thy training hath been noble.
Hold, here's more gold for thee.   [*He gives gold.*]
A curse upon him, die he like a thief,

---

30 what 'tis to say what I'm trying to say   **34 but** (To catch the sexual innuendo of this remark, compare the completed phrase, "No roses without prickles.")   **37–9 That . . . chaste** i.e., Modesty in speech gives good reputation to a bawd, as well as attesting to the chastity of many women who deserve no such reputation.   **43–4 she . . . sea** i.e., She is just the thing for a man who is sexually ravenous.   **45 a word** i.e., to say a few words in private to her   **46 have done presently** be done in a moment.   **50–1 I . . . him** I hope to find him truly honorable (not merely *honorable* in the sense used in line 49, "of high rank").   **53, 54 bound** (1) obligated (2) subject   **63 paced** broken in. (A term from horse training.)   **64 manage** handling. (Again from horse training.)   **69 but . . . offend** without offending.

75 go to't i.e., practice sexual acts   **76 gamester** wanton woman   **80–1 of such resort** to be visited for such a purpose   **82 parts** qualities   **90 my authority . . . thee** i.e., I'll wink at your offenses, not enforce the laws against prostitutes   **94 If put upon you** i.e., if your high position was conferred after birth, not through inheritance   **99 Diseases . . . physic** venereal diseases have been transmitted for higher prices than their curative remedies would cost   **102 meanest** lowest   **106 had** would have   **107 clear** virtuous   **110 be you thoughten** assure yourself

That robs thee of thy goodness! If thou dost
Hear from me, it shall be for thy good.

    [Enter Bolt.]

BOLT   I beseech Your Honor, one piece for me.
LYSIMACHUS   Avaunt, thou damnèd doorkeeper!
Your house, but for this virgin that doth prop it,
Would sink and overwhelm you. Away!   *[Exit.]*
BOLT   How's this? We must take another course with
you. If your peevish chastity, which is not worth a
breakfast in the cheapest country under the cope, shall 125
undo a whole household, let me be gelded like a span-
iel. Come your ways.
MARINA   Whither would you have me?
BOLT   I must have your maidenhead taken off, or the 129
common hangman shall execute it. Come your ways. 130
We'll have no more gentlemen driven away. Come
your ways, I say.

    Enter bawds [Bawd and Pander].

BAWD   How now, what's the matter?
BOLT   Worse and worse, mistress. She has here spoken
holy words to the Lord Lysimachus.
BAWD   Oh, abominable!
BOLT   She makes our profession as it were to stink afore
the face of the gods.
BAWD   Marry, hang her up forever!
BOLT   The nobleman would have dealt with her like a 140
nobleman, and she sent him away as cold as a snow- 141
ball, saying his prayers too.
BAWD   Bolt, take her away. Use her at thy pleasure.
Crack the glass of her virginity and make the rest
malleable.
BOLT   An if she were a thornier piece of ground than 146
she is, she shall be plowed.
MARINA   Hark, hark, you gods!
BAWD   She conjures. Away with her! Would she had
never come within my doors!—Marry, hang you!—
She's born to undo us.—Will you not go the way of
womenkind? Marry, come up, my dish of chastity 152
with rosemary and bays!   *[Exeunt Bawd and Pander.]* 153
BOLT   Come, mistress, come your ways with me.
MARINA   Whither wilt thou have me?
BOLT   To take from you the jewel you hold so dear.
MARINA   Prithee, tell me one thing first.
BOLT   Come now, your one thing.   158
MARINA
What canst thou wish thine enemy to be?   159
BOLT   Why, I could wish him to be my master, or
rather, my mistress.

MARINA
Neither of these are so bad as thou art,
Since they do better thee in their command.   163
Thou hold'st a place for which the pained'st fiend   164
Of hell would not in reputation change.
Thou art the damnèd doorkeeper to every
Coistrel that comes inquiring for his Tib.   167
To the choleric fisting of every rogue   168
Thy ear is liable; thy food is such
As hath been belched on by infected lungs.
BOLT   What would you have me do? Go to the wars,
would you, where a man may serve seven years for 172
the loss of a leg and have not money enough in the
end to buy him a wooden one?
MARINA
Do anything but this thou doest. Empty
Old receptacles, or common shores, of filth;   176
Serve by indenture to the common hangman.   177
Any of these ways are yet better than this;
For what thou professest, a baboon, could he speak,   179
Would own a name too dear. That the gods   180
Would safely deliver me from this place!
Here, here's gold for thee.   *[She gives gold.]*
If that thy master would gain by me,   183
Proclaim that I can sing, weave, sew, and dance,
With other virtues, which I'll keep from boast,   185
And will undertake all these to teach.
I doubt not but this populous city will
Yield many scholars.   188
BOLT   But can you teach all this you speak of?
MARINA
Prove that I cannot, take me home again   190
And prostitute me to the basest groom   191
That doth frequent your house.
BOLT   Well, I will see what I can do for thee. If I can
place thee, I will.
MARINA   But amongst honest women.
BOLT   Faith, my acquaintance lies little amongst them.
But since my master and mistress hath bought you,
there's no going but by their consent. Therefore I will
make them acquainted with your purpose, and I
doubt not but I shall find them tractable enough.
Come, I'll do for thee what I can. Come your ways.
    Exeunt.

[5. Chorus]

    Enter Gower.

125 **cope** firmament   **129–30 or . . . execute it** (As if taking the maidenhead were a kind of beheading.)   **140–1 like a nobleman** i.e., as a
nobleman would have done, using her and rewarding her   **146 An if**
Even if   **152 Marry, come up** i.e., Hoity-toity   **153 rosemary and
bays** (Customary garnishes for certain foods; the Bawd sees Marina
as a fancy dish.)   **158 thing** (Bolt plays on Marina's *one thing* [line
157] in a lewd sense, referring to her sexual anatomy.)   **159 What . . .
to be?** i.e., Who is your worst enemy imaginable? (Marina means the
devil. Bolt, in reply, can think only in terms of his master and mistress, who presumably make his life miserable.)

163 **Since . . . command** i.e., since they give the orders but you do the
actual dirty work.   **164 pained'st** most tormented   **167 Coistrel**
knave. **Tib** common woman.   **168 choleric fisting** angry blows
172 would you would you have me.   **for** i.e., to end up with
176 shores sewers, or, garbage dumps at the water's edge   **177 by
indenture** i.e., as an apprentice   **179 what thou professest** your profession   **180 Would . . . dear** would consider himself and his reputation too good for that.   **That** Would that   **183 If that** If   **185 virtues**
accomplishments   **188 scholars** pupils.   **190 Prove** If you find
191 groom menial
5.0.

GOWER

Marina thus the brothel scapes and chances
Into an honest house, our story says.
She sings like one immortal, and she dances
As goddesslike to her admirèd lays.   4
Deep clerks she dumbs, and with her neele
composes   5
Nature's own shape, of bud, bird, branch, or
berry,
That even her art sisters the natural roses;   7
Her inkle, silk, twin with the rubied cherry,   8
That pupils lacks she none of noble race,   9
Who pour their bounty on her, and her gain
She gives the cursèd bawd. Here we her place,
And to her father turn our thoughts again,
Where we left him, on the sea. We there him lost,
Where, driven before the winds, he is arrived
Here where his daughter dwells; and on this coast
Suppose him now at anchor. The city strived
God Neptune's annual feast to keep, from whence
Lysimachus our Tyrian ship espies,
His banners sable, trimmed with rich expense,
And to him in his barge with fervor hies.
In your supposing once more put your sight;   21
Of heavy Pericles think this his bark,   22
Where what is done in action—more, if might—   23
Shall be discovered. Please you, sit and hark.   24
                                              Exit.

❖

[5.1]

*Enter Helicanus. To him two Sailors, [one
belonging to the Tyrian vessel, the other to a barge
of Mytilene that is evidently alongside, out of
view].*

TYRIAN SAILOR [*to the Sailor of Mytilene*]
Where is Lord Helicanus? He can resolve you.   1
Oh, here he is.—
Sir, there is a barge put off from Mytilene,
And in it is Lysimachus the Governor,
Who craves to come aboard. What is your will?
HELICANUS
That he have his. Call up some gentlemen.
TYRIAN SAILOR   Ho, gentlemen! My lord calls.

Enter two or three Gentlemen.

FIRST GENTLEMAN   Doth Your Lordship call?

HELICANUS   Gentlemen,
There is some of worth would come aboard.   10
I pray, greet him fairly.   11
                  [*The Gentlemen and the two Sailors
                        go to greet Lysimachus.*]

Enter [as from the barge] Lysimachus, [escorted].

TYRIAN SAILOR [*to Lysimachus*]   Sir,
This is the man that can, in aught you would,   13
Resolve you.
LYSIMACHUS
Hail, reverend sir! The gods preserve you!
HELICANUS   And you, to outlive the age I am,
And die as I would do.
LYSIMACHUS   You wish me well.   17
Being on shore, honoring of Neptune's triumphs,   18
Seeing this goodly vessel ride before us,
I made to it, to know of whence you are.
HELICANUS   First, what is your place?   21
LYSIMACHUS
I am the governor of this place you lie before.   22
HELICANUS   Sir,
Our vessel is of Tyre, in it the King,
A man who for this three months hath not spoken
To anyone, nor taken sustenance
But to prorogue his grief.   27
LYSIMACHUS
Upon what ground is his distemperature?   28
HELICANUS
'Twould be too tedious to repeat,
But the main grief springs from the loss
Of a belovèd daughter and a wife.
LYSIMACHUS   May we not see him?
HELICANUS   You may,
But bootless is your sight. He will not speak   34
To any.
LYSIMACHUS   Yet let me obtain my wish.
HELICANUS
Behold him. [*Pericles is discovered to view, in rough
clothing and with long hair and beard.*]
This was a goodly person,
Till the disaster that, one mortal night,   38
Drove him to this.
LYSIMACHUS [*to Pericles*]
Sir King, all hail! The gods preserve you!
Hail, royal sir!
HELICANUS
It is in vain. He will not speak to you.
A LORD   Sir,
We have a maid in Mytilene, I durst wager,
Would win some words of him.
LYSIMACHUS   'Tis well bethought.
She questionless, with her sweet harmony

---

4 lays songs.   **5 Deep . . . dumbs** She silences profound scholars.
neele needle   **7 That . . . roses** in such a way that her embroidery is
just as natural as real roses are   **8 inkle** linen thread or yarn.   **twin
with** resemble closely   **9 race** class, family   **21 In . . . sight** Visualize
the scene again in your imagination   **22 heavy** sorrowful   **23 if
might** if we could   **24 discovered** revealed, shown.
5.1. Location: On board Pericles's ship, off Mytilene. A pavilion for
Pericles is provided onstage, with a curtain before it, perhaps by
means of a "discovery space"; Pericles, reclining within, is "discovered" at line 37 by the drawing back of the curtain.
1 resolve answer, satisfy

10 some of worth some nobleman (who)   **11 fairly** courteously.
13 in aught you would in whatever you wish to know   **17 as I
would do** i.e., at the end of a long and honorable life.   **18 honoring
. . . triumphs** celebrating a festival in honor of Neptune   **21 place**
office.   **22 lie** lie at anchor   **27 prorogue** prolong   **28 Upon . . . distemperature?** What is the cause of his disturbance of mind?
34 bootless fruitless   **38 mortal** fatal

And other chosen attractions, would allure,   47
And make a batt'ry through his deafened ports,   48
Which now are midway stopped.   49
She is all happy as the fairest of all   50
And, with her fellow maids, is now upon
The leafy shelter that abuts against
The island's side.   *[He signals to the Lord, who goes*
                                  off to bring Marina.]

HELICANUS
Sure, all effectless; yet nothing we'll omit   54
That bears recovery's name. But since your kindness   55
We have stretched thus far, let us beseech you
That for our gold we may provision have,
Wherein we are not destitute for want,
But weary for the staleness.

LYSIMACHUS   Oh, sir, a courtesy   59
Which if we should deny, the most just gods
For every graft would send a caterpillar,   61
And so inflict our province. Yet once more   62
Let me entreat to know at large the cause   63
Of your king's sorrow.

HELICANUS
Sit, sir, I will recount it to you.—
But, see, I am prevented.   66

        [Enter, as though from the barge, the Lord, with
        Marina, and a young lady.]

LYSIMACHUS
Oh, here's the lady that I sent for.—
Welcome, fair one!—Is't not a goodly presence?   68
HELICANUS   She's a gallant lady.   69
LYSIMACHUS
She's such a one that, were I well assured
Came of a gentle kind and noble stock,   71
I'd wish no better choice, and think me rarely wed.—   72
Fair one, all goodness that consists in bounty   73
Expect even here, where is a kingly patient;
If that thy prosperous and artificial feat   75
Can draw him but to answer thee in aught,
Thy sacred physic shall receive such pay   77
As thy desires can wish.

MARINA   Sir, I will use
My utmost skill in his recovery, provided
That none but I and my companion maid
Be suffered to come near him.

LYSIMACHUS   Come, let us leave her; 81
And the gods make her prosperous!   82
        [They stand aside.] The song [by Marina].

LYSIMACHUS *[advancing]*
Marked he your music?
MARINA   No, nor looked on us.
LYSIMACHUS *[to Helicanus]*   See, she will speak to him.
MARINA *[to Pericles]*   Hail, sir! My lord, lend ear.
PERICLES   Hum, ha!   *[He pushes her away.]*
MARINA
I am a maid, my lord, that ne'er before
Invited eyes, but have been gazèd on   88
Like a comet. She speaks,   89
My lord, that maybe hath endured a grief
Might equal yours, if both were justly weighed.
Though wayward fortune did malign my state,   92
My derivation was from ancestors
Who stood equivalent with mighty kings;
But time hath rooted out my parentage,
And to the world and awkward casualties   96
Bound me in servitude. *[Aside]* I will desist;
But there is something glows upon my cheek,
And whispers in mine ear, "Go not till he speak."
PERICLES
My fortunes—parentage—good parentage—
To equal mine!—Was it not thus? What say you?
MARINA
I said, my lord, if you did know my parentage,
You would not do me violence.
PERICLES
I do think so. Pray you, turn your eyes upon me.   104
You're like something that—What countrywoman?
Here of these shores?
MARINA   No, nor of any shores.
Yet I was mortally brought forth, and am   107
No other than I appear.
PERICLES
I am great with woe and shall deliver weeping.   109
My dearest wife was like this maid, and such a one
My daughter might have been. My queen's square
   brows;
Her stature to an inch; as wandlike straight;
As silver-voiced; her eyes as jewel-like
And cased as richly; in pace another Juno;   114
Who starves the ears she feeds, and makes them
   hungry
The more she gives them speech.—Where do you
   live?
MARINA
Where I am but a stranger. From the deck
You may discern the place.
PERICLES
Where were you bred? And how achieved you these
Endowments which you make more rich to owe?   120
MARINA
If I should tell my history, it would seem

---

47 **chosen** choice   48 **make . . . ports** i.e., force an entrance through his deafened sense of hearing   49 **midway stopped** shut so that communications get only halfway through.   50 **all happy** completely fortunate (in having such beauty)   54 **effectless** useless   55 **bears recovery's name** deserves the name of cure.   59 **for** because of   61 **graft** scion, shoot, grafted plant   62 **inflict** afflict   63 **at large** in detail   66 **prevented** forestalled.   68 **Is't . . . presence?** Isn't her demeanor fine?   69 **gallant** splendid   71 **gentle kind** noble kindred   72 **rarely** excellently   73 **all . . . bounty** (In the Quarto, which reads "beautie" for "bounty," this phrase could mean: You, Marina, possessed of all good that beauty can contain.)   75 **prosperous** producing favorable results.   **artificial** skillful   77 **physic** medicine   81 **suffered** permitted.   82.1 *The song* (Not given in the Quarto.)

88 **Invited eyes** asked to be looked at   88–9 **gazèd . . . comet** i.e., stared at in astonishment.   92 **wayward** contrary.   **did . . . state** has dealt malignantly with my condition   96 **awkward casualties** adverse misfortunes   104 **I do think so** I agree.   107 **mortally** humanly   109 **great** (1) pregnant (2) heavy.   **deliver** (1) give birth (2) speak   114 **cased** enclosed, framed.   **pace** gait, carriage   120 **to owe** by possessing.

Like lies disdained in the reporting.
PERICLES   Prithee, speak.   122
Falseness cannot come from thee, for thou lookest
Modest as Justice, and thou seemest a palace
For the crowned Truth to dwell in. I will believe thee
And make my senses credit thy relation   126
To points that seem impossible, for thou lookest
Like one I loved indeed. What were thy friends?   128
Didst thou not say, when I did push thee back—
Which was when I perceived thee—that thou cam'st
From good descending?
MARINA   So indeed I did.   131
PERICLES
Report thy parentage. I think thou said'st
Thou hadst been tossed from wrong to injury,
And that thou thought'st thy griefs might equal mine,
If both were opened.
MARINA   Some such thing   135
I said, and said no more but what my thoughts
Did warrant me was likely.
PERICLES   Tell thy story.
If thine, considered, prove the thousand part   138
Of my endurance, thou art a man, and I   139
Have suffered like a girl. Yet thou dost look
Like Patience gazing on kings' graves and smiling   141
Extremity out of act. What were thy friends?   142
How lost thou them? Thy name, my most kind virgin?
Recount, I do beseech thee. Come, sit by me.
MARINA [sitting]   My name is Marina.
PERICLES   Oh, I am mocked,
And thou by some incensèd god sent hither   147
To make the world to laugh at me.
MARINA   Patience, good sir, or here I'll cease.
PERICLES
Nay, I'll be patient. Thou little know'st how thou
Dost startle me to call thyself Marina.
MARINA   The name
Was given me by one that had some power:
My father, and a king.
PERICLES   How, a king's daughter?
And called Marina?
MARINA   You said you would believe me;
But, not to be a troubler of your peace,
I will end here.
PERICLES   But are you flesh and blood?
Have you a working pulse, and are no fairy?   158
Motion? Well, speak on. Where were you born?   159
And wherefore called Marina?
MARINA   Called Marina
For I was born at sea.
PERICLES   At sea! What mother?   161

MARINA
My mother was the daughter of a king,
Who died the minute I was born,
As my good nurse Lychorida hath oft
Delivered weeping.
PERICLES   Oh, stop there a little!   165
This is the rarest dream that e'er dull sleep
Did mock sad fools withal. This cannot be   167
My daughter—buried!—Well, where were you bred?
I'll hear you more, to th' bottom of your story,
And never interrupt you.
MARINA
You scorn. Believe me, 'twere best I did give o'er.   171
PERICLES
I will believe you by the syllable   172
Of what you shall deliver. Yet give me leave:
How came you in these parts? Where were you bred?
MARINA
The King my father did in Tarsus leave me,
Till cruel Cleon, with his wicked wife,
Did seek to murder me; and having wooed
A villain to attempt it, who having drawn to do't,   178
A crew of pirates came and rescued me,
Brought me to Mytilene. But, good sir,
Whither will you have me? Why do you weep? It may
  be   181
You think me an impostor. No, good faith,
I am the daughter to King Pericles,
If good King Pericles be.   184
PERICLES [calling]   Ho, Helicanus!
HELICANUS   Calls my lord?
PERICLES
Thou art a grave and noble counselor,
Most wise in general. Tell me, if thou canst,
What this maid is, or what is like to be,   189
That thus hath made me weep?
HELICANUS   I know not,
But here's the regent, sir, of Mytilene
Speaks nobly of her.
LYSIMACHUS   She never would tell   192
Her parentage; being demanded that,
She would sit still and weep.
PERICLES
Oh, Helicanus, strike me, honored sir,
Give me a gash, put me to present pain,
Lest this great sea of joys rushing upon me
O'erbear the shores of my mortality,   198
And drown me with their sweetness.—Oh, come
  hither,
Thou that beget'st him that did thee beget,   200
Thou that wast born at sea, buried at Tarsus,
And found at sea again!—Oh, Helicanus,

---

122 **in the reporting** even as I spoke them.   126 **credit thy relation**
believe your account   128 **friends** relatives.   131 **descending**
descent.   135 **opened** revealed.   138 **thousand** thousandth   139 **my**
endurance what I have endured   141–2 **gazing . . . act** i.e., viewing
with equanimity the evidence that all human greatness ends in death
and disarming with a smile the worst that fortune can do.   147 **sent**
are sent   158 **working** beating   159 **Motion?** Have you motion?
161 **For** because

165 **Delivered** recited, told. (Similarly in line 173.)   167 **withal** with.
171 **give o'er** cease.   172 **by the syllable** i.e., to the letter   178 **drawn**
drawn his sword   181 **Whither . . . me?** Where are you leading me in
this interrogation?   184 **be** is alive.   189 **what . . . to be** who she
might be   192 **Speaks** who speaks   198 **O'erbear . . . mortality** overwhelm my mortal senses   200 **Thou . . . beget** i.e., you who renew
the life of your own father

Down on thy knees! Thank the holy gods as loud   203
As thunder threatens us. This is Marina.—   204
What was thy mother's name? Tell me but that,
For truth can never be confirmed enough,
Though doubts did ever sleep.   207

MARINA
First, sir, I pray, what is your title?

PERICLES
I am Pericles of Tyre. But tell me now
My drowned queen's name, as in the rest you said
Thou hast been godlike perfect, the heir of kingdoms,   211
And another life to Pericles thy father.   212

MARINA
Is it no more to be your daughter than   213
To say my mother's name was Thaisa?
Thaisa was my mother, who did end
The minute I began.

PERICLES
Now, blessing on thee! Rise, thou'rt my child.—
Give me fresh garments.—Mine own Helicanus,   218
She is not dead at Tarsus, as she should have been,   219
By savage Cleon. She shall tell thee all,   220
When thou shalt kneel, and justify in knowledge   221
She is thy very princess.—Who is this?

HELICANUS
Sir, 'tis the Governor of Mytilene,
Who, hearing of your melancholy state,
Did come to see you.

PERICLES [to Lysimachus]   I embrace you.
Give me my robes. I am wild in my beholding.   227
                    [He is freshly attired.]
O heavens bless my girl! But, hark, what music?
Tell Helicanus, my Marina, tell him
O'er, point by point, for yet he seems to doubt,   230
How sure you are my daughter. But, what music?   231

HELICANUS   My lord, I hear none.

PERICLES   None?
The music of the spheres! List, my Marina.   233

LYSIMACHUS
It is not good to cross him. Give him way.

PERICLES   Rarest sounds! Do ye not hear?

LYSIMACHUS
Music, my lord? I hear.

PERICLES   Most heavenly music!   236

It nips me unto list'ning, and thick slumber   237
Hangs upon mine eyes. Let me rest.   [He sleeps.]

LYSIMACHUS
A pillow for his head. So, leave him all.
Well, my companion friends,
If this but answer to my just belief,   241
I'll well remember you.   [Exeunt all but Pericles.]   242

        Diana [appears to Pericles as in a vision].

DIANA
My temple stands in Ephesus. Hie thee thither
And do upon mine altar sacrifice.
There, when my maiden priests are met together
Before the people all,
Reveal how thou at sea didst lose thy wife.
To mourn thy crosses, with thy daughter's, call   248
And give them repetition to the life.   249
Or perform my bidding, or thou livest in woe;   250
Do't, and happy, by my silver bow!
Awake, and tell thy dream.   [She disappears.]

PERICLES
Celestial Dian, goddess argentine,   253
I will obey thee.—Helicanus!

        [Enter Helicanus, Lysimachus, and Marina.]

HELICANUS   Sir?

PERICLES
My purpose was for Tarsus, there to strike
The inhospitable Cleon, but I am
For other service first. Toward Ephesus
Turn our blown sails; eftsoons I'll tell thee why.   258
[To Lysimachus] Shall we refresh us, sir, upon your
        shore
And give you gold for such provision
As our intents will need?

LYSIMACHUS   Sir,
With all my heart; and, when you come ashore,
I have another suit.

PERICLES   You shall prevail,
Were it to woo my daughter, for it seems
You have been noble towards her.

LYSIMACHUS   Sir, lend me your arm.

PERICLES   Come, my Marina.   Exeunt.

[5.2]

        [Enter Gower, before the temple of Diana of
        Ephesus; Thaisa standing near the altar, as high
        priestess; a number of virgins on each side;
        Cerimon and other inhabitants of Ephesus
        attending.]

203–4 **as loud . . . us** i.e., with hosannas as loud as the thunder with which the gods threaten us.   **207 Though . . . sleep** i.e., even though all doubts were laid to rest forever.   **211 godlike perfect** all-knowing like a god.   **the heir** i.e., if you can do this, you will show yourself to be the heir   **212 another life** i.e., the bringer of a new life   **213 Is it no more** Is nothing more required   **218 Mine own Helicanus** (Perhaps this should read "Mine own, Helicanus!"—i.e., she is my own daughter.)   **219 should have been** was thought to be, or, was intended to have been   **220 By** at the hands of   **221 justify in knowledge** acknowledge   **227 wild . . . beholding** elated and delirious in everything I see, or, possibly, unkempt, savage in appearance.   **230 doubt** (Or perhaps *dote*, be in a daze; the Quarto reads "doat.")   **231 sure** certainly   **233 music of the spheres** celestial harmony, supposedly produced by the ordered movements of the heavenly bodies. (Whether the music is to be heard in the theater is not clear.)   **236 I hear** (Lysimachus may hear music or may say this to humor Pericles and *give him way* [line 234]. Editors sometimes regard the word *music* in line 236 as a stage direction or assign *I hear* to Pericles.)

237 nips overpowers and compels   **241 but . . . belief** turns out as I expect it to   **242 remember** reward.   **242.1 Diana** (Perhaps she descends from the heavens and reascends at line 252.)   **248 crosses** misfortunes.   **call** lift your voice   **249 give . . . life** repeat them point for point.   **250 Or** Either   **253 argentine** silvery in appearance (as appropriate to the moon goddess)   **258 blown** inflated by the wind.   **eftsoons** shortly, later on
5.2. Location: The temple of Diana at Ephesus.
0.1 before the temple (Perhaps Gower reveals this scene, by means of a curtain, at line 17.)

GOWER

   Now our sands are almost run;
   More a little, and then dumb.   2
   This my last boon give me,
   For such kindness must relieve me:
   That you aptly will suppose   5
   What pageantry, what feats, what shows,
   What minstrelsy, and pretty din
   The regent made in Mytilin
   To greet the King. So he thrived   9
   That he is promised to be wived
   To fair Marina, but in no wise
   Till he had done his sacrifice   12
   As Dian bade; whereto being bound,   13
   The interim, pray you, all confound.   14
   In feathered briefness sails are filled,   15
   And wishes fall out as they're willed.
   At Ephesus the temple see,
   Our King and all his company.
   That he can hither come so soon
   Is by your fancies' thankful doom.   [*Exit.*]   20

❖

[5.3]

     [*Enter Pericles, with his train; Lysimachus,*
     Helicanus, Marina, and a lady.]

PERICLES

   Hail, Dian! To perform thy just command,
   I here confess myself the King of Tyre,
   Who, frighted from my country, did wed
   At Pentapolis the fair Thaisa.
   At sea in childbed died she, but brought forth
   A maid child called Marina, who, O goddess,   6
   Wears yet thy silver livery. She at Tarsus   7
   Was nursed with Cleon, who at fourteen years   8
   He sought to murder; but her better stars
   Brought her to Mytilene, 'gainst whose shore
   Riding, her fortunes brought the maid aboard us,   11
   Where, by her own most clear remembrance, she
   Made known herself my daughter.

THAISA   Voice and favor!   13
   You are, you are—O royal Pericles!   [*She faints.*]

PERICLES

   What means the nun? She dies! Help, gentlemen!

CERIMON   Noble sir,
   If you have told Diana's altar true,
   This is your wife.

PERICLES   Reverend appearer, no;   18
   I threw her overboard with these very arms.

CERIMON
   Upon this coast, I warrant you.

PERICLES   'Tis most certain.

CERIMON
   Look to the lady; Oh, she's but overjoyed.
   Early one blustering morn this lady was
   Thrown upon this shore. I oped the coffin,
   Found there rich jewels, recovered her, and placed her   24
   Here in Diana's temple.

PERICLES   May we see them?

CERIMON
   Great sir, they shall be brought you to my house,
   Whither I invite you. Look, Thaisa is
   Recovered.

THAISA [*rising*]   Oh, let me look!
   If he be none of mine, my sanctity   30
   Will to my sense bend no licentious ear,   31
   But curb it, spite of seeing.—O my lord,   32
   Are you not Pericles? Like him you spake,
   Like him you are. Did you not name a tempest,
   A birth, and death?

PERICLES   The voice of dead Thaisa!

THAISA
   That Thaisa am I, supposèd dead
   And drowned.

PERICLES
   Immortal Dian!

THAISA   Now I know you better.
   When we with tears parted Pentapolis,   39
   The King my father gave you such a ring.   40
                  [*She points to his ring.*]

PERICLES
   This, this! No more, you gods! Your present kindness
   Makes my past miseries sports. You shall do well   42
   That on the touching of her lips I may   43
   Melt and no more be seen.—Oh, come, be buried   44
   A second time within these arms!   [*They embrace.*]

MARINA [*kneeling*]   My heart
   Leaps to be gone into my mother's bosom.

PERICLES
   Look who kneels here! Flesh of thy flesh, Thaisa,
   Thy burden at the sea, and called Marina
   For she was yielded there.

THAISA   Blest, and mine own!   49
                  [*They embrace.*]

HELICANUS
   Hail, madam, and my queen!

THAISA   I know you not.

PERICLES
   You have heard me say, when I did fly from Tyre

---

2 **More . . . dumb** A little more of the story, and then I shall be silent.
5 **aptly** readily   9 **So he thrived** He (Lysimachus) fared so well
12 **he** i.e., Pericles   13 **bade** commanded   14 **confound** do away
with, omit.   15 **feathered** winged   20 **Is . . . doom** is thanks to the
consent (and willing participation) of your imaginations.
5.3. Location: Scene continues; the temple, as before.
6 **maid child** baby girl   7 **Wears . . . livery** i.e., is still a virgin.
8 **with Cleon** under Cleon's care   11 **Riding** (we) riding at anchor
13 **favor** face, appearance.   18 **Reverend appearer** You who appear
reverend

24 **recovered** revived   30–2 **If . . . seeing** If he is not my husband, my
holy way of life will lend no credence to my physical sense of sight
and my sensual inclination but will curb my longings (for marriage,
my lost life of domestic pleasure), despite what I see before me.
39 **parted** departed from   40.1 *She points to his ring* (Possibly Pericles included this ring among the jewels he laid in Thaisa's casket, or,
more probably, she may recognize it on his finger now.)   42 **sports**
mere amusements.   42–4 **You . . . seen** You gods would give me a
good death if, when I touch her lips with mine, I should die of happiness.   49 **For** because.   **yielded** brought forth, born

I left behind an ancient substitute.
Can you remember what I called the man?
I have named him oft.
THAISA   'Twas Helicanus then.
PERICLES   Still confirmation!
Embrace him, dear Thaisa, this is he.   [*They embrace.*]
Now do I long to hear how you were found,
How possibly preserved, and who to thank,   59
Besides the gods, for this great miracle.
THAISA
Lord Cerimon, my lord; this man,
Through whom the gods have shown their power,
     that can
From first to last resolve you.
PERICLES [*to Cerimon*]   Reverend sir,   63
The gods can have no mortal officer   64
More like a god than you. Will you deliver   65
How this dead queen re-lives?
CERIMON   I will, my lord.
Beseech you, first go with me to my house,
Where shall be shown you all was found with her,   68
How she came placed here in the temple,
No needful thing omitted.
PERICLES
Pure Dian, I bless thee for thy vision, and   71
Will offer night oblations to thee. Thaisa,   72
This prince, the fair betrothèd of your daughter,   73
Shall marry her at Pentapolis. And now
This ornament   75
Makes me look dismal will I clip to form;   76
And what this fourteen years no razor touched,
To grace thy marriage day, I'll beautify.

THAISA
Lord Cerimon hath letters of good credit, sir,   79
My father's dead.
PERICLES
Heavens make a star of him! Yet there, my queen,   81
We'll celebrate their nuptials, and ourselves
Will in that kingdom spend our following days.
Our son and daughter shall in Tyrus reign.
Lord Cerimon, we do our longing stay   85
To hear the rest untold. Sir, lead 's the way.   86
                                                       [*Exeunt.*]

[*Enter Gower.*]

GOWER
In Antiochus and his daughter you have heard
Of monstrous lust the due and just reward.
In Pericles, his queen, and daughter seen,
Although assailed with fortune fierce and keen,
Virtue preserved from fell destruction's blast,   91
Led on by heaven, and crowned with joy at last.
In Helicanus may you well descry
A figure of truth, of faith, of loyalty.
In reverend Cerimon there well appears
The worth that learnèd charity aye wears.
For wicked Cleon and his wife, when fame   97
Had spread his cursèd deed to the honored name   98
Of Pericles, to rage the city turn,   99
That him and his they in his palace burn;   100
The gods for murder seemèd so content
To punish—although not done, but meant.   102
So, on your patience evermore attending,
New joy wait on you! Here our play has ending.
                                                          [*Exit.*]

---

59 **possibly** by what possible means   63 **resolve you** satisfy your curiosity.   64 **mortal officer** human agent   65 **deliver** recount   68 **all was** all that was   71 **thy vision** appearing to me in a vision   72 **night oblations** nightly sacrifices, evening prayers   73 **This prince** Lysimachus   75 **ornament** i.e., hair and beard   76 **Makes** which makes.   **to form** to proper shape

79 **of good credit** trustworthy   81 **there** i.e., in Pentapolis   85 **do . . . stay** merely postpone the completion of our desires   86 **untold** that is not yet told.   91 **fell** cruel   97 **fame** report; common talk   98 **his . . . deed** i.e., the deed done by him and his family, especially Dionyza, against   99 **turn** did turn   100 **That** so that.   **and his** and his family, notably Dionyza   102 **although . . . meant** i.e., even though the crime was only intended and not actually carried out.

Cymbeline

Cymbeline's remarkable blending of romantic narrative and quasi-history urges us to think about the play as a genealogical fantasy about British origins. By choosing a setting in ancient Britain, the play searches for a national identity through a rediscovered national history. To be truly British, Britain must have a history, a story about its origins. Chroniclers since Geoffrey of Monmouth (c. 1136) had undertaken to provide Britain with a mythical past, from the supposed settlement of the British Isles by a great-grandson of Aeneas down through the days of Roman occupation around the beginning of the Christian Era. The accounts were by and large fabulous, and were under increasing pressure of skepticism in Shakespeare's day. Perhaps for those very reasons, they offered rich material for poetic and dramatic exploration. How do these myths of origin enter into the dramatic world of *Cymbeline*?

One possible line of inquiry is to ask how the play dramatizes anxieties about national identity in relation to gender identities. As Coppélia Kahn, Janet Adelman, and others have argued, Imogen's sufferings of virtual rape and subsequent slander by a scheming Italian (Iachimo) may suggest the island nation's fear of invasion and mistrust of Catholic Italy. Conversely, the saga of Posthumus Leonatus, as he loses faith in his wife, attempts to arrange her murder, and eventually repents what he has done, suggests a testing and definition of British manhood through which the final emergence of Posthumus as Britain's martial champion is emblematic of the emergence of Britain as a specifically masculine nation. (Imogen's prospects of inheriting the kingdom from her father, Cymbeline, are set aside by the rediscovery of her two lost brothers.) The vexed relationship of Britain to Rome points to an ambivalent feeling about the period of Roman occupation, and, more generally, to Britain's indebtedness to the cultural legacy of ancient Rome as opposed to its own nascent literary nationalism. The Roman presence may also have prompted Shakespeare's

audience to think of their own monarch, James I, and his aspirations to a kind of neo-Augustan empire in the shape of a united Britain and a pan-European peace. In a period of difficult transition, we see glimmerings at least of an emerging Britain that is able to appropriate the virtues of Rome for its own national identity.

The genre of *Cymbeline* can be suggested by such critical terms as romance, tragicomedy, and the comedy of forgiveness. As in *Pericles, The Winter's Tale*, and other late plays, Shakespeare turns to the improbable fictions of romance: a stepmother-queen skilled in the use of poisons and envious of her fair and virtuous stepdaughter (as in *Snow White*), lost sons recognized by the inevitable birthmark, the reunion of many persons long separated by exile and wandering, the intervention of the gods by means of a riddling and inane prophecy. These are the distinguishing features of English romance in the 1580s, a titillating vogue exploited by Robert Greene and other professional writers of the period. From two romantic plays of the 1580s—*Sir Clyomon and Sir Clamydes* and *The Rare Triumphs of Love and Fortune*—Shakespeare may, in fact, have drawn source material. Why did he turn to such old-fashioned models in 1608–1610? The choice has puzzled many critics and has prompted them to speak condescendingly of Shakespeare's dotage or to assign parts of the play (notably the descent of Jupiter) to some other dramatist.

Shakespeare nevertheless courted the improbabilities, even the deliberate absurdities, of romance with a serious artistic purpose. In part, he was responding to a new literary fashion, evident especially in the private theaters, for a tragicomedy of refined sensibility—a literary fashion that produced Francis Beaumont and John Fletcher's *Philaster*. This play of about 1609 features, like *Cymbeline*, a rapidly moving and ingeniously woven plot of separation and reunion, a king's daughter betrothed by her father to a churl and then wrongly accused of infidelity, a young maiden in male disguise, and other comparable details. Whether *Cymbeline* preceded or followed *Philaster* is a matter that is difficult to determine, since *Cymbeline* can be dated only approximately as from 1608–1610 on grounds of style; in any case, Shakespeare's fascination with romance goes back at least to *All's Well That Ends Well* (c. 1601–1604) and *Pericles* (c. 1606–1608). His experiments in the genre must be viewed as innovative and unique. Despite the affinities to Fletcherian tragicomedy, Shakespeare never indulges in the cloying sensationalism, the exaggerated heightening of exotic emotion, and (except in *The Winter's Tale*) the trickery of concealing essential information from the audience, such as we find in works of Beaumont and Fletcher. Shakespeare's interest in romantic improbability is related to the serious motif of redemption, of an unexpected and undeserved second chance for erring humanity.

The tragic possibilities are manifold. Cymbeline, like Lear (another king from British legendary history in Raphael Holinshed's *Chronicles*, 1578), tyrannically repulses a virtuous daughter and rewards the vicious members of his family, with predictably unhappy consequences. Posthumus Leonatus, like Othello, commands the death of his beloved mistress because he believes a groundless but cunningly presented accusation of her infidelity; finally, concluding that he has destroyed the only person capable of giving order to his life, he despairingly longs for death. Whereas in a similar situation Lear and Othello suffer the tragic consequences of their choice, Cymbeline and Posthumus are spared. Some benign force, integral to the world of this play, prevents fallible mortals from pursuing their misguided intentions to the point of irreversible injury. Posthumus relies for his vengeance on the virtuous Pisanio, who cannot bring himself to slay Imogen. The Queen's box of "poison," given ultimately to Imogen by the well-meaning but duped Pisanio, is only a sleeping potion concocted by that kindly manipulator behind the scenes, Doctor Cornelius. These fortunate avoidances of disaster recall other such narrow escapes in *Much Ado About Nothing, All's Well That Ends Well*, and *Measure for Measure*. They also anticipate similar events in *The Winter's Tale*.

Because *Cymbeline* begins with dilemmas like those of *King Lear* and *Othello*, the prevailing tone is at first serious. (The editors of the 1623 First Folio printed the play among the tragedies.) The King's behavior toward Imogen and her virtuous but nonaristocratic husband, Posthumus, is tyrannical. Disinterested observers condemn the wicked Queen's dominance over Cymbeline and laugh privately at the Queen's cowardly and ridiculous son Cloten. A good man like Belarius suffers lifelong banishment from the envious court and spends his exile dwelling in caves. Many conventional features of romantic narrative—wandering and return, loss and rediscovery, apparent death and rebirth—are set in motion by the need to escape from a court dominated by the wicked Queen. One by one, honest persons of the play—Posthumus, Imogen, Pisanio—leave society in disfavor to be reunited in the wild landscape of Belarius and his foster sons. Italy is no better a place than the English court. Its evil genius is Iachimo, apostle of animal appetite, duplicity, and cynical indifference to human values.

Despite the prevailing tragic mood at first, there are promises of brighter prospects. Posthumus's birth is attended by wondrous circumstances that would appear to single him out for an extraordinary career. In the first scene, moreover, we learn that the King's only two sons were stolen from their nursery in their infancy—an obvious hint that they will turn up sooner or later. Cloten, too, strikes us as a ludicrous suitor for Imogen, the type of buffoonish rival appropriate to a love comedy. Because he is witless, superficial, and preoccupied with clothes, he deserves to be exposed and ridiculed. Even his death is grotesquely comic. He acts as a foil or caricature to Posthumus, in whose clothes he is erroneously taken by Imogen to be her dead husband; the outward resemblance of the two men suggests to us that Posthumus has not been unlike Cloten when he has suspected Imogen of betraying him and has vowed revenge. Cloten's death signals an end to Posthumus's disposition to be fooled by appearances.

The initial somber mood, with its threat of tragic outcome, is further lightened by the juxtaposition of sorrow and hope. When Arviragus and Guiderius mourn the "death" of Imogen with an exquisite song on the vanity of human striving, we respond to the appropriateness of the sentiment and yet qualify our sorrow with our consoling knowledge that she has really taken a sleeping potion. Similarly, when Posthumus jests eloquently about death with his jailer and prepares to find his only freedom in surcease, we cannot ignore Jupiter's assurance of eventual redress. As in *Measure for Measure*, suffering and regret are framed in the benign context of a providential design that the audience alone can fully appreciate.

Tragicomedy threatens and consoles at the same time. The chief source of anxiety is Posthumus's renunciation of Imogen. The sensationalism of the plot derives in part from the use of the "wager" motif found in several Italianate *novelle*, such as the ninth tale of the second day in Giovanni Boccaccio's *Decameron*. The psychological portrait of Posthumus's wavering and fall, like that of Othello or Leontes, is intense and ugly, fraught with grotesque images of sexual coupling. As with Othello and Leontes, Posthumus is threatened by his wife's sexuality and is unable to respond securely to her offered love that is appropriately sensual and spiritual. He is comfortable only when he thinks of her as sexually restrained even in her marriage bed, praying forbearance of her husband with "A pudency so rosy the sweet view on't / Might well have warmed old Saturn" (2.5.11–12). He is aroused by virginal unresponsiveness but repelled by too great a responsiveness. Such unbalanced expectations leave him prone to insinuations that women practice deception. Once Imogen has been made to appear carnal to him, she becomes monstrous and insatiable in his imagination. He conjures up the imagined sexual triumph of Iachimo in animalistic terms: "Perchance he spoke not, but, / Like a full-acorned boar, a German one, / Cried 'Oh!' and mounted" (lines 15–17). Like Othello, he insists on being proved a cuckold; once he has experienced jealousy, he can expect only one conclusion. He longs "to tear her limbmeal," and like Lear he would violently destroy "The woman's part in me" (2.4.150; 2.5.20).

Posthumus suffers from dark fantasies about women such as we find elsewhere in Shakespeare. Because he regards women as male property, he is all too ready to engage in a contest with other males "in praise of our country mistresses" and to boast that Imogen is (in the terms of the contest) "more fair, virtuous, wise, chaste, constant, qualified, and less attemptable" than any other lady alive (1.4.57–61). The results are predictably disastrous, as they were earlier in Shakespeare's *The Rape of Lucrece*. By engaging in the objectification of women, Posthumus betrays his emotional kinship to Iachimo, who takes advantage of his concealment in Imogen's bedchamber to catalogue in clinical detail her physical charms along with the furniture of the room itself (2.2). Posthumus's misogynistic outburst against women as "half-workers" in the act of generation (2.5.1 ff.) reveals his fear of betrayal by all women (including his own mother) and hence his own helpless vulnerability to what he supposes to be women's lying, flattering, deceiving, "Lust and rank thoughts," revenges, "Nice longing, slanders, mutability, / All faults that have a name, nay, that hell knows" (lines 22–7). This male phobia is deeply sculpted in the male world of *Cymbeline*, for we see it also in Cloten's warped desire to possess Imogen and in Cymbeline's troubled patriarchal relations with his daughter and his domineering wife. In Posthumus, this typically male perversity threatens disaster and demands either a tragic ending or the contrived happy ending of tragicomedy. His failure places a special burden on Imogen to endure his frailty and to redeem it; only through her can Posthumus receive a second chance. Meantime, his failure has raised a familiarly Shakespearean question about his responsibility for his fall. How could he have avoided accusing Imogen falsely?

Powerful forces militate against Posthumus. Iachimo is a plausible villain, in the vein of Don John (*Much Ado About Nothing*), Iago (*Othello*), and Edmund (*King Lear*). Like them, he plots to arouse envy and dissension in others, by means of appearances falsely presented to the senses. We can readily understand him in human terms as a quarrelsome and lecherous man, and yet his sinister delight in mischief also suggests a more all-encompassing and diabolical evil. His contention is that every woman has her price (and every man, too). When he discovers in Imogen a wholesomeness that will not yield to his insinuations, he seeks to destroy her as a dangerous refutation of his low premise about human nature. He states the confrontation between them in cosmic terms: "Though this a heavenly angel, hell is here" (2.2.50). He does not, to be sure, boast gleefully to the audience or dominate the play as Iago does; moreover, he himself experiences the beneficent change brought about by the play's happy ending and speaks in praise of Imogen's virtue. As befits a tragicomedy, he is more sinister than potent, almost at times a travesty of a tragic villain. Nevertheless, in his scenes of villainy, his function is that of a diabolical tempter working through humanity's frail senses. His use of the ring as evidence recalls the handkerchief in *Othello*. Iachimo creates a minutely circumstantial inference of Imogen's transgression and lets Posthumus's inclination to believe the worst do the rest.

Like Othello, then, Posthumus must bear the blame for his loss of faith. The tempter can prevail upon his senses, but humanity's own wavering heart chooses evil. Trustworthy observers perceive Posthumus's fallacy and indicate the correct response; as Philario says, "This is not strong enough to be believed / Of one persuaded well of" (2.4.134–5). True faith urges that, being what she is, Imogen could not do the thing alleged. She is, like Helena and Desdemona before her, a virtuous woman who responds to her undeserved tribulations with forbearance (though even her patience has a limit, and she, too, is capable of overreacting and misjudging). She overbalances male faithlessness with her forgiveness. Her perseverance in virtue confounds Iachimo's thesis and rescues Posthumus from his worst self. Iachimo and she are spiritual contestants for the allegiance of Posthumus's faith. She triumphs, not through Posthumus's choice (which is for evil), but through her own unassailable goodness. Belatedly, too, Posthumus makes the amends that are necessary if we are to accept him as the restored hero. He forgives Imogen even before he knows of her innocence, seeks death as an atonement, and moves by degrees through sin to regret, confession of guilt, and penance. His peasant costume in Act 5 signals the resignation of worldly desire he must achieve to be worthy of an almost miraculous second chance. As fallen man, he can never truly deserve that mercy, but he can strive at least to atone for what he has done.

The story of King Cymbeline's long-lost sons is similarly tragicomic and is even more explicitly indebted to the conventions of romance with its motifs of banishment, wandering, and eventual recognition and reunion. The sylvan setting of this romantic narrative lends to the second half of the play a primal vigor and mystery (as also in *The Winter's Tale*). Arviragus and Guiderius remind us of medieval legends about Parzival; that is, like Parzival, they are young princes raised in a wilderness, lacking courtly training and yet possessing an "invisible instinct" (4.2.179) that prompts them to assert their royal blood. Ignoring their stepfather's warnings about the ingratitude and decadence of the courtly society he has abandoned, the princes long to prove themselves in deeds of chivalry. They are a rejuvenating force in this play, bringing together the ideals of medieval knighthood and the unsullied strength of their sylvan world. Cloten, that effete semblance of a courtier and their foil in every respect, is appropriately killed by these agents of "divine Nature" (line 172). They cherish Imogen as one of their own and grieve for her seeming death with the vivid immediacy of those who have lived with nature. Her seeming death and reawakening is for them something like the restorative cycle of the seasons, bringing a renewal of natural vigor that nicely complements the spiritual grace she embodies for Posthumus. Her name to them is appropriately "Fidele." Old Belarius's reconciliation with Cymbeline signals an end to political injustice, still another consequence of humanity's fallen condition for which grace must be provided.

The story of the war between Britain and Rome, derived in part from Holinshed's *Chronicles*, contributes also to the process of spiritual rebirth. The war sets in motion a series of apparently unrelated events, including the return to Britain of Posthumus and Iachimo, without which the play's happy conclusion would be impossible. Although the war itself is destructive and is supported chiefly by Cloten and the Queen (whose patriotic speeches show us just how hollow a thing patriotism can be), the war does lead ultimately to new life for Britain, as well as for the romantic lovers. Sudden turns in the battle, especially when an old man and two boys defend a narrow lane against an army, are seen as marvels directed by some higher power. In the benign aftermath of peace, the King, no longer misled by evil counselors, finds reconciliation with his daughter and her husband, as well as with Rome. The final scene, in which the seeming accidents of fortune are unraveled, is a structural tour de force of comic discovery.

The three main plots of *Cymbeline*—of Posthumus and Imogen, of the King's lost sons, and of the war between Britain and Rome—may seem outwardly unconnected with one another. Certainly, the play ranges over a wide geographical space and introduces a host of characters, many of whom never meet until the final scene. Yet the three plots are unified by being structurally like one another. In each, we perceive a pattern of fall from innocence, followed by conflict and eventual redemption. Posthumus is tempted into a loss of faith and attempted murder, from which he recovers through penance. The saga of the King's sons provides a secular equivalent in its story of estrangement, mistaken identity, and eventual recovery of loss. Politically, Britain is alienated from Rome through the machinations of the Queen only to rediscover

after many years a new harmony. The plots impinge on one another in ways that seem contrived (as, for example, when the accidents of war finally bring together Imogen, Posthumus, and Iachimo in the presence of Cymbeline), and yet we understand at last that the contrivance is providential and benign, intended to test humanity and then reward those who have persevered or at least have found true contrition.

Despite the symmetries of structure among the various plots of *Cymbeline*, the play manages to keep us constantly off balance. Its tragicomic pattern of innocence, conflict, and eventual redemption is repeatedly disturbed by the odd juxtapositions of imperial Rome, Renaissance Rome, and prehistoric Britain contrived from chronicle, romance, and pastoral. The play yields weird moments, such as Imogen's awakening near Milford Haven to find herself next to Cloten's headless body and to mistake it for Posthumus's body (4.2.294–335), or Jupiter's descent to earth on the back of an eagle (5.4.92 ff.). The play's denouement relies on the unraveling of an absurdly infantile riddle. The final accommodation of Britain into the Roman empire may add topical complexity by casting oblique glances in the direction of King James I of England and his dream of assuming a central role in the forging of a pacified Europe. Generically, the play is a deliberate mingling of history and romance, however successfully it may attempt to harmonize these genres; formally, it opts for instability through the intrusion of the comic into the serious. An implicit relationship between the psychosexual in the private realm and the political in the public realm is everywhere apparent and yet elusive.

Through such boldly experimental means, Shakespeare creates his dramatic world of accident and design, of odd juxtapositions and symmetry. The dramatist chooses by experimental and outrageous means to bring together disparate elements and to flaunt the lack of a perfectly smooth resolution, even while suggesting an overall sense of purpose and harmony that human witnesses can only imperfectly comprehend. Jupiter becomes the spokesman for a providential view in his role as *deus ex machina*—literally illustrating that term, since he "descends" from the stage roof by means of some mechanical device. The scene of this divine intervention (5.4) is so blatantly unrealistic that, as we have seen, many critics have wished to exonerate Shakespeare of having written it, but this very unreality is the key to the play's ending. Jupiter places the human suffering of the play in a larger perspective: "Whom best I love I cross, to make my gift, / The more delayed, delighted. Be content" (5.4.101–2). In the tragicomic view, suffering is the manifestation of a design engineered and supervised by a loving deity to test and strengthen humankind. Understood as such, the test affirms Imogen's strength, shows Posthumus a reason to cherish what he would otherwise destroy, and even reclaims the evil agent by whom the test had been put in operation. As Caius Lucius insists to the long-suffering Fidele, "Some falls are means the happier to arise" (4.2.406).

In the theater, *Cymbeline* calls for sensational effects. The nineteenth century often went for opulent splendor, as in Henry Irving's expensively realistic renditions of Celtic Britain and ancient Rome in his 1896 production at the Lyceum Theater, London. More recent interpretations have preferred theatrical wizardry of a more updated sort. Robin Phillips, at Stratford, Canada, in 1986, set the battle scenes in World War I garb, with Jupiter as a flying ace in goggles, appearing from above in a burst of light.

Wales was the primitive land of Tarzan. Directors have to choose whether to play Jupiter's epiphany as straight romance, emphasizing the wonder of it, or send the scene up as campy impossibility; if audiences laugh, the actors will go for parody and exaggeration. Since the play itself daringly courts improbability, styles of performance are likely to succeed best when the production is consciously aware of its own contrivances. Romance becomes metatheater; the theatrical space becomes one of magical virtuosity, inspiring in audiences an assent to the "truth" of the story as one of theatrical artifice at its best and as its own best excuse.

Cymbeline

[*Dramatis Personae*

CYMBELINE, *King of Britain*
QUEEN, *wife of Cymbeline*
CLOTEN, *her son by a former husband*
IMOGEN, *daughter of Cymbeline by a former queen*
POSTHUMUS LEONATUS, *a gentleman, Imogen's husband*
BELARIUS, *a banished lord, disguised as Morgan*
GUIDERIUS, ⎫ *sons of Cymbeline, disguised as Polydore*
ARVIRAGUS, ⎭ *and Cadwal, supposed sons of Morgan*

PISANIO, *servant of Posthumus*
CORNELIUS, *a physician*
Two LORDS *attending Cloten*
Two GENTLEMEN *of Cymbeline's court*
HELEN, *a lady attending Imogen*
Another LADY *attending Imogen, or possibly the same*
A LADY *attending the Queen*
A British LORD
Two British CAPTAINS
Two JAILERS
Two MESSENGERS

PHILARIO, *friend of Posthumus,* ⎫
IACHIMO, *friend of Philario,*   ⎬ *Italians*
A FRENCHMAN, *friend of Philario* ⎭

CAIUS LUCIUS, *general of the Roman forces*
Two Roman SENATORS
A TRIBUNE
A Roman CAPTAIN
Philharmonus, *a* SOOTHSAYER

JUPITER
The Ghost of SICILIUS *Leonatus, father of Posthumus*
The Ghost of Leonatus's MOTHER
The Ghosts of Leonatus's two BROTHERS

Lords, Ladies, Attendants, Musicians attending Cloten, a Dutchman, a Spaniard, Senators, Tribunes, Captains, and Soldiers

SCENE: *Britain; Italy*]

1.1

Enter two Gentlemen.

FIRST GENTLEMAN
You do not meet a man but frowns. Our bloods   1
No more obey the heavens than our courtiers'
Still seem as does the King's.

SECOND GENTLEMAN   But what's the matter?   3

FIRST GENTLEMAN
His daughter, and the heir of 's kingdom, whom
He purposed to his wife's sole son—a widow   5
That late he married—hath referred herself   6
Unto a poor but worthy gentleman. She's wedded,
Her husband banished, she imprisoned. All
Is outward sorrow, though I think the King   9
Be touched at very heart.

SECOND GENTLEMAN   None but the King?

FIRST GENTLEMAN
He that hath lost her, too. So is the Queen,   11
That most desired the match. But not a courtier,
Although they wear their faces to the bent   13
Of the King's looks, hath a heart that is not
Glad at the thing they scowl at.

SECOND GENTLEMAN   And why so?

FIRST GENTLEMAN
He that hath missed the Princess is a thing
Too bad for bad report, and he that hath her—
I mean, that married her, alack, good man!
And therefore banished—is a creature such
As, to seek through the regions of the earth
For one his like, there would be something failing   21
In him that should compare. I do not think   22
So fair an outward and such stuff within   23
Endows a man but he.

SECOND GENTLEMAN   You speak him far.   24

FIRST GENTLEMAN
I do extend him, sir, within himself,   25
Crush him together rather than unfold   26
His measure duly.

SECOND GENTLEMAN What's his name and birth?   27

FIRST GENTLEMAN
I cannot delve him to the root. His father   28
Was called Sicilius, who did join his honor   29
Against the Romans with Cassibelan,   30

But had his titles by Tenantius, whom   31
He served with glory and admired success,
So gained the sur-addition Leonatus;   33
And had, besides this gentleman in question,
Two other sons, who in the wars o'th' time
Died with their swords in hand; for which their father,
Then old and fond of issue, took such sorrow   37
That he quit being, and his gentle lady,   38
Big of this gentleman our theme, deceased   39
As he was born. The King he takes the babe   40
To his protection, calls him Posthumus Leonatus,
Breeds him and makes him of his bedchamber,   42
Puts to him all the learnings that his time   43
Could make him the receiver of, which he took,
As we do air, fast as 'twas ministered,
And in 's spring became a harvest, lived in court—   46
Which rare it is to do—most praised, most loved,
A sample to the youngest, to th' more mature   48
A glass that feated them, and to the graver   49
A child that guided dotards. To his mistress,   50
For whom he now is banished, her own price   51
Proclaims how she esteemed him; and his virtue
By her election may be truly read   53
What kind of man he is.

SECOND GENTLEMAN   I honor him
Even out of your report. But pray you, tell me,   55
Is she sole child to th' King?

FIRST GENTLEMAN   His only child.
He had two sons; if this be worth your hearing,
Mark it: The eldest of them at three years old,
I'th' swaddling-clothes the other, from their nursery
Were stol'n, and to this hour no guess in knowledge   60
Which way they went.

SECOND GENTLEMAN   How long is this ago?

FIRST GENTLEMAN Some twenty years.

SECOND GENTLEMAN
That a king's children should be so conveyed,
So slackly guarded, and the search so slow
That could not trace them!

FIRST GENTLEMAN   Howso'er 'tis strange,
Or that the negligence may well be laughed at,
Yet is it true, sir.

SECOND GENTLEMAN   I do well believe you.

FIRST GENTLEMAN
We must forbear. Here comes the gentleman,   69
The Queen, and Princess.   *Exeunt.*

Enter the Queen, Posthumus, and Imogen.

1.1. Location: Britain. At the court of King Cymbeline.
1–3 Our . . . King's The constitutions and dispositions of us mortals are not more obedient to the influence of the heavenly bodies than our courtiers' demeanors and looks follow those of the King. **5 purposed to** intended for **6 late** lately. **referred** given (in marriage) **9 outward** mere pretense of (as explained in lines 12–22) **11 He . . . her** i.e., Cloten, the Queen's son, Imogen's unsuccessful wooer. (Also in line 16.) **13 bent** inclination **21 his like** like him **22 him . . . compare** anyone chosen for comparison. **23 stuff** (1) substance (2) fabric (as the imagery of lines 26–7 further suggests) **24 speak him far** go far in praising him. **25 I . . . himself** I expand his virtues within the limits of what he actually is **26–7 unfold . . . duly** disclose his dimensions to the degree that he merits. **28 delve . . . root** i.e., account fully for his lineage. **29 join his honor** give his honorable assistance in arms **30 Cassibelan** Cymbeline's uncle; see 3.1.5. (According to Holinshed, Cassibelan was Cymbeline's great-uncle, being younger brother and successor to King Lud.)

31 Tenantius Cymbeline's father, son of King Lud. (In Holinshed, Tenantius is Cassibelan's nephew.) **33 sur-addition** additional title, surname. **Leonatus** lion-born **37 fond of issue** devoted to his children **38 quit being** died. **gentle** noble **39 Big . . . theme** pregnant with this Posthumus we are talking about **40 King he** i.e., King **42 Breeds** raises, educates. **of his bedchamber** one of his intimate retinue **43 Puts to** sets before. **time** time of life, age **46 in 's . . . harvest** i.e., in his youth became ripe in learning **48 sample** example **49 A glass . . . them** a mirror that furnished them an image of virtue **49–50 to . . . dotards** i.e., to older courtiers he offered wise example as if a child were to instruct doddering old men. **50 To** As for; or, In the eyes of **51 her own price** the price she willingly paid (of her father's hostility) **53 election** choice (of him) **55 out of** judging by **60 guess in knowledge** credible conjecture **69 forbear** stop talking and withdraw.

QUEEN
 No, be assured you shall not find me, daughter,
 After the slander of most stepmothers,   72
 Evil-eyed unto you. You're my prisoner, but
 Your jailer shall deliver you the keys
 That lock up your restraint. For you, Posthumus, 75
 So soon as I can win th'offended King
 I will be known your advocate. Marry, yet   77
 The fire of rage is in him, and 'twere good
 You leaned unto his sentence with what patience 79
 Your wisdom may inform you.
POSTHUMUS   Please Your Highness, 80
 I will from hence today.
QUEEN   You know the peril.
 I'll fetch a turn about the garden, pitying
 The pangs of barred affections, though the King
 Hath charged you should not speak together. *Exit.*
IMOGEN   Oh,
 Dissembling courtesy! How fine this tyrant
 Can tickle where she wounds! My dearest husband,
 I something fear my father's wrath, but nothing— 87
 Always reserved my holy duty—what   88
 His rage can do on me. You must be gone,
 And I shall here abide the hourly shot
 Of angry eyes, not comforted to live   91
 But that there is this jewel in the world
 That I may see again.
POSTHUMUS   My queen, my mistress!
 Oh, lady, weep no more, lest I give cause   94
 To be suspected of more tenderness   95
 Than doth become a man. I will remain   96
 The loyal'st husband that did e'er plight troth;
 My residence in Rome at one Philario's,
 Who to my father was a friend, to me
 Known but by letter; thither write, my queen,
 And with mine eyes I'll drink the words you send,
 Though ink be made of gall.

     Enter Queen.

QUEEN   Be brief, I pray you.
 If the King come, I shall incur I know not
 How much of his displeasure. [*Aside*] Yet I'll move him
 To walk this way. I never do him wrong   105
 But he does buy my injuries, to be friends, 106
 Pays dear for my offenses.   [*Exit.*] 107
POSTHUMUS [*to Imogen*] Should we be taking leave
 As long a term as yet we have to live,
 The loathness to depart would grow. Adieu!
IMOGEN Nay, stay a little!
 Were you but riding forth to air yourself, 112

Such parting were too petty. Look here, love:
This diamond was my mother's. Take it, heart,
But keep it till you woo another wife
When Imogen is dead.
   [*She gives a ring, or puts it on his finger.*]
POSTHUMUS   How, how? Another?
 You gentle gods, give me but this I have,
 And cere up my embracements from a next 118
 With bonds of death! Remain, remain thou here 119
 While sense can keep it on. And, sweetest, fairest, 120
 As I my poor self did exchange for you   121
 To your so infinite loss, so in our trifles   122
 I still win of you. For my sake wear this.   123
 It is a manacle of love; I'll place it
 Upon this fairest prisoner.
   [*He puts a bracelet upon her arm.*]
IMOGEN   O the gods!
 When shall we see again?

   Enter Cymbeline and lords.

POSTHUMUS   Alack, the King!   126
CYMBELINE [*to Posthumus*]
 Thou basest thing, avoid hence, from my sight! 127
 If after this command thou freight the court 128
 With thy unworthiness, thou diest. Away!
 Thou'rt poison to my blood.
POSTHUMUS   The gods protect you,
 And bless the good remainders of the court! 131
 I am gone.   *Exit.*
IMOGEN There cannot be a pinch in death 132
 More sharp than this is.
CYMBELINE   O disloyal thing,
 That shouldst repair my youth, thou heap'st 134
 A year's age on me.
IMOGEN   I beseech you, sir, 135
 Harm not yourself with your vexation.
 I am senseless of your wrath; a touch more rare 137
 Subdues all pangs, all fears.
CYMBELINE   Past grace? Obedience?
IMOGEN
 Past hope and in despair; that way past grace. 139
CYMBELINE
 That mightst have had the sole son of my queen!
IMOGEN
 O blessèd, that I might not! I chose an eagle 141

---

72 After the slander according to what is slanderously told **75 For** As for **77 Marry** i.e., Indeed. (Originally, "by the Virgin Mary.") **79 leaned unto** deferred to **80 inform** instill in **87 something** somewhat. **nothing** not in the least **88 Always . . . duty** although never forgetting my sacred duty to him. (Though dutiful and even fearful, Imogen will not let her father's rage alter her determination.) **91 not . . . live** finding no comfort in living **94–6 lest . . . man** i.e., lest I, too, shed tears, which would be unmanly in me. **105–7 I . . . offenses** Whenever I wrong him, he interprets those injuries as kindnesses and submits to them in order to remain on good terms. **112 air yourself** take some fresh air

118 cere up wrap in cerecloth or waxed cloth used for wrapping a dead body; perhaps with a play on sealing a document with wax. (See *bonds* in the next line.) **a next** another wife **119 Remain** (The ring will remind him of Imogen always.) **120 sense** sensory feeling. **it** (Said of the ring.) **121 exchange** (In their wedding vows, they have given themselves to each other.) **122 trifles** i.e., love tokens **123 I . . . you** I still am enriched in the exchange, receive better than I give. **126 see** see each other **127 avoid hence** begone **128 freight** burden **131 remainders of** those who remain at **132 pinch** pang **134 repair** restore **134–5 thou . . . on me** you've added a year to my age. **137 senseless of** insensible to. **a touch** a feeling (of love for Posthumus and pain at his banishment) **139 despair . . . grace** (Imogen puns bitterly on grace, by which the King meant "gracious dutifulness"; in her religious metaphor, to despair is to be beyond God's grace.) **141 blessèd** (Imogen continues the religious paradox: she is *blessèd* in her love, though *past grace*, or damned, in terms of the King's favor.)

And did avoid a puttock.   142

CYMBELINE
  Thou took'st a beggar, wouldst have made my throne
  A seat for baseness.

IMOGEN   No, I rather added
  A luster to it.

CYMBELINE   O thou vile one!

IMOGEN   Sir,
  It is your fault that I have loved Posthumus.
  You bred him as my playfellow, and he is
  A man worth any woman, overbuys me   148
  Almost the sum he pays.

CYMBELINE   What, art thou mad?   149

IMOGEN
  Almost, sir. Heaven restore me! Would I were
  A neatherd's daughter, and my Leonatus   151
  Our neighbor shepherd's son!

        Enter Queen.

CYMBELINE   Thou foolish thing!—
  [To the Queen] They were again together. You have
      done
  Not after our command. Away with her   154
  And pen her up.

QUEEN   Beseech your patience.—Peace,   155
  Dear lady daughter, peace!—Sweet sovereign,
  Leave us to ourselves, and make yourself some
      comfort
  Out of your best advice.

CYMBELINE   Nay, let her languish   158
  A drop of blood a day, and, being aged,   159
  Die of this folly!   Exit [with lords].

QUEEN   Fie, you must give way.   160

        Enter Pisanio.

  Here is your servant.—How now, sir? What news?

PISANIO
  My lord your son drew on my master.

QUEEN   Ha?   162
  No harm, I trust, is done?

PISANIO   There might have been,
  But that my master rather played than fought
  And had no help of anger. They were parted   165
  By gentlemen at hand.

QUEEN   I am very glad on't.   166

IMOGEN
  Your son's my father's friend; he takes his part   167
  To draw upon an exile. Oh, brave sir!   168

I would they were in Afric both together,   169
  Myself by with a needle, that I might prick   170
  The goer-back.—Why came you from your master?

PISANIO
  On his command. He would not suffer me   172
  To bring him to the haven, left these notes
  Of what commands I should be subject to
  When't pleased you to employ me.

QUEEN [to Imogen]   This hath been
  Your faithful servant. I dare lay mine honor   176
  He will remain so.

PISANIO   I humbly thank Your Highness.

QUEEN [to Imogen]   Pray, walk awhile.   179

IMOGEN [to Pisanio]   About some half hour hence,
  Pray you, speak with me. You shall at least
  Go see my lord aboard. For this time leave me.

                                        Exeunt.

                    ❧

1.[2]

        Enter Cloten and two Lords.

FIRST LORD   Sir, I would advise you to shift a shirt. The   1
  violence of action hath made you reek as a sacrifice.
  Where air comes out, air comes in; there's none
  abroad so wholesome as that you vent.   4

CLOTEN   If my shirt were bloody, then to shift it. Have   5
  I hurt him?

SECOND LORD [aside]   No, faith, not so much as his   7
  patience.   8

FIRST LORD   Hurt him? His body's a passable carcass if   9
  he be not hurt. It is a thoroughfare for steel if it be not   10
  hurt.

SECOND LORD [aside]   His steel was in debt; it went o'th'   12
  backside the town.   13

CLOTEN   The villain would not stand me.   14

SECOND LORD [aside]   No, but he fled forward still,   15
  toward your face.   16

FIRST LORD   Stand you? You have land enough of your
  own, but he added to your having, gave you some   18
  ground.   19

SECOND LORD [aside]   As many inches as you have   20
  oceans. Puppies!   21

---

142 **puttock** kite, bird of prey.   148–9 **overbuys . . . pays** pays more
for me than I am worth by almost as much as the price he pays
(which is his banishment).   149 **mad** insane. (But Imogen uses the
word to mean "mad with grief"; compare with her pun on *grace* in
line 139.)   151 **neatherd's** cowherd's   154 **after** according to
155 **Beseech** I beseech   158 **best advice** most mature reflection.
languish pine away   159 **drop of blood** (Each sigh was supposed to
deprive the heart of a drop of blood.)   160 **Fie . . . way** (Said to the
departing King as a way of pretending, for Imogen's benefit, the
Queen's concern for her.)   162 **My . . . master** i.e., Cloten drew his
sword on Posthumus.   165 **had . . . anger** was not whetted on by
anger.   166 **on't** of it.   167 **takes his part** sides with the King, or,
plays the role one would expect of him   168 **To draw** in drawing

169 **in Afric** i.e., in some deserted spot   170 **prick** urge forward
172 **suffer** allow   176 **lay** wager   179 **walk awhile** i.e., walk with
me awhile.
**1.2. Location: Britain. At the court of Cymbeline, as before. The time
is virtually continuous; Cloten still sweats from his duel (1.1.162).**
1 **shift** change   4 **abroad** outside you. (The First Lord flatteringly suggests that the outside air is not as wholesome as that of Cloten's own
sweet body, as though the outside air were the cause of the odor of
perspiration, but the effect of *reek* and *vent* is to inform us at any rate
that the odor is rank.)   5 **then to shift it** in that case, I would change
it.   7–8 **his patience** (Posthumus's patience has been sorely tried by
this encounter, but little else.)   9 **passable** (1) penetrable (2) tolerably
good   9–10 **if . . . hurt** i.e., I don't know what you mean by "hurt"
otherwise.   12–13 **His . . . town** ie., Cloten's rapier avoided the fight
in a cowardly fashion, as a debtor hides in back streets. (With an antithetical play on *backside / thoroughfare*.)   14 **stand me** stand up to me.
15–16 **No . . . face** i.e., What you call fleeing looked instead like his
charging relentlessly toward you. (Said sardonically.)   18–19 **gave . . .
ground** fell back before your advance. (With pun on literal meaning.)
20–1 **As . . . oceans** i.e., None.   21 **Puppies!** Arrogant, vain cubs!

CLOTEN   I would they had not come between us.

SECOND LORD [*aside*]   So would I, till you had measured how long a fool you were upon the ground.

CLOTEN   And that she should love this fellow and refuse me!

SECOND LORD [*aside*]   If it be a sin to make a true election, she is damned.   28

FIRST LORD   Sir, as I told you always, her beauty and her brain go not together. She's a good sign, but I have   30 seen small reflection of her wit.   31

SECOND LORD [*aside*]   She shines not upon fools, lest the reflection should hurt her.   33

CLOTEN   Come, I'll to my chamber. Would there had been some hurt done!

SECOND LORD [*aside*]   I wish not so, unless it had been the fall of an ass, which is no great hurt.

CLOTEN   You'll go with us?   38

FIRST LORD   I'll attend Your Lordship.

CLOTEN   Nay, come, let's go together.

SECOND LORD   Well, my lord.   *Exeunt.*

❧

1.[3]

Enter Imogen and Pisanio.

IMOGEN
I would thou grew'st unto the shores o'th' haven
And questioned'st every sail. If he should write
And I not have it, 'twere a paper lost   3
As offered mercy is. What was the last   4
That he spake to thee?

PISANIO   It was his queen, his queen!

IMOGEN
Then waved his handkerchief?

PISANIO   And kissed it, madam.

IMOGEN
Senseless linen, happier therein than I!   7
And that was all?

PISANIO   No, madam; for so long
As he could make me with this eye or ear
Distinguish him from others, he did keep
The deck, with glove, or hat, or handkerchief
Still waving, as the fits and stirs of 's mind
Could best express how slow his soul sailed on,
How swift his ship.

IMOGEN   Thou shouldst have made him
As little as a crow, or less, ere left   15
To after-eye him.

PISANIO   Madam, so I did.   16

IMOGEN
I would have broke mine eyestrings, cracked them, but   17
To look upon him till the diminution   18
Of space had pointed him sharp as my needle—   19
Nay, followed him till he had melted from
The smallness of a gnat to air, and then
Have turned mine eye and wept. But, good Pisanio,
When shall we hear from him?

PISANIO   Be assured, madam,
With his next vantage.   24

IMOGEN
I did not take my leave of him, but had
Most pretty things to say. Ere I could tell him
How I would think on him at certain hours
Such thoughts and such; or I could make him swear
The shes of Italy should not betray   29
Mine interest and his honor; or have charged him   30
At the sixth hour of morn, at noon, at midnight
T'encounter me with orisons, for then   32
I am in heaven for him; or ere I could   33
Give him that parting kiss which I had set
Betwixt two charming words, comes in my father,   35
And like the tyrannous breathing of the north   36
Shakes all our buds from growing.

Enter a Lady.

LADY   The Queen, madam,
Desires Your Highness' company.

IMOGEN
Those things I bid you do, get them dispatched.   39
I will attend the Queen.

PISANIO   Madam, I shall.   *Exeunt.*

❧

1.[4]

*Enter Philario, Iachimo, a Frenchman, a
Dutchman, and a Spaniard.*

IACHIMO   Believe it, sir, I have seen him in Britain. He was then of a crescent note, expected to prove so   2 worthy as since he hath been allowed the name of. But   3 I could then have looked on him without the help of admiration, though the catalogue of his endowments   5 had been tabled by his side and I to peruse him by   6 items.

28 **election** choice. (With a pun on the theological meaning.)   **30 go not together** do not match.   **sign** semblance, appearance   **31 wit** intelligence.   **33 reflection** (The Second Lord plays on *reflection,* "shining," in line 31, suggesting here that, if Imogen were to show favor to fools, it would *reflect on,* or bring reproach on, her character.) **38 You'll . . . us?** (Addressed to the Second Lord or to both.) **1.3. Location:** Britain. At the court of Cymbeline. **3–4 'twere . . . is** i.e., the loss of such a letter would be as unfortunate as a pardon offered but failing to arrive before the execution, or as God's mercy similarly having no effect.   **7 Senseless** Unfeeling **15–16 ere . . . him** before you left off following him with your gaze.

17 eyestrings the muscles, nerves, or tendons of the eye, thought to break or crack at loss of sight.   **but** merely   **18–19 till . . . needle** until the increase of distance had made him appear as small as my needle's point   **24 next vantage** first opportunity.   **29 shes** women **30 Mine interest** my legitimate claim to his loyalty   **32 T'encounter** to join.   **orisons** prayers   **33 in heaven** i.e., praying   **35 charming** having magical potency (to protect Posthumus from evil)   **36 north** north wind   **39 bid** bade, ordered **1.4. Location:** Rome. Philario's house. Perhaps a feast is in progress; see 5.5.157. **2 crescent note** growing reputation   **3 allowed the name of** granted to have the reputation for.   **5 admiration** wonder. (Iachimo insists he was not dazzled by Posthumus.)   **6 tabled** set down in a list

PHILARIO   You speak of him when he was less furnished
than now he is with that which makes him both with-   9
out and within.   10

FRENCHMAN   I have seen him in France. We had very
many there could behold the sun with as firm eyes   12
as he.

IACHIMO   This matter of marrying his king's daughter,
wherein he must be weighed rather by her value than
his own, words him, I doubt not, a great deal from the   16
matter.   17

FRENCHMAN   And then his banishment.

IACHIMO   Ay, and the approbation of those that weep   19
this lamentable divorce under her colors are wonder-   20
fully to extend him, be it but to fortify her judgment,   21
which else an easy battery might lay flat for taking a   22
beggar without less quality. But how comes it he is to   23
sojourn with you? How creeps acquaintance?   24

PHILARIO   His father and I were soldiers together, to
whom I have been often bound for no less than my
life.

Enter Posthumus.

Here comes the Briton. Let him be so entertained
amongst you as suits, with gentlemen of your know-   29
ing, to a stranger of his quality.—I beseech you all, be   30
better known to this gentleman, whom I commend to
you as a noble friend of mine. How worthy he is I will
leave to appear hereafter rather than story him in his   33
own hearing.

FRENCHMAN   Sir, we have known together in Orleans.   35

POSTHUMUS   Since when I have been debtor to you for
courtesies which I will be ever to pay and yet pay still.   37

FRENCHMAN   Sir, you o'errate my poor kindness. I was
glad I did atone my countryman and you. It had been   39
pity you should have been put together with so mortal   40
a purpose as then each bore, upon importance of so   41
slight and trivial a nature.

POSTHUMUS   By your pardon, sir, I was then a young
traveler; rather shunned to go even with what I heard
than in my every action to be guided by others'
experiences. But upon my mended judgment—if I   46
offend not to say it is mended—my quarrel was not
altogether slight.

FRENCHMAN   Faith, yes, to be put to the arbitrament of   49
swords, and by such two that would by all likelihood   50
have confounded one the other or have fallen both.   51

IACHIMO   Can we, with manners, ask what was the
difference?   53

FRENCHMAN   Safely, I think; 'twas a contention in
public, which may without contradiction suffer the   55
report. It was much like an argument that fell out last   56
night, where each of us fell in praise of our country   57
mistresses, this gentleman at that time vouching—and   58
upon warrant of bloody affirmation—his to be more   59
fair, virtuous, wise, chaste, constant, qualified, and less   60
attemptable than any the rarest of our ladies in France.   61

IACHIMO   That lady is not now living, or this gentleman's opinion by this worn out.   63

POSTHUMUS   She holds her virtue still, and I my mind.   64

IACHIMO   You must not so far prefer her 'fore ours of   65
Italy.

POSTHUMUS   Being so far provoked as I was in France,
I would abate her nothing, though I profess myself   68
her adorer, not her friend.   69

IACHIMO   As fair and as good—a kind of hand-in-hand   70
comparison—had been something too fair and too   71
good for any lady in Britain. If she went before others   72
I have seen, as that diamond of yours outlusters many   73
I have beheld, I could not but believe she excelled
many. But I have not seen the most precious diamond
that is, nor you the lady.

POSTHUMUS   I praised her as I rated her. So do I my
stone.

IACHIMO   What do you esteem it at?

POSTHUMUS   More than the world enjoys.   80

IACHIMO   Either your unparagoned mistress is dead, or   81
she's outprized by a trifle.   82

POSTHUMUS   You are mistaken. The one may be sold or
given, or if there were wealth enough for the purchase   84
or merit for the gift. The other is not a thing for sale,
and only the gift of the gods.   86

IACHIMO   Which the gods have given you?

POSTHUMUS   Which, by their graces, I will keep.

IACHIMO   You may wear her in title yours; but you   89
know strange fowl light upon neighboring ponds.   90

9–10 makes . . . within establishes him as regards both his fortune
and his character.   12 behold the sun i.e., like an eagle, a royal bird
supposedly able to stare at the sun unblinkingly   16–17 words . . .
matter causes him to be described in accounts that go beyond the
truth.   19–23 Ay . . . quality Yes, and those who weep for this lamentable forced separation, taking Imogen's side in the matter (literally,
carrying her banner), approvingly seek every means possible to
praise Posthumus beyond his merit, if only to justify her choice of
him, which otherwise would be vulnerable to attack for having chosen a beggar of no rank or merit.   24 How creeps acquaintance?
How has he crept into your favor?   29–30 knowing knowledge of
affairs, *savoir faire*   30 stranger foreigner.   quality rank.   33 story
give an account of   35 known together been acquainted   37 which
. . . still which I will always be indebted to you for, even if I go on
paying forever.   39 atone, reconcile   40 put together set opposite
one another in a duel.   mortal deadly   41 importance matter, occasion   44 shunned . . . even declined to agree   46 upon even upon.
mended improved

49–50 arbitrament of swords settlement by a duel   51 confounded
destroyed   53 difference quarrel.   55–6 without . . . report without
objection be reported or told.   57–8 our country mistresses the lady
each of us loves in his native land   59 bloody affirmation affirming
the truth in a duel   60 qualified having fine qualities   61 attemptable open to attempts on her virtue.   any the rarest any of the finest
63 by this by now   64 mind opinion.   65 prefer her advance her
claims   68 would abate her nothing would not lower my estimate of
her in the slightest   68–9 though . . . friend even though I should (as
at that time, in France) profess myself to be her adorer or worshiper
in the "courtly" sense, not her accepted lover.   70–1 hand-in-hand
comparison comparison claiming equality only, not superiority
71 had would have   72 went before excelled   73 diamond i.e., the
ring Imogen gave Posthumus   80 the world enjoys anything in the
world.   81–2 Either . . . trifle (In that case, jests Iachimo, you must
love your jewel more than her, for if she is alive she is "in the
world.")   84 or if if either   86 only . . . gods the gift of the gods
alone.   89 wear . . . yours possess her in name, claim title to her
90 strange . . . ponds i.e., claiming possession doesn't prevent
strangers from infiltrating one's private domain.

Your ring may be stolen too. So your brace of unpriz- 91
able estimations, the one is but frail and the other ca- 92
sual. A cunning thief or a that-way-accomplished cour- 93
tier would hazard the winning both of first and last.

POSTHUMUS   Your Italy contains none so accomplished a
courtier to convince the honor of my mistress if, in 96
the holding or loss of that, you term her frail. I do
nothing doubt you have store of thieves; notwith- 98
standing, I fear not my ring. 99

PHILARIO   Let us leave here, gentlemen. 100

POSTHUMUS   Sir, with all my heart. This worthy signor,
I thank him, makes no stranger of me; we are familiar 102
at first. 103

IACHIMO   With five times so much conversation I
should get ground of your fair mistress, make her go 105
back even to the yielding, had I admittance and 106
opportunity to friend. 107

POSTHUMUS   No, no.

IACHIMO   I dare thereupon pawn the moiety of my estate 109
to your ring, which in my opinion o'ervalues it some- 110
thing. But I make my wager rather against your confi- 111
dence than her reputation, and, to bar your offense 112
herein too, I durst attempt it against any lady in the
world.

POSTHUMUS   You are a great deal abused in too bold a 115
persuasion, and I doubt not you sustain what you're 116
worthy of by your attempt.

IACHIMO   What's that?

POSTHUMUS   A repulse—though your attempt, as you
call it, deserve more: a punishment too.

PHILARIO   Gentlemen, enough of this. It came in too
suddenly; let it die as it was born, and, I pray you, be
better acquainted.

IACHIMO   Would I had put my estate and my neighbor's 124
on th'approbation of what I have spoke! 125

POSTHUMUS   What lady would you choose to assail?

IACHIMO   Yours, whom in constancy you think stands
so safe. I will lay you ten thousand ducats to your ring 128
that, commend me to the court where your lady is, 129
with no more advantage than the opportunity of a
second conference, and I will bring from thence that
honor of hers which you imagine so reserved. 132

POSTHUMUS   I will wage against your gold, gold to it. 133
My ring I hold dear as my finger; 'tis part of it.

IACHIMO   You are a friend, and therein the wiser. If you 135
buy ladies' flesh at a million a dram, you cannot 136
preserve it from tainting. But I see you have some
religion in you, that you fear. 138

POSTHUMUS   This is but a custom in your tongue. You
bear a graver purpose, I hope.

IACHIMO   I am the master of my speeches and would
undergo what's spoken, I swear. 142

POSTHUMUS   Will you? I shall but lend my diamond till
your return. Let there be covenants drawn between 's.
My mistress exceeds in goodness the hugeness of your
unworthy thinking. I dare you to this match; here's
my ring.   [He wagers his ring.] 147

PHILARIO   I will have it no lay. 148

IACHIMO   By the gods, it is one. If I bring you no
sufficient testimony that I have enjoyed the dearest
bodily part of your mistress, my ten thousand ducats
are yours; so is your diamond too. If I come off and
leave her in such honor as you have trust in, she your
jewel, this your jewel, and my gold are yours—
provided I have your commendation for my more free 155
entertainment. 156

POSTHUMUS   I embrace these conditions. Let us have
articles betwixt us. Only, thus far you shall answer: if
you make your voyage upon her and give me directly 159
to understand you have prevailed, I am no further your
enemy; she is not worth our debate. If she remain un-
seduced, you not making it appear otherwise, for your
ill opinion and th'assault you have made to her chastity you shall answer me with your sword.

IACHIMO   Your hand; a covenant. [They shake hands.]
We will have these things set down by lawful counsel,
and straight away for Britain, lest the bargain should
catch cold and starve. I will fetch my gold and have 168
our two wagers recorded.

POSTHUMUS   Agreed.   [Exeunt Posthumus and Iachimo.]

FRENCHMAN   Will this hold, think you?

PHILARIO   Signor Iachimo will not from it. Pray let us 172
follow 'em.   Exeunt.

❧

1.[5]

Enter Queen, Ladies, and Cornelius.

QUEEN
Whiles yet the dew's on ground, gather those flowers.
Make haste. Who has the note of them?

A LADY   I, madam.   2

---

91 **ring** (Often, as here, symbolic of a chastity that can be lost.)
91–2 **your . . . estimations** of the pair of objects (lady and ring) that
you esteem beyond value   92–3 **casual** susceptible to accident (such
as theft).   93 **that-way-accomplished** i.e., accomplished in seducing
women   96 **to convince** as to overcome   98 **nothing** not at all.
store plenty   99 **fear not** fear not for   100 **leave** leave off, cease
102–3 **familiar at first** on familiar terms right from the start.   105 **get
ground** gain the advantage   105–6 **go back** succumb, give way. (The
metaphor is from fencing, with sexual suggestion.)   107 **to friend** to
assist me.   109 **moiety** half   110–11 **something** somewhat.   112 **bar
your offense** avoid offending you individually   115–16 **abused . . .
persuasion** deceived in your excessively bold belief   116 **sustain**
will sustain, receive   124 **put** wagered   125 **th'approbation** the
attestation, confirmation   128 **lay** wager   129 **commend me** provide
me a letter of introduction   132 **reserved** kept safe.   133 **to it** in
equal amount.

135 **You . . . wiser** i.e., You know her too well, being her lover, to bet
your ring on her.   136 **at . . . dram** i.e., at an inordinately high price
for a very small amount   138 **that** since.   **fear** (1) experience "the
fear of the Lord" that is the beginning of true wisdom (2) are fearful.
142 **undergo** undertake   147 s.d. *wagers his ring* (Possibly Posthumus hands the ring to Iachimo or to Philario as official of the wager,
or perhaps he still keeps it himself; see 2.4.108.)   148 **I . . . lay** I will
not let it be a wager.   155 **commendation** introduction (to Imogen)
155–6 **free entertainment** ready welcome.   159 **directly** straightfor-
wardly, unequivocally   168 **starve** die (through second thoughts and
cooling of resolve).   172 **from it** depart from it.
1.5. Location: Britain. At the court of Cymbeline.
2 note list

QUEEN   Dispatch.   *Exeunt Ladies.*
  Now, Master Doctor, have you brought those drugs?
CORNELIUS
  Pleaseth Your Highness, ay. Here they are, madam.   5
                              [*He presents a small box.*]
  But I beseech Your Grace, without offense—
  My conscience bids me ask—wherefore you have   7
  Commanded of me these most poisonous
      compounds,
  Which are the movers of a languishing death,
  But though slow, deadly.
QUEEN   I wonder, Doctor,
  Thou ask'st me such a question. Have I not been
  Thy pupil long? Hast thou not learned me how   12
  To make perfumes? Distill? Preserve? Yea, so
  That our great king himself doth woo me oft
  For my confections? Having thus far proceeded—   15
  Unless thou think'st me devilish—is't not meet   16
  That I did amplify my judgment in   17
  Other conclusions? I will try the forces   18
  Of these thy compounds on such creatures as
  We count not worth the hanging—but none human—
  To try the vigor of them and apply   21
  Allayments to their act, and by them gather   22
  Their several virtues and effects.
CORNELIUS   Your Highness   23
  Shall from this practice but make hard your heart.   24
  Besides, the seeing these effects will be
  Both noisome and infectious.
QUEEN   Oh, content thee.   26

            Enter Pisanio.

  [*Aside*] Here comes a flattering rascal; upon him
  Will I first work. He's for his master,   28
  And enemy to my son.—How now, Pisanio?—
  Doctor, your service for this time is ended;
  Take your own way.
CORNELIUS [*aside*]   I do suspect you, madam,   31
  But you shall do no harm.
QUEEN [*to Pisanio*]   Hark thee, a word.
CORNELIUS [*aside*]
  I do not like her. She doth think she has
  Strange ling'ring poisons. I do know her spirit
  And will not trust one of her malice with
  A drug of such damned nature. Those she has
  Will stupefy and dull the sense awhile,
  Which first, perchance, she'll prove on cats and dogs,   38
  Then afterward up higher; but there is
  No danger in what show of death it makes
  More than the locking-up the spirits a time,

To be more fresh, reviving. She is fooled
With a most false effect, and I the truer   43
So to be false with her.
QUEEN   No further service, Doctor,
  Until I send for thee.
CORNELIUS   I humbly take my leave.   *Exit.*
QUEEN [*to Pisanio*]
  Weeps she still, say'st thou? Dost thou think in time
  She will not quench, and let instructions enter   49
  Where folly now possesses? Do thou work.
  When thou shalt bring me word she loves my son,
  I'll tell thee on the instant thou art then
  As great as is thy master; greater, for
  His fortunes all lie speechless, and his name   54
  Is at last gasp. Return he cannot, nor
  Continue where he is. To shift his being   56
  Is to exchange one misery with another,
  And every day that comes comes to decay   58
  A day's work in him. What shalt thou expect   59
  To be depender on a thing that leans,   60
  Who cannot be new built, nor has no friends,
  So much as but to prop him? [*The Queen drops the box:
      Pisanio takes it up.*] Thou tak'st up
  Thou know'st not what; but take it for thy labor.
  It is a thing I made, which hath the King
  Five times redeemed from death. I do not know
  What is more cordial. Nay, I prithee, take it;   66
  It is an earnest of a farther good   67
  That I mean to thee. Tell thy mistress how
  The case stands with her; do't as from thyself.   69
  Think what a chance thou changest on, but think   70
  Thou hast thy mistress still—to boot, my son,   71
  Who shall take notice of thee. I'll move the King   72
  To any shape of thy preferment such   73
  As thou'lt desire; and then myself, I chiefly,
  That set thee on to this desert, am bound   75
  To load thy merit richly. Call my women.
  Think on my words.   *Exit Pisanio.*
                    A sly and constant knave,
  Not to be shaked; the agent for his master,   78
  And the remembrancer of her to hold   79
  The handfast to her lord. I have given him that   80
  Which, if he take, shall quite unpeople her   81
  Of liegers for her sweet, and which she after,   82

5 Pleaseth If it please   **5.1 He presents . . . box** (Perhaps Cornelius hesitates before actually giving it to her; she may snatch it from him.)   **7 wherefore** why   **12 learned** taught   **15 confections** compounds (of drugs)   **16 meet** fitting   **17 did** should   **18 conclusions** experiments.   **try** test   **21–3 To try . . . effects** to test their efficacy and apply antidotes to their action, and by these experiments determine their various operative powers and effects.   **24 but** only   **26 noisome** noxious, foul-smelling.   **content thee** do not trouble yourself.   **28 He's for** i.e., He's an agent for   **31 Take your own way** Be off, go about your business.   **38 prove** test

43 truer more honest   **49 quench** become cool.   **instructions** good counsel   **54 name** reputation   **56 shift his being** change his abode   **58–9 And . . . him** i.e., and every new day that arrives means the undoing of a day's fruitful endeavor as far as he's concerned.   **59 What . . . expect** What can you expect for yourself   **60 To . . . leans** to be a dependent of a creature (Posthumus) who is about to fall   **66 cordial** restorative (literally, to the heart).   **67 earnest** first payment   **69 as from thyself** as if from your own advice.   **70 Think . . . on** Think what an improvement in your fortunes you come upon in this change of service   **71 Thou . . . still** i.e., you will have Imogen as your patroness still, as the wife of Cloten, your new lord.   **to boot** and besides her (you will have)   **72 take notice of thee** look out for you, offer advancement to you.   **73 preferment** advancement   **75 That . . . desert** who urged you to take this action for which you will be rewarded   **78 shaked** shaken (in his loyalty)   **79 remembrancer of her** one who reminds her   **80 handfast** marriage contract   **81–2 shall . . . sweet** will thoroughly deprive her of the services of any ambassadors to her sweet Posthumus

Except she bend her humor, shall be assured 83
To taste of too.

Enter Pisanio, and Ladies [with flowers].

So, so. Well done, well done.
The violets, cowslips, and the primroses
Bear to my closet. Fare thee well, Pisanio; 86
Think on my words. *Exeunt Queen and Ladies.*

PISANIO And shall do.
But when to my good lord I prove untrue,
I'll choke myself. There's all I'll do for you. *Exit.*

❧

1.[6]

Enter Imogen alone.

IMOGEN
A father cruel and a stepdame false,
A foolish suitor to a wedded lady
That hath her husband banished. Oh, that husband! 3
My supreme crown of grief, and those repeated 4
Vexations of it! Had I been thief-stol'n,
As my two brothers, happy! But most miserable 6
Is the desire that's glorious. Blest be those, 7
How mean soe'er, that have their honest wills, 8
Which seasons comfort.—Who may this be? Fie! 9

Enter Pisanio and Iachimo.

PISANIO
Madam, a noble gentleman of Rome,
Comes from my lord with letters.
IACHIMO Change you, madam? 11
The worthy Leonatus is in safety
And greets Your Highness dearly.
[He presents a letter.]
IMOGEN Thanks, good sir.
You're kindly welcome. *[She reads.]*
IACHIMO *[aside]*
All of her that is out of door most rich! 15
If she be furnished with a mind so rare,
She is alone th'Arabian bird, and I 17
Have lost the wager. Boldness be my friend!
Arm me, audacity, from head to foot!
Or, like the Parthian, I shall flying fight— 20
Rather, directly fly.
IMOGEN *(reads)* "He is one of the noblest note, to 22
whose kindnesses I am most infinitely tied. Reflect 23

upon him accordingly, as you value your trust—
Leonatus."
So far I read aloud.
But even the very middle of my heart
Is warmed by th' rest and takes it thankfully.
You are as welcome, worthy sir, as I
Have words to bid you, and shall find it so
In all that I can do.
IACHIMO Thanks, fairest lady.
What, are men mad? Hath nature given them eyes
To see this vaulted arch and the rich crop 33
Of sea and land, which can distinguish twixt
The fiery orbs above and the twinned stones 35
Upon th'unnumbered beach, and can we not 36
Partition make with spectacles so precious 37
Twixt fair and foul?
IMOGEN What makes your admiration? 38
IACHIMO
It cannot be i'th'eye, for apes and monkeys
Twixt two such shes would chatter this way and 40
Contemn with mows the other; nor i'th' judgment, 41
For idiots in this case of favor would 42
Be wisely definite; nor i'th'appetite: 43
Sluttery, to such neat excellence opposed, 44
Should make desire vomit emptiness, 45
Not so allured to feed. 46
IMOGEN
What is the matter, trow?
IACHIMO The cloyèd will— 47
That satiate yet unsatisfied desire, that tub 48
Both filled and running—ravening first the lamb, 49
Longs after for the garbage.
IMOGEN What, dear sir,
Thus raps you? Are you well? 51
IACHIMO
Thanks, madam, well. *[To Pisanio]* Beseech you, sir,
Desire my man's abode where I did leave him. 53
He's strange and peevish.
PISANIO I was going, sir, 54
To give him welcome. *Exit.*
IMOGEN
Continues well my lord? His health, beseech you?
IACHIMO Well, madam.
IMOGEN
Is he disposed to mirth? I hope he is.
IACHIMO
Exceeding pleasant; none a stranger there 59

---

83 **Except . . . humor** unless she changes her mind (about not accepting Cloten) 86 **closet** private chamber.
1.6. Location: Britain. At the court.
3 **That . . . banished** whose husband is banished. 4 **repeated** already enumerated 6 **happy!** how happy and fortunate would I be! 7 **the desire . . . glorious** i.e., the ungratified yearnings of those of us who are born to high social station—in this case my yearning for Posthumus. 8 **mean** lowly. **honest wills** simple desires 9 **seasons** adds relish to 11 **Comes** who comes. **letters** i.e., (probably) a letter.
Change you, Madam? Does your expression change at news of letters from Rome? 15 **out of door** external 17 **th'Arabian bird** i.e., the phoenix, therefore unique 20 **Parthian** (The Parthians were proverbial in ancient times for discharging a flight of arrows as they fled.)
22 **note** reputation 23 **Reflect** Bestow favor

33 **vaulted arch** sky. **crop** harvest, produce 35 **fiery orbs** stars. **twinned** exactly alike 36 **th'unnumbered** the numberless 37 **Partition** distinction. **with . . . precious** i.e., with organs of vision so acutely sensitive 38 **admiration** wonder. 40 **chatter this way** i.e., indicate approval of Imogen 41 **Contemn** scorn. **mows** grimaces, wry faces 42 **in . . . favor** in question concerning a face of such grace and beauty 43 **Be wisely definite** choose wisely 44–6 **Sluttery . . . feed** sluttishness itself, confronted with such pure excellence, would void its own empty desire, not being tempted to feed its lust.
47 **trow** do you think. **will** lustful appetite 48 **satiate** glutted, *cloyèd*, as in line 47. (The perverted sexual appetite is at once glutted and insatiable.) 49 **running** emptying itself. **ravening** devouring greedily 51 **raps** transports, makes rapt 53 **Desire . . . abode** bid my servant remain 54 **strange and peevish** a foreigner and easily upset. 59 **none a stranger** no other foreigner

So merry and so gamesome. He is called   60
The Briton reveler.
IMOGEN   When he was here
He did incline to sadness, and ofttimes   62
Not knowing why.
IACHIMO   I never saw him sad.
There is a Frenchman his companion, one
An eminent monsieur that, it seems, much loves
A Gallian girl at home. He furnaces   66
The thick sighs from him, whiles the jolly Briton—   67
Your lord, I mean—laughs from 's free lungs, cries
"Oh,   68
Can my sides hold, to think that man, who knows
By history, report, or his own proof   70
What woman is, yea, what she cannot choose
But must be, will 's free hours languish   72
For assurèd bondage?"
IMOGEN   Will my lord say so?   73
IACHIMO
Ay, madam, with his eyes in flood with laughter.
It is a recreation to be by
And hear him mock the Frenchman. But heavens
    know
Some men are much to blame.
IMOGEN   Not he, I hope.
IACHIMO
Not he; but yet heaven's bounty towards him might   78
Be used more thankfully. In himself, 'tis much;   79
In you, which I account his, beyond all talents.   80
Whilst I am bound to wonder, I am bound   81
To pity too.
IMOGEN   What do you pity, sir?   82
IACHIMO
Two creatures heartily.
IMOGEN   Am I one, sir?   83
You look on me. What wrack discern you in me   84
Deserves your pity?
IACHIMO   Lamentable! What,   85
To hide me from the radiant sun, and solace   86
I'th' dungeon by a snuff?
IMOGEN   I pray you, sir,   87
Deliver with more openness your answers
To my demands. Why do you pity me?   89
IACHIMO   That others do—
I was about to say—enjoy your—But

It is an office of the gods to venge it,   92
Not mine to speak on't.
IMOGEN   You do seem to know   93
Something of me, or what concerns me. Pray you—
Since doubting things go ill often hurts more   95
Than to be sure they do; for certainties
Either are past remedies, or, timely knowing,   97
The remedy then born—discover to me   98
What both you spur and stop.
IACHIMO   Had I this cheek   99
To bathe my lips upon; this hand, whose touch,
Whose every touch, would force the feeler's soul
To th'oath of loyalty; this object, which
Takes prisoner the wild motion of mine eye,
Fixing it only here; should I, damned then,
Slaver with lips as common as the stairs
That mount the Capitol; join grips with hands   106
Made hard with hourly falsehood—falsehood as   107
With labor; then by-peeping in an eye   108
Base and illustrous as the smoky light   109
That's fed with stinking tallow—it were fit
That all the plagues of hell should at one time
Encounter such revolt.
IMOGEN   My lord, I fear,   112
Has forgot Britain.
IACHIMO   And himself. Not I,   113
Inclined to this intelligence, pronounce   114
The beggary of his change, but 'tis your graces   115
That from my mutest conscience to my tongue   116
Charms this report out.
IMOGEN   Let me hear no more.
IACHIMO
O dearest soul, your cause doth strike my heart
With pity that doth make me sick. A lady
So fair, and fastened to an empery   120
Would make the great'st king double—to be partnered   121
With tomboys hired with that self exhibition   122
Which your own coffers yield; with diseased ventures   123
That play with all infirmities for gold   124
Which rottenness can lend nature; such boiled stuff   125
As well might poison poison! Be revenged,
Or she that bore you was no queen, and you
Recoil from your great stock.   128

---

60 gamesome sportive. (With a sexual suggestion, as also, in the following lines, in *reveler, jolly, free,* etc.)   **62 sadness** seriousness   **66 Gallian** Gallic, French.   **furnaces** gives forth like a furnace   **67 thick** coming thick and fast   **68 from 's free lungs** i.e., without restraint, heartily   **70 proof** experience   **72 will 's . . . languish** will give up his free time and licentious opportunities   **73 assurèd** (1) certain (2) betrothed   **78–82 heaven's . . . pity too** i.e., the graces that heaven has lent him might be more thankfully acknowledged and employed. His own graces are considerable; but his having you as his wife (or so I understand) bestows on him a gift of such rarity that I am bound to wonder at and at the same time to pity.   **83 two creatures** (Iachimo implies that he pities Imogen for having a faithless husband and, in a different sense, pities Posthumus for abusing such a rich gift.)   **84 wrack** ruin   **85 Deserves** that deserves   **86 hide me** i.e., hide.   **solace** take delight   **87 snuff** smoking candlewick.   **89 demands** inquiries.

92 office function   **93 on't** of it.   **95 doubting** fearing (that)   **97 timely knowing** if one knows in time   **98 then born** i.e., is then born.   **discover** reveal   **99 What . . . stop** i.e., what you simultaneously urge toward disclosure and then conceal, as if spurring and then reining in a horse.   **106 grips** claspings   **107–8 as With labor** as much as if they had been made hard by actual labor   **108 by-peeping** giving sidelong glances   **109 illustrous** not lustrous   **112 Encounter . . . revolt** confront and punish such infidelity.   **113–15 Not . . . change** It is not through any inclination to disclose this information that I report his contemptible alteration   **116 mutest conscience** most silent inner being   **120–1 fastened . . . double** endowed with an empire (of graces and inheritance) that would make any king's wealth twice what it was before   **121–3 to be . . . yield** to be made to share him as sexual partner with wantons paid for with that very allowance of money that he received from your own treasure chests   **123–5 with diseased . . . nature** with diseased prostitutes who, for gold, play around with all the infirmities that rottenness (venereal disease) can lend to human nature.   **125 boiled stuff** i.e., women treated by "sweating" for venereal disease   **128 Recoil** fall away, degenerate

IMOGEN   Revenged?
How should I be revenged? If this be true—
As I have such a heart that both mine ears   131
Must not in haste abuse—if it be true,   132
How should I be revenged?
IACHIMO   Should he make me
Live like Diana's priest betwixt cold sheets   134
Whiles he is vaulting variable ramps,   135
In your despite, upon your purse? Revenge it.   136
I dedicate myself to your sweet pleasure,
More noble than that runagate to your bed,   138
And will continue fast to your affection,   139
Still close as sure.
IMOGEN [calling]   What, ho, Pisanio!   140
IACHIMO
Let me my service tender on your lips.
IMOGEN
Away! I do condemn mine ears that have
So long attended thee. If thou wert honorable,   143
Thou wouldst have told this tale for virtue, not
For such an end thou seek'st—as base as strange.
Thou wrong'st a gentleman who is as far
From thy report as thou from honor, and
Solicits here a lady that disdains
Thee and the devil alike.—What ho, Pisanio!—
The King my father shall be made acquainted
Of thy assault. If he shall think it fit
A saucy stranger in his court to mart   152
As in a Romish stew and to expound   153
His beastly mind to us, he hath a court
He little cares for and a daughter who
He not respects at all.—What, ho, Pisanio!
IACHIMO
O happy Leonatus! I may say
The credit that thy lady hath of thee   158
Deserves thy trust, and thy most perfect goodness
Her assured credit.—Blessèd live you long,   160
A lady to the worthiest sir that ever
Country called his, and you his mistress, only   162
For the most worthiest fit! Give me your pardon.
I have spoke this to know if your affiance   164
Were deeply rooted, and shall make your lord   165
That which he is new o'er; and he is one   166
The truest mannered, such a holy witch   167
That he enchants societies into him.   168
Half all men's hearts are his.
IMOGEN   You make amends.   169

IACHIMO
He sits 'mongst men like a descended god.
He hath a kind of honor sets him off   171
More than a mortal seeming. Be not angry,   172
Most mighty Princess, that I have adventured
To try your taking of a false report, which hath
Honored with confirmation your great judgment
In the election of a sir so rare,   176
Which you know cannot err. The love I bear him   177
Made me to fan you thus, but the gods made you,   178
Unlike all others, chaffless. Pray, your pardon.   179
IMOGEN
All's well, sir. Take my power i'th' court for yours.
IACHIMO
My humble thanks. I had almost forgot
T'entreat Your Grace but in a small request,
And yet of moment too, for it concerns   183
Your lord, myself, and other noble friends
Are partners in the business.
IMOGEN   Pray, what is't?   185
IACHIMO
Some dozen Romans of us and your lord—
The best feather of our wing—have mingled sums   187
To buy a present for the Emperor;
Which I, the factor for the rest, have done   189
In France. 'Tis plate of rare device, and jewels   190
Of rich and exquisite form, their values great,
And I am something curious, being strange,   192
To have them in safe stowage. May it please you
To take them in protection?
IMOGEN   Willingly;
And pawn mine honor for their safety. Since
My lord hath interest in them, I will keep them   196
In my bedchamber.
IACHIMO   They are in a trunk,
Attended by my men. I will make bold
To send them to you, only for this night;
I must aboard tomorrow.
IMOGEN   Oh, no, no.
IACHIMO
Yes, I beseech, or I shall short my word   201
By length'ning my return. From Gallia   202
I crossed the seas on purpose and on promise
To see Your Grace.
IMOGEN   I thank you for your pains.
But not away tomorrow!
IACHIMO   Oh, I must, madam.
Therefore I shall beseech you, if you please
To greet your lord with writing, do't tonight.
I have outstood my time, which is material   208

131 As i.e., I say "if," since   132 Must . . . abuse must not overhastily
wrong (by being too credulous)   134 Diana's priest i.e., priestess
devoted to the goddess of chastity   135 vaulting . . . ramps mounting various prostitutes   136 In . . . purse treating you contemptuously, while spending your money.   138 runagate renegade
139 fast firm   140 Still . . . sure always as secret as I am true.
143 attended listened to   152 to mart should bargain   153 Romish
stew Roman house of prostitution   158 credit faith.   of in   160 Her
assured credit deserves her faith in you, Leonatus.   162 called his
called its own   164 affiance fidelity   165–6 and shall . . . o'er and
my report will confirm anew in Leonatus an assurance that he is
indeed your lord   166–7 one . . . mannered uniquely, above all others
honorably disposed   167–8 such . . . him such a virtuous yet charming man that he draws all sorts of people to him as if by magic.
169 Half . . . his All persons give him half their hearts.

171–2 sets . . . seeming that sets him apart as if he were a god.
176 election choice   177 Which who   178 fan test. (A metaphor
from winnowing of grain.)   179 chaffless without chaff, i.e., perfect.
183 moment importance   185 Are who are   187 The best . . . wing
i.e., the choicest spirit of our company   189 factor agent   190 plate
ware plated with precious metal.   192 something curious somewhat
anxious.   strange a foreigner   196 interest a stake   201 short fall
short of   202 Gallia Gaul, France   208 outstood overstayed

To th' tender of our present.

IMOGEN   I will write.   209
Send your trunk to me; it shall safe be kept
And truly yielded you. You're very welcome. *Exeunt.* 211

❖

2.1

Enter Cloten and the two Lords.

CLOTEN   Was there ever man had such luck? When I
kissed the jack upon an upcast, to be hit away! I had   2
a hundred pound on't. And then a whoreson jacka-   3
napes must take me up for swearing, as if I borrowed   4
mine oaths of him and might not spend them at my
pleasure.

FIRST LORD   What got he by that? You have broke his   7
pate with your bowl.   8

SECOND LORD [*aside*]   If his wit had been like him that
broke it, it would have run all out.

CLOTEN   When a gentleman is disposed to swear, it is
not for any standers-by to curtail his oaths, ha?   12

SECOND LORD   No, my lord; [*aside*] nor crop the ears of
them.

CLOTEN   Whoreson dog! I gave him satisfaction? Would   15
he had been one of my rank!   16

SECOND LORD [*aside*]   To have smelled like a fool.

CLOTEN   I am not vexed more at anything in the earth. A   18
pox on't! I had rather not be so noble as I am. They   19
dare not fight with me because of the Queen my
mother. Every jack-slave hath his bellyful of fighting,   21
and I must go up and down like a cock that nobody   22
can match.   23

SECOND LORD [*aside*]   You are cock and capon too, and   24
you crow, cock, with your comb on.   25

CLOTEN   Sayest thou?   26

SECOND LORD   It is not fit Your Lordship should under-   27
take every companion that you give offense to.   28

CLOTEN   No, I know that, but it is fit I should commit   29
offense to my inferiors.   30

SECOND LORD   Ay, it is fit for Your Lordship only.

CLOTEN   Why, so I say.

FIRST LORD   Did you hear of a stranger that's come to
court tonight?   34

CLOTEN   A stranger, and I not know on't?

SECOND LORD [*aside*]   He's a strange fellow himself,
and knows it not.

FIRST LORD   There's an Italian come, and, 'tis thought,
one of Leonatus' friends.

CLOTEN   Leonatus? A banished rascal; and he's another,
whatsoever he be. Who told you of this stranger?

FIRST LORD   One of Your Lordship's pages.

CLOTEN   Is it fit I went to look upon him? Is there no
derogation in't?   44

SECOND LORD   You cannot derogate, my lord.   45

CLOTEN   Not easily, I think.

SECOND LORD [*aside*]   You are a fool granted; therefore   47
your issues, being foolish, do not derogate.   48

CLOTEN   Come, I'll go see this Italian. What I have lost
today at bowls I'll win tonight of him. Come, go.

SECOND LORD   I'll attend Your Lordship.
                              Exeunt [*Cloten and First Lord*].
That such a crafty devil as is his mother
Should yield the world this ass! A woman that
Bears all down with her brain, and this her son   54
Cannot take two from twenty, for his heart,   55
And leave eighteen. Alas, poor Princess,
Thou divine Imogen, what thou endur'st,
Betwixt a father by thy stepdame governed,
A mother hourly coining plots, a wooer
More hateful than the foul expulsion is
Of thy dear husband, than that horrid act   61
Of the divorce he'd make! The heavens hold firm   62
The walls of thy dear honor, keep unshaked
That temple, thy fair mind, that thou mayst stand
T'enjoy thy banished lord and this great land!   *Exit.*

❖

2.2

*Enter Imogen in her bed, and a lady [Helen,
attending. A trunk is brought on.]*

IMOGEN
Who's there? My woman Helen?

HELEN   Please you, madam.

---

209 tender of our present offering of our gift.   **211 truly yielded you**
duly returned to you.
2.1. Location: Britain. At the court.
2 kissed the jack touched and lay near the small bowl used as target
in the game of bowls.   **upcast** i.e., crucial throw in the game of bowls
3–4 whoreson jackanapes wretched coxcomb   **4 take me up** take me
to task   **7–8 broke his pate** i.e., given him a blow to the head. (But
the Second Lord jokes as though a *broken* head would allow brains to
run out.)   **12 curtail** shorten, as one might bob the tail (and sometimes the ears) of a curtal dog; hence, *crop the ears* (of the *oaths*) in the
next speech   **15 gave** was to give. (To *give satisfaction* is to accept a
challenge to a duel from one who feels himself insulted—something
that Cloten professes himself unwilling to do because the opponent is
of lower social rank, though Cloten's real motive appears to have
been cowardice.)   **16 rank** social class. (But the Second Lord takes it
in the sense of "rankness of smell.")   **18–19 A pox on't!** i.e., A plague
on it!   **21 jack-slave** lowborn fellow   **22–3 like a cock . . . match**
(Like the champion cock in cockfighting, complains Cloten, I am
unchallenged because all are socially unequal to me.)   **24 capon** castrated rooster. (Used quibblingly for *cap-on*, i.e., with fool's cap or
coxcomb.)   **25 with your comb on** (There is a play here on "coxcomb" and "cock's comb.")   **26 Sayest thou?** What do you say?
27–8 undertake engage with, give satisfaction to   **28 companion** fellow.   **give offense to** attack or insult in the code of dueling. (But the
speaker also suggests that Cloten gives offense to virtually everyone
by being who he is. The insinuation is present in line 31 as well: no
one but Your Lordship is so adept at giving offense.)

29–30 commit offense to attack, initiate action against. (With unin-
tended sense of "defecate upon.")   **34 tonight** last night.   **44 derogation** loss of dignity   **45 cannot derogate** (1) cannot do anything
undignified (2) have no dignity to lose.   **47 a fool granted** an
acknowledged fool   **48 issues** offspring, i.e., deeds, actions
54 Bears all down carries all before her, triumphs over everyone
55 for his heart for the life of him   **61–2 than . . . make** more hateful
than his horrid undertaking to separate Imogen from Posthumus.
2.2 Location: Britain. Imogen's bedchamber in Cymbeline's palace.
0.1. in her bed (On the Elizabethan stage, a curtain presumably would
be withdrawn from a recessed area backstage, revealing a bed and
trunk within. Alternatively, a bed could be "thrust out" at this point
and the trunk carried on containing Iachimo, unless he uses the
trapdoor or other such device. Imogen has a book; a lighted candle
is provided.)

IMOGEN
    What hour is it?
HELEN   Almost midnight, madam.
IMOGEN
    I have read three hours then. Mine eyes are weak.
                    [*She gives her the book.*]
    Fold down the leaf where I have left. To bed.
    Take not away the taper; leave it burning.
    And if thou canst awake by four o'th' clock,
    I prithee, call me. Sleep hath seized me wholly.
                    [*Exit Helen, leaving the book beside the bed.*]
    To your protection I commend me, gods.
    From fairies and the tempters of the night   9
    Guard me, beseech ye!
                    Sleeps. Iachimo [*comes*] *from the trunk.*

IACHIMO
    The crickets sing, and man's o'erlabored sense
    Repairs itself by rest. Our Tarquin thus   12
    Did softly press the rushes ere he wakened   13
    The chastity he wounded. Cytherea,   14
    How bravely thou becom'st thy bed, fresh lily,   15
    And whiter than the sheets! That I might touch!
    But kiss, one kiss! Rubies unparagoned,   17
    How dearly they do't! 'Tis her breathing that   18
    Perfumes the chamber thus. The flame o'th' taper
    Bows toward her and would underpeep her lids
    To see th'enclosèd lights, now canopied
    Under these windows, white and azure-laced   22
    With blue of heaven's own tinct. But my design—   23
    To note the chamber. I will write all down.
                    [*He writes.*]
    Such and such pictures; there the window; such
    Th'adornment of her bed; the arras, figures,   26
    Why, such and such; and the contents o'th' story. 27
    Ah, but some natural notes about her body   28
    Above ten thousand meaner movables   29
    Would testify t'enrich mine inventory.
    O sleep, thou ape of death, lie dull upon her,   31
    And be her sense but as a monument   32
    Thus in a chapel lying! Come off, come off;
                    [*taking off her bracelet*]
    As slippery as the Gordian knot was hard!   34
    'Tis mine; and this will witness outwardly,
    As strongly as the conscience does within,   36
    To th' madding of her lord. On her left breast   37
    A mole cinque-spotted, like the crimson drops   38
    I'th' bottom of a cowslip. Here's a voucher

Stronger than ever law could make. This secret
Will force him think I have picked the lock and ta'en
The treasure of her honor. No more. To what end?
Why should I write this down that's riveted,
Screwed to my memory? She hath been reading late
The tale of Tereus; here the leaf's turned down   45
Where Philomel gave up. I have enough.
To th' trunk again, and shut the spring of it.
Swift, swift, you dragons of the night, that dawning
May bare the raven's eye! I lodge in fear;   49
Though this a heavenly angel, hell is here.
                    Clock strikes.
One, two, three. Time, time!   51
                    [*He goes into the trunk.*] *Exeunt.*

❖

2.3

    Enter Cloten and Lords.

FIRST LORD   Your Lordship is the most patient man in
    loss, the most coldest that ever turned up ace.   2
CLOTEN   It would make any man cold to lose.   3
FIRST LORD   But not every man patient after the noble
    temper of Your Lordship. You are most hot and furious
    when you win.
CLOTEN   Winning will put any man into courage. If I
    could get this foolish Imogen, I should have gold
    enough. It's almost morning, is't not?
FIRST LORD   Day, my lord.
CLOTEN   I would this music would come. I am advised
    to give her music o' mornings; they say it will pene- 12
    trate.   13

    Enter Musicians.

Come on, tune. If you can penetrate her with your
fingering, so; we'll try with tongue too. If none will 15
do, let her remain, but I'll never give o'er. First, a very
excellent good-conceited thing; after, a wonderful   17
sweet air, with admirable rich words to it—and then   18
let her consider.   [*Music plays.*]
MUSICIAN [*sings*]

            Song.

    Hark, hark, the lark at heaven's gate sings,
        And Phoebus 'gins arise,   21

---

9 **fairies** i.e., evil spirits   12 **Our Tarquin** the Roman Sextus Tarquinius, who raped Lucrece   13 **rushes** (Elizabethan floors were
strewn with rushes or reeds.)   14 **Cytherea** Venus   15 **bravely** handsomely   17 **Rubies** Red lips   18 **do't** i.e., kiss each other.   22 **windows** i.e., eyelids   23 **tinct** color, hue.   26 **arras** tapestry.   **figures**
carvings   27 **contents . . . story** narrative represented in the tapestry (?).
28 **notes** marks   29 **meaner movables** less important furnishings
31 **ape** i.e., imitator.   **dull** heavy   32 **be . . . monument** let her be as
insensible as a horizontal effigy on a tomb   34 **slippery** easy to slip
off.   **Gordian knot** (According to prophecy, whoever untied the knot
binding the yoke to the pole of the chariot of Gordius, peasant King
of Phrygia, should be king of all Asia. Alexander severed the knot
with his sword.)   36 **conscience** consciousness, internal conviction
37 **madding** maddening   38 **cinque-spotted** with five spots

45 **Tereus** mythical king of Thrace, who raped Philomela, sister of his
wife, Procne. (He had Philomela's tongue cut out so that she could
not tell the story, but she wove it into a tapestry.)   49 **raven's eye**
(The raven was supposed to wake at early dawn.)   51.1 **Exeunt** (Presumably the bed, and trunk with Iachimo inside, are carried offstage,
unless Iachimo exits by a trapdoor or other means as a way of reen-
tering the "trunk.")
**2.3. Location: Britain. Adjoining Imogen's apartments. The sense of
time is nearly continuous, since it is early morn.**
2 **the most . . . ace** the least impatient person that ever threw the lowest throw of one at dice. (With a pun on *ass*.)   3 **cold** gloomy, dispir-
ited   12–13 **penetrate** affect the feelings. (With suggestion of
penetrating her sexually; continued in *fingering* and *tongue*, line 15.
See also lines 72, 77, and notes.)   15 **so it** is well   17 **good-conceited**
imaginatively invented   18 **air** accompanied song for single voice
21 **Phoebus** i.e., the sun-god with his chariot and horses

His steeds to water at those springs
    On chaliced flowers that lies;   23
And winking marybuds begin   24
    To ope their golden eyes.
With everything that pretty is,
    My lady sweet, arise,
        Arise, arise!

CLOTEN   So, get you gone. If this penetrate, I will con- 29
sider your music the better; if it do not, it is a vice in 30
her ears, which horsehairs and calves' guts, nor the 31
voice of unpaved eunuch to boot, can never amend. 32
                          [*Exeunt Musicians.*]

Enter Cymbeline and Queen.

SECOND LORD   Here comes the King.
CLOTEN   I am glad I was up so late, for that's the reason
I was up so early. He cannot choose but take this ser-
vice I have done fatherly.—Good morrow to Your 36
Majesty, and to my gracious mother.
CYMBELINE
Attend you here the door of our stern daughter?
Will she not forth?
CLOTEN   I have assailed her with musics, but she vouch-
safes no notice.
CYMBELINE
The exile of her minion is too new;   42
She hath not yet forgot him. Some more time   43
Must wear the print of his remembrance on't,   44
And then she's yours.
QUEEN   You are most bound to th' King,
Who lets go by no vantages that may   46
Prefer you to his daughter. Frame yourself   47
To orderly solicits, and be friended   48
With aptness of the season; make denials   49
Increase your services; so seem as if
You were inspired to do those duties which
You tender to her; that you in all obey her,
Save when command to your dismission tends,   53
And therein you are senseless.   54
CLOTEN   Senseless? Not so.

[*Enter a Messenger.*]

MESSENGER
So like you, sir, ambassadors from Rome;   56
The one is Caius Lucius.
CYMBELINE   A worthy fellow,   57
Albeit he comes on angry purpose now;
But that's no fault of his. We must receive him

According to the honor of his sender;
And towards himself, his goodness forespent on us, 61
We must extend our notice. Our dear son,   62
When you have given good morning to your mistress,
Attend the Queen and us. We shall have need
T'employ you towards this Roman.—Come, our
    queen.   *Exeunt [all but Cloten].*
CLOTEN
If she be up, I'll speak with her; if not,
Let her lie still and dream.—By your leave, ho!—
I know her women are about her. What
If I do line one of their hands? 'Tis gold   69
Which buys admittance—oft it doth—yea, and makes 70
Diana's rangers false themselves, yield up   71
Their deer to th' stand o'th' stealer; and 'tis gold 72
Which makes the true man killed and saves the thief, 73
Nay, sometimes hangs both thief and true man. What 74
Can it not do and undo? I will make
One of her women lawyer to me, for   76
I yet not understand the case myself.—   77
By your leave.   *Knocks.*

Enter a Lady.

LADY
Who's there that knocks?
CLOTEN   A gentleman.
LADY   No more?
CLOTEN
Yes, and a gentlewoman's son.
LADY [*aside*]   That's more
Than some, whose tailors are as dear as yours, 81
Can justly boast of.—What's Your Lordship's
    pleasure?
CLOTEN
Your lady's person. Is she ready?
LADY   Ay,   83
[*Aside*] To keep her chamber.
CLOTEN   There is gold for you;
Sell me your good report.   [*He offers money.*] 85
LADY
How? My good name? Or to report of you
What I shall think is good?—The Princess!   87
                          [*Exit Lady.*]

Enter Imogen.

61 his . . . us in light of the honorable conduct he has shown on past occasions **62 extend our notice** show special attentiveness. **69 line** i.e., with gold **70–2 makes . . . stealer** prompts the nymphs who serve as Diana's chaste gamekeepers to falsify their oaths by betraying the deer to the marauding huntsman—i.e., they admit a would-be seducing male in return for a bribe. (*Deer* puns on "dear"; *stand*, meaning the station for the huntsman waiting to shoot the game, has erotic connotations of male erection.) **73–4 Which . . . true man** (Gold can corrupt justice, sometimes with wantonly arbitrary consequences.) **76 her** Imogen's. **lawyer to** advocate for **77 understand the case** know how to conduct my suit. (With bawdy pun on *stand* again, line 72, and on *case*, meaning "vagina," as well as a legal *case* requiring a *lawyer*.) **81 dear** costly. (The Lady jests that expensive clothes are no guarantee of gentility.) **83 person** (1) presence (2) body. **ready** dressed. (But the Lady quibbles in another sense of "prepared, inclined.") **85 Sell . . . report** i.e., Let me offer this money in return for your speaking favorably on my behalf to Imogen. (But the Lady quibbles on *report* in the sense of "reputation, good name.") **87 What . . . good** what seems good to me to report (favorable or unfavorable).

23 chaliced with cuplike blossoms **24 winking marybuds** closed buds of marigolds, as though with closed eyes **29–30 consider** reward, value **31 horsehairs and calves' guts** i.e., bow hair and fiddle strings **32 unpaved** unstoned, castrated **36 fatherly** as a father would receive it, graciously and thankfully. **42 minion** darling **43–4 more . . . on't** more time must elapse, erasing the image of him on the memory **46 vantages** favorable occasions **47 Prefer** recommend. **Frame** Prepare **48 To** with. **solicits** soliciting, importunings **48–9 be . . . season** make timely use of your best opportunity **49 denials** i.e., Imogen's refusals **53–4 Save . . . senseless** except when she orders you to leave—a command you profess not to understand. (Cloten, however, understands *senseless* as meaning "stupid.") **56 So like you** If you please **57 The one** the chief one

CLOTEN
Good morrow, fairest. Sister, your sweet hand.

IMOGEN
Good morrow, sir. You lay out too much pains
For purchasing but trouble. The thanks I give
Is telling you that I am poor of thanks
And scarce can spare them.

CLOTEN   Still, I swear I love you.

IMOGEN
If you but said so, 'twere as deep with me.   93
If you swear still, your recompense is still   94
That I regard it not.

CLOTEN   This is no answer.

IMOGEN
But that you shall not say I yield being silent,   96
I would not speak. I pray you, spare me. Faith,
I shall unfold equal discourtesy   98
To your best kindness. One of your great knowing   99
Should learn, being taught, forbearance.

CLOTEN
To leave you in your madness, 'twere my sin.
I will not.

IMOGEN
Fools are not mad folks.

CLOTEN   Do you call me fool?   103

IMOGEN   As I am mad, I do.   104
If you'll be patient, I'll no more be mad;
That cures us both. I am much sorry, sir,
You put me to forget a lady's manners
By being so verbal; and learn now for all   108
That I, which know my heart, do here pronounce,   109
By th' very truth of it, I care not for you,
And am so near the lack of charity   111
To accuse myself I hate you—which I had rather   112
You felt than make 't my boast.

CLOTEN   You sin against   113
Obedience, which you owe your father. For   114
The contract you pretend with that base wretch,   115
One bred of alms and fostered with cold dishes,
With scraps o'th' court, it is no contract, none.
And though it be allowed in meaner parties—   118
Yet who than he more mean?—to knit their souls,

On whom there is no more dependency   120
But brats and beggary, in self-figured knot,   121
Yet you are curbed from that enlargement by   122
The consequence o'th' crown, and must not foil   123
The precious note of it with a base slave,   124
A hilding for a livery, a squire's cloth,   125
A pantler—not so eminent.

IMOGEN   Profane fellow!   126
Wert thou the son of Jupiter and no more
But what thou art besides, thou wert too base
To be his groom. Thou wert dignified enough,   129
Even to the point of envy, if 'twere made   130
Comparative for your virtues, to be styled   131
The underhangman of his kingdom, and hated
For being preferred so well.

CLOTEN   The south fog rot him!   133

IMOGEN
He never can meet more mischance than come
To be but named of thee. His mean'st garment   135
That ever hath but clipped his body is dearer   136
In my respect than all the hairs above thee,   137
Were they all made such men.—How now, Pisanio!   138

Enter Pisanio.

CLOTEN   "His garment!" Now the devil—

IMOGEN
To Dorothy my woman hie thee presently.   140

CLOTEN
"His garment!"

IMOGEN   I am sprited with a fool,   141
Frighted, and angered worse. Go bid my woman
Search for a jewel that too casually
Hath left mine arm. It was thy master's. 'Shrew me   144
If I would lose it for a revenue
Of any king's in Europe. I do think
I saw 't this morning; confident I am
Last night 'twas on mine arm; I kissed it.
I hope it be not gone to tell my lord
That I kiss aught but he.

PISANIO   'Twill not be lost.

IMOGEN
I hope so. Go and search.   [*Exit Pisanio.*]

CLOTEN   You have abused me.
"His meanest garment!"

IMOGEN   Ay, I said so, sir.

---

93 **deep** binding, efficacious. (Imogen's point is that Cloten's oath adds nothing to his unwelcome protestation of love.)   94 **still** constantly. (Imogen puns on Cloten's *Still,* "nonetheless," in line 92.)
96 **But . . . silent** If it were not for the fact that you might interpret my silence as giving consent   98 **unfold equal discourtesy** display discourtesy equal   99 **knowing** knowledge, discernment. (Said with tactful irony.)   103 **Fools . . . folks** i.e., I may seem a fool to refuse you or to waste time talking with you, but that doesn't make me mad (?), or, if I'm mad, as you say, at least I'm not a fool like you (?)
104 **As I am mad** Insofar as I am mad (and you, after all, were the one who said I was mad)   108 **By . . . verbal** (If the phrase refers to Cloten, the meaning of *verbal* is "verbose"; if it refers to Imogen, "plainspoken.")   **for all** once and for all   109 **which** who
111–13 **And . . . boast** and am so nearly lacking in Christian charity as to be obliged to accuse myself of hating you—which I would rather you perceived without my having to say it.   114 **For** As for
115 **pretend** allege   118 **meaner parties** persons of lower social rank, who, says Cloten, are allowed to choose in marriage because the only consequence is their own child-burdened poverty

120–1 **On . . . knot** from whose marriage there are no consequences other than many children and poverty, in a self-contracted union
122 **enlargement** liberty, freedom of action   123 **consequence** succession, all that follows as a result of your being heir to the throne.   **foil** defile, foul   124 **note** reputation   125 **hilding for a livery** good-for-nothing fellow fit only for wearing a servant's uniform.   **cloth** uniform, livery   126 **pantler** pantry-servant.   **not** not even   129 **his** Posthumus's   129–33 **Thou wert . . . so well** If you and Posthumus were to be compared in virtue, you would be given high enough status, even to the point of being envied and hated for your promotion, if you were given the title of assistant hangman of his kingdom.   133 **south fog** (The south wind was supposed to be laden with poisonous vapors and diseases.)   135 **of** by   136 **clipped** embraced   137 **respect** regard.   **above thee** on your head   138 **such men** such men as you are.
140 **hie thee presently** go at once.   141 **sprited with** haunted by
144 **'Shrew me** Beshrew me. (A mild oath.)

If you will make 't an action, call witness to't.   153

CLOTEN
I will inform your father.

IMOGEN   Your mother too.
She's my good lady and will conceive, I hope,   155
But the worst of me. So, I leave you, sir,
To th' worst of discontent.   *Exit.*

CLOTEN   I'll be revenged.
"His mean'st garment!" Well.   *Exit.*

❖

2.4

Enter Posthumus and Philario.

POSTHUMUS
Fear it not, sir. I would I were so sure
To win the King as I am bold her honor   2
Will remain hers.

PHILARIO   What means do you make to him?   3

POSTHUMUS
Not any, but abide the change of time,
Quake in the present winter's state, and wish
That warmer days would come. In these feared hopes   6
I barely gratify your love; they failing,   7
I must die much your debtor.

PHILARIO   Your very goodness and your company
O'erpays all I can do. By this, your king   10
Hath heard of great Augustus; Caius Lucius   11
Will do 's commission throughly. And I think   12
He'll grant the tribute, send th'arrearages,   13
Or look upon our Romans, whose remembrance   14
Is yet fresh in their grief.

POSTHUMUS   I do believe,   15
Statist though I am none, nor like to be,   16
That this will prove a war; and you shall hear
The legions now in Gallia sooner landed
In our not-fearing Britain than have tidings
Of any penny tribute paid. Our countrymen
Are men more ordered than when Julius Caesar   21
Smiled at their lack of skill but found their courage
Worthy his frowning at. Their discipline,   23
Now mingled with their courages, will make known

To their approvers they are people such   25
That mend upon the world.

Enter Iachimo.

PHILARIO   See! Iachimo!   26

POSTHUMUS
The swiftest harts have posted you by land,   27
And winds of all the corners kissed your sails,   28
To make your vessel nimble.

PHILARIO   Welcome, sir.

POSTHUMUS
I hope the briefness of your answer made   30
The speediness of your return.

IACHIMO   Your lady
Is one of the fairest that I have looked upon.

POSTHUMUS
And therewithal the best, or let her beauty
Look through a casement to allure false hearts   34
And be false with them.

IACHIMO   Here are letters for you.
[*He gives a letter or letters.*]

POSTHUMUS
Their tenor good, I trust.

IACHIMO   'Tis very like.   36

PHILARIO
Was Caius Lucius in the Briton court
When you were there?

IACHIMO   He was expected then,
But not approached.   39

POSTHUMUS   All is well yet.   40
Sparkles this stone as it was wont, or is 't not
Too dull for your good wearing? [*Indicating the ring.*]

IACHIMO   If I have lost it,   42
I should have lost the worth of it in gold.
I'll make a journey twice as far t'enjoy
A second night of such sweet shortness which
Was mine in Britain, for the ring is won.

POSTHUMUS
The stone's too hard to come by.

IACHIMO   Not a whit,
Your lady being so easy.

POSTHUMUS   Make not, sir,
Your loss your sport. I hope you know that we
Must not continue friends.

IACHIMO   Good sir, we must,
If you keep covenant. Had I not brought
The knowledge of your mistress home, I grant   52

---

153 action action at law   **155 good lady** i.e., patroness. (Said ironically.)   **conceive** believe, think.   **hope** (Continues the irony, though it can also mean "expect.")
2.4. Location: Rome. Philario's house.
2 bold confident   **3 means** overtures.   **him** i.e., the King.   **6 feared** mixed with fear   **7 gratify** repay   **10 this** this time   **11 of** from
12 do 's do his.   **throughly** thoroughly.   **13 He'll** i.e., Cymbeline will.
13–15 send . . . grief (and) send the part of the tribute still in arrears, sooner than face the Romans, the remembrance of whom is yet fresh in the Britons' grief. (*Or* can mean "ere," "sooner than," or possibly "or else"; *grief* could refer to the grief inflicted by the Romans.)
16 Statist statesman.   **like** likely   **21 more ordered** better disciplined and governed.   **Julius Caesar** (As proconsul in Gaul in 58–49 B.C., Caesar extended Roman dominion into Britain.)   **23 frowning** i.e., in stern military resolve and concern, not disapproval

25 their approvers those who test their courage   **25–6 such . . . world** such as are able to improve their standing in the world's estimation.
27 The swiftest . . . land i.e., You have made speed as if conveyed on land by the swiftest of deer   **28 of all the corners** from every corner
30 hope expect.   **your answer** the answer you were given   **34 Look through a casement** (As a whore might show herself to attract customers. The *casement* here is her body or perhaps her laced bodice.)
36 like likely.   **39 not** had not   **40 All is well yet** (Posthumus is evidently reassured by what he has read of the letter.)   **42 s.d. Indicating the ring** (The ring possibly is in the custody of Philario as official of the wager; although Posthumus appears to have it himself at line 108, he may then take it from Philario and give it to Iachimo.)
52 knowledge i.e., carnal knowledge

We were to question farther; but I now 53
Profess myself the winner of her honor,
Together with your ring, and not the wronger
Of her or you, having proceeded but
By both your wills.

POSTHUMUS　　　　If you can make 't apparent
That you have tasted her in bed, my hand
And ring is yours; if not, the foul opinion
You had of her pure honor gains or loses 60
Your sword or mine, or masterless leaves both 61
To who shall find them.

IACHIMO　　　　　Sir, my circumstances, 62
Being so near the truth as I will make them,
Must first induce you to believe; whose strength
I will confirm with oath, which I doubt not
You'll give me leave to spare when you shall find 66
You need it not.

POSTHUMUS　　　　Proceed.

IACHIMO　　　　　First, her bedchamber—
Where, I confess, I slept not, but profess
Had that was well worth watching—it was hanged 69
With tapestry of silk and silver; the story
Proud Cleopatra when she met her Roman,
And Cydnus swelled above the banks, or for 72
The press of boats or pride. A piece of work
So bravely done, so rich, that it did strive 74
In workmanship and value, which I wondered 75
Could be so rarely and exactly wrought,
Since the true life on't was—

POSTHUMUS　　　　　This is true; 77
And this you might have heard of here, by me
Or by some other.

IACHIMO　　　　More particulars
Must justify my knowledge.

POSTHUMUS　　　　So they must, 80
Or do your honor injury.

IACHIMO　　　　The chimney 81
Is south the chamber, and the chimneypiece 82
Chaste Dian bathing. Never saw I figures 83
So likely to report themselves. The cutter 84
Was as another nature, dumb; outwent her, 85
Motion and breath left out.

POSTHUMUS　　　　This is a thing 86
Which you might from relation likewise reap, 87
Being, as it is, much spoke of.

IACHIMO　　　　The roof o'th' chamber
With golden cherubins is fretted. Her andirons— 89

I had forgot them—were two winking Cupids 90
Of silver, each on one foot standing, nicely 91
Depending on their brands.

POSTHUMUS　　　　This is her honor! 92
Let it be granted you have seen all this—and praise
Be given to your remembrance—the description 94
Of what is in her chamber nothing saves 95
The wager you have laid.

IACHIMO　　　　Then, if you can 96
Be pale, I beg but leave to air this jewel. See! 97
　　　　　　　　[He shows the bracelet.]
And now 'tis up again. It must be married 98
To that your diamond; I'll keep them.

POSTHUMUS　　　　Jove!
Once more let me behold it. Is it that
Which I left with her?

IACHIMO　　　　Sir—I thank her—that.
She stripped it from her arm; I see her yet;
Her pretty action did outsell her gift, 103
And yet enriched it too. She gave it me
And said she prized it once.

POSTHUMUS　Maybe she plucked it off
To send it me.

IACHIMO　　　　She writes so to you, doth she?

POSTHUMUS
Oh, no, no, no! 'Tis true. Here, take this too.
　　　　　　　　[He gives the ring.]
It is a basilisk unto mine eye, 109
Kills me to look on't. Let there be no honor
Where there is beauty, truth where semblance, love 111
Where there's another man. The vows of women
Of no more bondage be to where they are made
Than they are to their virtues, which is nothing. 114
Oh, above measure false!

PHILARIO　　　　Have patience, sir,
And take your ring again; 'tis not yet won.
It may be probable she lost it; or
Who knows if one her women, being corrupted, 118
Hath stolen it from her?

POSTHUMUS　Very true,
And so, I hope, he came by't. Back my ring!
　　　　　　　　[He takes back the ring.]
Render to me some corporal sign about her
More evident than this; for this was stolen. 123

IACHIMO
By Jupiter, I had it from her arm.

POSTHUMUS
Hark you, he swears; by Jupiter he swears.
'Tis true—nay, keep the ring—'tis true. I am sure
She would not lose it. Her attendants are
All sworn and honorable. They induced to steal it? 128

---

53 **question** dispute, i.e., settle matters by a duel　**60–1 gains . . . mine** i.e., means that we must fight a duel　**62 who** whoever.　**circumstances** detailed observations　**66 spare** leave out　**69 that** that which.　**watching** remaining awake (for)　**72 Cydnus** a river in Cilicia, or modern-day southern Turkey, the scene of the meeting of Antony and Cleopatra. (See *Antony and Cleopatra,* 2.2.196–236.)　**or for** either because of　**74 bravely** handsomely　**74–5 it did . . . value** it was a question whether the workmanship or the monetary value was the greater　**77 on't** of it　**80 justify** confirm　**81 chimney** fireplace　**82 chimneypiece** sculptured mantelpiece　**83 Dian** Diana, goddess of chastity　**84 So . . . themselves** so like what they purported to represent, speaking likenesses.　**84–6 The cutter . . . out** The sculptor rivaled nature in creative power, albeit mute; indeed, he outwent nature, except that his creation lacked motion and the ability to breathe.　**87 relation** hearsay, report　**89 fretted** carved.

90 winking i.e., blind　**91–2 nicely . . . brands** ingeniously leaning on their torches.　**92 This . . . honor!** i.e., Is this what you can allege to impugn her honor? (Said sarcastically.)　**94 remembrance** ability to remember　**95 nothing** not at all　**96–7 if . . . pale** if you are prepared to look aghast　**98 up** put up, pocketed　**103 outsell** exceed in value　**109 basilisk** fabulous serpent or dragon whose look was fatal　**111 semblance** mere seeming　**114 Than . . . virtues** than women are bound to their virtuousness　**118 one** one of　**123 evident** conclusive　**128 sworn** bound by oath

And by a stranger? No, he hath enjoyed her.
The cognizance of her incontinency   130
Is this. She hath bought the name of whore thus
     dearly.
There, take thy hire, and all the fiends of hell   132
Divide themselves between you!
                              [*He gives the ring again.*]
PHILARIO   Sir, be patient.   133
This is not strong enough to be believed
Of one persuaded well of.
POSTHUMUS   Never talk on't.   135
She hath been colted by him.
IACHIMO   If you seek   136
For further satisfying, under her breast—
Worthy the pressing—lies a mole, right proud
Of that most delicate lodging. By my life,
I kissed it, and it gave me present hunger
To feed again, though full. You do remember
This stain upon her?
POSTHUMUS   Ay, and it doth confirm
Another stain, as big as hell can hold,
Were there no more but it.
IACHIMO   Will you hear more?
POSTHUMUS
Spare your arithmetic! Never count the turns.   145
Once, and a million!
IACHIMO   I'll be sworn—
POSTHUMUS   No swearing.   146
If you will swear you have not done't, you lie,
And I will kill thee if thou dost deny
Thou'st made me cuckold.
IACHIMO   I'll deny nothing.
POSTHUMUS
Oh, that I had her here, to tear her limbmeal!   150
I will go there and do't, i'th' court, before
Her father. I'll do something—   *Exit.*
PHILARIO   Quite besides   152
The government of patience! You have won.
Let's follow him and pervert the present wrath   154
He hath against himself.
IACHIMO   With all my heart.   *Exeunt.*

❧

[2.5]

Enter Posthumus.

POSTHUMUS
Is there no way for men to be, but women   1
Must be half-workers? We are all bastards,   2
And that most venerable man which I
Did call my father was I know not where

When I was stamped. Some coiner with his tools   5
Made me a counterfeit; yet my mother seemed
The Dian of that time. So doth my wife   7
The nonpareil of this. Oh, vengeance, vengeance!   8
Me of my lawful pleasure she restrained
And prayed me oft forbearance; did it with
A pudency so rosy the sweet view on't   11
Might well have warmed old Saturn, that I thought
     her   12
As chaste as unsunned snow. Oh, all the devils!
This yellow Iachimo, in an hour, was't not?   14
Or less? At first? Perchance he spoke not, but,   15
Like a full-acorned boar, a German one,   16
Cried "Oh!" and mounted; found no opposition
But what he looked for should oppose and she   18
Should from encounter guard. Could I find out
The woman's part in me! For there's no motion   20
That tends to vice in man but I affirm
It is the woman's part. Be it lying, note it,
The woman's; flattering, hers; deceiving, hers;
Lust and rank thoughts, hers, hers; revenges, hers;
Ambitions, covetings, change of prides, disdain,   25
Nice longing, slanders, mutability,   26
All faults that have a name, nay, that hell knows,
Why, hers, in part or all, but rather all.
For even to vice
They are not constant, but are changing still   30
One vice but of a minute old for one
Not half so old as that. I'll write against them,   32
Detest them, curse them. Yet 'tis greater skill   33
In a true hate to pray they have their will;   34
The very devils cannot plague them better.   *Exit.*

❧

3.1

*Enter in state, Cymbeline, Queen, Cloten, and
lords at one door, and at another, Caius Lucius
and attendants.*

CYMBELINE
Now say, what would Augustus Caesar with us?
LUCIUS
When Julius Caesar, whose remembrance yet   2

---

130 cognizance token   **132–3 all . . . you**! i.e., may you and Imogen suffer equal torments in hell!   **135 persuaded well of** well thought of.   **on't** of it.   **136 colted** enjoyed sexually   **145 turns** (With a bitter suggestion of "tricks," sexual encounters with a customer.)   **146 Once, and a million** i.e., What does it matter if once or a million times; it's all the same.   **150 limbmeal** limb from limb.   **152 besides** beyond   **154 pervert** divert
2.5. Location: Philario's house, as before. The scene may be virtually continuous.
1 be exist   **2 half-workers** partners, collaborators.

5 stamped (The image of procreation as an act of coinage by the father occurs often in Shakespeare.)   **tools** (With bitter suggestion of the male sexual organ.)   **7 Dian** Diana, goddess of chastity   **8 nonpareil** one who has no equal.   **this** this time.   **11 pudency** modesty.   **rosy** blushing (that).   **on't** of it   **12 Saturn** father of Jupiter, associated with old age   **14 yellow** sallow   **15 At first?** Right at first?   **16 full-acorned** full of acorns, favorite food of boars. (In German, *eichel*, "acorn," also means "penis" because of its glanslike shape.)   **18 But . . . oppose** i.e., except for the pleasant physical friction or barrier (the hymen) he expected in entering. (Imogen is no longer a virgin, being married, but the hymen still symbolizes what she should *guard* from *encounter*, line 19.)   **20 part** (With bitter sexual suggestion.)   **motion** impulse   **25 change of prides** varying vanities (in dress, etc.)   **26 Nice** fastidious, wanton.   **mutability** inconstancy   **30 still** continuously   **32 write against** denounce   **33–4 Yet . . . will** Yet the best way to damn women in a spirit of true hatred is simply to pray that they be encouraged to have their desire (since they will proceed then to damn themselves).
3.1. Location: Britain. At the court of Cymbeline.
2 whose remembrance the remembrance of whom

Lives in men's eyes, and will to ears and tongues
Be theme and hearing ever, was in this Britain
And conquered it, Cassibelan, thine uncle—
Famous in Caesar's praises no whit less
Than in his feats deserving it—for him
And his succession granted Rome a tribute,   8
Yearly three thousand pounds, which by thee lately
Is left untendered.
QUEEN   And, to kill the marvel,   10
Shall be so ever.
CLOTEN   There be many Caesars
Ere such another Julius. Britain's a world
By itself, and we will nothing pay
For wearing our own noses.
QUEEN   That opportunity   14
Which then they had to take from 's, to resume   15
We have again. Remember, sir, my liege,   16
The kings your ancestors, together with
The natural bravery of your isle, which stands
As Neptune's park, ribbed and paled in   19
With rocks unscalable and roaring waters,
With sands that will not bear your enemies' boats,
But suck them up to th' topmast. A kind of conquest
Caesar made here, but made not here his brag
Of "Came and saw and overcame." With shame—
The first that ever touched him—he was carried
From off our coast, twice beaten; and his shipping,
Poor ignorant baubles, on our terrible seas   27
Like eggshells moved upon their surges, cracked   28
As easily 'gainst our rocks. For joy whereof
The famed Cassibelan, who was once at point—   30
O giglot fortune!—to master Caesar's sword,   31
Made Lud's Town with rejoicing fires bright   32
And Britons strut with courage.
CLOTEN   Come, there's no more tribute to be paid. Our
kingdom is stronger than it was at that time; and, as I
said, there is no more such Caesars. Other of them may
have crooked noses, but to owe such straight arms,   37
none.
CYMBELINE   Son, let your mother end.   39
CLOTEN   We have yet many among us can grip as hard   40
as Cassibelan. I do not say I am one; but I have a hand.
Why tribute? Why should we pay tribute? If Caesar
can hide the sun from us with a blanket, or put the
moon in his pocket, we will pay him tribute for light;
else, sir, no more tribute, pray you now.
CYMBELINE [to Lucius] You must know,
Till the injurious Romans did extort   47
This tribute from us, we were free. Caesar's ambition,

Which swelled so much that it did almost stretch
The sides o'th' world, against all color here   50
Did put the yoke upon 's, which to shake off
Becomes a warlike people, whom we reckon
Ourselves to be. We do say then to Caesar,
Our ancestor was that Mulmutius which   54
Ordained our laws, whose use the sword of Caesar   55
Hath too much mangled, whose repair and franchise   56
Shall, by the power we hold, be our good deed,
Though Rome be therefore angry. Mulmutius made
   our laws,
Who was the first of Britain which did put
His brows within a golden crown and called
Himself a king.
LUCIUS   I am sorry, Cymbeline,
That I am to pronounce Augustus Caesar—
Caesar, that hath more kings his servants than
Thyself domestic officers—thine enemy.
Receive it from me, then: war and confusion   65
In Caesar's name pronounce I 'gainst thee. Look
For fury not to be resisted. Thus defied,   67
I thank thee for myself.
CYMBELINE   Thou art welcome, Caius.   68
Thy Caesar knighted me; my youth I spent
Much under him. Of him I gathered honor,
Which he to seek of me again perforce   71
Behooves me keep at utterance. I am perfect   72
That the Pannonians and Dalmatians for   73
Their liberties are now in arms, a precedent   74
Which not to read would show the Britons cold.   75
So Caesar shall not find them.
LUCIUS   Let proof speak.   76
CLOTEN   His Majesty bids you welcome. Make pastime
with us a day or two, or longer. If you seek us after-
wards in other terms, you shall find us in our saltwater   79
girdle. If you beat us out of it, it is yours; if you fall in   80
the adventure, our crows shall fare the better for you,   81
and there's an end.
LUCIUS   So, sir.
CYMBELINE
I know your master's pleasure and he mine.
All the remain is "Welcome!"   *Exeunt.*   85

8 **succession** heirs   10 **untendered** unpaid.   **to kill . . . marvel** to
end the suspense   14 **our own noses** i.e., British, not Roman, noses.
(See Cloten's gibe at the Romans' *crooked noses* in line 37.)   15–16 **to
resume . . . again** we now have the opportunity to take back.
19 **ribbed and palèd in** enclosed and fenced in   27 **ignorant baubles**
silly trifles   28 **their surges** the waves of the sea   30 **Cassibelan**
(The incident referred to is recorded of Nennius, brother of Cassibelan, in Holinshed.)   30 **at point** ready   31 **giglot** lewd, wanton
32 **Lud's Town** London (supposedly named after King Lud, Cymbe-
line's grandfather)   37 **owe** own.   **straight** i.e., strong   39 **end** finish speaking.   40 **can grip** who can grasp (a sword)   47 **injurious**
insolent

50 **against all color** in defiance of all rightful claim. (*Color*, "arguable
ground or claim," may also pun on *yoke*, "collar," in the next line.)
54 **Mulmutius** (according to legend, the first King of Britain)
55 **whose use** the exercise of which laws   56 **whose . . . franchise** the
repair and free exercise of which laws   65 **confusion** destruction
67 **Thus defied** You having been thus defied   68 **thank . . . myself**
thank you personally for this welcome.   71–2 **Which . . . utterance**
which honor, since he seeks to take it away from me, I must defend to
the last extremity of death. (From the French *à l'outrance*.)   72 **perfect**
well aware   73–4 **That . . . liberties** that the inhabitants of Hungary
and Dalmatia (along the Adriatic coast), in order to defend their liberties   74–5 **a precedent . . . cold** (Cymbeline implies that Britons should
be quick to see the military advantage to them of Rome's facing an
insurrection in the Balkans, draining off military resources and thus
providing Britons a *precedent* in refusing to pay tribute. *Cold* means
"lacking spirit.")   76 **proof** the outcome. (The proof of the pudding is
in the eating.)   79–80 **our saltwater girdle** our ocean-surrounded
island.   81 **crows** i.e., scavenger birds, like vultures   85 **All the
remain** All that remains (to be said)

3.2

Enter Pisanio, reading of a letter.

PISANIO
How? Of adultery? Wherefore write you not
What monster's her accuser? Leonatus,
Oh, master, what a strange infection
Is fall'n into thy ear! What false Italian,
As poisonous-tongued as handed, hath prevailed   5
On thy too ready hearing? Disloyal? No.   6
She's punished for her truth, and undergoes,   7
More goddesslike than wifelike, such assaults
As would take in some virtue. O my master,   9
Thy mind to her is now as low as were   10
Thy fortunes. How? That I should murder her,
Upon the love and truth and vows which I
Have made to thy command? I, her? Her blood?
If it be so to do good service, never
Let me be counted serviceable. How look I,
That I should seem to lack humanity
So much as this fact comes to? [*He reads.*] "Do't. The
    letter   17
That I have sent her, by her own command
Shall give thee opportunity." O damned paper,
Black as the ink that's on thee! Senseless bauble,   20
Art thou a fedarie for this act, and look'st   21
So virginlike without? Lo, here she comes.

Enter Imogen.

I am ignorant in what I am commanded.   23
IMOGEN   How now, Pisanio?
PISANIO
Madam, here is a letter from my lord.
IMOGEN [*taking the letter*]
Who, thy lord that is my lord, Leonatus?
Oh, learned indeed were that astronomer   27
That knew the stars as I his characters;   28
He'd lay the future open. You good gods,
Let what is here contained relish of love,   30
Of my lord's health, of his content—yet not   31
That we two are asunder; let that grieve him.
Some griefs are med'cinable; that is one of them,   33
For it doth physic love—of his content   34
All but in that! Good wax, thy leave. [*She breaks the
    seal.*] Blest be
You bees that make these locks of counsel! Lovers   36

And men in dangerous bonds pray not alike;   37
Though forfeiters you cast in prison, yet   38
You clasp young Cupid's tables. Good news, gods!   39
    [*She reads.*] "Justice and your father's wrath, should
he take me in his dominion, could not be so cruel to me 41
as you, O the dearest of creatures, would even renew   42
me with your eyes. Take notice that I am in Cambria,   43
at Milford Haven. What your own love will out of this
advise you, follow. So he wishes you all happiness
that remains loyal to his vow, and your increasing in   46
love.   Leonatus Posthumus."   47
Oh, for a horse with wings! Hear'st thou, Pisanio?
He is at Milford Haven. Read, and tell me
How far 'tis thither. If one of mean affairs   50
May plod it in a week, why may not I
Glide thither in a day? Then, true Pisanio,
Who long'st like me to see thy lord, who long'st—
Oh, let me bate—but not like me, yet long'st,   54
But in a fainter kind—oh, not like me,
For mine's beyond beyond; say, and speak thick—   56
Love's counselor should fill the bores of hearing,   57
To th' smothering of the sense—how far it is   58
To this same blessèd Milford. And by th' way   59
Tell me how Wales was made so happy as
T'inherit such a haven. But first of all,   61
How we may steal from hence, and for the gap
That we shall make in time from our hence-going
And our return, to excuse. But first, how get hence?
Why should excuse be born or ere begot?   65
We'll talk of that hereafter. Prithee, speak,
How many score of miles may we well ride
Twixt hour and hour?
PISANIO   One score twixt sun and sun, 68
Madam, 's enough for you—and too much too.   69
IMOGEN
Why, one that rode to 's execution, man,
Could never go so slow. I have heard of riding wagers   71
Where horses have been nimbler than the sands
That run i'th' clock's behalf. But this is fool'ry.   73

3.2. Location: Britain. At the court of Cymbeline.
0.1 *reading of* reading   **5 As . . . handed** as skilled in slander as in the
art of secret poisoning (for which the Italians were notorious)
6 ready credulous   **7 truth** fidelity   **9 take in** cause to yield   **10 to
her** compared to hers   **17 fact** deed   **20 Senseless bauble** Trifle incapable of feeling   **21 fedarie** accomplice   **23 am ignorant in** will
pretend not to know   **27 astronomer** astrologer   **28 characters** handwriting. (With a suggestion, too, of astrological symbols.)   **30 relish**
taste   **31 not** i.e., not content   **33 med'cinable** curative, health-giv-
ing   **34 physic** make healthy, strong   **36 locks of counsel** waxen
seals enclosing confidential matters.

36–9 Lovers . . . tables People in love don't address the same prayers to
you wax-making bees as do men at risk of penalties for contracts
they've signed; your beeswax, used to seal documents, puts forfeiters
of contracts in prison, whereas you bees seal with wax the writing
tablets or love letters used in the affairs of Cupid.   **41 take** apprehend
42 as but that. (The letter, however, is studiously ambiguous and suggests also that no one can be so cruel as she.)   **43 Cambria** Wales
46 that remains loyal more ambiguity: (1) to you who remain loyal
(2) on condition that you remain loyal   **46–7 your increasing in love**
(he wishes) your advancement and prosperity in love. (Suggesting, too,
he wishes your love for your husband were greater.)   **50 mean affairs**
ordinary business   **54 bate** moderate my speech   **56 beyond beyond**
i.e., even greater than something already great.   **thick** many words
quickly   **57 the bores of hearing** the ears   **58 To . . . sense** to the point
of overwhelming the sense of hearing   **59 by th' way** as we go
61 T'inherit to come to possess   **65 Why . . . begot?** i.e., Why worry
about how to excuse our absence before we've figured how to get
away?   **68 Twixt hour and hour** in an hour.   **One . . . and sun** twenty
miles a day   **69 too much too** i.e., even that would exhaust you. (But
suggesting also that she will arrive too soon at her fatal destiny. Her
answer unconsciously picks up the irony.)   **71 riding** racing   **73 That
. . . behalf** that run in the hourglass, doing the service of a clock.

Go bid my woman feign a sickness, say
She'll home to her father; and provide me presently   75
A riding suit no costlier than would fit
A franklin's huswife.

PISANIO   Madam, you're best consider.   77

IMOGEN
I see before me, man. Nor here, nor here,   78
Nor what ensues, but have a fog in them   79
That I cannot look through. Away, I prithee!
Do as I bid thee. There's no more to say.
Accessible is none but Milford way.
                              Exeunt [separately].

❧

3.3

*Enter [from the cave] Belarius; Guiderius, and
Arviragus [following].*

BELARIUS
A goodly day not to keep house with such   1
Whose roof's as low as ours. Stoop, boys; this gate
Instructs you how t'adore the heavens and bows you   3
To a morning's holy office. The gates of monarchs   4
Are arched so high that giants may jet through   5
And keep their impious turbans on, without
Good morrow to the sun.—Hail, thou fair heaven!
We house i'th' rock, yet use thee not so hardly   8
As prouder livers do.

GUIDERIUS   Hail, heaven!

ARVIRAGUS   Hail, heaven!   9

BELARIUS
Now for our mountain sport. Up to yond hill;
Your legs are young. I'll tread these flats. Consider,
When you above perceive me like a crow,   12
That it is place which lessens and sets off,   13
And you may then revolve what tales I have told you   14
Of courts, of princes, of the tricks in war.
This service is not service, so being done,   16
But being so allowed. To apprehend thus   17
Draws us a profit from all things we see;
And often, to our comfort, shall we find

The sharded beetle in a safer hold   20
Than is the full-winged eagle. Oh, this life
Is nobler than attending for a check,   22
Richer than doing nothing for a bauble,   23
Prouder than rustling in unpaid-for silk;   24
Such gain the cap of him that makes him fine,   25
Yet keeps his book uncrossed. No life to ours.   26

GUIDERIUS
Out of your proof you speak. We poor unfledged   27
Have never winged from view o'th' nest, nor know
   not
What air's from home. Haply this life is best,   29
If quiet life be best, sweeter to you
That have a sharper known, well corresponding
With your stiff age; but unto us it is
A cell of ignorance, traveling abed,   33
A prison for a debtor that not dares
To stride a limit.

ARVIRAGUS   What should we speak of   35
When we are old as you? When we shall hear
The rain and wind beat dark December, how,   37
In this our pinching cave, shall we discourse   38
The freezing hours away? We have seen nothing.
We are beastly: subtle as the fox for prey,
Like warlike as the wolf for what we eat.   41
Our valor is to chase what flies. Our cage   42
We make a choir, as doth the prisoned bird,
And sing our bondage freely.

BELARIUS   How you speak!   44
Did you but know the city's usuries
And felt them knowingly; the art o'th' court,
As hard to leave as keep, whose top to climb   47
Is certain falling, or so slipp'ry that
The fear's as bad as falling, the toil o'th' war,   49
A pain that only seems to seek out danger   50
I'th' name of fame and honor, which dies i'th' search
And hath as oft a slanderous epitaph
As record of fair act; nay, many times
Doth ill deserve by doing well; what's worse,   54
Must curtsy at the censure. Oh, boys, this story
The world may read in me. My body's marked
With Roman swords, and my report was once   57
First with the best of note. Cymbeline loved me,   58

---

75 She'll . . . father (The waiting woman's pretended emergency will justify her asking for a riding habit that Imogen can then use.) **77 franklin's** yeoman's. (A franklin was a farmer who owned his own land but was not of noble birth.)   **you're best** you had better **78 before me** immediately in front of me.   **Nor . . . here** (She gestures: not to this side, not to that.)   **79 ensues** happens later. (Imogen can only look directly ahead to Milford Haven, nowhere else and not beyond.)
3.3. Location: Wales. Before the cave of Belarius.
1 keep house stay at home   **3 bows you** makes you bow   **4 holy office** i.e., a morning prayer.   **5 jet** strut   **8 use . . . hardly** treat you not so badly, do not offend heaven as much. (With a play on the idea of *rock* and *hard*.)   **9 prouder livers** those who live more proudly and magnificently   **12 like a crow** appearing through distance as small as a crow   **13 place** position.   **sets off** enhances   **14 revolve** ponder **16–17 This . . . allowed** i.e., Any act of service is valued not for itself, but is valued as proof of the greatness of the person for whom the service is performed.

20 sharded living in dung, or, covered with the sheaths of insects' wings.   **hold** stronghold   **22 attending . . . check** doing service (at court) only to be rewarded with a rebuke   **23 bauble** trifle **24 unpaid-for** for which the wearer is in debt to his tailor **25–6 Such . . . uncrossed** such finery wins the respectful greeting of his tailor, but does nothing to cancel his record of debts.   **26 to** compared with   **27 proof** experience.   **unfledged** not yet feathered **29 What . . . home** what things are like away from home.   **Haply** Perhaps   **33 abed** i.e., in imagination only, in dreams   **35 stride a limit** overpass a bound (where the debtor will be liable for arrest). **37 beat dark December** beat down, as befitting dark December **38 pinching** nippingly cold, or, confining   **41 Like** as   **42 flies** flees. **44 freely** (Said ironically: the only freedom is to sing of one's bondage.)   **47 keep** dwell in   **49 the toil o'th' war** i.e., did you but know the toil of war   **50 pain** labor   **54 Doth . . . deserve** earns ungrateful treatment   **57 report** reputation   **58 the best of note** persons of the highest distinction.

And when a soldier was the theme, my name
Was not far off. Then was I as a tree
Whose boughs did bend with fruit. But in one night,   61
A storm, or robbery, call it what you will,
Shook down my mellow hangings, nay, my leaves,   63
And left me bare to weather.
GUIDERIUS   Uncertain favor!   64
BELARIUS
My fault being nothing—as I have told you oft—
But that two villains, whose false oaths prevailed
Before my perfect honor, swore to Cymbeline
I was confederate with the Romans. So
Followed my banishment, and this twenty years
This rock and these demesnes have been my world,   70
Where I have lived at honest freedom, paid   71
More pious debts to heaven than in all
The fore-end of my time. But up to th' mountains!   73
This is not hunters' language. He that strikes
The venison first shall be the lord o'th' feast;
To him the other two shall minister,
And we will fear no poison, which attends   77
In place of greater state. I'll meet you in the valleys.
                     Exeunt [Guiderius and Arviragus].
How hard it is to hide the sparks of nature!
These boys know little they are sons to th' King,
Nor Cymbeline dreams that they are alive.
They think they are mine; and though trained up thus
        meanly
I'th' cave wherein they bow, their thoughts do hit
The roofs of palaces, and nature prompts them
In simple and low things to prince it much   85
Beyond the trick of others. This Polydore,   86
The heir of Cymbeline and Britain, who
The King his father called Guiderius—Jove!
When on my three-foot stool I sit and tell
The warlike feats I have done, his spirits fly out
Into my story; say, "Thus mine enemy fell,
And thus I set my foot on 's neck," even then
The princely blood flows in his cheek, he sweats,
Strains his young nerves, and puts himself in posture   94
That acts my words. The younger brother, Cadwal,
Once Arviragus, in as like a figure   96
Strikes life into my speech and shows much more   97
His own conceiving. [_Sounds of hunting are heard._]
        Hark, the game is roused!—   98
O Cymbeline, heaven and my conscience knows
Thou didst unjustly banish me; whereon,
At three and two years old, I stole these babes,
Thinking to bar thee of succession as
Thou refts me of my lands. Euriphile,   103
Thou wast their nurse; they took thee for their mother,

And every day do honor to her grave.   105
Myself, Belarius, that am Morgan called,
They take for natural father.—The game is up.   107
                                              Exit.

3.4

Enter Pisanio and Imogen.

IMOGEN
Thou toldst me, when we came from horse, the place   1
Was near at hand. Ne'er longed my mother so
To see me first as I have now. Pisanio, man,   3
Where is Posthumus? What is in thy mind
That makes thee stare thus? Wherefore breaks that
        sigh
From th'inward of thee? One but painted thus
Would be interpreted a thing perplexed   7
Beyond self-explication. Put thyself   8
Into a havior of less fear, ere wildness   9
Vanquish my staider senses. What's the matter?   10
                        [_He offers her a letter._]
Why tender'st thou that paper to me with   11
A look untender? If't be summer news,
Smile to't before; if winterly, thou need'st
But keep that countenance still. My husband's hand?
That drug-damned Italy hath outcrafted him,   15
And he's at some hard point. Speak, man. Thy tongue   16
May take off some extremity, which to read   17
Would be even mortal to me.
PISANIO   Please you, read,   18
And you shall find me, wretched man, a thing
The most disdained of fortune.
IMOGEN (_reads_) "Thy mistress, Pisanio, hath played the
        strumpet in my bed, the testimonies whereof lies
        bleeding in me. I speak not out of weak surmises but
        from proof as strong as my grief and as certain as I
        expect my revenge. That part thou, Pisanio, must act
        for me, if thy faith be not tainted with the breach of
        hers. Let thine own hands take away her life. I shall
        give thee opportunity at Milford Haven—she hath
        my letter for the purpose—where, if thou fear to strike
        and to make me certain it is done, thou art the pander
        to her dishonor and equally to me disloyal."
PISANIO
What shall I need to draw my sword? The paper
Hath cut her throat already. No, 'tis slander,
Whose edge is sharper than the sword, whose tongue
Outvenoms all the worms of Nile, whose breath   35

---

61 Whose . . . fruit laden with rewards, the harvest of my efforts.
63 hangings hanging fruit   **64 Uncertain favor!** How unreliable is
the favor bestowed on one by great men!   **70 demesnes** domains,
regions   **71 at honest freedom** (Compare the phrases "at peace," "at
liberty.")   **73 fore-end** earlier part   **77 attends** is present, renders
service   **85 prince it** play the prince   **86 trick** manner   **94 nerves**
sinews   **96 in . . . figure** acting his part equally well   **97–8 shows . . .
conceiving** i.e., adds to my story his own conception.   **103 Thou
refts** you have bereft, deprived

105 her (Belarius shifts easily from apostrophizing the dead Euriphile
to speaking about her.)   **107 up** roused. (Belarius hears a hunting cry.)
3.4. Location: Wales. Country near Milford Haven.
1 came from horse dismounted   **3 have** i.e., have longing to see
Posthumus   **7–8 perplexed . . . self-explication** bewildered beyond
the ability to express his condition.   **9 havior of less fear** less fearsome behavior   **9–10 ere . . . senses** before frenzy and panic overcome my calm.   **11 tender'st** offerest. (With a play on _untender_ in the
next line.)   **15 That . . . him** That country notorious for its poisons
has overcome him by craft   **16 hard point** dangerous crisis.   **17 take
. . . extremity** reduce somewhat the shock   **18 mortal** fatal
35 worms serpents

Rides on the posting winds and doth belie   36
All corners of the world. Kings, queens, and states,   37
Maids, matrons, nay, the secrets of the grave
This viperous slander enters.—What cheer, madam?

IMOGEN
False to his bed? What is it to be false?
To lie in watch there and to think on him?   41
To weep twixt clock and clock? If sleep charge nature,   42
To break it with a fearful dream of him   43
And cry myself awake? That's false to's bed, is it?

PISANIO   Alas, good lady!

IMOGEN
I false? Thy conscience witness, Iachimo,   46
Thou didst accuse him of incontinency.
Thou then looked'st like a villain; now methinks
Thy favor's good enough. Some jay of Italy,   49
Whose mother was her painting, hath betrayed him.   50
Poor I am stale, a garment out of fashion,   51
And, for I am richer than to hang by th' walls,   52
I must be ripped. To pieces with me! Oh,   53
Men's vows are women's traitors! All good seeming,
By thy revolt, O husband, shall be thought   55
Put on for villainy; not born where't grows,   56
But worn a bait for ladies.

PISANIO   Good madam, hear me.

IMOGEN
True honest men being heard like false Aeneas   58
Were in his time thought false, and Sinon's weeping   59
Did scandal many a holy tear, took pity   60
From most true wretchedness. So thou, Posthumus,   61
Wilt lay the leaven on all proper men;   62
Goodly and gallant shall be false and perjured   63
From thy great fail.—Come, fellow, be thou honest;   64
Do thou thy master's bidding. When thou see'st him,
A little witness my obedience. Look,   66
         [drawing her sword and offering it to him]

I draw the sword myself. Take it, and hit
The innocent mansion of my love, my heart.
Fear not; 'tis empty of all things but grief.
Thy master is not there, who was indeed
The riches of it. Do his bidding; strike.
Thou mayst be valiant in a better cause,   72
But now thou seem'st a coward.

PISANIO [rejecting the sword]   Hence, vile instrument!
Thou shalt not damn my hand.

IMOGEN   Why, I must die;
And if I do not by thy hand, thou art
No servant of thy master's. Against self-slaughter
There is a prohibition so divine
That cravens my weak hand. Come, here's my heart.   78
Something's afore't. Soft, soft! We'll no defense;   79
Obedient as the scabbard. What is here?   80
         [She takes letters from her bodice.]
The scriptures of the loyal Leonatus,   81
All turned to heresy? Away, away,
Corrupters of my faith! [She throws away the letters.]
   You shall no more
Be stomachers to my heart. Thus may poor fools   84
Believe false teachers. Though those that are betrayed
Do feel the treason sharply, yet the traitor
Stands in worse case of woe. And thou, Posthumus,   87
That didst set up   88
My disobedience 'gainst the King my father
And make me put into contempt the suits
Of princely fellows, shalt hereafter find   91
It is no act of common passage, but   92
A strain of rareness; and I grieve myself   93
To think, when thou shalt be disedged by her   94
That now thou tirest on, how thy memory   95
Will then be panged by me.—Prithee, dispatch.   96
The lamb entreats the butcher. Where's thy knife?
Thou art too slow to do thy master's bidding
When I desire it too.

PISANIO   Oh, gracious lady,
Since I received command to do this business
I have not slept one wink.

IMOGEN
                          Do't, and to bed then.

PISANIO
I'll wake mine eyeballs blind first.

IMOGEN   Wherefore then   102
Didst undertake it? Why hast thou abused
So many miles with a pretense? This place?
Mine action and thine own? Our horses' labor?
The time inviting thee? The perturbed court,

36 posting hastening. belie spread lies throughout 37 states statesmen 41 in watch awake 42 twixt . . . clock from hour to hour. charge nature i.e., overcome wakefulness 43 fearful dream of him fearful dream about his safety 46 Thy conscience witness Let your conscience bear me witness. (She apostrophizes the absent Iachimo; see next note.) 49 Thy . . . enough your appearance is good enough (since what you said about Posthumus must sadly be true after all.) (Imogen thinks that some whore of Italy, not Iachimo, is to blame for this.) jay i.e., flashy or light woman 50 Whose . . . painting i.e., who owed her beauty to cosmetics 51 stale no longer fresh. (But with bitter suggestion of "harlot.") 52 And . . . walls and, because I am too expensive to hang up idly like discarded clothing 53 ripped torn apart (1) in murder (2) like rich garments unsewn to recover the cloth. 55 revolt inconstancy 56 born i.e., innate 58 being heard like when they were heard to speak like. Aeneas (Thought of as the pattern of faithless love because of his desertion of Dido.) 59 Were . . . false i.e., were mistrusted because of Aeneas's deceptive speech, which was indeed false; his smooth falsehood cast doubt even on perfectly honest professions of love. Sinon Greek who by his guile persuaded the Trojans to introduce within the walls of Troy the wooden horse filled with armed men 60 scandal bring scandal to, discredit 60–1 took pity From prevented the bestowing of well-deserved pity upon 62 lay . . . men take credit away from all well-deserving and honorable men (just as sour leaven or fermenting dough causes more dough to ferment and spoil) 63 be be thought 64 fail fault, offense. honest loyal to your vow of obedience. (Said with bitter irony.) 66 A little witness testify somewhat to

72 Thou mayst be Maybe you are 78 cravens makes cowardly 79 Something's i.e., Posthumus's letter is. Soft i.e., Wait a minute 80 Obedient i.e., as willing to receive the sword 81 scriptures writings, letters. (With a play on "Holy Scriptures.") 84 stomachers ornamental coverings for the breast worn by women under their bodices 87 Stands . . . woe i.e., risks the penalty of damnation. 88 set up incite, encourage 91 princely fellows those of equal social rank with me 92–3 It . . . rareness that my choice (of you) was no act of a common sort but a rare trait 94 disedged surfeited, having the edge of appetite taken off 95 thou tirest on you tear or devour ravenously (as a bird of prey) 96 panged pierced by thought of 102 wake . . . blind remain awake until I can no longer see

For my being absent, whereunto I never
Purpose return? Why hast thou gone so far,
To be unbent when thou hast ta'en thy stand,   109
Th'elected deer before thee?
PISANIO   But to win time   110
To lose so bad employment, in the which   111
I have considered of a course. Good lady,
Hear me with a patience.
IMOGEN   Talk thy tongue weary. Speak.
I have heard I am a strumpet, and mine ear,
Therein false struck, can take no greater wound,   115
Nor tent to bottom that. But speak.
PISANIO   Then, madam,   116
I thought you would not back again.
IMOGEN   Most like,   117
Bringing me here to kill me.
PISANIO   Not so, neither.
But if I were as wise as honest, then   119
My purpose would prove well. It cannot be   120
But that my master is abused. Some villain,   121
Ay, and singular in his art, hath done   122
You both this cursèd injury.
IMOGEN
Some Roman courtesan.
PISANIO   No, on my life.
I'll give but notice you are dead, and send him
Some bloody sign of it, for 'tis commanded
I should do so. You shall be missed at court,
And that will well confirm it.
IMOGEN   Why, good fellow,
What shall I do the while? Where bide? How live?
Or in my life what comfort, when I am
Dead to my husband?
PISANIO   If you'll back to th' court—
IMOGEN
No court, no father, nor no more ado
With that harsh, noble, simple nothing,
That Cloten, whose love suit hath been to me
As fearful as a siege.
PISANIO   If not at court,
Then not in Britain must you bide.
IMOGEN   Where, then?
Hath Britain all the sun that shines? Day, night,
Are they not but in Britain? I'th' world's volume   138
Our Britain seems as of it but not in't,   139
In a great pool a swan's nest. Prithee, think
There's livers out of Britain.
PISANIO   I am most glad   141
You think of other place. Th'ambassador,
Lucius the Roman, comes to Milford Haven

Tomorrow. Now, if you could wear a mind   144
Dark as your fortune is, and but disguise   145
That which, t'appear itself, must not yet be   146
But by self-danger, you should tread a course   147
Pretty and full of view; yea, haply near   148
The residence of Posthumus, so nigh at least
That, though his actions were not visible, yet
Report should render him hourly to your ear
As truly as he moves.
IMOGEN   Oh, for such means!
Though peril to my modesty, not death on't,   153
I would adventure.
PISANIO   Well, then, here's the point.
You must forget to be a woman, change
Command into obedience; fear and niceness—   156
The handmaids of all women, or, more truly,
Woman its pretty self—into a waggish courage;   158
Ready in gibes, quick-answered, saucy, and
As quarrelous as the weasel. Nay, you must   160
Forget that rarest treasure of your cheek,
Exposing it—but oh, the harder heart!   162
Alack, no remedy—to the greedy touch
Of common-kissing Titan, and forget   164
Your laborsome and dainty trims, wherein   165
You made great Juno angry.
IMOGEN   Nay, be brief.   166
I see into thy end and am almost
A man already.
PISANIO   First, make yourself but like one.
Forethinking this, I have already fit—   169
'Tis in my cloak bag—doublet, hat, hose, all
That answer to them. Would you in their serving,   171
And with what imitation you can borrow
From youth of such a season, 'fore noble Lucius   173
Present yourself, desire his service, tell him   174
Wherein you're happy—which will make him know,   175
If that his head have ear in music—doubtless   176
With joy he will embrace you, for he's honorable,   177
And, doubling that, most holy. Your means abroad,   178

---

109 **To be unbent** to unbend your bow again (and thus refuse to shoot). **stand** place from which to shoot game   110 **Th'elected** the chosen.   **But** Only   111 **which** which time   115 **take** receive   116 **tent . . . that** probe that wound to the bottom.   117 **back** go back (to court).   **like** likely   119–20 **But . . . well** (Pisanio hopes the plan he is going to propose will be as clever as he is honest in intent.)   121 **abused** deceived.   122 **singular** unexcelled   138 **but** except   139 **as . . . in't** i.e., as part of it but a small and relatively insignificant part, on the periphery, like a page torn out of a volume   141 **livers** persons living

144–7 **if . . . self-danger** if you could adapt your spirit to the obscurity of your fortune and simply disguise your womanhood, which, if it were to reveal itself for what it truly is, remains full of self-danger for the present   148 **Pretty . . . view** advantageous and promising, affording a fair prospect.   **haply** perhaps. (With a suggestion also of "happily" [the Folio spelling], "fortunately.")   153 **Though . . . on't** As long as the risk to my modesty would not be fatal to it   156 **Command into obedience** i.e., as befitting one of royal birth. (Imogen will be disguising her royal birth and assuming the guise of one who must obey orders.) **niceness** daintiness   158 **waggish** roguish, masculine   160 **quarrelous** quarrelsome   162 **harder** too hard. (Pisanio is either reproaching the cruel necessity of his speaking so, or blaming Posthumus, or suggesting that Imogen must harden her heart.)   164 **common-kissing Titan** the sun god who kisses (i.e., shines on) everybody and everything   165 **laborsome . . . trims** elaborate and dainty apparel   166 **angry** i.e., jealous.   169 **Forethinking** Anticipating.   **fit** ready   171 **answer to** go along with.   **Would . . . serving** If you would, assisted by them   173 **of . . . season** of such an age as you will represent   174 **his service** employment in his service   175 **happy** gifted, skillful.   **make him know** convince him   176 **If . . . music** i.e., if he has an ear for music, since he then cannot fail to appreciate your voice   177 **embrace you** take you in (to his service)   178 **doubling that** twice as important.   **Your means abroad** As for your financial means while you are abroad

You have me, rich, and I will never fail   179
Beginning nor supplyment.   [*He gives her a cloak bag.*]

IMOGEN   Thou art all the comfort   180
The gods will diet me with. Prithee, away.   181
There's more to be considered, but we'll even   182
All that good time will give us. This attempt
I am soldier to, and will abide it with   184
A prince's courage. Away, I prithee.

PISANIO
Well, madam, we must take a short farewell,
Lest, being missed, I be suspected of
Your carriage from the court. My noble mistress,   188
Here is a box; I had it from the Queen.
                                    [*He gives a box.*]
What's in't is precious. If you are sick at sea
Or stomach-qualmed at land, a dram of this
Will drive away distemper. To some shade,   192
And fit you to your manhood. May the gods
Direct you to the best!

IMOGEN   Amen. I thank thee.
                                    Exeunt [*separately*].

❧

3.5

Enter Cymbeline, Queen, Cloten, Lucius,
[*Attendants,*] *and Lords.*

CYMBELINE
Thus far, and so farewell.

LUCIUS   Thanks, royal sir.   1
My emperor hath wrote I must from hence;   2
And am right sorry that I must report ye
My master's enemy.

CYMBELINE   Our subjects, sir,
Will not endure his yoke, and for ourself
To show less sovereignty than they must needs
Appear unkinglike.

LUCIUS   So, sir. I desire of you   7
A conduct overland to Milford Haven.   8
Madam, all joy befall Your Grace, and you!   9

CYMBELINE
My lords, you are appointed for that office;   10
The due of honor in no point omit.
So farewell, noble Lucius.

LUCIUS [*to Cloten*]   Your hand, my lord.

CLOTEN
Receive it friendly; but from this time forth

I wear it as your enemy.

LUCIUS   Sir, the event   14
Is yet to name the winner. Fare you well.

CYMBELINE
Leave not the worthy Lucius, good my lords,
Till he have crossed the Severn. Happiness!   17
                                    Exeunt Lucius etc.

QUEEN
He goes hence frowning, but it honors us
That we have given him cause.

CLOTEN   'Tis all the better;
Your valiant Britons have their wishes in it.

CYMBELINE
Lucius hath wrote already to the Emperor
How it goes here. It fits us therefore ripely   22
Our chariots and our horsemen be in readiness.
The powers that he already hath in Gallia   24
Will soon be drawn to head, from whence he moves   25
His war for Britain.

QUEEN   'Tis not sleepy business,
But must be looked to speedily and strongly.

CYMBELINE
Our expectation that it would be thus
Hath made us forward. But, my gentle queen,   29
Where is our daughter? She hath not appeared
Before the Roman, nor to us hath tendered
The duty of the day. She looks us like   32
A thing more made of malice than of duty.
We have noted it.—Call her before us, for
We have been too slight in sufferance.
                                    [*Exit an Attendant.*]

QUEEN   Royal sir,   35
Since the exile of Posthumus, most retired
Hath her life been; the cure whereof, my lord,
'Tis time must do. Beseech Your Majesty,
Forbear sharp speeches to her. She's a lady
So tender of rebukes that words are strokes
And strokes death to her.

Enter [*Attendant as*] *a messenger.*

CYMBELINE   Where is she, sir? How
Can her contempt be answered?

ATTENDANT   Please you, sir,   42
Her chambers are all locked, and there's no answer
That will be given to th' loud'st of noise we make.

QUEEN
My lord, when last I went to visit her,
She prayed me to excuse her keeping close,   46
Whereto constrained by her infirmity
She should that duty leave unpaid to you   48
Which daily she was bound to proffer. This
She wished me to make known, but our great court   50

---

179 **rich** adequately supplied with funds   180 **Beginning nor sup-**
plyment from first to last in supplying your needs.   181 **diet** feed
182 **even** keep pace with, profit by   184 **soldier to** enlisted in, courageously prepared for.   **abide it** sustain it, stick with it   188 **Your car-**
riage having removed you   192 **distemper** illness.   **shade** secluded
and protected spot
3.5. Location: At the court of Cymbeline.
1 **Thus far** Thus far we can escort you   2 **wrote** written. (Also in line
21.)   7 **So** i.e., Very good. (A polite way of closing the discussion.)
8 **conduct** safe-conduct, escort   9 **and you** (Possibly addressed to
Cloten, or, more probably, to the King. Lucius bids farewell to Cloten
in line 12.)   10 **office** duty (as escorts of Lucius)

14 **event** outcome   17 **Severn** river between England and Wales.
22 **fits** befits.   **ripely** speedily   24 **powers** armed forces   25 **drawn**
to head brought together, assembled   29 **forward** well prepared.
32 **looks us** seems to me   35 **slight in sufferance** permissive.
42 **answered** accounted for.   46 **close** in private   48 **She . . . leave**
she found herself obliged to leave that duty   50 **great court** important courtly business

Made me to blame in memory.

CYMBELINE   Her doors locked?
Not seen of late? Grant, heavens, that which I fear
Prove false!   *Exit.*

QUEEN   Son, I say, follow the King.

CLOTEN
That man of hers, Pisanio, her old servant,
I have not seen these two days.

QUEEN   Go, look after.
                                         Exit [Cloten].

Pisanio, thou that stand'st so for Posthumus!   56
He hath a drug of mine; I pray his absence
Proceed by swallowing that, for he believes   58
It is a thing most precious. But for her,
Where is she gone? Haply despair hath seized her,
Or, winged with fervor of her love, she's flown
To her desired Posthumus. Gone she is
To death or to dishonor, and my end   63
Can make good use of either. She being down,
I have the placing of the British crown.

        Enter Cloten.

How now, my son?

CLOTEN   'Tis certain she is fled.
Go in and cheer the King. He rages; none
Dare come about him.

QUEEN   All the better. May
This night forestall him of the coming day!   69
                                         Exit Queen.

CLOTEN
I love and hate her. For she's fair and royal,   70
And that she hath all courtly parts more exquisite   71
Than lady, ladies, woman—from every one   72
The best she hath, and she, of all compounded,   73
Outsells them all—I love her therefore. But   74
Disdaining me and throwing favors on   75
The low Posthumus slanders so her judgment   76
That what's else rare is choked; and in that point   77
I will conclude to hate her, nay, indeed,
To be revenged upon her. For when fools
Shall—

        Enter Pisanio. [He attempts to avoid Cloten.]

             Who is here? What, are you packing, sirrah?   80
Come hither. Ah, you precious pander! Villain,
Where is thy lady? In a word, or else
Thou art straightway with the fiends.
                    [He threatens him with his sword.]

PISANIO   Oh, good my lord!

CLOTEN
Where is thy lady? Or, by Jupiter,
I will not ask again. Close villain,   85

---

56 **thou that stand'st so** you who stand up so for, look out for the interests of   58 **Proceed by** results from   63 **end** intent   69 **forestall** deprive (i.e., bring about his death)   70 **For** Because   71 **that** because. **parts** endowments, graces   72 **Than lady, ladies, woman** than any lady, or all ladies, or indeed womankind   72–3 **from . . . she hath** she has the best qualities of each   74 **Outsells** outvalues, excels   75 **Disdaining** her disdaining   76 **slanders** discredits   77 **rare** excellent   80 **packing** plotting and sneaking away.   **sirrah** (Form of address to a social inferior; also in lines 106 and 108.)   85 **Close** Secretive

I'll have this secret from thy heart or rip
Thy heart to find it. Is she with Posthumus,
From whose so many weights of baseness cannot   88
A dram of worth be drawn?

PISANIO   Alas, my lord,   89
How can she be with him? When was she missed?
He is in Rome.

CLOTEN   Where is she, sir? Come nearer.   91
No farther halting. Satisfy me home   92
What is become of her.

PISANIO
Oh, my all-worthy lord!

CLOTEN   All-worthy villain!
Discover where thy mistress is at once,   95
At the next word. No more of "worthy lord"!
Speak, or thy silence on the instant is
Thy condemnation and thy death.

PISANIO   Then, sir,
This paper is the history of my knowledge
Touching her flight.   *[He presents a letter.]*

CLOTEN   Let's see't. I will pursue her
Even to Augustus' throne.

PISANIO *[aside]*   Or this or perish.   101
She's far enough, and what he learns by this
May prove his travel, not her danger.

CLOTEN *[reading]*   Hum!

PISANIO *[aside]*
I'll write to my lord she's dead. O Imogen,
Safe mayst thou wander, safe return again!

CLOTEN   Sirrah, is this letter true?

PISANIO   Sir, as I think.

CLOTEN   It is Posthumus' hand, I know't. Sirrah, if thou
wouldst not be a villain, but do me true service, un-   109
dergo those employments wherein I should have   110
cause to use thee with a serious industry—that is,
what villainy soe'er I bid thee do, to perform it directly
and truly—I would think thee an honest man. Thou
shouldst neither want my means for thy relief nor my
voice for thy preferment.   115

PISANIO   Well, my good lord.

CLOTEN   Wilt thou serve me? For since patiently and
constantly thou hast stuck to the bare fortune of that
beggar Posthumus, thou canst not, in the course of
gratitude, but be a diligent follower of mine. Wilt thou
serve me?

PISANIO   Sir, I will.

CLOTEN   Give me thy hand; here's my purse. *[He gives*   123
money.] Hast any of thy late master's garments in thy   124
possession?

PISANIO   I have, my lord, at my lodging the same suit
he wore when he took leave of my lady and mistress.

CLOTEN   The first service thou dost me, fetch that suit
hither. Let it be thy first service. Go.

88–9 **From . . . drawn** from whom not even a tiny amount of worthiness can be extracted, so heavy is the preponderance of baseness.   91 **Come nearer** Answer more to the point.   92 **home** completely   95 **Discover** Disclose   101 **Or** Either   109–10 **undergo** undertake   115 **preferment** advancement.   123 **purse** (Cloten is not giving Pisanio salary but making him his purse bearer.)   124 **late** recent. (Not "dead.")

PISANIO   I shall, my lord.   *Exit.*

CLOTEN   Meet thee at Milford Haven!—I forgot to ask
him one thing; I'll remember't anon.—Even there,
thou villain Posthumus, will I kill thee. I would these
garments were come. She said upon a time—the bitterness of it I now belch from my heart—that she held
the very garment of Posthumus in more respect than   136
my noble and natural person, together with the adorn-
ment of my qualities. With that suit upon my back
will I ravish her; first kill him, and in her eyes. There
shall she see my valor, which will then be a torment to
her contempt. He on the ground, my speech of insult-   141
ment ended on his dead body, and when my lust hath   142
dined—which, as I say, to vex her I will execute in the
clothes that she so praised—to the court I'll knock her
back, foot her home again. She hath despised me re-   145
joicingly, and I'll be merry in my revenge.

   Enter Pisanio [with the clothes].

Be those the garments?

PISANIO   Ay, my noble lord.

CLOTEN   How long is't since she went to Milford
Haven?

PISANIO   She can scarce be there yet.

CLOTEN   Bring this apparel to my chamber; that is the
second thing that I have commanded thee. The third
is that thou wilt be a voluntary mute to my design. Be
but duteous, and true preferment shall tender itself to
thee. My revenge is now at Milford. Would I had
wings to follow it! Come, and be true.   *Exit.*

PISANIO

Thou bidd'st me to my loss; for true to thee
Were to prove false, which I will never be,
To him that is most true. To Milford go,
And find not her whom thou pursuest. Flow, flow,
You heavenly blessings, on her! This fool's speed   162
Be crossed with slowness; labor be his meed!   *Exit.*   163

3.6

   Enter Imogen alone [in boy's clothes].

IMOGEN

I see a man's life is a tedious one.
I have tired myself, and for two nights together
Have made the ground my bed. I should be sick   2
But that my resolution helps me. Milford,
When from the mountain top Pisanio showed thee,
Thou wast within a ken. O Jove, I think   6
Foundations fly the wretched—such, I mean,   7
Where they should be relieved. Two beggars told me
I could not miss my way. Will poor folks lie,
That have afflictions on them, knowing 'tis

A punishment or trial? Yes; no wonder,   11
When rich ones scarce tell true. To lapse in fullness   12
Is sorer than to lie for need, and falsehood   13
Is worse in kings than beggars. My dear lord!
Thou art one o'th' false ones. Now I think on thee,
My hunger's gone; but even before I was   16
At point to sink for food. [*She sees the cave.*] But what
   is this?   17
Here is a path to't. 'Tis some savage hold.   18
I were best not call; I dare not call. Yet famine,
Ere clean it o'erthrow nature, makes it valiant.   20
Plenty and peace breeds cowards; hardness ever   21
Of hardiness is mother.—Ho! Who's here?   22
If anything that's civil, speak; if savage,   23
Take or lend. Ho!—No answer? Then I'll enter.   24
Best draw my sword; an if mine enemy   25
But fear the sword like me, he'll scarcely look on't.
Such a foe, good heavens!   27

   *[She draws her sword, and]
   exit [into the cave].*

   Enter Belarius, Guiderius, and Arviragus.

BELARIUS

You, Polydore, have proved best woodman and   28
Are master of the feast. Cadwal and I
Will play the cook and servant; 'tis our match.   30
The sweat of industry would dry and die   31
But for the end it works to. Come, our stomachs   32
Will make what's homely savory; weariness   33
Can snore upon the flint, when resty sloth   34
Finds the down pillow hard. Now peace be here,
Poor house, that keep'st thyself!

GUIDERIUS   I am throughly weary.   36

ARVIRAGUS

I am weak with toil, yet strong in appetite.

GUIDERIUS

There is cold meat i'th' cave. We'll browse on that   38
Whilst what we have killed be cooked.

BELARIUS [*looking into the cave*]   Stay, come not in.
But that it eats our victuals, I should think
Here were a fairy.

GUIDERIUS   What's the matter, sir?

BELARIUS

By Jupiter, an angel! Or, if not,
An earthly paragon! Behold divineness
No elder than a boy!

   Enter Imogen.

---

136 **more respect** higher regard   141–2 **insultment** contemptuous triumph   145 **foot** kick   162 **This fool's** May this fool's   163 **crossed**
thwarted.   **meed** reward.
3.6. Location: Wales. Before the cave of Belarius.
2 **tired** (1) exhausted (2) attired   6 **within a ken** within sight.
7 **Foundations** (1) certainties, fixed places (2) charitable institutions.
fly the wretched i.e., are never there when most needed

11 **trial** test of virtue. (Poverty may be a Job-like affliction visited on
those God wishes to test, in which case lying is dangerously sinful.)
12 **lapse in fullness** lie and commit other sins in a state of prosperity
13 **sorer** worse, more wicked   16 **but even before** just now   17 **for**
for lack of   18 **hold** stronghold, fastness.   20 **clean** altogether
21 **hardness** hardship   22 **Of hardiness is mother** breeds courage.
23 **civil** civilized   24 **Take or lend** rob me (or something worse), or
give me food.   25 **Best** It were best to.   **an if** if   27 **Such . . . heavens!** May the heavens grant me a foe as timid as myself!   28 **woodman** woodsman, huntsman   30 **match** agreement, bargain.
31–2 **The sweat . . . works to** Human labor would dry up and cease if
it were not for the desired end.   33 **homely** plain   34 **resty** sluggish,
indolent   36 **keep'st thyself** i.e., is untended, empty.   **throughly**
thoroughly   38 **browse** nibble

IMOGEN   Good masters, harm me not.   45
Before I entered here, I called, and thought
To have begged or bought what I have took. Good   47
    troth,
I have stol'n naught, nor would not, though I had
    found
Gold strewed i'th' floor. Here's money for my meat.
                              [*She offers money.*]
I would have left it on the board so soon
As I had made my meal, and parted
With prayers for the provider.
GUIDERIUS   Money, youth?
ARVIRAGUS
All gold and silver rather turn to dirt,   53
As 'tis no better reckoned but of those   54
Who worship dirty gods.
IMOGEN   I see you're angry.
Know, if you kill me for my fault, I should
Have died had I not made it.
BELARIUS   Whither bound?   57
IMOGEN   To Milford Haven.
BELARIUS   What's your name?
IMOGEN
Fidele, sir. I have a kinsman who
Is bound for Italy. He embarked at Milford,   61
To whom being going, almost spent with hunger,
I am fall'n in this offense.
BELARIUS   Prithee, fair youth,   63
Think us no churls, nor measure our good minds
By this rude place we live in. Well encountered!
'Tis almost night. You shall have better cheer
Ere you depart, and thanks to stay and eat it.
Boys, bid him welcome.
GUIDERIUS   Were you a woman, youth,
I should woo hard but be your groom in honesty,   69
Ay, bid for you as I do buy.   70
ARVIRAGUS [*to Guiderius*]   I'll make't my comfort
He is a man; I'll love him as my brother.
[*To Imogen*] And such a welcome as I'd give to him   73
After long absence, such is yours. Most welcome!
Be sprightly, for you fall 'mongst friends.
IMOGEN   'Mongst friends,   75
If brothers. [*Aside*] Would it had been so that they   76
Had been my father's sons! Then had my prize   77
Been less, and so more equal ballasting   78
To thee, Posthumus.
BELARIUS   He wrings at some distress.   79

GUIDERIUS
Would I could free't!
ARVIRAGUS   Or I; whate'er it be,
What pain it cost, what danger! Gods!
BELARIUS   Hark, boys.   81
                              [*He whispers to them.*]
IMOGEN [*to herself*]   Great men
That had a court no bigger than this cave,
That did attend themselves and had the virtue   84
Which their own conscience sealed them, laying by   85
That nothing-gift of differing multitudes,   86
Could not outpeer these twain. Pardon me, gods!   87
I'd change my sex to be companion with them,
Since Leonatus's false.
BELARIUS   It shall be so.   89
Boys, we'll go dress our hunt. Fair youth, come in.   90
Discourse is heavy, fasting; when we have supped,   91
We'll mannerly demand thee of thy story,
So far as thou wilt speak it.
GUIDERIUS   Pray draw near.
ARVIRAGUS
The night to th'owl and morn to th' lark less welcome.
IMOGEN   Thanks, sir.
ARVIRAGUS   I pray, draw near.   *Exeunt.*

❖

3.[7]

Enter two Roman Senators and Tribunes.

FIRST SENATOR
This is the tenor of the Emperor's writ:
That since the common men are now in action
'Gainst the Pannonians and Dalmatians,
And that the legions now in Gallia are
Full weak to undertake our wars against
The fall'n-off Britons, that we do incite   6
The gentry to this business. He creates
Lucius proconsul, and to you the tribunes,   8
For this immediate levy, he commends   9
His absolute commission. Long live Caesar!   10
A TRIBUNE
Is Lucius general of the forces?
SECOND SENATOR   Ay.
A TRIBUNE
Remaining now in Gallia?
FIRST SENATOR   With those legions
Which I have spoke of, whereunto your levy

---

45 masters i.e., sirs. (A form of address to ordinary folk.)   **47 Good
troth** In truth   **53 All gold** Let all gold   **54 but of** except by
57 made committed   **61 embarked** was to have embarked   **63 in**
into   **69–70 I . . . buy** I would woo earnestly rather than fail to be
your swain in all honesty, yes, and propose marriage to you as if
offering to buy something precious.   **73 him** i.e., such a brother
75–6 'Mongst . . . brothers i.e., Certainly I am among friends, if the
three of us are to be like brothers.   **77–9 Then . . . Posthumus** Then
my value would be less (since my brothers would take my place as
heirs to the throne) and thus more equal in social station and wealth
to that of you, Posthumus. (*Prize* also suggests a captured vessel at
sea, in the nautical metaphor continued with *ballasting,* which gives a
ship stability).   **79 wrings** writhes

81 What whatever   **84–6 That . . . multitudes** who had no one to
attend them but themselves and no moral excellence to boast of other
than what their own self-knowledge could swear to, disregarding the
valueless gift of adulation from the fickle populace   **87 outpeer** excel
89 It shall be so (Belarius finishes his conversation apart with Arviragus and Guiderius.)   **90 hunt** game taken in the hunt.   **91 Discourse
. . . fasting** Conversation is difficult when one has not eaten.
3.7. Location: Rome. A public place, perhaps the Senate House.
6 fall'n-off revolted   **8 proconsul** provincial governor   **9 commends**
entrusts   **10 absolute commission** unlimited authority.

Must be supplyant. The words of your commission   14
Will tie you to the numbers and the time   15
Of their dispatch.
A TRIBUNE   We will discharge our duty.
                                                            Exeunt.

❖

4.1

Enter Cloten alone, [dressed in Posthumus's garments].

CLOTEN   I am near to th' place where they should meet, if Pisanio have mapped it truly. How fit his garments   2
serve me! Why should his mistress, who was made by Him that made the tailor, not be fit too? The   4
rather—saving reverence of the word—for 'tis said a   5
woman's fitness comes by fits. Therein I must play the   6
workman. I dare speak it to myself, for it is not vain-glory for a man and his glass to confer in his own   8
chamber—I mean, the lines of my body are as well drawn as his; no less young, more strong, not beneath him in fortunes, beyond him in the advantage of the   11
time, above him in birth, alike conversant in general   12
services, and more remarkable in single oppositions.   13
Yet this imperceiverant thing loves him in my despite.   14
What mortality is! Posthumus, thy head, which now is   15
growing upon thy shoulders, shall within this hour be off, thy mistress enforced, thy garments cut to pieces before her face; and all this done, spurn her home to her father, who may haply be a little angry for my so rough   19
usage; but my mother, having power of his testiness,   20
shall turn all into my commendations. My horse is tied up safe. Out, sword, and to a sore purpose! [*He draws.*]   22
Fortune put them into my hand! This is the very description of their meeting place, and the fellow dares not deceive me.   *Exit.*

❖

4.2

Enter Belarius, Guiderius, Arviragus, and Imogen from the cave.

BELARIUS [*to Imogen*]
    You are not well. Remain here in the cave;
    We'll come to you after hunting.
ARVIRAGUS [*to Imogen*]   Brother, stay here.

Are we not brothers?
IMOGEN   So man and man should be,   3
    But clay and clay differs in dignity,   4
    Whose dust is both alike. I am very sick.   5
GUIDERIUS [*to Arviragus and Belarius*]
    Go you to hunting. I'll abide with him.
IMOGEN
    So sick I am not, yet I am not well;   7
    But not so citizen a wanton as   8
    To seem to die ere sick. So please you, leave me;   9
    Stick to your journal course. The breach of custom   10
    Is breach of all. I am ill, but your being by me
    Cannot amend me; society is no comfort
    To one not sociable. I am not very sick,
    Since I can reason of it. Pray you, trust me here—   14
    I'll rob none but myself—and let me die,   15
    Stealing so poorly.
GUIDERIUS   I love thee—I have spoke it—   16
    How much the quantity, the weight as much,   17
    As I do love my father.
BELARIUS   What? How? How?
ARVIRAGUS
    If it be sin to say so, sir, I yoke me   19
    In my good brother's fault. I know not why
    I love this youth; and I have heard you say
    Love's reason's without reason. The bier at door,
    And a demand who is't shall die, I'd say
    "My father, not this youth."
BELARIUS [*aside*]   Oh, noble strain!   24
    Oh, worthiness of nature! Breed of greatness!
    Cowards father cowards and base things sire base;
    Nature hath meal and bran, contempt and grace.   27
    I'm not their father; yet who this should be   28
    Doth miracle itself, loved before me.   29
    [*Aloud*] 'Tis the ninth hour o'th' morn.
ARVIRAGUS [*to Imogen*]   Brother, farewell.
IMOGEN
    I wish ye sport.
ARVIRAGUS   You health. [*To Belarius*] So please you, sir.   31
IMOGEN [*aside*]
    These are kind creatures. Gods, what lies I have heard!
    Our courtiers say all's savage but at court.
    Experience, oh, thou disprov'st report!
    Th'imperious seas breeds monsters; for the dish,   35
    Poor tributary rivers as sweet fish.   36

14 **supplyant** reinforcing, auxiliary.   15 **tie you to** specify for you
4.1. Location: Wales. Near the cave of Belarius.
2 **his** Posthumus's   4 **Him** i.e., God   5 **saving reverence** asking pardon (i.e., for the indecent punning on *fitness* and *fit.*)   **for** because
6 **fitness** sexual inclination.   **fits** fits and starts.   8 **glass** mirror
11–12 **the advantage of the time** superiority in social opportunity
12–13 **alike . . . services** equally versed in military matters   13 **single oppositions** single combat.   14 **imperceiverant** dull of perception.
in my despite to spite me.   15 **What mortality is!** What a thing life is!   19 **haply** perchance   20 **power of** control over   22 **sore** grievous
4.2. Location: Before the cave of Belarius. The scene may be virtually continuous.

3–5 **So . . . alike** i.e., We are brothers, as all humans should be, being made out of the same dust, though social distinctions impose their artificial differences.   7 **So sick I am not** I am not that sick   8–9 **But . . . sick** but I am not so city-bred a weakling as to fear I am dying when I am not even really sick yet.   10 **journal** daily   14 **reason of it** talk coherently about it.   15–16 **I'll . . . poorly** (Imogen's witticism is that, since she will only be robbing herself of their company, not taking their food as in 3.6, only she should pay the penalty of loneliness for such a petty "crime.")   17 **How . . . as much** just as much in quantity and weight   19 **yoke me** join company   24 **strain** inherited disposition.   27 **Nature . . . grace** in human nature we find both flour and husks, the worthy and the contemptible.   28–9 **who . . . before me** it is miraculous that this youth, whoever he is, should be loved in preference to me.   31 **You** i.e., I wish you.   **So please you** At your service   35 **Th'imperious** The imperial, as contrasted with *tributary*
35–6 **for . . . fish** when it comes to providing delicious fish to eat, small tributaries do at least as well as the sea. (By analogy, humble surroundings breed at least as great virtue as can be found at court.)

I am sick still, heartsick. Pisanio,
I'll now taste of thy drug.
      [*She swallows some. The men speak apart.*]
GUIDERIUS   I could not stir him.   38
He said he was gentle, but unfortunate;   39
Dishonestly afflicted, but yet honest.   40
ARVIRAGUS
Thus did he answer me, yet said hereafter
I might know more.
BELARIUS   To th' field, to th' field!—
We'll leave you for this time. Go in and rest.
ARVIRAGUS
We'll not be long away.
BELARIUS   Pray be not sick,
For you must be our huswife.
IMOGEN   Well or ill,
I am bound to you.   *Exit* [*to the cave*].
BELARIUS   And shalt be ever.   47
This youth, howe'er distressed, appears he hath had   48
Good ancestors.
ARVIRAGUS   How angel-like he sings!
GUIDERIUS
But his neat cookery! He cut our roots in characters   50
And sauced our broths as Juno had been sick   51
And he her dieter.
ARVIRAGUS   Nobly he yokes   52
A smiling with a sigh, as if the sigh
Was that it was for not being such a smile;   54
The smile mocking the sigh, that it would fly
From so divine a temple to commix   56
With winds that sailors rail at.
GUIDERIUS   I do note   57
That grief and patience, rooted in him both,
Mingle their spurs together.
ARVIRAGUS   Grow, patience,   59
And let the stinking elder, grief, untwine   60
His perishing root with the increasing vine!   61
BELARIUS
It is great morning. Come, away!—Who's there?   62

    Enter Cloten, [*not seeing them at first*].

CLOTEN
I cannot find those runagates. That villain   63
Hath mocked me. I am faint.
BELARIUS   "Those runagates"?
Means he not us? I partly know him. 'Tis
Cloten, the son o' th' Queen. I fear some ambush.
I saw him not these many years, and yet
I know 'tis he. We are held as outlaws. Hence!

GUIDERIUS
He is but one. You and my brother search
What companies are near. Pray you, away.   70
Let me alone with him.
      [*Exeunt Belarius and Arviragus.*]
CLOTEN   Soft, what are you   71
That fly me thus? Some villain mountaineers?
I have heard of such. What slave art thou?
GUIDERIUS   A thing
More slavish did I ne'er than answering
A slave without a knock.
CLOTEN   Thou art a robber,   75
A lawbreaker, a villain. Yield thee, thief.
GUIDERIUS
To who? To thee? What art thou? Have not I
An arm as big as thine? A heart as big?
Thy words, I grant, are bigger, for I wear not
My dagger in my mouth. Say what thou art,
Why I should yield to thee.
CLOTEN   Thou villain base,
Know'st me not by my clothes?   82
GUIDERIUS   No, nor thy tailor, rascal,   83
Who is thy grandfather. He made those clothes,   84
Which, as it seems, make thee.
CLOTEN   Thou precious varlet,   85
My tailor made them not.
GUIDERIUS   Hence, then, and thank
The man that gave them thee. Thou art some fool;
I am loath to beat thee.
CLOTEN   Thou injurious thief,   88
Hear but my name, and tremble.
GUIDERIUS   What's thy name?
CLOTEN   Cloten, thou villain.
GUIDERIUS
Cloten, thou double villain, be thy name,
I cannot tremble at it. Were it toad, or adder, spider,
'Twould move me sooner.
CLOTEN   To thy further fear,
Nay, to thy mere confusion, thou shalt know   94
I am son to th' Queen.
GUIDERIUS   I am sorry for't; not seeming
So worthy as thy birth.
CLOTEN   Art not afeard?
GUIDERIUS
Those that I reverence, those I fear—the wise.   97
At fools I laugh, not fear them.
CLOTEN   Die the death!   98
When I have slain thee with my proper hand,   99
I'll follow those that even now fled hence
And on the gates of Lud's Town set your heads.
Yield, rustic mountaineer!   *Fight, and exeunt.*

    Enter Belarius and Arviragus.

---

38 stir him persuade him to tell about himself. **39 gentle** wellborn
40 Dishonestly afflicted afflicted by adverse and ignominious fortune **47 bound** obligated. (But Belarius answers in the sense of
"bound by affection.") **48 he hath had** i.e., to have had **50 characters** letters, designs **51 as** as if **52 dieter** cook. **54 that** what
56 commix join **57 winds . . . at** i.e., the rude wind, so infinitely
rougher than the sigh. **59 spurs** roots **60–1 And let . . . vine!** and
let the strong-smelling elder tree (on which Judas is supposed to have
hanged himself after betraying Jesus) cease to twine its deadly root
around that of the bounteous vine! i.e., may grief cease to afflict
Fidele's well-being! **62 great morning** broad day. **63 runagates**
renegades, runaways. **That villain** Pisanio

70 companies companions **71 Let . . . him** Leave me alone to deal
with him. **Soft** i.e., Wait a minute **75 without a knock** without giving him a blow. **82 Know'st . . . clothes?** (Cloten is dressed as one
from the court.) **83–5 No . . . thee** (A jest on the proverbial idea that
"The tailor makes the man.") **85 precious varlet** arrant rascal
88 injurious insulting, malicious **94 mere confusion** utter ruin
97 fear regard with awe **98 Die the death!** (A solemn pronounce-
ment of the sentence of death.) **99 proper** own

BELARIUS   No company's abroad?

ARVIRAGUS
None in the world. You did mistake him, sure.

BELARIUS
I cannot tell. Long is it since I saw him,
But time hath nothing blurred those lines of favor   106
Which then he wore. The snatches in his voice   107
And burst of speaking were as his. I am absolute   108
'Twas very Cloten.

ARVIRAGUS   In this place we left them.   109
I wish my brother make good time with him,   110
You say he is so fell.

BELARIUS   Being scarce made up,   111
I mean to man, he had not apprehension   112
Of roaring terrors; for defect of judgment   113
Is oft the cause of fear.

Enter Guiderius [with Cloten's head].

                              But see, thy brother.   114

GUIDERIUS
This Cloten was a fool, an empty purse;
There was no money in't. Not Hercules
Could have knocked out his brains, for he had none.
Yet I not doing this, the fool had borne   118
My head as I do his.

BELARIUS   What hast thou done?

GUIDERIUS
I am perfect what: cut off one Cloten's head,   120
Son to the Queen, after his own report,   121
Who called me traitor, mountaineer, and swore
With his own single hand he'd take us in,   123
Displace our heads where—thanks, ye gods!—they
       grow,   124
And set them on Lud's Town.

BELARIUS   We are all undone.

GUIDERIUS
Why, worthy father, what have we to lose
But that he swore to take, our lives? The law   127
Protects not us. Then why should we be tender   128
To let an arrogant piece of flesh threat us,   129
Play judge and executioner all himself,
For we do fear the law? What company   131
Discover you abroad?

BELARIUS   No single soul
Can we set eye on; but in all safe reason
He must have some attendants. Though his humor   134
Was nothing but mutation—ay, and that   135
From one bad thing to worse—not frenzy,

Not absolute madness could so far have raved
To bring him here alone. Although perhaps
It may be heard at court that such as we
Cave here, hunt here, are outlaws, and in time
May make some stronger head, the which he
       hearing—   141
As it is like him—might break out and swear   142
He'd fetch us in, yet is't not probable   143
To come alone, either he so undertaking   144
Or they so suffering. Then on good ground we fear,   145
If we do fear this body hath a tail
More perilous than the head.

ARVIRAGUS   Let ord'nance   147
Come as the gods foresay it. Howsoe'er,   148
My brother hath done well.

BELARIUS   I had no mind   149
To hunt this day. The boy Fidele's sickness
Did make my way long forth.

GUIDERIUS   With his own sword,   151
Which he did wave against my throat, I have ta'en
His head from him. I'll throw't into the creek
Behind our rock, and let it to the sea
And tell the fishes he's the Queen's son, Cloten.
That's all I reck.   *Exit.*   156

BELARIUS   I fear 'twill be revenged.
Would, Polydore, thou hadst not done't, though valor
Becomes thee well enough.

ARVIRAGUS   Would I had done't,
So the revenge alone pursued me! Polydore,   159
I love thee brotherly, but envy much
Thou hast robbed me of this deed. I would revenges   161
That possible strength might meet would seek us
       through   162
And put us to our answer.

BELARIUS   Well, 'tis done.   163
We'll hunt no more today, nor seek for danger
Where there's no profit. I prithee, to our rock.
You and Fidele play the cooks. I'll stay
Till hasty Polydore return, and bring him   167
To dinner presently.

ARVIRAGUS   Poor sick Fidele!
I'll willingly to him. To gain his color   169
I'd let a parish of such Clotens blood,   170
And praise myself for charity.   *Exit [into the cave].*

BELARIUS   O thou goddess,
Thou divine Nature, how thyself thou blazon'st   172
In these two princely boys! They are as gentle
As zephyrs blowing below the violet,

---

106 nothing not at all.   lines of favor facial features   107 snatches
hesitations   108 absolute positive   109 very Cloten Cloten himself.
110 make good time acquit himself well   111 fell fierce.   111–14
Being . . . fear Even when he was barely full-grown, Cloten had no
clear apprehension of danger, for a defective judgment like his often
produces a recklessness that is to be feared (as evidenced in Cloten's
behavior as reported in lines 120–43 below).   118 Yet . . . this Yet if I
had not done this.   had would have   120 perfect well aware
121 after according to   123 take us in capture us   124 where from
where   127 that that which   128–9 be . . . let be so meek as to allow
131 For simply because   134 humor disposition   135 mutation
changeability

141 make assemble.   head armed force   142 break out burst out (in
speech)   143 fetch us in capture us   144 To come that he would
come   145 suffering permitting.   147 ord'nance what is ordained
148 foresay predetermine   149 mind inclination   151 Did . . . forth
made my wanderings (from the cave) seem long.   his i.e., Cloten's
156 reck care.   159 alone . . . me would have pursued me only.
161 Thou that thou   161–3 I would . . . answer I wish that revenges
equal to all the human strength that we could muster would seek us
out and put us to the test.   167 hasty rash   169 gain his color restore
the color (to his cheeks)   170 I'd . . . blood I'd drain the blood from a
parish full of such Clotens   172 how . . . blazon'st how you proudly
display yourself

Not wagging his sweet head; and yet as rough,
Their royal blood enchafed, as the rud'st wind   176
That by the top doth take the mountain pine
And make him stoop to th' vale. 'Tis wonder
That an invisible instinct should frame them   179
To royalty unlearned, honor untaught,
Civility not seen from other, valor   181
That wildly grows in them but yields a crop   182
As if it had been sowed. Yet still it's strange
What Cloten's being here to us portends,
Or what his death will bring us.

Enter Guiderius.

GUIDERIUS   Where's my brother?
I have sent Cloten's clodpoll down the stream   186
In embassy to his mother. His body's hostage   187
For his return.   *Solemn music.*
BELARIUS   My ingenious instrument!   188
Hark, Polydore, it sounds. But what occasion
Hath Cadwal now to give it motion? Hark!
GUIDERIUS
Is he at home?
BELARIUS   He went hence even now.
GUIDERIUS
What does he mean? Since death of my dear'st mother
It did not speak before. All solemn things   193
Should answer solemn accidents. The matter?   194
Triumphs for nothing and lamenting toys   195
Is jollity for apes and grief for boys.   196
Is Cadwal mad?

*Enter Arviragus, with Imogen, [as] dead, bearing
her in his arms.*

BELARIUS   Look, here he comes,
And brings the dire occasion in his arms
Of what we blame him for.
ARVIRAGUS   The bird is dead
That we have made so much on. I had rather   200
Have skipped from sixteen years of age to sixty,
To have turned my leaping-time into a crutch,   202
Than have seen this.
GUIDERIUS   O sweetest, fairest lily!
My brother wears thee not the one half so well   204
As when thou grew'st thyself.
BELARIUS   O Melancholy,   205

Who ever yet could sound thy bottom, find   206
The ooze to show what coast thy sluggish crare   207
Might eas'liest harbor in?—Thou blessèd thing,   208
Jove knows what man thou mightst have made; but I,   209
Thou diedst, a most rare boy, of melancholy.—
How found you him?
ARVIRAGUS   Stark, as you see,   211
Thus smiling, as some fly had tickled slumber,   212
Not as death's dart being laughed at; his right cheek   213
Reposing on a cushion.
GUIDERIUS   Where?
ARVIRAGUS   O'th' floor,
His arms thus leagued. I thought he slept, and put   215
My clouted brogues from off my feet, whose rudeness   216
Answered my steps too loud.
GUIDERIUS   Why, he but sleeps.
If he be gone, he'll make his grave a bed;
With female fairies will his tomb be haunted,
And worms will not come to thee.
ARVIRAGUS   With fairest flowers   220
Whilst summer lasts and I live here, Fidele,
I'll sweeten thy sad grave. Thou shalt not lack
The flower that's like thy face, pale primrose, nor
The azured harebell, like thy veins, no, nor   224
The leaf of eglantine, whom, not to slander,   225
Outsweetened not thy breath. The ruddock would   226
With charitable bill—O bill sore shaming
Those rich-left heirs that let their fathers lie
Without a monument!—bring thee all this,
Yea, and furred moss besides, when flowers are none,
To winter-ground thy corpse.
GUIDERIUS   Prithee, have done,   231
And do not play in wenchlike words with that   232
Which is so serious. Let us bury him
And not protract with admiration what   234
Is now due debt. To th' grave!
ARVIRAGUS   Say, where shall 's lay him?   235
GUIDERIUS
By good Euriphile, our mother.
ARVIRAGUS   Be't so.
And let us, Polydore, though now our voices
Have got the mannish crack, sing him to th' ground,
As once to our mother; use like note and words,   239

---

176 **enchafed** being heated (with anger). **rud'st** roughest
179 **frame** shape, direct 181 **not seen from other** not learned by
observing it in some other persons 182 **wildly grows** grows wild
186 **clodpoll** blockhead, head. (With a play on Cloten's name.)
187–8 **His . . . return** Cloten's body will be held as hostage to ensure
the safe return of his head, which is being sent as though it were the
ambassador to a parley. (That return will of course never occur;
Guiderius speaks sardonically.) 188 **ingenious** skillfully made
193 **did not speak** has not sounded 194 **answer** correspond to.
accidents events. 195–6 **Triumphs . . . boys** Holding ceremonies
about nothing and grieving over trivialities are foolish and jejune.
200 **on** of. 202 **leaping-time** time of energetic youth 204–5 **My . . .
thyself** i.e., It is not even half so beautiful a sight to see you carried
by my brother, as though he were wearing a lily, as when you lived
and grew.

206–8 **find . . . harbor in**? dredge up muddy bottoms to show where
your sluggish skiff might best seek quiet harbor? (Who can ever
know where Melancholy will lodge, says Belarius, when she afflicts
even so fair a youth as this? They all conclude that "Fidele" died of
melancholy.) 208 **thing** i.e., Fidele 209 **but I** i.e., but I know that
211 **Stark** Stiff 212 **as** as if 213 **Not as . . . laughed at** not as though
laughing at death's dart (which Arviragus believes Fidele to be
doing) 215 **leagued** folded. 216 **clouted brogues** hobnailed boots
220 **to thee** (Addressed to Imogen.) 224 **The azured . . . veins** the
blue hyacinth, as blue as the blood in your veins 225 **eglantine** i.e.,
the sweetbrier rose or honeysuckle 225–6 **whom . . . breath** it is no
slander to the eglantine to say that its fragrance was not sweeter than
your breath. 226–31 **The ruddock . . . corpse** (According to fable the
ruddock or robin redbreast would cover graves with flowers and
moss, thus showing more tenderness and reverence than forgetful
humans. To *winter-ground* is to cover protectively against frost.)
231 **have done** stop 232 **wenchlike** womanish 234 **admiration**
wonder 235 **due debt** i.e., a ceremonial obligation (of burial) that
must be paid now. **shall 's** shall we 239 **like note** a similar tune

Save that "Euriphile" must be "Fidele."

GUIDERIUS   Cadwal,
I cannot sing. I'll weep, and word it with thee;   242
For notes of sorrow out of tune are worse
Than priests and fanes that lie.

ARVIRAGUS   We'll speak it, then.   244

BELARIUS
Great griefs, I see, med'cine the less, for Cloten   245
Is quite forgot. He was a queen's son, boys,
And, though he came our enemy, remember
He was paid for that. Though mean and mighty,
        rotting   248
Together, have one dust, yet reverence,   249
That angel of the world, doth make distinction   250
Of place 'tween high and low. Our foe was princely,
And though you took his life as being our foe,
Yet bury him as a prince.

GUIDERIUS   Pray you, fetch him hither.
Thersites' body is as good as Ajax'   255
When neither are alive.

ARVIRAGUS   If you'll go fetch him,
We'll say our song the whilst. Brother, begin.
                                    [Exit Belarius.]

GUIDERIUS
Nay, Cadwal, we must lay his head to th'east.   258
My father hath a reason for't.

ARVIRAGUS   'Tis true.

GUIDERIUS
Come on, then, and remove him.
            [They lay out Imogen with her head to the east.]

ARVIRAGUS   So. Begin.

                    Song.

GUIDERIUS
        Fear no more the heat o'th' sun,
            Nor the furious winter's rages;
        Thou thy worldly task hast done,
            Home art gone, and ta'en thy wages.
        Golden lads and girls all must,
            As chimney sweepers, come to dust.

ARVIRAGUS
        Fear no more the frown o'th' great;
            Thou art past the tyrant's stroke.
        Care no more to clothe and eat;
            To thee the reed is as the oak.   270
        The scepter, learning, physic, must   271
            All follow this and come to dust.

GUIDERIUS
        Fear no more the lightning flash,

ARVIRAGUS
        Nor th'all-dreaded thunderstone.   274

GUIDERIUS
Fear not slander, censure rash;

ARVIRAGUS
Thou hast finished joy and moan.

BOTH
        All lovers young, all lovers must
        Consign to thee and come to dust.   278

GUIDERIUS
No exorciser harm thee!   279

ARVIRAGUS
Nor no witchcraft charm thee!

GUIDERIUS
Ghost unlaid forbear thee!   281

ARVIRAGUS
Nothing ill come near thee!

BOTH
        Quiet consummation have,   283
        And renownèd be thy grave!

    Enter Belarius, with the [headless] body of Cloten.

GUIDERIUS
We have done our obsequies. Come, lay him down.
                [Cloten is laid next to Imogen.]

BELARIUS
Here's a few flowers, but 'bout midnight, more.
                    [They strew flowers.]
The herbs that have on them cold dew o'th' night
Are strewings fitt'st for graves. Upon their faces.   288
You were as flowers, now withered; even so
These herblets shall, which we upon you strew.   290
Come on, away; apart upon our knees.   291
The ground that gave them first has them again.
Their pleasures here are past, so is their pain.
            Exeunt [Belarius, Guiderius, and Arviragus].

IMOGEN (awakes)
Yes, sir, to Milford Haven. Which is the way?
I thank you. By yond bush? Pray, how far thither?
Ods pittikins! Can it be six mile yet?   296
I have gone all night. Faith, I'll lie down and sleep. 297
But soft, no bedfellow? [She sees or touches Cloten's
        body.] O gods and goddesses!
These flowers are like the pleasures of the world,
This bloody man the care on't. I hope I dream,   300
For so I thought I was a cave keeper   301
And cook to honest creatures. But 'tis not so.
'Twas but a bolt of nothing, shot of nothing,   303
Which the brain makes of fumes. Our very eyes   304
Are sometimes like our judgments, blind. Good faith,
I tremble still with fear; but if there be

242 word speak   244 fanes temples   245 med'cine cure   248 mean
those lowly born   249–50 reverence . . . world i.e., the great principle
of reverence, through which the hierarchy of order and degree in
human affairs mirrors that of the angels   255 Thersites' . . . Ajax'
(Thersites was the base scoffer in the *Iliad*; Ajax, a Greek hero.)
258 lay . . . east (Opposite to the Christian custom and hence suggestive here of Celtic pre-Christian worship.)   270 reed, oak (Contrasting symbols of a fragility that survives by being flexible and a
mightiness often overthrown. Fidele is past caring for the lesson contained in this contrast.)   271 physic medical learning   274 thunder-
stone (The supposed solid body accompanying a stroke of lightning.)

278 Consign to co-sign with, share a similar fate with, submit to the
same terms with   279 exorciser conjurer   281 unlaid not laid to rest
283 consummation end, death   288 Upon their faces i.e., Strew flowers on the dead persons' faces or perhaps on the front of their bodies,
since Cloten is headless. (The line may be corrupt.)   290 shall shall
wither   291 apart let us depart   296 Ods pittikins! God's pity! (A
diminutive oath.)   297 gone walked   300 the care on't i.e., is like the
troubles of this world.   301 For so for then.   cave keeper dweller in
a cave   303 bolt arrow.   shot of nothing shot from nowhere
304 fumes vapors engendered of humors which, according to current
theory, rose up into the brain and, by affecting imagination in the
forechamber of the brain, caused dreams.

Yet left in heaven as small a drop of pity
As a wren's eye, feared gods, a part of it!   308
The dream's here still. Even when I wake, it is
Without me, as within me; not imagined, felt.   310
A headless man? The garments of Posthumus?
I know the shape of 's leg; this is his hand,
His foot Mercurial, his Martial thigh,   313
The brawns of Hercules; but his Jovial face—   314
Murder in heaven? How? 'Tis gone. Pisanio,
All curses madded Hecuba gave the Greeks,   316
And mine to boot, be darted on thee! Thou,
Conspired with that irregulous devil, Cloten,   318
Hath here cut off my lord. To write and read   319
Be henceforth treacherous! Damned Pisanio
Hath with his forgèd letters—damned Pisanio—
From this most bravest vessel of the world
Struck the maintop! O Posthumus! Alas,   323
Where is thy head? Where's that? Ay me, where's
    that?
Pisanio might have killed thee at the heart
And left this head on. How should this be? Pisanio?
'Tis he and Cloten. Malice and lucre in them   327
Have laid this woe here. Oh, 'tis pregnant, pregnant!   328
The drug he gave me, which he said was precious
And cordial to me, have I not found it   330
Murd'rous to th' senses? That confirms it home.   331
This is Pisanio's deed, and Cloten.—Oh,   332
Give color to my pale cheek with thy blood,   333
That we the horrider may seem to those
Which chance to find us. Oh, my lord, my lord!

          [*She falls on the body.*]

        Enter Lucius, Captains, and a Soothsayer.

CAPTAIN
To them the legions garrisoned in Gallia,   336
After your will, have crossed the sea, attending   337
You here at Milford Haven with your ships.
They are in readiness.
LUCIUS   But what from Rome?
CAPTAIN
The Senate hath stirred up the confiners   340
And gentlemen of Italy, most willing spirits,
That promise noble service, and they come
Under the conduct of bold Iachimo,
Siena's brother.
LUCIUS   When expect you them?   344

CAPTAIN
With the next benefit o'th' wind.
LUCIUS   This forwardness
Makes our hopes fair. Command our present numbers
Be mustered; bid the captains look to't.—Now, sir,
What have you dreamed of late of this war's purpose? 348
SOOTHSAYER
Last night the very gods showed me a vision—
I fast and prayed for their intelligence—thus: 350
I saw Jove's bird, the Roman eagle, winged
From the spongy south to this part of the west,   352
There vanished in the sunbeams, which portends—
Unless my sins abuse my divination—   354
Success to th' Roman host.
LUCIUS   Dream often so,
And never false. [*He sees Cloten and Imogen.*] Soft, ho,
    what trunk is here
Without his top? The ruin speaks that sometime
It was a worthy building. How? A page?
Or dead or sleeping on him? But dead rather;   359
For nature doth abhor to make his bed
With the defunct, or sleep upon the dead.
Let's see the boy's face.
CAPTAIN   He's alive, my lord.
LUCIUS
He'll then instruct us of this body.—Young one,
Inform us of thy fortunes, for it seems
They crave to be demanded. Who is this   365
Thou mak'st thy bloody pillow? Or who was he
That, otherwise than noble nature did,   367
Hath altered that good picture? What's thy interest
In this sad wrack? How came't? Who is't?   369
What art thou?
IMOGEN   I am nothing; or if not,   370
Nothing to be were better. This was my master,   371
A very valiant Briton and a good,
That here by mountaineers lies slain. Alas,
There is no more such masters. I may wander
From east to occident, cry out for service,
Try many, all good, serve truly, never
Find such another master.
LUCIUS   'Lack, good youth!
Thou mov'st no less with thy complaining than   378
Thy master in bleeding. Say his name, good friend.
IMOGEN
Richard du Champ. [*Aside*] If I do lie and do
No harm by it, though the gods hear, I hope
They'll pardon it.—Say you, sir?
LUCIUS   Thy name?
IMOGEN   Fidele, sir.
LUCIUS
Thou dost approve thyself the very same;   383
Thy name well fits thy faith, thy faith thy name.
Wilt take thy chance with me? I will not say

---

308 **wren's eye** i.e., a very small eye, rendering a small teardrop.
a part i.e., give me a part   310 **Without me** outside of me, externally
real and not just imagined (within)   313 **Mercurial** nimble and swift
like the foot of Mercury.   **Martial** powerful for war like that of Mars
314 **brawns** muscles.   **Jovial** Jove-like   316 **madded Hecuba** the
widow of King Priam of Troy, driven insane by her longing for
revenge on the Greeks who had killed her husband and sacked Troy
318 **Conspired** conspiring.   **irregulous** lawless   319 **Hath** hast   323
maintop top of mainmast, i.e., head.   327 **lucre** greed   328 **pregnant**
evident   330 **cordial** restorative to the heart   331 **home** utterly.   332
Cloten i.e., Cloten's.   333 **Give . . . blood** (Imogen may daub her
cheeks with what she supposes to be Posthumus's blood, or she may
simply fall on the body.)   336 **To them** i.e., In addition to the forces
we've already mentioned   337 **After** according to   340 **confiners**
inhabitants   344 **Siena's** the Duke of Siena's

348 **purpose** effect, outcome.   350 **fast** fasted   352 **spongy** damp
354 **abuse** falsify   359 **Or** Either   365 **demanded** asked about.
367 **That . . . did** who, in a manner different from the way that noble
nature fashioned him   369 **wrack** ruin.   370–1 **or . . . better** or if I am
not nothing, it would be better to be nothing.   378 **mov'st** i.e., to pity
383 **approve** prove.   **the very same** (*Fidele* means "faithful.")

Thou shalt be so well mastered, but be sure
No less beloved. The Roman Emperor's letters
Sent by a consul to me should not sooner
Than thine own worth prefer thee. Go with me.   389

IMOGEN
I'll follow, sir. But first, an't please the gods,   390
I'll hide my master from the flies as deep
As these poor pickaxes can dig; and when   392
With wild-wood leaves and weeds I ha' strewed his
    grave
And on it said a century of prayers,   394
Such as I can, twice o'er I'll weep and sigh,
And leaving so his service, follow you,
So please you entertain me.

LUCIUS   Ay, good youth,   397
And rather father thee than master thee.—
My friends,
The boy hath taught us manly duties. Let us
Find out the prettiest daisied plot we can
And make him with our pikes and partisans   402
A grave. Come, arm him. Boy, he's preferred   403
By thee to us, and he shall be interred
As soldiers can. Be cheerful; wipe thine eyes.
Some falls are means the happier to arise.
                         Exeunt, [bearing Cloten's body].

❧

4.3

*Enter Cymbeline, Lords, [Attendants,] and
Pisanio.*

CYMBELINE
Again, and bring me word how 'tis with her.
                         [Exit an Attendant.]
A fever with the absence of her son,   2
A madness, of which her life's in danger. Heavens,
How deeply you at once do touch me! Imogen,   4
The great part of my comfort, gone; my queen
Upon a desperate bed, and in a time
When fearful wars point at me; her son gone,
So needful for this present! It strikes me past
The hope of comfort. [*To Pisanio*] But for thee, fellow,
Who needs must know of her departure and
Dost seem so ignorant, we'll enforce it from thee   11
By a sharp torture.

PISANIO   Sir, my life is yours;
I humbly set it at your will. But for my mistress,
I nothing know where she remains, why gone,
Nor when she purposes return. Beseech Your
    Highness,
Hold me your loyal servant.

A LORD   Good my liege,   16

The day that she was missing he was here.
I dare be bound he's true and shall perform
All parts of his subjection loyally. For Cloten,   19
There wants no diligence in seeking him,   20
And will no doubt be found.

CYMBELINE   The time is troublesome.   21
[*To Pisanio*] We'll slip you for a season, but our jealousy   22
Does yet depend.

A LORD   So please Your Majesty,   23
The Roman legions, all from Gallia drawn,
Are landed on your coast with a supply
Of Roman gentlemen by the Senate sent.

CYMBELINE
Now for the counsel of my son and queen!   27
I am amazed with matter.

A LORD   Good my liege,   28
Your preparation can affront no less   29
Than what you hear of. Come more, for more you're
    ready.   30
The want is but to put those powers in motion   31
That long to move.

CYMBELINE   I thank you. Let's withdraw,
And meet the time as it seeks us. We fear not
What can from Italy annoy us, but   34
We grieve at chances here. Away!   35
                         Exeunt [all but Pisanio].

PISANIO
I heard no letter from my master since
I wrote him Imogen was slain. 'Tis strange.
Nor hear I from my mistress, who did promise
To yield me often tidings. Neither know I
What is betid to Cloten, but remain   40
Perplexed in all. The heavens still must work.
Wherein I am false I am honest; not true, to be true.
These present wars shall find I love my country,
Even to the note o'th' King, or I'll fall in them.   44
All other doubts, by time let them be cleared;   45
Fortune brings in some boats that are not steered.
                         Exit.

❧

4.4

Enter Belarius, Guiderius, and Arviragus.

GUIDERIUS
The noise is round about us.

BELARIUS   Let us from it.

---

389 prefer recommend   **390 an't** if it   **392 pickaxes** i.e., fingers
394 century of hundred   **397 entertain** employ   **402 partisans** long-
handled weapons, halberds   **403 arm him** lift him up.   **preferred**
recommended
4.3. Location: Britain. At the court of Cymbeline.
2 with brought on by   **4 touch** wound, afflict   **11 seem** pretend to be
13 for as for. (Also in line 19.)   **16 Hold me** regard me as

19 subjection duty as a subject   **20 wants** is lacking   **21 will** he will.
troublesome filled with deep troubles.   **22 slip you** let you go.
22–3 but . . . depend but our suspicions still hold.   **27 Now for** If
only I now had   **28 amazed with matter** confused and overwhelmed
by the pressure of affairs.   **29–30 Your . . . . hear of** your military
force already mustered can confront as large an army as you hear
reported.   **30 Come more** If more (enemy) come   **31 want is but**
sole thing needed is.   **powers** armed forces   **34 annoy** injure
35 chances accidents (the Queen's illness, etc.)   **40 is betid** has happened   **44 Even . . . King** to the extent of attracting the favorable
notice of the King (for my bravery)   **45 let them** i.e., let us pray
that they
4.4. Location: Wales. Before the cave of Belarius.

ARVIRAGUS
   What pleasure, sir, find we in life, to lock it
   From action and adventure?
GUIDERIUS   Nay, what hope
   Have we in hiding us? This way the Romans   4
   Must or for Britons slay us or receive us   5
   For barbarous and unnatural revolts   6
   During their use, and slay us after.
BELARIUS   Sons,   7
   We'll higher to the mountains, there secure us.
   To the King's party there's no going. Newness
   Of Cloten's death—we being not known, not
      mustered
   Among the bands—may drive us to a render   11
   Where we have lived, and so extort from 's that
   Which we have done, whose answer would be death   13
   Drawn on with torture.
GUIDERIUS   This is, sir, a doubt   14
   In such a time nothing becoming you   15
   Nor satisfying us.
ARVIRAGUS   It is not likely
   That when they hear the Roman horses neigh,
   Behold their quartered fires, have both their eyes   18
   And ears so cloyed importantly as now,   19
   That they will waste their time upon our note,   20
   To know from whence we are.
BELARIUS   Oh, I am known
   Of many in the army. Many years,
   Though Cloten then but young, you see, not wore him   23
   From my remembrance. And besides, the King
   Hath not deserved my service nor your loves,
   Who find in my exile the want of breeding,   26
   The certainty of this hard life, aye hopeless   27
   To have the courtesy your cradle promised,   28
   But to be still hot summer's tanlings and   29
   The shrinking slaves of winter.
GUIDERIUS   Than be so,   30
   Better to cease to be. Pray, sir, to th'army.
   I and my brother are not known; yourself   32
   So out of thought, and thereto so o'ergrown,   33
   Cannot be questioned.
ARVIRAGUS   By this sun that shines,   34
   I'll thither. What thing is't that I never   35
   Did see man die, scarce ever looked on blood
   But that of coward hares, hot goats, and venison!   37

   Never bestrid a horse, save one that had
   A rider like myself, who ne'er wore rowel   39
   Nor iron on his heel! I am ashamed
   To look upon the holy sun, to have
   The benefit of his blest beams, remaining
   So long a poor unknown.
GUIDERIUS   By heavens, I'll go.
   If you will bless me, sir, and give me leave,
   I'll take the better care, but if you will not,   45
   The hazard therefore due fall on me by   46
   The hands of Romans!
ARVIRAGUS   So say I. Amen.
BELARIUS
   No reason I, since of your lives you set
   So slight a valuation, should reserve
   My cracked one to more care. Have with you, boys!   50
   If in your country wars you chance to die,   51
   That is my bed too, lads, and there I'll lie.
   Lead, lead. [*Aside*] The time seems long; their blood
      thinks scorn   53
   Till it fly out and show them princes born.   *Exeunt.*

❖

5.1

Enter Posthumus alone [in Italian dress, with a bloody handkerchief].

POSTHUMUS
   Yea, bloody cloth, I'll keep thee, for I wished
   Thou shouldst be colored thus. You married ones,
   If each of you should take this course, how many
   Must murder wives much better than themselves
   For wrying but a little! O Pisanio!   5
   Every good servant does not all commands;
   No bond but to do just ones. Gods, if you   7
   Should have ta'en vengeance on my faults, I never   8
   Had lived to put on this; so had you saved   9
   The noble Imogen to repent, and struck
   Me, wretch, more worth your vengeance. But alack,
   You snatch some hence for little faults; that's love,   12
   To have them fall no more; you some permit   13
   To second ills with ills, each elder worse,   14
   And make them dread it, to the doers' thrift.   15
   But Imogen is your own. Do your best wills,
   And make me blest to obey! I am brought hither
   Among th'Italian gentry, and to fight
   Against my lady's kingdom. 'Tis enough

4 This way i.e., If we take such a course of conduct   **5 Must or** must either   **6 revolts** deserters, rebels   **7 During their use** as long as they find us useful   **11 bands** troops.   **render** rendering of an account **13 answer** consequence   **14 Drawn on with** brought about and lengthened by   **15 nothing** not at all   **18 quartered fires** campfires **19 cloyed importantly** filled with urgent business   **20 upon our note** in observing us   **23 then** was then.   **not wore him** did not erase him **26–8 Who . . . promised** you who find in exile with me a lack of proper education and hardship from which there is no escape, without hope of ever achieving the cultivated existence promised you by your gentle birth (as sons of a onetime courtier and soldier)   **29 But** i.e., but destined instead.   **tanlings** those tanned by the sun **30 shrinking** i.e., shrinking from the cold and cowering in servitude **32–3 yourself . . . o'ergrown** yourself so forgotten by now, and besides that overgrown with hair and beard as well as years   **34 questioned** looked at with suspicion.   **35 What thing** What a disgraceful thing **37 hot** lecherous

39 rowel wheel of a spur   **45 take . . . care** be more careful, proceed with better prospects of success   **46 The hazard therefore due** may the danger resulting from disobedience and lack of parental blessing **50 cracked** i.e., weakened with age.   **Have with you** Come on, then **51 country** country's   **53 The time . . . scorn** i.e., They are eager to go. Their blood disdains itself
5.1. Location: Britain. An open place.
5 wrying swerving from the right course   **7 bond but** obligation except   **8 Should have** had, as you should have   **9 put on this** undertake this deed   **12–13 that's . . . more** that is a loving act, since it makes them sin no more   **14 second** follow up.   **elder** subsequent (sin)   **15 and make . . . thrift** and make those evildoers repent their deeds, to their ultimate spiritual profit.

That, Britain, I have killed thy mistress; peace,   20
I'll give no wound to thee. Therefore, good heavens,
Hear patiently my purpose: I'll disrobe me
Of these Italian weeds and suit myself   23
As does a Briton peasant; so I'll fight
Against the part I come with; so I'll die   25
For thee, O Imogen, even for whom my life
Is every breath a death; and thus, unknown,   27
Pitied nor hated, to the face of peril   28
Myself I'll dedicate. Let me make men know
More valor in me than my habits show.   30
Gods, put the strength o'th' Leonati in me!
To shame the guise o'th' world, I will begin   32
The fashion: less without and more within.   *Exit.*   33

❖

5.2

*Enter Lucius, Iachimo, and the Roman army at
one door, and the Briton army at another,
Leonatus Posthumus following like a poor soldier.
They march over and go out. Then enter again, in
skirmish, Iachimo and Posthumus; he vanquisheth
and disarmeth Iachimo, and then leaves him.*

IACHIMO
The heaviness and guilt within my bosom
Takes off my manhood. I have belied a lady,
The princess of this country, and the air on't   3
Revengingly enfeebles me; or could this carl,   4
A very drudge of nature's, have subdued me   5
In my profession? Knighthoods and honors borne
As I wear mine are titles but of scorn.
If that thy gentry, Britain, go before   8
This lout as he exceeds our lords, the odds
Is that we scarce are men and you are gods.   *Exit.*

*The battle continues; the Britons fly; Cymbeline is
taken. Then enter, to his rescue, Belarius,
Guiderius, and Arviragus.*

BELARIUS
Stand, stand! We have th'advantage of the ground;
The lane is guarded. Nothing routs us but
The villainy of our fears.
GUIDERIUS, ARVIRAGUS   Stand, stand, and fight!

*Enter Posthumus, and seconds the Britons. They
rescue Cymbeline, and exeunt. Then enter Lucius,
Iachimo, and Imogen.*

LUCIUS
Away, boy, from the troops, and save thyself!
For friends kill friends, and the disorder's such

As war were hoodwinked.
IACHIMO   'Tis their fresh supplies.   16
LUCIUS
It is a day turned strangely. Or betimes   17
Let's reinforce, or fly.   *Exeunt.*

❖

5.3

*Enter Posthumus [dressed as a British peasant
still], and a Briton Lord.*

LORD
Cam'st thou from where they made the stand?
POSTHUMUS   I did,
Though you, it seems, come from the fliers?
LORD   I did.
POSTHUMUS
No blame be to you, sir, for all was lost,
But that the heavens fought. The King himself   4
Of his wings destitute, the army broken,   5
And but the backs of Britons seen, all flying
Through a strait lane; the enemy fullhearted,   7
Lolling the tongue with slaught'ring, having work   8
More plentiful than tools to do't, struck down
Some mortally, some slightly touched, some falling   10
Merely through fear, that the strait pass was dammed
With dead men hurt behind, and cowards living   12
To die with lengthened shame.
LORD   Where was this lane?   13
POSTHUMUS
Close by the battle, ditched, and walled with turf;
Which gave advantage to an ancient soldier,
An honest one, I warrant, who deserved   16
So long a breeding as his white beard came to,   17
In doing this for's country. Athwart the lane,
He, with two striplings—lads more like to run   19
The country base than to commit such slaughter,   20
With faces fit for masks, or rather fairer   21
Than those for preservation cased or shame—   22
Made good the passage, cried to those that fled,   23
"Our Britain's harts die flying, not our men.
To darkness fleet souls that fly backwards. Stand!   25
Or we are Romans and will give you that   26

---

16 As as if.   **hoodwinked** blindfolded. (War swings his weapons blindly, without looking to see who is struck.)   **17 Or betimes** Either swiftly
5.3. Location: The field of battle, as before.
4 But that if it had not been for the fact that   **5 wings** flanks of the army   **7 strait** narrow.   **fullhearted** full of courage and confidence   **8 Lolling** letting hang out   **10 touched** wounded   **12 behind** from the rear (while running away)   **13 lengthened** lingering (for the rest of their lives)   **16 honest** worthy   **16–17 who ... to** to whose white beard betokened the length of years that he deserves to live still in honor   **19 like** likely   **20 base** prisoner's base, a game in which rapid running is the means to victory   **21 fit for masks** refined enough to deserve sheltering from the elements   **22 Than ... shame** than ladies' faces masked (*cased*) either for protection against the elements or for modesty   **23 Made good** secured   **25 darkness** i.e., ignominy, hell.   **fleet** hasten   **26 we are Romans** i.e., we three will act like Romans.   **that** i.e., death blows

---

20 peace i.e., calm yourself, be reassured   **23 suit** clothe   **25 part** party, side   **27 Is ... death** i.e., is like dying again and again, every instant, from painful remorse   **28 Pitied** neither pitied   **30 habits** clothes   **32 guise** custom   **33 The fashion: less without** the fashion of relying less on outward show
5.2. Location: Britain. Field of battle. The scene is probably continuous with the previous.
0.3 *poor* of low rank and poorly outfitted   **3 on't** of it   **4 or** otherwise.   **carl** churl, peasant   **5 drudge** slave   **8 go before** excel

Like beasts which you shun beastly, and may save   27
But to look back in frown. Stand, stand!" These three,   28
Three thousand confident, in act as many—   29
For three performers are the file when all   30
The rest do nothing—with this word "Stand, stand,"
Accommodated by the place, more charming   32
With their own nobleness, which could have turned   33
A distaff to a lance, gilded pale looks,   34
Part shame, part spirit renewed, that some, turned
      coward   35
But by example—oh, a sin in war,   36
Damned in the first beginners!—'gan to look   37
The way that they did and to grin like lions   38
Upon the pikes o'th' hunters. Then began   39
A stop i'th' chaser, a retire, anon   40
A rout, confusion thick. Forthwith they fly   41
Chickens, the way which they stooped eagles; slaves,   42
The strides they victors made. And now our cowards,   43
Like fragments in hard voyages, became   44
The life o'th' need. Having found the back door open   45
Of the unguarded hearts, heavens, how they wound!
Some slain before, some dying, some their friends   47
O'erborne i'th' former wave, ten chased by one,   48
Are now each one the slaughterman of twenty.
Those that would die or ere resist are grown   50
The mortal bugs o'th' field.

LORD   This was strange chance: 51
A narrow lane, an old man, and two boys!

POSTHUMUS
Nay, do not wonder at it. You are made
Rather to wonder at the things you hear
Than to work any. Will you rhyme upon't   55
And vent it for a mockery? Here is one: 56
"Two boys, an old man twice a boy, a lane,   57
Preserved the Britons, was the Romans' bane."

LORD
Nay, be not angry, sir.
POSTHUMUS   'Lack, to what end?   59
Who dares not stand his foe, I'll be his friend;   60
For if he'll do as he is made to do,   61
I know he'll quickly fly my friendship too.   62
You have put me into rhyme.
LORD   Farewell. You're angry.
                                          Exit.

POSTHUMUS
Still going? This is a lord! Oh, noble misery,   64
To be i'th' field, and ask "What news?" of me!
Today how many would have given their honors
To have saved their carcasses! Took heel to do't,
And yet died too! I, in mine own woe charmed,   68
Could not find Death where I did hear him groan,
Nor feel him where he struck. Being an ugly monster,
'Tis strange he hides him in fresh cups, soft beds,   71
Sweet words, or hath more ministers than we   72
That draw his knives i'th' war. Well, I will find him;   73
For being now a favorer to the Briton,   74
      [*removing his British garb*]
No more a Briton, I have resumed again   75
The part I came in. Fight I will no more,   76
But yield me to the veriest hind that shall   77
Once touch my shoulder. Great the slaughter is   78
Here made by th' Roman; great the answer be   79
Britons must take. For me, my ransom's death.
On either side I come to spend my breath,   81
Which neither here I'll keep nor bear again,
But end it by some means for Imogen.

      Enter two [British] Captains and soldiers.

FIRST CAPTAIN
Great Jupiter be praised! Lucius is taken.
'Tis thought the old man and his sons were angels.
SECOND CAPTAIN
There was a fourth man, in a silly habit,   86
That gave th'affront with them.
FIRST CAPTAIN   So 'tis reported,   87
But none of 'em can be found.—Stand! Who's there?
POSTHUMUS   A Roman,
Who had not now been drooping here if seconds   90
Had answered him.
SECOND CAPTAIN   Lay hands on him; a dog!   91

27 Like beasts i.e., like savage lions.   **beastly** like cowards   **27–8 and may . . . frown** and which you may prevent only by turning and facing us in defiance.   **29 Three . . . many** as confident as if they were three thousand men, doing the deeds of that many   **30 file** i.e., entire force (as in "rank and file")   **32–9 Accommodated . . . hunters** assisted by the place, casting a spell on their fellow soldiers by exemplary action so noble that it could have inspired even a housewife to become a soldier, imparted a flush of color to the cheeks of palefaced men, partly through shame and partly through a renewing of courage, so that some soldiers who had turned coward only by others' display of cowardice—oh, a terrible sin in war, damnable in those who first cower in time of danger!—now began to model themselves on the looks and actions of the three brave warriors and to bare their teeth like lions at the weapons of those who hunted them down.   **40 stop i'th' chaser** stopping of those who had been the pursuers, i.e., the Romans.   **retire** retreat   **41–3 Forthwith . . . made** Immediately the Romans fled like chickens along the narrow passage down which they had just swooped down like eagles, retracing, like slaves, the steps thay had taken as victors.   **44 fragments** scraps, fragments of food, something to fall back on as a last resort   **45 The life o'th' need** vital support in time of necessity.   **back door** i.e., vulnerable soft spot of the Romans   **47–8 Some . . . by one** i.e., some who were given up for dead or dying, and some comrades overwhelmed in the previous Roman assault who had yielded by the tens to each Roman soldier   **50 would . . . ere** previously were ready to die rather than   **51 mortal bugs** deadly bugbears, terrors   **55 work any** perform any such wonders yourself. (Said reproachfully.)   **55–6 Will . . . one** i.e., Would you like to compose rhymes on this event in ballad fashion and thus make a mockery of it with your cheap exploitation? Here is a sample. (*Vent* means "air, circulate.")   **57 twice a boy** in his second childhood

59 'Lack . . . end? Alack, why should I be angry?   **60–2 Who . . . too** i.e., I can put up with the friendship of any coward (like yourself), for, if he is true to his colors, he'll run away and rid me of his company. (*Who* means "whoever," *stand* "stand against," *made* "inclined.")   **64 Still . . . misery** Still running away? This is a fine lord! What a miserable specimen of the nobility   **68 too** anyway.   **charmed** made invulnerable as if by a spell   **71 cups** cups of wine   **72–3 Sweet . . . war** sweet whisperings of lovers, and yet has more agents to carry out his (Death's) work than we soldiers have weapons.   **74 For . . . Briton** for since Death now favors the British side   **75 No . . . Briton** I remaining no longer a Briton   **76 The part . . . in** i.e., my Roman guise (in which my capture and execution seem assured).   **77 hind** peasant   **78 touch my shoulder** i.e., place me under arrest.   **79 answer be** retaliation is that   **81 spend my breath** give up my life   **86 silly** simple, rustic   **87 th'affront** the attack   **90 drooping** languishing.   **seconds** supporters   **91 answered him** followed his lead, or answered his call for help.

A leg of Rome shall not return to tell   92
What crows have pecked them here. He brags his
   service
As if he were of note. Bring him to th' King.

Enter Cymbeline, Belarius, Guiderius, Arvira-
gus, Pisanio, [soldiers, attendants,] and Roman
captives. The Captains present Posthumus to
Cymbeline, who delivers him over to a Jailer.

[Then exeunt.]

5.4

Enter Posthumus [in chains] and [two] Jailer[s].

FIRST JAILER
You shall not now be stol'n; you have locks upon you.
So graze as you find pasture.

SECOND JAILER   Ay, or a stomach.   2
                              [Exeunt Jailers.]

POSTHUMUS
Most welcome, bondage! For thou art a way,
I think, to liberty. Yet am I better
Than one that's sick o'th' gout, since he had rather
Groan so in perpetuity than be cured
By th' sure physician, Death, who is the key
T'unbar these locks. My conscience, thou art fettered
More than my shanks and wrists. You good gods,
   give me
The penitent instrument to pick that bolt,   10
Then, free forever! Is't enough I am sorry?
So children temporal fathers do appease;
Gods are more full of mercy. Must I repent,   13
I cannot do it better than in gyves,   14
Desired more than constrained. To satisfy,   15
If of my freedom 'tis the main part, take   16
No stricter render of me than my all.   17
I know you are more clement than vile men,
Who of their broken debtors take a third,   19
A sixth, a tenth, letting them thrive again
On their abatement. That's not my desire.   21
For Imogen's dear life take mine; and though
'Tis not so dear, yet 'tis a life; you coined it.   23

'Tween man and man they weigh not every stamp;   24
Though light, take pieces for the figure's sake;   25
You rather mine, being yours. And so, great powers,   26
If you will take this audit, take this life   27
And cancel these cold bonds. O Imogen!   28
I'll speak to thee in silence.   *[He sleeps.]*

Solemn music. Enter, as in an apparition, Sicilius
Leonatus, father to Posthumus, an old man, attired
like a warrior; leading in his hand an ancient
matron, his wife, and mother to Posthumus, with
music before them. Then, after other music, follows
the two young Leonati, brothers to Posthumus,
with wounds as they died in the wars. They circle
Posthumus round, as he lies sleeping.

SICILIUS
No more, thou Thunder-master, show   30
   Thy spite on mortal flies.   31
With Mars fall out, with Juno chide,
   That thy adulteries   33
   Rates and revenges.   34
Hath my poor boy done aught but well,
   Whose face I never saw?
I died whilst in the womb he stayed
   Attending nature's law;   38
Whose father then—as men report   39
   Thou orphans' father art—   40
Thou shouldst have been, and shielded him
   From this earth-vexing smart.   42

MOTHER
Lucina lent not me her aid,   43
   But took me in my throes,
That from me was Posthumus ripped,
   Came crying 'mongst his foes,
      A thing of pity!

SICILIUS
Great nature, like his ancestry,   48
   Molded the stuff so fair   49
That he deserved the praise o'th' world
   As great Sicilius' heir.

FIRST BROTHER
When once he was mature for man,   52
   In Britain where was he   53
That could stand up his parallel,
   Or fruitful object be
In eye of Imogen, that best
   Could deem his dignity?   57

---

92 leg i.e., one of the lower extremities, one who does the walking
(and the running away)
5.4. Location: A British prison or stockade. Possibly the scene is
continuous; see the next note.
0.1 *Enter* (The scene may be continuous, with Posthumus and the jailers remaining onstage, though the Folio does mark an entrance for
Posthumus and one jailer, and the scene does appear to call for manacles [lines 9, 191]. On the unlocalized Elizabethan stage, the change
of scene is achieved chiefly by the actors and their dialogue.) **2 graze
. . . pasture** i.e., like a horse, fettered by one leg. **10 The penitent . . .
bolt** the penitence to unlock the fetters encumbering my conscience
and to find the death I seek **13 Must I** If I must **14 gyves** fetters
15 constrained forced (upon me). **satisfy** make atonement **16 If . . .
part** i.e., if such atonement is essential to freeing my conscience
17 stricter render sterner repayment **19 broken** bankrupt **21 abatement** diminished principal. **23 so dear** as valuable as hers

24–6 'Tween . . . yours In commercial transactions, men do not weigh
each coin exactly; even if some coins may be under the exact weight,
men accept them for the sake of the image stamped thereon of the
King; you gods should all the more readily take my coin (i.e., me),
even though I am a light (worthless) coin, since I am stamped in your
image. **27 take this audit** accept this accounting **28 bonds** (1) fetters, both literal and figurative (2) legal contracts. **30 Thunder-master** i.e., Jupiter **31 mortal flies** i.e., petty creatures, mere humans.
33 That who (i.e., Juno) **34 Rates** scolds **38 Attending nature's law**
i.e., awaiting the completion of his term in the womb **39–40 Whose
father . . . art** (Psalm 68:5 praises God as "A father of the fatherless.")
42 earth-vexing smart suffering to which all life is prone. **43 Lucina**
goddess of childbirth **48 like** acting in concert with, or, taking the
part of **49 stuff** substance **52 mature for man** grown to manhood
53 he any man **57 deem his dignity** judge his worth.

MOTHER
 With marriage wherefore was he mocked,
  To be exiled and thrown
 From Leonati seat, and cast
  From her his dearest one,
  Sweet Imogen?
SICILIUS
 Why did you suffer Iachimo,
  Slight thing of Italy,   64
 To taint his nobler heart and brain
  With needless jealousy,
 And to become the geck and scorn   67
  O'th'other's villainy?
SECOND BROTHER
 For this from stiller seats we came, 69
  Our parents and us twain,
 That striking in our country's cause 71
  Fell bravely and were slain,
 Our fealty and Tenantius' right   73
  With honor to maintain.
FIRST BROTHER
 Like hardiment Posthumus hath 75
  To Cymbeline performed.
 Then, Jupiter, thou king of gods,
  Why hast thou thus adjourned 78
 The graces for his merits due,
  Being all to dolors turned?
SICILIUS
 Thy crystal window ope; look out.
  No longer exercise
 Upon a valiant race thy harsh
  And potent injuries.
MOTHER
 Since, Jupiter, our son is good,
  Take off his miseries.
SICILIUS
 Peep through thy marble mansion. Help,
  Or we poor ghosts will cry
 To th' shining synod of the rest   89
  Against thy deity.
BROTHERS
 Help, Jupiter, or we appeal,
  And from thy justice fly.

 Jupiter descends in thunder and lightning, sitting
 upon an eagle. He throws a thunderbolt. The
 ghosts fall on their knees.

JUPITER
 No more, you petty spirits of region low,
  Offend our hearing. Hush! How dare you ghosts
 Accuse the Thunderer, whose bolt, you know,
  Sky-planted, batters all rebelling coasts? 96
 Poor shadows of Elysium, hence, and rest
  Upon your never-withering banks of flowers.
 Be not with mortal accidents oppressed. 99

No care of yours it is; you know 'tis ours.
 Whom best I love I cross, to make my gift, 101
  The more delayed, delighted. Be content. 102
Your low-laid son our godhead will uplift. 103
 His comforts thrive, his trials well are spent. 104
Our Jovial star reigned at his birth, and in 105
 Our temple was he married. Rise, and fade. 106
He shall be lord of Lady Imogen,
 And happier much by his affliction made.
This tablet lay upon his breast, wherein 109
 Our pleasure his full fortune doth confine. 110
     [He delivers a tablet.]
And so away! No farther with your din
 Express impatience, lest you stir up mine.
 Mount, eagle, to my palace crystalline. *Ascends.*
SICILIUS
 He came in thunder; his celestial breath
 Was sulfurous to smell. The holy eagle
 Stooped, as to foot us. His ascension is 116
 More sweet than our blest fields. His royal bird 117
 Prunes the immortal wing and cloys his beak, 118
 As when his god is pleased.
ALL   Thanks, Jupiter!
SICILIUS
 The marble pavement closes; he is entered 120
 His radiant roof. Away! And, to be blest,
 Let us with care perform his great behest.
   [The ghosts place the tablet on
   Posthumus's breast, and] vanish.
POSTHUMUS *[waking]*
 Sleep, thou hast been a grandsire and begot
 A father to me; and thou hast created
 A mother and two brothers. But, oh scorn, 125
 Gone! They went hence so soon as they were born.
 And so I am awake. Poor wretches that depend
 On greatness' favor dream as I have done,
 Wake and find nothing. But, alas, I swerve! 129
     [He sees the tablet.]
 Many dream not to find, neither deserve, 130
 And yet are steeped in favors; so am I,
 That have this golden chance and know not why.
 What fairies haunt this ground? A book? Oh, rare one! 133
 Be not, as is our fangled world, a garment 134
 Nobler than that it covers. Let thy effects
 So follow, to be most unlike our courtiers, 136
 As good as promise.

64 Slight worthless **67 geck** dupe **69 stiller seats** quieter abodes (i.e., the Elysian Fields) **71 That** who **73 Tenantius'** Cymbeline's father's **75 Like hardiment** Similar bold exploits **78 adjourned** deferred **89 synod of the rest** assembly of the gods **96 Sky-planted** growing out of the sky **99 accidents** events

101 cross thwart **102 delighted** (the more) delighted in. **103 Your . . . uplift** I, in my godhead, will raise up your humbled son. **104 spent** ended. **105 Jovial star** the planet Jupiter **106 fade** vanish. **109–10 wherein . . . confine** wherein I am pleased to set forth precisely his happy fortune to come. **116 Stooped . . . us** swooped down, as if to seize us in his talons. **116–17 His . . . fields** His ascent gives a favorable aspect and a sweet odor surpassing that of the Elysian Fields. **118 Prunes** preens. **cloys** claws, strokes with the claw **120 The marble pavement** i.e., the aperture giving access to the hut over the stage in which machinery for ascents and descents was housed. The floor of this hut, serving as a roof over the stage, was decorated with celestial emblems to represent the heavens. (Compare with *marble mansion* in line 87.) **125 scorn** mockery **129 swerve** mistake, go astray. **130 to find** of finding **133 book** i.e., the tablet or scroll. **rare** excellent **134 fangled** characterized by fripperies or gaudiness **136 to** so as to

(*Reads.*) "Whenas a lion's whelp shall, to himself 138
unknown, without seeking find and be embraced by
a piece of tender air; and when from a stately cedar
shall be lopped branches which, being dead many
years, shall after revive, be jointed to the old stock, and
freshly grow; then shall Posthumus end his miseries,
Britain be fortunate and flourish in peace and plenty."
'Tis still a dream, or else such stuff as madmen 145
Tongue and brain not; either both or nothing, 146
Or senseless speaking or a speaking such 147
As sense cannot untie. Be what it is, 148
The action of my life is like it, which
I'll keep, if but for sympathy. 150

Enter [First] Jailer.

FIRST JAILER   Come, sir, are you ready for death?
POSTHUMUS   Overroasted rather; ready long ago.
FIRST JAILER   Hanging is the word, sir. If you be ready 153
for that, you are well cooked.
POSTHUMUS   So, if I prove a good repast to the spectators, the dish pays the shot. 156
FIRST JAILER   A heavy reckoning for you, sir. But the
comfort is, you shall be called to no more payments,
fear no more tavern bills, which are often the sadness 159
of parting as the procuring of mirth. You come in faint
for want of meat, depart reeling with too much drink;
sorry that you have paid too much, and sorry that you
are paid too much; purse and brain both empty; the 163
brain the heavier for being too light, the purse too 164
light, being drawn of heaviness. Of this contradiction 165
you shall now be quit. Oh, the charity of a penny cord! 166
It sums up thousands in a trice. You have no true 167
debitor and creditor but it; of what's past, is, and to 168
come, the discharge. Your neck, sir, is pen, book, and 169
counters; so the acquittance follows. 170
POSTHUMUS   I am merrier to die than thou art to live.
FIRST JAILER   Indeed, sir, he that sleeps feels not the
toothache. But a man that were to sleep your sleep, 173
and a hangman to help him to bed, I think he would
change places with his officer; for, look you, sir, you 175
know not which way you shall go. 176
POSTHUMUS   Yes, indeed do I, fellow.

FIRST JAILER   Your death has eyes in 's head then; I
have not seen him so pictured. You must either be 179
directed by some that take upon them to know, or to 180
take upon yourself that which I am sure you do not
know, or jump the after-inquiry on your own peril. 182
And how you shall speed in your journey's end, I 183
think you'll never return to tell one.
POSTHUMUS   I tell thee, fellow, there are none want eyes 185
to direct them the way I am going but such as wink 186
and will not use them.
FIRST JAILER   What an infinite mock is this, that a man
should have the best use of eyes to see the way of 189
blindness! I am sure hanging's the way of winking. 190

Enter a Messenger.

MESSENGER   Knock off his manacles. Bring your prisoner to the King.
POSTHUMUS   Thou bring'st good news. I am called to
be made free.   [*He is freed from his irons.*] 194
FIRST JAILER   I'll be hanged then. 195
POSTHUMUS   Thou shalt be then freer than a jailer; no
bolts for the dead.   *Exeunt [all but the First Jailer].*
FIRST JAILER   Unless a man would marry a gallows and
beget young gibbets, I never saw one so prone. Yet, 199
on my conscience, there are verier knaves desire to 200
live, for all he be a Roman; and there be some of them 201
too that die against their wills. So should I, if I were 202
one. I would we were all of one mind, and one mind 203
good. Oh, there were desolation of jailers and gal- 204
lowses! I speak against my present profit, but my wish 205
hath a preferment in't.   [*Exit.*] 206

5.5

Enter Cymbeline, Belarius, Guiderius, Arviragus,
Pisanio, [officers, attendants,] and lords.

CYMBELINE
Stand by my side, you whom the gods have made
Preservers of my throne. Woe is my heart
That the poor soldier that so richly fought,
Whose rags shamed gilded arms, whose naked breast 4
Stepped before targes of proof, cannot be found. 5

---

138 Whenas When   **145–8 'Tis . . . untie** It is a dream or else the sort
of thing that madmen speak without understanding; either it is the
senseless babbling of a madman or a language that reason cannot
unravel; it may be both of these things, or neither.   **150 sympathy**
i.e., resemblance (between my life and this mystery).   **153 Hanging**
(1) Hanging up like cooking meat (2) Being hanged as a criminal
156 the dish . . . shot (1) the food is worth the tavern reckoning
(2) my death settles my account.   **159 often** as often   **163 are paid**
are subdued (by excessive drink)   **164 light** foolish   **165 being . . .**
heaviness being emptied of the money that weighed it down.
166 charity benevolent action, one that settles all debts   **167 sums up**
(1) totals up a reckoning (2) collects, summarizes.   **trice** (1) instant
(2) tricing up, hauling up by a rope.   **168 debitor and creditor**
account book   **169 discharge** (1) payment of debt (2) disburdening,
release, as in death.   **170 counters** metal disks used for calculating.
acquittance (1) discharge of an account (2) deliverance   **173 a man**
that were to if there were a man who was sentenced to   **175 officer**
i.e., the hangman   **176 which . . . go** i.e., to heaven or hell; but
Posthumus answers in the sense of knowing that death will release
all sorrows.

179 so pictured (The traditional death's-head is an eyeless skull.)
180 take upon them undertake, profess   **182 jump** finesse   **183 speed**
succeed   **185 want** lacking   **186 wink** close the eyes   **189–90 the**
way of blindness i.e., the way to death.   **190 hanging's . . . winking**
hanging will close up the eyes.   **194 made free** i.e., executed and
thereby freed from existence.   **195 I'll be hanged then** (The jailer is
using a conventional expression, like "I'll be damned if that's so," but
Posthumus replies that he means *free* in a spiritual sense.)   **199 prone**
ready, eager.   **200–3 there . . . were one** i.e., he's not such a bad fellow, even if he is a Roman; worse men than he desire to live when
they're to be executed, as I would in such a plight. (Romans were
supposed to be stoical in the face of death.)   **204–5 there . . . gal-**
lowses! i.e., if all men were good, there would be no work left for jailers and gallows!   **206 a preferment** i.e., a preference for us all to live
in a better world (with a hope that this pious wish may stand me in
good stead at my day of reckoning and thus "prefer" me to bliss). Possibly, the jailer thinks of more worldly promotion to a better office.
5.5. Location: Britain. The camp of King Cymbeline.
4 gilded arms glittering armor   **5 targes of proof** shields hardened to
withstand tests

He shall be happy that can find him, if
Our grace can make him so.
BELARIUS   I never saw   7
Such noble fury in so poor a thing,
Such precious deeds in one that promised naught
But beggary and poor looks.
CYMBELINE   No tidings of him?
PISANIO
He hath been searched among the dead and living,
But no trace of him.
CYMBELINE   To my grief, I am
The heir of his reward, [*to Belarius, Guiderius, and*
   Arviragus] which I will add
To you, the liver, heart, and brain of Britain,   14
By whom I grant she lives. 'Tis now the time
To ask of whence you are. Report it.
BELARIUS   Sir,
In Cambria are we born, and gentlemen.
Further to boast were neither true nor modest,
Unless I add we are honest.
CYMBELINE   Bow your knees.
                                              [*They kneel.*]
Arise my knights o'th' battle. I create you   20
Companions to our person and will fit you
With dignities becoming your estates.   [*They rise.*] 22

        Enter Cornelius and Ladies.

There's business in these faces. Why so sadly
Greet you our victory? You look like Romans,
And not o'th' court of Britain.
CORNELIUS   Hail, great King!
To sour your happiness, I must report
The Queen is dead.
CYMBELINE   Who worse than a physician   27
Would this report become? But I consider   28
By med'cine life may be prolonged, yet death
Will seize the doctor too. How ended she?
CORNELIUS
With horror, madly dying, like her life,
Which, being cruel to the world, concluded
Most cruel to herself. What she confessed
I will report, so please you. These her women
Can trip me, if I err, who with wet cheeks   35
Were present when she finished.
CYMBELINE   Prithee, say.
CORNELIUS
First, she confessed she never loved you, only
Affected greatness got by you, not you;   38
Married your royalty, was wife to your place,
Abhorred your person.
CYMBELINE   She alone knew this;
And, but she spoke it dying, I would not   41
Believe her lips in opening it. Proceed.   42

CORNELIUS
Your daughter, whom she bore in hand to love   43
With such integrity, she did confess
Was as a scorpion to her sight, whose life,
But that her flight prevented it, she had   46
Ta'en off by poison.
CYMBELINE   Oh, most delicate fiend!   47
Who is't can read a woman? Is there more?
CORNELIUS
More, sir, and worse. She did confess she had
For you a mortal mineral which, being took,   50
Should by the minute feed on life and, ling'ring,   51
By inches waste you. In which time she purposed,
By watching, weeping, tendance, kissing, to   53
O'ercome you with her show and, in fine,   54
When she had fitted you with her craft, to work   55
Her son into th'adoption of the crown;   56
But, failing of her end by his strange absence,
Grew shameless desperate; opened, in despite   58
Of heaven and men, her purposes; repented   59
The evils she hatched were not effected; so
Despairing died.
CYMBELINE   Heard you all this, her women?
LADIES   We did, so please Your Highness.
CYMBELINE   Mine eyes
Were not in fault, for she was beautiful;
Mine ears, that heard her flattery; nor my heart,
That thought her like her seeming. It had been vicious 66
To have mistrusted her. Yet, O my daughter,
That it was folly in me thou mayst say,
And prove it in thy feeling. Heaven mend all!   69

        Enter Lucius, Iachimo, [the Soothsayer,] and other
        Roman prisoners, [guarded; Posthumus] Leonatus
        behind, and Imogen [disguised as Fidele].

Thou com'st not, Caius, now for tribute. That
The Britons have rased out, though with the loss   71
Of many a bold one, whose kinsmen have made suit
That their good souls may be appeased with slaughter
Of you their captives, which ourself have granted.
So think of your estate.   75
LUCIUS
Consider, sir, the chance of war. The day
Was yours by accident. Had it gone with us,
We should not, when the blood was cool, have
   threatened
Our prisoners with the sword. But since the gods
Will have it thus, that nothing but our lives
May be called ransom, let it come. Sufficeth

---

43 bore in hand pretended   **46 had** would have   **47 Ta'en off**
ended.   **delicate** subtle   **50 mortal mineral** deadly poison   **51 by
the minute** minute by minute   **53 watching** staying awake (as
nurse).   **tendance** attentiveness   **54 in fine** in conclusion   **55 fitted
you** shaped you to her wish   **56 th'adoption** the right of an adopted
heir   **58 opened** revealed   **59 repented** regretted   **66 That . . .
vicious** that thought her to be what she appeared to be. It would have
been wrong   **69 in thy feeling** by feeling it, by what you have suffered. (Cymbeline apostrophizes the absent Imogen, who then ironically enters in disguise.)   **71 rased out** erased   **75 estate** spiritual
estate (in preparation for your death).

---

7 grace favor   **14 liver, heart, and brain** i.e., heart and soul
20 knights o'th' battle knights created on the battlefield.   **22 estates**
i.e., new status.   **27–8 Who . . . become?** i.e., A report of death does
not speak well for the doctor, of all people.   **35 trip** refute, contradict
38 Affected desired   **41 but** were it not that   **42 opening** revealing

A Roman with a Roman's heart can suffer.
Augustus lives to think on't; and so much   83
For my peculiar care. This one thing only   84
I will entreat: my boy, a Briton born,
Let him be ransomed. Never master had
A page so kind, so duteous, diligent,
So tender over his occasions, true,   88
So feat, so nurselike. Let his virtue join   89
With my request, which I'll make bold Your Highness   90
Cannot deny. He hath done no Briton harm,
Though he have served a Roman. Save him, sir,
And spare no blood beside.
CYMBELINE   I have surely seen him;   93
His favor is familiar to me.—Boy,   94
Thou hast looked thyself into my grace   95
And art mine own. I know not why, wherefore,
To say "Live, boy." Ne'er thank thy master. Live,   97
And ask of Cymbeline what boon thou wilt,   98
Fitting my bounty and thy state, I'll give it,
Yea, though thou do demand a prisoner,
The noblest ta'en.
IMOGEN   I humbly thank Your Highness.
LUCIUS
I do not bid thee beg my life, good lad,
And yet I know thou wilt.
IMOGEN   No, no, alack,
There's other work in hand. I see a thing   104
Bitter to me as death. Your life, good master,
Must shuffle for itself.
LUCIUS   The boy disdains me,
He leaves me, scorns me. Briefly die their joys   107
That place them on the truth of girls and boys.   108
Why stands he so perplexed?   [She studies Iachimo.]
CYMBELINE   What wouldst thou, boy?
I love thee more and more. Think more and more
What's best to ask. Know'st him thou look'st on?
Speak,
Wilt have him live? Is he thy kin? Thy friend?
IMOGEN
He is a Roman, no more kin to me
Than I to Your Highness; who, being born your vassal,   114
Am something nearer.
CYMBELINE   Wherefore ey'st him so?   115
IMOGEN
I'll tell you, sir, in private, if you please
To give me hearing.
CYMBELINE   Ay, with all my heart,
And lend my best attention. What's thy name?
IMOGEN
Fidele, sir.
CYMBELINE   Thou'rt my good youth, my page;

I'll be thy master. Walk with me; speak freely.
            [Cymbeline and Imogen converse apart.]
BELARIUS [to Arviragus and Guiderius]
Is not this boy revived from death?
ARVIRAGUS   One sand another   122
Not more resembles that sweet rosy lad   123
Who died, and was Fidele. What think you?   124
GUIDERIUS   The same dead thing alive.
BELARIUS
Peace, peace! See further. He eyes us not; forbear.
Creatures may be alike. Were't he, I am sure
He would have spoke to us.
GUIDERIUS   But we saw him dead.
BELARIUS
Be silent; let's see further.
PISANIO [aside]   It is my mistress.
Since she is living, let the time run on   130
To good or bad. [Cymbeline and Imogen come forward.]
CYMBELINE [to Imogen] Come, stand thou by our side.   131
Make thy demand aloud. [To Iachimo] Sir, step you
forth;
Give answer to this boy, and do it freely,
Or, by our greatness and the grace of it,   134
Which is our honor, bitter torture shall
Winnow the truth from falsehood.—On, speak to him.
IMOGEN
My boon is that this gentleman may render   137
Of whom he had this ring.
            [She points to the ring Iachimo wears.]
POSTHUMUS [aside]   What's that to him?
CYMBELINE [to Iachimo]
That diamond upon your finger, say
How came it yours?
IACHIMO
Thou'lt torture me to leave unspoken that   141
Which, to be spoke, would torture thee.
CYMBELINE   How? Me?
IACHIMO
I am glad to be constrained to utter that
Which torments me to conceal. By villainy
I got this ring. 'Twas Leonatus' jewel,
Whom thou didst banish; and—which more may
grieve thee,
As it doth me—a nobler sir ne'er lived
Twixt sky and ground. Wilt thou hear more, my lord?
CYMBELINE
All that belongs to this.
IACHIMO   That paragon, thy daughter,
For whom my heart drops blood and my false spirits   150
Quail to remember—Give me leave; I faint.
CYMBELINE
My daughter? What of her? Renew thy strength.
I had rather thou shouldst live while nature will   153

---

83 **think on't** i.e., consider what revenge to take   84 **my peculiar care** my concern for myself.   88 **tender . . . occasions** solicitous of his master's needs   89 **feat** graceful   90 **make bold** venture   93 **And** even if (you)   94 **favor** face   95 **looked . . . grace** won my favor by your appearance   97 **Ne'er thank thy master** i.e., Don't attribute your being saved to Lucius's request.   98 **ask** if you ask   104 **thing** i.e., the ring on Iachimo's finger   107–8 **Briefly . . . That** Swiftly die the joys of those who   108 **truth** fidelity   114 **who** i.e., I, Fidele   115 **something** somewhat

122–4 **One . . . died** One grain of sand does not resemble another more than this youth resembles the sweet rose-cheeked lad who died   130–1 **let . . . bad** i.e., let come what must come.   134 **the grace of it** that which adorns it   137 **render** give account   141 **to leave** for leaving, if I leave.   150 **and** and whom   153 **live . . . will** continue to live as long as nature permits (with your death sentence forgiven)

Than die ere I hear more. Strive, man, and speak.

IACHIMO
Upon a time—unhappy was the clock
That struck the hour!—it was in Rome—accurst
The mansion where!—'twas at a feast—Oh, would
Our viands had been poisoned, or at least
Those which I heaved to head!—the good
    Posthumus—   159
What should I say? He was too good to be
Where ill men were, and was the best of all
Amongst the rar'st of good ones—sitting sadly,
Hearing us praise our loves of Italy   163
For beauty that made barren the swelled boast   164
Of him that best could speak; for feature, laming   165
The shrine of Venus or straight-pight Minerva,   166
Postures beyond brief nature; for condition,   167
A shop of all the qualities that man   168
Loves woman for, besides that hook of wiving,   169
Fairness which strikes the eye—

CYMBELINE   I stand on fire.   170
Come to the matter.

IACHIMO   All too soon I shall,
Unless thou wouldst grieve quickly. This Posthumus,
Most like a noble lord in love and one
That had a royal lover, took his hint,   174
And not dispraising whom we praised—therein
He was as calm as virtue—he began
His mistress' picture; which by his tongue being
    made,
And then a mind put in't, either our brags   178
Were cracked of kitchen trulls, or his description   179
Proved us unspeaking sots.

CYMBELINE   Nay, nay, to th' purpose.   180
IACHIMO
Your daughter's chastity—there it begins.
He spake of her as Dian had hot dreams   182
And she alone were cold; whereat I, wretch,
Made scruple of his praise and wagered with him   184
Pieces of gold 'gainst this which then he wore
Upon his honored finger, to attain
In suit the place of 's bed and win this ring   187
By hers and mine adultery. He, true knight,
No lesser of her honor confident
Than I did truly find her, stakes this ring;
And would so, had it been a carbuncle   191
Of Phoebus' wheel, and might so safely, had it   192
Been all the worth of 's car. Away to Britain   193
Post I in this design. Well may you, sir,   194

Remember me at court, where I was taught
Of your chaste daughter the wide difference   196
Twixt amorous and villainous. Being thus quenched
Of hope, not longing, mine Italian brain   198
'Gan in your duller Britain operate   199
Most vilely; for my vantage, excellent.   200
And, to be brief, my practice so prevailed   201
That I returned with simular proof enough   202
To make the noble Leonatus mad
By wounding his belief in her renown   204
With tokens thus and thus; averring notes   205
Of chamber hanging, pictures, this her bracelet—   206
        [*showing the bracelet*]
Oh, cunning, how I got it!—nay, some marks
Of secret on her person, that he could not
But think her bond of chastity quite cracked,
I having ta'en the forfeit. Whereupon—   210
Methinks, I see him now—
POSTHUMUS [*advancing*]   Ay, so thou dost,
Italian fiend! Ay me, most credulous fool,
Egregious murderer, thief, anything
That's due to all the villains past, in being,
To come! Oh, give me cord, or knife, or poison,
Some upright justicer! Thou, King, send out   216
For torturers ingenious! It is I
That all th'abhorred things o'th'earth amend   218
By being worse than they. I am Posthumus,
That killed thy daughter—villain-like, I lie—
That caused a lesser villain than myself,
A sacrilegious thief, to do't. The temple
Of virtue was she, yea, and she herself.   223
Spit, and throw stones, cast mire upon me, set
The dogs o'th' street to bay me! Every villain
Be called Posthumus Leonatus, and
Be "villainy" less than 'twas! O Imogen!   227
My queen, my life, my wife! O Imogen,
Imogen, Imogen!
IMOGEN   Peace, my lord. Hear, hear—
POSTHUMUS
Shall 's have a play of this? Thou scornful page,   230
There lie thy part.   [*He strikes her; she falls.*]
PISANIO   Oh, gentlemen, help!   231
        [*He goes to her assistance.*]
Mine and your mistress! Oh, my lord Posthumus,
You ne'er killed Imogen till now. Help, help!
Mine honored lady!
CYMBELINE   Does the world go round?   234

---

159 **heaved to head** raised to my lips   163–70 **Hearing . . . eye** hearing us praise our Italian mistresses for beauty that surpassed even the exaggerated boast of the most eloquent speaker, attributing to them graces surpassing those of ordinary mortals and able indeed to make the enshrined Venus and stately, straight-backed Minerva seem lame by comparison, praising these women for qualities that are the sum of all that men love women for, and in addition the physical attractiveness that serves as a bait to inveigle men into marriage   174 **hint** occasion   178 **put in't** inserted into the picture   179 **cracked of kitchen trulls** boastfully offered in praise of kitchen maids   180 **unspeaking sots** inarticulate blockheads   182 **as** as if   184 **Made scruple of** expressed doubts as to   187 **In suit** by urging my suit   191 **would so** would have done so   192 **Phoebus' wheel** i.e., the wheel of the sungod's chariot   193 **'s car** his chariot   194 **Post** hasten

196 **Of** by   198 **not longing** though not of my desire   199 **duller** i.e., slower-minded (supposedly caused by the northern climate)   200 **vantage** profit   201 **practice** scheming   202 **simular** simulated, or, pretended, plausible   204 **renown** good name   205 **averring** avouching, citing   206 **hanging** hangings   210 **the forfeit** i.e., what was forfeited by the breaking of her bond of chaste loyalty.   216 **justicer** judge.   218 **That . . . amend** who make all loathsome things seem better in comparison   223 **she herself** she was Virtue herself.   227 **Be . . . 'twas!** let the name "villainy" signify something less heinous than it used to!   230 **Shall 's** Shall we   231 **There lie thy part** Your part is to lie there on the ground.   234 **Does . . . round?** i.e., Is the ground turning under my feet? (An expression of dizziness.)

POSTHUMUS
How comes these staggers on me?
PISANIO   Wake, my mistress! 235
CYMBELINE
If this be so, the gods do mean to strike me
To death with mortal joy.
PISANIO   How fares my mistress?
IMOGEN   Oh, get thee from my sight!
Thou gav'st me poison. Dangerous fellow, hence!
Breathe not where princes are.
CYMBELINE   The tune of Imogen! 241
PISANIO   Lady,
The gods throw stones of sulfur on me if 243
That box I gave you was not thought by me
A precious thing. I had it from the Queen.
CYMBELINE
New matter still?
IMOGEN   It poisoned me.
CORNELIUS   O gods!
I left out one thing which the Queen confessed,
[To Pisanio] Which must approve thee honest. "If
    Pisanio 248
Have," said she, "given his mistress that confection 249
Which I gave him for cordial, she is served
As I would serve a rat."
CYMBELINE   What's this, Cornelius?
CORNELIUS
The Queen, sir, very oft importuned me
To temper poisons for her, still pretending 253
The satisfaction of her knowledge only
In killing creatures vile, as cats and dogs,
Of no esteem. I, dreading that her purpose
Was of more danger, did compound for her
A certain stuff which, being ta'en, would cease 258
The present power of life, but in short time
All offices of nature should again
Do their due functions.—Have you ta'en of it?
IMOGEN
Most like I did, for I was dead.
BELARIUS [to Guiderius and Arviragus]   My boys, 262
There was our error.
GUIDERIUS   This is, sure, Fidele.
IMOGEN [to Posthumus]
Why did you throw your wedded lady from you?
                        [She embraces him.]
Think that you are upon a rock, and now 265
Throw me again.   [They embrace.]
POSTHUMUS   Hang there like fruit, my soul,
Till the tree die!
CYMBELINE   How now, my flesh, my child?
What, mak'st thou me a dullard in this act? 268
Wilt thou not speak to me?
IMOGEN [kneeling]   Your blessing, sir.
BELARIUS [to Guiderius and Arviragus]
Though you did love this youth, I blame ye not;

You had a motive for't.
CYMBELINE   My tears that fall
Prove holy water on thee! Imogen,
Thy mother's dead.
IMOGEN [rising]   I am sorry for't, my lord.
CYMBELINE
Oh, she was naught; and long of her it was 274
That we meet here so strangely. But her son
Is gone, we know not how nor where.
PISANIO   My lord,
Now fear is from me, I'll speak truth. Lord Cloten,
Upon my lady's missing, came to me
With his sword drawn, foamed at the mouth, and
    swore
If I discovered not which way she was gone 280
It was my instant death. By accident
I had a feignèd letter of my master's 282
Then in my pocket, which directed him
To seek her on the mountains near to Milford;
Where, in a frenzy, in my master's garments,
Which he enforced from me, away he posts
With unchaste purpose and with oath to violate
My lady's honor. What became of him
I further know not.
GUIDERIUS   Let me end the story:
I slew him there.
CYMBELINE   Marry, the gods forfend! 290
I would not thy good deeds should from my lips 291
Pluck a hard sentence. Prithee, valiant youth,
Deny't again. 293
GUIDERIUS   I have spoke it, and I did it.
CYMBELINE   He was a prince.
GUIDERIUS
A most incivil one. The wrongs he did me
Were nothing princelike, for he did provoke me
With language that would make me spurn the sea
If it could so roar to me. I cut off 's head,
And am right glad he is not standing here
To tell this tale of mine.
CYMBELINE   I am sorrow for thee. 301
By thine own tongue thou art condemned and must
Endure our law. Thou'rt dead.
IMOGEN   That headless man
I thought had been my lord.
CYMBELINE   Bind the offender,
And take him from our presence.
                [Guards start to bind Guiderius.]
BELARIUS   Stay, sir King.
This man is better than the man he slew,
As well descended as thyself, and hath
More of thee merited than a band of Clotens
Had ever scar for. [To the Guard] Let his arms alone; 309

235 staggers dizziness, bewilderment   241 tune accent, voice
243 stones of sulfur thunderbolts   248 approve prove   249 confection composition of drugs   253 temper mix   258 cease cause to
cease   262 like likely   265 a rock i.e., solid ground (?) (Some editors
conjecture lock, "a wrestling embrace.")   268 dullard sluggish performer

274 naught wicked.   long of on account of   280 discovered disclosed   282 feignèd (Pisanio would not have wished to show Cloten
the real letter, since it ordered Pisanio to kill Imogen.)   290 forfend
forbid.   291 thy good deeds i.e., that you, who fought so valiantly
against the Romans   293 Deny't again take back what you just said.
301 tell . . . mine i.e., tell of cutting off my head.   sorrow sorry
309 Had ever scar for ever merited by their battle scars.

They were not born for bondage.
CYMBELINE   Why, old soldier,
Wilt thou undo the worth thou art unpaid for
By tasting of our wrath? How of descent
As good as we?
ARVIRAGUS   In that he spake too far.
CYMBELINE [to Belarius]
And thou shalt die for't.
BELARIUS   We will die all three
But I will prove that two on 's are as good   315
As I have given out him. My sons, I must   316
For mine own part unfold a dangerous speech,   317
Though, haply, well for you.
ARVIRAGUS   Your danger's ours.
GUIDERIUS
And our good his.
BELARIUS   Have at it then, by leave.   319
Thou hadst, great King, a subject who
Was called Belarius.
CYMBELINE   What of him? He is
A banished traitor.
BELARIUS   He it is that hath
Assumed this age; indeed a banished man,   323
I know not how a traitor.
CYMBELINE   Take him hence!
The whole world shall not save him.
BELARIUS   Not too hot.
First pay me for the nursing of thy sons,
And let it be confiscate all so soon
As I have received it.
CYMBELINE   Nursing of my sons?
BELARIUS
I am too blunt and saucy. Here's my knee. [He kneels.]
Ere I arise, I will prefer my sons;   330
Then spare not the old father. Mighty sir,
These two young gentlemen, that call me father
And think they are my sons, are none of mine;
They are the issue of your loins, my liege,
And blood of your begetting.
CYMBELINE   How? My issue?
BELARIUS
So sure as you your father's. I, old Morgan,
Am that Belarius whom you sometime banished.
Your pleasure was my mere offense, my punishment   338
Itself, and all my treason; that I suffered   339
Was all the harm I did. These gentle princes—   340
For such and so they are—these twenty years   341
Have I trained up; those arts they have as I
Could put into them. My breeding was, sir, as
Your Highness knows. Their nurse, Euriphile,
Whom for the theft I wedded, stole these children

Upon my banishment. I moved her to't,   346
Having received the punishment before
For that which I did then. Beaten for loyalty   348
Excited me to treason. Their dear loss,
The more of you 'twas felt, the more it shaped   350
Unto my end of stealing them. But, gracious sir,   351
Here are your sons again, and I must lose
Two of the sweet'st companions in the world.
The benediction of these covering heavens
Fall on their heads like dew! For they are worthy
To inlay heaven with stars.
CYMBELINE   Thou weep'st and speak'st.   356
The service that you three have done is more   357
Unlike than this thou tell'st. I lost my children;   358
If these be they, I know not how to wish
A pair of worthier sons.
BELARIUS [rising]   Be pleased awhile.   360
This gentleman, whom I call Polydore,
Most worthy prince, as yours, is true Guiderius;
This gentleman, my Cadwal, Arviragus,
Your younger princely son. He, sir, was lapped   364
In a most curious mantle, wrought by th' hand   365
Of his queen mother, which for more probation   366
I can with ease produce.
CYMBELINE   Guiderius had
Upon his neck a mole, a sanguine star;   368
It was a mark of wonder.
BELARIUS   This is he,   369
Who hath upon him still that natural stamp.
It was wise nature's end in the donation   371
To be his evidence now.
CYMBELINE   Oh, what, am I   372
A mother to the birth of three? Ne'er mother   373
Rejoiced deliverance more. Blest pray you be,   374
That, after this strange starting from your orbs,   375
You may reign in them now! O Imogen,   376
Thou hast lost by this a kingdom.
IMOGEN   No, my lord,
I have got two worlds by't. O my gentle brothers,
Have we thus met? Oh, never say hereafter
But I am truest speaker. You called me brother,
When I was but your sister; I you brothers,
When ye were so indeed.
CYMBELINE   Did you e'er meet?
ARVIRAGUS
Ay, my good lord.
GUIDERIUS   And at first meeting loved;
Continued so until we thought he died.

---

315 **But I will** if I do not.   **on 's** of us   316 **given out** reported
317 **For . . . speech** unfold a speech that is dangerous for me   319 **And
our good his** i.e., and whatever fortune comes to us we share with
him, Belarius.   **Have . . . leave** Here goes, with your permission.
323 **Assumed** reached, attained   330 **prefer** promote   338–40 **Your . . .
did** Your displeasure toward me was all the offense I committed; so,
too, my punishment and my supposed treason were the creation of
your royal whim; what I suffered was the extent of my wrongdoing.
340 **gentle** nobly born   341 **such and so** i.e., both princes and gentle

346 **moved** persuaded   348 **Beaten** Being beaten   350 **of** by
350–1 **shaped . . . of** fitted my purpose in   356 **To . . . stars** to be
inlaid in heaven, like stars.   356–8 **Thou . . . tell'st** i.e., Your weeping
seems a testimony of the truth of what you speak, and your story is,
in any event, more credible—strange though it seems—than the
brave service you three did in battle.   360 **Be pleased awhile** i.e., Be
so kind as to listen a while longer.   364 **lapped** enfolded   365 **curious** exquisitely made   366 **probation** proof   368 **sanguine** blood-red
369 **of wonder** to be wondered at.   371 **end in the donation** aim in
giving it to him   372 **his evidence** evidence of his identity
373–4 **Ne'er . . . more** Never did deliverance (in childbed) more
rejoice a mother.   375 **starting . . . orbs** shooting from your orbits,
i.e., leaving your places at court   376 **reign** i.e., both as royal persons
and as planets with influence

CORNELIUS
By the Queen's dram she swallowed.

CYMBELINE   Oh, rare instinct!
When shall I hear all through? This fierce abridgement 386
Hath to it circumstantial branches, which 387
Distinction should be rich in. Where, how lived you? 388
And when came you to serve our Roman captive?
How parted with your brothers? How first met them?
Why fled you from the court? And whither? These,
And your three motives to the battle, with 392
I know not how much more, should be demanded, 393
And all the other by-dependencies 394
From chance to chance; but nor the time nor place 395
Will serve our long interrogatories. See,
Posthumus anchors upon Imogen,
And she, like harmless lightning, throws her eye
On him, her brothers, me, her master, hitting 399
Each object with a joy; the counterchange 400
Is severally in all. Let's quit this ground 401
And smoke the temple with our sacrifices. 402
[To Belarius] Thou art my brother; so we'll hold thee
    ever.

IMOGEN [to Belarius]
You are my father too, and did relieve me 404
To see this gracious season.

CYMBELINE   All o'erjoyed,
Save these in bonds. Let them be joyful too,
For they shall taste our comfort.

IMOGEN [to Lucius]   My good master,
I will yet do you service.

LUCIUS   Happy be you!

CYMBELINE
The forlorn soldier, that so nobly fought, 409
He would have well becomed this place and graced 410
The thankings of a king.

POSTHUMUS   I am, sir,
The soldier that did company these three
In poor beseeming; 'twas a fitment for 413
The purpose I then followed. That I was he,
Speak, Iachimo. I had you down and might
Have made you finish.

IACHIMO [kneeling]   I am down again; 416
But now my heavy conscience sinks my knee, 417
As then your force did. Take that life, beseech you,
Which I so often owe; but your ring first; 419
And here the bracelet of the truest princess
That ever swore her faith. [He gives ring and bracelet.]

POSTHUMUS   Kneel not to me.
The power that I have on you is to spare you;

The malice towards you to forgive you. Live,
And deal with others better.   [Iachimo rises.]

CYMBELINE   Nobly doomed! 424
We'll learn our freeness of a son-in-law; 425
Pardon's the word to all.

ARVIRAGUS [to Posthumus]   You holp us, sir, 426
As you did mean indeed to be our brother; 427
Joyed are we that you are.

POSTHUMUS
Your servant, princes. [To Lucius] Good my lord of
    Rome,
Call forth your soothsayer. As I slept, methought
Great Jupiter, upon his eagle backed,
Appeared to me, with other spr-itely shows 432
Of mine own kindred. When I waked, I found
This label on my bosom [showing tablet], whose
    containing 434
Is so from sense in hardness that I can 435
Make no collection of it. Let him show 436
His skill in the construction.

LUCIUS   Philharmonus! 437

SOOTHSAYER
Here, my good lord.

LUCIUS   Read, and declare the meaning.

SOOTHSAYER (reads) "Whenas a lion's whelp shall, to
    himself unknown, without seeking find and be em-
    braced by a piece of tender air; and when from a stately
    cedar shall be lopped branches which, being dead
    many years, shall after revive, be jointed to the old
    stock and freshly grow; then shall Posthumus end his
    miseries, Britain be fortunate and flourish in peace
    and plenty."
Thou, Leonatus, art the lion's whelp;
The fit and apt construction of thy name,
Being Leo-natus, doth import so much. 449
[To Cymbeline] The piece of tender air, thy virtuous
    daughter,
Which we call "mollis aer," and "mollis aer" 451
We term it "mulier"; which "mulier" I divine
Is this most constant wife; who, even now, 453
Answering the letter of the oracle,   [to Posthumus] 454
Unknown to you, unsought, were clipped about 455
With this most tender air.

CYMBELINE   This hath some seeming. 456

SOOTHSAYER
The lofty cedar, royal Cymbeline,
Personates thee, and thy lopped branches point
Thy two sons forth; who, by Belarius stol'n,
For many years thought dead, are now revived,

---

386 **fierce abridgment** drastically compressed account   387–8 **circumstantial . . . in** details and ramifications to be distinguished in all
their abundance.   392 **your three motives** the motives of you three
393 **demanded** inquired into   394 **by-dependencies** attendant circumstances   395 **chance to chance** event to event.   **nor** the neither
the   399 **her master** i.e., Lucius   400–1 **the counterchange . . . all** the
exchange (of happy glances) involves each of us to everyone else.
402 **smoke** fill with incense   404 **relieve** save   409 **forlorn** missing,
or, poorly dressed   410 **graced** adorned   413 **beseeming** appearance.   **fitment** makeshift disguise   416 **made you finish** put an end
to you.   417 **sinks** causes to sink   419 **often** many times over

424 **doomed** decreed, judged.   425 **freeness** liberality, generosity
426 **holp** helped   427 **As** as if   432 **sprutely shows** ghostly appearances   434 **label** tablet, paper   434–5 **whose . . . hardness** whose
meaning is so remote from sense in its difficulty   436 **collection**
interpretation   437 **construction** construing of it.   449 **Leo-natus**
one born of the lion   451 *mollis aer* tender air. (A fanciful derivation
of Latin *mulier*, "woman.")   453 **who** (Perhaps referring to Posthumus, but the grammar is loose and the point of reference may shift
after line 454.)   454 **Answering . . . of** fulfilling the exact terms of
455 **were clipped about** i.e., you were embraced   456 **seeming**
plausibility.

To the majestic cedar joined, whose issue
Promises Britain peace and plenty.

CYMBELINE   Well,
My peace we will begin. And, Caius Lucius,
Although the victor, we submit to Caesar
And to the Roman empire, promising
To pay our wonted tribute, from the which
We were dissuaded by our wicked queen,
Whom heavens in justice both on her and hers   468
Have laid most heavy hand.

SOOTHSAYER
The fingers of the powers above do tune
The harmony of this peace. The vision
Which I made known to Lucius ere the stroke
Of this yet scarce-cold battle at this instant
Is full accomplished; for the Roman eagle,
From south to west on wing soaring aloft,

Lessened herself, and in the beams o'th' sun   476
So vanished; which foreshowed our princely eagle,   477
Th'imperial Caesar, should again unite
His favor with the radiant Cymbeline,
Which shines here in the west.

CYMBELINE   Laud we the gods, 480
And let our crooked smokes climb to their nostrils   481
From our blest altars. Publish we this peace
To all our subjects. Set we forward. Let
A Roman and a British ensign wave
Friendly together. So through Lud's Town march,
And in the temple of great Jupiter
Our peace we'll ratify, seal it with feasts.
Set on there! Never was a war did cease,   488
Ere bloody hands were washed, with such a peace.   489
                                              Exeunt.

---

468 Whom on whom.   **hers** i.e., Cloten

476 Lessened herself i.e., grew smaller to sight   **477 foreshowed**
foreshowed that   **480 Laud** Praise   **481 crooked** curling, twining
488 Set on there Forward march.   **was a war** was there a war that
489 Ere . . . washed before hands were washed in blood or free of
blood

The Winter's Tale

The Winter's Tale (c. 1609–1611), with its almost symmetrical division into two halves of bleak tragedy and comic romance, illustrates perhaps more clearly than any other Shakespearean play the genre of tragicomedy. To be sure, all the late romances feature journeys of separation, apparent deaths, and tearful reconciliations. Marina and Thaisa in *Pericles*, Imogen in *Cymbeline*, and Ferdinand in *The Tempest*, all supposed irrecoverably lost, are brought back to life by apparently miraculous devices. Of the four late romances, however, *The Winter's Tale* uses the most formal structure to evoke the antithesis of tragedy and romance. It is sharply divided into contrasting halves by a gap of sixteen years. The tragic first half takes place almost entirely in Sicilia, whereas the action of the second half is limited for the most part to Bohemia. At the court of Sicilia, we see tyrannical jealousy producing a spiritual climate of "winter / In storm perpetual"; in Bohemia, we witness a pastoral landscape and a sheepshearing evoking "the sweet o'th' year," "When daffodils begin to peer" (3.2.212–13; 4.3.1–3). Paradoxically, the contrast between the two halves is intensified by parallels between the two: both begin with Camillo onstage and proceed to scenes of confrontation and jealousy in which, ironically, the innocent cause of jealousy in the first half, Polixenes, becomes the jealous tyrant of the second half. The mirroring reminds us of the cyclical nature of time and the hope it brings of renewal as we move from tragedy to romantic comedy.

Although this motif of a renewing journey from jaded court to idealized countryside reminds us of *As You Like It* and other early comedies, we sense in the late romances and especially in *The Winter's Tale* a new preoccupation with humanity's tragic folly. The vision of human depravity is world-weary and pessimistic, as though infected by the gloomy spirit of the great tragedies. And because humanity is so bent on destroying itself, the restoration is at once more urgently needed and more miraculous than in the "festive" world of early comedy. Renewal is mythically associated with the seasonal cycle from winter to summer.

King Leontes's tragedy seems at first irreversible and terrifying, like that of Shakespeare's greatest tragic protagonists. He suffers from irrational jealousy, as does Othello, and attempts to destroy the person on whom all his happiness depends. As with Othello, his jealousy stems from a characteristically male fear of inadequacy and rejection. Unlike Othello, however, Leontes needs no diabolical tempter such as Iago to poison his mind against Queen Hermione. Leontes is undone by his own fantasies. No differences in race or age can explain Leontes's fears of estrangement from Hermione. She is not imprudent in her conduct, like her counterpart in Robert Greene's *Pandosto* (1588), the prose romance from which Shakespeare drew his narrative. Although Hermione is graciously fond of Leontes's dear friend Polixenes and urges him to stay longer in Sicilia, she does so only with a hospitable warmth demanded by the occasion and encouraged by her husband. In every way, then, Shakespeare strips away from Leontes the motive and the occasion for plausible doubting of his wife. All observers in the Sicilian court are incredulous and shocked at the King's accusations. Even so, Leontes is neither an unsympathetic nor an unbelievable character. Like Othello, Leontes cherishes his wife and perceives with a horrifying intensity what a fearful cost they both must pay for his suspicions. Not only his marriage, but also his lifelong friendship with Polixenes, his sense of pride in his children, and his enjoyment of his subjects' warm regard, all must be sacrificed to a single overwhelming compulsion.

Whatever may be the psychological cause of this obsession, it manifests itself as a revulsion against all sexual behavior. Like mad Lear, Leontes imagines lechery to be the unavoidable fact of the cosmos and of the human condition, the lowest common denominator to which all persons (including Hermione) must stoop. He is persuaded that "It is a bawdy planet," in which cuckolded man has "his pond fished by his next neighbor, by / Sir Smile, his neighbor" (1.2.195–201). Leontes's tortured soliloquies are laden with sexual images, of unattended "gates" letting in and out the enemy "With bag and baggage," and of a "dagger" that must be "muzzled / Lest it should bite its master" (lines 197, 206, 156–7). As in *King Lear*, order is inverted to disorder, sanity to madness, legitimacy to illegitimacy. Sexual misconduct is emblematic of a universal malaise: "Why, then the world and all that's in 't is nothing, / The covering sky is nothing, Bohemia nothing, / My wife is nothing" (lines 292–4). Other characters, too, see the trial of Hermione as a testing of humanity's worth: if Hermione proves false, Antigonus promises, he will treat his own wife as a stable horse and will "geld" his three daughters (2.1.148). Prevailing images are of spiders, venom, infection, sterility, and the "dungy earth" (line 158).

Cosmic order is never really challenged, however, even though the human suffering is very real and the injustice to women especially apparent. Leontes's fantasies of universal disorder are chimerical. His wife is, in fact, chaste, Polixenes true, and the King's courtiers loyal. Camillo refuses to carry out Leontes's order to murder Polixenes, not only because he knows murder to be wrong, but also because history offers not one example of a man "that had struck anointed kings / And flourished after" (1.2.357–8). The cosmos of this play is one in which crimes are invariably and swiftly punished. The Delphic oracle vindicates Hermione and gives Leontes stern warning. When Leontes persists in his madness, his son Mamillius's death follows as an immediate consequence. As Leontes at once perceives, "Apollo's angry, and the heavens themselves / Do strike at my injustice" (3.2.146–7). Leontes paradoxically welcomes the lengthy contrition he must undergo, for it confirms a pattern in the universe of just cause and effect. Although as tragic protagonist he has discovered the truth about Hermione moments too late and so must pay richly for his error, Leontes has at least recovered faith in Hermione's transcendent goodness. His nightmare now over, he accepts and embraces suffering as a necessary atonement.

The transition to romance is therefore anticipated to an extent by the play's first half, even though the tone of the last two acts is strikingly different. The old Shepherd signals a momentous change when he speaks to his son of a cataclysmic storm and a ravenous bear set in opposition to the miraculous discovery of a child: "Now bless thyself. Thou mett'st with things dying, I with things newborn" (3.3.110–11). Time comes onstage as Chorus, like Gower in *Pericles*, to remind us of the conscious artifice of the dramatist. He can "o'erthrow law" and carry us over sixteen years as if we had merely dreamed out the interim (4.1). Shakespeare flaunts the improbability

of his story by giving Bohemia a seacoast (much to the distress of Ben Jonson) and by bringing onstage either a live bear or an actor costumed as one ("*Exit, pursued by a bear*"; 3.3.57 s.d.). The narrative uses many typical devices of romance: a babe abandoned to the elements, a princess brought up by shepherds, a prince disguised as a swain, a sea voyage, and a recognition scene. Love is threatened, not by the internal psychic obstacle of jealousy, but by the external obstacles of parental opposition and a seeming disparity of social rank between the lovers. Comedy easily finds solutions for such difficulties by the unraveling of illusion. This comic world also properly includes clownish shepherds, coy shepherdesses, and Autolycus, the roguish peddler, whose machinations contribute in an unforeseen manner to the working out of the love plot. Autolycus is in many ways the presiding genius of the play's second half, as dominant a character as Leontes in the first half and one whose delightful function is to do good "against my will" (5.2.125). In this paradox of knavery converted surprisingly to benign ends, we see how the comic providence of Shakespeare's tragicomic world makes use of the most implausible and outrageous happenings in pursuit of its own inscrutable design.

The conventional romantic ending is infused, however, with a sadness and a mystery that take the play well beyond what is usual in comedy. Mamillius and Antigonus are really dead, and that irredeemable fact is not forgotten in the play's final happy moments. Hermione, although vindicated by the gods, has suffered public shame, the death of one child, separation from her other child, and prolonged isolation from her husband; like Imogen in *Cymbeline*, she has had to endure the consequences of male frailty and thereby redeem her husband through her suffering. Her husband, having thrown her aside, must, like Pericles, rediscover and learn to cherish the woman he once chose who now has aged; he must reconfirm his marriage to her, even as he learns to accept the marriage of his daughter to a younger man. All of these crucial turnings hinge upon Shakespeare's most notable departure from his source, Greene's *Pandosto*: Hermione is brought back to life. All observers regard this event, and the rediscovery of Perdita, as grossly implausible, "so like an old tale that the verity of it is in strong suspicion" (5.2.29–30). The play's very title, *The Winter's Tale*, reinforces this sense of naive improbability. Why does Shakespeare stress this riddling paradox of an unbelievable reality, and why does he deliberately mislead his audience into believing that Hermione has, in fact, died (3.3.15–45), using a kind of theatrical trickery found in no other Shakespearean play? The answer may well be that, in Paulina's words, we must awake our faith, accepting a narrative of death and return to life that cannot ultimately be comprehended by reason. On the rational level, we are told that Hermione has been kept in hiding for sixteen years, in order to fulfill the condition of the oracle that Leontes is to live without an heir (and hence without a wife) until Perdita is found. Such an explanation seems psychologically incomprehensible, however, for it demands that Hermione live in extended isolation and that Paulina serve as the King's conscience for such a long period of time without any way for the participants to know when their suffering will end. Instead, we are drawn toward an emblematic interpretation, bearing in mind that it is more an evocative hint than a complete truth. Throughout the play, Hermione has been repeatedly associated with "Grace" and with the goddess Proserpina, whose return from the underworld, after "Three crabbèd months had soured themselves to death" (1.2.102), signals the coming of spring. Perdita, also associated with Proserpina (4.4.116), is welcomed by her father "As is the spring to th' earth" (5.1.152). The emphasis on the bond of father and daughter, so characteristic of Shakespeare's late plays and especially his romances, goes importantly beyond the patriarchalism of Shakespeare's earlier history plays in its exploration of family relationships. Paulina has a similarly emblematic role, that of Conscience, patiently guiding the King to a divinely appointed renewal of his joy. Paulina speaks of herself as an artist figure, like Prospero in *The Tempest*, performing wonders of illusion, though she rejects the assistance of wicked powers. These emblematic hints do not rob the story of its human drama, but they do lend a transcendent significance to Leontes's bittersweet story of sinful error, affliction, and an unexpected second happiness.

On stage in recent decades, the play has shown its remarkable dramaturgic effectiveness, especially in the restoration of Hermione to her husband as a living and breathing statue. Peter Brook, at the Phoenix Theatre in London, 1951, chose a permanent set to underscore the play's malleable swift action and its need for the audience to participate imaginatively in the fashioning of theatrical illusion. Trevor Nunn's set at Stratford-upon-Avon in 1969 was a three-sided white box in which nothing was realistically represented. Nunn and John Barton, at Stratford-upon-Avon in 1976, visualized bears everywhere: in motifs of wall hangings and carpets, in a bearskin draped on a couch. The violent irrationality of Ian McKellen's Leontes seemed plausible in such a symbolic and mythic landscape. In Terry Hands's 1986 production also at Stratford-upon-Avon, a huge bear rug on the cool marble floor of Leontes's Regency palace during the play's first half became, in Bohemia, the live bear that tore into the shoulder of Antigonus. Above all, the apparent bringing back to life of Hermione's statue in the final scene has proven again and again to be a masterful *coup de théâtre*. What we see in the theater is of course an illusion, but at what level? Are we to understand that a statue comes to life? Much depends on the actress's skill in appearing motionless and then warm to her husband's touch. The moment is indeed one calculated to awaken our faith in the miracle of renewal and in the power of art to confound illusion and reality. We are led to ponder deeply the mysteries of our own uncertain existence.

The Winter's Tale

The Names of the Actors

LEONTES, *King of Sicilia*
MAMILLIUS, *young prince of Sicilia*
CAMILLO,
ANTIGONUS,
CLEOMENES,
DION, } *four Lords of Sicilia*

HERMIONE, *Queen to Leontes*
PERDITA, *daughter to Leontes and Hermione*
PAULINA, *wife to Antigonus*
EMILIA, *a lady [attending on Hermione]*

POLIXENES, *King of Bohemia*
FLORIZEL, *Prince of Bohemia*
ARCHIDAMUS, *a lord of Bohemia*
Old SHEPHERD, *reputed father of Perdita*
CLOWN, *his son*
AUTOLYCUS, *a rogue*

[MOPSA,
[DORCAS, } *Shepherdesses.]*

[A MARINER
A JAILER
Two LADIES *attending Hermione*
Two SERVANTS *attending Leontes*
One or more LORDS *attending Leontes*
An OFFICER *of the court*
A GENTLEMAN *attending Leontes*
Three GENTLEMEN *of the court of Sicilia*
A SERVANT *of the Old Shepherd*

TIME, *as Chorus]*

Other Lords and Gentlemen, [Ladies, Officers,] and
Servants; Shepherds and Shepherdesses; [Twelve
Countrymen disguised as Satyrs]

[SCENE: *Sicilia, and Bohemia.]*

1.1

Enter Camillo and Archidamus.

ARCHIDAMUS   If you shall chance, Camillo, to visit Bohemia on the like occasion whereon my services are   2
now on foot, you shall see, as I have said, great   3
difference betwixt our Bohemia and your Sicilia.
CAMILLO   I think this coming summer the King of Sicilia
means to pay Bohemia the visitation which he justly   6
owes him.
ARCHIDAMUS   Wherein our entertainment shall shame   8
us, we will be justified in our loves; for indeed—   9
CAMILLO   Beseech you—

ARCHIDAMUS   Verily, I speak it in the freedom of my   11
knowledge. We cannot with such magnificence—in   12
so rare—I know not what to say. We will give you
sleepy drinks, that your senses, unintelligent of our   14
insufficience, may, though they cannot praise us, as
little accuse us.
CAMILLO   You pay a great deal too dear for what's
given freely.
ARCHIDAMUS   Believe me, I speak as my understanding
instructs me and as mine honesty puts it to utterance.
CAMILLO   Sicilia cannot show himself overkind to Bo-   21
hemia. They were trained together in their childhoods,
and there rooted betwixt them then such an affection
which cannot choose but branch now. Since their   24
more mature dignities and royal necessities made
separation of their society, their encounters, though   26

1.1 Location: Sicilia. The court of Leontes.
2–3 on the . . . foot on an occasion like this one that I am engaged in
(attending on King Polixenes)   **6 Bohemia** the King of Bohemia.
(Also at lines 21–2.)   **8–9 Wherein . . . loves** In whatever way our
attempts to entertain you will shame us by falling short, we will
make up for by our affection

11–12 in . . . knowledge as my knowledge entitles me to speak.
14 sleepy sleep-inducing.   **unintelligent** unaware   **21 Sicilia** The
King of Sicilia   **24 branch** put forth new growth, flourish. (Also perhaps with opposite and unconscious suggestion of "divide.")
26 their society their being together

not personal, hath been royally attorneyed with   27
interchange of gifts, letters, loving embassies, that
they have seemed to be together though absent,
shook hands as over a vast, and embraced as it were   30
from the ends of opposed winds. The heavens con-   31
tinue their loves!

ARCHIDAMUS   I think there is not in the world either
malice or matter to alter it. You have an unspeakable
comfort of your young prince Mamillius. It is a   35
gentleman of the greatest promise that ever came into
my note.   37

CAMILLO   I very well agree with you in the hopes of
him. It is a gallant child, one that indeed physics the   39
subject, makes old hearts fresh. They that went on   40
crutches ere he was born desire yet their life to see him   41
a man.

ARCHIDAMUS   Would they else be content to die?

CAMILLO   Yes, if there were no other excuse why they
should desire to live.

ARCHIDAMUS   If the King had no son, they would desire   46
to live on crutches till he had one.   *Exeunt.*   47

❖

1.2

*Enter Leontes, Hermione, Mamillius, Polixenes,
Camillo.*

POLIXENES
Nine changes of the wat'ry star hath been   1
The shepherd's note since we have left our throne   2
Without a burden. Time as long again   3
Would be filled up, my brother, with our thanks,
And yet we should for perpetuity   5
Go hence in debt. And therefore, like a cipher,   6
Yet standing in rich place, I multiply   7
With one "We thank you" many thousands more
That go before it.

LEONTES   Stay your thanks awhile
And pay them when you part.

POLIXENES   Sir, that's tomorrow.
I am questioned by my fears of what may chance   11
Or breed upon our absence, that may blow   12
No sneaping winds at home to make us say,   13
"This is put forth too truly." Besides, I have stayed   14

To tire your royalty.

LEONTES   We are tougher, brother,
Than you can put us to't.

POLIXENES   No longer stay.   16

LEONTES
One sev'nnight longer.

POLIXENES   Very sooth, tomorrow.   17

LEONTES
We'll part the time between 's, then, and in that   18
I'll no gainsaying.

POLIXENES   Press me not, beseech you, so.   19
There is no tongue that moves, none, none i' th' world
So soon as yours could win me. So it should now,
Were there necessity in your request, although
'Twere needful I denied it. My affairs
Do even drag me homeward, which to hinder
Were in your love a whip to me, my stay   25
To you a charge and trouble. To save both,   26
Farewell, our brother.

LEONTES   Tongue-tied, our Queen? Speak you.

HERMIONE
I had thought, sir, to have held my peace until   28
You had drawn oaths from him not to stay. You, sir,   29
Charge him too coldly. Tell him you are sure
All in Bohemia's well; this satisfaction   31
The bygone day proclaimed. Say this to him,   32
He's beat from his best ward.

LEONTES   Well said, Hermione.   33

HERMIONE
To tell he longs to see his son were strong.   34
But let him say so then, and let him go.
But let him swear so and he shall not stay;   36
We'll thwack him hence with distaffs.   37
[*To Polixenes*] Yet of your royal presence I'll adventure   38
The borrow of a week. When at Bohemia   39
You take my lord, I'll give him my commission
To let him there a month behind the gest   41
Prefixed for 's parting.—Yet, good deed, Leontes,   42
I love thee not a jar o' th' clock behind   43
What lady she her lord.—You'll stay?

POLIXENES   No, madam.   44

HERMIONE
Nay, but you will?

POLIXENES   I may not, verily.

HERMIONE   Verily?

---

27 **personal** in person.   **attorneyed** carried out by deputy   **30 vast**
boundless space   **31 ends . . . winds** i.e., opposite ends of the earth.
The heavens May the heavens   **35 of** in the person of   **37 note**
observation.   **39–40 physics the subject** brings health to the subjects
of this kingdom   **41 their life** to continue living   **46–7 If . . . one**
Even if there were no living heir to the throne, these old people
would still wish to go on living in hopes of one.
1.2. Location: The same.   1 wat'ry star moon   **2 note** observation.
we I. (The royal "we.")   **3 burden** occupant.   **5 for perpetuity** forever   **6–7 like . . . place** like a zero at the end of a number, increasing
its value by powers of ten, though of itself without value   **11–14 I am
. . . truly** I am anxious about what may happen in my absence, especially a stirring up of envy and backbiting that would cause me to say
my fears were all too plausible.

16 Than . . . to't than anything you can do to try me.   **17 sev'nnight**
week.   **Very sooth** Truly   **18 part the time** split the difference, i.e.,
divide a week in two   **19 I'll no gainsaying** I won't take "no" for an
answer.   **25 Were . . . whip** would be a punishment to me, though
done through love   **26 charge** expense, burden   **28–9 I . . . to stay**
i.e., I almost thought that you were going to get him to swear he *won't*
stay, before I got a chance to say anything.   **31–2 this . . . proclaimed**
yesterday brought news to satisfy on that score.   **32 Say** If you say
33 ward defensive posture. (A fencing term.)   **34 tell** tell us that.
strong a strong argument.   **36 he shall not stay** i.e., we wouldn't let
him stay even if he wanted to.   **37 distaffs** sticks used in spinning,
here employed as a domestic kind of weapon.   **38 adventure** risk
39 borrow borrowing   **41–2 To . . . parting** to let him stay there a
month longer than the originally agreed-upon time for his departure.
42 good deed indeed   **43–4 I love . . . lord** I love you not even a tiny
bit (literally, a tick of the clock) less than any noble lady loves her
husband.

You put me off with limber vows; but I,   47
Though you would seek t'unsphere the stars with
    oaths,
Should yet say, "Sir, no going." Verily,
You shall not go. A lady's "verily" is
As potent as a lord's. Will you go yet?
Force me to keep you as a prisoner,
Not like a guest: so you shall pay your fees   53
When you depart, and save your thanks. How say
    you?
My prisoner or my guest? By your dread "verily,"
One of them you shall be.

POLIXENES   Your guest, then, madam.
To be your prisoner should import offending,   57
Which is for me less easy to commit
Than you to punish.

HERMIONE   Not your jailer, then,
But your kind hostess. Come, I'll question you
Of my lord's tricks and yours when you were boys.
You were pretty lordings then?

POLIXENES   We were, fair Queen,
Two lads that thought there was no more behind   63
But such a day tomorrow as today,
And to be boy eternal.

HERMIONE   Was not my lord
The verier wag o'th' two?   66

POLIXENES
We were as twinned lambs that did frisk i'th' sun
And bleat the one at th'other. What we changed   68
Was innocence for innocence; we knew not
The doctrine of ill-doing, nor dreamed
That any did. Had we pursued that life,
And our weak spirits ne'er been higher reared
With stronger blood, we should have answered
    heaven   73
Boldly "Not guilty," the imposition cleared   74
Hereditary ours.

HERMIONE   By this we gather   75
You have tripped since.

POLIXENES   Oh, my most sacred lady,
Temptations have since then been born to 's, for
In those unfledged days was my wife a girl;   78
Your precious self had then not crossed the eyes
Of my young playfellow.

HERMIONE   Grace to boot!   80
Of this make no conclusion, lest you say   81
Your queen and I are devils. Yet go on.
Th'offenses we have made you do we'll answer,
If you first sinned with us, and that with us
You did continue fault, and that you slipped not

With any but with us.

LEONTES   Is he won yet?   86

HERMIONE
He'll stay, my lord.

LEONTES   At my request he would not.
Hermione, my dearest, thou never spok'st
To better purpose.

HERMIONE   Never?

LEONTES   Never but once.

HERMIONE
What? Have I twice said well? When was 't before?
I prithee, tell me. Cram 's with praise and make 's
As fat as tame things. One good deed dying
    tongueless   92
Slaughters a thousand waiting upon that.   93
Our praises are our wages. You may ride 's
With one soft kiss a thousand furlongs ere
With spur we heat an acre. But to th' goal: 96
My last good deed was to entreat his stay.
What was my first? It has an elder sister,
Or I mistake you. Oh, would her name were Grace!
But once before I spoke to the purpose. When?
Nay, let me have't; I long.

LEONTES   Why, that was when
Three crabbèd months had soured themselves to
    death
Ere I could make thee open thy white hand
And clap thyself my love. Then didst thou utter,   104
"I am yours forever."

HERMIONE   'Tis grace indeed.
Why, lo you now, I have spoke to th' purpose twice:
The one forever earned a royal husband,
Th'other for some while a friend.
                            [She gives her hand to Polixenes.]

LEONTES [aside]   Too hot, too hot!
To mingle friendship far is mingling bloods.   109
I have *tremor cordis* on me. My heart dances,   110
But not for joy, not joy. This entertainment   111
May a free face put on, derive a liberty   112
From heartiness, from bounty, fertile bosom,   113
And well become the agent. 'T may, I grant.   114
But to be paddling palms and pinching fingers,
As now they are, and making practiced smiles
As in a looking glass, and then to sigh, as 'twere
The mort o'th' deer; oh, that is entertainment   118
My bosom likes not, nor my brows.—Mamillius,   119
Art thou my boy?

MAMILLIUS   Ay, my good lord.

LEONTES   I'fecks,   120

---

47 **limber** limp   53 **fees** payments demanded by jailers of prisoners
at the time of their release   57 **import offending** imply my having
offended   63 **behind** still to come   66 **The verier wag** truly the more
mischievous   68 **changed** exchanged   73 **stronger blood** mature
sexual passions   74–5 **the imposition . . . ours** i.e., being freed from
original sin itself (if we had continued in that state); or, excepting of
course the original sin that is the common condition of all mortals.
78 **unfledged** not yet feathered, i.e., immature   80 **Grace to boot!**
Heaven help me!   81 **Of . . . conclusion** Don't follow your implied
line of reasoning to its logical conclusion

86 **Is he won yet?** (Leontes has been out of hearing for much of their
conversation.)   92 **tongueless** unpraised, unsung   93 **Slaughters . . .
that** i.e., will inhibit many other good deeds that would have been
inspired by that praise.   96 **heat** traverse as in a race.   **to th' goal** to
come to the point   104 **clap** clasp hands, pledge   109 **mingling
bloods** (Sexual intercourse was thought to produce a mingling of
bloods.)   110 *tremor cordis* fluttering of the heart   111 **entertainment** i.e., of Polixenes by Hermione   112 **free face** innocent appearance   113 **fertile bosom** i.e., generous affection   114 **well . . . agent**
do credit to the doer.   118 **mort** note sounded on a horn at the death
of the hunted deer   119 **brows** (Alludes to cuckolds' horns, the supposed badge of men whose wives are unfaithful.)   120 **I'fecks** in
faith

Why, that's my bawcock. What, hast smutched thy
    nose?   121
They say it is a copy out of mine. Come, captain,
We must be neat; not neat, but cleanly, captain.   123
And yet the steer, the heifer, and the calf
Are all called neat.—Still virginaling   125
Upon his palm?—How now, you wanton calf?   126
Art thou my calf?

MAMILLIUS   Yes, if you will, my lord.

LEONTES
Thou want'st a rough pash and the shoots that I have   128
To be full like me. Yet they say we are   129
Almost as like as eggs. Women say so,
That will say anything. But were they false
As o'erdyed blacks, as wind, as waters, false   132
As dice are to be wished by one that fixes   133
No bourn twixt his and mine, yet were it true   134
To say this boy were like me. Come, sir page,
Look on me with your welkin eye. Sweet villain!   136
Most dear'st! My collop! Can thy dam?—may't be?—   137
Affection, thy intention stabs the center.   138
Thou dost make possible things not so held,   139
Communicat'st with dreams—how can this be?—   140
With what's unreal thou coactive art,   141
And fellow'st nothing. Then 'tis very credent   142
Thou mayst cojoin with something; and thou dost,   143
And that beyond commission, and I find it,   144
And that to the infection of my brains
And hard'ning of my brows.

POLIXENES   What means Sicilia?   146

HERMIONE
He something seems unsettled.

POLIXENES   How, my lord?   147
What cheer? How is't with you, best brother?

HERMIONE   You look
As if you held a brow of much distraction.
Are you moved, my lord?

LEONTES   No, in good earnest.   150
How sometimes nature will betray its folly,   151
Its tenderness, and make itself a pastime   152
To harder bosoms! Looking on the lines   153

Of my boy's face, methoughts I did recoil   154
Twenty-three years, and saw myself unbreeched,   155
In my green velvet coat, my dagger muzzled   156
Lest it should bite its master and so prove,
As ornaments oft do, too dangerous.
How like, methought, I then was to this kernel,
This squash, this gentleman.—Mine honest friend,   160
Will you take eggs for money?   161

MAMILLIUS   No, my lord, I'll fight.

LEONTES
You will? Why, happy man be 's dole!—My brother,   163
Are you so fond of your young prince as we
Do seem to be of ours?

POLIXENES   If at home, sir,
He's all my exercise, my mirth, my matter,   166
Now my sworn friend and then mine enemy,
My parasite, my soldier, statesman, all.
He makes a July's day short as December,
And with his varying childness cures in me   170
Thoughts that would thick my blood.

LEONTES   So stands this squire   171
Officed with me. We two will walk, my lord,   172
And leave you to your graver steps. Hermione,
How thou lov'st us, show in our brother's welcome.   174
Let what is dear in Sicily be cheap.   175
Next to thyself and my young rover, he's
Apparent to my heart.

HERMIONE   If you would seek us,   177
We are yours i'th' garden. Shall 's attend you there?   178

LEONTES
To your own bents dispose you. You'll be found,   179
Be you beneath the sky. [*Aside*] I am angling now,
Though you perceive me not how I give line.   181
Go to, go to!   182
How she holds up the neb, the bill to him,   183
And arms her with the boldness of a wife   184
To her allowing husband!

          [*Exeunt Polixenes and Hermione.*]
          Gone already!   185
Inch thick, knee-deep, o'er head and ears a forked
    one!—   186
Go play, boy, play. Thy mother plays, and I   187
Play too, but so disgraced a part, whose issue   188

---

121 bawcock i.e., fine fellow. (French *beau coq*.)   **123 not . . . cleanly**
(Leontes changes the word because *neat* also means "cattle" and hence
reminds him of cuckolds' horns.)   **125 virginaling** touching hands, as
in playing on the virginals, a keyboard instrument   **126 wanton** frisky
128 Thou . . . have You lack a shaggy head and the horns that I have.
(Again alluding to cuckolds' horns.)   **129 full** fully   **132 o'erdyed
blacks** black garments that have been weakened by too much dye or
that have been dyed over another color (thereby betraying a falseness
in the mourner)   **132–4 false . . . mine** as false as dice are wished false
by one who intends to cheat me, and who respects no boundary
between what is his and mine   **136 welkin** sky-blue   **137 collop** small
piece of meat; i.e., of my own flesh.   **dam** mother   **138–43 Affection
. . . something** Strong passion, your intense power pierces to the very
center, the soul. You make possible things normally considered fantastic, partaking as you do of the nature of dreams. How can this be?
You collaborate with unreality and imagined fantasies. It's all the
likelier, then, that such imaginings may also fasten on a real object
144 commission what is lawful   **146 What means Sicilia?** Why is the
King of Sicilia looking so distracted?   **147 something** somewhat
150 moved angry   **151 nature** i.e., affectionate feeling between parent and child   **152 pastime** occasion for amusement   **153 To harder
bosoms** for persons who are less tender-hearted.

154 methoughts it seemed to me.   **recoil** i.e., go back in memory
155 unbreeched not yet wearing breeches   **156 muzzled** i.e., sheathed.
(With phallic suggestion.)   **160 squash** unripe peascod or pea pod.
honest worthy   **161 take eggs for money** i.e., be imposed upon,
taken advantage of, cheated. (Proverbial.)   **163 happy . . . dole** may good
fortune be his lot. (Proverbial.)   **166 matter** concern   **170 childness**
childlike ways   **171 thick my blood** (Melancholy thoughts were supposed to thicken the blood.)   **172 Officed** placed in particular function
174–5 How . . . cheap (A hidden second meaning in these lines may be
intentional: show just how much you love me by the way you encourage Polixenes's attentions and thereby cheapen the most precious thing
in Sicily.)   **177 Apparent** heir apparent (perhaps with a suggestion too
of "evident, revealed")   **178 Shall 's** Shall we   **179 To . . . dispose you**
Act according to your inclinations. (With more bitter double meaning,
continued in *You'll be found*, i.e., found out.)   **181 give line** pay out line
(to let the fish hook itself well).   **182 Go to** (An expression of remonstrance.)   **183 neb** beak, i.e., nose, mouth   **184 arms her with** assumes
185 allowing approving   **186 forked** horned   **187 play** play games.
plays i.e., in a sexual liaison   **188 Play** play a role.   **issue** outcome.
(With a pun on the sense of "offspring" and "theatrical exit.")

Will hiss me to my grave. Contempt and clamor
Will be my knell. Go play, boy, play. There have been,
Or I am much deceived, cuckolds ere now;
And many a man there is, even at this present,
Now while I speak this, holds his wife by th' arm,
That little thinks she has been sluiced in 's absence   194
And his pond fished by his next neighbor, by
Sir Smile, his neighbor. Nay, there's comfort in 't
Whiles other men have gates and those gates opened,   197
As mine, against their will. Should all despair
That have revolted wives, the tenth of mankind   199
Would hang themselves. Physic for 't there's none.   200
It is a bawdy planet, that will strike   201
Where 'tis predominant; and 'tis powerful, think it,   202
From east, west, north, and south. Be it concluded,
No barricado for a belly. Know 't,   204
It will let in and out the enemy
With bag and baggage. Many thousand on 's   206
Have the disease and feel 't not.—How now, boy?

MAMILLIUS
I am like you, they say.

LEONTES   Why, that's some comfort.
What, Camillo there?

CAMILLO [coming forward]   Ay, my good lord.

LEONTES
Go play, Mamillius; thou'rt an honest man.
                         [Exit Mamillius.]
Camillo, this great sir will yet stay longer.

CAMILLO
You had much ado to make his anchor hold.
When you cast out, it still came home.

LEONTES   Didst note it?   213

CAMILLO
He would not stay at your petitions, made
His business more material.

LEONTES   Didst perceive it?   215
[Aside] They're here with me already, whisp'ring,
   rounding,   216
"Sicilia is a so-forth." 'Tis far gone   217
When I shall gust it last.—How came 't, Camillo,   218
That he did stay?

CAMILLO   At the good Queen's entreaty.

LEONTES
"At the Queen's" be 't. "Good" should be pertinent,   220
But so it is, it is not. Was this taken   221
By any understanding pate but thine?

For thy conceit is soaking, will draw in   223
More than the common blocks. Not noted, is 't,   224
But of the finer natures? By some severals   225
Of headpiece extraordinary? Lower messes   226
Perchance are to this business purblind? Say.   227

CAMILLO
Business, my lord? I think most understand
Bohemia stays here longer.

LEONTES
Ha?

CAMILLO   Stays here longer.

LEONTES   Ay, but why?

CAMILLO
To satisfy Your Highness and the entreaties
Of our most gracious mistress.

LEONTES   Satisfy?   232
Th'entreaties of your mistress? Satisfy?
Let that suffice. I have trusted thee, Camillo,
With all the nearest things to my heart, as well   235
My chamber councils, wherein, priestlike, thou   236
Hast cleansed my bosom. I from thee departed
Thy penitent reformed. But we have been
Deceived in thy integrity, deceived
In that which seems so.

CAMILLO   Be it forbid, my lord!   240

LEONTES
To bide upon 't, thou art not honest; or,   241
If thou inclin'st that way, thou art a coward,   242
Which hoxes honesty behind, restraining   243
From course required; or else thou must be counted   244
A servant grafted in my serious trust   245
And therein negligent; or else a fool
That see'st a game played home, the rich stake drawn,   247
And tak'st it all for jest.

CAMILLO   My gracious lord,
I may be negligent, foolish, and fearful;
In every one of these no man is free
But that his negligence, his folly, fear,
Among the infinite doings of the world
Sometime puts forth. In your affairs, my lord,   253
If ever I were willful-negligent,
It was my folly; if industriously   255
I played the fool, it was my negligence,
Not weighing well the end; if ever fearful
To do a thing where I the issue doubted,   258

---

194 **sluiced** drawn off, as by a sluice. (The water in his pond, so to speak, has been drawn off by a cheating neighbor.)   197 **gates** sluice gates, suggestive of the wife's chastity that has been opened and robbed   199 **revolted** unfaithful   200 **Physic** Medicine   201 **It . . . planet** i.e., This unchastity is like the planet Venus.   **strike** blast, destroy by a malign influence   202 **predominant** in the ascendant. (Said of a planet.)   **think it** be assured of this   204 **barricado** barricade.   **Know 't** Be certain of this   206 **bag and baggage** (With sexual suggestion, as earlier in *dagger* [line 156], *sluiced, gates, let in and out,* etc.)   **on 's** of us   213 **still came home** always came back to the ship, failed to hold.   215 **material** important.   216 **They're . . . already** People are already onto my situation.   **rounding** whispering, gossiping   217 **a so-forth** a so-and-so, a you-know-what.   218 **gust** taste, i.e., hear of   220 **pertinent** i.e., appropriately applied   221 **so it is** as things stand.   **taken** perceived

223 **conceit is soaking** understanding is receptive   224 **blocks** blockheads.   225 **But . . . natures** except by those of rarefied intellect.   **severals** individuals   226 **Lower messes** Those who sit lower at table, i.e., inferior persons   227 **purblind** totally blind.   232 **Satisfy?** (Leontes takes the word in a sexual sense.)   235–6 **as well . . . councils** as well as with my private affairs   240 **Be it forbid** i.e., God forbid I should do such a thing   241–4 **To bide . . . required** If you hold back from saying what you think, you are not being honest; or, if you would like to speak but remain silent, you are a coward, allowing frankness to be hamstrung or shackled from carrying out the duty it should perform   245 **grafted . . . trust** taken into my complete confidence. (*Grafted* means "deeply embedded," like a graft.)   247 **home** i.e., for keeps, in earnest. (With perhaps a sexual double meaning, continued in *rich stake drawn*.)   **drawn** won   253 **Sometime puts forth** sometimes shows itself.   255 **industriously** deliberately   258 **the issue doubted** feared the outcome

Whereof the execution did cry out   259
Against the nonperformance, 'twas a fear   260
Which oft infects the wisest. These, my lord,
Are such allowed infirmities that honesty   262
Is never free of. But, beseech Your Grace,
Be plainer with me. Let me know my trespass
By its own visage. If I then deny it,   265
'Tis none of mine.

LEONTES   Ha' not you seen, Camillo—
But that's past doubt; you have, or your eyeglass   267
Is thicker than a cuckold's horn—or heard—   268
For to a vision so apparent, rumor   269
Cannot be mute—or thought—for cogitation
Resides not in that man that does not think—   271
My wife is slippery? If thou wilt confess,
Or else be impudently negative   273
To have no eyes nor ears nor thought, then say   274
My wife's a hobbyhorse, deserves a name   275
As rank as any flax-wench that puts to   276
Before her trothplight. Say't and justify't.   277

CAMILLO
I would not be a stander-by to hear
My sovereign mistress clouded so without
My present vengeance taken. 'Shrew my heart,   280
You never spoke what did become you less
Than this, which to reiterate were sin   282
As deep as that, though true.

LEONTES   Is whispering nothing?   283
Is leaning cheek to cheek? Is meeting noses?
Kissing with inside lip? Stopping the career   285
Of laughter with a sigh—a note infallible
Of breaking honesty? Horsing foot on foot?   287
Skulking in corners? Wishing clocks more swift,
Hours minutes, noon midnight? And all eyes   289
Blind with the pin and web but theirs, theirs only,   290
That would unseen be wicked? Is this nothing?
Why, then the world and all that's in't is nothing,
The covering sky is nothing, Bohemia nothing,
My wife is nothing, nor nothing have these nothings,
If this be nothing.

CAMILLO   Good my lord, be cured
Of this diseased opinion, and betimes,   296
For 'tis most dangerous.

LEONTES   Say it be, 'tis true.   297

CAMILLO
No, no, my lord.

LEONTES   It is. You lie, you lie!
I say thou liest, Camillo, and I hate thee,
Pronounce thee a gross lout, a mindless slave,
Or else a hovering temporizer, that   301
Canst with thine eyes at once see good and evil,
Inclining to them both. Were my wife's liver   303
Infected as her life, she would not live   304
The running of one glass.

CAMILLO   Who does infect her?   305

LEONTES
Why, he that wears her like her medal, hanging   306
About his neck, Bohemia—who, if I
Had servants true about me, that bare eyes   308
To see alike mine honor as their profits,
Their own particular thrifts, they would do that   310
Which should undo more doing. Ay, and thou,   311
His cupbearer—whom I from meaner form   312
Have benched and reared to worship, who mayst see 313
Plainly as heaven sees earth and earth sees heaven
How I am galled—mightst bespice a cup   315
To give mine enemy a lasting wink,   316
Which draft to me were cordial.

CAMILLO   Sir, my lord,   317
I could do this, and that with no rash potion,   318
But with a ling'ring dram that should not work
Maliciously like poison. But I cannot   320
Believe this crack to be in my dread mistress,   321
So sovereignly being honorable.   322
I have loved thee—

LEONTES   Make that thy question, and go rot!   323
Dost think I am so muddy, so unsettled,   324
To appoint myself in this vexation, sully   325
The purity and whiteness of my sheets—
Which to preserve is sleep, which being spotted
Is goads, thorns, nettles, tails of wasps—
Give scandal to the blood o' th' prince my son,
Who I do think is mine and love as mine,
Without ripe moving to't? Would I do this?   331
Could man so blench?

CAMILLO   I must believe you, sir.   332
I do, and will fetch off Bohemia for't;   333
Provided that, when he's removed, Your Highness
Will take again your queen as yours at first,

259–60 Whereof . . . nonperformance in which the completion of the task showed how wrong I was in being reluctant to undertake it **262 allowed** acknowledged.   **that** as   **265 visage** face, i.e., plain appearance.   **267 eyeglass** lens of the eye   **268 cuckold's horn** (A thin sheet of horn can be seen through like a lens, though a cuckold's horn is another matter.)   **269 to a vision so apparent** about something so plainly visible   **271 think** i.e., think so   **273–4 Or . . . eyes** or, as the only possible alternative, insist impudently that you have neither eyes   **275 hobbyhorse** wanton woman   **276 flax-wench** common slut.   **puts to** engages in sex   **277 justify't** affirm it. **280 present** immediate.   **'Shrew** Beshrew, curse   **282–3 which . . . true** i.e., to repeat which accusation would be to sin as deeply as her supposed adultery, even if it were true (which it isn't).   **285 career** full gallop   **287 honesty** chastity.   **Horsing foot on foot** Placing one's foot on that of another person and then moving the feet up and down together.   **289 Hours minutes** wishing hours were minutes **290 pin and web** cataract of the eye. (The lovers wish to think themselves unobserved.)   **296 betimes** quickly   **297 Say it be** Even if it is dangerous

301 hovering wavering   **303 Inclining . . . both** being tolerant of evil along with the good.   **304 Infected as her life** as full of disease as is her moral conduct   **305 glass** hourglass.   **306 like her medal** like a miniature portrait of her, worn in a locket   **308 bare** bore, had **310 thrifts** gains   **311 undo** prevent   **312 meaner form** humbler station   **313 benched** placed on the bench of authority.   **worship** dignity, honor   **315 galled** rubbed, chafed   **316 lasting wink** everlasting closing of the eyes (in death)   **317 were cordial** would be restorative.   **318 rash** quick-acting (and therefore easily detected) **320 Maliciously** virulently   **321 crack** flaw.   **dread** worthy of awe **322 sovereignly** supremely   **323 Make . . . rot!** i.e., If you're going to question my accusations, may you rot in hell!   **324 muddy** muddleheaded   **325 To . . . vexation** to give myself this vexation   **331 ripe** ample, urgent   **332 blench** swerve (from sensible conduct). **333 fetch off** do away with; or, with deliberate ambiguity, rescue. (As also in *removed* in the next line.)

Even for your son's sake, and thereby for sealing   336
The injury of tongues in courts and kingdoms
Known and allied to yours.

LEONTES   Thou dost advise me
Even so as I mine own course have set down.
I'll give no blemish to her honor, none.

CAMILLO   My lord,
Go then, and with a countenance as clear
As friendship wears at feasts, keep with Bohemia   343
And with your queen. I am his cupbearer.
If from me he have wholesome beverage,
Account me not your servant.

LEONTES   This is all.
Do't and thou hast the one half of my heart;
Do't not, thou splitt'st thine own.

CAMILLO   I'll do't, my lord.

LEONTES
I will seem friendly, as thou hast advised me.   *Exit.*

CAMILLO
Oh, miserable lady! But, for me,
What case stand I in? I must be the poisoner
Of good Polixenes, and my ground to do't
Is the obedience to a master, one
Who in rebellion with himself will have
All that are his so too. To do this deed,   355
Promotion follows. If I could find example   356
Of thousands that had struck anointed kings
And flourished after, I'd not do't; but since   358
Nor brass, nor stone, nor parchment bears not one,   359
Let villainy itself forswear't. I must
Forsake the court. To do't or no is certain   361
To me a breakneck. Happy star reign now!   362
Here comes Bohemia.

Enter Polixenes.

POLIXENES [*to himself*]   This is strange. Methinks
My favor here begins to warp. Not speak?—   364
Good day, Camillo.

CAMILLO   Hail, most royal sir!

POLIXENES
What is the news i'th' court?

CAMILLO   None rare, my lord.   366

POLIXENES
The King hath on him such a countenance
As he had lost some province and a region   368
Loved as he loves himself. Even now I met him
With customary compliment, when he,
Wafting his eyes to th' contrary and falling   371
A lip of much contempt, speeds from me, and

So leaves me to consider what is breeding   373
That changeth thus his manners.

CAMILLO   I dare not know, my lord.

POLIXENES
How, dare not? Do not? Do you know, and dare not?   376
Be intelligent to me. 'Tis thereabouts,   377
For to yourself what you do know you must,   378
And cannot say you dare not. Good Camillo,   379
Your changed complexions are to me a mirror
Which shows me mine changed too; for I must be   381
A party in this alteration, finding   382
Myself thus altered with't.

CAMILLO   There is a sickness
Which puts some of us in distemper, but
I cannot name the disease; and it is caught
Of you that yet are well.

POLIXENES   How? Caught of me?   386
Make me not sighted like the basilisk.   387
I have looked on thousands who have sped the better   388
By my regard, but killed none so. Camillo,   389
As you are certainly a gentleman, thereto   390
Clerklike experienced, which no less adorns   391
Our gentry than our parents' noble names,   392
In whose success we are gentle, I beseech you,   393
If you know aught which does behoove my
     knowledge
Thereof to be informed, imprison't not
In ignorant concealment.

CAMILLO   I may not answer.   396

POLIXENES
A sickness caught of me, and yet I well?
I must be answered. Dost thou hear, Camillo?
I conjure thee, by all the parts of man   399
Which honor does acknowledge, whereof the least   400
Is not this suit of mine, that thou declare   401
What incidency thou dost guess of harm   402
Is creeping toward me; how far off, how near;
Which way to be prevented, if to be;   404
If not, how best to bear it.

CAMILLO   Sir, I will tell you,
Since I am charged in honor and by him   406
That I think honorable. Therefore mark my counsel,
Which must be even as swiftly followed as
I mean to utter it, or both yourself and me

---

336 for sealing for the sake of silencing. (Some editors prefer *forsealing*, sealing up tight.) **343 keep** remain in company **355 All . . . too** i.e., all his followers like him in rebelling against the best in themselves and in obeying his worst self. **To do** If I do **356 If** Even if **358–9 but . . . one** but since recorded history shows no instances of persons who have killed a king and prospered afterwards **361 To do 't or no** i.e., Either to kill Polixenes or not to kill him **362 breakneck** destruction, ruin. **Happy** Propitious, favorable **364 warp** change, shrivel, grow askew (as wood warps). **Not speak?** (Leontes has just passed by Polixenes without speaking.) **366 rare** noteworthy **368 As** as if **371 Wafting . . . contrary** averting his eyes. **falling** letting fall

373 breeding hatching **376 Do not?** i.e., Or do you mean you don't know? **377 intelligent** intelligible. **'Tis thereabouts** It must be something of this sort, i.e., that you know and dare not tell **378–9 For . . . dare not** i.e., for in your heart, whatever it is you know, you must in fact know, and can't claim it's a matter of not daring to know. **381–2 for . . . alteration** i.e., for my looks must have changed, too, reflecting this change in my position **386 Of** from **387 sighted** provided with a gaze. **basilisk** a fabled serpent whose gaze was fatal. **388 sped** prospered **389 regard** look **390–3 thereto . . . gentle** in addition to which you are a cultivated and educated person—something that graces our gentlemanlike condition no less than the worthy name of our ancestors, by succession from whom we are made noble **396 ignorant concealment** concealment that would keep me ignorant or that would proceed from pretended ignorance on your part. **399 parts** obligations **400–1 whereof . . . not** not the least of which is (to answer) **402 incidency** likely incident **404 if to be** if it can be (prevented) **406 by him** i.e., by you yourself

Cry lost, and so good night!

POLIXENES   On, good Camillo.   410

CAMILLO

I am appointed him to murder you.   411

POLIXENES

By whom, Camillo?

CAMILLO   By the King.

POLIXENES   For what?

CAMILLO

He thinks, nay, with all confidence he swears,
As he had seen't or been an instrument
To vice you to't, that you have touched his queen   415
Forbiddenly.

POLIXENES   Oh, then my best blood turn
To an infected jelly, and my name
Be yoked with his that did betray the Best!   418
Turn then my freshest reputation to
A savor that may strike the dullest nostril   420
Where I arrive, and my approach be shunned,
Nay, hated too, worse than the great'st infection
That e'er was heard or read!

CAMILLO   Swear his thought over   423
By each particular star in heaven and
By all their influences, you may as well
Forbid the sea for to obey the moon   426
As or by oath remove or counsel shake   427
The fabric of his folly, whose foundation   428
Is piled upon his faith and will continue   429
The standing of his body.

POLIXENES   How should this grow?   430

CAMILLO

I know not. But I am sure 'tis safer to
Avoid what's grown than question how 'tis born.
If therefore you dare trust my honesty,
That lies enclosèd in this trunk which you   434
Shall bear along impawned, away tonight!   435
Your followers I will whisper to the business,   436
And will by twos and threes at several posterns   437
Clear them o'th' city. For myself, I'll put
My fortunes to your service, which are here
By this discovery lost. Be not uncertain,   440
For, by the honor of my parents, I
Have uttered truth, which if you seek to prove,   442
I dare not stand by; nor shall you be safer   443
Than one condemned by the King's own mouth,
  thereon
His execution sworn.

POLIXENES   I do believe thee;

I saw his heart in 's face. Give me thy hand.
Be pilot to me, and thy places shall   447
Still neighbor mine. My ships are ready, and   448
My people did expect my hence departure
Two days ago. This jealousy
Is for a precious creature. As she's rare,
Must it be great; and as his person's mighty,
Must it be violent; and as he does conceive
He is dishonored by a man which ever
Professed to him, why, his revenges must   455
In that be made more bitter. Fear o'ershades me.
Good expedition be my friend, and comfort   457
The gracious Queen, part of his theme, but nothing   458
Of his ill-ta'en suspicion! Come, Camillo,   459
I will respect thee as a father if
Thou bear'st my life off. Hence! Let us avoid.   461

CAMILLO

It is in mine authority to command
The keys of all the posterns. Please Your Highness
To take the urgent hour. Come, sir, away.   *Exeunt.*

❖

2.1

Enter Hermione, Mamillius, [and] Ladies.

HERMIONE

Take the boy to you. He so troubles me,
'Tis past enduring.

FIRST LADY [*taking Mamillius from the Queen*]
                          Come, my gracious lord,
Shall I be your playfellow?

MAMILLIUS

No, I'll none of you.

FIRST LADY   Why, my sweet lord?   4

MAMILLIUS

You'll kiss me hard and speak to me as if
I were a baby still.—I love you better.

SECOND LADY

And why so, my lord?

MAMILLIUS   Not for because   7
Your brows are blacker; yet black brows, they say,
Become some women best, so that there be not   9
Too much hair there, but in a semicircle,
Or a half-moon made with a pen.

SECOND LADY   Who taught' this?   11

MAMILLIUS

I learned it out of women's faces. Pray now,
What color are your eyebrows?

FIRST LADY   Blue, my lord.

MAMILLIUS

Nay, that's a mock. I have seen a lady's nose

---

410 **good night** i.e., this is the end.   411 **him** by him (Leontes), or, the one   415 **vice** force, as with a carpenter's tool, or, impel, tempt. (The *Vice* was a tempter in the morality play.)   418 **his . . . Best** the name of him (Judas) who betrayed Christ.   420 **savor** stench   423 **Swear . . . over** i.e., Even if you should deny his suspicion with oaths   426 **for to** to   427 **or . . . or** either . . . or   428 **fabric** edifice   428–30 **whose . . . body** the foundation of which is built upon an unshaken conviction and which will last as long as his body exists.   430 **How . . . grow?** How could this suspicion have arisen?   434 **trunk** body. (With a suggestion too of a traveling trunk.)   435 **impawned** i.e., as a pledge of good faith   436 **whisper to** secretly inform of and urge   437 **posterns** rear gates   440 **discovery** revelation, disclosure   442 **prove** test   443 **stand by** affirm publicly; stay

447–8 **thy . . . mine** your official position will always be near to me.   455 **Professed** openly professed friendship   457–9 **Good . . . suspicion!** May good speed befriend me, and may my quick departure ease the predicament of the gracious Queen, who is the object of the King's suspicions but who is guiltless of them!   461 **bear'st my life off** can get me out of this alive.   **avoid** depart.
2.1. Location: Sicilia. The royal court.
4 **none of you** have nothing to do with you.   7 **for because** because   9 **so** provided   11 **taught'** taught you

That has been blue, but not her eyebrows.
FIRST LADY   Hark ye,
The Queen your mother rounds apace. We shall
Present our services to a fine new prince
One of these days, and then you'd wanton with us,   18
If we would have you.
SECOND LADY   She is spread of late
Into a goodly bulk. Good time encounter her!   20
HERMIONE [*calling to her women*]
What wisdom stirs amongst you?—Come, sir, now
I am for you again. Pray you, sit by us   22
And tell 's a tale.
MAMILLIUS   Merry or sad shall 't be?
HERMIONE   As merry as you will.
MAMILLIUS
A sad tale's best for winter. I have one
Of sprites and goblins.
HERMIONE   Let's have that, good sir.
Come on, sit down. Come on, and do your best
To fright me with your sprites. You're powerful at it.
MAMILLIUS
There was a man—
HERMIONE   Nay, come sit down, then on.
                                        [*Mamillius sits.*]
MAMILLIUS
Dwelt by a churchyard. I will tell it softly;
Yond crickets shall not hear it.   31
HERMIONE
Come on, then, and give't me in mine ear.
                              [*They converse privately.*]

        [*Enter*] Leontes, Antigonus, Lords, [*and others*].

LEONTES
Was he met there? His train? Camillo with him?
A LORD
Behind the tuft of pines I met them. Never
Saw I men scour so on their way. I eyed them   35
Even to their ships.
LEONTES   How blest am I
In my just censure, in my true opinion!   37
Alack, for lesser knowledge! How accurst   38
In being so blest! There may be in the cup   39
A spider steeped, and one may drink, depart,   40
And yet partake no venom, for his knowledge
Is not infected; but if one present
Th'abhorred ingredient to his eye, make known
How he hath drunk, he cracks his gorge, his sides,   44
With violent hefts. I have drunk, and seen the spider. 45
Camillo was his help in this, his pander.
There is a plot against my life, my crown.
All's true that is mistrusted. That false villain   48

Whom I employed was pre-employed by him.
He has discovered my design, and I   50
Remain a pinched thing, yea, a very trick   51
For them to play at will. How came the posterns   52
So easily open?
A LORD   By his great authority,
Which often hath no less prevailed than so
On your command.
LEONTES   I know't too well.
[*To Hermione*] Give me the boy. I am glad you did not
    nurse him.
Though he does bear some signs of me, yet you
Have too much blood in him.
HERMIONE   What is this? Sport?   59
LEONTES [*to a Lord*]
Bear the boy hence; he shall not come about her.
Away with him! And let her sport herself
With that she's big with, [*to Hermione*] for 'tis Polixenes
Has made thee swell thus.   [*Mamillius is led out.*]
HERMIONE   But I'd say he had not,   63
And I'll be sworn you would believe my saying,
Howe'er you lean to th' nayward.
LEONTES   You, my lords,   65
Look on her, mark her well. Be but about
To say "She is a goodly lady," and   67
The justice of your hearts will thereto add
"'Tis pity she's not honest, honorable."   69
Praise her but for this her without-door form,   70
Which on my faith deserves high speech, and straight 71
The shrug, the hum or ha, these petty brands   72
That calumny doth use—oh, I am out,   73
That mercy does, for calumny will sear   74
Virtue itself—these shrugs, these hums and ha's,
When you have said she's goodly, come between   76
Ere you can say she's honest. But be't known,
From him that has most cause to grieve it should be,
She's an adulteress.
HERMIONE   Should a villain say so,
The most replenished villain in the world,   80
He were as much more villain. You, my lord,   81
Do but mistake.
LEONTES   You have mistook, my lady, 82
Polixenes for Leontes. Oh, thou thing!
Which I'll not call a creature of thy place,   84
Lest barbarism, making me the precedent,
Should a like language use to all degrees   86
And mannerly distinguishment leave out   87

50 **discovered** disclosed   51 **pinched** tortured, ridiculous.   **trick**
plaything   52 **play** play with   59 **Sport?** A joke?   63 **I'd** I need only
65 **th' nayward** the contrary.   67 **goodly** attractive   69 **honest** chaste
70 **without-door** outward, external   71 **straight** straightaway, at once
72 **brands** i.e., signs, stigmas   73 **out** wrong, in error   74 **does** uses.
(Leontes's point is that no one commits calumny by suggesting with a
shrug that Hermione is unchaste; calumny attacks *virtue itself*, whereas
Hermione has only the false appearance of virtue.)   76 **come between**
interrupt   80 **replenished** complete   81 **He . . . villain** his saying so
would double his villainy.   82 **mistook** taken wrongfully. (Playing
bitterly on *mistake*, "misapprehend.")   84 **Which . . . place** whose
exalted rank I will not desecrate by calling you what you really are
86 **like** similar.   **degrees** social ranks   87 **And . . . out** and leave out
proper distinctions

18 **wanton** sport, play   20 **Good . . . her!** May she have a happy
issue!   22 **for you** ready for you   31 **crickets** i.e., the court ladies, tit-
tering and laughing   35 **scour** scurry   37 **censure** judgment
38 **Alack . . . knowledge!** Would that there were less for me to know!
39 **blest** i.e., with knowledge (that causes unhappiness).   40 **A spider**
(The superstition referred to here is that the drinker is not poisoned
by the spider in the cup unless the spider is known to be there.)
44 **gorge** throat   45 **hefts** heavings, retchings.   48 **mistrusted** suspected.

Betwixt the prince and beggar. I have said
She's an adult'ress; I have said with whom.
More, she's a traitor, and Camillo is
A fedarie with her, and one that knows   91
What she should shame to know herself   92
But with her most vile principal, that she's   93
A bed-swerver, even as bad as those   94
That vulgars give bold'st titles, ay, and privy   95
To this their late escape.

HERMIONE   No, by my life,   96
Privy to none of this. How will this grieve you,
When you shall come to clearer knowledge, that
You thus have published me! Gentle my lord,   99
You scarce can right me throughly then to say   100
You did mistake.

LEONTES   No. If I mistake
In those foundations which I build upon,
The center is not big enough to bear   103
A schoolboy's top.—Away with her to prison!
He who shall speak for her is afar off guilty   105
But that he speaks.

HERMIONE   There's some ill planet reigns.   106
I must be patient till the heavens look
With an aspect more favorable. Good my lords,
I am not prone to weeping, as our sex
Commonly are, the want of which vain dew   110
Perchance shall dry your pities; but I have
That honorable grief lodged here which burns
Worse than tears drown. Beseech you all, my lords,
With thoughts so qualified as your charities   114
Shall best instruct you, measure me; and so   115
The King's will be performed!

LEONTES   Shall I be heard?   116

HERMIONE
Who is't that goes with me? Beseech Your Highness
My women may be with me, for you see
My plight requires it.—Do not weep, good fools;   119
There is no cause. When you shall know your mistress
Has deserved prison, then abound in tears
As I come out. This action I now go on   122
Is for my better grace.—Adieu, my lord.   123
I never wished to see you sorry; now
I trust I shall. My women, come, you have leave.   125

LEONTES   Go, do our bidding. Hence!
            [*Exit Queen, guarded, with Ladies.*]

A LORD
Beseech Your Highness, call the Queen again.

ANTIGONUS
Be certain what you do, sir, lest your justice

Prove violence, in the which three great ones suffer:
Yourself, your queen, your son.

A LORD   For her, my lord,
I dare my life lay down and will do't, sir,
Please you t'accept it, that the Queen is spotless
I'th'eyes of heaven and to you—I mean
In this which you accuse her.

ANTIGONUS   If it prove
She's otherwise, I'll keep my stables where   135
I lodge my wife. I'll go in couples with her;   136
Than when I feel and see her no farther trust her.   137
For every inch of woman in the world,
Ay, every dram of woman's flesh is false,
If she be.

LEONTES   Hold your peaces.

A LORD   Good my lord—   140

ANTIGONUS
It is for you we speak, not for ourselves.
You are abused, and by some putter-on   142
That will be damned for't. Would I knew the villain;
I would land-damn him. Be she honor-flawed,   144
I have three daughters—the eldest is eleven,
The second and the third, nine and some five—   146
If this prove true, they'll pay for't. By mine honor,
I'll geld 'em all! Fourteen they shall not see   148
To bring false generations. They are co-heirs,   149
And I had rather glib myself than they   150
Should not produce fair issue.

LEONTES   Cease, no more!   151
You smell this business with a sense as cold
As is a dead man's nose; but I do see't and feel't
As you feel doing thus, and see withal   154
The instruments that feel.

ANTIGONUS   If it be so,   155
We need no grave to bury honesty;
There's not a grain of it the face to sweeten
Of the whole dungy earth.

LEONTES   What? Lack I credit?   158

A LORD
I had rather you did lack than I, my lord,
Upon this ground; and more it would content me   160
To have her honor true than your suspicion,
Be blamed for't how you might.

LEONTES   Why, what need we   162
Commune with you of this, but rather follow

---

91 fedarie confederate   **92–3 to know . . . principal** to acknowledge privately even with her contemptible partner   **94 bed-swerver** adulteress   **95 That . . . titles** that common people call by the rudest names.   **privy** in on the secret   **96 late** recent   **99 published** proclaimed.   **Gentle my** My noble   **100 You . . . say** you scarcely can do me full justice then merely by saying   **103 center** earth   **105 afar off** indirectly   **106 But . . . speaks** merely by speaking.   **110 want** lack   **114 qualified** tempered   **115 measure** judge   **116 heard** i.e., obeyed.   **119 fools** (Here, a term of endearment.)   **122 come out** am released from prison.   **122–3 The action . . . grace** What I now must undergo will ultimately make me seem more gracious in others' eyes and ennoble me by suffering.   **125 leave** permission (to attend me).

135–6 I'll . . . wife (If Hermione is an adulteress, says Antigonus, then all women are no better than animals, to be penned up and guarded suspiciously.)   **136 in couples** i.e., like two hounds leashed together and hence inseparable   **137 Than . . . her** trust her no further than I can feel her next to me and actually see her.   **140 she** i.e., Hermione   **142 abused** deceived.   **putter-on** instigator   **144 land-damn** lambaste (? Meaning uncertain.)   **146 some** about   **148 geld** sterilize, de-sex   **149 bring false generations** have illegitimate children.   **They are co-heirs** i.e., They will share my inheritance (since I have no son to inherit all)   **150 glib** castrate, geld   **151 fair issue** legitimate offspring.   **154 thus** (Leontes presumably grasps Antigonus by the arm or pinches him or tweaks his nose.)   **154–5 and see . . . feel** i.e., just as you and I see these fingers that pinch, I see in my mind's eye the amorous touching of Hermione and Polixenes. (*Withal* means "in addition.")   **158 credit** credibility.   **160 Upon this ground** in this matter   **162 we** I. (The royal "we.")

Our forceful instigation? Our prerogative 164
Calls not your counsels, but our natural goodness 165
Imparts this; which if you—or stupefied 166
Or seeming so in skill—cannot or will not 167
Relish a truth like us, inform yourselves 168
We need no more of your advice. The matter,
The loss, the gain, the ordering on't, is all 170
Properly ours.

ANTIGONUS   And I wish, my liege,
You had only in your silent judgment tried it,
Without more overture.

LEONTES   How could that be? 173
Either thou art most ignorant by age, 174
Or thou wert born a fool. Camillo's flight,
Added to their familiarity—
Which was as gross as ever touched conjecture, 177
That lacked sight only, naught for approbation 178
But only seeing, all other circumstances
Made up to th' deed—doth push on this proceeding. 180
Yet, for a greater confirmation—
For in an act of this importance 'twere
Most piteous to be wild—I have dispatched in post 183
To sacred Delphos, to Apollo's temple, 184
Cleomenes and Dion, whom you know
Of stuffed sufficiency. Now from the oracle 186
They will bring all, whose spiritual counsel had 187
Shall stop or spur me. Have I done well?

A LORD   Well done, my lord.

LEONTES
Though I am satisfied, and need no more
Than what I know, yet shall the oracle
Give rest to th' minds of others, such as he 192
Whose ignorant credulity will not
Come up to th' truth. So have we thought it good 194
From our free person she should be confined, 195
Lest that the treachery of the two fled hence
Be left her to perform. Come, follow us.
We are to speak in public, for this business
Will raise us all.

ANTIGONUS [aside]   To laughter, as I take it, 199
If the good truth were known.   Exeunt.

❖

2.2

Enter Paulina, a Gentleman, [and attendants].

PAULINA
The keeper of the prison, call to him.
Let him have knowledge who I am.
                    [*The Gentleman goes to the door.*]
                         Good lady, 2
No court in Europe is too good for thee;
What dost thou then in prison?

          [*Enter*] *Jailer.*

                         Now, good sir,
You know me, do you not?

JAILER   For a worthy lady
And one who much I honor.

PAULINA   Pray you then,
Conduct me to the Queen.

JAILER   I may not, madam.
To the contrary I have express commandment.

PAULINA
Here's ado, to lock up honesty and honor from
Th'access of gentle visitors! Is't lawful, pray you,
To see her women? Any of them? Emilia?

JAILER   So please you, madam,
To put apart these your attendants, I 13
Shall bring Emilia forth.

PAULINA   I pray now, call her.—
Withdraw yourselves.
                    [*Gentleman and attendants withdraw.*]

JAILER   And, madam,
I must be present at your conference.

PAULINA   Well, be't so, prithee.   [*Exit Jailer.*]
Here's such ado, to make no stain a stain 19
As passes coloring.

          [*Enter Jailer, with*] *Emilia.*

                    Dear gentlewoman, 20
How fares our gracious lady?

EMILIA
As well as one so great and so forlorn
May hold together. On her frights and griefs— 23
Which never tender lady hath borne greater— 24
She is something before her time delivered. 25

PAULINA
A boy?

EMILIA   A daughter, and a goodly babe,
Lusty and like to live. The Queen receives 27
Much comfort in't, says, "My poor prisoner,
I am innocent as you."

PAULINA   I dare be sworn.
These dangerous unsafe lunes i'th' King, beshrew
them! 30
He must be told on't, and he shall. The office 31
Becomes a woman best; I'll take't upon me. 32

---

164 **Our ... instigation** my own strong inclination.   164–6 **Our prerogative ... this** My royal prerogative is under no obligation to consult you, but rather out of natural generosity I inform you of the matter   166 **or** either   167 **Or ... skill** or pretending to be stupefied out of cunning   168 **Relish** savor, appreciate   170 **on't** of it   173 **overture** public disclosure.   174 **by age** through the folly of old age   177 **as gross ... conjecture** as palpably evident as any conjecture ever touched upon and verified   178 **approbation** proof   180 **Made up** added up.   **push on** urge onward   183 **wild** rash.   **post** haste   184 **Delphos** (See note at 3.1.2.)   186 **Of stuffed sufficiency** abundantly qualified and trustworthy.   187 **all** the whole truth.   **had** having been obtained   192 **he** any person (such as Antigonus)   194 **Come up to** face   195 **From** away from.   **free** accessible   199 **raise** rouse
2.2 Location: Sicilia. A prison.

2 **Good lady** (Addressed to the absent Hermione.)   13 **put apart** dismiss   19–20 **to make ... coloring** to make out of no stain at all a besmirching of honor that surpasses any justification. (Expressed in a metaphor of dyeing and painting.)   23 **On** In consequence of   24 **Which** than which   25 **something** somewhat. (Also in line 55.)   27 **Lusty** vigorous.   **like** likely   30 **lunes** fits of lunacy   31 **on't** of it   32 **Becomes** suits

If I prove honeymouthed, let my tongue blister   33
And never to my red-looked anger be   34
The trumpet any more. Pray you, Emilia,
Commend my best obedience to the Queen.   36
If she dares trust me with her little babe,
I'll show't the King and undertake to be
Her advocate to th' loud'st. We do not know   39
How he may soften at the sight o'th' child.
The silence often of pure innocence
Persuades when speaking fails.

EMILIA   Most worthy madam,
Your honor and your goodness is so evident
That your free undertaking cannot miss   44
A thriving issue. There is no lady living   45
So meet for this great errand. Please Your Ladyship   46
To visit the next room, I'll presently   47
Acquaint the Queen of your most noble offer,
Who but today hammered of this design,   49
But durst not tempt a minister of honor   50
Lest she should be denied.

PAULINA   Tell her, Emilia,
I'll use that tongue I have. If wit flow from't   52
As boldness from my bosom, let 't not be doubted
I shall do good.

EMILIA   Now be you blest for it!
I'll to the Queen.—Please you, come something nearer.   55

JAILER
Madam, if't please the Queen to send the babe,
I know not what I shall incur to pass it,   57
Having no warrant.

PAULINA   You need not fear it, sir.
This child was prisoner to the womb and is
By law and process of great Nature thence
Freed and enfranchised, not a party to
The anger of the King nor guilty of—
If any be—the trespass of the Queen.

JAILER   I do believe it.

PAULINA
Do not you fear. Upon mine honor, I
Will stand betwixt you and danger.   *Exeunt.*

❧

2.3

Enter Leontes.

LEONTES
Nor night nor day, no rest! It is but weakness
To bear the matter thus, mere weakness. If
The cause were not in being—part o'th' cause,   3
She th'adulteress, for the harlot King   4

Is quite beyond mine arm, out of the blank   5
And level of my brain, plot-proof, but she   6
I can hook to me—say that she were gone,   7
Given to the fire, a moiety of my rest   8
Might come to me again.—Who's there?

        [Enter a] Servant.

SERVANT   My lord?
LEONTES   How does the boy?
SERVANT
He took good rest tonight; 'tis hoped   11
His sickness is discharged.

LEONTES   To see his nobleness!
Conceiving the dishonor of his mother,   13
He straight declined, drooped, took it deeply,   14
Fastened and fixed the shame on't in himself,   15
Threw off his spirit, his appetite, his sleep,
And downright languished.—Leave me solely. Go,   17
See how he fares.   *[Exit Servant.]*
                  Fie, fie! No thought of him.   18
The very thought of my revenges that way
Recoil upon me—in himself too mighty,
And in his parties, his alliance. Let him be,   21
Until a time may serve. For present vengeance,
Take it on her. Camillo and Polixenes
Laugh at me, make their pastime at my sorrow.
They should not laugh if I could reach them, nor
Shall she, within my power.

        *Enter Paulina [with a baby]; Antigonus and Lords
        [trying to hold her back].*

A LORD   You must not enter.
PAULINA
Nay, rather, good my lords, be second to me.   27
Fear you his tryannous passion more, alas,
Than the Queen's life? A gracious innocent soul,
More free than he is jealous.

ANTIGONUS   That's enough.   30
SERVANT
Madam, he hath not slept tonight, commanded
None should come at him.

PAULINA   Not so hot, good sir.
I come to bring him sleep. 'Tis such as you,
That creep like shadows by him and do sigh
At each his needless heavings, such as you   35
Nourish the cause of his awaking. I   36
Do come with words as medicinal as true,
Honest as either, to purge him of that humor   38
That presses him from sleep.

LEONTES   What noise there, ho?

---

33 blister (It was popularly supposed that lying blistered the tongue.)
34 red-looked red-faced   **36 Commend** deliver   **39 to th' loud'st** as
loudly as I can.   **44 free** generous   **45 thriving issue** successful outcome.   **46 meet** suited.   **Please** If it please   **47 presently** at once
49 hammered of mused upon   **50 tempt** solicit (to serve as ambassador in such a case)   **52 wit** wisdom   **55 come . . . nearer** i.e., come
into the next room (as in lines 46–7).   **57 to pass it** if I let it pass
2.3. Location: Sicilia. The royal court.
3 not in being dead   **4 harlot** lewd. (Originally applied to either sex.)

5–6 out . . . level beyond the range. (Archery terms: *blank* is the center
of the target or the close range needed for a direct shot at it, as in
"point-blank"; *level* is the action of aiming.)   **7 hook** (As with grappling hooks.)   **8 Given to the fire** burned at the stake (as a traitor
conspiring against the King).   **moiety** portion   **11 tonight** last night
13 Conceiving Grasping the enormity of   **14 straight** immediately
15 on't of it   **17 solely** alone.   **18 him** i.e., Polixenes.   **21 his parties**
. . . alliance his supporters and allies.   **27 be second to** aid, second
30 free innocent   **35 heavings** sighs or groans   **36 awaking** inability
to sleep.   **38 humor** distemper

PAULINA
No noise, my lord, but needful conference
About some gossips for Your Highness.
LEONTES   How?   41
Away with that audacious lady! Antigonus,
I charged thee that she should not come about me.
I knew she would.
ANTIGONUS   I told her so, my lord,
On your displeasure's peril and on mine,
She should not visit you.
LEONTES   What, canst not rule her?
PAULINA
From all dishonesty he can. In this,
Unless he take the course that you have done—
Commit me for committing honor—trust it,   49
He shall not rule me.
ANTIGONUS   La you now, you hear!   50
When she will take the rein I let her run,
But she'll not stumble.
PAULINA   Good my liege, I come—
And, I beseech you hear me, who professes
Myself your loyal servant, your physician,
Your most obedient counselor, yet that dares
Less appear so in comforting your evils   56
Than such as most seem yours—I say, I come   57
From your good queen.
LEONTES   Good queen?
PAULINA
Good queen, my lord, good queen, I say good queen,
And would by combat make her good, so were I   61
A man, the worst about you.
LEONTES [to Lords]   Force her hence.   62
PAULINA
Let him that makes but trifles of his eyes
First hand me. On mine own accord I'll off,
But first I'll do my errand. The good Queen,
For she is good, hath brought you forth a daughter—
Here 'tis—commends it to your blessing.
                        [She lays down the baby.]
LEONTES   Out!
A mankind witch! Hence with her, out o' door!   68
A most intelligencing bawd!
PAULINA   Not so.   69
I am as ignorant in that as you
In so entitling me, and no less honest
Than you are mad; which is enough, I'll warrant,
As this world goes, to pass for honest.
LEONTES [to Lords]   Traitors!
Will you not push her out? [To Antigonus] Give her the
    bastard.
Thou dotard, thou art woman-tired, unroosted   75

By thy Dame Partlet here. Take up the bastard!   76
Take't up, I say. Give't to thy crone.
PAULINA [to Antigonus]   Forever
Unvenerable be thy hands if thou
Tak'st up the Princess by that forcèd baseness   79
Which he has put upon't!
LEONTES   He dreads his wife.
PAULINA
So I would you did. Then 'twere past all doubt
You'd call your children yours.
LEONTES   A nest of traitors!
ANTIGONUS
I am none, by this good light.
PAULINA   Nor I, nor any   83
But one that's here, and that's himself; for he
The sacred honor of himself, his queen's,
His hopeful son's, his babe's, betrays to slander,
Whose sting is sharper than the sword's; and will
    not—
For, as the case now stands, it is a curse   88
He cannot be compelled to't—once remove   89
The root of his opinion, which is rotten   90
As ever oak or stone was sound.
LEONTES   A callet   91
Of boundless tongue, who late hath beat her husband 92
And now baits me! This brat is none of mine;   93
It is the issue of Polixenes.
Hence with it, and together with the dam
Commit them to the fire!
PAULINA   It is yours;
And, might we lay th'old proverb to your charge,
So like you, 'tis the worse. Behold, my lords,   98
Although the print be little, the whole matter
And copy of the father—eye, nose, lip,
The trick of 's frown, his forehead, nay, the valley, 101
The pretty dimples of his chin and cheek, his smiles,
The very mold and frame of hand, nail, finger.
And thou, good goddess Nature, which hast made it
So like to him that got it, if thou hast   105
The ordering of the mind too, 'mongst all colors
No yellow in't, lest she suspect, as he does,   107
Her children not her husband's!
LEONTES   A gross hag!
And, lozel, thou art worthy to be hanged,   109
That wilt not stay her tongue.
ANTIGONUS   Hang all the husbands   110
That cannot do that feat, you'll leave yourself

41 **gossips** godparents for the baby at its baptism   49 **Commit** i.e., to prison   50 **La . . . hear!** i.e., There now, you hear how she will go on talking!   56–7 **in comforting . . . yours** when it comes to encouraging your evil courses than those flatterers who seem to be your most loyal servants   61 **by combat** by trial by combat.   **make** prove   62 **worst** least manly, or, lowest in rank   68 **mankind** masculine, behaving like a man   69 **intelligencing bawd** acting as go-between and spy (for the Queen and Polixenes).   75 **woman-tired** henpecked. (From *tire* in falconry, meaning "tear with the beak.")   **unroosted** driven from perch

76 **Partlet** or Pertilote, a common name for a hen (as in *Reynard the Fox* and in Chaucer's "Nun's Priest's Tale")   79 **by that forcèd baseness** under that wrongfully imposed name of bastard   83 **by this good light** by the light of day. (A common oath.)   88–90 **as . . . opinion** i.e., since he is King, he regrettably can't be compelled to change his deeply rooted opinion   91 **callet** scold   92 **late** recently   93 **baits** (With a pun on *beat* in the previous line, pronounced "bate.")   98 **So . . . worse** he's so like you that he fares the worse for it.   101 **trick** characteristic expression.   **valley** cleft above the upper lip   105 **got** begot   107 **No yellow** let there be no yellow, i.e., the color of jealousy. (A chaste woman could hardly expect that her own children are illegitimate, but Paulina may be hyperbolically ridiculing Leontes's suspicions.)   109 **lozel** worthless person, scoundrel. (Addressed to Antigonus.)   110 **stay** restrain

Hardly one subject.

LEONTES　　　　　　　　　Once more, take her hence.

PAULINA
A most unworthy and unnatural lord
Can do no more.

LEONTES　　　　　　　　　I'll ha' thee burnt.

PAULINA　　　　　　　　　　　　　　　I care not.
It is an heretic that makes the fire,　　　　　　　115
Not she which burns in 't. I'll not call you tyrant;　116
But this most cruel usage of your queen,
Not able to produce more accusation　　　　　　118
Than your own weak-hinged fancy, something savors
Of tyranny and will ignoble make you,
Yea, scandalous to the world.

LEONTES [to Antigonus]　　　　On your allegiance,
Out of the chamber with her! Were I a tyrant,
Where were her life? She durst not call me so　　123
If she did know me one. Away with her!

PAULINA
I pray you, do not push me; I'll be gone.
Look to your babe, my lord; 'tis yours. Jove send her
A better guiding spirit!—What needs these hands?　127
You that are thus so tender o'er his follies
Will never do him good, not one of you.
So, so. Farewell, we are gone.　　　　　　Exit.

LEONTES [to Antigonus]
Thou, traitor, hast set on thy wife to this.
My child? Away with 't! Even thou, that hast
A heart so tender o'er it, take it hence
And see it instantly consumed with fire;
Even thou and none but thou. Take it up straight.
Within this hour bring me word 'tis done,
And by good testimony, or I'll seize thy life,
With what thou else call'st thine. If thou refuse
And wilt encounter with my wrath, say so;
The bastard brains with these my proper hands　　140
Shall I dash out. Go, take it to the fire,
For thou set'st on thy wife.

ANTIGONUS　　　　　　　　I did not, sir.
These lords, my noble fellows, if they please,
Can clear me in 't.

LORDS　　　　　　　We can. My royal liege,
He is not guilty of her coming hither.

LEONTES　You're liars all.

A LORD
Beseech Your Highness, give us better credit.　　147
We have always truly served you, and beseech'　148
So to esteem of us; and on our knees we beg,
As recompense of our dear services　　　　　　150
Past and to come, that you do change this purpose,
Which being so horrible, so bloody, must
Lead on to some foul issue. We all kneel.

LEONTES
I am a feather for each wind that blows.
Shall I live on to see this bastard kneel
And call me father? Better burn it now
Than curse it then. But be it; let it live.
It shall not neither. [To Antigonus] You, sir, come you
　　hither,
You that have been so tenderly officious
With Lady Margery, your midwife there,　　　　160
To save this bastard's life—for 'tis a bastard,
So sure as this beard's gray. What will you adventure 162
To save this brat's life?

ANTIGONUS　　　　　　Anything, my lord,
That my ability may undergo
And nobleness impose. At least thus much:
I'll pawn the little blood which I have left
To save the innocent—anything possible.

LEONTES [holding his sword]
It shall be possible. Swear by this sword
Thou wilt perform my bidding.

ANTIGONUS [his hand on the hilt]　　I will, my lord.

LEONTES
Mark and perform it, see'st thou; for the fail　　170
Of any point in 't shall not only be
Death to thyself but to thy lewd-tongued wife,
Whom for this time we pardon. We enjoin thee,
As thou art liegeman to us, that thou carry　　　174
This female bastard hence, and that thou bear it
To some remote and desert place quite out
Of our dominions, and that there thou leave it,
Without more mercy, to it own protection　　　　178
And favor of the climate. As by strange fortune
It came to us, I do in justice charge thee,
On thy soul's peril and thy body's torture,
That thou commend it strangely to some place　　182
Where chance may nurse or end it. Take it up.

ANTIGONUS [taking up the baby]
I swear to do this, though a present death
Had been more merciful.—Come on, poor babe.
Some powerful spirit instruct the kites and ravens
To be thy nurses! Wolves and bears, they say,
Casting their savageness aside, have done
Like offices of pity.—Sir, be prosperous
In more than this deed does require!—And blessing　190
Against this cruelty fight on thy side,
Poor thing, condemned to loss!　　Exit [with the baby].

LEONTES　　　　　　　　　　　No, I'll not rear　192
Another's issue.

　　　　　　　　Enter a Servant.

SERVANT　　　　　　Please Your Highness, posts　193
From those you sent to th'oracle are come
An hour since. Cleomenes and Dion,

115–16 It is . . . in 't i.e., In burning me, you who would be making or
building the fire are the heretic, not me (since loss of faith in innocence is a kind of heresy), or, you can burn a woman if you like, but
it's a heretic's fire only if she is, in fact, a heretic.　118 Not able you
not being able　123 Where . . . life? how could she escape execution
at my command?　127 What . . . hands? What need is there to push
me?　140 proper own　147 credit belief.　148 beseech' beseech you
150 dear loyal, heartfelt

160 Margery (A derisive term, evidently equivalent to Partlet in line
76.)　162 this beard's (Probably Antigonus's.)　170 see'st thou i.e.,
do you hear.　fail failure　174 liegeman loyal subject　178 it its
182 commend . . . place commit it to some foreign place　190 more
i.e., more ways, more extent.　require deserve.　192 loss destruction.　193 posts messengers

Being well arrived from Delphos, are both landed,
Hasting to th' court.
A LORD   So please you, sir, their speed
Hath been beyond account.
LEONTES   Twenty-three days   198
They have been absent. 'Tis good speed, foretells
The great Apollo suddenly will have   200
The truth of this appear. Prepare you, lords.
Summon a session, that we may arraign   202
Our most disloyal lady; for, as she hath
Been publicly accused, so shall she have
A just and open trial. While she lives
My heart will be a burden to me. Leave me,
And think upon my bidding.   *Exeunt [separately].*

❖

3.1

Enter Cleomenes and Dion.

CLEOMENES
The climate's delicate, the air most sweet,
Fertile the isle, the temple much surpassing   2
The common praise it bears.
DION   I shall report,
For most it caught me, the celestial habits—   4
Methinks I so should term them—and the reverence
Of the grave wearers. Oh, the sacrifice!
How ceremonious, solemn, and unearthly
It was i'th'offering!
CLEOMENES   But of all, the burst
And the ear-deaf'ning voice o'th'oracle,
Kin to Jove's thunder, so surprised my sense   10
That I was nothing.
DION   If th'event o'th' journey   11
Prove as successful to the Queen—O, be't so!—
As it hath been to us rare, pleasant, speedy,
The time is worth the use on't.
CLEOMENES   Great Apollo   14
Turn all to th' best! These proclamations,
So forcing faults upon Hermione,
I little like.
DION   The violent carriage of it   17
Will clear or end the business. When the oracle,
Thus by Apollo's great divine sealed up,   19
Shall the contents discover, something rare   20
Even then will rush to knowledge. Go. Fresh horses!
And gracious be the issue!   *Exeunt.*

❖

3.2

Enter Leontes, Lords, [and] Officers.

LEONTES
This sessions, to our great grief we pronounce,
Even pushes 'gainst our heart: the party tried
The daughter of a king, our wife, and one
Of us too much beloved. Let us be cleared   4
Of being tyrannous, since we so openly
Proceed in justice, which shall have due course
Even to the guilt or the purgation.   7
Produce the prisoner.
OFFICER
It is His Highness' pleasure that the Queen
Appear in person here in court. Silence!

    *[Enter] Hermione, as to her trial, [Paulina, and]
    Ladies.*

LEONTES   Read the indictment.
OFFICER *[reads]* "Hermione, Queen to the worthy
Leontes, King of Sicilia, thou art here accused and ar-
raigned of high treason, in committing adultery with
Polixenes, King of Bohemia, and conspiring with
Camillo to take away the life of our sovereign lord the
King, thy royal husband; the pretense whereof being   17
by circumstances partly laid open, thou, Hermione,
contrary to the faith and allegiance of a true subject,
didst counsel and aid them, for their better safety, to
fly away by night."
HERMIONE
Since what I am to say must be but that
Which contradicts my accusation, and
The testimony on my part no other
But what comes from myself, it shall scarce boot me   25
To say "not guilty." Mine integrity,
Being counted falsehood, shall, as I express it,
Be so received. But thus: if powers divine
Behold our human actions, as they do,
I doubt not then but innocence shall make
False accusation blush and tyranny
Tremble at patience. You, my lord, best know,
Who least will seem to do so, my past life
Hath been as continent, as chaste, as true
As I am now unhappy; which is more
Than history can pattern, though devised   36
And played to take spectators. For behold me—   37
A fellow of the royal bed, which owe   38
A moiety of the throne, a great king's daughter,   39
The mother to a hopeful prince—here standing
To prate and talk for life and honor 'fore

198 beyond account unprecedented, or, beyond explanation.
200 suddenly at once   **202 session** trial
3.1. Location: Sicilia. On the way to Leontes's court.
2 isle (Shakespeare follows Greene's *Pandosto* in fictitiously placing
Delphi on an island. Delphi, sometimes known as Delphos [see
2.1.184, 2.3.196, and 3.2.126], was often confused with Delos, the
island birthplace of Apollo and location also of an oracle.)   **4 habits**
vestments   **10 surprised** overwhelmed   **11 th'event** the outcome
14 is worth . . . on't has been well employed.   **17 carriage** execution,
management   **19 great divine** chief priest   **20 discover** reveal

3.2. Location: Sicilia. A place of justice, probably at court.
4 Of us by me   **7 purgation** acquittal.   **17 pretense** purpose, design
25 boot avail   **36 history** story, drama.   **pattern** show a similar
example for   **37 take** please, charm   **38 which owe** who owns
39 moiety share

Who please to come and hear. For life, I prize it   42
As I weigh grief, which I would spare. For honor,   43
'Tis a derivative from me to mine,   44
And only that I stand for. I appeal   45
To your own conscience, sir, before Polixenes   46
Came to your court, how I was in your grace,
How merited to be so; since he came,
With what encounter so uncurrent I   49
Have strained t'appear thus; if one jot beyond   50
The bound of honor, or in act or will
That way inclining, hardened be the hearts   52
Of all that hear me, and my near'st of kin
Cry "Fie" upon my grave!

LEONTES   I ne'er heard yet
That any of these bolder vices wanted   55
Less impudence to gainsay what they did   56
Than to perform it first.

HERMIONE   That's true enough,
Though 'tis a saying, sir, not due to me.   58

LEONTES
You will not own it.

HERMIONE   More than mistress of   59
Which comes to me in name of fault, I must not   60
At all acknowledge. For Polixenes,   61
With whom I am accused, I do confess
I loved him as in honor he required;   63
With such a kind of love as might become
A lady like me; with a love even such,
So, and no other, as yourself commanded;
Which not to have done I think had been in me
Both disobedience and ingratitude
To you and toward your friend, whose love had
   spoke,   69
Even since it could speak, from an infant, freely   70
That it was yours. Now, for conspiracy,   71
I know not how it tastes, though it be dished   72
For me to try how. All I know of it
Is that Camillo was an honest man;
And why he left your court, the gods themselves,
Wotting no more than I, are ignorant.   76

LEONTES
You knew of his departure, as you know
What you have underta'en to do in 's absence.

HERMIONE   Sir,
You speak a language that I understand not.
My life stands in the level of your dreams,   81

Which I'll lay down.

LEONTES   Your actions are my dreams.   82
You had a bastard by Polixenes,
And I but dreamed it. As you were past all shame—
Those of your fact are so—so past all truth,   85
Which to deny concerns more than avails; for as   86
Thy brat hath been cast out, like to itself,   87
No father owning it—which is indeed
More criminal in thee than it—so thou
Shalt feel our justice, in whose easiest passage   90
Look for no less than death.

HERMIONE   Sir, spare your threats.   91
The bug which you would fright me with I seek.   92
To me can life be no commodity.   93
The crown and comfort of my life, your favor,
I do give lost, for I do feel it gone,   95
But know not how it went. My second joy
And firstfruits of my body, from his presence
I am barred, like one infectious. My third comfort,
Starred most unluckily, is from my breast,   99
The innocent milk in it most innocent mouth,   100
Haled out to murder; myself on every post   101
Proclaimed a strumpet; with immodest hatred   102
The childbed privilege denied, which longs   103
To women of all fashion; lastly, hurried   104
Here to this place, i'th'open air, before
I have got strength of limit. Now, my liege,   106
Tell me what blessings I have here alive
That I should fear to die? Therefore proceed.
But yet hear this; mistake me not. No life,   109
I prize it not a straw. But for mine honor,
Which I would free, if I shall be condemned   111
Upon surmises, all proofs sleeping else
But what your jealousies awake, I tell you
'Tis rigor and not law. Your Honors all,   114
I do refer me to the oracle.
Apollo be my judge!

A LORD   This your request
Is altogether just. Therefore bring forth,
And in Apollo's name, his oracle.

                [*Exeunt certain Officers.*]

HERMIONE
The Emperor of Russia was my father.
Oh, that he were alive and here beholding
His daughter's trial! That he did but see

---

42 Who please whoever chooses   **42–5 For . . . stand for** As for life, I value it as I value grief, and would as willingly do without; as for honor, it is transmitted from me to my descendants, and that only I make a stand for.   **46 conscience** consideration, inward knowledge   **49–50 With . . . thus** (I ask) by what behavior so unacceptable I have transgressed so that I appear thus (in disgrace and on trial)   **52 hardened** hardened against me   **55–6 wanted Less** were more lacking in   **58 due** applicable   **59–61 More . . . acknowledge** I must not acknowledge more faults than I actually have.   **61 For** As for   **63 required** deserved   **69–71 your friend . . . yours** i.e., Polixenes, who professed love for you from earliest childhood (as you for him).   **71 for** as for   **72 though . . . dished** even if it were to be served up   **76 Wotting** supposing they know   **81 level** aim, range

82 Which i.e., my life.   **Your . . . dreams** i.e., You have performed what I have fantasized, and what you have done preys on my mind.   **85 Those of your fact** All those who do what you did   **86 Which . . . avails** your denial of which is understandable, but it won't do you any good   **87 like to itself** as an outcast, fatherless brat ought to be   **90–1 in whose . . . death** i.e., which will impose the death sentence at least, perhaps torture also.   **92 bug** bugbear, bogey, imaginary object of terror   **93 commodity** asset   **95 give** reckon as, or give up for   **99 Starred most unluckily** born under a most unlucky star   **100 it** its   **101 post** posting place for public notices   **102 immodest** immoderate   **103 The childbed . . . longs** denied the privilege of bedrest after giving birth, something that is the right   **104 all fashion** every rank   **106 got . . . limit** regained my strength after having borne a child.   **109 No life** i.e., I do not ask for life   **111 free** vindicate   **114 rigor** tyranny

The flatness of my misery, yet with eyes 122
Of pity, not revenge!

[*Enter Officers, with*] Cleomenes [*and*] Dion.

OFFICER [*holding a sword*]
You here shall swear upon this sword of justice
That you, Cleomenes and Dion, have
Been both at Delphos, and from thence have brought
This sealed up oracle, by the hand delivered
Of great Apollo's priest, and that since then
You have not dared to break the holy seal
Nor read the secrets in't.
CLEOMENES, DION   All this we swear.
LEONTES
Break up the seals and read.   131
OFFICER [*reads*]   "Hermione is chaste, Polixenes blame-
less, Camillo a true subject, Leontes a jealous tyrant,
his innocent babe truly begotten, and the King shall
live without an heir if that which is lost be not
found."
LORDS
Now blessèd be the great Apollo!
HERMIONE   Praised!
LEONTES
Hast thou read truth?
OFFICER   Ay, my lord, even so
As it is here set down.
LEONTES
There is no truth at all i'th'oracle.
The sessions shall proceed. This is mere falsehood.

[*Enter a Servant.*]

SERVANT
My lord the King, the King!
LEONTES   What is the business?
SERVANT
Oh, sir, I shall be hated to report it!   143
The Prince your son, with mere conceit and fear   144
Of the Queen's speed, is gone.
LEONTES   How? Gone?
SERVANT   Is dead.   145
LEONTES
Apollo's angry, and the heavens themselves
Do strike at my injustice. [*Hermione swoons.*] How now
    there?
PAULINA
This news is mortal to the Queen. Look down
And see what death is doing.
LEONTES   Take her hence.
Her heart is but o'ercharged; she will recover.
I have too much believed mine own suspicion.
Beseech you, tenderly apply to her
Some remedies for life.
          [*Exeunt Paulina and Ladies, with Hermione.*]
                              Apollo, pardon
My great profaneness 'gainst thine oracle!
I'll reconcile me to Polixenes,

New woo my queen, recall the good Camillo,
Whom I proclaim a man of truth, of mercy;
For, being transported by my jealousies
To bloody thoughts and to revenge, I chose
Camillo for the minister to poison
My friend Polixenes; which had been done,
But that the good mind of Camillo tardied   162
My swift command, though I with death and with
Reward did threaten and encourage him,
Not doing it and being done. He, most humane   165
And filled with honor, to my kingly guest
Unclasped my practice, quit his fortunes here,   167
Which you knew great, and to the hazard
Of all incertainties himself commended   169
No richer than his honor. How he glisters   170
Through my rust! And how his piety   171
Does my deeds make the blacker!

[*Enter Paulina.*]

PAULINA   Woe the while!
Oh, cut my lace, lest my heart, cracking it,   173
Break too!
A LORD   What fit is this, good lady?
PAULINA
What studied torments, tyrant, hast for me?   175
What wheels, racks, fires? What flaying, boiling 176
In leads or oils? What old or newer torture
Must I receive, whose every word deserves   178
To taste of thy most worst? Thy tyranny,   179
Together working with thy jealousies—
Fancies too weak for boys, too green and idle   181
For girls of nine—oh, think what they have done,
And then run mad indeed, stark mad! For all
Thy bygone fooleries were but spices of it.   184
That thou betrayed'st Polixenes, 'twas nothing;
That did but show thee, of a fool, inconstant   186
And damnable ingrateful. Nor was 't much
Thou wouldst have poisoned good Camillo's honor,
To have him kill a king—poor trespasses,   189
More monstrous standing by; whereof I reckon   190
The casting forth to crows thy baby daughter   191
To be or none or little, though a devil   192
Would have shed water out of fire ere done't.   193
Nor is't directly laid to thee, the death
Of the young Prince, whose honorable thoughts,
Thoughts high for one so tender, cleft the heart 196
That could conceive a gross and foolish sire   197

122 **flatness** boundlessness   131 **up** open   143 **to report** for reporting
144 **conceit and fear** i.e., anxious concern   145 **speed** fate, fortune

162 **tardied** delayed   165 **Not . . . done** i.e., death if he did not do it
and reward if he did.   167 **Unclasped my practice** disclosed my plot
169 **himself commended** entrusted himself   170 **No richer than** with
no riches except   170–1 **How . . . rust!** How he shines in contrast with
my fault!   173 **my lace** the lace of my stays   175 **studied** ingeniously
devised   176 **wheels . . . flaying** (Various methods of torture: being
stretched on a wheel or rack until the bones are broken or pulled
apart at the joints, being burned or skinned alive.)   178–9 **whose . . .
worst?** I, whose every word seems to invite your severest punishment?   181 **idle** foolish   184 **spices** foretastes, samples   186 **of** for
189 **To have** by having.   **poor** slight   190 **More . . . by** when more
monstrous sins are at hand for comparison   191 **crows** carrion birds
192 **or none** either none   193 **shed . . . fire** wept from his fiery eyes or
while surrounded by hellfire   196 **tender** young   197 **conceive**
apprehend that

Blemished his gracious dam. This is not, no,   198
Laid to thy answer. But the last—Oh, lords,   199
When I have said, cry woe! The Queen, the Queen,   200
The sweet'st, dear'st creature's dead, and vengeance
   for't
Not dropped down yet.

A LORD   The higher powers forbid!

PAULINA
I say she's dead. I'll swear't. If word nor oath
Prevail not, go and see. If you can bring
Tincture or luster in her lip, her eye,   205
Heat outwardly or breath within, I'll serve you
As I would do the gods. But, O thou tyrant!
Do not repent these things, for they are heavier
Than all thy woes can stir. Therefore betake thee   209
To nothing but despair. A thousand knees
Ten thousand years together, naked, fasting,
Upon a barren mountain, and still winter   212
In storm perpetual, could not move the gods
To look that way thou wert.

LEONTES   Go on, go on.   214
Thou canst not speak too much. I have deserved
All tongues to talk their bitt'rest.

A LORD [to Paulina]   Say no more.
Howe'er the business goes, you have made fault
I'th' boldness of your speech.

PAULINA   I am sorry for't.
All faults I make, when I shall come to know them,   219
I do repent. Alas, I have showed too much
The rashness of a woman! He is touched
To th' noble heart. What's gone and what's past help
Should be past grief.—Do not receive affliction   223
At my petition. I beseech you, rather   224
Let me be punished, that have minded you   225
Of what you should forget. Now, good my liege,
Sir, royal sir, forgive a foolish woman.
The love I bore your queen—lo, fool again!
I'll speak of her no more, nor of your children;
I'll not remember you of my own lord,   230
Who is lost too. Take your patience to you,   231
And I'll say nothing.

LEONTES   Thou didst speak but well
When most the truth, which I receive much better
Than to be pitied of thee. Prithee, bring me
To the dead bodies of my queen and son.
One grave shall be for both. Upon them shall
The causes of their death appear, unto
Our shame perpetual. Once a day I'll visit
The chapel where they lie, and tears shed there
Shall be my recreation. So long as nature   240
Will bear up with this exercise, so long

I daily vow to use it. Come and lead me
To these sorrows.   Exeunt.

❖

3.3

Enter Antigonus [and] a Mariner, [with a] babe.

ANTIGONUS
Thou art perfect then, our ship hath touched upon   1
The deserts of Bohemia?

MARINER   Ay, my lord, and fear   2
We have landed in ill time. The skies look grimly
And threaten present blusters. In my conscience,   4
The heavens with that we have in hand are angry
And frown upon 's.

ANTIGONUS   Their sacred wills be done! Go, get aboard;
Look to thy bark. I'll not be long before   8
I call upon thee.

MARINER   Make your best haste, and go not
Too far i'th' land. 'Tis like to be loud weather.   10
Besides, this place is famous for the creatures
Of prey that keep upon't.

ANTIGONUS   Go thou away.   12
I'll follow instantly.

MARINER   I am glad at heart
To be so rid o'th' business.   Exit.

ANTIGONUS   Come, poor babe.
I have heard, but not believed, the spirits o'th' dead
May walk again. If such thing be, thy mother
Appeared to me last night, for ne'er was dream
So like a waking. To me comes a creature,
Sometimes her head on one side, some another;   19
I never saw a vessel of like sorrow,
So filled and so becoming. In pure white robes,   21
Like very sanctity, she did approach
My cabin where I lay, thrice bowed before me,
And, gasping to begin some speech, her eyes
Became two spouts. The fury spent, anon
Did this break from her: "Good Antigonus,
Since fate, against thy better disposition,
Hath made thy person for the thrower-out
Of my poor babe, according to thine oath,
Places remote enough are in Bohemia;
There weep and leave it crying. And, for the babe   31
Is counted lost forever, Perdita,   32
I prithee, call't. For this ungentle business   33
Put on thee by my lord, thou ne'er shalt see
Thy wife Paulina more." And so, with shrieks,
She melted into air. Affrighted much,
I did in time collect myself and thought
This was so and no slumber. Dreams are toys;   38

---

198 dam mother.   199 Laid ... answer presented as a charge that
you must answer.   200 said finished speaking   205 Tincture color
209 woes can stir penance can remove.   212 still always   214 To look
... wert to regard you.   219 I make that I make   223–4 Do ... petition Do not afflict yourself with remorse at my urging.   225 minded
you put you in mind   230 remember remind   231 Take ... you Arm
yourself with patience   240 my recreation (1) my sole diversion (2) my
spiritual regeneration.   nature my physical being

3.3 Location: Bohemia. The seacoast.
1 perfect certain   2 deserts of Bohemia i.e., deserted region on the
coast. (Shakespeare follows Greene's *Pandosto* in giving Bohemia a
seacoast.)   4 present immediate.   conscience opinion   8 bark ship.
10 like likely.   loud stormy   12 keep upon't inhabit it.   19 some
another sometimes the other   21 So ... becoming i.e., so filled with
sorrow and able to bear it so gracefully.   31 for because   32 Perdita
i.e., the lost one   33 ungentle ignoble   38 toys trifles

Yet for this once, yea, superstitiously,
I will be squared by this. I do believe   40
Hermione hath suffered death, and that
Apollo would, this being indeed the issue
Of King Polixenes, it should here be laid,
Either for life or death, upon the earth
Of its right father. Blossom, speed thee well!
              [*He lays down the baby.*]
There lie, and there thy character; there these,   46
       [*He places a box and a fardel beside the baby.*]
Which may, if fortune please, both breed thee, pretty,   47
And still rest thine. [*Thunder.*] The storm begins. Poor
      wretch,   48
That for thy mother's fault art thus exposed
To loss and what may follow! Weep I cannot,   50
But my heart bleeds; and most accurst am I
To be by oath enjoined to this. Farewell!
The day frowns more and more. Thou'rt like to have
A lullaby too rough. I never saw
The heavens so dim by day. A savage clamor!
Well may I get aboard! This is the chase.
I am gone forever!   *Exit, pursued by a bear.*

       [*Enter a*] *Shepherd.*

SHEPHERD   I would there were no age between ten and
three-and-twenty, or that youth would sleep out the
rest, for there is nothing in the between but getting
wenches with child, wronging the ancientry, stealing,   61
fighting—Hark you now, would any but these boiled   62
brains of nineteen and two-and-twenty hunt this   63
weather? They have scared away two of my best sheep,
which I fear the wolf will sooner find than the master.
If anywhere I have them, 'tis by the seaside, browsing
of ivy. Good luck, an't be thy will! [*Seeing the child.*]   67
What have we here? Mercy on 's, a bairn, a very pretty   68
bairn! A boy or a child, I wonder? A pretty one, a very   69
pretty one. Sure some scape. Though I am not bookish,   70
yet I can read waiting-gentlewoman in the scape.
This has been some stair-work, some trunk-work,   72
some behind-door-work. They were warmer that got   73
this than the poor thing is here. I'll take it up for pity.
Yet I'll tarry till my son come; he hallooed but even
now.—Whoa, ho, hoa!   76

       Enter Clown.

CLOWN   Hilloa, loa!

SHEPHERD   What, art so near? If thou'lt see a thing to
talk on when thou art dead and rotten, come hither.
What ail'st thou, man?
CLOWN   I have seen two such sights, by sea and by
land! But I am not to say it is a sea, for it is now the sky;
betwixt the firmament and it you cannot thrust a
bodkin's point.   84
SHEPHERD   Why, boy, how is it?
CLOWN   I would you did but see how it chafes, how it
rages, how it takes up the shore! But that's not to the   87
point. Oh, the most piteous cry of the poor souls! Sometimes to see 'em, and not to see 'em; now the ship
boring the moon with her mainmast, and anon swallowed with yeast and froth, as you'd thrust a cork into   91
a hogshead. And then for the land service, to see how   92
the bear tore out his shoulder bone; how he cried to
me for help and said his name was Antigonus, a nobleman. But to make an end of the ship: to see how
the sea flapdragoned it! But first, how the poor souls   96
roared and the sea mocked them, and how the poor
gentleman roared and the bear mocked him, both
roaring louder than the sea or weather.
SHEPHERD   Name of mercy, when was this, boy?
CLOWN   Now, now. I have not winked since I saw these   101
sights. The men are not yet cold under water, nor the
bear half dined on the gentleman. He's at it now.
SHEPHERD   Would I had been by, to have helped the
old man!
CLOWN   I would you had been by the ship side, to have
helped her. There your charity would have lacked
footing.   108
SHEPHERD   Heavy matters, heavy matters! But look thee
here, boy. Now bless thyself. Thou met'st with things
dying, I with things newborn. Here's a sight for thee;
look thee, a bearing cloth for a squire's child! Look   112
thee here; take up, take up, boy. Open't. So, let's see.
It was told me I should be rich by the fairies. This is
some changeling. Open't. What's within, boy?   115
                   [*The Clown opens the box.*]
CLOWN   You're a made old man. If the sins of your
youth are forgiven you, you're well to live. Gold, all   117
gold!
SHEPHERD   This is fairy gold, boy, and 'twill prove so.
Up with't, keep it close. Home, home, the next way.   120
We are lucky, boy, and to be so still requires nothing   121
but secrecy. Let my sheep go. Come, good boy, the   122
next way home.

---

40 squared directed in my course   **46 thy character** the written account of you (i.e., the one that subsequently will serve to identify Perdita).   **these** i.e., the gold and jewels found by the Shepherd, also later used to identify her.   **46.1 box, fardel** (The box, containing gold and jewels, is later produced by the old Shepherd and the Clown; see 4.4.758–9. They also have a *fardel*, or "bundle," consisting evidently of the bearing cloth [3.3.112] and/or mantle [5.2.34] in which the babe was found.)   **47 breed thee** keep you, pay for your support.   **pretty pretty one**   **48 And still rest thine** i.e., and still provide a heritage with what is unspent.   **50 Weep I cannot** i.e., I cannot weep as the Queen instructed me (line 31)   **61 ancientry** old people   **62–3 boiled brains** addlepated youths   **67 Good . . . will!** i.e., May God grant me good luck in finding my sheep!   **68 bairn** child   **69 child** i.e., female infant **70 scape** sexual escapade.   **72–3 stair-work . . . behind-door-work** i.e., sexual liaisons under or behind the stairs or using a room or a trunk for concealment.   **73 got** begot   **76.1 Clown** country fellow, rustic.

84 bodkin's needle's. (A *bodkin* can also be a dagger, awl, etc.)   **87 takes up** (1) contends with, rebukes (2) swallows   **91 yeast** foam   **92 hogshead** large barrel. (The image is of a cork swimming in a turbulent expanse of frothing liquid.)   **land service** (1) dish of food served on land (2) military service on land (as distinguished from naval service); here, the doings on land   **96 flapdragoned** swallowed as one would a flapdragon, i.e., a raisin or the like swallowed out of burning brandy in the game of snapdragon   **101 winked** blinked an eye   **108 footing** (1) foothold (2) establishment of a charitable foundation, one that would provide *charity* (line 107).   **112 bearing cloth** rich cloth or mantle in which a child was carried to its baptism   **115 changeling** child left or taken by fairies.   **117 well to live** well-to-do.   **120 close** secret.   **next** nearest   **121–2 to be . . . secrecy** (To talk about fairy gifts would be to insure bad luck.)   **121 still** on a continuing basis

CLOWN   Go you the next way with your findings. I'll go
see if the bear be gone from the gentleman, and how
much he hath eaten. They are never curst but when 126
they are hungry. If there be any of him left, I'll bury it.

SHEPHERD   That's a good deed. If thou mayest discern
by that which is left of him what he is, fetch me to th' 129
sight of him.

CLOWN   Marry, will I; and you shall help to put him i'th' 131
ground.

SHEPHERD   'Tis a lucky day, boy, and we'll do good
deeds on't.   *Exeut.*

4.1

Enter Time, the Chorus.

TIME

I, that please some, try all, both joy and terror   1
Of good and bad, that makes and unfolds error,   2
Now take upon me, in the name of Time,
To use my wings. Impute it not a crime
To me or my swift passage that I slide
O'er sixteen years and leave the growth untried   6
Of that wide gap, since it is in my power
To o'erthrow law and in one self-born hour   8
To plant and o'erwhelm custom. Let me pass   9
The same I am ere ancient'st order was   10
Or what is now received. I witness to   11
The times that brought them in; so shall I do   12
To th' freshest things now reigning, and make stale
The glistering of this present as my tale   14
Now seems to it. Your patience this allowing,   15
I turn my glass and give my scene such growing   16
As you had slept between. Leontes leaving   17
Th'effects of his fond jealousies, so grieving   18
That he shuts up himself, imagine me,
Gentle spectators, that I now may be
In fair Bohemia. And remember well
I mentioned a son o'th' King's, which Florizel
I now name to you; and with speed so pace   23
To speak of Perdita, now grown in grace   24
Equal with wond'ring. What of her ensues   25
I list not prophesy; but let Time's news   26
Be known when 'tis brought forth. A shepherd's
daughter,

And what to her adheres, which follows after,   28
Is th'argument of Time. Of this allow,   29
If ever you have spent time worse ere now;
If never, yet that Time himself doth say   31
He wishes earnestly you never may.   *Exit.*

4.2

Enter Polixenes and Camillo.

POLIXENES   I pray thee, good Camillo, be no more
importunate. 'Tis a sickness denying thee anything, a
death to grant this.

CAMILLO   It is fifteen years since I saw my country. 4
Though I have for the most part been aired abroad, I   5
desire to lay my bones there. Besides, the penitent
King, my master, hath sent for me, to whose feeling   7
sorrows I might be some allay—or I o'erween to think   8
so—which is another spur to my departure.

POLIXENES   As thou lov'st me, Camillo, wipe not out the
rest of thy services by leaving me now. The need I
have of thee thine own goodness hath made. Better
not to have had thee than thus to want thee. Thou,   13
having made me businesses which none without thee
can sufficiently manage, must either stay to execute
them thyself or take away with thee the very services
thou hast done; which if I have not enough
considered—as too much I cannot—to be more thank-   18
ful to thee shall be my study, and my profit therein the
heaping friendships. Of that fatal country, Sicilia, 20
prithee, speak no more, whose very naming punishes
me with the remembrance of that penitent, as thou
call'st him, and reconciled King, my brother, whose
loss of his most precious queen and children are even
now to be afresh lamented. Say to me, when saw'st
thou the Prince Florizel, my son? Kings are no less
unhappy, their issue not being gracious, than they are 27
in losing them when they have approved their virtues. 28

CAMILLO   Sir, it is three days since I saw the Prince.
What his happier affairs may be are to me unknown;
but I have missingly noted he is of late much retired 31
from court and is less frequent to his princely exercises 32
than formerly he hath appeared.

POLIXENES   I have considered so much, Camillo, and   34
with some care, so far that I have eyes under my ser- 35
vice which look upon his removedness; from whom I   36
have this intelligence, that he is seldom from the   37
house of a most homely shepherd—a man, they say,   38

126 curst mean, fierce   **129 what he is** what is his identity or rank
131 Marry i.e., Indeed. (Originally an oath, "by the Virgin Mary.")
4.1.
1 try test   **2 that . . . error** i.e., I who make error, thus bringing joy to
the bad and terror to the good, and then at last unfold or disclose error,
thus bringing joy to the good and terror to the bad   **6 growth untried**
developments unexplored   **8 law** any established order (including the
rule of the unity of time in a dramatic performance, conventionally
limiting the action to twenty-four hours).   **self-born** selfsame, or born
of myself (since hours are the creations of Time)   **9–11 Let . . . received**
Let me continue as I have been from before the beginning of time to the
present.   **12 them** i.e., law and custom   **14 glistering** glittering shine
15 seems to it seems (stale) when compared with the present.
16 glass hourglass   **17 As** as if   **18 fond** foolish   **23 pace** proceed
24–5 now . . . wondering now grown so gracious (and graceful) as to
inspire wonderment.   **26 list not** do not care to

28 to her adheres concerns her   **29 th'argument** the subject matter
31 yet that i.e., yet allow that
4.2. Location: Bohemia. The court of Polixenes.
4 fifteen (Compare "sixteen" at 4.1.6.)   **5 been aired abroad** lived
abroad   **7 feeling** heartfelt   **8 allay** means of abatement.   **o'erween**
am presumptuous enough   **13 want** lack   **18 considered** rewarded
20 heaping friendships accumulation of your kind services and our
mutual affection.   **27 their . . . gracious** if their children behave ungra-
ciously   **28 approved** proved   **31 missingly** being aware that he is
missing   **32 frequent to** devoted to   **34 so much** as much   **35–6 eyes
. . . removedness** spies who keep an eye on him in his absence
37 intelligence news.   **from** away from   **38 homely** simple

that from very nothing, and beyond the imagination
of his neighbors, is grown into an unspeakable estate. 40
CAMILLO   I have heard, sir, of such a man, who hath a
daughter of most rare note. The report of her is 42
extended more than can be thought to begin from
such a cottage.
POLIXENES   That's likewise part of my intelligence; but,
I fear, the angle that plucks our son thither. Thou shalt 46
accompany us to the place, where we will, not appearing what we are, have some question with the shep- 48
herd; from whose simplicity I think it not uneasy to 49
get the cause of my son's resort thither. Prithee, be my
present partner in this business, and lay aside the
thoughts of Sicilia.
CAMILLO   I willingly obey your command.
POLIXENES   My best Camillo! We must disguise ourselves.   *Exit* [*with Camillo*].

4.3

Enter Autolycus, singing.

AUTOLYCUS
    When daffodils begin to peer,   1
        With heigh, the doxy over the dale!   2
    Why, then comes in the sweet o'the year,
        For the red blood reigns in the winter's pale. 4

    The white sheet bleaching on the hedge,
        With heigh, the sweet birds, oh, how they
            sing!
    Doth set my pugging tooth on edge,   7
        For a quart of ale is a dish for a king.   8

    The lark, that tirralirra chants,
        With heigh, with heigh, the thrush and the jay!
    Are summer songs for me and my aunts,   11
        While we lie tumbling in the hay.

I have served Prince Florizel and in my time wore
three-pile, but now I am out of service.   14

    But shall I go mourn for that, my dear?   15
        The pale moon shines by night,
    And when I wander here and there,   17
        I then do most go right.   18

    If tinkers may have leave to live,   19
        And bear the sow-skin budget,   20

Then my account I well may give,   21
    And in the stocks avouch it.   22

My traffic is sheets; when the kite builds, look to lesser 23
linen. My father named me Autolycus, who, being, as 24
I am, littered under Mercury, was likewise a snap- 25
per-up of unconsidered trifles. With die and drab I 26
purchased this caparison, and my revenue is the silly 27
cheat. Gallows and knock are too powerful on the 28
highway; beating and hanging are terrors to me. For 29
the life to come, I sleep out the thought of it. A prize, 30
a prize!

Enter Clown.

CLOWN   Let me see: every 'leven wether tods; every tod 32
yields pound and odd shilling; fifteen hundred shorn,
what comes the wool to?
AUTOLYCUS [*aside*]   If the springe hold, the cock's mine. 35
CLOWN   I cannot do't without counters. Let me see; 36
what am I to buy for our sheepshearing feast? Three
pound of sugar, five pound of currants, rice—what
will this sister of mine do with rice? But my father hath
made her mistress of the feast, and she lays it on. She
hath made me four-and-twenty nosegays for the shear- 41
ers—three-man-song men all, and very good ones; 42
but they are most of them means and basses, but one 43
Puritan amongst them, and he sings psalms to horn- 44
pipes. I must have saffron to color the warden pies; 45
mace; dates?—none, that's out of my note; nutmegs, 46
seven; a race or two of ginger, but that I may beg; four 47
pound of prunes, and as many of raisins o'th' sun. 48
AUTOLYCUS   Oh, that ever I was born! [*He grovels on the
ground.*]
CLOWN   I'th' name of me!   50
AUTOLYCUS   Oh, help me, help me! Pluck but off these
rags, and then death, death!

21 my account an account of myself   **22 in . . . avouch it** i.e., affirm
that I am a tinker if I find myself sitting in the stocks, where vagabonds
often end up. (Autolycus passes himself off as a tinker to mask his real
calling of thief.)   **23–4 when . . . linen** (The kite, a bird of prey, was
thought to carry off small pieces of linen with which to construct its
nest, whereas Autolycus makes off with larger linen or sheets hung out
to dry.)   **24 Autolycus** (Like his namesake, Ulysses's grandfather, the
son of Mercury, this Autolycus is an expert thief.)   **who** (Refers
ambiguously to Autolycus and "My father"; see next note.)   **25 littered under Mercury** (1) sired by Mercury, the god of thieves (2) born
when the planet Mercury was in the ascendant   **26 unconsidered** left
unattended, not worth thinking about   **26–8 With . . . cheat** Gambling
and whoring have brought me to the wearing of these tattered rags,
and my source of income is petty trickery used to cheat simpletons.
28–9 Gallows . . . to me i.e., Hanging and being beaten, the ordinary
hazards of being a highwayman, are too much for me; I'll stick to being
a petty thief.   **29 For** As for   **30 sleep . . . it** i.e., don't give a thought to
punishment in the next world.   **prize** booty   **32 every . . . tods** every
eleven sheep yield a *tod*, i.e., a bulk of wool weighing twenty-eight
pounds   **35 springe** snare.   **cock** woodcock. (A proverbially stupid
bird.)   **36 counters** metal disks used in reckoning.   **41 made me**
made. (*Me* is used colloquially.)   **nosegays** bouquets   **42 three-man-
song men** singers of songs for three male voices: bass, tenor, and treble
43 means tenors   **43–5 but . . . hornpipes** (Puritans were often laughed
at for their pious singing; this Puritan is imagined as singing hymns
even to the sounds of raucous merriment at a fair.)   **45 warden** made
of the warden pear   **46 out of my note** not on my list   **47 race** root
48 o'th' sun dried in the sun.   **50 I'th' name of me!** (An unusual and
perhaps comic oath.)

40 unspeakable beyond description   **42 note** distinction.   **46 angle**
baited fishhook.   **our** (The royal plural; also in *us*, line 47.)   **48 question** talk   **49 uneasy** difficult
4.3. Location: Bohemia. A road near the Shepherd's cottage.
1 peer peep out, appear   **2 doxy** beggar's wench   **4 pale** (1) paleness
(2) domain, region of authority. (The image is of red blood restoring
vitality to a pale complexion.)   **7 set . . . on edge** i.e., whets the
appetite of my thieving tooth, my taste for thieving. (To *pug* is to
"pull, tug.")   **8 quart of ale** (To be paid for perhaps with profits from
theft of sheets.)   **11 aunts** i.e., whores   **14 three-pile** velvet having
very rich pile or nap   **15 for that** i.e., for being out of service
17 wander (i.e., as a thief)   **18 most go right** i.e., live the life that is
meant for me.   **19 leave to live** permission to practice their trade
20 budget tool bag

CLOWN Alack, poor soul! Thou hast need of more rags to lay on thee, rather than have these off.

AUTOLYCUS Oh, sir, the loathsomeness of them offend me more than the stripes I have received, which are mighty ones and millions.

CLOWN Alas, poor man! A million of beating may come to a great matter.

AUTOLYCUS I am robbed, sir, and beaten; my money and apparel ta'en from me, and these detestable things put upon me.

CLOWN What, by a horseman or a footman? 63

AUTOLYCUS A footman, sweet sir, a footman.

CLOWN Indeed, he should be a footman by the garments he has left with thee. If this be a horseman's coat, it hath seen very hot service. Lend me thy hand; I'll help thee. Come, lend me thy hand. [*He helps him up.*]

AUTOLYCUS Oh, good sir, tenderly. Oh!

CLOWN Alas, poor soul!

AUTOLYCUS Oh, good sir, softly, good sir! I fear, sir, my shoulder blade is out.

CLOWN How now? Canst stand?

AUTOLYCUS [*picking his pocket*] Softly, dear sir; good sir, softly. You ha' done me a charitable office.

CLOWN [*reaching for his purse*] Dost lack any money? I have a little money for thee. 76 / 77

AUTOLYCUS No, good sweet sir; no, I beseech you, sir. I have a kinsman not past three quarters of a mile hence, unto whom I was going; I shall there have money or anything I want. Offer me no money, I pray you. That kills my heart.

CLOWN What manner of fellow was he that robbed you?

AUTOLYCUS A fellow, sir, that I have known to go about with troll-my-dames. I knew him once a servant of the Prince. I cannot tell, good sir, for which of his virtues it was, but he was certainly whipped out of the court. 85

CLOWN His vices, you would say. There's no virtue whipped out of the court. They cherish it to make it stay there; and yet it will no more but abide. 90

AUTOLYCUS Vices, I would say, sir. I know this man well. He hath been since an ape bearer, then a process server, a bailiff. Then he compassed a motion of the Prodigal Son and married a tinker's wife within a mile where my land and living lies, and, having flown over many knavish professions, he settled only in rogue. Some call him Autolycus. 92 / 93 / 95

CLOWN Out upon him! Prig, for my life, prig! He haunts wakes, fairs, and bearbaitings. 98 / 99

AUTOLYCUS Very true, sir. He, sir, he. That's the rogue that put me into this apparel.

CLOWN Not a more cowardly rogue in all Bohemia. If you had but looked big and spit at him, he'd have run.

AUTOLYCUS I must confess to you, sir, I am no fighter. I am false of heart that way, and that he knew, I warrant him. 106

CLOWN How do you now?

AUTOLYCUS Sweet sir, much better than I was. I can stand and walk. I will even take my leave of you and pace softly towards my kinsman's. 111

CLOWN Shall I bring thee on the way? 112

AUTOLYCUS No, good-faced sir, no, sweet sir.

CLOWN Then fare thee well. I must go buy spices for our sheepshearing. *Exit.*

AUTOLYCUS Prosper you, sweet sir! Your purse is not hot enough to purchase your spice. I'll be with you at your sheep shearing too. If I make not this cheat bring out another, and the shearers prove sheep, let me be unrolled and my name put in the book of virtue! 116 / 117 / 118 / 119 / 120

Song.

Jog on, jog on, the footpath way,
  And merrily hent the stile-a; 122
A merry heart goes all the day,
  Your sad tires in a mile-a. *Exit.*

❖

4.4

Enter Florizel [in shepherd's garb, and] Perdita [in holiday attire].

FLORIZEL
These your unusual weeds to each part of you 1
Does give a life; no shepherdess, but Flora 2
Peering in April's front. This your sheepshearing 3
Is as a meeting of the petty gods, 4
And you the queen on't.

PERDITA Sir, my gracious lord,
To chide at your extremes it not becomes me. 6
Oh, pardon that I name them! Your high self,
The gracious mark o'th' land, you have obscured 8
With a swain's wearing, and me, poor lowly maid, 9

---

63 horseman highwayman.   **footman** footpad. (As the Clown observes in line 65, a common robber on foot would have poorer clothes than a mounted highwayman.)   **76–7 I have . . . thee** (The Clown reaches for his money and might have discovered the robbery if Autolycus had not quickly begged him not to bother.)   **85 troll-my-dames** or troll-madams (from the French *trou-madame*), a game in which the object was to *troll* balls through arches set on a board. (Autolycus uses the word to suggest women who *troll* or saunter about.)   **90 no more but abide** make only a temporary or unwilling stay.   **92 ape bearer** one who carries a trained monkey about for exhibition   **92–3 process server** sheriff's officer who serves processes or summonses   **93 compassed a motion** devised a puppet show   **95 living** property

98 Prig Thief   **99 wakes** village festivals   **106 false** cowardly
111 softly slowly   **112 bring . . . way** go part of the way with you.
116 Prosper . . . sir! (Said to the departing Clown.)   **116–17 Your . . . spice** i.e., You'll find but a cold purse to pay for your hot spices; an empty purse is a cold one. (Said after the Clown's departure.)
118–19 cheat bring out swindle lead to   **120 unrolled** taken off the roll (of rogues and vagabonds)   **122 hent** take hold of (as a means of leaping over)
4.4. Location: Bohemia. The Shepherd's cottage. (See lines 181–2, 187, etc.)
1 unusual weeds special, holiday attire   **2 Flora** goddess of flowers   **3 Peering . . . front** peeping forth in early April, or, in April's countenance or garb.   **4 petty** minor   **6 extremes** extravagant statements   **8 mark o'th' land** one who is noted and used as a model by everyone   **9 wearing** garb

Most goddesslike pranked up. But that our feasts   10
In every mess have folly, and the feeders   11
Digest it with a custom, I should blush   12
To see you so attired, swoon, I think,
To show myself a glass.

FLORIZEL   I bless the time   14
When my good falcon made her flight across
Thy father's ground.

PERDITA   Now Jove afford you cause!   16
To me the difference forges dread; your greatness   17
Hath not been used to fear. Even now I tremble
To think your father by some accident
Should pass this way as you did. Oh, the Fates!
How would he look to see his work, so noble,   21
Vilely bound up? What would he say? Or how   22
Should I, in these my borrowed flaunts, behold   23
The sternness of his presence?

FLORIZEL   Apprehend
Nothing but jollity. The gods themselves,
Humbling their deities to love, have taken
The shapes of beasts upon them. Jupiter   27
Became a bull, and bellowed; the green Neptune   28
A ram, and bleated; and the fire-robed god,   29
Golden Apollo, a poor humble swain,   30
As I seem now. Their transformations
Were never for a piece of beauty rarer,
Nor in a way so chaste, since my desires   33
Run not before mine honor, nor my lusts
Burn hotter than my faith.

PERDITA   Oh, but sir,
Your resolution cannot hold when 'tis
Opposed, as it must be, by th' power of the King.
One of these two must be necessities,
Which then will speak: that you must change this
    purpose
Or I my life.

FLORIZEL   Thou dearest Perdita,   40
With these forced thoughts, I prithee, darken not   41
The mirth o'th' feast. Or I'll be thine, my fair,   42
Or not my father's. For I cannot be
Mine own, nor anything to any, if
I be not thine. To this I am most constant,
Though destiny say no. Be merry, gentle!   46
Strangle such thoughts as these with anything   47
That you behold the while. Your guests are coming.   48

Lift up your countenance as it were the day   49
Of celebration of that nuptial which
We two have sworn shall come.

PERDITA   O Lady Fortune,
Stand you auspicious!

FLORIZEL   See, your guests approach.
Address yourself to entertain them sprightly,   53
And let's be red with mirth.

[Enter] Shepherd, Clown; Polixenes, Camillo
[disguised]; Mopsa, Dorcas; servants.

SHEPHERD
Fie, daughter! When my old wife lived, upon
This day she was both pantler, butler, cook,   56
Both dame and servant; welcomed all, served all;   57
Would sing her song and dance her turn; now here,
At upper end o'th' table, now i'th' middle;
On his shoulder, and his; her face afire   60
With labor, and the thing she took to quench it   61
She would to each one sip. You are retired,   62
As if you were a feasted one and not
The hostess of the meeting. Pray you, bid
These unknown friends to 's welcome, for it is   65
A way to make us better friends, more known.   66
Come, quench your blushes and present yourself
That which you are, mistress o'th' feast. Come on,
And bid us welcome to your sheepshearing,
As your good flock shall prosper.

PERDITA *[to Polixenes]*   Sir, welcome.
It is my father's will I should take on me
The hostess-ship o'th' day. *[To Camillo]* You're
    welcome, sir.—
Give me those flowers there, Dorcas.—Reverend sirs,
For you there's rosemary and rue; these keep
Seeming and savor all the winter long.   75
Grace and remembrance be to you both,   76
And welcome to our shearing!   *[Giving them flowers.]*

POLIXENES   Shepherdess—
A fair one are you—well you fit our ages
With flowers of winter.

PERDITA   Sir, the year growing ancient,   79
Not yet on summer's death nor on the birth
Of trembling winter, the fairest flow'rs o'th' season
Are our carnations and streaked gillyvors,   82
Which some call nature's bastards. Of that kind   83
Our rustic garden's barren, and I care not
To get slips of them.

POLIXENES   Wherefore, gentle maiden,   85
Do you neglect them?

PERDITA   For I have heard it said   86

---

10 **pranked up** bedecked. **10–12 But . . . custom** Were it not that whenever folks gather for merry feasting one encounters some folly, which the guests take in their stride as to be expected **14 To show . . . glass** if I were to see myself in a mirror. **16 Jove . . . cause!** May Jove grant that you have good reason to be thankful! **17 To me . . . dread** To me, the difference in our social rank is a source of dread **21–2 How . . . bound up?** What would he think to see the nobly-born son he created so vilely outfitted? (The *work,* Florizel, is metaphorically a piece of writing, and his garments are the binding of the book.) **23 flaunts** finery **27–30 Jupiter . . . swain** (Jupiter in the guise of a bull wooed Europa, Neptune disguised as a ram deceived Bisaltes or Theophane [Ovid, *Metamorphoses,* 6.117], and Apollo took the guise of a humble shepherd to enable Admetus to woo Alcestis.) **33 in a way** i.e., pursuing a purpose **40 Or I my life** i.e., or I will be threatened with loss of life (as Polixenes indeed threatens at lines 436–43). **41 forced** farfetched, unnatural **42 Or** Either **46 gentle** i.e., my gentle love. **47–8 Strangle . . . while** i.e., Put down such thoughts by attending to matters at hand.

49 as as if **53 Address** Prepare **56 pantler** pantry servant **57 dame** mistress of the household **60 On his . . . his** at one person's . . . another's **61–2 and . . . sip** and she would toast each one with the drink she took to quench the fire of her labor. **65 to 's** each to his **66 more known** better acquainted. **75 Seeming** outward appearance, color **76 Grace and remembrance** Divine grace and remembrance after death. (Equated respectively with rue and rosemary.) **79 the year . . . ancient** i.e., when autumn arrives **82 gillyvors** gillyflowers, a kind of carnation **83 nature's bastards** i.e., the result of artificial breeding. (See lines 86–8.) **85 slips** cuttings **86 For** Because

There is an art which in their piedness shares 87
With great creating nature.
POLIXENES   Say there be;
Yet nature is made better by no mean 89
But nature makes that mean. So, over that art 90
Which you say adds to nature is an art
That nature makes. You see, sweet maid, we marry
A gentler scion to the wildest stock, 93
And make conceive a bark of baser kind
By bud of nobler race. This is an art
Which does mend nature—change it, rather—but
The art itself is nature.
PERDITA   So it is.
POLIXENES
Then make your garden rich in gillyvors,
And do not call them bastards.
PERDITA   I'll not put
The dibble in earth to set one slip of them, 100
No more than, were I painted, I would wish 101
This youth should say 'twere well, and only therefore
Desire to breed by me. Here's flowers for you:
                            [giving them flowers]
Hot lavender, mints, savory, marjoram, 104
The marigold, that goes to bed wi'th' sun
And with him rises weeping. These are flowers
Of middle summer, and I think they are given 107
To men of middle age. You're very welcome.
CAMILLO
I should leave grazing, were I of your flock,
And only live by gazing.
PERDITA   Out, alas! 110
You'd be so lean that blasts of January
Would blow you through and through. [To Florizel]
      Now, my fair'st friend,
I would I had some flow'rs o'th' spring that might
Become your time of day; [to the Shepherdesses] and
      yours, and yours,
That wear upon your virgin branches yet
Your maidenheads growing. O Proserpina, 116
For the flow'rs now that, frighted, thou let'st fall
From Dis's wagon! Daffodils,
That come before the swallow dares, and take 119
The winds of March with beauty; violets dim, 120
But sweeter than the lids of Juno's eyes
Or Cytherea's breath; pale primroses, 122
That die unmarried ere they can behold

Bright Phoebus in his strength—a malady 124
Most incident to maids; bold oxlips and 125
The crown imperial; lilies of all kinds, 126
The flower-de-luce being one. Oh, these I lack 127
To make you garlands of, and my sweet friend, 128
To strew him o'er and o'er!
FLORIZEL   What, like a corpse?
PERDITA
No, like a bank for Love to lie and play on, 130
Not like a corpse; or if, not to be buried, 131
But quick and in mine arms. Come, take your flowers.
                            [Giving flowers.] 132
Methinks I play as I have seen them do
In Whitsun pastorals. Sure this robe of mine 134
Does change my disposition.
FLORIZEL   What you do
Still betters what is done. When you speak, sweet, 136
I'd have you do it ever. When you sing,
I'd have you buy and sell so, so give alms,
Pray so; and, for the ord'ring your affairs,
To sing them too. When you do dance, I wish you
A wave o'th' sea, that you might ever do
Nothing but that—move still, still so,
And own no other function. Each your doing, 143
So singular in each particular, 144
Crowns what you are doing in the present deeds, 145
That all your acts are queens.
PERDITA   Oh, Doricles, 146
Your praises are too large. But that your youth, 147
And the true blood which peeps fairly through't
Do plainly give you out an unstained shepherd, 149
With wisdom I might fear, my Doricles,
You wooed me the false way.
FLORIZEL   I think you have
As little skill to fear as I have purpose 152
To put you to't. But come, our dance, I pray. 153
Your hand, my Perdita. So turtles pair, 154
That never mean to part.
PERDITA   I'll swear for 'em. 155
                            [They speak apart.]
POLIXENES [to Camillo]
This is the prettiest lowborn lass that ever

---

87 **art** i.e., of crossbreeding.   **piedness** particolored appearance. (Perdita disclaims the art of crossbreeding, since it infringes on what nature itself does so well.)   89 **mean** means   90 **But** unless. (Polixenes's point is that the art of improving on nature is itself natural.) 93 **gentler** nobler, more cultivated   100 **dibble** trowel   101 **painted** made artificially beautiful by cosmetics   104 **Hot** eager, ardent, aromatic (?) (Spices were classified as hot or cold.)   107 **middle summer** (Having no autumn flowers in any case [lines 79–82], since it is too early in the season, Perdita flatters her older guests by giving them flowers appropriate to *middle age*.)   116 **Proserpina** daughter of Ceres, stolen away by Pluto (*Dis*) and taken to Hades when, according to Ovid, she was gathering flowers   119 **take** charm   120 **dim** with hanging heads 122 **Cytherea's** Venus's

124 **Phoebus** the sun-god   124–5 **a malady . . . maids** (Young maids, suffering from greensickness, a kind of anemia, are pale like the primrose.)   126 **crown imperial** flower from the Levant, cultivated in English gardens   127 **flower-de-luce** fleur-de-lis.   **I lack** (Because the season is too late for them.)   128 **To . . . friend** to make garlands of them for you (Polixenes and Camillo) and for my sweet friend (Florizel)   130 **like . . . play on** as if one were strewing a bank where Cupid himself might lie in amorous play   131 **or if** or if like a corpse, that is, a living body   132 **quick** alive   134 **Whitsun pastorals** plays (including Robin Hood plays) and English morris dances often performed at Whitsuntide, seven Sundays after Easter. (The part of Maid Marian strikes Perdita as immodest for her usual behavior.) 136 **Still . . . done** gets better and better.   143 **Each your doing** Each thing you do and how you do it   144 **singular** unique and peerless 145 **Crowns . . . deeds** makes whatever you are doing at the moment seem supremely wonderful   146 **Doricles** (Florizel's disguise name.) 147 **large** lavish.   **But that** Were it not that   149 **give you out** proclaim you to be   152 **skill** reason   153 **To . . . to't** i.e., to woo you "the false way," with intent to seduce you.   154 **turtles** turtledoves, as symbols of faithful love   155 **I'll swear for 'em** i.e., I'll be sworn they do.

Ran on the greensward. Nothing she does or seems   157
But smacks of something greater than herself,
Too noble for this place.
CAMILLO   He tells her something
That makes her blood look out. Good sooth, she is   160
The queen of curds and cream.
CLOWN   Come on, strike up!
DORCAS
Mopsa must be your mistress. Marry, garlic,   162
To mend her kissing with!
MOPSA   Now, in good time!   163
CLOWN
Not a word, a word. We stand upon our manners.   164
Come, strike up!   165

[Music.] Here a dance of shepherds and
shepherdesses.

POLIXENES
Pray, good shepherd, what fair swain is this
Which dances with your daughter?
SHEPHERD
They call him Doricles, and boasts himself   168
To have a worthy feeding; but I have it   169
Upon his own report and I believe it.
He looks like sooth. He says he loves my daughter.   171
I think so too, for never gazed the moon
Upon the water as he'll stand and read,
As 'twere, my daughter's eyes; and, to be plain,
I think there is not half a kiss to choose
Who loves another best.
POLIXENES   She dances featly.   176
SHEPHERD
So she does anything—though I report it
That should be silent. If young Doricles
Do light upon her, she shall bring him that   179
Which he not dreams of.

Enter Servant.

SERVANT   Oh, master, if you did but hear the peddler at
the door, you would never dance again after a tabor   182
and pipe; no, the bagpipe could not move you. He
sings several tunes faster than you'll tell money. He   184
utters them as he had eaten ballads and all men's ears   185
grew to his tunes.
CLOWN   He could never come better. He shall come in.   187
I love a ballad but even too well, if it be doleful matter   188
merrily set down, or a very pleasant thing indeed and   189
sung lamentably.   190
SERVANT   He hath songs for man or woman, of all sizes.   191
No milliner can so fit his customers with gloves. He   192

has the prettiest love songs for maids, so without
bawdry, which is strange, with such delicate burdens   194
of dildos and fadings, "Jump her and thump her"; and   195
where some stretchmouthed rascal would, as it were,   196
mean mischief and break a foul gap into the matter,   197
he makes the maid to answer, "Whoop, do me no
harm, good man"; puts him off, slights him, with
"Whoop, do me no harm, good man."
POLIXENES   This is a brave fellow.   201
CLOWN   Believe me, thou talkest of an admirable con-   202
ceited fellow. Has he any unbraided wares?   203
SERVANT   He hath ribbons of all the colors i'th'
rainbow; points more than all the lawyers in Bohemia   205
can learnedly handle, though they come to him by th'
gross; inkles, caddisses, cambrics, lawns. Why, he   207
sings 'em over as they were gods or goddesses; you
would think a smock were a she-angel, he so chants to   209
the sleevehand and the work about the square on't.   210
CLOWN   Prithee, bring him in, and let him approach
singing.
PERDITA   Forewarn him that he use no scurrilous words
in 's tunes.   *[The Servant goes to the door.]*
CLOWN   You have of these peddlers that have more in   215
them than you'd think, sister.
PERDITA   Ay, good brother, or go about to think.   217

Enter Autolycus, singing.

AUTOLYCUS
Lawn as white as driven snow,
Cyprus black as e'er was crow,   219
Gloves as sweet as damask roses,   220
Masks for faces and for noses,
Bugle bracelet, necklace amber,   222
Perfume for a lady's chamber,
Golden coifs and stomachers,   224
For my lads to give their dears,
Pins and poking-sticks of steel,   226
What maids lack from head to heel,
Come buy of me, come. Come buy, come buy.
Buy, lads, or else your lasses cry.
Come buy.
CLOWN   If I were not in love with Mopsa, thou shouldst

157 greensward grassy turf.   160 makes . . . out makes her blush.
162 mistress i.e., partner in the dance.   163 kissing i.e., bad breath.
(Dorcas jests that even garlic would improve Mopsa's breath.)   in
good time (An expression of indignation.)   164 stand upon set store
by   165.1 dance (Probably a morris dance.)   168 and i.e., and they
say he   169 feeding pasturage, lands   171 He . . . sooth He appears
to be honest.   176 another the other.   featly gracefully.   179 light
upon choose   182 tabor small drum   184 several various.   tell
count   185 as as if. (Also in line 208.)   187 better at a better time.
188 but even too well all too well   189 pleasant merry   190 lamentably mournfully.   191 sizes sorts.   192 milliner vendor of fancy
ware and apparel, including gloves, ribbons, and bonnets

194 burdens refrains   195 dildos and fadings words used as part of
the refrains of ballads. (But with bawdy double meaning unperceived
by the servant, as also in *jump her, thump her, do me no harm,* etc.)
196 stretchmouthed widemouthed, foulmouthed   197 break . . .
matter insert some gross obscenity into the song, or, act in a suggestive way   201 brave excellent   202–3 admirable conceited wonderfully witty and clever   203 unbraided not shopworn, new
205 points (1) laces for fastening clothes (2) headings in an argument
207 inkles . . . lawns linen tapes, worsted tape used for garters, fine
heavy linen fabrics, fine sheer linens.   209 smock petticoat
210 sleevehand wristband.   square on't embroidered bosom or yoke
of the garment.   215 You . . . peddlers You'll find peddlers   217 go
about intend, wish.   217.1 Enter Autolycus (Apparently he is wearing a false beard; later in this scene, he removes it to impersonate a
courtier to the Clown and Shepherd.)   219 Cyprus crepe   220 sweet
i.e., perfumed. (Also in line 249.)   222 Bugle bracelet bracelet of
black glossy beads   224 coifs close-fitting caps.   stomachers
embroidered fronts for ladies' dresses   226 poking-sticks rods used
for ironing and stiffening the plaits of ruffs. (With bawdy suggestion.)

take no money of me, but being enthralled as I am, it 232
will also be the bondage of certain ribbons and gloves. 233

MOPSA   I was promised them against the feast, but they 234
come not too late now.

DORCAS   He hath promised you more than that, or 236
there be liars. 237

MOPSA   He hath paid you all he promised you. Maybe
he has paid you more, which will shame you to give 239
him again. 240

CLOWN   Is there no manners left among maids? Will 241
they wear their plackets where they should bear their 242
faces? Is there not milking time, when you are going to 243
bed, or kilnhole, to whistle of these secrets, but you 244
must be tittle-tattling before all our guests? 'Tis well
they are whisp'ring. Clamor your tongues, and not a 246
word more.

MOPSA   I have done. Come, you promised me a tawdry 248
lace and a pair of sweet gloves. 249

CLOWN   Have I not told thee how I was cozened by the 250
way and lost all my money?

AUTOLYCUS   And indeed, sir, there are cozeners abroad;
therefore it behooves men to be wary.

CLOWN   Fear not thou, man, thou shalt lose nothing
here.

AUTOLYCUS   I hope so, sir, for I have about me many
parcels of charge. 257

CLOWN   What hast here? Ballads?

MOPSA   Pray now, buy some. I love a ballad in print
alife, for then we are sure they are true. 260

AUTOLYCUS   Here's one to a very doleful tune, how a
usurer's wife was brought to bed of twenty moneybags at a burden, and how she longed to eat adders' 263
heads and toads carbonadoed. 264

MOPSA   Is it true, think you?

AUTOLYCUS   Very true, and but a month old.

DORCAS   Bless me from marrying a usurer! 267

AUTOLYCUS   Here's the midwife's name to't, one
Mistress Taleporter, and five or six honest wives that 269
were present. Why should I carry lies abroad?

MOPSA   Pray you now, buy it.

CLOWN   Come on, lay it by, and let's first see more
ballads. We'll buy the other things anon.

AUTOLYCUS   Here's another ballad, of a fish that appeared upon the coast on Wednesday the fourscore of 275
April, forty thousand fathom above water, and sung 276
this ballad against the hard hearts of maids. It was

thought she was a woman and was turned into a cold
fish for she would not exchange flesh with one that 279
loved her. The ballad is very pitiful and as true.

DORCAS   Is it true too, think you?

AUTOLYCUS   Five justices' hands at it, and witnesses 282
more than my pack will hold.

CLOWN   Lay it by too. Another.

AUTOLYCUS   This is a merry ballad, but a very pretty
one.

MOPSA   Let's have some merry ones.

AUTOLYCUS   Why, this is a passing merry one and goes 288
to the tune of "Two Maids Wooing a Man." There's
scarce a maid westward but she sings it. 'Tis in 290
request, I can tell you.

MOPSA   We can both sing it. If thou'lt bear a part, thou
shalt hear; 'tis in three parts.

DORCAS   We had the tune on't a month ago. 294

AUTOLYCUS   I can bear my part; you must know 'tis my
occupation. Have at it with you. 296

Song.

AUTOLYCUS
Get you hence, for I must go
Where it fits not you to know.

DORCAS
      Whither?

MOPSA
            Oh, whither?

DORCAS
                   Whither?

MOPSA
It becomes thy oath full well,
Thou to me thy secrets tell.

DORCAS
      Me too. Let me go thither.

MOPSA
Or thou goest to th' grange or mill. 303

DORCAS
If to either, thou dost ill.

AUTOLYCUS
      Neither.

DORCAS
           What, neither?

AUTOLYCUS
                 Neither.

DORCAS
Thou hast sworn my love to be.

MOPSA
Thou hast sworn it more to me.
    Then whither goest? Say, whither?

CLOWN   We'll have this song out anon by ourselves. 309
My father and the gentlemen are in sad talk, and we'll 310
not trouble them. Come, bring away thy pack after
me. Wenches, I'll buy for you both. Peddler, let's have
the first choice. Follow me, girls.
                   [Exit with Dorcas and Mopsa.]

AUTOLYCUS   And you shall pay well for 'em.
                       [He follows singing.]

232–3 it will . . . bondage it will mean the taking into custody (by means of purchase and tying up into a parcel)   **234 against** in anticipation of, in time for   **236–7 He . . . liars** i.e., He promised to marry
you, too, or else rumor is a liar.   **239 paid you more** i.e., made you
pregnant   **239–40 which . . . again** i.e., which will shame you by giving birth to his child.   **241–3 Will . . . faces?** i.e., Will they always be
talking and revealing personal secrets?   **plackets** slits in petticoats.
(With bawdy suggestion of the pudendum, as in line 613.)   **244 kilnhole** fire hole of a baking oven (where maids might gossip).   **whistle**
whisper   **246 Clamor** i.e., Silence   **248–9 tawdry lace** cheap and
showy lace, or, neckerchief. (So called from St. Audrey's Fair.)
250 cozened cheated   **257 parcels of charge** valuable items.
260 alife on my life   **263 at a burden** in one childbirth   **264 carbonadoed** scored across and grilled.   **267 Bless** God protect, keep
269 Taleporter i.e., talebearer, gossip   **275 fourscore** eightieth (!)
276 forty thousand fathom 240,000 feet

279 exchange flesh have sex   **282 hands at it** signatures on it
288 passing surpassingly   **290 westward** in the West Country
294 on't of it   **296 Have at it** Here goes   **303 Or** Either.   **grange**
farm   **309 have this song out** finish this song   **310 sad** serious

Song.

Will you buy any tape,
Or lace for your cape,
My dainty duck, my dear-a?
  Any silk, any thread,
  And toys for your head,   319
Of the new'st and fin'st, fin'st wear-a?
  Come to the peddler;
  Money's a meddler,   322
That doth utter all men's ware-a.   *Exit.* 323

[*Enter a Servant.*]

SERVANT Master, there is three carters, three shep- 324
herds, three neatherds, three swineherds, that have 325
made themselves all men of hair. They call themselves 326
saultiers, and they have a dance which the wenches say 327
is a gallimaufry of gambols, because they are not in't; 328
but they themselves are o'th' mind, if it be not too
rough for some that know little but bowling, it will 330
please plentifully.

SHEPHERD Away! We'll none on't. Here has been too
much homely foolery already.—I know, sir, we 333
weary you.

POLIXENES You weary those that refresh us. Pray, let's
see these four threes of herdsmen.

SERVANT One three of them, by their own report, sir, 337
hath danced before the King, and not the worst of the
three but jumps twelve foot and a half by the square. 339

SHEPHERD Leave your prating. Since these good men 340
are pleased, let them come in; but quickly now.

SERVANT Why, they stay at door, sir.

[*He goes to the door.*]

Here a dance of twelve Satyrs.

POLIXENES [*to the Shepherd*]
Oh, father, you'll know more of that hereafter.   343
[*To Camillo*] Is it not too far gone? 'Tis time to part
  them.
He's simple and tells much. [*To Florizel*] How now, fair
  shepherd?   345
Your heart is full of something that does take
Your mind from feasting. Sooth, when I was young
And handed love as you do, I was wont   348
To load my she with knacks. I would have ransacked
The peddler's silken treasury and have poured it
To her acceptance; you have let him go,   351
And nothing marted with him. If your lass   352

Interpretation should abuse and call this   353
Your lack of love or bounty, you were straited   354
For a reply, at least if you make a care
Of happy holding her.
FLORIZEL   Old sir, I know   356
She prizes not such trifles as these are.
The gifts she looks from me are packed and locked   358
Up in my heart, which I have given already,
But not delivered. [*To Perdita*] Oh, hear me breathe my
  life   360
Before this ancient sir, who, it should seem,   361
Hath sometime loved! I take thy hand, this hand,
As soft as dove's down and as white as it,
Or Ethiopian's tooth, or the fanned snow that's bolted   364
By th' northern blasts twice o'er.   [*He takes her hand.*]
POLIXENES   What follows this?
How prettily the young swain seems to wash
The hand was fair before! I have put you out.   367
But to your protestation; let me hear   368
What you profess.
FLORIZEL   Do, and be witness to't.
POLIXENES
And this my neighbor too?
FLORIZEL   And he, and more
Than he, and men—the earth, the heavens, and all:
That, were I crowned the most imperial monarch,
Thereof most worthy, were I the fairest youth   373
That ever made eye swerve, had force and knowledge   374
More than was ever man's, I would not prize them
Without her love; for her employ them all,
Commend them and condemn them to her service   377
Or to their own perdition.
POLIXENES   Fairly offered.   378
CAMILLO
This shows a sound affection.
SHEPHERD   But, my daughter,
Say you the like to him?
PERDITA   I cannot speak
So well, nothing so well; no, nor mean better.
By th' pattern of mine own thoughts I cut out   382
The purity of his.
SHEPHERD   Take hands, a bargain!   383
And, friends unknown, you shall bear witness to't:
I give my daughter to him and will make
Her portion equal his.
FLORIZEL   Oh, that must be
I'th' virtue of your daughter. One being dead,   387

---

319 toys trifles   **322 meddler** i.e., go-between in commercial transactions   **323 utter** put on the market   **324 carters** cart drivers
325 neatherds cowherds   **326 of hair** dressed in skins.   **327 saultiers** leapers or vaulters. (With perhaps a play on *Saltiers* as a blunder for "satyrs.")   **328 gallimaufry** jumble   **330 bowling** (A more gentle sport than the vigorous satyr dancing.)   **333 homely** unpolished   **337 three** threesome   **339 by the square** precisely.   **340 Leave** Leave off   **343 Oh, . . . hereafter** (Polixenes completes the conversation he has been having with the old Shepherd during the dance. *Father* is a respectful term of address for older men.)   **345 He's simple** The old Shepherd is guileless   **348 handed** handled, dealt in   **351 To her acceptance** for her to choose   **352 nothing marted with** have done no business with

353 Interpretation should abuse should interpret wrongly   **354 were straited** would be hard-pressed   **356 happy holding her** keeping her happy.   **358 looks** looks for   **360 But not delivered** i.e., but I have not confirmed it by a solemn vow before witnesses, making binding the contract.   **breathe my life** i.e., pronounce eternal vows   **361 this ancient sir** Polixenes   **364 fanned** blown.   **bolted** sifted   **367 was** that was.   **put you out** interrupted what you were saying.   **368 to your protestation** on with your public affirmation   **373 Thereof most worthy** the most worthy of monarchs   **374 swerve** turn in my direction (out of awe and respect)   **377–8 Commend . . . perdition** either commend them to her service, or, failing that, condemn them to deserved destruction.   **382–3 By . . . of his** By the purity of my own thoughts I can define the purity of his. (A metaphor of clothesmaking; Perdita has formed her own thoughts on the model of his.)   **387 One being dead** When a certain person dies

I shall have more than you can dream of yet;
Enough then for your wonder. But come on: 389
Contract us 'fore these witnesses.
SHEPHERD   Come, your hand;
And, daughter, yours.
POLIXENES   Soft, swain, awhile, beseech you.   391
Have you a father?
FLORIZEL   I have, but what of him?
POLIXENES   Knows he of this?
FLORIZEL   He neither does nor shall.
POLIXENES   Methinks a father
Is at the nuptial of his son a guest
That best becomes the table. Pray you, once more,
Is not your father grown incapable
Of reasonable affairs? Is he not stupid   400
With age and altering rheums? Can he speak? Hear?   401
Know man from man? Dispute his own estate?   402
Lies he not bedrid, and again does nothing
But what he did being childish?
FLORIZEL   No, good sir,   404
He has his health and ampler strength indeed
Than most have of his age.
POLIXENES   By my white beard,
You offer him, if this be so, a wrong
Something unfilial. Reason my son   408
Should choose himself a wife, but as good reason
The father, all whose joy is nothing else
But fair posterity, should hold some counsel   411
In such a business.
FLORIZEL   I yield all this;   412
But for some other reasons, my grave sir,
Which 'tis not fit you know, I not acquaint
My father of this business.
POLIXENES   Let him know't.
FLORIZEL
He shall not.
POLIXENES   Prithee, let him.
FLORIZEL   No, he must not.
SHEPHERD
Let him, my son. He shall not need to grieve
At knowing of thy choice.
FLORIZEL   Come, come, he must not.
Mark our contract.
POLIXENES [discovering himself]   Mark your divorce,
     young sir,
Whom son I dare not call. Thou art too base
To be acknowledged. Thou a scepter's heir,
That thus affects a sheephook?—Thou old traitor,   422
I am sorry that by hanging thee I can
But shorten thy life one week.—And thou, fresh piece

Of excellent witchcraft, who of force must know   425
The royal fool thou cop'st with—
SHEPHERD   Oh, my heart!   426
POLIXENES
I'll have thy beauty scratched with briers and made
More homely than thy state.—For thee, fond boy,   428
If I may ever know thou dost but sigh
That thou no more shalt see this knack—as never   430
I mean thou shalt—we'll bar thee from succession,
Not hold thee of our blood, no, not our kin,
Farre than Deucalion off. Mark thou my words.   433
Follow us to the court.—Thou churl, for this time,   434
Though full of our displeasure, yet we free thee
From the dead blow of it.—And you, enchantment,   436
Worthy enough a herdsman—yea, him too,   437
That makes himself, but for our honor therein,   438
Unworthy thee—if ever henceforth thou   439
These rural latches to his entrance open,
Or hoop his body more with thy embraces,
I will devise a death as cruel for thee
As thou art tender to't.   *Exit.*
PERDITA   Even here undone!
I was not much afeard; for once or twice
I was about to speak and tell him plainly
The selfsame sun that shines upon his court
Hides not his visage from our cottage, but
Looks on alike. Will't please you, sir, begone?   448
I told you what would come of this. Beseech you,
Of your own state take care. This dream of mine—
Being now awake, I'll queen it no inch farther,
But milk my ewes and weep.
CAMILLO   Why, how now, father?
Speak ere thou diest.
SHEPHERD   I cannot speak, nor think,   453
Nor dare to know that which I know. [*To Florizel*] Oh,
     sir,
You have undone a man of fourscore three,
That thought to fill his grave in quiet, yea,
To die upon the bed my father died,   457
To lie close by his honest bones; but now
Some hangman must put on my shroud and lay me
Where no priest shovels in dust. [*To Perdita*] Oh,
     cursed wretch,
That knew'st this was the Prince, and wouldst adven-
     ture
To mingle faith with him! Undone, undone!   462
If I might die within this hour, I have lived
To die when I desire.   *Exit.*
FLORIZEL [*to Perdita*]   Why look you so upon me?

---

389 Enough . . . wonder there will be enough then for you to wonder at.   **391 Soft** Wait a minute   **400 reasonable affairs** matters requiring the use of reason.   **401 altering rheums** weakening catarrhs or other diseases.   **402 Dispute** Discuss.   **estate** affairs, condition.   **404 being childish** when he was a child.   **408 Something** somewhat.   **Reason my son** It is reasonable that my son. (The disguised Polixenes seems to be speaking hypothetically, using himself as an example, but of course the application to Florizel is direct.)   **411 hold some counsel** be consulted   **412 yield** concede   **422 affects** desires, shows inclination for

425 of force of necessity   **426 thou cop'st** you deal   **428 homely** (1) unattractive (2) humble.   **fond** foolish   **430 knack** trifle, schemer   **433 Farre . . . off** farther in kinship than Deucalion (the Noah of classical legend and hence the primal, distant ancestor of the whole human race).   **434 churl** i.e., the Shepherd   **436 dead** deadly.   **enchantment** i.e., Perdita   **437–9 him too . . . thee** worthy indeed of him (Florizel) whose behavior renders him unworthy even of you, if we were to set aside for the moment the question of the dignity of our royal house   **448 alike** both alike.   **453 ere thou diest** before you die of grief (?). (Although Polixenes has relented of his threat to hang the Shepherd, the Shepherd is gloomily sure it will come to a hanging, lines 459–60.)   **457 died** died on   **462 mingle faith** exchange pledges

I am but sorry, not afeard; delayed,
But nothing altered. What I was, I am,
More straining on for plucking back, not following   468
My leash unwillingly.

CAMILLO   Gracious my lord,
You know your father's temper. At this time
He will allow no speech, which I do guess
You do not purpose to him; and as hardly
Will he endure your sight as yet, I fear.
Then, till the fury of His Highness settle,
Come not before him.

FLORIZEL   I not purpose it.
I think Camillo?

CAMILLO   Even he, my lord.

PERDITA
How often have I told you 'twould be thus?
How often said my dignity would last   478
But till 'twere known?

FLORIZEL   It cannot fail but by
The violation of my faith; and then   480
Let nature crush the sides o'th'earth together
And mar the seeds within! Lift up thy looks.   482
From my succession wipe me, father; I   483
Am heir to my affection.

CAMILLO   Be advised.   484

FLORIZEL
I am, and by my fancy. If my reason   485
Will thereto be obedient, I have reason;   486
If not, my senses, better pleased with madness,
Do bid it welcome.

CAMILLO   This is desperate, sir.

FLORIZEL
So call it, but it does fulfill my vow;
I needs must think it honesty. Camillo,
Not for Bohemia nor the pomp that may
Be thereat gleaned, for all the sun sees or
The close earth wombs or the profound seas hides   493
In unknown fathoms, will I break my oath
To this my fair beloved. Therefore, I pray you,
As you have ever been my father's honored friend,
When he shall miss me—as, in faith, I mean not
To see him any more—cast your good counsels
Upon his passion. Let myself and fortune   499
Tug for the time to come. This you may know   500
And so deliver: I am put to sea   501
With her who here I cannot hold on shore;   502
And most opportune to our need I have
A vessel rides fast by, but not prepared   504

For this design. What course I mean to hold
Shall nothing benefit your knowledge nor   506
Concern me the reporting.

CAMILLO   Oh, my lord,   507
I would your spirit were easier for advice,   508
Or stronger for your need.

FLORIZEL   Hark, Perdita.
[To Camillo] I'll hear you by and by.
                        [He draws Perdita aside.]

CAMILLO [aside]   He's irremovable,   510
Resolved for flight. Now were I happy if
His going I could frame to serve my turn,   512
Save him from danger, do him love and honor,
Purchase the sight again of dear Sicilia
And that unhappy king, my master, whom
I so much thirst to see.

FLORIZEL   Now, good Camillo,
I am so fraught with curious business that   517
I leave out ceremony.

CAMILLO   Sir, I think   518
You have heard of my poor services i'th' love
That I have borne your father?

FLORIZEL   Very nobly
Have you deserved. It is my father's music
To speak your deeds, not little of his care
To have them recompensed as thought on.

CAMILLO   Well, my lord, 523
If you may please to think I love the King
And through him what's nearest to him, which is
Your gracious self, embrace but my direction,   526
If your more ponderous and settled project   527
May suffer alteration. On mine honor,   528
I'll point you where you shall have such receiving
As shall become Your Highness, where you may   530
Enjoy your mistress—from the whom I see
There's no disjunction to be made but by,
As heavens forfend, your ruin—marry her,   533
And, with my best endeavors in your absence   534
Your discontenting father strive to qualify   535
And bring him up to liking.

FLORIZEL   How, Camillo,   536
May this, almost a miracle, be done,
That I may call thee something more than man,
And after that trust to thee?

CAMILLO   Have you thought on   539
A place whereto you'll go?

FLORIZEL   Not any yet.
But as th'unthought-on accident is guilty   541
To what we wildly do, so we profess   542

468 **More . . . back** i.e., like a hound on the leash, all the more eager to go forward for being restrained   478 **my dignity** i.e., the new status this marriage would have offered   480 **then** when that happens   482 **mar the seeds within** i.e., destroy the very sources of life on earth (since all material life was thought to be derived from *seeds*).   483 **From . . . father** (Florizel apostrophizes the absent Polixenes.) 483–4 **I . . . affection** i.e., I will be content with my passionate love for Perdita in place of my inheritance.   **Be advised** Think carefully, be receptive to wise advice.   485 **fancy** love.   486 **have reason** (1) will be reasonable (2) will be sane.   493 **wombs** encloses, conceals 499 **passion** anger.   500 **Tug** contend   501 **deliver** report   502 **who** whom   504 **rides** that rides at anchor.   **but** though

506–7 **Shall . . . reporting** would not behoove you to know nor me to report.   508 **easier for** more open to   510 **irremovable** immovable 512 **frame** shape   517 **curious** demanding care   518 **I . . . ceremony** (Florizel apologizes for failing to observe proper ceremony toward Camillo under the pressures of the present crisis.)   523 **as thought on** as deservingly as they merit.   526 **embrace . . . direction** simply follow my advice   527 **ponderous** weighty   528 **suffer** permit   530 **become Your Highness** suit your royal rank, suit Your Highness   533 **forfend** forbid   534 **with** together with   535 **discontenting** discontented, displeased.   **qualify** appease, pacify   536 **bring . . . liking** get him to the point of approval.   539 **after** ever after   541–2 **as . . . wildly do** just as the unexpected happening (e.g., of our being discovered by the King) is responsible for what we rashly do at this point

Ourselves to be the slaves of chance and flies   543
Of every wind that blows.

CAMILLO   Then list to me.
This follows, if you will not change your purpose
But undergo this flight: make for Sicilia,
And there present yourself and your fair princess—
For so I see she must be—'fore Leontes.
She shall be habited as it becomes   549
The partner of your bed. Methinks I see
Leontes opening his free arms and weeping   551
His welcomes forth; asks thee there "Son,
   forgiveness!"
As 'twere i'th' father's person; kisses the hands
Of your fresh princess; o'er and o'er divides him   554
Twixt his unkindness and his kindness. Th'one   555
He chides to hell, and bids the other grow
Faster than thought or time.

FLORIZEL   Worthy Camillo,   557
What color for my visitation shall I   558
Hold up before him?

CAMILLO   Sent by the King your father   559
To greet him and to give him comforts. Sir,
The manner of your bearing towards him, with
What you, as from your father, shall deliver—   562
Things known betwixt us three—I'll write you down,
The which shall point you forth at every sitting   564
What you must say, that he shall not perceive
But that you have your father's bosom there   566
And speak his very heart.

FLORIZEL   I am bound to you.
There is some sap in this.

CAMILLO   A course more promising
Than a wild dedication of yourselves
To unpathed waters, undreamed shores, most certain
To miseries enough; no hope to help you,
But as you shake off one to take another;   572
Nothing so certain as your anchors, who   573
Do their best office if they can but stay you   574
Where you'll be loath to be. Besides, you know   575
Prosperity's the very bond of love,   576
Whose fresh complexion and whose heart together   577
Affliction alters.

PERDITA   One of these is true: 578
I think affliction may subdue the cheek,   579
But not take in the mind.

CAMILLO   Yea, say you so?   580

There shall not at your father's house these seven
   years   581
Be born another such.

FLORIZEL   My good Camillo,
She's as forward of her breeding as she is   583
I'th' rear 'our birth.   584

CAMILLO   I cannot say 'tis pity
She lacks instructions, for she seems a mistress   585
To most that teach.

PERDITA   Your pardon, sir; for this
I'll blush you thanks.

FLORIZEL   My prettiest Perdita!
But oh, the thorns we stand upon! Camillo,
Preserver of my father, now of me,
The medicine of our house, how shall we do?
We are not furnished like Bohemia's son,
Nor shall appear so in Sicilia.

CAMILLO   My lord,
Fear none of this. I think you know my fortunes
Do all lie there. It shall be so my care
To have you royally appointed as if   595
The scene you play were mine. For instance, sir,
That you may know you shall not want, one word.

                    [*They talk aside.*]

Enter Autolycus.

AUTOLYCUS   Ha, ha, what a fool Honesty is! And Trust,
his sworn brother, a very simple gentleman! I have
sold all my trumpery; not a counterfeit stone, not a
ribbon, glass, pomander, brooch, table book, ballad,   601
knife, tape, glove, shoe tie, bracelet, horn ring, to
keep my pack from fasting. They throng who should   603
buy first, as if my trinkets had been hallowed and   604
brought a benediction to the buyer; by which means
I saw whose purse was best in picture, and what I   606
saw, to my good use I remembered. My clown, who
wants but something to be a reasonable man, grew so   608
in love with the wenches' song that he would not stir
his pettitoes till he had both tune and words, which   610
so drew the rest of the herd to me that all their other
senses stuck in ears. You might have pinched a   612
placket, it was senseless. 'Twas nothing to geld a cod-   613
piece of a purse. I could have filed keys off that hung   614
in chains. No hearing, no feeling, but my sir's song,   615
and admiring the nothing of it. So that in this time of   616
lethargy I picked and cut most of their festival purses;
and had not the old man come in with hubbub

---

543 flies i.e., insignificant insects, blown about by the winds of chance
549 habited (richly) dressed   **551 free** generous, noble   **554 fresh**
young and beautiful   **554–5 divides . . . kindness** divides his speech
between his former unkindness (which he condemns) and his present
intention of kindness.   **557 Faster** firmer; also, more swiftly
558 color excuse, pretext   **559 Hold up before** present to.   **Sent** i.e.,
Say you are sent   **562 deliver** say   **564 point you forth** indicate to
you.   **sitting** conference   **566 bosom** inmost thoughts   **572 one** one
misery, one misfortune   **take** encounter   **573 Nothing** not at all.
573–5 who . . . to be which are doing as well as can be hoped if they
simply hold you in some undesirable place (rather than allowing you
to proceed on toward even greater disaster).   **576–8 Prosperity's . . .**
alters i.e., young love flourishes while things are going well but loses
its fresh complexion and strength of feeling under the test of adversity.   **579 subdue the cheek** make the complexion look pale and
wasted   **580 take in** overcome

581 your father's (Said either to Florizel or Perdita.)   **these seven**
years i.e., for a long time to come. (Camillo's point is that she is a
nonpareil.)   **583 forward . . . breeding** far in advance of her lowly
upbringing   **584 I'th' rear 'our** below me in   **585 instructions** formal
schooling.   **a mistress** a teacher   **595 appointed** equipped, outfitted
601 pomander scent-ball.   **table book** notebook   **603 from fasting**
i.e., from being empty.   **604 hallowed** made sacred, like a relic
606 best in picture i.e., best to look at, most promising   **608 wants**
but something lacks one thing only (i.e., intelligence)   **610 pettitoes**
pig's toes; here, toes   **612 stuck in ears** were occupied with hearing.
613 placket (Literally, slit in a petticoat; with bawdy suggestion.)
senseless insensible.   **613–14 geld . . . purse** cut a purse loose from
the pouch worn at the front of a man's breeches   **615 my sir's** i.e., the
Clown's   **616 nothing** (1) vacuity (2) noting, tune. (*Nothing* and
noting were sounded alike in Elizabethan English.)

against his daughter and the King's son and scared my
choughs from the chaff, I had not left a purse alive in 620
the whole army.

[*Camillo, Florizel, and Perdita come forward.*]

CAMILLO
Nay, but my letters, by this means being there
So soon as you arrive, shall clear that doubt.
FLORIZEL
And those that you'll procure from King Leontes—
CAMILLO
Shall satisfy your father.
PERDITA   Happy be you!
All that you speak shows fair.
CAMILLO [*seeing Autolycus*]   Who have we here?
We'll make an instrument of this, omit
Nothing may give us aid.   628
AUTOLYCUS [*aside*]   If they have overheard me now,
why, hanging.
CAMILLO   How now, good fellow? Why shak'st thou so?
Fear not, man, here's no harm intended to thee.
AUTOLYCUS   I am a poor fellow, sir.
CAMILLO   Why, be so still. Here's nobody will steal that
from thee. Yet for the outside of thy poverty we must 635
make an exchange. Therefore discase thee instantly— 636
thou must think there's a necessity in't—and change 637
garments with this gentleman. Though the penny- 638
worth on his side be the worst, yet hold thee, there's 639
some boot.   [*He gives money.*] 640
AUTOLYCUS   I am a poor fellow, sir. [*Aside*] I know ye
well enough.
CAMILLO   Nay, prithee, dispatch. The gentleman is half 643
flayed already.   644
AUTOLYCUS   Are you in earnest, sir? [*Aside*] I smell the
trick on't.
FLORIZEL   Dispatch, I prithee.
AUTOLYCUS   Indeed, I have had earnest, but I cannot 648
with conscience take it.
CAMILLO   Unbuckle, unbuckle.
        [*Florizel and Autolycus exchange garments.*]
Fortunate mistress—let my prophecy   651
Come home to ye!—you must retire yourself   652
Into some covert. Take your sweetheart's hat   653
And pluck it o'er your brows, muffle your face,
Dismantle you, and, as you can, disliken   655
The truth of your own seeming, that you may—   656
For I do fear eyes—over to shipboard   657
Get undescried.
PERDITA   I see the play so lies
That I must bear a part.
CAMILLO   No remedy.—

Have you done there?
FLORIZEL   Should I now meet my father,
He would not call me son.
CAMILLO   Nay, you shall have no hat.
                                    [*He gives it to Perdita.*]
Come, lady, come. Farewell, my friend.
AUTOLYCUS   Adieu, sir.
FLORIZEL
Oh, Perdita, what have we twain forgot?
Pray you, a word.   [*They speak aside.*]
CAMILLO [*aside*]
What I do next shall be to tell the King
Of this escape and whither they are bound;
Wherein my hope is I shall so prevail
To force him after, in whose company
I shall re-view Sicilia, for whose sight   670
I have a woman's longing.
FLORIZEL   Fortune speed us!
Thus we set on, Camillo, to th' seaside.
CAMILLO   The swifter speed the better.
                        Exit [*with Florizel and Perdita*].
AUTOLYCUS   I understand the business; I hear it. To
have an open ear, a quick eye, and a nimble hand is
necessary for a cutpurse; a good nose is requisite also,
to smell out work for th'other senses. I see this is the
time that the unjust man doth thrive. What an
exchange had this been without boot! What a boot is 679
here with this exchange! Sure the gods do this year
connive at us, and we may do anything extempore. 681
The Prince himself is about a piece of iniquity, stealing 682
away from his father with his clog at his heels. If I 683
thought it were a piece of honesty to acquaint the King
withal, I would not do't. I hold it the more knavery to 685
conceal it; and therein am I constant to my profession.

        Enter Clown and Shepherd [*carrying a bundle and
        a box*].

Aside, aside! Here is more matter for a hot brain.
Every lane's end, every shop, church, session, hang- 688
ing, yields a careful man work.   [*He stands aside.*]
CLOWN   See, see, what a man you are now! There is no
other way but to tell the King she's a changeling and 691
none of your flesh and blood.
SHEPHERD   Nay, but hear me.
CLOWN   Nay, but hear me.
SHEPHERD   Go to, then.   695
CLOWN   She being none of your flesh and blood, your
flesh and blood has not offended the King, and so
your flesh and blood is not to be punished by him.
Show those things you found about her, those secret
things, all but what she has with her. This being done,
let the law go whistle, I warrant you.
SHEPHERD   I will tell the King all, every word, yea, and
his son's pranks too; who, I may say, is no honest

---

620 **choughs** jackdaws   628 **Nothing** nothing that   635 **the outside . . .
poverty** i.e., your ragged clothing   636 **discase** undress   637 **think**
understand   638–9 **pennyworth** i.e., value of the bargain   640 **some
boot** something in addition.   643 **dispatch** hurry. (Also in line 647.)
644 **flayed** skinned, i.e., undressed   648 **earnest** advance payment.
(Playing on *in earnest* in line 645.)   651–2 **let . . . to ye!** i.e., let my
prophecy that you, Perdita, will be fortunate be fulfilled for you!
653 **covert** hidden place.   655–6 **as you . . . seeming** as much as you
can, disguise your outward appearance   657 **eyes** spying eyes

670 **re-view** see again   679 **without boot** i.e., even without added
payment.   **What a boot** What a profit   681 **connive at** look indul-
gently at   682 **about** engaged in   683 **clog** encumbrance (i.e.,
Perdita)   685 **withal** with it   688 **session** court session   691
changeling child left by the fairies   695 **Go to** Go ahead. (Or, an
expression of impatience.)

man, neither to his father nor to me, to go about to 704
make me the King's brother-in-law.

CLOWN   Indeed, brother-in-law was the farthest off you
could have been to him, and then your blood had
been the dearer by I know not how much an ounce.

AUTOLYCUS [*aside*]   Very wisely, puppies!

SHEPHERD   Well, let us to the King. There is that in this
fardel will make him scratch his beard.   711

AUTOLYCUS [*aside*]   I know not what impediment this
complaint may be to the flight of my master.   713

CLOWN   Pray heartily he be at' palace.   714

AUTOLYCUS [*aside*]   Though I am not naturally honest,
I am so sometimes by chance. Let me pocket up my
peddler's excrement. [*He takes off his false beard.*] How 717
now, rustics, whither are you bound?

SHEPHERD   To the palace, an it like Your Worship.   719

AUTOLYCUS   Your affairs there, what, with whom, the
condition of that fardel, the place of your dwelling, 721
your names, your ages, of what having, breeding, and 722
anything that is fitting to be known, discover.   723

CLOWN   We are but plain fellows, sir.   724

AUTOLYCUS   A lie; you are rough and hairy. Let me have
no lying. It becomes none but tradesmen, and they
often give us soldiers the lie, but we pay them for it 727
with stamped coin, not stabbing steel; therefore they
do not give us the lie.   729

CLOWN   Your Worship had like to have given us one, if 730
you had not taken yourself with the manner.   731

SHEPHERD   Are you a courtier, an't like you, sir?

AUTOLYCUS   Whether it like me or no, I am a courtier.
See'st thou not the air of the court in these enfoldings? 734
Hath not my gait in it the measure of the court? Re- 735
ceives not thy nose court odor from me? Reflect I not
on thy baseness court contempt? Think'st thou, for 737
that I insinuate to toze from thee thy business, I am 738
therefore no courtier? I am courtier cap-à-pie, and one 739
that will either push on or pluck back thy business
there. Whereupon I command thee to open thy affair. 741

SHEPHERD   My business, sir, is to the King.

AUTOLYCUS   What advocate hast thou to him?

SHEPHERD   I know not, an't like you.

CLOWN [*aside to Shepherd*]   "Advocate" 's the court
word for a pheasant. Say you have none.   746

SHEPHERD   None, sir. I have no pheasant, cock nor hen.

AUTOLYCUS [*aside*]
How blessed are we that are not simple men!
Yet nature might have made me as these are;
Therefore I will not disdain.

CLOWN [*to Shepherd*]   This cannot be but a great courtier.

SHEPHERD   His garments are rich, but he wears them
not handsomely.

CLOWN   He seems to be the more noble in being fantas- 755
tical. A great man, I'll warrant. I know by the picking 756
on's teeth.   757

AUTOLYCUS   The fardel there? What's i'th' fardel?
Wherefore that box?

SHEPHERD   Sir, there lies such secrets in this fardel and
box which none must know but the King, and which
he shall know within this hour if I may come to the
speech of him.

AUTOLYCUS   Age, thou hast lost thy labor.   764

SHEPHERD   Why, sir?

AUTOLYCUS   The King is not at the palace. He is gone
aboard a new ship to purge melancholy and air
himself; for, if thou be'st capable of things serious, 768
thou must know the King is full of grief.

SHEPHERD   So 'tis said, sir; about his son, that should
have married a shepherd's daughter.

AUTOLYCUS   If that shepherd be not in handfast, let him 772
fly. The curses he shall have, the tortures he shall feel,
will break the back of man, the heart of monster.

CLOWN   Think you so, sir?

AUTOLYCUS   Not he alone shall suffer what wit can make 776
heavy and vengeance bitter, but those that are ger- 777
mane to him, though removed fifty times, shall all 778
come under the hangman—which, though it be great
pity, yet it is necessary. An old sheep-whistling rogue, 780
a ram tender, to offer to have his daughter come into 781
grace? Some say he shall be stoned; but that death is 782
too soft for him, say I. Draw our throne into a sheep- 783
cote? All deaths are too few, the sharpest too easy.   784

CLOWN   Has the old man e'er a son, sir, do you hear,
an't like you, sir?

AUTOLYCUS   He has a son, who shall be flayed alive; then,
'nointed over with honey, set on the head of a wasp's
nest; then stand till he be three-quarters and a dram 789
dead; then recovered again with aqua vitae or some 790
other hot infusion; then, raw as he is, in the hot-
test day prognostication proclaims, shall he be set 792
against a brick wall, the sun looking with a southward
eye upon him, where he is to behold him with flies 794
blown to death. But what talk we of these traitorly ras- 795
cals, whose miseries are to be smiled at, their offenses

---

704 go about make it his object   **711 fardel** bundle   **713 my master**
i.e., Florizel. (See 4.3.13.)   **714 at'** at the   **717 excrement** outgrowth of
hair, beard.   **719 an it like** if it please   **721 condition** nature
722 having property   **723 discover** reveal.   **724 plain** simple. (But
Autolycus plays on the meaning "smooth.")   **727 give . . . lie** i.e.,
cheat us. (But *giving the lie* also means to accuse a person to his face of
lying, an affront which a soldier would repay with *stabbing steel*.)
729 give (Autolycus punningly observes that, since soldiers pay
tradesmen for their wares, the tradesmen cannot be said to have *given*
the lie, and so a duel is avoided.)   **730 had like** was about   **731 taken
. . . manner** i.e., caught yourself in the act, stopped short. (The Clown
observes that Autolycus has once again avoided the "giving of the lie"
and its consequences in a duel by his clever equivocation. Compare
with Touchstone in *As You Like It*, 5.4.)   **734 enfoldings** clothes.   **735
measure** stately tread   **737–8 for that . . . business** because I undertake to pry out of you what your business may be   **739 cap-à-pie**
from head to foot   **741 open** reveal   **746 pheasant** (The rustics suppose that Autolycus has asked them what gift they propose to present
as a bribe, as one might do to a judge in a court of law.)

755–6 fantastical eccentric.   **756–7 picking on's teeth** (A stylish
affectation in Shakespeare's time.)   **764 Age** Old man   **768 be'st
capable of** know anything about   **772 handfast** custody. (With a play
on "betrothal.")   **776 wit** ingenuity (in devising tortures)   **777–8 ger-
mane** related   **780 sheep-whistling** tending sheep by whistling after
them   **781 offer** dare   **782 grace** favor.   **783–4 sheepcote** pen for
sheep   **789 a dram** i.e., a small amount, a fraction   **790 aqua vitae**
brandy   **792 prognostication** forecasting (in the almanac)   **794 he**
i.e., the sun   **795 blown** swollen.   **what** i.e., why

being so capital? Tell me, for you seem to be honest
plain men, what you have to the King. Being some- 798
thing gently considered, I'll bring you where he is 799
aboard, tender your persons to his presence, whisper 800
him in your behalfs; and if it be in man besides the
King to effect your suits, here is man shall do it.

CLOWN [*to Shepherd*]   He seems to be of great authority.
Close with him, give him gold; and though authority 804
be a stubborn bear, yet he is oft led by the nose
with gold. Show the inside of your purse to the outside of his hand, and no more ado. Remember—
"stoned," and "flayed alive."

SHEPHERD   An't please you, sir, to undertake the
business for us, here is that gold I have. [*He offers
money.*] I'll make it as much more and leave this young
man in pawn till I bring it you.   812

AUTOLYCUS   After I have done what I promised?

SHEPHERD   Ay, sir.

AUTOLYCUS [*taking the money*]   Well, give me the moiety. 815
[*To the Clown*] Are you a party in this business?

CLOWN   In some sort, sir. But, though my case be a piti- 817
ful one, I hope I shall not be flayed out of it.

AUTOLYCUS   Oh, that's the case of the shepherd's son.
Hang him, he'll be made an example.

CLOWN [*to Shepherd*]   Comfort, good comfort! We must
to the King and show our strange sights. He must
know 'tis none of your daughter nor my sister; we are
gone else.—Sir, I will give you as much as this old 824
man does when the business is performed, and
remain, as he says, your pawn till it be brought you.

AUTOLYCUS   I will trust you. Walk before toward the
seaside; go on the right hand. I will but look upon the 828
hedge and follow you.   829

CLOWN [*to Shepherd*]   We are blessed in this man, as I
may say, even blessed.

SHEPHERD   Let's before, as he bids us. He was provided
to do us good.   *Exeunt* [*Shepherd and Clown*].

AUTOLYCUS   If I had a mind to be honest, I see Fortune
would not suffer me; she drops booties in my mouth.
I am courted now with a double occasion: gold, and a 836
means to do the Prince my master good, which who
knows how that may turn back to my advancement? I 838
will bring these two moles, these blind ones, aboard 839
him. If he think it fit to shore them again and that the 840
complaint they have to the King concerns him noth- 841
ing, let him call me rogue for being so far officious, for 842
I am proof against that title and what shame else 843
belongs to't. To him will I present them. There may be
matter in it.   [*Exit.*]

5.1

*Enter Leontes, Cleomenes, Dion, Paulina, [and]
servants.*

CLEOMENES
Sir, you have done enough, and have performed
A saintlike sorrow. No fault could you make
Which you have not redeemed—indeed, paid down
More penitence than done trespass. At the last,
Do as the heavens have done: forget your evil.
With them, forgive yourself.

LEONTES   Whilst I remember
Her and her virtues, I cannot forget
My blemishes in them, and so still think of   8
The wrong I did myself, which was so much
That heirless it hath made my kingdom and
Destroyed the sweet'st companion that e'er man
Bred his hopes out of. True?

PAULINA   Too true, my lord.
If one by one you wedded all the world,
Or from the all that are took something good   14
To make a perfect woman, she you killed
Would be unparalleled.

LEONTES   I think so. Killed?
She I killed? I did so, but thou strik'st me
Sorely to say I did. It is as bitter
Upon thy tongue as in my thought. Now, good now, 19
Say so but seldom.

CLEOMENES   Not at all, good lady.
You might have spoken a thousand things that would
Have done the time more benefit and graced
Your kindness better.

PAULINA   You are one of those
Would have him wed again.

DION   If you would not so,
You pity not the state nor the remembrance   25
Of his most sovereign name, consider little   26
What dangers by His Highness' fail of issue   27
May drop upon his kingdom and devour
Incertain lookers-on. What were more holy   29
Than to rejoice the former queen is well?   30
What holier than, for royalty's repair,
For present comfort and for future good,
To bless the bed of majesty again
With a sweet fellow to't?

PAULINA   There is none worthy,
Respecting her that's gone. Besides, the gods   35
Will have fulfilled their secret purposes;   36
For has not the divine Apollo said,
Is't not the tenor of his oracle,
That King Leontes shall not have an heir

---

798 what you have to what business you have with   **798–9 Being . . .
considered** i.e., (1) Being a gentleman of some influence (2) If I receive
a gentlemanly consideration, a bribe   **800 tender your persons** introduce you   **804 Close with him** Accept his offer   **812 in pawn** as
security   **815 moiety** half.   **817 case** (1) cause (2) skin   **824 gone
else** undone otherwise.   **828–9 look . . . hedge** i.e., relieve myself
836 occasion opportunity   **838 turn back** redound   **839–40 aboard
him** i.e., to him (Prince Florizel) aboard his ship.   **840 shore** put
ashore   **841–2 nothing** not at all   **843 proof against** invulnerable to

5.1. Location: Sicilia. The royal court.
8 in them in comparison with them   **14 the all that are** all the women
that there are   **19 good now** i.e., if you please   **25 nor the remembrance** i.e., nor give consideration to the perpetuation (through bearing a child and heir)   **26 consider** you consider   **27 fail of issue**
failure to produce an heir   **29 Incertain** not knowing what to think or
do (about the royal succession)   **30 well** happy, at rest (in heaven).
35 Respecting in comparison with   **36 Will . . . purposes** are determined to have their secret purposes fulfilled

Till his lost child be found? Which that it shall
Is all as monstrous to our human reason
As my Antigonus to break his grave   42
And come again to me, who, on my life,
Did perish with the infant. 'Tis your counsel   44
My lord should to the heavens be contrary,
Oppose against their wills. [*To Leontes*] Care not for
    issue.   46
The crown will find an heir. Great Alexander
Left his to th' worthiest; so his successor   48
Was like to be the best.

LEONTES   Good Paulina,
Who hast the memory of Hermione,
I know, in honor, oh, that ever I
Had squared me to thy counsel! Then even now   52
I might have looked upon my queen's full eyes,
Have taken treasure from her lips—

PAULINA   And left them
More rich for what they yielded.

LEONTES   Thou speak'st truth.
No more such wives, therefore no wife. One worse, 56
And better used, would make her sainted spirit   57
Again possess her corpse, and on this stage,   58
Where we're offenders now, appear soul-vexed,
And begin, "Why to me?"

PAULINA   Had she such power,   60
She had just cause.

LEONTES   She had, and would incense me   61
To murder her I married.

PAULINA   I should so.   62
Were I the ghost that walked, I'd bid you mark
Her eye and tell me for what dull part in't
You chose her. Then I'd shriek, that even your ears
Should rift to hear me, and the words that followed 66
Should be, "Remember mine."

LEONTES   Stars, stars,   67
And all eyes else dead coals! Fear thou no wife;   68
I'll have no wife, Paulina.

PAULINA   Will you swear
Never to marry but by my free leave?

LEONTES
Never, Paulina, so be blest my spirit!

PAULINA
Then, good my lords, bear witness to his oath.

CLEOMENES
You tempt him overmuch.

PAULINA   Unless another,   73
As like Hermione as is her picture,

Affront his eye.

CLEOMENES   Good madam—

PAULINA   I have done.   75
Yet if my lord will marry—if you will, sir,
No remedy, but you will—give me the office
To choose you a queen. She shall not be so young
As was your former, but she shall be such
As, walked your first queen's ghost, it should take joy 80
To see her in your arms.

LEONTES   My true Paulina,
We shall not marry till thou bidd'st us.

PAULINA   That
Shall be when your first queen's again in breath;
Never till then.   84

        Enter a Gentleman.

GENTLEMAN
One that gives out himself Prince Florizel,   85
Son of Polixenes, with his princess—she
The fairest I have yet beheld—desires access
To your high presence.

LEONTES   What with him? He comes not   88
Like to his father's greatness. His approach,   89
So out of circumstance and sudden, tells us   90
'Tis not a visitation framed, but forced   91
By need and accident. What train?

GENTLEMAN   But few,   92
And those but mean.

LEONTES   His princess, say you, with him? 93

GENTLEMAN
Ay, the most peerless piece of earth, I think,
That e'er the sun shone bright on.

PAULINA   Oh, Hermione,
As every present time doth boast itself   96
Above a better gone, so must thy grave   97
Give way to what's seen now! [*To the Gentleman*] Sir,
    you yourself   98
Have said and writ so, but your writing now
Is colder than that theme. She had not been   100
Nor was not to be equaled—thus your verse   101
Flowed with her beauty once. 'Tis shrewdly ebbed   102
To say you have seen a better.

GENTLEMAN   Pardon, madam.
The one I have almost forgot—your pardon!
The other, when she has obtained your eye,
Will have your tongue too. This is a creature,   106
Would she begin a sect, might quench the zeal

---

42 **As** as for   44 **'Tis your counsel** It's your advice that   46 **Oppose** oppose himself.   **Care not for** Do not be anxious about   48 **Left . . . worthiest** (When Alexander the Great died in 323 B.C., his son Alexander was yet unborn, necessitating the choice of an heir.)
52 **squared me** adjusted or regulated myself   56–7 **One . . . used** i.e., If I took a new, less excellent wife and treated her better   57 **her** Hermione's   58 **possess her corpse** i.e., return to earth (*this stage*) in Hermione's human shape   60 **Why to me?** Why this offense to me?
61 **had** would have.   **incense** stir up, incite   62 **should so** would similarly incite you.   66 **rift** rive, split   67 **mine** my eyes.   **Stars** i.e., Her eyes were stars   68 **all eyes else** all other eyes   73 **tempt** bear down on

75 **Affront** confront   80 **walked . . . ghost** if your first queen's ghost were to walk.   **take joy** be overjoyed   84.1 *Enter a Gentleman* (He is called a "Servant" in the Folio text, but his writing poetry in lines 100–4 is more consistent with his being a courtier. Any such person at court is a servant of the king.)   85 **gives out himself** reports himself to be   88 **What** What retinue   89 **Like to** in a manner consistent with   90 **out of circumstance** without ceremony   91 **framed** planned   92 **train** retinue.   93 **mean** lowly.   96–8 **As . . . now!** As every present age boasts its superiority to past times that were in point of fact better, so you, long dead, must give way to present fashion!   100 **that theme** i.e., Hermione, the subject of your verses.   100–1 **She . . . equaled** (Presumably, the poet wrote "She has not been nor is not to be equaled.")   102 **'Tis shrewdly ebbed** i.e., You've egregiously gone back on your word   106 **tongue** i.e., approval

Of all professors else, make proselytes   108
Of who she but bid follow.

PAULINA   How? Not women!   109

GENTLEMAN
Women will love her that she is a woman
More worth than any man; men, that she is
The rarest of all women.

LEONTES   Go, Cleomenes.
Yourself, assisted with your honored friends,
Bring them to our embracement.
                              Exit [Cleomenes with others].
                                     Still, 'tis strange
He thus should steal upon us.

PAULINA   Had our prince,
Jewel of children, seen this hour, he had paired
Well with this lord. There was not full a month
Between their births.

LEONTES   Prithee, no more, cease. Thou know'st
He dies to me again when talked of. Sure,
When I shall see this gentleman, thy speeches
Will bring me to consider that which may
Unfurnish me of reason. They are come.   123
            Enter Florizel, Perdita, Cleomenes, and others.
Your mother was most true to wedlock, Prince,
For she did print your royal father off,
Conceiving you. Were I but twenty-one,
Your father's image is so hit in you,   127
His very air, that I should call you brother,
As I did him, and speak of something wildly
By us performed before. Most dearly welcome!
And your fair princess—goddess! Oh! Alas,
I lost a couple that twixt heaven and earth
Might thus have stood begetting wonder as
You, gracious couple, do. And then I lost—
All mine own folly—the society,
Amity too, of your brave father, whom,   136
Though bearing misery, I desire my life   137
Once more to look on him.

FLORIZEL   By his command   138
Have I here touched Sicilia, and from him
Give you all greetings that a king, at friend,   140
Can send his brother; and but infirmity,   141
Which waits upon worn times, hath something seized 142
His wished ability, he had himself   143
The lands and waters twixt your throne and his
Measured to look upon you, whom he loves—   145
He bade me say so—more than all the scepters
And those that bear them living.

LEONTES   O my brother!   147
Good gentleman, the wrongs I have done thee stir

Afresh within me, and these thy offices,   149
So rarely kind, are as interpreters   150
Of my behindhand slackness. Welcome hither,   151
As is the spring to th'earth. And hath he too
Exposed this paragon to th' fearful usage—
At least ungentle—of the dreadful Neptune,   154
To greet a man not worth her pains, much less
Th'adventure of her person?

FLORIZEL   Good my lord,   156
She came from Libya.

LEONTES   Where the warlike Smalus,
That noble honored lord, is feared and loved?

FLORIZEL
Most royal sir, from thence, from him, whose daughter 159
His tears proclaimed his, parting with her. Thence,   160
A prosperous south wind friendly, we have crossed,
To execute the charge my father gave me
For visiting Your Highness. My best train
I have from your Sicilian shores dismissed,
Who for Bohemia bend, to signify   165
Not only my success in Libya, sir,
But my arrival and my wife's in safety
Here where we are.

LEONTES   The blessèd gods
Purge all infection from our air whilst you
Do climate here! You have a holy father,   170
A graceful gentleman, against whose person,   171
So sacred as it is, I have done sin,
For which the heavens, taking angry note,
Have left me issueless; and your father's blest,
As he from heaven merits it, with you,
Worthy his goodness. What might I have been,
Might I a son and daughter now have looked on,
Such goodly things as you?

            Enter a Lord.

LORD   Most noble sir,
That which I shall report will bear no credit
Were not the proof so nigh. Please you, great sir,
Bohemia greets you from himself by me;
Desires you to attach his son, who has—   182
His dignity and duty both cast off—   183
Fled from his father, from his hopes, and with
A shepherd's daughter.

LEONTES   Where's Bohemia? Speak.

LORD
Here in your city. I now came from him.
I speak amazedly, and it becomes   187
My marvel and my message. To your court   188
Whiles he was hast'ning—in the chase, it seems,
Of this fair couple—meets he on the way

---

108 professors else believers in other sects or deities   **109 Of . . . follow** of all those whom she merely told to follow her.   **How? Not women!** What do you mean? Surely women wouldn't become converts!   **123 Unfurnish** deprive, divest   **127 hit** exactly reproduced   **136 brave** noble   **137 my life** i.e., to live long enough   **138 him** (Redundant in modern syntax.)   **140 at friend** in friendship   **141 but** were it not that   **142 waits . . . times** attends old age   **142–3 something . . . ability** to some extent taken away his ability (to travel) as he wishes   **145 Measured** traversed   **147 those . . . living** those living kings who bear scepters.

149 offices messages of good will, courteous attentions   **150 rarely** exceptionally   **150–1 are . . . slackness** are like commentators on my slowness in greeting you.   **154 Neptune** god of the sea   **156 Th'adventure** the hazard   **159–60 whose . . . her** whose tears, as he parted with her, proclaimed her to be his daughter.   **165 bend** direct their course   **170 climate** dwell, reside (in this clime)   **171 graceful** full of grace, gracious   **182 attach** arrest   **183 dignity and duty** princely dignity and filial duty   **187–8 I . . . message** i.e., I speak perplexedly as befits my perplexity and my astonishing news.

The father of this seeming lady and
Her brother, having both their country quitted
With this young prince.

FLORIZEL   Camillo has betrayed me,
Whose honor and whose honesty till now
Endured all weathers.

LORD   Lay't so to his charge.   195
He's with the King your father.

LEONTES   Who? Camillo?

LORD
Camillo, sir. I spake with him, who now
Has these poor men in question. Never saw I   198
Wretches so quake. They kneel, they kiss the earth,
Forswear themselves as often as they speak.
Bohemia stops his ears and threatens them
With divers deaths in death.

PERDITA   Oh, my poor father!   202
The heaven sets spies upon us, will not have
Our contract celebrated.

LEONTES   You are married?

FLORIZEL
We are not, sir, nor are we like to be.   205
The stars, I see, will kiss the valleys first;
The odds for high and low's alike.

LEONTES   My lord,   207
Is this the daughter of a king?

FLORIZEL   She is,
When once she is my wife.

LEONTES
That "once," I see, by your good father's speed
Will come on very slowly. I am sorry,
Most sorry, you have broken from his liking
Where you were tied in duty, and as sorry
Your choice is not so rich in worth as beauty,   214
That you might well enjoy her.

FLORIZEL [to Perdita]   Dear, look up.
Though Fortune, visible an enemy,   216
Should chase us with my father, power no jot   217
Hath she to change our loves.—Beseech you, sir,
Remember since you owed no more to time   219
Than I do now. With thought of such affections,   220
Step forth mine advocate. At your request
My father will grant precious things as trifles.

LEONTES
Would he do so, I'd beg your precious mistress,
Which he counts but a trifle.

PAULINA   Sir, my liege,
Your eye hath too much youth in't. Not a month
'Fore your queen died, she was more worth such
    gazes
Than what you look on now.

LEONTES   I thought of her

Even in these looks I made. [*To Florizel*] But your
    petition
Is yet unanswered. I will to your father.
Your honor not o'erthrown by your desires,   230
I am friend to them and you. Upon which errand
I now go toward him. Therefore follow me,
And mark what way I make. Come, good my lord.   233
                            Exeunt.

❧

5.2

Enter Autolycus and a Gentleman.

AUTOLYCUS   Beseech you, sir, were you present at this
    relation?   2

FIRST GENTLEMAN   I was by at the opening of the fardel,
    heard the old shepherd deliver the manner how he   4
    found it; whereupon, after a little amazedness, we
    were all commanded out of the chamber. Only this,
    methought, I heard the shepherd say: he found the
    child.

AUTOLYCUS   I would most gladly know the issue of it.   9

FIRST GENTLEMAN   I make a broken delivery of the busi-   10
    ness, but the changes I perceived in the King and Cam-
    illo were very notes of admiration. They seemed al-   12
    most, with staring on one another, to tear the cases of   13
    their eyes. There was speech in their dumbness, lan-   14
    guage in their very gesture. They looked as they had   15
    heard of a world ransomed, or one destroyed. A notable
    passion of wonder appeared in them, but the wisest
    beholder, that knew no more but seeing, could not say   18
    if th'importance were joy or sorrow; but in the ex-   19
    tremity of the one it must needs be.   20

Enter another Gentleman.

Here comes a gentleman that haply knows more.—   21
The news, Rogero?

SECOND GENTLEMAN   Nothing but bonfires. The oracle
    is fulfilled; the King's daughter is found. Such a deal of   24
    wonder is broken out within this hour that ballad
    makers cannot be able to express it.

Enter another Gentleman.

Here comes the Lady Paulina's steward. He can deliver
    you more.—How goes it now, sir? This news which is
    called true is so like an old tale that the verity of it is in
    strong suspicion. Has the King found his heir?

THIRD GENTLEMAN   Most true, if ever truth were preg-   31
    nant by circumstance. That which you hear you'll   32

---

230 **Your . . . desires** If your chaste honor has not been overcome by
sexual desire, or, if what you want in this match is compatible with
your royal honor   233 **way** progress
5.2. Location: Sicilia. At court.
2 **relation** narrative, account.   4 **deliver** report   9 **issue** outcome
10 **broken** disjointed, fragmented   12 **very notes of admiration** veritable marks of wonderment.   13–14 **cases of their eyes** eyelids.   15 **as**
as if   18 **no . . . seeing** nothing except what he could see   19 **th'importance** the import, meaning   20 **of the one** of one or the other
21 **haply** perhaps   24 **deal** huge quantity   31–2 **pregnant by circumstance** made apparent by circumstantial evidence.

---

195 **Lay't . . . charge** Confront him with it directly.   198 **in question**
under interrogation.   202 **deaths** i.e., tortures   205 **like** likely   207
The odds . . . alike Fortune treats high and low alike.   214 **worth**
rank   216–17 **Though . . . father** Though the goddess Fortune herself
were to manifest herself as our enemy and join my father in chasing
us   219–20 **since . . . now** when you were no older than I am now.
220 **With . . . affections** Recalling what it was to be in love at that age

swear you see, there is such unity in the proofs. The mantle of Queen Hermione's, her jewel about the neck of it, the letters of Antigonus found with it which they know to be his character, the majesty of the creature in resemblance of the mother, the affection of nobleness which nature shows above her breeding, and many other evidences proclaim her with all certainty to be the King's daughter. Did you see the meeting of the two kings?

SECOND GENTLEMAN   No.

THIRD GENTLEMAN   Then have you lost a sight which was to be seen, cannot be spoken of. There might you have beheld one joy crown another, so and in such manner that it seemed Sorrow wept to take leave of them, for their joy waded in tears. There was casting up of eyes, holding up of hands, with countenance of such distraction that they were to be known by garment, not by favor. Our king, being ready to leap out of himself for joy of his found daughter, as if that joy were now become a loss, cries, "Oh, thy mother, thy mother!" then asks Bohemia forgiveness; then embraces his son-in-law; then again worries he his daughter with clipping her; now he thanks the old shepherd, which stands by like a weather-bitten conduit of many kings' reigns. I never heard of such another encounter, which lames report to follow it and undoes description to do it.

SECOND GENTLEMAN   What, pray you, became of Antigonus, that carried hence the child?

THIRD GENTLEMAN   Like an old tale still, which will have matter to rehearse though credit be asleep and not an ear open. He was torn to pieces with a bear. This avouches the shepherd's son, who has not only his innocence, which seems much, to justify him, but a handkerchief and rings of his that Paulina knows.

FIRST GENTLEMAN   What became of his bark and his followers?

THIRD GENTLEMAN   Wrecked the same instant of their master's death and in the view of the shepherd; so that all the instruments which aided to expose the child were even then lost when it was found. But oh, the noble combat that twixt joy and sorrow was fought in Paulina! She had one eye declined for the loss of her husband, another elevated that the oracle was fulfilled. She lifted the Princess from the earth, and so locks her in embracing as if she would pin her to her heart, that she might no more be in danger of losing.

FIRST GENTLEMAN   The dignity of this act was worth the audience of kings and princes, for by such was it acted.

THIRD GENTLEMAN   One of the prettiest touches of all, and that which angled for mine eyes—caught the water, though not the fish—was when, at the relation of the Queen's death, with the manner how she came to't bravely confessed and lamented by the King, how attentiveness wounded his daughter; till, from one sign of dolor to another, she did, with an "Alas!" I would fain say, bleed tears, for I am sure my heart wept blood. Who was most marble there changed color; some swooned, all sorrowed. If all the world could have seen't, the woe had been universal.

FIRST GENTLEMAN   Are they returned to the court?

THIRD GENTLEMAN   No. The Princess hearing of her mother's statue, which is in the keeping of Paulina—a piece many years in doing and now newly performed by that rare Italian master, Julio Romano, who, had he himself eternity and could put breath into his work, would beguile Nature of her custom, so perfectly he is her ape; he so near to Hermione hath done Hermione that they say one would speak to her and stand in hope of answer—thither with all greediness of affection are they gone, and there they intend to sup.

SECOND GENTLEMAN   I thought she had some great matter there in hand, for she hath privately twice or thrice a day, ever since the death of Hermione, visited that removed house. Shall we thither and with our company piece the rejoicing?

FIRST GENTLEMAN   Who would be thence that has the benefit of access? Every wink of an eye some new grace will be born. Our absence makes us unthrifty to our knowledge. Let's along.   *Exeunt* [*Gentlemen*].

AUTOLYCUS   Now, had I not the dash of my former life in me, would preferment drop on my head. I brought the old man and his son aboard the Prince, told him I heard them talk of a fardel and I know not what. But he at that time overfond of the shepherd's daughter—so he then took her to be—who began to be much seasick, and himself little better, extremity of weather continuing, this mystery remained undiscovered. But 'tis all one to me, for had I been the finder out of this secret, it would not have relished among my other discredits.

Enter Shepherd and Clown, [*dressed in finery*].

Here come those I have done good to against my will, and already appearing in the blossoms of their fortune.

SHEPHERD   Come, boy. I am past more children, but thy sons and daughters will be all gentlemen born.

36 character handwriting   **37 affection of** natural disposition to
38 breeding rearing   **48 countenance** bearing, demeanor   **50 favor**
features.   **54 worries he** he pesters   **55 clipping** embracing
56–7 which . . . reigns who stands by weeping like a weather-beaten
fountain that has stood there over the course of many kings' reigns.
58–9 which . . . do it which makes any account of it seem inadequate
and beggars the powers of description in an attempt to do justice to
it.   **63 rehearse** relate.   **credit** belief   **64 with** by   **65 avouches** confirms, corroborates   **66 innocence** simplemindedness (such that he
would seem unable to invent such a story)   **67 his** Antigonus's
75–6 She . . . fulfilled i.e., She wept and laughed at the same time.
79 losing being lost.

88 attentiveness listening to it   **89 dolor** grief   **91 Who . . . marble**
Even the most hardhearted   **97 performed** completed   **98 Julio
Romano** Italian painter and sculptor of the sixteenth century, better
known as a painter (and an anachronism in this play)   **100 beguile**
deprive, cheat.   **custom** trade   **101 ape** imitator   **103–4 greediness
of affection** eagerness born of love   **104 sup** i.e., feed their hungry
eyes (?) or, perhaps, have a commemorative banquet (?).
108 removed sequestered   **109 piece** add to, augment   **112 unthrifty
to** passing up an opportunity to increase   **114–15 had I . . . head** if it
weren't for the lingering reputation of petty thievery that hangs about
me, royal favor would be sure to fall to my lot.   **116 the Prince** the
Prince's ship   **122 'tis all one** it's all the same   **123 relished** tasted
well, suited

CLOWN [*to Autolycus*] You are well met, sir. You denied to fight
with me this other day because I was no gentleman 131
born. See you these clothes? Say you see them not and
think me still no gentleman born. You were best say
these robes are not gentlemen born. Give me the lie, 134
do, and try whether I am not now a gentleman born.

AUTOLYCUS   I know you are now, sir, a gentleman born.

CLOWN   Ay, and have been so any time these four
hours.

SHEPHERD   And so have I, boy.

CLOWN   So you have. But I was a gentleman born before
my father; for the King's son took me by the hand
and called me brother; and then the two kings called
my father brother; and then the Prince my brother and
the Princess my sister called my father father; and so
we wept, and there was the first gentlemanlike tears
that ever we shed.

SHEPHERD   We may live, son, to shed many more.

CLOWN   Ay, or else 'twere hard luck, being in so pre- 148
posterous estate as we are. 149

AUTOLYCUS   I humbly beseech you, sir, to pardon me
all the faults I have committed to Your Worship, and to
give me your good report to the Prince my master. 152

SHEPHERD   Prithee, son, do; for we must be gentle, now 153
we are gentlemen.

CLOWN [*to Autolycus*]   Thou wilt amend thy life?

AUTOLYCUS   Ay, an it like Your good Worship. 156

CLOWN   Give me thy hand. I will swear to the Prince
thou art as honest a true fellow as any is in Bohemia. 158

SHEPHERD   You may say it, but not swear it.

CLOWN   Not swear it, now I am a gentleman? Let boors 160
and franklins say it; I'll swear it. 161

SHEPHERD   How if it be false, son?

CLOWN   If it be ne'er so false, a true gentleman may
swear it in the behalf of his friend.—And I'll swear to
the Prince thou art a tall fellow of thy hands and that 165
thou wilt not be drunk; but I know thou art no tall
fellow of thy hands and that thou wilt be drunk. But
I'll swear it, and I would thou wouldst be a tall fellow
of thy hands.

AUTOLYCUS   I will prove so, sir, to my power. 170

CLOWN   Ay, by any means prove a tall fellow. If I do not
wonder how thou dar'st venture to be drunk, not
being a tall fellow, trust me not. Hark, the kings and
the princes, our kindred, are going to see the Queen's
picture. Come, follow us. We'll be thy good masters. 175
Exeunt.

❧

5.3

*Enter Leontes, Polixenes, Florizel, Perdita,
Camillo, Paulina, lords, etc.*

LEONTES
O grave and good Paulina, the great comfort
That I have had of thee!

PAULINA   What, sovereign sir, 2
I did not well, I meant well. All my services
You have paid home. But that you have vouchsafed, 4
With your crowned brother and these your contracted
Heirs of your kingdoms, my poor house to visit,
It is a surplus of your grace which never 7
My life may last to answer.

LEONTES   O Paulina, 8
We honor you with trouble. But we came 9
To see the statue of our queen. Your gallery
Have we passed through, not without much content
In many singularities; but we saw not 12
That which my daughter came to look upon,
The statue of her mother.

PAULINA   As she lived peerless,
So her dead likeness, I do well believe,
Excels whatever yet you looked upon
Or hand of man hath done. Therefore I keep it
Lonely, apart. But here it is. Prepare 18
To see the life as lively mocked as ever 19
Still sleep mocked death. Behold, and say 'tis well. 20
[*Paulina draws a curtain, and discovers*]
Hermione [*standing*] *like a statue.*
I like your silence; it the more shows off
Your wonder. But yet speak; first, you, my liege.
Comes it not something near?

LEONTES   Her natural posture! 23
Chide me, dear stone, that I may say indeed
Thou art Hermione; or rather, thou art she
In thy not chiding, for she was as tender
As infancy and grace. But yet, Paulina,
Hermione was not as much wrinkled, nothing 28
So agèd as this seems.

POLIXENES   Oh, not by much.

PAULINA
So much the more our carver's excellence,
Which lets go by some sixteen years and makes her
As she lived now.

LEONTES   As now she might have done, 32
So much to my good comfort as it is
Now piercing to my soul. Oh, thus she stood,
Even with such life of majesty—warm life,
As now it coldly stands—when first I wooed her!
I am ashamed. Does not the stone rebuke me
For being more stone than it? O royal piece! 38

131 this other the other   **134 Give me the lie** Accuse me to my face
of lying (an insult that requires a challenge to a duel)   **148–9 prepos-
terous** (Blunder for "prosperous.")   **152 me** on my behalf   **153 gentle** nobly generous   **156 an it like** if it please   **158 honest a true**
worthy an honest   **160 boors** peasants   **161 franklins** farmers owning their own small farms   **165 tall . . . hands** brave fellow   **170 my
power** the best of my ability. (Autolycus slyly promises to use his hands
well—in picking pockets.)   **175 picture** i.e., likeness, painted statue.

5.3. Location: Sicilia. Paulina's house.
2 What Whatever   **4 home** fully.   **7–8 which . . . answer** which I can
never live long enough to be able to repay.   **9 We . . . trouble** i.e., we
trouble you with the demands of hospitality, though you are kind
enough to call it an honor.   **12 singularities** rarities, curiosities
18 Lonely isolated   **19 as lively mocked** as realistically counterfeited
20 Still motionless   **23 something** somewhat   **28 nothing** not at all
32 As she as if she   **38 piece** work of art.

There's magic in thy majesty, which has
My evils conjured to remembrance and
From thy admiring daughter took the spirits,   41
Standing like stone with thee.

PERDITA   And give me leave,
And do not say 'tis superstition, that
I kneel and then implore her blessing. Lady,
                                              [kneeling]
Dear Queen, that ended when I but began,
Give me that hand of yours to kiss.

PAULINA   Oh, patience!
The statue is but newly fixed; the color's   47
Not dry.

CAMILLO
My lord, your sorrow was too sore laid on,   49
Which sixteen winters cannot blow away,
So many summers dry. Scarce any joy   51
Did ever so long live; no sorrow
But killed itself much sooner.

POLIXENES   Dear my brother,
Let him that was the cause of this have power   54
To take off so much grief from you as he
Will piece up in himself.

PAULINA   Indeed, my lord,   56
If I had thought the sight of my poor image
Would thus have wrought you—for the stone is
    mine—   58
I'd not have showed it.

LEONTES   Do not draw the curtain.

PAULINA
No longer shall you gaze on't, lest your fancy
May think anon it moves.

LEONTES   Let be, let be.
Would I were dead but that methinks already—
What was he that did make it? See, my lord,
Would you not deem it breathed? And that those veins
Did verily bear blood?

POLIXENES   Masterly done.
The very life seems warm upon her lip.

LEONTES
The fixture of her eye has motion in't,   67
As we are mocked with art.

PAULINA   I'll draw the curtain.   68
My lord's almost so far transported that
He'll think anon it lives.

LEONTES   Oh, sweet Paulina,
Make me to think so twenty years together!
No settled senses of the world can match   72
The pleasure of that madness. Let't alone.

PAULINA
I am sorry, sir, I have thus far stirred you; but

I could afflict you farther.

LEONTES   Do, Paulina;
For this affliction has a taste as sweet
As any cordial comfort. Still methinks   77
There is an air comes from her. What fine chisel
Could ever yet cut breath? Let no man mock me,
For I will kiss her.

PAULINA   Good my lord, forbear.
The ruddiness upon her lip is wet;
You'll mar it if you kiss it, stain your own
With oily painting. Shall I draw the curtain?   83

LEONTES
No, not these twenty years.

PERDITA   So long could I
Stand by, a looker on.

PAULINA   Either forbear,
Quit presently the chapel, or resolve you   86
For more amazement. If you can behold it,
I'll make the statue move indeed, descend
And take you by the hand. But then you'll think—
Which I protest against—I am assisted
By wicked powers.

LEONTES   What you can make her do
I am content to look on, what to speak
I am content to hear; for 'tis as easy
To make her speak as move.

PAULINA   It is required
You do awake your faith. Then all stand still.
On; those that think it is unlawful business   96
I am about, let them depart.

LEONTES   Proceed.
No foot shall stir.

PAULINA   Music, awake her; strike!   [Music.] 98
'Tis time. Descend. Be stone no more. Approach.
Strike all that look upon with marvel. Come,   100
I'll fill your grave up. Stir, nay, come away,
Bequeath to death your numbness, for from him   102
Dear life redeems you.—You perceive she stirs.
                                    [Hermione comes down.]
Start not. Her actions shall be holy as
You hear my spell is lawful. Do not shun her   105
Until you see her die again, for then   106
You kill her double. Nay, present your hand.   107
When she was young you wooed her. Now in age
Is she become the suitor?   [Leontes touches her.]

LEONTES   Oh, she's warm!
If this be magic, let it be an art
Lawful as eating.

POLIXENES   She embraces him.

CAMILLO   She hangs about his neck.
If she pertain to life, let her speak too.   114

POLIXENES
Ay, and make it manifest where she has lived,
Or how stol'n from the dead.

PAULINA   That she is living,

41 **admiring** filled with wonder.   **spirits** vital spirits   47 **fixed** made
fast in its color   49 **sore** heavily   51 **So . . . dry** i.e., and sixteen summers cannot dry up. (Camillo tells the King that he has imposed too
heavy a sorrow on himself if even sixteen years' time cannot end it.)
54 **him** i.e., myself (as an innocent cause, but still a cause)   56 **piece
up in himself** add to his own burden.   58 **wrought** affected   67 **The
fixture . . . in't** i.e., Her eye, though motionless, gives the appearance
of motion   68 **As . . . art** in such a way that we are fooled by artistic
illusion   72 **No settled . . . world** No calm mind in the world

77 **cordial** restorative, heartwarming   83 **painting** paint.
86 **presently** immediately   96 **On; those** (Often emended to *Or
those.*)   98 **strike** strike up.   100 **upon** on   102 **him** i.e., death
105–7 **Do . . . double** i.e., If you ever shun her during the rest of her
life, you will kill her again.   114 **pertain to life** be truly alive

Were it but told you, should be hooted at
Like an old tale; but it appears she lives,
Though yet she speak not. Mark a little while.
[*To Perdita*] Please you to interpose, fair madam. Kneel,   120
And pray your mother's blessing.—Turn, good lady;
Our Perdita is found.

HERMIONE   You gods, look down
And from your sacred vials pour your graces
Upon my daughter's head!—Tell me, mine own,
Where hast thou been preserved? Where lived? How
    found
Thy father's court? For thou shalt hear that I,
Knowing by Paulina that the oracle
Gave hope thou wast in being, have preserved
Myself to see the issue.   129

PAULINA   There's time enough for that,
Lest they desire upon this push to trouble   131
Your joys with like relation. Go together,   132
You precious winners all; your exultation
Partake to everyone. I, an old turtle,   134
Will wing me to some withered bough and there

My mate, that's never to be found again,   136
Lament till I am lost.

LEONTES   Oh, peace, Paulina!   137
Thou shouldst a husband take by my consent,
As I by thine a wife. This is a match,
And made between 's by vows. Thou hast found
    mine,
But how is to be questioned, for I saw her,
As I thought, dead, and have in vain said many
A prayer upon her grave. I'll not seek far—
For him, I partly know his mind—to find thee   144
An honorable husband. Come, Camillo,
And take her by the hand, whose worth and honesty   146
Is richly noted and here justified   147
By us, a pair of kings. Let's from this place.
[*To Hermione*] What? Look upon my brother. Both your
    pardons,
That e'er I put between your holy looks
My ill suspicion. This' your son-in-law   151
And son unto the King, whom, heavens directing,
Is trothplight to your daughter. Good Paulina,   153
Lead us from hence, where we may leisurely
Each one demand and answer to his part
Performed in this wide gap of time since first
We were dissevered. Hastily lead away.   *Exeunt.*

---

120 madam (Addressed to Perdita as Princess and affianced to be married.) **129 the issue** (1) the outcome (2) my child. **131–2 Lest ... relation** lest they (bystanders) insist, at this critical juncture, on interrupting this moment of joy with your relating of your story or with their telling what has happened to them. **134 Partake to** share with, communicate. **turtle** turtledove

136–7 My mate ... lost grieve for my lost mate until I die. **144 For** as for **146 whose** i.e., Camillo's **147 richly noted** abundantly acknowledged. **justified** avouched **151 This'** This is **153 troth-plight** betrothed

The Tempest

Shakespeare creates in *The Tempest* a world of the imagination, a place of conflict and ultimately of magical rejuvenation, like the forests of *A Midsummer Night's Dream* and *As You Like It*. The journey to Shakespeare's island is to a realm of art where everything is controlled by the artist-figure. Yet the journey is no escape from reality, for the island shows people what they are, as well as what they ought to be. Even its location juxtaposes the "real" world with an idealized landscape: like Plato's New Atlantis or Thomas More's Utopia, Shakespeare's island is to be found both somewhere and nowhere. On the narrative level, it is located in the Mediterranean Sea. Yet there are overtones of the New World, the Western Hemisphere, where Thomas More had situated his island of Utopia. Ariel fetches dew at Prospero's command from the "Bermudas" (1.2.230). Caliban when prostrate reminds Trinculo of a "dead Indian" (2.2.33) who might be displayed before gullible crowds eager to see such a prodigious creature from across the seas, and Caliban's god, Setebos, was, according to Richard Eden's account of Magellan's circumnavigation of the globe (in *History of Travel*, 1577), worshiped by South American natives. An inspiration for Shakespeare's story (for which no direct literary source is known) may well have been various accounts of the shipwreck in the Bermudas in 1609 of the *Sea Venture*, which was carrying settlers to the new Virginian colony. Shakespeare borrowed details from Sylvester Jourdain's *A Discovery of the Bermudas, Otherwise Called the Isle of Devils*, published in 1610, and from William Strachey's *A True Reportory of the Wreck and Redemption . . . from the Islands of the Bermudas*, which Shakespeare must have seen in manuscript since it was not published until after his death. He wrote the play shortly after reading these works, for *The Tempest* was acted at court in 1611. He may also have known or heard of various accounts of Magellan's circumnavigation of the world in 1519–1522 (including Richard Eden's shortened English version, as part of his *History of Travel*,

of an Italian narrative by Antonio Pigafetta), Francis Fletcher's journal of Sir Francis Drake's circumnavigation in 1577–1580, Richard Rich's *News from Virginia* (1610), and still other potential sources of information. Shakespeare's fascination with the Western Hemisphere gave him, not the actual location of his story, which remains Mediterranean, but a state of mind associated with newness and the unfamiliar. From this strange and unknown place, we gain a radical perspective on the old world of European culture. Miranda sees on the island a "new world" in which humankind appears "brave" (5.1.185), and, although her wonder must be tempered by Prospero's rejoinder that "'Tis new to thee" (line 186) and by Aldous Huxley's still more ironic use of her phrase in the title of his satirical novel *Brave New World*, the island endures as a restorative vision. Even though we experience it fleetingly, as in a dream, this nonexistent realm assumes a permanence enjoyed by all great works of art.

Prospero rules autocratically as artist-king and patriarch over this imaginary world, conjuring up trials and visions to test people's intentions and awaken their consciences. To the island come an assortment of persons who, because they require varied ordeals, are separated by Prospero and Ariel into three groups: King Alonso and those accompanying him; Alonso's son, Ferdinand; and Stephano and Trinculo. Prospero's authority over them, though strong, has limits. As Duke of Milan, he was bookishly inattentive to political matters and thus vulnerable to the Machiavellian conniving of his younger brother, Antonio. Only in this world apart, the artist's world, do his powers derived from learning find their proper sphere. Because he cannot control the world beyond his isle, he must wait for "strange, bountiful Fortune, / Now my dear lady" (1.2.179–80) to bring his enemies near his shore. He eschews, moreover, the black arts of diabolism. His is a white magic, devoted ultimately to what he considers moral ends: rescuing Ariel from the spell of the witch Sycorax, curbing the appetite of Caliban, spying on Antonio and Sebastian in the role of Conscience. He thus comes to see Fortune's gift of delivering his enemies into his hands as an opportunity for him to forgive and restore them, not be revenged.

Such an assumption of godlike power is close to arrogance, even blasphemy, for Prospero is no god. His chief power, learned from books and exercised through Ariel, is to control the elements so as to create illusion—of separation, of death, of the gods' blessing. Yet, since he is human, even this power is an immense burden and temptation. Prospero has much to learn, like those whom he controls. He must subdue his anger, his self-pity, his readiness to blame others, his domineering over Miranda. He must overcome the vengeful impulse he experiences toward those who have wronged him, and he must conquer the longing many a father feels to hold on to his daughter when she is desired by another man. He struggles with these problems through his art, devising games and shows in which his angry self-pity and jealousy are transmuted into playacting scenes of divine warning and forgiveness toward his enemies and watchful parental austerity toward Miranda and Ferdinand. Prospero's responsibilities cause him to behave magisterially and to be resented by the spirits of the isle. His authority is problematic to us because he seems so patriarchal, colonialist, even sexist and racist in his arrogating to himself the right and responsibility to control others in the name of values they may not share. Ariel longs to be free of this authority. Perhaps our sympathy for Prospero is greatest when we perceive that he, too, with mixed feelings of genuine relief and melancholy, is ready to lay aside his demanding and self-important role as creative moral intelligence.

Alonso and his court party variously illustrate the unregenerate world left behind in Naples and Milan. We first see them on shipboard, panicky and desperate, their titles and finery mocked by roaring waves. Futile ambition seems destined for a watery demise. Yet death by water in this play is a transfiguration rather than an end, a mystical rebirth, as in the regenerative cycle of the seasons from winter to summer. Ariel suggests as much in his song about a drowned father: "Those are pearls that were his eyes. / Nothing of him that doth fade / But doth suffer a sea change / Into something rich and strange" (1.2.402–5). Still, this miracle is not apparent at first to those who are caught in the illusion of death. As in T. S. Eliot's The Waste Land, which repeatedly alludes to The Tempest, self-blinded human beings fear a disaster that is ironically the prelude to reawakening.

The illusions created on the island serve to test these imperfect men and to make them reveal their true selves. Only Gonzalo, who long ago aided Prospero and Miranda when they were banished from Milan, responds affirmatively to illusion. In his eyes, their having been saved from drowning is a miracle: they breathe fresh air, the grass is green on the island, and their very garments appear not to have been stained by the salt water. His ideal commonwealth (2.1.150–71), which Shakespeare drew in part from an essay by Montaigne, postulates a natural goodness in humanity and makes no allowance for the darker propensities of human behavior, but at least Gonzalo's cheerfulness is in refreshing contrast to the jaded sneers of some of his companions. Sebastian and Antonio react to the magic isle, as to Gonzalo's commonwealth, by cynically refusing to believe in miracles. They scoff at Gonzalo for insistently looking on the bright side; if he were to examine his supposedly unstained clothes more carefully, they jest, he would discover that his pockets are filled with mud. Confident that they are unobserved, they seize the opportunity afforded by Alonso's being asleep to plot a murder and political coup. This attempt is not only despicable but also madly ludicrous, for they are all shipwrecked and no longer have kingdoms over which to quarrel. Even more ironically, Sebastian and Antonio, despite their insolent belief in their self-sufficiency, are being observed. The villains must be taught that an unseen power keeps track of their misdeeds. However presumptuous Prospero may be to assume through Ariel's means the role of godlike observer, he does awaken conscience and prevent murder. The villains may revert to type when returned to their usual habitat, but even they are at least briefly moved to an awareness of the unseen (3.3.21–7). Alonso, more worthy than they, though burdened, too, with sin, responds to his situation with guilt and despair, for he assumes that his son Ferdinand's death is the just punishment of the gods for Alonso's part in the earlier overthrow of Prospero. Alonso must be led, by means of curative illusions, through the purgative experience of contrition to the reward he thinks impossible and undeserved: reunion with his lost son.

Alonso is thus, like Posthumus in Cymbeline or Leontes in The Winter's Tale, a tragicomic figure—sinful, contrite, forgiven. Alonso's son Ferdinand must also undergo ordeals and visions devised by Prospero to test his worth, but more on the level of romantic comedy. Ferdinand is young, innocent, and hopeful, well-matched to Miranda. From the start, Prospero obviously approves of his prospective son-in-law. Yet even Prospero, needing to prepare himself for a life in which Miranda will no longer be solely his, is not ready to lay aside at least the comic fiction of parental opposition. He invents difficulties, imposes tasks of logbearing (like those assigned Caliban), and issues stern warnings against premarital lust. In the comic mode, parents are expected to cross their children in matters of the heart. Prospero is so convincing in his role of overbearing parent, insisting on absolute unthinking obedience from his daughter, that we remain unsure whether he is truly like that or whether we are meant to sense in his performance a grappling with his own deepest feelings of possessiveness and autocratic authority, tempered finally by his awareness of the arbitrariness of such a role and his readiness to let Miranda decide for herself. As a teacher of youth, moreover, Prospero is convinced by long experience that prizes too easily won are too lightly esteemed. Manifold are the temptations urging Ferdinand to surrender to the natural rhythms of the isle as Caliban would. In place of ceremonies conducted in civilized societies by the church, Prospero must create the illusion of ceremony by his art. The betrothal of Ferdinand and Miranda accordingly unites the best of both worlds: the natural innocence of the island, which teaches them to avoid the corruptions of civilization at its worst, and the higher law of nature achieved through moral wisdom at its best. To this marriage, the goddesses Iris, Ceres, and Juno bring promises of bounteous harvest, "refreshing showers," celestial harmony, and a springtime brought back to the earth by Proserpina's return from Hades (4.1.76–117). In Ferdinand and Miranda, "nurture" is wedded to "nature." This bond unites spirit and flesh, legitimizing erotic pleasure by incorporating it within Prospero's vision of a cosmic moral order.

At the lowest level of this traditional cosmic and moral framework, in Prospero's view, are Stephano and Trinculo. Their comic scenes juxtapose them with Caliban, for he represents untutored Nature, whereas they represent the unnatural depths to which human beings brought up in civilized society can fall. In this they resemble Sebastian and Antonio, who have learned in supposedly civilized Italy arts of intrigue and political murder. The antics of Stephano and Trinculo burlesque the conduct of their presumed betters, thereby exposing to ridicule the self-deceptions of ambitious men. The clowns desire to exploit the natural wonders of the isle by taking Caliban back to civilization to be shown in carnivals or by plying him with strong drink and whetting his resentment against authority. These plottings are in vain, however, for, like Sebastian and Antonio, the clowns are being watched. The clowns teach Caliban to cry out for "freedom" (2.2.184), by which they mean license to do as one pleases, but are foiled by Ariel as comic nemesis. Because they are degenerate buffoons, Prospero as satirist devises for them an exposure that is appropriately humiliating and satirical.

In contrast with them, Caliban is in many ways a sympathetic character. His sensitivity to natural beauty, as in his descriptions of the "nimble marmoset" or the dreaming music he so often hears (2.2.168; 3.2.137–45), is entirely appropriate to this child of nature. He is, to be sure, the child of a witch and is called many harsh names by Miranda and Prospero, such as "Abhorrèd slave" and "a born devil, on whose nature / Nurture can never stick" (1.2.354; 4.1.188–9). Yet he protests with some justification that the island was his in the first place and that Prospero and Miranda are interlopers. His very existence calls radically into question the value of civilization, which has shown itself capable of limitless depravity. What profit has

Caliban derived from learning Prospero's language other than, as he puts it, to "know how to curse" (1.2.367)? With instinctive cunning, he senses that books are his chief enemy and plots to destroy them first in his attempt at rebellion. The unspoiled natural world does indeed offer civilization a unique perspective on itself. In this it resembles Gonzalo's ideal commonwealth, which, no matter how laughably implausible from the cynic's point of view, does at least question some assumptions—economic, political, and social—common in western societies.

Radical perspectives of this kind invite consideration of many unsettling questions about exploration, colonialist empire building, and sexual imperialism. The fleeting comparison of Caliban to an indigenous native (2.2.33), although ignored in stage productions of the play until the late nineteenth century, suggests a discourse on colonialism in *The Tempest* that anticipates to a remarkable degree a doleful history of exploitation, of providing rum and guns to the natives, and of taking away land through violent expropriation in the name of bringing civilization and God to the New World. Stephano and Trinculo, pouring wine down Caliban's throat and thus reducing him to a worshiping slave, show exploitation at its worst, but surely the play allows us to wonder also if Prospero's enslavement of Caliban, however high-minded in its claims of preventing disorder and rape, is not tainted by the same imperatives of possession and control. The issue is wonderfully complex. Caliban is a projection of both the naturally depraved savage described in many explorers' accounts and the nobly innocent savage described by Montaigne. By dramatizing the conflict without taking sides, Shakespeare leaves open a debate about the worth of Prospero's endeavor to contain Caliban's otherness and produces an ambivalent result in which the apparent victory of colonialism and censorship does not entirely conceal the contradictory struggle through which those values are imposed. The play's many open-ended questions apply not only to the New World but also, nearer at hand, to Ireland—an island on the margins of Britain that was regarded as both savage and threatening.

The play's discourse also raises issues of class and political justice. The battle between Prospero and Caliban is one of "master" and "man" (2.2.183); even if Caliban's cry of "freedom" leads him only into further enslavement by Stephano and Trinculo (who are themselves masterless men), the play does not resolve the conflict by simply reimposing social hierarchy. Caliban, Stephano, and Trinculo are all taught a lesson and are satirically punished for their rebellious behavior, but Caliban at least is pardoned and is left behind on the island at the play's end where presumably he will no longer be a slave. In political terms, Prospero resolves the long-standing hostilities between Milan and Naples by his astute arranging of the betrothal of Miranda to Ferdinand. However much it is idealized as a romantic match presided over harmoniously by the gods, it is also a political union aimed at bringing together the ruling families of those two city states. Prospero's masque, his ultimate vision of the triumph of civilization, transforms the myth of the rape of a daughter (Proserpina) in such a way as to preserve the daughter's chaste honor in a union that will repair the political and social damage done by the ouster of Prospero from his dukedom of Milan. For these reasons, the betrothal of Ferdinand and Miranda must have seemed politically relevant to Shakespeare's audience when *The Tempest* was performed before King James at Whitehall in November of 1611 and then again at court in 1613 in celebration of the marriage of James's daughter Elizabeth to Frederick, the Elector Palatine.

The play's ending is far from perfectly stable. Antonio never repents, and we cannot be sure what the island will be like once Prospero has disappeared from the scene. Since Prospero's occupation of the island replicates in a sense the process by which he himself was overthrown, we cannot know when the cycle of revolution will ever cease. We cannot even be sure of the extent to which Shakespeare is master of his own colonial debate in *The Tempest* or, conversely, the extent to which today we should feel ourselves free to relativize, ironize, or in other ways criticize this play for apparent or probable prejudices. Not even a great author like Shakespeare can escape the limits of his own time, any more than we can escape the limits of our own. Perhaps we can nonetheless project ourselves, as spectators and readers, into Shakespeare's attempt to celebrate humanity's highest achievement in the union of the island with the civilized world. Miranda and Ferdinand have bright hopes for the future, even if those hopes must be qualified by Prospero's melancholic observation that the "brave new world" with "such people in't" is only "new to thee," to those who are young and not yet experienced in the world's vexations. Even Caliban may be at last reconciled to Prospero's insistent idea of a harmony between will and reason, no matter how perilously and delicately achieved. Prospero speaks of Caliban as a "thing of darkness I / Acknowledge mine," and Caliban vows to "be wise hereafter / And seek for grace" (5.1.278–9, 298–9). Prospero's view is that the natural human within is more contented, better understood, and more truly free when harmonized with reason.

Caliban is a part of humanity; Ariel is not. Ariel can comprehend what compassion and forgiveness would be like, "were I human" (5.1.20), and can take good-natured part in Prospero's designs to castigate or reform his fellow mortals, but Ariel longs to be free in quite another sense from that meant by Caliban. Ariel takes no part in the final integration of human society. This spirit belongs to a magic world of song, music, and illusion that the artist borrows for his use but that exists eternally outside of him. Like the elements of air, earth, fire, and water in which it mysteriously dwells, this spirit is morally neutral but incredibly vital. From it the artist achieves powers of imagination, enabling him to bedim the noontide sun or call forth the dead from their graves. These visions are illusory in the profound sense that all life is illusory, an "insubstantial pageant" melted into thin air (4.1.150–5). Prospero the artist cherishes his own humanity, as a promise of surcease from his labors. Yet the artifact created by the artist endures, existing apart from time and place, as does Ariel: "Then to the elements / Be free, and fare thou well!" (5.1.321–2). No doubt it is a romantic fiction to associate the dramatist Shakespeare with Prospero's farewell to his art, but it is an almost irresistible idea, because we are so moved by the sense of completion and yet humility, the exultation and yet the calm contained in this leave-taking.

As though to demonstrate the summation of his artistry as magician-poet in what he may indeed have designed as his farewell to the stage, Shakespeare puts on a dazzling display of the verbal artistry for which he had already become famous. His command of blank verse is, by this time, more flexible and protean than ever before, with a marked increase in run-on lines, caesuras in mid line, the sharing of blank verse lines between two or more speakers, feminine endings, and other features of the late Shakespearean style. (See General Introduction, pp. lxxx–lxxxi). The play is notable for its bravura passages, such as those that begin "Our revels now are ended" (4.1.148–58) and "Ye elves of hills" (5.1.33–57). With its opening storm scene and its solemn shows and masques—the *several strange shapes* bringing in a banquet and the appearance of Ariel *like a harpy* in 3.3, the masque of Iris, Ceres, and Juno in 4.1, and Prospero's confining the Neapolitans to a charmed circle in 5.1—*The Tempest* presents itself as a tour de force of spectacle and grandeur in which all of these dazzling events are also astutely interrupted by the resurgence of human appetite and by satiric correction. At every turn the drama manifests a deft compression of time and event. The tone is masterfully assured, in prose as in verse. Images of a dreamlike world come together in a remarkable amalgam whereby the characters participate in a fluid world that moves through them even as they move through it, becoming one with the tempest of time.

In performance, *The Tempest* reveals an extraordinary range of interpretive possibilities. Caliban, in nineteenth-century stage versions, was apt to be a grotesque specimen of Darwinian evolution, outfitted with gills, fishy scales, and long fingernails for prying shellfish out of rocks (the long fingernails are in fact mentioned, at 2.2.166). Herbert Beerbohm Tree, in 1904, saw Caliban as hairy from head to foot, with unkempt beard, pointed ears, sinister eyes, and long fingernails. To Frank Benson, at Stratford-upon-Avon in 1891, Caliban (played by Benson himself) was the missing link in an evolutionary chain of monkeys, baboons, and other presumably human ancestors; the Caliban of this production climbed a tree on stage, hung upside down, and gibbered. More recently, in accord with critical interest in the play as a potential critique of colonialism, Caliban has often been seen as a Caribbean native, physically imposing and even handsome, restive under his slavery, a man of immense human dignity. An example is that of David Suchet in Clifford Williams's 1987 production for the Royal Shakespeare Company; Suchet's Caliban, a sympathetic victim of imperialism, evoked unmistable echoes of third-world exploited populations from the West Indies and sub-Saharan Africa. Prospero has undergone no less of a sea change, from the benign authorial stand-in of traditional nineteenth-century productions to a man who can be tyrannical, arbitrary, menacing, close to violence, deeply angry, as in Derek Jarman's 1980 film. Interpretations of Ariel have varied from saccharine sweetness to the punk-haired and drug-inebriated, as in Mark Rylance's Ariel in Ron Daniels's 1982 RSC production. Underlying sexual tensions are evident on all sides in recent productions. Some of the most remarkable versions of the play have abandoned Shakespeare's script to varying degrees, as in Peter Brook's Round House production of 1968 featuring an enormous Sycorax giving birth to Caliban, a takeover of the island and capture of Prospero by Caliban, and a wild orgy. Derek Jarman's film version of 1980 saw the play as dominantly gay, with Caliban as an aging "queen." Giorgio Strehler's *La Tempesta*, Milan, 1977, pictured Ariel as a commedia dell'arte Pierrot attached to a wire, soaring through the air and landing as though on Prospero's raised finger. Peter Greenaway's 1991 film called *Prospero's Books* presented the entire play through Prospero's eyes; John Gielgud, as Prospero, spoke virtually all the lines. The extraordinary range of theatrical innovations that has been brought to this play testifies to the script's own remarkable theatrical self-consciousness and its delight in magic and illusion.

The Tempest

Names of the Actors

ALONSO, *King of Naples*
SEBASTIAN, *his brother*
PROSPERO, *the right Duke of Milan*
ANTONIO, *his brother, the usurping Duke of Milan*
FERDINAND, *son to the King of Naples*
GONZALO, *an honest old counselor*
ADRIAN *and*
FRANCISCO, } *lords*
CALIBAN, *a savage and deformed slave*
TRINCULO, *a jester*
STEPHANO, *a drunken butler*
MASTER *of a ship*

BOATSWAIN
MARINERS

MIRANDA, *daughter to Prospero*

ARIEL, *an airy spirit*
IRIS,
CERES,
JUNO, } *[presented by] spirits*
NYMPHS,
REAPERS,

[*Other Spirits attending on Prospero*]

THE SCENE: *An uninhabited island*

1.1

*A tempestuous noise of thunder and lightning
heard. Enter a Shipmaster and a Boatswain.*

MASTER   Boatswain!

BOATSWAIN   Here, Master. What cheer?

MASTER   Good, speak to th' mariners. Fall to't yarely,
or we run ourselves aground. Bestir, bestir!   *Exit.*   3

Enter Mariners.

BOATSWAIN   Heigh, my hearts! Cheerly, cheerly, my
hearts! Yare, yare! Take in the topsail. Tend to th' Mas-   6
ter's whistle.—Blow till thou burst thy wind, if room   7
enough!   8

*Enter Alonso, Sebastian, Antonio, Ferdinand,
Gonzalo, and others.*

ALONSO   Good Boatswain, have care. Where's the Master? Play the men.   10

BOATSWAIN   I pray now, keep below.

ANTONIO   Where is the Master, Boatswain?

BOATSWAIN   Do you not hear him? You mar our labor.
Keep your cabins! You do assist the storm.   14

GONZALO   Nay, good, be patient.   15

BOATSWAIN   When the sea is. Hence! What cares these
roarers for the name of king? To cabin! Silence! Trou-   17
ble us not.

GONZALO   Good, yet remember whom thou hast
aboard.

BOATSWAIN   None that I more love than myself. You are
a councillor; if you can command these elements to
silence and work the peace of the present, we will not   23
hand a rope more. Use your authority. If you cannot,   24
give thanks you have lived so long and make yourself
ready in your cabin for the mischance of the hour, if it
so hap.—Cheerly, good hearts!—Out of our way,   27
I say.   *Exit.*

GONZALO   I have great comfort from this fellow. Methinks he hath no drowning mark upon him; his com-   30
plexion is perfect gallows. Stand fast, good Fate, to his   31
hanging! Make the rope of his destiny our cable, for
our own doth little advantage. If he be not born to be   33

hanged, our case is miserable.   *Exeunt [courtiers].*   34

Enter Boatswain.

BOATSWAIN   Down with the topmast! Yare! Lower,
lower! Bring her to try wi'th' main course. (*A cry*   36
within.) A plague upon this howling! They are louder
than the weather or our office.   38

Enter Sebastian, Antonio, and Gonzalo.

Yet again? What do you here? Shall we give o'er and   39
drown? Have you a mind to sink?

SEBASTIAN   A pox o'your throat, you bawling, blasphe-
mous, incharitable dog!

BOATSWAIN   Work you, then.

ANTONIO   Hang, cur! Hang, you whoreson, insolent
noisemaker! We are less afraid to be drowned than
thou art.

GONZALO   I'll warrant him for drowning, though the   47
ship were no stronger than a nutshell and as
leaky as an unstanched wench.   49

BOATSWAIN   Lay her ahold, ahold! Set her two courses.   50
Off to sea again! Lay her off!

Enter Mariners, wet.

MARINERS   All lost! To prayers, to prayers! All lost!
[*The Mariners run about in confusion, exiting at
random.*]

BOATSWAIN   What, must our mouths be cold?   53

GONZALO
The King and Prince at prayers! Let's assist them,
For our case is as theirs.

SEBASTIAN   I am out of patience.

ANTONIO
We are merely cheated of our lives by drunkards.   56
This wide-chapped rascal! Would thou mightst lie
drowning   57
The washing of ten tides!

GONZALO   He'll be hanged yet,   58
Though every drop of water swear against it
And gape at wid'st to glut him.
(*A confused noise within:*)   "Mercy on us!"—   60
"We split, we split!"—"Farewell my wife and
children!"—   61
"Farewell, brother!"—"We split, we split, we split!"
[*Exit Boatswain.*]

ANTONIO   Let's all sink wi'th' King.

SEBASTIAN   Let's take leave of him.

Exit [with Antonio].

GONZALO   Now would I give a thousand furlongs of sea

Names of the Actors This list appears at the end of the play in the
First Folio, in this order, with Miranda's name below that of the men,
as was conventional in lists of the period.   **PROSPERO, *the right***
the rightful   **CALIBAN . . . *slave*** The Folio reads "*saluage*," a common alternative spelling of *savage* but perhaps also with a resonance
of being salvaged from shipwreck. *Slave* has a range of meanings:
wretch, rascal, servile creature, one who is owned by another person,
one who is divested of freedom and personal rights.
1.1 Location: On board ship, off the island's coast.
3 Good i.e., It's good you've come, or, my good fellow.   **yarely** nimbly   **6 Tend** Attend   **7 Blow** (Addressed to the wind.)   **7–8 if room
enough** as long as we have sea room enough.   **10 Play the men** Act
like men, with spirit.   **14 Keep** Remain in   **15 good** good fellow
17 roarers waves or winds, or both; spoken to as though they were
"bullies" or "blusterers"   **23 work . . . present** bring calm to our present circumstances   **24 hand** handle   **27 hap** happen.   **30–1 complexion . . . gallows** appearance shows he was born to be hanged
(and therefore, according to the proverb, in no danger of drowning).
33 our . . . advantage our own cable is of little benefit.

34 case is miserable circumstances are desperate.   **36 Bring . . .
course** Sail her close to the wind by means of the mainsail.   **38 our
office** i.e., the noise we make at our work.   **39 give o'er** give up
47 warrant him for drowning guarantee that he will never be
drowned   **49 unstanched** insatiable, loose, unrestrained. (Suggesting
also "incontinent" and "menstrual.")   **50 ahold** ahull, close to the
wind.   **courses** sails, i.e., foresail as well as mainsail, set in an
attempt to get the ship back out into open water.   **53 must . . . cold?**
i.e., must we drown in the cold sea?   **56 merely** utterly   **57 wide-
chapped** big-mouthed   **57–8 Would . . . tides!** (Pirates were hanged
on the shore and left until three tides had come in.)   **60 at wid'st**
wide open.   **glut** swallow   **61 split** break apart.

for an acre of barren ground: long heath, brown furze,   66
anything. The wills above be done! But I would fain   67
die a dry death.   *Exit.*

❧

1.2

Enter Prospero [in his magic cloak] and Miranda.

MIRANDA
If by your art, my dearest father, you have   1
Put the wild waters in this roar, allay them.   2
The sky, it seems, would pour down stinking pitch,
But that the sea, mounting to th' welkin's cheek,   4
Dashes the fire out. Oh, I have suffered
With those that I saw suffer! A brave vessel,   6
Who had, no doubt, some noble creature in her,
Dashed all to pieces. Oh, the cry did knock
Against my very heart! Poor souls, they perished.
Had I been any god of power, I would
Have sunk the sea within the earth or ere   11
It should the good ship so have swallowed and
The freighting souls within her.
PROSPERO   Be collected.   13
No more amazement. Tell your piteous heart   14
There's no harm done.
MIRANDA   Oh, woe the day!
PROSPERO   No harm.
I have done nothing but in care of thee,   16
Of thee, my dear one, thee, my daughter, who
Art ignorant of what thou art, naught knowing
Of whence I am, nor that I am more better   19
Than Prospero, master of a full poor cell,   20
And thy no greater father.
MIRANDA   More to know
Did never meddle with my thoughts.
PROSPERO   'Tis time   22
I should inform thee farther. Lend thy hand
And pluck my magic garment from me. So,
    [laying down his magic cloak and staff]
Lie there, my art.—Wipe thou thine eyes. Have
    comfort.
The direful spectacle of the wreck, which touched   26
The very virtue of compassion in thee,   27
I have with such provision in mine art
So safely ordered that there is no soul—
No, not so much perdition as an hair   30
Betid to any creature in the vessel   31
Which thou heard'st cry, which thou saw'st sink. Sit
    down,   32

For thou must now know farther.
MIRANDA *[sitting]*   You have often
Begun to tell me what I am, but stopped
And left me to a bootless inquisition,   35
Concluding, "Stay, not yet."
PROSPERO   The hour's now come;
The very minute bids thee ope thine ear.
Obey, and be attentive. Canst thou remember
A time before we came unto this cell?
I do not think thou canst, for then thou wast not
Out three years old.
MIRANDA   Certainly, sir, I can.   41
PROSPERO
By what? By any other house or person?
Of anything the image, tell me, that
Hath kept with thy remembrance.
MIRANDA   'Tis far off,
And rather like a dream than an assurance   45
That my remembrance warrants. Had I not   46
Four or five women once that tended me?
PROSPERO
Thou hadst, and more, Miranda. But how is it
That this lives in thy mind? What see'st thou else
In the dark backward and abysm of time?   50
If thou rememb'rest aught ere thou cam'st here,   51
How thou cam'st here thou mayst.
MIRANDA   But that I do not.
PROSPERO
Twelve year since, Miranda, twelve year since,
Thy father was the Duke of Milan and
A prince of power.
MIRANDA   Sir, are not you my father?
PROSPERO
Thy mother was a piece of virtue, and   56
She said thou wast my daughter; and thy father
Was Duke of Milan, and his only heir
And princess no worse issued.
MIRANDA   Oh, the heavens!   59
What foul play had we, that we came from thence?
Or blessèd was't we did?
PROSPERO   Both, both, my girl.
By foul play, as thou say'st, were we heaved thence,
But blessedly holp hither.
MIRANDA   Oh, my heart bleeds   63
To think o'th' teen that I have turned you to,   64
Which is from my remembrance! Please you, farther.   65
PROSPERO
My brother and thy uncle, called Antonio—
I pray thee mark me—that a brother should
Be so perfidious!—he whom next thyself   68
Of all the world I loved, and to him put
The manage of my state, as at that time   70
Through all the seigniories it was the first,   71

---

66 **heath** heather.   **furze** gorse, a weed growing on wasteland
67 **fain** rather
1.2 Location: The island, near Prospero's cell. On the Elizabethan
stage, this cell is implicitly at hand throughout the play, although
in some scenes the convention of flexible distance allows us to
imagine characters in other parts of the island.
1 **art** magic   2 **allay** pacify   4 **welkin's cheek** sky's face   6 **brave**
gallant, splendid   11 **or ere** before   13 **freighting souls** cargo of
souls.   **collected** calm, composed.   14 **amazement** consternation.
piteous pitying   16 **but** except   19 **more better** of higher rank
20 **full** very   22 **meddle** mingle   26 **wreck** shipwreck   27 **virtue**
essence   30 **perdition** loss   31 **Betid** happened   32 **Which** whom

35 **bootless inquisition** profitless inquiry   41 **Out** fully   45–6 **assurance . . . warrants** certainty that my memory guarantees.   50 **backward
. . . time** abyss of the past.   51 **aught** anything   56 **piece** masterpiece,
exemplar   59 **no worse issued** no less nobly born, descended.   63 **holp**
helped   64 **teen . . . to** trouble I've caused you to remember or put you
to   65 **from** out of   68 **next** next to   70 **manage** management, administration   71 **seigniories** i.e., city-states of northern Italy

And Prospero the prime duke, being so reputed   72
In dignity, and for the liberal arts
Without a parallel; those being all my study,
The government I cast upon my brother
And to my state grew stranger, being transported   76
And rapt in secret studies. Thy false uncle—
Dost thou attend me?

MIRANDA   Sir, most heedfully.

PROSPERO
Being once perfected how to grant suits,   79
How to deny them, who t'advance and who
To trash for overtopping, new created   81
The creatures that were mine, I say, or changed 'em,   82
Or else new formed 'em; having both the key   83
Of officer and office, set all hearts i'th' state   84
To what tune pleased his ear, that now he was   85
The ivy which had hid my princely trunk
And sucked my verdure out on't. Thou attend'st not.   87

MIRANDA
Oh, good sir, I do.

PROSPERO   I pray thee, mark me.
I, thus neglecting worldly ends, all dedicated
To closeness and the bettering of my mind   90
With that which, but by being so retired,   91
O'erprized all popular rate, in my false brother   92
Awaked an evil nature; and my trust,
Like a good parent, did beget of him   94
A falsehood in its contrary as great
As my trust was, which had indeed no limit,
A confidence sans bound. He being thus lorded   97
Not only with what my revenue yielded
But what my power might else exact, like one   99
Who, having into truth by telling of it,   100
Made such a sinner of his memory   101
To credit his own lie, he did believe   102
He was indeed the Duke, out o'th' substitution   103
And executing th'outward face of royalty   104
With all prerogative. Hence his ambition growing—   105
Dost thou hear?

MIRANDA   Your tale, sir, would cure deafness.

PROSPERO
To have no screen between this part he played   107
And him he played it for, he needs will be   108
Absolute Milan. Me, poor man, my library   109
Was dukedom large enough. Of temporal royalties   110
He thinks me now incapable; confederates—   111
So dry he was for sway—wi'th' King of Naples   112
To give him annual tribute, do him homage,   113
Subject his coronet to his crown, and bend   114
The dukedom yet unbowed—alas, poor Milan!—   115
To most ignoble stooping.

MIRANDA   O the heavens!

PROSPERO
Mark his condition and th'event, then tell me   117
If this might be a brother.

MIRANDA   I should sin
To think but nobly of my grandmother.   119
Good wombs have borne bad sons.

PROSPERO   Now the condition.
This King of Naples, being an enemy
To me inveterate, hearkens my brother's suit,   122
Which was that he, in lieu o'th' premises   123
Of homage and I know not how much tribute,
Should presently extirpate me and mine   125
Out of the dukedom and confer fair Milan,
With all the honors, on my brother. Whereon,
A treacherous army levied, one midnight
Fated to th' purpose did Antonio open
The gates of Milan, and, i'th' dead of darkness,
The ministers for th' purpose hurried thence   131
Me and thy crying self.

MIRANDA   Alack, for pity!
I, not remembering how I cried out then,
Will cry it o'er again. It is a hint   134
That wrings mine eyes to 't.

PROSPERO   Hear a little further,   135
And then I'll bring thee to the present business
Which now's upon 's, without the which this story
Were most impertinent.

MIRANDA   Wherefore did they not   138
That hour destroy us?

PROSPERO   Well demanded, wench.   139
My tale provokes that question. Dear, they durst
    not,
So dear the love my people bore me, nor set   141
A mark so bloody on the business, but   142

---

72 prime first in rank and importance   **76 to . . . stranger** i.e., withdrew from my responsibilities as duke.   **transported** carried away   **79 perfected** grown skillful   **81 trash** check a hound by tying a cord or weight to its neck.   **overtopping** running too far ahead of the pack; surmounting, exceeding one's authority   **81–3 new . . . formed 'em** won the loyalty of my officers by appointing them to new posts, or replaced them with others who would be loyal to Antonio, or else redefined the positions and their occupants   **83–5 having . . . ear** having now under his control both the officers and the positions, he set a tone for his rule according to his own inclination. (*Key* is also a metaphor for tuning stringed instruments.)   **87 verdure** vitality.   **on't** of it.   **90 closeness** retirement, seclusion   **91–2 but . . . rate** i.e., were it not that its private nature caused me to neglect my public responsibilities, had a value far beyond what public opinion could appreciate, or, simply because it was done in such seclusion, had a value not appreciated by popular opinion   **94 good parent** (Alludes to the proverb that good parents often bear bad children; see also line 120.)   **of** in   **97 sans** without.   **lorded** raised to lordship, with power and wealth   **99 else** otherwise, additionally   **100–2 Who . . . lie** i.e., who, by repeatedly telling the lie (that he was indeed Duke of Milan), made his memory such a confirmed sinner against truth that he began to believe his own lie   **103–5 out . . . prerogative** as a result of his making himself my substitute and carrying out all the visible functions of royalty with all its rights and privileges.

107–9 To have . . . Milan In order to eliminate all separation between his role and himself, he insisted on becoming the Duke of Milan in name as well as in fact.   **110 temporal royalties** practical prerogatives and responsibilities of a sovereign   **111 confederates** conspires, allies himself   **112 dry** thirsty.   **sway** power   **113 him** i.e., the King of Naples   **114 his . . . his** Antonio's . . . the King of Naples'.   **bend** make bow down   **115 yet** hitherto   **117 condition** pact.   **th'event** the outcome   **119 but** other than   **122 hearkens** listens to   **123 he** the King of Naples.   **in . . . premises** in return for the stipulation   **125 presently extirpate** at once remove   **131 ministers . . . purpose** agents employed to do this.   **thence** from there   **134 hint** prompting   **135 wrings** (1) constrains (2) wrings tears from   **138 impertinent** irrelevant.   **Wherefore** Why   **139 demanded** asked.   **wench** (Here a term of endearment.)   **141–2 set . . . bloody** i.e., make obvious their murderous intent. (From the practice of marking with the blood of the prey those who have participated in a successful hunt.)

With colors fairer painted their foul ends.   143
In few, they hurried us aboard a bark,   144
Bore us some leagues to sea, where they prepared
A rotten carcass of a butt, not rigged,   146
Nor tackle, sail, nor mast; the very rats   147
Instinctively have quit it. There they hoist us,   148
To cry to th' sea that roared to us, to sigh
To th' winds whose pity, sighing back again,
Did us but loving wrong.

MIRANDA   Alack, what trouble   151
Was I then to you!

PROSPERO   Oh, a cherubin
Thou wast that did preserve me. Thou didst smile,
Infusèd with a fortitude from heaven,   154
When I have decked the sea with drops full salt,   155
Under my burden groaned, which raised in me   156
An undergoing stomach, to bear up   157
Against what should ensue.

MIRANDA   How came we ashore?

PROSPERO   By Providence divine.
Some food we had, and some fresh water, that
A noble Neapolitan, Gonzalo,
Out of his charity, who being then appointed
Master of this design, did give us, with
Rich garments, linens, stuffs, and necessaries,   165
Which since have steaded much. So, of his
     gentleness,   166
Knowing I loved my books, he furnished me
From mine own library with volumes that
I prize above my dukedom.

MIRANDA   Would I might   169
But ever see that man!

PROSPERO   Now I arise.   170
         [*He puts on his magic cloak.*]
Sit still, and hear the last of our sea sorrow.   171
Here in this island we arrived; and here
Have I, thy schoolmaster, made thee more profit   173
Than other princes can, that have more time   174
For vainer hours and tutors not so careful.   175

MIRANDA
Heavens thank you for't! And now, I pray you, sir—
For still 'tis beating in my mind—your reason
For raising this sea storm?

PROSPERO   Know thus far forth:
By accident most strange, bountiful Fortune,
Now my dear lady, hath mine enemies   180
Brought to this shore; and by my prescience
I find my zenith doth depend upon   182

A most auspicious star, whose influence   183
If now I court not, but omit, my fortunes   184
Will ever after droop. Here cease more questions.
Thou art inclined to sleep. 'Tis a good dullness,   186
And give it way. I know thou canst not choose.   187
         [*Miranda sleeps.*]
Come away, servant, come! I am ready now.   188
Approach, my Ariel, come.

Enter Ariel.

ARIEL
All hail, great master, grave sir, hail! I come
To answer thy best pleasure; be't to fly,
To swim, to dive into the fire, to ride
On the curled clouds, to thy strong bidding task   193
Ariel and all his quality.

PROSPERO   Hast thou, spirit,   194
Performed to point the tempest that I bade thee?   195

ARIEL   To every article.
I boarded the King's ship. Now on the beak,   197
Now in the waist, the deck, in every cabin,   198
I flamed amazement. Sometime I'd divide   199
And burn in many places; on the topmast,
The yards, and bowsprit would I flame distinctly,   201
Then meet and join. Jove's lightning, the precursors
O'th' dreadful thunderclaps, more momentary
And sight-outrunning were not. The fire and cracks   204
Of sulfurous roaring the most mighty Neptune   205
Seem to besiege and make his bold waves tremble,
Yea, his dread trident shake.

PROSPERO   My brave spirit!   207
Who was so firm, so constant, that this coil   208
Would not infect his reason?

ARIEL   Not a soul
But felt a fever of the mad and played   210
Some tricks of desperation. All but mariners
Plunged in the foaming brine and quit the vessel,
Then all afire with me. The King's son, Ferdinand,
With hair up-staring—then like reeds, not hair—   214
Was the first man that leapt; cried, "Hell is empty,
And all the devils are here!"

PROSPERO   Why, that's my spirit!
But was not this nigh shore?

ARIEL   Close by, my master.

PROSPERO
But are they, Ariel, safe?

ARIEL   Not a hair perished.
On their sustaining garments not a blemish,   219
But fresher than before; and, as thou bad'st me,   220

---

143 fairer apparently more attractive   **144 few** few words.   **bark** ship   **146 butt** cask, tub   **147 Nor tackle** neither rigging   **148 quit** abandoned   **151 Did . . . wrong** i.e., pitied us even as they drove us on.   **154 Infusèd** filled, suffused   **155 decked** covered (with salt tears); adorned   **156 which** i.e., the smile   **157 undergoing stomach** courage to go on   **165 stuffs** supplies   **166 steaded much** been of much use.   **So, of** Similarly, out of   **169 Would** I wish   **170 But ever** i.e., someday   **171 sea sorrow** sorrowful adventure at sea.   **173–4 made . . . can** provided a more valuable education than other royal children (of either sex) can enjoy   **175 vainer** more foolishly spent   **180 my dear lady** (Refers to Fortune, not Miranda.)   **182 zenith** height of fortune. (Astrological term.)

183 influence astrological power   **184 but omit** but ignore instead   **186 dullness** drowsiness   **187 give it way** let it happen (i.e., don't fight it).   **188 Come away** Come   **193 task** make demands upon   **194 quality** (1) fellow spirits (2) abilities.   **195 to point** to the smallest detail   **197 beak** prow   **198 waist** midships.   **deck** poop deck at the stern   **199 flamed amazement** struck terror in the guise of fire, i.e., Saint Elmo's fire.   **201 distinctly** in different places   **204 sight-outrunning** swifter than sight.   **were not** could not have been.   **205 Neptune** Roman god of the sea   **207 trident** three-pronged weapon   **208 coil** tumult   **210 of the mad** such as madmen feel   **214 up-staring** standing on end   **219 sustaining** protecting   **220 bad'st** ordered

In troops I have dispersed them 'bout the isle.   221
The King's son have I landed by himself,
Whom I left cooling of the air with sighs   223
In an odd angle of the isle, and sitting,   224
His arms in this sad knot.   [*He folds his arms.*]
PROSPERO   Of the King's ship,   225
The mariners, say how thou hast disposed,
And all the rest o'th' fleet.
ARIEL   Safely in harbor
Is the King's ship; in the deep nook, where once   228
Thou called'st me up at midnight to fetch dew   229
From the still-vexed Bermudas, there she's hid;   230
The mariners all under hatches stowed,
Who, with a charm joined to their suffered labor,   232
I have left asleep. And for the rest o'th' fleet,
Which I dispersed, they all have met again
And are upon the Mediterranean float   235
Bound sadly home for Naples,
Supposing that they saw the King's ship wrecked
And his great person perish.
PROSPERO   Ariel, thy charge
Exactly is performed. But there's more work.
What is the time o'th' day?
ARIEL   Past the mid season.   240
PROSPERO
At least two glasses. The time twixt six and now   241
Must by us both be spent most preciously.
ARIEL
Is there more toil? Since thou dost give me pains,   243
Let me remember thee what thou hast promised,   244
Which is not yet performed me.
PROSPERO   How now? Moody?
What is't thou canst demand?
ARIEL   My liberty.
PROSPERO
Before the time be out? No more!
ARIEL   I prithee,
Remember I have done thee worthy service,
Told thee no lies, made thee no mistakings, served
Without or grudge or grumblings. Thou did promise
To bate me a full year.
PROSPERO   Dost thou forget   251
From what a torment I did free thee?
ARIEL   No.
PROSPERO
Thou dost, and think'st it much to tread the ooze
Of the salt deep,
To run upon the sharp wind of the north,
To do me business in the veins o'th' earth   256

When it is baked with frost.
ARIEL   I do not, sir.   257
PROSPERO
Thou liest, malignant thing! Hast thou forgot
The foul witch Sycorax, who with age and envy   259
Was grown into a hoop? Hast thou forgot her?   260
ARIEL   No, sir.
PROSPERO
Thou hast. Where was she born? Speak. Tell me.
ARIEL
Sir, in Argier.
PROSPERO   Oh, was she so? I must   263
Once in a month recount what thou hast been,
Which thou forget'st. This damned witch Sycorax,
For mischiefs manifold and sorceries terrible
To enter human hearing, from Argier,
Thou know'st, was banished. For one thing she did   268
They would not take her life. Is not this true?
ARIEL   Ay, sir.
PROSPERO
This blue-eyed hag was hither brought with child   271
And here was left by th' sailors. Thou, my slave,
As thou report'st thyself, was then her servant;
And, for thou wast a spirit too delicate   274
To act her earthy and abhorred commands,
Refusing her grand hests, she did confine thee,   276
By help of her more potent ministers
And in her most unmitigable rage,
Into a cloven pine, within which rift
Imprisoned thou didst painfully remain
A dozen years; within which space she died
And left thee there, where thou didst vent thy
     groans
As fast as mill wheels strike. Then was this island—   283
Save for the son that she did litter here,   284
A freckled whelp, hag-born—not honored with   285
A human shape.
ARIEL   Yes, Caliban her son.   286
PROSPERO
Dull thing, I say so: he, that Caliban   287
Whom now I keep in service. Thou best know'st
What torment I did find thee in. Thy groans
Did make wolves howl, and penetrate the breasts
Of ever-angry bears. It was a torment
To lay upon the damned, which Sycorax
Could not again undo. It was mine art,
When I arrived and heard thee, that made gape   294
The pine and let thee out.
ARIEL   I thank thee, master.

---

221 **troops** groups   223 **cooling of** cooling   224 **angle** corner
225 **sad knot** (Folded arms are indicative of melancholy.)   228 **nook**
bay   229 **dew** (Collected at midnight for magical purposes; compare
with line 324.)   230 **still-vexed Bermudas** ever stormy Bermudas.
(Perhaps refers to the then recent Bermuda shipwreck; see play Introduction. The Folio text reads "*Bermoothes.*")   232 **with . . . labor** by
means of a spell added to all the labor they have undergone
235 **float** sea   240 **mid season** noon.   241 **glasses** hourglasses.
243 **pains** labors   244 **remember** remind   251 **bate** remit, deduct
256 **do me** do for me.   **veins** veins of minerals, or, underground
streams, thought to be analogous to the veins of the human body

257 **baked** hardened   259 **envy** malice   260 **grown into a hoop** i.e.,
so bent over with age as to resemble a hoop.   263 **Argier** Algiers
268 **one . . . did** (Perhaps a reference to her pregnancy, for which her
life would be spared.)   271 **blue-eyed** with dark circles under the
eyes or with blue eyelids, implying pregnancy.   **with child** pregnant
274 **for** because   276 **hests** commands   283 **as mill wheels strike** as
the blades of a mill wheel strike the water.   284 **Save** except.   **litter**
give birth to   285 **whelp** offspring. (Used of animals.)   **hag-born**
born of a female demon   286 **Yes . . . son** (Ariel is probably concur-
ring with Prospero's comment about a "freckled whelp," not contra-
dicting the point about "A human shape.")   287 **Dull . . . so** i.e.,
Exactly, that's what I said, you dullard   294 **gape** open wide

PROSPERO
　　If thou more murmur'st, I will rend an oak
　　And peg thee in his knotty entrails till   297
　　Thou hast howled away twelve winters.
ARIEL   Pardon, master.
　　I will be correspondent to command   299
　　And do my spriting gently.   300
PROSPERO   Do so, and after two days
　　I will discharge thee.
ARIEL   That's my noble master!
　　What shall I do? Say what? What shall I do?
PROSPERO
　　Go make thyself like a nymph o'th' sea. Be subject
　　To no sight but thine and mine, invisible
　　To every eyeball else. Go take this shape
　　And hither come in't. Go, hence with diligence!
　　　　　　　　　　　　　　　　　Exit [Ariel].
　　[To Miranda] Awake, dear heart, awake! Thou hast
　　　　slept well.
　　Awake!
MIRANDA   The strangeness of your story put
　　Heaviness in me.
PROSPERO   Shake it off. Come on,   310
　　We'll visit Caliban, my slave, who never
　　Yields us kind answer.
MIRANDA   'Tis a villain, sir,
　　I do not love to look on.
PROSPERO   But, as 'tis,
　　We cannot miss him. He does make our fire,   314
　　Fetch in our wood, and serves in offices   315
　　That profit us.—What ho! Slave! Caliban!
　　Thou earth, thou! Speak.
CALIBAN (within)   There's wood enough within.
PROSPERO
　　Come forth, I say! There's other business for thee.
　　Come, thou tortoise! When?   319

　　　　　Enter Ariel like a water nymph.

　　Fine apparition! My quaint Ariel,   320
　　Hark in thine ear.   [He whispers.]
ARIEL   My lord, it shall be done.   Exit.
PROSPERO
　　Thou poisonous slave, got by the devil himself   322
　　Upon thy wicked dam, come forth!   323

　　　　　Enter Caliban.

CALIBAN
　　As wicked dew as e'er my mother brushed   324
　　With raven's feather from unwholesome fen   325
　　Drop on you both! A southwest blow on ye   326
　　And blister you all o'er!
PROSPERO
　　For this, be sure, tonight thou shalt have cramps,

Side-stitches that shall pen thy breath up. Urchins   329
Shall forth at vast of night that they may work   330
All exercise on thee. Thou shalt be pinched
As thick as honeycomb, each pinch more stinging   332
Than bees that made 'em.
CALIBAN   I must eat my dinner.   333
　　This island's mine, by Sycorax my mother,
　　Which thou tak'st from me. When thou cam'st first,
　　Thou strok'st me and made much of me, wouldst give
　　　me
　　Water with berries in't, and teach me how
　　To name the bigger light, and how the less,   338
　　That burn by day and night. And then I loved thee
　　And showed thee all the qualities o'th'isle,
　　The fresh springs, brine pits, barren place and fertile.
　　Cursed be I that did so! All the charms   342
　　Of Sycorax, toads, beetles, bats, light on you!
　　For I am all the subjects that you have,
　　Which first was mine own king; and here you sty me 345
　　In this hard rock, whiles you do keep from me
　　The rest o'th'island.
PROSPERO   Thou most lying slave,
　　Whom stripes may move, not kindness! I have used
　　　thee,   348
　　Filth as thou art, with humane care, and lodged thee 349
　　In mine own cell, till thou didst seek to violate
　　The honor of my child.
CALIBAN
　　Oho, oho! Would't had been done!
　　Thou didst prevent me; I had peopled else   353
　　This isle with Calibans.
MIRANDA   Abhorrèd slave,   354
　　Which any print of goodness wilt not take,   355
　　Being capable of all ill! I pitied thee,
　　Took pains to make thee speak, taught thee each hour
　　One thing or other. When thou didst not, savage,
　　Know thine own meaning, but wouldst gabble like
　　A thing most brutish, I endowed thy purposes   360
　　With words that made them known. But thy vile race, 361
　　Though thou didst learn, had that in't which good
　　　natures
　　Could not abide to be with; therefore wast thou
　　Deservedly confined into this rock,
　　Who hadst deserved more than a prison.   365
CALIBAN
　　You taught me language, and my profit on't
　　Is I know how to curse. The red plague rid you   367

---

297 his its   299 correspondent responsive, submissive   300 spriting
gently duties as a spirit willingly.   310 Heaviness drowsiness
314 miss do without   315 offices functions, duties   319 When (An
exclamation of impatience.)   320 quaint ingenious   322 got begotten, sired   323 dam mother. (Used of animals.)   324 wicked mischievous, harmful   325 fen marsh, bog   326 southwest i.e., wind
thought to bring disease

329 Urchins Hedgehogs; here, suggesting goblins in the guise of
hedgehogs   330 vast lengthy, desolate time. (Malignant spirits were
thought to be restricted to the hours of darkness.)   332 as honeycomb i.e., as a honeycomb full of bees   333 'em i.e., the honeycomb.
338 the bigger . . . less i.e., the sun and the moon. (See Genesis 1:16:
"God then made two great lights: the greater light to rule the day, and
the less light to rule the night.")   342 charms spells   345 sty confine
as in a sty   348 stripes lashes   349 humane (Not distinguished as a
word from human.)   353 peopled else otherwise populated   354–65
Abhorrèd . . . prison (Sometimes assigned by editors to Prospero.)
355 print imprint, impression   360 purposes meanings, desires
361 race natural disposition; species, nature   367 red plague plague
characterized by red sores and evacuation of blood.   rid destroy

For learning me your language!

PROSPERO   Hagseed, hence!   368
Fetch us in fuel, and be quick, thou'rt best,   369
To answer other business. Shrugg'st thou, malice?   370
If thou neglect'st or dost unwillingly
What I command, I'll rack thee with old cramps,   372
Fill all thy bones with aches, make thee roar   373
That beasts shall tremble at thy din.

CALIBAN   No, pray thee.
[*Aside*]   I must obey. His art is of such power
It would control my dam's god, Setebos,   376
And make a vassal of him.

PROSPERO   So, slave, hence!   377

Exit Caliban.

*Enter Ferdinand; and Ariel, invisible, playing and
singing. [Ferdinand does not see Prospero and
Miranda.]*

Ariel's Song.

ARIEL

Come unto these yellow sands,
    And then take hands;
Curtsied when you have, and kissed   380
    The wild waves whist;   381
Foot it featly here and there,   382
    And, sweet sprites, bear   383
The burden. Hark, hark!   384
        Burden, dispersedly [*within*].Bow-wow. 385
    The watchdogs bark.
        [*Burden, dispersedly within*.] Bow-wow.
Hark, hark! I hear
The strain of strutting chanticleer
    Cry Cock-a-diddle-dow.

FERDINAND

Where should this music be? I'th'air or th'earth?
It sounds no more; and sure it waits upon   392
Some god o'th'island. Sitting on a bank,   393
Weeping again the King my father's wreck,
This music crept by me upon the waters,
Allaying both their fury and my passion   396
With its sweet air. Thence I have followed it, 397
Or it hath drawn me rather. But 'tis gone.
No, it begins again.

Ariel's Song.

ARIEL

Full fathom five thy father lies.
    Of his bones are coral made.

Those are pearls that were his eyes.
    Nothing of him that doth fade
But doth suffer a sea change
Into something rich and strange.
Sea nymphs hourly ring his knell.   406
        Burden [*within*]. Ding dong.
Hark, now I hear them, ding dong bell.

FERDINAND

The ditty does remember my drowned father.   409
This is no mortal business, nor no sound
That the earth owes. I hear it now above me. 411

PROSPERO [*to Miranda*]

The fringèd curtains of thine eye advance   412
And say what thou see'st yond.

MIRANDA   What is't? A spirit?
Lord, how it looks about! Believe me, sir,
It carries a brave form. But 'tis a spirit.   415

PROSPERO

No, wench, it eats and sleeps and hath such senses
As we have, such. This gallant which thou see'st
Was in the wreck; and, but he's something stained 418
With grief, that's beauty's canker, thou mightst
    call him   419
A goodly person. He hath lost his fellows
And strays about to find 'em.

MIRANDA   I might call him
A thing divine, for nothing natural
I ever saw so noble.

PROSPERO [*aside*]   It goes on, I see,
As my soul prompts it.—Spirit, fine spirit, I'll free thee
Within two days for this.

FERDINAND [*seeing Miranda*]   Most sure, the goddess
On whom these airs attend!—Vouchsafe my prayer 426
May know if you remain upon this island,   427
And that you will some good instruction give
How I may bear me here. My prime request,   429
Which I do last pronounce, is—O you wonder!—   430
If you be maid or no?

MIRANDA   No wonder, sir,   431
But certainly a maid.

FERDINAND   My language? Heavens!
I am the best of them that speak this speech,   433
Were I but where 'tis spoken.

PROSPERO [*coming forward*]   How? The best?
What wert thou if the King of Naples heard thee?

FERDINAND

A single thing, as I am now, that wonders   436
To hear thee speak of Naples. He does hear me, 437

---

368 **learning** teaching.   **Hagseed** Offspring of a female demon
369 **thou'rt best** you'd be well advised   370 **answer other business**
perform other tasks.   372 **old** such as old people suffer, or, plenty of
373 **aches** (Pronounced "aitches.")   376 **Setebos** (A god of the Patago-
nians, named in Richard Eden's *History of Travel*, 1577.)   377.2 *Ariel,
invisible* (Ariel wears a garment that by convention indicates he is invisible to Ferdinand and Miranda.)   380 **Curtsied . . . have** when you have
curtsied   380–1 **kissed . . . whist** kissed the waves into silence, or, kissed
while the waves are being hushed   382 **Foot it featly** dance nimbly
383 **sprites** spirits   384 **burden** refrain, undersong.   385 s.d. *dispersedly* i.e., from all directions, not in unison   392 **waits upon** serves,
attends   393 **bank** sandbank   396 **passion** grief   397 **Thence** i.e.,
From the bank on which I sat

406 **knell** announcement of a death by the tolling of a bell.
409 **remember** commemorate   411 **owes** owns.   412 **advance** raise
415 **brave** excellent   418 **but . . . stained** were it not that his luster is
somewhat darkened   419 **canker** cankerworm (feeding on buds and
leaves)   426 **airs** songs.   **Vouchsafe** Grant   427 **remain** dwell
429 **bear me** conduct myself.   **prime** chief   430 **wonder** (Miranda's
name means "to be wondered at.")   431 **maid** (1) a human maiden as
opposed to a goddess (2) unmarried (3) a virgin   433 **best** i.e., in
birth   436 **A single . . . now** (1) A single figure who combines into
one person both self and King of Naples (since Ferdinand believes he
has inherited the kingship) (2) A lonely shipwrecked figure
437 **Naples** the King of Naples.   **He . . . me** I who hear my own
words am the King of Naples

And that he does I weep. Myself am Naples,   438
Who with mine eyes, never since at ebb, beheld   439
The King my father wrecked.

MIRANDA   Alack, for mercy!

FERDINAND
Yes, faith, and all his lords, the Duke of Milan
And his brave son being twain.

PROSPERO [*aside*]   The Duke of Milan   442
And his more braver daughter could control thee,   443
If now 'twere fit to do't. At the first sight
They have changed eyes.—Delicate Ariel,   445
I'll set thee free for this. [*To Ferdinand*] A word, good
   sir.
I fear you have done yourself some wrong. A word!   447

MIRANDA [*aside*]
Why speaks my father so ungently? This
Is the third man that e'er I saw, the first
That e'er I sighed for. Pity move my father
To be inclined my way!

FERDINAND [*to Miranda*]   Oh, if a virgin,
And your affection not gone forth, I'll make you
The Queen of Naples.

PROSPERO   Soft, sir! One word more.
[*Aside*] They are both in either's powers; but this swift
   business
I must uneasy make, lest too light winning   454
Make the prize light. [*To Ferdinand*] One word more: I   455
   charge thee   456
That thou attend me. Thou dost here usurp   457
The name thou ow'st not, and hast put thyself   458
Upon this island as a spy, to win it
From me, the lord on't.

FERDINAND   No, as I am a man.   460

MIRANDA
There's nothing ill can dwell in such a temple.
If the ill spirit have so fair a house,
Good things will strive to dwell with't.

PROSPERO   Follow me.—   463
Speak not you for him; he's a traitor.—Come,
I'll manacle thy neck and feet together.
Seawater shalt thou drink; thy food shall be
The fresh-brook mussels, withered roots, and husks
Wherein the acorn cradled. Follow.

FERDINAND   No!
I will resist such entertainment till   469
Mine enemy has more pow'r.   470
             He draws, and is charmed from moving.

MIRANDA   O dear father,
Make not too rash a trial of him, for   471

He's gentle, and not fearful.

PROSPERO   What, I say,   472
My foot my tutor?—Put thy sword up, traitor,   473
Who mak'st a show but dar'st not strike, thy
   conscience
Is so possessed with guilt. Come, from thy ward,   475
For I can here disarm thee with this stick
And make thy weapon drop. [*He brandishes his staff.*]

MIRANDA [*trying to hinder him*]   Beseech you, father!

PROSPERO
Hence! Hang not on my garments.

MIRANDA   Sir, have pity!
I'll be his surety.

PROSPERO   Silence! One word more   479
Shall make me chide thee, if not hate thee. What,
An advocate for an impostor? Hush!
Thou think'st there is no more such shapes as he,
Having seen but him and Caliban. Foolish wench,
To th' most of men this is a Caliban,   484
And they to him are angels.

MIRANDA   My affections
Are then most humble; I have no ambition
To see a goodlier man.

PROSPERO [*to Ferdinand*]   Come on, obey.
Thy nerves are in their infancy again   488
And have no vigor in them.

FERDINAND   So they are.
My spirits, as in a dream, are all bound up.   490
My father's loss, the weakness which I feel,
The wreck of all my friends, nor this man's threats
To whom I am subdued, are but light to me,   493
Might I but through my prison once a day
Behold this maid. All corners else o'th'earth   495
Let liberty make use of; space enough
Have I in such a prison.

PROSPERO [*aside*]   It works. [*To Ferdinand*] Come on.—
Thou hast done well, fine Ariel! [*To Ferdinand*] Follow
   me.
[*To Ariel*] Hark what thou else shalt do me.

MIRANDA [*to Ferdinand*]   Be of comfort.   499
My father's of a better nature, sir,
Than he appears by speech. This is unwonted   501
Which now came from him.

PROSPERO [*to Ariel*]   Thou shalt be as free
As mountain winds; but then exactly do   503
All points of my command.

ARIEL   To th' syllable.

PROSPERO [*to Ferdinand*]
Come, follow. [*To Miranda*] Speak not for him.
                                              Exeunt.

❖

---

438 And . . . weep i.e., and I weep at this reminder that my father is seemingly dead, leaving me heir.   **439 never . . . ebb** never dry, continually weeping   **442 son** (The only reference in the play to a son of Antonio.)   **443 more braver** more splendid.   **control** refute   **445 changed eyes** exchanged amorous glances.   **447 done . . . wrong** i.e., spoken falsely.   **454 both in either's** each in the other's   **455 uneasy** difficult   **456 light** cheap. (Playing on *light*, "easy," in 455.)   **457 attend** follow, obey   **458 ow'st** ownest   **460 on't** of it.   **463 strive . . . with't** i.e., expel the evil and occupy the *temple*, the body.   **469 entertainment** treatment   **470 s.d. charmed** magically prevented   **471 rash** harsh

472 gentle (1) wellborn (2) easily managed.   **fearful** frightening, dangerous.   **473 My . . . tutor?** i.e., Do you, as my daughter and thus bound to me by obedience, dare presume to teach me what to do?   **475 ward** defensive posture (in fencing)   **479 surety** guarantee.   **484 To** compared with   **488 nerves** sinews   **490 spirits** vital powers   **493 light** unimportant   **495 corners else** other corners, regions   **499 me** for me.   **501 unwonted** unusual   **503 then** if so, then

2.1

*Enter Alonso, Sebastian, Antonio, Gonzalo,
Adrian, Francisco, and others.*

GONZALO [*to Alonso*]
Beseech you, sir, be merry. You have cause,
So have we all, of joy, for our escape
Is much beyond our loss. Our hint of woe   3
Is common; every day some sailor's wife,
The masters of some merchant, and the merchant,   5
Have just our theme of woe. But for the miracle,   6
I mean our preservation, few in millions
Can speak like us. Then wisely, good sir, weigh   8
Our sorrow with our comfort.

ALONSO   Prithee, peace.   9

SEBASTIAN [*aside to Antonio*]   He receives comfort like
cold porridge.   11

ANTONIO [*aside to Sebastian*]   The visitor will not give   12
him o'er so.   13

SEBASTIAN   Look, he's winding up the watch of his wit;
by and by it will strike.

GONZALO [*to Alonso*]   Sir—

SEBASTIAN [*aside to Antonio*]   One. Tell.   17

GONZALO   When every grief is entertained   18
That's offered, comes to th'entertainer—   19

SEBASTIAN   A dollar.   20

GONZALO   Dolor comes to him, indeed. You have spoken truer than you purposed.

SEBASTIAN   You have taken it wiselier than I meant you
should.

GONZALO [*to Alonso*]   Therefore, my lord—

ANTONIO   Fie, what a spendthrift is he of his tongue!

ALONSO [*to Gonzalo*]   I prithee, spare.   27

GONZALO   Well, I have done. But yet—

SEBASTIAN [*aside to Antonio*]   He will be talking.

ANTONIO [*aside to Sebastian*]   Which, of he or Adrian,   30
for a good wager, first begins to crow?   31

SEBASTIAN   The old cock.   32

ANTONIO   The cockerel.   33

SEBASTIAN   Done. The wager?

ANTONIO   A laughter.   35

SEBASTIAN   A match!   36

ADRIAN   Though this island seem to be desert—   37

ANTONIO   Ha, ha, ha!

SEBASTIAN   So, you're paid.   39

ADRIAN   Uninhabitable and almost inaccessible—

SEBASTIAN   Yet—

ADRIAN   Yet—

ANTONIO   He could not miss't.   43

ADRIAN   It must needs be of subtle, tender, and delicate   44
temperance.   45

ANTONIO   Temperance was a delicate wench.   46

SEBASTIAN   Ay, and a subtle, as he most learnedly   47
delivered.   48

ADRIAN   The air breathes upon us here most sweetly.

SEBASTIAN   As if it had lungs, and rotten ones.

ANTONIO   Or as 'twere perfumed by a fen.   51

GONZALO   Here is everything advantageous to life.

ANTONIO   True, save means to live.   53

SEBASTIAN   Of that there's none, or little.

GONZALO   How lush and lusty the grass looks! How   55
green!

ANTONIO   The ground indeed is tawny.   57

SEBASTIAN   With an eye of green in't.   58

ANTONIO   He misses not much.

SEBASTIAN   No. He doth but mistake the truth totally.   60

GONZALO   But the rarity of it is—which is indeed
almost beyond credit—

SEBASTIAN   As many vouched rarities are.   63

GONZALO   That our garments, being, as they were,
drenched in the sea, hold notwithstanding their fresh-
ness and glosses, being rather new-dyed than stained
with salt water.

ANTONIO   If but one of his pockets could speak, would   68
it not say he lies?   69

SEBASTIAN   Ay, or very falsely pocket up his report.   70

GONZALO   Methinks our garments are now as fresh as
when we put them on first in Afric, at the marriage of
the King's fair daughter Claribel to the King of Tunis.

SEBASTIAN   'Twas a sweet marriage, and we prosper
well in our return.

ADRIAN   Tunis was never graced before with such a
paragon to their queen.   77

2.1. Location: Another part of the island.
3 hint occasion   **5 The masters . . . the merchant** the officers or owners of some merchant vessel and the merchant who owns the cargo
6 for as for   **8–9 weigh . . . comfort** balance our sorrow against our
comfort.   **11 porridge** (Punningly suggested by *peace*, i.e., "peas" or
"pease," a common ingredient of porridge.)   **12 visitor** one bringing
nourishment and comfort to the sick, as Gonzalo is doing   **12–13 give
him o'er** abandon him   **17 Tell** Keep count.   **18–19 When . . . entertainer** When every sorrow that presents itself is accepted without
resistance, there comes to the recipient   **20 dollar** widely circulated
coin, the German thaler and the Spanish piece of eight. (Sebastian
puns on *entertainer* in the sense of paid performer or innkeeper; to
Gonzalo, *dollar* suggests "dolor," grief.)   **27 spare** forbear, cease.
30–1 Which . . . crow? Which of the two, Gonzalo or Adrian, do you
bet will speak (crow) first?   **32 The old cock** Gonzalo.   **33 The cockerel** Adrian.   **35 laughter** (1) burst of laughter (2) sitting of eggs.
(When Adrian, the *cockerel*, begins to speak two lines later, Sebastian
loses the bet. The Folio speech prefixes in lines 38–9 are here reversed
so that Antonio enjoys his laugh as the prize for winning, in the
proverb "He who laughs last laughs best" or "He laughs that wins."
The Folio assignment can work in the theater, however, if Sebastian
pays for losing with a sardonic laugh of concession.)

36 A match! A bargain; agreed!   **37 desert** uninhabited   **39 you're
paid** i.e., you've had your laugh.   **43 miss't** (1) avoid saying "Yet"
(2) miss the island.   **44 must needs be** has to be   **45 temperance**
mildness of climate.   **46 Temperance** a girl's name.   **delicate** (Here
it means "given to pleasure, voluptuous"; in line 44, "pleasant."
Antonio is evidently suggesting that *tender, and delicate temperance*
sounds like a Puritan phrase, which Antonio then mocks by applying
the words to a woman rather than an island. He began this bawdy
comparison with a double entendre on *inaccessible*, line 40.)   **47 subtle** (Here it means "tricky, sexually crafty"; in line 44, "delicate.")
48 delivered uttered. (Sebastian joins Antonio in baiting the Puritans
with his use of the pious cant phrase *learnedly delivered*.)   **51 fen** evil-
smelling marshland.   **53 save** except   **55 lusty** healthy   **57 tawny**
dull brown, yellowish.   **58 eye** tinge, or spot. (Sebastian is mocking
Gonzalo's optimism by saying there's precious little green to see anywhere. Antonio echoes him in line 59 with similar sarcasm.)   **60 He
. . . totally** i.e., He's only a tiny 100% wrong. (Sarcastic.)   **63 As . . . are**
(More sarcasm: Just as many alleged strange sights are doubtful,
including this one.)   **68–70 If . . . report** (More wisecracking: Gonzalo's mud-filled pockets would surely give the lie to his talk of clean
fresh garments, thereby *pocketing up* or tabling the *report*.)   **77 to** for

GONZALO   Not since widow Dido's time.   78

ANTONIO   [*aside to Sebastian*]   Widow? A pox o' that!
How came that "widow" in? Widow Dido!

SEBASTIAN   What if he had said "widower Aeneas"
too? Good Lord, how you take it!   82

ADRIAN   [*to Gonzalo*]   "Widow Dido" said you? You make
me study of that. She was of Carthage, not of Tunis.   84

GONZALO   This Tunis, sir, was Carthage.

ADRIAN   Carthage?

GONZALO   I assure you, Carthage.

ANTONIO   His word is more than the miraculous harp.   88

SEBASTIAN   He hath raised the wall, and houses too.

ANTONIO   What impossible matter will he make easy
next?

SEBASTIAN   I think he will carry this island home in his
pocket and give it his son for an apple.

ANTONIO   And, sowing the kernels of it in the sea,   94
bring forth more islands.

GONZALO   Ay.   96

ANTONIO   Why, in good time.   97

GONZALO   [*to Alonso*]   Sir, we were talking that our
garments seem now as fresh as when we were at Tunis
at the marriage of your daughter, who is now queen.

ANTONIO   And the rarest that e'er came there.   101

SEBASTIAN   Bate, I beseech you, widow Dido.   102

ANTONIO   Oh, widow Dido? Ay, widow Dido.

GONZALO   Is not, sir, my doublet as fresh as the first   104
day I wore it? I mean, in a sort.   105

ANTONIO   That "sort" was well fished for.   106

GONZALO   When I wore it at your daughter's marriage.

ALONSO
You cram these words into mine ears against
The stomach of my sense. Would I had never   109
Married my daughter there! For, coming thence,   110
My son is lost and, in my rate, she too,   111
Who is so far from Italy removed
I ne'er again shall see her. O thou mine heir
Of Naples and of Milan, what strange fish
Hath made his meal on thee?

FRANCISCO   Sir, he may live.
I saw him beat the surges under him   116
And ride upon their backs. He trod the water,

Whose enmity he flung aside, and breasted
The surge most swoll'n that met him. His bold head
'Bove the contentious waves he kept, and oared   120
Himself with his good arms in lusty stroke   121
To th' shore, that o'er his wave-worn basis bowed,   122
As stooping to relieve him. I not doubt   123
He came alive to land.

ALONSO   No, no, he's gone.

SEBASTIAN   [*to Alonso*]
Sir, you may thank yourself for this great loss,
That would not bless our Europe with your daughter,   126
But rather loose her to an African,   127
Where she at least is banished from your eye,   128
Who hath cause to wet the grief on't.

ALONSO   Prithee, peace.   129

SEBASTIAN
You were kneeled to and importuned otherwise   130
By all of us, and the fair soul herself   131
Weighed between loathness and obedience at   132
Which end o'th' beam should bow. We have lost your
son,   133
I fear, forever. Milan and Naples have
More widows in them of this business' making   135
Than we bring men to comfort them.
The fault's your own.

ALONSO   So is the dear'st o'th' loss.   138

GONZALO   My lord Sebastian,
The truth you speak doth lack some gentleness
And time to speak it in. You rub the sore   141
When you should bring the plaster.

SEBASTIAN   Very well.   142

ANTONIO   And most chirurgeonly.   143

GONZALO   [*to Alonso*]
It is foul weather in us all, good sir,
When you are cloudy.

SEBASTIAN   [*to Antonio*]   Fowl weather?

ANTONIO   [*to Sebastian*]   Very foul.   145

GONZALO
Had I plantation of this isle, my lord—   146

ANTONIO   [*to Sebastian*]
He'd sow't with nettle seed.

SEBASTIAN   Or docks, or mallows.   147

GONZALO
And were the king on't, what would I do?

---

78 widow Dido Queen of Carthage, deserted by Aeneas. (She was, in fact, a widow when Aeneas, a widower, met her, but Antonio may be amused at Gonzalo's prudish use of the term "widow" to describe a woman deserted by her lover.)   **82 take** understand, respond to, interpret   **84 study of** think about   **88 miraculous harp** (Alludes to Amphion's harp, with which he raised the walls of Thebes; Gonzalo has exceeded that deed by recreating ancient Carthage—*wall and houses*—mistakenly on the site of modern-day Tunis. Some Renaissance commentators believed, like Gonzalo, that the two sites were near each other.)   **94 kernels** seeds   **96 Ay** (Gonzalo may be reasserting his point about Carthage, or he may be responding ironically to Antonio, who, in turn, answers sarcastically.)   **97 in good time** (An expression of ironical acquiescence or amazement, i.e., "sure, right away.")   **101 rarest** most remarkable, beautiful   **102 Bate** Abate, except, leave out. (Sebastian says sardonically, surely you should allow widow Dido to be an exception.)   **104 doublet** close-fitting jacket   **105 in a sort** in a way.   **106 sort** (Antonio plays on the idea of drawing lots and on "fishing" for something to say.)   **109 The stomach . . . sense** my appetite for hearing them.   **110 Married** given in marriage   **111 rate** estimation, opinion   **116 surges** waves

120 oared propelled as by an oar   **121 lusty** vigorous   **122 that . . . bowed** that projected out over its (*his*) surf-eroded base, bending down toward the sea   **123 As** as if   **126 That** you who   **127 But . . . her** but would rather turn her loose (or, "lose her")   **128–9 Where . . . on't** where at least she is not a constant reproach in your eye, which has good reason to weep sorrowfully for this unhappy development.   **130 importuned** urged, implored   **131–3 the fair . . . bow** Claribel herself was poised uncertainly, as in a balancing scale, between being unwilling to marry and yet wishing to obey her father.   **135 of . . . making** on account of this marriage and subsequent shipwreck   **138 dear'st** heaviest, most costly   **141 time** appropriate time   **142 plaster** (A medical application.)   **143 chirurgeonly** like a skilled surgeon. (Antonio mocks Gonzalo's medical analogy of a *plaster* applied curatively to a wound.)   **145 Fowl** (With a pun on *foul*, returning to the imagery of lines 30–5.)   **146 plantation** colonial settlement. (With subsequent wordplay on the literal meaning, "planting.")   **147 docks . . . mallows** (Weeds; the first was used as an antidote for nettle stings.)

SEBASTIAN   Scape being drunk for want of wine.   149

GONZALO
I'th' commonwealth I would by contraries   150
Execute all things; for no kind of traffic   151
Would I admit; no name of magistrate;
Letters should not be known; riches, poverty,   153
And use of service, none; contract, succession,   154
Bourn, bound of land, tilth, vineyard, none;   155
No use of metal, corn, or wine, or oil;   156
No occupation; all men idle, all,
And women too, but innocent and pure;
No sovereignty—

SEBASTIAN   Yet he would be king on't.

ANTONIO   The latter end of his commonwealth forgets
the beginning.

GONZALO
All things in common nature should produce
Without sweat or endeavor. Treason, felony,
Sword, pike, knife, gun, or need of any engine   164
Would I not have; but nature should bring forth,
Of it own kind, all foison, all abundance,   166
To feed my innocent people.

SEBASTIAN   No marrying 'mong his subjects?

ANTONIO   None, man, all idle—whores and knaves.

GONZALO
I would with such perfection govern, sir,
T'excel the Golden Age.

SEBASTIAN   'Save His Majesty!   171

ANTONIO
Long live Gonzalo!

GONZALO   And—do you mark me, sir?

ALONSO
Prithee, no more. Thou dost talk nothing to me.

GONZALO   I do well believe Your Highness, and did it
to minister occasion to these gentlemen, who are of   175
such sensible and nimble lungs that they always use   176
to laugh at nothing.

ANTONIO   'Twas you we laughed at.

GONZALO   Who in this kind of merry fooling am nothing
to you; so you may continue, and laugh at nothing still.

ANTONIO   What a blow was there given!

SEBASTIAN   An it had not fallen flat-long.   182

GONZALO   You are gentlemen of brave mettle; you   183
would lift the moon out of her sphere if she would   184

continue in it five weeks without changing.

Enter Ariel [invisible] playing solemn music.

SEBASTIAN   We would so, and then go a-batfowling.   186

ANTONIO   Nay, good my lord, be not angry.

GONZALO   No, I warrant you, I will not adventure my   188
discretion so weakly. Will you laugh me asleep? For I   189
am very heavy.   190

ANTONIO   Go sleep, and hear us.   191
[*All sleep except Alonso, Sebastian, and Antonio.*]

ALONSO
What, all so soon asleep? I wish mine eyes
Would, with themselves, shut up my thoughts. I find   193
They are inclined to do so.

SEBASTIAN   Please you, sir,
Do not omit the heavy offer of it.   195
It seldom visits sorrow; when it doth,
It is a comforter.

ANTONIO   We two, my lord,
Will guard your person while you take your rest,
And watch your safety.

ALONSO   Thank you. Wondrous heavy.
[*Alonso sleeps. Exit Ariel.*]

SEBASTIAN
What a strange drowsiness possesses them!

ANTONIO
It is the quality o'th' climate.

SEBASTIAN   Why
Doth it not then our eyelids sink? I find not
Myself disposed to sleep.

ANTONIO   Nor I. My spirits are nimble.
They fell together all, as by consent;   204
They dropped, as by a thunderstroke. What might,
Worthy Sebastian, oh, what might—? No more.
And yet methinks I see it in thy face
What thou shouldst be. Th'occasion speaks thee, and   208
My strong imagination sees a crown
Dropping upon thy head.

SEBASTIAN   What, art thou waking?

ANTONIO
Do you not hear me speak?

SEBASTIAN   I do, and surely
It is a sleepy language, and thou speak'st   212
Out of thy sleep. What is it thou didst say?
This is a strange repose, to be asleep
With eyes wide open—standing, speaking, moving—
And yet so fast asleep.

ANTONIO   Noble Sebastian,
Thou let'st thy fortune sleep—die, rather; wink'st   217

---

149 Scape Escape.   **want** lack. (Sebastian jokes sarcastically that this
hypothetical ruler would be saved from dissipation only by the bar-
renness of the island.)   **150 by contraries** by what is directly opposite to usual custom   **151 traffic** trade   **153 Letters** learning
154 use of service custom of employing servants.   **succession** holding of property by right of inheritance   **155 Bourn . . . tilth** boundaries, property limits, tillage of soil   **156 corn** grain   **164 pike** lance.
engine instrument of warfare   **166 it** its.   **foison** plenty   **171 the
Golden Age** an age of prelapsarian abundance and peace; the first of
four "ages" of human history, followed by silver, bronze, and lead.
'Save God save   **175 minister occasion** furnish opportunity (for
laughter)   **176 sensible** sensitive.   **use** are accustomed   **182 An** If.
flat-long with the flat of the sword, i.e., ineffectually.   **183 mettle**
temperament, courage. (The sense of *metal*, indistinguishable as a
form from *mettle*, continues the metaphor of the sword. F reads
"mettal.")   **184 sphere** orbit. (Literally, one of the concentric zones
occupied by planets in Ptolemaic astronomy.)

186 a-batfowling hunting birds at night with lantern and *bat*, or
"stick"; also, gulling a simpleton. (Gonzalo is the simpleton, or fowl,
and Sebastian will use the moon as his lantern.)   **188–9 adventure . . .
weakly** risk my reputation for discretion for so trivial a cause (by getting angry).   **190 heavy** sleepy.   **191 Go . . . us** i.e., Get ready for
sleep, and we'll do our part by laughing.   **193 Would . . . thoughts**
would shut off my melancholy brooding when they (my eyes) close
themselves in sleep.   **195 Do . . . it** do not decline the invitation to
drowsiness.   **204 They . . . consent** The others all fell asleep simultaneously, as if by common agreement   **208 Th' occasion . . . thee** The
opportunity of the moment calls upon you   **212 sleepy** dreamlike,
fantastic   **217 wink'st** (you) shut your eyes

Whiles thou art waking.

SEBASTIAN   Thou dost snore distinctly;   218
There's meaning in thy snores.

ANTONIO
I am more serious than my custom. You
Must be so too if heed me, which to do   221
Trebles thee o'er.

SEBASTIAN   Well, I am standing water.   222

ANTONIO
I'll teach you how to flow.

SEBASTIAN   Do so. To ebb   223
Hereditary sloth instructs me.

ANTONIO   Oh,   224
If you but knew how you the purpose cherish   225
Whiles thus you mock it! How, in stripping it,   226
You more invest it! Ebbing men, indeed,   227
Most often do so near the bottom run   228
By their own fear or sloth.

SEBASTIAN   Prithee, say on.
The setting of thine eye and cheek proclaim   230
A matter from thee, and a birth indeed   231
Which throes thee much to yield.

ANTONIO   Thus, sir: 232
Although this lord of weak remembrance, this   233
Who shall be of as little memory   234
When he is earthed, hath here almost persuaded—   236
For he's a spirit of persuasion, only   236
Professes to persuade—the King his son's alive,   237
'Tis as impossible that he's undrowned
As he that sleeps here swims.

SEBASTIAN   I have no hope
That he's undrowned.

ANTONIO   Oh, out of that "no hope"
What great hope have you! No hope that way is   241
Another way so high a hope that even   242
Ambition cannot pierce a wink beyond,   243
But doubt discovery there. Will you grant with me   244
That Ferdinand is drowned?

SEBASTIAN   He's gone.

ANTONIO   Then tell me,
Who's the next heir of Naples?

SEBASTIAN   Claribel.

ANTONIO
She that is Queen of Tunis; she that dwells
Ten leagues beyond man's life; she that from Naples   248
Can have no note, unless the sun were post—   249
The Man i'th' Moon's too slow—till newborn chins
Be rough and razorable; she that from whom   251
We all were sea-swallowed, though some cast again,   252
And by that destiny to perform an act
Whereof what's past is prologue, what to come
In yours and my discharge.   255

SEBASTIAN   What stuff is this? How say you?
'Tis true my brother's daughter's Queen of Tunis,
So is she heir of Naples, twixt which regions
There is some space.

ANTONIO   A space whose ev'ry cubit   259
Seems to cry out, "How shall that Claribel
Measure us back to Naples? Keep in Tunis,   261
And let Sebastian wake." Say this were death   262
That now hath seized them, why, they were no worse
Than now they are. There be that can rule Naples   264
As well as he that sleeps, lords that can prate   265
As amply and unnecessarily
As this Gonzalo. I myself could make   267
A chough of as deep chat. Oh, that you bore   268
The mind that I do! What a sleep were this
For your advancement! Do you understand me?

SEBASTIAN
Methinks I do.

ANTONIO   And how does your content   271
Tender your own good fortune?

SEBASTIAN   I remember   272
You did supplant your brother Prospero.

ANTONIO   True.
And look how well my garments sit upon me,
Much feater than before. My brother's servants   275
Were then my fellows. Now they are my men.

SEBASTIAN   But, for your conscience?   277

ANTONIO
Ay, sir, where lies that? If 'twere a kibe,   278
'Twould put me to my slipper; but I feel not   279
This deity in my bosom. Twenty consciences   280
That stand twixt me and Milan, candied be they   281
And melt ere they molest! Here lies your brother,   282
No better than the earth he lies upon,
If he were that which now he's like—that's dead,
Whom I, with this obedient steel, three inches of it,

218 distinctly articulately   **221 if heed** if you heed   **222 Trebles thee o'er** makes you three times as great and rich.   **standing water** water that neither ebbs nor flows, at a standstill.   **223 ebb** recede, decline **224 Hereditary sloth** i.e., natural laziness and the position of younger brother, one who cannot inherit   **225–6 If . . . mock it!** If you only knew how much you secretly cherish ambition even while your words mock it!   **226–7 How . . . invest it!** How the more you speak flippantly of ambition, the more you, in effect, affirm it, clothing what you have stripped!   **228 the bottom** i.e., on which unadventurous men may go aground and miss the tide of fortune   **230 setting** set expression (of earnestness)   **231 matter** matter of importance   **232 throes** causes pain, as in giving birth.   **yield** give forth, speak about.   **233–7 Although . . . alive** although this owner of weak memory, he who will be only weakly remembered when he is dead, has nearly persuaded— since he's a mind or soul devoted solely to persuade—King Alonso that Ferdinand lives   **241 that way** i.e., in regard to Ferdinand's being saved   **242–4 that . . . there** that even ambition for high status cannot see anything higher, and even there it doubts the reality of what it sees (because the place is so supremely high). (What then follows is Antonio's analysis of why they can proceed without fear.)

248 Ten . . . life i.e., further than the journey of a lifetime   **249 note** news, intimation.   **post** messenger   **251 razorable** ready for shaving. **from** on our voyage from   **252 cast** were disgorged. (With a pun on *casting* of parts for a play.)   **255 discharge** part to play.   **259 cubit** ancient measure of length of about twenty inches   **261 Measure us** retrace our journey.   **Keep** You, Claribel, stay   **262 wake** i.e., to his good fortune.   **264 There be** There are those   **265 prate** speak foolishly   **267–8 I . . . chat** I could teach a jackdaw to talk as wisely, or, be such a garrulous talker myself.   **271–2 And . . . fortune?** And how does your contentment with what I've just said further your good fortune?   **275 feater** more becomingly, fittingly   **277 for** as for **278 kibe** chilblain, here a sore on the heel   **279 put me to** oblige me to wear   **280–2 Twenty . . . molest!** Even if there were twenty consciences between me and the dukedom of Milan, may they be lumped together or crystallized like candy and then melted down before I'd let them interfere!

Can lay to bed forever; whiles you, doing thus, 286
To the perpetual wink for aye might put 287
This ancient morsel, this Sir Prudence, who
Should not upbraid our course. For all the rest, 289
They'll take suggestion as a cat laps milk; 290
They'll tell the clock to any business that 291
We say befits the hour.

SEBASTIAN   Thy case, dear friend,
Shall be my precedent. As thou got'st Milan,
I'll come by Naples. Draw thy sword. One stroke
Shall free thee from the tribute which thou payest, 295
And I the king shall love thee.

ANTONIO   Draw together;
And when I rear my hand, do you the like
To fall it on Gonzalo.   [*They draw.*]

SEBASTIAN   Oh, but one word. 298
                              [*They talk apart.*]

Enter Ariel [invisible], with music and song.

ARIEL [*to Gonzalo*]
My master through his art foresees the danger
That you, his friend, are in, and sends me forth—
For else his project dies—to keep them living.
                              Sings in Gonzalo's ear.
While you here do snoring lie,
Open-eyed conspiracy
    His time doth take. 304
If of life you keep a care,
Shake off slumber, and beware.
    Awake, awake!

ANTONIO   Then let us both be sudden.
GONZALO [*waking*]   Now, good angels preserve the King!
                              [*The others wake.*]

ALONSO
Why, how now, ho, awake? Why are you drawn?
Wherefore this ghastly looking?
GONZALO   What's the matter?
SEBASTIAN
Whiles we stood here securing your repose, 312
Even now, we heard a hollow burst of bellowing
Like bulls, or rather lions. Did 't not wake you?
It struck mine ear most terribly.
ALONSO   I heard nothing.
ANTONIO
Oh, 'twas a din to fright a monster's ear,
To make an earthquake! Sure it was the roar
Of a whole herd of lions.
ALONSO   Heard you this, Gonzalo?
GONZALO
Upon mine honor, sir, I heard a humming,
And that a strange one too, which did awake me.
I shaked you, sir, and cried. As mine eyes opened, 322
I saw their weapons drawn. There was a noise,

That's verily. 'Tis best we stand upon our guard, 324
Or that we quit this place. Let's draw our weapons.
ALONSO
Lead off this ground, and let's make further search
For my poor son.
GONZALO   Heavens keep him from these beasts!
For he is, sure, i'th'island.
ALONSO   Lead away.
ARIEL [*aside*]
Prospero my lord shall know what I have done.
So, King, go safely on to seek thy son.
                              Exeunt [separately].

                              ❖

2.2

*Enter Caliban with a burden of wood. A noise
of thunder heard.*

CALIBAN
All the infections that the sun sucks up
From bogs, fens, flats, on Prosper fall, and make him 2
By inchmeal a disease! His spirits hear me, 3
And yet I needs must curse. But they'll nor pinch, 4
Fright me with urchin shows, pitch me i'th' mire, 5
Nor lead me, like a firebrand, in the dark 6
Out of my way, unless he bid 'em. But
For every trifle are they set upon me,
Sometimes like apes, that mow and chatter at me 9
And after bite me; then like hedgehogs, which
Lie tumbling in my barefoot way and mount
Their pricks at my footfall. Sometime am I
All wound with adders, who with cloven tongues 13
Do hiss me into madness.

Enter Trinculo.

                      Lo, now, lo!
Here comes a spirit of his, and to torment me
For bringing wood in slowly. I'll fall flat.
Perchance he will not mind me.   [*He lies down.*] 17
TRINCULO   Here's neither bush nor shrub to bear off 18
any weather at all. And another storm brewing; I hear
it sing i'th' wind. Yond same black cloud, yond huge
one, looks like a foul bombard that would shed his 21
liquor. If it should thunder as it did before, I know not
where to hide my head. Yond same cloud cannot
choose but fall by pailfuls. [*Seeing Caliban*] What have
we here, a man or a fish? Dead or alive? A fish, he
smells like a fish; a very ancient and fishlike smell; a
kind of not-of-the-newest Poor John. A strange fish! 27
Were I in England now, as once I was, and had but
this fish painted, not a holiday fool there but would 29

---

286 **thus** similarly. (The actor makes a stabbing gesture.)   287 **wink** sleep, closing of eyes.   **aye** ever   289 **Should not** must not be allowed to   290 **take suggestion** respond to prompting   291 **tell the clock** i.e., agree, answer appropriately, chime   295 **tribute** (See 1.2.113–24.)   298 **fall it** let it fall   304 **time** opportunity   312 **securing** standing guard over   322 **cried** called out.

324 **verily** true.
2.2. Location: Another part of the island.
2 **flats** swamps   3 **By inchmeal** inch by inch   4 **needs must** have to.
nor neither   5 **urchin shows** elvish apparitions shaped like hedgehogs   6 **like a firebrand** they in the guise of a will-o'-the-wisp
9 **mow** make faces   13 **wound with** entwined by   17 **mind** notice
18 **bear off** keep off   21 **foul bombard** dirty leather jug.   **his** its
27 **Poor John** salted fish, type of poor fare.   29 **painted** i.e., painted on a sign set up outside a booth or tent at a fair

give a piece of silver. There would this monster make   30
a man. Any strange beast there makes a man. When   31
they will not give a doit to relieve a lame beggar, they   32
will lay out ten to see a dead Indian. Legged like a
man, and his fins like arms! Warm, o' my troth! I do   34
now let loose my opinion, hold it no longer: this is no   35
fish, but an islander, that hath lately suffered by a
thunderbolt. [*Thunder.*] Alas, the storm is come again!
My best way is to creep under his gaberdine. There is   38
no other shelter hereabout. Misery acquaints a man
with strange bedfellows. I will here shroud till the   40
dregs of the storm be past.   41

[*He creeps under Caliban's garment.*]

Enter Stephano, singing, [*a bottle in his hand*].

STEPHANO
"I shall no more to sea, to sea,
    Here shall I die ashore—"
This is a very scurvy tune to sing at a man's funeral.
Well, here's my comfort.   *Drinks.*
(*Sings.*)
"The master, the swabber, the boatswain, and I,   46
    The gunner and his mate,
Loved Mall, Meg, and Marian, and Margery,
    But none of us cared for Kate.
For she had a tongue with a tang,   50
    Would cry to a sailor, 'Go hang!'
She loved not the savor of tar nor of pitch,
Yet a tailor might scratch her where'er she did itch.   53
    Then to sea, boys, and let her go hang!"
This is a scurvy tune too. But here's my comfort.
    Drinks.

CALIBAN   Do not torment me! Oh!   56
STEPHANO   What's the matter? Have we devils here? Do   57
you put tricks upon 's with savages and men of Ind,   58
ha? I have not scaped drowning to be afeard now of
your four legs. For it hath been said, "As proper a man   60
as ever went on four legs cannot make him give   61
ground"; and it shall be said so again while Stephano
breathes at' nostrils.   63
CALIBAN   This spirit torments me! Oh!
STEPHANO   This is some monster of the isle with four
legs, who hath got, as I take it, an ague. Where the   66
devil should he learn our language? I will give him   67
some relief, if it be but for that. If I can recover him   68
and keep him tame and get to Naples with him, he's

a present for any emperor that ever trod on neat's   70
leather.   71
CALIBAN   Do not torment me, prithee. I'll bring my
wood home faster.
STEPHANO   He's in his fit now and does not talk after   74
the wisest. He shall taste of my bottle. If he have never   75
drunk wine afore, it will go near to remove his fit. If I   76
can recover him and keep him tame, I will not take too   77
much for him. He shall pay for him that hath him, and   78
that soundly.
CALIBAN   Thou dost me yet but little hurt; thou wilt
anon, I know it by thy trembling. Now Prosper works
upon thee.
STEPHANO   Come on your ways. Open your mouth. Here
is that which will give language to you, cat. Open your   84
mouth. This will shake your shaking, I can tell you,   85
and that soundly. [*Giving Caliban a drink.*] You cannot   86
tell who's your friend. Open your chaps again.   87
TRINCULO   I should know that voice. It should be—but
he is drowned, and these are devils. Oh, defend me!
STEPHANO   Four legs and two voices—a most delicate   90
monster! His forward voice now is to speak well of his
friend; his backward voice is to utter foul speeches and   92
to detract. If all the wine in my bottle will recover him,   93
I will help his ague. Come. [*Giving a drink.*] Amen! I
will pour some in thy other mouth.
TRINCULO   Stephano!
STEPHANO   Doth thy other mouth call me? Mercy,
mercy! This is a devil, and no monster. I will leave
him. I have no long spoon.   99
TRINCULO   Stephano! If thou be'st Stephano, touch me
and speak to me, for I am Trinculo—be not afeard—
thy good friend Trinculo.
STEPHANO   If thou be'st Trinculo, come forth. I'll pull
thee by the lesser legs. If any be Trinculo's legs, these
are they. [*Pulling him out.*] Thou art very Trinculo
indeed! How cam'st thou to be the siege of this   106
mooncalf? Can he vent Trinculos?   107
TRINCULO   I took him to be killed with a thunderstroke.
But art thou not drowned, Stephano? I hope now thou
art not drowned. Is the storm overblown? I hid me   110
under the dead mooncalf's gaberdine for fear of the
storm. And art thou living, Stephano? Oh, Stephano,
two Neapolitans scaped!   [*He capers with Stephano.*]

30–1 make a man (1) make a man's fortune (2) pass for a human being.   **32 doit** small coin   **34 o' my troth** by my faith.   **35 hold it** hold it in   **38 gaberdine** cloak, loose upper garment.   **40 shroud** take shelter   **41 dregs** i.e., last remains (as in a *bombard* or jug, line 21)   **46 swabber** crew member whose job is to wash the decks   **50 tang** sting   **53 tailor . . . itch** (A dig at tailors for their supposed effeminacy and a bawdy suggestion of satisfying a sexual craving.)   **56 Do . . . me!** (Caliban assumes that one of Prospero's spirits has come to punish him.)   **57 What's the matter?** What's going on here?   **58 put tricks upon 's** trick us with conjuring shows.   **Ind** India   **60 proper** handsome   **61 four legs** (The conventional phrase would supply *two legs*, but the creature Stephano thinks he sees has four.)   **63 at'** at the   **66 ague** fever. (Probably both Caliban and Trinculo are quaking; see lines 56 and 81.)   **67 should he learn** could he have learned   **68 for that** i.e., for knowing our language.   **recover** revive

70–1 neat's leather cowhide.   **74–5 after the wisest** in the wisest fashion.   **76 afore** before.   **go near to** be in a fair way to   **77 recover** restore   **77–8 I will . . . much** i.e., no sum can be too much   **78 He shall . . . hath him** Anyone who wants him will have to pay dearly for him   **84–5 cat . . . mouth** (Allusion to the proverb "Good liquor will make a cat speak.")   **85 shake** shake off   **86–7 You . . . friend** i.e., You can't tell who's your friend until someone like me provides you with a drink.   **87 chaps** jaws   **90 delicate** ingenious   **92 backward voice** (Trinculo and Caliban are facing in opposite directions. Stephano supposes the monster to have a rear end that can emit *foul speeches* or foul-smelling wind at the monster's *other mouth*, line 95.)   **93 If . . . him** Even if it takes all the wine in my bottle to cure him   **99 long spoon** (Allusion to the proverb "He that sups with the devil has need of a long spoon.")   **106 siege** excrement   **107 mooncalf** monstrous or misshapen creature (whose deformity is caused by the malignant influence of the moon).   **vent** excrete, defecate   **110 overblown** blown over.

STEPHANO   Prithee, do not turn me about. My stomach
is not constant.   115

CALIBAN

These be fine things, an if they be not spirits.   116
That's a brave god, and bears celestial liquor.   117
I will kneel to him.

STEPHANO   How didst thou scape? How cam'st thou
hither? Swear by this bottle how thou cam'st hither. I
escaped upon a butt of sack which the sailors heaved   121
o'erboard—by this bottle, which I made of the bark of   122
a tree with mine own hands since I was cast ashore.

CALIBAN [*kneeling*]   I'll swear upon that bottle to be
thy true subject, for the liquor is not earthly.

STEPHANO   Here. Swear then how thou escaped'st.

TRINCULO   Swum ashore, man, like a duck. I can swim
like a duck, I'll be sworn.

STEPHANO   Here, kiss the book. Though thou canst   129
swim like a duck, thou art made like a goose.
                                        [*Giving him a drink.*]

TRINCULO   Oh, Stephano, hast any more of this?

STEPHANO   The whole butt, man. My cellar is in a rock
by th' seaside, where my wine is hid.—How now,
mooncalf? How does thine ague?

CALIBAN   Hast thou not dropped from heaven?

STEPHANO   Out o'th' moon, I do assure thee. I was the
man i'th' moon when time was.   137

CALIBAN

I have seen thee in her, and I do adore thee.
My mistress showed me thee, and thy dog, and thy
bush.   139

STEPHANO   Come, swear to that. Kiss the book. I will
furnish it anon with new contents. Swear.
                                        [*Giving him a drink.*]

TRINCULO   By this good light, this is a very shallow   142
monster! I afeard of him? A very weak monster! The
man i'th' moon? A most poor credulous monster!
Well drawn, monster, in good sooth!   145

CALIBAN [*to Stephano*]

I'll show thee every fertile inch o'th'island,
And I will kiss thy foot. I prithee, be my god.

TRINCULO   By this light, a most perfidious and drunken
monster! When 's god's asleep, he'll rob his bottle.   149

CALIBAN

I'll kiss thy foot. I'll swear myself thy subject.

STEPHANO   Come on then. Down, and swear.
                                        [*Caliban kneels.*]

TRINCULO   I shall laugh myself to death at this puppy-
headed monster. A most scurvy monster! I could find
in my heart to beat him—

STEPHANO   Come, kiss.

TRINCULO   But that the poor monster's in drink. An   156
abominable monster!

CALIBAN

I'll show thee the best springs. I'll pluck thee berries.
I'll fish for thee and get thee wood enough.
A plague upon the tyrant that I serve!
I'll bear him no more sticks, but follow thee,
Thou wondrous man.

TRINCULO   A most ridiculous monster, to make a
wonder of a poor drunkard!

CALIBAN

I prithee, let me bring thee where crabs grow,   165
And I with my long nails will dig thee pignuts,   166
Show thee a jay's nest, and instruct thee how
To snare the nimble marmoset. I'll bring thee   168
To clust'ring filberts, and sometimes I'll get thee
Young scamels from the rock. Wilt thou go with me?   170

STEPHANO   I prithee now, lead the way without any
more talking.—Trinculo, the King and all our com-   172
pany else being drowned, we will inherit here.—   173
Here, bear my bottle.—Fellow Trinculo, we'll fill him
by and by again.

CALIBAN (*sings drunkenly*)
Farewell, master, farewell, farewell!

TRINCULO   A howling monster; a drunken monster!

CALIBAN

No more dams I'll make for fish,
Nor fetch in firing   179
At requiring,
Nor scrape trenchering, nor wash dish.   181
'Ban, 'Ban, Ca–Caliban
Has a new master. Get a new man!   183
Freedom, high-day! High-day, freedom! Freedom   184
high-day, freedom!

STEPHANO   O brave monster! Lead the way.   *Exeunt.*

3.1

Enter Ferdinand, bearing a log.

FERDINAND

There be some sports are painful, and their labor   1
Delight in them sets off. Some kinds of baseness   2
Are nobly undergone, and most poor matters   3
Point to rich ends. This my mean task   4
Would be as heavy to me as odious, but   5

115 **constant** steady.   116 **an if** if   117 **brave** fine, magnificent
121 **butt of sack** barrel of Canary wine   122 **by this bottle** i.e., I swear
by this bottle   129 **book** i.e., bottle. (But with ironic reference to the
practice of kissing the Bible in swearing an oath; see *I'll be sworn* in line
128.)   137 **when time was** once upon a time.   139 **dog . . . bush** (The
man in the moon was popularly imagined to have with him a dog and
a bush of thorn.)   142 **By . . . light** By God's light, by this good light
from heaven   145 **Well . . . sooth!** Well pulled on the bottle, truly!
149 **When . . . bottle** i.e., Caliban wouldn't even stop at robbing his
god (i.e., Stephano) of his bottle if he could catch him asleep.

156 **But that** were it not that.   **in drink** drunk.   165 **crabs** crab apples,
or crabs   166 **pignuts** earthnuts, edible tuberous roots   168 **marmoset** small monkey.   170 **scamels** (Possibly *seamews*, mentioned in
Strachey's letter, or shellfish, or perhaps from *squamelle*, "furnished
with little scales." Contemporary French and Italian travel accounts
report that the natives of Patagonia in South America ate small fish
described as *fort scameux* and *squame*.)   172–3 **all . . . else** all the rest
of our shipboard companions   173 **inherit** take possession   179 **firing** firewood   181 **trenchering** trenchers, wooden plates   183 **Get a
new man** (Addressed to Prospero.)   184 **high-day** holiday.
3.1. Location: Before Prospero's cell.
1–2 **There . . . sets off** Some pastimes are laborious, but the pleasure
we get from them compensates for the effort. (Pleasure is *set off* by
labor as a jewel is set off by its foil.)   2 **baseness** menial activity
3 **undergone** undertaken.   **most poor** poorest   4 **mean** lowly   5 **but**
were it not that

The mistress which I serve quickens what's dead   6
And makes my labors pleasures. Oh, she is
Ten times more gentle than her father's crabbed,
And he's composed of harshness. I must remove
Some thousands of these logs and pile them up,
Upon a sore injunction. My sweet mistress   11
Weeps when she sees me work and says such baseness
Had never like executor. I forget;   13
But these sweet thoughts do even refresh my labors,
Most busy lest when I do it.

> *Enter Miranda; and Prospero [at a distance, unseen].*

MIRANDA   Alas now, pray you,   15
Work not so hard. I would the lightning had
Burnt up those logs that you are enjoined to pile!   17
Pray, set it down and rest you. When this burns,   18
'Twill weep for having wearied you. My father   19
Is hard at study. Pray now, rest yourself.
He's safe for these three hours.
FERDINAND   O most dear mistress,   21
The sun will set before I shall discharge   22
What I must strive to do.
MIRANDA   If you'll sit down,
I'll bear your logs the while. Pray, give me that.
I'll carry it to the pile.
FERDINAND   No, precious creature,
I had rather crack my sinews, break my back,
Than you should such dishonor undergo
While I sit lazy by.
MIRANDA   It would become me
As well as it does you; and I should do it
With much more ease, for my good will is to it,
And yours it is against.
PROSPERO [*aside*]   Poor worm, thou art infected!
This visitation shows it.
MIRANDA   You look wearily.   32
FERDINAND
No, noble mistress, 'tis fresh morning with me
When you are by at night. I do beseech you—   34
Chiefly that I might set it in my prayers—
What is your name?
MIRANDA   Miranda.—O my father,
I have broke your hest to say so.
FERDINAND   Admired Miranda!   37
Indeed the top of admiration, worth
What's dearest to the world! Full many a lady   39
I have eyed with best regard, and many a time   40
The harmony of their tongues hath into bondage

Brought my too diligent ear. For several virtues   42
Have I liked several women, never any
With so full soul but some defect in her
Did quarrel with the noblest grace she owed   45
And put it to the foil. But you, oh, you,   46
So perfect and so peerless, are created
Of every creature's best!
MIRANDA   I do not know   48
One of my sex; no woman's face remember,
Save, from my glass, mine own. Nor have I seen
More that I may call men than you, good friend,
And my dear father. How features are abroad   52
I am skilless of; but, by my modesty,   53
The jewel in my dower, I would not wish
Any companion in the world but you;
Nor can imagination form a shape,
Besides yourself, to like of. But I prattle   57
Something too wildly, and my father's precepts   58
I therein do forget.
FERDINAND   I am in my condition   59
A prince, Miranda; I do think, a king—
I would, not so!—and would no more endure   61
This wooden slavery than to suffer   62
The flesh-fly blow my mouth. Hear my soul speak: 63
The very instant that I saw you did
My heart fly to your service, there resides
To make me slave to it, and for your sake
Am I this patient log-man.
MIRANDA   Do you love me?
FERDINAND
O heaven, O earth, bear witness to this sound,
And crown what I profess with kind event   69
If I speak true! If hollowly, invert   70
What best is boded me to mischief! I   71
Beyond all limit of what else i'th' world   72
Do love, prize, honor you.
MIRANDA [*weeping*]   I am a fool
To weep at what I am glad of.
PROSPERO [*aside*]   Fair encounter
Of two most rare affections! Heavens rain grace
On that which breeds between 'em!
FERDINAND   Wherefore weep you?
MIRANDA
At mine unworthiness, that dare not offer
What I desire to give, and much less take
What I shall die to want. But this is trifling,   79
And all the more it seeks to hide itself
The bigger bulk it shows. Hence, bashful cunning,   81

---

6 quickens gives life to   **11 sore injunction** severe command.
13 Had . . . executor was never before undertaken by so noble a
being.   **I forget** i.e., I forget that I'm supposed to be working
15 Most . . . do it (Ferdinand seems to say that the busier he is, the
less likely he is to forget the sweet thoughts that make his labors
pleasant. The line may be in need of emendation.)   **17 enjoined** commanded   **18 this** i.e., the log   **19 weep** i.e., exude resin   **21 these** the
next   **22 discharge** complete   **32 visitation** (1) Miranda's visit to
Ferdinand (2) visitation of the plague, i.e., infection of love   **34 by**
nearby   **37 hest** command.   **Admired Miranda** (Her name means
"to be admired or wondered at.")   **39 dearest** most treasured
40 best regard thoughtful and approving attention

42 diligent attentive.   **several** various. (Also in line 43.)   **45 owed**
owned   **46 put . . . foil** (1) overthrew it (as in fencing or wrestling)
(2) served as a *foil*, or "contrast," to set it off.   **48 Of** out of   **52 How . . .
abroad** What people look like in other places   **53 skilless** ignorant.
modesty virginity   **57 like of** be pleased with, be fond of.   **58 Something** somewhat   **59 condition** rank   **61 I would** I wish it were
62 wooden slavery being compelled to carry wood   **62–3 than . . .
mouth** than I would allow flying insects to deposit their eggs in my
mouth as if in decaying flesh.   **69 kind event** favorable outcome
70 hollowly insincerely, falsely.   **invert** turn   **71 boded** in store for.
mischief harm.   **72 what** whatever   **79 die** (Probably with an
unconscious sexual meaning that underlies all of lines 77–81.)   **to
want** through lacking.   **81 bashful cunning** coyness

And prompt me, plain and holy innocence!
I am your wife, if you will marry me;
If not, I'll die your maid. To be your fellow   84
You may deny me, but I'll be your servant
Whether you will or no.

FERDINAND   My mistress, dearest,   86
And I thus humble ever.

MIRANDA   My husband, then?

FERDINAND   Ay, with a heart as willing   89
As bondage e'er of freedom. Here's my hand.

MIRANDA [*clasping his hand*]
And mine, with my heart in't. And now farewell
Till half an hour hence.

FERDINAND   A thousand thousand!   92
           Exeunt [*Ferdinand and Miranda, separately*].

PROSPERO
So glad of this as they I cannot be,
Who are surprised with all; but my rejoicing   94
At nothing can be more. I'll to my book,
For yet ere suppertime must I perform
Much business appertaining.   *Exit.*   97

❖

3.2

Enter Caliban, Stephano, and Trinculo.

STEPHANO   Tell not me. When the butt is out, we will   1
drink water, not a drop before. Therefore bear up and   2
board 'em. Servant monster, drink to me.   3

TRINCULO   Servant monster? The folly of this island!   4
They say there's but five upon this isle. We are three
of them; if th'other two be brained like us, the state   6
totters.

STEPHANO   Drink, servant monster, when I bid thee.
Thy eyes are almost set in thy head.   [*Giving a drink.*]   9

TRINCULO   Where should they be set else? He were a   10
brave monster indeed if they were set in his tail.   11

STEPHANO   My man-monster hath drowned his tongue
in sack. For my part, the sea cannot drown me. I   13
swam, ere I could recover the shore, five and thirty   14
leagues off and on. By this light, thou shalt be my   15
lieutenant, monster, or my standard.   16

TRINCULO   Your lieutenant, if you list; he's no standard.   17

STEPHANO   We'll not run, Monsieur Monster.   18

TRINCULO   Nor go neither, but you'll lie like dogs and   19
yet say nothing neither.

STEPHANO   Mooncalf, speak once in thy life, if thou
be'st a good mooncalf.

CALIBAN
How does Thy Honor? Let me lick thy shoe.
I'll not serve him. He is not valiant.

TRINCULO   Thou liest, most ignorant monster, I am in   25
case to jostle a constable. Why, thou deboshed fish,   26
thou, was there ever man a coward that hath drunk so   27
much sack as I today? Wilt thou tell a monstrous lie,
being but half a fish and half a monster?

CALIBAN
Lo, how he mocks me! Wilt thou let him, my lord?

TRINCULO   "Lord," quoth he? That a monster should be
such a natural!   32

CALIBAN
Lo, lo, again! Bite him to death, I prithee.

STEPHANO   Trinculo, keep a good tongue in your head.
If you prove a mutineer—the next tree! The poor mon-   35
ster's my subject, and he shall not suffer indignity.

CALIBAN
I thank my noble lord. Wilt thou be pleased
To hearken once again to the suit I made to thee?

STEPHANO   Marry, will I. Kneel and repeat it. I will   39
stand, and so shall Trinculo.   [*Caliban kneels.*]   40

Enter Ariel, invisible.

CALIBAN
As I told thee before, I am subject to a tyrant,
A sorcerer, that by his cunning hath
Cheated me of the island.

ARIEL [*mimicking Trinculo*]
Thou liest.

CALIBAN   Thou liest, thou jesting monkey, thou!
I would my valiant master would destroy thee.
I do not lie.

STEPHANO   Trinculo, if you trouble him any more in 's
tale, by this hand, I will supplant some of your teeth.   48

TRINCULO   Why, I said nothing.

STEPHANO   Mum, then, and no more.—Proceed.

CALIBAN
I say by sorcery he got this isle;
From me he got it. If Thy Greatness will
Revenge it on him—for I know thou dar'st,
But this thing dare not—   54

STEPHANO   That's most certain.

CALIBAN
Thou shalt be lord of it, and I'll serve thee.

---

84 maid handmaiden, servant.   **fellow** mate   **86 will** desire it.   **My mistress** i.e., The woman I adore and serve (not an illicit sexual partner)   **89 willing** desirous   **92 A thousand thousand!** A thousand thousand farewells!   **94 with all** by everything that has happened, or, *withal,* "by it"   **97 appertaining** related to this.
3.2 Location: Another part of the island.
1 out empty   **2–3 bear . . . 'em** (Stephano uses the terminology of maneuvering at sea and boarding a vessel under attack as a way of urging an assault on the liquor supply.)   **4 folly of** i.e., stupidity found on   **6 be brained** are endowed with intelligence   **9 set . . . head** fixed in a drunken stare. (But Trinculo answers in a literal sense.)   **10 set** placed   **11 brave** fine, splendid   **13 sack** Spanish white wine. (Also in line 28.)   **14 recover** gain, reach   **14–15 five . . . on** i.e., a little over a hundred miles, give or take, or, off and on, intermittently. (A drunken hyperbole.)   **15 By this light** (An oath: By the light of the sun.)   **16 standard** standard-bearer, ensign. (But Trinculo answers in the literal sense: Caliban is *no standard,* not able to stand up because he's so drunk.)   **17 list** prefer

18 run run away, retreat (as a standard-bearer should not do)
19 Nor . . . dogs i.e., You won't even walk, much less run; you'll lie down in the field like the proverbial cowardly dog. (With a play on *lie,* tell falsehoods.)   **25–6 in case** ready, valiant enough
26 deboshed debauched, drunken   **27 ever . . . coward** ever a coward. (Trinculo appeals to his gargantuan drinking as refutation of the charge that he is *not valiant,* line 24.   **32 natural** fool, idiot.   **35 the next tree** i.e., you'll hang.   **39 Marry** i.e., Indeed. (Originally an oath, "by the Virgin Mary.")   **40.1 invisible** i.e., wearing a garment to connote invisibility, as at 1.2.377.2.   **48 supplant** uproot, displace
54 this thing i.e., Trinculo

STEPHANO   How now shall this be compassed? Canst 57
thou bring me to the party?

CALIBAN
Yea, yea, my lord. I'll yield him thee asleep,
Where thou mayst knock a nail into his head.

ARIEL [*mimicking Trinculo*]   Thou liest; thou canst not.

CALIBAN
What a pied ninny's this! Thou scurvy patch!—   62
I do beseech Thy Greatness, give him blows
And take his bottle from him. When that's gone
He shall drink naught but brine, for I'll not show
    him
Where the quick freshes are.   66

STEPHANO   Trinculo, run into no further danger. Interrupt the monster one word further and, by this hand,
I'll turn my mercy out o' doors and make a stockfish of 69
thee.

TRINCULO   Why, what did I? I did nothing. I'll go farther
off.

STEPHANO   Didst thou not say he lied?

ARIEL [*mimicking Trinculo*]   Thou liest.

STEPHANO   Do I so? Take thou that.   [*He beats Trinculo.*]
As you like this, give me the lie another time.   76

TRINCULO   I did not give the lie. Out o' your wits and
hearing too? A pox o' your bottle! This can sack and 78
drinking do. A murrain on your monster, and the 79
devil take your fingers!

CALIBAN   Ha, ha, ha!

STEPHANO   Now, forward with your tale. [*To Trinculo*]
Prithee, stand further off.

CALIBAN
Beat him enough. After a little time
I'll beat him too.

STEPHANO   Stand farther.—Come, proceed.

CALIBAN
Why, as I told thee, 'tis a custom with him
I'th'afternoon to sleep. There thou mayst brain him,
Having first seized his books; or with a log
Batter his skull, or paunch him with a stake,   90
Or cut his weasand with thy knife. Remember   91
First to possess his books, for without them
He's but a sot, as I am, nor hath not   93
One spirit to command. They all do hate him
As rootedly as I. Burn but his books.
He has brave utensils—for so he calls them—   96
Which, when he has a house, he'll deck withal.   97
And that most deeply to consider is
The beauty of his daughter. He himself
Calls her a nonpareil. I never saw a woman
But only Sycorax my dam and she;
But she as far surpasseth Sycorax
As great'st does least.

STEPHANO   Is it so brave a lass?   104

CALIBAN
Ay, lord. She will become thy bed, I warrant,   105
And bring thee forth brave brood.

STEPHANO   Monster, I will kill this man. His daughter
and I will be king and queen—save Our Graces!—and
Trinculo and thyself shall be viceroys. Dost thou like
the plot, Trinculo?

TRINCULO   Excellent.

STEPHANO   Give me thy hand. I am sorry I beat thee;
but, while thou liv'st, keep a good tongue in thy head.

CALIBAN
Within this half hour will he be asleep.
Wilt thou destroy him then?

STEPHANO   Ay, on mine honor.

ARIEL [*aside*]   This will I tell my master.

CALIBAN
Thou mak'st me merry; I am full of pleasure.
Let us be jocund. Will you troll the catch   119
You taught me but whilere?   120

STEPHANO   At thy request, monster, I will do reason, 121
any reason.—Come on, Trinculo, let us sing.   *Sings.* 122
    "Flout 'em and scout 'em   123
    And scout 'em and flout 'em!
        Thought is free."

CALIBAN   That's not the tune.   126
        Ariel plays the tune on a tabor and pipe.

STEPHANO   What is this same?

TRINCULO   This is the tune of our catch, played by the
picture of Nobody.   129

STEPHANO   If thou be'st a man, show thyself in thy
likeness. If thou be'st a devil, take't as thou list.   131

TRINCULO   Oh, forgive me my sins!

STEPHANO   He that dies pays all debts. I defy thee. 133
Mercy upon us!

CALIBAN   Art thou afeard?

STEPHANO   No, monster, not I.

CALIBAN
Be not afeard. The isle is full of noises,
Sounds, and sweet airs, that give delight and hurt not.
Sometimes a thousand twangling instruments
Will hum about mine ears, and sometimes voices
That, if I then had waked after long sleep,
Will make me sleep again; and then, in dreaming,
The clouds methought would open and show riches
Ready to drop upon me, that when I waked
I cried to dream again.   145

STEPHANO   This will prove a brave kingdom to me,
where I shall have my music for nothing.

CALIBAN   When Prospero is destroyed.

---

57 compassed achieved.   **62 pied ninny** fool in motley.   **patch** fool.
66 quick freshes running springs   **69 turn . . . o' doors** banish all
merciful feelings.   **stockfish** dried cod beaten before cooking
76 give me the lie call me a liar to my face   **78 A pox** i.e., A plague.
(A curse.)   **79 murrain** plague. (Literally, a cattle disease.)   **90 paunch**
stab in the belly   **91 weasand** windpipe   **93 sot** fool   **96 brave utensils** fine furnishings   **97 deck withal** furnish it with.

104 brave splendid, attractive   **105 become** suit (sexually)   **119 jocund**
jovial, merry.   **troll the catch** sing the round   **120 but whilere** only a
short time ago.   **121–2 reason, any reason** anything reasonable.
123 Flout Scoff at.   **scout** deride   **126.1 *tabor*** small drum   **129 picture of Nobody** (Refers to a familiar figure with head, arms, and legs
but no trunk.)   **131 take't . . . list** (A proverbial formula of bravado
and defiance, as in *Romeo and Juliet*, 1.1.40–1.)   **133 He . . . debts**
(Another proverbial swagger: Death settles all scores, I'm not afraid
to fight.)   **145 to dream** desirous of dreaming

STEPHANO   That shall be by and by. I remember the   149
story.

TRINCULO   The sound is going away. Let's follow it,
and after do our work.

STEPHANO   Lead, monster; we'll follow. I would I could
see this taborer! He lays it on.   154

TRINCULO   Wilt come? I'll follow, Stephano.
Exeunt [following Ariel's music].

♣

3.3

*Enter Alonso, Sebastian, Antonio, Gonzalo,
Adrian, Francisco, etc.*

GONZALO
By'r lakin, I can go no further, sir.   1
My old bones aches. Here's a maze trod indeed
Through forthrights and meanders! By your patience,   3
I needs must rest me.

ALONSO   Old lord, I cannot blame thee,
Who am myself attached with weariness,   5
To th' dulling of my spirits. Sit down and rest.   6
Even here I will put off my hope, and keep it
No longer for my flatterer. He is drowned
Whom thus we stray to find, and the sea mocks
Our frustrate search on land. Well, let him go.   10
[Alonso and Gonzalo sit.]

ANTONIO *[aside to Sebastian]*
I am right glad that he's so out of hope.
Do not, for one repulse, forgo the purpose   12
That you resolved t'effect.

SEBASTIAN *[to Antonio]*   The next advantage
Will we take throughly.

ANTONIO *[to Sebastian]*   Let it be tonight,   14
For, now they are oppressed with travel, they   15
Will not, nor cannot, use such vigilance   16
As when they are fresh.

SEBASTIAN *[to Antonio]*   I say tonight. No more.   17

*Solemn and strange music; and Prospero on
the top, invisible.*

ALONSO
What harmony is this? My good friends, hark!

GONZALO   Marvelous sweet music!

*Enter several strange shapes, bringing in a ban-
quet, and dance about it with gentle actions of
salutations; and, inviting the King, etc., to eat,
they depart.*

ALONSO
Give us kind keepers, heavens! What were these?   20

SEBASTIAN
A living drollery. Now I will believe   21
That there are unicorns; that in Arabia
There is one tree, the phoenix' throne, one phoenix   23
At this hour reigning there.

ANTONIO   I'll believe both;
And what does else want credit, come to me   25
And I'll be sworn 'tis true. Travelers ne'er did lie,
Though fools at home condemn 'em.

GONZALO   If in Naples
I should report this now, would they believe me
If I should say I saw such islanders?
For, certes, these are people of the island,   30
Who, though they are of monstrous shape, yet note,
Their manners are more gentle, kind, than of
Our human generation you shall find
Many, nay, almost any.

PROSPERO *[aside]*   Honest lord,
Thou hast said well, for some of you there present
Are worse than devils.

ALONSO   I cannot too much muse   36
Such shapes, such gesture, and such sound,
expressing—
Although they want the use of tongue—a kind   38
Of excellent dumb discourse.

PROSPERO *[aside]*   Praise in departing.   39

FRANCISCO
They vanished strangely.

SEBASTIAN   No matter, since
They have left their viands behind, for we have
stomachs.   41
Will 't please you taste of what is here?

ALONSO   Not I.

GONZALO
Faith, sir, you need not fear. When we were boys,
Who would believe that there were mountaineers   44
Dewlapped like bulls, whose throats had hanging at
'em   45
Wallets of flesh? Or that there were such men   46
Whose heads stood in their breasts? Which now we
find   47
Each putter-out of five for one will bring us   48
Good warrant of.

ALONSO   I will stand to and feed,   49

149 **by and by** very soon.   154 **lays it on** i.e., plays the drum vigorously.
3.3. Location: Another part of the island.
1 **By'r lakin** By our Ladykin, by our Lady   3 **forthrights and meanders** paths straight and crooked.   5 **attached with** seized by   6 **To . . .
spirits** to the point of being dull-spirited.   10 **frustrate** frustrated
12 **for** because of   14 **throughly** thoroughly.   15 **now** now that.
travel (Spelled "trauaile" in the Folio and carrying the sense of labor
as well as traveling.)   16 **use such vigilance** be as vigilant   17.1–2 *on
the top* at some high point of the tiring-house or the theater, on a
third level above the gallery

20 **kind keepers** guardian angels   21 **living drollery** comic entertainment, caricature, or puppet show put on by live actors.   23 **phoenix**
mythical bird consumed to ashes every five hundred to six hundred
years, only to be renewed into another cycle   25 **want credit** lack
credibility   30 **certes** certainly   36 **muse** wonder at   38 **want** lack
39 **Praise in departing** i.e., Save your praise until the end of the performance. (Proverbial.)   41 **viands** provisions.   **stomachs** appetites.
44 **mountaineers** mountain dwellers   45 **Dewlapped** having a
dewlap, or fold of skin hanging from the neck, like cattle   46 **Wallets**
pendent folds of skin, wattles   47 **in their breasts** (i.e., like the
Anthropophagi described in *Othello*, 1.3.146.)   48 **putter-out . . . one**
one who invests money or gambles on the risks of travel on the condition that the traveler who returns safely is to receive five times the
amount deposited; hence, any traveler   49 **Good warrant** assurance.
stand to come forward, fall to. (Also in line 52.)

Although my last—no matter, since I feel 50
The best is past. Brother, my lord the Duke, 51
Stand to, and do as we.   [*They approach the table.*] 52

> *Thunder and lightning. Enter Ariel, like a harpy,*
> *claps his wings upon the table, and with a quaint*
> *device the banquet vanishes.*

ARIEL

You are three men of sin, whom Destiny— 53
That hath to instrument this lower world 54
And what is in't—the never-surfeited sea 55
Hath caused to belch up you, and on this island 56
Where man doth not inhabit, you 'mongst men
Being most unfit to live. I have made you mad;
And even with suchlike valor men hang and drown 59
Their proper selves.   [*Alonso, Sebastian, and Antonio*
                                   draw their swords.]
                         You fools! I and my fellows 60
Are ministers of Fate. The elements
Of whom your swords are tempered may as well 62
Wound the loud winds, or with bemocked-at stabs 63
Kill the still-closing waters, as diminish 64
One dowl that's in my plume. My fellow ministers 65
Are like invulnerable. If you could hurt, 66
Your swords are now too massy for your strengths 67
And will not be uplifted. But remember—
For that's my business to you—that you three
From Milan did supplant good Prospero;
Exposed unto the sea, which hath requit it, 71
Him and his innocent child; for which foul deed
The powers, delaying, not forgetting, have
Incensed the seas and shores, yea, all the creatures,
Against your peace. Thee of thy son, Alonso,
They have bereft; and do pronounce by me
Ling'ring perdition, worse than any death 77
Can be at once, shall step by step attend
You and your ways; whose wraths to guard you
      from— 79
Which here, in this most desolate isle, else falls 80
Upon your heads—is nothing but heart's sorrow 81
And a clear life ensuing. 82

> *He vanishes in thunder; then, to soft music,*
> *enter the shapes again, and dance, with mocks*
> *and mows, and carrying out the table.*

PROSPERO 50
Bravely the figure of this harpy hast thou 83
Performed, my Ariel; a grace it had devouring. 84
Of my instruction hast thou nothing bated 85
In what thou hadst to say. So, with good life 86
And observation strange, my meaner ministers 87
Their several kinds have done. My high charms work, 88
And these mine enemies are all knit up
In their distractions. They now are in my power; 90
And in these fits I leave them, while I visit
Young Ferdinand, whom they suppose is drowned,
And his and mine loved darling.   [*Exit above.*]
GONZALO
I'th' name of something holy, sir, why stand you 94
In this strange stare?
ALONSO   Oh, it is monstrous, monstrous! 95
Methought the billows spoke and told me of it; 96
The winds did sing it to me, and the thunder,
That deep and dreadful organ pipe, pronounced
The name of Prosper; it did bass my trespass. 99
Therefor my son i'th'ooze is bedded; and
I'll seek him deeper than e'er plummet sounded, 101
And with him there lie mudded.   *Exit.*
SEBASTIAN   But one fiend at a time, 103
I'll fight their legions o'er.
ANTONIO   I'll be thy second. 104
                    Exeunt [*Sebastian and Antonio*].
GONZALO
All three of them are desperate. Their great guilt, 105
Like poison given to work a great time after, 106
Now 'gins to bite the spirits. I do beseech you, 107
That are of suppler joints, follow them swiftly, 108
And hinder them from what this ecstasy 109
May now provoke them to.
ADRIAN   Follow, I pray you.
                            Exeunt omnes.

❖

4.1

> *Enter Prospero, Ferdinand, and Miranda.*

PROSPERO
If I have too austerely punished you,
Your compensation makes amends, for I

50 Although my last even if this were to be my last meal   **51 best** best part of life   **52.1 harpy** a fabulous monster with a woman's face and breasts and a vulture's body, supposed to be a minister of divine vengeance   **52.2–3 with . . . vanishes** by means of some ingenious stage contrivance, the food vanishes. (The table remains until line 82.)   **53–6 whom . . . up you** you whom Destiny, acting through this sublunary world as its instrument, has caused the ever-hungry sea to belch up   **59 suchlike valor** i.e., the reckless valor derived from madness   **60 proper** own   **62 whom** which.   **tempered** made hard   **63 bemocked-at** scorned   **64 still-closing** always closing again when parted   **65 dowl** soft, fine feather   **66 like** likewise, similarly.   **If** Even if   **67 massy** heavy   **71 requit** requited, avenged   **77 perdition** ruin, destruction   **79 whose . . . from** to guard you from which heavenly wrath   **80 else** otherwise   **81 is nothing** there is no way   **82 clear** unspotted, innocent   **82.2–3 mocks and mows** mocking gestures and grimaces

83 Bravely Finely, dashingly   **84 a grace . . . devouring** your impersonation displayed a ravishing grace. (With a punning suggestion of having caused the banquet to disappear as if by consuming it.)   **85 bated** abated, omitted   **86–8 So . . . done** Similarly, my lesser spirits assisting you have done their various tasks with observant care and attention to detail.   **90 distractions** trancelike state.   **94–5 why . . . stare?** (Gonzalo was not addressed in Ariel's speech to the *three men of sin*, line 53, and is not, as they are, in a maddened state; see lines 105–7.)   **95 it** i.e., my sin. (Also in line 96.)   **96 billows** waves   **99 bass my trespass** proclaim my trespass like a bass note in the music.   **101 than . . . sounded** than ever a lead weight attached to a line tested the depth   **103–4 But . . . o'er** If the demons come at me one at a time, I'll fight them all.   **105 desperate** despairing and reckless.   **106 Like . . . after** like poison, starting to work long after it has been administered   **107 bite the spirits** sap their vital powers through anguish.   **107–8 you . . . joints** Adrian, Francisco, and others not under Ariel's numbing spell   **109 ecstasy** mad frenzy
4.1. Location: Before Prospero's cell.

Have given you here a third of mine own life,   3
Or that for which I live; who once again
I tender to thy hand. All thy vexations   5
Were but my trials of thy love, and thou
Hast strangely stood the test. Here, afore heaven,   7
I ratify this my rich gift. O Ferdinand,
Do not smile at me that I boast her off,   9
For thou shalt find she will outstrip all praise
And make it halt behind her.

FERDINAND   I do believe it   11
Against an oracle.   12

PROSPERO
Then, as my gift and thine own acquisition
Worthily purchased, take my daughter. But
If thou dost break her virgin-knot before
All sanctimonious ceremonies may   16
With full and holy rite be ministered,
No sweet aspersion shall the heavens let fall   18
To make this contract grow; but barren hate,
Sour-eyed disdain, and discord shall bestrew
The union of your bed with weeds so loathly   21
That you shall hate it both. Therefore take heed,
As Hymen's lamps shall light you.

FERDINAND   As I hope   23
For quiet days, fair issue, and long life,   24
With such love as 'tis now, the murkiest den,
The most opportune place, the strong'st suggestion   26
Our worser genius can, shall never melt   27
Mine honor into lust, to take away   28
The edge of that day's celebration   29
When I shall think or Phoebus' steeds are foundered   30
Or Night kept chained below.

PROSPERO   Fairly spoke.
Sit then and talk with her. She is thine own.
        [Ferdinand and Miranda sit and talk together.]
What, Ariel! My industrious servant, Ariel!   33

        Enter Ariel.

ARIEL
What would my potent master? Here I am.

PROSPERO
Thou and thy meaner fellows your last service   35
Did worthily perform, and I must use you
In such another trick. Go bring the rabble,   37

O'er whom I give thee power, here to this place.
Incite them to quick motion, for I must
Bestow upon the eyes of this young couple
Some vanity of mine art. It is my promise,   41
And they expect it from me.

ARIEL   Presently?   42

PROSPERO   Ay, with a twink.   43

ARIEL
Before you can say "Come" and "Go,"
And breathe twice, and cry "So, so,"
Each one, tripping on his toe,
Will be here with mop and mow.   47
Do you love me, master? No?

PROSPERO
Dearly, my delicate Ariel. Do not approach
Till thou dost hear me call.

ARIEL   Well; I conceive.   Exit.   50

PROSPERO
Look thou be true; do not give dalliance   51
Too much the rein. The strongest oaths are straw
To th' fire i'th' blood. Be more abstemious,
Or else good night your vow!

FERDINAND   I warrant you, sir,   54
The white cold virgin snow upon my heart   55
Abates the ardor of my liver.

PROSPERO   Well.   56
Now come, my Ariel! Bring a corollary,   57
Rather than want a spirit. Appear, and pertly!—   58
No tongue! All eyes! Be silent.   Soft music.   59

        Enter Iris.

IRIS
Ceres, most bounteous lady, thy rich leas   60
Of wheat, rye, barley, vetches, oats, and peas;   61
Thy turfy mountains, where live nibbling sheep,
And flat meads thatched with stover, them to keep;   63
Thy banks with pionèd and twillèd brims,   64
Which spongy April at thy hest betrims   65
To make cold nymphs chaste crowns; and thy
        broom groves,   66
Whose shadow the dismissèd bachelor loves,   67
Being lass-lorn; thy poll-clipped vineyard;   68
And thy sea marge, sterile and rocky hard,   69
Where thou thyself dost air: the queen o'th' sky,   70

---

3 a third i.e., Miranda, into whose education I have put a third of my life, or (less precisely) who represents a large part of what I have cared about, along with my dukedom and my magical art   5 tender offer   7 strangely exceptionally   9 boast her off i.e., praise her so, or, perhaps an error for "boast of her"; the Folio reads "boast her of"   11 halt limp   12 Against an oracle even if an oracle should declare otherwise.   16 sanctimonious sacred   18 aspersion dew, shower   21 weeds (In place of the flowers customarily strewn on the marriage bed.)   23 As . . . you i.e., as you long for happiness and concord in your marriage. (Hymen was the Greek and Roman god of marriage; his symbolic torches, the wedding torches, were supposed to burn brightly for a happy marriage and smokily for a troubled one.)   24 issue offspring   26–7 the strong'st . . . can the strongest temptation that the evil spirit within us can propose   28 to so as to   29 edge keen enjoyment, sexual ardor   30 or . . . foundered either that the horses of the sun's chariot have gone lame (thus delaying the night for which I will be so eager)   33 What Now then   35 meaner fellows subordinates   37 trick device. rabble band, i.e., the *meaner fellows* of line 35

41 vanity (1) illusion (2) trifle (3) desire for admiration, conceit   42 Presently? Immediately?   43 with a twink in the twinkling of an eye.   47 mop and mow grimaces.   50 conceive understand.   51 true true to your promise   54 good night i.e., say good-bye to. warrant guarantee   55 The white . . . heart i.e., the chaste ideal to which my heart is devoted   56 liver (The presumed seat of the passions.)   57 corollary surplus, extra supply   58 want lack.   pertly briskly.   59 No tongue! Quiet, everyone!   59.1 Iris goddess of the rainbow and Juno's messenger.   60 Ceres goddess of the generative power of nature.   leas meadows   61 vetches plants for forage, fodder   63 meads meadows.   stover winter fodder for cattle   64 pionèd and twillèd undercut by the swift current and protected by roots and branches that tangle to form a barricade   65 spongy wet.   hest command   66 broom groves clumps of broom, gorse, yellow-flowered shrub   67 dismissèd bachelor rejected male lover   68 poll-clipped pruned, lopped at the top, or *pole-clipped*, "hedged in with poles"   69 sea marge shore   70 thou . . . air you take the air, go for walks.   queen o'th' sky i.e., Juno

Whose wat'ry arch and messenger am I,   71
Bids thee leave these, and with her sovereign grace,   72
                    Juno descends [slowly in her car].
Here on this grass plot, in this very place,
To come and sport. Her peacocks fly amain.   74
Approach, rich Ceres, her to entertain.   75

               Enter Ceres.

CERES
Hail, many-colored messenger, that ne'er
Dost disobey the wife of Jupiter,
Who with thy saffron wings upon my flowers   78
Diffusest honeydrops, refreshing showers,
And with each end of thy blue bow dost crown   80
My bosky acres and my unshrubbed down,   81
Rich scarf to my proud earth. Why hath thy queen   82
Summoned me hither to this short-grassed green?

IRIS
A contract of true love to celebrate,
And some donation freely to estate   85
On the blest lovers.

CERES   Tell me, heavenly bow,
If Venus or her son, as thou dost know,   87
Do now attend the Queen? Since they did plot   88
The means that dusky Dis my daughter got,   89
Her and her blind boy's scandaled company   90
I have forsworn.

IRIS   Of her society   91
Be not afraid. I met Her Deity   92
Cutting the clouds towards Paphos, and her son   93
Dove-drawn with her. Here thought they to have
    done   94
Some wanton charm upon this man and maid,   95
Whose vows are that no bed-right shall be paid   96
Till Hymen's torch be lighted; but in vain.
Mars's hot minion is returned again;   98
Her waspish-headed son has broke his arrows,   99
Swears he will shoot no more, but play with
    sparrows   100
And be a boy right out.

         [Juno alights.]

CERES   Highest Queen of state,   101
Great Juno, comes; I know her by her gait.   102

JUNO
How does my bounteous sister? Go with me   103
To bless this twain, that they may prosperous be,
And honored in their issue.   *They sing:*   105

JUNO
    Honor, riches, marriage blessing,
    Long continuance, and increasing,
    Hourly joys be still upon you!   108
    Juno sings her blessings on you.

CERES
    Earth's increase, foison plenty,   110
    Barns and garners never empty,   111
    Vines with clust'ring bunches growing,
    Plants with goodly burden bowing;

    Spring come to you at the farthest
    In the very end of harvest!   115
    Scarcity and want shall shun you;
    Ceres' blessing so is on you.

FERDINAND
This is a most majestic vision, and
Harmonious charmingly. May I be bold   119
To think these spirits?

PROSPERO   Spirits, which by mine art
I have from their confines called to enact
My present fancies.

FERDINAND   Let me live here ever!
So rare a wondered father and a wise   123
Makes this place Paradise.

            *Juno and Ceres whisper, and send
                    Iris on employment.*

PROSPERO   Sweet now, silence!
Juno and Ceres whisper seriously;
There's something else to do. Hush and be mute,
Or else our spell is marred.

IRIS *[calling offstage]*
You nymphs, called naiads, of the windring brooks,   128
With your sedged crowns and ever-harmless looks,   129
Leave your crisp channels, and on this green land   130
Answer your summons; Juno does command.
Come, temperate nymphs, and help to celebrate   132
A contract of true love. Be not too late.

            Enter certain nymphs.

You sunburned sicklemen, of August weary,   134
Come hither from the furrow and be merry.   135

---

71 **wat'ry arch** rainbow   72.1 *Juno descends* i.e., starts her descent
from the "heavens" above the stage   74 **peacocks** birds sacred to
Juno and used to pull her chariot.   **amain** with full speed.   75 **entertain** receive.   78 **saffron** yellow   80 **bow** rainbow   81 **bosky**
wooded.   **unshrubbed down** open upland   82 **scarf** (The rainbow is
like a colored silk band adorning the earth.)   85 **estate** bestow   87
son i.e., Cupid.   **as** as far as   88–91 **Since . . . forsworn** Since Venus
and her blind son Cupid plotted the means by which Dis (Pluto) carried off my daughter Proserpina to be his bride in Hades, I have forsworn their scandalous company.   92 **Her Deity** i.e., Her Highness
93 **Paphos** place on the island of Cyprus, sacred to Venus   94 **Dove-
drawn** (Venus's chariot was drawn by doves.)   94–5 **done . . . charm**
inflicted some lustful spell   96 **that . . . paid** that their union will not
be sexually consummated   98 **Mars's hot minion** i.e., Venus, the
beloved of Mars.   **returned** i.e., returned to Paphos   99 **waspish-
headed** hotheaded, peevish   100 **sparrows** (Supposed lustful, and
sacred to Venus.)   101 **right out** outright.   **Highest . . . state** Most
majestic Queen   102 **gait** i.e., majestic bearing.

103 **sister** i.e., fellow goddess.   105 **issue** offspring.   108 **still** always
110 **foison plenty** plentiful harvest   111 **garners** granaries   115 **In . . .
harvest** i.e., with no winter in between.   119 **charmingly** enchant-
ingly.   123 **wondered** wonder-performing, wondrous.   **wise** (The
Folio appears to read "wise" here, but with a tall "s" that resembles an
"f," leading to much dispute over this reading. In some copies of the
Folio the "s" looks like an "f," perhaps damaged, but evidently as the
result of an inkblot, so that the true reading is "s." Even so, an error in
transmission would be easy, so that the author's intention is uncertain.
The matter bears importantly on whether or not Ferdinand includes
Miranda in his vision of paradise.)   128 **naiads** nymphs of springs,
rivers, or lakes.   **windring** wandering, winding (?)   129 **sedged**
made of reeds.   **ever-harmless** ever innocent   130 **crisp** curled, rip-
pled   132 **temperate** chaste   134 **sicklemen** harvesters, field workers who cut down grain and grass.   **of August weary** i.e., weary of
the hard work of the harvest   135 **furrow** i.e., plowed fields

Make holiday; your rye-straw hats put on,
And these fresh nymphs encounter every one   137
In country footing.   138

*Enter certain reapers, properly habited. They join
with the nymphs in a graceful dance, towards the
end whereof Prospero starts suddenly, and speaks;
after which, to a strange, hollow, and confused
noise, they heavily vanish.*

PROSPERO [*aside*]
I had forgot that foul conspiracy
Of the beast Caliban and his confederates
Against my life. The minute of their plot
Is almost come. [*To the Spirits*] Well done! Avoid; no
    more!   142
FERDINAND [*to Miranda*]
This is strange. Your father's in some passion
That works him strongly.
MIRANDA   Never till this day   144
Saw I him touched with anger so distempered.
PROSPERO
You do look, my son, in a moved sort,   146
As if you were dismayed. Be cheerful, sir.
Our revels now are ended. These our actors,   148
As I foretold you, were all spirits and
Are melted into air, into thin air;
And, like the baseless fabric of this vision,   151
The cloud-capped towers, the gorgeous palaces,
The solemn temples, the great globe itself,   153
Yea, all which it inherit, shall dissolve,   154
And, like this insubstantial pageant faded,
Leave not a rack behind. We are such stuff   156
As dreams are made on, and our little life   157
Is rounded with a sleep. Sir, I am vexed.   158
Bear with my weakness. My old brain is troubled.
Be not disturbed with my infirmity.   160
If you be pleased, retire into my cell   161
And there repose. A turn or two I'll walk
To still my beating mind.
FERDINAND, MIRANDA   We wish your peace.   163
                Exeunt [*Ferdinand and Miranda*].
PROSPERO
Come with a thought! I thank thee, Ariel. Come.   164

Enter Ariel.

ARIEL
Thy thoughts I cleave to. What's thy pleasure?   165
PROSPERO   Spirit,
We must prepare to meet with Caliban.

ARIEL
Ay, my commander. When I presented Ceres,   167
I thought to have told thee of it, but I feared
Lest I might anger thee.
PROSPERO
Say again, where didst thou leave these varlets?
ARIEL
I told you, sir, they were red-hot with drinking;
So full of valor that they smote the air
For breathing in their faces, beat the ground
For kissing of their feet; yet always bending   174
Towards their project. Then I beat my tabor,
At which, like unbacked colts, they pricked their ears,   176
Advanced their eyelids, lifted up their noses   177
As they smelt music. So I charmed their ears   178
That calflike they my lowing followed through   179
Toothed briers, sharp furzes, pricking gorse, and
    thorns,   180
Which entered their frail shins. At last I left them
I'th' filthy-mantled pool beyond your cell,   182
There dancing up to th' chins, that the foul lake
O'erstunk their feet.
PROSPERO   This was well done, my bird.   184
Thy shape invisible retain thou still.
The trumpery in my house, go bring it hither,   186
For stale to catch these thieves.
ARIEL   I go, I go.   *Exit.* 187
PROSPERO
A devil, a born devil, on whose nature
Nurture can never stick; on whom my pains,
Humanely taken, all, all lost, quite lost!
And as with age his body uglier grows,
So his mind cankers. I will plague them all,   192
Even to roaring.

Enter Ariel, loaden with glistering apparel, etc.

                Come, hang them on this line.   193

[*Ariel hangs up the showy finery; Prospero and
Ariel remain, invisible.*] *Enter Caliban, Stephano,
and Trinculo, all wet.*

CALIBAN
Pray you, tread softly, that the blind mole may
Not hear a foot fall. We now are near his cell.
STEPHANO Monster, your fairy, which you say is a
harmless fairy, has done little better than played the
jack with us.   198

---

137 **encounter** join   138 **country footing** country dancing.
138.1 *properly* suitably   138.5 *heavily* slowly, dejectedly   142 **Avoid**
Withdraw   144 **works** affects, agitates   146 **moved sort** troubled
state, condition   148 **revels** entertainment, pageant   151 **baseless
fabric** unsubstantial theatrical edifice or contrivance   153 **great
globe** (With a glance at the Globe Theatre.)   154 **which it inherit**
who subsequently occupy it   156 **rack** wisp of cloud   157 **on** of
158 **rounded** surrounded (before birth and after death), or crowned,
rounded off   160 **with** by   161 **retire** withdraw, go   163 **beating**
agitated   164 **with a thought** i.e., on the instant, or, summoned by
my thought, no sooner thought of than here.   165 **cleave** cling,
adhere

167 **presented** acted the part of, or, introduced   174 **bending** aiming
176 **unbacked** unbroken, unridden   177 **Advanced** lifted up   178 **As**
as if   179 **lowing** mooing   180 **furzes . . . gorse** prickly shrubs
182 **filthy-mantled** covered with a slimy coating   184 **O'erstunk**
smelled worse than, or, caused to stink terribly   186 **trumpery** cheap
goods, the *glistering apparel* mentioned in the following stage direction   187 **stale** (1) decoy (2) out-of-fashion garments. (With possible
further suggestions of "horse piss," as in line 199, and "steal," pronounced like *stale. For stale* could also mean "fit for a prostitute.")
192 **cankers** festers, grows malignant.   193 **line** lime tree or linden.
193.1–2 *Prospero and Ariel remain* (The staging is uncertain. They
may instead exit here and return with the spirits at line 256.)
198 **jack** (1) knave (2) will-o'-the-wisp

TRINCULO   Monster, I do smell all horse piss, at which
my nose is in great indignation.
STEPHANO   So is mine. Do you hear, monster? If I
should take a displeasure against you, look you—
TRINCULO   Thou wert but a lost monster.
CALIBAN
Good my lord, give me thy favor still.
Be patient, for the prize I'll bring thee to
Shall hoodwink this mischance. Therefore speak
softly.   206
All's hushed as midnight yet.
TRINCULO   Ay, but to lose our bottles in the pool—
STEPHANO   There is not only disgrace and dishonor in
that, monster, but an infinite loss.
TRINCULO   That's more to me than my wetting. Yet this
is your harmless fairy, monster!
STEPHANO   I will fetch off my bottle, though I be o'er   213
ears for my labor.   214
CALIBAN
Prithee, my king, be quiet. See'st thou here,
This is the mouth o'th' cell. No noise, and enter.
Do that good mischief which may make this island
Thine own forever, and I thy Caliban
For aye thy footlicker.
STEPHANO   Give me thy hand. I do begin to have bloody
thoughts.
TRINCULO [seeing the finery]   O King Stephano! O peer!   222
O worthy Stephano! Look what a wardrobe here is
for thee!
CALIBAN
Let it alone, thou fool, it is but trash.
TRINCULO   Oho, monster! We know what belongs to a
frippery. O King Stephano!   [He puts on a gown.] 227
STEPHANO   Put off that gown, Trinculo. By this hand,
I'll have that gown.
TRINCULO   Thy Grace shall have it.
CALIBAN
The dropsy drown this fool! What do you mean   231
To dote thus on such luggage? Let't alone   232
And do the murder first. If he awake,
From toe to crown he'll fill our skins with pinches,   234
Make us strange stuff.
STEPHANO   Be you quiet, monster.—Mistress line, is   236
not this my jerkin? [He takes it down.] Now is the jerkin 237
under the line. Now, jerkin, you are like to lose your   238
hair and prove a bald jerkin.   239

TRINCULO   Do, do! We steal by line and level, an't like 240
Your Grace.
STEPHANO   I thank thee for that jest. Here's a garment
for't. [He gives a garment.] Wit shall not go unrewarded
while I am king of this country. "Steal by line and
level" is an excellent pass of pate. There's another   245
garment for't.
TRINCULO   Monster, come, put some lime upon your   247
fingers, and away with the rest.
CALIBAN
I will have none on't. We shall lose our time,
And all be turned to barnacles, or to apes   250
With foreheads villainous low.   251
STEPHANO   Monster, lay to your fingers. Help to bear   252
this away where my hogshead of wine is, or I'll turn   253
you out of my kingdom. Go to, carry this.   254
TRINCULO   And this.
STEPHANO   Ay, and this.
        [They load Caliban with more and more garments.]

        A noise of hunters heard. Enter divers spirits, in
        shape of dogs and hounds, hunting them about,
        Prospero and Ariel setting them on.

PROSPERO   Hey, Mountain, hey!
ARIEL   Silver! There it goes, Silver!
PROSPERO   Fury, Fury! There, Tyrant, there! Hark! Hark!
        [Caliban, Stephano, and Trinculo are driven out.]
Go, charge my goblins that they grind their joints
With dry convulsions, shorten up their sinews   261
With agèd cramps, and more pinch-spotted make
them   262
Than pard or cat o' mountain.
ARIEL   Hark, they roar!   263
PROSPERO
Let them be hunted soundly. At this hour   264
Lies at my mercy all mine enemies.
Shortly shall all my labors end, and thou
Shalt have the air at freedom. For a little   267
Follow, and do me service.   Exeunt.

❧

5.1

        Enter Prospero in his magic robes, [with his
        staff,] and Ariel.

---

206 **hoodwink this mischance** cover up (literally, blindfold) this mistake.   213–14 **o'er ears** over my ears in the filthy horse pond (line 182)   222 **King . . . peer** (Alludes to the old ballad beginning, "King Stephen was a worthy peer.")   227 **frippery** second-hand-clothing shop. (Trinculo knows that what they have just found is much finer.)   231 **The dropsy drown** (An oath. *Dropsy* is a disease characterized by the accumulation of fluid in the connective tissue of the body.)   232 **luggage** cumbersome trash.   234 **crown** head   236 **Mistress line** (Addressed to the linden or lime tree upon which, at line 193, Ariel hung the *glistering apparel*.)   237 **jerkin** jacket made of leather   238 **under the line** under the lime tree. (With punning sense of being south of the equinoctial line or equator; sailors on long voyages to the southern regions were popularly supposed to lose their hair from scurvy or other diseases. Stephano also quibbles bawdily on losing hair through syphilis, and puns in *Mistress* and *jerkin*.)   **like** likely   239 **bald** (1) hairless, napless (2) meager

240 **Do, do!** i.e., Bravo! (Said in response to the jesting or to the taking of the jerkin, or both.)   **steal . . . level** i.e., steal by means of plumb line and carpenter's level, methodically. (With pun on *line*, "lime tree," line 238, and *steal*, pronounced like *stale*, i.e., prostitute, continuing Stephano's bawdy quibble.)   **an't like** if it please   245 **pass of pate** sally of wit. (The metaphor is from fencing.)   247 **lime** birdlime, sticky substance (to give Caliban sticky fingers)   250 **barnacles** barnacle geese, formerly supposed to be hatched from barnacles attached to trees or to rotting timber; here, evidently used, like *apes*, as types of simpletons   251 **villainous** vilely   252 **lay to** start using   253 **this** i.e., the *glistering apparel*.   **hogshead** large cask   254 **Go to** (An expression of exhortation or remonstrance.)   261 **dry convulsions** racking cramps   262 **agèd** characteristic of old age   263 **pard** panther or leopard.   **cat o' mountain** wildcat.   264 **soundly** severely.   267 **little** little while longer
5.1. Location: Before Prospero's cell.

PROSPERO

    Now does my project gather to a head.

    My charms crack not, my spirits obey, and Time   2

    Goes upright with his carriage. How's the day?   3

ARIEL

    On the sixth hour, at which time, my lord,   4

    You said our work should cease.

PROSPERO   I did say so,

    When first I raised the tempest. Say, my spirit,

    How fares the King and 's followers?

ARIEL   Confined together

    In the same fashion as you gave in charge,

    Just as you left them; all prisoners, sir,

    In the line grove which weather-fends your cell.   10

    They cannot budge till your release. The King,   11

    His brother, and yours abide all three distracted,   12

    And the remainder mourning over them,

    Brim full of sorrow and dismay; but chiefly

    Him that you termed, sir, the good old lord,

    Gonzalo.

    His tears runs down his beard like winter's drops

    From eaves of reeds. Your charm so strongly works

      'em   17

    That if you now beheld them your affections   18

    Would become tender.

PROSPERO   Dost thou think so, spirit?

ARIEL

    Mine would, sir, were I human.

PROSPERO   And mine shall.

    Hast thou, which art but air, a touch, a feeling   21

    Of their afflictions, and shall not myself,

    One of their kind, that relish all as sharply   23

    Passion as they, be kindlier moved than thou art?   24

    Though with their high wrongs I am struck to th'

      quick,

    Yet with my nobler reason 'gainst my fury

    Do I take part. The rarer action is   27

    In virtue than in vengeance. They being penitent,

    The sole drift of my purpose doth extend

    Not a frown further. Go release them, Ariel.

    My charms I'll break, their senses I'll restore,

    And they shall be themselves.

ARIEL   I'll fetch them, sir.

                        Exit.

    [*Prospero traces a charmed circle with his staff.*]

PROSPERO

    Ye elves of hills, brooks, standing lakes, and groves,   33

    And ye that on the sands with printless foot

    Do chase the ebbing Neptune, and do fly him

    When he comes back; you demi-puppets that   36

    By moonshine do the green sour ringlets make,   37

    Whereof the ewe not bites; and you whose pastime

    Is to make midnight mushrooms, that rejoice   39

    To hear the solemn curfew; by whose aid,   40

    Weak masters though ye be, I have bedimmed   41

    The noontide sun, called forth the mutinous winds,

    And twixt the green sea and the azured vault   43

    Set roaring war; to the dread rattling thunder   44

    Have I given fire, and rifted Jove's stout oak   45

    With his own bolt; the strong-based promontory   46

    Have I made shake, and by the spurs plucked up   47

    The pine and cedar; graves at my command

    Have waked their sleepers, oped, and let 'em forth

    By my so potent art. But this rough magic   50

    I here abjure, and when I have required   51

    Some heavenly music—which even now I do—

    To work mine end upon their senses that   53

    This airy charm is for, I'll break my staff,

    Bury it certain fathoms in the earth,

    And deeper than did ever plummet sound

    I'll drown my book.   *Solemn music.*

      Here enters Ariel before; then Alonso, with a

      frantic gesture, attended by Gonzalo; Sebastian and

      Antonio in like manner, attended by Adrian and

      Francisco. They all enter the circle which Prospero

      had made, and there stand charmed; which

      Prospero observing, speaks:

    [*To Alonso*] A solemn air, and the best comforter   58

    To an unsettled fancy, cure thy brains,   59

    Now useless, boiled within thy skull! [*To Sebastian*

      and Antonio] There stand,   60

    For you are spell-stopped.—

    Holy Gonzalo, honorable man,

    Mine eyes, e'en sociable to the show of thine,   63

    Fall fellowly drops. [*Aside*] The charm dissolves

      apace,   64

    And as the morning steals upon the night,

    Melting the darkness, so their rising senses

    Begin to chase the ignorant fumes that mantle   67

    Their clearer reason.—O good Gonzalo,   68

    My true preserver, and a loyal sir

    To him thou follow'st! I will pay thy graces   70

    Home both in word and deed.—Most cruelly   71

    Didst thou, Alonso, use me and my daughter.

    Thy brother was a furtherer in the act.—   73

---

2 crack collapse, fail. (The metaphor is probably alchemical, as in *project* and *gather to a head*, line 1.)   **3 his carriage** its burden. (Time is no longer heavily burdened and so can go *upright*, standing straight and unimpeded.)   **4 On** Approaching   **10 line grove** grove of lime trees.   **weather-fends** protects from the weather   **11 your release** you release them.   **12 distracted** out of their wits   **17 eaves of reeds** thatched roofs.   **18 affections** disposition, feelings   **21 touch** sense, apprehension   **23–4 that . . . they** I who experience human passions as acutely as they   **24 kindlier** (1) more sympathetically (2) more naturally, humanly   **27 rarer** nobler   **33 Ye . . . groves** (This passage, down through line 50, is an embellished paraphrase of Golding's translation of Ovid's *Metamorphoses*, 7.197–219.)

36 demi-puppets puppets of half size, i.e., elves and fairies   **37 green sour ringlets** fairy rings, circles in grass (actually produced by mushrooms)   **39 midnight mushrooms** mushrooms appearing overnight   **40 curfew** evening bell, usually rung at nine o'clock, ushering in the time when spirits are abroad   **41 Weak masters** i.e., subordinate spirits, as in 4.1.35   **43 the azured vault** i.e., the sky   **44–5 to . . . fire** I have discharged the dread rattling thunderbolt   **45 rifted** riven, split.   **oak** a tree that was sacred to Jove   **46 bolt** thunderbolt   **47 spurs** roots   **50 rough** violent   **51 required** demanded   **53 their senses that** the senses of those whom   **58 air** song.   **and** i.e., which is   **59 fancy** imagination   **60 boiled** i.e., extremely agitated   **63 sociable** sympathetic.   **show** appearance   **64 Fall** let fall   **67 ignorant fumes** fumes that render them incapable of comprehension.   **mantle** envelop   **68 clearer** growing clearer   **70 pay thy graces** requite your favors and virtues   **71 Home** fully   **73 furtherer** accomplice

Thou art pinched for't now, Sebastian. [*To Antonio*]
    Flesh and blood,   74
You, brother mine, that entertained ambition,
Expelled remorse and nature, whom, with Sebastian,   76
Whose inward pinches therefore are most strong,
Would here have killed your king, I do forgive thee,
Unnatural though thou art.—Their understanding
Begins to swell, and the approaching tide
Will shortly fill the reasonable shore   81
That now lies foul and muddy. Not one of them
That yet looks on me, or would know me.—Ariel,
Fetch me the hat and rapier in my cell.
        [*Ariel goes to the cell and returns immediately.*]
I will discase me and myself present   85
As I was sometime Milan. Quickly, spirit!   86
Thou shalt ere long be free.
               Ariel sings and helps to attire him.

ARIEL
    Where the bee sucks, there suck I.
    In a cowslip's bell I lie;
    There I couch when owls do cry.   90
    On the bat's back I do fly
    After summer merrily.   92
    Merrily, merrily shall I live now
    Under the blossom that hangs on the bough.

PROSPERO
Why, that's my dainty Ariel! I shall miss thee,
But yet thou shalt have freedom. So, so, so.   96
To the King's ship, invisible as thou art!
There shalt thou find the mariners asleep
Under the hatches. The Master and the Boatswain
Being awake, enforce them to this place,
And presently, I prithee.   101

ARIEL
I drink the air before me, and return
Or ere your pulse twice beat.   *Exit.* 103

GONZALO
All torment, trouble, wonder, and amazement
Inhabits here. Some heavenly power guide us
Out of this fearful country!

PROSPERO   Behold, sir King,   106
The wrongèd Duke of Milan, Prospero.
For more assurance that a living prince
Does now speak to thee, I embrace thy body;
And to thee and thy company I bid
A hearty welcome.   [*Embracing him.*]

ALONSO   Whe'er thou be'st he or no,
Or some enchanted trifle to abuse me,   112
As late I have been, I not know. Thy pulse   113
Beats as of flesh and blood; and, since I saw thee,
Th' affliction of my mind amends, with which

I fear a madness held me. This must crave—   116
An if this be at all—a most strange story.   117
Thy dukedom I resign, and do entreat   118
Thou pardon me my wrongs. But how should
    Prospero   119
Be living, and be here?

PROSPERO [*to Gonzalo*]   First, noble friend,
Let me embrace thine age, whose honor cannot   121
Be measured or confined.   [*Embracing him.*]

GONZALO   Whether this be
Or be not, I'll not swear.

PROSPERO   You do yet taste
Some subtleties o'th'isle, that will not let you   124
Believe things certain. Welcome, my friends all!
[*Aside to Sebastian and Antonio*] But you, my brace of
    lords, were I so minded,   126
I here could pluck His Highness' frown upon you
And justify you traitors. At this time   128
I will tell no tales.

SEBASTIAN   The devil speaks in him.

PROSPERO   No.
[*To Antonio*] For you, most wicked sir, whom to call
    brother
Would even infect my mouth, I do forgive
Thy rankest fault—all of them; and require
My dukedom of thee, which perforce I know
Thou must restore.

ALONSO   If thou be'st Prospero,
Give us particulars of thy preservation,
How thou hast met us here, whom three hours since   136
Were wrecked upon this shore; where I have lost—
How sharp the point of this remembrance is!—
My dear son Ferdinand.

PROSPERO   I am woe for't, sir.   139

ALONSO
Irreparable is the loss, and Patience
Says it is past her cure.

PROSPERO   I rather think
You have not sought her help, of whose soft grace
For the like loss I have her sovereign aid   143
And rest myself content.

ALONSO   You the like loss?

PROSPERO
As great to me as late, and supportable   145
To make the dear loss, have I means much weaker   146
Than you may call to comfort you; for I   147
Have lost my daughter.

ALONSO   A daughter?
O heavens, that they were living both in Naples,

---

74 pinched punished, afflicted   **76 remorse and nature** pity and natural feeling.   **whom** you who   **81 reasonable shore** shores of reason, i.e., minds. (Their reason returns, like the incoming tide.)
85 discase disrobe   **86 As . . . Milan** in my former appearance as
Duke of Milan.   **90 couch** lie   **92 After summer** following summer
as it moves to various parts of the world   **96 So, so, so** (Expresses
approval of Ariel's help as valet.)   **101 presently** immediately
103 Or ere before   **106 fearful** frightening   **112 trifle** trick of magic.
abuse deceive   **113 late** lately

116 crave require   **117 An . . . all** if this is actually happening.   **story**
i.e., explanation.   **118 Thy . . . resign** (Alonso made arrangement
with Antonio at the time of Prospero's banishment for Milan to pay
tribute to Naples; see 1.2.113–27.)   **119 wrongs** wrongdoings.
121 thine age your venerable self   **124 subtleties** illusions, magical
powers. (Playing on the idea of "pastries, concoctions.")   **126 brace**
pair   **128 justify you** prove you to be   **136 whom** we who   **139 woe**
sorry   **143 sovereign** efficacious   **145 late** recent   **145–7 and supportable . . . you** and I have much weaker means to make my loss
supportable than you can call upon to comfort you

The king and queen there! That they were, I wish   151
Myself were mudded in that oozy bed   152
Where my son lies. When did you lose your daughter?   153
PROSPERO
In this last tempest. I perceive these lords
At this encounter do so much admire   155
That they devour their reason and scarce think   156
Their eyes do offices of truth, their words   157
Are natural breath. But, howsoever you have   158
Been jostled from your senses, know for certain
That I am Prospero and that very duke
Which was thrust forth of Milan, who most strangely   161
Upon this shore, where you were wrecked, was
    landed
To be the lord on't. No more yet of this,
For 'tis a chronicle of day by day,   164
Not a relation for a breakfast nor
Befitting this first meeting. Welcome, sir.
This cell's my court. Here have I few attendants,
And subjects none abroad. Pray you, look in.   168
My dukedom since you have given me again,
I will requite you with as good a thing,   170
At least bring forth a wonder to content ye
As much as me my dukedom.   172

Here Prospero discovers Ferdinand and Miranda,
playing at chess.

MIRANDA   Sweet lord, you play me false.   173
FERDINAND   No, my dearest love,
I would not for the world.
MIRANDA
Yes, for a score of kingdoms you should wrangle,   176
And I would call it fair play.
ALONSO   If this prove   177
A vision of the island, one dear son   178
Shall I twice lose.
SEBASTIAN   A most high miracle!
FERDINAND [*approaching his father*]
Though the seas threaten, they are merciful;
I have cursed them without cause.   [*He kneels.*]
ALONSO   Now all the blessings
Of a glad father compass thee about!   182
Arise, and say how thou cam'st here.
                                         [*Ferdinand rises.*]
MIRANDA   Oh, wonder!
How many goodly creatures are there here!
How beauteous mankind is! Oh, brave new world   185

That has such people in't!
PROSPERO   'Tis new to thee.
ALONSO
What is this maid with whom thou wast at play?
Your eld'st acquaintance cannot be three hours.   188
Is she the goddess that hath severed us,
And brought us thus together?
FERDINAND   Sir, she is mortal;
But by immortal Providence she's mine.
I chose her when I could not ask my father
For his advice, nor thought I had one. She
Is daughter to this famous Duke of Milan,
Of whom so often I have heard renown,
But never saw before; of whom I have
Received a second life; and second father
This lady makes him to me.
ALONSO   I am hers.
But oh, how oddly will it sound that I
Must ask my child forgiveness!
PROSPERO   There, sir, stop.
Let us not burden our remembrances with
A heaviness that's gone.
GONZALO   I have inly wept,   202
Or should have spoke ere this. Look down, you gods,
And on this couple drop a blessèd crown!
For it is you that have chalked forth the way   205
Which brought us hither.
ALONSO   I say amen, Gonzalo!
GONZALO
Was Milan thrust from Milan, that his issue   207
Should become kings of Naples? Oh, rejoice
Beyond a common joy, and set it down
With gold on lasting pillars: in one voyage
Did Claribel her husband find at Tunis,
And Ferdinand, her brother, found a wife
Where he himself was lost; Prospero his dukedom
In a poor isle; and all of us ourselves   214
When no man was his own.
ALONSO [*to Ferdinand and Miranda*]   Give me your hands. 215
Let grief and sorrow still embrace his heart   216
That doth not wish you joy!
GONZALO   Be it so! Amen!

Enter Ariel, with the Master and Boatswain
amazedly following.

Oh, look, sir, look, sir! Here is more of us.
I prophesied, if a gallows were on land,
This fellow could not drown.—Now, blasphemy,   220
That swear'st grace o'erboard, not an oath on shore?   221
Hast thou no mouth by land? What is the news?
BOATSWAIN
The best news is that we have safely found

151–3 That . . . lies I would wish myself buried in that muddy bed where my son's body lies drowned if that would somehow make them alive and reigning in Naples.   **155 admire** wonder   **156 devour their reason** i.e., are openmouthed, dumbfounded   **156–8 and scarce . . . breath** and scarcely can believe their eyes or their own words. **161 of** from   **164 of day by day** requiring days to tell, or covering a long span of time   **168 abroad** anywhere else.   **170 requite** repay **172.1 discovers** i.e., by opening a curtain, presumably rearstage **173 play me false** cheat.   **176–7 Yes . . . play** i.e., Yes, even if we were playing for twenty kingdoms, something less than the whole world, you would still press your advantage against me, and I would lovingly let you do it as though it were fair play.   **178 vision** illusion **182 compass** encompass, embrace   **185 brave** splendid, gorgeously appareled, handsome

188 eld'st longest   **202 heaviness** sadness.   **inly** inwardly **205 chalked . . . way** marked as with a piece of chalk the pathway **207 Was Milan** Was the Duke of Milan.   **issue** child   **214–15 all . . . own** all of us have found ourselves and our sanity when we all had lost our senses.   **216 still** always.   **his** that person's   **220 blasphemy** i.e., blasphemer   **221 That swear'st grace o'erboard** i.e., you who expel heavenly grace from the ship by your blasphemies.   **not an oath** aren't you going to swear an oath

Our King and company; the next, our ship—
Which, but three glasses since, we gave out split— 225
Is tight and yare and bravely rigged as when 226
We first put out to sea.

ARIEL [*aside to Prospero*]   Sir, all this service
Have I done since I went.

PROSPERO [*aside to Ariel*]   My tricksy spirit! 228

ALONSO
These are not natural events; they strengthen 229
From strange to stranger. Say, how came you hither?

BOATSWAIN
If I did think, sir, I were well awake,
I'd strive to tell you. We were dead of sleep, 232
And—how we know not—all clapped under hatches,
Where but even now, with strange and several noises 234
Of roaring, shrieking, howling, jingling chains,
And more diversity of sounds, all horrible,
We were awaked; straightway at liberty;
Where we, in all her trim, freshly beheld
Our royal, good, and gallant ship, our Master
Cap'ring to eye her. On a trice, so please you, 240
Even in a dream, were we divided from them 241
And were brought moping hither.

ARIEL [*aside to Prospero*]   Was't well done? 242

PROSPERO [*aside to Ariel*]
Bravely, my diligence. Thou shalt be free.

ALONSO
This is as strange a maze as e'er men trod,
And there is in this business more than nature
Was ever conduct of. Some oracle 246
Must rectify our knowledge.

PROSPERO   Sir, my liege,
Do not infest your mind with beating on 248
The strangeness of this business. At picked leisure, 249
Which shall be shortly, single I'll resolve you, 250
Which to you shall seem probable, of every 251
These happened accidents; till when, be cheerful 252
And think of each thing well. [*Aside to Ariel*] Come
hither, spirit. 253
Set Caliban and his companions free.
Untie the spell.   [*Exit Ariel.*]
    [*To Alonso*]   How fares my gracious sir?
There are yet missing of your company
Some few odd lads that you remember not. 257

Enter Ariel, driving in Caliban, Stephano, and
Trinculo, in their stolen apparel.

STEPHANO   Every man shift for all the rest, and let no 258
man take care for himself; for all is but fortune. *Corag-* 259

gio, bully monster, *coraggio!* 260

TRINCULO   If these be true spies which I wear in my 261
head, here's a goodly sight.

CALIBAN
O Setebos, these be brave spirits indeed! 263
How fine my master is! I am afraid 264
He will chastise me.

SEBASTIAN   Ha, ha!
What things are these, my lord Antonio?
Will money buy 'em?

ANTONIO   Very like. One of them
Is a plain fish, and no doubt marketable.

PROSPERO
Mark but the badges of these men, my lords, 270
Then say if they be true. This misshapen knave, 271
His mother was a witch, and one so strong
That could control the moon, make flows and ebbs,
And deal in her command without her power. 274
These three have robbed me, and this demidevil—
For he's a bastard one—had plotted with them 276
To take my life. Two of these fellows you
Must know and own. This thing of darkness I 278
Acknowledge mine.

CALIBAN   I shall be pinched to death.

ALONSO
Is not this Stephano, my drunken butler?

SEBASTIAN   He is drunk now. Where had he wine?

ALONSO
And Trinculo is reeling ripe. Where should they 282
Find this grand liquor that hath gilded 'em? 283
[*To Trinculo*] How cam'st thou in this pickle? 284

TRINCULO   I have been in such a pickle since I saw you
last that, I fear me, will never out of my bones. I shall
not fear flyblowing. 287

SEBASTIAN   Why, how now, Stephano?

STEPHANO   Oh, touch me not! I am not Stephano, but a
cramp.

PROSPERO   You'd be king o'the isle, sirrah? 291

STEPHANO   I should have been a sore one, then. 292

ALONSO [*pointing to Caliban*]
This is a strange thing as e'er I looked on.

PROSPERO
He is as disproportioned in his manners
As in his shape.—Go, sirrah, to my cell.
Take with you your companions. As you look
To have my pardon, trim it handsomely. 297

---

225 **glasses** hourglasses. **gave out split** reported shipwrecked, gave up for lost **226 yare** ready. **bravely** splendidly **228 tricksy** ingenious, sportive **229 strengthen** increase **232 dead of sleep** deep in sleep **234 several** diverse **240 Cap'ring to eye** dancing for joy to see. **On a trice** In an instant **241 them** i.e., the other crew members **242 moping** in a daze **246 conduct** director **248 infest** harass, disturb. **beating on** worrying about **249 picked** chosen, convenient **250 single** privately. **resolve** satisfy, explain to **251 probable** plausible **251–2 of every These** about every one of these **252 accidents** occurrences **253 well** favorably. **257 odd** unaccounted for **258–9 Every . . . himself** (Stephano drunkenly inverts the saying "Every man for himself.")

259–60 Coraggio . . . monster Have courage, gallant monster **261 true spies** accurate observers (i.e., sharp eyes) **263 brave** handsome **264 fine** splendidly attired **270 badges** emblems worn by servants to indicate whom they serve **271 say . . . true** say if they are worthy and loyal servants. **274 And . . . power** and usurp the moon's command (over tides) without her authority. (Sycorax could control the moon and hence the tides.) **276 bastard** counterfeit **278 own** acknowledge. **282 reeling ripe** staggeringly drunk. **283 gilded 'em** flushed their complexion (from the drink), giving them a ruddy or gilded appearance. **284 pickle** (1) fix, predicament (2) pickling brine (in this case, horse urine). **287 flyblowing** i.e., being fouled by fly eggs (from which he is saved by being pickled). **291 sirrah** (Standard form of address to an inferior, here expressing reprimand.) **292 sore** (1) tyrannical (2) sorry, inept (3) wracked by pain **297 trim** prepare, decorate

CALIBAN
　Ay, that I will; and I'll be wise hereafter
　And seek for grace. What a thrice-double ass　299
　Was I to take this drunkard for a god
　And worship this dull fool!
PROSPERO　　　　　　　　　　　Go to. Away!
ALONSO
　Hence, and bestow your luggage where you found it.
SEBASTIAN　　Or stole it, rather.
　　　　　　　[Exeunt Caliban, Stephano, and Trinculo.]
PROSPERO
　Sir, I invite Your Highness and your train
　To my poor cell, where you shall take your rest
　For this one night; which, part of it, I'll waste　306
　With such discourse as, I not doubt, shall make it
　Go quick away: the story of my life,
　And the particular accidents gone by　309
　Since I came to this isle. And in the morn
　I'll bring you to your ship, and so to Naples,
　Where I have hope to see the nuptial
　Of these our dear-belovèd solemnized;
　And thence retire me to my Milan, where
　Every third thought shall be my grave.
ALONSO　　　　　　　　　　　　　　I long
　To hear the story of your life, which must
　Take the ear strangely.
PROSPERO　　　　　　　　I'll deliver all;　317
　And promise you calm seas, auspicious gales,
　And sail so expeditious that shall catch　319
　Your royal fleet far off. [Aside to Ariel] My Ariel, chick,　320

That is thy charge. Then to the elements
Be free, and fare thou well!
　　　　　　[To the others] Please you, draw near.　322
　　　　　　　Exeunt omnes [except Prospero].

Epilogue　　Spoken by PROSPERO.

Now my charms are all o'erthrown,
And what strength I have 's mine own,
Which is most faint. Now, 'tis true,
I must be here confined by you
Or sent to Naples. Let me not,
Since I have my dukedom got
And pardoned the deceiver, dwell
In this bare island by your spell,
But release me from my bands　9
With the help of your good hands.　10
Gentle breath of yours my sails　11
Must fill, or else my project fails,
Which was to please. Now I want　13
Spirits to enforce, art to enchant,
And my ending is despair,
Unless I be relieved by prayer,　16
Which pierces so that it assaults　17
Mercy itself, and frees all faults.　18
As you from crimes would pardoned be,　19
Let your indulgence set me free.　　　Exit.　20

299 grace pardon, favor.　306 waste spend　309 accidents occurrences　317 Take take effect upon, enchant.　deliver declare, relate
319–20 catch . . . far off enable you to catch up with the main part of
your royal fleet, now afar off en route to Naples. (See 1.2.235–6.)

322 draw near i.e., enter my cell.
Epilogue.
9 bands bonds　10 hands i.e., applause (the noise of which could
break a charm).　11 Gentle breath Favorable breeze (produced by
hands clapping or favorable comment)　13 want lack　16 prayer i.e.,
Prospero's petition to the audience　17 assaults penetrates the heart
of　18 frees obtains forgiveness for　19 crimes sins　20 indulgence
(1) humoring, lenient approval (2) remission of punishment for sin

The Two Noble Kinsmen

The Two Noble Kinsmen, seemingly the very last play in which Shakespeare had a hand, returns to a theme he had pursued in *The Two Gentlemen of Verona*, one of his early plays and possibly even the first. As in that early comedy, two friends vie for the affection of a lady in such a way as to put their warm friendship to a severe test. In the late play, as Bruce Smith, Jeffrey Masten, and others have observed, the famous friendship of Palamon and Arcite is rich in a sexual innuendo of which they seem innocently unaware until they both fall in love with Emilia. "We are one another's wife, ever begetting / New births of love," declares Arcite to his cousin as they find themselves imprisoned together in Athens. "We are father, friends, acquaintance; / We are in one another, families; / I am your heir, and you are mine" (2.2.80–3). The sentiment is close to that of Aufidius in *Coriolanus*, when he says of his former enemy, Coriolanus: "that I see thee here, / Thou noble thing, more dances my rapt heart / Than when I first wedded mistress saw / Bestride my threshold" (4.5.120–3). This is not to argue that Palamon and Arcite become lovers in their imprisonment. Nonetheless, at its most exalted, same-sex friendship fulfills the emotional role expected of matrimony and is indeed put in conflict with matrimonial intent.

The Two Noble Kinsmen was probably first performed in 1613 or 1614, and was revived for performance at court in 1619 and again seemingly in 1625–1626. Rights were subsequently assigned to the publisher of the so-called Beaumont and Fletcher Folio, 1646. The play actually appeared in print in a second edition, entitled *Fifty Comedies and Tragedies, Written by Francis Beaumont, and John Fletcher, Gentlemen*, 1679—of which, in fact, a good number were by Beaumont or by Fletcher alone, with many others by Fletcher in collaboration with other dramatists. The play did not appear in the First Folio of Shakespeare's plays in 1623 or in subsequent editions of that work. Perhaps for these reasons, *The Two Noble Kinsmen* was for

centuries excluded from the Shakespeare canon and is still only occasionally studied or performed. Shakespeare was so famous that his name was often attached to plays in which he had no part; was *The Two Noble Kinsmen* one of these? Why would Shakespeare want to collaborate when his name was so well known?

Whatever his personal reasons, however, Shakespeare does seem to have done just that. Perhaps his own retirement, seemingly announced in *The Tempest*, turned out to be a semi-retirement. John Fletcher was his younger colleague and, in effect, successor as playwright for the King's Men. The two seemingly collaborated in writing *Henry VIII* at about the same time, although there the evidence is less certain and Shakespeare's role in any case more dominant. He appears to have collaborated with Thomas Middleton in the writing of *Timon of Athens*. Earlier, in the 1590s, Shakespeare had agreed to help revise a controversial play by writing a new scene for *The Book of Sir Thomas More*, originally perhaps by Anthony Munday and others. Shakespeare's name was linked with that of Fletcher in the authorship of the seemingly lost play *Cardenio*, c. 1612–1613. Shakespeare was loyal to his acting company and may have helped them out with collaborations on other occasions. And, as Jeffrey Masten has suggested, the dominant theme of male friendship in *The Two Noble Kinsmen* is one that offers itself as an apt subject for authors working in collaboration.

On the basis of style, metrics, distinctive rhythms, vocabulary, linguistic preferences for forms like *ye* and *'em* (both of these characteristic of Fletcher), tone, characterization, and a kind of theatrical abruptness that Fletcher seems to have cultivated, many editors and critics come to a general consensus, not shared by all, that Shakespeare seems to have written all of Act 1, the first scene of Act 2, the first two scenes of Act 3, scene 3 of Act 4, and most of the final act except scene 2. This division would give to Shakespeare the scenes that dramatize Duke Theseus's resolve to defend the cause of three slain kings against Creon of Thebes, Palamon and Arcite's dilemma in serving the tyrant Creon and their brave defeat in battle by Theseus's Athenian army, Emilia's defense of friendship between women, Arcite and Palamon's quarrel in the forest after one has been released from captivity by Theseus and the other freed from prison by the Jailer's enamored daughter, the Jailer's Daughter's forlorn lament at Palamon's neglect of her, a touching scene in which the Jailer and a Doctor overhear manifestations of the Jailer's Daughter's mad affliction, and the long concluding action in which Palamon and Arcite's rival claims to Emilia are sorted out by divine will.

Fletcher is then left with the bulk of the play's middle action, including the startling scene (2.2) in which the imprisoned Palamon and Arcite declare their love for each other but then fall instantly into bitter enmity once they have both seen Emilia, Arcite's encounter (after he has been released from prison) with some country rustics who tell him of public games in which Arcite resolves to compete, his success there in winning the right to be Emilia's "servant," several scenes of the Jailer's Daughter's increasing madness, some broadly comic subplot business in which a pedantic schoolmaster and his rustic companions prepare a Morris dance to be performed in Theseus's presence, Palamon and Arcite's determination to fight each other even at the certain cost of their being captured and sentenced to death by Theseus, Emilia's inability to choose between Palamon and Arcite even when it appears that her choice would save one of them from death, and still more.

Even a quick outline suggests how Fletcher seems to have preferred the scenes of unexpected reversals of the action in which plausibility of motivation yields precedence to self-conscious theatrical artifice. Some of the scenes assigned to Fletcher exploit sexuality in novel situations, as when the Doctor advises the Wooer of the Jailer's Daughter to disguise himself as Palamon, for whose love the Daughter has lost her wits. The Doctor insists that her whim is to be indulged in every detail, even if the Wooer must climb into bed with her. When the father protests that marriage should come before sexual fulfillment, the Doctor is curt with such a prudish idea: "Nev'r cast away your child for honesty [chastity]," he admonishes (5.2.22). This droll exploitation of a tittilating situation is characteristic of Fletcher. The Prologue and Epilogue are almost certainly by him.

Whatever their mode of collaboration in writing *The Two Noble Kinsmen*, Shakespeare and Fletcher chose to dramatize a tale from Chaucer's *Canterbury Tales*, the Knight's tale, which is about noble friendship. Palamon and Arcite are cousins and devoted friends, "dearer in

love than blood" (1.2.1). When we first see them, they are considering what guidance their friendship can provide them in the corrupted world of Thebes. Under the rule of their uncle Creon, "a most unbounded tyrant" (line 63), Thebes is a place of carnal temptation and political favoritism. Their virtuous behavior makes them aliens and the subjects of mockery. "Not to be ev'n jump / As they are here were to be strangers" (lines 40–1), Arcite insists, and yet the alternative of swimming along in "The common stream" would be enough to turn them both into "mere monsters" (lines 10, 42). They resolve not to ape the mannerisms and dress of their contemporaries, and long for war as a means of purging the enervating softness of peace. Yet war, when it comes, provides only another dilemma, for military action in support of a tyrant undermines the very purpose for which they wish to fight. Ultimately the calling of military duty prevails, and they are captured by Theseus's Athenian army after having surpassed all others in the battle.

The mutual fondness of these cousins is not the only study in this play of friendship under duress. Duke Theseus of Athens and his general, Pirithous, are friends in the tradition of Alexander and Hephaestion, Damon and Pythias, and other figures from classical legend and history. Pirithous is reputed to have descended into Hades with Theseus to help carry off Persephone. "How his longing / Follows his friend!" exclaims Theseus's sister-in-law Emilia as she sees Pirithous eagerly depart to join Theseus in the military campaign against Thebes (1.3.26–7). Delayed for a time by Theseus's command that he see to the ceremonies that the war has interrupted, Pirithous cannot devote his full energies to matters of peace; his heart is with Theseus on the field of battle. Theseus's bride, Hippolyta, quite agrees with her sister Emilia: Theseus and Pirithous have shared so many dangers, she says, that "Their knot of love, / Tied, weaved, entangled . . . May be outworn, never undone" (lines 41–4). As is always the case in such conventional debates about friendship and love, or love and honor, rival claims test friendship to prove its durability. Pirithous's loyalty to Theseus overcomes all other considerations.

Emilia and Hippolyta, as sisters, discuss friendship between women, comparing it to friendship between men. "Theirs has more ground," concedes Emilia, "is more maturely seasoned, / More buckled with strong judgment." Yet Emilia's own love for the now-dead Flavina, whom she once enjoyed as a playfellow, had qualities of innocence, of mutual devotion to chastity, and of intermingling of souls that men seemingly cannot match. "Like the elements / That know not what nor why, yet do effect / Rare issues by their operance, our souls / Did so to one another," Emilia longingly recalls. Their tastes were instinctively identical; their mannerisms and garments were so alike that neither could discern who had begun the fashion. Emilia's conclusion is that "true love 'tween maid and maid may be / More than in sex divid-ual"—that is, between persons of the opposite sex (1.3.55–82). At first, then, both men and women in this play find bonding to a person of the same sex more per-fect and fulfilling than heterosexual love. The situation recalls that of *A Midsummer Night's Dream*, where that play's Duke Theseus also marries Hippolyta, Queen of the Amazons. The very image of the Amazonian maiden is of a woman armed to defend herself against men.

These familiar topics of love versus honor and the battle of the sexes, eloquently set up by Shakespeare in the first act, inevitably lead to complications and testings in the second and third acts. Even in the first act, choices must be faced in terms of a code of chivalric honor. The-seus, about to marry Hippolyta but petitioned by three widows to avenge the dishonor done to their royal hus-bands by Creon, postpones his marital happiness to march against Thebes. Pirithous must reconcile the claims of duty and of his longing to be with Theseus on the field of battle. Palamon and Arcite seek ways to jus-tify their military service in support of a tyrant and a cor-rupt state. Emilia announces her resolution to live and die a virgin, while her sister Hippolyta determines to go ahead with her marriage to Theseus, in a sisterly debate that reminds us of Luciana and her married sister Adri-ana in *The Comedy of Errors*.

Fletcher's theatrical strategy in the middle acts of the play is to subject these conventional polarities of love and honor to surprising and disarmingly improbable turns of events. In the prison where Palamon and Arcite lie lan-guishing after their capture by Theseus's army, the Jailer's Daughter falls immediately and disastrously in love with Palamon, even though she readily concedes that Arcite is as handsome (2.4.16) and that "To marry him [Palamon] is hopeless, / To be his whore is witless" (lines 4–5). For their part, the two young men, resolving in the best stoical fashion to embrace their imprisonment as a way to repu-diate a bad world and rely instead on their own sustain-ing friendship, fall instantly to quarreling when Emilia appears in the courtyard below their window (2.2.1–284). Palamon claims precedence because he has seen Emilia first. Whereas they previously regarded women as "The poison of pure spirits" and worse than a distraction (1line 75), they now devote their loyalties to love alone and look upon each other as villains worthy only of sudden death. Neither has yet spoken a word with the lady in question.

The pattern of flamboyant theatrical artifice continues to unfold. Once Arcite is released from prison for some unexplained reason and banished from Athens (lines 251–2), his only wish is to return in some disguise so that he may be near Emilia; once Palamon in turn is freed by the lovesick Jailer's Daughter at considerable risk to her-self and her poor father, Palamon's sole hope is to see

Emilia again. When the two cousins encounter one another by chance in the forest near Athens (another rec-ollection of *A Midsummer Night's Dream*), their fierce determination to undo each other is almost comically mediated by the solicitude of each warrior that the other be properly armed. The hyperbolic vaunting, the unex-pected coincidences, the lack of plausible motivation are highly theatrical and self-conscious in a way that is char-acteristic not only of Fletcher's other plays but of Jacobean drama in the 1610s and indeed of some of Shakespeare's own final work.

Throughout, the major characters operate in response to a code of aristocratic behavior that is eminently suited to a play about heroic chivalry. Arcite, in disguise as one who is competing in the "pastimes" devised to entertain Theseus and his court (2.3.78), amply displays his "noble qualities" to all who see him, even though they suppose him a stranger. "His body / And fiery mind illustrate a brave father," says Hippolyta; that is, he is nobly descended (2.5.21–2). He speaks well: "All his words are worthy" (line 29). With a modesty and *sprezzatura* aptly suited to his noble station, he allows that he knows well the aristocratic pursuits of hawking and hunting, and most of all horsemanship. "I dare not praise / My feat in horsemanship," he says, "yet they that know me / Would say it was my best piece" (lines 11–14). Elsewhere, as often is the case in Shakespeare, horsemanship is a sure sign of aristocratic bearing, as when Pirithous describes Arcite as able to hold his saddle "bravely" even on a vicious horse that eventually topples over backward on its rider and crushes him (5.4.48–84). Arcite is "as brave a knight as e'er / Did spur a noble steed" (5.3.115–16). Palamon and Arcite's insistence on duelling even at the risk of the law's judgment is another mark of their inherent nobleness, even if the play also dramatizes the conflict between that aristocratic code of duelling and Theseus's insistence (reflecting Elizabethan and Jacobean official policy) that quarrels must be submitted to the authority of the state (3.6.132 ff.). Palamon and Arcite's followers in the climactic trial by combat in Act 5 are elaborately described as worthy of their greatness, with "all the ornament of honor" in their outward appearance and behavior; they "are all the sons of honor" (4.2.75–141). Theseus too is governed by the code of aris-tocratic honor, and his final resolution to allow Palamon and Arcite to settle their differences in a state-sponsored public arena through trial by combat is presented as a suitable solution for chivalric strife.

Even the comedy of this play, chiefly by Fletcher, is well suited to the aristocratic presuppositions of the main plot. The countrymen who tell Arcite about the upcom-ing pastimes in which he can compete to win the favor of Theseus and Emilia are country rustics whose rude man-nerisms are contrasted at every turn with those of Arcite.

Their conversation is often about sexuality, about jealous wives who must be "boarded" and "stowed" in suitable fashion, about the "wenches" with whom they will dance before the Duke, and so on (2.3.25–66). Like the shipwrecked hero of *Pericles*, who similarly obtains from poor country folk a means of competing in courtly games as a stranger, Arcite is beholden to these good-natured bumpkins and immeasurably far above them in noble graces. "'Tis a pretty fellow," one of them allows (line 79). The pedantic Schoolmaster Gerald, who, with his tedious Latinisms, presents a Morris dance before the Duke, reminds us of the schoolmaster Holofernes in *Love's Labor's Lost* and Peter Quince in *A Midsummer Night's Dream*; indeed, the business of devising a play within the play, witnessed by an amused critical audience onstage, is a medley of motifs out of Shakespeare. The plot line of the distraught Jailer's Daughter, sometimes comic, sometimes touching, borrows elements of mad talk from Ophelia in *Hamlet* and of medical eavesdropping from Lady Macbeth's sleepwalking in *Macbeth*. The Jailer's Daughter's song of "Willow, willow, willow" (4.1.80) would appear to be an explicit allusion to Desdemona's song in *Othello*. At every point, the play's subplot material seems intended to reflect through parody and comic exaggeration the heroic themes of love versus honor and the display of chivalric nobility. At the same time, the play's depiction of madness and erotic desire is serious and even clinical, in much the way that madness and desire come together in *Hamlet*'s depiction of the deranged Ophelia.

Staging is appropriately ceremonial and elaborate. The play opens with a procession headed by Hymen, god of marriage, and including a courtly entourage of Theseus, his bride-to-be, and others, all elaborately robed in costumes and garlands symbolic of their ceremonial roles. A boy sings a hymn to love and marriage. The interruption of this grand entrance by the three widowed petitioners signals the sorts of conflicts that will continue to challenge the courtly ideals of perfect love, friendship, and honor. The battle between Thebes and Athens and later athletic contests are decorously conducted offstage (1.4.0.1–5, 2.5.0.1–3), but the entrances of Theseus and other dignitaries continue to be heralded by the blaze of cornets and other flourishes. Repeated kneelings underscore the hierarchical structure of the Athenian court and the obedience that Theseus expects to his authority. Music accompanies the ceremonials of interment devised for the three dead kings (1.5.0.1–3). The theater building is used to its fullest extent, as when Palamon and Arcite appear in prison "*above*" (2.0.51.1) and look down upon Emilia on the main stage gathering flowers as though in a garden adjacent to the prison. The sounds of cornets and halooing are heard from various directions to signify the celebration of May Day (3.1.0.1–2).

Doors are used to suggest locations: Palamon enters, presumably in the forest, "*as out of a bush*" (3.1.30.1), and Palamon and Arcite enter to their final trial at opposite doors (5.1.7.1–2). A Morris dance provides opportunity for numerous quaint characters in costume, including a baboon, the Lord and Lady of May (i.e., Robin Hood and Maid Marian), the Chambermaid, the Servingman, mine Host and his fat Spouse, the rustic countryman called the Clown, and the Fool (3.5.128–35). The dance itself is an elaborate if lower-class entertainment that is hard to recapture through reading the play text, and it certainly required music, including a taborer or player on pipe and drum. Palamon and Arcite fight a duel in full armor; the dialogue makes much of the stage business of their dressing each other for the encounter (3.6.16–131).

The play's last act is especially ceremonial, as though calling upon ceremony as a visual language of closure. Palamon and Arcite are brought onstage from opposite doors at the beginning of Act 5 to "tender their holy prayers" before the gods, asking for divine judgment in their strife. First Arcite and then Palamon approach the altars of their respective immortal patrons, Mars and Venus. The staging is uncertain. Conceivably, one altar is to stand in turn for the altar of Mars and Venus, and then for Diana when Emilia in her turn implores the gods' assistance; the elaborate stage business requires a trapdoor, of which the theater where the play was performed might have provided only one. Still, it is quite possible that three altars were provided onstage at once, giving the balanced, antithetical, and symbolic sense of location that the last act visually demands. Mars's altar answers Arcite's entreaties with "*clanging of armor, with a short thunder*" (5.1.61.2) in an auspicious sign that Mars will grant Arcite the desired ascendancy. Palamon and his followers hear "*music*" at Venus's altar and see doves (line 129.1) as a "fair token" of truth in love. Emilia's ceremonial at Diana's altar is the most elaborate, requiring as it does "*still music*," garlands and flowers, and a "*silver hind, in which is conveyed incense and sweet odors*." The oblation being set afire on the altar, "*the hind vanishes under the altar, and in the place ascends a rose tree, having one rose upon it*." This rose subsequently falls from a tree to the accompaniment of "*a sudden twang of instruments*" (lines 136.1–8, 168.1–2). These symbolic actions, signifying that virginity will yield chastely to love's erotic fulfillment, demand the services of a trapdoor, but the first two ceremonies do not. Perhaps then Diana's altar is centrally placed and is flanked by the representations of war and love. Such a configuration would give visual confirmation to the last act's movement toward a reconciliation in which the seemingly competing demands of military prowess, eros, and chaste denial are finally given their respective places in the crowning ceremonial of marriage. Staging thus embodies the antitheses of this chivalric play by visually juxtaposing male and female, friendship and love, love and honor, and by seeking a way to bring these opposites together.

Whatever Shakespeare's exact share may have been, *The Two Noble Kinsmen* displays many of the characteristics of the late Shakespeare, not only in the freedom of the verse, with its run-on lines and hypermetric effects, but also in the play's fascination with romantic plotting. The play that Shakespeare and Fletcher fashioned out of an old Chaucerian tale is one that portrays chivalric ideals through the medium of theatrical artifice. Like *Pericles*, whose narrator is Chaucer's contemporary John Gower, *The Two Noble Kinsmen* goes back to a quaint and improbable fiction of medieval times where fancy and imagination can do their work of theatrical transformation. Staging is elaborate, especially at the close, as in *Cymbeline*. The gods intervene directly in the play's denouement, as in all the late romances (though the gods in *The Tempest* are of Prospero's devising).

As in the romances as a group, the audience is asked to approach, in a spirit of wonder combined perhaps with ironic detachment, a work that is self-consciously theatrical in its depiction of supernatural effects. The gods have their way in *The Two Noble Kinsmen*. The human protagonists stand in awe at their final deliverance from their own worst selves. Palamon and Arcite, in their perverse but noble attempts to destroy each other for love, fulfill the will of destiny that is revealed to them at the altars of Mars, Venus, and Diana: the brave Arcite is to die on horseback, the lover Palamon is to win the lady Emilia, and she is to find marital happiness even while preserving her ideal of chaste marriage. The ending is contrived to a striking degree, in that it depends on a physical accident; and yet it is no more arbitrary than the ending of *Cymbeline*. What seems accident to mere mortals is seen finally by the play's protagonists as part of a deeper heavenly design. "O you heavenly charmers," Theseus apostrophizes the gods in a choric close, "What things you make of us! For what we lack / We laugh, for what we have are sorry, still / Are children in some kind." Theseus's conclusion from this is one of pious acceptance: "Let us be thankful / For that which is" (5.4.131–5). The audience, even while it is openly encouraged to see the play's romantic structure as theatrical artifice, is also invited to ponder what deeper ideologies may be embodied in Shakespeare's and Fletcher's depiction of dramatic art as pattern, order, ornament, contrivance, and vision.

The Two Noble Kinsmen has been seen on stage only occasionally, more so in recent decades than in the preceding centuries. Productions have tended to focus on the play's fairy-tale-like qualities, its fascination with sexual ambiguities, and its penchant for the theatrically surprising. A French version, *Deux Nobles Cousins,* for the Centre Dramatique de Courneuve in 1979, directed by Pierre Constant, saw the play as an extended debate about heterosexual versus homosexual love. Barry Kyle, directing the play in 1986 for the Royal Shakespeare Theatre, chose a large Japanese decor to emphasize a culture of chivalric warriors locked into an antique code of honor. Theseus has sometimes been seen as a problematic and tyrannical figure of authority, browbeating Emilia into making her difficult choice between Palamon and Arcite. The Jailer's Daughter has come into her own as perhaps the most believable character in the play, with her forthright sexuality and her Ophelia-like pathos.

The Two Noble Kinsmen

[*Dramatis Personae*

PROLOGUE

THESEUS, *Duke of Athens*
HIPPOLYTA, *Queen of the Amazons, later married to Theseus*
EMILIA, *her sister*
PIRITHOUS, *friend of Theseus*

PALAMON ⎫ *the two noble kinsmen, cousins, nephews*
ARCITE ⎭ *of Creon, the King of Thebes*

HYMEN, *god of marriage*
A BOY
ARTESIUS, *an Athenian soldier*
Three QUEENS, *widows of three kings killed at the siege of Thebes*
VALERIUS, *a Theban*
A HERALD
A WOMAN *attending Emilia*
An Athenian GENTLEMAN
MESSENGERS

SCENE: *Athens and Thebes.*]

Six KNIGHTS, *three following Palamon and three Arcite*
A SERVANT
THE JAILER *in charge of Theseus's prison*
THE JAILER'S DAUGHTER
THE JAILER'S BROTHER
THE WOOER *of the Jailer's Daughter*
Two FRIENDS *of the Jailer*
A DOCTOR
Six COUNTRYMEN, *one dressed as a babion, or baboon*
A SCHOOLMASTER *named Gerald*
NELL, *a country wench*
Four other country wenches: Friz, Maudline, Luce, and Barbery
A TABORER *named Timothy*
Nymphs, attendants, maids, executioner, guard

EPILOGUE

Prologue

Flourish. [*Enter Prologue.*]

PROLOGUE
New plays and maidenheads are near akin:
Much followed both, for both much money gi'en, 2
If they stand sound and well. And a good play, 3
Whose modest scenes blush on his marriage day 4
And shake to lose his honor, is like her 5
That after holy tie and first night's stir 6

Yet still is modesty, and still retains 7
More of the maid to sight than husband's pains. 8
We pray our play may be so; for I am sure
It has a noble breeder and a pure, 10
A learnèd, and a poet never went 11
More famous yet 'twixt Po and silver Trent. 12
Chaucer, of all admired, the story gives; 13
There, constant to eternity, it lives. 14

0.1 *Flourish* fanfare to announce the arrival or departure of a notable person   2 **Much followed** eagerly sought after   3 **stand sound** seem healthy   4 **his marriage day** i.e., its first day of performance   5 **shake . . . honor** (1) tremble at the thought of loss of virginity (2) fear disgrace at the hands of the audience   6 **holy . . . stir** marriage and sexual consummation that night

7 **is modesty** (1) remains chaste (2) is modest about the play's success   7–8 **still retains . . . pains** still appears more like a virgin than like a woman transformed into a wife by her husband's exertions. (The moral edge that is given to virginity over married chastity is characteristic of the play as a whole.)   10 **breeder** (1) sire (2) author   11–12 **a poet . . . Trent** there never was a more famous poet anywhere in Europe (literally, between the river Po in northern Italy and the Trent in England).   13 **of** by   14 **There** i.e., in "The Knight's Tale" of *The Canterbury Tales*

If we let fall the nobleness of this,   15
And the first sound this child hear be a hiss,   16
How will it shake the bones of that good man,
And make him cry from under ground, "Oh, fan
From me the witless chaff of such a writer
That blasts my bays and my famed works makes
    lighter   20
Than Robin Hood!" This is the fear we bring;   21
For, to say truth, it were an endless thing,
And too ambitious, to aspire to him,   23
Weak as we are, and almost breathless swim
In this deep water. Do but you hold out
Your helping hands, and we shall tack about   26
And something do to save us. You shall hear
Scenes, though below his art, may yet appear   28
Worth two hours' travail. To his bones sweet sleep;   29
Content to you. If this play do not keep   30
A little dull time from us, we perceive   31
Our losses fall so thick we must needs leave.

Flourish. [Exit.]

❖

1.1

*[Music.] Enter Hymen with a torch burning; a boy
in a white robe before, singing and strewing
flowers; after Hymen a nymph, encompassed in her
tresses, bearing a wheaten garland; then Theseus
between two other nymphs with wheaten chaplets
on their heads; then Hippolyta, the bride, led by
Pirithous, and another holding a garland over her
head, her tresses likewise hanging; after her,
Emilia, holding up her train; [Artesius and
attendants].*

BOY *[singing as they enter]*
        Roses, their sharp spines being gone,
        Not royal in their smells alone,
            But in their hue;
        Maiden pinks, of odor faint,
        Daisies smell-less, yet most quaint,   5
            And sweet thyme true;

        Primrose, firstborn child of Ver,   7
        Merry springtime's harbinger,
            With her bells dim;   9
        Oxlips, in their cradles growing,   10

Marigolds, on deathbeds blowing,   11
    Lark's-heels trim;   12

(Strew flowers) All dear Nature's children sweet
Lie 'fore bride and bridegroom's feet,
    Blessing their sense.   15
Not an angel of the air,
Bird melodious or bird fair,
    Is absent hence.

The crow, the sland'rous cuckoo, nor   19
The boding raven, nor chough hoar   20
    Nor chatt'ring pie,   21
May on our bridehouse perch or sing,
Or with them any discord bring,
But from it fly.   24

*Enter three Queens in black, with veils stained,
with imperial crowns. The first Queen falls down
at the foot of Theseus; the second falls down at the
foot of Hippolyta; the third before Emilia.*

FIRST QUEEN *[to Theseus]*
    For pity's sake and true gentility's,   25
    Hear and respect me.
SECOND QUEEN *[to Hippolyta]*   For your mother's sake,   26
    And as you wish your womb may thrive with fair
        ones,
    Hear and respect me.
THIRD QUEEN *[to Emilia]*
    Now for the love of him whom Jove hath marked   29
    The honor of your bed, and for the sake   30
    Of clear virginity, be advocate   31
    For us and our distresses. This good deed
    Shall raze you out o'th' book of trespasses   33
    All you are set down there.   34
THESEUS *[to First Queen]*
    Sad lady, rise.
HYPPOLYTA *[to Second Queen]*   Stand up.
EMILIA *[to Third Queen]*   No knees to me.
    What woman I may stead that is distressed   36
    Does bind me to her.   37
                        [The Second and Third Queens rise.]
THESEUS *[to First Queen]*
    What's your request? Deliver you for all.   38
FIRST QUEEN *[kneeling still]*
    We are three queens whose sovereigns fell before
    The wrath of cruel Creon; who endured   40
    The beaks of ravens, talons of the kites,

---

15 **let fall** allow to collapse   16 **child** i.e., play   20 **blasts my bays** withers my poetic reputation   21 **Than Robin Hood** i.e., than popular ballad material.   23 **him** Chaucer   26 **tack about** turn about in the water, as though sailing, in response to the wind generated by the audience's applause   28 **his** Chaucer's.   **may** which may   29 **travail** (Spelled *"travell"* in the original Quarto, suggesting [1] the actors' exertions [2] the audience's journey of imagination.)   30–1 **If . . . from us** i.e., If we don't manage to be entertaining and thereby able to fend off boredom   **1.1 Location**: Athens. Enroute to the temple where the marriage is to take place.   0.1 *Hymen* god of marriage.   0.3–4 *a nymph . . . tresses* a young woman with her hair unbound, as a token of virginity   0.4 *wheaten garland* symbol of fecundity   0.5 *chaplets* garlands   5 **quaint** beautiful, trim   7 **Ver** spring personified   9 **bells dim** pale bell-shaped flowers   10 **Oxlips . . . growing** cowslip-like flowers with the bud cradled by surrounding petals and leaves

11 **on deathbeds blowing** flowering on graves   12 **Lark's-heels** larkspur   15 **Blessing their sense** pleasing all their senses.   19 **sland'rous cuckoo** (The cuckoo was despised for seeming to mock married men as potential cuckolds and for laying its eggs in other birds' nests.)   20 **boding** prophesying bad fortune.   **chough hoar** gray-feathered jackdaw   21 **pie** magpie   24.1 *stained* dyed black to betoken mourning   25 **gentility's** nobility's   26 **respect** pay considerate attention to   29–30 **marked . . . bed** destined to be your honorable husband   31 **clear** pure   33–4 **raze . . . there** erase from the book of heaven's judgment all your sins set down there.   36–7 **What . . . to her** Whatsoever woman in distress that I can assist will by her very situation obligate me to her (without further kneeling on her part).   37.1 *rise* (The stage directions to rise and kneel again are conjectural in their placement.)   38 **Deliver** Speak   40 **who** i.e., our three husbands

And pecks of crows in the foul fields of Thebes. 42
He will not suffer us to burn their bones,
To urn their ashes, nor to take th'offense
Of mortal loathsomeness from the blest eye 45
Of holy Phoebus, but infects the winds 46
With stench of our slain lords. Oh, pity, Duke!
Thou purger of the earth, draw thy feared sword 48
That does good turns to th' world; give us the bones
Of our dead kings, that we may chapel them; 50
And of thy boundless goodness take some note 51
That for our crownèd heads we have no roof
Save this, which is the lion's and the bear's, 53
And vault to everything.

THESEUS   Pray you, kneel not; 54
I was transported with your speech and suffered
Your knees to wrong themselves. I have heard the
    fortunes
Of your dead lords, which gives me such lamenting
As wakes my vengeance and revenge for 'em.
[*To the First Queen*] King Capaneus was your lord; the
    day
That he should marry you, at such a season 60
As now it is with me, I met your groom 61
By Mars's altar. You were that time fair—
Not Juno's mantle fairer than your tresses,
Nor in more bounty spread her. Your wheaten wreath 64
Was then nor threshed nor blasted; Fortune at you 65
Dimpled her cheek with smiles. Hercules, our
    kinsman—
Then weaker than your eyes—laid by his club; 67
He tumbled down upon his Nemean hide 68
And swore his sinews thawed. O Grief and Time, 69
Fearful consumers, you will all devour! 70

FIRST QUEEN   Oh, I hope some god,
Some god hath put his mercy in your manhood,
Whereto he'll infuse power and press you forth 73
Our undertaker.

THESEUS   Oh, no knees, none, widow; 74
Unto the helmeted Bellona use them 75
And pray for me, your soldier.
                              [*The First Queen rises.*]
Troubled I am.   [*He*] *turns away.*

SECOND QUEEN [*kneeling*]   Honored Hippolyta,
Most dreaded Amazonian, that hast slain 78
The scythe-tusked boar; that with thy arm, as strong 79

As it is white, wast near to make the male 80
To thy sex captive, but that this thy lord,
Born to uphold creation in that honor 82
First nature styled it in, shrunk thee into 83
The bound thou wast o'erflowing, at once subduing 84
Thy force and thy affection; soldieress
That equally canst poise sternness with pity, 86
Whom now I know hast much more power on him 87
Then ever he had on thee, who ow'st his strength 88
And his love too, who is a servant for 89
The tenor of thy speech: dear glass of ladies, 90
Bid him that we, whom flaming war doth scorch,
Under the shadow of his sword may cool us!
Require him he advance it o'er our heads. 93
Speak 't in a woman's key, like such a woman 94
As any of us three; weep ere you fail. 95
Lend us a knee;
But touch the ground for us no longer time 97
Than a dove's motion when the head's plucked off. 98
Tell him if he i'th' blood-sized field lay swoll'n, 99
Showing the sun his teeth, grinning at the moon, 100
What you would do.

HIPPOLYTA   Poor lady, say no more.
I had as lief trace this good action with you 102
As that whereto I am going, and never yet 103
Went I so willing way. My lord is taken 104
Heart-deep with your distress. Let him consider.
I'll speak anon.   [*The Second Queen rises.*]

THIRD QUEEN [*kneel to Emilia*]   Oh, my petition was 106
Set down in ice, which by hot grief uncandied 107
Melts into drops; so sorrow, wanting form, 108
Is pressed with deeper matter.

EMILIA   Pray stand up; 109
Your grief is written in your cheek.

THIRD QUEEN   Oh, woe!
You cannot read it there; there through my tears, 111
Like wrinkled pebbles in a glassy stream, 112
You may behold 'em. Lady, lady, alack! 113
He that will all the treasure know o'th'earth

---

80 wast near to make was on the verge of making   **82–3 Born . . . it in**
i.e., destined to restore and maintain the natural hierarchy of the sexes,
as ordained since the beginning of time   **84 The bound . . . o'erflowing** the circumscribed limits that you were attempting to exceed, like a
river overflowing its banks   **86 poise** counterpoise, balance   **87 on**
over   **88 who ow'st** you who now own or control   **89–90 who . . .
ladies** i.e., Theseus, who is obedient in love to your every command:
you who are a mirror or model for all ladies   **93 Require . . . it**
Request of him that he hold it aloft   **94 key** tone, style   **95 weep . . .
fail** weep rather than give up.   **97–8 But . . . off** i.e., we ask that you
touch your knee to the ground for us only for a moment or two, in the
time it would take a beheaded dove to cease moving.   **99 blood-sized
field** blood-soaked battlefield. (*Size* is a gelatinous glue-like coating
that soaks into a wall, paper, leather, etc. as a way of filling pores.)
100 Showing . . . moon grinning as a skull does   **102–4 I had . . . way**
I would just as gladly speak on your behalf as go ahead with my
impending marriage, which I look forward to more willingly than
anything I've ever done.   **104 taken** struck, afflicted   **106–9 my petition . . . matter** i.e., my petition, coldly formal when expressed in mere
words, is melted by my hot grief into teardrops; thus my sorrow, lacking shape or power of expression, is pressed out in tears by the deep
cause of my grief.   **111–13 You . . . 'em** i.e., You cannot read my grief
truly on my cheek, in the external sign; look through my tears into my
eyes, as you would look at pebbles distorted in their shape through
the rippling water of a clear stream.

---

42 fields battlefields   **45–6 from . . . Phoebus** out of the sun (which
hastens the process of putrefaction)   **48 Thou . . . earth** You who are
renowned for defending the innocent against monsters and evil-doers
50 chapel inter in a chapel   **51 of** out of   **53 this** the sky   **54 vault**
roof   **60 should** was about to   **61 groom** bridegroom   **64 Nor . . .
her** nor enveloped her in more luxuriant tresses.   **64–5 Your . . .
blasted** Your garland woven of wheat (a token of fecundity, as at
1.1.0.4) was neither threshed (punning on "thrashed," beaten) nor
withered   **67 weaker than your eyes** subdued by your gaze
68 Nemean hide (One of Hercules's twelve labors was to kill and
skin the Nemean lion.)   **69 thawed** i.e., rendered powerless (by love).
70 all devour devour all things.   **73–4 press . . . undertaker** press
you into service as our champion.   **75 Bellona** goddess of war
78–9 that . . . boar (Atalanta, a huntress like Hippolyta, helped kill the
fearful wild boar of Calydon; see Chaucer's "The Knight's Tale" and
Ovid, *Metamorphoses*, Book 8.)

Must know the center too; he that will fish   115
For my least minnow, let him lead his line   116
To catch one at my heart. Oh, pardon me!
Extremity, that sharpens sundry wits,   118
Makes me a fool.

                    [The Third Queen rises.]

EMILIA   Pray you say nothing, pray you.   119
Who cannot feel nor see the rain, being in't,   120
Knows neither wet nor dry. If that you were   121
The ground-piece of some painter, I would buy you   122
T'instruct me 'gainst a capital grief, indeed   123
Such heart-pierced demonstration; but alas,   124
Being a natural sister of our sex,   125
Your sorrow beats so ardently upon me   126
That it shall make a counter-reflect 'gainst   127
My brother's heart and warm it to some pity,   128
Though it were made of stone. Pray have good
    comfort.

THESEUS
Forward to th' temple. Leave not out a jot
O'th' sacred ceremony.

FIRST QUEEN   Oh, this celebration   131
Will longer last and be more costly than   132
Your suppliants' war. Remember that your fame   133
Knolls in the ear o'th' world; what you do quickly   134
Is not done rashly; your first thought is more
Than others' labored meditance, your premeditating   136
More than their actions. But, O Jove, your actions,
Soon as they move, as ospreys do the fish,   138
Subdue before they touch. Think, dear Duke, think   139
What beds our slain kings have.

SECOND QUEEN   What griefs our beds,   140
That our dear lords have none.

THIRD QUEEN   None fit for th' dead.   141
Those that with cords, knives, drams, precipitance,   142
Weary of this world's light, have to themselves
Been death's most horrid agents, human grace
Affords them dust and shadow.

FIRST QUEEN   But our lords   145

Lie blist'ring 'fore the visitating sun,   146
And were good kings when living.   147

THESEUS
It is true, and I will give you comfort
To give your dead lords graves;   149
The which to do must make some work with Creon.   150

FIRST QUEEN
And that work presents itself to th' doing.   151
Now 'twill take form; the heats are gone tomorrow.   152
Then, bootless toil must recompense itself   153
With its own sweat. Now he's secure,   154
Not dreams we stand before your puissance,   155
Rinsing our holy begging in our eyes
To make petition clear.

SECOND QUEEN   Now you may take him,   157
Drunk with his victory.

THIRD QUEEN   And his army full
Of bread and sloth.

THESEUS *[to Artesius]*   Artesius, that best knowest
How to draw out, fit to this enterprise,   160
The prim'st for this proceeding, and the number   161
To carry such a business: forth and levy   162
Our worthiest instruments, whilst we dispatch   163
This grand act of our life, this daring deed   164
Of fate in wedlock.

FIRST QUEEN *[to the other Queens]*   Dowagers, take hands.   165
Let us be widows to our woes; delay   166
Commends us to a famishing hope.

ALL *[THE QUEENS]*   Farewell.   167

SECOND QUEEN
We come unseasonably; but when could grief
Cull forth, as unpanged judgment can, fitt'st time   169
For best solicitation?

THESEUS   Why, good ladies,
This is a service, whereto I am going,
Greater than any was; it more imports me   172
Than all the actions that I have foregone,   173
Or futurely can cope.

FIRST QUEEN   The more proclaiming   174
Our suit shall be neglected, when her arms,   175
Able to lock Jove from a synod, shall   176
By warranting moonlight corslet thee. Oh, when   177

---

115 Must . . . too must mine deeply   **116 lead** attach a lead weight to (so that the fishing gear may sink deeply)   **118–19 Extremity . . . fool** Extremity of grief, which sharpens some people's minds, prompts me to speak distractedly.   **120–1 Who . . . dry** i.e., Anyone who would not be moved by your eloquence simply has no feeling.   **121–4 If that . . . demonstration** If you were merely depicted by some painter as an image intended to provide moral example, I would buy the painting to help me anticipate and thus ward off a deadly grief, indeed just such a heart-piercing instance as your sad case represents   **125 Being . . . sex** i.e., since you are a living woman, not a painting   **126 ardently** burningly, sunlike in intensity   **127 make a counter-reflect** reflect back from me as from a mirror   **128 My brother's** my prospective brother-in-law's, Theseus'   **131–3 Oh, this . . . war** (The First Queen urges Theseus to consider that the wedding ceremony will consume precious time, during which the queens' supplications and their struggle with Creon will languish.)   **134 Knolls** tolls   **136 labored meditance** laborious thought   **138–9 as ospreys . . . touch** (Osprey hawks, which dive spectacularly on fish in the water, were thought to subdue their prey with a powerful emanating influence even before they struck.)   **140 What griefs our beds** i.e., Think in what beds of grief we lie, so to speak   **141 None . . . dead** i.e., the cold ground on which they lie is no fit bed for a dead warrior.   **142 drams** poisons. **precipitance** suicidal leaps. (The Third Queen's point is that even suicides are allowed some kind of burial.)   **145 dust and shadow** i.e., to lie in quiet darkness in the earth.

146 visitating surveying, overseeing   **147 And** i.e., and yet, unlike suicides   **149 To give** by giving   **150 must . . . work** necessitates dealing **151–4 presents . . . sweat** calls for action immediately. It can be shaped, like heated metal, now, but will soon cool. Tomorrow, all effort will be fruitless and will have to be content with the effort itself.   **154 he's** i.e., Creon is   **155 your puissance** your mighty self   **157 To . . . clear** to purify our supplication and stress our point.   **160 draw out** choose **161 prim'st** best   **162 carry** carry out. **forth** go forth   **163 instruments** agents, i.e., soldiers   **164–5 This . . . wedlock** (Theseus's view here of his marriage as a heroic deed, a counter-adventure, is quite different from the view that the queens are presenting [e.g., lines 174 ff.].) **166–7 delay . . . hope** the delay (occasioned by this marriage) commits us to a dying hope.   **169 Cull forth** choose, select. **unpanged** unafflicted by the pangs of sorrow   **172 more imports me** is more important to me   **173 foregone** previously achieved   **174 futurely can cope** can achieve in the future.   **The more proclaiming** Making it all the more clear that   **175–7 when . . . thee** when the arms of her (Hippolyta) whose charms would keep Jupiter himself from an assembly of the gods will, by the light of the love-authorizing moon, encircle you like close-fitting armor.

Her twinning cherries shall their sweetness fall   178
Upon thy tasteful lips, what wilt thou think   179
Of rotten kings or blubbered queens? What care   180
For what thou feel'st not, what thou feel'st being able   181
To make Mars spurn his drum? Oh, if thou couch   182
But one night with her, every hour in't will
Take hostage of thee for a hundred, and   184
Thou shalt remember nothing more than what
That banquet bids thee to.

HIPPOLYTA [to Theseus]   Though much unlike   186
You should be so transported, as much sorry   187
I should be such a suitor, yet I think,   188
Did I not, by th'abstaining of my joy—   189
Which breeds a deeper longing—cure their surfeit   190
That craves a present med'cine, I should pluck   191
All ladies' scandal on me. [She kneels.] Therefore, sir,   192
As I shall here make trial of my prayers,
Either presuming them to have some force,
Or sentencing for aye their vigor dumb,   195
Prorogue this business we are going about, and hang   196
Your shield afore your heart, about that neck
Which is my fee, and which I freely lend   198
To do these poor queens service.

ALL [THE] QUEENS [to Emilia]   Oh, help now!
Our cause cries for your knee.

EMILIA [to Theseus, kneeling]   If you grant not
My sister her petition in that force,   201
With that celerity and nature which   202
She makes it in, from henceforth I'll not dare   203
To ask you anything, nor be so hardy
Ever to take a husband.

THESEUS   Pray stand up.
                [Hippolyta and Emilia rise.]
I am entreating of myself to do
That which you kneel to have me.—Pirithous,   207
Lead on the bride; get you and pray the gods   208
For success and return; omit not anything   209
In the pretended celebration.—Queens,   210
Follow your soldier. [To Artesius] As before, hence you,   211
And at the banks of Aulis meet us with
The forces you can raise, where we shall find

The moiety of a number for a business   214
More bigger looked.   [Exit Artesius.]
[To Hippolyta]   Since that our theme is haste,   215
I stamp this kiss upon thy current lip;   216
Sweet, keep it as my token.—Set you forward,   217
For I will see you gone.
                [The marriage procession moves] towards the temple.
[To Emilia] Farewell, my beauteous sister.—Pirithous,   219
Keep the feast full; bate not an hour on't.

PIRITHOUS   Sir,   220
I'll follow you at heels. The feast's solemnity   221
Shall want till your return.

THESEUS   Cousin, I charge you,   222
Budge not from Athens. We shall be returning
Ere you can end this feast, of which I pray you
Make no abatement.—Once more, farewell all.
                Exeunt [in procession, all but Theseus
                and the Queens].

FIRST QUEEN
Thus dost thou still make good the tongue o'th' world.   226

SECOND QUEEN
And earn'st a deity equal with Mars.

THIRD QUEEN   If not above him, for
Thou, being but mortal, makest affections bend   229
To godlike honors; they themselves, some say,   230
Groan under such a mast'ry.   231

THESEUS   As we are men,
Thus should we do; being sensually subdued,   232
We lose our human title. Good cheer, ladies!   233
Now turn we towards your comforts.
                Flourish. Exeunt.

❖

1.2

Enter Palamon and Arcite.

ARCITE
Dear Palamon, dearer in love than blood,   1
And our prime cousin, yet unhardened in   2
The crimes of nature, let us leave the city   3
Thebes, and the temptings in't, before we further   4
Sully our gloss of youth.   5

---

178 **twinning cherries** cherry lips.   **fall** let fall   179 **tasteful** capable of tasting   180 **rotten** with decaying flesh.   **blubbered** tear-stained   180–2 **What . . . drum?** Why should you care for something that does not touch you personally, at a time when your sexual desire is enough to make you set aside military duty?   182 **couch** lie   184 **Take . . . hundred** i.e., commit you to a hundred more such hours   186–8 **Though . . . suitor** Even though it would be much unlike you to be lifted into transports thus, and as much as I regret being the one to request (that you postpone the wedding)   189 **of** from   190 **Which . . . longing** Hippolyta's point is that by abstaining virtuously from the joys of marriage, she (and Theseus, too) can engender a deeper longing by making more precious and well-earned the reward. **surfeit** excess (of grief)   191 **present** immediate   191–2 **I should . . . on me** I should invite the scorn of all ladies for my scandalous behavior.   195 **Or . . . dumb** or condemning them forever as ineffectual (if they fail), as if they had never been spoken   196 **Prorogue** postpone   198 **my fee** due to me (in marriage)   201–3 **in that force . . . it in** with the same intensity, speed, and natural feeling she uses in making her petition   207 **have me** have me do.   208 **get you** get you hence, depart   209 **return** our victorious return   210 **pretended** intended   211 **your soldier** i.e., Theseus himself.

214–15 **The moiety . . . looked** a part of an armed force raised to deal with a larger enterprise. (An army, raised for some other campaign, is now to be turned against Thebes.)   215 **Since that our theme** Since our business   216 **current** (1) legal and genuine, like a coin stamped with the royal image (2) currant-red. (The Quarto spelling, "currant," allows for both meanings.)   217 **token** (1) keepsake (2) stamped coin   219 **sister** sister-in-law-to-be.   220 **full** fully.   **bate . . . on't** don't abate one hour of it.   221 **solemnity** ceremonial dignity   222 **want** be lacking.   **Cousin** (A term used by royal figures to address their courtiers.)   226 **the tongue o'th' world** your reputation among all peoples.   229–31 **makest . . . mast'ry** subdue your passions to your godlike sense of honor; the gods themselves, some people say, suffer under passions that master them.   232 **being sensually subdued** if we allow ourselves to be subdued by our sensual natures   233 **human title** claim to be called human.
1.2 Location: Thebes.
1 **blood** kinship   2 **prime cousin** nearest kin   3 **The crimes of nature** those vices to which the human race is prone   4 **temptings** temptations   5 **Sully . . . youth** stain the luster of our youth.

And here to keep in abstinence we shame 6
As in incontinence; for not to swim 7
I'th'aid o'th' current were almost to sink, 8
At least to frustrate striving; and to follow 9
The common stream, 'twould bring us to an eddy 10
Where we should turn or drown; if labor through, 11
Our gain but life and weakness. 12

PALAMON   Your advice
Is cried up with example. What strange ruins, 13
Since first we went to school, may we perceive
Walking in Thebes? Scars and bare weeds 15
The gain o'th' martialist, who did propound 16
To his bold ends honor and golden ingots, 17
Which though he won, he had not, and now flirted 18
By peace for whom he fought. Who then shall offer 19
To Mars's so scorned altar? I do bleed 20
When such I meet, and wish great Juno would 21
Resume her ancient fit of jealousy 22
To get the soldier work, that peace might purge 23
For her repletion, and retain anew 24
Her charitable heart, now hard and harsher 25
Than strife or war could be.

ARCITE   Are you not out? 26
Meet you no ruin but the soldier in
The cranks and turns of Thebes? You did begin 28
As if you met decays of many kinds.
Perceive you none that do arouse your pity
But th'unconsidered soldier?

PALAMON   Yes, I pity 31
Decays where'er I find them, but such most
That, sweating in an honorable toil,
Are paid with ice to cool 'em.

ARCITE   'Tis not this 34
I did begin to speak of; this is virtue 35
Of no respect in Thebes. I spake of Thebes, 36
How dangerous, if we will keep our honors, 37
It is for our residing, where every evil
Hath a good color; where ev'ry seeming good's 39

A certain evil; where not to be ev'n jump 40
As they are here were to be strangers, and 41
Such things to be, mere monsters.

PALAMON   'Tis in our power 42
(Unless we fear that apes can tutor's) to 43
Be masters of our manners. What need I
Affect another's gait, which is not catching 45
Where there is faith? Or to be fond upon 46
Another's way of speech, when by mine own
I may be reasonably conceived—saved, too— 48
Speaking it truly? Why am I bound 49
By any generous bond to follow him 50
Follows his tailor, haply so long until 51
The followed make pursuit? Or let me know 52
Why mine own barber is unblessed, with him 53
My poor chin too, for 'tis not scissored just 54
To such a favorite's glass? What canon is there 55
That does command my rapier from my hip 56
To dangle't in my hand, or to go tip-toe 57
Before the street be foul? Either I am 58
The fore-horse in the team, or I am none
That draw i'th' sequent trace. These poor slight sores 60
Need not a plantain. That which rips my bosom 61
Almost to th' heart's—

ARCITE   Our uncle Creon.
PALAMON   He,
A most unbounded tyrant, whose successes
Makes heaven unfeared and villainy assured 64
Beyond its power there's nothing; almost puts 65
Faith in a fever, and deifies alone 66
Voluble chance; who only attributes 67
The faculties of other instruments 68
To his own nerves and act; commands men service, 69
And what they win in't, boot and glory; one 70

6–12 And . . . weakness And we shame ourselves as much by practicing abstinence here in this corrupt city as we would by indulging in licentious conduct; the first is to resist the current at the risk of drowning or frustration at the very least, whereas the second is to go with the flow and thereby either fall into deadly sin or eddy about aimlessly, or, at best, be weakened by sinfulness.   13 cried up with example proclaimed by many instances.   ruins persons ruined by extravagance   15–20 Scars . . . altar? Scars and threadbare garments are the reward of the soldier, who had proposed instead as a reward for his martial deeds honor and wealth, which, though he had indeed earned in battle, he had not received, and instead was jeered at by the very peace-loving (and craven) citizens for whom he fought. Who now would wish to be a soldier?   20 I do bleed i.e., my heart bleeds   21–6 wish . . . could be (Palamon wishes that war might break out again, renewing the conflict that came about when Juno vented her hatred on Thebes in retaliation for her husband Jupiter's affair with Alcmena in that city. War would put honorable soldiers to work. Peace, purging herself through war of her own excesses of decadent indolence, would paradoxically be more charitable than the harsh present reality of unchaste behavior.)   26 out mistaken (in pitying only the soldier).   28 cranks winding streets   31 th'unconsidered the neglected   34 Are . . . 'em i.e., are treated coldly.   35–6 this . . . respect i.e., no one cares for military honor   37 will wish to   39 Hath a good color assumes a pleasant appearance

40–2 where . . . monsters where not to go along exactly with Theban customs will brand us as strangers; yet to be as the Thebans are would make us utter monsters.   43 Unless . . . tutor's unless we are so insecure as to copy the behavior of those who are themselves mere imitators of others   45–6 Affect . . . faith model myself on another person's bearing, which should have no attraction for me when I practice self-reliance.   46 fond upon infatuated with   48 conceived understood   48–9 saved . . . truly i.e., I can reasonably hope to be saved from eternal damnation by my own speech, if I speak the truth.   50 generous bond honorable and gentlemanly obligation   50–2 to follow . . . pursuit to follow one who puts himself in obligation to his tailor, perchance until the tailor ends up pursuing that gentleman in order to recover what that gentleman owes.   53 unblessed not in favor   54 for because   54–5 just . . . glass precisely according to the latest fashion as reflected in the mirror of one who is much in favor.   55 canon law   56–8 That . . . foul (Carrying one's rapier in one's hand and tiptoeing even when the streets are not dirty are here seen as affectations of the dandy.)   60 That . . . trace that pull in the traces among a team of horses following behind the leader. (Palamon insists on being the leader or else no part of the team.)   60–1 These . . . plantain i.e., These social inanities are not what really needs curing. (Plantain is a plant used in healing wounds.)   64–5 Makes . . . nothing seem to suggest that villains need not fear heaven's justice and that no superior divine authority exists beyond human power   65–7 puts . . . chance undermines religious faith and makes mutable Chance the only goddess   67–9 who . . . act who attributes the capabilities and achievements of those who serve him to his own sinews (nerves) and deeds alone   69–70 commands . . . glory forces men to follow him and then arrogates to himself both the glory and the spoils they have won in battle

That fears not to do harm; good, dares not. Let   71
The blood of mine that's sib to him be sucked   72
From me with leeches! Let them break and fall   73
Off me with that corruption.
ARCITE   Clear-spirited cousin,   74
Let's leave his court, that we may nothing share
Of his loud infamy; for our milk   76
Will relish of the pasture, and we must   77
Be vile or disobedient, not his kinsmen   78
In blood unless in quality.
PALAMON   Nothing truer.   79
I think the echoes of his shames have deafed   80
The ears of heav'nly justice: widows' cries
Descend again into their throats, and have not
Due audience of the gods.

Enter Valerius.

Valerius!   83
VALERIUS
The King calls for you; yet be leaden-footed   84
Till his great rage be off him. Phoebus, when   85
He broke his whipstock and exclaimed against   86
The horses of the sun, but whispered to   87
The loudness of his fury.
PALAMON   Small winds shake him.   88
But what's the matter?
VALERIUS
Theseus, who where he threats appalls, hath sent   90
Deadly defiance to him and pronounces
Ruin to Thebes, who is at hand to seal   92
The promise of his wrath.
ARCITE   Let him approach.
But that we fear the gods in him, he brings not   94
A jot of terror to us. Yet what man   95
Thirds his own worth—the case is each of ours—   96
When that his action's dregged with mind assured   97
'Tis bad he goes about.
PALAMON   Leave that unreasoned.   98
Our services stand now for Thebes, not Creon.
Yet to be neutral to him were dishonor,   100
Rebellious to oppose; therefore we must   101

With him stand to the mercy of our fate,   102
Who hath bounded our last minute.
ARCITE   So we must.   103
Is't said this war's afoot, or it shall be   104
On fail of some condition?
VALERIUS   'Tis in motion;   105
The intelligence of state came in the instant   106
With the defier.
PALAMON   Let's to the King, who, were he   107
A quarter carrier of that honor which   108
His enemy come in, the blood we venture   109
Should be as for our health, which were not spent,   110
Rather laid out for purchase. But alas,   111
Our hands advanced before our hearts, what will   112
The fall o'th' stroke do damage?
ARCITE   Let th'event,   113
That never-erring arbitrator, tell us
When we know all ourselves, and let us follow
The becking of our chance.   *Exeunt.*   116

❖

1.3

Enter Pirithous, Hippolyta, Emilia.

PIRITHOUS
No further.
HIPPOLYTA   Sir, farewell. Repeat my wishes   1
To our great lord, of whose success I dare not
Make any timorous question; yet I wish him
Excess and overflow of power, an't might be,   4
To dure ill-dealing fortune. Speed to him!   5
Store never hurts good governors.
PIRITHOUS   Though I know   6
His ocean needs not my poor drops, yet they   7
Must yield their tribute there. [*To Emilia*] My precious
     maid,
Those best affections that the heaven infuse   9
In their best-tempered pieces keep enthroned   10
In your dear heart!
EMILIA   Thanks, sir. Remember me
To our all-royal brother, for whose speed   12

71 **good, dares not** dares not do any good (lest it leave him vulnerable to those he might trust).   72 **sib** akin   73 **leeches . . . break** (These bloodsucking worms, used by physicians to purge the blood, were allowed to fill to bursting and then fall off.)   74 **Clear-spirited** Noble-minded   76 **loud** notorious   76–9 **our . . . quality** our milk (like that of cows) will acquire the flavor of what we have eaten, so that we must either be vile like him or resist his corrupt authority; to be his kinsman in blood is to risk becoming like him in quality.   80 **deafed** deafened   83 **Due audience of** proper attention from   84 **be leaden-footed** answer the summons slowly   85–8 **Phoebus . . . fury** The sun god, when he vented his fury on the horses that drew his chariot (after his son Phaethon had had to be destroyed for misgoverning his father's chariot), merely whispered compared to the loudness of Creon's present anger. (See Ovid, *Metamorphoses*, 2.398 ff.)   88 **Small . . . him** The most trivial things put him in a rage.   90 **appalls** makes pale, terrifies   92 **who** i.e., Theseus.   **seal** ratify, carry out   94 **But** Were it not that   95–8 **Yet . . . about** Yet any man whatever cuts down by one third his own worth as a soldier—as we all do—when what he is about to do seems to him unworthy.   98 **Leave that unreasoned** Consider it not so deeply.   100 **Yet to be** To continue to be.   **were** would be   101 **Rebellious** treasonous

102–3 **stand . . . minute** submit to our fate, which has determined when we will die.   104–5 **or . . . condition?** is war contingent on Thebes's accepting or refusing certain conditions?   106–7 **The intelligence . . . defier** the tidings of Creon's decision to fight were virtually synchronous with the arrival of Theseus's challenge.   108–9 **A quarter . . . come in** possessed of a mere fourth of the honor that his enemy (Theseus) brings to the battle   110–11 **Should . . . purchase** would be therapeutic, like a medical bloodletting, the blood being not wasted but put to profitable use (in defending an honorable cause).   112–13 **Our . . . damage?** if we lift our hands in battle before our hearts are engaged, what can our half-hearted blows be expected to accomplish?   113 **th'event** the outcome   116 **The becking . . . chance** the beckoning of our destiny (which will reveal all to us in the fullness of time).
1.3 Location: Athens, at the edge of the city, toward Thebes.
1 **No further** (Hippolyta and Emilia have escorted Pirithous to the city gates for his departure; here they must stay behind.)   4 **an't . . . be** if it (such an overflow of power) were possible   5 **dure** endure   5–6 **Speed . . . governors** May he prosper! Abundance (the "overflow of power" in line 4) never hurts those who manage things well.   7 **drops** i.e., drops of blood   9 **affections** good dispositions   10 **their best-tempered pieces** those persons whom the heavens have made of best temper or quality   12 **speed** success

The great Bellona I'll solicit; and   13
Since in our terrene state petitions are not   14
Without gifts understood, I'll offer to her
What I shall be advised she likes. Our hearts
Are in his army, in his tent.
HIPPOLYTA   In 's bosom.
We have been soldiers, and we cannot weep
When our friends don their helms, or put to sea,
Or tell of babes broached on the lance, or women   20
That have sod their infants in—and after ate them—   21
The brine they wept at killing 'em; then if
You stay to see of us such spinsters, we   23
Should hold you here forever.
PIRITHOUS   Peace be to you
As I pursue this war, which shall be then   25
Beyond further requiring.   *Exit Pirithous.*
EMILIA   How his longing   26
Follows his friend! Since his depart, his sports,   27
Though craving seriousness and skill, passed slightly   28
His careless execution, where nor gain   29
Made him regard, or loss consider, but
Playing one business in his hand, another
Directing in his head, his mind nurse equal   32
To these so diff'ring twins. Have you observed him   33
Since our great lord departed?
HIPPOLYTA   With much labor;
And I did love him for't. They two have cabined   35
In many as dangerous as poor a corner,   36
Peril and want contending; they have skiffed   37
Torrents whose roaring tyranny and power   38
I'th' least of these was dreadful, and they have   39
Fought out together where Death's self was lodged;   40
Yet fate hath brought them off. Their knot of love,   41
Tied, weaved, entangled, with so true, so long,
And with a finger of so deep a cunning,   43
May be outworn, never undone. I think   44
Theseus cannot be umpire to himself,
Cleaving his conscience into twain and doing
Each side like justice, which he loves best.
EMILIA   Doubtless   47
There is a best, and reason has no manners   48

To say it is not you. I was acquainted
Once with a time when I enjoyed a playfellow;
You were at wars when she the grave enriched,
Who made too proud the bed; took leave o'th' moon—   52
Which then looked pale at parting—when our count   53
Was each eleven.
HIPPOLYTA   'Twas Flavina.
EMILIA   Yes.
You talk of Pirithous' and Theseus' love.
Theirs has more ground, is more maturely seasoned,   56
More buckled with strong judgment, and their needs   57
The one of th'other may be said to water
Their intertangled roots of love. But I,
And she I sigh and spoke of, were things innocent;   60
Loved for we did, and, like the elements   61
That know not what nor why, yet do effect   62
Rare issues by their operance, our souls   63
Did so to one another. What she liked   64
Was then of me approved, what not, condemned—
No more arraignment. The flower that I would pluck   66
And put between my breasts—Oh, then but beginning
To swell about the blossom—she would long   68
Till she had such another, and commit it
To the like innocent cradle, where, phoenix-like,   70
They died in perfume. On my head no toy   71
But was her pattern; her affections—pretty,   72
Though happily her careless wear—I followed   73
For my most serious decking. Had mine ear   74
Stol'n some new air, or at adventure hummed one   75
From musical coinage, why, it was a note   76
Whereon her spirits would sojourn—rather dwell
    on—
And sing it in her slumbers. This rehearsal—   78
Which seely innocence wots well, comes in   79
Like old importment's bastard—has this end: 80
That the true love 'tween maid and maid may be   81
More than in sex dividual.
HIPPOLYTA   You're out of breath,   82
And this high-speeded pace is but to say

---

13 Bellona goddess of war   **14 terrene** earthly   **20 broached** spitted, impaled   **21 sod** boiled   **23 spinsters** women involved solely in domestic chores   **25 As** while, as long as   **25–6 which . . . requiring** which war, when I have triumphed, will no longer require your prayers.   **27 his depart** Theseus's departure.   **his sports** Pirithous's amusements, diversions   **28–9 passed . . . execution** received only Pirithous's cursory attention   **29 nor** neither   **32–3 nurse . . . twins** i.e., evenly divided between his caring for his sports (such as hunting and martial practice) and his longing to be with Theseus   **35–7 have . . . contending** have shared soldiers' quarters in many a place that was as dangerous as poorly furnished, the danger and the paucity of comfort contending as to which was more oppressive   **37–8 skiffed Torrents** braved turbulent waters in light skiffs   **39 I'th' least of these** at their least threatening   **40 Fought . . . lodged** battled it out with Death itself in Death's own dominion. (According to legend; Theseus descended with Pirithous, King of the Lapithae, to Hades to help him carry off Persephone, for which crime he suffered imprisonment in Hades until rescued by Hercules.)   **41 brought them off** rescued them.   **43 cunning** skill   **44 outworn** worn out (by death)   **47 like** equal.   **which** i.e., Hippolyta or Pirithous   **48 There is a best** (Emilia responds to Hippolyta's modest disclaimer by insisting that of course Theseus loves his bride best.)

52 Who . . . moon who was too fine to grace the bed of death; who departed from this mortal sublunary sphere and from the service of the goddess of chastity   **53 count** age   **56 ground** firm foundation   **57 buckled with** joined together, held in by   **60 things innocent** innocent young beings   **61 for** simply because.   **61–4 like . . . another** like the four elements of earth, water, air, and fire, out of which the universe is composed, which, acting instinctively in obedience to some higher law of nature, bring about amazing results by their interaction, our souls responded to each other.   **66 No more arraignment** without needing any further inquiry or trial.   **68 To swell . . . blossom** (The image applies to the flower and to Emilia's breasts.)   **70–1 phoenix-like . . . perfume** (The phoenix was said to build a nest of "sweet-smelling sticks" that was then set on fire by the sun, consuming the mythical bird to ashes from which arose a new and unique phoenix. An emblem of immortality.)   **71–2 no toy . . . pattern** no bit of finery that was not emulated by her   **72–3 her affections . . . wear** what she chose to wear—pretty even when perchance casual   **74 serious decking** carefully thought out attire.   **75–6 Stol'n . . . coinage** caught some new tune, or randomly hummed an improvised one of my own   **78–82 This . . . dividual** This narrative of mine, which blissful innocence recognizes as the imperfect representation (as if it were an illegitimate child) of some meaningful old tale, is meant to show that true love between two young women can be greater than the love between persons of the opposite sex.

That you shall never—like the maid Flavina—
Love any that's called man.
EMILIA   I am sure I shall not.
HIPPOLYTA   Now alack, weak sister,
I must no more believe thee in this point—
Though in't I know thou dost believe thyself—
Than I will trust a sickly appetite,
That loathes even as it longs. But sure, my sister,
If I were ripe for your persuasion, you   92
Have said enough to shake me from the arm
Of the all-noble Theseus, for whose fortunes
I will now in and kneel, with great assurance
That we, more than his Pirithous, possess
The high throne in his heart.
EMILIA   I am not
Against your faith, yet I continue mine.   *Exeunt.*

❧

1.4

Cornets. A battle struck within; then a retreat.
Flourish. Then enter [from one door] Theseus,
victor. [A Herald follows with attendants bearing
Palamon and Arcite. From another door] the three
Queens meet him and fall on their faces before him.

FIRST QUEEN
To thee no star be dark!
SECOND QUEEN   Both heaven and earth   1
Friend thee forever!
THIRD QUEEN   All the good that may
Be wished upon thy head, I cry amen to't!
THESEUS
Th'impartial gods, who, from the mounted heavens,   4
View us their mortal herd, behold who err
And in their time chastise. Go and find out
The bones of your dead lords, and honor them
With treble ceremony; rather than a gap
Should be in their dear rites, we would supply't.
But those we will depute, which shall invest   10
You in your dignities, and even each thing   11
Our haste does leave imperfect. So adieu,
And heaven's good eyes look on you.
                              Exeunt Queens.
              [*Theseus points to Palamon and Arcite.*]
                              What are those?

HERALD
Men of great quality, as may be judged   14
By their appointment. Some of Thebes have told 's   15

They are sisters' children, nephews to the King.
THESEUS
By th' helm of Mars, I saw them in the war,
Like to a pair of lions, smeared with prey,
Make lanes in troops aghast. I fixed my note   19
Constantly on them, for they were a mark   20
Worth a god's view. What prisoner was't that told me
When I inquired their names?
HERALD   Wi' leave, they're called   22
Arcite and Palamon.
THESEUS   'Tis right; those, those.
They are not dead?
HERALD
Nor in a state of life. Had they been taken
When their last hurts were given, 'twas possible
They might have been recovered. Yet they breathe
And have the name of men.
THESEUS   Then like men use 'em.   28
The very lees of such, millions of rates,   29
Exceed the wine of others. All our surgeons   30
Convent in their behoof; our richest balms,   31
Rather than niggard, waste; their lives concern us   32
Much more than Thebes is worth. Rather than have
  'em   33
Freed of this plight, and in their morning state,   34
Sound and at liberty, I would 'em dead;   35
But forty-thousandfold we had rather have 'em
Prisoners to us than death. Bear 'em speedily
From our kind air, to them unkind, and minister   38
What man to man may do—for our sake more,
Since I have known frights, fury, friends' behests,   40
Love's provocations, zeal, a mistress' task,   41
Desire of liberty, a fever, madness,   42
Hath set a mark which nature could not reach to   43
Without some imposition, sickness in will   44
O'er-wrestling strength in reason. For our love   45
And great Apollo's mercy, all our best   46
Their best skill tender.—Lead into the city,
Where, having bound things scattered, we will post   48
To Athens 'fore our army.   *Flourish. Exeunt.*

❧

92 **ripe . . . persuasion** disposed to be won over by your argument
1.4 Location: At the siege of Thebes.
0.1 *Cornets* trumpet calls signifying battle.   *within* offstage, behind
the stage façade.   *retreat* withdrawal after combat, not necessarily in
flight.   **1 no star be dark** may no planet or heavenly body be obscure
and unfavorable.   **4 mounted** high   **10–11 But . . . dignities** But I
will deputize others to perform these ceremonies which will clothe
you in the dignities that you and your dead husbands have deserved.
(Having performed his vow to guarantee the burial of the dead kings,
Theseus is eager to return to his marriage.)   **11 even** make even,
complete   **14 quality** rank   **15 appointment** accouterment, armor.

19 Make . . . aghast hew their way through troops that were aghast.
note attention   **20 mark** object of attention   **22 Wi' leave** By your
leave, if you'll allow me to say so   **28 have . . . men** are nominally
still alive.   **29 The very . . . rates** The mere dregs or last physical remnants of such men, by millions of times   **30–1 All . . . behoof** Call
together all our surgeons on their behalf   **32 Rather . . . waste** rather
than be niggardly with, expend lavishly   **33–5 Rather . . . dead** i.e., If
it were the previous morning, before the battle began, I would have
wished them dead rather than healthy and free, ready to fight on the
enemy side   **38 kind . . . unkind** (The air that Theseus cherishes is
dangerous to his enemies, especially since air was thought to be
infectious to open wounds.)   **40–5 Since . . . reason** Theseus has
known men like Palamon and Arcite to strive for something nearly
impossible and quite unreasonable, when their natural common
sense is overwhelmed by some compelling desire to please friends,
lovers, or country, or in response to some equally impulsive emotion.
46 Apollo here invoked as god of healing.   **all our best** let all our
best surgeons   **48 post** hasten

1.5

Music. Enter the Queens with [attendants bearing]
the hearses of their knights in a funeral solemnity,
etc.

[*Song*]

Urns and odors bring away;   1
Vapors, sighs darken the day;
   Our dole more deadly looks than dying;   3
Balms and gums and heavy cheers,   4
Sacred vials filled with tears,
   And clamors through the wild air flying.

Come all sad and solemn shows
That are quick-eyed Pleasure's foes;
We convent naught else but woes,   9
We convent naught else but woes.

THIRD QUEEN
This funeral path brings to your household's grave;   11
Joy seize on you again; peace sleep with him!

SECOND QUEEN
And this to yours.

FIRST QUEEN   Yours this way. Heavens lend   13
A thousand differing ways to one sure end.

THIRD QUEEN
This world's a city full of straying streets,
And death's the market-place where each one meets.   16
Exeunt severally.

❧

2.1

Enter Jailer and Wooer.

JAILER   I may depart with little while I live; something I   1
may cast to you, not much. Alas, the prison I keep,   2
though it be for great ones, yet they seldom come;
before one salmon you shall take a number of min-
nows. I am given out to be better lined than it can   5
appear to me report is a true speaker. I would I were   6
really that I am delivered to be. Marry, what I   7

have—be it what it will—I will assure upon my   8
daughter at the day of my death.

WOOER   Sir, I demand no more than your own offer,
and I will estate your daughter in what I have   11
promised.

JAILER   Well, we will talk more of this when the   13
solemnity is past. But have you a full promise of her?   14
When that shall be seen, I tender my consent.   15

WOOER   I have, sir.

Enter [Jailer's] Daughter [with rushes].

Here she comes.

JAILER [*to Daughter*]   Your friend and I have chanced
to name you here, upon the old business; but no
more of that now. So soon as the court hurry is over
we will have an end of it. I'th' meantime look   21
tenderly to the two prisoners. I can tell you they are   22
princes.

JAILER'S DAUGHTER   These strewings are for their cham-   24
ber. 'Tis pity they are in prison, and 'twere pity they   25
should be out. I do think they have patience to make   26
any adversity ashamed. The prison itself is proud   27
of 'em, and they have all the world in their chamber.   28

JAILER   They are famed to be a pair of absolute men.   29

JAILER'S DAUGHTER   By my troth, I think fame but stam- 30
mers 'em; they stand a grece above the reach of report.   31

JAILER   I heard them reported in the battle to be the   32
only doers.   33

JAILER'S DAUGHTER   Nay, most likely, for they are
noble suff'rers. I marvel how they would have looked
had they been victors, that with such a constant
nobility enforce a freedom out of bondage, making   37
misery their mirth and affliction a toy to jest at.   38

JAILER   Do they so?

JAILER'S DAUGHTER   It seems to me they have no more
sense of their captivity than I of ruling Athens. They
eat well, look merrily, discourse of many things, but
nothing of their own restraint and disasters. Yet sometime a divided sigh, martyred as 'twere i'th' deliver-   44
ance, will break from one of them, when the other
presently gives it so sweet a rebuke that I could   46
wish myself a sigh to be so chid, or at least a sigher to
be comforted.

WOOER   I never saw 'em.

JAILER   The Duke himself came privately in the night,   50

1.5. Location: Outside Thebes. A marginal note in the Quarto speci-
fies at line 26 in the previous scene that the "hearses" are to be made
"ready" for this present scene.
0.2 their knights their husband kings. **0.3 *etc.*** This notation invites
the use of extras, conventional props, and blocking through which
the acting company is to stage a solemn procession suitable to the
weight of the occasion. **0.4 *Song*** The song may be sung by the three
queens, but possibly by attendant singers. **1 odors** incense. **away**
along **3 Our . . . dying** our mourning has a more grim appearance
than death itself **4 gums** resins burned to produce incense. **heavy
cheers** sad countenances **9 convent** (1) assemble (2) suit **11 brings**
leads. **household's grave** family monument and burial plot
13 And this And this path **16.1 *severally*** separately. (The funeral
procession divides into three, each queen going through a stage door
accompanied by the hearse of her dead husband.)
**2.1. Location: Athens. A prison garden, on the main stage, with the
prison cell above in the theater gallery.**
1 depart with part with, give away **2 cast to** confer upon (in the
way of dowry) **5–6 I . . . speaker** I am reputed to have more wealth
than I can see any reason for the rumor of it to be believed. **7 that**
that which. **delivered** rumored, said. **Marry** an oath, originally
"by the Virgin Mary"

8 assure guarantee to settle **11 estate** settle an estate upon **13–14 the
solemnity** i.e., the royal wedding of Theseus and Hippolyta; the "court
hurry" of line 20 **14 of** from **15 seen** understood to have occurred.
tender offer **21–2 look tenderly to** tend carefully **24 strewings**
rushes or reeds strewn on the floor and changed from time to time
25 pity . . . pity (The Jailer's Daughter takes pity on them as prisoners,
but would hate to see them set free.) **26–7 to make . . . ashamed** to
put to shame any adversity by their noble resolution. **28 they have . . .
chamber** i.e., their friendship is a world unto itself. **29 absolute men**
complete gentlemen. **30–1 stammers** describes only haltingly
31 grece step. (They stand above anything reputation can say of them.)
32–3 the only doers the ones whose brave feats immeasurably outdid
those of any others. **37 enforce . . . bondage** manage to make themselves free in spirit even in their captivity **38 toy** trifle **44 divided**
broken, incomplete **46 presently** instantly **50 privately** secretly. (The
Duke returned home with his prisoners at night; unobserved.)

and so did they; what the reason of it is, I know not.   51

Enter Palamon and Arcite above [in shackles].

Look, yonder they are. That's Arcite looks out.   52

JAILER'S DAUGHTER   No, sir, no, that's Palamon. Arcite
is the lower of the twain; you may perceive a part of   54
him.

JAILER   Go to, leave your pointing. They would not   56
make us their object. Out of their sight!   57

JAILER'S DAUGHTER   It is a holiday to look on them.
Lord, the diff'rence of men!   59

Exeunt [Jailer, Wooer, and Daughter].

❖

2.2

PALAMON
How do you, noble cousin?

ARCITE   How do you, sir?

PALAMON
Why, strong enough to laugh at misery
And bear the chance of war; yet we are prisoners
I fear forever, cousin.

ARCITE   I believe it,
And to that destiny have patiently
Laid up my hour to come.

PALAMON   Oh, cousin Arcite,   6
Where is Thebes now? Where is our noble country?
Where are our friends and kindreds? Never more
Must we behold those comforts, never see
The hardy youths strive for the games of honor,
Hung with the painted favors of their ladies,   11
Like tall ships under sail; then start amongst 'em
And, as an east wind, leave 'em all behind us,
Like lazy clouds, whilst Palamon and Arcite,
Even in the wagging of a wanton leg,   15
Outstripped the people's praises, won the garlands
Ere they have time to wish 'em ours. Oh, never
Shall we two exercise, like twins of honor,
Our arms again, and feel our fiery horses   19
Like proud seas under us. Our good swords, now—
Better the red-eyed god of war nev'r wore—   21
Ravished our sides, like age must run to rust   22
And deck the temples of those gods that hate us;
These hands shall never draw 'em out like lightning
To blast whole armies more.

ARCITE   No, Palamon,   25
Those hopes are prisoners with us. Here we are,
And here the graces of our youths must wither
Like a too-timely spring. Here age must find us,   28
And—which is heaviest, Palamon—unmarried.   29
The sweet embraces of a loving wife,
Loaden with kisses, armed with thousand Cupids,   31
Shall never clasp our necks; no issue know us;   32
No figures of ourselves shall we ev'r see   33
To glad our age, and, like young eagles, teach 'em   34
Boldly to gaze against bright arms, and say   35
"Remember what your fathers were, and conquer!"
The fair-eyed maids shall weep our banishments
And in their songs curse ever-blinded Fortune,
Till she for shame see what a wrong she has done
To youth and nature. This is all our world;
We shall know nothing here but one another;
Hear nothing but the clock that tells our woes.   42
The vine shall grow, but we shall never see it;
Summer shall come, and with her all delights,
But dead-cold winter must inhabit here still.

PALAMON
'Tis too true, Arcite. To our Theban hounds
That shook the agèd forest with their echoes
No more now must we hollo; no more shake   48
Our pointed javelins, whilst the angry swine   49
Flies like a Parthian quiver from our rages,   50
Struck with our well-steeled darts. All valiant uses—   51
The food and nourishment of noble minds—
In us two here shall perish; we shall die—
Which is the curse of honor—lastly,   54
Children of grief and ignorance.

ARCITE   Yet, cousin,   55
Even from the bottom of these miseries,
From all that fortune can inflict upon us,
I see two comforts rising, two mere blessings,   58
If the gods please: to hold here a brave patience,
And the enjoying of our griefs together.
Whilst Palamon is with me, let me perish
If I think this our prison.

PALAMON   Certainly
'Tis a main goodness, cousin, that our fortunes   63
Were twinned together. 'Tis most true, two souls   64
Put in two noble bodies, let 'em suffer   65
The gall of hazard, so they grow together,   66
Will never sink; they must not, say they could.   67
A willing man dies sleeping and all's done.   68

ARCITE
Shall we make worthy uses of this place

51.1 *above* in the gallery over the stage.   52 **looks out** who looks out.
54 **lower** less tall   56 **Go to** i.e., Come, come, enough of that
56–7 **They . . . object** They wouldn't be so rude as to point to us; they
have no wish to see us.   59 **the diff'rence of men!** how much finer
some men are than others!
2.2. Palamon and Arcite probably remain onstage in a continuation
of scene 1, but since the Quarto explicitly has them *"Exeunt"* and
then *"Enter . . . in prison,"* the Q scene division is retained.
6 **Laid up . . . come** devoted the rest of my life.   11 **painted favors**
brightly colored tokens of favor in love, such as a scarf or glove
15 **Even . . . leg** i.e., with seemingly effortless motion, sportively
19 **arms** armor, weapons   21 **red-eyed god of war** Mars, red-eyed with
fury   22 **Ravished** seized violently from   25 **blast** blight, destroy

28 **too-timely** prematurely blooming   29 **heaviest** most burdensome
31 **Loaden** loaded   32 **issue** offspring   33 **figures** likenesses
34 **glad** gladden   34–5 **like . . . arms** we will never be able to teach
our children to look fearlessly at the arms of opponents, much as
eagles are reputed to be able to gaze directly at the sun   42 **tells**
counts   48 **hollo** cry encouragement   49 **swine** wild boar
50 **Parthian** (The Parthians, fierce warriors, were famed for their ability to shoot while in real or feigned retreat.)   51 **uses** pursuits (such
as hunting)   54 **lastly** finally   55 **Children . . . ignorance** i.e., sadly
and forgotten.   58 **mere** unmixed   63 **main goodness** major blessing, piece of good luck   64 **twinned** (The Quarto spelling, "twyn'd,"
suggests [1] paired inseparably [2] entwined.)   65–6 **let . . . hazard**
even if they should suffer the rubs of misfortune   66 **so** provided
that   67 **say** even if   68 **A willing . . . sleeping** One who is stoically
prepared for death dies as though going gently to sleep

That all men hate so much?
PALAMON   How, gentle cousin?   70
ARCITE
Let's think this prison holy sanctuary,
To keep us from corruption of worse men.
We are young and yet desire the ways of honor
That liberty and common conversation,   74
The poison of pure spirits, might, like women,   75
Woo us to wander from. What worthy blessing   76
Can be but our imaginations   77
May make it ours? And here being thus together,   78
We are an endless mine to one another.   79
We are one another's wife, ever begetting
New births of love; we are father, friends,
    acquaintance;
We are in one another, families;
I am your heir, and you are mine. This place
Is our inheritance; no hard oppressor
Dare take this from us. Here, with a little patience,
We shall live long and loving. No surfeits seek us;
The hand of war hurts none here, nor the seas
Swallow their youth. Were we at liberty,
A wife might part us lawfully, or business;
Quarrels consume us; envy of ill men   90
Crave our acquaintance. I might sicken, cousin,   91
Where you should never know it, and so perish
Without your noble hand to close mine eyes,
Or prayers to the gods. A thousand chances,
Were we from hence, would sever us.
PALAMON   You have made me—
I thank you, cousin Arcite—almost wanton   96
With my captivity. What a misery
It is to live abroad, and everywhere!   98
'Tis like a beast, methinks. I find the court here,   99
I am sure, a more content; and all those pleasures   100
That woo the wills of men to vanity
I see through now, and am sufficient
To tell the world 'tis but a gaudy shadow
That old Time, as he passes by, takes with him.
What had we been, old in the court of Creon,   105
Where sin is justice, lust and ignorance
The virtues of the great ones? Cousin Arcite,
Had not the loving gods found this place for us,
We had died as they do, ill old men, unwept,   109
And had their epitaphs, the people's curses.   110
Shall I say more?
ARCITE   I would hear you still.
PALAMON   Ye shall.

Is there record of any two that loved
Better than we do, Arcite?
ARCITE   Sure there cannot.
PALAMON
I do not think it possible our friendship
Should ever leave us.
ARCITE   Till our deaths it cannot.

        Enter Emilia and her Woman [below].

And after death our spirits shall be led
To those that love eternally.
              [*Palamon sees Emilia and is speechless.*]
                          Speak on, sir.   117
EMILIA [*as she and her Woman gather flowers*]
This garden has a world of pleasures in't.
What flower is this?
WOMAN   'Tis called narcissus, madam.   119
EMILIA
That was a fair boy, certain, but a fool   120
To love himself. Were there not maids enough?   121
ARCITE [*to Palamon*]
Pray, forward.
PALAMON   Yes.
EMILIA [*to her Woman*]   Or were they all hard-hearted?   122
WOMAN
They could not be to one so fair.
EMILIA   Thou wouldst not.
WOMAN
I think I should not, madam.
EMILIA   That's a good wench;
But take heed to your kindness, though.
WOMAN   Why, madam?
EMILIA
Men are mad things.
ARCITE [*to Palamon*]   Will ye go forward, cousin?   126
EMILIA [*to her Woman*]
Canst not thou work such flowers in silk, wench?
WOMAN   Yes.   127
EMILIA
I'll have a gown full of 'em, and of these.
This is a pretty color; will't not do
Rarely upon a skirt, wench?
WOMAN   Dainty, madam.   130
ARCITE [*to Palamon*]
Cousin, cousin, how do you, sir? Why, Palamon!
PALAMON
Never till now was I in prison, Arcite.
ARCITE
Why, what's the matter, man?
PALAMON [*indicating Emilia*]   Behold and wonder!

---

70 gentle well-born, gracious   **74 common conversation** indiscrimi-
nate dealings with people   **75 like women** as if they were women.
(Liberty and common conversation are personified as temptresses
wooing the young men away from honor.)   **76–8 What . . . ours?**
What worthy blessing can there be that in our imaginations we cannot make ours?   **79 mine** resource   **90–1 Quarrels . . . acquaintance**
becoming involved in the quarrels might destroy our friendship; we
might succumb to the vice of envying or imitating bad men   **96 wanton** sportive   **98 abroad** at liberty   **99 the court** i.e., the court that we
create for ourselves, as distinguished from the courts of Creon or Theseus   **100 more** greater   **105 What . . . old** What would we have
been like, if we had grown old   **109 they** i.e., the "great ones" of line
107.   **ill** evil   **110 their epitaphs** i.e., the same remembrance they got

117 To . . . eternally to those lovers whose spirits dwell in the Elysian
Fields.   **119–21 narcissus . . . himself** (As punishment for his refusal
to return the love of the nymph Echo, Narcissus fell fruitlessly in love
with his own image in a fountain; eventually he was transformed into
the flower that bears his name. Ovid, *Metamorphoses*, 3.)   **122 forward** continue with what you were saying. (Also in line 126.)
126 Men are mad things (Emilia warns her Woman that a kindly disposition toward handsome young men, however indicative of goodness of heart, may get a young woman into trouble.)   **127 work**
embroider   **130 Rarely** excellently

By heaven, she is a goddess.
ARCITE [*seeing Emilia*]   Ha!
PALAMON   Do reverence;
She is a goddess, Arcite.
EMILIA [*to her Woman*]   Of all flowers
Methinks a rose is best.
WOMAN   Why, gentle madam?
EMILIA
It is the very emblem of a maid;
For when the west wind courts her gently,
How modestly she blows, and paints the sun   139
With her chaste blushes! When the north comes near
      her,   140
Rude and impatient, then, like chastity,
She locks her beauties in her bud again,
And leaves him to base briers.
WOMAN   Yet, good madam,   143
Sometimes her modesty will blow so far   144
She falls for't; a maid,   145
If she have any honor, would be loath
To take example by her.
EMILIA   Thou art wanton.   147
ARCITE [*to Palamon*]
She is wondrous fair.
PALAMON   She is all the beauty extant.
EMILIA [*to her Woman*]
The sun grows high; let's walk in. Keep these flowers;
We'll see how near art can come near their colors. 150
I am wondrous merry-hearted; I could laugh now.   151
WOMAN
I could lie down, I am sure.
EMILIA   And take one with you?   152
WOMAN
That's as we bargain, madam.
EMILIA   Well, agree then.
      Exeunt Emilia and [her] Woman.
PALAMON
What think you of this beauty?
ARCITE   'Tis a rare one.
PALAMON
Is't but a rare one?
ARCITE   Yes, a matchless beauty.
PALAMON
Might not a man well lose himself and love her?
ARCITE
I cannot tell what you have done; I have,
Beshrew mine eyes for't! Now I feel my shackles.   158
PALAMON   You love her, then?
ARCITE   Who would not?
PALAMON   And desire her?

ARCITE   Before my liberty.
PALAMON   I saw her first.
ARCITE   That's nothing.
PALAMON   But it shall be.
ARCITE   I saw her too.
PALAMON   Yes, but you must not love her.
ARCITE
I will not, as you do, to worship her
As she is heavenly and a blessèd goddess.
I love her as a woman, to enjoy her;
So both may love.
PALAMON   You shall not love at all.
ARCITE   Not love at all? Who shall deny me?
PALAMON
I, that first saw her; I, that took possession
First with mine eye of all those beauties
In her revealed to mankind. If thou lov'st her,
Or entertain'st a hope to blast my wishes,   177
Thou art a traitor, Arcite, and a fellow
False as thy title to her. Friendship, blood,
And all the ties between us I disclaim
If thou once think upon her.
ARCITE   Yes, I love her,
And if the lives of all my name lay on it,   182
I must do so. I love her with my soul;
If that will lose ye, farewell, Palamon.
I say again I love, and, in loving her, maintain
I am as worthy and as free a lover,   186
And have as just a title to her beauty,
As any Palamon or any living
That is a man's son.
PALAMON   Have I called thee friend?
ARCITE
Yes, and have found me so. Why are you moved thus? 190
Let me deal coldly with you. Am not I   191
Part of your blood, part of your soul? You have told
      me
That I was Palamon, and you were Arcite.
PALAMON   Yes.
ARCITE
Am not I liable to those affections,   194
Those joys, griefs, angers, fears, my friend shall suffer?
PALAMON
Ye may be.
ARCITE   Why then would you deal so cunningly,
So strangely, so unlike a noble kinsman,
To love alone? Speak truly, do you think me
Unworthy of her sight?
PALAMON   No, but unjust
If thou pursue that sight.
ARCITE   Because another
First sees the enemy, shall I stand still
And let mine honor down, and never charge?
PALAMON
Yes, if he be but one.
ARCITE   But say that one   203

---

139 **she blows . . . sun** the rose blooms, and adds color to the sun's rays **140 north** north wind **143 And . . . briers** and leaves the north wind with nothing but her briers. **144–45 Sometimes . . . for't** (The Woman observes that the rose eventually blooms so openly, in despite of modesty, that it goes past its prime and decays. *Blow* can suggest being puffed up with vanity. A woman following such an example might well fall into temptation.) **147 Thou art wanton** You're being witty. **150 art** i.e., embroidery. (See line 127.) **151–2 laugh . . . lie down** The Woman continues the sexual joking with her reference to a proverb and a card game called "Laugh and lay (or lie) down." **152 one** someone, a man **158 Beshrew** i.e., May the devil take. (A mild curse.)

177 **blast** blight, destroy **182 name** family. **lay** depended **186 free** noble **190 moved** angered **191 coldly** calmly **194 affections** feelings **203 but one** (The code of chivalry would forbid Arcite to join Palamon in engaging with a single opponent, two against one.)

Had rather combat me?

PALAMON   Let that one say so,   204
And use thy freedom; else, if thou pursuest her,   205
Be as that cursèd man that hates his country,
A branded villain.

ARCITE   You are mad.

PALAMON   I must be.
Till thou art worthy, Arcite, it concerns me;   208
And in this madness if I hazard thee   209
And take thy life, I deal but truly.

ARCITE   Fie, sir!
You play the child extremely. I will love her,
I must, I ought to do so, and I dare,
And all this justly.

PALAMON   Oh, that now, that now   213
Thy false self and thy friend had but this fortune   214
To be one hour at liberty, and grasp   215
Our good swords in our hands! I would quickly teach
   thee
What 'twere to filch affection from another.
Thou art baser in it than a cutpurse.
Put but thy head out of this window more,
And, as I have a soul, I'll nail thy life to't.   220

ARCITE
Thou dar'st not, fool, thou canst not, thou art feeble.
Put my head out? I'll throw my body out
And leap the garden, when I see her next,   223

          Enter Jailer [above].

And pitch between her arms to anger thee.   224

PALAMON
No more; the keeper's coming. I shall live
To knock thy brains out with my shackles.

ARCITE   Do.

JAILER
By your leave, gentlemen.

PALAMON   Now, honest keeper?   227

JAILER
Lord Arcite, you must presently to th' Duke.
The cause I know not yet.

ARCITE   I am ready, keeper.

JAILER
Prince Palamon, I must awhile bereave you
Of your fair cousin's company.
                    Exeunt Arcite and Jailer.

PALAMON   And me too,
Even when you please, of life. Why is he sent for?
It may be he shall marry her; he's goodly,   233
And like enough the Duke hath taken notice   234

Both of his blood and body. But his falsehood!   235
Why should a friend be treacherous? If that
Get him a wife so noble and so fair,
Let honest men ne'er love again. Once more
I would but see this fair one. Blessèd garden,
And fruit and flowers more blessèd, that still blossom
As her bright eyes shine on ye! Would I were,
For all the fortune of my life hereafter,
Yon little tree, yon blooming apricot.
How I would spread and fling my wanton arms
In at her window! I would bring her fruit
Fit for the gods to feed on; youth and pleasure
Still as she tasted should be doubled on her,   247
And, if she be not heavenly, I would make her   248
So near the gods in nature they should fear her;

          Enter Jailer [above].

And then I am sure she would love me.—How now,
   keeper?
Where's Arcite?

JAILER   Banished. Prince Pirithous
Obtained his liberty; but never more,
Upon his oath and life, must he set foot
Upon this kingdom.

PALAMON   He's a blessèd man.
He shall see Thebes again, and call to arms
The bold young men that, when he bids 'em charge,
Fall on like fire. Arcite shall have a fortune,   257
If he dare make himself a worthy lover,
Yet in the field to strike a battle for her;   259
And if he lose her then, he's a cold coward.
How bravely may he bear himself to win her
If he be noble Arcite—thousand ways!
Were I at liberty, I would do things
Of such a virtuous greatness that this lady,
This blushing virgin, should take manhood to her   265
And seek to ravish me.

JAILER   My lord, for you
I have this charge too.

PALAMON   To discharge my life.   267

JAILER
No, but from this place to remove Your Lordship;
The windows are too open.

PALAMON   Devils take 'em
That are so envious to me! Prithee kill me.

JAILER
And hang for't afterward.

PALAMON   By this good light,
Had I a sword I would kill thee.

JAILER   Why, my lord?

PALAMON
Thou bring'st such pelting scurvy news continually, 273
Thou art not worthy life. I will not go.

204–5 Let . . . freedom If that opponent were to indicate a preference for engaging with you, not me, you could go ahead and exercise your free choice by engaging with that person. (The "opponent" in this argument has become Emilia, not a hypothetical warrior.)   **208 Till . . . me** i.e., Until you behave worthily to me once again, by forgoing your claim to Emilia, the issue engages my honor   **209 hazard thee** put your life at hazard   **213–15 Oh . . . liberty** Would that you and I had but one hour of freedom from this prison   **220 to't** i.e., to the window frame. (Palamon will not allow Arcite to gaze any more at Emilia in the garden below their window.)   **223 leap** leap down into   **224 pitch** thrust myself   **227 honest** worthy   **233 goodly** handsome   **234 like** likely

235 blood breeding, lineage   **247 Still as** whenever   **248 be not** is not already   **257 Fall on** begin the battle.   **fortune** chance   **259 strike a battle** fight a battle, engage the enemy force   **265 take manhood to her** go on the offensive, like a male. (Palamon pictures himself here as the raped object of desire.)   **267 discharge my life** release me from life. (Playing sardonically on the Jailer's *charge*, "order," and on the idea of discharging a firearm.)   **273 pelting** paltry, contemptible

JAILER
Indeed you must, my lord.

PALAMON May I see the garden?

JAILER
No.

PALAMON Then I am resolved, I will not go.

JAILER
I must constrain you then; and, for you are dangerous, 277
I'll clap more irons on you.

PALAMON Do, good keeper.
I'll shake 'em so, ye shall not sleep;
I'll make ye a new morris. Must I go? 280

JAILER
There is no remedy.

PALAMON Farewell, kind window;
May rude wind never hurt thee.—Oh, my lady,
If ever thou hast felt what sorrow was,
Dream how I suffer!—Come, now bury me. 284

Exeunt Palamon and Jailer.

❧

2.3

Enter Arcite.

ARCITE
Banished the kingdom? 'Tis a benefit,
A mercy I must thank 'em for; but banished
The free enjoying of that face I die for, 3
Oh, 'twas a studied punishment, a death 4
Beyond imagination—such a vengeance
That, were I old and wicked, all my sins
Could never pluck upon me. Palamon,
Thou hast the start now; thou shalt stay and see
Her bright eyes break each morning 'gainst thy
window
And let in life into thee; thou shalt feed
Upon the sweetness of a noble beauty
That nature nev'r exceeded, nor nev'r shall.
Good gods, what happiness has Palamon!
Twenty to one he'll come to speak to her, 14
And if she be as gentle as she's fair,
I know she's his; he has a tongue will tame
Tempests and make the wild rocks wanton.
Come what can come,
The worst is death. I will not leave the kingdom.
I know mine own is but a heap of ruins, 20
And no redress there; if I go, he has her.
I am resolved another shape shall make me 22
Or end my fortunes. Either way I am happy;
I'll see her, and be near her or no more. 24

*Enter four Country people and one with a garland
before them. [Arcite stands apart.]*

FIRST COUNTRYMAN My masters, I'll be there, that's 25
certain.

SECOND COUNTRYMAN And I'll be there.

THIRD COUNTRYMAN And I.

FOURTH COUNTRYMAN Why then, have with ye, boys! 29
'Tis but a chiding. Let the plough play today; I'll 30
tickle't out of the jades' tails tomorrow. 31

FIRST COUNTRYMAN I am sure to have my wife as
jealous as a turkey; but that's all one. I'll go through; 33
let her mumble.

SECOND COUNTRYMAN Clap her aboard tomorrow 35
night, and stow her, and all's made up again.

THIRD COUNTRYMAN Ay, do but put a fescue in her 37
fist, and you shall see her take a new lesson out and be 38
a good wench. Do we all hold against the maying? 39

FOURTH COUNTRYMAN Hold? What should ail us? 40

THIRD COUNTRYMAN Arcas will be there.

SECOND COUNTRYMAN And Sennois and Rycas, and
three better lads nev'r danced under green tree; and
ye know what wenches, ha! But will the dainty 44
dominie, the schoolmaster, keep touch, do you think? 45
For he does all, ye know. 46

THIRD COUNTRYMAN He'll eat a hornbook e'er he fail. 47
Go to, the matter's too far driven between him and the 48
tanner's daughter to let slip now; and she must see the 49
Duke, and she must dance too. 50

FOURTH COUNTRYMAN Shall we be lusty? 51

SECOND COUNTRYMAN All the boys in Athens blow 52
wind i'th' breech on 's! And here I'll be and there 53
I'll be, for our town, and here again and there again. 54
Ha, boys, hey for the weavers! 55

FIRST COUNTRYMAN This must be done i'th' woods.

FOURTH COUNTRYMAN Oh, pardon me. 57

SECOND COUNTRYMAN By any means, our thing of 58
learning says so; where he himself will edify the Duke 59
most parlously in our behalfs. He's excellent i'th' 60

---

277 for since **280 morris** a morris dance, in which the dancers wore bells around their legs; the sound might be thought to resemble the clanking of chains. **284 bury me** i.e., remove me where I cannot see Emilia, which will be tantamount to death.
2.3. Location: Outside Athens.
3 die would die **4 studied** premeditated **14 come** find occasion **20 mine own** my own kingdom (Thebes) **22 another shape** i.e., a disguise **24 no more** be no more, perish.

25 masters sirs. (Used often among workmen and citizens.) **29–30 have . . . chiding** I'll join you, boys; the worst thing that can happen to me is a scolding (for not ploughing). **30–1 I'll . . . tomorrow** i.e., I'll make up for lost time tomorrow by whipping the old horses into working faster. **33 that's all one** no matter. **35 Clap her aboard** Board her. The sexual wordplay continues in *stow her*, "place your cargo belowdecks in her," and in *all's made up*: (1) all's supplied for a journey (2) the quarrel is patched up (3) the hole is stopped up. **37 a fescue** a pointer used in pointing out letters for children learning to read **38 take . . . out** learn a new lesson **39 hold against the maying** hold to our intention with respect to the May Day celebration. **40 ail us** prevent us from taking part. **44–5 dainty dominie** fastidious schoolmaster **45 keep touch** keep faith, keep his promise **46 he does all** all depends on him **47 hornbook** an alphabet, etc. protected by a layer of cowhorn or similar animal horn cut thin enough to be virtually transparent, used in classrooms **48 Go to** (An expression of impatience.) **the matter's . . . driven** things have gone too far **49–50 she must see . . . too** she insists on seeing the Duke and dancing too. **51 lusty** jolly, lively. **52–3 All . . . on 's!** i.e., May all the lads of Athens have to pant and puff to keep up with us! **53–4 And . . . town** And I'll be here, there, and everywhere in the morris dance, for honor of our town **55 hey . . . weavers!** hooray for the weavers! (the guild to which the First Countryman evidently belongs) **57 Oh, pardon me** i.e., I beg to differ. **58–9 By . . . so** In the woods, certainly; our schoolmaster says so. (The morris dance will be more fitting as part of the hunt in the woods; it is too rustic for performance at court.) **60 parlously** cleverly, amazingly

woods; bring him to th' plains, his learning makes no   61
cry.   62

THIRD COUNTRYMAN   We'll see the sports, then every
man to 's tackle. And, sweet companions, let's re-   64
hearse, by any means, before the ladies see us, and do
sweetly, and God knows what may come on't.   66

FOURTH COUNTRYMAN   Content. The sports once
ended, we'll perform. Away, boys, and hold!   68

[*They start to go.*]

ARCITE [*coming forward*]   By your leaves, honest   69
friends; pray you, whither go you?

FOURTH COUNTRYMAN   Whither? Why, what a question's that?

ARCITE   Yes, 'tis a question to me that know not.

THIRD COUNTRYMAN   To the games, my friend.

SECOND COUNTRYMAN [*to Arcite*]
Where were you bred, you know it not?

ARCITE   Not far, sir.
Are there such games today?

FIRST COUNTRYMAN   Yes, marry, are there,
And such as you never saw. The Duke himself
Will be in person there.

ARCITE   What pastimes are they?

SECOND COUNTRYMAN
Wrestling and running. [*To his companions*] 'Tis a
pretty fellow.

THIRD COUNTRYMAN [*to Arcite*]
Thou wilt not go along?

ARCITE   Not yet, sir.

FOURTH COUNTRYMAN   Well, sir,
Take your own time.—Come, boys.

FIRST COUNTRYMAN   My mind misgives me,   81
This fellow has a vengeance trick o'th' hip;   82
Mark how his body's made for't.

SECOND COUNTRYMAN   I'll be hanged, though,
If he dare venture. Hang him, plum porridge!   84
He wrestle? He roast eggs! Come, let's be gone, lads.   85

Exeunt four. [*Arcite remains.*]

ARCITE
This is an offered opportunity
I durst not wish for. Well I could have wrestled—   87
The best men called it excellent—and run
Swifter than wind upon a field of corn,   89
Curling the wealthy ears, never flew. I'll venture,   90
And in some poor disguise be there. Who knows
Whether my brows may not be girt with garlands,
And happiness prefer me to a place   93
Where I may ever dwell in sight of her?

Exit Arcite.

❖

61–2 **bring . . . cry** if we were to bring this morris dance and the
schoolmaster's presentation of it to court, his learning would look out
of place, like confused hunting dogs no longer yelping after their
prey.   64 **tackle** i.e., bells and other gear for the morris dance.
66 **on't** of it.   68 **hold** hold to your promise.   69 **honest** worthy
81–2 **My mind . . . hip** I suspect that this fellow may have a fearsome
ability to catch his opponent on the hip in wrestling   84 **plum porridge** i.e., weakling, milksop. (Literally, stewed fruit.)   85 **He roast
eggs!** i.e., He might as soon turn cook as wrestler.   87 **Well . . . wrestled** I used to know how to wrestle well   89–90 **Swifter . . . flew**
swifter than the wind ever flew through a grainfield, curling back the
fruitful ears of the grain.   93 **happiness prefer** good fortune advance

2.4

Enter Jailer's Daughter, alone.

JAILER'S DAUGHTER
Why should I love this gentleman? 'Tis odds   1
He never will affect me. I am base,   2
My father the mean keeper of his prison,   3
And he a prince. To marry him is hopeless,
To be his whore is witless. Out upon't,   5
What pushes are we wenches driven to   6
When fifteen once has found us! First I saw him;   7
I, seeing, thought he was a goodly man;
He has as much to please a woman in him—
If he please to bestow it so—as ever
These eyes yet looked on. Next I pitied him,
And so would any young wench, o' my conscience,   12
That ever dreamed, or vowed her maidenhead   13
To a young handsome man. Then I loved him,
Extremely loved him, infinitely loved him,
And yet he had a cousin, fair as he too.
But in my heart was Palamon, and there,
Lord, what a coil he keeps! To hear him   18
Sing in an evening, what a heaven it is!
And yet his songs are sad ones. Fairer spoken
Was never gentleman. When I come in
To bring him water in a morning, first
He bows his noble body, then salutes me thus: 23
"Fair, gentle maid, good morrow; may thy goodness
Get thee a happy husband." Once he kissed me;
I loved my lips the better ten days after.
Would he would do so ev'ry day! He grieves much,
And me as much to see his misery.
What should I do to make him know I love him?
For I would fain enjoy him. Say I ventured   30
To set him free? What says the law then? [*She snaps her
fingers*] Thus much
For law or kindred! I will do it,
And this night; ere tomorrow he shall love me.

Exit.

❖

2.5

[*A*] *short flourish of cornets, and shouts within.
Enter Theseus, Hippolyta, Pirithous, Emilia,
Arcite* [*disguised*] *with a garland, etc.*

THESEUS [*to Arcite*]
You have done worthily. I have not seen,
Since Hercules, a man of tougher sinews.
Whate'er you are, you run the best and wrestle   3
That these times can allow.

ARCITE   I am proud to please you.   4

2.4. Location: Somewhere near the prison.
1 **'Tis odds** The likelihood is that   2 **affect** love.   **base** of low social
station   3 **mean** lowly   5 **Out upon't** (An expression of dismay.)
6 **pushes** exertions, extremes   7 **fifteen** the age of fifteen   12 **o' my
conscience** on my word of honor   13 **vowed** dedicated   18 **coil he
keeps** tumult he stirs up.   23 **salutes** greets   30 **fain** willingly
2.5. Location: The arena for wrestling, running, etc., near Athens.
3 **run . . . wrestle** are the best runner and wrestler   4 **allow** boast of.

THESEUS
    What country bred you?
ARCITE   This; but far off, prince.
THESEUS
    Are you a gentleman?
ARCITE   My father said so,
    And to those gentle uses gave me life.   7
THESEUS
    Are you his heir?
ARCITE   His youngest, sir.
THESEUS   Your father
    Sure is a happy sire, then. What proves you?   9
ARCITE
    A little of all noble qualities.   10
    I could have kept a hawk and well have hallooed   11
    To a deep cry of dogs; I dare not praise   12
    My feat in horsemanship, yet they that knew me   12
    Would say it was my best piece; last, and greatest,   14
    I would be thought a soldier.
THESEUS   You are perfect.   15
PIRITHOUS
    Upon my soul, a proper man.
EMILIA   He is so.   16
PIRITHOUS [to Hippolyta]
    How do you like him, lady?
HIPPOLYTA   I admire him.   17
    I have not seen so young a man, so noble—
    If he say true—of his sort.
EMILIA   Believe,   19
    His mother was a wondrous handsome woman;
    His face, methinks, goes that way.
HIPPOLYTA   But his body
    And fiery mind illustrate a brave father.
PIRITHOUS
    Mark how his virtue, like a hidden sun,   23
    Breaks through his baser garments.
HIPPOLYTA   He's well got, sure.   24
THESEUS [to Arcite]
    What made you seek this place, sir?
ARCITE   Noble Theseus,
    To purchase name, and do my ablest service   26
    To such a well-found wonder as thy worth;   27
    For only in thy court, of all the world,
    Dwells fair-eyed honor.
PIRITHOUS   All his words are worthy.
THESEUS [to Arcite]
    Sir, we are much indebted to your travel,   30
    Nor shall you lose your wish.—Pirithous,

    Dispose of this fair gentleman.
PIRITHOUS   Thanks, Theseus.   32
    [To Arcite] Whate'er you are, you're mine, and I shall
        give you
    To a most noble service, to this lady,
    This bright young virgin; pray observe her goodness.   35
    You have honored her fair birthday with your virtues,
    And as your due you're hers. Kiss her fair hand, sir.
ARCITE
    Sir, you're a noble giver. [To Emilia] Dearest beauty,
    Thus let me seal my vowed faith.
                            [He kisses her hand.]
                            When your servant,
    Your most unworthy creature, but offends you,   40
    Command him die, he shall.
EMILIA   That were too cruel.
    If you deserve well, sir, I shall soon see't.
    You're mine, and somewhat better than your rank
    I'll use you.
PIRITHOUS [to Arcite]
    I'll see you furnished, and because you say
    You are a horseman, I must needs entreat you
    This afternoon to ride—but 'tis a rough one.   47
ARCITE
    I like him better, prince; I shall not then
    Freeze in my saddle.
THESEUS [to Hippolyta]   Sweet, you must be ready—
    And you, Emilia, and you, friend, and all—
    Tomorrow by the sun, to do observance   51
    To flow'ry May in Dian's wood.—Wait well, sir,
    Upon your mistress.—Emily, I hope
    He shall not go afoot.
EMILIA   That were a shame, sir,
    While I have horses. [To Arcite] Take your choice; and
        what
    You want at any time, let me but know it.   56
    If you serve faithfully, I dare assure you
    You'll find a loving mistress.
ARCITE   If I do not,
    Let me find that my father ever hated: 59
    Disgrace and blows.
THESEUS   Go lead the way; you have won it. 60
    It shall be so: you shall receive all dues
    Fit for the honor you have won; 'twere wrong else.—
    Sister, beshrew my heart, you have a servant   63
    That, if I were a woman, would be master;
    But you are wise.
EMILIA   I hope too wise for that, sir.
                            Flourish. Exeunt omnes.

                            ❖

7 **to . . . life** my father bred me to the accomplishments of a gentleman.   9 **What proves you?** What accomplishments do you have to
demonstrate your gentlemanly breeding?   10 **qualities** accomplishments.   11 **could have kept** was trained to keep   12 **deep cry** deep-
mouthed yelping (of hounds in pursuit of game)   13 **feat** skill
14 **piece** example, accomplishment   15 **would be thought** profess
myself to be   16 **proper** excellent, handsome   17 **admire** marvel at
19 **sort** class, rank.   **Believe** You may rest assured that   23 **virtue**
moral and personal excellence, strength   24 **got** begotten, born
26 **purchase name** gain reputation   27 **well-found** well-deserved
30 **travel** (1) coming to this court (2) endeavoring so nobly (in the
contests)

32 **Dispose of** make provision for, find a place for   35 **observe** show
respect for, honor   40 **but offends you** offends you in the smallest
way   47 **a rough one** i.e., a temperamental horse.   51 **by the sun** at
dawn   56 **want** lack   59 **that** that which   60 **it** i.e., the honor of
leading the return to court.   63 **Sister** Sister-in-law.   **servant** (Arcite
has formally become Emilia's "servant" in the sense of being her
courtly admirer, devoted to the service of his "mistress," line 58, not
her lover in an explicitly sexual sense.)

2.6

Enter Jailer's Daughter, alone.

JAILER'S DAUGHTER
Let all the dukes and all the devils roar!
He is at liberty. I have ventured for him,   2
And out I have brought him. To a little wood
A mile hence I have sent him, where a cedar,
Higher than all the rest, spreads like a plane,   5
Fast by a brook, and there he shall keep close   6
Till I provide him files and food, for yet
His iron bracelets are not off. O Love,   8
What a stout-hearted child thou art! My father
Durst better have endured cold iron than done it.   10
I love him beyond love and beyond reason,   11
Or wit, or safety. I have made him know it;   12
I care not, I am desperate. If the law
Find me and then condemn me for't, some wenches,
Some honest-hearted maids, will sing my dirge,
And tell to memory my death was noble,
Dying almost a martyr. That way he takes   17
I purpose is my way too. Sure, he cannot
Be so unmanly as to leave me here.
If he do, maids will not so easily
Trust men again. And yet he has not thanked me
For what I have done; no, not so much as kissed me,
And that, methinks, is not so well; nor scarcely
Could I persuade him to become a free man,
He made such scruples of the wrong he did
To me and to my father. Yet I hope,
When he considers more, this love of mine
Will take more root within him. Let him do
What he will with me, so he use me kindly;   29
For use me so he shall, or I'll proclaim him,
And to his face, no man. I'll presently   31
Provide him necessaries and pack my clothes up,
And where there is a path of ground I'll venture,   33
So he be with me. By him, like a shadow   34
I'll ever dwell. Within this hour the hubbub
Will be all o'er the prison; I am then
Kissing the man they look for. Farewell, father!
Get many more such prisoners, and such daughters,   38
And shortly you may keep yourself. Now to him.   39
                                                        [Exit.]

2.6. Location: Athens. Somewhere near the prison.
2 He Palamon.   **ventured** risked dangers   **5 plane** plane tree,
sycamore   **6 Fast by** near by.   **close** concealed   **8 Love** Cupid
10 Durst . . . it would rather have encountered armed assailants than
to have done this deed.   **11 him** Palamon   **12 wit** human understanding   **17 way** direction, path   **29 so** provided.   **kindly**
(1) benevolently (2) as my sexual nature requires   **31 no man** (1) no
gentleman (2) impotent.   **33 a path of ground** a path to be found
anywhere (in the forest)   **34 So** provided that   **38 Get** (1) Acquire
(2) Beget   **39 And . . . yourself** i.e., and soon you can have the jail to
yourself, with neither prisoners nor daughter.   **him** Palamon.

3.1

*Cornets in sundry places. Noise and hallooing as
people a-maying. Enter Arcite, alone.*

ARCITE
The Duke has lost Hippolyta; each took   1
A several laund. This is a solemn rite   2
They owe bloomed May, and the Athenians pay it   3
To th' heart of ceremony. O Queen Emilia,   4
Fresher than May, sweeter
Than her gold buttons on the boughs, or all   6
Th'enameled knacks o'th' mead or garden—yea,   7
We challenge too the bank of any nymph   8
That makes the stream seem flowers; thou, O jewel   9
O'th' wood, o'th' world, hast likewise blessed a pace   10
With thy sole presence; in thy rumination   11
That I, poor man, might eftsoons come between   12
And chop on some cold thought! Thrice blessèd
   chance   13
To drop on such a mistress, expectation   14
Most guiltless on't! Tell me, O Lady Fortune,   15
Next after Emily my sovereign, how far   16
I may be proud. She takes strong note of me,   17
Hath made me near her, and this beauteous morn,
The prim'st of all the year, presents me with   19
A brace of horses; two such steeds might well
Be by a pair of kings backed, in a field   21
That their crowns' titles tried. Alas, alas,   22
Poor cousin Palamon, poor prisoner, thou
So little dream'st upon my fortune that
Thou think'st thyself the happier thing, to be
So near Emilia! Me thou deem'st at Thebes,
And therein wretched, although free; but if
Thou knew'st my mistress breathed on me, and that
I eared her language, lived in her eye, O coz,   29
What passion would enclose thee!

*Enter Palamon as out of a bush, with his shackles;
[he] bends his fist at Arcite.*

PALAMON   Traitor kinsman,   30

3.1. Location: A forest near Athens.
0.1 in sundry places i.e., from various locations offstage.   **1–2 took . . .
laund** headed for a different glade.   **3 bloomed** in full blossom   **4 To
. . . ceremony** with full ceremony.   **6 buttons** buds   **7 Th'enameled
knacks** the ornamental delicacies (i.e., flowers).   **mead** meadow
8–9 We . . . flowers i.e., I dare compare my mistress's beauty with any
bank of a stream belonging to a guardian spirit (or nymph) and reflecting its flowered beauty in the water   **10 pace** narrow passage (through
the woods)   **11–15 in thy . . . on't!** O, would that I, poor man, meditat-
ing on you, might enter into your thoughts from time to time and, by
interrupting them, bring about an exchange of some cold thought for
thoughts of love! What a thrice blessed fortune, to happen upon such a
mistress, when least expecting to do so!   **16–17 how . . . proud** i.e., how
far may I bask in good fortune like this without growing worrisomely
overconfident.   **17 She . . . me** Emilia pays a lot of attention to me
19 prim'st finest   **21 backed** mounted   **21–2 field . . . tried** battlefield
on which their titles to their crowns were being contested.   **29 eared . . .
eye** took in her speech at my ear and lived under her gaze.   **coz** cousin
30 passion anger.   **enclose thee** enfold you in its grasp.   **s.d. as out of
a bush** i.e., either through a door understood to represent a hiding place
in the forest, or possibly out of a stage structure provided for this act.
bends shakes, aims

Thou shouldst perceive my passion if these signs
Of prisonment were off me, and this hand
But owner of a sword. By all oaths in one,
I and the justice of my love would make thee
A confessed traitor, O thou most perfidious
That ever gently looked, the void'st of honor   36
That ev'r bore gentle token, falsest cousin   37
That ever blood made kin! Call'st thou her thine?
I'll prove it in my shackles, with these hands,   39
Void of appointment, that thou liest, and art   40
A very thief in love, a chaffy lord,   41
Not worth the name of villain. Had I a sword,
And these house-clogs away—

ARCITE   Dear cousin Palamon—   43

PALAMON
Cozener Arcite, give me language such   44
As thou hast showed me feat.

ARCITE   Not finding in   45
The circuit of my breast any gross stuff   46
To form me like your blazon holds me to   47
This gentleness of answer: 'tis your passion   48
That thus mistakes, the which, to you being enemy,   49
Cannot to me be kind. Honor and honesty   50
I cherish and depend on, howsoev'r
You skip them in me, and with them, fair coz,   52
I'll maintain my proceedings. Pray be pleased   53
To show in generous terms your griefs, since that   54
Your question's with your equal, who professes   55
To clear his own way with the mind and sword   56
Of a true gentleman.

PALAMON   That thou durst, Arcite!   57

ARCITE
My coz, my coz, you have been well advertised   58
How much I dare; you've seen me use my sword
Against th'advice of fear. Sure of another   60
You would not hear me doubted, but your silence   61
Should break out, though i'th' sanctuary.

PALAMON   Sir,   62
I have seen you move in such a place which well   63
Might justify your manhood; you were called

A good knight and a bold. But the whole week's not
fair   65
If any day it rain; their valiant temper   66
Men lose when they incline to treachery,
And then they fight like compelled bears—would fly   68
Were they not tied.

ARCITE   Kinsman, you might as well
Speak this and act it in your glass as to   70
His ear which now disdains you.

PALAMON   Come up to me;
Quit me of these cold gyves, give me a sword,   72
Though it be rusty, and the charity
Of one meal lend me. Come before me then,
A good sword in thy hand, and do but say
That Emily is thine, I will forgive
The trespass thou hast done me—yea, my life,   77
If then thou carry't; and brave souls in shades   78
That have died manly, which will seek of me
Some news from earth, they shall get none but this:
That thou art brave and noble.

ARCITE   Be content;
Again betake you to your hawthorn house.   82
With counsel of the night I will be here   83
With wholesome viands. These impediments   84
Will I file off. You shall have garments and
Perfumes to kill the smell o'th' prison. After,
When you shall stretch yourself and say but "Arcite,   87
I am in plight," there shall be at your choice   88
Both sword and armor.

PALAMON   O you heavens, dares any   89
So noble bear a guilty business? None   90
But only Arcite; therefore none but Arcite
In this kind is so bold.

ARCITE   Sweet Palamon—

PALAMON
I do embrace you and your offer; for   93
Your offer do't I only; sir, your person   94
Without hypocrisy I may not wish   95
More than my sword's edge on't.

Wind horns off. Cornets [sounded].

ARCITE   You hear the horns.   96
Enter your muset, lest this match between 's   97

---

36 **gently looked** had the appearance of a gentleman   37 **bore gentle token** wore signs of gentility   39 **in my shackles** even with these shackles on   40 **Void of appointment** lacking accouterments of arms   41 **chaffy** worthless as chaff   43 **house-clogs** shackles confining the prisoner to his cell   44 **Cozener** Deceiver. (With a familiar pun on *cousin* in line 43.)   44–5 **give . . . feat** match your words to your (perfidious) deeds. (*Feat* means "apt, apropos.")   45–8 **Not . . . answer** Not finding anything base in my conduct that corresponds to your accusation, I answer gently. (A *blazon* is a description or catalogue, as on a shield in heraldry.)   48 **passion** anger   49–50 **the which . . . kind** which show of anger, wherein you are your own worst enemy, makes you also unfair to me.   52 **skip** fail to see   53–6 **Pray . . . way** Please use courteous speech in setting forth your grievances, since your dispute is with one who is your equal, and who affirms his intention of vindicating his own behavior   57 **That thou durst** If only you would dare to do that   58 **advertised** informed, put on notice   60–2 **Against . . . sanctuary** when prudence would advise caution. Surely you would not permit my honor to be doubted by some other person; you would break silence to defend me even if you were in hiding.   63 **place** i.e., field of battle or lists for a tournament

65–6 **But . . . rain** i.e., Unless you are perfectly consistent all the time in honorable behavior, the evidence of your bravery at other times proves nothing about the present instance   66 **temper** temperament   68 **compelled bears** (In bear-baiting, bears were tied to a stake and attacked by dogs.)   **would** who would   70 **in your glass** to yourself, in your mirror   72 **Quit me of** release me from.   **gyves** shackles   77 **trespass** insult, wrong   78 **carry't** win the fight between us.   **shades** the dark world of Hades, the abode of the dead   82 **betake . . . house** i.e., go to your place of hiding in the woods.   83 **With . . . night** Under cover of darkness, witnessed only by the night   84 **viands** food.   87 **stretch** rouse   88 **in plight** in readiness   89–90 **dares . . . business?** dare anyone venture so nobly in a cause so guilty?   93–6 **for . . . on't** (Palamon accepts Arcite's offer, but without acknowledging any personal thanks to one whom he frankly wishes only to kill.)   96 **s.d. *Wind horns off*** Sound horns offstage (indicative of a hunt).   97 **muset** meuse or opening in a hedge used by hunted game for concealment

Be crossed ere met. Give me your hand; farewell.   98
I'll bring you every needful thing; I pray you,
Take comfort and be strong.

PALAMON   Pray hold your promise,
And do the deed with a bent brow. Most certain   101
You love me not; be rough with me, and pour
This oil out of your language. By this air,   103
I could for each word give a cuff, my stomach   104
Not reconciled by reason.

ARCITE   Plainly spoken.
Yet pardon me hard language. When I spur   106
My horse, I chide him not; content and anger
In me have but one face.

Wind horns.

                              Hark, sir, they call   108
The scattered to the banquet. You must guess   109
I have an office there.

PALAMON   Sir, your attendance   110
Cannot please heaven, and I know your office
Unjustly is achieved.

ARCITE   'Tis a good title.   112
I am persuaded this question, sick between's,   113
By bleeding must be cured. I am a suitor   114
That to your sword you will bequeath this plea,   115
And talk of it no more.

PALAMON   But this one word:
You are going now to gaze upon my mistress—
For note you, mine she is—

ARCITE   Nay then—

PALAMON   Nay, pray you—
You talk of feeding me to breed me strength;
You are going now to look upon a sun
That strengthens what it looks on. There you have
A vantage o'er me, but enjoy't till
I may enforce my remedy. Farewell.

*Exeunt [separately, Palamon as into his hawthorn
house].*

❖

3.2

Enter Jailer's Daughter alone [with a file].

JAILER'S DAUGHTER
He has mistook the brake I meant, is gone   1
After his fancy. 'Tis now well-nigh morning.   2
No matter; would it were perpetual night,
And darkness lord o'th' world. Hark, 'tis a wolf!

In me hath grief slain fear, and but for one thing,
I care for nothing, and that's Palamon.
I reck not if the wolves would jaw me, so   7
He had this file. What if I hallooed for him?
I cannot halloo. If I whooped, what then?
If he not answered, I should call a wolf,
And do him but that service. I have heard   11
Strange howls this livelong night; why may't not be
They have made prey of him? He has no weapons;
He cannot run; the jingling of his gyves
Might call fell things to listen, who have in them   15
A sense to know a man unarmed, and can
Smell where resistance is. I'll set it down   17
He's torn to pieces; they howled many together,
And then they fed on him. So much for that.
Be bold to ring the bell. How stand I then?   20
All's chared when he is gone. No, no, I lie;   21
My father's to be hanged for his escape,   22
Myself to beg, if I prized life so much   23
As to deny my act, but that I would not,   24
Should I try death by dozens. I am moped;   25
Food took I none these two days,
Sipped some water. I have not closed mine eyes
Save when my lids scoured off their brine. Alas,   28
Dissolve, my life! Let not my sense unsettle,   29
Lest I should drown, or stab, or hang myself.
O state of nature, fail together in me,   31
Since thy best props are warped! So which way now?   32
The best way is the next way to a grave;   33
Each errant step beside is torment. Lo,   34
The moon is down, the crickets chirp, the screech owl
Calls in the dawn. All offices are done   36
Save what I fail in; but the point is this—
An end, and that is all.   38

                              Exit.

❖

3.3

Enter Arcite with meat, wine, and files.

ARCITE
I should be near the place.—Ho! Cousin Palamon!
PALAMON [*from the bush*]
Arcite?
ARCITE   The same. I have brought you food and files.

---

98 **crossed ere met** thwarted before it takes place.   101 **bent** frowning   103 **oil** i.e., calming and reconciling words   104 **stomach** anger   106 **pardon . . . language** pardon me if I refrain from using harsh speech.   108 **have but one face** look outwardly alike.   109 **The scattered** the hunters, who have separated during the hunt   110 **office** function (of waiting on Emilia)   112 '**Tis . . . title** It is a title I have justly earned.   113–15 **I am . . . plea** I am convinced that the contention that afflicts us both can be cured only by our swords, drawing blood as a doctor bleeds patients to effect a cure. I beg of you to refer this lawsuit to your sword   **3.2. Location: The forest.**
1 **brake** thicket   2 **After his fancy** as his wishes prompt him.

7 **reck** care.   **jaw** gnaw.   **so** provided   11 **And . . . service** i.e., and accomplish nothing more than to bring a wolf who would then threaten Palamon's life as well as mine.   15 **fell things** savage beasts   17 **set it down** record it as for a fact that   20 **the bell** i.e., the bell rung by the bellman to announce a person's death.   **How stand I** What plight am I in   21 **chared** done for. (To *chare* is to accomplish a turn of work, a chore.)   22 **his** Palamon's   23 **Myself to beg** I would be forced to beg for my living (as the daughter of an executed man)   24 **deny my act** deny allowing Palamon to escape   25 **Should . . . dozens** even if I had to suffer death many times or in many forms.   **moped** stupefied, dazed   28 **scoured . . . brine** skimmed off the briny tears from my eyes.   29 **sense** sanity   31 **state of nature** existence.   **together** altogether   32 **props** supports   33 **next** nearest   34 **Each . . . beside** each step that deviates from the quickest way to the grave   36 **offices** duties   38 **An end** i.e., death   **3.3. Location: The forest, as before.**

Come forth and fear not. Here's no Theseus.

Enter Palamon [as out of a bush].

PALAMON
Nor none so honest, Arcite.

ARCITE   That's no matter;
We'll argue that hereafter. Come, take courage;
You shall not die thus beastly. Here, sir, drink;
I know you are faint. Then I'll talk further with you.

PALAMON
Arcite, thou mightst now poison me.

ARCITE   I might;
But I must fear you first. Sit down and, good now,   9
No more of these vain parleys. Let us not,
Having our ancient reputation with us,   11
Make talk for fools and cowards. To your health, sir!
                                        [*He drinks.*]

PALAMON
Do.

ARCITE   Pray sit down, then, and let me entreat you,
By all the honesty and honor in you,
No mention of this woman; 'twill disturb us.
We shall have time enough.

PALAMON   Well, sir, I'll pledge you.   16
                                        [*He drinks.*]

ARCITE
Drink a good hearty draught; it breeds good blood,
    man.   17
Do not you feel it thaw you?

PALAMON
Stay, I'll tell you after a draught or two more.

ARCITE
Spare it not; the Duke has more, coz. Eat now.

PALAMON
Yes.   [*He eats.*]

ARCITE   I am glad you have so good a stomach.   21

PALAMON
I am gladder I have so good meat to't.

ARCITE
Is't not mad lodging here in the wild woods, cousin?

PALAMON
Yes, for them that have wild consciences.

ARCITE   How tastes your victuals?
Your hunger needs no sauce, I see.

PALAMON   Not much.
But if it did, yours is too tart, sweet cousin.   27
What is this?

ARCITE   Venison.

PALAMON   'Tis a lusty meat.   28
Give me more wine. Here, Arcite, to the wenches
We have known in our days!   [*He drinks.*]
                      The Lord Steward's daughter—
Do you remember her?

ARCITE   After you, coz.   31

PALAMON
She loved a black-haired man.

ARCITE   She did so. Well, sir?

PALAMON
And I have heard some call him Arcite, and—

ARCITE
Out with't, faith.

PALAMON   She met him in an arbor.
What did she there, coz? Play o'th' virginals?   35

ARCITE
Something she did, sir.

PALAMON   Made her groan a month for't—   36
Or two, or three, or ten.

ARCITE   The marshal's sister   37
Had her share, too, as I remember, cousin,
Else there be tales abroad. You'll pledge her?

PALAMON   Yes.   39
                                        [*They drink.*]

ARCITE
A pretty brown wench 'tis. There was a time   40
When young men went a-hunting—and a wood,
And a broad beech—and thereby hangs a tale.
Heigh ho!

PALAMON   For Emily, upon my life! Fool,
Away with this strained mirth. I say again,
That sigh was breathed for Emily. Base cousin,
Dar'st thou break first?

ARCITE   You are wide.

PALAMON   By heaven and earth,   46
There's nothing in thee honest.

ARCITE   Then I'll leave you;
You are a beast now.

PALAMON   As thou mak'st me, traitor.

ARCITE
There's all things needful: files, and shirts, and
    perfumes.
I'll come again some two hours hence and bring
That that shall quiet all.

PALAMON   A sword and armor.   51

ARCITE
Fear me not. You are now too foul. Farewell.   52
Get off your trinkets; you shall want naught.

PALAMON   Sirrah—   53

ARCITE
I'll hear no more.   *Exit.*

PALAMON   If he keep touch, he dies for't.   54
                      Exit, [as into the bush].

❖

9 **must** should have to.   **good now** i.e., please, for goodness' sake
11 **ancient** long-established   16 **pledge** drink a toast to   17 **breeds good blood** (Wine was thought to resupply the blood.)   21 **stomach** appetite.   27 **yours . . . tart** (1) your sauce is too sharp (2) your insolence is too keen   28 **lusty** agreeable, fortifying; lust-provoking
31 **After you** i.e., Go ahead with your toast, and I'll reciprocate

35 **virginals** a spinet-like keyboard instrument. (With sexual suggestion here.)   36–7 **groan . . . ten** i.e., suffer a pregnancy. (*Ten* is an approximation for nine).   39 **tales** false rumors   40 **brown** dark-complexioned, brunette   46 **break** i.e., break our convenant not to speak of Emilia.   **wide** wide of the mark.   51 **quiet** put an end to
52 **Fear me not** i.e., Don't worry about my not doing all I promised. (Palamon has just reiterated his demands.)   **foul** beastly.   53 **trinkets** i.e., the shackles, still to be filed off.   **want naught** lack nothing.
54 **keep touch** keeps his promise

3.4

Enter Jailer's Daughter.

JAILER'S DAUGHTER
I am very cold, and all the stars are out too,
The little stars and all, that look like aglets.   2
The sun has seen my folly.—Palamon!—
Alas, no; he's in heaven. Where am I now?
Yonder's the sea, and there's a ship. How't tumbles!
And there's a rock lies watching under water.
Now, now, it beats upon it; now, now, now,
There's a leak sprung, a sound one. How they cry!   8
Open her before the wind, you'll lose all else.   9
Up with a course or two, and tack about, boys.   10
Good night, good night, you're gone. I am very
    hungry;
Would I could find a fine frog! He would tell me
News from all parts o'th' world. Then would I make
A carrack of a cockleshell, and sail   14
By east and north-east to the king of pygmies,
For he tells fortunes rarely. Now my father,   16
Twenty to one, is trussed up in a trice   17
Tomorrow morning. I'll say never a word.
(Sing)
        For I'll cut my green coat a foot above my knee,
        And I'll clip my yellow locks an inch below
            mine e'e;
        Hey, nonny, nonny, nonny.
        He s' buy me a white cut, forth for to ride,   22
        And I'll go seek him through the world that is
            so wide;
        Hey, nonny, nonny, nonny.
Oh, for a prick now, like a nightingale,   25
To put my breast against! I shall sleep like a top else.
                                                Exit.

❖

3.[5]

*Enter a schoolmaster [Gerald], six Countrymen,
[one of whom is dressed as a] babion, five
Wenches, with a taborer [Timothy].*

SCHOOLMASTER   Fie, Fie,
What tediosity and disinsanity   2
Is here among ye? Have my rudiments   3

Been labored so long with ye, milked unto ye,
And, by a figure, even the very plum broth   5
And marrow of my understanding laid upon ye?   6
And do you still cry "Where?" and "How?" and
    "Wherefore?"
You most coarse frieze capacities, ye jean judgments, 8
Have I said, "Thus let be," and "There let be,"
And "Then let be," and no man understand me?
Proh deum, medius fidius, ye are all dunces!   11
Forwhy, here stand I. Here the Duke comes. There are
    you,   12
Close in the thicket. The Duke appears. I meet him,   13
And unto him I utter learnèd things
And many figures. He hears, and nods, and hums,   15
And then cries, "Rare!", and I go forward. At length   16
I fling my cap up; mark there! Then do you,
As once did Meleager and the boar,   18
Break comely out before him. Like true lovers,
Cast yourselves in a body decently,
And sweetly, by a figure, trace and turn, boys.   21
FIRST COUNTRYMAN
And sweetly we will do it, Master Gerald.
SECOND COUNTRYMAN
Draw up the company. Where's the taborer?
THIRD COUNTRYMAN [*calling*]
Why, Timothy!
TABORER   Here, my mad boys. Have at ye!   24
SCHOOLMASTER
But I say, where's their women?
FOURTH COUNTRYMAN   Here's Friz and Maudline.
SECOND COUNTRYMAN
And little Luce with the white legs, and bouncing
    Barbery.   26
FIRST COUNTRYMAN
And freckled Nell, that never failed her master.
SCHOOLMASTER
Where be your ribbons, maids? Swim with your
    bodies,   28
And carry it sweetly and deliverly,   29
And now and then a favor and a frisk.   30
NELL
Let us alone, sir.
SCHOOLMASTER   Where's the rest o'th' music?   31

3.4. Location: The forest, as before.
2 aglets spangles, ornamental studs peeping through eyelet-holes.
8 sound robust   **9 Open her** Unfurl her sails. (The talk of storms and
sailing vessels is indicative of the Daughter's madness and is filled
with sexual double meanings, as in the leaky vessel of line 8.)
10 course sails furled on the lower yard until they are hauled up and
unfurled   **14 carrack** large merchant ship or fighting vessel
16 rarely excellently.   **17 is . . . trice** will be hanged quickly
22 s' buy shall buy.   **cut** common laboring horse (with cut tail or a
gelding). Also a slang word suggesting the female sexual anatomy.
25 prick thorn, against which the nightingale was thought to lean in
order to stay awake. (With bawdy suggestion.)
3.5. Location: The forest still.
0.2 babion baboon   **0.3 *taborer*** player on the tabor or small drum
(and probably on the pipe as well)   **2 tediosity and disinsanity**
pedantic Latinisms for *tediousness and complete folly*   **3 rudiments**
basic teachings

5 by a figure to use a figure of speech   **5–6 plum . . . marrow** i.e.,
essence   **8 frieze capacities** persons with homespun mental capacities.   **jean** made of twilled cotton (named originally for Genoa)
11 Proh . . . fidius So help me the God of faith   **12 Forwhy** Wherefore, because   **13 Close** hidden   **15 figures** figures of speech.
16 Rare! Remarkable, excellent!   **18 Meleager and the boar** Evidently the Schoolmaster instructs the rustics to present themselves
before Duke Theseus as though acting out the story of the Greek warrior's slaying of the Calydonian boar; Hippolyta, at 1.1.78–9, is seemingly associated with the story. They are to come forward gracefully
(*break comely out*), arrange themselves in order (*cast . . . decently*), and
dance (*by a figure, trace and turn*). To trace is to step, "tread a measure," dance.   **21 trace** step, "tread a measure," dance   **24 Have at
ye!** i.e., Here we go, have a go at it.   **26 bouncing** strapping, plump
28 Swim Move gracefully   **29 carry it** execute the dance movement.
deliverly nimbly   **30 favor** gesture of friendly regard, such as bow-
ing or blowing a kiss.   **frisk** caper, jig.   **31 Let us alone** Leave it to
us.   **music** musicians.

THIRD COUNTRYMAN
  Dispersed, as you commanded.
SCHOOLMASTER   Couple then,   32
  And see what's wanting. Where's the babion?—   33
  My friend, carry your tail without offense
  Or scandal to the ladies; and be sure
  You tumble with audacity and manhood,
  And when you bark, do it with judgment.
BABION   Yes, sir.
SCHOOLMASTER
  Quousque tandem? Here is a woman wanting.   38
FOURTH COUNTRYMAN
  We may go whistle; all the fat's i'th' fire.   39
SCHOOLMASTER   We have,
  As learnèd authors utter, washed a tile;   40
  We have been *fatuus* and labored vainly.   41
SECOND COUNTRYMAN
  This is that scornful piece, that scurvy hilding   42
  That gave her promise faithfully she would be here—
  Cicely, the seamster's daughter.   44
  The next gloves that I give her shall be dogskin.   45
  Nay, an she fail me once—you can tell, Arcas,
  She swore by wine and bread she would not break.   47
SCHOOLMASTER   An eel and woman,
  A learnèd poet says, unless by th' tail
  And with thy teeth thou hold, will either fail.   50
  In manners this was false position.   51
FIRST COUNTRYMAN
  A fire ill take her! Does she flinch now?
THIRD COUNTRYMAN   What   52
  Shall we determine, sir?
SCHOOLMASTER   Nothing;   53
  Our business is become a nullity,
  Yea, and a woeful and a piteous nullity.
FOURTH COUNTRYMAN
  Now, when the credit of our town lay on it,
  Now to be frampold, now to piss o'th' nettle!   57
  Go thy ways, I'll remember thee, I'll fit thee!   58

        Enter Jailer's Daughter.

JAILER'S DAUGHTER [*sings*]
        The *George Alow* came from the south,   59
          From the coast of Barbary-a;
        And there he met with brave gallants of war,   61
          By one, by two, by three-a.

"Well hailed, well hailed, you jolly gallants,
  And whither now are you bound-a?
Oh, let me have your company
  Till I come to the sound-a."

There was three fools fell out about an owlet—

    [*She sings*]
  The one he said it was an owl,   68
    The other he said nay,
  The third he said it was a hawk,
    And her bells were cut away.   71
THIRD COUNTRYMAN
  There's a dainty madwoman, master,
  Comes i'th' nick, as mad as March hare.   73
  It we can get her dance, we are made again.   74
  I warrant her, she'll do the rarest gambols.   75
FIRST COUNTRYMAN
  A madwoman? We are made, boys!
SCHOOLMASTER [*to the Jailer's Daughter*]
  And are you mad, good woman?
JAILER'S DAUGHTER
  I would be sorry else. Give me your hand.
SCHOOLMASTER   Why?
JAILER'S DAUGHTER   I can tell your fortune.
  You are a fool. Tell ten; I have posed him. Buzz!   81
  Friend, you must eat no white bread; if you do,
  Your teeth will bleed extremely. Shall we dance, ho?
  I know you, you're a tinker. Sirrah tinker,   84
  Stop no more holes but what you should.
SCHOOLMASTER   *Dii boni!*   85
  A tinker, damsel?
JAILER'S DAUGHTER   Or a conjurer.
  Raise me a devil now, and let him play   87
  Qui passa o'th' bells and bones.
SCHOOLMASTER   Go take her,   88
  And fluently persuade her to a peace.   89
  Et opus exegi, quod nec Iovis ira, nec ignis.
  Strike up, and lead her in.
SECOND COUNTRYMAN   Come, lass, let's trip it.   91
JAILER'S DAUGHTER   I'll lead.
THIRD COUNTRYMAN   Do, do.
SCHOOLMASTER
  Persuasively and cunningly.
                        Wind horns.
                Away, boys!   94
  I hear the horns. Give me some meditation,   95

---

32 **Couple** Arrange yourself in pairs   33 **wanting** lacking.
38 *Quousque tandem?* How long, then? (From the beginning of
Cicero's Latin oration *Contra Catiline*: "How long, then, Catiline, will
you abuse our patience?")   39 **We . . . fire** i.e., We are out of luck,
all's come to nothing.   40 **washed a tile** i.e., striven in vain
41 *fatuus* foolish   42 **This . . . hilding** That's a scornful wench, that
wretched jade   44 **seamster's** tailor's   45 **dogskin** cheap leather.
47 **by wine and bread** by the Mass.   **break** break her promise.
50 **either fail** both prove too slippery. (Proverbial.)   51 **In . . . position** i.e., Cicely's failed promise was like a false assertion in logic.
52 **A fire . . . her!** (1) May a fire consume her! (2) May venereal disease infect her!   53 **determine** decide to do   57 **be frampold . . . piss
o'th' nettle** be ill-tempered . . . recalcitrant.   58 **Go . . . fit thee** Go
right ahead, I'll be even with you. (Said to the absent Cicely.)   59 **The
George Alow** (This ship was featured in a popular ballad, of which
the Jailer's Daughter sings a fragment.)   61 **gallants of war** warships

68–71 **The one . . . away** (A nursery rhyme.)   71 **bells** (In falconry,
the birds flew with bells hung from their legs.)   73 **th' nick** the nick
of time   74 **dance** to dance.   **we are made again** our fortunes are
restored.   75 **rarest gambols** most elegant leaps in dancing.   81 **Tell
. . . Buzz!** Count to ten; he can't, I've stumped him. Pshaw!   84 **tinker**
itinerant peddlers who mended kitchenware and the like were
thought of as rogues and vagabonds. (The reference to stopping holes
[line 85] is given a sexual double meaning.)   85 *Dii boni!* Good gods!
87–8 **let . . . bones** let him play a popular dance tune, *Qui (Chi) passa
per questa strada* ("Who passes through this street"), using bells and
bones as musical and percussion instruments.   89–91 **fluently . . .
Strike up** with graceful speech, persuade her to dance peacefully
with us. "And I have completed a work which neither the anger of
love nor fire [shall undo]." Start the music. (The Latin quotation is
from Ovid's *Metamorphoses*.)   94 **s.d. Wind** Sound   95 **meditation**
time to think

And mark your cue.

Exeunt all but [the] Schoolmaster.
Pallas, inspire me!   96

Enter Theseus, Pirithous, Hippolyta, Emilia,
Arcite, and train.

THESEUS   This way the stag took.
SCHOOLMASTER   Stay and edify.   98
THESEUS   What have we here?
PIRITHOUS   Some country sport, upon my life, sir.
THESEUS *[to the Schoolmaster]*
Well, sir, go forward; we will edify.
[Seats are brought for Theseus and the ladies.]
Ladies, sit down; we'll stay it.   *[They sit.]* 102
SCHOOLMASTER
Thou doughty Duke, all hail! All hail, sweet ladies! 103
THESEUS *[to Pirithous and the ladies]*
This is a cold beginning.   104
SCHOOLMASTER
If you but favor, our country pastime made is.   105
We are a few of those collected here
That ruder tongues distinguish "villager";   107
And to say verity, and not to fable,
We are a merry rout, or else a rabble,   109
Or company, or, by a figure, chorus,   110
That 'fore thy dignity will dance a morris.   111
And I that am the rectifier of all,   112
By title *pedagogus*, that let fall   113
The birch upon the breeches of the small ones,
And humble with a ferula the tall ones,   115
Do here present this machine, or this frame;   116
And, dainty Duke, whose doughty dismal fame   117
From Dis to Daedalus, from post to pillar,   118
Is blown abroad, help me, thy poor well-willer,
And with thy twinkling eyes, look right and straight
Upon this mighty "Morr" of mickle weight.   121
"Is" now comes in, which, being glued together,   122
Makes "Morris," and the cause that we came hither.   123
The body of our sport, of no small study,   124
I first appear, though rude, and raw, and muddy,
To speak before thy noble grace this tenner,   126

At whose great feet I offer up my penner.   127
The next, the Lord of May and Lady bright;   128
The Chambermaid and Servingman, by night
That seek out silent hanging; then mine Host   130
And his fat Spouse, that welcomes to their cost   131
The gallèd traveller, and with a beck'ning   132
Informs the tapster to inflame the reck'ning;   133
Then the beest-eating Clown; and next the Fool;   134
The Babion with long tail and eke long tool,   135
Cum multis aliis that make a dance;   136
Say "ay," and all shall presently advance.   137
THESEUS
Ay, ay, by any means, dear dominie.
PIRITHOUS   Produce!   138
SCHOOLMASTER *(knock for [the] school)*
Intrate, filii; come forth and foot it.   139

Music.

Enter the [Countrymen, the Taborer, the Wenches,
and the Jailer's Daughter. They] dance [a morris].

Ladies, if we have been merry,
And have pleased ye with a derry,   141
And a derry and a down,
Say the schoolmaster's no clown.
Duke, if we have pleased thee too,
And have done as good boys should do,
Give us but a tree or twain
For a maypole, and again,
Ere another year run out,
We'll make thee laugh, and all this rout.
THESEUS
Take twenty, dominie. *[To Hippolyta]* How does my
sweetheart?
HIPPOLYTA
Never so pleased, sir.
EMILIA   'Twas an excellent dance,
And for a preface, I never heard a better.   152
THESEUS
Schoolmaster, I thank you.—One see 'em all
rewarded.   153
PIRITHOUS
And here's something to paint your pole withal.
[He gives them money.]
THESEUS   Now to our sports again.   155
SCHOOLMASTER
May the stag thou hunt'st stand long,   156
And thy dogs be swift and strong;

96 Pallas Pallas Athene   **98 edify** be instructed.   **102 stay it** stay to attend the presentation.   **103 doughty** valiant, worthy   **104 cold** (Theseus puns on the meteorological meaning of "hail.")   **105 favor** grant the favor of your attention   **107 ruder** county-bred.   **distinguish** classify or characterize as   **109 rout** assembly   **110 figure** figure of speech   **111 'fore thy dignity** in your royal presence   **112 rectifier** one who corrects, the director, but also the one who corrects and spanks students (in lines 113–15)   **113 pedagogus** schoolmaster **115 ferula** cane used to punish older students   **116 this machine . . . frame** this device, this construction (the entertainment)   **117 dainty** gracious.   **dismal** unpropitious (to your enemies). (The words are chosen partly for their alliteration.)   **118 From Dis to Daedalus** from the underworld to the labyrinth of Daedalus. (Again with alliterative effect.)   **121–3 "Morr" . . . "Is" . . . "Morris"** To achieve this pedantry, the Schoolmaster has evidently outfitted two of his dancers to depict "Morr" (perhaps signifying "Moor") and "Is" (perhaps "ice"); when they stand together, the result is "Morris."   **121 mickle** much **124 The body . . . study** (1) The substance of our entertainment, mastered with no small amount of effort (2) I, as the structural centerpiece of our entertainment, a person of considerable learning **126 tenner** i.e., ten-syllable line. (Punning also on *tenor*, purport.)

127 penner leather sheath for pens.   **128 Lady** i.e., Queen of May, Maid Marian   **130 silent hanging** wall or bed curtains behind which to seek concealment   **131–2 to their . . . traveller** chafed and weary travelers, who find their welcome a costly one   **133 inflame the reck'ning** inflate the bill   **134 beest-eating** eating the first milk to be drawn from a cow after it gives birth. (Such a diet characterizes the Clown as a country bumpkin.)   **135 tool** penis.   **136 Cum multis aliis** with many others   **137 presently** immediately   **138 dominie** schoolmaster.   **Produce!** Bring them forth!   **139 s.d. knock for [the] school** The schoolmaster signals for those under his tutelage to enter. **139 Intrate, filii** Come in, my boys.   **foot it** dance.   **141 derry** ballad, refrain. ("Derry down derry" is a common nonsense refrain.) **152 for** as for   **153 One** Someone   **155 sports** hunting   **156 stand long** hold out a long time (thus providing good sport)

May they kill him without lets,   158
And the ladies eat his dowsets.   159
          Wind horns [within. Exeunt Theseus and train.]
Come, we are all made. *Dii deaeque omnes!*   160
Ye have danced rarely, wenches.   *Exeunt.*

❧

3.[6]

Enter Palamon from the bush.

PALAMON
About this hour my cousin gave his faith
To visit me again, and with him bring
Two swords and two good armors. If he fail,   3
He's neither man nor soldier. When he left me,
I did not think a week could have restored
My lost strength to me, I was grown so low
And crest-fall'n with my wants. I thank thee, Arcite,
Thou art yet a fair foe; and I feel myself,
With this refreshing, able once again
To outdure danger. To delay it longer   10
Would make the world think, when it comes to
     hearing,   11
That I lay fatting like a swine to fight,   12
And not a soldier. Therefore this blest morning
Shall be the last; and that sword he refuses,   14
If it but hold, I kill him with; 'tis justice.   15
So, love and fortune for me!

Enter Arcite with [suits of] armor and swords.

                         Oh, good morrow.

ARCITE
Good morrow, noble kinsman.
PALAMON   I have put you
To too much pains, sir.
ARCITE   That too much, fair cousin,
Is but a debt to honor and my duty.
PALAMON
Would you were so in all, sir. I could wish ye   20
As kind a kinsman as you force me find   21
A beneficial foe, that my embraces   22
Might thank ye, not my blows.
ARCITE   I shall think either,
Well done, a noble recompense.
PALAMON   Then I shall quit you. 24
ARCITE
Defy me in these fair terms, and you show   25

More than a mistress to me. No more anger,
As you love anything that's honorable!
We were not bred to talk, man; when we are armed,
And both upon our guards, then let our fury,
Like meeting of two tides, fly strongly from us,
And then to whom the birthright of this beauty   31
Truly pertains—without upbraidings, scorns,   32
Despisings of our persons, and such poutings,
Fitter for girls and schoolboys—will be seen,
And quickly, yours or mine. Will't please you arm, sir?
Or if you feel yourself not fitting yet   36
And furnished with your old strength, I'll stay, cousin,
And ev'ry day discourse you into health,
As I am spared. Your person I am friends with,   39
And I could wish I had not said I loved her,
Though I had died; but loving such a lady,   41
And justifying my love, I must not fly from't.
PALAMON
Arcite, thou art so brave an enemy
That no man but thy cousin's fit to kill thee.
I am well and lusty; choose your arms.
ARCITE   Choose you, sir. 45
PALAMON
Wilt thou exceed in all, or dost thou do it   46
To make me spare thee?
ARCITE   If you think so, cousin,
You are deceivèd, for, as I am a soldier,
I will not spare you.
PALAMON   That's well said.
ARCITE   You'll find it.   49
PALAMON
Then, as I am an honest man, and love
With all the justice of affection,
I'll pay thee soundly.   *[He chooses one suit of armor.]*
                 This I'll take.
ARCITE *[indicating the other suit]*   That's mine, then. 52
I'll arm you first.
PALAMON   Do. Pray thee tell me, cousin,
Where got'st thou this good armor?
ARCITE *[arming Palamon]*   'Tis the Duke's,
And to say true, I stole it. Do I pinch you?
PALAMON
No.
ARCITE   Is't not too heavy?
PALAMON   I have worn a lighter,
But I shall make it serve.
ARCITE   I'll buckle't close.
PALAMON
By any means.
ARCITE   You care not for a grand guard?   58
PALAMON
No, no, we'll use no horses. I perceive

---

158 lets hindrances   **159 dowsets** testicles—considered a delicacy.
160 *Dii deaeque omnes!* All gods and goddesses!
**3.6. Location: The forest still. Palamon's entrance "from the bush"
suggests some sort of visual indication at a stage door or structure.**
3 armors suits of armor.   **10 outdure** endure, outlast
11 when . . . hearing when the matter is generally known   **12 fatting
. . . fight** lazing about in my preparations for fighting like a swine
being fattened for the kill   **14–15 that sword . . . hold** the sword he
brings for me to use (having chosen the other one for himself), so
long as it remains whole. (At line 45 Palamon offers Arcite his choice
of weapons.)   **20–2 Would . . . foe** I wish you were as honorable in all
things as you are in providing these weapons and armor. I could wish
you were as kind a kinsman as what you oblige me to find you are
instead: an enemy who does me this benefit (of providing armor and
food.)   **24 quit** repay   **25 show** show yourself to be

31–2 to whom . . . pertains the one who can claim the beautiful
Emilia by right of birth   **36 fitting** prepared   **39 As I am spared** as
far as I have time.   **41 Though I had died** even if my remaining
silent had killed me   **45 lusty** healthy, strong   **46 exceed in all** go
beyond me in everything that is chivalrous   **49 You'll find it** i.e., I
mean to do what I've said I'll do.   **52 pay** reward, punish   **58 grand
guard** armor plate covering the breast and left shoulder, used in tour-
naments and hence appropriate for tilting on horseback (as Palamon
implies in line 59).

You would fain be at that fight.
ARCITE   I am indifferent.   60
PALAMON
Faith, so am I. Good cousin, thrust the buckle
Through far enough.
ARCITE   I warrant you.
PALAMON   My casque now.   62
ARCITE
Will you fight bare-armed?
PALAMON   We shall be the nimbler.
ARCITE
But use your gauntlets, though. Those are o'th' least.   64
Prithee take mine, good cousin
PALAMON   Thank you, Arcite.
How do I look? Am I fall'n much away?   66
ARCITE
Faith, very little; love has used you kindly.
PALAMON
I'll warrant thee, I'll strike home.
ARCITE   Do, and spare not.   68
I'll give you cause, sweet cousin.
PALAMON   Now to you, sir.
[Arming Arcite] Methinks this armor's very like that,
    Arcite,
Thou wor'st that day the three kings fell, but lighter.
ARCITE
That was a very good one, and that day,
I well remember, you outdid me, cousin;
I never saw such valor. When you charged
Upon the left wing of the enemy,
I spurred hard to come up, and under me   76
I had a right good horse.
PALAMON   You had indeed;
A bright bay, I remember.
ARCITE   Yes, but all   78
Was vainly labored in me; you outwent me,
Nor could my wishes reach you. Yet a little
I did by imitation.
PALAMON   More by virtue.   81
You are modest, cousin.
ARCITE   When I saw you charge first,
Methought I heard a dreadful clap of thunder
Break from the troop.
PALAMON   But still before that flew
The lightning of your valor. Stay a little;
Is not this piece too strait?
ARCITE   No, no, 'tis well.   86
PALAMON
I would have nothing hurt thee but my sword;
A bruise would be dishonor.
ARCITE   Now I am perfect.   88
PALAMON
Stand off, then.
ARCITE   Take my sword; I hold it better.   89

PALAMON
I thank ye. No, keep it; your life lies on it.   90
Here's one; if it but hold, I ask no more
For all my hopes. My cause and honor guard me!
ARCITE
And me my love!

They bow several ways, then advance and stand.

                Is there aught else to say?   93
PALAMON
This only, and no more: thou art mine aunt's son,
And that blood we desire to shed is mutual—
In me, thine, and in thee, mine. My sword
Is in my hand, and if thou kill'st me,
The gods and I forgive thee! If there be
A place prepared for those that sleep in honor,
I wish his weary soul that falls may win it.
Fight bravely, cousin. Give me thy noble hand.
ARCITE [as they clasp hands]
Here, Palamon. This hand shall never more
Come near thee with such friendship.
PALAMON   I commend thee.   103
ARCITE
If I fall, curse me, and say I was a coward,
For none but such dare die in these just trials.   105
Once more farewell, my cousin.
PALAMON   Farewell, Arcite.

        [They] fight. Horns within. They stand.

ARCITE
Lo, cousin, lo, our folly has undone us.
PALAMON   Why?
ARCITE
This is the Duke, a-hunting, as I told you.
If we be found, we are wretched. Oh, retire
For honor's sake, and safely, presently,
Into your bush again. Sir, we shall find
Too many hours to die in. Gentle cousin,
If you be seen, you perish instantly
For breaking prison, and I, if you reveal me,
For my contempt. Then all the world will scorn us,   115
And say we had a noble difference,   116
But base disposers of it.
PALAMON   No, no, cousin,   117
I will no more be hidden, nor put off
This great adventure to a second trial.   119
I know your cunning, and I know your cause;
He that faints now, shame take him! Put thyself   121
Upon thy present guard.
ARCITE   You are not mad?   122
PALAMON
Or I will make th'advantage of this hour

---

60 would . . . fight would prefer to fight that way, mounted.   62 warrant promise.   casque helmet   64 gauntlets plated gloves.   o'th'
least too small.   66 fall'n much away much thinner.   68 home to the
heart.   76 come up come up from the rear   78 bay reddish brown
81 virtue manliness.   86 strait tight-fitting.   88 perfect i.e., correctly
armed in every detail.   89 hold it better regard it as the better one.

90 lies depends   93 s.d. *several ways* in various directions, as
though to those witnessing a tournament   103 commend thee commend you to the gods.   105 For none . . . trials i.e., only the unworthy are sure to lose in trial by combat, since the gods will give victory
to the just.   115 contempt i.e., disobedience of the decree of banishment.   116–17 we had . . . of it we had a noble quarrel but were
guilty of conducting it in defiance of royal command.   119 adventure venture   121 faints proves fainthearted   122 Upon . . . guard on
guard at once.

Mine own, and what to come shall threaten me 124
I fear less than my fortune. Know, weak cousin, 125
I love Emilia, and in that I'll bury
Thee and all crosses else.

ARCITE   Then come what can come, 127
Thou shalt know, Palamon, I dare as well
Die as discourse or sleep. Only this fears me: 129
The law will have the honor of our ends. 130
Have at thy life!

PALAMON   Look to thine own well, Arcite!

[They] fight again.

*Horns. Enter Theseus, Hippolyta, Emilia,
Pirithous, and train. [Palamon and Arcite are
separated.]*

THESEUS
What ignorant and mad malicious traitors
Are you, that 'gainst the tenor of my laws
Are making battle, thus like knights appointed, 134
Without my leave and officers of arms? 135
By Castor, both shall die.

PALAMON   Hold thy word, Theseus. 136
We are certainly both traitors, both despisers
Of thee and of thy goodness. I am Palamon,
That cannot love thee, he that broke thy prison;
Think well what that deserves. And this is Arcite;
A bolder traitor never trod thy ground,
A falser nev'r seemed friend. This is the man
Was begged and banished, this is he contemns thee 143
And what thou dar'st do, and in this disguise,
Against thine own edict, follows thy sister,
That fortunate bright star, the fair Emilia,
Whose servant—if there be a right in seeing, 147
And first bequeathing of the soul to—justly
I am; and, which is more, dares think her his.
This treachery, like a most trusty lover,
I called him now to answer. If thou be'st
As thou art spoken, great and virtuous,
The true decider of all injuries, 153
Say "Fight again," and thou shalt see me, Theseus,
Do such a justice thou thyself wilt envy.
Then take my life; I'll woo thee to't.

PIRITHOUS   O heaven, 156
What more than man is this!

THESEUS   I have sworn.

ARCITE   We seek not
Thy breath of mercy, Theseus. 'Tis to me 158
A thing as soon to die as thee to say it,
And no more moved. Where this man calls me traitor, 160

Let me say thus much: if in love be treason,
In service of so excellent a beauty,
As I love most, and in that faith will perish,
As I have brought my life here to confirm it,
As I have served her truest, worthiest,
As I dare kill this cousin that denies it,
So let me be most traitor, and ye please me. 167
For scorning thy edict, Duke, ask that lady 168
Why she is fair, and why her eyes command me
Stay here to love her; and if she say "traitor,"
I am a villain fit to lie unburied.

PALAMON
Thou shalt have pity of us both, O Theseus,
If unto neither thou show mercy. Stop,
As thou art just, thy noble ear against us;
As thou art valiant, for thy cousin's soul, 175
Whose twelve strong labors crown his memory,
Let's die together at one instant, Duke. 177
Only a little let him fall before me,
That I may tell my soul he shall not have her.

THESEUS
I grant your wish, for to say true, your cousin
Has ten times more offended, for I gave him
More mercy than you found, sir, your offenses 182
Being no more than his.—None here speak for 'em,
For ere the sun set both shall sleep for ever.

HIPPOLYTA *[to Emilia]*
Alas, the pity! Now or never, sister,
Speak not to be denied. That face of yours
Will bear the curses else of after ages
For these lost cousins.

EMILIA   In my face, dear sister,
I find no anger to 'em, nor no ruin;
The misadventure of their own eyes kill 'em. 190
Yet that I will be woman and have pity, *[kneeling]*
My knees shall grow to th' ground but I'll get mercy. 192
Help me, dear sister; in a deed so virtuous,
The powers of all women will be with us.—
Most royal brother—

HIPPOLYTA *[kneeling]*   Sir, by our tie of marriage—

EMILIA
By your own spotless honor—

HIPPOLYTA   By that faith,
That fair hand, and that honest heart you gave me—

EMILIA
By that you would have pity in another, 198
By your own virtues infinite—

HIPPOLYTA   By valor,
By all the chaste nights I have ever pleased you— 200

THESEUS
These are strange conjurings.

PIRITHOUS *[kneeling]*   Nay then, I'll in too.

124–5 **what . . . fortune** I fear whatever the future may threaten me with less than the outcome of this present fight.   127 **crosses else** other thwartings or afflictions.   129 **fears** frightens   130 **The law . . . ends** The law will execute us rather than allowing us to settle this matter honorably.   134 **appointed** accoutered in arms   135 **officers of arms** referees of chivalric combat.   136 **Castor** one of Jupiter's sons, twin brother of Pollux.   **Hold** Keep   143 **Was begged** whose life was begged of you. (See 2.2.251–4.)   **contemns** scorns   147 **servant** knight devoted to the service of the lady he loves. (Palamon claims a prior right to be Emilia's "servant" by virtue of having seen her first and having given his soul to her, lines 147–8.)   153 **injuries** wrongful acts   156 **Then** After that   158–60 **'Tis . . . moved** My death would mean no more to me than it would to you in uttering the judgment.

167 **So . . . me** if that is what "traitor" means, you will gratify me by calling me such.   168 **For** As for   175 **thy cousin's** Hercules's, who was famous for his twelve labors (line 176)   177 **Let's** let the two of us   182 **More . . . found** (Theseus released Arcite from prison, though banishing him, while Palamon remained in prison.)   190 **The misadventure . . . 'em** i.e., they are sentenced to die not by my anger but by their own rash quarreling over me.   192 **but** unless and until   198 **that** your hope that.   **in** from   200 **chaste nights** nights spent in monogamous wedded happiness

By all our friendship, sir, by all our dangers,
By all you love most, wars and this sweet lady—
EMILIA
By that you would have trembled to deny   204
A blushing maid—
HIPPOLYTA   By your own eyes, by strength,   205
In which you swore I went beyond all women,   206
Almost all men, and yet I yielded, Theseus—
PIRITHOUS
To crown all this, by your most noble soul,
Which cannot want due mercy, I beg first—   209
HIPPOLYTA
Next hear my prayers—
EMILIA   Last let me entreat, sir—
PIRITHOUS
For mercy.
HIPPOLYTA   Mercy.
EMILIA   Mercy on these princes.
THESEUS
Ye make my faith reel. [*To Emilia*] Say I felt   212
Compassion to 'em both, how would you place it?
                                    [*They rise.*]
EMILIA
Upon their lives—but with their banishments.
THESEUS
You are a right woman, sister; you have pity,   215
But want the understanding where to use it.
If you desire their lives, invent a way
Safer than banishment. Can these two live,
And have the agony of love about 'em,
And not kill one another? Every day
They'd fight about you, hourly bring your honor   221
In public question with their swords. Be wise, then, 222
And here forget 'em; it concerns your credit
And my oath equally. I have said they die;
Better they fall by th' law than one another.
Bow not my honor.
EMILIA   O my noble brother,   226
That oath was rashly made, and in your anger;
Your reason will not hold it. If such vows   228
Stand for express will, all the world must perish. 229
Beside, I have another oath 'gainst yours,
Of more authority, I am sure more love,
Not made in passion neither, but good heed.   232
THESEUS
What is it, sister?
PIRITHOUS   Urge it home, brave lady.   233
EMILIA
That you would nev'r deny me anything
Fit for my modest suit and your free granting.
I tie you to your word now; if ye fail in't,

Think how you maim your honor—
For now I am set a-begging, sir, I am deaf
To all but your compassion—how their lives   239
Might breed the ruin of my name, opinion.   240
Shall anything that loves me perish for me?
That were a cruel wisdom. Do men prune
The straight young boughs that blush with thousand
     blossoms
Because they may be rotten? O Duke Theseus,   244
The goodly mothers that have groaned for these,   245
And all the longing maids that ever loved,
If your vow stand, shall curse me and my beauty,
And in their funeral songs for these two cousins
Despise my cruelty, and cry woe worth me,   249
Till I am nothing but the scorn of women.
For heaven's sake, save their lives and banish 'em.
THESEUS
On what conditions?
EMILIA   Swear 'em never more   252
To make me their contention, or to know me,   253
To tread upon thy dukedom, and to be,
Wherever they shall travel, ever strangers
To one another.
PALAMON   I'll be cut a-pieces
Before I take this oath. Forget I love her?
O all ye gods, despise me then. Thy banishment   258
I not mislike, so we may fairly carry   259
Our swords and cause along; else never trifle,
But take our lives, Duke. I must love and will,
And for that love must and dare kill this cousin
On any piece the earth has.
THESEUS   Will you, Arcite,   263
Take these conditions?
PALAMON   He's a villain, then.
PIRITHOUS   These are men!
ARCITE
No, never, Duke. 'Tis worse to me than begging
To take my life so basely. Though I think
I never shall enjoy her, yet I'll preserve
The honor of affection, and die for her,   268
Make death a devil.   269
THESEUS
What may be done? For now I feel compassion.
PIRITHOUS
Let it not fall again, sir.
THESEUS   Say, Emilia,   271
If one of them were dead, as one must, are you
Content to take th'other to your husband?   273
They cannot both enjoy you. They are princes
As goodly as your own eyes, and as noble
As ever fame yet spoke of. Look upon 'em,

204–5 By . . . maid by the chivalrous obligations that you would not wish to deny to a maiden in distress   **206 went beyond** excelled   **209 want** be lacking in   **212 Ye . . . reel** You shake my hitherto unwavering oath.   **215 right** veritable, typical.   **sister** sister-in-law   **221–2 bring . . . question** fight publicly over the honor of being your servant   **226 Bow . . . honor** Do not oblige me to yield dishonorably.   **228 hold it** keep to it.   **229 Stand . . . will** are to be taken as unshakable resolve   **232 passion** anger.   **good heed** thoughtfully.   **233 home** to the quick

239 their lives i.e., their deaths   **240 name, opinion** reputation.   **244 be** become in time   **245 groaned** groaned in childbearing   **249 worth** befall, betide   **252 Swear 'em** Oblige them to swear   **253 know** acknowledge   **258 Thy banishment** The banishment you propose   **259 so** provided.   **fairly** fitly, justly   **263 piece** piece of ground   **268 The honor of affection** the honor of devoting my love and service to her   **269 Make . . . devil** no matter how horrible a death I must die.   **271 fall** diminish, fail   **273 to your** for, as your

And, if you can love, end this difference.
I give consent.—Are you content too, princes?

PALAMON AND ARCITE
With all our souls.

THESEUS   He that she refuses
Must die, then.

PALAMON AND ARCITE   Any death thou canst invent, Duke.

PALAMON
If I fall from that mouth, I fall with favor,   281
And lovers yet unborn shall bless my ashes.

ARCITE
If she refuse me, yet my grave will wed me,
And soldiers sing my epitaph.

THESEUS [to Emilia]   Make choice, then.

EMILIA
I cannot, sir; they are both too excellent.
For me, a hair shall never fall of these men.   286

HIPPOLYTA
What will become of 'em?

THESEUS   Thus I ordain it,
And by mine honor, once again, it stands,
Or both shall die. [To Palamon and Arcite] You shall
    both to your country,
And each, within this month, accompanied
With three fair knights, appear again in this place,
In which I'll plant a pyramid; and whether,   292
Before us that are here, can force his cousin
By fair and knightly strength to touch the pillar,
He shall enjoy her; the other lose his head,
And all his friends; nor shall he grudge to fall,   296
Nor think he dies with interest in this lady.   297
Will this content ye?

PALAMON   Yes. Here, cousin Arcite,
I am friends again till that hour.

ARCITE   I embrace ye.
                                    [They embrace.]

THESEUS
Are you content, sister?

EMILIA   Yes, I must, sir,
Else both miscarry.

THESEUS [to Palamon and Arcite]
                          Come, shake hands again, then,
And take heed, as you are gentlemen, this quarrel
Sleep till the hour prefixed, and hold your course.

PALAMON
We dare not fail thee, Theseus.

THESEUS   Come, I'll give ye
Now usage like to princes and to friends.
When ye return, who wins I'll settle here;   306
Who loses yet I'll weep upon his bier.
                                              Exeunt.

281 **from that mouth** as a result of the decision she pronounces
286 **For me** On my account   292 **plant a pyramid** erect an obelisk or
pillar.   **whether** whichever of you two   296–7 **And . . . lady** and all
his followers shall die also; nor shall he protest that the sentence is
unjust, or that he continues to have a claim upon Emilia.   306 **who . . .
here** whoever wins I'll make a member of my court here in Athens

4.1

Enter Jailer and his Friend.

JAILER
Hear you no more? Was nothing said of me
Concerning the escape of Palamon?
Good sir, remember.

FIRST FRIEND   Nothing that I heard,
For I came home before the business
Was fully ended. Yet I might perceive,
Ere I departed, a great likelihood
Of both their pardons; for Hippolyta
And fair-eyed Emily, upon their knees,
Begged with such handsome pity that the Duke,
Methought, stood staggering whether he should
    follow
His rash oath or the sweet compassion
Of those two ladies; and to second them
That truly noble prince, Pirithous—
Half his own heart—set in too, that I hope   14
All shall be well; neither heard I one question
Of your name or his scape.

Enter Second Friend.

JAILER   Pray heaven it hold so.

SECOND FRIEND
Be of good comfort, man! I bring you news,
Good news.

JAILER   They are welcome.

SECOND FRIEND   Palamon has cleared you,   18
And got your pardon, and discovered how   19
And by whose means he escaped, which was your
    daughter's,
Whose pardon is procured too, and the prisoner,
Not to be held ungrateful to her goodness,
Has given a sum of money to her marriage—
A large one, I'll assure you.

JAILER   Ye are a good man
And ever bring good news.

FIRST FRIEND   How was it ended?

SECOND FRIEND
Why, as it should be: they that nev'r begged
But they prevailed had their suits fairly granted;
The prisoners have their lives.

FIRST FRIEND   I knew 'twould be so.

SECOND FRIEND
But there be new conditions, which you'll hear of
At better time.

JAILER   I hope they are good.

SECOND FRIEND   They are honorable;
How good they'll prove I know not.

Enter Wooer.

FIRST FRIEND   'Twill be known.

WOOER
Alas, sir, where's your daughter?

JAILER   Why do you ask?

4.1. Location: The prison.
14 that so that   **18 They** The news   **19 discovered** revealed

WOOER
    Oh, sir, when did you see her?
SECOND FRIEND [*aside*]   How he looks!
JAILER
    This morning.
WOOER   Was she well? Was she in health?
    Sir, when did she sleep?
FIRST FRIEND   These are strange questions.
JAILER
    I do not think she was very well, for now
    You make me mind her, but this very day   37
    I asked her questions, and she answered me
    So far from what she was, so childishly,   39
    So sillily, as if she were a fool,
    An innocent, and I was very angry.   41
    But what of her, sir?
WOOER   Nothing but my pity;
    But you must know it, and as good by me
    As by another that less loves her.
JAILER
    Well, sir?
FIRST FRIEND   Not right?
SECOND FRIEND   Not well?
WOOER   No, sir, not well.   45
    'Tis too true, she is mad.
FIRST FRIEND   It cannot be.
WOOER
    Believe you'll find it so.
JAILER   I half suspected
    What you told me. The gods comfort her!
    Either this was her love to Palamon,
    Or fear of my miscarrying on his scape,   50
    Or both.
WOOER   'Tis likely.
JAILER   But why all this haste, sir?
WOOER
    I'll tell you quickly. As I late was angling   52
    In the great lake that lies behind the palace,
    From the far shore, thick set with reeds and sedges,
    As patiently I was attending sport,   55
    I heard a voice—a shrill one; and attentive,
    I gave my ear, when I might well perceive
    'Twas one that sung, and by the smallness of it   58
    A boy or woman. I then left my angle   59
    To his own skill, came near, but yet perceived not 60
    Who made the sound, the rushes and the reeds
    Had so encompassed it. I laid me down
    And listened to the words she sung, for then,
    Through a small glade cut by the fishermen,   64
    I saw it was your daughter.
JAILER   Pray go on, sir.
WOOER
    She sung much, but no sense, only I heard her
    Repeat this often: "Palamon is gone,

    Is gone to th' wood to gather mulberries;
    I'll find him out tomorrow."
FIRST FRIEND   Pretty soul!
WOOER
    "His shackles will betray him; he'll be taken,
    And what shall I do then? I'll bring a bevy,
    A hundred black-eyed maids that love as I do,
    With chaplets on their heads of daffadillies,   73
    With cherry lips and cheeks of damask roses,   74
    And all we'll dance an antic 'fore the Duke,   75
    And beg his pardon." Then she talked of you, sir— 76
    That you must lose your head tomorrow morning,
    And she must gather flowers to bury you,
    And see the house made handsome. Then she sung
    Nothing but "Willow, willow, willow," and between
    Ever was "Palamon, fair Palamon,"
    And "Palamon was a tall young man." The place 82
    Was knee-deep where she sat. Her careless tresses 83
    A wreath of bulrush rounded; about her stuck   84
    Thousand freshwater flowers of several colors,
    That methought she appeared like the fair nymph
    That feeds the lake with waters, or as Iris,   87
    Newly dropped down from heaven. Rings she made
    Of rushes that grew by, and to 'em spoke
    The prettiest posies: "Thus our true love's tied," 90
    "This you may lose, not me," and many a one;
    And then she wept, and sung again, and sighed,
    And with the same breath smiled and kissed her hand.
SECOND FRIEND
    Alas, what pity it is!
WOOER   I made in to her.   94
    She saw me, and straight sought the flood. I saved her 95
    And set her safe to land, when presently
    She slipped away, and to the city made
    With such a cry and swiftness that, believe me,
    She left me far behind her. Three or four
    I saw from far off cross her—one of 'em   100
    I knew to be your brother—where she stayed   101
    And fell, scarce to be got away. I left them with her 102

    Enter [Jailer's] Brother, [Jailer's] Daughter, and
    others.

    And hither came to tell you. Here they are.
JAILER'S DAUGHTER [*sings*]
    May you never more enjoy the light . . . (etc.)
    Is not this a fine song?
JAILER'S BROTHER   Oh, a very fine one.
JAILER'S DAUGHTER
    I can sing twenty more.
JAILER'S BROTHER   I think you can.
JAILER'S DAUGHTER
    Yes, truly can I; I can sing "The Broom,"

---

37 **mind** think of. **but** only 39 **So far . . . was** so differently from
her usual way 41 **innocent** simpleton 45 **right** in her right mind.
50 **miscarrying on** suffering misfortune on account of 52 **late**
recently. **angling** fishing 55 **attending sport** i.e., waiting for a bite
58 **smallness** high pitch 59 **angle** fishing tackle. 60 **To his own
skill** to manage itself 64 **glade** clearing

73 **chaplets** garlands of flowers 74 **of damask roses** rose-colored
75 **antic** quaint or grotesque pageant 76 **beg his pardon** beg the life
of Palamon. 82 **tall** handsome, valiant 83–4 **Her . . . rounded** A
garland of bulrushes encircled her disheveled tresses 87 **Iris** goddess of the rainbow and messenger of Hera 90 **posies** short mottoes,
often inscribed within rings 94 **made in to** advanced toward
95 **straight . . . flood** immediately got in the water 100 **cross** inter-
cept 101 **stayed** halted 102 **scarce . . . away** almost unremovable.

And "Bonny Robin." Are not you a tailor?
JAILER'S BROTHER
Yes.
JAILER'S DAUGHTER
    Where's my wedding gown?
JAILER'S BROTHER   I'll bring it tomorrow.
JAILER'S DAUGHTER
Do, very rarely; I must be abroad else   110
To call the maids and pay the minstrels,
For I must lose my maidenhead by cocklight;   112
'Twill never thrive else.
(*Sings*)   O fair, O sweet . . . (etc.)
JAILER'S BROTHER [*to the Jailer*]
You must ev'n take it patiently.
JAILER   'Tis true.
JAILER'S DAUGHTER
Good ev'n, good men. Pray, did you ever hear
Of one young Palamon?
JAILER   Yes, wench, we know him.
JAILER'S DAUGHTER
Is't not a fine young gentleman?
JAILER   'Tis, love.
JAILER'S BROTHER [*to the others*]
By no mean cross her; she is then distempered   119
Far worse than now she shows.
FIRST FRIEND [*to the Jailer's Daughter*]
    Yes, he's a fine man.
JAILER'S DAUGHTER
Oh, is he so? You have a sister.
FIRST FRIEND   Yes.
JAILER'S DAUGHTER
But she shall never have him, tell her so,
For a trick that I know. You'd best look to her,   123
For if she see him once, she's gone—she's done
And undone in an hour. All the young maids
Of our town are in love with him, but I laugh at 'em
And let 'em all alone. Is't not a wise course?
FIRST FRIEND   Yes.   127
JAILER'S DAUGHTER
There is at least two hundred now with child by him—
There must be four; yet I keep close for all this,   129
Close as a cockle; and all these must be boys—   130
He has the trick on't—and at ten years old   131
They must be all gelt for musicians,   132
And sing the wars of Theseus.
SECOND FRIEND [*to the others*]   This is strange.
JAILER'S BROTHER [*to the Second Friend*]
As ever you heard; but say nothing.
FIRST FRIEND   No.
JAILER'S DAUGHTER
They come from all parts of the dukedom to him.

I'll warrant ye, he had not so few last night   136
As twenty to dispatch. He'll tickle't up   137
In two hours, if his hand be in.
JAILER [*to the others*]   She's lost   138
Past all cure.
JAILER'S BROTHER   Heaven forbid, man!
JAILER'S DAUGHTER [*to the Jailer*]
Come hither; you are a wise man.
FIRST FRIEND [*to the Second Friend*]   Does she know him?
SECOND FRIEND [*to the First Friend*]
No; would she did.
JAILER'S DAUGHTER   You are master of a ship?
JAILER   Yes.
JAILER'S DAUGHTER   Where's your compass?
JAILER   Here.
JAILER'S DAUGHTER   Set it to th' north;   145
And now direct your course to th' wood, where Palamon
Lies longing for me. For the tackling,   147
Let me alone. Come, weigh, my hearts, cheerly all.   148
Owgh, owgh, owgh! 'Tis up.   149
The wind's fair. Top the bowline.   150
Out with the mainsail! Where's your whistle, master?
JAILER'S BROTHER   Let's get her in.
JAILER   Up to the top, boy!
JAILER'S BROTHER   Where's the pilot?
FIRST FRIEND   Here.
JAILER'S DAUGHTER   What kenn'st thou?   156
SECOND FRIEND   A fair wood.
JAILER'S DAUGHTER   Bear for it, master. Tack about.   158
(*Sings*)
    When Cynthia with her borrowed light . . . (etc.)
    Exeunt.

❧

4.2

Enter Emilia alone with two pictures.

EMILIA
Yet I may bind those wounds up, that must open
And bleed to death for my sake else; I'll choose,
And end their strife. Two such young handsome men
Shall never fall for me; their weeping mothers,
Following the dead cold ashes of their sons,
Shall never curse my cruelty. Good heaven,
What a sweet face has Arcite! If wise Nature,
With all her best endowments, all those beauties
She sows into the births of noble bodies,
Were here a mortal woman, and had in her   10
The coy denials of young maids, yet doubtless   11

136–7 not so few . . . As no fewer than   **137 tickle't up** finish up. (With sexual suggestion.)   **138 if . . . in** if he's in good form. (With sexual suggestion.)   **145 Set** Orient   **147–8 For . . . alone** As for the rigging, leave it to me.   **148 weigh** weigh anchor   **149 Owgh** a grunting sound of exertion   **150 Top the bowline** Haul in on the line used to hold steady the edge of a square sail in sailing close to the wind.   **156 kenn'st thou** do you discern.   **158 Bear** Head **4.2 Location: Theseus's palace, Athens.**
10–11 and had . . . maids and possessed the modest inclination of virtuous young maids to resist male blandishments

110 rarely early; excellently.   **abroad else** away from home otherwise   **112 cocklight** dawn   **119 mean** means.   **cross** contradict.   **distempered** mentally disordered   **123 For** because of   **127 let . . . alone** pay no attention to them.   **129 keep close** keep to myself, keep still   **130 cockle** clam-like mollusk   **131 on't** i.e., of begetting sons   **132 gelt for musicians** castrated before puberty to preserve the soprano or contralto voice

She would run mad for this man. What an eye,
Of what a fiery sparkle and quick sweetness,   13
Has this young prince! Here Love himself sits smiling;   14
Just such another wanton Ganymede   15
Set Jove afire with, and enforced the god
Snatch up the goodly boy and set him by him,
A shining constellation. What a brow,   18
Of what a spacious majesty, he carries,
Arched like the great-eyed Juno's, but far sweeter,
Smoother than Pelops' shoulder! Fame and Honor,   21
Methinks, from hence, as from a promontory   22
Pointed in heaven, should clap their wings and sing   23
To all the under world the loves and fights   24
Of gods and such men near 'em. Palamon   25
Is but his foil, to him a mere dull shadow;
He's swart and meager, of an eye as heavy   27
As if he had lost his mother, a still temper,   28
No stirring in him, no alacrity,
Of all this sprightly sharpness not a smile.   30
Yet these that we count errors may become him;
Narcissus was a sad boy but a heavenly.   32
Oh, who can find the bent of woman's fancy?   33
I am a fool; my reason is lost in me;
I have no choice, and I have lied so lewdly   35
That women ought to beat me. On my knees
I ask thy pardon! Palamon, thou art alone
And only beautiful, and these the eyes,
These the bright lamps of beauty, that command
And threaten love, and what young maid dare cross
    'em?   40
What a bold gravity, and yet inviting,
Has this brown manly face! O Love, this only   42
From this hour is complexion. Lie there, Arcite;   43
Thou art a changeling to him, a mere gypsy,   44
And this the noble body. I am sotted,   45
Utterly lost; my virgin's faith has fled me.
For if my brother but even now had asked me
Whether I loved, I had run mad for Arcite;   48
Now if my sister, more for Palamon.
Stand both together. Now come ask me, brother;

Alas, I know not! Ask me now, sweet sister;
I may go look. What a mere child is Fancy,   52
That, having two fair gauds of equal sweetness,   53
Cannot distinguish, but must cry for both!

Enter a Gentleman.

How now, sir?
GENTLEMAN   From the noble Duke, your brother,
Madam, I bring you news: the knights are come.
EMILIA
To end the quarrel?
GENTLEMAN   Yes.
EMILIA   Would I might end first!
What sins have I committed, chaste Diana,   58
That my unspotted youth must now be soiled
With blood of princes, and my chastity
Be made the altar where the lives of lovers—
Two greater and two better never yet
Made mothers joy—must be the sacrifice   63
To my unhappy beauty?

    Enter Theseus, Hippolyta, Pirithous, and
    attendants.

THESEUS   Bring 'em in   64
Quickly, by any means; I long to see 'em.
                         [*Exit one or more.*]
[*To Emilia*] Your two contending lovers are returned,
And with them their fair knights. Now, my fair sister,
You must love one of them.
EMILIA   I had rather both,
So neither for my sake should fall untimely.
THESEUS
Who saw 'em?
PIRITHOUS   I awhile.
GENTLEMAN   And I.   70

    Enter a Messenger.

THESEUS
From whence come you, sir?
MESSENGER   From the knights.
THESEUS   Pray speak,
You that have seen them, what they are.
MESSENGER   I will, sir,
And truly what I think. Six braver spirits
Than these they have brought, if we judge by the
    outside,
I never saw nor read of. He that stands
In the first place with Arcite, by his seeming   76
Should be a stout man, by his face a prince;   77
His very looks so say him, his complexion   78
Nearer a brown than black—stern and yet noble—
Which shows him hardy, fearless, proud of dangers.
The circles of his eyes show fire within him,
And as a heated lion, so he looks.   82

---

13 quick lively   **14 Love himself** Cupid. (Emilia is comparing the two portraits; see also lines 43 and 50.)   **15 Ganymede** the young man whom Jove, infatuated, took to be his cupbearer   **18 constellation** (The zodiacal sign Aquarius was often thought to have been Ganymede transported to the sky.)   **21 Pelops' shoulder** (Pelops's father, Tantalus, served the child to the gods in a banquet to see if they could tell the flesh from that of some animal. He managed to fool Demeter into eating part of the shoulder. The gods restored Pelops to life with the missing shoulder replaced by ivory.)   **22 hence** Arcite's brow   **23 Pointed** coming to a point   **24 the under world** the earth as seen from the heavens   **25 near 'em** close to the gods in achievement. **27 He's . . . meager** Palamon is swarthy and of deficient build.   **heavy** sad   **28 still temper** lethargic temperament   **30 Of . . . smile** with not even a smile to match Arcite's sprightly keenness.   **32 Narcissus . . . heavenly** i.e., Narcissus too had a sad look about him (owing to his being punished for repulsing the love of Echo by becoming enamored of his own image in a fountain), and yet he was immortalized. **33 bent** inclination   **35 choice** ability to choose.   **lewdly** basely, ignorantly   **40 cross** encounter, oppose   **42–3 this only . . . complexion** from this day forth, Palamon's dark complexion is the only one for me.   **44 a changeling** a child (usually stupid or ugly) thought to have been left by fairies in exchange for one stolen   **45 sotted** besotted **48 Whether** which of the two.   **had** would have

52 I . . . look i.e., for all my looking, I find no answer.   **Fancy** love **53 gauds** toys, baubles   **58 Diana** goddess associated with the moon and with chastity   **63 joy** rejoice   **64 unhappy** causing misfortune **70 awhile** recently.   **76 seeming** appearance   **77 stout** valiant **78 say** proclaim   **82 heated** angry

His hair hangs long behind him, black and shining
Like ravens' wings; his shoulders broad and strong,
Armed long and round; and on his thigh a sword   85
Hung by a curious baldric, when he frowns,   86
To seal his will with. Better, o' my conscience,   87
Was never soldier's friend.

THESEUS
Thou hast well described him.

PIRITHOUS   Yet a great deal short,
Methinks, of him that's first with Palamon.

THESEUS
Pray speak him, friend.

PIRITHOUS   I guess he is a prince too,   91
And, if it may be, greater, for his show   92
Has all the ornament of honor in't.
He's somewhat bigger than the knight he spoke of,   94
But of a face far sweeter; his complexion
Is, as a ripe grape, ruddy. He has felt
Without doubt what he fights for, and so apter   97
To make this cause his own. In 's face appears
All the fair hopes of what he undertakes,
And when he's angry, then a settled valor,
Not tainted with extremes, runs through his body,
And guides his arm to brave things. Fear he cannot;
He shows no such soft temper. His head's yellow,
Hard-haired and curled, thick-twined like ivy-tods,   104
Not to undo with thunder. In his face   105
The livery of the warlike maid appears,   106
Pure red and white, for yet no beard has blessed him;
And in his rolling eyes sits Victory,
As if she ever meant to court his valor.   109
His nose stands high, a character of honor;   110
His red lips, after fights, are fit for ladies.

EMILIA
Must these men die too?

PIRITHOUS   When he speaks, his tongue
Sounds like a trumpet. All his lineaments
Are as a man would wish 'em—strong and clean.
He wears a well-steeled ax, the staff of gold;
His age some five-and-twenty.

MESSENGER   There's another—
A little man, but of a tough soul, seeming
As great as any. Fairer promises
In such a body yet I never looked on.

PIRITHOUS
Oh, he that's freckle-faced?

MESSENGER   The same, my lord.
Are they not sweet ones?

PIRITHOUS   Yes, they are well.

MESSENGER   Methinks,   121
Being so few, and well disposed, they show   122

Great and fine art in nature. He's white-haired—   123
Not wanton white, but such a manly color   124
Next to an auburn; tough and nimble-set,   125
Which shows an active soul. His arms are brawny,
Lined with strong sinews. To the shoulder-piece   127
Gently they swell, like women new-conceived,   128
Which speaks him prone to labor, never fainting   129
Under the weight of arms; stout-hearted still,   130
But when he stirs, a tiger. He's grey-eyed,   131
Which yields compassion where he conquers; sharp   132
To spy advantages, and where he finds 'em,
He's swift to make 'em his. He does no wrongs,
Nor takes none. He's round-faced, and when he
    smiles   135
He shows a lover, when he frowns, a soldier.   136
About his head he wears the winner's oak,   137
And in it stuck the favor of his lady;   138
His age some six-and-thirty. In his hand
He bears a charging-staff embossed with silver.   140

THESEUS
Are they all thus?

PIRITHOUS   They are all the sons of honor.

THESEUS
Now, as I have a soul, I long to see 'em.
[*To Hippolyta*] Lady, you shall see men fight, now.

HIPPOLYTA   I wish it,
But not the cause, my lord. They would show   144
Bravely about the titles of two kingdoms;   145
'Tis pity love should be so tyrannous.
                                        [*Emilia weeps.*]
Oh, my soft-hearted sister, what think you?
Weep not till they weep blood. Wench, it must be.

THESEUS [*to Emilia*]
You have steeled 'em with your beauty. [*To Pirithous*]
    Honored friend,   149
To you I give the field; pray order it   150
Fitting the persons that must use it.

PIRITHOUS   Yes, sir.

THESEUS
Come, I'll go visit 'em; I cannot stay,   152
Their fame has fired me so. Till they appear,
Good friend, be royal.

PIRITHOUS   There shall want no bravery.   154

EMILIA [*to herself*]
Poor wench, go weep, for whosoever wins
Loses a noble cousin for thy sins.
                                        Exeunt.

85 **Armed . . . round** with long, well-shaped arms   86–7 **Hung . . . with** hung from an intricately designed sword belt (worn across one shoulder), which he uses to execute his furious will.   91 **speak** describe   92 **show** appearance   94 **he** the messenger   97 **what . . . for** i.e., love   104 **Hard-haired and curled** tightly curled.   **ivy-tods** ivy bushes   105 **undo** be undone or destroyed   106 **the warlike maid** Athene, warlike goddess, protector of Athens   109 **As . . . valor** as if Victory were constantly drawn to woo him for his valor.   110 **His . . . honor** (The prominent Roman nose was thought to indicate honorableness.)   121 **they** the freckles   122 **disposed** placed, situated

123 **white-haired** blond   124 **wanton** effeminate   125 **nimble-set** nimble of build   127 **Lined** fortified   128 **new-conceived** newly pregnant   129 **speaks . . . labor** bespeaks one willing to strive hard. (With a pun on the "labor" of pregnancy.)   130 **still** (1) always, under any conditions (2) at rest   131 **grey-eyed** blue-eyed   132 **Which . . . conquers** which indicates his inclination to be compassionate to those he conquers   135 **Nor takes none** and does not tolerate anyone injuring him.   136 **shows** looks like   137 **oak** garland of oak leaves   138 **favor** glove, scarf or other token   140 **charging-staff** tilting lance   144–5 **They . . . kingdoms** Their splendor would be well suited to a contention between two kingdoms   149 **steeled** hardened   150 **the field** the management of the contest   152 **stay** wait   154 **be royal** arrange matters with royal generosity.   **want no bravery** lack no splendor.

4.3

Enter Jailer, Wooer, Doctor.

DOCTOR   Her distraction is more at some time of the
 moon than at other some, is it not?   2

JAILER   She is continually in a harmless distemper,   3
 sleeps little; altogether without appetite, save often
 drinking; dreaming of another world, and a better;
 and what broken piece of matter soe'er she's about,
 the name "Palamon" lards it, that she farces ev'ry   7
 business withal, fits it to every question.

Enter [Jailer's] Daughter.

Look where she comes. You shall perceive her behavior.   *[They stand apart.]*

JAILER'S DAUGHTER   I have forgot it quite; the burden   11
 on't was "Down-a, down-a," and penned by no   12
 worse man than Geraldo, Emilia's schoolmaster. He's
 as fantastical, too, as ever he may go upon 's legs; for   14
 in the next world will Dido see Palamon, and then will   15
 she be out of love with Aeneas.

DOCTOR   What stuff's here! Poor soul!

JAILER   Ev'n thus all day long.

JAILER'S DAUGHTER   Now for this charm that I told you
 of, you must bring a piece of silver on the tip of your
 tongue, or no ferry; then if it be your chance to come   21
 where the blessèd spirits are—there's a sight now!
 We maids that have our livers perished, cracked to   23
 pieces with love, we shall come there, and do nothing
 all day long but pick flowers with Proserpine. Then   25
 will I make Palamon a nosegay, then let him mark me,   26
 then—

DOCTOR   How prettily she's amiss! Note her a little
 further.

JAILER'S DAUGHTER   Faith, I'll tell you: sometime we go
 to barley-break, we of the blessèd. Alas, 'tis a sore   31
 life they have i'th'other place. Such burning, frying,   32
 boiling, hissing, howling, chatt'ring, cursing—Oh,
 they have shrewd measure, take heed! If one be mad,   34
 or hang or drown themselves, thither they go, Jupiter
 bless us, and there shall we be put in a cauldron of
 lead and usurers' grease, amongst a whole million of   37
 cutpurses, and there boil like a gammon of bacon that   38
 will never be enough.   39

DOCTOR   How her brain coins!   40

JAILER'S DAUGHTER   Lords and courtiers that have got
 maids with child, they are in this place; they shall
 stand in fire up to the navel and in ice up to th' heart,
 and there th'offending part burns and the deceiving part freezes—in truth a very grievous punishment,
 as one would think, for such a trifle. Believe me,
 one would marry a leprous witch to be rid on't, I'll
 assure you.

DOCTOR   How she continues this fancy! 'Tis not an en-   49
 grafted madness, but a most thick and profound   50
 melancholy.   51

JAILER'S DAUGHTER   To hear there a proud lady and a
 proud city wife howl together! I were a beast an I'd call   53
 it good sport. One cries, "Oh, this smoke!," th'other,
 "This fire!"; one cries, "Oh, that ever I did it behind
 the arras!", and then howls; th'other curses a   56
 suing fellow and her garden house.   57
 (Sings)
  I will be true, my stars, my fate . . . (etc.)
        Exit [Jailer's] Daughter.

JAILER   What think you of her, sir?

DOCTOR   I think she has a perturbed mind, which I
 cannot minister to.

JAILER   Alas, what then?

DOCTOR   Understand you she ever affected any man   63
 ere she beheld Palamon?

JAILER   I was once, sir, in great hope she had fixed her
 liking on this gentleman, my friend.

WOOER   I did think so too, and would account I had a   67
 great penn'orth on 't to give half my state that both she   68
 and I, at this present, stood unfeignedly on the same
 terms.

DOCTOR   That intemp'rate surfeit of her eye hath distempered the other senses. They may return and
 settle again to execute their preordained faculties, but
 they are now in a most extravagant vagary. This you   74
 must do: confine her to a place where the light may
 rather seem to steal in than be permitted. Take upon
 you, young sir, her friend, the name of Palamon; say
 you come to eat with her, and to commune of love.
 This will catch her attention, for this her mind beats
 upon; other objects that are inserted 'tween her mind
 and eye become the pranks and friskins of her   81
 madness. Sing to her such green songs of love as she   82
 says Palamon hath sung in prison; come to her stuck   83
 in as sweet flowers as the season is mistress of, and
 thereto make an addition of some other compounded
 odors which are grateful to the sense. All this shall
 become Palamon, for Palamon can sing, and Palamon   87
 is sweet and ev'ry good thing. Desire to eat with her,
 carve her, drink to her, and still among intermingle   89

4.3. Location: The prison.
2 at other some at other times   **3 distemper** state of mental disorder
7 lards is inserted into.   **farces** stuffs. (Cooking terms.)   **11–12 burden on't** refrain of it   **14 fantastical** filled with lively imagination.
ever . . . legs anyone who can walk, any person   **15 Dido** Queen of
Carthage, deserted by Aeneas in Virgil's *Aeneid*   **21 or no ferry** (A
coin was placed on the tongue of a deceased person as fare for being
ferried across the Styx to the underworld by Charon.)   **23 livers** supposed seat of the passions   **25 Proserpine** (As this beautiful goddess
was picking flowers in Sicily, she was carried off by Hades to be his
queen in the lower world.)   **26 nosegay** bouquet of flowers.   **mark
me** pay attention to me   **31 barley-break** a game played by various
couples, one couple in the center (called "hell") trying to catch the
others   **32 i'th'other place** i.e., in hell.   **34 shrewd measure** dire
punishment   **37 grease** i.e., sweat   **38 gammon** ham   **38–9 that . . .
enough** i.e., the torment will never cease.   **40 coins** fabricates.

49–51 'Tis . . . melancholy It's not insanity in the psychotic sense, but
a profound lovesickness.   **53 I . . . an** I would be a beast if   **56 arras**
hanging screen placed in front of walls, allowing space behind for
concealment and assignations   **57 suing fellow** suitor.   **garden
house** (A suitable place for a seduction.)   **63 affected** felt passion for
67–8 would . . . on 't would consider it a great bargain   **68 state**
estate   **74 in . . . vagary** wandering out of bounds.   **81 friskins** playful encounters   **82 green** youthful   **83 stuck** decked out   **87 become**
suit your role as   **89 carve** carve meat for.   **still among** mingled
with these activities

your petition of grace and acceptance into her favor.
Learn what maids have been her companions and
playferes, and let them repair to her with "Palamon"   92
in their mouths, and appear with tokens, as if they   93
suggested for him. It is a falsehood she is in, which is   94
with falsehoods to be combatted. This may bring her
to eat, to sleep, and reduce what's now out of square   96
in her into their former law and regiment. I have seen   97
it approved, how many times I know not; but, to   98
make the number more, I have great hope in this. I
will between the passages of this project come in   100
with my appliance. Let us put it in execution, and   101
hasten the success, which doubt not will bring forth   102
comfort.

Exeunt.

❖

5.1

*Flourish. Enter Theseus, Pirithous, Hippolyta,
attendants. [Three altars are visible.]*

THESEUS
Now let 'em enter, and before the gods
Tender their holy prayers. Let the temples
Burn bright with sacred fires, and the altars
In hallowed clouds commend their swelling incense
To those above us. Let no due be wanting;
They have a noble work in hand, will honor   6
The very powers that love 'em.

*Flourish of cornets. Enter Palamon and Arcite
and their knights [at opposite doors].*

PIRITHOUS   Sir, they enter.
THESEUS
You valiant and strong-hearted enemies,
You royal german foes, that this day come   9
To blow that nearness out that flames between ye,   10
Lay by your anger for an hour, and, dove-like,
Before the holy altars of your helpers,
The all-feared gods, bow down your stubborn bodies.
Your ire is more than mortal; so your help be,   14
And as the gods regard ye, fight with justice.   15
I'll leave you to your prayers, and betwixt ye
I part my wishes.
PIRITHOUS   Honor crown the worthiest!
*Exeunt Theseus and his train, [including Pirithous
and Hippolyta].*
PALAMON *[to Arcite]*
The glass is running now that cannot finish   18
Till one of us expire. Think you but thus,

That were there aught in me which strove to show   20
Mine enemy in this business, were't one eye
Against another, arm oppressed by arm,
I would destroy th'offender, coz—I would,
Though parcel of myself. Then from this gather   24
How I should tender you.
ARCITE   I am in labor   25
To push your name, your ancient love, our kindred,   26
Out of my memory, and i'th' selfsame place
To seat something I would confound. So hoist we   28
The sails that must these vessels port even where   29
The heavenly limiter pleases.
PALAMON   You speak well.   30
Before I turn, let me embrace thee, cousin.   31
                    [They embrace.]
This I shall never do again.
ARCITE   One farewell.
PALAMON
Why, let it be so; farewell, coz.
ARCITE   Farewell, sir.
                    Exeunt Palamon and his knights.
Knights, kinsmen, lovers, yea, my sacrifices,
True worshipers of Mars, whose spirit in you
Expels the seeds of fear and th'apprehension   36
Which still is father of it: go with me   37
Before the god of our profession. There   38
Require of him the hearts of lions and   39
The breath of tigers, yea, the fierceness too,   40
Yea, the speed also—to go on, I mean;
Else wish we to be snails. You know my prize
Must be dragged out of blood; force and great feat
Must put my garland on, where she sticks,   44
The queen of flowers. Our intercession, then,   45
Must be to him that makes the camp a cistern   46
Brimmed with the blood of men. Give me your aid,   47
And bend your spirits towards him.

*They [advance to Mars's altar, fall prostrate, and]
kneel.*

Thou mighty one, that with thy power hast turned
Green Neptune into purple;   50
Whose havoc in vast field comets prewarn,   51
Unearthèd skulls proclaim; whose breath blows down
The teeming Ceres' foison; who dost pluck   53
With hand armipotent from forth blue clouds   54
The masoned turrets, that both mak'st and break'st   55
The stony girths of cities: me thy pupil,   56

---

92 **playferes** playfellows.   **repair** come   93 **tokens** love tokens
94 **suggested** pleaded.   **falsehood** delusion   96 **reduce** lead back
97 **regiment** order.   98 **it approved** this course of treatment confirmed in practice   100 **passages** transactions   101 **appliance** application, administering.   102 **success** outcome
5.1. Location: The forest, where Palamon and Arcite fought (in 3.6)
and where the tournament is now to be held. Visible onstage are
temples to Mars, Venus, and Diana, each with an altar.
6 **will** that will   9 **german** cousin   10 **blow that nearness out** blow
out or extinguish the friendship and nearness of blood   14 **be** must
be   15 **regard** watch over   18 **glass** hourglass

20 **show** appear as   24 **parcel** part   25 **tender** behave toward, treat
26 **kindred** kinship   28 **confound** destroy.   29 **port** transport, convey to port   30 **The heavenly limiter** the god who controls all life
31 **turn** turn away   36–7 **th'apprehension . . . of it** the anticipation or
perception of danger which is ever the cause of fear   38 **of our profession** to whom we offer our services and who is patron of our military calling.   39 **Require** request   40 **breath** endurance, "wind"
44–5 **Must . . . flowers** flowers must win for me the victory laurel wreath, of
which Emilia, who already reigns in my heart, is the chiefest flower.
46 **him** Mars   47 **Brimmed** filled to the brim   50 **Green Neptune** i.e.,
the sea   51 **field** battlefield   53 **The . . . foison** the teeming crops
ready for harvesting, the gift of Ceres, goddess of agriculture
53–5 **pluck . . . turrets** pull down with your mighty arm, from out of
the sky, the stone-built fortifications
56 **girths** walls

Youngest follower of thy drum, instruct this day
With military skill, that to thy laud   58
I may advance my streamer, and by thee   59
Be styled the lord o'th' day. Give me, great Mars,   60
Some token of thy pleasure.   61

*Here they fall on their faces as formerly, and there
is heard clanging of armor, with a short thunder,
as the burst of a battle, whereupon they all rise and
bow to the altar.*

O great corrector of enormous times,   62
Shaker of o'er-rank states, thou grand decider   63
Of dusty and old titles, that heal'st with blood   64
The earth when it is sick, and cur'st the world
O'th' plurisy of people, I do take   66
Thy signs auspiciously, and in thy name
To my design march boldly. [*To his knights*] Let us go.
                                                        Exeunt.   68

*Enter Palamon and his knights, with the former
observance.*

PALAMON

Our stars must glister with new fire, or be   69
Today extinct. Our argument is love,
Which, if the goddess of it grant, she gives
Victory too. Then blend your spirits with mine,
You whose free nobleness do make my cause
Your personal hazard. To the goddess Venus
Commend we our proceeding, and implore
Her power unto our party.

*Here they [advance to Venus's altar, prostrate
themselves, and] kneel as formerly.*

Hail, sovereign queen of secrets, who hast power
To call the fiercest tyrant from his rage
And weep unto a girl; that hast the might   79
Even with an eye-glance to choke Mars's drum
And turn th'alarm to whispers; that canst make   81
A cripple flourish with his crutch, and cure him   82
Before Apollo; that mayst force the king   83
To be his subject's vassal, and induce
Stale gravity to dance! The polled bachelor—   85
Whose youth, like wanton boys through bonfires,
Have skipped thy flame—at seventy thou canst catch,
And make him, to the scorn of his hoarse throat,
Abuse young lays of love. What godlike power   89
Hast thou not power upon? To Phoebus thou
Add'st flames hotter than his; the heavenly fires

Did scorch his mortal son, thine him. The huntress,   92
All moist and cold, some say, began to throw
Her bow away and sigh. Take to thy grace
Me, thy vowed soldier, who do bear thy yoke
As 'twere a wreath of roses, yet is heavier   96
Than lead itself, stings more than nettles.
I have never been foul-mouthed against thy law;
Nev'r revealed secret, for I knew none; would not,
Had I kenned all that were. I never practiced   100
Upon man's wife, nor would the libels read   101
Of liberal wits. I never at great feasts   102
Sought to betray a beauty, but have blushed   103
At simp'ring sirs that did. I have been harsh
To large confessors, and have hotly asked them   105
If they had mothers; I had one, a woman,
And women 'twere they wronged. I knew a man
Of eighty winters—this I told them—who
A lass of fourteen brided; 'twas thy power   109
To put life into dust. The agèd cramp
Had screwed his square foot round;   111
The gout had knit his fingers into knots;
Torturing convulsions from his globy eyes   113
Had almost drawn their spheres, that what was life   114
In him seemed torture. This anatomy   115
Had by his young fair fere a boy, and I   116
Believed it was his, for she swore it was,
And who would not believe her? Brief, I am   118
To those that prate and have done, no companion;   119
To those that boast and have not, a defier;
To those that would and cannot, a rejoicer.
Yea, him I do not love that tells close offices   122
The foulest way, nor names concealments in
The boldest language. Such a one I am,   124
And vow that lover never yet made sigh
Truer than I. Oh, then, most soft sweet goddess,
Give me the victory of this question, which   127
Is true love's merit, and bless me with a sign   128
Of thy great pleasure.

*Here music is heard. Doves are seen to flutter.
They fall again upon their faces, then on their
knees.*

O thou that from eleven to ninety reign'st
In mortal bosoms, whose chase is this world   131
And we in herds thy game, I give thee thanks   132
For this fair token, which, being laid unto

---

58 **to thy laud** in praise of thee   59 **streamer** banner   60 **styled** titled
61.3 **burst** eruption   62 **enormous** abnormal, monstrous   63 **o'er-**
rank overripe, decadent   64 **with blood** through bloodletting (a
common medical treatment for sickness)   66 **plurisy** diseased super-
abundance. (Pleurisy, an inflammation of the lung sacks or pleura,
was wrongly thought to be derived from the Latin *plus, plur-*,
"more.")   68.1–2 *the former observance*. Palamon and his knights
fulfill ceremonies at Venus's altar like those performed by Arcite and
his knights at Mars's altar.   69 **stars** fortunes   79 **weep unto** make
him weep before, imploring the favor of   81 **th'alarm** the alarum,
call to arms   82 **flourish with** wave about vigorously   83 **Before**
Apollo even sooner than Apollo, the god of medicine   85 **polled**
bald   89 **Abuse** butcher (with his hoarse singing)

92 **his mortal son** Phaethon, who drove the sun god Phoebus's chariot too near the sun.   **The huntress** Diana or Artemis, goddess
of chastity and of the moon, who fell in love with a shepherd
(Endymion)   96 **is** it is   100 **kenned** known   100–1 **practiced Upon**
attempted to seduce   102 **liberal** licentious   103 **betray** (1) tattle
about (2) seduce   105 **large confessors** men who boast unre-
strainedly of their sexual prowess with many women   109 **brided**
took as his bride   111 **Had . . . round** had twisted his well-
proportioned foot into a gouty misshapen mass   113 **globy** protrud-
ing   114 **drawn their spheres** popped out the eyeballs.   **that** so that
115 **anatomy** mere skeleton   116 **fere** partner (in marriage)
118 **Brief** In brief   119 **and have done** and did what they boast about
122 **close offices** secret affairs   124 **Such a one** i.e., One who condemns male boastfulness   127 **question** contention   128 **Is . . . merit**
is the reward of the true lover   131 **chase** hunting-ground
132 **game** quarry

Mine innocent true heart, arms in assurance
My body to this business. [*To his knights*] Let us rise
And bow before the goddess.   *They* [*rise and*] *bow.*
                              Time comes on.   *Exeunt.* 136

Still music of record[*er*]*s. Enter Emilia in white,*
her hair about her shoulders, [*wearing*] *a wheaten*
wreath; one in white holding up her train, her hair
stuck with flowers; one before her carrying a silver
hind, in which is conveyed incense and sweet
odors; which being set upon the altar [*of Diana*]*,*
her maids standing aloof, she sets fire to it. Then
they curtsy and kneel.

EMILIA

O sacred, shadowy, cold, and constant queen,   137
Abandoner of revels, mute contemplative,
Sweet, solitary, white as chaste, and pure
As wind-fanned snow, who to thy female knights
Allow'st no more blood than will make a blush,
Which is their order's robe: I here, thy priest,   142
Am humbled 'fore thine altar. Oh, vouchsafe
With that thy rare green eye, which never yet   144
Beheld thing maculate, look on thy virgin!   145
And, sacred silver mistress, lend thine ear—
Which nev'r heard scurril term, into whose port   147
Ne'er entered wanton sound—to my petition,
Seasoned with holy fear. This is my last
Of vestal office; I am bride-habited,   150
But maiden-hearted. A husband I have 'pointed,   151
But do not know him. Out of two I should
Choose one, and pray for his success, but I
Am guiltless of election. Of mine eyes   154
Were I to lose one—they are equal precious—
I could doom neither; that which perished should   156
Go to't unsentenced. Therefore, most modest queen,   157
He of the two pretenders that best loves me   158
And has the truest title in't, let him
Take off my wheaten garland, or else grant   160
The file and quality I hold I may   161
Continue in thy band.   162

Here the hind vanishes under the altar, and in the
place ascends a rose tree, having one rose upon it.

See what our general of ebbs and flows   163
Out from the bowels of her holy altar
With sacred act advances—but one rose!   165
If well inspired, this battle shall confound   166

Both these brave knights, and I, a virgin flower,
Must grow alone, unplucked.

Here is heard a sudden twang of instruments, and
the rose falls from the tree.   [*The tree descends.*]

The flower is fall'n, the tree descends. Oh, mistress,
Thou here dischargest me. I shall be gathered;   170
I think so, but I know not thine own will.
Unclasp thy mystery!—I hope she's pleased;
Her signs were gracious.

                              They curtsy and exeunt.

5.2

Enter Doctor, Jailer, and Wooer in [*the*] *habit of*
Palamon.

DOCTOR   Has this advice I told you done any good
upon her?

WOOER   Oh, very much. The maids that kept her company have half persuaded her that I am Palamon.
Within this half-hour she came smiling to me, and
asked me what I would eat, and when I would kiss
her. I told her presently, and kissed her twice.

DOCTOR
'Twas well done. Twenty times had been far better,
For there the cure lies mainly.

WOOER   Then she told me
She would watch with me tonight, for well she knew   10
What hour my fit would take me.

DOCTOR   Let her do so.   11
And when your fit comes, fit her home,   12
And presently.

WOOER   She would have me sing.

DOCTOR
You did so?

WOOER   No.

DOCTOR   'Twas very ill done, then;
You should observe her ev'ry way.

WOOER   Alas,   15
I have no voice, sir, to confirm her that way.   16

DOCTOR
That's all one, if ye make a noise.   17
If she entreat again, do anything;
Lie with her if she ask you.

JAILER   Whoa there, doctor!

DOCTOR
Yes, in the way of cure.

JAILER   But first, by your leave,
I'th' way of honesty.

DOCTOR   That's but a niceness.   21
Nev'r cast your child away for honesty.   22

136.1 *Still* Quiet   **136.2 *her hair ... shoulders*** (Betokening a virginal
and yet-unmarried woman.)   **136.2–3 *wheaten wreath*** symbol of
fecundity and of marriage, as at 1.1.0.4   **136.5 *hind*** doe. (Also at 162.1.)
136.7 *aloof* apart   **137 *shadowy*** associated with the night.   **cold** chaste
142 *Which ... robe* which blush is the visible garb of those who worship you   **144 *rare*** excellent   **145 *maculate*** spotted, defiled   **147 *scurril*** scurrilous.   **port** portal (of the ear)   **150 *bride-habited*** dressed as a
bride   **151 *I have 'pointed*** has been appointed for me   **154 *election***
having made a choice.   **156 *doom*** condemn   **157 *Go to't*** go to execution   **158 *pretenders*** suitors   **160 *Take ... garland*** take my virginity.
(See 136.2–3.)   **161–2 *The file ... band*** that the position and status I
hold (as a virgin) may continue, with me as a valued and ranking member of your entourage   **163 *our general ... flows*** our goddess of the
moon and of tides   **165 *advances*** lifts up   **166 *If well inspired*** If this
omen and my prophetic reading of it are true.   **confound** destroy

170 *Thou ... me* you release me from your service.   **gathered** harvested, i.e., married and thus be a virgin no longer
5.2. Location: The prison.
0.1 *habit* garb   **10 *watch*** stay awake   **11 *fit*** sudden inclination
12 *fit her home* humor her in every way   **15 *observe*** humor   **16 *confirm*** fortify, encourage   **17 *That's all one*** It's all the same   **21 *honesty***
chaste marriage.   **niceness** fastidiousness.   **22 *Nev'r ... honesty*** Don't
abandon her to her affliction merely out of regard for her chastity.

Cure her first this way; then if she will be honest,   23
She has the path before her.
JAILER
Thank ye, doctor.
DOCTOR   Pray bring her in,
And let's see how she is.
JAILER   I will, and tell her
Her Palamon stays for her. But, doctor,   27
Methinks you are i'th' wrong still.   *Exit Jailer.*
DOCTOR   Go, go;
You fathers are fine fools! Her honesty?
An we should give her physic till we find that—   30
WOOER
Why, do you think she is not honest, sir?
DOCTOR
How old is she?
WOOER   She's eighteen.
DOCTOR   She may be,
But that's all one; 'tis nothing to our purpose.
Whate'er her father says, if you perceive
Her mood inclining that way that I spoke of,
Videlicet, the way of flesh—you have me?   36
WOOER
Yes, very well, sir.
DOCTOR   Please her appetite,
And do it home; it cures her, *ipso facto*,   38
The melancholy humor that infects her.
WOOER
I am of your mind, doctor.

Enter Jailer [and his] Daughter, [mad].

DOCTOR
You'll find it so. She comes; pray humor her.
                    [*Doctor and Wooer stand aside.*]
JAILER
Come, your love Palamon stays for you, child,
And has done this long hour, to visit you.
JAILER'S DAUGHTER
I thank him for his gentle patience.
He's a kind gentleman, and I am much bound to him.
Did you nev'r see the horse he gave me?
JAILER   Yes.
JAILER'S DAUGHTER
How do you like him?
JAILER   He's a very fair one.   47
JAILER'S DAUGHTER
You never saw him dance?
JAILER   No.
JAILER'S DAUGHTER   I have, often.
He dances very finely, very comely,
And for a jig, come cut and long tail to him,   50
He turns ye like a top.
JAILER   That's fine indeed.   51

JAILER'S DAUGHTER
He'll dance the morris twenty mile an hour,
And that will founder the best hobby-horse,   53
If I have any skill, in all the parish;   54
And gallops to the tune of "Light o' love."   55
What think you of this horse?
JAILER   Having these virtues,
I think he might be brought to play at tennis.
JAILER'S DAUGHTER
Alas, that's nothing.
JAILER   Can he write and read too?   58
JAILER'S DAUGHTER
A very fair hand, and casts himself th'accounts   59
Of all his hay and provender. That hostler   60
Must rise betime that cozens him. You know   61
The chestnut mare the Duke has?
JAILER   Very well.
JAILER'S DAUGHTER
She is horribly in love with him, poor beast,   63
But he is like his master, coy and scornful.   64
JAILER
What dowry has she?
JAILER'S DAUGHTER   Some two hundred bottles,   65
And twenty strike of oats, but he'll ne'er have her.   66
He lisps in 's neighing able to entice   67
A miller's mare. He'll be the death of her.   68
DOCTOR   What stuff she utters!
                    [*The Wooer approaches her.*]
JAILER
Make curtsy; here your love comes.
WOOER   Pretty soul,
How do ye? [*She curtsies*] That's a fine maid; there's a
    curtsy!
JAILER'S DAUGHTER
Yours to command i'th' way of honesty.
How far is't now to th' end o'th' world, my masters?   73
DOCTOR
Why, a day's journey, wench.
JAILER'S DAUGHTER [*to the Wooer*]
                    Will you go with me?
WOOER
What shall we do there, wench?
JAILER'S DAUGHTER   Why, play at stool-ball.   75
What is there else to do?
WOOER   I am content,
If we shall keep our wedding there.
JAILER'S DAUGHTER   'Tis true,   77

---

23 will wishes to be   **27 stays** waits   **30 An . . . that** If we were to give her medical treatment until we were assured of her chastity   **36 *Videlicet*** namely.   **have** understand   **38 home** thoroughly.   **cures her** cures her of.   ***ipso facto*** by that very act   **47 fair** good-looking   **50 come . . . to him** i.e., no matter what other kinds of horse (with docked or long tails) there are to compete with him. (With sexual double entendres, as throughout this scene.)   **51 ye** for you

53 founder lame, disable, cause to collapse.   **hobby-horse** a morris dancer with a figure of a horse fastened around his waist, or a toy horse   **54 skill** judgment   **55 "Light o' love"** a ballad on the subject of inconstancy in love   **58 that's nothing** that's easy, he can do that already.   **59 A very . . . accounts** He writes with beautiful penmanship and keeps track of his own expenses   **60–1 That hostler . . . him** Any caretaker of horses who wants to cheat this horse will have to get up early to do so.   **63 She . . . him** The mare is horribly in love with the talented stallion   **64 his master** i.e., Palamon, who is imagined to have given the Jailer's Daughter this horse.   **coy** disdainful   **65 bottles** bundles   **66 strike** bundles, usually bushel or half-bushel   **67–8 He lisps . . . mare** This stallion has an ingratiating manner of speech able to seduce even the most plodding and stolid of mares.   **73 my masters** my good sirs.   **75 stool-ball** a cricket-like game with a stool-like wicket.   **77 keep** celebrate

For there, I will assure you, we shall find
Some blind priest for the purpose, that will venture
To marry us; for here they are nice, and foolish.   80
Besides, my father must be hanged tomorrow,
And that would be a blot i'th' business.
Are not you Palamon?
WOOER   Do not you know me?
JAILER'S DAUGHTER
  Yes, but you care not for me. I have nothing
  But this poor petticoat and two coarse smocks.   85
WOOER
  That's all one; I will have you.
JAILER'S DAUGHTER   Will you surely?   86
WOOER
  Yes, by this fair hand, will I.
JAILER'S DAUGHTER   We'll to bed then.
WOOER Ev'n when you will.   [He kisses her.]
JAILER'S DAUGHTER [wiping her mouth]
                    Oh, sir, you would fain be nibbling.
WOOER
  Why do you rub my kiss off?
JAILER'S DAUGHTER   'Tis a sweet one,
  And will perfume me finely against the wedding.   90
  [Pointing to the Doctor] Is not this your cousin Arcite?
DOCTOR   Yes, sweetheart,
  And I am glad my cousin Palamon
  Has made so fair a choice.
JAILER'S DAUGHTER   Do you think he'll have me?
DOCTOR
  Yes, without doubt.
JAILER'S DAUGHTER [to the Jailer]   Do you think so too?
JAILER   Yes.
JAILER'S DAUGHTER
  We shall have many children. [To the Doctor] Lord,
    how you're grown!
  My Palamon, I hope, will grow too, finely,
  Now he's at liberty. Alas, poor chicken,
  He was kept down with hard meat and ill lodging,   98
  But I'll kiss him up again.

              Enter a Messenger.

MESSENGER
  What do you here? You'll lose the noblest sight
  That ev'r was seen.
JAILER   Are they i'th' field?
MESSENGER   They are.
  You bear a charge there too.
JAILER   I'll away straight.   102
  [To the others] I must ev'n leave you here.
DOCTOR   Nay, we'll go with you.
  I will not lose the fight.
JAILER   How did you like her?   104
DOCTOR
  I'll warrant you, within these three or four days

I'll make her right again. [To the Wooer] You must not
    from her,
  But still preserve her in this way.
WOOER   I will.
DOCTOR
  Let's get her in.
WOOER [to the Jailer's Daughter]
                Come, sweet, we'll go to dinner,
  And then we'll play at cards.
JAILER'S DAUGHTER   And shall we kiss too?
WOOER
  A hundred times.
JAILER'S DAUGHTER   And twenty.
WOOER   Ay, and twenty.
JAILER'S DAUGHTER
  And then we'll sleep together.
DOCTOR [to the Wooer]   Take her offer.
WOOER [to the Jailer's Daughter]
  Yes, marry, will we.
JAILER'S DAUGHTER   But you shall not hurt me.
WOOER
  I will not, sweet.
JAILER'S DAUGHTER   If you do, love, I'll cry.   Exeunt.

                        ❧

5.3

     Flourish. Enter Theseus, Hippolyta, Emilia,
     Pirithous, and some attendants.

EMILIA [to Pirithous]
  I'll no step further.
PIRITHOUS   Will you lose this sight?
EMILIA
  I had rather see a wren hawk at a fly   2
  Than this decision. Ev'ry blow that falls   3
  Threats a brave life; each stroke laments
  The place whereon it falls, and sounds more like
  A bell than blade. I will stay here.   6
  It is enough my hearing shall be punished
  With what shall happen, 'gainst the which there is
  No deafing, but to hear; not taint mine eye   9
  With dread sights it may shun.
PIRITHOUS [to Theseus]   Sir, my good lord,
  Your sister will no further.
THESEUS   Oh, she must.
  She shall see deeds of honor in their kind,   12
  Which sometime show well, pencilled. Nature now   13
  Shall make and act the story, the belief   14
  Both sealed with eye and ear. [To Emilia] You must be
    present;   15
  You are the victor's meed—the prize and garland   16
  To crown the question's title.
EMILIA   Pardon me;

---

80 nice fastidious   85 smocks petticoats, undergarments.   86 That's
all one It doesn't matter   90 against in preparation for   98 kept . . .
meat kept from growing by harsh fare. (And with sexual meaning in
kept down, kiss him up [line 99], and throughout this passage.)
102 bear a charge have official responsibilities   104 lose the fight
lose the chance to see this armed encounter.   like find (medically)

5.3. Location: Near the tournament field, as in 5.1.
2 hawk fly on the attack   3 decision contest through which the
rivalry will be decided.   6 bell bell toll announcing a death   9 No . . .
hear no way of preventing one's hearing.   not I will not   12–15 deeds
. . . ear those honorable deeds in real life which are often so well represented in art. Nature now will both create and enact the story, so
that belief in it will be confirmed by eye and ear.   16 meed prize

If I were there, I'd wink.

THESEUS   You must be there;   18
This trial is as 'twere i'th' night, and you
The only star to shine.

EMILIA   I am extinct.   20
There is but envy in that light which shows   21
The one the other. Darkness, which ever was   22
The dam of Horror, who does stand accurst   23
Of many mortal millions, may even now,   24
By casting her black mantle over both,
That neither could find other, get herself   26
Some part of a good name, and many a murder   27
Set off whereto she's guilty.

HIPPOLYTA   You must go.   28

EMILIA
In faith, I will not.

THESEUS   Why, the knights must kindle
Their valor at your eye. Know, of this war
You are the treasure, and must needs be by
To give the service pay.

EMILIA   Sir, pardon me;   32
The title of a kingdom may be tried   33
Out of itself.

THESEUS   Well, well, then; at your pleasure.   34
Those that remain with you could wish their office   35
To any of their enemies.

HIPPOLYTA [to Emilia]   Farewell, sister.   36
I am like to know your husband 'fore yourself   37
By some small start of time. He whom the gods
Do of the two know best, I pray them he   39
Be made your lot.

Exeunt Theseus, Hippolyta, Pirithous, etc. [Emilia
remains, attended, comparing two pictures of Palamon
and Arcite.]

EMILIA
Arcite is gently visaged, yet his eye
Is like an engine bent, or a sharp weapon   42
In a soft sheath; mercy and manly courage
Are bedfellows in his visage. Palamon   44
Has a most menacing aspect; his brow
Is graved, and seems to bury what it frowns on;   46
Yet sometime 'tis not so, but alters to   47
The quality of his thoughts. Long time his eye   48
Will dwell upon his object. Melancholy   49
Becomes him nobly; so does Arcite's mirth;   50
But Palamon's sadness is a kind of mirth,

So mingled as if mirth did make him sad
And sadness merry. Those darker humors that   53
Stick misbecomingly on others, on him   54
Live in fair dwelling.   55

Cornets. Trumpets sound as to a charge.

Hark how yon spurs to spirit do incite   56
The princes to their proof! Arcite may win me,   57
And yet may Palamon wound Arcite to   58
The spoiling of his figure. Oh, what pity   59
Enough for such a chance? If I were by,   60
I might do hurt, for they would glance their eyes
Toward my seat, and in that motion might
Omit a ward or forfeit an offense   63
Which craved that very time. It is much better   64
I am not there. Oh, better never born
Than minister to such harm!

Cornets. A great cry and noise within,
crying "A Palamon!"

Enter Servant.

                          What is the chance?   66
SERVANT   The cry's "A Palamon!"
EMILIA
Then he has won. 'Twas ever likely;
He looked all grace and success, and he is
Doubtless the prim'st of men. I prithee run   70
And tell me how it goes.

Shout and cornets, crying "A Palamon!"

SERVANT   Still "Palamon."
EMILIA
Run and inquire.   [*Exit Servant.*]
                    [*To the picture in her right hand*]
                    Poor servant, thou hast lost.
Upon my right side still I wore thy picture,   73
Palamon's on the left—why so, I know not;
I had no end in't else; chance would have it so.   75
On the sinister side the heart lies; Palamon   76
Had the best-boding chance.

Another cry and shout within, and cornets.

                          This burst of clamor   77
Is sure th'end o'th' combat.

Enter Servant.

SERVANT
They said that Palamon had Arcite's body
Within an inch o'th' pyramid, that the cry

Was general "A Palamon!" But anon
Th'assistants made a brave redemption, and   82
The two bold titlers at this instant are
Hand to hand at it.
EMILIA   Were they metamorphosed   84
Both into one!—Oh, why? There were no woman   85
Worth so composed a man; their single share,   86
Their nobleness peculiar to them, gives   87
The prejudice of disparity, value's shortness   88
To any lady breathing.   89

Cornets. Cry within, "Arcite, Arcite!"

                    More exulting?
"Palamon" still?
SERVANT   Nay, now the sound is "Arcite."
EMILIA
I prithee lay attention to the cry;   91
Set both thine ears to th' business.

Cornets. A great shout and cry, "Arcite! Victory!"

SERVANT   The cry is
"Arcite" and "Victory!" Hark, "Arcite, victory!"
The combat's consummation is proclaimed   94
By the wind instruments.
EMILIA   Half-sights saw   95
That Arcite was no babe. God's lid, his richness   96
And costliness of spirit looked through him; it could   97
No more be hid in him that fire in flax,
Than humble banks can go to law with waters   99
That drift-winds force to raging. I did think   100
Good Palamon would miscarry, yet I knew not
Why I did think so. Our reasons are not prophets
When oft our fancies are. They are coming off.   103
Alas, poor Palamon!

Cornets. Enter Theseus, Hippolyta, Pirithous,
Arcite as victor, and attendants, etc.

THESEUS
Lo, where our sister is in expectation,
Yet quaking and unsettled! Fairest Emily,
The gods by their divine arbitrament   107
Have given you this knight; he is a good one
As ever struck at head. [*To Emilia and Arcite*] Give me
     your hands.
[*To Arcite*] Receive you her, [*to Emilia*] you him; be
     plighted with
A love that grows as you decay.
ARCITE   Emily,

To buy you I have lost what's dearest to me   112
Save what is bought, and yet I purchase cheaply,   113
As I do rate your value.
THESEUS   O loved sister,   114
He speaks now of as brave a knight as e'er
Did spur a noble steed. Surely the gods
Would have him die a bachelor, lest his race   117
Should show i'th' world too godlike. His behavior
So charmed me that methought Alcides was   119
To him a sow of lead. If I could praise   120
Each part of him to th'all I have spoke, your Arcite   121
Did not lose by't; for he that was thus good   122
Encountered yet his better. I have heard
Two emulous Philomels beat the ear o'th' night   124
With their contentious throats, now one the higher,
Anon the other, then again the first,
And by and by out-breasted, that the sense   127
Could not be judge between 'em. So it fared
Good space between these kinsmen, till heavens did   129
Make hardly one the winner. [*To Arcite*] Wear the
     garland   130
With joy that you have won.—For the subdued,   131
Give them our present justice, since I know   132
Their lives but pinch 'em. Let it here be done.   133
The scene's not for our seeing; go we hence
Right joyful, with some sorrow. [*To Arcite*] Arm your
     prize;   135
I know you will not lose her.
          [*Arcite takes Emilia's arm in his.*]
                    Hippolyta,   136
I see one eye of yours conceives a tear,
The which it will deliver.
EMILIA   Is this winning?
O all you heavenly powers, where is your mercy?
But that your wills have said it must be so,
And charge me live to comfort this unfriended,   141
This miserable prince, that cuts away
A life more worthy from him than all women,
I should and would die too.
HIPPOLYTA   Infinite pity
That four such eyes should be so fixed on one
That two must needs be blind for't.
THESEUS   So it is.
          Flourish. Exeunt.

❧

82 **Th'assistants** the knights seconding Arcite.   **redemption** rescue
84 **Were they** Would that they   85 **were** would be, could be   86 **so**
composed a man a man thus made of both their best qualities
86–9 **their . . . breathing** the worthiness of either and the nobleness
unique to each puts any woman at a disadvantage by comparison.
91 **lay** apply   94 **consummation** completion   95 **Half-sights** Even a
quick glance   96 **God's lid** By God's eyelid. (An oath.)   97 **looked**
through shone out of   99 **humble** low.   **go to law** i.e., contend
100 **drift-winds** driving winds   103 **off** off the field.   107 **arbitra-**
ment decision, deciding of a dispute

112–14 **To buy . . . value** to win you I have lost Palamon, dearest of all
persons excepting only yourself, and yet the cost is comparatively little since I value you so highly.   117 **his race** his descendants
119–20 **that . . . lead** that I thought Hercules himself a mere ingot of
lead (i.e., dull and heavy) compared with Palamon.   121 **to . . . spoke**
to the extent that I have praised all of him   122 **Did** would
124 **emulous Philomels** contending nightingales   127 **out-breasted**
outsung.   **sense** sense of hearing   129 **Good space** for some length
of time   130 **hardly** by a close judgment call; or, after hard fighting
131 **For** As for   132 **our present justice** immediate execution
133 **but pinch** only torment   135 **Arm** Give your arm to   136 **lose**
(1) lose possession of (2) forget (3) release (spelled "loose" in the
Quarto)   141 **this unfriended** Arcite, who has lost his best friend

5.4

*Enter, [guarded,] Palamon and his knights pin-
ioned; Jailer, Executioner, etc.*

PALAMON
  There's many a man alive that hath outlived
  The love o'th' people; yea, i'th' selfsame state
  Stands many a father with his child. Some comfort
  We have by so considering. We expire,
  And not without men's pity; to live still,
  Have their good wishes. We prevent   6
  The loathsome misery of age, beguile
  The gout and rheum that in lag hours attend   8
  For grey approachers. We come towards the gods
  Young and unwappered, not halting under crimes   10
  Many and stale. That sure shall please the gods   11
  Sooner than such, to give us nectar with 'em,   12
  For we are more clear spirits. My dear kinsmen,   13
  Whose lives for this poor comfort are laid down,
  You have sold 'em too too cheap.
FIRST KNIGHT   What ending could be
  Of more content? O'er us the victors have
  Fortune, whose title is as momentary
  As to us death is certain. A grain of honor
  They not o'erweigh us.
SECOND KNIGHT   Let us bid farewell,
  And with our patience anger tott'ring Fortune,
  Who at her certain'st reels.
THIRD KNIGHT   Come, who begins?   21
PALAMON
  Ev'n he that led you to this banquet shall
  Taste to you all. [*To the Jailer*] Aha, my friend, my
    friend,   23
  Your gentle daughter gave me freedom once;
  You'll see't done now forever. Pray, how does she?   25
  I heard she was not well; her kind of ill   26
  Gave me some sorrow.
JAILER   Sir, she's well restored,
  And to be married shortly.
PALAMON   By my short life,
  I am most glad on't; 'tis the latest thing   29
  I shall be glad of. Prithee tell her so.
  Commend me to her, and to piece her portion   31

  Tender her this.   [*He gives the Jailer his purse.*]
FIRST KNIGHT   Nay, let's be offerers all.
SECOND KNIGHT
  Is it a maid?
PALAMON   Verily, I think so—
  A right good creature, more to me deserving
  Than I can quit or speak of.
ALL THE KNIGHTS   Commend us to her.   35
                      They give their purses.
JAILER
  The gods requite you all, and make her thankful!
PALAMON
  Adieu, and let my life be now as short
  As my leave-taking!
      [*He mounts the scaffold and*] lays [*his head*] *on
                                      the block.*
FIRST KNIGHT   Lead, courageous cousin.
SECOND *AND* THIRD KNIGHTS
  We'll follow cheerfully.

    *A great noise within, crying "Run!" "Save!"
    "Hold!" Enter in haste a Messenger.*

MESSENGER
  Hold, hold! Oh, hold, hold, hold!

      Enter Pirithous in haste.

PIRITHOUS
  Hold, ho! It is a cursèd haste you made   41
  If you have done so quickly. Noble Palamon,   42
  The gods will show their glory in a life
  That thou art yet to lead.
PALAMON   Can that be,
  When Venus, I have said, is false? How do things fare?
PIRITHOUS
  Arise, great sir, and give the tidings ear
  That are most rarely sweet and bitter.
PALAMON [*rising and descending from the scaffold*] What
  Hath waked us from our dream?
PIRITHOUS   List, then. Your cousin,
  Mounted upon a steed that Emily
  Did first bestow on him, a black one, owing   50
  Not a hair-worth of white—which some will say   51
  Weakens his price, and many will not buy
  His goodness with this note, which superstition   53
  Here finds allowance—on this horse is Arcite   54
  Trotting the stones of Athens, which the calkins   55
  Did rather tell than trample, for the horse   56
  Would make his length a mile, if't pleased his rider 57
  To put pride in him. As he thus went counting   58

---

6 **prevent** forestall   8 **rheum . . . approachers** catarrh and rheumatic
pains that in the lag end of life await grey-haired old persons
approaching their sickly end.   10 **unwappered** unwearied. **halting**
limping   11 **stale** out of date.   11–13 **That . . . spirits** Such youthful
service offered to the gods will surely please them sooner than the
service of those who are old and sin-ridden, prompting the gods to
invite us to feed on nectar with them, since we are more unsullied
spirits.   21 **Who . . . reels** who is unstable even when she seems most
favoring.   23 **Taste . . . all** i.e., go first, like the official taster whose
assignment it was to taste food before distinguished persons ate to
see if the food was poisoned.   25 **You'll . . . forever** you will now
give me freedom forever, in death.   26 **her kind of ill** her distressing
madness   29 **latest** last   31 **piece her portion** piece out her dowry

35 **quit** requite, repay   41 **made** would have made   42 **have done** had
completed the execution   50 **owing** owning, having   51–3 **which . . .
note** (A uniformly dark color was widely regarded as a sign of
viciousness in horses.)   53 **note** distinguishing feature, stigma
54 **allowance** approbation, confirmation   55 **calkins** turned-down
edges of a horseshoe that raise the horse's foot and heel from the
ground and help prevent skidding   56 **tell** count, i.e., enumerate as
markers in the horse's swift and feathery touch   57 **make . . . mile**
make each stride a mile in length   58 **put pride in him** i.e., give him
his head, let him show his stuff.

5.4. Location: Near the tournament field, as in 3.6, 5.1, and 5.3. A
scaffold is visible onstage.

The flinty pavement, dancing, as 'twere, to th' music
His own hooves made—for, as they say, from iron   60
Came music's origin—what envious flint,   61
Cold as old Saturn, and like him possessed   62
With fire malevolent, darted a spark,   63
Or what fierce sulfur else, to this end made,   64
I comment not—the hot horse, hot as fire,   65
Took toy at this and fell to what disorder   66
His power could give his will; bounds, comes on end,   67
Forgets school-doing, being therein trained   68
And of kind manège. Pig-like he whines
At the sharp rowel, which he frets at rather   70
Than any jot obeys; seeks all foul means   71
Of boist'rous and rough jadery to disseat   72
His lord, that kept it bravely. When naught served,   73
When neither curb would crack, girth break, nor
    diff'ring plunges   74
Disroot his rider whence he grew, but that
He kept him 'tween his legs, on his hind hooves
On end he stands,
That Arcite's legs, being higher than his head,
Seemed with strange art to hang. His victor's wreath
Even then fell off his head; and presently
Backward the jade comes o'er, and his full poise   81
Becomes the rider's load. Yet is he living,   82
But such a vessel 'tis that floats but for   83
The surge that next approaches. He much desires   84
To have some speech with you. Lo, he appears.

*Enter Theseus, Hippolyta, Emilia, [with] Arcite in
a chair [carried by attendants. Palamon approaches
Arcite.]*

PALAMON
  Oh, miserable end of our alliance!
  The gods are mighty, Arcite. If thy heart,
  Thy worthy, manly heart, be yet unbroken,
  Give me thy last words. I am Palamon,

One that yet loves thee dying.
ARCITE   Take Emilia,
  And with her all the world's joy. Reach thy hand;   91
  Farewell. I have told my last hour. I was false,   92
  Yet never treacherous. Forgive me, cousin.
  One kiss from fair Emilia. [*Kisses her.*] 'Tis done.
  Take her; I die.   [*He dies.*]
PALAMON   Thy brave soul seek Elysium!
EMILIA
  I'll close thine eyes, prince. Blessèd souls be with thee!
  Thou art a right good man, and while I live,
  This day I give to tears.
PALAMON   And I to honor.   98
THESEUS [*to Palamon*]
  In this place first you fought; ev'n very here
  I sundered you. Acknowledge to the gods   100
  Our thanks that you are living.
  His part is played, and, though it were too short,
  He did it well. Your day is lengthened, and
  The blissful dew of heaven does arrose you.   104
  The powerful Venus well hath graced her altar,
  And given you your love. Our master, Mars,
  Hath vouched his oracle, and to Arcite gave   107
  The grace of the contention. So the deities   108
  Have showed due justice. [*To the attendants*] Bear this
    hence.   [*Exeunt attendants with Arcite's body.*]
PALAMON   Oh, cousin,
  That we should things desire which do cost us
  The loss of our desire! That naught could buy
  Dear love but loss of dear love!
THESEUS   Never Fortune
  Did play a subtler game: the conquered triumphs,
  The victor has the loss. Yet in the passage   114
  The gods have been most equal. Palamon,   115
  Your kinsman hath confessed the right o'th' lady
  Did lie in you, for you first saw her and
  Even then proclaimed your fancy. He restored her
  As your stol'n jewel, and desired your spirit
  To send him hence forgiven. The gods my justice
  Take from my hand, and they themselves become
  The executioners. Lead your lady off,
  And call your lovers from the stage of death, 123
  Whom I adopt my friends.
            [*The knights approach from the scaffold.*]
              A day or two
  Let us look sadly, and give grace unto
  The funeral of Arcite, in whose end   126
  The visages of bridegrooms we'll put on
  And smile with Palamon, for whom an hour,
  But one hour since, I was as dearly sorry
  As glad of Arcite, and am now as glad

60–1 **from iron . . . origin** (Pythagoras supposedly came upon the idea of harmonic relationships in music by observing how hammers of differing sizes produced pure intervals of fourths, fifths, and octaves when struck upon an anvil. Tubalcain, the first "artificer in brass and iron" [Genesis 4:22], was popularly credited with earlier discoveries of this sort.)   61–5 **what . . . not** whatever malicious flint it was, or else some other violent sulfurous device make for this purpose, cold as the gloomy saturnine god associated with the cold and moist "humour" in the body called phlegm and yet filled with burning malevolence (like Saturn in Chaucer's "The Knight's Tale," who sends a fury to goad Arcite's horse into wild action) that sent out a hot spark, I do not care to speculate   66 **Took toy at** took a capricious dislike to.   **fell to what** started acting out whatever   67 **comes on end** rears straight up   68 **school-doing** the *kind manège* or trained movements he has been schooled in (lines 68–9)   70 **rowel** sharp-pointed disk on a spur   71 **jot** slightest bit   72 **jadery** tricks characteristic of a vicious horse   73 **that . . . bravely** who nonetheless kept in his saddle superbly.   74 **curb** strap attached to the bit to control the horse.   **girth** belt under the horse's belly to hold the saddle in place.   **diff'ring** different kinds of   81–2 **his full . . . load** the full weight of the horse now becomes the rider's load to be carried, as though the rider were the horse.   82 **Yet** (1) Still (2) Nonetheless   83–4 **But . . . approaches** but Arcite is like a ship that needs only one more big wave to founder.

91 **Reach** Extend   92 **told** counted out   98 **to honor** i.e., to honor the memory of Arcite.   100 **Acknowledge** Let us acknowledge   104 **arrose** bedew, sprinkle   107 **vouched** affirmed, guaranteed the truth of   108 **grace** honor   114 **passage** (1) occurrence (2) exchange of blows   115 **equal** impartial, fair and balanced.   123 **lovers** devoted followers   126 **in whose end** after which

As for him sorry. O you heavenly charmers, 131
What things you make of us! For what we lack
We laugh, for what we have are sorry, still
Are children in some kind. Let us be thankful
For that which is, and with you leave dispute 135
That are above our question. Let's go off, 136
And bear us like the time. *Flourish. Exeunt.* 137

Epilogue

[*Enter Epilogue.*]

EPILOGUE
I would now ask ye how ye like the play,
But, as it is with schoolboys, cannot say; 2

---

131 **charmers** i.e., gods, with their magical powers capable of
enchanting us   135–6 **and . . . question** and leave off disputing with
you, whose high will we must not question.   137 **bear . . . time** bear
ourselves in a matter suitable to the sad and yet joyful occasion.
Epilogue
2 **schoolboys** (Probably it is a juvenile actor who speaks.)   **say** speak

---

I am cruel fearful. Pray yet stay awhile, 3
And let me look upon ye. No man smile?
Then it goes hard, I see. He that has
Loved a young handsome wench, then, show his
    face—
'Tis strange if none be here—and if he will,
Against his conscience, let him hiss, and kill 8
Our market. 'Tis in vain, I see, to stay ye. 9
Have at the worst can come, then! Now, what say ye? 10
And yet mistake me not; I am not bold:
We have no such cause. If the tale we have told—
For 'tis no other—any way content ye,
For to that honest purpose it was meant ye,
We have our end; and ye shall have ere long, 15
I dare say, many a better to prolong
Your old loves to us. We and all our might
Rest at your service. Gentlemen, good night.
                              Flourish. [*Exit.*]

---

3 **cruel** extremely   8–9 **kill Our market** spoil the demand for this
play.   9 **stay** restrain   10 **Have . . . then!** Go ahead, then, do your
damnedst!   15 **end** intent, wish

The Poems

Venus and Adonis

Like most of his contemporaries, Shakespeare apparently did not regard the writing of plays as an elegant literary pursuit. He must have known that he was good at it, and he certainly became famous in his day as a playwright, but he took no pains over the publication of his plays. We have no literary prefaces for them, no indication that Shakespeare saw them through the press. Writing for the theater was rather like writing for the movies today: a profitable and even glamorous venture but subliterary. When Ben Jonson brought out his collected *Works* (mostly plays) during his lifetime, he was jeered at for his pretensions.

The writing of sonnets and other "serious" poetry, on the other hand, was conventionally a bid for true literary fame. Shakespeare's prefatory epistle to his *Venus and Adonis* betrays an eagerness for recognition. Deferentially, he seeks the sponsorship of the Earl of Southampton, in hopes of literary prestige as well as financial support. He speaks of *Venus and Adonis* as "the first heir of my invention," as though he had written no plays earlier, and promises Southampton a "graver labor" to appear shortly. *Venus and Adonis* in 1593 and *The Rape of Lucrece* in 1594 were, in fact, Shakespeare's first publications. Both were carefully and correctly printed. They were probably composed between June of 1592 and May of 1594, a period when the theaters were closed because of the plague. Shakespeare's belief in their importance to his literary career is confirmed by the reports of his contemporaries. Richard Barnfield singled them out as the works most likely to assure a place for Shakespeare in "fame's immortal book." Francis Meres, in his *Palladis Tamia: Wit's Treasury*, exclaimed in 1598 that "the sweet witty soul of Ovid lives in mellifluous and honey-tongued Shakespeare: witness his *Venus and Adonis*, his *Lucrece*, his sugared sonnets among his private friends, etc." Gabriel Harvey, although preferring *Lucrece* and *Hamlet* as more pleasing to "the wiser sort," conceded that "the younger sort takes much delight in Shakespeare's *Venus and Ado-*

nis." John Weever and still others add further testimonials to the extraordinary reputation of Shakespeare's nondramatic poems.

As Gabriel Harvey's puritanical comment on *Venus and Adonis* suggests, this poem was regarded as amatory and even risqué. It mirrored a current vogue for Ovidian erotic poetry, as exemplified by Thomas Lodge's *Scilla's Metamorphosis*, 1589 (in which an amorous nymph courts a reluctant young man), and by Christopher Marlowe's *Hero and Leander*. This latter poem, left unfinished at Marlowe's death in 1593 and published in 1598 with a continuation by George Chapman, was evidently circulated in manuscript, as were so many poems of this sophisticated sort, including Shakespeare's sonnets. Shakespeare may well have been influenced by Marlowe's tone of wryly comic detachment and sensuous grace. He may also have read Michael Drayton's *Endymion and Phoebe* (published in 1595 but written earlier), in which the erotic tradition is somewhat idealized into moral allegory. Most important, however, Shakespeare knew his Ovid, both firsthand and in Golding's English translation (1567). He appears to have combined three mythical tales from the *Metamorphoses*. The narrative outline is to be found in Venus's pursuit of Adonis (Book 10), but the bashful reluctance of the young man is more reminiscent of Hermaphroditus (Book 4) and Narcissus (Book 3). Hermaphroditus pleads youth as his reason for wishing to escape the clutches of the water nymph Salmacis and so is transformed with her into a single body containing both sexes; Narcissus evades the nymph Echo out of self-infatuation. Shakespeare has thus drawn a composite portrait of male coyness, a subject he was to explore further in the sonnets. Such a theme was suited to a nobleman of Southampton's youth and prospects. In tone it was also well suited to the aristocratic and intellectual set who read such poetry. Shakespeare here aimed at a more refined audience than that for which he wrote plays, though his theatrical audience must also have been generally intelligent. The ornate qualities of

Venus and Adonis should be judged in the fashionable context of a sophisticated audience.

The poem is, among other things, a tour de force of stylized poetic techniques. The story itself is relatively uneventful, and the characters are static. For two-thirds of the poem, very little happens other than a series of amorous claspings, from which Adonis feebly attempts to extricate himself. Even his subsequent fight with the boar and his violent death are occasions for rhetorical pathos rather than for vivid narrative description. The story is essentially a frame. Similarly, we must not expect psychological insight or meaningful self-discovery. The conventions of amatory verse do not encourage a serious interest in character. Venus and Adonis are mouthpieces for contrasting attitudes toward love. They debate a favorite courtly topic in the style of John Lyly. Both appeal to conventional wisdom and speak in *sententiae*, or aphoristic pronouncements. Venus, for example, warning Adonis of the need for caution in pursuing the boar, opines that "Danger deviseth shifts; wit waits on fear" (line 690). Adonis, pleading his unreadiness for love, cites commonplace analogies: "No fisher but the ungrown fry forbears. / The mellow plum doth fall, the green sticks fast" (lines 526–7). In substance, their arguments are equally conventional. Venus urges a carpe diem philosophy of seizing the moment of pleasure. "Make use of time, let not advantage slip; / Beauty within itself should not be wasted" (lines 129–30). She bolsters her claim with an appeal to the "law of nature," according to which all living things are obliged to reproduce themselves; only by begetting can humans conquer time and death. Yet, however close this position may be to a major theme of the sonnets, it does not go unchallenged. Adonis charges vigorously that Venus is only rationalizing her lust: "O strange excuse, / When reason is the bawd to lust's abuse!" (lines 791–2). His plea for more time in which to mature and prove his manliness is understandable, however much we may smile at his inability to be aroused by Venus's blandishments. Thus, neither contestant wins the argument. Venus is proved right in her fear that Adonis will be killed by the boar he hunts, but Adonis's rejection of idle lust for manly activity affirms a conventional idea of masculinity that requires the fleshing of one's killing sword as ritual prerequisite to the fleshing of one's phallic sword. The debate is, in a sense, an ingeniously elaborate literary exercise, yet it also allows for reflection on contrasting views of love as sensual and spiritual, absurd and magnificent, funny and serious.

The narrator's persona is central to the ambivalence in the debate. He, too, speaks in *sententiae*, and his aphorisms appear to sympathize with both contestants. At times, he affirms the irresistible force of love: "What though the rose have prickles, yet 'tis plucked" (line 574). At other times, he laughs at Venus for her vacillation of mood: "Thy weal and woe are both of them extremes. /

Despair and hope makes thee ridiculous" (lines 987–8). Like Ovid's usual persona, the speaker here is both intrigued and amused by love, compelled to heed its power and yet aware of the absurdities. The result is a characteristic Ovidian blend of irony and pathos. The irony is especially evident in the delightful comic touches that undermine the potential seriousness of the action: Venus like an Amazon pulling Adonis off his mount and tucking him under one arm, pouting and blushing; Adonis's horse chasing away after a mare in heat, leaving Adonis to fend for himself; Venus fainting at the thought of the boar and pulling Adonis right on top of her, "in the very lists of love, / Her champion mounted for the hot encounter" (lines 595–6). These devices distance us from the action and create an atmosphere of elegant if prurient entertainment. Yet the poem is also suffused with the rich pathos of sensuous emotion. Venus's sorrow over the death of Adonis is quite genuine. The sensuousness would cloy without the ironic humor, whereas the humor would seem frivolous without the pathos.

The poem hints at moral allegory, in the manner of Ovidian mythologizing. Venus represents herself as the goddess, not only of erotic passion, but also of eternal love conquering time and death. Because Adonis perversely spurns this ideal, Venus concludes that human beauty must perish and that human happiness must be subject to mischance. Yet this reading is only one part of the argument and is contradicted by an opposing suggestion that Adonis is the rational principle attempting unsuccessfully to govern human lust (the boar and Adonis's unbridled horse). These contradictions, which derive from the structure of the poem as a debate and also from Renaissance Neoplatonism, confirm our impression that the allegory is not the true "meaning" of the poem but is part of an ambiguous view of love as both exalted and earthly, a mystery that we will never comprehend in single terms. The allegory elevates the seriousness, adding poetic dignity to what might otherwise appear to be an unabashedly erotic poem. We should not minimize the sexual teasing or fail to acknowledge our own erotic pleasure in it. Venus's repeated encounters with Adonis take the form of ingeniously varied positions, ending in coital embrace, although without consummation. Adonis's passive role invites the male reader to fantasize himself in Adonis's place, being seduced by the goddess of beauty. The famous passage comparing Venus's body to a deer park with "pleasant fountains," "sweet bottom grass," and "round rising hillocks" (lines 229–40) is graphic through the use of double entendre without being pornographic. The poem is equally explicit in its "banquet" of the five senses (lines 433–50). This is the "naughty" Ovid of the *Ars Amatoria*.

Shakespeare's poem is an embroidery of poetic flourishes, of "conceits" or ingeniously wrought similes, of artfully constructed digressions, such as the narrative of

Adonis's horse, and of color symbolism. Images usually are drawn from nature (eagles, birds caught in nets, wolves, berries) or connote burning, blazing, and shining (torches, jewels). The dominant colors are red and white, usually paired antithetically: the red of the rising sun or Adonis's blushing face or Mars's ensign, the white of an alabaster hand or fresh bed linen or "ashy-pale" anger. Ironically, too, the boar's frothy-white mouth is stained with red, and Adonis's red blood blemishes his "wonted lily white." Adonis's flower, the anemone, is reddish-purple and white. A similarly balanced antithesis pervades the poem's rhetorical figures, as in the symmetrical repetition of words in grammatically parallel phrases (*parison*), or in phrases of equal length (*isocolon*), or in inverted order (*antimetabole*), or at the beginning and ending of a line (*epanalepsis*), and so on. These pyrotechnics may at first seem mechanical, but they, too, have a place in a work of art that celebrates both the erotic and the spiritual in love. Decoration has its function and is not mere embellishment for its own sake. At all events Shakespeare has created a powerful poetic variation on an ancient myth that is at the same time a rhetorical tour de force.

Venus and Adonis

*"Vilia miretur vulgus; mihi flavus Apollo
Pocula Castalia plena ministret aqua."*

To the RIGHT HONORABLE HENRY WRIOTHESLEY, *Earl of Southampton, and Baron of Titchfield.*

RIGHT HONORABLE,

   I know not how I shall offend in dedicating my unpolished lines to Your Lordship, nor how the world will censure me for choosing so strong a prop to support so weak a burden; only if Your Honor seem but pleased, I account myself highly praised, and vow to take advantage of all idle hours, till I have honored you with some graver labor. But if the first heir of my invention prove deformed, [7] I shall be sorry it had so noble a godfather, and never after ear so barren a land, for fear it yield me still so bad a harvest. [9] I leave it to your honorable survey, and Your Honor to your heart's content, which I wish may always answer your own wish and the world's hopeful expectation.

Your Honor's in all duty,

William Shakespeare.

Motto: *Vilia miretur,* etc. Let the base vulgar admire trash; may golden-haired Apollo serve me goblets filled from the Castalian spring. (Ovid, *Amores*, 1.15.35–6.)
Dedication: Henry Wriothesley, Earl of Southampton (A popular and brilliant young gentleman of nineteen years, already prominent at court. Subsequent dedications by Shakespeare and others indicate that he was a genuinely devoted patron of literature throughout his life.)

7 the first . . . invention (This phrase has been variously interpreted to mean Shakespeare's first written work, his first printed work, his first "invented" work in the sense that the plots of his plays were usually not original with him, his first work independent of collaborators, or his first "literary" work, since plays were unliterary in the Elizabethan sense. The second and last are the most probable.)   **9 ear** sow, cultivate

Even as the sun with purple-colored face
Had ta'en his last leave of the weeping morn,
Rose-cheeked Adonis hied him to the chase.
Hunting he loved, but love he laughed to scorn.
    Sick-thoughted Venus makes amain unto him,
    And like a boldfaced suitor 'gins to woo him.

"Thrice-fairer than myself," thus she began,
"The field's chief flower, sweet above compare,
Stain to all nymphs, more lovely than a man,
More white and red than doves or roses are:
    Nature that made thee, with herself at strife,
    Saith that the world hath ending with thy life.

"Vouchsafe, thou wonder, to alight thy steed,
And rein his proud head to the saddlebow.
If thou wilt deign this favor, for thy meed
A thousand honey secrets shalt thou know.
    Here come and sit, where never serpent hisses,
    And being set, I'll smother thee with kisses;

"And yet not cloy thy lips with loathed satiety,
But rather famish them amid their plenty,
Making them red and pale with fresh variety—
Ten kisses short as one, one long as twenty.
    A summer's day will seem an hour but short,
    Being wasted in such time-beguiling sport."

With this she seizeth on his sweating palm,
The precedent of pith and livelihood,
And, trembling in her passion, calls it balm,
Earth's sovereign salve, to do a goddess good.
    Being so enraged, desire doth lend her force
    Courageously to pluck him from his horse.

Over one arm the lusty courser's rein,
Under her other was the tender boy,
Who blushed and pouted in a dull disdain,
With leaden appetite, unapt to toy;
    She red and hot as coals of glowing fire,
    He red for shame, but frosty in desire.

The studded bridle on a ragged bough
Nimbly she fastens. Oh, how quick is love!

The steed is stallèd up, and even now
To tie the rider she begins to prove.
    Backward she pushed him, as she would be thrust,
    And governed him in strength, though not in lust.

So soon was she along as he was down,
Each leaning on their elbows and their hips.
Now doth she stroke his cheek, now doth he frown,
And 'gins to chide, but soon she stops his lips
    And kissing speaks, with lustful language broken,
    "If thou wilt chide, thy lips shall never open."

He burns with bashful shame; she with her tears
Doth quench the maiden burning of his cheeks.
Then with her windy sighs and golden hairs
To fan and blow them dry again she seeks.
    He saith she is immodest, blames her miss;
    What follows more, she murders with a kiss.

Even as an empty eagle, sharp by fast,
Tires with her beak on feathers, flesh, and bone,
Shaking her wings, devouring all in haste,
Till either gorge be stuffed or prey be gone,
    Even so she kissed his brow, his cheek, his chin,
    And where she ends she doth anew begin.

Forced to content, but never to obey,
Panting he lies and breatheth in her face.
She feedeth on the steam as on a prey,
And calls it heavenly moisture, air of grace,
    Wishing her cheeks were gardens full of flowers,
    So they were dewed with such distilling showers.

Look how a bird lies tangled in a net,
So fastened in her arms Adonis lies;
Pure shame and awed resistance made him fret,
Which bred more beauty in his angry eyes.
    Rain added to a river that is rank
    Perforce will force it overflow the bank.

Still she entreats, and prettily entreats,
For to a pretty ear she tunes her tale.
Still is he sullen, still he lours and frets,
Twixt crimson shame and anger ashy-pale.
    Being red, she loves him best; and being white,
    Her best is bettered with a more delight.

Look how he can, she cannot choose but love;
And by her fair immortal hand she swears
From his soft bosom never to remove,
Till he take truce with her contending tears,

Line numbers (left column): 1, 2, 3, 5, 9, 11, 12, 13, 14, 15, 16, 24, 25, 26, 28, 29, 30, 31, 33, 34

Line numbers (right column): 39, 40, 43, 47, 53, 55, 56, 58, 61, 66, 67, 69, 71, 77, 78, 81, 82

1 **purple-colored** red, blushing   2 **the weeping morn** the goddess of the dawn, Aurora, weeping tears (i.e., the dew of morning) at being left by the sun-god. (In the Greek myth, she weeps for the death of her lover, Tithonus.)   3 **hied him** betook himself, hastened   5 **Sick-thoughted** lovesick. **makes amain** hastens   9 **Stain . . . nymphs** eclipsing in beauty all young beautiful women   11–12 **Nature . . . life** Nature, having striven to surpass herself in making you her masterpiece, says that if you die the world will cease. (The story of Adonis's death, and of the anemone that springs from his blood, is a vegetation myth.)   13 **Vouchsafe** Deign. **alight** alight from   14 **the saddlebow** the arch in, or the pieces forming, the front of the saddle. (The image is of reining the horse's head sharply back.)   15 **meed** reward   16 **honey** sweet   24 **wasted** spent   25 **sweating** i.e., indicative of youth; not dried with age   26 **The precedent . . . livelihood** the sign of sexual strength and vitality   28 **sovereign** efficacious   29 **enraged** ardent   30 **Courageously** lustfully and boldly   31 **lusty courser's** vigorous horse's   33 **dull** moody, listless   34 **unapt to toy** undisposed to dally amorously

39 **stallèd** fastened, secured (as in a stall)   40 **prove** try.   43 **along** lying at his side   47 **broken** interrupted   53 **miss** offense, misconduct   55 **sharp by fast** hungry for lack of food   56 **Tires** tears, feeds ravenously   58 **gorge** bird's crop   61 **content** acquiesce. **obey** i.e., answer her lust   66 **So** provided that. **distilling** gently falling, in fine droplets   67 **Look how** Just as   69 **awed** daunted, overborne   71 **rank** full to overflowing   77 **Being** i.e., He being   78 **more** greater   81 **remove** move, remove herself   82 **take truce** come to terms

Which long have rained, making her cheeks all wet;
And one sweet kiss shall pay this countless debt.   84

Upon this promise did he raise his chin,
Like a divedapper peering through a wave,   86
Who, being looked on, ducks as quickly in.
So offers he to give what she did crave;
    But when her lips were ready for his pay,   89
    He winks and turns his lips another way.   90

Never did passenger in summer's heat   91
More thirst for drink than she for this good turn.
Her help she sees, but help she cannot get;
She bathes in water, yet her fire must burn.   94
    "Oh, pity," 'gan she cry, "flint-hearted boy!
    'Tis but a kiss I beg. Why art thou coy?

"I have been wooed, as I entreat thee now,
Even by the stern and direful god of war,   98
Whose sinewy neck in battle ne'er did bow,
Who conquers where he comes in every jar;   100
    Yet hath he been my captive and my slave,
    And begged for that which thou unasked shalt have.

"Over my altars hath he hung his lance,
His battered shield, his uncontrollèd crest,   104
And for my sake hath learned to sport and dance,
To toy, to wanton, dally, smile, and jest,   106
    Scorning his churlish drum and ensign red,
    Making my arms his field, his tent my bed.   108

"Thus he that overruled I overswayed,
Leading him prisoner in a red-rose chain.
Strong-tempered steel his stronger strength obeyed,
Yet was he servile to my coy disdain.   112
    Oh, be not proud, nor brag not of thy might,
    For mastering her that foiled the god of fight!   114

"Touch but my lips with those fair lips of thine—   115
Though mine be not so fair, yet are they red—
The kiss shall be thine own as well as mine.   117
What see'st thou in the ground? Hold up thy head.
    Look in mine eyeballs, there thy beauty lies;   119
    Then why not lips on lips, since eyes in eyes?

"Art thou ashamed to kiss? Then wink again,   121
And I will wink; so shall the day seem night.
Love keeps his revels where there are but twain;
Be bold to play, our sport is not in sight.   124

These blue-veined violets whereon we lean
Never can blab, nor know not what we mean.   126

"The tender spring upon thy tempting lip   127
Shows thee unripe, yet mayst thou well be tasted.
Make use of time, let not advantage slip;   129
Beauty within itself should not be wasted.   130
    Fair flowers that are not gathered in their prime
    Rot and consume themselves in little time.

"Were I hard-favored, foul, or wrinkled old,   133
Ill-nurtured, crooked, churlish, harsh in voice,
O'erworn, despisèd, rheumatic, and cold,   135
Thick-sighted, barren, lean, and lacking juice,   136
    Then mightst thou pause, for then I were not for thee;
    But having no defects, why dost abhor me?

"Thou canst not see one wrinkle in my brow;
Mine eyes are gray and bright and quick in turning;   140
My beauty as the spring doth yearly grow,   141
My flesh is soft and plump, my marrow burning;   142
    My smooth moist hand, were it with thy hand felt,   143
    Would in thy palm dissolve, or seem to melt.

"Bid me discourse, I will enchant thine ear,
Or like a fairy, trip upon the green,   146
Or like a nymph, with long disheveled hair,
Dance on the sands, and yet no footing seen.   148
    Love is a spirit all compact of fire,   149
    Not gross to sink, but light, and will aspire.   150

"Witness this primrose bank whereon I lie;
These forceless flowers like sturdy trees support me.   152
Two strengthless doves will draw me through the sky,   153
From morn till night, even where I list to sport me.   154
    Is love so light, sweet boy, and may it be   155
    That thou shouldst think it heavy unto thee?   156

"Is thine own heart to thine own face affected?   157
Can thy right hand seize love upon thy left?   158
Then woo thyself, be of thyself rejected;   159
Steal thine own freedom and complain on theft.   160

126 **mean** intend.   127 **spring** growth (i.e., downy hair)   129 **advantage** opportunity   130 **Beauty . . . wasted** beauty should not be wasted by being kept to itself.   133 **hard-favored** ugly.   **foul** ugly   135 **O'erworn** worn by time   136 **Thick-sighted** dim-eyed   140 **gray** i.e., blue.   **quick in turning** animated   141 **as . . . grow** is perennially renewed, like spring   142 **marrow** vital animal spirit.   **burning** sexually ardent   143 **moist** (Indicative of youth and passion, as with *sweating* in line 25.)   146 **trip** dance   148 **footing** footprint   149 **compact** composed   150 **gross** heavy. (The heavy elements, earth and water, sink; fire and air rise.)   **aspire** rise.   152 **forceless** frail   153 **doves** (Venus's chariot was depicted as being drawn by doves.)   154 **list** desire   155 **light** (1) rising, weightless (2) wanton   156 **heavy** (1) weighty (2) troublous   157 **affected** drawn by affection.   **158–60 Can . . . theft** i.e., Do you think you can you find love by having one hand woo the other, as if love were wholly contained within oneself? Then go ahead, play all the roles of love yourself: woo yourself, find yourself rejected by yourself, make captive your own heart to yourself and complain of yourself as the thief of love.   159 **of** by

84 **countless** beyond reckoning   86 **divedapper** dabchick, a common English waterbird   89 **for his pay** to be paid by him (with a kiss)   90 **winks** shuts his eyes (and winces)   91 **passenger** wayfarer   94 **water** i.e., her tears.   **fire** (of passion)   98 **direful** inspiring dread.   **god of war** Mars   100 **where** wherever.   **jar** fight   104 **uncontrollèd** unconquered, unbowed.   **crest** i.e., of helmet   106 **toy, wanton, dally** sport amorously   108 **arms** (With a pun on "weapons.")   112 **coy** aloof, teasing   114 **foiled** vanquished   115 **Touch** If you touch   117 **thine . . . mine** i.e., mutual, shared.   119 **there . . . lies** i.e., (1) see your beauty reflected there (2) your beauty lies in my beholding   121 **wink** close the eyes   124 **not in sight** observed by no one.

Narcissus so himself himself forsook, 161
And died to kiss his shadow in the brook. 162

"Torches are made to light, jewels to wear,
Dainties to taste, fresh beauty for the use,
Herbs for their smell, and sappy plants to bear. 165
Things growing to themselves are growth's abuse. 166
    Seeds spring from seeds, and beauty breedeth beauty.
    Thou wast begot; to get it is thy duty. 168

"Upon the earth's increase why shouldst thou feed,
Unless the earth with thy increase be fed?
By law of nature thou art bound to breed,
That thine may live when thou thyself art dead; 172
    And so, in spite of death, thou dost survive,
    In that thy likeness still is left alive."

By this the lovesick queen began to sweat, 175
For where they lay the shadow had forsook them,
And Titan, tirèd in the midday heat, 177
With burning eye did hotly overlook them, 178
    Wishing Adonis had his team to guide, 179
    So he were like him, and by Venus' side. 180

And now Adonis, with a lazy sprite, 181
And with a heavy, dark, disliking eye,
His louring brows o'erwhelming his fair sight, 183
Like misty vapors when they blot the sky,
    Souring his cheeks, cries, "Fie, no more of love! 185
    The sun doth burn my face; I must remove." 186

"Ay me," quoth Venus, "young, and so unkind? 187
What bare excuses mak'st thou to be gone!
I'll sigh celestial breath, whose gentle wind
Shall cool the heat of this descending sun.
    I'll make a shadow for thee of my hairs;
    If they burn too, I'll quench them with my tears.

"The sun that shines from heaven shines but warm, 193
And, lo, I lie between that sun and thee.
The heat I have from thence doth little harm;
Thine eye darts forth the fire that burneth me,
    And were I not immortal, life were done 197
    Between this heavenly and earthly sun.

"Art thou obdurate, flinty, hard as steel?
Nay, more than flint, for stone at rain relenteth. 200
Art thou a woman's son, and canst not feel
What 'tis to love, how want of love tormenteth? 202
    Oh, had thy mother borne so hard a mind,
    She had not brought forth thee, but died unkind. 204

"What am I, that thou shouldst contemn me this? 205
Or what great danger dwells upon my suit? 206
What were thy lips the worse for one poor kiss? 207
Speak, fair, but speak fair words, or else be mute. 208
    Give me one kiss, I'll give it thee again, 209
    And one for interest, if thou wilt have twain.

"Fie, lifeless picture, cold and senseless stone, 211
Well-painted idol, image dull and dead,
Statue contenting but the eye alone,
Thing like a man, but of no woman bred!
    Thou art no man, though of a man's complexion, 215
    For men will kiss even by their own direction." 216

This said, impatience chokes her pleading tongue,
And swelling passion doth provoke a pause.
Red cheeks and fiery eyes blaze forth her wrong; 219
Being judge in love, she cannot right her cause. 220
    And now she weeps, and now she fain would speak, 221
    And now her sobs do her intendments break. 222

Sometime she shakes her head and then his hand, 223
Now gazeth she on him, now on the ground;
Sometime her arms enfold him like a band. 225
She would, he will not in her arms be bound;
    And when from thence he struggles to be gone,
    She locks her lily fingers one in one.

"Fondling," she saith, "since I have hemmed thee here 229
Within the circuit of this ivory pale, 230
I'll be a park, and thou shalt be my deer. 231
Feed where thou wilt, on mountain or in dale;
    Graze on my lips; and if those hills be dry,
    Stray lower, where the pleasant fountains lie. 234

"Within this limit is relief enough, 235
Sweet bottom grass and high delightful plain, 236

---

161 Narcissus a beautiful youth in classical mythology who, leaning over a pool to drink, fell in love with his reflection and stayed there until he died. He was afterward changed into a flower. (Ovid, *Metamorphoses*, 3.339–510.) **himself himself forsook** i.e., abandoned himself to a hopeless passion for himself **162 to kiss his shadow** seeking fruitlessly to kiss his own reflection **165 sappy plants** sap-bearing fruit trees **166 Things . . . abuse** Things that grow solely for their own use abuse the very purpose of growth. **168 get** beget, procreate **172 thine** your progeny **175 By this** By this time **177 Titan** the sun-god. **tirèd** (1) attired (2) weary **178 overlook** look upon **179 his team** i.e., Titan's team of horses **180 So . . . side** i.e., so that he, Titan, might be in Adonis's place. **181 lazy sprite** dull spirit **183 o'erwhelming** overhanging so as to cover. **sight** eyes **185 Souring his cheeks** scowling **186 remove** move. **187 unkind** unrelenting; unnatural. **193 shines but warm** merely makes me warm (whereas you burn me up) **197 were done** would be done for, finished

200 relenteth wears slowly away. **202 want of love** being denied reciprocal love **204 unkind** unnaturally unrelenting, not fulfilling her natural function. **205 contemn me this** scornfully refuse me this request, or, scorn me thus. **206 dwells upon** attends **207 What** In what way **208 Speak, fair** Speak, handsome youth. **fair words** kind words **209 Give** If you give **211 senseless** insensible **215 complexion** outward appearance **216 direction** inclination. **219 blaze forth** proclaim. (With a metaphorical sense of "seem to burn," "show by their flaming.") **220 Being . . . cause** although goddess and hence arbiter of love, Venus cannot prevail in her own case. **221 fain** gladly **222 do . . . break** interrupt what she intends to say. **223 his hand** (i.e., not in a handshake but in a gesture of frustration) **225 like a band** as in a bond or fetter. **229 Fondling** Foolish one **230 pale** fence (i.e., her arms; the sexual topography is continued in *fountains, bottom grass, hillocks, brakes*, etc.) **231 park** deer preserve. **deer** (With a pun on *dear*.) **234 fountains** (1) springs (2) breasts **235 limit** boundary. **relief** (1) pasture (2) sexual pleasure (3) variety of landscape **236 bottom grass** valley grass. (With an allusion to pubic hair.) **plain** i.e., mons veneris or the stomach (?)

Round rising hillocks, brakes obscure and rough, 237
To shelter thee from tempest and from rain.
    Then be my deer, since I am such a park;
    No dog shall rouse thee, though a thousand bark." 240

At this Adonis smiles as in disdain,
That in each cheek appears a pretty dimple. 242
Love made those hollows, if himself were slain, 243
He might be buried in a tomb so simple, 244
    Foreknowing well, if there he came to lie,
    Why, there Love lived; and there he could not die. 246

These lovely caves, these round enchanting pits,
Opened their mouths to swallow Venus' liking. 248
Being mad before, how doth she now for wits? 249
Struck dead at first, what needs a second striking?
    Poor queen of love, in thine own law forlorn, 251
    To love a cheek that smiles at thee in scorn!

Now which way shall she turn? What shall she say?
Her words are done, her woes the more increasing;
The time is spent; her object will away,
And from her twining arms doth urge releasing.
    "Pity," she cries, "some favor, some remorse!" 257
    Away he springs and hasteth to his horse.

But, lo, from forth a copse that neighbors by, 259
A breeding jennet, lusty, young, and proud, 260
Adonis' trampling courser doth espy,
And forth she rushes, snorts, and neighs aloud.
    The strong-necked steed, being tied unto a tree,
    Breaketh his rein, and to her straight goes he. 264

Imperiously he leaps, he neighs, he bounds,
And now his woven girths he breaks asunder. 266
The bearing earth with his hard hoof he wounds, 267
Whose hollow womb resounds like heaven's thunder.
    The iron bit he crusheth 'tween his teeth,
    Controlling what he was controllèd with.

His ears up-pricked, his braided hanging mane
Upon his compassed crest now stand on end; 272
His nostrils drink the air, and forth again,
As from a furnace, vapors doth he send.
    His eye, which scornfully glisters like fire,
    Shows his hot courage and his high desire. 276

Sometime he trots, as if he told the steps, 277
With gentle majesty and modest pride;
Anon he rears upright, curvets, and leaps, 279
As who should say, "Lo, thus my strength is tried, 280
    And this I do to captivate the eye
    Of the fair breeder that is standing by."

What recketh he his rider's angry stir, 283
His flattering "Holla," or his "Stand, I say"? 284
What cares he now for curb or pricking spur?
For rich caparisons or trappings gay? 286
    He sees his love, and nothing else he sees,
    For nothing else with his proud sight agrees.

Look when a painter would surpass the life, 289
In limning out a well-proportioned steed, 290
His art with nature's workmanship at strife,
As if the dead the living should exceed, 292
    So did this horse excel a common one
    In shape, in courage, color, pace, and bone. 294

Round-hoofed, short-jointed, fetlocks shag and long, 295
Broad breast, full eye, small head, and nostril wide,
High crest, short ears, straight legs and passing strong, 297
Thin mane, thick tail, broad buttock, tender hide: 298
    Look what a horse should have he did not lack, 299
    Save a proud rider on so proud a back.

Sometime he scuds far off, and there he stares;
Anon he starts at stirring of a feather;
To bid the wind a base he now prepares, 303
And whe'er he run or fly they know not whether; 304
    For through his mane and tail the high wind sings,
    Fanning the hairs, who wave like feathered wings.

He looks upon his love and neighs unto her;
She answers him as if she knew his mind.
Being proud, as females are, to see him woo her,
She puts on outward strangeness, seems unkind, 310
    Spurns at his love and scorns the heat he feels, 311
    Beating his kind embracements with her heels. 312

Then, like a melancholy malcontent,
He vails his tail that, like a falling plume, 314

---

277 **told** numbered   279 **curvets** raises his forelegs and then springs with his hind legs before the forelegs reach the ground   280 **As who should** as one might. **tried** tested   283 **What recketh he** What does he care about or pay attention to. **stir** bustle, agitation   284 **flattering** cajoling. **Holla** Stop   286 **caparisons** gaily ornamental cloth coverings for the saddle and harness   289 **Look when** Just as when   290 **limning out** portraying, drawing   292 **dead** inanimate   294 **bone** frame.   295 **short-jointed** with short pasterns, the part of the horse's foot between the hoof and the fetlock. **fetlocks** lower part of horses' legs where the tuft of hair grows behind, just above the hoof. **shag** shaggy   297 **crest** ridge of the neck. **passing** surpassingly   298 **tender hide** i.e., delicate of hide, not coarse   299 **Look what** whatever   303 **bid the wind a base** challenge the wind to a contest. (From the children's game of prisoner's base.)   304 **whe'er** whether. **whether** which of the two   310 **outward strangeness** seeming indifference. **unkind** unattracted sexually, not responding to natural feeling   311 **Spurns at** (1) kicks at (2) repels   312 **kind** (1) affectionate, passionate (2) prompted by nature   314 **vails** lowers

237 **hillocks** buttocks (?) **brakes** patches of dense fern and bracken. (Again with sexual suggestion.) **obscure** dark. **rough** shaggy, dense   240 **rouse** cause to start from cover   242 **That** so that 243 **Love** Cupid. **if** so that if   244 **simple** unadorned   246 **Love** (1) the essence of love, loveliness (2) Cupid himself   248 **Opened . . . liking** i.e., looked so winsome in their dimpling that Venus was engulfed, swallowed up, by love. **liking** desire.   249 **how . . . wits?** how may she keep her sanity now?   251 **in . . . forlorn** condemned to suffer under your own rule of love   257 **remorse** compassion. 259 **copse . . . by** neighboring thicket   260 **breeding jennet** small Spanish mare in heat. **lusty** spirited   264 **straight** straightway 266 **girths** cloth belts securing the saddle   267 **bearing** receiving 272 **compassed crest** arched ridge of the neck. **stand on end** (The hairs of the mane stand on end.)   276 **courage** passion

Cool shadow to his melting buttock lent;
He stamps and bites the poor flies in his fume.   316
  His love, perceiving how he was enraged,
  Grew kinder, and his fury was assuaged.

His testy master goeth about to take him,   319
When, lo, the unbacked breeder, full of fear,   320
Jealous of catching, swiftly doth forsake him,   321
With her the horse, and left Adonis there.   322
  As they were mad, unto the wood they hie them,   323
  Outstripping crows that strive to overfly them.   324

All swoll'n with chafing, down Adonis sits,   325
Banning his boisterous and unruly beast;   326
And now the happy season once more fits   327
That lovesick Love by pleading may be blest;   328
  For lovers say the heart hath treble wrong
  When it is barred the aidance of the tongue.   330

An oven that is stopped, or river stayed,   331
Burneth more hotly, swelleth with more rage;
So of concealèd sorrow may be said.   333
Free vent of words love's fire doth assuage;   334
  But when the heart's attorney once is mute,   335
  The client breaks, as desperate in his suit.   336

He sees her coming and begins to glow,
Even as a dying coal revives with wind,
And with his bonnet hides his angry brow,   339
Looks on the dull earth with disturbèd mind,
  Taking no notice that she is so nigh,   341
  For all askance he holds her in his eye.   342

Oh, what a sight it was, wistly to view   343
How she came stealing to the wayward boy!
To note the fighting conflict of her hue,
How white and red each other did destroy!
  But now her cheek was pale, and by and by   347
  It flashed forth fire, as lightning from the sky.

Now was she just before him as he sat,
And like a lowly lover down she kneels;
With one fair hand she heaveth up his hat,
Her other tender hand his fair cheek feels.
  His tenderer cheek receives her soft hand's print,   353
  As apt as new-fall'n snow takes any dint.   354

Oh, what a war of looks was then between them!
Her eyes petitioners to his eyes suing,
His eyes saw her eyes as they had not seen them;   357
Her eyes wooed still, his eyes disdained the wooing;
  And all this dumb play had his acts made plain   359
  With tears which, choruslike, her eyes did rain.   360

Full gently now she takes him by the hand,
A lily prisoned in a jail of snow,
Or ivory in an alabaster band;
So white a friend engirts so white a foe.   364
  This beauteous combat, willful and unwilling,
  Showed like two silver doves that sit a-billing.   366

Once more the engine of her thoughts began: 367
"O fairest mover on this mortal round,   368
Would thou wert as I am, and I a man,
My heart all whole as thine, thy heart my wound!   370
  For one sweet look thy help I would assure thee,   371
  Though nothing but my body's bane would cure thee."   372

"Give me my hand," saith he. "Why dost thou feel it?"   373
"Give me my heart," saith she, "and thou shalt have it.   374
Oh, give it me, lest thy hard heart do steel it,   375
And being steeled, soft sighs can never grave it.   376
  Then love's deep groans I never shall regard,
  Because Adonis' heart hath made mine hard."

"For shame," he cries, "let go, and let me go!
My day's delight is past, my horse is gone,   339
And 'tis your fault I am bereft him so.   381
I pray you hence, and leave me here alone;   382
  For all my mind, my thought, my busy care,
  Is how to get my palfrey from the mare."   384

Thus she replies: "Thy palfrey, as he should,
Welcomes the warm approach of sweet desire.
Affection is a coal that must be cooled,   387
Else, suffered, it will set the heart on fire.   388
  The sea hath bounds, but deep desire hath none;
  Therefore no marvel though thy horse be gone.

"How like a jade he stood, tied to the tree,   391
Servilely mastered with a leathern rein!
But when he saw his love, his youth's fair fee,   393

---

316 **fume** anger.   319 **testy** irritated.   **goeth about** makes an effort
320 **unbacked breeder** unbroken and riderless mare in heat
321 **Jealous of catching** wary of being caught   322 **horse** i.e., stallion
323 **As** As if.   **hie them** hasten   324 **overfly them** fly faster than
they can run, or, keep pace above them in flight.   325 **swoll'n with**
chafing puffed with anger   326 **Banning** cursing   327 **fits** is fitting,
is suited   328 **Love** i.e., Venus, the goddess of love (not Cupid, as in
lines 243–6)   330 **aidance** help   331 **stopped** stopped up.   **stayed**
dammed   333 **may** it may   334 **love's . . . assuage** assuages love's fire
335 **the heart's attorney** i.e., the tongue   336 **breaks** (1) goes bankrupt
(2) breaks asunder, as the heart is said to break in rejected love
339 **And . . . brow** and pulls his hat down over his frowning brows
341 **Taking** i.e., pretending to take   342 **all . . . eye** he watches her out
of the corner of his eye.   343 **wistly** earnestly, attentively   347 **But**
now A short time ago   353 **tenderer** i.e., even more tender than her
hand   354 **dint** impression.

357 **as** as if   359–60 **And . . . rain** and all this silent action, as if in a
dumbshow preceding a play, was interpreted by her choruslike tears.
(In line 359, *his* means "its.")   364 **engirts** surrounds   366 **Showed**
looked   367 **the engine of her thoughts** her tongue   368 **mover** one
who moves or walks; also, one who imparts motion to the universe
itself.   **mortal round** earth   370 **thy heart my wound** would that
your heart suffered my wound.   371 **For** In return for.   **thy help . . .**
thee I would promise to help you   372 **bane** ruin, death. (With a suggestion of sexual surrender.)   373 **Give me** Let go   374 **it** your hand.
375 **give . . . it** give me back my heart, lest your hardness of heart turn
it to steel. (With a suggestion of *steal:* don't steal my heart from me.)
376 **grave** engrave, make an impression on   381 **bereft** deprived of
382 **hence** go away   384 **palfrey** saddle horse   387 **Affection . . .**
cooled Passion is an ember that must be quenched through satisfaction of desire   388 **suffered** permitted to continue   391 **jade** spirit-
less, worn-out nag   393 **fair fee** due reward

He held such petty bondage in disdain,
    Throwing the base thong from his bending crest,   395
    Enfranchising his mouth, his back, his breast.   396

"Who sees his true love in her naked bed,   397
Teaching the sheets a whiter hue than white,
But when his glutton eye so full hath fed,   399
His other agents aim at like delight?   400
    Who is so faint that dares not be so bold
    To touch the fire, the weather being cold?

"Let me excuse thy courser, gentle boy;
And learn of him, I heartily beseech thee,
To take advantage on presented joy.   405
Though I were dumb, yet his proceedings teach thee.   406
    Oh, learn to love; the lesson is but plain,
    And once made perfect, never lost again."   408

"I know not love," quoth he, "nor will not know it,
Unless it be a boar, and then I chase it;
'Tis much to borrow, and I will not owe it;   411
My love to love is love but to disgrace it;   412
    For I have heard it is a life in death,
    That laughs and weeps, and all but with a breath.   414

"Who wears a garment shapeless and unfinished?
Who plucks the bud before one leaf put forth?
If springing things be any jot diminished,   417
They wither in their prime, prove nothing worth.
    The colt that's backed and burdened being young   419
    Loseth his pride and never waxeth strong.

"You hurt my hand with wringing. Let us part
And leave this idle theme, this bootless chat.   422
Remove your siege from my unyielding heart;
To love's alarms it will not ope the gate.   424
    Dismiss your vows, your feignèd tears, your flatt'ry;
    For where a heart is hard they make no batt'ry."   426

"What, canst thou talk?" quoth she. "Hast thou a
    tongue?
Oh, would thou hadst not, or I had no hearing!
Thy mermaid's voice hath done me double wrong;   429
I had my load before, now pressed with bearing: 430
    Melodious discord, heavenly tune harsh sounding,
    Ear's deep sweet music, and heart's deep sore
      wounding.

"Had I no eyes but ears, my ears would love
That inward beauty and invisible;   434
Or were I deaf, thy outward parts would move   435
Each part in me that were but sensible.   436
    Though neither eyes nor ears, to hear nor see,
    Yet should I be in love by touching thee.

"Say that the sense of feeling were bereft me,
And that I could not see, nor hear, nor touch,
And nothing but the very smell were left me,
Yet would my love to thee be still as much;
    For from the stillitory of thy face excelling   443
    Comes breath perfumed that breedeth love by smelling.

"But oh, what banquet wert thou to the taste,
Being nurse and feeder of the other four!
Would they not wish the feast might ever last,
And bid Suspicion double-lock the door,   448
    Lest Jealousy, that sour unwelcome guest,
    Should, by his stealing in, disturb the feast?"

Once more the ruby-colored portal opened,   451
Which to his speech did honey passage yield,   452
Like a red morn, that ever yet betokened
Wreck to the seaman, tempest to the field,   454
    Sorrow to shepherds, woe unto the birds,
    Gusts and foul flaws to herdmen and to herds.   456

This ill presage advisedly she marketh.   457
Even as the wind is hushed before it raineth,
Or as the wolf doth grin before he barketh,   459
Or as the berry breaks before it staineth,
    Or like the deadly bullet of a gun,
    His meaning struck her ere his words begun.

And at his look she flatly falleth down,
For looks kill love, and love by looks reviveth;
A smile recures the wounding of a frown.   465
But blessèd bankrupt, that by love so thriveth!   466
    The silly boy, believing she is dead,   467
    Claps her pale cheek, till clapping makes it red;

And all amazed brake off his late intent,   469
For sharply he did think to reprehend her,
Which cunning Love did wittily prevent.
Fair fall the wit that can so well defend her!   472
    For on the grass she lies as she were slain,   473
    Till his breath breatheth life in her again.

395 base worthless, paltry.   **bending crest** arching ridge of the neck **396 Enfranchising** freeing   **397 in . . . bed** naked in her bed   **399 But when** but that when   **400 agents** organs, senses   **405 on presented joy** of joy that presents itself.   **406 dumb** unable to speak   **408 made perfect** learned completely   **411 borrow** assume as an obligation. **owe** obligate myself to repay   **412 My . . . disgrace it** my only inclination toward love is a desire to render it contemptible, discredit it **414 all . . . breath** all in the same breath.   **417 springing** sprouting, immature   **419 backed** broken in   **422 idle** useless.   **bootless** profitless   **424 alarms** signals of attack   **426 batt'ry** breach in a fortified wall.   **429 mermaid's** siren's   **430 I . . . bearing** I was already burdened with desire; now I am oppressed by the weight of it, hearing your voice

434 That . . . invisible i.e., the unseen beauty of your voice   **435 deaf** i.e., deaf as well as blind.   **outward parts** i.e., tangible body   **436 sensible** susceptible to sensual impressions.   **443 For . . . excelling** for from the distillery of your unmatchable face   **448 Suspicion** watchfulness against danger   **451 portal** i.e., mouth   **452 honey** sweet   **454 Wreck** shipwreck. (A red sun at sunrise proverbially betokens a storm.)   **tempest to the field** a heavy storm that beats down the grain   **456 flaws** gusts of wind   **457 ill presage** prediction of storm.   **advisedly** attentively   **459 grin** bare its teeth   **465 recures** cures   **466 blessèd bankrupt** (In becoming like a bankrupt, she paradoxically regains a fortune, i.e., Adonis's attention.)   **467 silly** naive   **469 amazed** perplexed, distraught.   **brake** broke   **472 Fair fall** Good luck befall. (With a pun on the idea of her falling down without hurting herself.)   **473 as** as if

He wrings her nose, he strikes her on the cheeks,   475
He bends her fingers, holds her pulses hard,   476
He chafes her lips; a thousand ways he seeks
To mend the hurt that his unkindness marred.   478
   He kisses her, and she, by her good will,   479
   Will never rise, so he will kiss her still.   480

The night of sorrow now is turned to day.
Her two blue windows faintly she upheaveth,
Like the fair sun, when in his fresh array
He cheers the morn and all the earth relieveth;
   And as the bright sun glorifies the sky,
   So is her face illumined with her eye,

Whose beams upon his hairless face are fixed,
As if from thence they borrowed all their shine.
Were never four such lamps together mixed,   489
Had not his clouded with his brow's repine;   490
   But hers, which through the crystal tears gave light,
   Shone like the moon in water seen by night.

"Oh, where am I?" quoth she, "in earth or heaven,
Or in the ocean drenched, or in the fire?   494
What hour is this? Or morn or weary even?   495
Do I delight to die, or life desire?
   But now I lived, and life was death's annoy;   497
   But now I died, and death was lively joy.   498

"Oh, thou didst kill me; kill me once again!
Thy eyes' shrewd tutor, that hard heart of thine,   500
Hath taught them scornful tricks and such disdain
That they have murdered this poor heart of mine;
   And these mine eyes, true leaders to their queen,   503
   But for thy piteous lips no more had seen.   504

"Long may they kiss each other, for this cure!   505
Oh, never let their crimson liveries wear!   506
And as they last, their verdure still endure,   507
To drive infection from the dangerous year,
   That the stargazers, having writ on death,   509
   May say the plague is banished by thy breath!

"Pure lips, sweet seals in my soft lips imprinted,   511
What bargains may I make, still to be sealing?   512
To sell myself I can be well contented,

So thou wilt buy and pay and use good dealing,   514
   Which purchase if thou make, for fear of slips   515
   Set thy seal manual on my wax-red lips.   516

"A thousand kisses buys my heart from me;
And pay them at thy leisure, one by one.
What is ten hundred touches unto thee?   519
Are they not quickly told and quickly gone?   520
   Say for nonpayment that the debt should double,
   Is twenty hundred kisses such a trouble?"

"Fair queen," quoth he, "if any love you owe me,   523
Measure my strangeness with my unripe years.   524
Before I know myself, seek not to know me.   525
No fisher but the ungrown fry forbears.   526
   The mellow plum doth fall; the green sticks fast,
   Or being early plucked is sour to taste.

"Look the world's comforter, with weary gait,   529
His day's hot task hath ended in the west;
The owl, night's herald, shrieks; 'tis very late;
The sheep are gone to fold, birds to their nest,
   And coal-black clouds that shadow heaven's light
   Do summon us to part and bid good night.

"Now let me say 'Good night,' and so say you;
If you will say so, you shall have a kiss."
"Good night," quoth she, and, ere he says "Adieu,"
The honey fee of parting tendered is.   538
   Her arms do lend his neck a sweet embrace;
   Incorporate then they seem; face grows to face;   540

Till, breathless, he disjoined, and backward drew
The heavenly moisture, that sweet coral mouth,
Whose precious taste her thirsty lips well knew,
Whereon they surfeit, yet complain on drouth.   544
   He with her plenty pressed, she faint with dearth,   545
   Their lips together glued, fall to the earth.

Now quick desire hath caught the yielding prey,
And gluttonlike she feeds, yet never filleth;
Her lips are conquerors, his lips obey,
Paying what ransom the insulter willeth,   550
   Whose vulture thought doth pitch the price so high   551
   That she will draw his lips' rich treasure dry.

And having felt the sweetness of the spoil,   553
With blindfold fury she begins to forage;

475 He . . . nose (A standard first-aid remedy; briefly stopping the air supply can induce the patient to resume breathing.)   **476 bends her fingers** (as a stimulus or test of consciousness).   **holds . . . hard** takes her pulse   **478 marred** caused to her detriment.   **479 good will** consent   **480 so** so that, or, provided.   **still** continually.   **489 Were never** Never before were   **490 repine** vexation   **494 drenched** drowned   **495 Or** Either   **497 death's annoy** i.e., as wretched as death   **498 lively joy** i.e., as joyous as life.   **500 shrewd** sharp, harsh   **503 leaders** guides.   **queen** i.e., the heart   **504 But for** were it not for.   **seen** had the power of sight.   **505 they** i.e., your lips.   **for** in payment for, as a means of effecting   **506 crimson liveries** uniforms or costumes of crimson.   **wear** wear out.   **507 their verdure** may their fresh fragrance. (Alludes to belief in the efficacy of certain herbs to ward off contagion.)   **509 writ on death** predicted (by means of astrology) an epidemic of deadly plague   **511 seals . . . imprinted** stamps that have left their impression on my soft lips   **512 still to be sealing** (1) to continue kissing always (2) to seal a bargain.

514 So provided that   **515 slips** errors or fraudulent payment (which Venus suggests they avoid by means of a *seal manual* or seal placed on the contract of their love)   **516 wax-red** (since wax would be used in sealing)   **519 touches** i.e., kisses   **520 told** counted   **523 owe** bear   **524 Measure . . . with** i.e., explain my reserve by   **525 to know me** (With erotic suggestion of carnal knowledge.)   **526 No . . . forbears** There is no fisherman who does not throw back immature fish.   **529 Look . . . comforter** See how the sun   **538 honey** sweet.   **tendered is** is given.   **540 Incorporate** united into one body   **544 on drouth** of drought, of not having enough.   **545 with . . . pressed** oppressed with the plenty she has bestowed on him   **550 insulter** boasting conqueror   **551 Whose . . . high** whose ravenous desire demands so high a price (in kisses)   **553 spoil** plunder, conquest

Her face doth reek and smoke, her blood doth boil,   555
And careless lust stirs up a desperate courage,   556
   Planting oblivion, beating reason back,   557
   Forgetting shame's pure blush and honor's wrack.   558

Hot, faint, and weary with her hard embracing,
Like a wild bird being tamed with too much handling,
Or as the fleet-foot roe that's tired with chasing,   561
Or like the froward infant stilled with dandling,   562
   He now obeys, and now no more resisteth,
   While she takes all she can, not all she listeth.   564

What wax so frozen but dissolves with temp'ring   565
And yields at last to every light impression?
Things out of hope are compassed oft with vent'ring,   567
Chiefly in love, whose leave exceeds commission.   568
   Affection faints not like a pale-faced coward,   569
   But then woos best when most his choice is froward.   570

When he did frown, oh, had she then gave over,   571
Such nectar from his lips she had not sucked.
Foul words and frowns must not repel a lover.   573
What though the rose have prickles, yet 'tis plucked.
   Were beauty under twenty locks kept fast,
   Yet love breaks through and picks them all at last.   576

For pity now she can no more detain him;   577
The poor fool prays her that he may depart.   578
She is resolved no longer to restrain him,
Bids him farewell, and look well to her heart,   580
   The which, by Cupid's bow she doth protest,   581
   He carries thence encagèd in his breast.

"Sweet boy," she says, "this night I'll waste in sorrow,   583
For my sick heart commands mine eyes to watch.   584
Tell me, Love's master, shall we meet tomorrow?
Say, shall we, shall we? Wilt thou make the match?"
   He tells her no, tomorrow he intends
   To hunt the boar with certain of his friends.

"The boar!" quoth she, whereat a sudden pale,   589
Like lawn being spread upon the blushing rose,   590
Usurps her cheek. She trembles at his tale,
And on his neck her yoking arms she throws.
   She sinketh down, still hanging by his neck;
   He on her belly falls, she on her back.

Now is she in the very lists of love,   595
Her champion mounted for the hot encounter.
All is imaginary she doth prove.   597
He will not manage her, although he mount her,   598
   That worse than Tantalus' is her annoy,   599
   To clip Elysium and to lack her joy.   600

Even so poor birds, deceived with painted grapes,   601
Do surfeit by the eye and pine the maw;   602
Even so she languisheth in her mishaps,
As those poor birds that helpless berries saw.   604
   The warm effects which she in him finds missing   605
   She seeks to kindle with continual kissing.

But all in vain; good queen, it will not be.
She hath assayed as much as may be proved.   608
Her pleading hath deserved a greater fee;   609
She's Love, she loves, and yet she is not loved.
   "Fie, fie," he says, "you crush me, let me go!
   You have no reason to withhold me so."

"Thou had'st been gone," quoth she, "sweet boy, ere this,
But that thou told'st me thou wouldst hunt the boar.
Oh, be advised! Thou know'st not what it is   615
With javelin's point a churlish swine to gore,
   Whose tushes, never sheathed, he whetteth still,   617
   Like to a mortal butcher bent to kill.   618

"On his bow-back he hath a battle set   619
Of bristly pikes, that ever threat his foes;   620
His eyes like glowworms shine when he doth fret;   621
His snout digs sepulchers where'er he goes;
   Being moved, he strikes whate'er is in his way,   623
   And whom he strikes his crooked tushes slay.

"His brawny sides, with hairy bristles armed,
Are better proof than thy spear's point can enter;   626
His short thick neck cannot be easily harmed;
Being ireful, on the lion he will venter.   628
   The thorny brambles and embracing bushes,
   As fearful of him, part, through whom he rushes.   630

"Alas, he naught esteems that face of thine,
To which Love's eyes pays tributary gazes,

---

555 **reek** i.e., steam   556 **careless** heedless   557 **Planting oblivion**
implanting or causing forgetfulness of all that she ought to remember
558 **wrack** ruin.   561 **with chasing** with being chased   562 **froward**
fretful   564 **listeth** desires.   565 **temp'ring** heating and working
with the fingers   567 **out of** beyond.   **compassed** encompassed,
accomplished   568 **whose . . . commission** which intemperately goes
beyond its instructions.   569 **Affection . . . not** Passion does not
relent   570 **when . . . froward** when the object of its choice is unwilling.   571 **gave** given   573 **Foul** Hostile, disagreeable   576 **picks
them all** (Picking a lock often has sexual meaning in Shakespeare.)
577 **For pity** Appealing to his sense of pity   578 **fool** (An affectionate
term.)   580 **and look well to** i.e., and bids him take good care of
581 **protest** vow, affirm   583 **waste** spend   584 **watch** stay awake.
589 **pale** pallor   590 **lawn** fine linen

595 **lists** tournament field (here a site of sexual encounter)   597 **All . . .
prove** She finds out, however, that the hot encounter is merely in her
imagination.   598 **manage** control, ride (as one manages a horse)
599 **Tantalus** a son of Zeus who was punished by perpetual hunger
and thirst with food and drink always in sight yet untouchable.
annoy vexation, torment   600 **To clip Elysium and** to embrace the
joys of afterlife of classical mythology and yet   601 **birds . . . grapes**
(Allusion to Zeuxis, a Greek painter of the fifth century B.C., so skillful an artist that birds were said to peck at his picture of a bunch of
grapes.)   602 **Do . . . maw** gorge themselves visually but starve the
stomach   604 **As** like.   **helpless** affording no sustenance   605 **warm
effects** sexual response   608 **assayed** tried.   **proved** experienced,
tried.   609 **Her pleading . . . fee** (A legal metaphor; she is *pleading*
her own case.)   615 **advised** warned.   617 **tushes** tusks.   **still** continually   618 **Like . . . kill** like a deadly butcher intent on killing.
619 **bow-back** arched back, but suggestive also of a bowman's quiver.
battle i.e., martial array   620 **ever threat** continually threaten
621 **fret** i.e., gnash his teeth   623 **moved** angered   626 **proof** armor
628 **ireful** wrathful.   **venter** venture.   630 **As** as if

Nor thy soft hands, sweet lips, and crystal eyne,   633
Whose full perfection all the world amazes;
    But having thee at vantage—wondrous dread!—   635
    Would root these beauties as he roots the mead.   636

"Oh, let him keep his loathsome cabin still!   637
Beauty hath naught to do with such foul fiends.
Come not within his danger by thy will;   639
They that thrive well take counsel of their friends.
    When thou didst name the boar, not to dissemble,   641
    I feared thy fortune, and my joints did tremble.   642

"Didst thou not mark my face? Was it not white?
Sawest thou not signs of fear lurk in mine eye?
Grew I not faint, and fell I not downright?   645
Within my bosom, whereon thou dost lie,
    My boding heart pants, beats, and takes no rest,
    But, like an earthquake, shakes thee on my breast.

"For where Love reigns, disturbing Jealousy   649
Doth call himself Affection's sentinel,
Gives false alarms, suggesteth mutiny,   651
And in a peaceful hour doth cry 'Kill, kill!',   652
    Distemp'ring gentle Love in his desire,   653
    As air and water do abate the fire.   654

"This sour informer, this bate-breeding spy,   655
This canker that eats up Love's tender spring,   656
This carry-tale, dissentious Jealousy,   657
That sometime true news, sometime false doth bring,
    Knocks at my heart and whispers in mine ear
    That if I love thee, I thy death should fear;

"And more than so, presenteth to mine eye   661
The picture of an angry chafing boar,
Under whose sharp fangs on his back doth lie
An image like thyself, all stained with gore,
    Whose blood upon the fresh flowers being shed
    Doth make them droop with grief and hang the head.

"What should I do, seeing thee so indeed,   667
That tremble at th'imagination?   668
The thought of it doth make my faint heart bleed,
And fear doth teach it divination.   670
    I prophesy thy death, my living sorrow,
    If thou encounter with the boar tomorrow.

"But if thou needs wilt hunt, be ruled by me;   673
Uncouple at the timorous flying hare,   674
Or at the fox which lives by subtlety,
Or at the roe which no encounter dare.
    Pursue these fearful creatures o'er the downs,   677
    And on thy well-breathed horse keep with thy hounds.   678

"And when thou hast on foot the purblind hare,   679
Mark the poor wretch, to overshoot his troubles   680
How he outruns the wind, and with what care
He cranks and crosses with a thousand doubles.   682
    The many musets through the which he goes   683
    Are like a labyrinth to amaze his foes.   684

"Sometime he runs among a flock of sheep,
To make the cunning hounds mistake their smell,
And sometime where earth-delving coneys keep,   687
To stop the loud pursuers in their yell,   688
    And sometime sorteth with a herd of deer.   689
    Danger deviseth shifts; wit waits on fear.   690

"For there his smell with others being mingled,
The hot scent-snuffing hounds are driven to doubt,
Ceasing their clamorous cry till they have singled
With much ado the cold fault cleanly out.   694
    Then do they spend their mouths; echo replies,   695
    As if another chase were in the skies.

"By this, poor Wat, far off upon a hill,   697
Stands on his hinder legs with list'ning ear,
To hearken if his foes pursue him still.
Anon their loud alarums he doth hear,
    And now his grief may be comparèd well
    To one sore sick that hears the passing bell.   702

"Then shalt thou see the dew-bedabbled wretch
Turn, and return, indenting with the way;   704
Each envious brier his weary legs do scratch,   705
Each shadow makes him stop, each murmur stay;
    For misery is trodden on by many,
    And, being low, never relieved by any.

"Lie quietly, and hear a little more.
Nay, do not struggle, for thou shalt not rise.
To make thee hate the hunting of the boar,
Unlike myself thou hear'st me moralize,   712
    Applying this to that, and so to so;
    For love can comment upon every woe.

633 eyne eyes   635 at vantage at a disadvantage   636 root root up.
mead meadow.   637 keep occupy.   cabin den   639 Come . . . will
Do not willingly come within reach of his ability to harm you
641 not to dissemble to tell the truth   642 feared feared for
645 downright right down.   649 Jealousy apprehension   651 suggesteth mutiny incites dissension   652 in a i.e., disturbing a
653 Distemp'ring quenching   654 abate extinguish   655 bate-
breeding strife-breeding   656 canker cankerworm.   spring young
shoot of a plant   657 carry-tale rumormonger   661 more than so
even more than that   667–8 seeing . . . th'imagination if I should
actually see you dead, when merely imagining it makes me tremble.
670 divination power to prophesy.

673 needs wilt hunt insist upon hunting   674 Uncouple unleash the
hounds.   flying fleeing pursuit   677 fearful full of fears.   downs
rolling hills   678 well-breathed not easily winded, in good condition
679 on foot in chase.   purblind dim-sighted   680 overshoot run
beyond   682 cranks and crosses twists and turns   683 musets gaps
in hedge or fence   684 amaze bewilder   687 coneys rabbits.   keep
dwell   688 yell cry   689 sorteth consorts, mingles   690 shifts tricks.
wit waits intelligence attends   694 cold fault cold or lost scent
695 spend their mouths give tongue   697 Wat (A common name
applied to the hare.)   702 sore very.   passing bell bell tolled for a
person who has just died.   704 indenting zigzagging   705 envious
malicious   712 Unlike . . . moralize contrary to the usual way of the
goddess of love, you hear me point out a moral application

"Where did I leave?" "No matter where," quoth he,   715
"Leave me, and then the story aptly ends;
The night is spent." "Why, what of that?" quoth she.
"I am," quoth he, "expected of my friends,   718
    And now 'tis dark, and going I shall fall."
    "In night," quoth she, "desire sees best of all.

"But if thou fall, oh, then imagine this,
The earth, in love with thee, thy footing trips,
And all is but to rob thee of a kiss.
Rich preys make true men thieves; so do thy lips   724
    Make modest Dian cloudy and forlorn,   725
    Lest she should steal a kiss and die forsworn.   726

"Now of this dark night I perceive the reason: 727
Cynthia for shame obscures her silver shine   728
Till forging Nature be condemned of treason   729
For stealing molds from heaven that were divine,
    Wherein she framed thee, in high heaven's despite,   731
    To shame the sun by day and her by night.   732

"And therefore hath she bribed the Destinies
To cross the curious workmanship of Nature,   734
To mingle beauty with infirmities,
And pure perfection with impure defeature,   736
    Making it subject to the tyranny
    Of mad mischances and much misery;

"As burning fevers, agues pale and faint,   739
Life-poisoning pestilence and frenzies wood,   740
The marrow-eating sickness, whose attaint   741
Disorder breeds by heating of the blood;
    Surfeits, impostumes, grief, and damned despair   743
    Swear Nature's death for framing thee so fair.   744

"And not the least of all these maladies
But in one minute's fight brings beauty under.   746
Both favor, savor, hue, and qualities,   747
Whereat th'impartial gazer late did wonder,   748
    Are on the sudden wasted, thawed, and done,   749
    As mountain snow melts with the midday sun.

"Therefore, despite of fruitless chastity,   751
Love-lacking vestals and self-loving nuns,

715 **leave** leave off. (But Adonis answers with another sense, "go away from.")   718 **of** by   724 **Rich . . . thieves** The chance of rich spoils (*preys*) will make thieves even of honest (*true*) men   725 **Dian** Diana, goddess of the moon, chastity, and the hunt. (Even Diana would fall in love with Adonis.)   **cloudy** obscured with clouds; sorrowful   726 **forsworn** having broken her vow as the goddess of chastity.   727 **of** for   728 **Cynthia** Diana, the moon   729 **forging** counterfeiting   731 **she** Nature.   **in . . . despite** in defiance of high heaven   732 **her** the moon   734 **cross** thwart.   **curious** ingenious   736 **defeature** disfigurement   739 **As** such as   740 **frenzies wood** mad seizures   741 **The marrow-eating sickness** (Probably venereal disease; love is said to burn or melt the marrow, as in line 142; hence the *heating of the blood* in line 742.)   **attaint** infection   743 **impostumes** abscesses   744 **Swear . . . fair** (all these diseases) swear to undo Nature because she formed you so beautiful.   746 **brings beauty under** subdues beauty.   747 **Both . . . qualities** Beauty of feature, sweetness of smell, color and shape, and other qualities   748 **late** lately   749 **wasted** wasted away.   **done** destroyed   751 **despite of fruitless** in defiance of barren

That on the earth would breed a scarcity
And barren dearth of daughters and of sons,
    Be prodigal. The lamp that burns by night
    Dries up his oil to lend the world his light.   756

"What is thy body but a swallowing grave,
Seeming to bury that posterity
Which by the rights of time thou needs must have,
If thou destroy them not in dark obscurity?
    If so, the world will hold thee in disdain,
    Sith in thy pride so fair a hope is slain.   762

"So in thyself thyself art made away,   763
A mischief worse than civil homebred strife,   764
Or theirs whose desperate hands themselves do slay,
Or butcher sire that reaves his son of life.   766
    Foul cank'ring rust the hidden treasure frets,   767
    But gold that's put to use more gold begets."

"Nay, then," quoth Adon, "you will fall again
Into your idle overhandled theme.   770
The kiss I gave you is bestowed in vain,
And all in vain you strive against the stream;   772
    For, by this black-faced night, desire's foul nurse,   773
    Your treatise makes me like you worse and worse.   774

"If love have lent you twenty thousand tongues,
And every tongue more moving than your own,
Bewitching like the wanton mermaids' songs,   777
Yet from mine ear the tempting tune is blown;
    For know, my heart stands armèd in mine ear
    And will not let a false sound enter there,

"Lest the deceiving harmony should run
Into the quiet closure of my breast;   782
And then my little heart were quite undone,
In his bedchamber to be barred of rest.
    No, lady, no. My heart longs not to groan,
    But soundly sleeps, while now it sleeps alone.

"What have you urged that I cannot reprove?   787
The path is smooth that leadeth on to danger.
I hate not love, but your device in love,   789
That lends embracements unto every stranger.
    You do it for increase. Oh, strange excuse,
    When reason is the bawd to lust's abuse!   792

"Call it not love, for Love to heaven is fled
Since sweating Lust on earth usurped his name,
Under whose simple semblance he hath fed   795
Upon fresh beauty, blotting it with blame;   796

756 **Dries up** expends.   **his** its   762 **Sith** since   763 **thyself art made away** i.e., your futurity is destroyed   764 **mischief** evil   766 **reaves** bereaves   767 **cank'ring** consuming (like the cankerworm).   **frets** eats away   770 **idle** profitless   772 **stream** current   773 **night . . . nurse** i.e., night, the foul nourisher of evil desire   774 **treatise** discourse   777 **mermaids'** i.e., sirens'   782 **closure** enclosure   787 **urged** argued for.   **reprove** refute.   789 **device** cunning, deceitful conduct   792 **bawd** procuress   795 **Under . . . fed** and under the guileless appearance of Love, Lust has fed   796 **blotting** soiling

Which the hot tyrant stains and soon bereaves,   797
As caterpillars do the tender leaves.

"Love comforteth like sunshine after rain,
But Lust's effect is tempest after sun.
Love's gentle spring doth always fresh remain;
Lust's winter comes ere summer half be done.
　　Love surfeits not, Lust like a glutton dies;
　　Love is all truth, Lust full of forgèd lies.

"More I could tell, but more I dare not say;
The text is old, the orator too green.   806
Therefore, in sadness, now I will away.   807
My face is full of shame, my heart of teen;   808
　　Mine ears, that to your wanton talk attended
　　Do burn themselves for having so offended."   810

With this, he breaketh from the sweet embrace
Of those fair arms which bound him to her breast
And homeward through the dark laund runs apace,   813
Leaves Love upon her back deeply distressed.
　　Look how a bright star shooteth from the sky,
　　So glides he in the night from Venus' eye;

Which after him she darts, as one on shore
Gazing upon a late-embarkèd friend,   818
Till the wild waves will have him seen no more,   819
Whose ridges with the meeting clouds contend.
　　So did the merciless and pitchy night
　　Fold in the object that did feed her sight.   822

Whereat amazed, as one that unaware   823
Hath dropped a precious jewel in the flood,   824
Or stonished as night wand'rers often are,   825
Their light blown out in some mistrustful wood,   826
　　Even so confounded in the dark she lay,   827
　　Having lost the fair discovery of her way.   828

And now she beats her heart, whereat it groans,
That all the neighbor caves, as seeming troubled,
Make verbal repetition of her moans.
Passion on passion deeply is redoubled: 832
　　"Ay me!" she cries, and twenty times "Woe, woe!"
　　And twenty echoes twenty times cry so.

She marking them begins a wailing note
And sings extemporally a woeful ditty
How love makes young men thrall and old men dote,   837
How love is wise in folly, foolish witty.

Her heavy anthem still concludes in woe,   839
And still the choir of echoes answer so.

Her song was tedious and outwore the night,
For lovers' hours are long, though seeming short.
If pleased themselves, others, they think, delight
In suchlike circumstance, with suchlike sport.
　　Their copious stories, oftentimes begun,
　　End without audience and are never done.

For who hath she to spend the night withal   847
But idle sounds resembling parasits,   848
Like shrill-tongued tapsters answering every call,   849
Soothing the humor of fantastic wits?   850
　　She says " 'Tis so," they answer all " 'Tis so,"
　　And would say after her, if she said "No."

Lo here the gentle lark, weary of rest,
From his moist cabinet mounts up on high,   854
And wakes the morning, from whose silver breast   855
The sun ariseth in his majesty,
　　Who doth the world so gloriously behold   857
　　That cedar tops and hills seem burnished gold.

Venus salutes him with this fair good morrow:
"O thou clear god, and patron of all light,   860
From whom each lamp and shining star doth borrow
The beauteous influence that makes him bright,   862
　　There lives a son that sucked an earthly mother   863
　　May lend thee light, as thou dost lend to other."   864

This said, she hasteth to a myrtle grove,
Musing the morning is so much o'erworn,   866
And yet she hears no tidings of her love.
She hearkens for his hounds and for his horn.
　　Anon she hears them chant it lustily,   869
　　And all in haste she coasteth to the cry.   870

And as she runs, the bushes in the way
Some catch her by the neck, some kiss her face,
Some twine about her thigh to make her stay.
She wildly breaketh from their strict embrace,   874
　　Like a milch doe, whose swelling dugs do ache,   875
　　Hasting to feed her fawn hid in some brake.   876

By this, she hears the hounds are at a bay,   877
Whereat she starts, like one that spies an adder

797 **bereaves** spoils   806 **The text** the point being explicated (like the *text* of a sermon).   **green** young, unpracticed.   807 **in sadness** seriously, truly   808 **teen** grief, vexation.   810 **burn themselves** blush   813 **laund** glade   818 **late-embarkèd** having recently taken ship   819 **have him seen** allow him to be seen   822 **Fold in** enfold, close in   823 **amazed** dazed, confused.   **unaware** inadvertently   824 **flood** body of flowing water   825 **stonished** bewildered   826 **mistrustful** causing apprehension   827 **confounded** bewildered   828 **the fair . . . way** i.e., the best way for her to go, or, him by whose light she could make her way.   832 **Passion** Lamentation   837 **thrall** captive

839 **heavy** melancholy.   **still** continually   847 **withal** with   848 **parasits** parasites, flattering attendants   849 **tapsters** waiters in taverns   850 **Soothing . . . wits** i.e., complying with the whim of capricious tavern customers.   854 **moist cabinet** dewy dwelling, nest   855 **whose silver breast** (Aurora, the dawn, is personified as a goddess bidding farewell to her lover, the sun.)   857 **behold** i.e., shine upon   860 **clear** bright   862 **influence** a supposed flowing or streaming of an ethereal fluid from a celestial body. (An astrological term.)   863 **a son** i.e., Adonis.   **sucked** suckled from   864 **May** who may   866 **Musing** wondering (that).   **o'erworn** advanced   869 **chant it lustily** baying eagerly   870 **coasteth to** runs toward   874 **strict** tight   875 **milch doe** female deer producing milk.   **dugs** udders   876 **brake** thicket.   877 **By this** By this time.   **at a bay** i.e., faced by their quarry, which, being cornered, has turned to make its stand

Wreathed up in fatal folds just in his way,   879
The fear whereof doth make him shake and shudder;
    Even so the timorous yelping of the hounds
    Appalls her senses and her spirit confounds.

For now she knows it is no gentle chase,
But the blunt boar, rough bear, or lion proud,
Because the cry remaineth in one place,
Where fearfully the dogs exclaim aloud.
    Finding their enemy to be so curst,   887
    They all strain court'sy who shall cope him first.   888

This dismal cry rings sadly in her ear,   889
Through which it enters to surprise her heart,   890
Who, overcome by doubt and bloodless fear,   891
With cold-pale weakness numbs each feeling part.   892
    Like soldiers, when their captain once doth yield,   893
    They basely fly and dare not stay the field.   894

Thus stands she in a trembling ecstasy,   895
Till, cheering up her senses all dismayed,
She tells them 'tis a causeless fantasy   897
And childish error that they are afraid;
    Bids them leave quaking, bids them fear no more—
    And with that word she spied the hunted boar,

Whose frothy mouth, bepainted all with red,
Like milk and blood being mingled both together,
A second fear through all her sinews spread,
Which madly hurries her she knows not whither.
    This way she runs, and now she will no further,
    But back retires to rate the boar for murther.   906

A thousand spleens bear her a thousand ways;   907
She treads the path that she untreads again;   908
Her more than haste is mated with delays,   909
Like the proceedings of a drunken brain,
    Full of respects, yet naught at all respecting,   911
    In hand with all things, naught at all effecting.   912

Here kenneled in a brake she finds a hound,   913
And asks the weary caitiff for his master,   914
And there another licking of his wound,
'Gainst venomed sores the only sovereign plaster;   916
    And here she meets another sadly scowling,
    To whom she speaks, and he replies with howling.

When he hath ceased his ill-resounding noise,   879
Another flapmouthed mourner, black and grim,   920
Against the welkin volleys out his voice;   921
Another and another answer him,
    Clapping their proud tails to the ground below,
    Shaking their scratched ears, bleeding as they go.

Look how the world's poor people are amazed   925
At apparitions, signs, and prodigies,
Whereon with fearful eyes they long have gazed,
Infusing them with dreadful prophecies;   928
    So she at these sad signs draws up her breath
    And, sighing it again, exclaims on Death.   930

"Hard-favored tyrant, ugly, meager, lean,   931
Hateful divorce of love!"—thus chides she Death—   932
"Grim-grinning ghost, earth's worm, what dost thou mean   933
To stifle beauty and to steal his breath,
    Who, when he lived, his breath and beauty set
    Gloss on the rose, smell to the violet?

"If he be dead—Oh, no, it cannot be,
Seeing his beauty, thou shouldst strike at it!
Oh, yes, it may; thou hast no eyes to see,   939
But hatefully at random dost thou hit.
    Thy mark is feeble age, but thy false dart   941
    Mistakes that aim and cleaves an infant's heart.

"Hadst thou but bid beware, then he had spoke,   943
And, hearing him, thy power had lost his power.   944
The Destinies will curse thee for this stroke;
They bid thee crop a weed, thou pluck'st a flower.
    Love's golden arrow at him should have fled,
    And not Death's ebon dart, to strike him dead.   948

"Dost thou drink tears, that thou provok'st such weeping?
What may a heavy groan advantage thee?
Why hast thou cast into eternal sleeping
Those eyes that taught all other eyes to see?
    Now Nature cares not for thy mortal vigor,   953
    Since her best work is ruined with thy rigor."   954

Here overcome, as one full of despair,
She vailed her eyelids, who, like sluices, stopped   956
The crystal tide that from her two cheeks fair
In the sweet channel of her bosom dropped;   958
    But through the floodgates breaks the silver rain,
    And with his strong course opens them again.   960

---

879 folds coils   **887 curst** savage   **888 strain court'sy** are punctiliously polite, stand upon ceremony; i.e., they hold back.   **cope** cope with   **889 dismal** foreboding ill   **890 surprise** assail suddenly   **891 bloodless fear** i.e., fear that causes the blood to draw to the heart and desert the features, leaving one *cold, pale,* and *weak* (line 892)   **892 feeling part** bodily part and organ of sense.   **893 when . . . yield** once their commanding officer has yielded   **894 stay the field** remain in the battlefield.   **895 ecstasy** agitated state   **897 them** i.e., her senses   **906 rate** berate   **907 spleens** impulses   **908 untreads** retraces   **909 mated** confounded, checked   **911–12 Full . . . effecting** full of considerations yet not considering anything at all, preoccupied with everything yet attending to nothing.   **913 kenneled** hiding as if in its kennel   **914 caitiff** wretch   **916 only sovereign plaster** best all-curing application

920 flapmouthed having broad, hanging lips or jowls   **921 welkin** sky   **925 Look how** Just as   **928 Infusing** imbuing.   **prophecies** prophetic qualities   **930 exclaims on** denounces   **931 Hard-favored** Ugly-faced   **932 divorce** terminator   **933 Grim-grinning** i.e., grinning like a skull.   **worm** i.e., cankerworm, consumer of flowers. (With the suggestion also of worms that devour corpses.)   **939 no eyes** (The eye sockets of the skull of Death are empty.)   **941 mark** target   **943 bid beware** i.e., issued a warning of your approach.   **he** Adonis   **944 his** its   **948 ebon** ebony, black   **953 cares . . . vigor** does not fear your deadly power   **954 with** by   **956 vailed** lowered.   **who . . . stopped** which, like floodgates, stopped up   **958 channel** i.e., cleavage   **960 his** its

Oh, how her eyes and tears did lend and borrow!   961
Her eye seen in the tears, tears in her eye,
Both crystals, where they viewed each other's sorrow,   963
Sorrow that friendly sighs sought still to dry;   964
　　But like a stormy day, now wind, now rain,
　　Sighs dry her cheeks, tears make them wet again.

Variable passions throng her constant woe,
As striving who should best become her grief.   968
All entertained, each passion labors so   969
That every present sorrow seemeth chief,
　　But none is best; then join they all together,   971
　　Like many clouds consulting for foul weather.   972

By this, far off she hears some huntsman hallow;   973
A nurse's song ne'er pleased her babe so well.
The dire imagination she did follow   975
This sound of hope doth labor to expel;
　　For now reviving joy bids her rejoice
　　And flatters her it is Adonis' voice.

Whereat her tears began to turn their tide,   979
Being prisoned in her eye like pearls in glass;
Yet sometimes falls an orient drop beside,   981
Which her cheek melts, as scorning it should pass,   982
　　To wash the foul face of the sluttish ground,   983
　　Who is but drunken when she seemeth drowned.   984

O hard-believing love, how strange it seems   985
Not to believe, and yet too credulous!   986
Thy weal and woe are both of them extremes.
Despair and hope makes thee ridiculous: 988
　　The one doth flatter thee in thoughts unlikely;   989
　　In likely thoughts the other kills thee quickly.

Now she unweaves the web that she hath wrought;
Adonis lives, and Death is not to blame;
It was not she that called him all to naught.   993
Now she adds honors to his hateful name:
　　She clepes him king of graves and grave for kings,   995
　　Imperious supreme of all mortal things.   996

"No, no," quoth she, "sweet Death, I did but jest.
Yet pardon me, I felt a kind of fear
Whenas I met the boar, that bloody beast,   999
Which knows no pity, but is still severe.   1000

Then, gentle shadow—truth I must confess—   1001
I railed on thee, fearing my love's decesse.   1002

" 'Tis not my fault; the boar provoked my tongue.
Be wreaked on him, invisible commander.   1004
'Tis he, foul creature, that hath done thee wrong;
I did but act, he's author of thy slander.   1006
　　Grief hath two tongues, and never woman yet   1007
　　Could rule them both without ten women's wit."

Thus hoping that Adonis is alive,
Her rash suspect she doth extenuate;   1010
And that his beauty may the better thrive,   1011
With Death she humbly doth insinuate;   1012
　　Tells him of trophies, statues, tombs, and stories   1013
　　His victories, his triumphs, and his glories.

"O Jove," quoth she, "how much a fool was I
To be of such a weak and silly mind
To wail his death who lives and must not die
Till mutual overthrow of mortal kind!   1018
　　For, he being dead, with him is beauty slain,
　　And, beauty dead, black chaos comes again.

"Fie, fie, fond love, thou art as full of fear   1021
As one with treasure laden, hemmed with thieves;   1022
Trifles, unwitnessèd with eye or ear,   1023
Thy coward heart with false bethinking grieves."   1024
　　Even at this word she hears a merry horn,
　　Whereat she leaps that was but late forlorn.   1026

As falcon to the lure, away she flies—
The grass stoops not, she treads on it so light—
And in her haste unfortunately spies
The foul boar's conquest on her fair delight;
　　Which seen, her eyes, as murdered with the view,   1031
　　Like stars ashamed of day, themselves withdrew;   1032

Or, as the snail, whose tender horns being hit,
Shrinks backward in his shelly cave with pain,
And there, all smothered up, in shade doth sit,
Long after fearing to creep forth again;
　　So, at his bloody view, her eyes are fled
　　Into the deep dark cabins of her head,

Where they resign their office and their light
To the disposing of her troubled brain,   1040

---

961 **lend and borrow** i.e., reflect each other. 963 **crystals** i.e., mirrors or magic crystals 964 **friendly** i.e., consoling 968 **As** as if. **who** which (passion). **become** suit 969 **entertained** having been admitted 971 **best** supreme 972 **consulting for** gathering and conspiring to produce 973 **By this** By this time. **hallow** halloo 975 **dire imagination** tragic train of thought. **follow** pursue in her thoughts 979 **turn their tide** ebb 981 **orient** shining. **beside** to one side 982 **melts** i.e., dries. **as** as if 983 **foul** dirty 984 **Who . . . drowned** i.e., the earth greedily drinks up her tears while she seems drowned in grief. 985–6 **O . . . credulous!** O suspicious love, how strange it appears that you don't believe, even though you are too credulous! 988 **Despair and hope** i.e., The rapid oscillation between despair and hope 989 **The one** i.e., hope 993 **called . . . naught** called Death wholly evil. 995 **clepes** names, calls 996 **Imperious supreme** imperial ruler 999 **Whenas** when 1000 **still severe** incessantly ruthless.

1001 **shadow** specter 1002 **railed on** reviled. **decesse** decease. 1004 **wreaked** revenged. **invisible commander** i.e., Death, a specter that orders our final destiny. 1006 **act** i.e., act as agent 1007 **two tongues** i.e., a double tongue, twice as loud and hard to control as a usual tongue. (Women are conventionally unable to rule their tongues in any case.) 1010 **rash suspect** too hasty suspicion (of Death). **extenuate** excuse 1011 **his** Adonis's 1012 **insinuate** ingratiate herself 1013 **trophies** memorial monuments. **stories** narrates 1018 **mutual** i.e., universal 1021 **fond** foolish 1022 **hemmed with** hemmed about by 1023–4 **Trifles . . . grieves** mere trifles, not actually seen by eye or heard by ear, grieve your cowardly heart with false imaginings. 1026 **leaps** leaps for joy. **late** lately 1031 **as** as if 1032 **ashamed of day** ashamed to be seen by daylight. **themselves withdrew** shut themselves up. **withdrew** i.e., closed 1040 **disposing** direction, ordering

Who bids them still consort with ugly night   1041
And never wound the heart with looks again—   1042
    Who, like a king perplexèd in his throne,   1043
    By their suggestion gives a deadly groan.   1044

Whereat each tributary subject quakes,   1045
As when the wind, imprisoned in the ground,   1046
Struggling for passage, earth's foundation shakes,
Which with cold terror doth men's minds confound.
    This mutiny each part doth so surprise   1049
    That from their dark beds once more leap her eyes;

And, being opened, threw unwilling light
Upon the wide wound that the boar had trenched
In his soft flank, whose wonted lily white   1053
With purple tears, that his wound wept, was drenched.
    No flower was nigh, no grass, herb, leaf, or weed,
    But stole his blood and seemed with him to bleed.   1056

This solemn sympathy poor Venus noteth.
Over one shoulder doth she hang her head.
Dumbly she passions, franticly she doteth;   1059
She thinks he could not die, he is not dead.
    Her voice is stopped, her joints forget to bow;   1061
    Her eyes are mad that they have wept till now.   1062

Upon his hurt she looks so steadfastly
That her sight, dazzling, makes the wound seem three; 1064
And then she reprehends her mangling eye,
That makes more gashes where no breach should be.
    His face seems twain, each several limb is doubled;
    For oft the eye mistakes, the brain being troubled.

"My tongue cannot express my grief for one,
And yet," quoth she, "behold two Adons dead!
My sighs are blown away, my salt tears gone;
Mine eyes are turned to fire, my heart to lead.
    Heavy heart's lead, melt at mine eyes' red fire!   1073
    So shall I die by drops of hot desire.   1074

"Alas, poor world, what treasure hast thou lost!
What face remains alive that's worth the viewing?
Whose tongue is music now? What canst thou boast
Of things long since, or anything ensuing?   1078
    The flowers are sweet, their colors fresh and trim,
    But true sweet beauty lived and died with him.

"Bonnet nor veil henceforth no creature wear!   1081
Nor sun nor wind will ever strive to kiss you.
Having no fair to lose, you need not fear;   1083
The sun doth scorn you, and the wind doth hiss you.
    But when Adonis lived, sun and sharp air
    Lurked like two thieves, to rob him of his fair.

"And therefore would he put his bonnet on,
Under whose brim the gaudy sun would peep;
The wind would blow it off and, being gone,   1089
Play with his locks. Then would Adonis weep;
    And straight, in pity of his tender years,   1091
    They both would strive who first should dry his tears.

"To see his face the lion walked along
Behind some hedge, because he would not fear him; 1094
To recreate himself when he hath song,   1095
The tiger would be tame and gently hear him;
    If he had spoke, the wolf would leave his prey
    And never fright the silly lamb that day.   1098

"When he beheld his shadow in the brook,   1099
The fishes spread on it their golden gills;
When he was by, the birds such pleasure took
That some would sing, some other in their bills   1102
    Would bring him mulberries and ripe-red cherries;
    He fed them with his sight, they him with berries.

"But this foul, grim, and urchin-snouted boar,   1105
Whose downward eye still looketh for a grave,   1106
Ne'er saw the beauteous livery that he wore—   1107
Witness the entertainment that he gave.   1108
    If he did see his face, why then I know
    He thought to kiss him, and hath killed him so.

" 'Tis true, 'tis true! Thus was Adonis slain:
He ran upon the boar with his sharp spear,
Who did not whet his teeth at him again,   1113
But by a kiss thought to persuade him there;   1114
    And, nuzzling in his flank, the loving swine
    Sheathed unaware the tusk in his soft groin.

"Had I been toothed like him, I must confess,   1117
With kissing him I should have killed him first;
But he is dead, and never did he bless

1041 **still consort** always remain   1042 **with looks** by looking
1043 **Who** which, i.e., the heart   1044 **By their suggestion** incited by
the eyes   1045 **tributary subject** i.e., subordinate part of the body
1046 **wind . . . ground** (The common Elizabethan explanation of
earthquakes; compare with *1 Henry IV*, 3.1.30.)   1049 **surprise** attack
suddenly   1053 **wonted** customary   1056 **But stole** that did not steal
1059 **passions** shows grief   1061 **forget to bow** cannot bend
1062 **till now** before now (in a lesser cause).   1064 **dazzling** being
dazzled   1073–4 **Heavy . . . desire** i.e., May my leaden heart be
melted by my hot tears! In that way I will die, as my desire melts me.
1078 **long . . . ensuing** past or to come.

1081 **Bonnet nor veil** Neither hat nor veil (worn to guard a fair complexion, regarded as particularly beautiful, against the sun)
1083 **fair** beauty. (Also in line 1086.)   1089 **being gone** it (the hat)
being gone   1091 **straight** at once   1094 **would not fear** did not wish
to frighten   1095 **To recreate . . . song** whenever he sang for his own
recreation   1098 **silly** innocent   1099 **shadow** reflected image
1102 **other** others   1105 **urchin-snouted** having a snout like a hedge-
hog   1106 **still** continually.   **for a grave** i.e., as if for a grave in which
to bury victims. (Compare with line 622, where the boar's snout *digs
sepulchers* as it roots in the earth.)   1107 **livery** i.e., outside appearance.   **he** Adonis   1108 **entertainment** treatment, reception
1113 **again** in return   1114 **persuade** win over, or, persuade to stay
1117 **toothed** tusked

My youth with his—the more am I accurst."
    With this, she falleth in the place she stood, 1121
    And stains her face with his congealèd blood.

She looks upon his lips, and they are pale;
She takes him by the hand, and that is cold;
She whispers in his ears a heavy tale, 1125
As if they heard the woeful words she told;
    She lifts the coffer-lids that close his eyes, 1127
    Where, lo, two lamps, burnt out, in darkness lies;

Two glasses, where herself herself beheld 1129
A thousand times, and now no more reflect,
Their virtue lost, wherein they late excelled, 1131
And every beauty robbed of his effect. 1132
    "Wonder of time," quoth she, "this is my spite, 1133
    That, thou being dead, the day should yet be light.

"Since thou art dead, lo, here I prophesy:
Sorrow on love hereafter shall attend.
It shall be waited on with jealousy, 1137
Find sweet beginning but unsavory end,
    Ne'er settled equally, but high or low, 1139
    That all love's pleasure shall not match his woe. 1140

"It shall be fickle, false, and full of fraud,
Bud and be blasted in a breathing while; 1142
The bottom poison, and the top o'erstrawed 1143
With sweets that shall the truest sight beguile.
    The strongest body shall it make most weak,
    Strike the wise dumb and teach the fool to speak.

"It shall be sparing and too full of riot, 1147
Teaching decrepit age to tread the measures; 1148
The staring ruffian shall it keep in quiet, 1149
Pluck down the rich, enrich the poor with treasures;
    It shall be raging mad and silly mild, 1151
    Make the young old, the old become a child.

"It shall suspect where is no cause of fear; 1153
It shall not fear where it should most mistrust;
It shall be merciful and too severe,

And most deceiving when it seems most just; 1156
    Perverse it shall be where it shows most toward, 1157
    Put fear to valor, courage to the coward.

"It shall be cause of war and dire events
And set dissension twixt the son and sire,
Subject and servile to all discontents, 1161
As dry combustious matter is to fire.
    Sith in his prime Death doth my love destroy, 1163
    They that love best their loves shall not enjoy."

By this, the boy that by her side lay killed 1165
Was melted like a vapor from her sight,
And in his blood that on the ground lay spilled
A purple flow'r sprung up, checkered with white, 1168
    Resembling well his pale cheeks and the blood
    Which in round drops upon their whiteness stood.

She bows her head, the new-sprung flower to smell,
Comparing it to her Adonis' breath,
And says within her bosom it shall dwell,
Since he himself is reft from her by death. 1174
    She crops the stalk, and in the breach appears
    Green dropping sap, which she compares to tears.

"Poor flower," quoth she, "this was thy father's guise— 1177
Sweet issue of a more sweet-smelling sire— 1178
For every little grief to wet his eyes; 1179
To grow unto himself was his desire, 1180
    And so 'tis thine; but know, it is as good
    To wither in my breast as in his blood.

"Here was thy father's bed, here in my breast;
Thou art the next of blood, and 'tis thy right.
Lo, in this hollow cradle take thy rest;
My throbbing heart shall rock thee day and night.
    There shall not be one minute in an hour
    Wherein I will not kiss my sweet love's flower."

Thus, weary of the world, away she hies
And yokes her silver doves, by whose swift aid
Their mistress mounted through the empty skies 1191
In her light chariot quickly is conveyed, 1192
    Holding their course to Paphos, where their queen 1193
    Means to immure herself and not be seen.

1121 place place where **1125 heavy** sad **1127 coffer-lids** lids covering chests of treasure, i.e., eyelids **1129 glasses** mirrors **1131 virtue** power (to see and to reflect) **1132 his** its **1133 time** i.e., the ages, human existence. **spite** torment, vexation **1137 It** Love. **with** by **1139 Ne'er . . . low** i.e., (love will be) never equal between the two lovers; they will be from high and low social stations, or of different intensities **1140 his** its **1142 blasted** blighted. **breathing while** moment **1143 The bottom . . . o'erstrawed** the inner substance poison, and the surface strewn over **1147 sparing . . . riot** i.e., both niggardly and excessive **1148 tread the measures** dance. (An inappropriate action for the old.) **1149 staring** looking savage, glaring **1151 silly** innocently, feebly, humbly, weak-mindedly **1153 is** there is

1156 just trustworthy **1157 Perverse** stubborn, contrary. **shows** looks. **toward** tractable **1161 Subject . . . discontents** (love will be) both the cause and the unwilling slave of every kind of dissension **1163 Sith** Since **1165 By this** By this time **1168 flow'r** anemone **1174 reft** torn **1177 guise** manner, way **1178 Sweet issue** i.e., you, the anemone, who are the sweet offspring **1179 For . . . eyes** to weep compassionately at every little sorrow **1180 To grow unto himself** to mature self-made and independent **1191–2 mounted . . . conveyed** is quickly conveyed, mounted in her light chariot, through the empty skies **1193 Paphos** Venus's dwelling in Cyprus

The Rape of Lucrece

The Rape of Lucrece is closely related to *Venus and Adonis*. The two were published about a year apart, in 1594 and 1593, respectively, and both were printed by Richard Field. Both are dedicated to the young Earl of Southampton, Henry Wriothesley, whose confidence and friendship Shakespeare appears to have gained during the interim between the two poems; the dedicatory preface to *The Rape of Lucrece* expresses assurance that the poem will be accepted. Stylistically, the two poems are of a piece: both are reliant on Petrarchan ornament and rhetorical showmanship and are steeped in Ovidian pathos. Yet they are complementary rather than similar in attitude and subject. *The Rape of Lucrece* appears to be the "graver labor" promised to Southampton in the dedication of the earlier poem, a planned sequel in which love would be subjected to a darker treatment. *Venus and Adonis* is chiefly about sensual pleasure, whereas *The Rape of Lucrece* is about heroic chastity. The first poem is amatory, erotic, and amusing, despite its sad end; the second is moral, declamatory, and lugubrious. As Gabriel Harvey observed (c. 1598–1601), "The younger sort takes much delight in Shakespeare's *Venus and Adonis*, but his *Lucrece* and his *Tragedy of Hamlet, Prince of Denmark*, have it in them to please the wiser sort."

Harvey's pairing of this poem with *Hamlet* suggests that, to Harvey at least, Shakespeare aspires to sublime effects in *Lucrece*. For his verse pattern, Shakespeare chooses the seven-line rhyme royal stanza, traditionally used for tragic expression, as in Geoffrey Chaucer's *Troilus and Criseyde* and several of the more formal *Canterbury Tales*, in John Lydgate's *The Fall of Princes* (1430–1438) and its continuation in *A Mirror for Magistrates* (1559), in Samuel Daniel's *The Complaint of Rosamond*, and others. Although Shakespeare turns to Ovid once again as his chief source, he chooses a tale of ravishment, suicide, and vengeance rather than one of titillating amatory pursuit. The story of Lucrece had gained wide currency in the ancient and medieval worlds as an exemplum of chaste conduct in women. Shakespeare seems to have known Livy's *History of Rome* (Book 1, chaps. 57–59), though he relied primarily on Ovid's *Fasti* (2.721–852). Among later versions, he may have known Chaucer's *The Legend of Good Women* and a translation of Livy in William Painter's *The Palace of Pleasure* (1566, 1575). He encountered other "complaints" in *A Mirror for Magistrates* and in Daniel's *The Complaint of Rosamond*, and it is to this well-established genre that *Lucrece* belongs. The poem had the desired effect of enhancing Shakespeare's reputation for elegant poetry; it was reprinted five times during his lifetime and was frequently admired by his contemporaries. *Venus and Adonis* was, to be sure, more popular still (it was reprinted nine times during Shakespeare's lifetime), but no one in Shakespeare's day seems to have regarded *Lucrece* as anything other than a noble work.

To understand the poem in terms of its own generic sense of form, we must recognize its conventions and not expect it to be other than what it professes to be. As in *Venus and Adonis*, plot and character are secondary. Although the story outlined in "The Argument" is potentially sensational and swift-moving, Shakespeare deliberately cuts away most of the action. We do not see Lucius Tarquinius's murder of his father-in-law and tyrannical seizure of Rome, or Collatinus's rash boasting of his wife Lucrece's virtue in the presence of the King's lustful son Sextus Tarquinius, nor, at the conclusion of the story, do we learn much about the avenging of Lucrece's rape. Shakespeare's focus is on the attitudes of the two protagonists immediately before and after the ravishment. Even here, despite opportunities for psychological probing, Shakespeare's real interest is not in the characters themselves so much as in the social ramifications of their actions. As Coppélia Kahn has shown (in *Shakespeare Studies 9*), the rape serves as a means of examining the nature of marriage in a patriarchal society in which competition for ownership and struggles for power characterize men's attitudes toward politics and sex. Using Rome as a familiar mirror for English customs, Shakespeare presents Lucrece as a heroine acting to uphold the institution of marriage. However innocently, she is the one who acquires the stain through being violated and must pay the cost of wifely duty in marriage. Her husband accepts the decorousness of her suicide as necessary for the preservation of his honor, however much he may grieve over her wrong. Like a number of Shakespeare's later heroines, such as Imogen in *Cymbeline*, Lucrece is portrayed as beautiful but not alluring, restrained even in her marriage bed. She arranges her death so as to make the most of its social implications.

Along with his interest in patriarchy and violence, Shakespeare frames the story of *The Rape of Lucrece* in terms of the political events that lead to the founding of the Roman republic. The corruption of the Tarquin dynasty raises issues about Roman values generally, and the poem ends with a strong repudiation of the old order. The villain of the poem is at once rapist and tyrant; the resolution is both a vindication of women as victims and a movement toward republicanism. To be sure, the patriarchy that has dictated the conditions of Lucrece's life and honor will remain intact in the republic; the wife is still her husband's possession, and her greatest obligation to state and family must be to ensure that the husband's honor remains unbesmirched. Nonetheless, the assumptions of Roman hierarchy have been held up to scrutiny.

Shakespeare casts his narrative in the form of a series of rhetorical disputations, each a set piece presented as a debate or as a formal declamation. The debates are built around familiar antitheses: honor versus lust, rude will versus conscience, "affection" versus reason, nobility versus baseness, and so on. Many of the images are similarly arranged in contrasting pairs: dove and owl, daylight and darkness, clear and cloudy weather, white and red. Tarquin debates with himself the reasons for and against rape; Lucrece tries to persuade him of the depravity of his course; Lucrece ponders suicide. These debates generate, in turn, a number of rhetorical apostrophes to marital fidelity (lines 22–8), to the ideal of kingship as a moral example to others (lines 610–37), to Night (lines 764–812), to Opportunity (lines 876–924), and to Time (lines 925–1022). Another rhetorical formula, perhaps the most successful in the poem, is the use of structural digression. The most notable describes a painting or tapestry of Troy with obvious relevance to Lucrece's sad fate: Troy is a city destroyed by a rape, Paris achieves his selfish pleasure at the expense of the public good, and Sinon wins his sinister victory through deceitful appearance (lines 1366–1568).

Throughout, the poem's ornament strives after heightened and elaborate effects. The comparisons, or "conceits," as the Elizabethans called them, are intentionally contrived and reliant on ingenious wordplay. Shakespeare puns on the word *will*, for example, as he does in his sonnets, where he takes advantage of his own first name being Will (see sonnet 135), and in *Venus and Adonis* (see line 365). In *The Rape of Lucrece*, the word is central to Shakespeare's depiction of Tarquin, as we see the ravisher holding a disputation between "frozen conscience and hot-burning will" (line 247), forcing the locks "between her chamber and his will" (line 302), feeding ravenously "in his will his willful eye" (line 417), and the like. These and other passages often frame the word in a polarity of "will" and "heart," and range over numerous meanings that include inclination, desire, appetite, sexual lust, request or command, volition, pleasure, permission, good will, and spontaneity. The fact that the word rhymes with "kill" and "ill" adds to its usefulness. Another kind of "conceit" found throughout *The Rape of Lucrece*—one that arises integrally from the poem's deepest concerns—is the extended military metaphor of a city under siege. Tarquin's heart beats an alarum, Lucrece's breasts are "round turrets" made pale by the assault (lines 432–41), and, in her subsequent death, she is likened to a "late-sacked island" surrounded by rivers of her own blood (line 1740). Elsewhere she is a house that has been pillaged, "Her mansion battered by the enemy" (lines 1170–1). Classical allusions are, of course, common, notably to the story of the rape of Philomel or Philomela (lines 1079, 1128, etc.). Rhetorical devices of antithesis are displayed with the same ornate versatility as in *Venus and Adonis*. In a poem on a serious subject, these devices may seem overly contrived to us. We should nevertheless recognize them as conventional in the genre to which *The Rape of Lucrece* belongs. We find a similar blending of the sensuous and the moral in the sometimes grotesque conceits of the Catholic poet Robert Southwell (d. 1595) and in the later baroque paradoxes of Richard Crashaw (d. 1649). Among Shakespeare's dramatic works, *Titus Andronicus* seems closest to *The Rape of Lucrece* in its pathos, refined sensationalism, and use of classical allusion, and specifically in the character of Lavinia, whose misfortunes and chaste dignity so much resemble those of Lucrece.

Throughout *The Rape of Lucrece*, we find a consciousness of the poem's own artistry. In Lucrece's tragic plight, Shakespeare explores art's ability to communicate through its various means of expression. Especially in the long passage on the painting of the fall of Troy (lines 1366–1568), Lucrece shows an understandable anxiety about art's ability to deceive. The painting is in some ways more realistic than life itself; the figures in the painting seem to move and are so cunningly rendered that they "mock the mind" (line 1414). The imaginary work is "conceit deceitful" (line 1423), able through synecdoche (using the part to represent the whole) to suggest a series of general truths lying behind the particulars that are shown. This power of art to deceive is most troublesome in the case of Sinon, the betrayer of Troy—"In him the painter labored with his skill / To hide deceit" (lines 1506–7)—and has succeeded with such devastating effect that the viewer cannot tell from Sinon's mild appearance that he is, in fact, capable of lim-

itless evil. In his capacity for deception, Sinon is like Tarquin, the seemingly attractive prince who has ravaged Lucrece. Art is thus capable of misrepresentation for purposes of evil; its persuasive power, its imaginative vision, can be perverted to wrong ends. Seen through such art, Rome, too, is at once a great source of civilization and a nation whose values are cast seriously in doubt. *The Rape of Lucrece* thus grapples with issues of serious consequences—ones that also concerned Shakespeare in his early plays (such as *Titus Andronicus*) and indeed throughout his career as a dramatist.

The Rape of Lucrece

To the RIGHT HONORABLE HENRY WRIOTHESLEY, *Earl of Southampton, and Baron of Titchfield.*

  The love I dedicate to Your Lordship is without end; whereof this pamphlet without beginning is but a superfluous moiety. The warrant I have of your honorable disposition, not the worth of my untutored lines, makes it assured of acceptance. What I have done is yours; what I have to do is yours; being part in all I have, devoted yours. Were my worth greater, my duty would show greater; meantime, as it is, it is bound to Your Lordship, to whom I wish long life still lengthened with all happiness.

2

3

6

9

Your Lordship's in all duty,

William Shakespeare.

The Argument

  Lucius Tarquinius, for his excessive pride surnamed Superbus, after he had caused his own father-in-law Servius Tullius to be cruelly murdered and, contrary to the Roman laws and customs, not requiring or staying for the people's suffrages, had possessed himself of the kingdom, went, accompanied with his sons and other noblemen of Rome, to besiege Ardea. During which siege, the principal men of the army meeting one evening at the tent of Sextus Tarquinius, the King's son, in their discourses after supper everyone commended the virtues of his own wife; among whom Collatinus extolled the incomparable chastity of his wife Lucretia. In that pleasant humor they all posted to Rome; and intending, by their secret and sudden arrival, to make trial of that which everyone had before avouched, only Collatinus finds his wife,

2

5

6

15

18

Dedication.
2 without beginning i.e., beginning *in medias res,* in the middle of the action   **3 moiety** part.   **warrant** assurance   **6 being . . . have** since you are part of everything I have done and have to do   **9 still** continually

The Argument.
2 Superbus "the Proud"   **5 requiring** requesting   **6 suffrages** consent   **15 pleasant** merry.   **posted** hastened   **18 avouched** affirmed

though it were late in the night, spinning amongst her maids; the other ladies were all found dancing and reveling, or in several dis-²¹ ports. Whereupon the noblemen yielded Collat-²² inus the victory and his wife the fame. At that time Sextus Tarquinius, being inflamed with Lucrece' beauty, yet smothering his passions for the present, departed with the rest back to the camp; from whence he shortly after privily²⁷ withdrew himself and was, according to his estate, royally entertained and lodged by Lu-²⁹ crece at Collatium. The same night he treacher- ously stealeth into her chamber, violently rav- ished her, and early in the morning speedeth away. Lucrece, in this lamentable plight, hastily dispatcheth messengers, one to Rome for her father, another to the camp for Collatine. They came, the one accompanied with Junius Brutus, the other with Publius Valerius; and finding Lucrece attired in mourning habit, demanded³⁸ the cause of her sorrow. She, first taking an oath of them for her revenge, revealed the actor and⁴⁰ whole manner of his dealing, and withal sud- denly stabbed herself. Which done, with one consent they all vowed to root out the whole hated family of the Tarquins; and, bearing the dead body to Rome, Brutus acquainted the people with the doer and manner of the vile deed, with a bitter invective against the tyranny of the King, wherewith the people were so moved that with one consent and a general acclamation the Tarquins were all exiled and the state government changed from kings to consuls.

From the besieged Ardea all in post,   1
Borne by the trustless wings of false desire,   2
Lust-breathèd Tarquin leaves the Roman host   3
And to Collatium bears the lightless fire   4
Which, in pale embers hid, lurks to aspire   5
    And girdle with embracing flames the waist
    Of Collatine's fair love, Lucrece the chaste.

Haply that name of "chaste" unhapp'ly set   8
This bateless edge on his keen appetite,   9
When Collatine unwisely did not let   10
To praise the clear unmatchèd red and white
Which triumphed in that sky of his delight,   12
    Where mortal stars, as bright as heaven's beauties, 13
    With pure aspects did him peculiar duties.   14

For he the night before, in Tarquin's tent,
Unlocked the treasure of his happy state,   16
What priceless wealth the heavens had him lent
In the possession of his beauteous mate,
Reck'ning his fortune at such high-proud rate
    That kings might be espousèd to more fame,   20
    But king nor peer to such a peerless dame.   21

Oh, happiness enjoyed but of a few!
And, if possessed, as soon decayed and done   23
As is the morning's silver melting dew
Against the golden splendor of the sun!
An expired date, canceled ere well begun.   26
    Honor and beauty in the owner's arms
    Are weakly fortressed from a world of harms.   28

Beauty itself doth of itself persuade   29
The eyes of men without an orator;
What needeth then apology be made
To set forth that which is so singular?
Or why is Collatine the publisher   33
    Of that rich jewel he should keep unknown
    From thievish ears, because it is his own?

Perchance his boast of Lucrece' sovereignty   36
Suggested this proud issue of a king,   37
For by our ears our hearts oft tainted be.
Perchance that envy of so rich a thing,   39
Braving compare, disdainfully did sting   40
    His high-pitched thoughts, that meaner men should
      vaunt   41
    That golden hap which their superiors want.   42

But some untimely thought did instigate
His all too timeless speed, if none of those.   44
His honor, his affairs, his friends, his state   45
Neglected all, with swift intent he goes
To quench the coal which in his liver glows.   47
    O rash false heat, wrapped in repentant cold,
    Thy hasty spring still blasts and ne'er grows old! 49

When at Collatium this false lord arrived,
Well was he welcomed by the Roman dame,
Within whose face beauty and virtue strived
Which of them both should underprop her fame.
When virtue bragged, beauty would blush for shame;
    When beauty boasted blushes, in despite   55
    Virtue would stain that o'er with silver white. 56

21–2 **several disports** various pastimes. 27 **privily** secretly 29 **estate** rank 38 **habit** attire 40 **actor** doer
1 **Ardea** a city twenty-four miles south of Rome. **post** haste 2 **trust- less** treacherous 3 **Lust-breathèd** excited by lust 4 **Collatium** a city about ten miles east of Rome. **lightless** i.e., smoldering invisibly 5 **aspire** rise, i.e., break into flames 8 **Haply** Perchance. **unhapp'ly** (1) unhappily (2) by mischance 9 **bateless** not to be blunted 10 **let** forbear 12 **sky** i.e., Lucrece's face 13 **mortal stars** i.e., Lucrece's eyes 14 **aspects** (1) looks (2) astrologically favorable position. **peculiar** exclusively for him

16 **Unlocked the treasure** i.e., opened and revealed (in conversation) the riches 20 **espousèd** i.e., joined, linked 21 **But king** but neither king 23 **done** done with 26 **date** period of time 28 **fortressed from** defended against 29 **of itself** by its own nature 33 **publisher** publicizer 36 **sovereignty** supremacy 37 **Suggested** tempted. **issue** offspring, son (i.e., Tarquin) 39 **Perchance that** Perhaps it was that 40 **Braving compare** defying comparison 41 **meaner** less nobly born 42 **hap** fortune. **want** lack. 44 **timeless** unseemly, unseasonable 45 **state** position 47 **liver** (Regarded as the seat of the passions.) 49 **blasts** is nipped by frost 55 **When … despite** when beauty boasted of its rosy blushing countenance, in defiance of that beauty 56 **o'er** (Perhaps with a pun on *or*, "gold.")

But beauty, in that white entituled 57
From Venus' doves, doth challenge that fair field. 58
Then virtue claims from beauty beauty's red, 59
Which virtue gave the golden age to gild 60
Their silver cheeks, and called it then their shield,
    Teaching them thus to use it in the fight:
    When shame assailed, the red should fence the white. 63

This heraldry in Lucrece' face was seen,
Argued by beauty's red and virtue's white. 65
Of either's color was the other queen,
Proving from world's minority their right. 67
Yet their ambition makes them still to fight, 68
    The sovereignty of either being so great
    That oft they interchange each other's seat. 70

This silent war of lilies and of roses,
Which Tarquin viewed in her fair face's field,
In their pure ranks his traitor eye encloses, 73
Where, lest between them both it should be killed,
The coward captive vanquishèd doth yield 75
    To those two armies, that would let him go
    Rather than triumph in so false a foe. 77

Now thinks he that her husband's shallow tongue,
The niggard prodigal that praised her so, 79
In that high task hath done her beauty wrong,
Which far exceeds his barren skill to show. 81
Therefore that praise which Collatine doth owe 82
    Enchanted Tarquin answers with surmise, 83
    In silent wonder of still-gazing eyes.

This earthly saint, adorèd by this devil,
Little suspecteth the false worshiper,
For unstained thoughts do seldom dream on evil;
Birds never limed no secret bushes fear. 88
So, guiltless, she securely gives good cheer 89
    And reverend welcome to her princely guest, 90
    Whose inward ill no outward harm expressed.

For that he colored with his high estate, 92
Hiding base sin in pleats of majesty, 93

That nothing in him seemed inordinate 94
Save sometimes too much wonder of his eye,
Which, having all, all could not satisfy;
    But, poorly rich, so wanteth in his store 97
    That, cloyed with much, he pineth still for more.

But she, that never coped with stranger eyes, 99
Could pick no meaning from their parling looks, 100
Nor read the subtle shining secrecies
Writ in the glassy margins of such books. 102
She touched no unknown baits, nor feared no hooks,
    Nor could she moralize his wanton sight 104
    More than his eyes were opened to the light. 105

He stories to her ears her husband's fame, 106
Won in the fields of fruitful Italy,
And decks with praises Collatine's high name,
Made glorious by his manly chivalry
With bruisèd arms and wreaths of victory. 110
    Her joy with heaved-up hand she doth express
    And, wordless, so greets heaven for his success.

Far from the purpose of his coming thither
He makes excuses for his being there.
No cloudy show of stormy blust'ring weather
Doth yet in his fair welkin once appear, 116
Till sable Night, mother of dread and fear, 117
    Upon the world dim darkness doth display
    And in her vaulty prison stows the day.

For then is Tarquin brought unto his bed,
Intending weariness with heavy sprite; 121
For, after supper, long he questionèd 122
With modest Lucrece, and wore out the night.
Now leaden slumber with life's strength doth fight,
    And everyone to rest himself betakes,
    Save thieves and cares and troubled minds that wakes.

As one of which doth Tarquin lie revolving 127
The sundry dangers of his will's obtaining; 128
Yet ever to obtain his will resolving,
Though weak-built hopes persuade him to abstaining. 130
Despair to gain doth traffic oft for gaining; 131
    And when great treasure is the meed proposed, 132
    Though death be adjunct, there's no death supposed. 133

57–8 But . . . field But beauty, asserting title to that white from the whiteness of Venus's turtledoves that draw her chariot, lays claim to Lucrece's face, which is both a battlefield for the contest of beauty and virtue and a heraldic shield where armorial devices are displayed in red and white. **59 Then . . . red** Then modesty claims that the color red really belongs to it, not to beauty (since modesty blushes) **60 gave the golden age** i.e., bestowed on those who live innocently and purely, as in ancient times before the world grew corrupt. **gild** i.e., cover with a blush of modesty. (Gold and red were often considered interchangeable as colors.) **63 fence** defend **65 Argued** disputed and demonstrated **67 from world's minority** from the beginning of time **68 still** always **70 seat** throne. **73 In . . . encloses** virtue and beauty, arrayed in battle formation, close in on Tarquin's eye, that is treacherously willing to come to terms with either side **75 coward captive** Tarquin's eye **77 in** over **79 niggard prodigal** unwisely lavish yet coming too short in praise **81 show** describe. **82 doth owe** must still render, having fallen short on previous occasions **83 answers with surmise** makes up for with wondering admiration **88 limed** snared with birdlime, a sticky substance placed on branches **89 she . . . cheer** she unsuspectingly provides hospitable entertainment **90 reverend** respectful **92 that he colored** i.e., he disguised his harmful intent **93 pleats** cunning folds, concealments

94 That so that **97 so . . . store** feels such a craving despite the abundance **99 stranger eyes** eyes of a stranger **100 parling** speaking **102 glassy . . . books** (Refers to the custom of printing explanatory comments in book margins; compare *Romeo and Juliet*, 1.3.87.) **104 moralize** interpret. **sight** looking **105 More . . . light** i.e., other than to see that his eyes were open and seemingly without concealing a hidden motive. **106 stories** relates **110 bruisèd arms** armor battered in combat **116 welkin** sky, i.e., appearance, face **117 sable** black **121 Intending** pretending. **sprite** spirit **122 questionèd** conversed **127 revolving** considering **128 his will's obtaining** obtaining his will **130 weak-built hopes** the fact that his hopes are built on a weak foundation **131 Despair . . . gaining** i.e., Even a despairing hope often perversely undertakes to venture for gain; or, though frail hopes of wooing her urge him to hold back, despair of gaining her unviolently often urges him (bargains with him) to gain her violently. **132 meed** reward **133 adjunct** adjoined, resultant. **supposed** thought of.

Those that much covet are with gain so fond 134
That what they have not, that which they possess 135
They scatter and unloose it from their bond, 136
And so, by hoping more, they have but less;
Or, gaining more, the profit of excess 138
    Is but to surfeit, and such griefs sustain 139
      That they prove bankrupt in this poor-rich gain.

The aim of all is but to nurse the life 141
With honor, wealth, and ease in waning age;
And in this aim there is such thwarting strife 143
That one for all or all for one we gage: 144
As life for honor in fell battle's rage, 145
    Honor for wealth; and oft that wealth doth cost
      The death of all, and all together lost.

So that in vent'ring ill we leave to be 148
The things we are for that which we expect; 149
And this ambitious foul infirmity, 150
In having much, torments us with defect 151
Of that we have. So then we do neglect
    The thing we have, and, all for want of wit, 153
      Make something nothing by augmenting it.

Such hazard now must doting Tarquin make,
Pawning his honor to obtain his lust,
And for himself himself he must forsake. 157
Then where is truth, if there be no self-trust?
When shall he think to find a stranger just,
    When he himself himself confounds, betrays
      To sland'rous tongues and wretched hateful days?

Now stole upon the time the dead of night,
When heavy sleep had closed up mortal eyes.
No comfortable star did lend his light; 164
No noise but owls' and wolves' death-boding cries
Now serves the season, that they may surprise
    The silly lambs. Pure thoughts are dead and still, 167
      While lust and murder wakes to stain and kill.

And now this lustful lord leapt from his bed,
Throwing his mantle rudely o'er his arm;
Is madly tossed between desire and dread;
Th'one sweetly flatters, th'other feareth harm; 172
But honest fear, bewitched with lust's foul charm,
    Doth too too oft betake him to retire, 174
      Beaten away by brainsick rude desire.

His falchion on a flint he softly smiteth, 176
That from the cold stone sparks of fire do fly,
Whereat a waxen torch forthwith he lighteth,
Which must be lodestar to his lustful eye; 179
And to the flame thus speaks advisedly: 180
    "As from this cold flint I enforced this fire,
      So Lucrece must I force to my desire."

Here pale with fear he doth premeditate
The dangers of his loathsome enterprise,
And in his inward mind he doth debate
What following sorrow may on this arise.
Then, looking scornfully, he doth despise
    His naked armor of still-slaughtered lust, 188
      And justly thus controls his thoughts unjust: 189

"Fair torch, burn out thy light, and lend it not
To darken her whose light excelleth thine;
And die, unhallowed thoughts, before you blot
With your uncleanness that which is divine.
Offer pure incense to so pure a shrine.
    Let fair humanity abhor the deed
      That spots and stains love's modest snow-white weed. 196

"Oh, shame to knighthood and to shining arms!
Oh, foul dishonor to my household's grave! 198
Oh, impious act, including all foul harms! 199
A martial man to be soft fancy's slave! 200
True valor still a true respect should have; 201
    Then my digression is so vile, so base, 202
      That it will live engraven in my face.

"Yea, though I die, the scandal will survive
And be an eyesore in my golden coat; 205
Some loathsome dash the herald will contrive 206
To cipher me how fondly I did dote; 207
That my posterity, shamed with the note, 208
    Shall curse my bones, and hold it for no sin
      To wish that I their father had not been.

"What win I, if I gain the thing I seek?
A dream, a breath, a froth of fleeting joy.
Who buys a minute's mirth to wail a week?
Or sells eternity to get a toy? 214
For one sweet grape who will the vine destroy?
    Or what fond beggar, but to touch the crown,
      Would with the scepter straight be strucken down? 217

---

134 fond infatuated   **135 what** for what   **136 bond** possession
138 profit of excess only advantage of having more than enough
139 such griefs sustain i.e., to sustain such griefs as accompany surfeit   **141 The aim . . . life** The ultimate aim of the good life should be
to sustain that life   **143 And** yet   **144 gage** stake, risk   **145 As** such
as. **fell** fierce   **148 leave to be** cease being   **149 expect** i.e., hope to
be   **150 infirmity** i.e., covetousness   **151 In having much** though we
have much. **defect** the imagined deficiency   **153 want of wit** lack
of common sense   **157 for . . . forsake** i.e., he must forsake his honorable self to satisfy his lustful self.   **164 comfortable** cheering, benevolent. **his** its   **167 silly** helpless, defenseless   **172 Th'one . . . flatters**
i.e., desire deceives him into thinking he can go ahead safely
174 retire withdraw, retreat

176 falchion curved sword   **179 lodestar** the guiding polestar
180 advisedly deliberately   **188 His . . . lust** the armor supplied by
lust that effectively leaves him naked and unprotected, the lust that
continually undoes itself   **189 controls** rebukes   **196 weed** garment
(i.e., chastity).   **198 my household's grave** memorial tomb of my
forebears.   **199 including** encompassing   **200 fancy's** love's, infatua-
tion's   **201 true respect** i.e., proper consideration for virtue
202 digression transgression   **205 coat** coat of arms   **206 dash** bar,
stroke (devised by the heralds to indicate something dishonorable in
the pedigree)   **207 cipher** express in characters, indicate. **fondly**
foolishly   **208 note** stigma, the heraldic bar (line 206)   **214 toy** trifle.
217 straight at once

"If Collatinus dream of my intent,
Will he not wake and in a desp'rate rage
Post hither, this vile purpose to prevent?—
This siege that hath engirt his marriage,
This blur to youth, this sorrow to the sage,
    This dying virtue, this surviving shame,
    Whose crime will bear an ever-during blame.

"Oh, what excuse can my invention make
When thou shalt charge me with so black a deed?
Will not my tongue be mute, my frail joints shake,
Mine eyes forgo their light, my false heart bleed?
The guilt being great, the fear doth still exceed;
    And extreme fear can neither fight nor fly,
    But cowardlike with trembling terror die.

"Had Collatinus killed my son or sire,
Or lain in ambush to betray my life,
Or were he not my dear friend, this desire
Might have excuse to work upon his wife,
As in revenge or quittal of such strife;
    But as he is my kinsman, my dear friend,
    The shame and fault finds no excuse nor end.

"Shameful it is; ay, if the fact be known,
Hateful it is. There is no hate in loving.
I'll beg her love. But she is not her own.
The worst is but denial and reproving.
My will is strong, past reason's weak removing.
    Who fears a sentence or an old man's saw
    Shall by a painted cloth be kept in awe."

Thus, graceless, holds he disputation
'Tween frozen conscience and hot-burning will,
And with good thoughts makes dispensation,
Urging the worser sense for vantage still,
Which in a moment doth confound and kill
    All pure effects, and doth so far proceed
    That what is vile shows like a virtuous deed.

Quoth he, "She took me kindly by the hand
And gazed for tidings in my eager eyes,
Fearing some hard news from the warlike band
Where her belovèd Collatinus lies.
Oh, how her fear did make her color rise!
    First red as roses that on lawn we lay,
    Then white as lawn, the roses took away.

"And how her hand, in my hand being locked,
Forced it to tremble with her loyal fear!

Which struck her sad, and then it faster rocked,
Until her husband's welfare she did hear;
Whereat she smilèd with so sweet a cheer
    That had Narcissus seen her as she stood
    Self-love had never drowned him in the flood.

"Why hunt I then for color or excuses?
All orators are dumb when beauty pleadeth;
Poor wretches have remorse in poor abuses;
Love thrives not in the heart that shadows dreadeth.
Affection is my captain, and he leadeth;
    And when his gaudy banner is displayed,
    The coward fights and will not be dismayed.

"Then, childish fear, avaunt! Debating, die!
Respect and reason, wait on wrinkled age!
My heart shall never countermand mine eye.
Sad pause and deep regard beseems the sage;
My part is youth, and beats these from the stage.
    Desire my pilot is, beauty my prize;
    Then who fears sinking where such treasure lies?"

As corn o'ergrown by weeds, so heedful fear
Is almost choked by unresisted lust.
Away he steals with open list'ning ear,
Full of foul hope and full of fond mistrust,
Both which, as servitors to the unjust,
    So cross him with their opposite persuasion
    That now he vows a league, and now invasion.

Within his thought her heavenly image sits,
And in the selfsame seat sits Collatine.
That eye which looks on her confounds his wits;
That eye which him beholds, as more divine,
Unto a view so false will not incline,
    But with a pure appeal seeks to the heart,
    Which once corrupted takes the worser part;

And therein heartens up his servile powers,
Who, flattered by their leader's jocund show,
Stuff up his lust, as minutes fill up hours;
And as their captain, so their pride doth grow,

220
221
222
224

226
228

236

239
241

244
245

248

251

258

264
265

267
269
270
271
273

274
275
276
277
278

281
284
286
287

290
291
293

295
296

220 Post hasten   221 engirt engirdled, as in a siege   222 blur blot, disgrace   224 ever-during everlasting   226 thou i.e., Collatinus   228 forgo their light lose their power of vision   236 quittal requital   239 fact deed   241 she . . . own i.e., she is not entirely independent, since she has duties to her husband.   244 Who Whoever.   sentence moral sentiment.   saw saying, proverb   245 painted cloth wall hanging in which moral tales and maxims were sometimes depicted. (Compare with lines 1366–1456, where such a painted cloth is described.)   248 makes dispensation dispenses, sets aside   251 effects intents and consequences   258 lawn fine white linen

264 a cheer an expression   265 Narcissus youth who fell in love with his own reflection in the water (but who would have fallen in love with Lucrece if he had seen her)   267 color pretext   269 Poor . . . abuses lowborn, cowardly men feel remorse for their paltry misdeeds   270 shadows i.e., the chimeras of conscience   271 Affection Passion   273 The coward i.e., even the coward   274 avaunt begone.   275 Respect Circumspection.   wait on attend, accompany   276 heart (Here, "moral sense"; compare with lines 293 ff., where the heart is corrupted.)   277 Sad Serious, reflective   278 My . . . stage (Tarquin visualizes himself as taking the role of hotheaded Youth in a morality play, driving away [offstage] his wise older counselors.)   281 corn grain   284 fond foolish   286 cross thwart   287 league treaty (of peace)   290 eye eye of lust.   confounds his wits overwhelms his reason with lust.   291 That eye . . . divine The eye of divine reason, reflecting on Collatine   293 seeks to looks to (for moral support)   295 his servile powers i.e., the heart's servants, i.e., appetites. (The image is the common one of the faculties as an army: the heart as captain of the sensible soul commands all the affections to serve him. Compare with lines 433 ff., below.)   296 jocund sprightly

Paying more slavish tribute than they owe.
　　By reprobate desire thus madly led,
　　The Roman lord marcheth to Lucrece' bed.

The locks between her chamber and his will,
Each one by him enforced, retires his ward;　303
But, as they open, they all rate his ill,　304
Which drives the creeping thief to some regard.　305
The threshold grates the door to have him heard;
　　Night-wand'ring weasels shriek to see him there;　307
　　They fright him, yet he still pursues his fear.　308

As each unwilling portal yields him way,
Through little vents and crannies of the place
The wind wars with his torch to make him stay,
And blows the smoke of it into his face,
Extinguishing his conduct in this case;　313
　　But his hot heart, which fond desire doth scorch,
　　Puffs forth another wind that fires the torch.

And being lighted, by the light he spies
Lucretia's glove, wherein her needle sticks.
He takes it from the rushes where it lies,　318
And gripping it, the needle his finger pricks,
As who should say, "This glove to wanton tricks　320
　　Is not inured. Return again in haste;　321
　　Thou see'st our mistress' ornaments are chaste."

But all these poor forbiddings could not stay him;　323
He in the worst sense consters their denial.　324
The doors, the wind, the glove that did delay him
He takes for accidental things of trial,　326
Or as those bars which stop the hourly dial,　327
　　Who with a ling'ring stay his course doth let　328
　　Till every minute pays the hour his debt.

"So, so," quoth he, "these lets attend the time,　330
Like little frosts that sometime threat the spring,
To add a more rejoicing to the prime,　332
And give the sneapèd birds more cause to sing.　333
Pain pays the income of each precious thing;　334
　　Huge rocks, high winds, strong pirates, shelves, and
　　　　sands　335
　　The merchant fears, ere rich at home he lands."

Now is he come unto the chamber door　299
That shuts him from the heaven of his thought,
Which with a yielding latch, and with no more,
Hath barred him from the blessèd thing he sought.
So from himself impiety hath wrought　341
　　That for his prey to pray he doth begin,
　　As if the heavens should countenance his sin.

But in the midst of his unfruitful prayer,
Having solicited th'eternal power
That his foul thoughts might compass his fair fair,　346
And they would stand auspicious to the hour,　347
Even there he starts. Quoth he, "I must deflower.　348
　　The powers to whom I pray abhor this fact;　349
　　How can they then assist me in the act?

"Then Love and Fortune be my gods, my guide!
My will is backed with resolution.
Thoughts are but dreams till their effects be tried;
The blackest sin is cleared with absolution;
Against love's fire fear's frost hath dissolution.
　　The eye of heaven is out, and misty night　356
　　Covers the shame that follows sweet delight."

This said, his guilty hand plucked up the latch,
And with his knee the door he opens wide.
The dove sleeps fast that this night owl will catch.
Thus treason works ere traitors be espied.
Who sees the lurking serpent steps aside;　362
　　But she, sound sleeping, fearing no such thing,
　　Lies at the mercy of his mortal sting.　364

Into the chamber wickedly he stalks,　365
And gazeth on her yet unstainèd bed.
The curtains being close, about he walks,　367
Rolling his greedy eyeballs in his head.
By their high treason is his heart misled,
　　Which gives the watchword to his hand full soon
　　To draw the cloud that hides the silver moon.　371

Look as the fair and fiery-pointed sun,　372
Rushing from forth a cloud, bereaves our sight,
Even so, the curtain drawn, his eyes begun
To wink, being blinded with a greater light.　375
Whether it is that she reflects so bright　376
　　That dazzleth them, or else some shame supposed;
　　But blind they are, and keep themselves enclosed.

Oh, had they in that darksome prison died,
Then had they seen the period of their ill!　380
Then Collatine again by Lucrece' side

299 Paying . . . owe i.e., paying tribute to the heart as its vassals, and doing so in an overdone and corrupting way. **303 retires his ward** draws back its guard, i.e., the locking mechanism **304 rate his ill** chide his evil (by creaking) **305 regard** caution. **307 weasels** (Weasels were sometimes kept in houses as rat catchers.) **308 his fear** i.e., the cause of his fear. **313 conduct** conductor, i.e., his torch. (With a play on "behavior.") **318 rushes** reeds used as floor covering **320 who should** one might **320–1 to wanton . . . inured** has not become habituated to lascivious stratagems. **323 stay** restrain **324 consters** construes **326 accidental . . . trial** i.e., accidents that test his resolve, not portents **327 bars . . . dial** minute marks on a clock face at which the minute hand seems to pause slightly **328 Who** which. **his** its. **let** hinder **330 these . . . time** i.e., these hindrances (like the minute marks) are part of the passage of time **332 more** greater. **prime** spring **333 sneapèd** nipped or pinched with cold **334 pays . . . of** is the price of obtaining, or, pays court to, as though attending the arrival of **335 shelves** sandbars

341 So . . . wrought Impiety has so wrested him away from his better nature **346 compass** encompass, possess. **fair fair** virtuous fair one **347 they** i.e., that they, the eternal powers of heaven **348 starts** i.e., is startled, taken aback. **349 fact** deed **356 The eye . . . out** i.e., The sun is set **362 Who** Whoever **364 mortal** deadly. **sting** bite. (Suggesting also "lust" and "penis.") **365 stalks** steals **367 close** (around a four-poster bed) **371 draw the cloud** i.e., draw back the bedcurtains **372 Look as** See how, just as **375 wink** shut **376 reflects** shines **380 period** end. **ill** wrongdoing.

In his clear bed might have reposèd still.   382
But they must ope, this blessèd league to kill,   383
   And holy-thoughted Lucrece to their sight   384
   Must sell her joy, her life, her world's delight.

Her lily hand her rosy cheek lies under,
Cozening the pillow of a lawful kiss,   387
Who, therefore angry, seems to part in sunder,
Swelling on either side to want his bliss;   389
Between whose hills her head entombèd is;
   Where, like a virtuous monument, she lies,   391
   To be admired of lewd unhallowed eyes.

Without the bed her other fair hand was,   393
On the green coverlet, whose perfect white
Showed like an April daisy on the grass,
With pearly sweat resembling dew of night.
Her eyes, like marigolds, had sheathed their light,
   And canopied in darkness sweetly lay,
   Till they might open to adorn the day.

Her hair, like golden threads, played with her breath—
Oh, modest wantons, wanton modesty!—
Showing life's triumph in the map of death   402
And death's dim look in life's mortality.   403
Each in her sleep themselves so beautify   404
   As if between them twain there were no strife,
   But that life lived in death and death in life.

Her breasts like ivory globes circled with blue,
A pair of maiden worlds unconquerèd,
Save of their lord no bearing yoke they knew,
And him by oath they truly honorèd.
These worlds in Tarquin new ambition bred,
   Who, like a foul usurper, went about
   From this fair throne to heave the owner out.

What could he see but mightily he noted?
What did he note but strongly he desired?
What he beheld, on that he firmly doted,
And in his will his willful eye he tired.   417
With more than admiration he admired
   Her azure veins, her alabaster skin,
   Her coral lips, her snow-white dimpled chin.

As the grim lion fawneth o'er his prey,   421
Sharp hunger by the conquest satisfied,
So o'er this sleeping soul doth Tarquin stay,
His rage of lust by gazing qualified—   424
Slacked, not suppressed, for, standing by her side,   425

His eye, which late this mutiny restrains,   426
Unto a greater uproar tempts his veins.

And they, like straggling slaves for pillage fighting,   428
Obdurate vassals fell exploits effecting,   429
In bloody death and ravishment delighting,
Nor children's tears nor mothers' groans respecting,   431
Swell in their pride, the onset still expecting.   432
   Anon his beating heart, alarum striking,
   Gives the hot charge and bids them do their liking.

His drumming heart cheers up his burning eye,
His eye commends the leading to his hand;   436
His hand, as proud of such a dignity,
Smoking with pride, marched on to make his stand
On her bare breast, the heart of all her land;
   Whose ranks of blue veins, as his hand did scale,   440
   Left their round turrets destitute and pale.

They, must'ring to the quiet cabinet   442
Where their dear governess and lady lies,
Do tell her she is dreadfully beset,
And fright her with confusion of their cries.
She, much amazed, breaks ope her locked-up eyes,
   Who, peeping forth this tumult to behold,
   Are by his flaming torch dimmed and controlled.   448

Imagine her as one in dead of night
From forth dull sleep by dreadful fancy waking,
That thinks she hath beheld some ghastly sprite,
Whose grim aspect sets every joint a-shaking.
What terror 'tis! But she, in worser taking,   453
   From sleep disturbèd, heedfully doth view
   The sight which makes supposèd terror true.

Wrapped and confounded in a thousand fears,
Like to a new-killed bird she trembling lies.
She dares not look; yet, winking, there appears   458
Quick-shifting antics, ugly in her eyes.   459
Such shadows are the weak brain's forgeries,
   Who, angry that the eyes fly from their lights,   461
   In darkness daunts them with more dreadful sights.

His hand, that yet remains upon her breast—
Rude ram, to batter such an ivory wall!—   464
May feel her heart—poor citizen!—distressed,
Wounding itself to death, rise up and fall,
Beating her bulk, that his hand shakes withal.   467
   This moves in him more rage and lesser pity
   To make the breach and enter this sweet city.

---

382 clear pure, innocent   **383 league** i.e., marriage   **384 to their
sight** for the sake of what they (his eyes) will see   **387 Cozening**
cheating   **389 to want his** i.e., protesting the lack of its   **391 monument** effigy on a tomb   **393 Without the bed** Outside the bedclothes
402 the map of death i.e., sleep. (*Map* means "image, picture.")
403 life's mortality life's least-living aspect, i.e., sleep.   **404 Each** i.e.,
Life and death   **417 will** lust.   **tired** (1) exhausted (2) glutted, fed
ravenously. (A term from falconry.)   **421 fawneth** shows delight
424 qualified softened, abated   **425 Slacked** moderated. (The Quarto
reading, "Slakt," could be modernized as "Slaked," with the same
meaning.)

426 late lately, a moment ago   **428 slaves** i.e., base-born soldiers
429 fell fierce.   **effecting** carrying out   **431 Nor** neither   **432 pride**
lust.   **still** continually   **436 commends** entrusts, commissions
440 scale ascend (as in military attack)   **442 mustering** gathering.
cabinet i.e., heart   **448 controlled** overpowered.   **453 taking** plight
458 winking closing the eyes   **459 antics** phantoms, fantastic appearances, shapes   **461 angry . . . lights** i.e., angry that the eyes abandon
their stations as guardians of light   **464 ram** battering ram   **467 bulk**
i.e., chest, breast.   **that** so that

First, like a trumpet, doth his tongue begin
To sound a parley to his heartless foe,   471
Who o'er the white sheet peers her whiter chin,   472
The reason of this rash alarm to know,
Which he by dumb demeanor seeks to show;   474
    But she with vehement prayers urgeth still   475
    Under what color he commits this ill.   476

Thus he replies: "The color in thy face,   477
That even for anger makes the lily pale,   478
And the red rose blush at her own disgrace,
Shall plead for me and tell my loving tale.
Under that color am I come to scale   481
    Thy never-conquered fort; the fault is thine,
    For those thine eyes betray thee unto mine.

"Thus I forestall thee, if thou mean to chide:
Thy beauty hath ensnared thee to this night,   485
Where thou with patience must my will abide—
My will that marks thee for my earth's delight,
Which I to conquer sought with all my might.
    But as reproof and reason beat it dead,   489
    By thy bright beauty was it newly bred.

"I see what crosses my attempt will bring;   491
I know what thorns the growing rose defends;
I think the honey guarded with a sting;   493
All this beforehand counsel comprehends.   494
But will is deaf and hears no heedful friends;
    Only he hath an eye to gaze on beauty
    And dotes on what he looks, 'gainst law or duty.   497

"I have debated even in my soul
What wrong, what shame, what sorrow I shall breed,
But nothing can affection's course control   500
Or stop the headlong fury of his speed.
I know repentant tears ensue the deed,   502
    Reproach, disdain, and deadly enmity;
    Yet strive I to embrace mine infamy."

This said, he shakes aloft his Roman blade,
Which, like a falcon towering in the skies,
Coucheth the fowl below with his wings' shade,   507
Whose crooked beak threats if he mount he dies.   508
So under his insulting falchion lies   509
    Harmless Lucretia, marking what he tells
    With trembling fear, as fowl hear falcon's bells.   511

"Lucrece," quoth he, "this night I must enjoy thee.
If thou deny, then force must work my way,
For in thy bed I purpose to destroy thee.
That done, some worthless slave of thine I'll slay,
To kill thine honor with thy life's decay;   516
    And in thy dead arms do I mean to place him,
    Swearing I slew him, seeing thee embrace him.

"So thy surviving husband shall remain
The scornful mark of every open eye,   520
Thy kinsmen hang their heads at this disdain,
Thy issue blurred with nameless bastardy;   522
And thou, the author of their obloquy,
    Shalt have thy trespass cited up in rhymes   524
    And sung by children in succeeding times.

"But if thou yield, I rest thy secret friend.   526
The fault unknown is as a thought unacted;
A little harm done to a great good end
For lawful policy remains enacted.   529
The poisonous simple sometime is compacted   530
    In a pure compound; being so applied,   531
    His venom in effect is purified.

"Then, for thy husband and thy children's sake,
Tender my suit. Bequeath not to their lot   534
The shame that from them no device can take,   535
The blemish that will never be forgot,
Worse than a slavish wipe or birth hour's blot.   537
    For marks descried in men's nativity
    Are nature's faults, not their own infamy."

Here with a cockatrice' dead-killing eye   540
He rouseth up himself and makes a pause,
While she, the picture of pure piety,
Like a white hind under the gripe's sharp claws,   543
Pleads, in a wilderness where are no laws,   544
    To the rough beast that knows no gentle right,   545
    Nor aught obeys but his foul appetite.

But when a black-faced cloud the world doth threat,
In his dim mist th'aspiring mountains hiding,   548
From earth's dark womb some gentle gust doth get,   549
Which blows these pitchy vapors from their biding,   550
Hind'ring their present fall by this dividing;   551

471 a parley a summoning of the defenders to a negotiation.   heartless terrified   472 peers causes to peep out (as a defender would peer out over the fortifications)   474 dumb demeanor mute gesture   475 urgeth cries out to know   476 color pretext   477 color hue. (Punning on the previous line.)   478 That . . . pale that makes even the lily turn pale in anger (at being surpassed in paleness)   481 color banner. (Punning on lines 476 and 477.)   485 ensnared thee to led you into the trap of   489 as as soon as.   it my will or passion   491 crosses vexations   493 think the honey know the honey to be   494 counsel wisdom, reason   497 looks sees   500 affection's passion's   502 ensue follow upon   507 Coucheth causes to couch, i.e., remain concealed.   his i.e., the falcon's (whose shadow frightens the fowl)   508 Whose . . . dies (The crooked beak of the falcon threatens that if the fowl dare emerge from hiding, it dies.)   509 insulting falchion triumphantly exulting sword   511 bells (Falcons had bells attached to their feet.)

516 To kill . . . decay i.e., to destroy your honor even while also taking your life   520 open eye i.e., observer   522 Thy . . . bastardy your children sullied with the suspicion of being bastards of some unknown father   524 in rhymes i.e., in ballads   526 rest remain. friend lover.   529 For . . . enacted is accepted as a lawful expedient. 530 simple ingredient, drug.   compacted mixed   531 pure i.e., benign, medically efficacious   534 Tender my suit regard my plea. 535 device (1) contrivance (2) heraldic motto   537 slavish wipe brand with which slaves were marked.   birth hour's blot unsightly birthmark.   540 cockatrice the basilisk, said to be hatched by a serpent from a cock's egg and to kill by its breath and the rays it emitted from its eyes   gripe's vulture's, or griffin's   543 hind female deer. 544 Pleads (With play on legal meaning.)   545 gentle right law of gentility   548 th'aspiring the high-rising   549 doth get comes into being   550 pitchy black.   their biding where they hang   551 their present fall i.e., the imminent onset of the storm

So his unhallowed haste her words delays, 552
And moody Pluto winks while Orpheus plays. 553

Yet, foul night-waking cat, he doth but dally,
While in his hold-fast foot the weak mouse panteth.
Her sad behavior feeds his vulture folly, 556
A swallowing gulf that even in plenty wanteth. 557
His ear her prayers admits, but his heart granteth
    No penetrable entrance to her plaining; 559
    Tears harden lust, though marble wear with raining.

Her pity-pleading eyes are sadly fixed
In the remorseless wrinkles of his face; 562
Her modest eloquence with sighs is mixed,
Which to her oratory adds more grace.
She puts the period often from his place, 565
    And midst the sentence so her accent breaks 566
    That twice she doth begin ere once she speaks.

She conjures him by high almighty Jove,
By knighthood, gentry, and sweet friendship's oath, 569
By her untimely tears, her husband's love, 570
By holy human law and common troth, 571
By heaven and earth, and all the power of both,
    That to his borrowed bed he make retire 573
    And stoop to honor, not to foul desire. 574

Quoth she, "Reward not hospitality
With such black payment as thou hast pretended. 576
Mud not the fountain that gave drink to thee; 577
Mar not the thing that cannot be amended. 578
End thy ill aim before thy shoot be ended; 579
    He is no woodman that doth bend his bow 580
    To strike a poor unseasonable doe. 581

"My husband is thy friend; for his sake spare me.
Thyself art mighty; for thine own sake leave me.
Myself a weakling; do not then ensnare me.
Thou look'st not like deceit; do not deceive me.
My sighs, like whirlwinds, labor hence to heave thee.
    If ever man were moved with woman's moans,
    Be movèd with my tears, my sighs, my groans;

"All which together, like a troubled ocean,
Beat at thy rocky and wreck-threat'ning heart,
To soften it with their continual motion;

For stones dissolved to water do convert. 592
Oh, if no harder than a stone thou art,
    Melt at my tears, and be compassionate!
    Soft pity enters at an iron gate.

"In Tarquin's likeness I did entertain thee.
Hast thou put on his shape to do him shame?
To all the host of heaven I complain me.
Thou wrong'st his honor, wound'st his princely name.
Thou art not what thou seem'st; and if the same, 600
    Thou seem'st not what thou art, a god, a king;
    For kings like gods should govern everything.

"How will thy shame be seeded in thine age, 603
When thus thy vices bud before thy spring?
If in thy hope thou dar'st do such outrage, 605
What dar'st thou not when once thou art a king?
Oh, be remembered, no outrageous thing 607
    From vassal actors can be wiped away; 608
    Then kings' misdeeds cannot be hid in clay. 609

"This deed will make thee only loved for fear, 610
But happy monarchs still are feared for love. 611
With foul offenders thou perforce must bear, 612
When they in thee the like offenses prove.
If but for fear of this, thy will remove; 614
    For princes are the glass, the school, the book, 615
    Where subjects' eyes do learn, do read, do look.

"And wilt thou be the school where Lust shall learn?
Must he in thee read lectures of such shame?
Wilt thou be glass wherein it shall discern
Authority for sin, warrant for blame,
To privilege dishonor in thy name? 621
    Thou back'st reproach against long-living laud 622
    And mak'st fair reputation but a bawd.

"Hast thou command? By Him that gave it thee, 624
From a pure heart command thy rebel will.
Draw not thy sword to guard iniquity,
For it was lent thee all that brood to kill. 627
Thy princely office how canst thou fulfill,
    When, patterned by thy fault, foul Sin may say 629
    He learned to sin, and thou didst teach the way?

"Think but how vile a spectacle it were
To view thy present trespass in another.
Men's faults do seldom to themselves appear;

---

552 So . . . delays thus her words delay his unhallowed haste
553 winks closes his eyes.   **Orpheus** husband of Eurydice, who went
to the underworld for her and charmed Pluto, ruler of the underworld,
with his playing the lyre   **556 vulture folly** ravenous lewdness and
madness   **557 gulf** maw, belly.   **wanteth** craves insatiably.
559 plaining lamentation   **562 wrinkles** i.e., frowns   **565 his place** its
place (in the sentence; i.e., she speaks in broken phrases)   **566 accent**
speech   **569 gentry** nobleness of birth and breeding   **570 untimely
tears** i.e., tears occasioned by an inopportune and unwelcome happening   **571 troth** good faith   **573 borrowed** lent him for the night
574 stoop to (1) subject himself to (2) pursue (3) swoop down to (as to
the lure or prey, like a falcon)   **576 pretended** proposed.   **577 Mud**
Muddy   **578 amended** returned to its former purity.   **579 shoot** shooting, hunting   **580 woodman** huntsman   **581 unseasonable** in foal or
not yet bearing, out of the hunting season

592 stones . . . convert stones are worn away in time by water.
convert change.   **600 if the same** i.e., if you are actually Tarquin
603 be seeded ripen   **605 in thy hope** i.e., while you are yet only heir
to the kingdom   **607 be remembered** bear in mind   **608 vassal
actors** vassals or ordinary subjects who commit crimes   **609 in clay**
i.e., even in death.   **610 loved for fear** obeyed out of fear   **611 still . . .
love** always are regarded with reverential awe stemming from love.
612 With . . . bear You will have to put up with others' foul offenses
614 but only.   **thy will remove** dissuade your lust   **615 glass** mirror
and paradigm   **621 privilege** license   **622 Thou back'st** You support.   **laud** praise   **624 Him** i.e., God   **627 that brood** i.e., the progeny of evil   **629 patterned** shown a precedent

Their own transgressions partially they smother.   634
This guilt would seem death-worthy in thy brother.
    Oh, how are they wrapped in with infamies
    That from their own misdeeds askance their eyes!   637

"To thee, to thee, my heaved-up hands appeal,   638
Not to seducing lust, thy rash relier.   639
I sue for exiled majesty's repeal;   640
Let him return, and flatt'ring thoughts retire.   641
His true respect will prison false desire   642
    And wipe the dim mist from thy doting eyne,   643
    That thou shalt see thy state and pity mine."

"Have done," quoth he. "My uncontrollèd tide   645
Turns not, but swells the higher by this let.   646
Small lights are soon blown out; huge fires abide,
And with the wind in greater fury fret.
The petty streams that pay a daily debt
    To their salt sovereign, with their fresh falls' haste   650
    Add to his flow but alter not his taste."

"Thou art," quoth she, "a sea, a sovereign king;
And lo, there falls into thy boundless flood
Black lust, dishonor, shame, misgoverning,
Who seek to stain the ocean of thy blood.   655
If all these petty ills shall change thy good,
    Thy sea within a puddle's womb is hearsed,   657
    And not the puddle in thy sea dispersed.   658

"So shall these slaves be king, and thou their slave;   659
Thou nobly base, they basely dignified;
Thou their fair life, and they thy fouler grave;
Thou loathèd in their shame, they in thy pride.
The lesser thing should not the greater hide;
    The cedar stoops not to the base shrub's foot,
    But low shrubs wither at the cedar's root.

"So let thy thoughts, low vassals to thy state—"
"No more," quoth he, "by heaven, I will not hear thee.
Yield to my love; if not, enforcèd hate,   668
Instead of love's coy touch, shall rudely tear thee.   669
That done, despitefully I mean to bear thee
    Unto the base bed of some rascal groom,   671
    To be thy partner in this shameful doom."

This said, he sets his foot upon the light,
For light and lust are deadly enemies;
Shame folded up in blind concealing night,
When most unseen, then most doth tyrannize.
The wolf hath seized his prey, the poor lamb cries;

Till with her own white fleece her voice controlled   678
Entombs her outcry in her lips' sweet fold.   679

For with the nightly linen that she wears
He pens her piteous clamors in her head,
Cooling his hot face in the chastest tears
That ever modest eyes with sorrow shed.
Oh, that prone lust should stain so pure a bed!   684
    The spots whereof could weeping purify,   685
    Her tears should drop on them perpetually.

But she hath lost a dearer thing than life,
And he hath won what he would lose again.   688
This forcèd league doth force a further strife;
This momentary joy breeds months of pain;
This hot desire converts to cold disdain.   691
    Pure Chastity is rifled of her store,   692
    And Lust, the thief, far poorer than before.

Look as the full-fed hound or gorgèd hawk,   694
Unapt for tender smell or speedy flight,   695
Make slow pursuit, or altogether balk   696
The prey wherein by nature they delight,
So surfeit-taking Tarquin fares this night.
    His taste delicious, in digestion souring,
    Devours his will, that lived by foul devouring.

Oh, deeper sin than bottomless conceit   701
Can comprehend in still imagination!   702
Drunken Desire must vomit his receipt   703
Ere he can see his own abomination.
While Lust is in his pride, no exclamation   705
    Can curb his heat or rein his rash desire,
    Till like a jade Self-will himself doth tire.   707

And then with lank and lean discolored cheek,
With heavy eye, knit brow, and strengthless pace,
Feeble Desire, all recreant, poor, and meek,   710
Like to a bankrupt beggar wails his case.   711
The flesh being proud, Desire doth fight with Grace,   712
    For there it revels, and when that decays,   713
    The guilty rebel for remission prays.   714

So fares it with this faultful lord of Rome,
Who this accomplishment so hotly chased;
For now against himself he sounds this doom,   717

---

634 **partially . . . smother** they hide from themselves.   637 **askance** avert   638 **heaved-up** raised   639 **thy rash relier** on which you rashly rely.   640 **repeal** recall from exile   641 **and flatt'ring thoughts retire** and let those thoughts that flatter and egg on lust go away.   642 **His . . . respect** His true authority and concern for truth.   **prison** imprison   643 **eyne** eyes   645 **Have done** Cease talking   646 **let** hindrance.   650 **salt sovereign** i.e., the sea   655 **blood** heritage; character.   657–8 **Thy . . . dispersed** in that case your royal sea is now buried in a foul puddle, rather than the puddle being dispersed in your royal sea.   659 **these slaves** i.e., lust, dishonor, etc.; see line 654   668 **enforcèd hate** force impelled by hatred   669 **coy** gentle   671 **groom** servant

678–9 **Till . . . fold** until, overmastering her voice with her own night-wear or bedlinen, he buries her outcry as though in the fold of her sweet lips. (*Fold* refers to her folded or compressed lips and to a sheep-fold; hence *pens* in line 681.)   684 **prone** eager, headlong   685 **could weeping** if weeping could   688 **what . . . again** what he soon wished he could undo.   691 **converts** changes   692 **Pure . . . store** i.e., Pure chastity loses all that it has, loses all itself   694 **Look as** Just as   695 **tender smell** delicate scent   696 **balk** turn away from, let slip   701 **bottomless conceit** limitless imagination   702 **in still imagination** in imagination alone.   703 **his receipt** what it has swallowed   705 **exclamation** protest   707 **jade** recalcitrant horse   710 **recreant** craven, cowed   711 **Like to** like   712 **proud** stubborn, willful   713 **there** i.e., in the flesh.   **when that decays** when the reveling in pleasure subsides   714 **The guilty . . . prays** the flesh prays for forgiveness.   717 **sounds this doom** pronounces this judgment

That through the length of times he stands disgraced.
Besides, his soul's fair temple is defaced,
    To whose weak ruins muster troops of cares
    To ask the spotted princess how she fares.   721

She says her subjects with foul insurrection   722
Have battered down her consecrated wall,
And by their mortal fault brought in subjection   724
Her immortality, and made her thrall
To living death and pain perpetual,
    Which in her prescience she controllèd still,   727
    But her foresight could not forestall their will.   728

Ev'n in this thought through the dark night he stealeth,
A captive victor that hath lost in gain,   730
Bearing away the wound that nothing healeth,
The scar that will, despite of cure, remain,
Leaving his spoil perplexed in greater pain.   733
    She bears the load of lust he left behind,
    And he the burden of a guilty mind.

He like a thievish dog creeps sadly thence;
She like a wearied lamb lies panting there.
He scowls and hates himself for his offense;
She, desperate, with her nails her flesh doth tear.
He faintly flies, sweating with guilty fear;   740
    She stays, exclaiming on the direful night;   741
    He runs, and chides his vanished, loathed delight.

He thence departs a heavy convertite;   743
She there remains a hopeless castaway.
He in his speed looks for the morning light;
She prays she never may behold the day.
"For day," quoth she, "night's scapes doth open lay,   747
    And my true eyes have never practiced how
    To cloak offenses with a cunning brow.

"They think not but that every eye can see
The same disgrace which they themselves behold;
And therefore would they still in darkness be,
To have their unseen sin remain untold.
For they their guilt with weeping will unfold,   754
    And grave, like water that doth eat in steel,   755
    Upon my cheeks what helpless shame I feel."

Here she exclaims against repose and rest   757
And bids her eyes hereafter still be blind.   758
She wakes her heart by beating on her breast,
And bids it leap from thence, where it may find

Some purer chest to close so pure a mind.   761
    Frantic with grief thus breathes she forth her spite   762
    Against the unseen secrecy of night:

"O comfort-killing Night, image of hell,
Dim register and notary of shame,   765
Black stage for tragedies and murders fell,   766
Vast sin-concealing chaos, nurse of blame!   767
Blind muffled bawd, dark harbor for defame,   768
    Grim cave of death, whisp'ring conspirator
    With close-tongued treason and the ravisher!   770

"O hateful, vaporous, and foggy Night,
Since thou art guilty of my cureless crime,
Muster thy mists to meet the eastern light,
Make war against proportioned course of time;   774
Or if thou wilt permit the sun to climb
    His wonted height, yet ere he go to bed
    Knit poisonous clouds about his golden head.

"With rotten damps ravish the morning air;
Let their exhaled unwholesome breaths make sick
The life of purity, the supreme fair,   780
Ere he arrive his weary noontide prick;   781
And let thy musty vapors march so thick
    That in their smoky ranks his smothered light
    May set at noon and make perpetual night.

"Were Tarquin Night, as he is but Night's child,
The silver-shining queen he would distain;   786
Her twinkling handmaids too, by him defiled,   787
Through Night's black bosom should not peep again.
So should I have copartners in my pain;
    And fellowship in woe doth woe assuage,
    As palmers' chat makes short their pilgrimage.   791

"Where now I have no one to blush with me,   792
To cross their arms and hang their heads with mine,   793
To mask their brows and hide their infamy;   794
But I alone alone must sit and pine,   795
Seasoning the earth with showers of silver brine,
    Mingling my talk with tears, my grief with groans,
    Poor wasting monuments of lasting moans.   798

"O Night, thou furnace of foul reeking smoke!
Let not the jealous Day behold that face
Which underneath thy black all-hiding cloak
Immodestly lies martyred with disgrace!   802
Keep still possession of thy gloomy place,

---

721 **spotted princess** i.e., his contaminated soul, of whom the *temple*, line 719, is the body.   722 **subjects** i.e., the senses or passions 724 **mortal** deadly   727–8 **Which . . . will** i.e., which senses or passions she theoretically governed in anticipation of any act but could not, despite her foresight, restrain in their state of sexual arousal. 730 **A captive . . . gain** one who has gained the prize at the cost of perpetual durance in sin   733 **spoil** prey, i.e., Lucrece   740 **faintly** cowardly   741 **exclaiming on** denouncing   743 **heavy convertite** sad penitent   747 **night's . . . lay** exposes night's transgressions to view   754 **unfold** reveal   755 **grave** engrave. **water** i.e., aqua fortis, nitric acid   757 **exclaims against** reproaches   758 **still** forever

761 **close** enclose   762 **spite** vexation   765 **register** registrar. **notary** recorder   766 **Black stage** (Referring seemingly to a practice of hanging the stage with black for the performance of a tragedy.) **fell** savage   767 **blame** evil.   768 **defame** infamy   770 **close-tongued** closemouthed, secretive of speech   774 **proportioned** i.e., orderly in the regulated interchange of day and night   780 **supreme fair** i.e., the sun   781 **arrive** arrive at. **prick** mark (as on a dial)   786 **queen** i.e., moon. **distain** stain, soil   787 **handmaids** i.e., stars   791 **palmers'** pilgrims'   792 **Where** Whereas   793–4 **To cross . . . infamy** (Folding the arms and pulling the hat over the brows were conventional gestures of grief.)   795 **I alone alone** only I alone   798 **monuments** tokens, mementos   802 **martyred** i.e., disfigured

That all the faults which in thy reign are made
May likewise be sepulch'red in thy shade.

"Make me not object to the telltale Day. 806
The light will show charactered in my brow 807
The story of sweet chastity's decay, 808
The impious breach of holy wedlock vow.
Yea, the illiterate, that know not how
    To cipher what is writ in learnèd books, 811
    Will quote my loathsome trespass in my looks. 812

"The nurse, to still her child, will tell my story,
And fright her crying babe with Tarquin's name;
The orator, to deck his oratory, 815
Will couple my reproach to Tarquin's shame;
Feast-finding minstrels, tuning my defame, 817
    Will tie the hearers to attend each line,
    How Tarquin wrongèd me, I Collatine.

"Let my good name, that senseless reputation, 820
For Collatine's dear love be kept unspotted.
If that be made a theme for disputation, 822
The branches of another root are rotted, 823
And undeserved reproach to him allotted
    That is as clear from this attaint of mine 825
    As I, ere this, was pure to Collatine.

"O unseen shame, invisible disgrace!
O unfelt sore, crest-wounding, private scar! 828
Reproach is stamped in Collatinus' face,
And Tarquin's eye may read the mot afar, 830
How he in peace is wounded, not in war.
    Alas, how many bear such shameful blows,
    Which not themselves but he that gives them knows!

"If, Collatine, thine honor lay in me,
From me by strong assault it is bereft;
My honey lost, and I, a dronelike bee,
Have no perfection of my summer left, 837
But robbed and ransacked by injurious theft.
    In thy weak hive a wand'ring wasp hath crept
    And sucked the honey which thy chaste bee kept.

"Yet am I guilty of thy honor's wrack;
Yet for thy honor did I entertain him.
Coming from thee, I could not put him back,
For it had been dishonor to disdain him.
Besides, of weariness he did complain him,
    And talked of virtue. Oh, unlooked-for evil,
    When virtue is profaned in such a devil!

"Why should the worm intrude the maiden bud?
Or hateful cuckoos hatch in sparrows' nests?
Or toads infect fair founts with venom mud?
Or tyrant folly lurk in gentle breasts? 851
Or kings be breakers of their own behests? 852
    But no perfection is so absolute
    That some impurity doth not pollute.

"The agèd man that coffers up his gold
Is plagued with cramps and gouts and painful fits,
And scarce hath eyes his treasure to behold,
But like still-pining Tantalus he sits, 858
And useless barns the harvest of his wits, 859
    Having no other pleasure of his gain
    But torment that it cannot cure his pain.

"So then he hath it when he cannot use it,
And leaves it to be mastered by his young, 863
Who in their pride do presently abuse it. 864
Their father was too weak, and they too strong, 865
To hold their cursèd-blessèd fortune long.
    The sweets we wish for turn to loathèd sours
    Even in the moment that we call them ours.

"Unruly blasts wait on the tender spring;
Unwholesome weeds take root with precious flowers;
The adder hisses where the sweet birds sing;
What virtue breeds, iniquity devours.
We have no good that we can say is ours
    But ill-annexèd Opportunity 874
    Or kills his life or else his quality. 875

"O Opportunity, thy guilt is great!
'Tis thou that execut'st the traitor's treason; 877
Thou sets the wolf where he the lamb may get;
Whoever plots the sin, thou 'point'st the season. 879
'Tis thou that spurn'st at right, at law, at reason;
    And in thy shady cell, where none may spy him,
    Sits Sin, to seize the souls that wander by him.

"Thou makest the vestal violate her oath; 883
Thou blowest the fire when temperance is thawed;
Thou smother'st honesty, thou murderest troth. 885
Thou foul abettor, thou notorious bawd,
Thou plantest scandal and displacest laud. 887
    Thou ravisher, thou traitor, thou false thief,
    Thy honey turns to gall, thy joy to grief!

806 **object** a thing exposed to sight, object of gossip   807 **charactered** inscribed   808 **decay** ruin   811 **cipher** decipher, read   812 **quote** note, observe   815 **deck** adorn   817 **Feast-finding** searching out feasts at which to sing   820 **senseless** impalpable   822–3 **If . . . rotted** i.e., If my reputation comes in question, then Collatine's will also be attacked   825 **attaint** stain, imputation of dishonor   828 **crest-wounding** disgraceful to the crest or device above the shield in one's coat of arms   830 **mot** motto   837 **Have . . . left** have nothing left of the honey I perfected in the summer

851 **folly** sensuality.   **gentle** noble (in rank and temperament)   852 **behests** biddings, injunctions.   858 **still-pining** continually starving.   **Tantalus** a son of Zeus who was punished by perpetual hunger and thirst with unreachable food and drink always in sight. (Renaissance commentators on Ovid glossed Tantalus as a usurer; hence the image of lines 859 ff.)   859 **barns** stores, as in a barn   863 **mastered** possessed.   **young** heirs   864 **presently** immediately   865 **strong** headstrong   874–5 **But . . . quality** but circumstance, joining itself to evil purpose at the critical moment, either kills the good entirely or at least destroys its nature.   877 **'Tis . . . treason** It is you that fulfills the traitor's treasonous plan by providing the opportunity   879 **thou . . . season** you appoint the time.   883 **vestal** vestal virgin, priestess of Vesta, the Roman goddess of hearth and home   885 **honesty** chastity.   **troth** honesty.   887 **laud** praise.

"Thy secret pleasure turns to open shame,
Thy private feasting to a public fast,
Thy smoothing titles to a ragged name,   892
Thy sugared tongue to bitter wormwood taste.
Thy violent vanities can never last.
    How comes it then, vile Opportunity,
    Being so bad, such numbers seek for thee?

"When wilt thou be the humble suppliant's friend,
And bring him where his suit may be obtained?
When wilt thou sort an hour great strifes to end?   899
Or free that soul which wretchedness hath chained?
Give physic to the sick, ease to the pained?   901
    The poor, lame, blind, halt, creep, cry out for thee,
    But they ne'er meet with Opportunity.

"The patient dies while the physician sleeps;
The orphan pines while the oppressor feeds;   905
Justice is feasting while the widow weeps;   906
Advice is sporting while infection breeds.   907
Thou grant'st no time for charitable deeds.
    Wrath, envy, treason, rape, and murder's rages,   909
    Thy heinous hours wait on them as their pages.   910

"When Truth and Virtue have to do with thee,
A thousand crosses keep them from thy aid.   912
They buy thy help; but Sin ne'er gives a fee;   913
He gratis comes; and thou art well apaid   914
As well to hear as grant what he hath said.   915
    My Collatine would else have come to me
    When Tarquin did, but he was stayed by thee.

"Guilty thou art of murder and of theft,
Guilty of perjury and subornation,
Guilty of treason, forgery, and shift,   920
Guilty of incest, that abomination—
An accessory by thine inclination   922
    To all sins past and all that are to come,
    From the creation to the general doom.   924

"Misshapen Time, copesmate of ugly Night,   925
Swift subtle post, carrier of grisly care,   926
Eater of youth, false slave to false delight,
Base watch of woes, sin's packhorse, virtue's snare!   928
Thou nursest all, and murd'rest all that are.
    Oh, hear me then, injurious, shifting Time!   930
    Be guilty of my death, since of my crime.   931

"Why hath thy servant Opportunity
Betrayed the hours thou gav'st me to repose,
Canceled my fortunes, and enchainèd me
To endless date of never-ending woes?   935
Time's office is to fine the hate of foes,   936
    To eat up errors by opinion bred,   937
    Not spend the dowry of a lawful bed.

"Time's glory is to calm contending kings,
To unmask falsehood and bring truth to light,
To stamp the seal of time in agèd things,
To wake the morn and sentinel the night,   942
To wrong the wronger till he render right,
    To ruinate proud buildings with thy hours,
    And smear with dust their glitt'ring golden towers;

"To fill with wormholes stately monuments,
To feed oblivion with decay of things,
To blot old books and alter their contents,   948
To pluck the quills from ancient ravens' wings,   949
To dry the old oak's sap and cherish springs,   950
    To spoil antiquities of hammered steel,
    And turn the giddy round of Fortune's wheel;

"To show the beldam daughters of her daughter,   953
To make the child a man, the man a child,   954
To slay the tiger that doth live by slaughter,
To tame the unicorn and lion wild,
To mock the subtle in themselves beguiled,   957
    To cheer the plowman with increaseful crops,   958
    And waste huge stones with little waterdrops.   959

"Why work'st thou mischief in thy pilgrimage,
Unless thou couldst return to make amends?
One poor retiring minute in an age   962
Would purchase thee a thousand thousand friends,
Lending him wit that to bad debtors lends.   964
    O, this dread night, wouldst thou one hour come back,
    I could prevent this storm and shun thy wrack!   966

"Thou ceaseless lackey to Eternity,   967
With some mischance cross Tarquin in his flight!   968
Devise extremes beyond extremity
To make him curse this cursèd crimeful night.
Let ghastly shadows his lewd eyes affright,
    And the dire thought of his committed evil
    Shape every bush a hideous shapeless devil.

---

892 **smoothing** flattering. **ragged** faulty, irregular **899 sort** choose, appoint **901 physic** medicine **905 pines** starves **906 Justice** i.e., wealthy, complacent Justices of the Peace **907 Advice** i.e., doctors who enjoy the idle pleasures of wealth gained from the medical advice they give **909–10 Wrath . . . pages** The heinous hours that you, Opportunity, give over to crime are like page boys serving wrath, envy, treason, rape, and murder. **912 crosses** hindrances **913–15 They . . . said** Truth and Virtue have to pay for any opportunity they get, whereas Sin never has to pay; Opportunity comes free to Sin. You, contrastingly, have to be satisfied to listen to and obey whatever conditions Opportunity lays down for you. **920 shift** fraud **922 inclination** natural disposition **924 general doom** Doomsday, Day of Judgment. **925 copesmate** companion, accomplice **926 post** messenger **928 watch** crier, one who announces woes **930 shifting** ever changing and treacherous **931 since of** since you are guilty of

935 date duration **936 Time's . . . foes** Time's function should be to end or punish hatred **937 opinion** popular rumor **942 sentinel** stand guard over **948 blot** erase, obliterate **949 To pluck . . . wings** i.e., to end even the existence of long-lived ravens **950 springs** new growth, shoots **953 To . . . daughter** to show to the aging women her granddaughters **954 a child** i.e., in the second childishness of old age **957 subtle . . . beguiled** crafty who are foiled by their own cleverness **958 increaseful** fruitful **959 waste** wear away **962 retiring** returning (thereby allowing sinners an opportunity to undo their evil) **964 Lending . . . lends** giving the would-be lender the foresight and second chance to avoid the mistake he has made. **966 prevent** anticipate, forestall **967 ceaseless lackey** untiring and relentless servant **968 cross** thwart

"Disturb his hours of rest with restless trances; 974
Afflict him in his bed with bedrid groans; 975
Let there bechance him pitiful mischances
To make him moan, but pity not his moans.
Stone him with hardened hearts harder than stones,
    And let mild women to him lose their mildness, 979
    Wilder to him than tigers in their wildness.

"Let him have time to tear his curlèd hair,
Let him have time against himself to rave,
Let him have time of Time's help to despair,
Let him have time to live a loathèd slave,
Let him have time a beggar's orts to crave, 985
    And time to see one that by alms doth live 986
    Disdain to him disdainèd scraps to give. 987

"Let him have time to see his friends his foes,
And merry fools to mock at him resort; 989
Let him have time to mark how slow time goes
In time of sorrow, and how swift and short
His time of folly and his time of sport;
    And ever let his unrecalling crime 933
    Have time to wail th'abusing of his time.

"O Time, thou tutor both to good and bad,
Teach me to curse him that thou taught'st this ill! 996
At his own shadow let the thief run mad,
Himself himself seek every hour to kill!
Such wretched hands such wretched blood should spill;
    For who so base would such an office have
    As sland'rous deathsman to so base a slave? 1001

"The baser is he, coming from a king,
To shame his hope with deeds degenerate. 1003
The mightier man, the mightier is the thing
That makes him honored or begets him hate;
For greatest scandal waits on greatest state. 1006
    The moon being clouded presently is missed, 1007
    But little stars may hide them when they list.

"The crow may bathe his coal-black wings in mire,
And unperceived fly with the filth away,
But if the like the snow-white swan desire,
The stain upon his silver down will stay.
Poor grooms are sightless night, kings glorious day. 1013
    Gnats are unnoted wheresoe'er they fly,
    But eagles gazed upon with every eye.

"Out, idle words, servants to shallow fools, 1016
Unprofitable sounds, weak arbitrators!

Busy yourselves in skill-contending schools; 1018
Debate where leisure serves with dull debaters;
To trembling clients be you mediators.
    For me, I force not argument a straw, 1021
    Since that my case is past the help of law. 1022

"In vain I rail at Opportunity,
At Time, at Tarquin, and uncheerful Night;
In vain I cavil with mine infamy, 1025
In vain I spurn at my confirmed despite. 1026
This helpless smoke of words doth me no right. 1027
    The remedy indeed to do me good
    Is to let forth my foul-defilèd blood. 1029

"Poor hand, why quiver'st thou at this decree?
Honor thyself to rid me of this shame!
For if I die, my honor lives in thee,
But if I live, thou liv'st in my defame.
Since thou couldst not defend thy loyal dame,
    And wast afeard to scratch her wicked foe,
    Kill both thyself and her for yielding so."

This said, from her betumbled couch she starteth,
To find some desp'rate instrument of death;
But this, no slaughterhouse, no tool imparteth 1039
To make more vent for passage of her breath,
Which, thronging through her lips, so vanisheth
    As smoke from Etna, that in air consumes, 1042
    Or that which from dischargèd cannon fumes.

"In vain," quoth she, "I live, and seek in vain
Some happy means to end a hapless life. 1045
I feared by Tarquin's falchion to be slain, 1046
Yet for the selfsame purpose seek a knife;
But when I feared, I was a loyal wife.
    So am I now.—Oh, no, that cannot be!
    Of that true type hath Tarquin rifled me. 1050

"Oh, that is gone for which I sought to live,
And therefore now I need not fear to die.
To clear this spot by death, at least I give 1053
A badge of fame to slander's livery, 1054
A dying life to living infamy.
    Poor helpless help, the treasure stol'n away,
    To burn the guiltless casket where it lay!

---

974 **trances** visions, fits   975 **bedrid** bedridden   979 **to** confronted with   985 **orts** refuse, fragments of food   986–7 **And . . . give** and may he live long enough to see the most miserable charity-supported beggar disdain to give him the leftover scraps from that beggar's meal.   989 **And . . . resort** and merry fools gather (*resort*) to mock him   993 **unrecalling crime** crime that cannot be undone   996 **that** to whom   1001 **sland'rous deathsman** despised executioner   1003 **his hope** the hope people had of him as heir to the crown   1006 **waits . . . state** potentially attends those of most exalted rank.   1007 **presently** at once   1013 **Poor . . . night** Poor lowly commoners are like pitch-dark night, unnoticed   1016 **Out** (An exclamation of disapproval.)

1018 **in . . . schools** i.e., among scholars who perennially debate with words   1021 **For . . . straw** As for me, I do not value argument as worth so much as a straw   1022 **Since that** since   1025 **cavil with** raise objections to   1026 **spurn at** (Literally, kick against.) **confirmed despite** unrecoverable injury.   1027 **helpless . . . words** unavailing rhetoric   1029 **let . . . blood** bleed (1) as a *remedy* (line 1028) for illness, a standard form of medical treatment (2) as a means of death.   1039 **no slaughterhouse** being no slaughterhouse. **imparteth** provides   1042 **Etna** famous volcano in northeast Sicily. **consumes** vanishes   1045 **happy** fit. (With a play of antithesis on *hapless*.)   1046 **falchion** curved sword   1050 **type** pattern (of virtue)   1053 **To clear** i.e., in clearing.   **spot** stain   1054 **fame** good reputation.   **livery** clothing or uniform worn by those in service, bearing a heraldic *badge* on the sleeve to indicate in whose service the livery is worn. (Lucrece says that the livery of shame will be partially redeemed by the badge of an honorable death.)

"Well, well, dear Collatine, thou shalt not know
The stainèd taste of violated troth;
I will not wrong thy true affection so
To flatter thee with an infringèd oath; 1061
This bastard graft shall never come to growth. 1062
    He shall not boast who did thy stock pollute
    That thou art doting father of his fruit.

"Nor shall he smile at thee in secret thought,
Nor laugh with his companions at thy state,
But thou shalt know thy int'rest was not bought 1067
Basely with gold, but stol'n from forth thy gate.
For me, I am the mistress of my fate, 1069
    And with my trespass never will dispense 1070
    Till life to death acquit my forced offense. 1071

"I will not poison thee with my attaint, 1072
Nor fold my fault in cleanly coined excuses; 1073
My sable ground of sin I will not paint, 1074
To hide the truth of this false night's abuses.
My tongue shall utter all; mine eyes, like sluices,
    As from a mountain spring that feeds a dale,
    Shall gush pure streams to purge my impure tale."

By this, lamenting Philomel had ended 1079
The well-tuned warble of her nightly sorrow,
And solemn night with slow sad gait descended
To ugly hell, when, lo, the blushing morrow
Lends light to all fair eyes that light will borrow. 1083
    But cloudy Lucrece shames herself to see, 1084
    And therefore still in night would cloistered be.

Revealing day through every cranny spies
And seems to point her out where she sits weeping,
To whom she sobbing speaks: "O eye of eyes,
Why pry'st thou through my window? Leave thy peeping.
Mock with thy tickling beams eyes that are sleeping.
    Brand not my forehead with thy piercing light,
    For day hath naught to do what's done by night." 1092

Thus cavils she with everything she sees.
True grief is fond and testy as a child 1094
Who, wayward once, his mood with naught agrees. 1095
Old woes, not infant sorrows, bear them mild: 1096
Continuance tames the one; the other, wild,
    Like an unpracticed swimmer plunging still,
    With too much labor drowns for want of skill.

So she, deep-drenchèd in a sea of care,
Holds disputation with each thing she views,
And to herself all sorrow doth compare;
No object but her passion's strength renews, 1103
And as one shifts, another straight ensues. 1104
    Sometimes her grief is dumb and hath no words,
    Sometimes 'tis mad and too much talk affords.

The little birds that tune their morning's joy
Make her moans mad with their sweet melody,
For mirth doth search the bottom of annoy; 1109
Sad souls are slain in merry company.
Grief best is pleased with grief's society.
    True sorrow then is feelingly sufficed 1112
    When with like semblance it is sympathized. 1113

'Tis double death to drown in ken of shore; 1114
He ten times pines that pines beholding food; 1115
To see the salve doth make the wound ache more; 1116
Great grief grieves most at that would do it good; 1117
Deep woes roll forward like a gentle flood,
    Who, being stopped, the bounding banks o'erflows; 1119
    Grief dallied with nor law nor limit knows. 1120

"You mocking birds," quoth she, "your tunes entomb
Within your hollow-swelling feathered breasts,
And in my hearing be you mute and dumb.
My restless discord loves no stops nor rests; 1124
A woeful hostess brooks not merry guests. 1125
    Relish your nimble notes to pleasing ears; 1126
    Distress likes dumps, when time is kept with tears. 1127

"Come, Philomel, that sing'st of ravishment,
Make thy sad grove in my disheveled hair.
As the dank earth weeps at thy languishment,
So I at each sad strain will strain a tear 1131
And with deep groans the diapason bear; 1132
    For burden-wise I'll hum on Tarquin still, 1133
    While thou on Tereus descants better skill. 1134

"And whiles against a thorn thou bear'st thy part 1135
To keep thy sharp woes waking, wretched I,
To imitate thee well, against my heart
Will fix a sharp knife to affright mine eye,

1061 **To flatter . . . oath** i.e., to deceive you by presenting you with a bastard child, born through an enforced violation of my vow of chastity, as though the child were your own   1062 **graft** scion   1067 **int'rest** claim, property   1069 **For** As for   1070 **with . . . dispense** never will pardon my offense. (To *dispense* is to grant dispensation.)   1071 **acquit** atone for   1072 **attaint** infection   1073 **fold** wrap up, conceal.   **cleanly coined** cleverly counterfeited   1074 **sable ground** dark surface on a heraldic device   1079 **Philomel** i.e., the nightingale. (Philomela was raped by her brother-in-law, Tereus, who cut out her tongue so that she could not disclose his villainy; she was changed into a nightingale.)   1083 **that . . . borrow** that wish to behold the light of dawn and reflect the light in their eyes.   1084 **cloudy** sorrowful.   **shames** is ashamed   1092 **to do** to do with   1094 **fond** foolish   1095 **wayward once** once in a peevish mood   1096 **bear . . . mild** behave themselves mildly

1103 **No . . . renews** everything she considers renews the strength of her sorrows   1104 **shifts** moves, yields place.   **straight** at once   1109 **search** probe.   **annoy** grief, injury   1112 **sufficed** contented   1113 **sympathized** matched.   1114 **ken** sight   1115 **He** Anyone.   **pines** hungers   1117 **would** which would   1119 **Who . . . o'erflows** which, being dammed up, overflows the banks that should contain it   1120 **dallied** trifled.   **nor . . . nor** neither . . . nor   1124 **restless** agitated. (With a pun on the musical sense of having no *stops* or *rests*, i.e., being ceaseless, without pause.)   1125 **brooks** enjoys   1126 **Relish** (1) Warble, make attractive (2) Elaborate with musical ornamentation.   **pleasing** capable of being pleased   1127 **dumps** mournful songs   1131 **strain . . . strain** melody . . . force, squeeze   1132 **diapason** bass accompaniment below the melody   1133 **burden-wise** in the manner of an undersong or bass. (With a play on *burden*, meaning "sorrow.")   1134 **While . . . skill** while, singing of Philomel's ravisher (see note 1079), you warble your musical elaboration in the upper register with better skill (than my bass accompaniment).   1135 **against a thorn** (According to popular belief, the nightingale perched deliberately with a thorn against her breast to keep herself awake.)

Who, if it wink, shall thereon fall and die.   1139
   These means, as frets upon an instrument,   1140
   Shall tune our heartstrings to true languishment.

"And for, poor bird, thou sing'st not in the day,   1142
As shaming any eye should thee behold,   1143
Some dark deep desert seated from the way,   1144
That knows not parching heat nor freezing cold,
Will we find out; and there we will unfold
   To creatures stern sad tunes, to change their kinds.   1147
   Since men prove beasts, let beasts bear gentle minds."

As the poor frighted deer, that stands at gaze,   1149
Wildly determining which way to fly,
Or one encompassed with a winding maze,
That cannot tread the way out readily,
So with herself is she in mutiny,
   To live or die which of the twain were better
   When life is shamed and death reproach's debtor.   1155

"To kill myself," quoth she, "alack, what were it
But with my body my poor soul's pollution?   1157
They that lose half with greater patience bear it
Than they whose whole is swallowed in confusion.   1159
That mother tries a merciless conclusion   1160
   Who, having two sweet babes, when death takes one,
   Will slay the other and be nurse to none.

"My body or my soul, which was the dearer,
When the one pure, the other made divine?
Whose love of either to myself was nearer,   1165
When both were kept for heaven and Collatine?
Ay me! The bark pilled from the lofty pine,   1167
   His leaves will wither and his sap decay;
   So must my soul, her bark being pilled away.

"Her house is sacked, her quiet interrupted,
Her mansion battered by the enemy,
Her sacred temple spotted, spoiled, corrupted,
Grossly engirt with daring infamy.   1173
Then let it not be called impiety
   If in this blemished fort I make some hole   1175
   Through which I may convey this troubled soul.   1176

"Yet die I will not till my Collatine
Have heard the cause of my untimely death,

That he may vow, in that sad hour of mine,
Revenge on him that made me stop my breath.
My stainèd blood to Tarquin I'll bequeath,
   Which, by him tainted, shall for him be spent,
   And as his due writ in my testament.   1183

"My honor I'll bequeath unto the knife
That wounds my body so dishonorèd.
'Tis honor to deprive dishonored life;   1186
The one will live, the other being dead.   1187
So of shame's ashes shall my fame be bred,   1188
   For in my death I murder shameful scorn;
   My shame so dead, mine honor is new born.

"Dear lord of that dear jewel I have lost,   1191
What legacy shall I bequeath to thee?
My resolution, love, shall be thy boast,
By whose example thou revenged mayst be.
How Tarquin must be used, read it in me:
   Myself, thy friend, will kill myself, thy foe,
   And for my sake serve thou false Tarquin so.

"This brief abridgment of my will I make:
My soul and body to the skies and ground;
My resolution, husband, do thou take;
Mine honor be the knife's that makes my wound;
My shame be his that did my fame confound;
   And all my fame that lives disbursèd be   1203
   To those that live and think no shame of me.

"Thou, Collatine, shalt oversee this will.
How was I overseen that thou shalt see it!   1206
My blood shall wash the slander of mine ill;
My life's foul deed my life's fair end shall free it.   1208
Faint not, faint heart, but stoutly say 'So be it.'
   Yield to my hand; my hand shall conquer thee.
   Thou dead, both die, and both shall victors be."

This plot of death when sadly she had laid,
And wiped the brinish pearl from her bright eyes,
With untuned tongue she hoarsely calls her maid,   1214
Whose swift obedience to her mistress hies;   1215
For fleet-winged duty with thought's feathers flies.
   Poor Lucrece' cheeks unto her maid seem so
   As winter meads when sun doth melt their snow.

Her mistress she doth give demure good morrow   1219
With soft slow tongue, true mark of modesty,
And sorts a sad look to her lady's sorrow,   1221
Forwhy her face wore sorrow's livery;   1222

1139 **Who** which, i.e., my heart.   **if it wink** i.e., if my eye should close in sleep   1140 **frets** bars placed on the fingerboards of stringed instruments to regulate the fingering. (With a pun on *frets,* meaning "vexations.")   1142 **for** because.   **sing'st not in the day** (One of the common errors of the time; nightingales sing both day and night.) 1143 **As shaming** as though being ashamed that, or, since you are ashamed that   1144 **desert** deserted place.   **seated from** situated away from   1147 **at gaze** transfixed, bewildered   1155 **death reproach's debtor** i.e., death by suicide would incur reproach.   1157 **But . . . pollution** but to add my poor soul's pollution (through suicide) to that of my body (through the rape). 1159 **confusion** ruin.   1160 **conclusion** experiment   1165 **Whose . . . either** Love of which of the two   1167 **pilled** peeled, stripped off, rifled   1173 **daring** audacious   1175 **fort** i.e., body   1176 **convey** spirit away

1183 **writ** written.   **testament** last will and testament.   1186 **deprive** take away   1187 **the one** honor.   **the other** life   1188 **So . . . bred** Thus will my fame be born out of the ashes of my shame, like the mythical Phoenix bird   1191 **that dear jewel** i.e., my chastity (which) 1203 **disbursèd** i.e., paid out as legacies   1206 **overseen** deluded, taken advantage of. (With quibble on *oversee,* line 1205, i.e., attend to as an executor of an estate.)   1208 **My . . . free it** my life's virtuous end will free my reputation of my life's foul deed.   1214 **untuned** discordant   1215 **Whose . . . hies** who in swift obedience hastens to her mistress   1219 **Her** To her   1221 **sorts** suits   1222 **Forwhy** because

But durst not ask of her audaciously
Why her two suns were cloud-eclipsèd so,
Nor why her fair cheeks over-washed with woe.

But as the earth doth weep, the sun being set,
Each flower moist'ned like a melting eye,
Even so the maid with swelling drops 'gan wet
Her circled eyne, enforced by sympathy   1229
Of those fair suns set in her mistress' sky,
Who in a salt-waved ocean quench their light,
Which makes the maid weep like the dewy night.

A pretty while these pretty creatures stand,   1233
Like ivory conduits coral cisterns filling.   1234
One justly weeps; the other takes in hand   1235
No cause but company of her drops' spilling.   1236
Their gentle sex to weep are often willing,
Grieving themselves to guess at others' smarts,   1238
And then they drown their eyes or break their hearts.

For men have marble, women waxen, minds,   1240
And therefore are they formed as marble will.   1241
The weak oppressed, th'impression of strange kinds   1242
Is formed in them by force, by fraud, or skill.   1243
Then call them not the authors of their ill,
No more than wax shall be accounted evil
Wherein is stamped the semblance of a devil.

Their smoothness, like a goodly champaign plain,   1247
Lays open all the little worms that creep;   1248
In men, as in a rough-grown grove, remain
Cave-keeping evils that obscurely sleep.   1250
Through crystal walls each little mote will peep.   1251
Though men can cover crimes with bold stern looks,
Poor women's faces are their own faults' books.

No man inveigh against the withered flower,   1254
But chide rough winter that the flower hath killed.
Not that devoured, but that which doth devour,
Is worthy blame. Oh, let it not be hild   1257
Poor women's faults that they are so fulfilled   1258
With men's abuses. Those proud lords, to blame,   1259
Make weak-made women tenants to their shame.   1260

The precedent whereof in Lucrece view,   1261
Assailed by night with circumstances strong   1262
Of present death, and shame that might ensue   1263

By that her death, to do her husband wrong.   1264
Such danger to resistance did belong   1265
That dying fear through all her body spread;   1266
And who cannot abuse a body dead?

By this, mild patience bid fair Lucrece speak   1268
To the poor counterfeit of her complaining: 1269
"My girl," quoth she, "on what occasion break
Those tears from thee, that down thy cheeks are raining?
If thou dost weep for grief of my sustaining,   1272
Know, gentle wench, it small avails my mood.   1273
If tears could help, mine own would do me good.

"But tell me, girl, when went"—and there she stayed
Till after a deep groan—"Tarquin from hence?"
"Madam, ere I was up," replied the maid,
"The more to blame my sluggard negligence.   1278
Yet with the fault I thus far can dispense: 1279
Myself was stirring ere the break of day,
And, ere I rose, was Tarquin gone away.

"But, lady, if your maid may be so bold,
She would request to know your heaviness."   1283
"Oh, peace!" quoth Lucrece. "If it should be told,
The repetition cannot make it less;   1285
For more it is than I can well express,
And that deep torture may be called a hell
When more is felt than one hath power to tell.

"Go, get me hither paper, ink, and pen.
Yet save that labor, for I have them here.
What should I say? One of my husband's men
Bid thou be ready by and by to bear
A letter to my lord, my love, my dear.
Bid him with speed prepare to carry it;
The cause craves haste, and it will soon be writ."

Her maid is gone, and she prepares to write,
First hovering o'er the paper with her quill.
Conceit and grief an eager combat fight;   1298
What wit sets down is blotted straight with will;   1299
This is too curious-good, this blunt and ill.   1300
Much like a press of people at a door
Throng her inventions, which shall go before.   1302

At last she thus begins: "Thou worthy lord
Of that unworthy wife that greeteth thee,
Health to thy person! Next vouchsafe t'afford—
If ever, love, thy Lucrece thou wilt see—

1229 **circled eyne** rounded eyes, or, circled with red.   **enforced** compelled   **1233 pretty while** considerable while   **1234 conduits** (Alludes to conduit spouts and fountains shaped in the form of human figures; the women's eyes run like conduits.)   **1235–6 takes . . . spilling** acknowledges no cause for the shedding of teardrops other than to keep her mistress company.   **1238 to guess at** merely when they conjecture **1240 waxen** i.e., soft, impressionable   **1241 will** wills, wishes. **1242 The weak** When the weak are.   **strange kinds** alien natures **1243 skill** cunning.   **1247 champaign** level, open   **1248 Lays open** reveals   **1250 Cave-keeping** concealed   **1251 mote** speck   **1254 No man** Let no one   **1257 worthy** deserving of.   **hild** held   **1258 fulfilled** filled to the brim   **1259 to blame** who are to blame   **1260 tenants . . . shame** i.e., occupying and sharing a shame that is properly men's. **1261 precedent** proof, example   **1262–3 circumstances . . . death** a situation strongly threatening immediate death

1264 **By that her death** by her very death   **1265 danger** i.e., the danger of being defamed by Tarquin   **1266 dying** i.e., paralyzing **1268 By this** By this time   **1269 counterfeit of her complaining** i.e., the maid, weeping like her   **1272 of my sustaining** borne by me **1273 small avails** little helps   **1278 to blame** at fault   **1279 dispense** give dispensation, find excuse   **1283 know your heaviness** know the reason for your sadness.   **1285 repetition** recital   **1298 Conceit** Thought (of what she will write).   **eager** fierce   **1299–1300 What . . . ill** i.e., whatever thought wishes to say is immediately ruled out as inadequate to express what she feels; one phrase is too fastidiously elaborate, another too blunt and ugly.   **1302 which . . . before** contending as to who is to enter first.

Some present speed to come and visit me. 1307
    So, I commend me from our house in grief. 1308
    My woes are tedious, though my words are brief." 1309

Here folds she up the tenor of her woe, 1310
Her certain sorrow writ uncertainly. 1311
By this short schedule Collatine may know 1312
Her grief, but not her grief's true quality.
She dares not thereof make discovery, 1314
    Lest he should hold it her own gross abuse, 1315
    Ere she with blood had stained her stained excuse. 1316

Besides, the life and feeling of her passion
She hoards, to spend when he is by to hear her,
When sighs and groans and tears may grace the fashion 1319
Of her disgrace, the better so to clear her
From that suspicion which the world might bear her.
    To shun this blot, she would not blot the letter 1322
    With words, till action might become them better.

To see sad sights moves more than hear them told,
For then the eye interprets to the ear
The heavy motion that it doth behold, 1326
When every part a part of woe doth bear. 1327
'Tis but a part of sorrow that we hear.
    Deep sounds make lesser noise than shallow fords, 1329
    And sorrow ebbs, being blown with wind of words.

Her letter now is sealed, and on it writ,
"At Ardea to my lord with more than haste."
The post attends, and she delivers it, 1333
Charging the sour-faced groom to hie as fast
As lagging fowls before the northern blast. 1335
    Speed more than speed but dull and slow she deems; 1336
    Extremity still urgeth such extremes. 1337

The homely villain curtsies to her low; 1338
And, blushing on her, with a steadfast eye
Receives the scroll without or yea or no, 1340
And forth with bashful innocence doth hie.
But they whose guilt within their bosoms lie
    Imagine every eye beholds their blame;
    For Lucrece thought he blushed to see her shame,

When, silly groom, God wot, it was defect 1345
Of spirit, life, and bold audacity.

Such harmless creatures have a true respect 1347
To talk in deeds, while others saucily 1348
Promise more speed, but do it leisurely.
    Even so this pattern of the worn-out age 1350
    Pawned honest looks but laid no words to gage. 1351

His kindled duty kindled her mistrust, 1352
That two red fires in both their faces blazed.
She thought he blushed as knowing Tarquin's lust,
And, blushing with him, wistly on him gazed. 1355
Her earnest eye did make him more amazed. 1356
    The more she saw the blood his cheeks replenish,
    The more she thought he spied in her some blemish.

But long she thinks till he return again, 1359
And yet the duteous vassal scarce is gone.
The weary time she cannot entertain, 1361
For now 'tis stale to sigh, to weep, and groan.
So woe hath wearied woe, moan tirèd moan,
    That she her plaints a little while doth stay, 1364
    Pausing for means to mourn some newer way.

At last she calls to mind where hangs a piece 1366
Of skillful painting, made for Priam's Troy, 1367
Before the which is drawn the power of Greece, 1368
For Helen's rape the city to destroy,
Threat'ning cloud-kissing Ilion with annoy, 1370
    Which the conceited painter drew so proud 1371
    As heaven, it seemed, to kiss the turrets bowed.

A thousand lamentable objects there,
In scorn of nature, art gave lifeless life. 1374
Many a dry drop seemed a weeping tear, 1375
Shed for the slaughtered husband by the wife.
The red blood reeked, to show the painter's strife, 1377
    And dying eyes gleamed forth their ashy lights
    Like dying coals burnt out in tedious nights.

There might you see the laboring pioneer 1380
Begrimed with sweat and smearèd all with dust;
And from the towers of Troy there would appear
The very eyes of men through loopholes thrust,
Gazing upon the Greeks with little lust. 1384
    Such sweet observance in this work was had 1385
    That one might see those far-off eyes look sad.

1307 present immediate **1308 commend me** ask to be remembered **1309 tedious** prolonged, painful **1310 tenor** gist, summary **1311 uncertainly** not in precise detail; in great uncertainty of feeling. **1312 schedule** document, summary **1314 thereof make discovery** reveal its true extent and nature **1315 abuse** wrongdoing **1316 Ere . . . excuse** before she had had a chance to put a better appearance on her unsatisfactory excuse by shedding her own blood. **1319 fashion** fashioning **1322 blot . . . blot** stain . . . mark **1326 heavy motion** sad action **1327 every part** i.e., of the body **1329 Deep sounds** Deep waters. (With pun on *sounds*, i.e., inlets of the sea, and "noise.") **1333 post** messenger **1335 lagging** falling behind in migratory flight **1336 Speed . . . deems** She considers even extraordinary speed too tedious and slow **1337 still** ever **1338 The homely . . . curtsies** The plain-mannered servant bows **1340 or . . . or** either . . . or **1345 silly groom** simple menial. **wot** knows

1347–8 have . . . deeds eagerly express their duty in their acts of service (rather than flowery speech) **1350–1 Even . . . gage** In just this fashion, this perfect model of old-fashioned loyalty pledged his service in wordless, honest looks. **1352 kindled duty** i.e., blushing obeisance. **mistrust** i.e., fear of her shame being known **1355 wistly** intently **1356 amazed** embarrassed. **1359 long she thinks** she thinks it long **1361 entertain** occupy **1364 stay** halt **1366 piece** picture (evidently in a tapestry) **1367 made for** depicting **1368 drawn** drawn up, arrayed. **power** army **1370 cloud-kissing Ilion** i.e., lofty-towered Troy. **annoy** harm **1371 conceited** ingenious **1374 In scorn of** i.e., defiantly rivaling. **lifeless** inanimate **1375 dry drop** i.e., drop of paint depicting a tear **1377 strife** rivalry, i.e., with Nature; also the strife depicted in the painting **1380 pioneer** digger of trenches and mines **1384 lust** pleasure, delight. **1385 sweet observance** i.e., verisimilitude created with loving attention to detail

In great commanders grace and majesty
You might behold, triumphing in their faces;
In youth, quick bearing and dexterity;   1389
And here and there the painter interlaces
Pale cowards marching on with trembling paces,
    Which heartless peasants did so well resemble   1392
    That one would swear he saw them quake and tremble.

In Ajax and Ulysses, oh, what art
Of physiognomy might one behold!
The face of either ciphered either's heart;   1396
Their face their manners most expressly told.
In Ajax' eyes blunt rage and rigor rolled,
    But the mild glance that sly Ulysses lent
    Showed deep regard and smiling government.   1400

There pleading might you see grave Nestor stand,   1401
As 'twere encouraging the Greeks to fight,
Making such sober action with his hand
That it beguiled attention, charmed the sight.
In speech, it seemed, his beard, all silver white,
    Wagged up and down, and from his lips did fly
    Thin winding breath, which purled up to the sky.   1407

About him were a press of gaping faces,
Which seemed to swallow up his sound advice,
All jointly list'ning, but with several graces,   1410
As if some mermaid did their ears entice;
Some high, some low, the painter was so nice.   1412
    The scalps of many, almost hid behind,   1413
    To jump up higher seemed, to mock the mind.   1414

Here one man's hand leaned on another's head,
His nose being shadowed by his neighbor's ear;
Here one being thronged bears back, all boll'n and red;   1417
Another, smothered, seems to pelt and swear;   1418
And in their rage such signs of rage they bear
    As, but for loss of Nestor's golden words,   1420
    It seemed they would debate with angry swords.

For much imaginary work was there,   1422
Conceit deceitful, so compact, so kind,   1423
That for Achilles' image stood his spear
Gripped in an armèd hand; himself, behind,
Was left unseen, save to the eye of mind.
    A hand, a foot, a face, a leg, a head,
    Stood for the whole to be imaginèd.

And from the walls of strong-besiegèd Troy,
When their brave hope, bold Hector, marched to field,
Stood many Trojan mothers, sharing joy
To see their youthful sons bright weapons wield;
And to their hope they such odd action yield   1433
    That through their light joy seemèd to appear,
    Like bright things stained, a kind of heavy fear.

And from the strand of Dardan where they fought   1436
To Simois' reedy banks the red blood ran,   1437
Whose waves to imitate the battle sought
With swelling ridges; and their ranks began
To break upon the gallèd shore and then   1440
    Retire again, till, meeting greater ranks,
    They join and shoot their foam at Simois' banks.

To this well-painted piece is Lucrece come,
To find a face where all distress is stelled.   1444
Many she sees where cares have carvèd some,
But none where all distress and dolor dwelled,
Till she despairing Hecuba beheld,   1447
    Staring on Priam's wounds with her old eyes,
    Which bleeding under Pyrrhus' proud foot lies.

In her the painter had anatomized   1450
Time's ruin, beauty's wrack, and grim care's reign.
Her cheeks with chaps and wrinkles were disguised;   1452
Of what she was no semblance did remain.
Her blue blood, changed to black in every vein,
    Wanting the spring that those shrunk pipes had fed,   1455
    Showed life imprisoned in a body dead.

On this sad shadow Lucrece spends her eyes,   1457
And shapes her sorrow to the beldam's woes,   1458
Who nothing wants to answer her but cries   1459
And bitter words to ban her cruel foes.   1460
The painter was no god to lend her those;
    And therefore Lucrece swears he did her wrong,
    To give her so much grief and not a tongue.

"Poor instrument," quoth she, "without a sound,
I'll tune thy woes with my lamenting tongue,   1465
And drop sweet balm in Priam's painted wound,
And rail on Pyrrhus that hath done him wrong,
And with my tears quench Troy that burns so long,
    And with my knife scratch out the angry eyes
    Of all the Greeks that are thine enemies.

"Show me the strumpet that began this stir,
That with my nails her beauty I may tear.
Thy heat of lust, fond Paris, did incur   1473

1389 **quick** lively   1392 **heartless** cowardly   1396 **ciphered** showed, expressed   1400 **deep . . . government** profound wisdom and calm self-control.   1401 **pleading** making a persuasive oration   1407 **purled** curled   1410 **with several graces** i.e., in differing attitudes   1412 **nice** accurate, particular.   1413 **scalps** heads of hair   1414 **To . . . mind** (The artistic illusion deceives the mind of the viewer into thinking he sees the movement of those in the back of the crowd who are jumping higher to catch Nestor's oration.)   1417 **thronged** crowded.   **bears** pushes.   **boll'n** swollen up   1418 **pelt** scold   1420 **but . . . words** were it not that they would thereby miss Nestor's speech   1422 **imaginary work** work of the imagination   1423 **Conceit . . . kind** a contrived artifice, so efficiently composed, so seemingly natural

1433 **they . . . yield** they add such actions and emotions at odds with the joy   1436 **strand** shore   1437 **Simois** river near Troy   1440 **gallèd** eroded   1444 **stelled** portrayed, engraved.   1447 **Hecuba** Queen of Troy, wife of King Priam   1450 **anatomized** laid open, dissected   1452 **chaps** cracks and lines in the skin.   **disguised** disfigured   1455 **spring** i.e., source of blood and life.   **pipes** i.e., veins   1457 **shadow** image, likeness   1458 **beldam's** old woman's   1459 **wants to answer her** lacks in order to be perfectly like Lucrece in her sorrow   1460 **ban** curse   1465 **tune** sing   1473 **fond** doting

This load of wrath that burning Troy doth bear.
Thine eye kindled the fire that burneth here,
    And here in Troy, for trespass of thine eye,
    The sire, the son, the dame, and daughter die.

"Why should the private pleasure of some one
Become the public plague of many moe?   1479
Let sin, alone committed, light alone   1480
Upon his head that hath transgressèd so;
Let guiltless souls be freed from guilty woe.
    For one's offense why should so many fall,
    To plague a private sin in general?   1484

"Lo, here weeps Hecuba, here Priam dies,
Here manly Hector faints, here Troilus swounds,   1486
Here friend by friend in bloody channel lies,   1487
And friend to friend gives unadvisèd wounds,   1488
And one man's lust these many lives confounds.
    Had doting Priam checked his son's desire,
    Troy had been bright with fame and not with fire."

Here feelingly she weeps Troy's painted woes,
For sorrow, like a heavy-hanging bell
Once set on ringing, with his own weight goes;   1494
Then little strength rings out the doleful knell.
So Lucrece, set a-work, sad tales doth tell
    To penciled pensiveness and colored sorrow;   1497
    She lends them words, and she their looks doth borrow.

She throws her eyes about the painting round,
And who she finds forlorn she doth lament.   1500
At last she sees a wretched image bound,   1501
That piteous looks to Phrygian shepherds lent.   1502
His face, though full of cares, yet showed content;
    Onward to Troy with the blunt swains he goes,   1504
    So mild that patience seemed to scorn his woes.   1505

In him the painter labored with his skill
To hide deceit and give the harmless show   1507
An humble gait, calm looks, eyes wailing still,   1508
A brow unbent that seemed to welcome woe;
Cheeks neither red nor pale, but mingled so
    That blushing red no guilty instance gave,   1511
    Nor ashy pale the fear that false hearts have.

But, like a constant and confirmèd devil,
He entertained a show so seeming just,   1514
And therein so ensconced his secret evil,   1515

That jealousy itself could not mistrust   1516
False-creeping craft and perjury should thrust
    Into so bright a day such black-faced storms,
    Or blot with hell-born sin such saintlike forms.

The well-skilled workman this mild image drew
For perjured Sinon, whose enchanting story   1521
The credulous old Priam after slew;   1522
Whose words like wildfire burnt the shining glory   1523
Of rich-built Ilion, that the skies were sorry,
    And little stars shot from their fixèd places
    When their glass fell wherein they viewed their faces.   1526

This picture she advisedly perused,   1527
And chid the painter for his wondrous skill,
Saying, some shape in Sinon's was abused;   1529
So fair a form lodged not a mind so ill.
And still on him she gazed, and gazing still,
    Such signs of truth in his plain face she spied   1532
    That she concludes the picture was belied.   1533

"It cannot be," quoth she, "that so much guile—"
She would have said "can lurk in such a look";
But Tarquin's shape came in her mind the while,
And from her tongue "can lurk" from "cannot" took.
"It cannot be" she in that sense forsook,
    And turned it thus: "It cannot be, I find,
    But such a face should bear a wicked mind.

"For even as subtle Sinon here is painted,
So sober-sad, so weary, and so mild,
As if with grief or travail he had fainted,   1543
To me came Tarquin armèd, too beguiled   1544
With outward honesty, but yet defiled
    With inward vice. As Priam him did cherish,
    So did I Tarquin; so my Troy did perish.

"Look, look, how list'ning Priam wets his eyes,
To see those borrowed tears that Sinon sheeds!   1549
Priam, why art thou old and yet not wise?
For every tear he falls, a Trojan bleeds.   1551
His eye drops fire, no water thence proceeds;
    Those round clear pearls of his, that move thy pity,
    Are balls of quenchless fire to burn thy city.

"Such devils steal effects from lightless hell,   1555
For Sinon in his fire doth quake with cold,

1479 **moe** more.   1480 **alone committed** committed by one person
alone.   **light** alight   1484 **in general** collectively, publicly.
1486 **swounds** swoons   1487 **channel** gutter   1488 **unadvisèd wounds**
wounds they never intended for each other   1494 **his** its   1497 **pen-
ciled** painted.   **colored** painted   1500 **who** whoever   1501 **image** i.e.,
of Sinon, betrayer of Troy.   **bound** onward bound   1502 **piteous . . .
lent** i.e., drew pitying looks from Phrygian shepherds. (Sinon deceived
humble Trojans into pitying him as a deserter from the Greeks, thereby
persuading them to admit the wooden horse.)   1504 **blunt swains** rustic peasants   1505 **patience** his patience.   **scorn** make light of
1507 **harmless show** outwardly harmless appearance   1508 **still** continually   1511 **guilty instance** symptom of guilt   1514 **entertained a
show** kept up an appearance   1515 **ensconced** hid

1516 **jealousy** suspicion.   **mistrust** suspect (that)   1521 **For** to represent.   **enchanting** bewitching   1522 **The . . . slew** subsequently
brought about the slaughter of credulous old Priam   1523 **wildfire** a
highly inflammable mixture of tar, sulfur, grease, etc., used in war
1526 **glass** mirror (i.e., rich-built Troy)   1527 **advisedly** studiously
1529 **some shape** i.e., the figure of some other person.   **abused** slanderously portrayed   1532 **plain** honest   1533 **belied** falsified.
1543 **travail** (The Quarto's "trauaile" also contains the idea of
"travel.")   1544 **armèd** equipped, accoutered.   **too beguiled** too
concealed or disguised by guile; or, "to beguile"   1549 **borrowed**
counterfeited.   **sheeds** sheds.   1551 **he falls** that Sinon lets fall
Such devils (The ability to weep without real tears—*effects*—was
attributed to devils.)   **effects** illusions. (Devils were supposedly able
to weep without real tears.)

And in that cold hot-burning fire doth dwell.
These contraries such unity do hold 1558
Only to flatter fools and make them bold. 1559
    So Priam's trust false Sinon's tears doth flatter 1560
    That he finds means to burn his Troy with water."

Here, all enraged, such passion her assails
That patience is quite beaten from her breast.
She tears the senseless Sinon with her nails, 1564
Comparing him to that unhappy guest 1565
Whose deed hath made herself herself detest.
    At last she smilingly with this gives o'er: 1567
    "Fool, fool!" quoth she, "his wounds will not be sore." 1568

Thus ebbs and flows the current of her sorrow,
And time doth weary time with her complaining. 1570
She looks for night, and then she longs for morrow,
And both she thinks too long with her remaining.
Short time seems long in sorrow's sharp sustaining; 1573
    Though woe be heavy, yet it seldom sleeps, 1574
    And they that watch see time how slow it creeps. 1575

Which all this time hath overslipped her thought
That she with painted images hath spent,
Being from the feeling of her own grief brought
By deep surmise of others' detriment, 1579
Losing her woes in shows of discontent. 1580
    It easeth some, though none it ever cured,
    To think their dolor others have endured.

But now the mindful messenger, come back, 1583
Brings home his lord and other company,
Who finds his Lucrece clad in mourning black,
And round about her tear-distainèd eye 1586
Blue circles streamed, like rainbows in the sky.
    These water galls in her dim element 1588
    Foretell new storms to those already spent. 1589

Which when her sad-beholding husband saw,
Amazedly in her sad face he stares.
Her eyes, though sod in tears, looked red and raw, 1592
Her lively color killed with deadly cares.
He hath no power to ask her how she fares;
    Both stood like old acquaintance in a trance,
    Met far from home, wond'ring each other's chance. 1596

At last he takes her by the bloodless hand
And thus begins: "What uncouth ill event 1598
Hath thee befall'n, that thou dost trembling stand?
Sweet love, what spite hath thy fair color spent? 1600
Why art thou thus attired in discontent? 1601
    Unmask, dear dear, this moody heaviness, 1602
    And tell thy grief, that we may give redress."

Three times with sighs she gives her sorrow fire 1604
Ere once she can discharge one word of woe. 1605
At length addressed to answer his desire, 1606
She modestly prepares to let them know
Her honor is ta'en prisoner by the foe,
    While Collatine and his consorted lords 1609
    With sad attention long to hear her words. 1610

And now this pale swan in her wat'ry nest 1611
Begins the sad dirge of her certain ending:
"Few words," quoth she, "shall fit the trespass best,
Where no excuse can give the fault amending.
In me more woes than words are now depending, 1615
    And my laments would be drawn out too long,
    To tell them all with one poor tirèd tongue.

"Then be this all the task it hath to say:
Dear husband, in the interest of thy bed 1619
A stranger came, and on that pillow lay
Where thou wast wont to rest thy weary head;
And what wrong else may be imaginèd
    By foul enforcement might be done to me,
    From that, alas, thy Lucrece is not free.

"For in the dreadful dead of dark midnight,
With shining falchion in my chamber came
A creeping creature with a flaming light,
And softly cried, 'Awake, thou Roman dame,
And entertain my love! Else lasting shame 1629
    On thee and thine this night I will inflict,
    If thou my love's desire do contradict.

" 'For some hard-favored groom of thine,' quoth he, 1632
'Unless thou yoke thy liking to my will,
I'll murder straight, and then I'll slaughter thee 1634
And swear I found you where you did fulfill
The loathsome act of lust, and so did kill
    The lechers in their deed. This act will be
    My fame and thy perpetual infamy.'

"With this, I did begin to start and cry;
And then against my heart he set his sword,

1558–9 These . . . bold This illusory corresponding of opposites serves to encourage and embolden such slaves to passion as Tarquin and Sinon. **1560 flatter** encourage **1564 senseless** inanimate; unfeeling **1565 unhappy** causing unhappiness and misfortune **1567 gives o'er** ceases **1568 his . . . sore** i.e., I am not hurting Tarquin in the least by this fruitless scratching at Sinon's picture with my fingernails. **1570 time . . . time** time seems to exhaust itself **1573 sharp sustaining** painful enduring **1574 heavy** exhausting; sorrowful **1575 watch** stay awake **1579 surmise** contemplation. **detriment** suffering **1580 shows of discontent** representations of sorrow, i.e., the painted scene of Troy's woe. **1583 mindful** diligent **1586 tear-distainèd** tear-stained **1588 water galls** fragments of rainbow, secondary rainbows (foretelling stormy weather). **dim** cloudy. **element** sky, i.e., face or eye **1589 to** besides **1592 sod** sodden, steeped **1596 wond'ring . . . chance** wondering at or about each other's fortune.

1598 uncouth unknown, strange **1600 spite** injury. **spent** expended, taken away. **1601 attired in discontent** (1) wrapped up in melancholy (2) dressed in mourning black (line 1585). **1602 Unmask** Reveal **1604–5 Three . . . woe** (The metaphor is that of discharging firearms by means of a match.) **1606 addressed** prepared **1609 consorted** companion **1610 sad** serious **1611 swan** (Alludes to the belief that the swan, ordinarily without a song, sings beautifully at its own death.) **1615 depending** belonging, impending. (With Latin sense of "weighing heavier.") **1619 in the interest** claiming possession **1629 entertain** receive **1632 hard-favored** ugly **1634 straight** at once

Swearing, unless I took all patiently,
I should not live to speak another word;
So should my shame still rest upon record,
    And never be forgot in mighty Rome
    Th'adulterate death of Lucrece and her groom.   1645

"Mine enemy was strong, my poor self weak,
And far the weaker with so strong a fear.
My bloody judge forbade my tongue to speak;
No rightful plea might plead for justice there.
His scarlet lust came evidence to swear   1650
    That my poor beauty had purloined his eyes;
    And when the judge is robbed the prisoner dies.

"Oh, teach me how to make mine own excuse!
Or at the least this refuge let me find:
Though my gross blood be stained with this abuse,
Immaculate and spotless is my mind.
That was not forced, that never was inclined
    To accessory yieldings, but still pure   1658
    Doth in her poisoned closet yet endure."   1659

Lo, here the hopeless merchant of this loss,   1660
With head declined and voice dammed up with woe,   1661
With sad set eyes and wreathèd arms across,   1662
From lips new waxen pale begins to blow   1663
The grief away that stops his answer so.
    But, wretched as he is, he strives in vain;
    What he breathes out his breath drinks up again.

As through an arch the violent roaring tide   1667
Outruns the eye that doth behold his haste,
Yet in the eddy boundeth in his pride
Back to the strait that forced him on so fast,
In rage sent out, recalled in rage, being past;
    Even so his sighs, his sorrows, make a saw,   1672
    To push grief on and back the same grief draw.   1673

Which speechless woe of his poor she attendeth,   1674
And his untimely frenzy thus awaketh: 1675
"Dear lord, thy sorrow to my sorrow lendeth
Another power; no flood by raining slaketh.   1677
My woe too sensible thy passion maketh   1678
    More feeling-painful. Let it then suffice   1679
    To drown one woe, one pair of weeping eyes.

"And for my sake, when I might charm thee so,   1681
For she that was thy Lucrece, now attend me:
Be suddenly revengèd on my foe,   1683
Thine, mine, his own. Suppose thou dost defend me   1684
From what is past. The help that thou shalt lend me
    Comes all too late, yet let the traitor die;
    For sparing justice feeds iniquity.   1687

"But ere I name him, you fair lords," quoth she,
Speaking to those that came with Collatine,
"Shall plight your honorable faiths to me,   1690
With swift pursuit to venge this wrong of mine;
For 'tis a meritorious fair design
    To chase injustice with revengeful arms.
    Knights, by their oaths, should right poor ladies'
        harms."

At this request, with noble disposition
Each present lord began to promise aid,
As bound in knighthood to her imposition,   1697
Longing to hear the hateful foe bewrayed.   1698
But she, that yet her sad task hath not said,   1699
    The protestation stops. "Oh, speak," quoth she,   1700
    "How may this forcèd stain be wiped from me?

"What is the quality of my offense,   1702
Being constrained with dreadful circumstance?   1703
May my pure mind with the foul act dispense,   1704
My low-declinèd honor to advance?   1705
May any terms acquit me from this chance?   1706
    The poisoned fountain clears itself again,
    And why not I from this compellèd stain?"

With this they all at once began to say
Her body's stain her mind untainted clears,
While with a joyless smile she turns away
The face, that map which deep impression bears   1712
Of hard misfortune, carved in it with tears.
    "No, no," quoth she, "no dame hereafter living
    By my excuse shall claim excuse's giving."   1715

Here with a sigh, as if her heart would break,
She throws forth Tarquin's name: "He, he," she says,
But more than "he" her poor tongue could not speak;
Till after many accents and delays,   1719
Untimely breathings, sick and short assays,
    She utters this: "He, he, fair lords, 'tis he,
    That guides this hand to give this wound to me."

1645 **Th'adulterate** the adulterous   1650 **came evidence** supplied
evidence   1658 **To accessory yieldings** to a yielding that would
make me an accessory to crime   1659 **poisoned closet** i.e., violated
body   1660 **merchant of this loss** i.e., owner who has sustained this
loss, Collatine   1661 **declined** bent down   1662 **wreathèd arms** (See
line 793–4 and note.)   1663 **new waxen** newly turned   1667 **arch** i.e.,
of a bridge, such as London Bridge or Clopton Bridge   1672 **saw** i.e.,
sawlike back-and-forth motion   1673 **and . . . draw** and draw the
same grief back. (Collatine breathes and sighs, in and out.)
1674 **Which . . . attendeth** To which speechless woe of Collatine poor
Lucrece pays heed   1675 **And . . . awaketh** and awakens him from
his ill-timed distraction   1677 **Another power** added strength.
no . . . slaketh no flood is lessened by more rain.   1678–9 **My . . .
painful** Your passionate grief makes my woe, already too keenly felt,
even more painfully perceived.

1681 **so** i.e., in the person of my former self, still unravished
1683 **suddenly** quickly   1684 **his own** i.e., his own worst enemy.
Suppose Imagine, think that   1687 **sparing** too lenient.   **feeds iniquity** encourages wrongdoing.   1690 **plight** pledge   1697 **imposition**
injunction   1698 **bewrayed** revealed, named.   1699 **her . . . said** had
not yet finished her sad task of speaking   1700 **The protestation**
their vows (to revenge her)   1702 **quality** nature   1703 **with dreadful circumstance** in a situation filled with dread.   1704 **with . . .
dispense** receive pardon for the foul deed   1705 **advance** raise up.
1706 **terms** mitigating grounds   1712 **map** i.e., image   1715 **By . . .
giving** will be able to claim the right to offer (give) an excuse using
my excuse as her precedent.   1719 **accents** sounds expressive of
emotion

Even here she sheathèd in her harmless breast
A harmful knife, that thence her soul unsheathed.
That blow did bail it from the deep unrest   1725
Of that polluted prison where it breathed.
Her contrite sighs unto the clouds bequeathed
    Her wingèd sprite, and through her wounds doth fly
    Life's lasting date from canceled destiny.   1729

Stone-still, astonished with this deadly deed,
Stood Collatine and all his lordly crew,
Till Lucrece' father, that beholds her bleed,
Himself on her self-slaughtered body threw,
And from the purple fountain Brutus drew   1734
    The murd'rous knife, and, as it left the place,
    Her blood, in poor revenge, held it in chase;

And bubbling from her breast, it doth divide
In two slow rivers, that the crimson blood
Circles her body in on every side,
Who, like a late-sacked island, vastly stood   1740
Bare and unpeopled in this fearful flood.
    Some of her blood still pure and red remained,
    And some looked black, and that false Tarquin stained.1743

About the mourning and congealèd face
Of that black blood a wat'ry rigol goes,   1745
Which seems to weep upon the tainted place;
And ever since, as pitying Lucrece' woes,
Corrupted blood some watery token shows,
    And blood untainted still doth red abide,
    Blushing at that which is so putrified.

"Daughter, dear daughter," old Lucretius cries,
"That life was mine which thou hast here deprived.   1752
If in the child the father's image lies,
Where shall I live now Lucrece is unlived?   1754
Thou wast not to this end from me derived.
    If children predecease progenitors,
    We are their offspring, and they none of ours.

"Poor broken glass, I often did behold   1758
In thy sweet semblance my old age new born;
But now that fair fresh mirror dim and old
Shows me a bare-boned death by time outworn.   1761
Oh, from thy checks my image thou hast torn,
    And shivered all the beauty of my glass,
    That I no more can see what once I was!

"O Time, cease thou thy course and last no longer,
If they surcease to be that should survive!   1766

Shall rotten Death make conquest of the stronger
And leave the faltering feeble souls alive?
The old bees die, the young possess their hive.   1725
    Then live, sweet Lucrece, live again and see
    Thy father die, and not thy father thee!"

By this, starts Collatine as from a dream,
And bids Lucretius give his sorrow place;   1773
And then in key-cold Lucrece' bleeding stream   1774
He falls, and bathes the pale fear in his face,   1775
And counterfeits to die with her a space,   1776
    Till manly shame bids him possess his breath
    And live to be revengèd on her death.

The deep vexation of his inward soul
Hath served a dumb arrest upon his tongue,   1780
Who, mad that sorrow should his use control
Or keep him from heart-easing words so long,
Begins to talk; but through his lips do throng
    Weak words, so thick come in his poor heart's aid   1784
    That no man could distinguish what he said.

Yet sometime "Tarquin" was pronouncèd plain,
But through his teeth, as if the name he tore.
This windy tempest, till it blow up rain,
Held back his sorrow's tide, to make it more.
At last it rains, and busy winds give o'er;
    Then son and father weep with equal strife
    Who should weep most, for daughter or for wife.

The one doth call her his, the other his,
Yet neither may possess the claim they lay.   1794
The father says, "She's mine." "Oh, mine she is,"
Replies her husband. "Do not take away
My sorrow's interest. Let no mourner say   1797
    He weeps for her, for she was only mine,
    And only must be wailed by Collatine."

"Oh," quoth Lucretius, "I did give that life
Which she too early and too late hath spilled."   1801
"Woe, woe," quoth Collatine, "She was my wife;
I owed her, and 'tis mine that she hath killed."   1803
"My daughter" and "my wife" with clamors filled
    The dispersed air, who, holding Lucrece' life,
    Answered their cries, "my daughter" and "my wife."   1806

Brutus, who plucked the knife from Lucrece' side,
Seeing such emulation in their woe,
Began to clothe his wit in state and pride,   1809
Burying in Lucrece' wound his folly's show.   1810

1725 **bail it** pay for its release   1729 **Life's . . . destiny** i.e., the life that now has a perpetual existence, its subjugation to corporeal existence having been canceled.   1734 **Brutus** Lucius Junius Brutus, whose brother had been put to death by the father of the Tarquin in this poem   1740 **Who** which.   **late-sacked** recently pillaged. **vastly** in desolation   1743 **and that . . . stained** and false Tarquin had stained that blood.   1745 **rigol** rim of pale serum that forms around congealing blood   1752 **deprived** taken away.   1754 **unlived** bereft of life.   1758 **glass** mirror (i.e., Lucrece, the image of her father) 1761 **death** death's-head, skull   1766 **surcease** cease

1773 **give . . . place** yield him precedence in sorrowing   1774 **key-cold** cold as steel   1775 **pale fear** fearful pallor   1776 **counterfeits to die** gives the appearance of dying.   **a space** for a period of time 1780 **dumb arrest** injunction to be silent   1784 **so . . . aid** coming too thick and fast to aid his heart   1794 **possess . . . lay** take possession of what they claim (since she is dead).   1797 **interest** claim to possession.   1801 **late** recently   1803 **owed** owned   1806 **Answered** echoed   1809 **state** dignity   1810 **folly's show** pretense of folly. (Lucius Junius Brutus had feigned madness to escape the fate of his brother; see the note for line 1734.)

He with the Romans was esteemèd so
   As silly jeering idiots are with kings,   1812
   For sportive words and uttering foolish things.

But now he throws that shallow habit by   1814
Wherein deep policy did him disguise,   1815
And armed his long-hid wits advisedly   1816
To check the tears in Collatinus' eyes.
"Thou wrongèd lord of Rome," quoth he, "arise!
   Let my unsounded self, supposed a fool,   1819
   Now set thy long-experienced wit to school.

"Why, Collatine, is woe the cure for woe?
Do wounds help wounds, or grief help grievous deeds?
Is it revenge to give thyself a blow
For his foul act by whom thy fair wife bleeds?
Such childish humor from weak minds proceeds.   1825
   Thy wretched wife mistook the matter so
   To slay herself, that should have slain her foe.

"Courageous Roman, do not steep thy heart
In such relenting dew of lamentations,
But kneel with me and help to bear thy part
To rouse our Roman gods with invocations
That they will suffer these abominations—   1832

Since Rome herself in them doth stand disgraced—
   By our strong arms from forth her fair streets chased. 1834

"Now, by the Capitol that we adore,
And by this chaste blood so unjustly stained,
By heaven's fair sun that breeds the fat earth's store,   1837
By all our country rights in Rome maintained,   1838
And by chaste Lucrece' soul that late complained
   Her wrongs to us, and by this bloody knife,
   We will revenge the death of this true wife."

This said, he struck his hand upon his breast,
And kissed the fatal knife, to end his vow;
And to his protestation urged the rest,   1844
Who, wond'ring at him, did his words allow.   1845
Then jointly to the ground their knees they bow,
   And that deep vow which Brutus made before
   He doth again repeat, and that they swore.

When they had sworn to this advisèd doom,   1849
They did conclude to bear dead Lucrece thence,
To show her bleeding body thorough Rome,   1851
And so to publish Tarquin's foul offense;   1852
Which being done with speedy diligence,
   The Romans plausibly did give consent   1854
   To Tarquin's everlasting banishment.

1812 **silly jeering idiots** i.e., innocent court jesters **1814 habit** cloak and disposition **1815 policy** cunning **1816 advisedly** with deliberation **1819 unsounded** unplumbed, unexplored **1825 humor** disposition **1832 suffer** permit

1834 **chased** i.e., to be chased away. **1837 fat** fertile. **store** abundance **1838 country rights** rights we have as a people **1844 to his protestation** to join in his vow **1845 wond'ring** marveling. **allow** approve. **1849 advisèd doom** considered judgment **1851 thorough** throughout **1852 publish** make public **1854 plausibly** with applause

The Phoenix and Turtle

"The Phoenix and Turtle" first appeared in a collection of poems called *Love's Martyr: Or, Rosalins Complaint* by Robert Chester (1601). This quarto volume offered various poetic exercises about the phoenix and the turtle "by the best and chiefest of our modern writers." The poem assigned to Shakespeare has been universally accepted as his and is one of his most remarkable productions. With a deceptively simple diction, in gracefully pure tetrameter quatrains and triplets, the poem effortlessly evokes the transcendental ideal of a love existing eternally beyond death. The occasion is an assembly of birds to observe the funeral rites of the phoenix (always found alone) and the turtledove (always found in pairs). The phoenix, legendary bird of resurrection from its own ashes, once more finds life through death in the company of the turtledove, emblem of pure constancy in affection. Their spiritual union becomes a mystical oneness in whose presence Reason stands virtually speechless. Baffled human discourse must resort to paradox in order to explain how two beings become one essence, "Hearts remote yet not asunder." Mathematics and logic are "confounded" by this joining of two spirits into a "concordant one." This paradox of oneness echoes scholastic theology and its expounding of the doctrine of the Trinity, in terms of persons, substance, accident, triunity, and the like, although, somewhat in the manner of John Donne's poetry, this allusion is more a part of the poem's serious wit than its symbolic meaning. The poignant brevity of this vision and its medieval bird-mass setting is rendered all the more mysterious by our not knowing what, if any, human tragedy may have prompted this metaphysical affirmation.

The Phoenix and Turtle

Let the bird of loudest lay 1
On the sole Arabian tree 2
Herald sad and trumpet be, 3
To whose sound chaste wings obey. 4

But thou shrieking harbinger, 5
Foul precurrer of the fiend, 6
Augur of the fever's end, 7
To this troop come thou not near.

From this session interdict
Every fowl of tyrant wing, 10
Save the eagle, feathered king;
Keep the obsequy so strict.

Let the priest in surplice white,
That defunctive music can, 14
Be the death-divining swan, 15
Lest the requiem lack his right. 16

And thou treble-dated crow, 17
That thy sable gender mak'st 18
With the breath thou giv'st and tak'st, 19
'Mongst our mourners shalt thou go.

Here the anthem doth commence.
Love and constancy is dead;

Phoenix and the turtle fled
In a mutual flame from hence.

So they loved, as love in twain 25
Had the essence but in one,
Two distincts, division none; 27
Number there in love was slain. 28

Hearts remote yet not asunder,
Distance and no space was seen
Twixt this turtle and his queen;
But in them it were a wonder. 32

So between them love did shine, 33
That the turtle saw his right 34
Flaming in the phoenix' sight; 35
Either was the other's mine. 36

Property was thus appalled 37
That the self was not the same; 38
Single nature's double name 39
Neither two nor one was called. 40

Reason, in itself confounded, 41
Saw division grow together, 42
To themselves yet either neither, 43
Simple were so well compounded, 44

Title: Phoenix mythical bird that was thought to be consumed in flame and reborn in its own ashes, symbol of immortality; here regarded as female, though traditionally of both sexes.   **Turtle** turtledove, symbol of constancy in love; here regarded as male (line 31)   **1 the bird . . . lay** the bird (possibly the nightingale) of loudest song   **2 sole Arabian tree** (The phoenix was thought to build its nest in a unique tree in Arabia.)   **3 sad** solemn.   **trumpet** trumpeter   **4 chaste wings** i.e., the wings of the good birds that are being summoned.   **obey** are obedient.   **5 shrieking harbinger** i.e., screech owl   **6 precurrer** forerunner   **7 Augur . . . end** i.e., prognosticator of death   **10 fowl . . . wing** bird of prey   **14 That . . . can** that is skilled in funereal music   **15 death-divining swan** (Alludes to the belief that the swan foresees its own death and sings when it is about to die.)   **16 his right** its proper ceremony, or, its proper due. (Referring either to the *requiem* or to the *swan*.)   **17 treble-dated** i.e., living thrice the normal span   **18–19 That . . . tak'st** (Compare with *Hortus Sanitatis*, Bk. 3, sec. 34, in Seager's *Natural History in Shakespeare's Time*: "They [ravens] are said to conceive and to lay eggs at the bill. The young become black on the seventh day.")   **sable gender** black offspring

25 So . . . as They so loved that   **27 distincts** separate or individual persons or things   **28 Number . . . slain** i.e., their love, being of one essence, paradoxically renders the very concept of number meaningless; "one [in the numerological tradition] is no number."   **32 But . . . wonder** this phenomenon, had it been seen anywhere but in them, would have seemed amazing.   **33 So** In such a way   **34 his right** his true nature, what pertained uniquely and rightly to him, or, what was due to him   **35 sight** eyes   **36 mine** i.e., very own. (The phoenix and turtle are so merged in one another's identity that each contains the other's being. *Mine* also suggests "source of each other's treasure.")   **37–8 Property . . . same** i.e., The very idea of a peculiar or essential quality was thus confounded by the paradoxical revelation here that each lover's identity was merged into the other's and was no longer itself   **39–40 Single . . . called** i.e., their nature was at once so single and double that it could not properly be called either one or two.   **40–4 Reason . . . compounded** i.e., Reason, which proceeds by making discriminations between separate entities, is confounded when it beholds a paradoxical union of such entities, each at once discrete and fused into a single being, at once simple (i.e., made of one substance) and a compound

That it cried, "How true a twain
Seemeth this concordant one!
Love hath reason, Reason none,
If what parts can so remain."

47
48

Whereupon it made this threne
To the phoenix and the dove,
Co-supremes and stars of love,
As chorus to their tragic scene.

49

51

THRENOS

Beauty, truth, and rarity,
Grace in all simplicity,
Here enclosed, in cinders lie.

53

55

Death is now the phoenix' nest,
And the turtle's loyal breast
To eternity doth rest,

45

58

Leaving no posterity;
'Twas not their infirmity,
It was married chastity.

60
61

Truth may seem, but cannot be;
Beauty brag, but 'tis not she;
Truth and beauty buried be.

62
63
64

To this urn let those repair
That are either true or fair;
For these dead birds sigh a prayer.

45 it i.e., Reason   **47–8 Love . . . remain** i.e., Love represents a higher reason than reason itself owing to its embodiment of the paradoxical unity of two in one.   **49 threne** lamentation, funeral song. (From Greek *threnos*.)   **51 Co-supremes** joint rulers   **53 truth** constancy in love. (Also in line 62.)   **55 enclosed** i.e., enclosed in *this urn* (line 65)

58 To eternity for all eternity   **60–1 'Twas . . . chastity** i.e., it was not a defect in them to leave no posterity but an emblem of their mystical eternal trothplight.   **62–4 Truth . . . be** Anything calling itself fidelity or beauty is only a shadow or approximation of the metaphysical reality hinted at in those words.

A Lover's Complaint

Thomas Thorpe published "A Lover's Complaint" in his 1609 Quarto of Shakespeare's *Sonnets*, ascribing the poem to "William Shakespeare" in its title heading (sig. Kᵛ). The ascription must not be given too much weight, for Thorpe evidently did not have Shakespeare's authorization to publish the sonnets and may possibly have added the last two sonnets from some other source. Yet the attribution of "A Lover's Complaint" to Shakespeare is entirely plausible and is refuted by no other claim. The poem was never assigned to any other author during Shakespeare's lifetime, and no convincing alternative candidate has come forward since then. Although some critics used to wonder if the poem were worthy of Shakespeare's genius, its density of metaphor and energy of wordplay are stylistically and intellectually very much like that of Shakespeare's mature work around or before the date of publication.

The poem takes as its point of departure the conventions of a familiar Elizabethan poetic genre: the "complaint." Often choosing as their setting a stylized pastoral landscape inhabited by rustic shepherds and shepherdesses, poems in this genre generally depicted the plaintive laments of deserted or unrequited lovers. Typically, the poet might catalogue the fickle lover's features and bewail in moralistic terms the dangerous consequences of blind passion. Elizabethans often expected this sort of didacticism in the genre and might, indeed, have been tempted to read Shakespeare's poem as a useful and moving object lesson to young women about the honeyed tongues of young wooers.

Yet the value of Shakespeare's poem goes far beyond the conventional demands of the genre, as did the contributions of other exceptional writers. Much as *As You Like It* shows us a complex, ironic vision of the pastoral, this poem explores the genre of the pastoral "complaint" with subtlety and range. Its multiple point of view is noteworthy. Beginning with the sympathetic voice of the poet-narrator, "A Lover's Complaint" introduces us to the forlorn maiden and then the old shepherd who becomes an audience for her tale of woe. He is a good listener, partly because he has sowed his own wild oats in his day (11. 58–60). The story he hears incorporates also the voice of the young man who has seduced the maiden; the passage in which the young man speaks directly to her, as reported to the old man and thus to us as readers, takes up much of the poem (11. 177–280).

Framed successively and concentrically by the points of view of the sad maiden, the old man, the poet, and ourselves, the male wooer is given free rein of expression in pleading for sympathy. The old man provides his own sympathy of regret and male acknowledgment of a kind of complicity, while the poet hovers in the background not simply as narrator but also as one who understands. The moralism is evident and yet is less important for us than the multiplicity of voices expressing in rich metaphorical language the tense and ultimately bitter struggle over sexuality that is so much a key to the "Dark Lady" sonnets as well. Thorpe's inclusion of the poem in his volume of the *Sonnets* suggests an integrity in that publishing venture.

A Lover's Complaint

From off a hill whose concave womb reworded 1
A plaintful story from a sist'ring vale, 2
My spirits t'attend this double voice accorded, 3
And down I laid to list the sad-tuned tale; 4
Ere long espied a fickle maid full pale, 5
Tearing of papers, breaking rings a-twain, 6
Storming her world with sorrow's wind and rain.

Upon her head a platted hive of straw, 8
Which fortified her visage from the sun, 9
Whereon the thought might think sometimes it saw 10
The carcass of a beauty spent and done. 11
Time had not scythèd all that youth begun, 12
Nor youth all quit, but spite of heaven's fell rage 13
Some beauty peeped through lattice of seared age. 14

Oft did she heave her napkin to her eyne, 15
Which on it had conceited characters, 16
Laund'ring the silken figures in the brine
That seasoned woe had pelleted in tears, 18
And often reading what contents it bears;
As often shrieking undistinguished woe, 20
In clamors of all size, both high and low.

Sometimes her leveled eyes their carriage ride, 22
As they did batt'ry to the spheres intend; 23
Sometimes diverted, their poor balls are tied 24
To th'orbèd earth; sometimes they do extend 25

Their view right on; anon their gazes lend 26
To every place at once, and, nowhere fixed, 27
The mind and sight distractedly commixed. 28

Her hair, nor loose nor tied in formal plat, 29
Proclaimed in her a careless hand of pride; 30
For some, untucked, descended her sheaved hat, 31
Hanging her pale and pinèd cheek beside; 32
Some in her threaden fillet still did bide, 33
And, true to bondage, would not break from thence,
Though slackly braided in loose negligence.

A thousand favors from a maund she drew 36
Of amber, crystal, and of beaded jet, 37
Which one by one she in a river threw,
Upon whose weeping margent she was set, 39
Like usury applying wet to wet, 40
Or monarch's hands that lets not bounty fall 41
Where want cries some, but where excess begs all. 42

Of folded schedules had she many a one, 43
Which she perused, sighed, tore, and gave the flood; 44
Cracked many a ring of posied gold and bone, 45
Bidding them find their sepulchers in mud;
Found yet more letters sadly penned in blood,
With sleided silk feat and affectedly 48
Enswathed and sealed to curious secrecy. 49

1 **concave womb** hollow-shaped hillside. **reworded** echoed
2 **plaintful story** i.e., mournful sound (which turns out to be the grieving of a maiden). **sist'ring** neighboring 3 **t'attend** to listen to. **double** (because echoed). **accorded** inclined, consented 4 **list** listen to. **sad-tuned** i.e., sung in a minor key 5 **fickle** i.e., perturbed, moody 6 **papers** i.e., love letters 8 **platted hive** i.e., woven hat 9 **fortified** protected 10 **the thought** the mind, the imagination 11 **carcass** decaying, lifeless remnant. **spent** consumed 12–13 **all . . . quit** all the beauty of her youth, nor had youth abandoned her entirely 13 **fell** deadly, cruel 14 **seared** dried up 15 **heave** lift. **napkin** handkerchief. **eyne** eyes 16 **conceited characters** fanciful or emblematic devices 18 **seasoned** (1) matured (2) salted. **pelleted** formed into small globules 20 **undistinguished woe** incoherent cries of grief 22 **her . . . ride** i.e., her eyes, directed and aimed like a cannon, swiveled about as on a gun carriage 23 **As . . . intend** as if they did intend to direct their fire against the heavens 24 **balls** eyeballs 24–5 **are . . . earth** seem fixed to the orb-shaped earth, to the ground

26 **right on** straight in front of her 26–7 **lend . . . once** i.e., roll distractedly everywhere 28 **The mind . . . commixed** her mind and sight wildly confused or mingled. 29 **nor . . . nor** neither . . . nor. **in formal plat** neatly braided 30 **careless . . . pride** hand careless of appearances 31 **descended** hung from. **sheaved** straw 32 **Hanging . . . beside** hanging beside her pale cheek wasted with pining 33 **threaden fillet** i.e., ribbon binding her hair 36 **favors** love tokens. **maund** woven basket with handles 37 **beaded jet** jet beads 39 **weeping margent** moist bank. (Though *weeping* also applies to her.) 40 **usury** i.e., adding money to money; she adds tears to the river's water 41–2 **Or . . . all** or like the monarch who distributes his bounty not among those whose need cries out for some aid, but among the excessively wealthy who beg for absolutely everything. 43 **schedules** papers containing writing, i.e., letters 44 **gave the flood** threw in the stream 45 **posied** inscribed with a motto 48 **sleided** separated into threads. **feat** featly, adroitly. **affectedly** lovingly 49 **Enswathed . . . secrecy** wrapped about (with the silk) and sealed (with wax) into careful secrecy.

These often bathed she in her fluxive eyes, 50
And often kissed, and often 'gan to tear;
Cried, "O false blood, thou register of lies, 52
What unapprovèd witness dost thou bear! 53
Ink would have seemed more black and damnèd here!"
This said, in top of rage the lines she rents, 55
Big discontent so breaking their contents. 56

A reverend man that grazed his cattle nigh— 57
Sometime a blusterer, that the ruffle knew 58
Of court, of city, and had let go by
The swiftest hours, observèd as they flew— 60
Towards this afflicted fancy fastly drew, 61
And, privileged by age, desires to know
In brief the grounds and motives of her woe.

So slides he down upon his grainèd bat, 64
And comely-distant sits he by her side, 65
When he again desires her, being sat, 66
Her grievance with his hearing to divide. 67
If that from him there may be aught applied 68
Which may her suffering ecstasy assuage, 69
'Tis promised in the charity of age. 70

"Father," she says, "though in me you behold 71
The injury of many a blasting hour, 72
Let it not tell your judgment I am old;
Not age, but sorrow, over me hath power.
I might as yet have been a spreading flower, 75
Fresh to myself, if I had self-applied 76
Love to myself and to no love beside.

"But, woe is me! Too early I attended 78
A youthful suit—it was to gain my grace— 79
Oh, one by nature's outwards so commended 80
That maidens' eyes stuck over all his face. 81
Love lacked a dwelling and made him her place; 82
And when in his fair parts she did abide,
She was new lodged and newly deified. 84

"His browny locks did hang in crooked curls,
And every light occasion of the wind 86

Upon his lips their silken parcels hurls. 87
What's sweet to do, to do will aptly find; 88
Each eye that saw him did enchant the mind,
For on his visage was in little drawn 90
What largeness thinks in Paradise was sawn. 91

"Small show of man was yet upon his chin;
His phoenix down began but to appear 93
Like unshorn velvet on that termless skin 94
Whose bare outbragged the web it seemed to wear. 95
Yet showed his visage by that cost more dear; 96
And nice affections wavering stood in doubt 97
If best were as it was, or best without. 98

"His qualities were beauteous as his form, 99
For maiden-tongued he was, and thereof free; 100
Yet, if men moved him, was he such a storm 101
As oft twixt May and April is to see, 102
When winds breathe sweet, unruly though they be.
His rudeness so with his authorized youth 104
Did livery falseness in a pride of truth. 105

"Well could he ride, and often men would say,
'That horse his mettle from his rider takes. 107
Proud of subjection, noble by the sway, 108
What rounds, what bounds, what course, what stop he
    makes!' 109
And controversy hence a question takes, 110
Whether the horse by him became his deed, 111
Or he his manage by th' well-doing steed. 112

"But quickly on this side the verdict went:
His real habitude gave life and grace 114
To appertainings and to ornament, 115
Accomplished in himself, not in his case. 116
All aids, themselves made fairer by their place, 117

---

50 **fluxive** flowing   52 **blood** i.e., the blood in which the letters were written (line 47), but with a sense also of the *blood* or passion that has played her false.   **register** record   53 **unapprovèd** unconfirmed, false   55 **in top of** in the height of.   rents rends, tears   56 **discontent . . . contents** (With a play of antithesis.)   57 **reverend** aged   58 **Sometime** at one time.   **blusterer** swaggerer.   **ruffle** commotion, bustle   60 **swiftest hours** i.e., time of youth.   **observèd as they flew** (This man has let his youth go by and disappear, but not without observing and learning from the years as they flew.)   61 **fancy** i.e., amorous passion and the person expressing it.   **fastly** (1) quickly (2) in close proximity   64 **So . . . bat** And so he lowers himself by means of his club or staff that is worn and showing the grain   65 **comely-distant** at a decorous distance   66 **being** he being   67 **divide** share.   68 **If that** If   69 **ecstasy** frenzy (of grief)   70 **in the charity of age** in the lovingkindness that old people can offer.   71 **Father** i.e., Old man   72 **blasting** blighting, withering   75 **spreading** unfolding   76 **Fresh to myself** i.e., like a flower that lives and dies unseen and unplucked   78 **attended** heeded   79 **grace** favor   80 **nature's outwards** the physical appearance given him by nature   81 **stuck over** i.e., were glued to   82 **Love** Venus   84 **She . . . deified** Love, already a goddess, was made doubly so when she dwelt with him.   86 **occasion** chance breath

87 **Upon . . . hurls** (the wind) tosses the *silken parcels*, the curls, against his lips.   88 **to do will aptly find** i.e., will find a doer or an occasion   90 **in little** in miniature   91 **What . . . sawn** what one supposes was seen in full scale in Paradise   93 **phoenix** i.e., suggesting his unique perfection (since only one phoenix, a mythical bird, exists at one time)   94 **Like . . . skin** like velvet with its nap not yet trimmed or shaved, on that skin which words are inadequate to describe   95 **Whose . . . wear** the unadorned surface of which could outboast in handsomeness the downy covering it seemed to wear.   96 **Yet . . . dear** Yet his face seemed all the lovelier for its rich covering   97 **nice affections** carefully discriminating tastes   98 **without** i.e., lacking the downy beard.   99 **qualities were** manner was as   100 **maiden-tongued** modest of speech, soft-spoken.   **free** eloquent, well-spoken   101 **moved** i.e., to anger   102 **to see** to be seen   104–5 **His . . . truth** His roughness, privileged by his youth, thereby did dress falseness in a magnificent garment or concealment of truth.   107 **mettle** vigor and strength of spirit   108 **noble by the sway** made noble by the way he's controlled   109 **stop** sudden check in a horse's "career" or trial gallop at full speed. (All the terms here are terms of *manage*, line 112, the schooling or handling of a horse.)   110 **takes** takes up, considers   111–12 **Whether . . . steed** whether it was owing to his horsemanship that his horse acted so becomingly or whether he seemed such a good rider because he had so good a horse.   114 **habitude** constitution, temperament   115 **appertainings** external attributes   116 **case** appearance and circumstances, e.g., the possession of so good a horse.   117 **place** i.e., place near to him or on his person

Came for additions, yet their purposed trim   118
Pieced not his grace, but were all graced by him.   119

"So on the tip of his subduing tongue
All kind of arguments and question deep,
All replication prompt and reason strong,   122
For his advantage still did wake and sleep.   123
To make the weeper laugh, the laugher weep,
He had the dialect and different skill,   125
Catching all passions in his craft of will,   126

"That he did in the general bosom reign   127
Of young, of old, and sexes both enchanted,
To dwell with him in thoughts, or to remain
In personal duty, following where he haunted.   130
Consents bewitched, ere he desire, have granted,   131
And dialogued for him what he would say,   132
Asked their own wills, and made their wills obey.   133

"Many there were that did his picture get
To serve their eyes, and in it put their mind,
Like fools that in th'imagination set   135
The goodly objects which abroad they find   136
Of lands and mansions, theirs in thought assigned,   137
And laboring in more pleasures to bestow them   138
Than the true gouty landlord which doth owe them;   139
                                                                      140

"So many have, that never touched his hand,   141
Sweetly supposed them mistress of his heart.   142
My woeful self, that did in freedom stand,
And was my own fee simple, not in part,   144
What with his art in youth, and youth in art,
Threw my affections in his charmèd power,   146
Reserved the stalk and gave him all my flower.

"Yet did I not, as some my equals did,   148
Demand of him, nor being desirèd yielded;   149
Finding myself in honor so forbid,   150

With safest distance I mine honor shielded.   151
Experience for me many bulwarks builded   152
Of proofs new-bleeding, which remained the foil   153
Of this false jewel and his amorous spoil.   154

"But, ah, who ever shunned by precedent
The destined ill she must herself assay?   156
Or forced examples, 'gainst her own content   157
To put the by-past perils in her way?   158
Counsel may stop awhile what will not stay;   159
For when we rage, advice is often seen   160
By blunting us to make our wits more keen.   161

"Nor gives it satisfaction to our blood   162
That we must curb it upon others' proof,   163
To be forbade the sweets that seems so good   164
For fear of harms that preach in our behoof.   165
O appetite, from judgment stand aloof!   166
The one a palate hath that needs will taste,   167
Though Reason weep and cry, 'It is thy last.'

"For further I could say 'This man's untrue,'   169
And knew the patterns of his foul beguiling;   170
Heard where his plants in others' orchards grew,   171
Saw how deceits were gilded in his smiling;   172
Knew vows were ever brokers to defiling;   173
Thought characters and words merely but art,   174
And bastards of his foul adulterate heart.

"And long upon these terms I held my city,   176
Till thus he 'gan besiege me: 'Gentle maid,
Have of my suffering youth some feeling pity,
And be not of my holy vows afraid.
That's to ye sworn to none was ever said;   180
For feasts of love I have been called unto,   181
Till now did ne'er invite, nor never woo.   182

" 'All my offenses that abroad you see   183
Are errors of the blood, none of the mind.

118–19 Came . . . him added to his attractiveness, yet their intended function as ornament did not so much augment his grace as take grace from him.   **122–3 All . . . sleep** all prompt riposte and persuasive argument served him at all hours, like servants always ready whenever called.   **125 dialect** manner of expression.   **different** varied, readily adaptable   **126 passions** (1) passions of his hearers (2) passions incorporated into his moving speech.   **craft of will** skill in persuasion   **127 That** so that.   **general bosom** hearts of all   **130 In personal duty** i.e., like a personal servant.   **haunted** frequented.   **131–3 Consents . . . obey** i.e., Women have consented to his will before he even asked them, have made up his love speeches to them for him, and have made themselves obey as if obeying their own desires.   **135 in it . . . mind** let their minds become engrossed with it   **136–40 Like . . . owe them** like fools who imagine certain goodly lands and mansions they have happened on in their travels to be their own, and try harder to make them habitable and pleasurable than does the gout-afflicted landlord who owns them   **141 So many** Thus many women   **142 them** themselves   **144 was . . . part** i.e., had total control of my own destiny, as of land held in perpetuity, not partial control   **146 charmèd power** power to charm or cast a spell   **148 my equals** i.e., of those equal to me in age and station   **149 Demand . . . yielded** i.e., ask him to take me, or, yield myself to him the moment he desired me to   **150 in honor so forbid** forbidden by (maidenly) honor to do so (i.e., to yield at once)

151 With safest distance by staying at a safe distance   **152–3 Experience . . . new-bleeding** i.e., The experience of those recently undone in love by him provided me with many defenses   **153 foil** dark background used to show off the brilliance of a jewel   **154 this false jewel** i.e., the young man.   **spoil** plunder; that which is spoiled.   **156 assay** learn by experience.   **157–8 Or . . . way?** Or, in order to deter her own present inclination, urged the dangers experienced by others in the past?   **159 stay** stop forever   **160 rage** i.e., in passion   **161 By . . . keen** in attempting to stop us, merely making us all the more ingenious and eager.   **162 blood** passion   **163 proof** experience   **164 seems** seem   **165 preach in our behoof** offer us good advice aimed at benefiting us.   **166 O appetite . . . aloof!** O desire, you will always remain distant from judgment!   **167 The one** i.e., Passion, *appetite*.   **needs will taste** insists upon gratification   **169 say . . . untrue** tell of this man's faithlessness   **170 knew . . . beguiling** had examples of his treachery before me   **171 plants** i.e., children illegitimately begotten.   **orchards** i.e., wombs   **172 gilded** given a gilded (false) surface   **173 brokers** panders   **174 characters and words** i.e., the written and spoken word.   **art** artifice   **176 city** citadel (of chastity)   **180 That's** That which is   **181–2 For . . . woo** I have been invited to other feasts of love before now, but never until now did I do the inviting and the wooing.   **183 abroad** in the world around us

Love made them not. With acture they may be, 185
Where neither party is nor true nor kind. 186
They sought their shame that so their shame did find;
And so much less of shame in me remains 188
By how much of me their reproach contains. 189

" 'Among the many that mine eyes have seen,
Not one whose flame my heart so much as warmed, 191
Or my affection put to th' smallest teen, 192
Or any of my leisures ever charmed. 193
Harm have I done to them, but ne'er was harmed;
Kept hearts in liveries, but mine own was free, 195
And reigned, commanding in his monarchy.

" 'Look here what tributes wounded fancies sent me, 197
Of pallid pearls and rubies red as blood,
Figuring that they their passions likewise lent me 199
Of grief and blushes, aptly understood
In bloodless white and the encrimsoned mood— 201
Effects of terror and dear modesty, 202
Encamped in hearts but fighting outwardly. 203

" 'And, lo, behold these talents of their hair, 204
With twisted metal amorously impleached, 205
I have received from many a several fair, 206
Their kind acceptance weepingly beseeched,
With th'annexions of fair gems enriched, 208
And deep-brained sonnets that did amplify 209
Each stone's dear nature, worth, and quality.

" 'The diamond? Why, 'twas beautiful and hard,
Whereto his invised properties did tend; 212
The deep-green emerald, in whose fresh regard 213
Weak sights their sickly radiance do amend; 214
The heaven-hued sapphire and the opal blend 215
With objects manifold—each several stone, 216
With wit well blazoned, smiled or made some moan. 217

" 'Lo, all these trophies of affections hot, 218
Of pensived and subdued desires the tender, 219
Nature hath charged me that I hoard them not,
But yield them up where I myself must render,
That is, to you, my origin and ender; 222
For these, of force, must your oblations be, 223
Since, I their altar, you enpatron me. 224

" 'Oh, then, advance of yours that phraseless hand, 225
Whose white weighs down the airy scale of praise! 226
Take all these similes to your own command, 227
Hallowed with sighs that burning lungs did raise; 228
What me, your minister for you, obeys, 229
Works under you; and to your audit comes 230
Their distract parcels in combinèd sums. 231

" 'Lo, this device was sent me from a nun,
Or sister sanctified of holiest note, 233
Which late her noble suit in court did shun, 234
Whose rarest havings made the blossoms dote; 235
For she was sought by spirits of richest coat, 236
But kept cold distance, and did thence remove 237
To spend her living in eternal love. 238

" 'But oh, my sweet, what labor is't to leave 239
The thing we have not, mast'ring what not strives, 240
Paling the place which did no form receive, 241
Playing patient sports in unconstrainèd gyves? 242
She that her fame so to herself contrives 243
The scars of battle scapeth by the flight,
And makes her absence valiant, not her might. 245

" 'Oh, pardon me, in that my boast is true! 246
The accident which brought me to her eye
Upon the moment did her force subdue, 248

185–6 With . . . kind They may be physically performed where neither partner is faithful or truly in love. 188–9 And . . . contains and I am all the less to blame by how little their reproaches really accuse me (rather than themselves). 191 Not one . . . warmed i.e., there is not one whose flame of passion so much as warmed my heart 192 Or . . . teen or gave my affection the least sorrow (teen) 193 Or . . . charmed or put a spell on any of my times of leisure. 195 in liveries in the uniform of a person in service, i.e., almost enslaved 197 wounded fancies i.e., doting young women 199 Figuring signifying 201 mood mode, form, emotional state (i.e., blushing) 202 Effects the signs or results. dear precious; deeply felt 203 Encamped . . . outwardly (White and red contend visually in the alternation of pallor and blushing cheeks, while fear and maidenly shame occupy the hearts of the women who have been seduced.) 204 talents i.e., treasures, riches 205 impleached intertwined 206 a several fair different beautiful young women 208 th'annexions the additions 209 deep-brained intricate. amplify enlarge upon, go into detail about 212 Whereto . . . tend toward which its invisible properties incline. (Invised, used nowhere else, may be an error for incised, "engraved.") The young man, too, is beautiful and hard. 213 regard aspect, sight 214 radiance power of vision. (The emerald helps repair weak vision in those who look at it, just as the young man refreshes the eyes by his beauty.) 215–16 blend . . . manifold blended of many colors (?), or, blended with (or that blends with) many objects presented to the sight (?) 216 several particular 217 blazoned proclaimed, cataloged (in the accompanying sonnets). smiled . . . moan symbolized joy or grief in love.

218 affections passions 219 pensived saddened. tender offering 222 ender end, conclusion. (You are the source of my life and that without which I cannot live.) 223 of force perforce. your oblations offerings made at the altar of love for you 224 Since . . . me since I am the altar (on which these gifts are offered) and you are my patron saint (to whom the altar is dedicated). 225 phraseless indescribable 226 weighs . . . praise outweighs in the scales any praise that can be offered to it in airy words. 227 similes i.e., symbolic love tokens or gems accompanied by symbolic explanation in the sonnets 228 Hallowed consecrated. burning i.e., hot with passion 229–30 What . . . you whatever is at the command of me, your minister or agent acting on your authority, is thus yours also 230 audit account 231 distract parcels component parts 233 note reputation 234 Which . . . shun who recently (before she became nun) shunned those who sued for her attention at court 235 Whose . . . dote whose rare gift of beauty made the young courtiers (in the blossom of their life) dote on her 236 spirits spirited young men. coat coat of arms, i.e., descent 237 remove depart 238 living lifetime. eternal love love of the eternal God (i.e., she became a nun). 239–42 what . . . gyves? how can it be called a difficult thing to give up something we haven't tried yet, mastering an emotion that offers no resistance, paling or fencing in the heart upon which no lover has yet made any impression, patiently pretending to endure restraints that, in fact, impose no restraint and that one is not obliged to endure? 243 her fame . . . contrives devises for herself a reputation (for renouncing love) 245 makes . . . might i.e., shows valor only in avoiding temptation, not in confronting it directly. 246 my boast i.e., that she could resist me only by fleeing, not when she saw me 248 Upon the moment at once

And now she would the cagèd cloister fly.   249
Religious love put out religion's eye.   250
Not to be tempted, would she be immured,   251
And now to tempt all liberty procured.   252

" 'How mighty then you are, oh, hear me tell!
The broken bosoms that to me belong   254
Have emptied all their fountains in my well,   255
And mine I pour your ocean all among.   256
I strong o'er them, and you o'er me being strong,   257
Must for your victory us all congest,   258
As compound love to physic your cold breast.   259

" 'My parts had power to charm a sacred nun,   260
Who, disciplined, ay, dieted in grace,   261
Believed her eyes when they t'assail begun,   262
All vows and consecrations giving place.
O most potential love! Vow, bond, nor space,   264
In thee hath neither sting, knot, nor confine,   265
For thou art all, and all things else are thine.

" 'When thou impressest, what are precepts worth   267
Of stale example? When thou wilt inflame,   268
How coldly those impediments stand forth
Of wealth, of filial fear, law, kindred, fame!
Love's arms are peace, 'gainst rule, 'gainst sense, 'gainst
      shame,   271
And sweetens, in the suff'ring pangs it bears,   272
The aloes of all forces, shocks, and fears.   273

" 'Now all these hearts that do on mine depend,
Feeling it break, with bleeding groans they pine,   275
And supplicant their sighs to you extend   276
To leave the batt'ry that you make 'gainst mine,   277

Lending soft audience to my sweet design,   278
And credent soul to that strong-bonded oath   279
That shall prefer and undertake my troth.'   280

"This said, his wat'ry eyes he did dismount,   281
Whose sights till then were leveled on my face;   282
Each cheek a river running from a fount
With brinish current downward flowed apace.
Oh, how the channel to the stream gave grace!   285
Who glazed with crystal gate the glowing roses   286
That flame through water which their hue encloses.   287

"Oh, father, what a hell of witchcraft lies   288
In the small orb of one particular tear!   289
But with the inundation of the eyes
What rocky heart to water will not wear?
What breast so cold that is not warmèd here?
Oh, cleft effect! Cold modesty, hot wrath,   293
Both fire from hence and chill extincture hath.   294

"For, lo, his passion, but an art of craft,   295
Even there resolved my reason into tears;   296
There my white stole of chastity I daffed,   297
Shook off my sober guards and civil fears;   298
Appear to him as he to me appears,   299
All melting, though our drops this difference bore: 300
His poisoned me, and mine did him restore.

"In him a plenitude of subtle matter,   302
Applied to cautels, all strange forms receives,   303
Of burning blushes, or of weeping water,
Or swooning paleness; and he takes and leaves,   305
In either's aptness, as it best deceives,   306
To blush at speeches rank, to weep at woes,   307
Or to turn white and swoon at tragic shows;

"That not a heart which in his level came   309
Could scape the hail of his all-hurting aim,   310
Showing fair nature is both kind and tame;   311

249 she would . . . fly she wished to flee the locked convent.
250 Religious . . . eye i.e., Love of me put out love of the divine.
251–2 Not . . . procured Before she wished to be shut up from temptation, but now she sought liberty to venture everything. (The Quarto reads "enur'd" for "immured" and perhaps should be "inured," habituated.)   **254 bosoms** hearts   **255–6 Have . . . among** have emptied all their affections into me as into a spring, and I in turn, like a river, pour all these fountains of affection into your ocean.
257 strong victorious   **258–9 Must . . . breast** must as a consequence of your victory gather together all of us (my admirers and myself) as a compound of various ingredients applied as a medicine to cure and thaw your resisting heart.   **260 parts** qualities   **261 dieted in** sustained by   **262 they t'assail begun** they (my qualities or *parts*) began to assail her heart   **264 potential** powerful   **264–5 Vow . . . confine** Against you vows have no strength (*sting*), bonds have no binding force (*knot*), and space is no barrier or impediment (*confine*)
267 thou impressest you make an impression on a heart or conscript it into your service   **267–8 what . . . example?** of what worth are moralistic warnings based on stale old instances?   **271 Love's . . . shame** Love's might enforces its own peace in the teeth of reason, good sense, and decorum   **272 pangs it bears** pangs that it (love) brings, the pangs that lovers must suffer   **273 aloes** bitter drugs, medicines   **275 break** i.e., break in disappointment at the threat of your rejecting me.   **bleeding groans** (Each groan was thought to cost the heart a drop of blood.)   **276 supplicant** as supplicants   **277 leave** leave off.   **mine** my heart

278–80 Lending . . . troth lending their support to my suit to you and credibility to the inviolable oath that thereby guarantees the truth of what I say.   **281 dismount** lower (as in dismounting an artillery piece)   **282 leveled on** aimed at   **285 channel . . . stream** cheek to the flow of tears   **286–7 Who . . . encloses** i.e., which river of tears glazed over the cheeks (the *roses*) with a kind of crystal covering, in such a way that the cheeks' rosy color shines through the water.
288 father i.e., the old man to whom she is talking   **289 particular** single   **293 cleft** twofold.   **293–4 Cold . . . hath** Cold modesty receives warmth and hot desire is cooled by such tears.   **295 passion** passionate wooing.   **but an art** merely an artifice   **296 resolved** dissolved   **297 stole** vestment.   **daffed** doffed, put off   **298 guards** defenses.   **civil** decorous, grave   **299 Appear** I did appear
300 drops teardrops   **302 subtle matter** malleable material and cunning   **303 cautels** crafty devices   **305 takes and leaves** uses one and avoids the other   **306 In either's aptness** whichever is more appropriate   **307 rank** gross   **309 That** So that.   **level** range and aim. (Continues the metaphor of siege.)   **310 hail** i.e., of artillery
311 Showing . . . tame i.e., his aim being to represent his true nature as loving and docile

And, veiled in them, did win whom he would maim.   312
Against the thing he sought he would exclaim;
When he most burnt in heart-wished luxury,   314
He preached pure maid and praised cold chastity.   315

"Thus merely with the garment of a grace   316
The naked and concealèd fiend he covered,   317
That th'unexperient gave the tempter place,   318
Which like a cherubin above them hovered.   319

Who, young and simple, would not be so lovered?   320
Ay me! I fell, and yet do question make   321
What I should do again for such a sake.   322

"Oh, that infected moisture of his eye,   323
Oh, that false fire which in his cheek so glowed,
Oh, that forced thunder from his heart did fly,   325
Oh, that sad breath his spongy lungs bestowed,   326
Oh, all that borrowed motion seeming owed,   327
Would yet again betray the fore-betrayed,
And new pervert a reconcilèd maid!"   329

312 And . . . maim and, disguised thus in kindness and docility, or in *blushes, weeping,* and *paleness* (lines 304–5), won the heart of the woman he intended to harm.   **314 heart-wished luxury** deeply desired lechery   **315 pure maid** as if he were an untouched virgin   **316 with . . . grace** with a charming outward show or appearance. (Perhaps suggesting also one of the three Graces.)   **317 The naked . . . covered** he covered his fiendish inner self   **318 th'unexperient** the inexperienced.   **place** entry   **319 Which . . . hovered** who, resembling a cherub, hovered over his victims as though offering them protection.

320 simple naive.   **be so lovered** surrender to a lover like him.   **321 question make** i.e., ask myself   **322 for such a sake** for someone like him, or, for the sake of falling into such pleasure, however brief.   **323 infected** infectious   **325 forced** feigned.   **from** that from   **326 spongy lungs** lungs that are spongelike (as all lungs are; perhaps with the suggestion of "blown up with flattery and pretended grief")   **327 all . . . owed** all that passion he seemed to possess himself but had, in fact, borrowed   **329 reconcilèd** penitent

Sonnets

Shakespeare seems to have cared more about his reputation as a lyric poet than as a dramatist. He contributed to the major nondramatic genres of his day: to amatory Ovidian narrative in *Venus and Adonis*, to the Complaint in *The Rape of Lucrece*, to philosophical poetry in "The Phoenix and Turtle." He cooperated in the publication of his first two important poems, dedicating them to the young Earl of Southampton with a plea to him for sponsorship. To write poetry in this vein was more fashionable than to write plays, which one did mainly for money.

A poet with ambitions of this sort simply had to write a sonnet sequence. Sonneteering was the rage in England in the early and mid 1590s. Based on the sonneteering tradition of Francesco Petrarch, Sir Thomas Wyatt, and others, and gaining new momentum in 1591 with the publication of Sir Philip Sidney's *Astrophel and Stella*, the vogue ended almost as suddenly as it began, in 1596 or 1597. The sonnet sequences of this brief period bear the names of most well-known and minor poets of the day: *Amoretti* by Edmund Spenser (1595), *Delia* by Samuel Daniel (1591 and 1592), *Caelica* by Fulke Greville (not published until 1633), *Idea's Mirror* by Michael Drayton (1594), *Diana* by Henry Constable (1592), *Phyllis* by Thomas Lodge (1593), and the more imitative sequences of Barnabe Barnes, Giles Fletcher, William Percy, Bartholomew Griffin, William Smith, and Robert Tofte.

Shakespeare wrote sonnets during the heyday of the genre, for in 1598 Francis Meres, in his *Palladis Tamia: Wit's Treasury*, praised Shakespeare's "sugared sonnets among his private friends." Even though they were not printed at the time, we know from Meres's remark that they were circulated in manuscript among the cognoscenti and commanded respect. Shakespeare may actually have preferred to delay the publication of his sonnets, not through indifference to their literary worth, but through a desire not to seem too professional. The "courtly makers" of the English Renaissance, those gentlemen whose chivalric accomplishments were supposed to include versifying, looked on the writing of poetry as an avocation designed to amuse one's peers or to court a lady. Publication was not quite genteel, and many such authors affected dismay when their verses were pirated into print. The young wits about London of the 1590s, whether aristocratic or not, sometimes imitated this fashion. Like young John Donne, they sought the favorable verdict of their fellow wits at the Inns of Court (where young men studied law) and professed not to care about wider recognition. Whether Shakespeare was motivated in this way we do not know, but, in any event, his much-sought-after sonnet sequence was not published until 1609, long after the vogue had passed. The publisher, Thomas Thorpe, seems not to have obtained Shakespeare's authorization. Two sonnets, numbers 138 and 144, had been pirated ten years earlier by William Jaggard in *The Passionate Pilgrim*, 1599, a little anthology with some poems by Shakespeare and some wrongly attributed to him. The sonnets were not reprinted until 1640, either because the sonnet vogue had passed or because Thorpe's edition had been suppressed.

The unexplained circumstances of publication have given rise to a host of vexing and apparently unanswerable questions. Probably no puzzle in all English literature has provoked so much speculation and produced so little agreement. To whom are the sonnets addressed? Do they tell a consistent story, and, if so, do they tell us anything about Shakespeare's life? The basic difficulty is that we cannot be sure that the order in which Thorpe published the sonnets represents Shakespeare's intention, nor can we assume that Thorpe spoke for Shakespeare when he dedicated the sonnets to "Mr. W. H." As they stand, most of the first 126 sonnets appear to be addressed in warm friendship to a handsome young aristocrat, whereas sonnets 127–52 mostly speak of the poet's dark-haired mistress. Yet the last two sonnets, 153–4, seem unrelated to anything previous and cast some doubt on the reliability of the ordering. Within each large grouping of the sonnets, moreover, we find evident inconsistencies: jealousies disappear and suddenly reappear, the poet bewails his absolute rejection by the friend and then speaks a few sonnets later of harmonious affection as though nothing had happened, and so on. Some sonnets are closely linked to their predecessors; some are apparently disconnected (although even here we must allow for the real possibility that Shakespeare intends juxtaposition and contrast). We cannot be sure if the friend of sonnets 1–126 is really one person or several. We can only speculate that the unhappy love triangle described in sonnets 40–2, in which the friend has usurped the poet's mistress, can be identified with the love triangle of the "Dark Lady" sonnets, 127–52. Most readers sense a narrative continuity of the whole yet find blocks of sonnets stubbornly out of place. The temptation to rearrange the order has proved irresistible, but no alternative order has ever won acceptance. The consensus is that Thorpe's order is at times suspect but may have more rationale than at first appears. It is, in any case, the only authoritative order we have.

No less frustrating is Thorpe's dedication "To the Only Begetter of These Ensuing Sonnets, Mr. W. H." Given the late and unauthorized publication, we cannot assume that Thorpe speaks for Shakespeare. Quite possibly he is only thanking the person who obtained the sonnets for him, making publication possible. Mundanely enough, Mr. W. H. could be William Hall, an associate of Thorpe's in the publishing business. Yet Elizabethan usage affords few instances of "begetter" in this sense of "obtainer." Donald Foster has offered new and persuasive arguments for the idea that "Mr. W. H." is only a typographical error of a common sort and that Thorpe meant to say "Mr. W. S.," Master William Shakespeare. In this case, "begetter" would mean simply "creator." This solution has a wonderful neatness about it, but other readers have wondered if it answers the seeming contradiction when Thorpe speaks of "Mr. W. H." and "our ever-living poet" in the dedication as though they are two people. Thorpe offers to Mr. W. H. "that eternity promised by our ever-living poet," as though Mr. W. H. were the very subject of those sonnets whom Shakespeare vows to immortalize.

This interpretation of "begetter" as "inspirer" has prompted many enthusiasts to search for a Mr. W. H. in Shakespeare's life, a nobleman who befriended him. The chief candidates are two. First is the young Earl of Southampton, to whom Shakespeare had dedicated *Venus and Adonis* and *The Rape of Lucrece*. The dedication to the second of these poems bespeaks a warmth and gratitude that had been less evident in the first. The Earl's name, Henry Wriothesley, yields initials that are the reverse of W. H. If this correspondence seems unconvincing, W. H. could stand for Sir William Harvey, third husband of Mary, Lady Southampton, the young Earl's

mother. Some researchers would have us believe that Shakespeare wrote the sonnets for Lady Southampton, especially those urging a young man (her son) to marry and procreate. This entire case is speculative, however, and we have no evidence that Shakespeare had any dealings with Southampton after *The Rape of Lucrece*. The plain ascription "Mr. W. H." seems an oddly uncivil way for Thorpe to have addressed an earl. If meant for Southampton, the sonnets must have been written fairly early in the 1590s, for they give no hint of Southampton's later career: his courtship of Elizabeth Vernon, her pregnancy and their secret marriage in 1598, and his later involvement in Essex's Irish campaign and abortive uprising against Queen Elizabeth. Those literary sleuths who stress similarities to the Southampton relationship are too willing to overlook dissimilarities.

The next chief candidate for Mr. W. H. is William Herbert, third Earl of Pembroke, to whom, along with his brother, Shakespeare's colleagues dedicated the First Folio of 1623. In 1595, Pembroke's parents were attempting to arrange his marriage with Lady Elizabeth Carey, granddaughter of the first Lord Hunsdon, who was Lord Chamberlain and patron of Shakespeare's company. In 1597, another alliance was attempted with Bridget Vere, granddaughter of Lord Burghley. In both negotiations, young Pembroke objected to the girl in question. This hypothesis requires, however, an uncomfortably late date for the sonnets and postulates a gap in age between Shakespeare and Pembroke that would have afforded little opportunity for genuine friendship. Pembroke was only fifteen in 1595; Shakespeare was thirty-one. Besides, no evidence supports the claim other than historical coincidence. The common initials W. H. can be made to produce other candidates as well, such as the Lincolnshire lawyer named William Hatcliffe proposed (to no one's satisfaction) by Leslie Hotson. Hotson wants to date most of the sonnets before 1589, since Hatcliffe came to London in 1587–1588. When such speculations are constructed on the single enigmatic testimonial of the dedication by Thomas Thorpe, who may well have had no connection with Shakespeare, we are left with a case that would not be worth describing had it not captured the imagination of so many researchers.

Biographical identifications have also been proposed for the various personages in the sonnet sequence, predictably with no better success. The rival poet, with "the proud full sail of his great verse" (sonnet 86), has been linked to Christopher Marlowe (who died in 1593), George Chapman, and others. The sequence gives us little to go on, other than that the rival poet possesses a considerable enough talent to intimidate the author of the sonnets and to ingratiate himself with the author's aristocratic friend. No biographical circumstances resembling this rivalry have come to light. Various candidates have also been found for the "Dark Lady." One is Mary

Fitton, a lady-in-waiting at court who bore a child by Pembroke in 1601. Again, we have no evidence that Shakespeare knew her, nor is he likely to have carried on an affair with one of such high rank. A. L. Rowse has proposed Emilia Lanier, wife of Alfonso Lanier and daughter of a court musician named Bassano, a woman of suitably dark complexion perhaps but whose presumed connection with Shakespeare rests only on the reported rumor that she was a mistress of Lord Hunsdon. We are left finally without knowing who any of these people were, or whether indeed Shakespeare was attempting to be biographical at all.

The same irresolution afflicts the dating of the sonnets. Do they give hints of a personal chronicle extending over some years, following Thorpe's arrangement of the sonnets or some alternative order? Sonnet 104 speaks of three years having elapsed since the poet met his friend. Are there other signposts that relate to contemporary events? A line in sonnet 107 ("The mortal moon hath her eclipse endured") is usually linked to the death of Queen Elizabeth (known as Diana or Cynthia) in 1603, though Leslie Hotson prefers to see in it an allusion to the Spanish Armada, shaped for sea battle in a moonlike crescent when it met defeat in 1588. The newly built pyramids in sonnet 123 remind Hotson of the obelisks built by Pope Sixtus V in Rome, 1586–1589; other researchers have discovered pyramids erected on London's streets in 1603 to celebrate the coronation of James I. As these illustrations suggest, speculative dating can be used to support a hypothesis of early or late composition. The wary consensus of most scholars is that the sonnets were written over a number of years; a large number, certainly, before 1598, but some perhaps later and even up to the date of publication in 1609.

However fruitless this quest for nonexistent certainties, it does at least direct us to a meaningful critical question: should we expect sonnets of this "personal" nature to be at least partly autobiographical? Shakespeare's sonnets have struck many readers as cries from the heart, voicing at times fears of rejection, self-hatred, and humiliation, and at other times a serene gratitude for reciprocated affection. This power of expression may, however, be a tribute to Shakespeare's dramatic gift rather than evidence of personal involvement. Earlier sonnet sequences, both Elizabethan and pre-Elizabethan, had established a variety of artistic conventions that tended to displace biography. Petrarch's famous *Rime,* or sonnets, later collected in his *Canzoniere,* though addressed to Laura in two sequences (during her life and after her death), idealized her into the unapproachable lady worshiped by the self-abasing and miserable lover. Petrarch's imitators—Serafino Aquilano, Pietro Bembo, Ludovico Ariosto, and Torquato Tasso among the Italians, Clement Marot, Joachim du Bellay, Pierre de Ronsard, and Philippe Desportes among the French Pléiade—reworked these conventions in countless variations. In England, the fashion was taken up by Sir Thomas Wyatt, the Earl of Surrey, George Gascoigne, Thomas Watson, and others. Spenser's *Amoretti* and Sidney's *Astrophel and Stella,* though inspired at least in part by real women in the poets' lives, are also deeply concerned with theories of writing poetry. Rejection of the stereotyped attitudes and relationships that had come to dominate the typical Petrarchan sonnet sequence is evidence not of biographical literalism in art but of a new insistence on lifelike emotion in art; as Sidney's muse urges him, "look in thy heart and write." Thus, both the Petrarchan and the anti-Petrarchan schools avoid biographical writing for its own sake. This is essentially true of all Elizabethan sonneteering, from Drayton's serious pursuit of platonic abstraction in his *Idea's Mirror* to the facile chorusing of lesser sonnet writers about Diana, Phyllis, Zepheria, or Fidessa.

The "story" connecting the individual poems of an Elizabethan sonnet sequence is never very important or consistent, even when we can be sure of the order in which the sonnets were written. Dante had used prose links in his *La Vita Nuova* (c. 1282) to stress narrative continuity, and so had Petrarch, but this sturdy framework had been abandoned by the late sixteenth century. Rather than telling a chronological story, the typical Elizabethan sonnet sequence offers a thematically connected series of lyrical meditations, chiefly on love but also on poetic theory, the adversities of fortune, death, or what have you. The narrative events mentioned from time to time are not the substance of the sequence but the occasion for meditative reflection. Attitudes need not be consistent throughout, and the characters need not be consistently motivated like dramatis personae in a play.

Shakespeare's sonnet sequence retains these conventions of Elizabethan sonneteering and employs many archetypal situations and themes that had been explored by his predecessors and contemporaries. His emphasis on friendship seems new, for no other sequence addressed a majority of its sonnets to a friend rather than to a mistress, but even here the anti-Petrarchan quest for spontaneity and candor is in the best Elizabethan tradition of Sidney and Spenser. Besides, the exaltation of friendship over love was itself a widespread Neoplatonic commonplace recently popularized in the writings of John Lyly. Shakespeare's sequence makes use of the structural design found in contemporary models. Even though we cannot reconstruct a rigorously consistent chronological narrative from the sonnets, we can discern overall patterns out of which the poet's emotional crises arise and upon which he constructs his meditative lyrics. Certain groupings, such as the sonnets addressed to the "Dark Lady," 127–52, in which individually they comment on one another through reinforcement or antithetical design and are thus enhanced by their context, achieve a plausible cohesion; a case can be made, in other words, for the order of the poems as Thorpe printed them. Even the last two sonnets, 153 and 154, have their defenders (see Michael J. B. Allen's essay in *Shakespeare Survey*, 1978). Juxtaposition is a favorite technique in Shakespeare's plays, and we must remember that he alone among the major Elizabethan sonneteers wrote for the stage.

Taking note of such considerations, we can account for most of the situations portrayed in Shakespeare's sonnets by postulating four figures: the poet-speaker himself, his friend, his mistress, and a rival poet. The order of events in this tangled relationship is not what the poet wishes to describe; instead, he touches upon this situation from time to time as he explores his own reaction to love in its various aspects.

The poet's relationship to his friend is a vulnerable one. This friend to whom he writes is aristocratic, handsome, and younger than he is. The poet is beholden to this friend as a sponsor and must consider himself as subservient, no matter how deep their mutual affection. Even at its happiest, their relationship is hierarchical. The poet abases himself in order to extol his friend's beauty and virtues (sonnets 52–4, 105–6). He confesses that his love would be idolatry, except that the friend's goodness excels all poetic hyperbole. As the older of the two, the poet sententiously urges his young friend to marry and eternize his beauty through the engendering of children (sonnets 1–17). Such a course, he argues, is the surest way to conquer devouring Time, the enemy of all earthly beauty and love. Yet elsewhere the poet exalts his own art as the surest defense against Time (sonnets 55, 60, 63–5, etc.). These conclusions are nominally contradictory, offering procreation in one instance and poetry in another as the best hope for immortality, but thematically the two are obviously related. In even the happiest of the sonnets, such as those giving thanks for "the marriage of true minds" (116, 123), the consciousness of devouring Time is inescapable. If love and celebratory poetry can sometimes triumph over Time, the victory is all the more precious because it is achieved in the face of such odds.

Love and perfect friendship are a refuge for the poet faced with hostile fortune and an indifferent world. He is too often "in disgrace with fortune and men's eyes" (sonnet 29), oppressed by his own failings, saddened by the facile success of opportunists (sonnets 66–8), ashamed of having sold himself cheap in his own profession (sonnets 110–11). If taken biographically, this could mean that Shakespeare was not happy about his career as actor and playwright, but the motif makes complete sense in the sonnet sequence without resort to biography. A biographical reading also raises the question of homosexual attraction, as urged by Joseph Pequigney in his *Such Is My Love* (University of Chicago Press, 1985). The bawdy reference in sonnet 20.12 to the friend's possession of "one thing to my purpose nothing" would seem to militate against the idea of a consummated homosexual relation-

ship, while conversely many sonnets (such as 138) do point to the poet's consummation with his mistress. Still, the bond between poet and friend is extraordinarily strong, and certainly there is a danger that traditional scholarship has minimized the erotic bond between the poet and his friend out of a distaste for the idea. Occasional absences torture the poet with the physical separation, even though he realizes that pure love of the spirit ought not to be hampered by distance or time (sonnets 43–51). The absence is especially painful when the poet must confess his own disloyalty (sonnets 117–18). The chronology of these absences cannot be worked out satisfactorily, but the haunting theme of separation is incessant and overwhelming. By extension, it includes the fear of separation through death (sonnets 71–3, 126). The concern with absence is closely related to the poet's obsession with devouring Time.

All the poet's misfortunes would be bearable if love were constant, but his dependency on the aristocratic friend leaves him at the mercy of that friend's changeable moods. The poet must not complain when his wellborn friend entertains a rival poet (sonnets 78–86) or forms other emotional attachments, even with the poet's own mistress (sonnets 40–2). These disloyalties evoke outbursts of jealousy. The poet vacillates between forgiveness and recrimination. Sometimes even his forgiveness is self-loathing, in which the poet confesses he would take back the friend on any terms (sonnets 93–5). At times the poet grovels, conceding that he deserves no better treatment (sonnets 57–8), but at other times his stored-up resentment bursts forth (sonnets 93–5). The poet's fears, though presented in no clear chronological order, run the gamut from a fatalistic sense that rejection will come one day (sonnet 49) to an abject and bitter final farewell (sonnet 87). Sometimes he is tormented by jealousy (sonnet 61) and sometimes by self-hate (sonnets 88–9).

The sonnets addressed to the poet's mistress, the "Dark Lady," similarly convey fear, self-abasement, and a panicky awareness of loss of self-control. In rare moments of happiness, the poet praises her dark features as proof of her being a real woman, not a Petrarchan goddess (sonnet 130). Too often, however, her lack of ideal beauty reminds the poet of his irrational enchantment (sonnets 148–50). She is tyrannous, disdainful, spiteful, disloyal, a "female evil" (sonnet 144) who has tempted away from the poet his better self, his friend. The poet is distressed not so much by her perfidy as by his own self-betrayal; he sees bitterly that he offends his nobler reason by his attachment to the rebellious flesh. He worships what others abhor and perjures himself by swearing to what he knows to be false (sonnets 150–2). His only hope for escape is to punish his flesh and renounce the vanity of all worldly striving (sonnet 146), but this solution evades him as he plunges helplessly back into the perverse enslavement of a sickened appetite.

This sketch of only some themes of the sequence may suggest the range and yet the interconnection of Shakespeare's meditations on love, friendship, and poetry. Patterns are visible, even if the exact chronology (never important in the Elizabethan sonnet sequence) cannot be determined. The pattern suggests a pivotal role for the sonnets in Shakespeare's development, as Richard Wheeler has urged in his *Shakespeare's Development* (University of California Press, 1981): the early sonnets about love and marriage pursue relationships central to the comedies, whereas subsequent sonnets move with increasing intensity toward the portrayal of promiscuity and degradation in erotic love and toward new assaults upon the binding power of friendship in such a way as to anticipate the darker vision of the tragedies. The playful and unthreatening heroine of the comedies gives way to a dark lady who inspires in the poet a compulsive and humiliating self-hatred; mutuality in friendship finds itself threatened by a one-sided relationship in which the abasement of the poet is answered by the indifference and infidelity of the friend. It as though in the sonnets Shakespeare opened the Pandora's box of hazardous erotic entanglements he was to dramatize in his late plays.

Shakespeare's concern with patterning is equally evident in matters of versification and imagery. The sonnets are written throughout in the "Shakespearean" or English form, *abab cdcd efef gg*. (Sonnet 126, written entirely in couplets, is an exception, perhaps because it was intended as the envoi to the series addressed to the poet's friend.) This familiar sonnet form, introduced by Wyatt and developed by Sidney, differs markedly from the octave-sestet division of the Petrarchan, or Italian, sonnet. The English form of three quatrains and a concluding couplet lends itself to a step-by-step development of idea and image, culminating in an epigrammatic two-line conclusion that may summarize the thought of the preceding twelve lines or give a sententious interpretation of the images developed up to this point. Sonnet 7 pursues the image of the sun at morning, noon, and evening through three quatrains, one for each phase of the day, and then in the couplet "applies" the image to the friend's unwillingness to beget children. Sonnet 29 moves from resentment of misfortune to a rejoicing in the friend's love and rhetorically mirrors this sudden elevation of mood in the image of the lark "at break of day arising / From sullen earth." Shakespeare's rhetorical and imagistic devices exploit the sonnet structure he inherited and perfected, and remind us again of the strong element of convention and artifice in these supremely "personal" sonnets. The recurring images—the canker on the rose, the pleading of a case at law, the seasonal rhythms of summer and winter, the alternations of day and night, the harmonies and dissonances of music—also testify to the artistic unity of the whole and to the artist's extraordinary discipline in evoking a sense of helpless loss of self-control.

Sonnets

To the Only Begetter of These Ensuing Sonnets

Mr. W. H.

All Happiness and That Eternity Promised
   by Our Ever-living Poet
Wisheth the Well-wishing Adventurer in
   Setting Forth

                     T. T.

1

From fairest creatures we desire increase,	1
That thereby beauty's rose might never die,	
But as the riper should by time decease,	3
His tender heir might bear his memory;	4
But thou, contracted to thine own bright eyes,	5
Feed'st thy light's flame with self-substantial fuel,	6
Making a famine where abundance lies,	
Thyself thy foe, to thy sweet self too cruel.	
Thou that art now the world's fresh ornament	
And only herald to the gaudy spring,	10
Within thine own bud buriest thy content,	11
And, tender churl, mak'st waste in niggarding.	12
Pity the world, or else this glutton be:	
To eat the world's due, by the grave and thee.	14

2

When forty winters shall besiege thy brow	
And dig deep trenches in thy beauty's field,	2

Thy youth's proud livery, so gazed on now,   3
Will be a tattered weed, of small worth held.   4
Then being asked where all thy beauty lies,
Where all the treasure of thy lusty days,   6
To say within thine own deep-sunken eyes
Were an all-eating shame and thriftless praise.   8
How much more praise deserved thy beauty's use   9
If thou couldst answer, "This fair child of mine
Shall sum my count and make my old excuse,"   11
Proving his beauty by succession thine.   12
   This were to be new made when thou art old,   13
   And see thy blood warm when thou feel'st it cold.

3

Look in thy glass, and tell the face thou viewest	1
Now is the time that face should form another,	
Whose fresh repair if now thou not renewest	3
Thou dost beguile the world, unless some mother.	4
For where is she so fair whose uneared womb	5
Disdains the tillage of thy husbandry?	6
Or who is he so fond will be the tomb	7
Of his self-love, to stop posterity?	
Thou art thy mother's glass, and she in thee	9
Calls back the lovely April of her prime;	
So thou through windows of thine age shalt see,	11
Despite of wrinkles, this thy golden time.	12
But if thou live remembered not to be,	13
Die single, and thine image dies with thee.	

1.1 **increase** procreation **3 as** just as, while **4 His** its, the ripening creation (including the young man). **bear his memory** i.e., immortalize it by bearing its features **5 contracted** (1) engaged, espoused (2) shrunk **6 self-substantial** of your own substance **10 only herald to** principal or unique messenger of **11 thy content** (1) that which is contained in you; potential fatherhood (2) your contentment **12 mak'st . . . niggarding** squander your substance by being miserly. (An oxymoron, like *tender churl*, "youthful old miser.") **14 the world's due** i.e., the offspring you owe to posterity. **by . . . thee** (consumed) by death and by your willfully remaining childless. **2.2 trenches** i.e., wrinkles. **field** (1) meadow (2) battlefield (3) heraldic background

3 **proud livery** handsome garments **4 weed** garment. (With a play on a *weed* growing in *beauty's field*, line 2.) **6 lusty** (1) vigorous (2) lustful **8 Were . . . praise** would be a shameful admission of gluttony and praise of idle extravagance. **9 deserved . . . use** would the proper investment and employment of your beauty deserve **11 Shall . . . excuse** will balance my account and make amends in my old age **12 thine** derived from you. **13 were** would be **3.1 glass** mirror **3 fresh repair** youthful condition **4 beguile** cheat. **unless some mother** withhold the happiness of childbearing from some woman. **5 uneared** untilled, uncultivated **6 husbandry** cultivation. (With obvious suggestion of "playing the husband.") **7 fond** foolish, (self-)loving. **will be** i.e., that he is willing to be **9 thy mother's glass** the image of your mother **11–12 So . . . time** in just the same way, you, looking through eyes dimmed by advancing years, and despite your own wrinkles of age, will see in your child an image of your own happy youth. **13 remembered not to be** in such a way as not to be remembered, without children

4

Unthrifty loveliness, why dost thou spend 1
Upon thyself thy beauty's legacy? 2
Nature's bequest gives nothing, but doth lend,
And being frank she lends to those are free. 4
Then, beauteous niggard, why dost thou abuse
The bounteous largess given thee to give?
Profitless usurer, why dost thou use 7
So great a sum of sums, yet canst not live? 8
For having traffic with thyself alone, 9
Thou of thyself thy sweet self dost deceive. 10
Then how, when Nature calls thee to be gone,
What acceptable audit canst thou leave?
    Thy unused beauty must be tombed with thee, 13
    Which, used, lives th'executor to be. 14

5

Those hours, that with gentle work did frame 1
The lovely gaze where every eye doth dwell, 2
Will play the tyrants to the very same 3
And that unfair which fairly doth excel; 4
For never-resting Time leads summer on 5
To hideous winter and confounds him there, 6
Sap checked with frost and lusty leaves quite gone, 7
Beauty o'ersnowed and bareness everywhere.
Then, were not summer's distillation left 9
A liquid prisoner pent in walls of glass, 10
Beauty's effect with beauty were bereft, 11
Nor it nor no remembrance what it was. 12
    But flowers distilled, though they with winter meet,
    Leese but their show; their substance still lives sweet. 14

6

Then let not winter's ragged hand deface 1
In thee thy summer ere thou be distilled.
Make sweet some vial; treasure thou some place 3
With beauty's treasure ere it be self-killed.
That use is not forbidden usury 5
Which happies those that pay the willing loan; 6
That's for thyself to breed another thee, 7

Or ten times happier, be it ten for one. 8
Ten times thyself were happier than thou art, 9
If ten of thine ten times refigured thee; 10
Then what could death do, if thou shouldst depart,
Leaving thee living in posterity?
    Be not self-willed, for thou art much too fair 13
    To be death's conquest and make worms thine heir.

7

Lo, in the orient when the gracious light 1
Lifts up his burning head, each under eye 2
Doth homage to his new-appearing sight,
Serving with looks his sacred majesty;
And having climbed the steep-up heavenly hill,
Resembling strong youth in his middle age,
Yet mortal looks adore his beauty still,
Attending on his golden pilgrimage;
But when from highmost pitch, with weary car, 9
Like feeble age, he reeleth from the day,
The eyes, 'fore duteous, now converted are 11
From his low tract and look another way. 12
    So thou, thyself outgoing in thy noon,
    Unlooked on diest, unless thou get a son. 14

8

Music to hear, why hear'st thou music sadly? 1
Sweets with sweets war not, joy delights in joy.
Why lov'st thou that which thou receiv'st not gladly, 3
Or else receiv'st with pleasure thine annoy? 4
If the true concord of well-tunèd sounds,
By unions married, do offend thine ear, 6
They do but sweetly chide thee, who confounds 7
In singleness the parts that thou shouldst bear. 8
Mark how one string, sweet husband to another, 9
Strikes each in each by mutual ordering, 10
Resembling sire and child and happy mother
Who, all in one, one pleasing note do sing;
    Whose speechless song, being many, seeming one, 13
    Sings this to thee: "Thou single wilt prove none." 14

4.1 Unthrifty (1) Prodigal (2) Unavailing   **2 thy beauty's legacy** the beauty you inherited (and should pass on to your children).   **4 frank** liberal, bounteous.   **are free** who are generous.   **7 use** (1) use up (2) fail to invest for profit. (See sonnet 6.5 and note.)   **8 live** (1) have a livelihood (2) live in your posterity.   **9 traffic** commerce. (The commercial and financial metaphor hints at sexual self-fascination.)   **10 deceive** cheat.   **13 unused** (1) unemployed (2) not invested for profit   **14 lives** would live (in your son)
5.1 frame make   **2 gaze** object of gazes   **3 play . . . to** oppress   **4 unfair** make unlovely.   **fairly** (1) in beauty (2) truly, honestly   **5 leads summer on** (1) guides the steps of summer (2) lures summer   **6 confounds** destroys   **7 lusty** vigorous   **9 summer's distillation** distilled perfume of flowers   **10 walls of glass** glass containers   **11 with . . . bereft** would be lost along with beauty itself   **12 Nor it nor no** (leaving behind) neither it (beauty) nor any   **14 Leese** lose.   **still** (1) notwithstanding (2) always
6.1 ragged rough   **3 vial** (With suggestion of a womb.)   **treasure** enrich   **5 use** lending money at interest   **6 happies** makes happy.   **pay . . . loan** willingly borrow on these terms and repay the loan   **7 That's . . . thee** i.e., such would be the case if you were to sire a child like you

8 Or . . . one i.e., or indeed the happy mother (of line 6) would be ten times happier were she to bear you ten children instead of one. (*Ten for one* alludes to the highest legal rate of interest, one for ten.)
9 Ten . . . art i.e., Ten children of yours would be a tenfold blessing and would make you happier   **10 refigured** duplicated, copied (producing one hundred grandchildren)   **13 self-willed** (1) obstinate (2) bequeathed to self
7.1 orient east.   **light** i.e., sun   **2 under** earthly   **9 pitch** highest point (as of a falcon's flight before it attacks).   **car** chariot (of the sungod)   **11 converted** turned away   **12 tract** course   **14 get** beget
8.1 Music to hear i.e., You whom it is music to hear.   **2 Sweets** Sweet things   **3–4 Why . . . annoy?** Why do you not gladly love the sweet things you hear, or find irksome that which is pleasurable?   **6 By unions married** perfectly blended in harmonious chords   **7–8 who . . . bear** you who destroy, by playing a single part only, the harmony (i.e., marriage) that you should sustain.   **9 sweet husband** i.e., paired, as on the double strings of the lute, one string vibrating sympathetically to the other   **10 each in each** i.e., with double resonance, sounding mutually   **13 Whose** i.e., the strings'.   **being . . . one** i.e., making harmony out of several voices   **14 Thou . . . none** (Alludes to the proverb, "One is no number." The single person who dies without posterity leaves nothing of himself behind.)

9

Is it for fear to wet a widow's eye   1
That thou consum'st thyself in single life?
Ah, if thou issueless shalt hap to die,   3
The world will wail thee like a makeless wife.   4
The world will be thy widow and still weep   5
That thou no form of thee hast left behind,
When every private widow well may keep,   7
By children's eyes, her husband's shape in mind.   8
Look what an unthrift in the world doth spend   9
Shifts but his place, for still the world enjoys it;   10
But beauty's waste hath in the world an end,
And, kept unused, the user so destroys it.   12
   No love toward others in that bosom sits
   That on himself such murd'rous shame commits.

10

For shame, deny that thou bear'st love to any,
Who for thyself art so unprovident!
Grant, if thou wilt, thou art beloved of many,
But that thou none lov'st is most evident;
For thou art so possessed with murd'rous hate
That 'gainst thyself thou stick'st not to conspire,   6
Seeking that beauteous roof to ruinate   7
Which to repair should be thy chief desire.
Oh, change thy thought, that I may change my mind!   9
Shall hate be fairer lodged than gentle love?
Be, as thy presence is, gracious and kind,   11
Or to thyself at least kindhearted prove:
   Make thee another self, for love of me,
   That beauty still may live in thine or thee.

11

As fast as thou shalt wane, so fast thou grow'st   1
In one of thine from that which thou departest;   2
And that fresh blood which youngly thou bestow'st   3
Thou mayst call thine when thou from youth convertest.   4
Herein lives wisdom, beauty, and increase;
Without this, folly, age, and cold decay.
If all were minded so, the times should cease   7
And threescore year would make the world away.   8
Let those whom Nature hath not made for store,   9
Harsh, featureless, and rude, barrenly perish;   10

Look whom she best endowed she gave the more,   11
Which bounteous gift thou shouldst in bounty cherish.
   She carved thee for her seal, and meant thereby   13
   Thou shouldst print more, not let that copy die.

12

When I do count the clock that tells the time,   1
And see the brave day sunk in hideous night;   2
When I behold the violet past prime,
And sable curls all silvered o'er with white;   4
When lofty trees I see barren of leaves
Which erst from heat did canopy the herd,   6
And summer's green, all girded up in sheaves,   7
Borne on the bier with white and bristly beard,   8
Then of thy beauty do I question make   9
That thou among the wastes of time must go,
Since sweets and beauties do themselves forsake
And die as fast as they see others grow;
   And nothing 'gainst Time's scythe can make defense
   Save breed, to brave him when he takes thee hence.   14

13

Oh, that you were yourself! But, love, you are   1
No longer yours than you yourself here live.   2
Against this coming end you should prepare,   3
And your sweet semblance to some other give.
So should that beauty which you hold in lease
Find no determination; then you were   6
Yourself again after yourself's decease,
When your sweet issue your sweet form should bear.
Who lets so fair a house fall to decay,
Which husbandry in honor might uphold   10
Against the stormy gusts of winter's day
And barren rage of death's eternal cold?
   Oh, none but unthrifts! Dear my love, you know
   You had a father; let your son say so.

14

Not from the stars do I my judgment pluck,   1
And yet methinks I have astronomy—   2
But not to tell of good or evil luck,
Of plagues, of dearths, or seasons' quality;   4
Nor can I fortune to brief minutes tell,   5
'Pointing to each his thunder, rain, and wind,   6

9.1 Is . . . eye Is it for fear of eventually leaving some woman a grieving widow when you die **3 issueless** without offspring **4 makeless** mateless, widowed **5 still** constantly, always **7 private** individual, as distinguished from the whole world **8 By** by means of **9 Look what** Whatever. **unthrift** spendthrift **10 his** its. **enjoys** uses, keeps in circulation **12 user** i.e., he who should use it. (With a suggestion of a *usurer* who is miserly.)
10.6 thou stick'st you scruple **7 that . . . roof** i.e., your aristocratic family **9 thought** intention. **my mind** my opinion. **11 presence** appearance, bearing
11.1–2 thou grow'st . . . departest i.e., you survive in a child of your own, though you leave the world behind **3 youngly** in youth **4 thou . . . convertest** you change from youth (to old age). **7 minded so** sharing your intention (to have no children). **times** succeeding generations **8 year** years **9 for store** for breeding **10 Harsh . . . rude** ugly, lacking attractive features or appearance, and rudely fashioned

11 Look . . . more to whomever Nature endowed with the greatest gifts, she gave even more **13 seal** stamp of authority, stamp from which impressions are made
12.1 tells (1) announces (2) counts **2 brave** splendid **4 sable** black **6 erst** formerly **7 girded** bundled **8 bier** i.e., harvest cart. (But with suggestion of funeral bier.) **beard** i.e., the tufted grain. (But suggesting also a dead man laid out for burial.) **9 do . . . make** I discuss with myself **14 breed** begetting offspring. **brave him** defy Time **13.1 yourself** i.e., your eternal self, not vulnerable to Time's decay. **2 here** i.e., here on earth **3 Against** In anticipation of **6 determination** end **10 husbandry** careful management. (With a pun on "being a husband.")
14.1 my judgment pluck derive my conclusions **2 have astronomy** am skilled in astrology **4 seasons' quality** what the weather of the seasons will be like **5 fortune . . . tell** foretell events to the precise minute **6 'Pointing** appointing, assigning. **each** each minute. **his** its

Or say with princes if it shall go well   7
By oft predict that I in heaven find.   8
But from thine eyes my knowledge I derive,
And, constant stars, in them I read such art   10
As truth and beauty shall together thrive   11
If from thyself to store thou wouldst convert.   12
  Or else of thee this I prognosticate:
  Thy end is truth's and beauty's doom and date.   14

15

When I consider every thing that grows
Holds in perfection but a little moment,
That this huge stage presenteth naught but shows   2
Whereon the stars in secret influence comment;   3
When I perceive that men as plants increase,   5
Cheerèd and checked even by the selfsame sky,   6
Vaunt in their youthful sap, at height decrease,   7
And wear their brave state out of memory;   8
Then the conceit of this inconstant stay   9
Sets you most rich in youth before my sight,
Where wasteful Time debateth with Decay   11
To change your day of youth to sullied night;
  And, all in war with Time for love of you,   13
  As he takes from you I engraft you new.   14

16

But wherefore do not you a mightier way
Make war upon this bloody tyrant, Time,
And fortify yourself in your decay
With means more blessèd than my barren rhyme?   4
Now stand you on the top of happy hours,
And many maiden gardens yet unset   6
With virtuous wish would bear your living flowers,   7
Much liker than your painted counterfeit.   8
So should the lines of life that life repair   9
Which this time's pencil, or my pupil pen,   10
Neither in inward worth nor outward fair   11
Can make you live yourself in eyes of men.   12
  To give away yourself keeps yourself still,   13
  And you must live, drawn by your own sweet skill. 14

17

Who will believe my verse in time to come
If it were filled with your most high deserts?
Though yet, heaven knows, it is but as a tomb   3
Which hides your life and shows not half your parts.   4
If I could write the beauty of your eyes
And in fresh numbers number all your graces,   6
The age to come would say, "This poet lies;
Such heavenly touches ne'er touched earthly faces."
So should my papers, yellowed with their age,
Be scorned like old men of less truth than tongue,   10
And your true rights be termed a poet's rage   11
And stretchèd meter of an antique song.   12
  But were some child of yours alive that time,
  You should live twice, in it and in my rhyme.

18

Shall I compare thee to a summer's day?
Thou art more lovely and more temperate.
Rough winds do shake the darling buds of May,
And summer's lease hath all too short a date.   4
Sometime too hot the eye of heaven shines,   5
And often is his gold complexion dimmed;
And every fair from fair sometimes declines,   7
By chance or nature's changing course untrimmed.   8
But thy eternal summer shall not fade
Nor lose possession of that fair thou ow'st;   10
Nor shall Death brag thou wand'r'st in his shade,
When in eternal lines to time thou grow'st.   12
  So long as men can breathe or eyes can see,
  So long lives this, and this gives life to thee.   14

19

Devouring Time, blunt thou the lion's paws,
And make the earth devour her own sweet brood;
Pluck the keen teeth from the fierce tiger's jaws,
And burn the long-lived phoenix in her blood;   4
Make glad and sorry seasons as thou fleet'st,   5
And do whate'er thou wilt, swift-footed Time,
To the wide world and all her fading sweets.
But I forbid thee one most heinous crime:
Oh, carve not with thy hours my love's fair brow,
Nor draw no lines there with thine antique pen;   10
Him in thy course untainted do allow   11
For beauty's pattern to succeeding men.

---

7 Or . . . well or say if things will go well for certain rulers   **8 oft predict** frequent predictions   **10–11 read . . . As** gather such learning as, in effect, that   **12 store** replenishment (through the begetting of children). **convert** turn.   **14 doom and date** limit of duration, destruction.
15.2 Holds in perfection maintains its prime   **3 stage** i.e., the world   **5 as** like   **6 Cheerèd and checked** (1) urged on, nourished, and held back, starved (2) applauded and hissed   **7 Vaunt** boast, exult.   **sap** vigor.   **at height decrease** i.e., no sooner reach full maturity but they (humans) start to decline   **8 brave** splendid.   **out of memory** until forgotten   **9 conceit** notion.   **inconstant stay** mutable brief time (on earth)   **11 debateth** competes   **13 all in war** I, fighting with might and main   **14 engraft you new** renew you by grafting, infusing new life into you (by means of my verse).
16.4 barren (1) unable to produce offspring (2) poetically sterile   **6 unset** (1) unplanted (2) unimpregnated   **7 virtuous wish** desire that is still chaste   **8 liker** more resembling you.   **painted** rendered by art (including poetry), artificial.   **counterfeit** portrait.   **9 lines of life** lineage, i.e., children (whose lineaments are more lifelike than lines of verse or of a portrait)   **10 this time's pencil** a portraiture done in this present age. **pupil** apprenticed, inexpert   **11 fair** beauty   **12 live** survive as   **13 give away yourself** i.e., marry and beget children.   **keeps** preserves   **14 skill** i.e., artistry in reproducing yourself, mightier than the poet's pen.

17.3 yet as yet   **4 parts** qualities.   **6 numbers** verses   **10 of . . . tongue** more garrulous than truthful   **11 rage** exaggerated inspiration   **12 stretchèd meter** overstrained poetry, poetic license
18.4 lease allotted time.   **date** duration.   **5 eye** i.e., sun   **7 fair from fair** beautiful thing from beauty   **8 untrimmed** stripped of ornament and beauty.   **10 fair thou ow'st** beauty you own   **12 lines** i.e., of poetry.   **to . . . grow'st** you become incorporated into time, engrafted upon it.   **14 this** i.e., this sonnet
19.4 phoenix legendary bird reputed to live for hundreds of years and then to be consumed alive (*in her blood*) in its own ashes, from which it is then reborn   **5 sorry** i.e., miserable, uncomfortable.   **thou fleet'st** you fleet, hurry   **10 antique** (1) old (2) antic, capricious, fantastic   **11 untainted** unsullied; uninjured

Yet, do thy worst, old Time. Despite thy wrong,
My love shall in my verse ever live young. 14

20

A woman's face with Nature's own hand painted 1
Hast thou, the master-mistress of my passion; 2
A woman's gentle heart, but not acquainted
With shifting change, as is false women's fashion; 4
An eye more bright than theirs, less false in rolling, 5
Gilding the object whereupon it gazeth; 6
A man in hue, all hues in his controlling, 7
Which steals men's eyes and women's souls amazeth.
And for a woman wert thou first created,
Till Nature, as she wrought thee, fell a-doting, 10
And by addition me of thee defeated, 11
By adding one thing to my purpose nothing. 12
    But since she pricked thee out for women's pleasure, 13
    Mine be thy love and thy love's use their treasure. 14

21

So is it not with me as with that muse, 1
Stirred by a painted beauty to his verse, 2
Who heaven itself for ornament doth use 3
And every fair with his fair doth rehearse, 4
Making a couplement of proud compare 5
With sun and moon, with earth and sea's rich gems,
With April's firstborn flowers, and all things rare
That heaven's air in this huge rondure hems. 8
Oh, let me, true in love, but truly write,
And then, believe me, my love is as fair
As any mother's child, though not so bright
As those gold candles fixed in heaven's air. 12
    Let them say more that like of hearsay well; 13
    I will not praise that purpose not to sell. 14

22

My glass shall not persuade me I am old 1
So long as youth and thou are of one date; 2
But when in thee Time's furrows I behold,
Then look I death my days should expiate. 4
For all that beauty that doth cover thee 5
Is but the seemly raiment of my heart, 6
Which in thy breast doth live, as thine in me. 7
How can I then be elder than thou art?
Oh, therefore, love, be of thyself so wary
As I, not for myself, but for thee will, 10
Bearing thy heart, which I will keep so chary 11
As tender nurse her babe from faring ill.
    Presume not on thy heart when mine is slain; 13
    Thou gav'st me thine, not to give back again.

23

As an unperfect actor on the stage 1
Who with his fear is put beside his part, 2
Or some fierce thing replete with too much rage, 3
Whose strength's abundance weakens his own heart, 4
So I, for fear of trust, forget to say 5
The perfect ceremony of love's rite,
And in mine own love's strength seem to decay,
O'ercharged with burden of mine own love's might.
Oh, let my books be then the eloquence 9
And dumb presagers of my speaking breast, 10
Who plead for love and look for recompense
More than that tongue that more hath more expressed. 12
    Oh, learn to read what silent love hath writ.
    To hear with eyes belongs to love's fine wit. 14

24

Mine eye hath played the painter and hath stelled 1
Thy beauty's form in table of my heart; 2
My body is the frame wherein 'tis held, 3
And perspective it is best painter's art. 4
For through the painter must you see his skill 5

14 My love (1) my beloved (2) my affection for him
20.1 with . . . hand i.e., naturally beautiful   **2 master-mistress** i.e.,
both master and mistress, male and female.   **passion** love   **4 as . . .
fashion** as is the way with women, who are false by nature
5 rolling i.e., roving   **6 Gilding** causing to shine brightly   **7 A man
. . . controlling** one who has a manly appearance surpassing all other
forms. (Suggesting, too, that he captivates all beholders and that his
hue is womanly as well as manly.)   **10 fell a-doting** fell infatuatedly
in love with you and so went mildly crazy   **11 defeated** defrauded,
deprived   **12 to my purpose nothing** out of line with my wishes
13 pricked designated. (With bawdy suggestion; the *thing* in line 12
is a phallus.)   **for women's pleasure** to give (sexual) pleasure to
women   **14 Mine . . . treasure** I will have your love in the truest
sense, while women will enjoy you sexually and bear you children.
(Expressed as a metaphor of financial capital or principal, which
belongs to the poet, versus the *use* or interest, which belongs to
women.)
21.1 muse i.e., poet   **2 Stirred** inspired.   **painted** artificial, created
by cosmetics   **3 Who . . . use** who does not scruple to invoke heaven
itself as an ornament of praise for his mistress   **4 every . . . rehearse**
compares his lady fair with every lovely thing   **5 Making . . . compare** joining (her) in proud comparison   **8 rondure** sphere.   **hems**
encloses, encircles.   **12 gold candles** i.e., stars. (The trite and exaggerated metaphor is of the sort the poet hopes to eschew.)   **13 like . . .
well** like to deal in secondhand or trite expressions   **14 I will . . . sell**
I, who do not intend to sell as a merchant might, will accordingly not
indulge in extravagant and empty praise.

22.1 glass mirror   **2 of one date** of an age, i.e., young   **4 look I** I
foresee that.   **expiate** end.   **5–7 For . . . me** Since my heart dwells in
your breast (and yours in me), your beauty is in effect a becoming
cover for my heart.   **10 will** i.e., will take wary care of myself for
your sake   **11 Bearing** since I bear.   **chary** carefully   **13 Presume . . .
slain** Do not expect to receive back your heart when mine is slain (as
would happen if you were to stop loving me)
23.1 unperfect one who has not learned his lines sufficiently   **2 is . . .
part** forgets his lines   **3 Or . . . rage** i.e., or some wild creature over-
filled with ungovernable rage   **4 Whose . . . heart** whose excess of
emotion collapses on itself   **5 for . . . trust** mistrusting myself and
fearful of not being trusted.   **forget** forget how   **9 books** (Possibly
refers to the sonnets or to *Venus and Adonis* and *The Rape of Lucrece* or,
more generally, the works of the persona poet.)   **10 dumb presagers**
silent messengers or presenters   **12 that tongue** the tongue of some
rival speaker.   **more hath more expressed** has more often or more
fully said more.   **14 fine wit** sharp intelligence.
24.1 played acted the part of.   **stelled** fixed, installed; or perhaps steeled,
i.e., engraved. (The Quarto reads "steeld.")   **2 table** tablet, wooden panel
used for painting   **3 frame** (1) picture frame (2) bodily frame   **4 perspective** an artist's method of producing a distorted picture that looks
right only from an oblique point of view; or, a painter's technique used
to produce the illusion of reality; or, the science of optics   **5 For . . .
skill** i.e., You must look through the eyes of me, the skillful painter

To find where your true image pictured lies,
Which in my bosom's shop is hanging still,
That hath his windows glazèd with thine eyes.   7
Now see what good turns eyes for eyes have done: 8
Mine eyes have drawn thy shape, and thine for me
Are windows to my breast, wherethrough the sun
Delights to peep, to gaze therein on thee.
    Yet eyes this cunning want to grace their art: 13
    They draw but what they see, know not the heart. 14

25

Let those who are in favor with their stars
Of public honor and proud titles boast,
Whilst I, whom fortune of such triumph bars,   3
Unlooked for joy in that I honor most.   4
Great princes' favorites their fair leaves spread   5
But as the marigold at the sun's eye,   6
And in themselves their pride lies burièd,   7
For at a frown they in their glory die.   8
The painful warrior famousèd for fight,   9
After a thousand victories once foiled,
Is from the book of honor rasèd quite,   11
And all the rest forgot for which he toiled.   12
    Then happy I, that love and am beloved
    Where I may not remove nor be removed.   14

26

Lord of my love, to whom in vassalage
Thy merit hath my duty strongly knit,
To thee I send this written embassage
To witness duty, not to show my wit—   4
Duty so great, which wit so poor as mine   5
May make seem bare, in wanting words to show it,   6
But that I hope some good conceit of thine   7
In thy soul's thought, all naked, will bestow it;   8
Till whatsoever star that guides my moving   9
Points on me graciously with fair aspect,   10
And puts apparel on my tattered loving
To show me worthy of thy sweet respect.
    Then may I dare to boast how I do love thee;
    Till then not show my head where thou mayst prove   14
      me.

27

Weary with toil, I haste me to my bed,
The dear repose for limbs with travel tirèd;   2
But then begins a journey in my head,
To work my mind when body's work's expirèd.
For then my thoughts, from far where I abide,   5
Intend a zealous pilgrimage to thee,   6
And keep my drooping eyelids open wide,
Looking on darkness which the blind do see;   8
Save that my soul's imaginary sight   9
Presents thy shadow to my sightless view,   10
Which, like a jewel hung in ghastly night,
Makes black night beauteous and her old face new.
    Lo, thus by day my limbs, by night my mind,
    For thee and for myself no quiet find.   14

28

How can I then return in happy plight
That am debarred the benefit of rest?
When day's oppression is not eased by night,
But day by night, and night by day, oppressed?   4
And each, though enemies to either's reign,
Do in consent shake hands to torture me,   6
The one by toil, the other to complain   7
How far I toil, still farther off from thee.
I tell the day, to please him, thou art bright
And dost him grace when clouds do blot the heaven;   10
So flatter I the swart-complexioned night,   11
When sparkling stars twire not, thou gild'st th' even. 12
    But day doth daily draw my sorrows longer,
    And night doth nightly make grief's strength seem
      stronger.

29

When, in disgrace with fortune and men's eyes,
I all alone beweep my outcast state,
And trouble deaf heaven with my bootless cries,   3
And look upon myself and curse my fate,   4
Wishing me like to one more rich in hope,   5
Featured like him, like him with friends possessed,   6
Desiring this man's art and that man's scope,   7

---

7 bosom's shop i.e., heart   **8 his** its.   **glazèd** fitted with glass, paned. (The friend, looking into the poet's eyes where his own eyes are reflected, sees into the poet's heart.)   **13 this cunning want** lack this skill.   **grace** enhance   **14 know not** do not perceive the thoughts of   **25.3 of** from   **4 Unlooked for** (1) unexpectedly (2) out of the public eye.   **that** that which   **5 their . . . spread** i.e., flourish, blossom, prosper   **6 But** only   **7 lies burièd** i.e., will die with the ending of their brief glory   **8 a frown** (1) a prince's frown (2) a cloud obscuring the sun   **9 painful** enduring much, striving.   **famousèd** renowned.   **fight** (Reads "worth" in the 1609 Quarto; some editors retain and emend "quite" in line 11 to "forth." Other editors prefer "might.")   **11 rasèd** erased (or *razèd*, scraped out)   **12 the rest** i.e., his *thousand victories*   **14 remove** i.e., be unfaithful.   **removed** i.e., removed from favor.
26.1 vassalage allegiance   **4 witness** bear witness to.   **wit** skill, literary ingenuity   **5 wit** intelligence and skill   **6 wanting** lacking   **7 good conceit** good conception, favorable opinion   **8 all naked** i.e., poor verse though it is.   **bestow** give lodging to   **9 moving** life and deeds   **10 Points on** directs its rays at.   **aspect** influence (as of a star)   **14 prove** test

27.2 travel (With connotation also of *travail*; spelled "trauaill" in the Quarto.)   **5 from far** i.e., far away from you   **6 Intend** (1) set out upon (2) have purposefully in mind   **8 Looking . . . see** while my thoughts try to peer (toward you) through the darkness, like the blind, who see only darkness   **9 Save** except   **10 thy shadow** the image of you   **14 For** on account of
28.4 But . . . oppressed i.e., but experiencing sleeplessness at night and fatigue during the day.   **6 in . . . hands** i.e., come to a mutual agreement   **7 the other to complain** i.e., the night by causing me to complain   **10 And . . . heaven** i.e., and that you shine in place of the sun when the sun is overclouded   **11 So flatter I** similarly I gratify.   **swart** dark   **12 When . . . even** i.e., by saying that, when sparkling stars do not twinkle or peep out, you make bright the evening.
29.3 bootless useless   **4 look upon myself** consider my predicament   **5 more rich in hope** with better prospects of success   **6 Featured** formed, i.e., having good looks.   **like him, like him** like a second man, like a third   **7 art** literary skill, learning.   **scope** range of powers

With what I most enjoy contented least;   8
Yet in these thoughts myself almost despising,
Haply I think on thee, and then my state,   10
Like to the lark at break of day arising
From sullen earth, sings hymns at heaven's gate;
    For thy sweet love remembered such wealth brings
    That then I scorn to change my state with kings.   14

30

When to the sessions of sweet silent thought   1
I summon up remembrance of things past,
I sigh the lack of many a thing I sought,   3
And with old woes new wail my dear time's waste.   4
Then can I drown an eye, unused to flow,   5
For precious friends hid in death's dateless night,   6
And weep afresh love's long-since-canceled woe,   7
And moan th'expense of many a vanished sight.   8
Then can I grieve at grievances foregone,   9
And heavily from woe to woe tell o'er   10
The sad account of fore-bemoanèd moan,   11
Which I new pay as if not paid before.
    But if the while I think on thee, dear friend,
    All losses are restored and sorrows end.

31

Thy bosom is endearèd with all hearts   1
Which I by lacking have supposèd dead,   2
And there reigns love and all love's loving parts,   3
And all those friends which I thought burièd.
How many a holy and obsequious tear   5
Hath dear religious love stol'n from mine eye   6
As interest of the dead, which now appear   7
But things removed that hidden in thee lie!   8
Thou art the grave where buried love doth live,
Hung with the trophies of my lovers gone,   10
Who all their parts of me to thee did give;   11
That due of many now is thine alone.   12
    Their images I loved I view in thee,   13
    And thou, all they, hast all the all of me.   14

32

If thou survive my well-contented day   1
When that churl Death my bones with dust shall cover,
And shalt by fortune once more re-survey   3
These poor rude lines of thy deceasèd lover,   4
Compare them with the bett'ring of the time,   5
And though they be outstripped by every pen,
Reserve them for my love, not for their rhyme,   7
Exceeded by the height of happier men.   8
Oh, then vouchsafe me but this loving thought: 9
"Had my friend's Muse grown with this growing age,
A dearer birth than this his love had brought   11
To march in ranks of better equipage;   12
    But since he died and poets better prove,   13
    Theirs for their style I'll read, his for his love."

33

Full many a glorious morning have I seen   1
Flatter the mountaintops with sovereign eye,   2
Kissing with golden face the meadows green,
Gilding pale streams with heavenly alchemy;
Anon permit the basest clouds to ride   5
With ugly rack on his celestial face,   6
And from the forlorn world his visage hide,
Stealing unseen to west with this disgrace.
Even so my sun one early morn did shine
With all-triumphant splendor on my brow.
But out, alack! He was but one hour mine;   11
The region cloud hath masked him from me now.   12
    Yet him for this my love no whit disdaineth;
    Suns of the world may stain when heaven's sun   14
      staineth.

34

Why didst thou promise such a beauteous day
And make me travel forth without my cloak,
To let base clouds o'ertake me in my way,   3
Hiding thy brav'ry in their rotten smoke?   4
'Tis not enough that through the cloud thou break,
To dry the rain on my storm-beaten face,
For no man well of such a salve can speak
That heals the wound and cures not the disgrace.   8

---

8 **most enjoy** possess most securely and take greatest pleasure in
10 **Haply** perchance; happily.   **state** state of mind. (Suggesting also
"fortunes.")   14 **change** exchange
30.1 **sessions** (The metaphor is that of a court of law, continued in
summon up, line 2.)   3 **sigh** sigh for   4 **new ... waste** lament anew
the wasting of precious time or time's erosion of those things held
precious.   5 **unused to flow** not prone to weep   6 **dateless** endless
7 **canceled** paid in full (by grieving)   8 **th'expense** the loss, expenditure   9 **grievances foregone** sorrows past   10 **heavily** sadly.   **tell**
count   11 **account** (1) narrative (2) financial reckoning.   **fore-
bemoanèd moan** previously uttered laments
31.1 **endearèd with all hearts** (1) beloved by all (2) made dear to me
by representing and including those I have loved   2 **lacking** not having   3 **parts** attributes   5 **obsequious** suitable to mourning   6 **religious** dutiful, reverent   7 **interest of** that which is rightfully due to.
which who   8 **But ... lie** i.e., no more than absent persons (now
dead), whose best qualities are to be found buried in you.
10 **Hung ... gone** festooned with symbolic memorials of my past triumphs in being loved by many   11 **parts** shares   12 **That due of
many** that which was both owed by, and paid to, many   13 **I loved**
which I loved   14 **all they** (you) who comprise all of them

32.1 **my ... day** i.e., the day of my death, which will content me well
3 **And ... fortune** and if by chance you happen   4 **rude** unpolished.
lover friend   5 **bett'ring** i.e., improved writing, greater cultural
sophistication   7 **Reserve** preserve.   **for my love** (1) out of love for
me (2) for the sake of my love for you.   **rhyme** i.e., poetic skill
8 **height** superiority, highest achievement.   **happier** more gifted or
fortunate   9 **vouchsafe me but** deign to bestow on me just   11 **dearer
birth** i.e., better poem, better artistic creation   12 **better equipage** i.e.,
more finely wrought verse   13 **better prove** turn out to be superior
33.1 **Full** Very   2 **sovereign eye** i.e., morning sunlight   5 **Anon** soon
afterward.   **basest** darkest   6 **rack** mass of cloud scudding before
the wind   11 **out, alack!** (An expression of dismay.)   12 **region** of the
upper air   14 **Suns** i.e., great men. (With a pun on *sons of the world*,
"mortal men.")   **stain** grow dim, be obscured, soiled.   **staineth** is
clouded over.
34.3 **To** only to   4 **brav'ry** finery.   **rotten smoke** foul vapors.   8 **disgrace** i.e., the scar, the disfigurement caused by his friend's neglect or
harsh treatment; the *loss* main mentioned in line 10.

Nor can thy shame give physic to my grief;   9
Though thou repent, yet I have still the loss.
Th'offender's sorrow lends but weak relief
To him that bears the strong offense's cross.   12
    Ah, but those tears are pearl which thy love sheds,
    And they are rich, and ransom all ill deeds.   14

35

No more be grieved at that which thou hast done.
Roses have thorns, and silver fountains mud,
Clouds and eclipses stain both moon and sun,   3
And loathsome canker lives in sweetest bud.   4
All men make faults, and even I in this,
Authorizing thy trespass with compare,   6
Myself corrupting, salving thy amiss,   7
Excusing thy sins more than thy sins are.   8
For to thy sensual fault I bring in sense—   9
Thy adverse party is thy advocate—   10
And 'gainst myself a lawful plea commence.
Such civil war is in my love and hate
    That I an accessary needs must be   13
    To that sweet thief which sourly robs from me.

36

Let me confess that we two must be twain,   1
Although our undivided loves are one;
So shall those blots that do with me remain,   3
Without thy help, by me be borne alone.
In our two loves there is but one respect,   5
Though in our lives a separable spite,   6
Which, though it alter not love's sole effect,   7
Yet doth it steal sweet hours from love's delight.
I may not evermore acknowledge thee,   9
Lest my bewailèd guilt should do thee shame,
Nor thou with public kindness honor me
Unless thou take that honor from thy name.   12
    But do not so; I love thee in such sort   13
    As, thou being mine, mine is thy good report.   14

37

As a decrepit father takes delight
To see his active child do deeds of youth,

So I, made lame by Fortune's dearest spite,   3
Take all my comfort of thy worth and truth.   4
For whether beauty, birth, or wealth, or wit,   5
Or any of these all, or all, or more,
Entitled in thy parts do crownèd sit,   7
I make my love engrafted to this store.   8
So then I am not lame, poor, nor despised,
Whilst that this shadow doth such substance give   10
That I in thy abundance am sufficed
And by a part of all thy glory live.
    Look what is best, that best I wish in thee.   13
    This wish I have; then ten times happy me!

38

How can my Muse want subject to invent   1
While thou dost breathe, that pour'st into my verse   2
Thine own sweet argument, too excellent   3
For every vulgar paper to rehearse?   4
Oh, give thyself the thanks, if aught in me   5
Worthy perusal stand against thy sight,   6
For who's so dumb that cannot write to thee,   7
When thou thyself dost give invention light?   8
Be thou the tenth Muse, ten times more in worth
Than those old nine which rhymers invoke;
And he that calls on thee, let him bring forth
Eternal numbers to outlive long date.   12
    If my slight Muse do please these curious days,   13
    The pain be mine, but thine shall be the praise.   14

39

Oh, how thy worth with manners may I sing,   1
When thou art all the better part of me?
What can mine own praise to mine own self bring?   3
And what is't but mine own when I praise thee?   4
Even for this let us divided live,   5
And our dear love lose name of single one,
That by this separation I may give
That due to thee which thou deserv'st alone.
O absence, what a torment wouldst thou prove,
Were it not thy sour leisure gave sweet leave   10
To entertain the time with thoughts of love,   11
Which time and thoughts so sweetly doth deceive,   12

---

9 **shame** repentance for the wrong done.   **physic** remedy   **12 cross** affliction.   **14 ransom** atone for
35.3 **stain** dim, obscure   **4 canker** cankerworm   **6 Authorizing** sanctioning, justifying.   **compare** comparisons (as in this sonnet)
7 **Myself . . . amiss** excusing your misdeed, thereby bringing blame on myself   **8 Excusing . . . are** going further to excuse your sins than they warrant, or, excusing you for even worse sins than you have actually committed.   **9 For . . . sense** I reason away your fleshly offenses   **10 Thy . . . advocate** I who profess to be your accuser find myself, instead, pleading your case   **13 That . . . be** that I am compelled (by my love) to be a guilty accomplice
36.1 **twain** parted   **3 blots** defects, stains of dishonor   **5 but one respect** a mutual regard, singleness of attitude   **6 separable spite** vexing separation   **7 sole effect** unique effect (of making the two of us into one)   **9 not evermore acknowledge** nevermore admit my acquaintance with   **12 Unless . . . from** without consequent loss of honor to   **13 in such sort** in such a way   **14 As . . . report** that since you are mine, your good reputation sustains me also.

37.3 **made lame** handicapped in life.   **dearest** most bitter   **4 of** in, from   **5 wit** intelligence   **7 Entitled . . . sit** sit enthroned among your qualities   **8 I make . . . store** I add my love to this abundance (and thereby flourish by drawing on their strength).   **10 shadow** idea (in the platonic sense).   **substance** actuality   **13 Look what** Whatever
38.1 **want . . . invent** lack something to write about   **2 that** you who   **3 Thine . . . argument** yourself as subject   **4 vulgar paper** common piece of writing.   **rehearse** recite, repeat.   **5–6 if . . . sight** if any of my writing strikes you as worthy of perusal   **7 dumb** silent, lacking in subject   **8 When . . . light** when you bring such a light of invention to yourself as poetic subject.   **12 numbers** verses.   **long date** even a very distant limit in time.   **13 curious** finicky   **14 pain** labor
39.1 **with manners** decently, becomingly   **3–4 What . . . thee?** i.e., Since my better self is entirely yours, what can I gain from praising you but a kind of vainglorious self-praise?   **5 Even for** Precisely because of   **10 not** not that   **11 entertain** pass, occupy   **12 Which . . . deceive** (thoughts of love), which sweetly beguile away time and (sad) thoughts

And that thou teachest how to make one twain
By praising him here who doth hence remain!   14

40

Take all my loves, my love, yea, take them all;   1
What hast thou then more than thou hadst before?
No love, my love, that thou mayst true love call;   3
All mine was thine before thou hadst this more.
Then if for my love thou my love receivest,   5
I cannot blame thee for my love thou usest;   6
But yet be blamed if thou this self deceivest   7
By willful taste of what thyself refusest.   8
I do forgive thy robb'ry, gentle thief,
Although thou steal thee all my poverty;   10
And yet love knows it is a greater grief
To bear love's wrong than hate's known injury.   12
    Lascivious grace, in whom all ill well shows,   13
    Kill me with spites; yet we must not be foes.

41

Those pretty wrongs that liberty commits   1
When I am sometime absent from thy heart,
Thy beauty and thy years full well befits,   3
For still temptation follows where thou art.   4
Gentle thou art, and therefore to be won;
Beauteous thou art, therefore to be assailed;
And when a woman woos, what woman's son   7
Will sourly leave her till he have prevailed?   8
Ay me, but yet thou mightst my seat forbear,   9
And chide thy beauty and thy straying youth,
Who lead thee in their riot even there   11
Where thou art forced to break a twofold truth: 12
    Hers, by thy beauty tempting her to thee,
    Thine, by thy beauty being false to me.

42

That thou hast her, it is not all my grief,
And yet it may be said I loved her dearly;
That she hath thee is of my wailing chief,
A loss in love that touches me more nearly.   3
Loving offenders, thus I will excuse ye:

Thou dost love her because thou know'st I love her,
And for my sake even so doth she abuse me,   7
Suff'ring my friend for my sake to approve her.   8
If I lose thee, my loss is my love's gain,   9
And, losing her, my friend hath found that loss;   10
Both find each other, and I lose both twain,
And both for my sake lay on me this cross.   12
    But here's the joy: my friend and I are one.
    Sweet flattery! Then she loves but me alone.   14

43

When most I wink, then do mine eyes best see,   1
For all the day they view things unrespected;   2
But when I sleep, in dreams they look on thee,
And, darkly bright, are bright in dark directed.   4
Then thou, whose shadow shadows doth make bright,   5
How would thy shadow's form form happy show   6
To the clear day with thy much clearer light,
When to unseeing eyes thy shade shines so!   8
How would, I say, mine eyes be blessèd made
By looking on thee in the living day,
When in dead night thy fair imperfect shade   11
Through heavy sleep on sightless eyes doth stay!   12
    All days are nights to see till I see thee,   13
    And nights bright days when dreams do show thee   14
    me.

44

If the dull substance of my flesh were thought,   1
Injurious distance should not stop my way;
For then despite of space I would be brought,
From limits far remote, where thou dost stay.   4
No matter then although my foot did stand
Upon the farthest earth removed from thee;   6
For nimble thought can jump both sea and land
As soon as think the place where he would be.   8
But, ah, thought kills me that I am not thought,   9
To leap large lengths of miles when thou art gone,
But that, so much of earth and water wrought,   11
I must attend time's leisure with my moan,   12

---

14 **here** (1) here where I am (2) here in this poem
40.1 all my loves (1) all those whom I love (2) all the love I have. (The young man addressed has taken away the poet's mistress.) **3 No . . . call** i.e., Any love more than you had already—my complete affection—cannot be called true love **5 my love . . . my love** love of me . . . her whom I love **6 for** because. **thou usest** you enjoy (sexually) **7 this self** i.e., me, your other self. (Often emended to "thyself.") **8 By . . . refusest** i.e., by tasting sexual pleasures that your best self would refuse. **10 steal . . . poverty** take for your own the poor little that I have **12 To . . . injury** to endure injuries arising out of a loving relationship than those stemming from calculated hatred. **13 Lascivious grace** i.e., You who are gracious even in your lasciviousness
41.1 pretty graciously committed, sportive. **liberty** licentiousness **3 befits** (The subject is *wrongs*, line 1.) **4 still** constantly **7–8 And . . . prevailed** i.e., When a woman woos, what man can resist until he has scored? (*He* is sometimes emended to "she.") **9 seat** place, that which belongs to me (i.e., my mistress) **11 Who** which. **riot** debauchery **12 twofold truth** i.e., her plighted love to me and your plighted friendship to me
42.3 is . . . chief is chief cause of my lamentation

7 abuse betray, wrong **8 Suff'ring** allowing. **approve** try, test (in a sexual sense) **9 my love's** hers whom I love, my mistress's **10 losing her** i.e., I losing her **12 for my sake** as though out of love for me. **cross** torment. **14 flattery** gratifying deception.
43.1 wink close my eyes in sleep **2 unrespected** unnoticed, unregarded; not deserving notice **4 And . . . directed** and, able to see in the darkness (though still shut), are directed toward your brightness in the dark. **5 whose . . . bright** whose image makes darkness bright **6 thy shadow's . . . show** the substance of the shadow, i.e., your presence, make a gladdening sight **8 unseeing eyes** i.e., closed eyes of the dreamer **11 imperfect** unsubstantial, indistinct as in a dream **12 stay** linger, dwell. **13 All . . . to see** All days are gloomy to behold **14 thee me** you to me. (But also suggesting "me to you.")
44.1 dull heavy **4 limits** regions, bounds. **where** to the place where **6 farthest earth removed** that part of the earth farthest removed **8 he** thought **9 ah, thought** ah, the thought **11 so . . . wrought** i.e., I, compounded to such an extent of the heavier elements, earth and water. (The lighter elements are fire and air.)
12 attend time's leisure i.e., wait until time has leisure to reunite us

Receiving naught by elements so slow   13
But heavy tears, badges of either's woe.   14

45

The other two, slight air and purging fire,   1
Are both with thee, wherever I abide;
The first my thought, the other my desire,
These present-absent with swift motion slide.   4
For when these quicker elements are gone
In tender embassy of love to thee,
My life, being made of four, with two alone   7
Sinks down to death, oppressed with melancholy;   8
Until life's composition be recured   9
By those swift messengers returned from thee,   10
Who even but now come back again, assured
Of thy fair health, recounting it to me.
　　This told, I joy; but then no longer glad,
　　I send them back again and straight grow sad.   14

46

Mine eye and heart are at a mortal war   1
How to divide the conquest of thy sight;   2
Mine eye my heart thy picture's sight would bar,   3
My heart mine eye the freedom of that right.   4
My heart doth plead that thou in him dost lie—
A closet never pierced with crystal eyes—   6
But the defendant doth that plea deny   7
And says in him thy fair appearance lies.
To 'cide this title is impanelèd   9
A quest of thoughts, all tenants to the heart,   10
And by their verdict is determinèd
The clear eye's moiety and the dear heart's part,   12
　　As thus: mine eye's due is thy outward part,   13
　　And my heart's right thy inward love of heart.

47

Betwixt mine eye and heart a league is took,   1
And each doth good turns now unto the other.
When that mine eye is famished for a look,   3
Or heart in love with sighs himself doth smother,   4

With my love's picture then my eye doth feast   5
And to the painted banquet bids my heart;   6
Another time mine eye is my heart's guest
And in his thoughts of love doth share a part.
So, either by thy picture or my love,
Thyself, away, are present still with me;
For thou no farther than my thoughts canst move,
And I am still with them and they with thee;   12
　　Or, if they sleep, thy picture in my sight
　　Awakes my heart to heart's and eye's delight.

48

How careful was I, when I took my way,   1
Each trifle under truest bars to thrust,   2
That to my use it might unusèd stay   3
From hands of falsehood, in sure wards of trust!   4
But thou, to whom my jewels trifles are,   5
Most worthy comfort, now my greatest grief,   6
Thou best of dearest and mine only care,
Art left the prey of every vulgar thief.   8
Thee have I not locked up in any chest,
Save where thou art not—though I feel thou art—
Within the gentle closure of my breast,
From whence at pleasure thou mayst come and part;   12
　　And even thence thou wilt be stol'n, I fear,
　　For truth proves thievish for a prize so dear.   14

49

Against that time, if ever that time come,   1
When I shall see thee frown on my defects,
Whenas thy love hath cast his utmost sum,   3
Called to that audit by advised respects;   4
Against that time when thou shalt strangely pass   5
And scarcely greet me with that sun, thine eye,
When love, converted from the thing it was,
Shall reasons find of settled gravity—   8
Against that time do I ensconce me here   9
Within the knowledge of mine own desart,   10
And this my hand against myself uprear,   11
To guard the lawful reasons on thy part.   12
　　To leave poor me thou hast the strength of laws,
　　Since why to love I can allege no cause.   14

13 by from　**14 badges** signs, tokens.　**either's** (1) both earth's and water's, because the earth is heavy and the sea is salt and wet like tears (2) both your and my
45.1 other two (i.e., of the four elements discussed in sonnet 44). **slight** insubstantial.　**purging** purifying　**4 present-absent** (1) now here and immediately gone (2) simultaneously both present and absent　**7 two alone** i.e., earth and water　**8 melancholy** a humor thought to be induced by an excess of earth and water　**9 composition** proper balance among the four elements.　**recured** restored
10 swift messengers i.e., fire and air, thought and desire　**14 straight** straightway
46.1 mortal deadly　**2 How . . . sight** how to divide the spoils of war, namely, the sight of you　**3–4 Mine . . . right** my eye wishes to bar my heart from seeing your image (perhaps a painting), and conversely my heart would like to deny my eye the free enjoyment of that right.　**6 closet** (1) small private room (2) cabinet　**7 the defendant** the eye　**9 'cide** decide　**10 quest** inquest, jury　**12 moiety** portion　**13 mine . . . part** i.e., the eye gets the outward appearance of you. (The jury, composed entirely of those who are loyal to the heart, being its *tenants*, awards true love to the heart.)
47.1 a league is took an agreement is reached　**3 When that** When **4 Or heart** or when my heart.　**himself** itself

5 With i.e., on　**6 painted banquet** i.e., visual feast, perhaps an actual picture of the friend　**12 still** constantly
48.1 took my way set out on my journey　**2 truest** most trusty　**3 to my use** for my own use and profit　**3–4 stay . . . falsehood** remain out of the hands of thieves　**5 to** compared to　**6 worthy** valuable. **grief** anxiety, cause of sorrow (i.e., because of your absence and likeliness of being stolen)　**8 vulgar** common　**12 part** depart　**14 truth** i.e., even honesty itself
49.1 Against In anticipation of　**3 Whenas** when.　**cast . . . sum** added up the sum total. (The metaphor is from closing accounts on a dissolution of partnership.)　**4 advised respects** careful consideration **5 strangely** as a stranger　**8 of settled gravity** (1) for a dignified reserve or continued coldness (2) of sufficient weight　**9 ensconce** fortify, shelter　**10 desart** i.e., deserving, such as it is. (This Quarto spelling of desert, "desart," indicates the rhyme with *part*.)　**11 this . . . uprear** I raise my own hand (as a witness) against my own interest **12 To . . . part** i.e., to testify in behalf of the lawful reasons on your side of the case.　**14 Since . . . cause** since I can urge no lawful cause why you should love me.

50

How heavy do I journey on the way,　　　　　　　1
When what I seek, my weary travel's end,　　　　2
Doth teach that ease and that repose to say,　　　3
"Thus far the miles are measured from thy friend!"　4
The beast that bears me, tirèd with my woe,
Plods dully on, to bear that weight in me,
As if by some instinct the wretch did know
His rider loved not speed being made from thee.
The bloody spur cannot provoke him on
That sometimes anger thrusts into his hide,
Which heavily he answers with a groan,
More sharp to me than spurring to his side;
　　For that same groan doth put this in my mind:
　　My grief lies onward and my joy behind.

51

Thus can my love excuse the slow offense　　　　1
Of my dull bearer when from thee I speed:　　　2
From where thou art why should I haste me thence?
Till I return, of posting is no need.　　　　　　　4
Oh, what excuse will my poor beast then find
When swift extremity can seem but slow?　　　　6
Then should I spur, though mounted on the wind;
In wingéd speed no motion shall I know.　　　　8
Then can no horse with my desire keep pace;
Therefore desire, of perfect'st love being made,
Shall neigh—no dull flesh—in his fiery race.　　11
But love, for love, thus shall excuse my jade:　12
　　Since from thee going he went willful slow,
　　Towards thee I'll run, and give him leave to go.　14

52

So am I as the rich whose blessèd key　　　　　1
Can bring him to his sweet up-lockèd treasure,
The which he will not ev'ry hour survey,
For blunting the fine point of seldom pleasure.　4
Therefore are feasts so solemn and so rare,　　5
Since, seldom coming, in the long year set,
Like stones of worth they thinly placèd are,
Or captain jewels in the carcanet.　　　　　　　8
So is the time that keeps you as my chest,　　　9
Or as the wardrobe which the robe doth hide,
To make some special instant special blest

By new unfolding his imprisoned pride.　　　　　12
　　Blessèd are you whose worthiness gives scope,　13
　　Being had, to triumph; being lacked, to hope.　14

53

What is your substance, whereof are you made,
That millions of strange shadows on you tend?　　2
Since everyone hath, every one, one shade,　　　3
And you, but one, can every shadow lend.　　　　4
Describe Adonis, and the counterfeit　　　　　　5
Is poorly imitated after you;
On Helen's cheek all art of beauty set,　　　　　7
And you in Grecian tires are painted new.　　　　8
Speak of the spring and foison of the year;　　　9
The one doth shadow of your beauty show,
The other as your bounty doth appear,
And you in every blessèd shape we know.　　　　12
　　In all external grace you have some part,
　　But you like none, none you, for constant heart.　14

54

Oh, how much more doth beauty beauteous seem
By that sweet ornament which truth doth give!　　2
The rose looks fair, but fairer we it deem
For that sweet odor which doth in it live.
The canker blooms have full as deep a dye　　　5
As the perfumèd tincture of the roses,
Hang on such thorns, and play as wantonly　　　7
When summer's breath their maskèd buds discloses;　8
But, for their virtue only is their show,　　　　9
They live unwooed and unrespected fade,　　　　10
Die to themselves. Sweet roses do not so;　　　11
Of their sweet deaths are sweetest odors made.　12
　　And so of you, beauteous and lovely youth,　　13
　　When that shall vade, by verse distills your truth.　14

55

Not marble nor the gilded monuments
Of princes shall outlive this powerful rhyme,

50.1 heavy sadly and slowly　**2–4 When . . . friend** when the ease and repose I seek at journey's end will merely remind me that I have gone so many miles from my friend.
51.1 slow offense offense consisting in slowness　**2 my dull bearer** i.e., the horse　**4 posting** riding swiftly　**6 swift extremity** extreme swiftness (in returning to you)　**8 In . . . know** even at the speed of flight I won't perceive the motion at all, won't feel as though I'm moving.　**11 Shall . . . race** i.e., shall neigh proudly in its fire-swift race, since it, composed like fire of a lighter element, is not held back by the heavy flesh. (See sonnet 45.)　**12 for love** for love's sake. **jade** nag　**14 go** travel on at his own pace.
52.1 as the rich like the rich man　**4 For . . . pleasure** lest he blunt the delicacy of pleasure sparingly enjoyed.　**5 feasts** feast days.　**solemn** ceremonious, festive.　**rare** excellent; uncommon　**8 captain** principal.　**carcanet** necklace of jewels.　**9 keeps you** (1) watches over you (2) keeps you from me.　**as** like

12 his its.　**pride** splendor, proud treasure.　**13–14 gives . . . hope** gives me opportunity, when you are with me, to rejoice, and when you are away from me, to hope for reunion.
53.2 strange (1) exotic (2) not belonging to you.　**tend** attend. **3 shade** shadow (as cast by the sun)　**4 And . . . lend** and yet you, being only one person, can cast all sorts of shadowy images or reflections (such as Adonis, Helen, etc.).　**5 Adonis** beautiful youth beloved of Venus.　**counterfeit** likeness, portrait　**7–8 On . . . new** set forth the entire art use to beautify the cheek of Helen of Troy, and the result will be a portrait of you in Grecian attire or headdress.
9 foison abundance, i.e., autumn　**12 you . . . know** we recognize you in every beautiful image.　**14 But . . . heart** but in the matter of constancy you resemble no one and no one can resemble you.
54.2 By by means of.　**truth** (1) constancy (2) substance, integrity　**5 canker blooms** dog roses (outwardly attractive but not as sweetly scented as the damask rose).　**dye** tincture　**7 wantonly** sportively　**8 discloses** causes to open　**9 for** because.　**their show** in their appearance　**10 unrespected** unregarded　**11 to themselves** i.e., without profit to others.　**12 Of . . . made** i.e., perfumes are made from the crushed petals of these roses.　**13 of you** (1) distilled from you (2) with regard to you.　**lovely** (1) lovable (2) handsome　**14 When . . . truth** when your physical beauty fades, your true substance will be distilled and preserved by (my) verse. (See sonnet 5.)　**vade** (1) fade (2) go away

But you shall shine more bright in these contents 3
Than unswept stone besmeared with sluttish time. 4
When wasteful war shall statues overturn, 5
And broils root out the work of masonry, 6
Nor Mars his sword nor war's quick fire shall burn 7
The living record of your memory.
'Gainst death and all-oblivious enmity 9
Shall you pace forth; your praise shall still find room
Even in the eyes of all posterity
That wear this world out to the ending doom. 12
    So, till the judgment that yourself arise, 13
    You live in this, and dwell in lovers' eyes.

56

Sweet love, renew thy force! Be it not said 1
Thy edge should blunter be than appetite, 2
Which but today by feeding is allayed, 3
Tomorrow sharpened in his former might. 4
So, love, be thou; although today thou fill
Thy hungry eyes even till they wink with fullness, 6
Tomorrow see again, and do not kill
The spirit of love with a perpetual dullness.
Let this sad interim like the ocean be 9
Which parts the shore where two contracted new 10
Come daily to the banks, that, when they see 11
Return of love, more blest may be the view; 12
    As call it winter, which being full of care 13
    Makes summer's welcome thrice more wished, more
      rare.

57

Being your slave, what should I do but tend 1
Upon the hours and times of your desire?
I have no precious time at all to spend,
Nor services to do, till you require.
Nor dare I chide the world-without-end hour 5
Whilst I, my sovereign, watch the clock for you, 6
Nor think the bitterness of absence sour 7
When you have bid your servant once adieu.
Nor dare I question with my jealous thought 9
Where you may be, or your affairs suppose, 10

But, like a sad slave, stay and think of naught
Save where you are how happy you make those.
    So true a fool is love that in your will, 13
    Though you do anything, he thinks no ill.

58

That god forbid, that made me first your slave,
I should in thought control your times of pleasure,
Or at your hand th'account of hours to crave, 3
Being your vassal, bound to stay your leisure! 4
Oh, let me suffer, being at your beck,
Th'imprisoned absence of your liberty, 6
And, patience-tame to sufferance, bide each check, 7
Without accusing you of injury.
Be where you list, your charter is so strong 9
That you yourself may privilege your time 10
To what you will; to you it doth belong
Yourself to pardon of self-doing crime. 12
    I am to wait, though waiting so be hell, 13
    Not blame your pleasure, be it ill or well.

59

If there be nothing new, but that which is 1
Hath been before, how are our brains beguiled,
Which, laboring for invention, bear amiss 3
The second burden of a former child! 4
Oh, that record could with a backward look, 5
Even of five hundred courses of the sun, 6
Show me your image in some antique book,
Since mind at first in character was done! 8
That I might see what the old world could say
To this composèd wonder of your frame; 10
Whether we are mended, or whe'er better they, 11
Or whether revolution be the same. 12
    Oh, sure I am the wits of former days 13
    To subjects worse have given admiring praise.

60

Like as the waves make towards the pebbled shore, 1
So do our minutes hasten to their end,
Each changing place with that which goes before, 3

55.3 these contents i.e., the contents of my poems written in praise of you   **4 Than unswept stone** than in a memorial stone that has been left unswept, unattended.   **sluttish** neglectful, slovenly, whorish   **5 wasteful** laying waste   **6 broils** uprisings, battles   **7 Nor Mars his sword** Neither Mars's sword (shall destroy)   **9 all-oblivious enmity** oblivion, at enmity with everything   **12 That . . . doom** that will last from now till doomsday. (*That* may refer to *eyes, praise,* or *posterity.*)   **13 till . . . arise** until the Judgment Day, when you will arise from the dead
56.1 love i.e., the spirit of love. (The friend is not directly mentioned in this sonnet.)   **1–2 Be . . . appetite** Let no one attempt to argue that true love should be any less sharp-edged in desire than sexual appetite   **3 but** only for   **4 his** its   **6 wink** shut   **9 sad interim** a period of love's abatement or absence   **10 parts the shore** separates the shores.   **contracted new** newly betrothed   **11 banks** shores
12 love the loved one   **13 As** just as appropriately
57.1 tend attend   **5 world-without-end** interminable   **6 Whilst . . . you** while I count the minutes, my sovereign, waiting for your command   **7 Nor think** nor dare I think   **9 question with** (1) debate with (2) seek to know by means of   **10 suppose** make conjectures about

13 true (1) constant (2) utter.   **in your will** with regard to your desire (with perhaps an allusion to "Will Shakespeare"; "will" is capitalized in the 1609 Quarto, as in sonnet 135)
58.3 th'account . . . crave should crave an accounting of how you spend your time   **4 stay** await   **6 Th'imprisoned . . . liberty** the lack of freedom I suffer in being absent from you, arising from (*of*) your freedom and licentious behavior   **7 And . . . check** and, trained to endure any suffering, let me put up with each rebuke   **9 list** please.   **charter** privilege   **10 privilege** authorize   **12 self-doing** committed by yourself   **13 am to** must
59.1 that everything   **3–4 laboring . . . child** striving to give birth to a new creation, merely miscarry with the repetition of something created before.   **5 record** memory, especially memory preserved in writing   **6 courses . . . sun** years   **8 Since . . . done** since thought was first expressed in writing.   **10 composèd wonder** wonderful composition   **11 mended** improved.   **whe'er** whether   **12 revolution . . . same** the revolving of the ages brings only repetition.   **13 wits** discerning persons; poets
60.1 Like . . . shore Just as waves move up the shingle beach
3 changing place with replacing

In sequent toil all forwards do contend. 4
Nativity, once in the main of light, 5
Crawls to maturity, wherewith being crowned,
Crookèd eclipses 'gainst his glory fight, 7
And Time that gave doth now his gift confound. 8
Time doth transfix the flourish set on youth 9
And delves the parallels in beauty's brow, 10
Feeds on the rarities of nature's truth, 11
And nothing stands but for his scythe to mow. 12
    And yet to times in hope my verse shall stand, 13
    Praising thy worth despite his cruel hand.

61

Is it thy will thy image should keep open
My heavy eyelids to the weary night?
Dost thou desire my slumbers should be broken
While shadows like to thee do mock my sight? 4
Is it thy spirit that thou send'st from thee
So far from home into my deeds to pry,
To find out shames and idle hours in me,
The scope and tenor of thy jealousy? 8
Oh, no, thy love, though much, is not so great;
It is my love that keeps mine eye awake,
Mine own true love that doth my rest defeat,
To play the watchman ever for thy sake.
    For thee watch I whilst thou dost wake elsewhere, 13
    From me far off, with others all too near.

62

Sin of self-love possesseth all mine eye,
And all my soul, and all my every part;
And for this sin there is no remedy,
It is so grounded inward in my heart.
Methinks no face so gracious is as mine, 5
No shape so true, no truth of such account,
And for myself mine own worth do define 7
As I all other in all worths surmount. 8
But when my glass shows me myself indeed, 9
Beated and chapped with tanned antiquity, 10
Mine own self-love quite contrary I read;
Self so self-loving were iniquity. 12
    'Tis thee, my self, that for myself I praise, 13
    Painting my age with beauty of thy days. 14

63

Against my love shall be, as I am now, 1
With Time's injurious hand crushed and o'erworn; 2
When hours have drained his blood and filled his brow
With lines and wrinkles; when his youthful morn
Hath traveled on to age's steepy night, 5
And all those beauties whereof now he's king
Are vanishing or vanished out of sight,
Stealing away the treasure of his spring;
For such a time do I now fortify 9
Against confounding age's cruel knife,
That he shall never cut from memory 11
My sweet love's beauty, though my lover's life. 12
    His beauty shall in these black lines be seen, 13
    And they shall live, and he in them still green. 14

64

When I have seen by Time's fell hand defaced 1
The rich proud cost of outworn buried age; 2
When sometime lofty towers I see down-razed 3
And brass eternal slave to mortal rage; 4
When I have seen the hungry ocean gain
Advantage on the kingdom of the shore,
And the firm soil win of the wat'ry main, 7
Increasing store with loss and loss with store; 8
When I have seen such interchange of state, 9
Or state itself confounded to decay, 10
Ruin hath taught me thus to ruminate
That Time will come and take my love away. 12
    This thought is as a death, which cannot choose 13
    But weep to have that which it fears to lose. 14

65

Since brass, nor stone, nor earth, nor boundless sea, 1
But sad mortality o'ersways their power,
How with this rage shall beauty hold a plea, 3
Whose action is no stronger than a flower? 4
Oh, how shall summer's honey breath hold out
Against the wrackful siege of batt'ring days, 6

---

4 In . . . contend one after another, all struggle onward.   5 Nativity . . .
light The newborn infant, no sooner born into the broad expanse of
this world and the light of day   7 Crookèd perverse, malignant
8 doth . . . confound now destroys what it gave.   9 doth . . . flourish
pierces through and destroys the ornament, i.e., the physical beauty
10 delves the parallels digs the wrinkles, furrows   11 Feeds . . . truth
consumes the most precious things created by the fidelity of nature
12 but . . . mow that can escape the mowing of Time's scythe.
13 times in hope times to come
61.4 shadows images. (But also suggesting spirits.)   8 The scope . . .
jealousy the aim and purport of your suspicion. (Probably in apposi-
tion to shames and idle hours.)   13 watch stay awake.   wake revel
62.5 Methinks It seems to me   7 for myself (1) by my own reckoning
(2) for my own pleasure   8 As as if.   other others   9 glass mirror.
indeed as I actually am   10 Beated battered, weather-beaten.   tanned
antiquity i.e., leathery old age   12 Self . . . iniquity it would be wicked
for the self to love such an aged and unattractive self.   13 thee, my
self you, with whom I identify myself.   for as   14 days i.e., youth.

63.1 Against Anticipating the time when.   love beloved   2 crushed
and o'erworn creased and worn threadbare (like a long-used garment)
5 traveled (1) journeyed (2) labored.   steepy precipitous, i.e., descending swiftly toward death   9 For such a time (Parallel in construction
with Against in line 1.)   fortify raise works of defense   10 confounding destroying   11 That so that   12 though i.e., though he cut
13 black (1) inscribed in ink (2) the opposite of fair or beautiful   14 still
(1) even in death (2) forever.   green i.e., as in springtime and youth.
64.1 fell cruel   2 The rich . . . age i.e., those monuments that were the
product of proud wealth and magnificent outlay in times now past
and forgotten   3 sometime formerly   4 brass . . . rage i.e., seemingly
indestructible brass subdued by the destructive power of decay   7 of
. . . main at the expense of the ocean   8 Increasing . . . store one gaining as the other loses, and losing as the other gains   9 state condition
10 state pomp, greatness; condition in the abstract.   confounded to
decay destroyed to the point of being in ruins   12 love beloved
13 which cannot choose (Modifies thought.)   14 to have at having
65.1 Since i.e., Since there is neither   3 How . . . plea how against this
destructive force can beauty hope to make its case   4 action (1) efficacy (2) case (in law)   6 wrackful destructive

When rocks impregnable are not so stout, 7
Nor gates of steel so strong, but Time decays? 8
Oh, fearful meditation! Where, alack, 9
Shall Time's best jewel from Time's chest lie hid? 10
Or what strong hand can hold his swift foot back?
Or who his spoil of beauty can forbid? 12
    Oh, none, unless this miracle have might,
    That in black ink my love may still shine bright. 14

66

Tired with all these, for restful death I cry: 1
As, to behold desert a beggar born, 2
And needy nothing trimmed in jollity, 3
And purest faith unhappily forsworn, 4
And gilded honor shamefully misplaced, 5
And maiden virtue rudely strumpeted, 6
And right perfection wrongfully disgraced, 7
And strength by limping sway disablèd, 8
And art made tongue-tied by authority, 9
And folly doctorlike controlling skill, 10
And simple truth miscalled simplicity, 11
And captive good attending captain ill. 12
    Tired with all these, from these would I be gone,
    Save that, to die, I leave my love alone. 14

67

Ah, wherefore with infection should he live, 1
And with his presence grace impiety,
That sin by him advantage should achieve 3
And lace itself with his society? 4
Why should false painting imitate his cheek
And steal dead seeming of his living hue? 6
Why should poor beauty indirectly seek 7
Roses of shadow, since his rose is true? 8

Why should he live, now Nature bankrupt is, 9
Beggared of blood to blush through lively veins, 10
For she hath no exchequer now but his, 11
And, proud of many, lives upon his gains? 12
    Oh, him she stores, to show what wealth she had 13
    In days long since, before these last so bad. 14

68

Thus is his cheek the map of days outworn, 1
When beauty lived and died as flowers do now,
Before these bastard signs of fair were born, 3
Or durst inhabit on a living brow; 4
Before the golden tresses of the dead, 5
The right of sepulchers, were shorn away 6
To live a second life on second head; 7
Ere beauty's dead fleece made another gay. 8
In him those holy antique hours are seen 9
Without all ornament, itself and true, 10
Making no summer of another's green,
Robbing no old to dress his beauty new;
    And him as for a map doth Nature store, 13
    To show false art what beauty was of yore.

69

Those parts of thee that the world's eye doth view
Want nothing that the thought of hearts can mend; 2
All tongues, the voice of souls, give thee that due, 3
Utt'ring bare truth, even so as foes commend. 4
Thy outward thus with outward praise is crowned, 5
But those same tongues that give thee so thine own 6
In other accents do this praise confound 7
By seeing farther than the eye hath shown.
They look into the beauty of thy mind,
And that, in guess, they measure by thy deeds; 10
Then, churls, their thoughts, although their eyes were
    kind,
To thy fair flower add the rank smell of weeds. 12

---

7 **stout** sturdy, impregnable 8 **decays** brings about their decay.
9–10 **Where . . . hid?** Where, alas, shall the youth and beauty of my friend (*Time's best jewel*) be hidden away from being deposited by Time in its repository of forgetfulness? 12 **spoil** despoliation, ravaging 14 **my love** (1) my beloved (2) the love I feel for him
66.1 **all these** i.e., the following 2 **As** for instance, namely. **desert** one who is deserving 3 **And needy . . . jollity** and empty worthlessness adorned in finery 4 **unhappily forsworn** wretchedly and evilly betrayed 5 **gilded** golden, splendid. (Not here suggesting mere appearance of splendor.) 6 **strumpeted** accused of profligacy, or violated 7 **right** true. **disgraced** banished from favor 8 **limping sway** halting leadership 9 **And art . . . authority** and literature and learning stifled by censorship 10 **doctorlike** assuming a learned bearing. **controlling** dominating, curbing 11 **miscalled simplicity** slandered as foolishness, naïveté 12 **attending** waiting on, subordinated to 14 **to die** in dying
67.1 **wherefore** why. **with infection** i.e., with the world's ills, as enumerated in the preceding sonnet. **he** i.e., the poet's friend
3 **That . . . achieve** with the result that sin should flourish by being associated with him 4 **lace . . . society** (1) adorn itself with his company (2) weave its way into his company. 6 **dead seeming of** lifeless appearance from 7 **poor** inferior. **indirectly** imitatively, or, falsely
8 **Roses of shadow** i.e., painted roses, cosmetically applied. **since** (1) just because (2) since after all

9–12 **Why . . . gains?** Why should he continue to live in this bad world, seeing that Nature has now squandered all her resources of beauty on him, with no genuine way left to produce a natural blush on the cheek, since she has no treasury of natural beauty other than what is vested in him, and, though (falsely) taking pride in her abundance (of offspring), lives solely on the wealth (of beauty) that he provides? 13 **stores** preserves, keeps in store 14 **last** i.e., recent days, the present
68.1 **map** embodiment, image 3 **bastard . . . fair** i.e., cosmetics. **born** (Suggesting also *borne*, "worn.") 4 **inhabit** dwell 5–7 **Before . . . head** i.e., before the deplorable current fad of making wigs out of dead persons' hair 8 **gay** lovely, gaudy. 9 **holy antique hours** blessed ancient times 10 **all** any 13 **store** stock (with beauty) and preserve
69.2 **Want** lack. **mend** improve upon 3–4 **the voice . . . commend** i.e., uttering heartfelt conviction, allow that as your due, thus saying what even your enemies would concede to be the bare truth. 5 **outward praise** the kind of praise suited to mere outward qualities
6 **thine own** your due 7 **In other accents** in other terms and with another emphasis. **confound** confute, destroy 10 **in guess** at a guess 12 **To . . . weeds** i.e., to the flower of your outward beauty, they contrastingly suggest something putrid within.

But why thy odor matcheth not thy show,   13
The soil is this, that thou dost common grow.   14

70

That thou art blamed shall not be thy defect,   1
For slander's mark was ever yet the fair;   2
The ornament of beauty is suspect,   3
A crow that flies in heaven's sweetest air.   4
So thou be good, slander doth but approve   5
Thy worth the greater, being wooed of time,   6
For canker vice the sweetest buds doth love,   7
And thou present'st a pure unstainèd prime.   8
Thou hast passed by the ambush of young days,   9
Either not assailed, or victor being charged;   10
Yet this thy praise cannot be so thy praise   11
To tie up envy, evermore enlarged.   12
    If some suspect of ill masked not thy show,   13
    Then thou alone kingdoms of hearts shouldst owe.   14

71

No longer mourn for me when I am dead
Than you shall hear the surly sullen bell   2
Give warning to the world that I am fled
From this vile world, with vilest worms to dwell.
Nay, if you read this line, remember not
The hand that writ it, for I love you so
That I in your sweet thoughts would be forgot
If thinking on me then should make you woe.   8
Oh, if, I say, you look upon this verse
When I perhaps compounded am with clay,   10
Do not so much as my poor name rehearse,   11
But let your love even with my life decay,   12
    Lest the wise world should look into your moan   13
    And mock you with me after I am gone.   14

72

Oh, lest the world should task you to recite   1
What merit lived in me that you should love,

After my death, dear love, forget me quite;   13
For you in me can nothing worthy prove—   14
Unless you would devise some virtuous lie
To do more for me than mine own desert,
And hang more praise upon deceasèd I   7
Than niggard truth would willingly impart.
Oh, lest your true love may seem false in this,
That you for love speak well of me untrue,   10
My name be buried where my body is,   11
And live no more to shame nor me nor you.   12
    For I am shamed by that which I bring forth,   13
    And so should you, to love things nothing worth.   14

73

That time of year thou mayst in me behold
When yellow leaves, or none, or few, do hang
Upon those boughs which shake against the cold,
Bare ruined choirs where late the sweet birds sang.   4
In me thou see'st the twilight of such day
As after sunset fadeth in the west,
Which by and by black night doth take away,
Death's second self, that seals up all in rest.   8
In me thou see'st the glowing of such fire
That on the ashes of his youth doth lie   10
As the deathbed whereon it must expire,
Consumed with that which it was nourished by.   12
    This thou perceiv'st, which makes thy love more strong,
    To love that well which thou must leave ere long.   14

74

But be contented when that fell arrest   1
Without all bail shall carry me away;
My life hath in this line some interest,   3
Which for memorial still with thee shall stay.   4
When thou reviewest this, thou dost review   5
The very part was consecrate to thee.   6
The earth can have but earth, which is his due;   7
My spirit is thine, the better part of me.

---

13 odor i.e., reputation   **14 soil** (1) blemish, fault (2) origin, source, ground.   **common** cheapened by being too familiar and available to all, inferior (like a weed)
70.1 defect fault   **2 mark** target   **3 The . . . suspect** i.e., Beauty is always attended by suspicion (*suspect*), as though suspicion were a necessary ornament to beauty   **5 So** Provided that.   **approve** prove   **6 being . . . time** i.e., since it shows you are courted by the world   **7 canker vice** i.e., slander, that is like the cankerworm   **8 unstainèd prime** unspotted youth (like the pure, unspoiled flower that attracts the cankerworm).   **9 ambush . . . days** temptations of youth   **10 being charged** when you were assailed   **11–12 Yet . . . enlarged** yet the praise you receive cannot be enough to silence malice, which is always at liberty to do its worst.   **13 If . . . show** If some suspicion (*suspect*) of ill doing did not partly obscure your outward attractiveness   **14 owe** own.
71.2 bell a passing bell for one who has died, rung once for each year of that person's life   **8 on** of, about.   **make you woe** cause you woe or make you woeful.   **10 compounded** mingled   **11 rehearse** repeat   **12 even with** at the same time as   **13 look . . . moan** investigate the cause of your sorrow   **14 with** because of; for loving; along with
72.1 recite tell

7 hang (as in hanging trophies on a funeral monument)   **10 of me untrue** (1) about me untruly (2) about me, flawed and inconstant as I am   **11 My name be** let my name be   **12 nor . . . nor** neither . . . nor   **13 that . . . forth** (Perhaps a deprecatory reference to the author's acting and writing of plays, but more probably his verse or his written work generally.)   **14 should you** i.e., you ought to be ashamed
73.4 Bare . . . sang (In their arched shape, the bare trees resemble the church choir where the service is sung; with a hint of *quires*, gatherings of *leaves* [see line 2] in a book or manuscript, and evoking memories of church buildings left in ruins by the dissolution of the monasteries in the English Reformation. *Late* means "lately.")   **8 seals** closes   **10 his** its   **12 with** (1) by (2) along with   **14 that** (1) me, your beloved (2) youth and life itself.   **leave** i.e., lose by the speaker's death
74.1 be contented . . . arrest do not be distressed when that cruel arrest (carried out by Death)   **3 line** verse.   **interest** legal concern, right, or title   **4 still** (1) always (2) despite death   **5 reviewest this** see this again (and view it with a critical eye)   **6 part was consecrate** part (of me) that was dedicated solemnly (as in a religious service)   **7 his** its

So then thou hast but lost the dregs of life,
The prey of worms, my body being dead,
The coward conquest of a wretch's knife,   11
Too base of thee to be rememberèd.   12
 The worth of that is that which it contains,   13
 And that is this, and this with thee remains.   14

75

So are you to my thoughts as food to life,   1
Or as sweet-seasoned showers are to the ground.   2
And for the peace of you I hold such strife   3
As twixt a miser and his wealth is found:
Now proud as an enjoyer, and anon
Doubting the filching age will steal his treasure;   6
Now counting best to be with you alone,   7
Then bettered that the world may see my pleasure;   8
Sometime all full with feasting on your sight,
And by and by clean starvèd for a look;   10
Possessing or pursuing no delight
Save what is had or must from you be took.   12
 Thus do I pine and surfeit day by day,   13
 Or gluttoning on all, or all away.   14

76

Why is my verse so barren of new pride?   1
So far from variation or quick change?   2
Why with the time do I not glance aside   3
To newfound methods and to compounds strange?   4
Why write I still all one, ever the same,   5
And keep invention in a noted weed,   6
That every word doth almost tell my name,
Showing their birth and where they did proceed?   8
Oh, know, sweet love, I always write of you,
And you and love are still my argument;   10
So all my best is dressing old words new,
Spending again what is already spent.
 For as the sun is daily new and old,
 So is my love still telling what is told.   14

77

Thy glass will show thee how thy beauties wear,   1
Thy dial how thy precious minutes waste;   2
The vacant leaves thy mind's imprint will bear,   3
And of this book this learning mayst thou taste: 4
The wrinkles which thy glass will truly show
Of mouthèd graves will give thee memory;   6
Thou by thy dial's shady stealth mayst know   7
Time's thievish progress to eternity.
Look what thy memory cannot contain   9
Commit to these waste blanks, and thou shalt find   10
Those children nursed, delivered from thy brain,   11
To take a new acquaintance of thy mind.   12
 These offices, so oft as thou wilt look,   13
 Shall profit thee and much enrich thy book.   14

78

So oft have I invoked thee for my Muse
And found such fair assistance in my verse   2
As every alien pen hath got my use   3
And under thee their poesy disperse.   4
Thine eyes, that taught the dumb on high to sing   5
And heavy ignorance aloft to fly,
Have added feathers to the learnèd's wing   7
And given grace a double majesty.   8
Yet be most proud of that which I compile,   9
Whose influence is thine and born of thee.   10
In others' works thou dost but mend the style,   11
And arts with thy sweet graces gracèd be;   12
 But thou art all my art, and dost advance   13
 As high as learning my rude ignorance.

79

Whilst I alone did call upon thy aid,
My verse alone had all thy gentle grace,
But now my gracious numbers are decayed,   3
And my sick Muse doth give another place.   4

11 **The coward . . . knife** i.e., the cowardly conquest that even such a poor wretch as Mortality, or Death, can make with his scythe   12 **of . . . rememberèd** to be remembered by you.   13–14 **The worth . . . remains** The only worth of my body is the spirit it contains, i.e., this verse, which will remain with you and endure through you.
75.1 as food to life what food is to life   2 **sweet-seasoned** of the sweet season, i.e., spring   3 **of you** to be found in loving you   6 **Doubting** suspecting, fearing that.   **filching** thieving   7 **counting** (1) thinking it (2) reckoning, like a miser   8 **bettered** made happier, better pleased. **see my pleasure** i.e., see me with you, enjoying your company   10 **clean** completely, absolutely.   **a look** (1) a glimpse of you (2) an exchange of glances   12 **Save . . . took** except what is had or must be received from you alone.   13 **pine and surfeit** starve and overeat   14 **Or . . . or** either . . . or.   **all away** i.e., all food being taken away.
76.1 pride ornament.   2 **quick change** fashionable innovation. 3 **time** way of the world, fashion   4 **compounds** strange literary inventions, or perhaps, compound words, neologisms.   5 **still all one** continually one way   6 **invention** literary creation.   **noted weed** familiar garment   8 **where** whence   10 **still** always. **argument** subject, theme   14 **telling** (1) retelling (2) counting over. (Continuing the financial wordplay of *Spending* and *spent* in line 12, and in 75.7.)

77.1 glass mirror.   **wear** wear away   2 **dial** sundial   3 **vacant leaves** blank pages. (Apparently these lines accompanied the gift of a book of blank pages, a memorandum book.)   **thy mind's imprint** i.e., your reflections and ideas, to be set down in the memorandum book   4 **this learning** i.e., mental profit derived from reflecting and keeping a journal, as explained in lines 9 ff.   6 **mouthèd** all-devouring, gaping.   **memory** reminder   7 **shady stealth** stealthy shadow   9 **Look what** Whatever   10 **waste blanks** blank pages   10–12 **thou . . . mind** you will see those thoughts, the children of your brain, nursed to maturity and ready to be newly reencountered by your mind.
13 **offices** duties (of meditation and reflection)   14 **thy book** i.e., the memorandum book, where these reflections are to be set down.
78.2 fair favorable   3 **As** that.   **alien** belonging to others.   **got my use** adopted my practice   4 **under thee** i.e., with you as their muse or patron; under your influence.   **disperse** circulate.   5 **on high** aloud. (Also anticipating *aloft.*)   7 **added . . . wing** i.e., enabled learned poets to fly higher still. (A falconry metaphor; birds could be given extra wing feathers.)   8 **And . . . majesty** and have added to the majesty of poets already capable of it.   9 **compile** compose, write   10 **influence** inspiration. (With suggestion of astrological meaning.)   11 **mend the style** correct or improve the style. (Also with a suggestion of repairing the point of a writing quill or stylus, continuing the metaphor of *pen* and *feathers.*)   12 **arts** learning, literary culture   13 **advance** lift up
79.3 numbers verse   4 **doth . . . place** yields place to another.

I grant, sweet love, thy lovely argument   5
Deserves the travail of a worthier pen,
Yet what of thee thy poet doth invent   7
He robs thee of and pays it thee again.   8
He lends thee virtue, and he stole that word
From thy behavior; beauty doth he give,
And found it in thy cheek; he can afford   11
No praise to thee but what in thee doth live.
    Then thank him not for that which he doth say,
    Since what he owes thee thou thyself dost pay.

80

Oh, how I faint when I of you do write,   1
Knowing a better spirit doth use your name,   2
And in the praise thereof spends all his might
To make me tongue-tied, speaking of your fame!
But since your worth, wide as the ocean is,   5
The humble as the proudest sail doth bear,   6
My saucy bark, inferior far to his,
On your broad main doth willfully appear.   8
Your shallowest help will hold me up afloat,   9
Whilst he upon your soundless deep doth ride;   10
Or, being wrecked, I am a worthless boat,   11
He of tall building and of goodly pride.   12
    Then if he thrive and I be cast away,   13
    The worst was this: my love was my decay.   14

81

Or I shall live your epitaph to make,   1
Or you survive when I in earth am rotten,
From hence your memory death cannot take,   3
Although in me each part will be forgotten.   4
Your name from hence immortal life shall have,   5
Though I, once gone, to all the world must die;
The earth can yield me but a common grave,
When you entombèd in men's eyes shall lie.
Your momument shall be my gentle verse,
Which eyes not yet created shall o'erread,
And tongues to be your being shall rehearse   11
When all the breathers of this world are dead.   12
    You still shall live—such virtue hath my pen—   13
    Where breath most breathes, even in the mouths of   14
        men.

82

I grant thou wert not married to my Muse,
And therefore mayst without attaint o'erlook   2
The dedicated words which writers use   3
Of their fair subject, blessing every book.   4
Thou art as fair in knowledge as in hue,   5
Finding thy worth a limit past my praise,   6
And therefore art enforced to seek anew
Some fresher stamp of these time-bettering days.   8
And do so, love; yet when they have devised
What strainèd touches rhetoric can lend,
Thou, truly fair, wert truly sympathized   11
In true plain words by thy true-telling friend;
    And their gross painting might be better used   13
    Where cheeks need blood; in thee it is abused.   14

83

I never saw that you did painting need,   1
And therefore to your fair no painting set;   2
I found, or thought I found, you did exceed
The barren tender of a poet's debt;   4
And therefore have I slept in your report,   5
That you yourself, being extant, well might show   6
How far a modern quill doth come too short,   7
Speaking of worth, what worth in you doth grow.   8
This silence for my sin you did impute,   9
Which shall be most my glory, being dumb;   10
For I impair not beauty, being mute,   11
When others would give life and bring a tomb.   12
    There lives more life in one of your fair eyes
    Than both your poets can in praise devise.   14

84

Who is it that says most which can say more
Than this rich praise: that you alone are you,   1
In whose confine immurèd is the store   2
Which should example where your equal grew?   3
        4

82.2 attaint blame, discredit. **o'erlook** look at, peruse **3 dedicated** devoted. (With suggestion of "dedicatory.") **writers** i.e., other writers **4 blessing every book** i.e., you bestowing favor thus on the writings presented to you, or, writers commending their own work. **5 hue** complexion, appearance **6 a limit . . . praise** an area extending beyond the capacities of my praise **8 Some . . . days** some more recently issued imprint, i.e., more up-to-date literary product of this culturally sophisticated age. **11 wert truly sympathized** would be faithfully matched and described **13 gross painting** flattery that is heavily laid on, like a cosmetic **14 abused** misused, misapplied.
83.1 painting i.e., artificial enhancement of beauty **2 fair** beauty. **set** applied **4 The barren . . . debt** the worthless homage that a poet can offer you **5 slept . . . report** been neglectful in writing praisingly of you **6 That** because, so that. **extant** still alive and much in the public eye **7 modern** (1) commonplace (2) up-to-date **7–8 doth come . . . grow** comes too short, in describing your worth, of the actual worth that flourishes in you. **9–10 This . . . dumb** You imputed my silence to willful failure when, in fact, it will prove most to my credit **11 being mute** (Modifies *I*.) **12 bring a tomb** i.e., instead, they bring an inadequate monument that conceals lifelessly rather than enhances. **14 both your poets** i.e., (probably,) I and the rival poet
84.1–2 Who . . . praise What extravagant writer of praise can say more than this in way of praise **3–4 In . . . grew** in whose person are contained all those rich qualities that would be needed as a model to produce again your equal in beauty.

---

5 thy lovely argument the theme of your lovable qualities **6 travail** labor **7–8 Yet . . . again** yet whatever a poet under your patronage discovers as a literary subject concerning you he merely robs from you and gives you back your own again. **11 afford** furnish, extend
80.1 faint grow weak, falter **2 better spirit** i.e., rival poet, whom the speaker admires **5 wide . . . is** as wide as is the ocean **6 as** as well as **8 main** ocean. **willfully** perversely, audaciously **9 Your . . . afloat** i.e., My genius is so slight that I derive only minimal benefit from the greatness of you as my subject **10 soundless** unfathomable **11 wrecked** shipwrecked **12 tall building** i.e., sturdy construction. **pride** splendor. **13 cast away** (1) shipwrecked (2) abandoned
14 my love (1) my love for you, which led me to be so reckless in my inferior boat (2) you, my beloved. **decay** ruin.
81.1 Or Whether **3 hence** (1) this poetry (2) the world **4 in . . . part** every quality of mine (as distinguished from the poetry) **5 from hence** (1) from this poetry (2) henceforth **11 to be** i.e., of persons yet unborn. **rehearse** recite **12 breathers** living people. **this world** this present time **13 virtue** power **14 even in the** in the very

Lean penury within that pen doth dwell   5
That to his subject lends not some small glory;   6
But he that writes of you, if he can tell
That you are you, so dignifies his story.   8
Let him but copy what in you is writ,
Not making worse what nature made so clear,   10
And such a counterpart shall fame his wit,   11
Making his style admirèd everywhere.
    You to your beauteous blessings add a curse,   13
    Being fond on praise, which makes your praises   14
       worse.

85

My tongue-tied Muse in manners holds her still,   1
While comments of your praise, richly compiled,   2
Reserve thy character with golden quill   3
And precious phrase by all the Muses filed.   4
I think good thoughts whilst other write good words,   5
And like unlettered clerk still cry "Amen"   6
To every hymn that able spirit affords   7
In polished form of well-refinèd pen.
Hearing you praised, I say "'Tis so, 'tis true,"
And to the most of praise add something more;   10
But that is in my thought, whose love to you,   11
Though words come hindmost, holds his rank before.   12
    Then others for the breath of words respect,   13
    Me for my dumb thoughts, speaking in effect.   14

86

Was it the proud full sail of his great verse,   1
Bound for the prize of all-too-precious you,   2
That did my ripe thoughts in my brain inhearse,   3
Making their tomb the womb wherein they grew?
Was it his spirit, by spirits taught to write   5
Above a mortal pitch, that struck me dead?   6
No, neither he, nor his compeers by night   7
Giving him aid, my verse astonishèd.   8
He, nor that affable familiar ghost   9

Which nightly gulls him with intelligence,   10
As victors of my silence cannot boast;
I was not sick of any fear from thence.   12
    But when your countenance filled up his line,   13
    Then lacked I matter; that enfeebled mine.   14

87

Farewell! Thou art too dear for my possessing,   1
And like enough thou know'st thy estimate.   2
The charter of thy worth gives thee releasing;   3
My bonds in thee are all determinate.   4
For how do I hold thee but by thy granting,
And for that riches where is my deserving?
The cause of this fair gift in me is wanting,
And so my patent back again is swerving.   8
Thyself thou gav'st, thy own worth then not knowing,
Or me, to whom thou gav'st it, else mistaking;   10
So thy great gift, upon misprision growing,   11
Comes home again, on better judgment making.   12
    Thus have I had thee as a dream doth flatter,
    In sleep a king, but waking no such matter.

88

When thou shalt be disposed to set me light   1
And place my merit in the eye of scorn,
Upon thy side against myself I'll fight   3
And prove thee virtuous, though thou art forsworn.
With mine own weakness being best acquainted,
Upon thy part I can set down a story
Of faults concealed, wherein I am attainted,   7
That thou in losing me shall win much glory.   8
And I by this will be a gainer too;
For, bending all my loving thoughts on thee,
The injuries that to myself I do,
Doing thee vantage, double-vantage me.   12
    Such is my love, to thee I so belong,
    That for thy right myself will bear all wrong.

89

Say that thou didst forsake me for some fault,   1
And I will comment upon that offense;   2
Speak of my lameness, and I straight will halt,   3

5–6 Lean . . . glory It is a poor piece of writing indeed that does not confer at least some glory on its subject   **8 so** sufficiently, thus   **10 clear** glorious, shining   **11 counterpart** copy, likeness.   **fame** endow with fame   **13 curse** (1) defect in character (2) burden for those seeking to praise you   **14 Being fond** doting.   **which . . . worse** (1) which encourages false flattery (2) which makes all praise seem inadequate in comparison to you.
85.1 in . . . still politely remains silent   **2 comments . . . compiled** eulogies of you composed in fine language   **3 Reserve thy character** store up praise of you in their writings.   **golden** aureate, affected   **4 precious** affected.   **filed** polished.   **5 other** others   **6–7 like . . . affords** like an illiterate assistant to a priest continually give my approval to every praising verse that the rival poet (and others like him) provides   **10 most** highmost   **11 that . . . thought** that which I add is added silently   **12 holds . . . before** is second to none in love.   **13 Then . . . respect** Then take notice of others for what they say   **14 speaking in effect** conveying what speech would say.
86.1 his i.e., an unidentified rival poet's   **2 prize** capture, booty (as in a seized cargo vessel)   **3 inhearse** coffin up   **5 spirits** i.e., literary ancestors or contemporaries. (With a suggestion also of *daemons*, attendant spirits.)   **6 pitch** height. (A term from falconry.)   **dead** i.e., dumb, silent.   **7 compeers by night** spirits (see line 5) visiting and aiding the poet in his dreams or nighttime reading   **8 astonishèd** struck dumb.   **9 ghost** spirit (as in lines 5 and 7)

10 gulls misleads.   **intelligence** information, ideas   **12 of** with   **13 countenance filled up** (1) approval repaired any defect in (2) beauty served as subject for   **14 lacked I matter** I had nothing left to write about
87.1 dear precious   **2 like** likely, probably.   **estimate** value.   **3 charter of** privilege derived from.   **releasing** i.e., release from obligations of love   **4 determinate** ended, expired. (A legal term, as throughout this sonnet.)   **8 my . . . swerving** my rights of possession revert to you.   **10 mistaking** i.e., overvaluing   **11 upon misprision growing** arising out of error   **12 on . . . making** on your forming a more accurate judgment.
88.1 set me light make light of me, value me slightingly   **3 Upon thy side** supporting your case. (Also *Upon thy part* in line 6.)   **7 concealed** not publicly known.   **attainted** dishonored   **8 That** so that.   **losing** i.e., separating from. (With a suggestion of "loosing," "setting free," the Quarto spelling.)   **12 vantage** advantage
89.1 Say Assert, claim   **2 comment** enlarge   **3 Speak . . . halt** i.e., If you ascribe to me any kind of handicap, I immediately will limp to show that you are right. (*Halt* also has the suggestion of ceasing to object, remaining silent.)

Against thy reasons making no defense.   4
Thou canst not, love, disgrace me half so ill,   5
To set a form upon desirèd change,   6
As I'll myself disgrace, knowing thy will.   7
I will acquaintance strangle and look strange,   8
Be absent from thy walks, and in my tongue   9
Thy sweet belovèd name no more shall dwell,
Lest I, too much profane, should do it wrong
And haply of our old acquaintance tell.   12
    For thee against myself I'll vow debate,   13
    For I must ne'er love him whom thou dost hate.

90

Then hate me when thou wilt; if ever, now;
Now, while the world is bent my deeds to cross,   2
Join with the spite of fortune, make me bow,
And do not drop in for an after-loss.   4
Ah, do not, when my heart hath scaped this sorrow,   5
Come in the rearward of a conquered woe;   6
Give not a windy night a rainy morrow,   7
To linger out a purposed overthrow.   8
If thou wilt leave me, do not leave me last,
When other petty griefs have done their spite,
But in the onset come; so shall I taste   11
At first the very worst of fortune's might,
    And other strains of woe, which now seem woe,   13
    Compared with loss of thee will not seem so.

91

Some glory in their birth, some in their skill,
Some in their wealth, some in their body's force,
Some in their garments, though newfangled ill,   3
Some in their hawks and hounds, some in their horse;   4
And every humor hath his adjunct pleasure,   5
Wherein it finds a joy above the rest.
But these particulars are not my measure;   7
All these I better in one general best.   8
Thy love is better than high birth to me,
Richer than wealth, prouder than garments' cost,   10
Of more delight than hawks or horses be;
And having thee, of all men's pride I boast—   12
    Wretched in this alone, that thou mayst take
    All this away and me most wretched make.

92

But do thy worst to steal thyself away,   1
For term of life thou art assurèd mine,   2
And life no longer than thy love will stay,
For it depends upon that love of thine.
Then need I not to fear the worst of wrongs,   5
When in the least of them my life hath end;   6
I see a better state to me belongs   7
Than that which on thy humor doth depend.   8
Thou canst not vex me with inconstant mind,
Since that my life on thy revolt doth lie.   10
Oh, what a happy title do I find,   11
Happy to have thy love, happy to die!
    But what's so blessèd-fair that fears no blot?   13
    Thou mayst be false, and yet I know it not.   14

93

So shall I live, supposing thou art true,   1
Like a deceivèd husband; so love's face   2
May still seem love to me, though altered new,   3
Thy looks with me, thy heart in other place.
For there can live no hatred in thine eye,   5
Therefore in that I cannot know thy change.   6
In many's looks the false heart's history
Is writ in moods and frowns and wrinkles strange,   8
But heaven in thy creation did decree
That in thy face sweet love should ever dwell;
Whate'er thy thoughts or thy heart's workings be,
Thy looks should nothing thence but sweetness tell.
    How like Eve's apple doth thy beauty grow,
    If thy sweet virtue answer not thy show!   14

94

They that have power to hurt and will do none,   1
That do not do the thing they most do show,   2
Who, moving others, are themselves as stone,
Unmovèd, cold, and to temptation slow,   4
They rightly do inherit heaven's graces   5
And husband nature's riches from expense;   6

---

4 **reasons** charges, arguments   5 **disgrace** discredit   6 **To . . . change** to provide a pretext for (in the interest of justifying) your change of affection and to set it in proper order   7 **As . . . disgrace** as I will disfigure and depreciate myself   8 **acquaintance strangle** put an end to familiarity (with you).   **strange** like a stranger   9 **walks** haunts   12 **haply** perchance   13 **vow debate** declare hostility, quarrel   90.2 **bent** determined.   **cross** thwart   4 **drop . . . after-loss** crushingly add to my sorrow.   5–6 **do not . . . woe** do not, when I have just recovered from my present grief, attack me from the rear   7 **windy, rainy** (Suggestive of sighs and tears.)   8 **linger out** protract.   **purposed** intended, inevitable   11 **in the onset** at the outset   13 **strains** (1) kinds (2) stresses   91.3 **newfangled ill** fashionably unattractive   4 **horse** horses   5 **humor** disposition, temperament.   **his adjunct** its corresponding   7 **measure** standard (of happiness); lot in life   8 **better** surpass, improve upon   10 **prouder** more splendid   12 **of . . . boast** I boast of having the equivalent of all that is a source of pride in other men

92.1 **But do** i.e., But even if you do   2 **term of life** i.e., my lifetime   5–6 **Then . . . end** I need not fear what most people would call the worst of misfortunes, since the seemingly lesser misfortune—loss of your friendship—would prove fatal to me   7–8 **I see . . . depend** i.e., I see that I am happier than most people whose happiness ends when they are cast from favor, since my very existence will cease when I am cast from favor and thus will end my misery.   **humor** whim, fancy   10 **Since . . . lie** since if you desert me it will cost me my life.   11 **happy title** right to be thought happy; fortunate legal right of ownership   13 **that fears** as to fear   14 **Thou . . . not** i.e., My worst fate would be to lose your affection without knowing it and thereby live on in an unloved state, unreleased by the death that certainty of your desertion would bring.   93.1 **So** (Continues the thought of sonnet 92.)   **supposing** I supposing (incorrectly)   2 **face** appearance   3 **new** to something new   5 **For** Since   6 **in . . . change** I won't be able to detect your changed affection from your eyes.   8 **moods** moody looks.   **strange** unfriendly   14 **answer . . . show** does not conform with your outward appearance.   94.1 **and . . . none** and do not willfully try to hurt   2 **show** i.e., show themselves capable of, or, seem to do   4 **cold** dispassionate   5 **inherit** (1) receive through inheritance (2) enjoy, make use of   6 **husband** carefully manage, preserve.   **expense** waste, expenditure.

They are the lords and owners of their faces, 7
Others but stewards of their excellence. 8
The summer's flower is to the summer sweet, 9
Though to itself it only live and die, 10
But if that flower with base infection meet,
The basest weed outbraves his dignity. 12
　　For sweetest things turn sourest by their deeds;
　　Lilies that fester smell far worse than weeds. 14

95

How sweet and lovely dost thou make the shame
Which, like a canker in the fragrant rose, 2
Doth spot the beauty of thy budding name! 3
Oh, in what sweets dost thou thy sins enclose!
That tongue that tells the story of thy days,
Making lascivious comments on thy sport, 6
Cannot dispraise, but, in a kind of praise,
Naming thy name, blesses an ill report. 8
Oh, what a mansion have those vices got
Which for their habitation chose out thee,
Where beauty's veil doth cover every blot,
And all things turns to fair that eyes can see! 12
　　Take heed, dear heart, of this large privilege; 13
　　The hardest knife ill used doth lose his edge. 14

96

Some say thy fault is youth, some wantonness; 1
Some say thy grace is youth and gentle sport; 2
Both grace and faults are loved of more and less; 3
Thou mak'st faults graces that to thee resort. 4
As on the finger of a thronèd queen
The basest jewel will be well esteemed,
So are those errors that in thee are seen
To truths translated and for true things deemed. 8
How many lambs might the stern wolf betray, 9
If like a lamb he could his looks translate! 10
How many gazers mightst thou lead away, 11
If thou wouldst use the strength of all thy state! 12
　　But do not so; I love thee in such sort 13
　　As, thou being mine, mine is thy good report. 14

97

How like a winter hath my absence been
From thee, the pleasure of the fleeting year!
What freezings have I felt, what dark days seen!
What old December's bareness everywhere!
And yet this time removed was summer's time, 5
The teeming autumn, big with rich increase, 6
Bearing the wanton burden of the prime, 7
Like widowed wombs after their lords' decease.
Yet this abundant issue seemed to me 9
But hope of orphans and unfathered fruit, 10
For summer and his pleasures wait on thee, 11
And, thou away, the very birds are mute;
　　Or, if they sing, 'tis with so dull a cheer 13
　　That leaves look pale, dreading the winter's near.

98

From you have I been absent in the spring,
When proud-pied April, dressed in all his trim, 2
Hath put a spirit of youth in everything,
That heavy Saturn laughed and leapt with him. 4
Yet nor the lays of birds nor the sweet smell 5
Of different flowers in odor and in hue 6
Could make me any summer's story tell, 7
Or from their proud lap pluck them where they grew. 8
Nor did I wonder at the lily's white,
Nor praise the deep vermilion in the rose;
They were but sweet, but figures of delight 11
Drawn after you, you pattern of all those. 12
　　Yet seemed it winter still, and, you away,
　　As with your shadow I with these did play. 14

99

The forward violet thus did I chide: 1
"Sweet thief, whence didst thou steal thy sweet that
　　smells, 2
If not from my love's breath? The purple pride 3
Which on thy soft cheek for complexion dwells
In my love's veins thou hast too grossly dyed." 5
The lily I condemnèd for thy hand, 6
And buds of marjoram had stol'n thy hair; 7
The roses fearfully on thorns did stand, 8

---

7 They . . . faces they are completely masters of themselves and of the qualities that appear in them　**8 but stewards** are merely custodians or dispensers　**9–10 The . . . die** i.e., Such self-contained persons may seem like flowers that live and die unto themselves, but, in fact, they have much sweetness and beauty to bestow　**12 outbraves his dignity** surpasses in show its worth.　**14 Lilies . . . weeds** (This line appears in the anonymous play *Edward III*, usually dated before 1595 and attributed in part by some editors to Shakespeare.)
95.2 canker cankerworm that destroys buds and leaves　**3 name** reputation.　**6 sport** amours　**8 blesses** graces　**12 all . . . fair** makes everything deceptively beautiful　**13 large** unlimited, licentious　**14 his** its
96.1 wantonness (1) exuberance (2) lechery　**2 gentle sport** gentle-manlike amorousness　**3 of more and less** by high and low　**4 Thou . . . resort** you convert into graces the faults that attend you.　**8 translated** transformed　**9 stern** cruel　**10 like** i.e., unto those of　**11 away** astray　**12 the strength . . . state** the full power at your command, i.e., your wealth, charm, and social rank.　**13–14 But . . . report** (The same couplet ends sonnet 36.)　**report** reputation.

97.5 time removed time of separation　**6 big** pregnant　**7 the wanton . . . prime** the fruit or offspring of wanton spring, i.e., the crops planted in springtime　**9 issue** offspring　**10 hope of orphans** orphaned hope　**11 his** its.　**wait on thee** attend on you, are at your disposal　**13 with . . . cheer** in so melancholy a fashion
98.2 proud-pied gorgeously multicolored.　**trim** finery　**4 That** so that.　**Saturn** (A planet associated with melancholy, *heavy*.)　**5 nor the lays** neither the songs　**6 different flowers** flowers differing　**7 any summer's story** i.e., any pleasant story　**8 proud lap** i.e., the earth　**11 but sweet . . . delight** mere sweetness, mere delightful forms or emblems　**12 after** resembling　**14 shadow** image, portrait.　**these** i.e., the flowers
99.1 forward early and presumptuous. (This sonnet has fifteen lines, the first being introductory.)　**2 thy sweet** your scent　**3 pride** splendor　**5 grossly** obviously and heavily　**6 for thy hand** i.e., because it has stolen its whiteness from your hand　**7 And . . . hair** i.e., and I condemned the buds of marjoram for having stolen your hair.　**buds of marjoram** (These are dark purple-red or auburn, and it may be that the reference is to color, although marjoram is noted for its sweet scent.)　**8 on thorns did stand** grew on thorny stems. (With a suggestion of being apprehensive.)

One blushing shame, another white despair; 9
A third, nor red nor white, had stol'n of both 10
And to his robbery had annexed thy breath, 11
But, for his theft, in pride of all his growth 12
A vengeful canker ate him up to death. 13
    More flowers I noted, yet I none could see 14
    But sweet or color it had stol'n from thee. 15

100

Where art thou, Muse, that thou forget'st so long
To speak of that which gives thee all thy might?
Spend'st thou thy fury on some worthless song, 3
Dark'ning thy pow'r to lend base subjects light? 4
Return, forgetful Muse, and straight redeem 5
In gentle numbers time so idly spent; 6
Sing to the ear that doth thy lays esteem 7
And gives thy pen both skill and argument. 8
Rise, resty Muse, my love's sweet face survey 9
If Time have any wrinkle graven there; 10
If any, be a satire to decay, 11
And make Time's spoils despisèd everywhere. 12
    Give my love fame faster than Time wastes life; 13
    So thou prevent'st his scythe and crooked knife. 14

101

O truant Muse, what shall be thy amends 1
For thy neglect of truth in beauty dyed? 2
Both truth and beauty on my love depends; 3
So dost thou too, and therein dignified. 4
Make answer, Muse. Wilt thou not haply say, 5
"Truth needs no color with his color fixed, 6
Beauty no pencil, beauty's truth to lay, 7
But best is best, if never intermixed"? 8
Because he needs no praise, wilt thou be dumb? 9
Excuse not silence so, for't lies in thee
To make him much outlive a gilded tomb
And to be praised of ages yet to be. 12
    Then do thy office, Muse; I teach thee how 13
    To make him seem, long hence, as he shows now. 14

102

My love is strengthened, though more weak in seeming; 1
I love not less, though less the show appear.
That love is merchandized whose rich esteeming 3
The owner's tongue doth publish everywhere. 4
Our love was new and then but in the spring 5
When I was wont to greet it with my lays, 6
As Philomel in summer's front doth sing 7
And stops her pipe in growth of riper days— 8
Not that the summer is less pleasant now
Than when her mournful hymns did hush the night,
But that wild music burdens every bough 11
And sweets grown common lose their dear delight.
    Therefore like her I sometime hold my tongue,
    Because I would not dull you with my song. 14

103

Alack, what poverty my Muse brings forth, 1
That, having such a scope to show her pride, 2
The argument all bare is of more worth 3
Than when it hath my added praise beside.
Oh, blame me not if I no more can write! 5
Look in your glass, and there appears a face 6
That overgoes my blunt invention quite, 7
Dulling my lines and doing me disgrace. 8
Were it not sinful then, striving to mend,
To mar the subject that before was well?
For to no other pass my verses tend 11
Than of your graces and your gifts to tell;
    And more, much more, than in my verse can sit 13
    Your own glass shows you when you look in it.

104

To me, fair friend, you never can be old,
For, as you were when first your eye I eyed,
Such seems your beauty still. Three winters cold
Have from the forests shook three summers' pride, 4
Three beauteous springs to yellow autumn turned
In process of the seasons have I seen, 6
Three April perfumes in three hot Junes burned
Since first I saw you fresh, which yet are green. 8

9 shame i.e., red for shame **10 nor red** neither (purely) red **11 to . . . annexed** to this robbery had added the robbery of **12 But, for** although, in punishment for. **in pride . . . growth** in his prime **13 canker** cankerworm **15 But** except. **sweet** scent (as in line 2)
100.3 fury poetic inspiration **4 Dark'ning** debasing **5 straight** straightway **6 gentle numbers** noble verses. **idly** foolishly **7 lays** songs **8 argument** subject. **9 resty** inactive, lazy **10 If** to see if **11 If any** if there are any. **satire to** satirist of, here one composing a satire on Time as a despoiler **12 spoils** acts of destruction, ravages **13 faster** (1) more quickly (2) more firmly **14 thou prevent'st** you forestall, thwart. **crooked knife** curved blade.
101.1 what . . . amends what reparation will you make **2 truth . . . dyed** truth made integrally a part of the beauty which it inhabits. **3–4 Both . . . dignified** i.e., Both faith and beauty depend on my love for their proper appreciation and recognition, and you, my Muse, depend for your very office and dignity on that same function. **5 haply** perhaps **6 no . . . fixed** no artificial color (with suggestion of *pretense*) added to its natural and permanent color or hue **7 pencil** paintbrush. **lay** apply color to, as with a brush **8 intermixed** adulterated. **9 dumb** silent. **12 of** by **13 office** function **14 long hence** long in the future. **shows** appears

102.1 seeming outward appearance **3 merchandized** degraded by being treated as a thing of sale. **esteeming** valuation **4 publish** announce, advertise **5 in the spring** only just beginning **6 wont . . . lays** accustomed to salute it (our love) with my song **7 Philomel** the nightingale. **front** forehead, beginning **8 stops her pipe** stops singing. **riper** i.e., those of late summer and autumn **11 But . . . music** i.e., but because a profusion of wild birds' singing. (Refers to other poets.) **burdens** weighs down. (But with a musical sense as well; a *burden* is a chorus.) **14 dull** surfeit
103.1 poverty poor stuff **2 pride** splendor **3 argument all bare** subject alone, unadorned **5 no more can write** i.e., (1) am silent (2) cannot go beyond what you yourself are, cannot excel my own poverty of invention. **6 glass** mirror **7 overgoes** surpasses; overwhelms. **blunt invention** unpolished style, writing **8 Dulling** i.e., making dull by comparison **11 pass** purpose, issue **13 sit** reside
104.4 pride splendor **6 process** the progression **8 which yet** who still

Ah, yet doth beauty, like a dial hand,   9
Steal from his figure and no pace perceived.   10
So your sweet hue, which methinks still doth stand,   11
Hath motion, and mine eye may be deceived,
    For fear of which, hear this, thou age unbred: 13
    Ere you were born was beauty's summer dead.

105

Let not my love be called idolatry,
Nor my belovèd as an idol show,   2
Since all alike my songs and praises be
To one, of one, still such, and ever so.   4
Kind is my love today, tomorrow kind,
Still constant in a wondrous excellence;
Therefore my verse, to constancy confined,
One thing expressing, leaves out difference.   8
"Fair, kind, and true" is all my argument,
"Fair, kind, and true" varying to other words;
And in this change is my invention spent,   11
Three themes in one, which wondrous scope affords.
    Fair, kind, and true have often lived alone,   13
    Which three till now never kept seat in one.   14

106

When in the chronicle of wasted time   1
I see descriptions of the fairest wights,   2
And beauty making beautiful old rhyme   3
In praise of ladies dead and lovely knights,
Then, in the blazon of sweet beauty's best,   5
Of hand, of foot, of lip, of eye, of brow,
I see their antique pen would have expressed
Even such a beauty as you master now.   8
So all their praises are but prophecies
Of this our time, all you prefiguring;
And, for they looked but with divining eyes,   11
They had not skill enough your worth to sing.
    For we, which now behold these present days,   13
    Have eyes to wonder, but lack tongues to praise.   14

107

Not mine own fears nor the prophetic soul   1
Of the wide world dreaming on things to come   2
Can yet the lease of my true love control,   3
Supposed as forfeit to a confined doom.   4
The mortal moon hath her eclipse endured,   5
And the sad augurs mock their own presage;   6
Incertainties now crown themselves assured,   7
And peace proclaims olives of endless age.   8
Now with the drops of this most balmy time   9
My love looks fresh, and Death to me subscribes,   10
Since, spite of him, I'll live in this poor rhyme,
While he insults o'er dull and speechless tribes;   12
    And thou in this shalt find thy monument,
    When tyrants' crests and tombs of brass are spent. 14

108

What's in the brain that ink may character   1
Which hath not figured to thee my true spirit?   2
What's new to speak, what now to register,   3
That may express my love or thy dear merit?
Nothing, sweet boy; but yet, like prayers divine,
I must each day say o'er the very same,
Counting no old thing old—thou mine, I thine—   7
Even as when first I hallowed thy fair name.   8
So that eternal love in love's fresh case   9
Weighs not the dust and injury of age,   10
Nor gives to necessary wrinkles place,
But makes antiquity for aye his page,   12
    Finding the first conceit of love there bred   13
    Where time and outward form would show it dead.   14

109

Oh, never say that I was false of heart,
Though absence seemed my flame to qualify.   2

9–10 **yet . . . perceived** yet beauty slips almost imperceptibly away, from you, like the dial hand of a watch making its stealthy progress away from number to number on the dial face.   **11 hue** appearance, complexion.   **still doth stand** remains seemingly unaltered   **13 unbred** not yet born
105.2 show appear   **4 To . . . so** (The poet loves his friend in phrases that recall the paradoxical and mysterious duality of two in one, as in "The Phoenix and Turtle." Such sacred love, by analogy, cannot be idolatry.)   **8 difference** diversity of theme and the seeming diversity of two persons (the poet and his friend) who are essentially one; also the seeming diversity of "Fair, kind, and true" which is also a variation on a single theme.   **11 this change** variations on this theme.   **invention** inventiveness.   **spent** expended
13 alone separately (in different people)   **14 kept seat** resided; sat enthroned
106.1 wasted past, used up   **2 wights** persons   **3 beauty** (1) beauty of style and language (2) beauty of the persons described   **5 blazon** i.e., glorification, cataloguing of qualities. (A heraldic metaphor.)
8 master possess, control   **11 for** because.   **divining** guessing or predicting as to the future   **13 For we** For even we   **14 praise** i.e., praise you worthily, sufficiently.

107.1–2 soul . . . world collective consciousness of humanity   **3–4 Can . . . doom** can set a limit to the time allotted to me to love you, though imagined to be destined to expire after a limited term.   **5 mortal moon** (Probably a reference to Queen Elizabeth, ill or deceased, most probably to her death in 1603; she was known as Diana, Cynthia, etc.)   **6 And . . . presage** and the solemn prophets of disaster now mock their earlier predictions   **7 Incertainties . . . assured** uncertainties have triumphantly given way to certainties. (Probably a reference to the accession and coronation of King James VI of Scotland and I of England.)   **8 olives** (Conventionally associated with peace and probably pointing here to King James I's resolutions of war with Spain and strife in Ireland.)   **of endless age** without foreseen end.   **9 with the drops** i.e., healed as though by a balmy dew. (Balm was employed in the coronation ceremony for James in 1603, as in all such coronations.)   **10 subscribes** yields   **12 insults . . . tribes** triumphs scornfully over endless generations of dead who have no poet to celebrate them   **14 crests** trophies adorning a tomb.   **spent** expended, wasted away.
108.1 character write   **2 figured** revealed, represented.   **true** constant   **3 register** record   **7 Counting . . . thine** dismissing no old truth as out of date or shopworn, such as the truth that you are mine and I yours   **8 hallowed** (As in "hallowed be thy name" from the Lord's Prayer.)   **9 fresh case** new exterior and circumstance
10 Weighs not is unconcerned about   **11 place** consideration, primacy   **12–14 But . . . dead** Love makes age serve its grand purposes, finding in age and antiquity the first stirrings of love, in a place where conventionally one would suppose it to be dead.
109.2 flame passion.   **qualify** temper, moderate.

As easy might I from myself depart
As from my soul, which in thy breast doth lie.
That is my home of love; if I have ranged,   5
Like him that travels I return again,
Just to the time, not with the time exchanged,   7
So that myself bring water for my stain.   8
Never believe, though in my nature reigned
All frailties that besiege all kinds of blood,   10
That it could so preposterously be stained
To leave for nothing all thy sum of good;   12
    For nothing this wide universe I call
    Save thou, my rose; in it thou art my all.

110

Alas, 'tis true, I have gone here and there
And made myself a motley to the view,   2
Gored mine own thoughts, sold cheap what is most dear,   3
Made old offenses of affections new;   4
Most true it is that I have looked on truth   5
Askance and strangely. But, by all above,   6
These blenches gave my heart another youth,   7
And worse essays proved thee my best of love.   8
Now all is done, have what shall have no end.   9
Mine appetite I never more will grind   10
On newer proof, to try an older friend,   11
A god in love, to whom I am confined.
    Then give me welcome, next my heaven the best,   13
    Even to thy pure and most most loving breast.

111

Oh, for my sake do you with Fortune chide,   1
The guilty goddess of my harmful deeds,   2
That did not better for my life provide
Than public means which public manners breeds.   4
Thence comes it that my name receives a brand,   5
And almost thence my nature is subdued
To what it works in, like the dyer's hand.   7
Pity me then, and wish I were renewed,   8
Whilst, like a willing patient, I will drink

Potions of eisel 'gainst my strong infection;   10
No bitterness that I will bitter think,   11
Nor double penance, to correct correction.   12
    Pity me then, dear friend, and I assure ye
    Even that your pity is enough to cure me.   14

112

Your love and pity doth th'impression fill   1
Which vulgar scandal stamped upon my brow;   2
For what care I who calls me well or ill,
So you o'ergreen my bad, my good allow?   4
You are my all the world, and I must strive   5
To know my shames and praises from your tongue;
None else to me, nor I to none alive,   7
That my steeled sense or changes, right or wrong.   8
In so profound abysm I throw all care   9
Of others' voices that my adder's sense   10
To critic and to flatterer stoppèd are.   11
Mark how with my neglect I do dispense: 12
    You are so strongly in my purpose bred   13
    That all the world besides, methinks, are dead.

113

Since I left you, mine eye is in my mind,   1
And that which governs me to go about   2
Doth part his function and is partly blind,   3
Seems seeing, but effectually is out;   4
For it no form delivers to the heart   5
Of bird, of flower, or shape, which it doth latch;   6
Of his quick objects hath the mind no part,   7
Nor his own vision holds what it doth catch;   8
For if it see the rud'st or gentlest sight,   9
The most sweet-favor or deformd'st creature,   10
The mountain or the sea, the day or night,
The crow or dove, it shapes them to your feature.   12

---

5 ranged traveled, wandered   **7 Just . . . exchanged** punctual to the minute, not changed by the period of separation   **8 water for my stain** i.e., repentant tears, to wash away the stain of my offense. **10 blood** temperament, sensual nature   **12 for** in exchange for **110.2 motley** jester, fool.   **to the view** in the eyes of the world **3 Gored** wounded   **4 Made . . . new** i.e., repeated old offenses or made offense against old friendship in forming new attachments **5 truth** constancy   **6 Askance and strangely** disdainfully, obliquely and at a distance.   **by all above** by heaven   **7 blenches** swervings. **another youth** i.e., a renewal of true friendship   **8 essays** experiments (in friendship)   **9 Now all** Now that all that.   **have what . . . end** take what is eternal (my friendship).   **10 grind** whet, sharpen **11 newer proof** further experiment, experience.   **try** test   **13 next my heaven** you, who are to me second only to heaven itself **111.1 do you** (A command: "Do")   **2 guilty goddess of** goddess responsible for   **3 life** livelihood   **4 Than . . . breeds** than providing me a means of livelihood that depends on catering to the public. (A probable reference to Shakespeare's career as an actor.)   **5 receives a brand** is disgraced (through prejudice against my occupation) **7 like the dyer's hand** (The dyer's hand is stained by the dye it handles, just as the dramatist's or actor's nature is almost overpowered by the medium in which he works—the theater.)   **8 renewed** restored to what I was by nature, cleansed

10 eisel vinegar, used as an antiseptic against the plague and also as an agent for removing stains   **11 No bitterness** there is no bitterness **12 Nor . . . correction** nor will I think it bitter to undertake a twofold penance in order to correct what must be doubly corrected.   **14 Even that your pity** that very pity of yours **112.1 doth th'impression fill** effaces the scar   **2 vulgar scandal** notoriety (for being an actor?)   **4 So you o'ergreen** provided that you cover as with green growth.   **allow** approve.   **5 my all the world** everything to me   **7–8 None . . . wrong** no one else but you affects my fixed and hardened sensibilities, whether for better or for worse. **9–11 In . . . are** Into so deep an abyss do I throw all concern as to what others may think that, adderlike, my ears are deaf to critic and flatterer alike. (Adders were popularly supposed to have no sense of hearing.)   **12 Mark . . . dispense** See how I justify my disregard of the opinion of others   **13 You . . . bred** you are so nurtured in my thoughts and are such a powerful influence over my intentions **113.1 mine . . . mind** i.e., I'm guided by my mind's eye   **2 that . . . about** i.e., my physical sight   **3 part** (1) divide (2) abandon.   **his** its, i.e., the physical eye's. (Also in lines 7 and 8.)   **4 Seems . . . out** seems to be seeing, but in reality is blind   **5 heart** (Here portrayed as capable of receiving sense impressions and of consciousness, as in sonnet 47.)   **6 latch** catch or receive the sight of   **7 Of . . . part** i.e., the mind, attuned to its inner eye, takes no part in the fleeting and lively (*quick*) things seen by the physical sight   **8 Nor . . . holds** nor does the eye itself retain.   **catch** see glimpsingly   **9 For . . . sight** for whether it see the most uncouth or most gracious sight   **10 sweet-favor** sweet-featured   **12 shapes . . . feature** makes them resemble you.

Incapable of more, replete with you,
My most true mind thus maketh mine eye untrue.

114

Or whether doth my mind, being crowned with you,   1
Drink up the monarch's plague, this flattery?   2
Or whether shall I say mine eye saith true,   3
And that your love taught it this alchemy,   4
To make of monsters and things indigest   5
Such cherubins as your sweet self resemble,   6
Creating every bad a perfect best   7
As fast as objects to his beams assemble?   8
Oh, 'tis the first, 'tis flatt'ry in my seeing,   9
And my great mind most kingly drinks it up;
Mine eye well knows what with his gust is greeing,   11
And to his palate doth prepare the cup.   12
      If it be poisoned, 'tis the lesser sin   13
      That mine eye loves it and doth first begin.   14

115

Those lines that I before have writ do lie,
Even those that said I could not love you dearer;
Yet then my judgment knew no reason why
My most full flame should afterwards burn clearer.
But reckoning Time, whose millioned accidents   5
Creep in twixt vows and change decrees of kings,   6
Tan sacred beauty, blunt the sharp'st intents,   7
Divert strong minds to th' course of alt'ring things—   8
Alas, why, fearing of Time's tyranny,   9
Might I not then say, "Now I love you best,"   10
When I was certain o'er incertainty,   11
Crowning the present, doubting of the rest?   12
      Love is a babe; then might I not say so,   13
      To give full growth to that which still doth grow.   14

116

Let me not to the marriage of true minds
Admit impediments. Love is not love   2

Which alters when it alteration finds,   3
Or bends with the remover to remove.   4
Oh, no, it is an ever-fixèd mark   5
That looks on tempests and is never shaken;
It is the star to every wand'ring bark,   7
Whose worth's unknown, although his height be taken.   8
Love's not Time's fool, though rosy lips and cheeks   9
Within his bending sickle's compass come;   10
Love alters not with his brief hours and weeks,
But bears it out even to the edge of doom.   12
      If this be error and upon me proved,
      I never writ, nor no man ever loved.

117

Accuse me thus: that I have scanted all   1
Wherein I should your great deserts repay,
Forgot upon your dearest love to call,   3
Whereto all bonds do tie me day by day;
That I have frequent been with unknown minds,   5
And given to time your own dear-purchased right;   6
That I have hoisted sail to all the winds
Which should transport me farthest from your sight.   8
Book both my willfulness and errors down,   9
And on just proof surmise accumulate;   10
Bring me within the level of your frown,   11
But shoot not at me in your wakened hate,
      Since my appeal says I did strive to prove   13
      The constancy and virtue of your love.

118

Like as to make our appetites more keen   1
With eager compounds we our palate urge;   2
As to prevent our maladies unseen   3
We sicken to shun sickness when we purge: 4
Even so, being full of your ne'er-cloying sweetness,   5
To bitter sauces did I frame my feeding   6
And, sick of welfare, found a kind of meetness   7

114.1, 3 Or whether (Indicates alternative possibilities.)   **1 crowned with you** elevated by possession of you   **2 the monarch's . . . flattery** this pleasing delusion to which all monarchs are prone.   **4 your love** my love of you.   **alchemy** science of transmuting base metals   **5 indigest** chaotic, formless   **6 cherubins** angelic forms (suggesting the youth and beauty of the friend)   **7 Creating** creating out of   **8 his beams** its (the eye's) gaze   **9 'tis flatt'ry . . . seeing** my eye is flattering my mind (see lines 1–2)   **11 what . . . greeing** what agrees with the mind's taste   **12 to** to suit   **13–14 'tis . . . begin** it extenuates the eye's sinful deed (of misleading the mind) that it tastes of the poison first, like an official taster sampling food before it is given to the king.
115.5 reckoning Time (1) Time, which we reckon up (2) Time, which demands a reckoning and settles all accounts.   **millioned accidents** multitudinous unforeseen occurrences   **6 twixt vows** i.e., between the making of vows and their fulfillment   **7 Tan** darken, i.e., coarsen   **8 Divert . . . things** divert the most resolute of intentions into the current of changing circumstances   **9 fearing of** fearing   **10 Might . . . say** i.e., wasn't it understandable for me to say then, when I wrote *Those lines* (line 1)   **11 certain o'er incertainty** i.e., certain of my love's perfection then, as contrasted with the uncertainty of the future   **12 Crowning** exalting.   **doubting of** fearing   **13 then might . . . so** i.e., therefore it was wrong of me to say, "Now I love you best" (line 10)   **14 To give** thereby giving
116.2 Admit concede that there might be, allow consideration of. (An echo of the marriage service.)

3 alteration i.e., in age, beauty, affection, health, circumstance   **4 Or . . . remove** or changes simply because there is change (by ill health, mental deterioration, death, absence, or inconstancy) in the person loved.   **5 mark** seamark, conspicuous object distinguishable at sea as an aid to navigation   **7 wand'ring bark** lost ship   **8 Whose . . . taken** whose value is beyond estimation, although its altitude above the horizon can be determined (for purposes of navigation).   **9 fool** plaything, laughingstock   **10 his** i.e., Time's. (Also in line 11.)   **bending** curved.   **compass** range   **12 bears . . . doom** endures or holds out to the very Day of Judgment.
117.1 scanted come short in   **3 Forgot . . . call** forgot to invoke or call upon your most precious love   **5 frequent** familiar.   **unknown minds** strangers of no consequence   **6 And . . . right** and wasted time that should have been devoted to you, to which you had every right   **8 should** were likely to   **9 Book . . . down** Record both my willful faults and errors   **10 on . . . accumulate** to sure proof add surmise, suspicion   **11 level** point-blank range, aim   **13 appeal** legal appealing of the case.   **I . . . prove** my intention was to test
118.1 Like as Just as   **2 eager compounds** pungent, bitter concoctions.   **urge** stimulate   **3 As** just as.   **prevent** anticipate, forestall   **4 We . . . purge** we induce a kind of sickness through purging (i.e., evacuation of stomach or bowel), in order to ward off greater sickness   **5 Even so** in just the same way   **6 bitter sauces** i.e., other loves, undesirable in comparison with you.   **frame** adapt, direct   **7 sick of welfare** surfeited by health and happiness (in love).   **meetness** suitability

To be diseased ere that there was true needing. 8
Thus policy in love, t'anticipate 9
The ills that were not, grew to faults assured, 10
And brought to medicine a healthful state 11
Which, rank of goodness, would by ill be cured. 12
    But thence I learn, and find the lesson true:
    Drugs poison him that so fell sick of you. 14

119

What potions have I drunk of siren tears, 1
Distilled from limbecks foul as hell within, 2
Applying fears to hopes and hopes to fears, 3
Still losing when I saw myself to win! 4
What wretched errors hath my heart committed,
Whilst it hath thought itself so blessèd never! 6
How have mine eyes out of their spheres been fitted 7
In the distraction of this madding fever! 8
Oh, benefit of ill! Now I find true
That better is by evil still made better;
And ruined love, when it is built anew,
Grows fairer than at first, more strong, far greater.
    So I return rebuked to my content,
    And gain by ills thrice more than I have spent.

120

That you were once unkind befriends me now, 1
And for that sorrow which I then did feel 2
Needs must I under my transgression bow, 3
Unless my nerves were brass or hammered steel. 4
For if you were by my unkindness shaken
As I by yours, you've passed a hell of time, 6
And I, a tyrant, have no leisure taken 7
To weigh how once I suffered in your crime. 8
Oh, that our night of woe might have remembered 9
My deepest sense how hard true sorrow hits, 10
And soon to you, as you to me then, tendered 11

The humble salve which wounded bosoms fits! 12
    But that your trespass now becomes a fee; 13
    Mine ransoms yours, and yours must ransom me. 14

121

'Tis better to be vile than vile esteemed 1
When not to be receives reproach of being, 2
And the just pleasure lost which is so deemed 3
Not by our feeling but by others' seeing. 4
For why should others' false adulterate eyes 5
Give salutation to my sportive blood? 6
Or on my frailties why are frailer spies, 7
Which in their wills count bad what I think good? 8
No, I am that I am, and they that level 9
At my abuses reckon up their own. 10
I may be straight though they themselves be bevel. 11
By their rank thoughts my deeds must not be shown, 12
    Unless this general evil they maintain:
    All men are bad, and in their badness reign. 14

122

Thy gift, thy tables, are within my brain 1
Full charactered with lasting memory, 2
Which shall above that idle rank remain 3
Beyond all date, even to eternity—
Or at the least, so long as brain and heart
Have faculty by nature to subsist; 6
Till each to razed oblivion yield his part 7
Of thee, thy record never can be missed. 8
That poor retention could not so much hold, 9
Nor need I tallies thy dear love to score; 10
Therefore to give them from me was I bold, 11

8 ere . . . needing before there was any real necessity for it. **9 policy** shortsighted calculation. **t'anticipate** to forestall **10 assured** actual **11 to medicine** into a state of needing medical care **12 rank of goodness** gorged and sickened by good health **14 Drugs . . . you** a rash and unnecessary course of treatment inflicted true sickness on one (myself) who had thought himself weary of your company.
119.1 siren i.e., deceitful. (The poet seems to speak of an affair.) **2 limbecks** vessels used in distillation. **foul as hell within** i.e., possessing an inner ugliness and evil contrasted with a beautiful and seductive appearance **3 Applying . . . fears** trying vainly to control my wild hopes with a sense of fear and to assuage my fears with hope **4 Still** always. **saw myself** vainly expected **6 so blessèd never** never before so fortunate. **7 How . . . fitted** How my eyes have popped out in convulsive fit **8 distraction** frenzy. **madding fever** fever that drives me mad.
120.1 befriends benefits (by giving me perspective on what I now need to do) **2–3 for . . . bow** i.e., realizing the sorrow I felt from your unkindness, I must now acknowledge my own guilt in being unkind to you **4 nerves** sinews **6 hell of** hellish **7 have . . . taken** have not taken the opportunity **8 weigh** consider. **in your crime** i.e., from your unkindness; or, from erring as you did. (If I suffered so, I should realize you've suffered, too, from my unkindness.) **9 that our night of woe** would that the dark and woeful time of our earlier estrangement. **remembered** reminded **10 sense** consciousness, apprehension **11 And . . . tendered** i.e., and would that I had quickly offered to you, as you did to me

12 humble salve i.e., apology and remorse. **which . . . fits** which is just what wounded hearts need. **13 that your trespass** that unkindness of yours. **fee** payment, compensation **14 ransoms** redeems, excuses **121.1 vile esteemed** (to be) considered vile **2 When . . . being** when not to be vile receives the reproach of vileness. (It's even worse to be unjustly accused of wickedness than to be reproved when one's conduct is truly vile.) **3–4 And . . . seeing** and to lose justifiable pleasure because its justification has to depend not on our feelings but on the censorious attitudes of others. **5 false adulterate eyes** i.e., the eyes of those whose own wickedness prompts them to misconstrue my innocent love **6 Give . . . blood** i.e., greet me, in my lusty merriment, with familiarity and with a knowing wink of the eye. **7 Or . . . spies** Or why should there be persons more faulty than I spying on my fleshly indulgences **8 Which in their wills** who by the measure of their prurient, licentious minds **9 am that** am what. **level** (1) aim (2) guess **10 abuses** misdoings. **reckon up their own** i.e., merely enumerate their own misdeeds. **11 bevel** out of square, crooked. **12 rank** ugly, foul. **shown** viewed, interpreted **14 reign** i.e., prosper. (Only a cynic would interpret my success in love as a paradoxical proof of my sharing in general human depravity.)
122.1 tables writing tablet, memorandum book **2 charactered with** written by **3 that idle rank** i.e., the relative unimportance of that memorandum book (as compared with the memory itself) **6 faculty . . . subsist** natural power to survive **7–8 Till . . . missed** until both heart and brain have given up their memory of you to the ravages of time, what you have written never can be lost. (Hence the memorandum book itself, which the poet has given away, is not essential.) **9 retention** i.e., the book, an instrument for retaining memoranda. **so much** i.e., as much as is in my memory **10 tallies** sticks notched to serve for reckoning. (The notebook is such a mere *tally*.) **score** reckon **11 to . . . me** i.e., to give away the writing tablet. **bold** i.e., bold in taking the liberty

To trust those tables that receive thee more. 12
   To keep an adjunct to remember thee 13
   Were to import forgetfulness in me. 14

123

No, Time, thou shalt not boast that I do change.
Thy pyramids built up with newer might 2
To me are nothing novel, nothing strange; 3
They are but dressings of a former sight. 4
Our dates are brief, and therefore we admire 5
What thou dost foist upon us that is old,
And rather make them born to our desire 7
Than think that we before have heard them told. 8
Thy registers and thee I both defy, 9
Not wond'ring at the present nor the past, 10
For thy records and what we see doth lie, 11
Made more or less by thy continual haste. 12
   This I do vow and this shall ever be:
   I will be true, despite thy scythe and thee.

124

If my dear love were but the child of state, 1
It might for Fortune's bastard be unfathered, 2
As subject to Time's love or to Time's hate,
Weeds among weeds, or flowers with flowers gathered. 4
No, it was builded far from accident; 5
It suffers not in smiling pomp, nor falls 6
Under the blow of thrallèd discontent, 7
Whereto th'inviting time our fashion calls. 8
It fears not Policy, that heretic, 9
Which works on leases of short-numbered hours, 10
But all alone stands hugely politic, 11
That it nor grows with heat nor drowns with showers. 12
   To this I witness call the fools of Time, 13
   Which die for goodness, who have lived for crime. 14

125

Were't aught to me I bore the canopy, 1
With my extern the outward honoring, 2
Or laid great bases for eternity 3
Which proves more short than waste or ruining? 4
Have I not seen dwellers on form and favor 5
Lose all, and more, by paying too much rent, 6
For compound sweet forgoing simple savor, 7
Pitiful thrivers, in their gazing spent? 8
No, let me be obsequious in thy heart, 9
And take thou my oblation, poor but free, 10
Which is not mixed with seconds, knows no art 11
But mutual render, only me for thee. 12
   Hence, thou suborned informer! A true soul 13
   When most impeached stands least in thy control. 14

126

O thou, my lovely boy, who in thy power 1
Dost hold Time's fickle glass, his sickle hour; 2
Who hast by waning grown, and therein show'st 3
Thy lovers withering as thy sweet self grow'st; 4
If Nature, sovereign mistress over wrack, 5
As thou goest onwards, still will pluck thee back, 6
She keeps thee to this purpose, that her skill 7
May Time disgrace and wretched minutes kill. 8
Yet fear her, O thou minion of her pleasure! 9
She may detain, but not still keep, her treasure. 10
Her audit, though delayed, answered must be, 11
And her quietus is to render thee. 12

---

12 those tables i.e., those of memory. **receive thee more** retain more of you. **13 adjunct** aid **14 Were** would be. **import** imply, impute **123.2 pyramids** (May refer to obelisks or other structures erected in Rome in 1586 or in London in 1603.) **3 nothing** not at all **4 dressings . . . sight** reconstructions in new form of things from the past. **5 dates** life spans **7 make . . . desire** consider them newly created to our liking and reinvented by us **8 told** reckoned, told about. **9 registers** visual records, monuments **10 wond'ring** marveling **11 doth lie** deceives us **12 Made . . . haste** i.e., raised one minute and ruined the next (by Time), and alternately overvalued and undervalued by us. **124.1–2 If . . . unfathered** If my love for you were merely the product of circumstances and your high position, we might disavow it as nothing but the bastard child of Fortune **4 Weeds . . . gathered** either despised as worthless like a weed or cherished like a flower as Fortune dictates. **5 accident** chance, fortune **6–8 It . . . calls** it does not grow acquiescent to the dictates of pomp and finery, nor does it weaken under the blows of slavish adversity, both of which the insidious mores of our present age tempt us to regard as fashionable. **9 Policy, that heretic** cunning expediency, false to the spirit of love **10 Which . . . hours** which thinks only shortsightedly of short-term gain and makes only short-term commitments **11 hugely politic** prudent in a long-term sense **12 That . . . showers** so that it neither pins its hopes unrealistically on rising fortunes nor grows desperate in times of adversity. **13–14 To . . . crime** I call as witnesses those creatures of Time who succumb to the moral weaknesses described in this sonnet, and who repent their evil ways only after having lived corruptly.

125.1–4 Were't . . . ruining? Would it mean anything to me if I did public homage to great persons by carrying over their heads a cloth of state as they go in procession, thereby honoring what is external by means of a purely external action, or if I laid foundations for supposedly eternal monuments which then prove to last no longer than the forces of decay and ruin allow? **5 dwellers . . . favor** those who depend on court etiquette and influence peddling; also, in figure and face **6 by paying . . . rent** i.e., by overdoing flattery and depending too much on hopes of obtaining favor **7 For . . . savor** i.e., foregoing wholesome sincerity for the sake of obsequious flattery **8 Pitiful . . . spent** pitiful in their unsuccessful attempts, their means consumed in their ineffectual fawning on greatness. **9 obsequious** (1) courtly (2) devoted **10 oblation** offering. **free** freely offered **11 seconds** inferior matter, adulterants. **art** artifice **12 render** exchange **13 suborned informer** perjured witness, the envious one who has charged the poet with self-interested flattery. **14 impeached** accused **126.1** (This sonnet is made up of six couplets.) **2 Time's . . . hour** Time's treacherous and inexorable hourglass, his reaping time **3 Who . . . grown** you who have grown more youthfully beautiful as you have aged. **show'st** show by way of contrast with yourself **4 Thy lovers** (including the poet) **5 wrack** ruin. (Nature is mistress over decay in that she decays and renews.) **6 onwards** i.e., in life's journey **7 to** for **8 May . . . kill** may put Time to shame and render powerless the passing of the minutes. **9 Yet . . . pleasure!** Yet fear Nature too, you who as her darling are subject to her will! **10 She . . . treasure** i.e., Nature may keep and restore you for a time, but Time will ultimately triumph. **11 Her audit** i.e., The proverbial paying of one's debt to Nature through death; also, Nature's account to Time. **answered** paid **12 quietus** discharge, quittance. **render** surrender

127

In the old age black was not counted fair,   1
Or if it were, it bore not beauty's name;   2
But now is black beauty's successive heir,   3
And beauty slandered with a bastard shame.   4
For since each hand hath put on nature's power,   5
Fairing the foul with art's false borrowed face,   6
Sweet beauty hath no name, no holy bower,   7
But is profaned, if not lives in disgrace.   8
Therefore my mistress' eyes are raven black,
Her brows so suited, and they mourners seem   10
At such who, not born fair, no beauty lack,   11
Sland'ring creation with a false esteem.   12
    Yet so they mourn, becoming of their woe,   13
    That every tongue says beauty should look so.

128

How oft, when thou, my music, music play'st
Upon that blessèd wood whose motion sounds   2
With thy sweet fingers when thou gently sway'st   3
The wiry concord that mine ear confounds,   4
Do I envy those jacks that nimble leap   5
To kiss the tender inward of thy hand,
Whilst my poor lips, which should that harvest reap,
At the wood's boldness by thee blushing stand!   8
To be so tickled, they would change their state   9
And situation with those dancing chips
O'er whom thy fingers walk with gentle gait,
Making dead wood more blest than living lips.
    Since saucy jacks so happy are in this,   13
    Give them thy fingers, me thy lips to kiss.

129

Th'expense of spirit in a waste of shame   1
Is lust in action; and, till action, lust   2

Is perjured, murd'rous, bloody, full of blame,   3
Savage, extreme, rude, cruel, not to trust,   4
Enjoyed no sooner but despisèd straight,   5
Past reason hunted, and no sooner had   6
Past reason hated, as a swallowed bait
On purpose laid to make the taker mad;
Mad in pursuit, and in possession so;
Had, having, and in quest to have, extreme;
A bliss in proof, and proved, a very woe;   11
Before, a joy proposed; behind, a dream.   12
    All this the world well knows; yet none knows well
    To shun the heaven that leads men to this hell. 14

130

My mistress' eyes are nothing like the sun;   1
Coral is far more red than her lips' red;
If snow be white, why then her breasts are dun;   3
If hairs be wires, black wires grow on her head.
I have seen roses damasked, red and white,   5
But no such roses see I in her cheeks;
And in some perfumes is there more delight
Than in the breath that from my mistress reeks.   8
I love to hear her speak, yet well I know
That music hath a far more pleasing sound.
I grant I never saw a goddess go;   11
My mistress, when she walks, treads on the ground.
    And yet, by heaven, I think my love as rare   13
    As any she belied with false compare.   14

131

Thou art as tyrannous, so as thou art,   1
As those whose beauties proudly make them cruel;
For well thou know'st to my dear doting heart   3
Thou art the fairest and most precious jewel.
Yet, in good faith, some say that thee behold
Thy face hath not the power to make love groan;
To say they err I dare not be so bold,
Although I swear it to myself alone.
And, to be sure that is not false I swear,   9
A thousand groans, but thinking on thy face,   10
One on another's neck, do witness bear   11
Thy black is fairest in my judgment's place.   12
    In nothing art thou black save in thy deeds,
    And thence this slander, as I think, proceeds.   14

127.1 old age olden times.   **black** darkness of hair and eyes.   **fair**
(1) beautiful (2) light-complexioned   **2 it bore . . . name** i.e., it was not
called so   **3 now . . . heir** nowadays black has been named lawful successor to the title of beauty   **4 beauty . . . shame** i.e., blonde beauty is
declared illegitimate, created artificially by cosmetics.   **5 put on** assumed
6 Fairing the foul making the ugly beautiful.   **borrowed face** i.e., cosmetics   **7 no name . . . bower** no reputation or pride of family, and no
sacred abode   **8 if not** or even   **10 so suited** decked out in the same
color and for the same reason   **11 At** for.   **no beauty lack** i.e., nonetheless make themselves attractive   **12 Sland'ring . . . esteem** i.e., dishonoring nature by blurring the distinction between real and false beauty.
13 they i.e., my mistress' eyes.   **becoming of** gracing or being graced by
128.2 wood keys of the spinet or virginal.   **motion** mechanism
3 thou gently sway'st you gently control   **4 wiry concord** harmony
produced by strings.   **confounds** i.e., pleasurably overwhelms
5 jacks (Literally, upright pieces of wood fixed to the key lever and
fitted with a quill that plucks the strings of the virginal; here used of
the keys and with a pun on *jacks* in the sense of "common fellows," as
in line 13.)   **8 by** beside, or, with. (The poet stands beside the lady as
she plays, blushing to his very lips; he blushes in vexation at the *jacks'*
boldness with her hand.)   **9 they** i.e., my lips   **13 jacks** (With a pun
on "knaves, fellows" as in line 5.)
129.1–2 Th'expense . . . action Lust being consummated is the expenditure or dissipation of vital energy in an orgy of shameful extravagance and guilt. (*Spirit* also suggests "sperm.")   **2 till action** until it
achieves consummation

3 blame (1) guilt (2) recrimination   **4 rude** brutal.   **to trust** to be
trusted   **5 straight** immediately   **6 Past reason** madly, intemperately
11 in proof while experienced.   **proved** i.e., afterward   **12 Before** in
prospect   **14 the heaven** the seeming bliss of sexual consummation.
hell (Often equated imagistically with the vagina.)
130.1 nothing not at all   **3 dun** dull grayish brown, mouse-colored
5 damasked mingled red and white   **8 reeks** emanates.   **11 go** walk
13 rare extraordinary and unique   **14 As . . . compare** as any woman
misrepresented with false comparison.
131.1 tyrannous pitiless and domineering.   **so as thou art** just as you
are (dark, not considered handsome)   **3 dear** fond   **9 to be sure** as
proof.   **false I** false that I   **10 but thinking on** when I do no more
than think of   **11 One . . . neck** one rapidly after another   **12 black**
dark complexion.   **my judgment's place** my opinion.   **14 this slander** (See lines 5–6.)   **proceeds** originates.

132

Thine eyes I love, and they, as pitying me,   1
Knowing thy heart torment me with disdain,   2
Have put on black, and loving mourners be,
Looking with pretty ruth upon my pain.   4
And truly not the morning sun of heaven
Better becomes the gray cheeks of the east,   6
Nor that full star that ushers in the even   7
Doth half that glory to the sober west   8
As those two mourning eyes become thy face.   9
Oh, let it then as well beseem thy heart   10
To mourn for me, since mourning doth thee grace,   11
And suit thy pity like in every part.   12
    Then will I swear beauty herself is black,
    And all they foul that thy complexion lack.   14

133

Beshrew that heart that makes my heart to groan   1
For that deep wound it gives my friend and me!
Is't not enough to torture me alone,
But slave to slavery my sweet'st friend must be?   4
Me from myself thy cruel eye hath taken,
And my next self thou harder hast engrossed.   6
Of him, myself, and thee I am forsaken—
A torment thrice threefold thus to be crossed.   8
Prison my heart in thy steel bosom's ward,   9
But then my friend's heart let my poor heart bail;   10
Whoe'er keeps me, let my heart be his guard;   11
Thou canst not then use rigor in my jail.   12
    And yet thou wilt; for I, being pent in thee,   13
    Perforce am thine, and all that is in me.   14

134

So, now I have confessed that he is thine,   1
And I myself am mortgaged to thy will,   2
Myself I'll forfeit, so that other mine   3
Thou wilt restore to be my comfort still.
But thou wilt not, nor he will not be free,   5
For thou art covetous and he is kind;

He learned but surety-like to write for me   7
Under that bond that him as fast doth bind.   8
The statute of thy beauty thou wilt take,   9
Thou usurer, that put'st forth all to use,   10
And sue a friend came debtor for my sake;   11
So him I lose through my unkind abuse.   12
    Him have I lost; thou hast both him and me;
    He pays the whole, and yet am I not free.   14

135

Whoever hath her wish, thou hast thy Will,   1
And Will to boot, and Will in overplus;
More than enough am I that vex thee still,   3
To thy sweet will making addition thus.
Wilt thou, whose will is large and spacious,
Not once vouchsafe to hide my will in thine?   6
Shall will in others seem right gracious,   7
And in my will no fair acceptance shine?
The sea, all water, yet receives rain still
And in abundance addeth to his store;   10
So thou, being rich in Will, add to thy Will
One will of mine, to make thy large Will more.
    Let no unkind no fair beseechers kill;   13
    Think all but one, and me in that one Will.   14

136

If thy soul check thee that I come so near,   1
Swear to thy blind soul that I was thy Will,   2
And will, thy soul knows, is admitted there;
Thus far for love my love suit, sweet, fulfill.   4
Will will fulfill the treasure of thy love,   5
Ay, fill it full with wills, and my will one.   6
In things of great receipt with ease we prove   7
Among a number one is reckoned none.   8
Then in the number let me pass untold,   9

132.1 **as** as if   **2 Knowing . . . torment** knowing that your heart torments   **4 ruth** pity   **6 becomes** adorns.   **cheeks** i.e., clouds   **7 that full star** the evening star, Hesperus, i.e., Venus.   **even** evening   **8 Doth** i.e., lends.   **sober** somber, subdued in color   **9 mourning** black. (Spelled "morning" in the Quarto, suggesting a pun on line 5.)   **10 beseem** suit   **11 since . . . grace** since you look very attractive in mourning black   **12 And suit . . . part** and dress your pity similarly, in your heart and eyes.   **14 And . . . that** and that all those are ugly who
133.1 **Beshrew** i.e., A plague upon   **4 slave to slavery** utterly enslaved   **6 And . . . engrossed** i.e., and you have put my dearest friend, my other self, under even greater restraint.   **engrossed** (1) driven into obsession (2) bought up wholesale.   **8 crossed** thwarted, afflicted.   **9 Prison** Imprison.   **thy . . . ward** the prison cell of your hard heart   **10 bail** set free by taking its place   **11 keeps** has custody of.   **his guard** my friend's guardhouse   **12 rigor** harshness.   **my jail** i.e., my heart, where my friend is kept (and where I can protect him from your harsh authority).   **13 pent** shut up   **14 and all** along with everything (including my friend's heart)
134.1 **now** now that   **2 will** (1) wishes (2) fleshly desire   **3 so . . . mine** provided that my other self, my friend   **5 will not** does not wish to, won't

7 surety-like as security, as guarantor.   **write** sign the bond, endorse (suggesting that the friend has taken the poet's place with the mistress)   **8 Under . . . bind** under that mortgage or bond (of sexual enslavement) that now binds him as securely as it does me.   **9 statute** a usurer's security or amount of money secured under his bond.   **take** call in, invoke. (The lady will exact the full forfeiture specified in the mortgage as the amount to which her beauty entitles her.)   **10 use** (1) usury (2) sexual pleasure   **11 sue** (With suggestion also of "woo.")   **came** i.e., who became   **12 my unkind abuse** your ill usage and unkind deceiving (of me).   **14 pays** (With sexual suggestion.)
135.1 **Will** (This and the following sonnet and sonnet 143 ring changes on the word *will*—sexual desire, temper, passion, and the poet's name; possibly also the friend's name. The word can also suggest the sexual organs, male and female.)   **3 vex** (by unwelcome wooing).   **still** continually   **6 hide . . . thine** (With sexual suggestion.)   **7 will in others** others' wills   **10 his** its   **13 Let . . . kill** Let no unkind word kill any who seek your favors, or, Let "no" unkind, etc., do not kill your wooers with the word no   **14 Think . . . Will** i.e., think all your wooers and their wills to be but one, all comprised in me.
136.1 **check** rebuke.   **come so near** i.e., come so near the truth about you (in my previous sonnet); with suggestion of physical nearness also   **2 blind** unperceptive; shut up in the body without sensory organs   **4 fulfill** grant.   **5 fulfill the treasure** fill full the treasury. (With suggestion of sexual entry.)   **6 my will** (Suggesting "my penis.")   **one** one of them.   **7 receipt** capacity. (Suggesting profligacy.)   **8 one . . . none** (A variant of the common saying "one is no number.")   **9 untold** uncounted

Though in thy store's account I one must be;   10
For nothing hold me, so it please thee hold   11
That nothing me, a something, sweet, to thee.   12
　　Make but my name thy love, and love that still,   13
　　And then thou lovest me for my name is Will.   14

137

Thou blind fool, Love, what dost thou to mine eyes   1
That they behold and see not what they see?   2
They know what beauty is, see where it lies,   3
Yet what the best is take the worst to be.   4
If eyes corrupt by overpartial looks   5
Be anchored in the bay where all men ride,   6
Why of eyes' falsehood hast thou forgèd hooks,   7
Whereto the judgment of my heart is tied?
Why should my heart think that a several plot   9
Which my heart knows the wide world's common place?   10
Or mine eyes seeing this, say this is not,   11
To put fair truth upon so foul a face?
　　In things right true my heart and eyes have erred,
　　And to this false plague are they now transferred.   14

138

When my love swears that she is made of truth   1
I do believe her, though I know she lies,   2
That she might think me some untutored youth,
Unlearnèd in the world's false subtleties.
Thus vainly thinking that she thinks me young,   5
Although she knows my days are past the best,
Simply I credit her false-speaking tongue;   7
On both sides thus is simple truth suppressed.
But wherefore says she not she is unjust?   9
And wherefore say not I that I am old?
Oh, love's best habit is in seeming trust,   11
And age in love loves not to have years told.   12

Therefore I lie with her, and she with me,   13
And in our faults by lies we flattered be.   14

139

Oh, call not me to justify the wrong   1
That thy unkindness lays upon my heart;   2
Wound me not with thine eye but with thy tongue;   3
Use power with power, and slay me not by art.   4
Tell me thou lov'st elsewhere, but in my sight,
Dear heart, forbear to glance thine eye aside;
What need'st thou wound with cunning when thy might   7
Is more than my o'erpressed defense can bide?   8
Let me excuse thee: "Ah, my love well knows
Her pretty looks have been mine enemies,
And therefore from my face she turns my foes,   11
That they elsewhere might dart their injuries."
　　Yet do not so; but since I am near slain,   13
　　Kill me outright with looks and rid my pain.   14

140

Be wise as thou art cruel; do not press
My tongue-tied patience with too much disdain,
Lest sorrow lend me words, and words express
The manner of my pity-wanting pain.   4
If I might teach thee wit, better it were,   5
Though not to love, yet, love, to tell me so,   6
As testy sick men, when their deaths be near,
No news but health from their physicians know.   8
For if I should despair, I should grow mad,
And in my madness might speak ill of thee.
Now this ill-wresting world is grown so bad,   11
Mad slanderers by mad ears believèd be.
　　That I may not be so, nor thou belied,   13
　　Bear thine eyes straight, though thy proud heart go
　　　　wide.   14

141

In faith, I do not love thee with mine eyes,
For they in thee a thousand errors note;   2
But 'tis my heart that loves what they despise,
Who in despite of view is pleased to dote.   4
Nor are mine ears with thy tongue's tune delighted,

10 in . . . account in your (huge) inventory (of lovers)   11–12 For . . .
thee i.e., consider me too insignificant to think of, provided that you
deign to hold insignificant me to you, my sweet, thereby making me
something of worth. (*Something* is sexually suggestive of "some
thing.")   13 my name i.e., "will," that is, desire.   still continually
14 for because
137.1 Love Cupid, portrayed as blind   2 see not do not comprehend
3 lies resides (and deceives through false appearance)   4 Yet . . . be
yet take the worst for the best.   5 corrupt by overpartial looks corrupted by doting and frankly prejudiced gazing   6 Be . . . ride seek
harbor where all men do so, i.e., *ride* in the arms of promiscuous
women   7 Why . . . hooks why have you, Love, fashioned snares out
of my eyes' delusion   9 think . . . plot think that to be a private field,
i.e., that woman to be the exclusive property of one man   10 knows
knows to be.   common place (1) a commons, a common pasture
(2) a woman's body that is open, promiscuous.   11 Or Or why
should.   not not so   14 false plague (1) plague of judging falsely
(2) false woman
138.1 (A version of this sonnet appears in *The Passionate Pilgrim*.)
truth fidelity, constancy   2 believe i.e., pretend to believe   5 vainly
thinking acting as though I thought   7 Simply (1) pretending to be
foolish (2) unconditionally.   credit give credence to   9 unjust
unfaithful, deceitful.   11 habit demeanor. (With, however, a suggestion of *garb*, i.e., "something put on.")   seeming trust apparent
fidelity   12 age in love an aging person in love, or, in matters of love.
told (1) counted (2) divulged.

13 lie with (1) deceive (2) have sex with   14 And . . . be and so by
lies we flatteringly deceive ourselves about our moral lapses.
139.1 call ask.   justify the wrong i.e., condone something actually
taking place under my eyes   2 unkindness i.e., flagrant infidelity
3 with thine eye i.e., with a roving eye. (See lines 5–6.)   4 with
power i.e., candidly, directly.   art artifice, cunning.   7 What why
8 bide abide, withstand.   11 foes i.e., the *pretty looks*, the beauty and
wanton glances of line 10   13 near nearly   14 rid end. (*Rid my pain*
also suggests "satiate my craving.")
140.4 pity-wanting (1) unpitied by you (2) pity-craving   5 wit wisdom, prudence   5–6 better . . . so (I would teach you that) even
though you don't love me, yet, dear friend, it would be better to tell
me that you do   8 know i.e., hear.   11 ill-wresting misinterpreting
in an evil sense.   bad bad (that)   13 so i.e., a *mad slanderer* who is
believèd.   belied slandered   14 Bear . . . straight keep your eyes on
me.   wide astray.
141.2 errors flaws in beauty   4 Who . . . view which (i.e., the heart),
in spite of what the eyes see

Nor tender feeling to base touches prone,   6
Nor taste, nor smell, desire to be invited
To any sensual feast with thee alone.
But my five wits nor my five senses can   9
Dissuade one foolish heart from serving thee,
Who leaves unswayed the likeness of a man,   11
Thy proud heart's slave and vassal wretch to be.
    Only my plague thus far I count my gain,   13
    That she that makes me sin awards me pain.   14

142

Love is my sin, and thy dear virtue hate,   1
Hate of my sin, grounded on sinful loving.   2
Oh, but with mine compare thou thine own state,
And thou shalt find it merits not reproving;   4
Or, if it do, not from those lips of thine
That have profaned their scarlet ornaments   6
And sealed false bonds of love as oft as mine,   7
Robbed others' beds' revenues of their rents.   8
Be it lawful I love thee as thou lov'st those   9
Whom thine eyes woo as mine importune thee.   10
Root pity in thy heart, that when it grows
Thy pity may deserve to pitied be.   12
    If thou dost seek to have what thou dost hide,   13
    By self-example mayst thou be denied.

143

Lo, as a careful huswife runs to catch   1
One of her feathered creatures broke away,   2
Sets down her babe and makes all swift dispatch
In pursuit of the thing she would have stay,
Whilst her neglected child holds her in chase,   5
Cries to catch her whose busy care is bent
To follow that which flies before her face,   7

Not prizing her poor infant's discontent: 8
So run'st thou after that which flies from thee,
Whilst I, thy babe, chase thee afar behind;
But if thou catch thy hope, turn back to me,
And play the mother's part: kiss me, be kind.
    So will I pray that thou mayst have thy Will,   13
    If thou turn back and my loud crying still.   14

144

Two loves I have, of comfort and despair,   1
Which like two spirits do suggest me still: 2
The better angel is a man right fair,   3
The worser spirit a woman colored ill.   4
To win me soon to hell, my female evil
Tempteth my better angel from my side,
And would corrupt my saint to be a devil,
Wooing his purity with her foul pride.
And whether that my angel be turned fiend
Suspect I may, yet not directly tell;
But being both from me, both to each friend,   11
I guess one angel in another's hell.   12
    Yet this shall I ne'er know, but live in doubt
    Till my bad angel fire my good one out.   14

145

Those lips that Love's own hand did make   1
Breathed forth the sound that said "I hate"
To me that languished for her sake;
But when she saw my woeful state,
Straight in her heart did mercy come,   5
Chiding that tongue that ever sweet
Was used in giving gentle doom,   7
And taught it thus anew to greet:
"I hate" she altered with an end,
That followed it as gentle day
Doth follow night, who like a fiend
From heaven to hell is flown away.
    "I hate" from hate away she threw,   13
    And saved my life, saying "not you."   14

---

6 Nor . . . prone nor (is) my delicate sense of touch inclined toward carnal contact (with you)   **9 my five wits** (neither) my five intellectual senses, i.e., the common sense, imagination, fancy, estimation (judgment), and memory   **11 Who . . . man** i.e., which heart abandons the proper government of my person, leaving me the mere likeness of a man   **13 thus far** to the following extent   **14 That . . . pain** i.e., that the sin brings with it its own punishment and contrition, thus presumably shortening my torment after death. (With a suggestion in *pain* of "sexual pleasure"; see sonnet 139.)
142.1–2 Love . . . loving My sin is to love you, and your best virtue is to hate—hate that sin in me, but also because of your uncontrolled sexual longing for other men. (The bitter paradox here is that hatred of sin must be virtue, and yet the lady is herself deeply implicated in this sin; her hatred is more a disdainful rejection of the poet's love than a noble virtue.)   **4 it** i.e., my state   **6–7 That . . . mine** i.e., that have forsworn themselves in love as often as my lips have. (The *scarlet ornaments* are lips and also red wax used to seal documents; they *seal* with a kiss.)   **8 Robbed . . . rents** i.e., and committed adultery with other women's husbands. (The metaphor is of income-yielding estates, *revenues*, whose *rents* or payments made by tenants are not properly paid; the husband does not pay what is owed to the wife in terms of marital affection and the producing of children.)
9–10 Be . . . thee i.e., I am as justified in loving you and imploring you with my eyes as you are in pursuing other men. (*Be it lawful* is a legal phrase meaning "Let it be considered lawful that.")   **12 deserve** make you deserving   **13 what . . . hide** what you withhold, i.e., pity
143.1 careful distressed, full of cares, busy.   **huswife** housewife
2 feathered . . . away domestic fowl which has broken away from the flock   **5 holds her in chase** chases after her   **7 flies** flees

8 Not prizing disregarding   **13 Will** (See sonnets 135, 136.)   **14 still** hush, make quiet.
144.1 (This sonnet appears, somewhat altered, in *The Passionate Pilgrim*.)   **2 suggest** urge, offer counsel, tempt.   **still** continually
3 right fair very handsome and blond   **4 ill** i.e., dark of complexion.
11 from me away from me. (The poet suspects they are together.)
both . . . friend friends to each other   **12 I . . . hell** I suspect that she (the evil angel) has him in her power (i.e., her sexual embracement; *hell* is slang for the pudenda).   **14 fire . . . out** drive out my good angel, stop seeing him. (With the suggestion of driving him out of the lady's sexual body as one would use fire and smoke to drive an animal out of its burrow, and with the further suggestion that the *fire* is venereal disease. *Bad angel* also hints at bad coinage driving out good money.)
145.1 (This sonnet is in eight-syllable meter.)   **5 Straight** at once
7 used . . . doom accustomed to passing a mild sentence   **13 "I hate" . . . threw** i.e., She separated the phrase "I hate" from the hatred I feared it expressed, from hateful meaning   **13–14 hate away . . . And** (Punning perhaps on the name of Shakespeare's wife, Anne Hathaway.)

146

Poor soul, the center of my sinful earth,   1
Thrall to these rebel powers that thee array,   2
Why dost thou pine within and suffer dearth,
Painting thy outward walls so costly gay?   4
Why so large cost, having so short a lease,   5
Dost thou upon thy fading mansion spend?   6
Shall worms, inheritors of this excess,
Eat up thy charge? Is this thy body's end?   8
Then, soul, live thou upon thy servant's loss,   9
And let that pine to aggravate thy store,   10
Buy terms divine in selling hours of dross;   11
Within be fed, without be rich no more.
    So shalt thou feed on Death, that feeds on men,
    And Death once dead, there's no more dying then.

147

My love is as a fever, longing still   1
For that which longer nurseth the disease,   2
Feeding on that which doth preserve the ill,   3
Th'uncertain sickly appetite to please.   4
My reason, the physician to my love,
Angry that his prescriptions are not kept,
Hath left me, and I desperate now approve   7
Desire is death, which physic did except.   8
Past cure I am, now reason is past care,   9
And frantic-mad with evermore unrest;   10
My thoughts and my discourse as madmen's are,
At random from the truth vainly expressed;   12
    For I have sworn thee fair and thought thee bright,
    Who art as black as hell, as dark as night.

148

Oh, me, what eyes hath love put in my head,
Which have no correspondence with true sight!
Or, if they have, where is my judgment fled,
That censures falsely what they see aright?   4
If that be fair whereon my false eyes dote,
What means the world to say it is not so?

If it be not, then love doth well denote   7
Love's eye is not so true as all men's "no."   8
How can it? Oh, how can love's eye be true,
That is so vexed with watching and with tears?   10
No marvel then though I mistake my view;   11
The sun itself sees not till heaven clears.
    O cunning love, with tears thou keep'st me blind,
    Lest eyes well-seeing thy foul faults should find.

149

Canst thou, O cruel, say I love thee not,
When I against myself with thee partake?   2
Do I not think on thee when I forgot   3
Am of myself, all tyrant for thy sake?   4
Who hateth thee that I do call my friend?
On whom frown'st thou that I do fawn upon?
Nay, if thou lour'st on me, do I not spend   7
Revenge upon myself with present moan?   8
What merit do I in myself respect   9
That is so proud thy service to despise,   10
When all my best doth worship thy defect,   11
Commanded by the motion of thine eyes?
    But, love, hate on, for now I know thy mind:
    Those that can see thou lov'st, and I am blind.   14

150

Oh, from what power hast thou this powerful might
With insufficiency my heart to sway?   2
To make me give the lie to my true sight   3
And swear that brightness doth not grace the day?   4
Whence hast thou this becoming of things ill,   5
That in the very refuse of thy deeds   6
There is such strength and warrantise of skill   7
That, in my mind, thy worst all best exceeds?
Who taught thee how to make me love thee more,
The more I hear and see just cause of hate?
Oh, though I love what others do abhor,
With others thou shouldst not abhor my state.   12
    If thy unworthiness raised love in me,
    More worthy I to be beloved of thee.

146.1 **sinful earth** body   2 **Thrall . . . array** made captive by the rebellious flesh that decks you in finery and lines you up in battle array. ("Thrall to" is one of several conjectures; the Quarto repeats "My sinfull earth" from line 1.)   4 **outward walls** i.e., the body, decked out in finery, cosmetics, etc.   5 **having . . . lease** having so brief a period of residence in this world   6 **mansion** dwelling, i.e., the body   8 **charge** expense, outlay.   **Is . . . end?** Is this what your body was intended to be used for?   9 **thy servant's** i.e., the body's   10 **let that . . . store** let the body starve to increase your stock of spiritual riches   11 **Buy . . . dross** i.e., purchase eternal life in return for giving up (selling) mere hours of wasteful pleasure; secure *terms* that only God can provide
147.1 **still** always   2 **nurseth** nourishes   3 **preserve the ill** sustain the illness   4 **Th'uncertain** the finicky   7–8 **and I . . . except** and I now, desperately sick and in desperation, discover by experience that desire, which rejected medicine (or, which medical advice warned against), is fatal.   9 **care** medical care. (The line is an inversion of the proverb, "things past cure are past care," i.e., don't worry about what can't be helped. Reason, the physician, has ceased to care for his patient.)   10 **evermore** constant and increasing   12 **vainly** to no sensible purpose
148.4 **censures** judges

7 **love** i.e., the self-deceiving nature of my love.   **denote** indicate, demonstrate (that)   8 **eye** (With a pun on "ay," yes.)   10 **vexed** troubled.   **watching** remaining awake   11 **I** (Punning on "eye.")   **mistake my view** err in what I see
149.2 **partake** take part (against myself).   3–4 **Do . . . sake?** Do I not put consideration of you foremost when I am tyrannously neglectful of, or oblivious of, myself and my best interests on your behalf?
7 **spend** vent   8 **present moan** immediate suffering and lamentation.   9 **respect** value   10 **thy . . . despise** as to think it demeaning to serve you   11 **all my best** all that is best in me.   **defect** flaws   14 **Those . . . blind** i.e., you scorn one who loves you in a blind passion, in defiance of reason, and are drawn instead to those who know you for what you are.
150.2 **With insufficiency** by means of all your shortcomings.   **sway** rule.   3 **give the lie to** accuse flatly of lying   4 **And . . . day** i.e., and swear that what is so is not so, that what is fair and beautiful is not fair and beautiful, since you are dark.   5 **becoming . . . ill** i.e., ability to show ill things in a becoming light   6 **in . . . deeds** in the most debased of your actions   7 **warrantise of skill** warrant or assurance of expertise   12 **state** i.e., condition of being helplessly in love.

151

Love is too young to know what conscience is;   1
Yet who knows not conscience is born of love?   2
Then, gentle cheater, urge not my amiss,   3
Lest guilty of my faults thy sweet self prove.
For, thou betraying me, I do betray   5
My nobler part to my gross body's treason.   6
My soul doth tell my body that he may   7
Triumph in love; flesh stays no farther reason,   8
But, rising at thy name, doth point out thee   9
As his triumphant prize. Proud of this pride,   10
He is contented thy poor drudge to be,
To stand in thy affairs, fall by thy side.   12
    No want of conscience hold it that I call   13
    Her "love" for whose dear love I rise and fall.

152

In loving thee thou know'st I am forsworn,   1
But thou art twice forsworn, to me love swearing:
In act thy bed-vow broke, and new faith torn   3
In vowing new hate after new love bearing.   4
But why of two oaths' breach do I accuse thee,
When I break twenty? I am perjured most,
For all my vows are oaths but to misuse thee,   7
And all my honest faith in thee is lost.   8
For I have sworn deep oaths of thy deep kindness,
Oaths of thy love, thy truth, thy constancy,
And, to enlighten thee, gave eyes to blindness,   11
Or made them swear against the thing they see;

For I have sworn thee fair. More perjured eye,   13
To swear against the truth so foul a lie!

153

Cupid laid by his brand and fell asleep.   1
A maid of Dian's this advantage found,   2
And his love-kindling fire did quickly steep
In a cold valley-fountain of that ground,   4
Which borrowed from this holy fire of Love
A dateless lively heat, still to endure,   6
And grew a seething bath, which yet men prove   7
Against strange maladies a sovereign cure.   8
But at my mistress' eye Love's brand new-fired,   9
The boy for trial needs would touch my breast;   10
I, sick withal, the help of bath desired,   11
And thither hied, a sad distempered guest,   12
    But found no cure. The bath for my help lies
    Where Cupid got new fire—my mistress' eyes.

154

The little love god lying once asleep
Laid by his side his heart-inflaming brand,
Whilst many nymphs that vowed chaste life to keep
Came tripping by; but in her maiden hand
The fairest votary took up that fire
Which many legions of true hearts had warmed,
And so the general of hot desire   7
Was, sleeping, by a virgin hand disarmed.
This brand she quenchèd in a cool well by,   9
Which from Love's fire took heat perpetual,
Growing a bath and healthful remedy   11
For men diseased; but I, my mistress' thrall,   12
    Came there for cure, and this by that I prove: 13
    Love's fire heats water, water cools not love.

151.1 too young (Love is personified as the young Cupid.)   **2 conscience** guilty knowing, carnal knowledge. (Playing on *conscience*, "moral sense," in line 1.)   **3 urge** stress, invoke.   **amiss** sin   **5 betraying** (1) cheating on (2) leading into temptation   **6 nobler part** i.e., soul   **7–8 that . . . in love** that he, the soul, may triumph in virtuous love. (But ambiguously misinterpretable as urging the flesh to triumph carnally.)   **8 flesh . . . reason** my flesh waits no longer to hear reason's lecture   **9 rising** (With bawdy suggestion of erection, continued in *point, Proud, stand, fall.* Metaphors of conjuration and of the compass needle's point are also invoked.)   **10 triumphant prize** spoils to be enjoyed in victory. **Proud of** Swelling with.   **pride** splendor; erection   **12 stand** (1) serve, undertake business (2) be erect.   **fall** (as in battle; with sexual suggestion of detumescence)   **13 want** lack

152.1 forsworn i.e., faithless to my vows of love (perhaps marriage vows)   **3 act** sexual act.   **bed-vow** marriage vows to your husband   **3–4 new . . . bearing** i.e., a new contract of fidelity is torn up by your swearing hatred toward me, to whom you have only recently professed love. (Or the *new faith* that is torn up may be that which the lady has sworn to the friend.)   **7 but to misuse** merely to deceive   **8 And . . . lost** i.e., all my professions of honesty are belied when I perjure myself by praising you for loving constancy.   **11 And . . . blindness** i.e., and, to invest you with brightness, I made my eyes testify to things they did not see

13 eye (With a pun on "I.")
153 (This sonnet and the following seemingly have no direct connection with those preceding. They are derived ultimately, through Renaissance adaptations, from an epigram by the fifth-century Byzantine poet Marianus Scholasticus in the Greek Anthology.)   **1 brand** torch. (With phallic suggestion.)   **2 maid** attendant virgin, votaress. **Dian** Diana, goddess of chastity   **4 of that ground** i.e., nearby. (*Valley-fountain* suggests the female sexual anatomy; compare with 154.9.) **6 dateless** endless, eternal.   **still** always   **7–8 And grew . . . cure** and became a spring of hot medicinal waters, which even today men discover to be an efficacious cure against strange maladies. (Syphilis was conventionally treated with hot medicinal baths.)   **9 new-fired** having been reignited   **10 for trial** by way of test   **11 withal** from it   **12 hied** hastened.   **distempered** sick. (The bath is suggestive again of the sweating cure for venereal disease.)

154.7 general inspirer and commander, i.e., Cupid   **9 by** nearby **11 Growing** becoming   **12 thrall** slave, bondman   **13 cure** (With suggestion of treatment for venereal disease, as in 153.7–14.)   **this** i.e., the following proposition.   **that** i.e., my coming, which failed to cure me

Appendix 1

Canon, Dates, and Early Texts

By "canon" we mean a listing of plays that can be ascribed to Shakespeare on the basis of reliable evidence. Such evidence is either "internal," derived from matters of style or poetics in the plays themselves (see General Introduction), or "external," derived from outside the play. The latter includes any reference by Shakespeare's contemporaries to his plays, any allusions in the plays themselves to contemporary events, the entering of Shakespeare's plays for publication in the Stationers' Register (S. R.), actual publication of the plays, and records of early performances. These matters of external evidence are also essential in attempting to date the plays.

The greatest single source of information is the First Folio text of Shakespeare's plays, sponsored by Shakespeare's fellow actors John Heminges and Henry Condell and published in 1623. It contains all the plays included in this present edition of Shakespeare except *Pericles* and *The Two Noble Kinsmen* and offers strong presumptive evidence of being a complete and accurate compilation of Shakespeare's work by men who knew him and cherished his memory. It provides the only texts we have for these eighteen plays: *The Comedy of Errors, The Two Gentlemen of Verona, The Taming of the Shrew, 1 Henry VI, King John, As You Like It, Twelfth Night, Julius Caesar, All's Well That Ends Well, Measure for Measure, Timon of Athens, Macbeth, Antony and Cleopatra, Coriolanus, Cymbeline, The Winter's Tale, The Tempest,* and *Henry VIII*. This includes nearly half the known canon of Shakespeare's plays. Our debt to the First Folio is incalculable and confirms our impression of its reliability.

The information of the First Folio is further confirmed by contemporary references. In 1598, a cleric and minor writer of the period named Francis Meres wrote in his *Palladis Tamia, Wit's Treasury*:

As the soul of Euphorbus was thought to live in Pythagoras, so the sweet, witty soul of Ovid lives in mellifluous and honey-tongued Shakespeare: witness his *Venus and Adonis*, his *Lucrece*, his sugared sonnets among his private friends, etc.

As Plautus and Seneca are accounted the best for comedy and tragedy among the Latins, so Shakespeare among the English is the most excellent in both kinds for the stage; for comedy, witness his *Gentlemen of Verona*, his *Errors*, his *Love's Labor's Lost*, his *Love's Labor's Won*, his *Midsummer's Night Dream*, and his *Merchant of Venice*; for tragedy his *Richard the II, Richard the III, Henry the IV, King John, Titus Andronicus* and his *Romeo and Juliet*.

Though this list was meant to offer praise, not to be an exhaustive catalogue, it is remarkably full. If the tantalizing *Love's Labor's Won* refers to *The Taming of the Shrew*, Meres's list of comedies is substantially complete down almost to 1598. It does not include the comedies that Shakespeare appears to have written around that date or soon afterward: *Much Ado About Nothing, The Merry Wives of Windsor, As You Like It,* and *Twelfth Night*. Meres correctly names all of Shakespeare's history plays except the *Henry VI* trilogy and of course the later histories, *Henry V* (1599) and *Henry VIII* (1613). He names both of Shakespeare's early tragedies that are not based on English history: *Titus Andronicus* and *Romeo and Juliet*. He tells us about the important nondramatic poems, which did not appear in the First Folio, since that volume is devoted exclusively to plays. Not much can be made of the order in which Meres names the plays, however, for we learn from other sources that *Richard III* clearly precedes *Richard II* in date of composition and that *King John* precedes the *Henry IV* plays.

Other writers of the 1590s add further confirming evidence. John Weever, in an epigram "*Ad Gulielmum Shakespeare*," published in 1599, refers to "Rose-cheeked Adonis" and "Fair fire-hot Venus," to "Chaste Lucretia" and "Proud lust-stung Tarquin," and to "*Romeo, Richard*—more whose names I know not." Richard Barnfield, in *Poems in*

Divers Humors (1598), praises Shakespeare for *"Venus"* and *"Lucrece."* Both Thomas Nashe and Robert Greene seemingly refer to the *Henry VI* plays, missing from Meres's list. Nashe, in his *Pierce Penniless* (1592), speculates how it would "have joyed brave Talbot (the terror of the French) to think that after he had lain two hundred years in his tomb, he should triumph again on the stage." Talbot is the hero of *1 Henry VI*, and we know of no other play on the subject. Greene, in his *Greene's Groats-worth of Wit* (1592), lashes out at an "upstart crow, beautified with our feathers, that with his *'Tiger's heart wrapped in a player's hide'* supposes he is as well able to bombast out a blank verse as the best of you, and, being an absolute *Johannes Factotum*, is in his own conceit the only Shake-scene in a country." The line about "Tiger's heart" is deliberately misquoted from *3 Henry VI*, 1.4.137. (It is possible that this famous attack on Shakespeare was actually written not by Greene himself but by Henry Chettle, his literary executor.)

Pericles (c. 1606–1608)

On May 20, 1608, Edward Blount entered in the Stationers' Register, the official record book of the London Company of Stationers (booksellers and printers), "A booke called. The booke of Pericles prynce of Tyre." He also entered *Antony and Cleopatra* at this time, possibly hoping to forestall unauthorized publishing of these two texts. If so, the plan succeeded with *Antony* but not with *Pericles*. A corrupt Quarto of this play was printed in 1609 by William White:

THE LATE, And much admired Play, Called Pericles, Prince of Tyre. With the true Relation of the whole Historie, aduentures, and fortunes of the said Prince: As also, The no lesse strange, and worthy accidents, in the Birth and Life, of his Daughter MARIANA. As it hath been diuers and sundry times acted by his Maiesties Seruants, at the Globe on the Banck-side. By William Shake-speare. Imprinted at London for *Henry Gosson*, and are to be sold at the signe of the Sunne in Pater-noster row, &c. 1609.

Blount was a friend of the players, and the text he registered is likely to have been the playbook. (This would explain why it is referred to as "A booke called the booke of Pericles" in the Stationers' Register, since playbooks were known technically as "books.") White's text, on the other hand, appears to be a memorially constructed text and at times it is unintelligible. Two reporters may have been at work, and the printing was done by at least three compositors. See the play's Introduction for some examples of inconsistency in the text. Unfortunately, this bad text is the best we have, though George Wilkins's *The Painful Adventures of Pericles* (see below) may have been influenced directly by the play and may well afford some clues as to the wording of the text; a recent and controversial hypothesis argues that *The Painful Adventures* is as much a "report" of the play as is the corrupt Quarto. Subsequent quartos

appeared in 1609, 1611, 1619, and 1630, but each was set up from the previous edition, and all attempts in them at improvement are editorial rather than authorial. *Pericles* did not appear at all in the First Folio of 1623, perhaps because the editors suspected it to be partly non-Shakespearean or because they did not possess a reliable text. Arguments for multiple authorship, though based essentially on internal evidence of the play's manifest inconsistencies, are still taken seriously by scholars. George Wilkins especially has been proposed as collaborator in the first two acts. The defects of the first two acts are generally more extensive than those found even in such unauthorized Quartos as *Hamlet* or *Romeo and Juliet*. Philip Edwards has argued, on the other hand (*Shakespeare Survey 5*, 1952), that the differences between the first two acts and the last three can be accounted for by memorial reporting and compositorial error. This matter is still in dispute.

Pericles (though probably differing textually from the play we have today) must have been in existence by the date of the Stationers' Register entry in May 1608. A play of *Pericles* was seen by the Venetian ambassador to England, Zorzi Giustinian, sometime during his official stay from January 5, 1606, to November 23, 1608. George Wilkins's *The Painful Adventures of Pericles, Prince of Tyre*, published in 1608, was certainly derived in part from a play about Pericles: its title page offers the work "as it was lately presented by the worthy and ancient poet John Gower," and the final sentence of the Argument urges the reader "to receive this history in the same manner as it was under the habit of ancient Gower, the famous English poet, by the Kings Majesty's players excellently presented." The play to which Wilkins refers may have been Shakespeare's or perhaps some earlier version—just how early, no one can say. As it stands, however, the play appears to represent the beginning of Shakespeare's fascination with the genre of romance. As such, its date is usually set between 1606 and 1608.

Cymbeline (c. 1608–1610)

Cymbeline was first printed in the First Folio of 1623, where it was included among the tragedies. The text, a good one, was evidently set from a careful transcript (perhaps by the scrivener Ralph Crane) of an earlier manuscript, one in which two copyists may have been involved, basing their work either on Shakespeare's own papers or on a theatrical playbook that had incorporated many authorial stage directions. The first recorded performance was in 1611. Dr. Simon Forman jotted down a description of *Cymbeline* in his commonplace book for that year; although he did not record the actual date he saw the play, he must have done so sometime between April and his sudden death on September 8 of that year. Stylistically, the play appears to follow *Pericles* (c. 1606–1608) and to precede *The Winter's Tale* (c. 1609–1611).

Cymbeline may also follow and imitate Beaumont and Fletcher's *Philaster*, produced with great success in 1609, although the relative order of these similar plays remains doubtful. If *Cymbeline* is the later of the two, it may have been written as late as 1610.

The Winter's Tale (c. 1609–1611)

The Winter's Tale was first printed in the First Folio of 1623. Its text is a good one, taken evidently from Ralph Crane's transcript of Shakespeare's own well-finished draft or possibly the playbook. As in most other Crane transcriptions, the stage directions are sparse, and the characters' names are grouped at the beginning of each scene. The first recorded performance was on May 15, 1611, when Simon Forman saw the play at the Globe Theater and recorded a summary of it in his commonplace book. Another performance that year at court, on November 5, is recorded in the *Revels Account* and still another, during the winter of 1612–1613. Quite possibly, the play was new at the time Forman saw it. It apparently contains an allusion to the dance of ten or twelve satyrs in Ben Jonson's *Masque of Oberon*, performed at court on January 1, 1611. A 1623 entry in the *Office book* of Sir Henry Herbert, Master of the Revels, refers to *The Winter's Tale* as "an old play . . . formerly allowed of by Sir George Bucke." Bucke (or Buc) was first appointed Master of the Revels in 1610 but had occasionally licensed plays before that date during his predecessor's illness, so that the backward limit of 1610 cannot be considered absolute. Still, matters of style confirm the likelihood that Forman was seeing a new play in 1611.

The Tempest (c. 1611)

The Tempest was first printed in the First Folio of 1623. It occupies first place in the volume and is a scrupulously prepared text from a transcript by Ralph Crane of a theater playbook or of Shakespeare's draft after it had been annotated for production; or, Crane may have provided some of the elaboration of stage directions. Shakespeare's colleagues may have placed *The Tempest* first in the Folio because they considered it his most recent complete play. The first recorded performance was at court on November 1, 1611: "Hallomas nyght was presented att Whithall before yᵉ kinges Maiestie a play Called the Tempest." The actors were "the Kings players" (*Revels Account*). The play was again presented at court during the winter of 1612–1613, this time "before the Princes Highnes the Lady Elizabeth and the Prince Pallatyne Elector." The festivities for this important betrothal and wedding were sumptuous and included at least thirteen other plays. Various arguments have been put forward that Shakespeare composed parts of *The Tempest*, especially the masque, for this occasion, but there is absolutely no evidence that the play

was singled out for special prominence among the many plays presented, and the masque is integral to the play as it stands. Probably the 1611 production was of a fairly new play. Simon Forman, who saw *Cymbeline* and *The Winter's Tale* in 1611, does not mention *The Tempest*. He died in September 1611. According to every stylistic test, such as run-on and hypermetric lines, the play is very late. Shakespeare probably knew Sylvester Jourdain's *A Discovery of the Bermudas*, published in 1610, and William Strachey's *A True Reportory of the Wreck and Redemption*, dated July 1610, although not published until 1625.

The Two Noble Kinsmen (1613–1614)

The Two Noble Kinsmen did not appear in the Shakespeare First Folio of 1623. Publishing rights were first assigned in the Stationers' Register to John Waterson on April 8, 1634, as "a TragiComedy called the two noble kinsmen by Jo: ffletcher & Wm. Shakespeare." It was first published in 1634 in quarto by John Waterson as:

THE TWO NOBLE KINSMEN: Presented at the Blackfriers by the Kings Maiesties servants, with great applause: Written by the memorable Worthies of their time; Mr. *John Fletcher*, and Mr. *William Shakspeare*, Gent. Printed at *London* by *Tho. Cotes*, for *Iohn Waterson*: and are to be sold at the signe of the *Crowne* in *Pauls* Church-yard. 1634.

Waterson transferred his rights in the play on October 31, 1646, to Humphrey Moseley, along with two other plays, as by "Mr fflesher." Moseley's first collection of plays by Beaumont and Fletcher in 1647 did not in fact include *The Two Noble Kinsmen*. It did appear finally in Moseley's 1679 edition of *Fifty Comedies and Tragedies, Written by Francis Beaumont, and John Fletcher, Gentlemen*. Despite the attribution to Fletcher and Shakespeare in 1634, the omission of the play from the Beaumont and Fletcher collected works led to its being excluded from the Shakespeare canon until well into the nineteenth century. Today nearly all editors view the play as a collaboration between Shakespeare, who was entering on his retirement, and the dramatist who succeeded him at the King's men.

The 1634 Quarto text is a good one, perhaps based on a scribal transcript and containing theatrical annotations by the "bookkeeper" or prompter in the form of marginal notes warning the acting company to get properties ready and naming minor actors.

The likely date of first performance is in 1613 or 1614. An expanded version of the morris dance in 3.5 had served as the antimasque (a kind of grotesque comic subplot) for Beaumont's *Masque of the Inner Temple and Gray's Inn* on February 20, 1613, presented at court during the marriage festivities for James I's daughter Elizabeth to Frederick, the Elector Palatine. It seems likely that this highly celebratory court occasion would have taken precedence over commercial performance. Ben Jonson's

Bartholomew Fair, first performed on October 31, 1614, alludes to a play called "Palamon." Shakespeare died in 1616 and may have been in failing health toward the very end; 1613 and 1614 seem to have been his last years of writing.

Venus and Adonis (1592–1593)

On April 18, 1593, "a booke intituled, Venus and Adonis" was entered by Richard Field in the Stationers' Register, the official record book of the London Company of Stationers (booksellers and printers), and was published by him the same year. The Quarto contains a dedication written by Shakespeare to the Earl of Southampton. The text seems to have been carefully supervised through the press and to have been based on the author's manuscript. The poem was very popular and was reprinted nine times before Shakespeare's death. The First Folio of 1623, being limited to plays, did not include it or any other non-dramatic poems. Contemporary references are numerous: Francis Meres and Richard Barnfield in 1598, Gabriel Harvey in 1598–1601, and John Weever in 1599, among others. Shakespeare probably wrote this poem shortly before its publication, since his intention was to present it to Southampton. The theaters closed from June 1592 to May 1594, giving Shakespeare a period of enforced leisure in which to write poetry.

The Rape of Lucrece (1593–1594)

Shakespeare promised a "graver labour" to Southampton in his dedication of *Venus and Adonis*, 1593, and *The Rape of Lucrece* is almost surely that promised sequel. It was registered in the Stationers' Register, the official record book of the London Company of Stationers (booksellers and printers), by John Harrison on May 9, 1594, and issued that same year as "printed by Richard Field, for Iohn Harrison." The printed text was probably based on Shakespeare's manuscript. Although not quite as popular as *Venus and Adonis*, the poem was reprinted five times during Shakespeare's lifetime. Contemporaries of Shakespeare who allude favorably to the poem include W. Har and Michael Drayton in 1594, William Covell in 1595, Francis Meres in 1598, Gabriel Harvey in 1598–1601, John Weever in 1599, and others. The date of composition of the poem is well fixed between the publication of *Venus and Adonis* in 1593 and that of *The Rape of Lucrece* itself in 1594.

The Phoenix and Turtle (by 1601)

"The Phoenix and Turtle" first appeared in a volume with the following title:

LOVES MARTYR: OR, ROSALINS COMPLAINT. *Allegorically shadowing the truth of Loue*, in the constant Fate of the Phoenix and Turtle….by ROBERT CHESTER….*To these are added some new compositions, of seuerall moderne Writers whose names are subscribed to their seuerall workes, vpon the first subiect: viz. the* Phoenix *and* Turtle.

The date 1601 appears on a separate title page. One poem is signed "William Shake-speare"; others are assigned to John Marston, George Chapman, and Ben Jonson.

A Lover's Complaint (c. 1601–1605)

A Lover's Complaint first appeared in Thomas Thorpe's 1609 edition of the sonnets. It may have been printed from the same transcript as that used to print the sonnets. The poem is not mentioned on the title page of the volume but has its own head-title on sig. K^v: "A Louers complaint. BY William Shake-speare." For the reliability of this attribution, see the Introduction to *A Lover's Complaint*. Stylistic tests suggest a date around the time of *Hamlet* and *All's Well That Ends Well*, though any such suggestion is approximate.

The Sonnets (c. 1593–1603)

On May 20, 1609, "Thomas Thorpe Entred for his copie vnder thandes of master Wilson and master Lownes Warden a Booke called Shakespeares sonnettes." In the same year appeared the following volume:

SHAKE-SPEARES SONNETS. Neuer before Imprinted. AT LONDON By *G. Eld* for *T. T.* [Thomas Thorpe] and are to be solde by *Iohn Wright*, dwelling at Christ Church gate. 1609.

Some copies of this same edition are marked to be sold by William Aspley rather than John Wright; evidently, Thorpe had set up two sellers to distribute the volume. The sonnets were not reprinted until John Benson's rearranged edition of 1640, possibly because the first edition had been suppressed or because sonnets were no longer in vogue. The 1609 edition may rest on a transcript of Shakespeare's sonnets by someone other than the author, and the edition itself is marred by misprints, though Thorpe was a reputable printer. Clearly, the collection was not supervised through the press as were *Venus and Adonis* and *The Rape of Lucrece*. All the evidence suggests that it was obtained without Shakespeare's permission from a manuscript that had been in private circulation (as we know from Francis Meres's 1598 allusion, in his *Palladis Tamia*, to Shakespeare's "sugared sonnets among his private friends"). Two sonnets, 138 and 144, had appeared in 1599 in *The Passionate Pilgrim*. On questions of dating and order of the sonnets, see the Introduction to *The Sonnets* in this volume.

Appendix 2

Sources

Pericles

This play, at least partly by Shakespeare, is based on the ancient Greek romance of Apollonius of Tyre. Shakespeare had used the story once before, in *The Comedy of Errors*. Medieval versions of this enduringly popular legend include the ninth-century Latin *Historia Apollonii Regis Tyri*, Godfrey of Viterbo's *Pantheon* (c. 1186), the *Gesta Romanorum* (a collection of ancient tales in Latin), John Gower's *Confessio Amantis* (c. 1383–1393), and an English chronicle of *Appolyn of Thyre* translated for the printer Wynkyn de Worde by Robert Copland from a French source (1510). Shakespeare, and perhaps a collaborator or the author of a lost earlier dramatic version, were chiefly indebted to Gower's *Confessio* and to Laurence Twine's *The Pattern of Painful Adventures*, a prose version registered in 1576 but existing today only in two editions from about 1594–1595 and 1607.

The order of events in Twine is much the same as in the play: the hero Apollonius's difficulty with the incestuous King Antiochus, his relieving of the city of Tharsus, his shipwreck at Pentapolis and his falling in love with the King's daughter Lucina (Thaisa in the play), her childbearing and apparent death at sea, the discovery of her floating casket at Ephesus, her revival by the physician Cerimon and her retirement to the Temple of Diana in Ephesus, her daughter Tharsia's (i.e., Marina's) capture by pirates and enslavement in a brothel, her conversion of Athanagoras (Lysimachus), the Governor of Machilenta (Mytilene), and Apollonius's eventual reunion with his daughter and wife. Gower's account, too, is much the same, with slightly different forms of the proper names: Appolinus's (Apollonius's) wife is referred to as the King's daughter, Appolinus's daughter is Thaise, the man she marries is Atenagoras (or Athenagoras) of Mytilene, and so on.

Other than changing some proper names, including that of the hero, Shakespeare did not introduce many significant alterations. To be sure, Shakespeare has given a more sordid impression of the brothel in which Marina must dwell, and has dignified the character of Lysimachus so as to render him worthy of marrying Marina. In Twine's prose account, Athanagoras actually tries to buy Tharsia from the pirates at an auction; when he is outbid by a bawd, he resolves to be the first to visit Tharsia in her new residence. Shakespeare has provided a more decorous action for Lysimachus, although traces of the older and more licentious character occasionally show through and create the impression of inconsistency. For the most part, however, Shakespeare's play stays unusually close to the episodic narrative structure of his sources.

The relationship of George Wilkins's *The Painful Adventures of Pericles, Prince of Tyre* (1608) to Shakespeare's play is complex and uncertain. Beyond doubt, Wilkins's prose account is based in part on a *Pericles* play; Wilkins acknowledges in his Argument that this same story has been recently presented "by the King's Majesty's Players." The play he used may, however, not have been the *Pericles* we know from the corrupt 1609 Quarto. Parts of Wilkins's narrative are very close to the earlier *Pattern of Painful Adventures* by Twine. Kenneth Muir suggests (*Shakespeare's Sources*, 1957) that because Wilkins's novel is closer to the first two acts of Shakespeare's play than to the last three acts, Wilkins may have been using an older play that Shakespeare then revised, substantially rewriting the last three acts but changing little in the first two. Whether the presumed *Ur-Pericles* might have been Wilkins's own play is a matter of conjecture. The very existence of an *Ur-Pericles* is by no means universally accepted but cannot be ruled out as a possibility.

Cymbeline

Cymbeline mingles legendary history with elements of romance. Traces of historical events lie dimly behind the narrative, but only insofar as they are incorporated in a much larger legendary purpose. A Cunobelinus, or Cymbeline, was leader of the Celtic chieftains in southeast England during the period of Roman hegemony there, following Julius Caesar's invasion of the island in 54 B.C. Cunobelinus ruled from about 5 to 40 A.D., with his capital at Camulodunum (Colchester). He was a friend and ally of Augustus Caesar and enjoyed a peaceful reign. When the Kingdom had passed to his sons (one of whom apparently was Caractacus), the Romans under Claudius pursued once again their conquest of England and subdued much of the southeast, though Caractacus escaped to Wales and became a leader of the resistance.

Beginning with Geoffrey of Monmouth's *Historia Regum Britanniae* (c. 1136), King Kymbelinus becomes a quasi-legendary figure. Geoffrey adds him to the genealogy of Kings (along with Leir, Locrine, etc.) descended from Aeneas's great-grandson Brut, the mythical founder of Britain. Kymbelinus's reign was peaceful, according to Geoffrey, since the King, having been raised in Augustus Caesar's household, willingly paid tribute to Rome without being asked. When Kymbelinus's elder son Guiderius succeeded to the throne, however, said Geoffrey, he defied the Emperor Claudius over the tribute. Guiderius fell in battle and was succeeded by his brother Arviragus, who more than held his own against Claudius, eventually settling matters by negotiation.

By the time of Raphael Holinshed's *Chronicles* (1587 edition), history is scarcely distinguishable from legend. Holinshed admits he cannot be sure whether Kymbeline or some other British leader fought against Augustus Caesar, or whether Kymbeline paid tribute; he does report that Guiderius fought Augustus Caesar (rather than Claudius) but is uncertain as to whether the Romans lost or won. Edmund Spenser's *The Faerie Queene* (2.10.50–1) affirms that Kimbeline fought the Romans over tribute and was slain in battle, whereupon his brother Arviragus took his place and compelled the Roman Claudius to a peace. (In other words, Spenser has conflated Cymbeline and Guiderius.) Shakespeare, like Spenser, imagines the great struggle with Rome and subsequent peace settlement to have taken place during Cymbeline's reign; following Holinshed, he assumes that Rome was then governed by Augustus Caesar. Shakespeare also seems to have consulted a vivid account of the battle in Thomas Blenerhasset's contribution to *The Second Part of the Mirror for Magistrates* (1578) and another account of Cymbeline's reign by John Higgins in the 1587 *Mirror for Magistrates*. Finally, Shakespeare turned for his background material to quite a different story in Holin-

shed, concerning a Scottish farmer named Hay who with his two sons helped defend Scotland against the Danes in 976. Shakespeare presumably found this story when reading for *Macbeth*, since it stands between the two accounts—Donwald's murder of Duff and Macbeth's murder of Duncan—that Shakespeare used in writing *Macbeth*. The exploits of Hay and his two sons resemble those of Belarius and the two princes in the final battle of *Cymbeline*.

The quasi-historical setting accounts for only a small part of *Cymbeline*, and Shakespeare had no special reason to regard the story of Cymbeline as historically "true." Most of his material is, after all, romantic. The central plot of a wager over a wife's virtue may have come from Giovanni Boccaccio's *Decameron*, Day 2, Story 9, although as a type this ancient story was widespread and presumably available to Shakespeare in many forms. Earlier versions include the thirteenth-century French *Roi Flore et la belle Jeanne*, the *Roman de la Violette* by Gerbert de Montreuil, a miracle play by Gautier de Coincy, and others. Boccaccio was available to Shakespeare in French translation but not in English.

A summary of Boccaccio's story suggests a number of particulars to which Shakespeare was indebted. Boccaccio tells of an Italian merchant, Bernabò of Genoa, who, at a gathering in Paris of fellow merchants discussing the wantonness of their wives, dares to affirm the absolute chastity of his own wife, Zinevra. A young merchant, Ambrogiuolo, makes a wager that he can seduce Zinevra and return with proof in three months. Going at once to Genoa, Ambrogiuolo discovers that Zinevra is indeed incorruptible. He therefore bribes an elderly lady, whom Zinevra has befriended, to convey him hidden in a chest to the lady's bedroom. When the lady is asleep, he steals forth from hiding, memorizes details of her room, notes particularly a mole upon her left breast, and takes with him a purse, gown, ring, and sash. Returning to Paris, he convinces his fellow merchants and Bernabò that he has succeeded. Bernabò hereupon travels to within a few miles of Genoa, summons his wife, and secretly orders his servant to kill her on the way. The servant is reluctant to do so, however, and gladly takes only her cloak as evidence of having finished the job. Zinevra now makes her way disguised as a man to Alexandria and enters the service of the Sultan. One day she happens to recognize her own purse and girdle in a Venetian clothes shop in Palestine, inquires as to their owner, meets Ambrogiuolo in this way (who has journeyed to Palestine selling merchandise), and hears from Ambrogiuolo's own boastful lips the story of his treachery. She cannily manages to bring Ambrogiuolo and Bernabò before the Sultan, throws off her male disguise, and reveals the whole story. She pardons Bernabò and is reunited with him, but Ambrogiuolo is sentenced by the

Sultan to be tied to a stake, smeared with honey, and left to be devoured by insects.

Shakespeare has altered the setting and has surrounded the story with other matters, such as King Cymbeline's lost sons, his quarrel with Rome, his difficulties with his Queen and her son, Cloten, and the like. Shakespeare's ending is much more forgiving toward Iachimo than in the narrative source. The circumstances of the denouement are changed. Still, the plot of Posthumus, Imogen, and Iachimo is extensively indebted to Boccaccio.

Shakespeare seems also to have known an English version, *Frederyke of Jennen* (Antwerp, 1518; London, 1520 and 1560), translated from the Dutch. In some details, it is closer to Shakespeare's play than is Boccaccio's story. For example, the merchants who witness the wager include a Spaniard, a Frenchman, a Florentine, and a Genoese (compare 1.4). Three of these merchants are not present when the villain returns to prove his victory, just as in 2.4 of Shakespeare's play. Also, the husband repents even before learning of his wife's innocence, as does Posthumus. Shakespeare greatly accentuates this motif of penance and forgiveness. Another source is a romantic play called *The Rare Triumphs of Love and Fortune*, acted before Queen Elizabeth in 1582, in which the princess Fidelia is banished by her father for falling in love, is betrayed and pursued by her boorish brother Armenio (compare Cloten), and is hospitably received by a banished courtier named Bomelio who lives hermitlike in a cave. "Fidele" is the name used by Shakespeare's Imogen to disguise her identity. Folk motifs are apparent throughout *Cymbeline*; the cruel Queen inevitably reminds us of Snow White's stepmother. Although Shakespeare may not have been acquainted with that particular story, he clearly was interested in folk legend when he wrote *Cymbeline*. One other anonymous romantic play, *Sir Clyomon and Sir Clamydes* (c. 1570–1583), may have given Shakespeare some suggestions for his Welsh scenes.

Francis Beaumont and John Fletcher's *Philaster* was written about the same time as *Cymbeline* and seems to bear a significant resemblance to Shakespeare's play. Philaster is, like Posthumus, in love with a princess whose father intends her for another suitor. Many of the similarities can be attributed to the conventions of the romance genre just then coming into vogue, and no one can be sure whether Shakespeare's play came after or before *Philaster*. If *Cymbeline* is the later of the two, however, *Philaster* must be considered as a source.

The Winter's Tale

Shakespeare based *The Winter's Tale* on Robert Greene's romantic novella called *Pandosto: The Triumph of Time* (1588), or *The History of Dorastus and Fawnia* in its running title. Shakespeare changes the names, reverses the two Kingdoms of Sicilia and Bohemia, and alters the unhappy ending that afflicts King Pandosto and Queen Bellaria of Bohemia (Leontes and Hermione of Sicilia). Otherwise, the narrative outline remains intact. The story begins with the state visit of King Egistus of Sicilia (Polixenes of Bohemia) to his boyhood companion, King Pandosto of Bohemia. Queen Bellaria entertains their guest with such warmth, "oftentimes coming herself into his bedchamber to see that nothing should be amiss to mislike him," that Pandosto grows jealous. He commands his cupbearer Franion (Camillo) to murder Egistus, and the latter seems to agree but instead warns his victim to flee with him. Their hasty departure appears to confirm Pandosto's worst suspicions. He sends the guard to arrest Bellaria as she plays with her young son Garinter (Mamillius). When the Queen gives birth to a daughter in prison, the King orders the child destroyed, but he relents upon the insistence of his courtiers and causes the infant to be set adrift in a small boat. The Queen nobly defends herself at her trial (in language that Shakespeare has copied in some detail). She herself requests that the oracle at Delphos be consulted. The oracle replies in words that Shakespeare has altered only slightly: "Bellaria is chaste, Egistus blameless, Franion a true subject, Pandosto treacherous, his babe an innocent; and the King shall live without an heir if that which is lost be not found." Pandosto is immediately stricken with remorse, and, when Queen Bellaria collapses at the news of her son Garinter's death, she is truly and irrecoverably dead.

A similarly close parallel in the narrative, along with telling changes in a number of details, characterizes the story's second half. The babe is conveyed by a tempest to the coast of Sicilia and is discovered by an impoverished shepherd named Porrus. He and his wife Mopsa adopt the child, naming her Fawnia. By the age of sixteen, Fawnia's natural beauty rivals that of the goddess Flora. At a meeting of the farmers' daughters of Sicilia, where she is chosen mistress of the feast, Fawnia is seen by the King's son Dorastus on his way home from hawking. She counters his importunate suit with the argument that she is too lowly a match for him, but he replies that the gods themselves sometimes take earthly lovers. Her foster father, distressed by the Prince's repeated visits (though he comes in shepherd's costume), resolves to carry the jewels he found with Fawnia to the King and reveal her story, thereby escaping blame for the goings-on. Dorastus escapes with Fawnia to a ship, aided by his servant Capnio (compare Camillo). Capnio also fulfills a role given by Shakespeare to Autolycus, for he manages to trick the shepherd Porrus into thinking he can see the King if he comes aboard Dorastus's ship. A storm drives these voyagers to Bohemia where, because of the ancient enmity between Egistus and Pandosto, they disguise themselves. Pandosto, happening to hear of Fawnia's beauty, orders her and the others to be arrested as spies and summoned to court, whereupon he falls incestuously in love with the disguised Fawnia. He promises to free the young man (who has taken the name of Meleagrus to conceal his identity) only if he will relinquish his claim to Fawnia. King Egistus meanwhile has discovered his son's whereabouts and sends ambassadors to Bohemia demanding the return of Dorastus and the execution of Fawnia, Capnio, and Porrus. Pandosto, his love for Fawnia having turned to hate, is about to comply when Porrus reveals the circumstances of Fawnia's infancy. Overjoyed to rediscover his daughter, Pandosto permits her to marry Dorastus but then falls into a melancholy fit and commits suicide.

Shakespeare has almost entirely created some characters, such as Paulina, Antigonus, the clownish shepherd's son, and Autolycus, though Capnio does perform one of Autolycus's functions by inveigling the old shepherd aboard ship. Antigonus's journey to the seacoast of Bohemia with the infant Perdita and his fatal exit *"pursued by a bear"* are Shakespearean additions. The character of Time is also added, and the shift in tone from tragedy to tragicomedy averts the catastrophe in Greene's novella (in which Pandosto commits suicide). The shepherdesses at the sheepshearing are Shakespearean. The old shepherd has a more substantial and comic role; Camillo is a stronger person than Capnio. Greene's Mopsa, the shrewish wife of old Porrus, disappears from the play. Shakespeare omits the incestuous love of Pandosto for his daughter and brings Hermione back to life. (For this motif of a statue made to breathe, he may well have recalled Ovid's account of Pygmalion in Ovid's *Metamorphoses*, Book 10.) Shakespeare's Leontes is more irrationally jealous than in Greene's account. Leontes's purgative sorrow is more intense and also more restorative than in the source; he is a truly noble and tragicomic figure, the center of a play about forgiveness and renewal.

Shakespeare may also have known Francis Sabie's *The Fisherman's Tale* (1595) and its continuation, *Flora's Fortune* (1595). From Greene's pamphlets, describing in vividly colloquial detail the life of London's underworld, Shakespeare probably derived many of Autolycus's tricks.

The Tempest

No direct literary source for the whole of *The Tempest* has been found. Shakespeare does seem to have drawn material from various accounts of the shipwreck of the *Sea Venture* in the Bermudas, in 1609, although the importance of these materials should not be overstated. Several of the survivors wrote narratives of the shipwreck itself and of their life on the islands for some nine months. Sylvester

Jourdain, in *A Discovery of the Bermudas*, published 1610, speaks of miraculous preservation despite the island's reputation for being "a most prodigious and enchanted place." William Strachey's letter, written in July of 1610 and published much later (1625) as *A True Reportory of the Wreck and Redemption . . . from the Islands of the Bermudas*, describes the panic among the passengers and crew, the much feared reputation of the island as the habitation of devils and wicked spirits, the actual beauty and fertility of the place with its abundance of wild life (compare Caliban's descriptions), and the treachery of the Indians they later encounter in Virginia. Shakespeare seems to have read Strachey's letter in manuscript and may have been acquainted with him. The storm scene in Chapter 4 of Laurence Twine's *The Pattern of Painful Adventures*, a major source for *Pericles*, may also have given Shakespeare material for the first scene of *The Tempest*. Shakespeare also kept up with travel accounts of Sir Walter Ralegh and Thomas Harriot, and knew various classical evocations of a New World. The name "Setebos" came from Richard Eden's *History of Travel* (1577), translated from Peter Martyr's *De Novo Orbe* and from other travel accounts of the period. (See the Introduction to *The Tempest* for the potential relevance of various journals of the circumnavigation of the globe.) All these hints are indeed suggestive, but they are scattered and relate more to the setting and general circumstance of Shakespeare's play than to the plot.

Shakespeare certainly consulted Michel de Montaigne's essay "Of the Cannibals," as translated by John Florio in 1603. Gonzalo's reverie on an ideal commonwealth (2.1.150–71) contains many verbal echoes of the essay. Montaigne's point is that supposedly civilized men who condemn as barbarous any society not conforming with their own are simply refusing to examine their own shortcomings. A supposedly primitive society may well embody perfect religion, justice, and harmony; civilized art can never rival the achievements of nature. The ideal commonwealth has no need of magistrates, riches, poverty, and contracts, all of which breed dissimulation and covetousness. The significance of these ideas for *The Tempest* extends well beyond the particular passage in which they are found. And Caliban himself, whose name is an anagram of "cannibal," illustrates (even though he is not an eater of human flesh) the truth of Montaigne's observation apropos of the intense and wanton cruelty he finds so widespread in so-called Western civilization: "I think there is more barbarism in eating men alive than to feed upon them being dead."

Prospero's famous valedictory speech to "Ye elves of hills, brooks, standing lakes, and groves" (5.1.33–57) owes its origin to Medea's similar invocation in Ovid's *Metamorphoses* (Book 7), which Shakespeare knew both in the Latin original and in Golding's translation: "Ye airs and winds, ye elves of hills, of brooks, of woods alone, / Of standing lakes . . ." Medea also anticipates Shakespeare's Sycorax. Medea thus provides material for the representation of both black and white magic in *The Tempest,* so carefully differentiated by Shakespeare. Ariel is part English fairy, like Puck, and part daemon. The pastoral situation in *The Tempest* is perhaps derived from Edmund Spenser's *The Faerie Queene,* Book 6 (with its distinctions between savage lust and true courtesy, between nature and art). Italian pastoral drama as practiced by Guarini and (in England) by John Fletcher may also have been an influence. The masque element in *The Tempest,* prominent as in much late Shakespeare, bears the imprint of the courtly masque tradition of Ben Jonson, Francis Beaumont, and John Fletcher. Virgil's *Aeneid* may have provided Shakespeare with a more indirect source, with its story of wandering in the Mediterranean and storm at sea, love in Carthage, the intervention of the gods, and the fulfillment of destiny in Italy. Donna Hamilton (*Virgil and "The Tempest,"* 1990) contends that Shakespeare "imitated" Virgil so as to argue for a politics of retrenchment.

A German play, *Die Schöne Sidea* by Jacob Ayrer, written before 1605, was once thought to have been based on an earlier version of *The Tempest* as performed by English players traveling in Germany. Today, the similarities between the two plays are generally attributed to conventions found everywhere in romance.

The Two Noble Kinsmen

For their chief source, John Fletcher and William Shakespeare turned to "The Knight's Tale" in Chaucer's *Canterbury Tales.* "Chaucer, of all admired, the story gives," the Prologue tells us (line 13). In general, the dramatists follow their source for their main plot, especially in the middle acts.

"The Knight's Tale" relates how Duke Theseus, "lord and governour" of Athens, conquers the reign of "Femenye" and leads home Queen Ipolita to be his wife in "greet solempnitee," bringing with them Ipolita's younger sister Emelye. Their approach to Athens is interrupted by the petitions of widowed Queens whose royal husbands have been slain at Thebes by the tyrant Creon. Complaining that their husbands' bodies have been desecrated, they implore Theseus to avenge the outrage. The Duke, filled with pity and anger, marches to battle forthwith and slays Creon, restoring to the widows the bones of their dead husbands.

On the field of battle are discovered two wounded cousins, Palamon and Arcite, nephews of the dead Creon. Taken back to Athens as prisoners for whom Theseus will accept no ransom, they languish in prison for some years, until it happens one May morning that they see Emelye from their prison tower as she gathers flowers. Palamon sees her first and is immediately stricken with love; Arcite, inquiring into his cousin's distress, soon follows his example. Despite their being sworn friends, they quarrel over her.

Arcite, it turns out, is a long-time acquaintance of Theseus's dearest friend, Perotheus, who many years ago made a dangerous journey to hell with Theseus. At Perotheus's behest, Arcite is freed but is also banished from Athens on pain of death. This condition of being separated from Emelye is a torment to him. The still-imprisoned Palamon is no less inconsolable, fearing that Arcite will assemble an army to attack Athens and thus gain his advantage with Emelye. The narrator asks: Which lover is in a worse plight?

After a year or two of this misery, Arcite, in Thebes, is visited by the god Mercury in a dream, bidding him return to Athens. He does so in disguise, and manages to obtain the office of chamberlain in Emelye's dwelling, where he remains "A yeer or two" as "Page of the chambre of Emelye the brighte." Theseus appoints the admirable young man as squire of his chamber as well. Three more years pass in this happy circumstance. Palamon meantime has been in his dark and horrible prison for seven years. At length, with the help of "a freend," he manages to break prison and flee Athens, hiding in a grove of trees until he can make his way to Thebes and obtain armed assistance in winning Emelye as his wife.

One May morning, out hunting with Theseus, Arcite happens upon Palamon's grove and encounters his furious cousin. Arcite agrees to bring arms and armor so that they can fight it out over Emelye. Their subsequent match is interrupted by Theseus, who objects that they may not fight thus "With-outen juge or other officere." Revealing their identities, the two cousins confess that they have incurred Theseus's just wrath. When the Duke condemns both to death, however, Ipolyta and Emelye intervene for mercy's sake until he relents. Theseus decrees that the cousins are to contend for Emelye, each with a hundred knights, in the lists, some fifty weeks hence. The cousins each repair to Thebes to prepare for the event.

The lists are set up in grand fashion, with three altars: for Venus, goddess of love, to the east; for Mars, god of war, to the west; and for Diana, goddess of chastity, to the north. Each altar is elaborately decorated with symbolic paintings, statuary, and the like. The contenders arrive with their supporting kings, who are presented to the reader in elaborate detail. The fateful day commences with prayers offered by the protagonists to their respective patron-gods: Palamon to Venus, Emelye to Diana, and Arcite to Mars. Each petitioner is answered with enigmatic but seemingly hopeful signs: Palamon is to have his love, Emelye is to have (though not the life of virginal purity she most wishes) the suitor who loves her most, and Arcite is to have the victory. Saturn will oversee the way in which these seemingly conflicting demands among mortals and gods alike can be amicably resolved.

All is fulfilled as destined. When Palamon falls in the lists, Theseus awards Emelye to Arcite—much to the distress of Venus, who complains to Saturn, only to be told to await the final end. Sure enough, an infernal fury, sent by Pluto at the behest of Saturn, causes Arcite's steed to shy and buck, throwing Arcite head-first to the ground. Dying, Arcite bestows Emelye on his dear cousin. Theseus orders an elaborate funeral for Arcite. After a decorous interval of some years, the Duke decrees an end to mourning so that the marriage of Palamon and Emelye can take place. They live happily ever afterward, with never a word of jealousy or other vexation.

The playwrights' alterations of this tale are revealing, especially in Shakespeare's contributions in the first and fifth act. Theseus's friend Pirithous plays a larger role at first than in Chaucer, giving Shakespeare opportunity to develop the motif of friendship in various guises. Emilia's loving remembrance of her dearest childhood friend is newly provided, for much the same thematic purpose. The extensive philosophical debate between Palamon and Arcite about the corruptions of Theban civic life and their need for stoical withdrawal is not even hinted at in Chaucer. In the play's last act, Shakespeare substitutes for Chaucer's rich description of the tournament a report of off-stage combat, so that the focus is on Emilia and her emotional response to the news of changing fortunes in the battle. Saturn's role is eliminated in the play; the one mention of his name (5.4.62) is an indirect reminder that he no longer controls the action. The fury that Saturn sends via Pluto to goad Arcite's horse becomes, in Shakespeare's account, a "fire malevolent" or "fierce sulfur," of hellish origin only in a metaphorical sense. Venus's direct intervention on behalf of Palamon forms no part of Shakespeare's dramatized account. The gods are still invoked as presiding deities over a destiny that humans cannot predict, but with a far less immediate role for the Olympians.

Time passes in Chaucer in narrative fashion over a succession of years. The playwrights are understandably more interested in a dramatic compression of events. Arcite's release from prison at Perotheus's (Pirithous's) behest is more carefully explained in Chaucer as the result of an old friendship. The appearance to Arcite of Mercury in a dream, urging him to return to Athens, has no counterpart in the play; throughout, actions of this sort are apt to be motivated more by human feeling than by divine ordinance. Palamon's escape from prison is accomplished with the help of a friend; it is at this point that the playwrights, especially Fletcher, devise a subplot of the infatuated Jailer's Daughter to assist in the escape.

Chaucer's interest is in chivalric pageantry and in the soliloquies of his protagonists, as they ponder the seeming cruelties of their fates. Chaucer focuses a good deal on Duke Theseus, as we might expect from a tale told by a knight in defense of knightly ideals. Theseus is a mighty warrior, a defender of the innocent, and an equitable judge. Chaucer seemingly does not hold it against Theseus that he condemns Arcite and Palamon to death for their crimes of disobedience, and in any case he listens mercifully to his petitioners. Theseus presides over a courtly world in which the god of love is mighty and that those who fall under love's spell, gods and humans alike, are likely to act with noble foolishness. The play's serious thematic treatment of friendship seems a conscious choice on the part of the dramatists, especially Shakespeare.

Occasional verbal echoes attest to the playwrights' direct acquaintance with "The Knight's Tale," perhaps in Thomas Speght's edition first published in 1598 and enlarged in 1602. They may also have known Chaucer's source, the *Teseida* of Boccaccio, in which that author undertook to acclimatize the Roman epic (especially Virgil's *Aeneid* and Statius's *Thebiad*) to Renaissance themes. Shakespeare made use of Sir Thomas North's translation of Plutarch's "Life of Theseus" for the friendship of Theseus and Pirithous. Shakespeare's own earlier *A Midsummer Night's Dream* afforded the playwrights a portrait of Duke Theseus as he sets about to marry Hippolyta and to adjudicate amorous conflicts among the courtiers.

The plot of the Jailer's Daughter is apparently an invention, albeit with generous infusions from earlier models in the depiction of the Daughter's madness, especially from the mad songs of Ophelia in *Hamlet*. The treatment of the Daughter's mental and emotional illness by a doctor in 4.3 (see especially lines 59–61) has some affinities to Lady Macbeth's plight; see *Macbeth*, 5.1 and 5.3.47–8. The Daughter's pathetic situation also recalls some earlier work of Fletcher, as for example *The Coxcomb* (c. 1609); the story is similar, too, to that of Mopsa in Book 4 of Philip Sidney's *Arcadia* (first printed in 1593).

Other elements of comic subplot material in *The Two Noble Kinsmen* borrow freely from Shakespeare's earlier plays and other materials. When Palamon returns to Athens and is helped by some countrymen to learn about the games in which he can compete (2.3 and 2.5), the story is close to that of Pericles's being assisted by some fishermen when he is washed ashore at Pentapolis (2.1). Fletcher's pedantic schoolmaster in 3.5 reminds us of Holofernes in *Love's Labor's Lost*, who, like Fletcher's Gerald, helps put on a ridiculous entertainment for royalty. *A Midsummer Night's Dream* presents a similar pageant devised by clownish countrymen, with a burgomask dance not unlike the antimasque of twelve dancers in *The*

Two Noble Kinsmen. Shakespeare and Fletcher took this antimasque, featuring a clown, a baboon, etc., and pedant as usher, from an antimasque devised for Francis Beaumont's *Masque of the Inner Temple*. Philip Sidney's entertainment, "The Lady of May," provides still another model for this buffoonish entertainment.

Two earlier plays on the subject of Palamon and Arcite have not survived. The first (in two parts) was written and staged in 1566 by Richard Edwards, whose surviving play about friendship, *Damon and Pythias* (c. 1560–1565), gives us some indication of the importance of friendship in Renaissance discourse. Castiglione's *The Courtier* and Sidney's *Arcadia* are but two of many models here. A second lost play about Palamon and Arcite was staged by the Admiral's men in 1594, and a lost play about Damon and Pythias by Henry Chettle was acted by the same company in 1600.

Venus and Adonis

Venus and Adonis was Shakespeare's contribution to the vogue of Ovidian and erotic poetry in the 1580s and 1590s that included Thomas Lodge's *Scilla's Metamorphosis* (1589), Michael Drayton's *Endimion and Phoebe* (published 1595), Christopher Marlowe's *Hero and Leander* (registered 1593), and John Marston's *Metamorphosis of Pygmalion's Image* (1598). On Shakespeare's combining of three passages from Ovid's *Metamorphoses*, see the Introduction to *Venus and Adonis*. A disdainful Adonis had evidently become a commonplace in the 1590s, for it appears in *Hero and Leander*, lines 12–14, Edmund Spenser's *Faerie Queene*, 3.1.35, and elsewhere.

The Rape of Lucrece

Shakespeare's chief source for *The Rape of Lucrece* was Ovid's *Fasti* (2, 721–852), which had not yet been translated into English. He also seems to have known Livy's *History of Rome* (1, 57–9), which had been translated by William Painter in his *The Palace of Pleasure* (1566), and Chaucer's *The Legend of Good Women* (which is, like Shakespeare's poem, indebted to Ovid and Livy). Shakespeare's version is considerably longer than any of these sources. Ovid, Livy, and Chaucer give narrative, swift-moving accounts; Shakespeare follows, instead, the literary tradition of the "Complaint," as in *A Mirror for Magistrates* and in Samuel Daniel's *The Complaint of Rosamond*.

The Phoenix and Turtle

"The Phoenix and Turtle" is sometimes related to Chaucer's *The Parlement of Fowles*, an allegorical treatment of an assembly of birds. No indebtedness can be proved, however. Instead, as F. T. Price has shown in his Arden edition of *The Poems*, Shakespeare's chief "source" was the very anthology to which he contributed this remarkable piece. Called *Love's Martyr*, assembled by one Robert Chester, it contains some execrable verse but was built around a single vivid and intriguing emblem: the union in death of two mythic birds expressing a love beyond human reason. The idea was sufficiently compelling to attract not only Shakespeare but Jonson, Chapman, and Marston. The cooperation of these highly sophisticated writers may have been prompted by some kind of private *jeu d'esprit*, but Shakespeare's venture into fantasy produced extraordinary results.

A Lover's Complaint

This poem resembles other complaints of forsaken women, as in Ovid's *Amores* and Chaucer's *Legend of Good Women*, but no specific source is known.

The Sonnets

See the Introduction to *The Sonnets* for a discussion of the sonnet vogue in England of the 1590s, and the previous history of the sonnet in England and on the Continent.

Appendix 3

Shakespeare in Performance

Lois Potter, University of Delaware

Although we know a good deal about the conditions of performance at the time Shakespeare's plays were first produced, much of this information (summarized in the Introduction, pp. xliv–xlvii) raises as many questions as it answers. We know, for example, that Shakespeare wrote most of his plays for the Lord Chamberlain's men, first formed in 1594 after a period of plague and theater closures, and that the company (officially servants of the courtier whose duties included supervising court entertainments) was honored with the title of the King's men at the accession of James I. Elizabethan acting companies were all male, with boys or young men playing women's roles, but we know almost nothing about how they acted, or who played which parts. We know that the stages of the public, partially roofed playhouses jutted into the yard where the audience stood on three sides, looking up at the actors; the rest of the spectators sat in covered galleries looking down on them. But we are not sure whether the gallery above the stage, pictured in the contemporary illustration of the Swan Theatre interior shown on page xlvi, was meant for musicians, spectators, or both. (And of course we do not know how much the Globe's interior resembled the Swan's.) If, as appears from the illustrations of theater interiors on pages xlvi and lxiv, some spectators normally watched the action from behind the stage, the actors would have had to move a great deal during a scene, as in modern theater-in-the-round productions, to make sure that they were visible and audible to all parts of their audience.

However much information we have, we still cannot know if aspects of the theater that were common then but unusual in our eyes were taken for granted by the spectators who watched the plays in the reigns of Elizabeth and James I. Did they think of the boy actresses as boys or believe in them as women? Those who had traveled to France and Italy would have known that women played women's parts in those countries and were often as famous as the male actors. What was the acting style for love scenes between a man and a cross-dressed boy, and what was the range of responses to it? The players in the open theaters performed by day (normally beginning at 2 P.M.), but used torches and candles to indicate when the action was supposed to be taking place at night. Did audiences find it difficult to accept a convention by which actors, fully visible to the audience, declare that they are unable to see anything? There is probably no single answer. It is likely that then, as always, audience members differed in the extent to which they preferred to believe in the performance or feel superior to it.

To the audiences of Shakespeare's time, the theaters were sumptuous and impressive buildings. Their wooden interiors were painted to look like marble, and the ceiling of the Globe was apparently decorated with the signs of the zodiac (perhaps, when Hamlet and Othello addressed the heavens, they looked at both a real and an artificial sky). Visitors from abroad were taken to see plays; actors traveled with them as far as Prague; versions of them were being translated into German as early as 1618. All this indicates how much English plays and players were respected. By about 1597, the company for which Shakespeare wrote was the one most frequently invited to perform at court, evidence that it was considered the best in London.

The theater in fact offered a great deal of visual and musical pleasure even for those who could not understand the language. Vast sums of money were spent on costumes. The most valuable surviving evidence, an account book of Philip Henslowe, manager of the Rose playhouse, shows that their bright or striking colors (often red and black, with silver and gold) allowed them to stand out on a stage that depended on daylight for most of its illumination. These were not "costumes" but clothes, sometimes bought in secondhand shops and sometimes donated or sold by gentlemen patrons. Characters normally wore contemporary dress, but with some indications of historical costume, like togas for classical characters (see the contemporary drawing, usually taken to be an illustration of *Titus Andronicus*, on p. lxi). Costumes and wigs, as well as false beards, were obviously important for a theater in which twelve to fourteen actors frequently doubled in as many as thirty roles. Music was frequently used in productions and a number of writers, including Shakespeare, incorporated popular contemporary songs into their plays. Robert Johnson, who is credited with the songs to a number of Jacobean plays, may have been the company's in-house composer. Some plays may have had as much music as a modern musical comedy, though very little of it has been identified.

Shakespeare's plays were designed to show off the actors' talents: singing, playing an instrument, dancing, and fencing. Most of his most popular plays end with either a dance or a fight, and nearly all of his tragic heroes (with the interesting exceptions of Othello and Antony) have at least one heroic fight scene. Since memorization and oratory were part of every grammar school education, audiences could recognize the superior memories of the actors who learned the long and complicated speeches that Shakespeare wrote for them. The combination of great actors and a dramatist who wrote great roles for them was attractive to other playwrights, and helped to ensure the company's continuing preeminence.

Shakespeare's practice of writing plays dominated by one very large starring role probably followed Richard Burbage's rise to stardom. Many contemporary references identify him with Richard III (see the anecdote on pp. lix–lx), and he is also known to have played Romeo, Hamlet, Othello, and Lear. John Lowin, who joined the company in 1602–1603, seems to have partnered Burbage in plays with two substantial roles. Shakespeare was unusual in that he wrote equally well for tragic and comic actors, and for the company clown, a type of performer traditionally famous for his ad-libs. Will Kemp, the most famous comedian of his day, certainly created the role of Dogberry—his name accidentally replaces the character's in one quarto of the play. It is not absolutely certain that he played Falstaff, but his departure from the Lord Chamberlain's men in 1599 is often linked with Shakespeare's writing the character out of *Henry V* after having apparently promised (at the end of *2 Henry IV*) to include him in the sequel. Those who think that Shakespeare was in agreement with Hamlet's advice to the players ("Let those that play your clowns speak no more than is set down for them") wonder whether Kemp's inability to refrain from "speaking" led to friction with his leading playwright.

Kemp's successor was Robert Armin, and it is often said that the more literary quality of Shakespeare's later fools resulted from their being tailored for the new actor.

Little is known about the other chief sharers in the company, though attempts have been made to identify them with, for example, references to exceptionally thin or exceptionally fat actors. It is not known whether any particular young actor inspired Shakespeare to write his best female roles, but many boys seem to have been good enough to have a personal following. A spectator who saw *Othello* in Oxford in 1610 mentions how moved the spectators were at the sight of Desdemona after her death.

It has often been suggested that Hamlet's insistence on naturalness, and the First Player's modest claim to have "reformed" the practice of overacting at least to some extent, reflect a perceived difference between the actors for whom Shakespeare wrote and the more melodramatic ones in the company led by Philip Henslowe and its leading actor Edward Alleyn. Yet Alleyn, who created the major Marlowe roles, was no less intelligent and talented than Burbage. It was Alleyn who retired early to live the life of a gentleman (in 1597, when he was only 31), with one brief comeback in 1601–1604. Burbage, on the other hand, went on acting up to his death at the age of 46, a fact that suggests a more theatrical personality than Alleyn's. If there was a movement toward greater naturalism in the 1590s, it probably resulted from greater professionalization and better training of actors, along with greater sophistication of the audiences themselves.

As the Lord Chamberlain's men grew more successful, they looked for a more select location. In 1597 James Burbage, Richard's father, purchased part of the disused monastic site of Blackfriars in the City of London. Protests from the local residents forced him to rent out the building to boys' companies (which performed less frequently) until, early in the reign of James I, times became more favorable. Finally moving into the new premises some time after 1607, the company was able to restrict its public to those who could afford the higher admission prices. In the indoor theaters, all the spectators were seated. Comfortable spectators cause less trouble than uncomfortable ones. The smaller size may have allowed for a more "realistic" style of playing. At the same time, the company continued to use the Globe throughout the period, as well as acting at court and elsewhere, so the actors must have been able to adapt their style to circumstances. In many ways, Shakespeare's last plays are his least "realistic," since they often involve magic, but the technology available in the Blackfriars playhouse may have made the magic convincing.

Besides, if realistic acting means acting that makes one forget that one is watching a play, it is unlikely that the drama was ever truly realistic. Other dramatists' allusions to Shakespeare are obviously meant to break the dramatic illusion: "What, Hamlet, are you mad?" asks a character in *Eastward Ho!* (1605), speaking to a servant who is named Hamlet only so that someone can ask him that question. Shakespeare himself also refers to his own plays. It is likely that the lovers' suicides in "Pyramus and This-be," performed at the end of *A Midsummer Night's Dream*, are meant as an absurd version of the end of *Romeo and Juliet*; Malvolio's madness, in *Twelfth Night*, probably parodies Hamlet's. Perhaps a comedy can make jokes about a tragedy without destroying the atmosphere, but *Hamlet* does the same thing. When Polonius tells Hamlet about playing Julius Caesar "at the university," and being killed by Brutus, many of their audience would remember that, not long before, the two actors speaking these lines had played Caesar and Brutus, respectively, in *Julius Caesar*.

The deaths of Shakespeare in 1616 and of Burbage in 1619 may have temporarily affected Shakespeare's theatrical popularity. Burbage was so much identified with the major roles that, according to one elegy, these characters seemed to have died with him. The Earl of Pembroke may have been typical when, in a letter, he expresses reluctance to go to the theater again. John Taylor, who replaced Burbage in 1619, inherited a number of his roles. He and Lowin led the company for the next twenty years, with first John Fletcher and then Philip Massinger as their leading dramatist. The company had been called the King's men since 1603, but the name was even more appropriate under Charles I than under his father, since the actors were much closer to the court. Taylor even served as acting coach to Queen Henrietta Maria and her ladies when they put on a pastoral tragicomedy in 1633.

Though not all Puritans or parliamentarians were hostile to the theater, and not all of Charles I's courtiers approved of it, the English civil war created a further association between theater and crown. Parliament closed the theaters at the start of the war in 1642, refusing to reopen them even when hostilities had ended. Performances continued nevertheless: professionals acted illegally in the theater buildings that were still usable, or, like amateurs, legally in private houses and inns. Some also went abroad and acted for English royalists in exile. Since the prohibition applied only to plays, scenes involving popular characters (Hamlet and the gravediggers, Falstaff, Bottom) were adapted and disguised as "drolls"—comic sketches—that could be performed in a mixed program of music, dance, and drama. The 1662 frontispiece to a collection of these drolls (p. lxiv) shows how Falstaff and Mrs. Quickly were probably costumed in this period.

The Restoration and the Eighteenth Century (1660–1776)

At the Restoration of 1660, one of Charles II's first acts was to establish two licensed acting companies, one patronized by him, the other by his brother the Duke of York. Each company was assigned a selection of plays from the prewar period. Shakespeare's were among the first to be revived; indeed, actors were already playing them in London before the new theaters had opened. Although one of the speakers in Dryden's dialogue on drama (*An Essay of Dramatic Poesy*, 1665) says that Beaumont and Fletcher's plays were more popular than Shakespeare's or Jonson's, the evidence indicates that Shakespeare went on being a frequently acted dramatist throughout this period. Since the King's company seems to have received preferential treatment, it is likely that the plays awarded to them—*1 Henry IV*, *The Merry Wives of Windsor*, and *Othello*—were the most popular of Shakespeare's works in 1660.

It was natural that Shakespeare's works would need updating; nearly fifty years after their author's death, their language, grammar, and jokes were already becoming obsolete. Audiences saw themselves as too refined for plays with clowns and devils. Both theater managers (Thomas Killigrew and William Davenant) had been playwrights before the war, and both produced the prewar drama with extensive alterations. *The Taming of the Shrew*, as produced in 1667 by the King's company under Killigrew, was called, improbably, *Sauny the Scot*, after the new comic servant who replaced Grumio; the actor John Lacy wrote the title role for himself, exploiting the anti-Scots feeling that had been exacerbated by the Civil War. "Scenes," or scenery, the norm in the theaters of France and Italy, had already been used in prewar masques, and in the 1630s Davenant had already been planning to open a theater equipped to use it for plays. As manager of the Duke's company, he set about revising old plays to create more possibilities for spectacle. His *The Law Against Lovers* (1662) conflated *Measure for Measure* and *Much Ado About Nothing*, neither of which was well known at the period. The result was an emphasis on the romantic part of both plays, as opposed to their low comedy. He added more music and scenery in his adaptations of *Macbeth* (1664) and *The Tempest* (1667); in later revivals, these two works became almost operatic. The new theaters were rather small, and actors still played at the front of the stage, with the wings and backdrop of the new scenery stretching away behind them. Scene changes could be made quickly by rolling away one sliding backdrop to reveal another one behind it, sometimes with a new set of characters already in place. The same painted wings and backdrop were expected to serve for a number of plays, acting as a kind of shorthand to distinguish indoor from outdoor settings. The idea that each play belonged to its own particular visual world did not gain currency until well into the nineteenth century.

Charles II had insisted, in his patent for the new theaters, that the custom of boy actors—unique to England—must end. Most of the women who became actresses during the early years of the Restoration were, inevitably, untrained. The famous Nell Gwyn, mistress of Charles II, was a star of the King's company. She was considered delightful in contemporary comedies, some of which were written especially for her; however, Pepys always insisted that she was disastrous in serious roles, and there is no record of her playing Shakespeare. The new actresses could exploit their natural gifts, their beauty, and their novelty, but no one wanted to see them in character parts, especially those of elderly women. As a result, roles like the witches in *Macbeth* were taken by men, often the company's low comedians, a practice that continued for centuries. The small number of parts for attractive young women in Shakespeare now became a problem. Davenant was skillful at multiplying them. He expanded the part of Lady Macduff; Miranda, no longer the only woman in *The Tempest*, acquired a naïve younger sister, while Caliban and Ariel were likewise paired off with a female monster and spirit respectively.

Some of these changes also had a moral purpose. Davenant balanced the wickedness of Macbeth and his Lady by developing the virtuous Macduffs as foils to them. He also gave Macbeth a death speech (only one line long) to show that the dying man recognized the vanity of his ambition. Later adaptations were still more concerned with "poetic justice." This term meant simply that art ought to reward virtue and punish vice, not because this is what happens in the real world, but because art's duty is to offer virtuous models whenever possible. John Dryden, who had worked with Davenant on *The Tempest*, later wrote free adaptations of both *Antony and Cleopatra* and *Troilus and Cressida*, in which the lovers, far from being unfaithful, are only sympathetic victims of misunderstanding. His version of *Antony and Cleopatra*, called *All for Love, or, the World Well Lost* (1675–1677), largely replaced its model for much of the next century, and was often played under Shakespeare's title. Though Dryden claimed that he had made Antony's wife Octavia a virtuous foil to Cleopatra, the play's success was due less to its superior morality (indeed, its most popular scene was one in which the two women insult each other) than to its simplification of the structure, which subordinated political history to the love story. Shadwell's *Timon of Athens* (1678) provided a faithful woman as well as a faithful steward, to contrast with the mercenary friends and mistress who desert the hero. Thomas Otway's *Caius Marius* (1679) made the suicides of Romeo and Juliet more acceptable by locating them in a classical world. One of Otway's other innovations—letting the heroine revive in time to converse with the hero before they die—was to outlast the adaptation itself. Nahum Tate's *King Lear* (1681) made the virtuous Cordelia a large and dramatic role, worthy of a star actress. He also added a love interest between her and Edgar, and provided a happy ending in which Lear is restored to his throne. The adaptation remained in the repertory for 150 years, and Samuel Johnson defended it in 1765 on the grounds that,

although the unjust tragic ending might be more true to life, "all reasonable beings naturally love justice." Tate's omission of the Fool, a character associated with old-fashioned theater, was not even noticed.

After 1679, the Popish Plot and uncertainty over the royal succession led to Shakespearean adaptations designed to score political points. In 1680, John Crowne wrote *The Misery of Civil War* (1680), the first of two adaptations based on the *Henry VI* plays, while Tate's *The Sicilian Usurper*, adapted from *Richard II*, fell foul of the censor, even though its deposed ruler was more sympathetic than Shakespeare's. In the following year, Tate reversed the order of scenes in *King Lear*, beginning with Edmund's first soliloquy: a bastard son claiming his right to inherit was bound to be topical in the reign of a king who had no legitimate children and whose next heir was a Roman Catholic brother. The turbulent political climate kept audiences away, and the two companies amalgamated in 1682. Very few plays of any kind survive from the last years of Charles II's reign and the three years of James II's leading to the revolution of 1688. In the reign of William and Mary (James's daughter), *King Lear* was once again so topical that it could not be staged. Mary and her sister Anne looked all too much like Lear's daughters, especially since Tate's version ends with the king's abdication in favor of his daughter and son-in-law.

Colley Cibber's *Richard III* (1699), the most successful of all adaptations, benefited from the fact that a number of Shakespeare's history plays had dropped out of the repertory by the end of the century, thus providing a quarry from which the adapter could borrow. Feeling that he had a free hand, Cibber removed Queen Margaret and, since he intended to play Richard himself, gave him some good lines from other histories, including (from *2 Henry IV*) the death speech that Shakespeare had neglected to write for his hero. This Richard, literally an actor's dream, was more theatrically popular than Shakespeare's had been, a fact that kept the version alive well into the twentieth century (the Olivier film, which also cut Margaret's role, used two recognizable Cibber lines). Cibber had some difficulties with the licenser just before the first performance because it was feared that his opening scene, showing the deposed Henry VI in the Tower, would remind its audiences of the deposed James II. He made sure to show his loyalty in his next adaptation— *King John*, under the title *Papal Tyranny*, coincided with the threatened invasion, in 1715, of James II's exiled Catholic son. As one of the managers of Drury Lane, and as poet laureate (from 1730), Cibber became a popular target for satire, and he is best remembered for Pope's attacks on him in *The Dunciad* (1743). But his entertaining autobiography, *An Apology for the Life of Colley Cibber, Comedian* (1740), is still the best source of information on the early eighteenth-century theater.

Indeed, without Cibber's book, it would be difficult to say much about Shakespearean acting at the turn of the eighteenth century. Though Thomas Betterton was recognized as the greatest actor of his age from the first years of the Restoration, those, like Samuel Pepys, who saw him at this time, praised him highly but in vague terms. Because of the division of the theatrical repertory, Betterton acquired some major Shakespearean roles, like Othello, only after the unification of the two companies in 1682, when senior actors of the King's company took the opportunity to retire. After this, he had virtually a monopoly, and went on playing a much-acclaimed Hamlet until he was seventy, as well as taking the role of Falstaff in what seems to have been his own adaptation of the *Henry IV* plays. Cibber's description of Betterton's Hamlet reacting to the first sight of his father's ghost became a point of comparison for later Hamlets well into the nineteenth century. It is clear that his effects had to do with "presence" rather than with movement—though, of course, Cibber was describing him in his last years, when he was presumably less active.

The early female performers are still more shadowy figures. Women had appeared on stage as singers, or singing actresses, in "operas" performed in the 1650s, and one of these, perhaps Margaret Hughes, may have been the first to play a Shakespearean role (probably Desdemona). Mary Sanderson, who became Mrs. Betterton, was the first Lady Macbeth. Her successor, Elizabeth Barry, was primarily a tragic actress. She is said to have owed her initial success to careful instruction by her lover, the Earl of Rochester, who recognized the importance of constant repetition and, like a modern director, insisted that she should rehearse in the dress that she was going to wear in performance. The best-loved comic actress of Cibber's youth, Anne Bracegirdle, played several Shakespearean comedy heroines alongside the Congreve roles for which she was famous. The popularity of *The Merry Wives of Windsor* may have been due not only to Betterton's playing of Falstaff but also to its two excellent roles for actresses past their first youth, probably the only women in the company experienced enough to do justice to Shakespearean comedy.

Though the history of Shakespeare editing begins in the early eighteenth century, the plays still belonged essentially to the theater; hence, the publication of acting editions, which allowed audiences to read what they were actually going to see in the theater, usually heavily cut and partially modernized. Even so, the first half of the century saw a steady return to original versions, as one role after another was suddenly revealed to be a superb vehicle for a particular actor. Shylock, for instance, had been a not-very-interesting comic miser in a not-very-interesting romantic comedy, often replaced by George Granville's adaptation, *The Jew of Venice* (1701). When Shakespeare's original was revived in 1741, Charles Macklin astonished his fellow-actors as much as the audience by emphasizing Shylock's terrifying malevolence.

Although later actors would play the character more sympathetically, Macklin made him what he has been ever since: a disturbing character who cannot be assimilated into a comic structure. Something of a theorist on acting, Macklin, in teaching other actors, insisted on clear and intelligent diction. Perhaps for that reason, his Iago was the most convincing of the period.

Richard III, in Cibber's version, was the role in which David Garrick made his London debut in 1741. The actor became famous almost instantly and went on to manage the Drury Lane Theatre from 1747 to 1776. Garrick was a self-proclaimed idolater of Shakespeare whose "Jubilee" at Stratford-upon-Avon in 1769 not only inaugurated the practice of celebrations and festivals but also led contemporaries to regard him as almost equal in importance with his author. Despite his reputation for restoring Shakespeare, Garrick was as much of an adapter as his famous predecessors, turning *The Taming of the Shrew* and the last part of *The Winter's Tale* into short three-act plays and making operas out of *A Midsummer Night's Dream* and *The Tempest*. His *Macbeth* had a death speech, much more dramatic and pathetic than the one-line moral that Davenant had given him. His *Romeo and Juliet* had a pathetic farewell scene based on the one in Otway's *Caius Marius*. In response to French criticisms, he even directed a *Hamlet* in 1771 with the low comedy of the gravediggers omitted. Yet he also revived many plays not seen in their Shakespearean form since the Restoration, showing by his acting what superb roles they contained. He was equally gifted at comedy and tragedy. Two of his most popular roles were Benedick and (Tate's) King Lear. *Julius Caesar* and *Othello,* plays in which Betterton had been particularly successful, were better acted by Garrick's chief rival, Spranger Barry, a tall and handsome actor with a beautiful voice. Garrick, shorter and less romantic in appearance, was famous for his mobile and expressive features that allowed him to delineate the transitions between the "passions." It was this grasp of human psychology that he praised in Shakespeare and that others praised in him. His most significant leading lady, Hannah Pritchard, must have been equally versatile, since she was famous both as Rosalind and as Lady Macbeth. It was, however, characteristic of Garrick that he was able to form an excellent company around himself, including a number of fine actresses and low comedians. Without these conditions, it would have been impossible to revive so many of the comedies.

The Romantic Period (1776–1850)

Between Garrick's retirement in 1776 and the end of the century, the theaters changed to the point where a rapid, subtle style like Garrick's was becoming almost impossible. The Licensing Act of 1737 had limited spoken drama to Drury Lane and Covent Garden, the descendents of the two London theaters licensed in 1660 by Charles II. The late eighteenth century saw the rapid growth of a London population in search of entertainment. The two theaters responded by increasing their audience capacity until, at the end of the century, Covent Garden held over 3,000 spectators, and Drury Lane 3,600. When much of the audience was too far from the stage to see facial expressions or hear the softer tones of an actor's voice, the most successful performers were those who could establish themselves through their volume or through visual effects. Two tall and statuesque actors, John Philip Kemble and his more gifted sister, Sarah Siddons, dominated the theater of this period. Siddons's Lady Macbeth was probably the finest performance of the age: when she said that she could smell blood, at least one contemporary spectator declared that he could smell it too. Her other finest Shakespearean roles were Isabella in *Measure for Measure* and Hermione in *The Winter's Tale*, both of them strong women whose sublime moral grandeur dwarfed everyone else. Kemble's attempt to impose greater discipline and unity on theatrical productions, with more historically "correct" sets and costumes, resulted in what must have been the most genuinely classical theater yet seen in Britain. *Coriolanus*, with Kemble in the title role and Siddons as a heroically obsessed Volumnia, was the triumph of their approach. It was ironic that it should have come in an age dominated by the spirit of revolution and of the complex attitudes that are summed up as Romanticism.

It was to this spirit that Edmund Kean appealed. Those who saw him make his famous London debut as Shylock in 1814, wearing a black wig instead of the traditional red one, would have realized at once that he was going to play, not a tragic villain, but a tragic victim. He had been a singer, dancer, and Harlequin before taking London by storm, and his acting benefited from these other skills. Unlike Kemble, who expressed authority and aristocratic dignity, he excelled as Shakespeare's outsiders and outlaws: the hunchbacked Richard III (still in Cibber's softened version), the Moor Othello, and the melancholy Hamlet. Knowing his gift for pathos, he starred in an adaptation of *3 Henry VI* (where York sobs over his murdered son) and attempted to bring back the original ending of *King Lear* (where Lear grieves over the dead Cordelia), but audiences were not yet ready for either. Those who saw him at his best never forgot his haunting delivery of Richard III's forebodings before Bosworth and Othello's farewell to arms, which provided the kind of appreciative, poetic commentary on Shakespeare that characterized the best contemporary criticism.

Kean's career was short, wrecked by drink and scandal. In 1833, just as he had reached his miserable end, another actor, using the stage name of Keane, made his Covent Garden debut in the role of Othello. Ira Aldridge, a black American, may have hoped to announce himself as Kean's successor, but racial prejudice in England prevented him from being accepted as a leading tragedian. He would, however, play Othello all over Europe, and especially in Russia, in bilingual productions with local casts. Like Kean, he sought out the roles of victims and social outcasts: Aaron in his own adaptation of *Titus Andronicus*, as well as (in white make-up) Macbeth, Shylock, and King Lear; like Kean, he was also capable of singing songs in dialect or even a Russian folksong. The excitement that German and Russian spectators felt at the sight of a black actor playing a black character would become an important part of theatrical experience a century later; at this point, it was a novelty. In the 1860s Aldridge finally acted in major London theaters and might have returned to the United States after the Civil War if he had not died unexpectedly while on tour in Poland.

Meanwhile, both of the unruly London theaters were managed, in turn, by William Macready, who, as his diary makes clear, took seriously his responsibility to a dramatist he worshipped. Still more than Kemble, he behaved like a modern director, with a vision of the production as a whole. His revivals of the history plays showed the possibilities of historical reconstruction. He is best known for restoring the Fool to *King Lear* in 1838, though he gave the role to a young woman to ensure that it would be played for pathos rather than low comic effects that might distract from his own scenes. A number of fine actresses played opposite him: Helen Faucit, young, fragile, refined, who would later write a perceptive if sentimental account of her approach to acting some of Shakespeare's female characters; Fanny Kemble, a member of the famous Kemble family, whose memoirs indicate the struggle involved for women in a star-dominated theater; Charlotte Cushman, a powerful visitor from America who sometimes played male roles. The plays were still heavily cut and showed the influence of earlier adaptations, but by the end of his career, Macready could fairly claim to have restored a good deal of Shakespeare's text and to have made the theater more respectable. The repeal of the Licensing Act in 1843, which allowed smaller theaters to cater to different publics, also encouraged gentrification. Samuel Phelps, who managed the working-class Sadler's Wells Theatre from 1844 to 1869, did even more than Macready had, performing thirty-four of Shakespeare's plays; he even restored the original *Richard III*, though other actors continued to prefer the Cibber version. Charles Kean (son of Edmund), at the Princess's Theatre from 1850 to 1859, carried the historicizing process still further; his "archaeological" productions were likely to be accompanied by notes explaining the reason for the choice of period, costumes, and props.

Still, it was only rarely that anyone had the opportunity to impose a concept of Shakespearean production on an acting company in his own theater. Star actors tended to spend much of their time on tour, both in England and America, performing their favorite roles after perhaps one rehearsal with the resident company. Far from seeking new ways to interpret a play, these actors had to rely on standardized stage business (when Mr. Wopsle plays Hamlet in Dickens's *Great Expectations*, an unsympathetic audience comments loudly on each theatrical cliché as it occurs). They naturally tended to conceive of their characters in isolation and to favor tragedy over comedy, which requires ensemble playing. (Similarly, nineteenth-century critics usually focus on the analysis of individual characters.) A common practice was the pitting of one actor against another in a famous role, arguing over which one was the "true" Hamlet or Lear. In one case, the rivalry developed a nationalistic dimension. Macready's visit to America, in 1849, is notorious for the riot at Astor Place in New York, when soldiers fired on and killed some of the crowd outside the theater. The rioters had been trying to drown out Macready's performance of *Macbeth* out of a mistaken loyalty to the American tragedian, Edwin Forrest. On a visit to Britain, Forrest had hissed Macready for some foppish business with a handkerchief that the actor, as Hamlet, had used to illustrate the phrase "I must be idle." Now his personal hostility became a quarrel about effete English acting versus the manly American tradition. In fact, the distinction was largely meaningless: many well-known American actors had begun their careers in England or Ireland. While some American Shakespeareans might have seen themselves as part of the Forrest tradition, and some (like the touring performers depicted by Mark Twain in *Huckleberry Finn*) were of no tradition at all, most American actors continued to look to Europe for models.

The Victorian Era and the Early Twentieth Century (1850–1912)

The greatest American actor of the next generation, Edwin Booth, was a refined and melancholy figure whose readings of the great Shakespearean roles were psychological and poetic. Booth was the son of Junius Brutus Booth, who had acted in London opposite Edmund Kean, and the brother of John Wilkes Booth, the assassin of Abraham Lincoln. (Ironically, all three members of this acting family had once performed together in the great assassination play, *Julius Caesar*.) Though Booth briefly attempted theater management, he spent much of his time in the exhausting business of touring. He clearly thought deeply about his own roles, and about the moments when other characters interacted with him. His correspondence with the New Variorum Shakespeare

editor, H.H. Furness, is quoted in many notes of that edition—an early example of successful communication between the theater and the scholarly world. Yet when Booth was alternating the two leading roles of *Othello* with Henry Irving in 1881, he sent his servant to take notes at rehearsal for him. Nothing in his experience had prepared him for a theater in which the actor-manager expected everyone to fit into a total artistic conception.

It was Irving, the first actor to be knighted, who dominated English Shakespearean acting in the late Victorian era. His pictorial sense was even stronger than that of the actor-managers who preceded him, and the technical means at his disposal in the Lyceum Theatre, which he began to manage in 1878, were much better. The old system of sliding screens in grooves, flanked by a series of wings, had been replaced by the "box set," which was built like a piece of architecture, creating a complete environment. Electric lighting, introduced in the 1880s, provided new, subtle visual effects. The elaborate and beautiful sets often required interminable scene changes and, sometimes, rearrangement of the plays to accommodate them. Irving's own performances were usually controversial. His Malvolio, like his Shylock, was a tragic figure, while his Iago was so witty and likeable that, playing opposite Booth's Othello, he stole all the sympathy from the hero. His theater offered a beautiful dream for the spectator to share: if it also disturbed the spectator, it was through its revelation of the psychological depths of character, never through its comments on social and political issues. Irving's leading lady, Ellen Terry, was both beautiful and brilliant; in most productions she was allowed to be only the former. Bernard Shaw, longing for her to appear in plays about "grownup" topics, by himself or Henrik Ibsen, resented her imprisonment in Irving's world. For Shaw and other modern thinkers, Shakespeare was becoming synonymous with nostalgia and with the moralistic and idealistic thinking that the new drama regarded as a vice. The early twentieth-century theater was finally affected by these critical attempts to reform it, but two kinds of production coexisted for some time. At His Majesty's Theatre, Herbert Beerbohm Tree, like Irving, offered psychologically based character acting in a beautiful scenic environment, recreating Cleopatra's Egypt and Henry VIII's England; having seen his lavish production of *Macbeth*, one critic commented that "Nature put up a pretty feeble imitation of what several barrels of stones and a few sheets of tin could do in His Majesty's." At the Savoy, on the other hand, Harley Granville Barker, a disciple of Bernard Shaw, developed a decorative visual style that was not tied to a specific historical period.

Meanwhile, a more experimental approach to acting was being developed in Germany. The country's unusual political structure, with small dukedoms and cities sponsoring their own theaters, made it possible for the

Duke of Saxe-Meiningen to sponsor his own company of players, sixty-six in all. His leading actors were unremarkable but, when he took them on tour in the 1880s, audiences were impressed by his handling of large groups. The Duke insisted that those who played major roles in one production should be walk-ons in another, so that crowds could be properly rehearsed instead of being assembled from those gathered around the stage door and drilled by the stage manager immediately before each performance.

Frank Benson, a young Oxford graduate, saw the Saxe-Meiningen company at Drury Lane in 1881, and was inspired to develop his own touring company—though, unlike the Duke, he acted in his own productions and consequently shaped them from a star's point of view. From 1886 on, the Bensonians became regular visitors at Stratford-upon-Avon. Shakespeare's birthplace had been briefly famous in 1769, the year of Garrick's Jubilee, but it was only in 1879, when the first Memorial Theatre was built, that tourists had any reason to visit for more than a few hours. Benson essentially created the first Stratford company, though it used the theater only during a short "Festival" season. Having a regular venue and a devoted audience enabled him to revive unusual works, if often drastically cut. In 1901 he inaugurated the new century with a "Grand Cycle" of Shakespeare's histories—the first English production of the plays as a group.

The desire to return to fuller texts and something like the original conditions of Shakespearean performance was initially associated with Germany and then with outsiders like William Poel, who founded the English Stage Society in 1894. Previously, Poel had given an experimental matinee of the First Quarto *Hamlet* at St. George's Hall in 1881. More surprisingly (though his friendship with Bernard Shaw in part explains it), the popular London actor Johnston Forbes-Robertson played an unusually full text of *Hamlet* in 1897, with characters like Reynaldo and Fortinbras appearing for the first time in centuries. Then Benson's company played an uncut *Hamlet* in 1899 and 1900. Poel, who often worked with amateurs, using all-purpose curtains rather than scenery on what was meant to be an Elizabethan stage, revived works previously considered unperformable, by Shakespeare's contemporaries as well as by Shakespeare. For example, he gave the first important *Troilus and Cressida* to be seen in London since 1734, dressing it in Elizabethan rather than classical costume. It was 1912. He had discovered the play's antiwar potential.

The Twentieth Century

World War I drastically curtailed many Shakespearean projects, including those for a gigantic celebration of the anniversary of his death in 1916, which at one point was intended to include the opening of a National Theatre. Although this theater did not come into existence until nearly 100 years after Irving had first suggested it, other developments were creating the conditions that would make Shakespeare plays, with their large casts, commercially viable.

One was the rise of repertory theaters, which could support a large company and a varied range of plays. The most famous of these was London's Royal Victoria, or "Old Vic," founded in 1914. Under a number of gifted directors (notably Robert Atkins, who had directed all the plays in the 1623 Folio by 1923, Harcourt Williams, and Tyrone Guthrie), it was the home to many legendary productions, including John Gielgud's first *Hamlet* (1929) and Olivier's first *Hamlet* (1937). At the Birmingham Repertory Theatre, Barry Jackson had already directed a modern-dress *Hamlet* in 1925. Modern dress had been common practice until the nineteenth century; it now seemed eccentric, but would by the end of the century become almost the norm. The Memorial Theatre at Stratford, after struggling to find its identity, saw some brilliant productions by Peter Brook in the 1940s and 1950s, including three plays traditionally considered minor: *Love's Labor's Lost* (1946), *Measure for Measure* (1948), and a *Titus Andronicus* (1955), starring Olivier, at which audience members regularly fainted at what was then unusual stage violence: the amputation of the hero's hand and the cutting of the villains' throats. Stratford and the Old Vic were becoming rival Shakespeare companies and in the 1960s each achieved a new status. The Memorial Theatre was renamed the Royal Shakespeare Theatre in 1960, with Peter Hall as director, whereas the Old Vic was designated the National Theatre in 1963. Olivier directed its opening production of *Hamlet*, with Peter O'Toole in the title role, and played a famous Othello in 1964. The National Theatre eventually moved into new premises in an arts complex, with three stages, on the South Bank of the Thames.

In the United States, the most exciting Shakespeare productions also occurred during a period of government subsidy: it was depression-era financing that enabled Orson Welles to direct Shakespeare on radio, and, for the Mercury Theatre, his "voodoo" *Macbeth* (1938) with an all-black cast, his anti-Fascist *Julius Caesar* (1937), and his condensation of the major history plays, *Five Kings*, which, although unsuccessful, later influenced his Falstaff film, *Chimes at Midnight* (1966). The other significant development in North America was the growth of summer Shakespeare festivals at outdoor Elizabethan-style theaters, beginning with the Elizabethan Stage at Ashland, Oregon (founded 1935), and the Guthrie-designed Festival Theatre at Stratford, Ontario (1953). Festival seasons allowed juxtapositions of related plays and the yearly performance of successive plays in a history cycle.

It was the English Stratford-upon-Avon, however, that fully seized on the history plays, performing the *Richard II–Henry V* group in 1951, during the Festival of Britain that celebrated the country's emergence from wartime and postwar rationing. For the rest of the century, the "cycle" of history plays would be recognized as a national epic, to be performed for special occasions. For the new Royal Shakespeare Company, Peter Hall and John Barton produced the *Henry VI–Richard III* group of plays— rewritten, reduced to three plays, and called *The Wars of the Roses*. They revived these, along with the other *Henry* plays, for the Shakespeare quatercentenary in 1964. The histories were produced again in 1975 by Terry Hands, with Alan Howard playing all the kings except Henry IV; in 1982 the *Henry IV* plays opened the company's new London theater at the Barbican under Trevor Nunn; and the company, now under Adrian Noble, marked the arrival of the millennium with a freshly conceived production of the *Richard II–Richard III* sequence. Just as the 1951 production showed the influence of Tillyard's essays on the histories as a unified cycle, the plays of the year 2000, deliberately disparate in style and even venue, were the product of a critical movement that emphasized discontinuity and diversity.

Contemporary Critical Approaches

By now, productions might require as much interpretation as plays. In the last half of the twentieth century, the spread of school and university education had created a substantial population that had studied at least one Shakespeare play and a smaller population, including some theater practitioners, that had read not only the plays but also the criticism. Stratford's John Barton, a former Cambridge don, directed *Twelfth Night* (1969) as if it were by Chekhov, encouraging the audience to imagine the unspoken feelings of the characters—not only Viola (Judi Dench), smiling through heartbreak, but Maria, in her apparently hopeless love for Sir Toby, and Sir Andrew in his even more hopeless love for Olivia. This attention to character, often created out of masses of tiny realistic details, informed some of the theater's most highly praised productions. Barton's *Richard II* (1973) worked very differently, externalizing the play's images in ways that were clearly independent of the characters' awareness: for instance, a glimpse of a melting snowman echoed Richard's wish that he were "a mockery king of snow" and linked the fall and rise of kings to a natural cycle of dissolution and renewal.

Other major critical approaches, easier to categorize, quickly found their way onto the stage. Political readings, often influenced by a Brechtian production style, dominated the 1960s and 1970s. These were usually Marxist and anti-authority: lines in which characters expressed high moral sentiments might be juxtaposed (legitimately) with those in which they showed themselves less noble, or (illegitimately) by setting them in a context that undermined them, as when, in Peter Zadek's *Held Henry* (Hero Henry), Henry V delivers the St. Crispin's Day speech to his bored mistress. Even before its first English publication in 1964, *Shakespeare Our Contemporary*, by the Polish critic Jan Kott, had powerfully influenced theater with his comparison of *Hamlet* and the histories to life under a totalitarian regime, *King Lear* to Theater of the Absurd, and the comedies to a Freudian nightmare. Both Brecht and Kott could be recognized behind Peter Brook's *King Lear* (1962), which, in place of the traditional sympathy with the king (a frighteningly harsh Paul Scofield), emphasized his and his followers' brutality toward Goneril's servants, and ruthlessly cut anything that might be cathartic; the Dover cliff meeting between Lear and Gloucester frankly drew on the stage imagery of Samuel Beckett's *Waiting for Godot*. Brook's *A Midsummer Night's Dream* (1970), which based its erotic treatment of Titania and Bottom on Kott's work, found a purely theatrical language for the critical commonplaces about the play's metatheatricality. Without makeup, under bright light, in a white-walled gymnasium that replaced the traditional moonlit forest, Oberon and Puck sat on trapezes and passed the aphrodisiac "flower," a metal plate, from one spinning metallic wand to another. The fact that this operation could, and occasionally did, go wrong was the point: it reminded the audience that the real magic lay in its own willingness to trust the actors. Even the "Pyramus and Thisbe" actors in the final scene were treated as serious artists, representatives of working-class culture who deserved respect. For many of his later productions, Peter Brook went abroad in search of a multilingual, multiethnic cast, searching for ways of escaping the "easy" assumptions about Shakespeare.

It was in fact race and gender rather than class that dominated Shakespeare production in the last quarter of the century. The concern with race began with the great American theatrical event of the 1940s, Margaret Webster's production of *Othello* with the charismatic Paul Robeson in the title role. After the longest run of any Shakespeare play on Broadway, it was taken on tour all over America in 1945, playing only in desegregated theaters. Although Robeson had already played Othello in London (1930), and would do so again at Stratford-upon-Avon, England, in 1959, his long period of disgrace in the politically polarized United States of the 1950s delayed the movement toward race-based casting as a norm. After initial embarrassment about racist language in Shakespeare, the theater began deliberately to explore its implications, as race became a subject for academic study. The range of *Othello* videos available by the 1990s indicates the play's performance history: besides Orson

Welles's film from 1952, these include the National Theatre production of 1964 starring Laurence Olivier and the BBC one with Antony Hopkins (1981), both with white actors in the title role; Trevor Nunn's Chekhovian version originally staged in 1989; the historic South African production by Janet Suzman, a political act at a time when apartheid still existed; and Oliver Parker's 1994 version, with Laurence Fishburne (opposite Kenneth Branagh's convincingly ordinary Iago), consciously conveying the concentrated power and sensuality associated with blackness. Confusion between "color-blind casting" (when the audience is supposed to ignore the race of both actor and character) and "race-based casting" (when the audience is being told something about race through the casting) was deliberately cultivated in Jude Kelly's *Othello* (Washington, D.C., 1997). This production enabled Patrick Stewart to achieve his otherwise unrealizable ambition of playing the title role by surrounding a white Othello with African American and Hispanic actors, yet with the play's racial references unaltered.

Just as some critics of racism felt that *Othello* and *The Merchant of Venice* had become theatrically unacceptable, some feminist responses to Shakespeare argued the same about *The Taming of the Shrew*, in which a female character is made to acquiesce in her humiliation by a husband who uses patriarchal arguments to justify his behavior. The play had usually been directed to soften its final moral, either by making it clear that the protagonists have fallen in love at first sight or by emphasizing its nature as a play within a play, safely distant from real life. A famous production by Michael Bogdanov (Royal Shakespeare Theatre, 1978) doubled the drunken tinker Sly with Petruchio and showed Kate being brutalized into a dazed submission that horrified even her husband. Obviously, the play in this version was no longer a comedy. A less obvious effect of feminism has been the increasing attention paid to Shakespeare's female characters. They tend now to be on stage more than the text directs, as when Ophelia stands appalled while her father reads Hamlet's love letters to the court or Gertrude enters in time to hear Claudius and Laertes plan to poison Hamlet, so that her decision to drink from the cup is recognized as a heroic device to save her son's life. The young Elizabeth of York, who does not appear in the text of *Richard III* although she is important to its plot, has frequently been seen and even heard in stage versions, as in the 1995 film by Richard Loncraine. The fact that women are often denied speech at crucial moments can be turned to an advantage, as when John Barton and a number of subsequent directors of *Measure for Measure* in the 1980s made Isabella silently refuse the Duke's proposal, which earlier actors and directors had assumed she would eagerly accept.

Still more important, in a theater in which women are far more likely than men to be underemployed, were devices that increased the number of Shakespearean roles for women. Cross-dressed performances, parallel to the productions focused on race, hovered between gender based and gender blind. Deborah Warner's *Richard II* in 1995, with Fiona Shaw as the title character (National Theatre, London), suggested a troubled and potentially erotic relationship between Richard and Bolingbroke without defining it further. In the all-male Cheek-by-Jowl production of *As You Like It* (1995), the audience was never certain whether it was meant to be thinking of Rosalind (Adrian Lester) as male or female. A similar confusion was exploited when Michael Kahn's *King Lear* (Washington, D.C., 1999) cast Cordelia as a deaf-mute, signing her lines, which were then interpreted by the Fool. This decision, which would have been meaningless if the audience had not known that the actress (Monique Holt) really was a deaf-mute, might be seen either as a return to the self-conscious theatricality of the Renaissance stage or as an example of identity politics.

Shakespeare on Film

Of course, the sense of identity between actor and role is strongest in the cinema, where physical appearance matters more and where audiences are particularly likely to bring with them recollections of an actor's previous roles. Films of Shakespeare plays are as old as film itself. Their transfer to videotape and then laserdisc and DVD, a process that began in the 1970s, has given them a much wider circulation and canonized some performances: Olivier's Richard III, for instance, now has much the same iconic status that Cibber gave to Betterton's Hamlet. Orson Welles's film versions of *Macbeth* (1947) and *Othello* (1952), visually remarkable as they were, have benefited from remastering to make their soundtracks more intelligible. The BBC made-for-TV versions of Shakespeare, 1979–1985, often disappointed both film and Shakespeare enthusiasts, though for different reasons, but have been widely used in schools. Kenneth Branagh's films, including a remarkable four-hour uncut *Hamlet* (1996), have been surprisingly successful in making the plays accessible to a popular audience. His *Henry V* (1989) was unfairly praised for being more "real" than Olivier's; both films were star-centered, with Olivier playing a more controlled king, Branagh a more vulnerable one. Whereas Olivier began his film with a view of an idealized Elizabethan London, then of a playhouse viewed from a superior perspective as old-fashioned and in some ways comic, Branagh introduced his Chorus (Derek Jacobi) in a room full of movie cameras, though he later allowed him to move among the actors in the film. As often in films, the moments most remembered were visual: Henry's (Branagh's) grief when, in order to enforce proper discipline, he is obliged to order the hanging of Bardolph, or the long shot, after the Battle of Agincourt, that shows Henry carrying the dead boy in a procession of English soldiers singing *Non nobis Domine.*

Branagh's youth was an asset in bringing Shakespeare to a young audience. Later filmmakers have aimed at a still younger group. *William Shakespeare's Romeo and Juliet* (directed by Baz Luhrmann, 1996), filled as it was with icons of contemporary youth culture, is perhaps the first of these, though it retains Shakespeare's language, juxtaposing it with contradictory images, so that it can be understood either as a complex visual-verbal experience or as a rather simple visual one. The *Hamlet* directed by Michael Almereyda (2000) represents its young characters as college students obsessed with modern technology: Hamlet (Ethan Hawke) is an amateur filmmaker and Ophelia is a photographer; "To be or not to be" is spoken in a video store against a background of videos labeled "Action." For students of the new field of Shakespeare in Popular Culture, Teenage Shakespeare, with the stories rewritten in contemporary language and settings, is becoming a genre in its own right. *Ten Things I Hate About You* (directed by Gil Junger, 1999) and *O* (directed by Tim Blake Nelson, 2001) retell *The Taming of the Shrew* and *Othello* in American high school settings. *The Children's Midsummer Night's Dream* (directed by Christine Edzard, 2001) has a cast of primary school children.

International Contexts and Contemporary Adaptations

Not only have the plays been adapted for every age group, they have turned out to speak an international language. This had not always been true, though English and French actors had visited each other's countries since the seventeenth century: in 1629 French actresses were booed by English audiences, still accustomed to an all-male stage; one group of English actors was booed in the Paris of 1818, but another visiting company in 1827 inspired French writers and actors to try to understand Shakespeare. English and American audiences saw *Othello* with new eyes when the Italian actor Tommaso Salvini, followed by several other famous Italians, performed on tour in the late nineteenth century. Along with the visit of the Berliner Ensemble to London in 1956, the most important influences in the late twentieth century came from Asian, especially Japanese, theater and from central and eastern Europe. Kurosawa's films, *Throne of Blood* (*Macbeth*, 1957) and *Ran* (*King Lear*, 1986), transpose Shakespearean plots into Japanese culture and images. Successful Russian films have ranged from the visually stunning colors of Yan Fried's *Twelfth Night* and Sergei Yutkevich's *Othello* (both 1955) to Grigori Kozintsev's black-and-white *Hamlet* (1964) and *King Lear* (1971).

The opening up of contacts with central and eastern Europe after 1989 has resulted in visits from theater companies of the former eastern bloc countries. When London audiences in 1990 saw *Hamlet* by the Bulandra Theatre of Romania (directed by Alexander Tocilescu), they discovered that plays often regarded in Britain and America as "conservative" tools of the "establishment" had elsewhere been a powerful vehicle for the expression of political dissent. When first produced in 1985, Tocilescu's *Hamlet* was clearly understood to be equating the rottenness of Elsinore with the world created by Nicolae Ceaucescu, the dictator executed in 1989; Ion Caramitru, the actor who played Hamlet, had been one of the leaders of the revolution. In Czech productions of Shakespeare, similarly, actors and audience had gathered in a deliberate act of misreading directed at the occupying Russians: in *Love's Labor's Lost*, of all plays, the princess's suggestion that the courtiers disguised as Muscovites should "be gone" was the high point of the evening.

Western directors have sometimes attempted to deal with a difficult text by interpreting it as "Other," particularly as Japanese: the samurai warrior culture was the background to Barry Kyle's *The Two Noble Kinsmen* (Swan Theatre, Stratford, 1986) and to David Farr's *Coriolanus* (Royal Shakespeare Theatre, 2002), whereas Ron Daniels's *Timon of Athens* (The Other Place, Stratford, 1980) drew on the concept of a society based on gift-giving. Conversely, Yukio Ninagawa's Japanese Shakespeare productions have combined Japanese costumes with a soundtrack of European music (*Macbeth*) and interpreted *The Tempest* through the story of the famous Japanese exile, Shunkan. Such cross-cultural borrowings have sometimes been denigrated as "cultural tourism," by which critics seem to mean that it is illegitimate to appropriate the merely visual aspects of a culture to which one does not belong.

Similarly, the reconstructed "Shakespeare's Globe" in London, which opened in 1997, was accused of attempting to appropriate the emotions of another historical period. Perhaps because the opening production was *Henry V*, the "groundlings" who stood in the yard for only £5 apiece seemed to be modeling themselves on their counterparts in the Globe sequence of Olivier's film, who boo when they hear that Falstaff has been banished. Their willingness to boo the French (and, in the next season, Shylock) at first shocked the critics, and it was suggested that this theater might be suited only to comedies and histories demanding a presentational style, but productions of *Hamlet* (2000) and *King Lear* (2001) showed that it was possible to control audience response to the tragedies. Mark Rylance's *Hamlet* skillfully played his line about groundlings "capable of nothing but inexplicable dumbshow," so that he could respond to their laughter by adding "*and* noise." Whether or not the theater can really tell anyone anything about Elizabethan stage conventions and audience response, it has given considerable pleasure. Other Globes, more and less historically based, now can be found in several countries (the United States, Japan, Poland, and the Czech Republic, among others), while the open stage of Stratford, Canada, remains one of the most successful modifications of the Elizabethan model. In a reversal of the search for authenticity, the Shakespeare Theatre in Washington, D.C., has abandoned its home in the reconstructed Fortune Theatre at the Folger Shakespeare Library for a purpose-built modern auditorium. In fact, the two kinds of theater can coexist. The well-established Shakespeare festivals of Stratford, Ontario; Ashland, Oregon; and Santa Cruz, California, have added well-equipped indoor theaters to their outdoor acting spaces, and an indoor auditorium is projected as an addition to Shakespeare's Globe in London. A reconstruction of the Blackfriars Playhouse opened in Staunton, Virginia, in 2001.

Although it has been impossible to discuss the theatrical fortunes of every Shakespeare play, it may be interesting to end by reflecting how greatly these have fluctuated. If some plays, like *Hamlet* and *Macbeth*, have always been popular, the history of others is more checkered. Some of the comedies most popular today, such as *As You Like It* and *Twelfth Night*, were regarded as insipid in the eighteenth century, redeemed only by their scenes of low comedy and occasional sententious speeches. *The Merry Wives of Windsor* was the most popular comedy during the Restoration; *King John* and *Henry VIII* were more popular in the nineteenth century than *Richard II* or *2 Henry IV*. *Othello* was acted without the "willow scene" (4.3) for most of the eighteenth and nineteenth centuries, and *Troilus and Cressida* and *Titus Andronicus* were performed, if at all, only in heavily adapted versions. It is arguable that the attitude to Shakespeare that Bernard Shaw ridiculed as "Bardolatry" reached its height, not in the Victorian age, but at the end of the twentieth century, a time when any Shakespeare play, however minor, was likely to find a director and an audience. One reason might be that the subsidized theaters had been giving fewer controversial productions since 1980, emphasizing instead what the plays have in common with musical comedies and films. An important American contribution to Shakespeare in performance has taken the form of musicals like *The Boys from Syracuse* (1938), *Kiss Me Kate* (1948), and *West Side Story* (1957), based respectively on *The Comedy of Errors*, *The Taming of the Shrew*, and *Romeo and Juliet*; now, many productions of the comedies followed the Restoration practice of filling them with popular music. What was new was not the practice of adaptation but the attitude toward it. In the mid century, the plays were taken to be fixed quantities: the job of the theater director, as of the critic, was to uncover the "real" work, whether through more authentic staging, a more accurate text, or a better understanding of its meaning. By the end of the millennium, when some theorists were insisting that the text itself was unknowable, it is not surprising to find a much greater tolerance for re-creations and explorations of the plays in other forms.

Bibliography

Abbreviations Used

English Literary History	*ELH*
Publications of the Modern	
Language Association of America	*PMLA*
Shakespeare Quarterly	*SQ*
Shakespeare Studies	*ShakS*
Shakespeare Survey	*ShS*

Works of Reference

Abbott, E. A. *A Shakespearian Grammar*. New ed., London, 1870.

Allen, Michael J. B., and Kenneth Muir, eds. *Shakespeare's Plays in Quarto*. Berkeley, 1981.

Bentley, G. E. *The Jacobean and Caroline Stage*. 7 vols. Oxford, 1941–1968.

Bergeron, David M. *Shakespeare: A Study and Research Guide*. New York, 1975; 2nd ed., rev. David Bergeron and Geraldo de Sousa. Lawrence, Kans., 1987.

Bullough, Geoffrey, ed. *Narrative and Dramatic Sources of Shakespeare*. 8 vols. London, 1957–1975.

Chambers, E.K. *The Elizabethan Stage*. 4 vols. Oxford, 1923; rev., 1945.

——. *The Mediaeval Stage*. 2 vols. Oxford, 1903.

——. *William Shakespeare: A Study of Facts and Problems*. 2 vols. Oxford, 1930.

Dent, R. W. *Shakespeare's Proverbial Language: An Index*. Berkeley, 1981.

Garland Shakespeare Bibliographies, gen. ed. William Godshalk. Published in separate volumes for various plays, at varying dates. Garland: New York.

Greg, W. W. *A Bibliography of the English Printed Drama to the Restoration*. 4 vols. London, 1939–1959.

——, ed. *Shakespeare Quarto Facsimiles*. London, 1939–. (An incomplete set; Greg's work has been supplemented by Charlton Hinman.)

Harbage, Alfred. *Annals of English Drama, 975–1700*. Rev. S. Schoenbaum.

Philadelphia, 1964; 3rd ed., Sylvia Stoler Wagonheim, 1989.

Hinman, Charlton, ed. *The Norton Facsimile: The First Folio of Shakespeare*. New York, 1968.

Hosley, Richard, ed. *Shakespeare's Holinshed*. New York, 1968.

Kökeritz, Helge. *Shakespeare's Names*. New Haven, 1959.

——. *Shakespeare's Pronunciation*. New Haven, 1953.

Long, John. *Shakespeare's Use of Music: Comedies*. Gainesville, Fla., 1955. *Final Comedies*, 1961; *Histories and Tragedies*, 1971.

McDonald, Russ. *The Bedford Companion to Shakespeare: An Introduction with Documents*. Boston, 1996; 2nd ed., 2001.

McManaway, James G., and Jeanne Addison Roberts, compilers. *A Selective Bibliography of Shakespeare*. Charlottesville, Va., 1975.

Muir, Kenneth. *Shakespeare's Sources*. 2 vols. London, 1957.

——, and S. Schoenbaum, eds. *A New Companion to Shakespeare Studies*. London and New York, 1971.

Munro, John, ed. *The Shakespeare Allusion Book*. 2 vols. London and New York, 1909; reissued 1932.

Naylor, Edward W. *Shakespeare and Music*. New ed., London, 1931.

Noble, Richmond. *Shakespeare's Biblical Knowledge*. London, 1935.

——. *Shakespeare's Use of Song*. London, 1923.

Onions, C. T. *A Shakespeare Glossary*. Rev. and enlgd. R. D. Eagleson. Oxford, 1986.

Pegasus Shakespeare Bibliographies. Annotated bibliographies of Shakespeare studies in a 12-volume series, gen. ed. Richard L. Nochimson, including *Love's Labor's Lost, A Midsummer Night's Dream*, and *The Merchant of Venice* (Clifford Chalmers Huffman), *Richard II, Henry IV, I and II*, and *Henry V* (Joseph Candido), *Hamlet* (Michael E. Mooney), *The Rape of Lucrece, Titus Andronicus, Julius Caesar,*

Antony and Cleopatra, and *Coriolanus* (Clifford Chalmers Huffman and John W. Velz), *King Lear* and *Macbeth* (Rebecca W. Bushnell), and *Shakespeare and the Renaissance Stage to 1616* and *Shakespearean Stage History 1616 to 1998* (Hugh Macrae Richmond). Binghamton, N.Y. (1995) and Asheville, N.C., 1996—.

Publications of the Modern Language Association of America (PMLA). Annual Bibliography.

Rothwell, Kenneth S., and Annabelle Henkin Melzer. *Shakespeare on Screen: An International Filmography and Videography*. New York and London, 1990.

Schmidt, Alexander. *Shakespeare-Lexicon*. 5th ed. Berlin, 1962.

Seager, H. W. *Natural History in Shakespeare's Time*. London, 1896.

Seng, Peter J. *The Vocal Songs in the Plays of Shakespeare*. Cambridge, Mass., 1967.

Shakespeare Bulletin.

Shakespeare-Jahrbuch.

Shakespeare Newsletter.

Shakespeare Quarterly. Annual Bibliography.

Shakespeare Studies.

Shakespeare Survey.

Spencer, T. J. B., ed. *Shakespeare's Plutarch*. Harmondsworth, Eng., 1964.

Spevack, Marvin. *The Harvard Concordance to Shakespeare*. Cambridge, Mass., 1973.

Sternfeld, Frederick W. *Music in Shakespearean Tragedy*. London, 1963, 1967.

Thomson, J. A. K. *Shakespeare and the Classics*. London, 1952.

Wells, Stanley, ed. *Shakespeare: Select Bibliographical Guides*. London, 1973.

——, ed. *The Cambridge Companion to Shakespeare Studies*. Cambridge, Eng., 1986.

Life in Shakespeare's England

Allen, Don Cameron. *The Star-Crossed Renaissance*. Durham, N.C., 1941.

Baker, Herschel. *The Image of Man: A Study of the Idea of Human Dignity in Classical Antiquity, the Middle Ages, and the Renaissance*. Cambridge, Mass., 1961. (First published in 1947 as *The Dignity of Man*.)

———. *The Wars of Truth: Studies in the Decay of Christian Humanism in the Earlier Seventeenth Century*. Cambridge, Mass., 1952.

Bakhtin, Mikhail M. *Rabelais and His World*, trans. H. Iswolsky. Cambridge, Mass., 1968.

Barkan, Leonard. *Nature's Work of Art: The Human Body as Image of the World*. New Haven, 1975.

———. *The Gods Made Flesh: Metamorphosis and the Pursuit of Paganism*. New Haven, 1986.

Barroll, J. Leeds. *Politics, Plague, and Shakespeare's Theater: The Stuart Years*. Ithaca, N.Y., 1991.

Bindoff, S. T., et al., eds. *Elizabethan Government and Society*. Essays presented to Sir John Neale. London, 1961.

Bush, Douglas. *The Renaissance and English Humanism*. Toronto, 1939.

Buxton, John. *Elizabethan Taste*. London, 1963.

Byrne, Muriel St. Clare. *Elizabethan Life in Town and Country*. 8th ed. London, 1970.

Camden, Carroll. *The Elizabethan Woman*. Houston, 1952.

Caspari, Fritz. *Humanism and the Social Order in Tudor England*. Chicago, 1954.

Cassirer, Ernst. *The Platonic Renaissance in England*, trans. J. E. Pettegrove. Austin, Tex., 1953.

De Grazia, Margreta, Maureen Quilligan, and Peter Stallybrass, eds. *Subject and Object in Renaissance Culture*. Cambridge, Eng., 1996.

Einstein, Lewis. *Tudor Ideals*. New York, 1921.

Elizabeth I. *Collected Works*, eds. Leah S. Marcus, Janel Mueller, and Mary Beth Rose. Chicago, 2000.

Elton, G. R. *The Tudor Revolution in Government*. Cambridge, Eng., 1959.

Fumerton, Patricia, and Simon Hunt, eds. *Renaissance Culture and the Everyday*. Philadelphia, 1999.

Gallagher, Lowell. *Medusa's Gaze: Casuistry and Conscience in the Renaissance*. Stanford, 1991.

Harrison, G. B. *An Elizabethan Journal*. London, 1928; supplements.

———. *A Jacobean Journal . . . 1603–1606*. London, 1941.

———. *A Second Jacobean Journal . . . 1607 to 1610*. Ann Arbor, Mich., 1958.

Haydn, Hiram. *The Counter-Renaissance*. New York, 1950.

Helgerson, Richard. *Forms of Nationhood: The Elizbethan Writing of England*. Chicago, 1992.

Heninger, S. K., Jr. *A Handbook of Renaissance Meteorology*. Durham, N.C., 1960.

Hirst, Derek. *Authority and Conflict: England, 1603–1658*. Cambridge, Mass., 1986.

Huizinga, Johan. *The Waning of the Middle Ages*. London, 1924; Baltimore, 1955.

Hurstfield, Joel, *Elizabeth I and the Unity of England*. London, 1960.

Jones, Ann Rosalind, and Peter Stallybrass. *Renaissance Clothing and the Materials of Memory*. Cambridge, Eng., 2000.

Jordan, Constance. *Renaissance Feminism: Literary Texts and Political Models*. Ithaca, N.Y., 1990.

Judges, A. V., ed. *The Elizabethan Underworld*. London and New York, 1930. Rpt., London, 1965.

Kewes, Paulina, ed. *Plagiarism in Early Modern England*. Basingstoke, Hampshire, Eng., 2003.

Knights, L. C. *Drama and Society in the Age of Jonson*. London, 1937.

Kocher, Paul. *Science and Religion in Elizabethan England*. San Marino, Calif., 1953.

Lee, Morris. *Great Britain's Solomon: James VI and I in His Three Kingdoms*. Urbana, Ill., 1990.

Lovejoy, A. O. *The Great Chain of Being*. Cambridge, Mass., 1936.

MacCaffrey, Wallace T. *The Shaping of the Elizabethan Regime*. Princeton, 1968.

Marotti, Arthur F., ed. *Catholicism and Anti-Catholicism in Early Modern English Texts*. Basingstoke, Hampshire, Eng., 1999.

Matar, Nabil. *Turks, Moors, and Englishmen in the Age of Discovery*. New York, 1999.

Mattingly, Garrett. *The Armada*. Boston, 1959.

McEachern, Claire, and Debora Shuger, eds. *Religion and Culture in Renaissance England*. Cambridge, Eng., 1997.

McElwee, W. *The Wisest Fool in Christendom*. [About James VI and I.] New York, 1958.

McPeek, James A. S. *The Black Book of Knaves and Unthrifts in Shakespeare and Other Renaissance Authors*. Storrs, Conn., 1969.

Neale, John E. *Elizabeth I and Her Parliaments*. 2 vols. London and New York, 1953–1958.

———. *The Elizabethan House of Commons*. London, 1949.

———. *Queen Elizabeth I*. London, 1934; New York, 1957.

Nichols, John, ed. *The Progresses and Public Processions of Queen Elizabeth*. 3 vols. London, 1823.

Patterson, Annabel M. *Reading Holinshed's Chronicles*. Chicago, 1994.

Peck, Linda Levy. *Court Patronage and Corruption in Early Stuart England*. Boston, 1990.

Penrose, Boies. *Travel and Discovery in the Renaissance, 1420–1620*. Cambridge, Mass., 1955.

Quinones, Ricardo J. *The Renaissance Discovery of Time*. Cambridge, Mass., 1972.

Rowse, A. L. *The England of Elizabeth: The Structure of Society*. London, 1951.

Stallybrass, Peter, and Allon White. *The Politics and Poetics of Transgression*. Ithaca, N.Y., and London, 1986.

Stone, Lawrence. *The Crisis of the Aristocracy, 1558–1641*. Oxford, 1965.

———. *The Family, Sex and Marriage in England, 1500–1800*. London, 1977.

Stow, John. *Survey of London*, ed. C. L. Kingsford. Oxford, 1971.

Targoff, Ramie. *Common Prayer: The Language of Public Devotion in Early Modern England*. Chicago, 2001.

Tawney, R. H. *Religion and the Rise of Capitalism*. New York, 1926, 1962.

Tillyard, E. M. W. *The Elizabethan World Picture*. London, 1943, 1967.

Underdown, David. *Revel, Riot, and Rebellion: Popular Politics and Culture in England, 1603–1660*. Oxford, 1985.

Whigham, Frank. *Ambition and Privilege: The Social Tropes of Elizabethan Courtesy Theory*. Berkeley, 1984.

Willson, David Harris. *King James VI & I*. New York, 1956.

Wilson, F. P. *Elizabethan and Jacobean*. Oxford, 1945.

Wilson, J. Dover, ed. *Life in Shakespeare's England*. Cambridge, Eng., 1911; 2nd ed., 1926.

Woodbridge, Linda. *Women and the English Renaissance*. Urbana, Ill., 1984.

Wright, Louis B. *Middle-Class Culture in Elizabethan England*. Chapel Hill, N.C., 1935.

Wrightson, Keith. *English Society, 1580–1680*. New Brunswick, N.J., 1982.

Zeeveld, W. Gordon. *Foundations of Tudor Policy*. Cambridge, Mass., 1948.

Shakespeare's Predecessors and Contemporaries

See also, under *Works of Reference*, Bentley, Chambers, Greg, and Harbage; under *London Theaters and Dramatic Companies*, McMillin and MacLean; and under *Shakespeare Criticism Since 1980*, Dollimore, Garber (*Cannibals*), Goldberg, Greenblatt, Jardine, Loomba, Mullaney, Newman, and Skura.

Altman, Joel B. *The Tudor Play of Mind: Rhetorical Inquiry and the Development of Elizabethan Drama*. Berkeley, 1978.

Bamford, Karen. *Sexual Violence on the Jacobean Stage*. New York, 2000.

Barber, C. L. *Creating Elizabethan Tragedy: The Theater of Kyd and Marlowe*. Chicago, 1988.

Bartels, Emily C. *Spectacles of Strangeness: Imperialism, Alienation, and Marlowe*. Philadelphia, 1993.

Bednarz, James P. *Shakespeare and the Poets' War*. New York, 2001.

Belsey, Catherine. *The Subject of Tragedy: Identity and Difference in Renaissance Drama*. London, 1985.

Berry, Philippa. *Of Chastity and Power: Elizabethan Literature and the Unmarried Queen*. London and New York, 1989.

Bevington, David. *From "Mankind" to Marlowe: Growth of Structure in the Popular Drama of Tudor England*. Cambridge, Mass., 1962.

———. *Tudor Drama and Politics*. Cambridge, Mass., 1968.

———, and Peter Holbrook, eds. *The Politics of the Stuart Court Masque*. Cambridge, Eng., 1991.

Bowers, Fredson T. *Elizabethan Revenge Tragedy, 1587–1642*. Princeton, 1940.

Braden, Gordon. *Renaissance Tragedy and the Senecan Tradition*. New Haven, 1985.

Braunmuller, A. R., and Michael Hattaway, eds. *The Cambridge Companion to English Renaissance Drama*. Cambridge, Eng., 1990.

Bristol, Michael D. *Carnival and Theater: Plebeian Culture and the Structure of Authority in Renaissance England.* London, 1985.

Brooke, C. F. Tucker, ed. *The Shakespeare Apocrypha.* Oxford, 1908.

Brooks, Douglas A. *From Playhouse to Printing House: Drama and Authorship in Early Modern England.* Cambridge, Eng., 2000.

Bruster, Douglas. *Drama and the Market in the Age of Shakespeare.* Cambridge, Eng., 1992.

Burt, Richard. *Licensed by Authority: Ben Jonson and the Discourses of Censorship.* Ithaca, N.Y., 1993.

Bushnell, Rebecca W. *Tragedies of Tyrants: Political Thought and Theater in the English Renaissance.* Ithaca, N.Y., 1990.

Butterworth, Philip. *Theatre of Fire: Special Effects in Early English and Scottish Theatre.* London, 1998.

Caputi, Anthony. *John Marston, Satirist.* Ithaca, N.Y., 1961.

Cohen, Walter. *Drama of a Nation: Public Theater in Renaissance England and Spain.* Ithaca, N.Y., 1985.

Comensoli, Viviana, and Anna Russell, eds. *Enacting Gender on the English Renaissance Stage.* Urbana, Ill., 1999.

Cox, John D., and David Scott Kastan, eds. *A New History of Early English Drama.* New York, 1997.

Craik, T. W. *The Tudor Interlude.* Leicester, 1958, 1962.

Dawson, Anthony B., and Paul Yachnin. *The Culture of Playgoing in Shakespeare's England: A Collaborative Debate.* Cambridge, Eng., 2001.

Deats, Sara Munson. *Sex, Gender, and Desire in the Plays of Christopher Marlowe.* Newark, Del., 1997.

Dessen, Alan C. *Elizabethan Drama and the Viewer's Eye.* Chapel Hill, N.C., 1977.

Diehl, Huston. *Staging Reform, Reforming the Stage: Protestantism and Popular Theater in Early Modern England.* Ithaca, N.Y., 1997.

Dillon, Janette. *Theatre, Court and City, 1595–1610: Drama and Social Space in London.* Cambridge, Eng., 2000.

DiGangi, Mario. *The Homoerotics of Early Modern Drama.* Cambridge, Eng., 1997.

Dolan, Frances E. *Dangerous Familiars: Representations of Domestic Crime in England, 1550–1700.* Ithaca, N.Y., 1994.

Doran, Madeleine. *Endeavors of Art: A Study of Form in Elizabethan Drama.* Madison, Wis., 1954, 1972.

Farley-Hills, David. *Shakespeare and the Rival Playwrights, 1600–1606.* London, 1990.

Findlay, Alison. *A Feminist Perspective on Renaissance Drama.* Oxford, 1999.

———. *Illegitimate Power: Bastards in Renaissance Drama.* Manchester, Eng., 1994.

Finkelpearl, Philip. *John Marston of the Middle Temple.* Cambridge, Mass., 1969.

Freer, Coburn. *The Poetics of Jacobean Drama.* Baltimore, 1981.

Gardiner, H. C. *Mysteries' End.* New Haven, 1946.

Gibbons, Brian. *Jacobean City Comedy.* London, 1968.

Hall, Kim F. *Things of Darkness: Economies of Race and Gender in Early Modern England.* Ithaca, N.Y., 1995.

Hardison, O. B., Jr. *Christian Rite and Christian Drama in the Middle Ages.* Baltimore, 1965.

Hassel, R. Chris. *Renaissance Drama and the English Church Year.* Lincoln, Neb., 1979.

Hattaway, Michael. *Elizabethan Popular Theatre: Plays in Performance.* London, 1982.

Hawkins, Harriett. *Likenesses of Truth in Elizabethan and Restoration Drama.* Oxford, 1972.

Helgerson, Richard. *Adulterous Alliances: Home, State, and History in Early Modern European Drama and Painting.* Chicago, 2000.

Hendricks, Margo, and Patricia Parker, eds. *Women, "Race," and Writing in the Early Modern Period.* London and New York, 1994.

Holbrook, Peter. *Literature and Degree in Renaissance England: Nashe, Bourgeois Tragedy, Shakespeare.* Newark, Del., 1994.

Howard, Jean. *The Stage and Social Struggle in Early Modern England.* London and New York, 1994.

Hunter, G. K. *John Lyly: The Humanist as Courtier.* Cambridge, Mass., 1962.

Kastan, David Scott, and Peter Stallybrass, eds. *Staging the Renaissance: Reinterpretations of Elizabethan and Jacobean Drama.* New York and London, 1991.

Kernan, Alvin. *The Cankered Muse: Satire of the English Renaissance.* New Haven, 1959.

Kiefer, Frederick. *Writing on the Renaissance Stage: Written Words, Printed Pages, Metaphoric Books.* Newark, Del., 1996.

Kirsch, Arthur C. *Jacobean Dramatic Perspectives.* Charlottesville, Va., 1972.

Kolve, V. A. *The Play Called Corpus Christi.* Palo Alto and London, 1966.

Leggatt, Alexander. *Citizen Comedy in the Age of Shakespeare.* Toronto, 1973.

———. *Jacobean Public Theatre.* London, 1992.

Leishman, J. B., ed. *The Three Parnassus Plays (1598–1601).* London, 1949.

Levin, Harry. *The Overreacher: A Study of Christopher Marlowe.* Cambridge, Mass., 1952, 1964.

Levin, Richard. *The Multiple Plot in English Renaissance Drama.* Chicago, 1971.

Margeson, J. M. R. *The Origins of English Tragedy.* Oxford, 1967.

Marrapodi, Michele, ed., with A. J. Hoenselaars. *The Italian World of English Renaissance Drama: Cultural Exchange and Intertextuality.* Newark, Del., 1998.

Maus, Katharine Eisaman. *Inwardness and Theater in the English Renaissance Drama.* Chicago, 1995.

McAlindon, T. *English Renaissance Tragedy.* London, 1986.

McLuskie, Kathleen. *Renaissance Dramatists.* (Feminist Readings.) Atlantic Highlands, N.J., 1989.

Orgel, Stephen. *The Illusion of Power: Political Theater in the English Renaissance.* Berkeley, 1975.

———. *Impersonations: The Performance of Gender in Shakespeare's England.* Cambridge, Eng., 1996.

Orgel, Stephen, and Roy Strong. *Inigo Jones: The Theatre of the Stuart Court.* 2 vols. London and Berkeley, 1973.

Ornstein, Robert. *The Moral Vision of Jacobean Tragedy.* Madison, Wis., 1960.

Rabkin, Norman, ed: *Reinterpretations of Elizabethan Drama.* New York, 1969.

Rasmussen, Mark David, ed. *Renaissance Literature and Its Formal Engagements.* Basingstoke, Hampshire, 2002.

Rose, Mary Beth. *The Expense of Spirit: Love and Sexuality in English Renaissance Drama.* Ithaca, N.Y., 1988.

———. *Gender and Heroism in Early Modern English Literature.* Chicago, 2002.

———. ed. *Renaissance Drama as Cultural History.* Evanston, Ill., 1990.

Sanders, Wilbur. *The Dramatist and the Received Idea: Studies in the Plays of Marlowe and Shakespeare.* Cambridge, Eng., 1968.

Shannon, Laurie. *Sovereign Amity: Figures of Friendship in Shakespearean Contexts.* Chicago, 2002.

Shapiro, James. *Rival Playwrights: Marlowe, Jonson, Shakespeare.* New York, 1991.

Smith, Bruce R. *The Acoustic World of Early Modern England.* Chicago, 1999.

Smith, David L., Richard Strier, and David Bevington, eds. *The Theatrical City: Culture, Theatre and Politics in London, 1567–1649.* Cambridge, Eng., 1995.

Southern, Richard. *The Medieval Theatre in the Round.* London, 1957.

Spivack, Bernard. *Shakespeare and the Allegory of Evil.* New York, 1958.

Traub, Valerie, M. Lindsay Kaplan, and Dympna C. Callaghan, eds. *Feminist Readings of Early Modern Culture: Emerging Subjects.* Cambridge, Eng., 1996.

Vickers, Brian. *"Counterfeiting" Shakespeare: Evidence, Authorship, and John Ford's "Funerall Elegye."* Cambridge, Eng., 2002.

Waith, Eugene M. *The Herculean Hero in Marlowe, Chapman, Shakespeare, and Dryden.* New York, 1962.

Whigham, Frank. *Seizures of the Will in Early Modern English Drama.* Cambridge, Eng., 1996.

White, Paul Whitfield. *Marlowe, History, and Sexuality: New Critical Essays on Christopher Marlowe.* New York, 1998.

———. *Theatre and Reformation: Protestantism, Patronage and Playing in Tudor England.* Cambridge, Eng., 1993.

Wickham, Glynne. *Early English Stages, 1300 to 1660.* 3 vols. London, 1959–1972.

Wilson, F. P. *Marlowe and the Early Shakespeare.* Oxford, 1953.

Woodbridge, Linda. *Women and the English Renaissance: Literature and the Nature of Womankind, 1540–1620.* Urbana, Ill., 1984.

Woolf, Rosemary. *The English Mystery Plays.* Berkeley and Los Angeles, 1972.

Yachnin, Paul. *Stage-Wrights: Shakespeare, Jonson, Middleton, and the Making of Theatrical Value.* Philadelphia, 1997.

Zimmerman, Susan, ed. *Erotic Politics: Desire on the Renaissance Stage.* London and New York, 1992.

London Theaters and Dramatic Companies

See also, under *Works of Reference*, Bentley, and Chambers (*Elizabethan Stage*).

Astington, John H., ed. *The Development of Shakespeare's Theater*. New York, 1992.

Beckerman, Bernard. *Shakespeare at the Globe, 1599–1609*. New York, 1962, 1967.

Bentley, Gerald Eades. *The Profession of Dramatist in Shakespeare's Time, 1590–1642*. Princeton, 1971.

———. *The Profession of Player in Shakespeare's Time, 1590–1642*. Princeton, 1984.

Berry, Herbert. *Shakespeare's Playhouses*. New York, 1987.

Bradley, David. *From Text to Performance in the Elizabethan Theatre: Preparing the Play for the Stage*. Cambridge, Eng., 1992.

Clare, Janet. *"Art Made Tongue-Tied by Authority": Elizabethan and Jacobean Dramatic Censorship*. Manchester, Eng., 1990.

Cook, Ann Jennalie. *The Privileged Playgoers of Shakespeare's London, 1576–1642*. Princeton, 1981.

Dutton, Richard. *Mastering the Revels: The Regulation and Censorship of English Renaissance Drama*. Iowa City, 1991.

Feuillerat, Albert, ed. *Documents Relating to the Office of the Revels in the Time of Queen Elizabeth*. Louvain (Louven), Belgium, 1908.

Foakes, R. A., ed. *The Henslowe Papers: The Diary, Theatre Papers, and Bear Garden Papers*. In full and in facsimile. 3 vols. in 2. London, 1976.

Foakes, R. A., and R. T. Rickert, eds. *Henslowe's Diary*. London, 1961.

Gair, W. Reavley. *The Children of Paul's*. Cambridge, Eng., 1982.

Greg, W. W., ed. *Dramatic Documents from the Elizabethan Playhouses: Stage Plots; Actors' Parts; Prompt Books*. 2 vols. Oxford, 1931.

Gurr, Andrew. *Playgoing in Shakespeare's London*. Cambridge, Eng., 1987; 2nd ed., 1996.

———. *The Shakespearian Playing Companies*. Oxford, 1996.

——— *The Shakespearean Stage, 1574–1642*. Cambridge, Eng., 1970; 2nd ed., 1980.

Gurr, Andrew, and John Orrell. *Rebuilding Shakespeare's Globe*. London and New York, 1989.

Harbage, Alfred. *Shakespeare's Audience*. New York, 1941.

Hodges, C. Walter. *The Globe Restored*. London, 1953; 2nd ed., New York, 1968.

Hosley, Richard. "Was There a Music-room in Shakespeare's Globe?" *ShS* 13 (1960), 113–23.

Ingram, William. *The Business of Playing: The Beginnings of the Adult Professional Theater in Elizabethan London*. Ithaca, N.Y., 1992.

King, T. J. *Casting Shakespeare's Plays: London Actors and Their Roles, 1590–1642*. Cambridge, Eng., 1992.

———. *Shakespearean Staging, 1599–1642*. Cambridge, Mass., 1971.

Knutson, Roslyn Lander. *The Repertory of Shakespeare's Company, 1594–1613*. Fayetteville, Ark., 1991.

———. *Playing Companies and Commerce in Shakespeare's Time*. Cambridge, Eng., 2001.

Linthicum, Marie C. *Costume in the Drama of Shakespeare and His Contemporaries*. Oxford, 1936.

Mann, David. *The Elizabethan Player: Contemporary Stage Representation*. London, 1991.

McMillin, Scott. *The Elizabethan Theatre and "The Book of Sir Thomas More."* Ithaca, N.Y., 1987.

McMillin, Scott, and Sally-Beth MacLean. *The Queen's Men and Their Plays*. Cambridge, Eng., 1998.

Nelson, Alan H. *Early Cambridge Theatres: College, University, and Town Stages, 1464–1720*. Cambridge, Eng., 1994.

Nungezer, Edwin. *A Dictionary of Actors*. London and New Haven, 1929.

Shapiro, Michael. *Children of the Revels: The Boys' Companies of Shakespeare's Time and Their Plays*. New York, 1977.

Wickham, Glynne. *Early English Stages, 1300 to 1660*. 3 vols. London, 1959–1972.

Shakespeare's Life and Work

Alexander, Peter. *Shakespeare's Life and Art*. New ed., New York, 1961.

Baldwin, T. W. *William Shakspere's Small Latine and Lesse Greeke*. 2 vols. Urbana, Ill., 1944.

Chambers, E. K. *William Shakespeare: A Study of Facts and Problems*. 2 vols. Oxford, 1930.

Eccles, Mark. *Shakespeare in Warwickshire*. Madison, Wis., 1961.

Honan, Park. *Shakespeare: A Life*. Oxford, 1998.

Matus, Irvin Leigh, *Shakespeare, In Fact*. New York, 1994.

Schoenbaum, S. *Shakespeare's Lives*. Oxford and New York, 1970.

———. *William Shakespeare: A Documentary Life*. Oxford, 1975. Also published with fewer illustrations and a slightly revised text as *A Compact Documentary Life*. 1977.

———. *William Shakespeare: Records and Images*. Oxford, 1981.

Wells, Stanley. *Shakespeare: A Life in Drama*. New York and London, 1995.

Wheeler, Richard P. "Deaths in the Family: The Loss of a Son and the Rise of Shakespearean Comedy," *SQ* 51 (2000), 127–53.

Shakespeare's Language: His Development as Poet and Dramatist

See also, under *Works of Reference*, Abbott, Onions, and Schmidt.

Byrne, Muriel St. Clare. "The Foundations of Elizabethan Language," *ShS* 17 (1964), 223–39.

Cercignani, Fausto. *Shakespeare's Works and Elizabethan Pronunciation*. Oxford, 1981.

Charney, Maurice. *Shakespeare's Roman Plays: The Function of Imagery in the Drama*. Cambridge, Mass., 1961.

———. *Style in Hamlet*. Princeton, 1969.

Clemen, Wolfgang H. *The Development of Shakespeare's Imagery*. Cambridge, Mass., 1951.

Cruttwell, Patrick. *The Shakespearean Moment and Its Place in the Poetry of the Seventeenth Century*. London, 1954.

Desmet, Christy. *Reading Shakespeare's Characters: Rhetoric, Ethics, and Identity*. Amherst, Mass., 1992.

Dobson, E. J. *English Pronunciation, 1500–1700*. 2 vols. 2nd ed. Oxford, 1968.

Donawerth, Jane. *Shakespeare and the Sixteenth-Century Study of Language*. Urbana, Ill., 1984.

Doran, Madeleine. *Shakespeare's Dramatic Language*. Madison, Wis., 1976.

Empson, William. *The Structure of Complex Words*. London, 1951; 3rd ed., 1977.

Hulme, Hilda M. *Explorations in Shakespeare's Language*. London, 1962.

Kermode, Frank. *Shakespeare's Language*. New York, 2000.

Kökeritz, Helge. *Shakespeare's Names*. New Haven, 1959.

———. *Shakespeare's Pronunciation*. New Haven, 1953.

Lanham, Richard A. *The Motives of Eloquence: Literary Rhetoric in the Renaissance*. New Haven, 1976.

Magnussen, Lynne. *Shakespeare and Social Dialogue: Dramatic Language and Elizabethan Letters*. Cambridge, Eng., 1999.

Mahood, M. M. *Shakespeare's Wordplay*. London, 1957.

Miriam Joseph, Sister. *Shakespeare's Use of the Arts of Language*. New York, 1947. Rpt. in part as *Rhetoric in Shakespeare's Time*. 1962.

Nares, Robert. *A Glossary . . . of Shakespeare and His Contemporaries*. New ed. J. O. Halliwell and Thomas Wright. 2 vols. London, 1859, 1905, Rpt. Detroit, 1966.

Partridge, Eric. *Shakespeare's Bawdy*. London, 1947, 1955.

Spurgeon, Caroline. *Shakespeare's Imagery and What it Tells Us*. Cambridge, Eng., 1935.

Thompson, Ann and John O. *Shakespeare: Meaning and Metaphor*. Iowa City, 1987.

Thorne, Alison. *Vision and Rhetoric in Shakespeare: Looking Through Language*. Basingstoke and New York, 2000.

Vickers, Brian. *The Artistry of Shakespeare's Prose*. London, 1968.

Willbern, David. *Poetic Will: Shakespeare and the Play of Language*. Philadelphia, 1997.

Willcock, Gladys D. "Shakespeare and Elizabethan English," *ShS* 7 (1954), 12–24.

Wright, George T. *Shakespeare's Metrical Art*. Berkeley, 1988.

Shakespeare Criticism to the 1930s

Badawi, M. M. *Coleridge: Critic of Shakespeare*. Cambridge, Eng., 1973.

Bradby, Anne, ed. *Shakespeare Criticism, 1919–35*. London, 1936.

Coleridge, S. T. *Coleridge on Shakespeare: The Text of the Lectures of 1811–12*, ed. R. A. Foakes. Charlottesville, Va., 1971.

———. *Coleridge's Writings on Shakespeare*, ed. Terence Hawkes. New York, 1959.

Evans, G. Blakemore, ed. *Shakespeare: Aspects of Influence*. Cambridge, Mass., 1976.

Hazlitt, William. *Characters of Shakespear's Plays*. London, 1817.

Johnson, Samuel. *Johnson on Shakespeare*, ed. Arthur Sherbo. Vol. 7 of *The Yale Edition of the Works of Samuel Johnson*. New Haven, 1968.

Kermode, Frank, ed. *Four Centuries of Shakespearean Criticism*. New York, 1965.

Knight, G. Wilson. *The Shakespearian Tempest*. London, 1932, 1953.

Muir, Kenneth. "Fifty Years of Shakespearian Criticism: 1900–1950," *ShS* 4 (1951), 1–25.

Rabkin, Norman, ed. *Approaches to Shakespeare*. New York, 1964.

Ralli, Augustus. *A History of Shakespearian Criticism*. 2 vols. London, 1932.

Raysor, T. M., ed. *Samuel Taylor Coleridge: Shakespearean Criticism*. 2 vols. 2nd ed. London, 1960.

Schlegel, August Wilhelm. *Lectures on Dramatic Art and Literature*, trans. John Black, 1846. Rpt., New York, 1965.

Schücking, Levin L. *Character Problems in Shakespeare's Plays*. London, 1917; trans., 1922.

Shaw, G. B. *Shaw on Shakespeare*, ed. Edwin Wilson. New York, 1961.

Sherbo, Arthur. *Samuel Johnson, Editor of Shakespeare*. Urbana, Ill., 1956.

Smith, David Nichol, ed. *Shakespeare Criticism: A Selection*. World's Classics, Oxford, 1916.

———, ed. *Eighteenth Century Essays on Shakespeare*. 2nd ed. Oxford, 1963.

Stoll, E. E. *Art and Artifice in Shakespeare*. Cambridge, Eng., 1933, 1962.

Vickers, Brian, ed. *Shakespeare: The Critical Heritage*. Several volumes. London and Boston, 1974—.

Welsford, Enid. *The Fool: His Social and Literary History*. London, 1935; rpt. 1966.

Westfall, A. V. *American Shakespearean Criticism, 1607–1865*. New York, 1939.

Shakespeare Criticism from the 1940s to the 1970s

Armstrong, Edward A. *Shakespeare's Imagination: A Study of the Psychology of Association and Inspiration*. London, 1946.

Bethell, S. L. *Shakespeare and the Popular Dramatic Tradition*. London and Durham, N.C., 1944.

Bevington, David, and Jay L. Halio, eds. *Shakespeare: Pattern of Excelling Nature*. Newark, Del., 1978.

Bloom, Allan, with Harry V. Jaffa. *Shakespeare's Politics*. New York and London, 1964.

Brown, John Russell. *Shakespeare's Plays in Performance*. London, 1966.

Bryant, J. A., Jr. *Hippolyta's View: Some Christian Aspects of Shakespeare's Plays*. Lexington, Ky., 1961.

Burckhardt, Sigurd. *Shakespearean Meanings*. Princeton, 1968.

Burke, Kenneth. *Language as Symbolic Action*. Berkeley, 1966.

Calderwood, James L. *Shakespearean Metadrama*. Minneapolis, 1971.

Coghill, Neville. *Shakespeare's Professional Skills*. Cambridge, Eng., 1964.

Colie, Rosalie L. *Shakespeare's Living Art*. Princeton, 1974.

Council, Norman. *When Honour's at the Stake: Ideas of Honour in Shakespeare's Plays*. London, 1973.

Danby, John F. *Poets on Fortune's Hill: Studies in Sidney, Shakespeare, and Beaumont and Fletcher*. London, 1952.

Dean, Leonard F., ed. *Shakespeare: Modern Essays in Criticism*. New York, 1967.

Driver, Tom F. *The Sense of History in Greek and Shakespearean Drama*. New York, 1960.

Dusinberre, Juliet. *Shakespeare and the Nature of Women*. New York, 1975. 2nd ed., 1996.

Eagleton, Terence. *Shakespeare and Society*. New York and London, 1967.

Edwards, Philip. *Shakespeare and the Confines of Art*. London and New York, 1968.

Empson, William. *The Structure of Complex Words*. London, 1951.

Fiedler, Leslie A. *The Stranger in Shakespeare*. New York, 1972.

Fly, Richard. *Shakespeare's Mediated World*. Amherst, Mass., 1976.

Frye, Roland M. *Shakespeare and Christian Doctrine*. Princeton, 1963.

Garber, Marjorie B. *Dream in Shakespeare: From Metaphor to Metamorphosis*. New Haven and London, 1974.

Goddard, Harold C. *The Meaning of Shakespeare*. Chicago, 1951.

Goldman, Michael. *Shakespeare and the Energies of Drama*. Princeton, 1972.

Granville-Barker, Harley. *Prefaces to Shakespeare*. 2 vols. Princeton, 1946–1947.

Harbage, Alfred. *As They Liked it*. New York, 1947.

———. *Shakespeare and the Rival Traditions*. New York, 1952.

Hawkes, Terence. *Shakespeare's Talking Animals: Language and Drama in Society*. London, 1973.

Hawkins, Harriett. *Poetic Freedom and Poetic Truth: Chaucer, Shakespeare, Marlowe, Milton*. Oxford, 1976.

Holland, Norman. *Psychoanalysis and Shakespeare*. New York, 1966.

———. *The Shakespearean Imagination*. New York, 1964.

Jones, Emrys. *The Origins of Shakespeare*. Oxford, 1977.

Jorgensen, Paul A. *Shakespeare's Military World*. Berkeley and Los Angeles, 1956.

Kernan, Alvin B. *The Playwright as Magician: Shakespeare's Image of the Poet in the English Public Theater*. New Haven, 1979.

———, ed. *Modern Shakespearean Criticism*. New York, 1970.

Kettle, Arnold, ed. *Shakespeare in a Changing World*. London and New York, 1964.

Knights, L. C. *Some Shakespearean Themes*. London, 1959.

Kott, Jan. *Shakespeare Our Contemporary*. New York, 1964.

Leavis, F. R. *The Common Pursuit*. London, 1952.

Levin, Richard. *New Readings vs. Old Plays: Recent Trends in the Reinterpretation of English Renaissance Drama*. Chicago, 1979.

McAlindon, T. *Shakespeare and Decorum*. London and New York, 1973.

Rabkin, Norman. *Shakespeare and the Common Understanding*. New York, 1967.

Righter, Anne. *Shakespeare and the Idea of the Play*. London, 1962.

Rossiter, A. P. *Angel with Horns*. London, 1961.

Sanders, Wilbur. *The Dramatist and the Received Idea: Studies in the Plays of Marlowe and Shakespeare*. Cambridge, Eng., 1968.

Sewell, Arthur. *Character and Society in Shakespeare*. London, 1951.

Soellner, Rolf. *Shakespeare's Patterns of Self-Knowledge*. Columbus, Ohio, 1972.

Spencer, Theodore. *Shakespeare and the Nature of Man*. New York, 1942.

Spivack, Bernard. *Shakespeare and the Allegory of Evil*. New York, 1958.

Stewart, J. I. M. *Character and Motive in Shakespeare*. London, 1949.

Stirling, Brents. *The Populace in Shakespeare*. New York, 1949.

Traversi, Derek. *An Approach to Shakespeare*. 2 vols. Rev. ed. London, 1968.

Van Laan, Thomas F. *Role-Playing in Shakespeare*. Toronto, 1978.

Watson, Curtis Brown. *Shakespeare and the Renaissance Concept of Honor*. Princeton, 1960.

Weimann, Robert. *Shakespeare and the Popular Tradition in the Theater*, ed. Robert Schwartz. Baltimore, 1978.

Whitaker, Virgil K. *Shakespeare's Use of Learning*. San Marino, Calif., 1953.

Zeeveld, W. Gordon. *The Temper of Shakespeare's Thought*. New Haven and London, 1974.

Shakespeare Criticism Since 1980, including New Historicism, Gender Studies, and Poststructuralism

See also, under *Shakespeare's Predecessors and Contemporaries*, Bednarz, Belsey, Braden, Bristol, Bruster, Cohen, Dolan, Farley-Hills, Findlay (two items), Freer, McLuskie, Orgel, Rasmussen, Rose, Shannon, and Vickers; and under *Shakespeare Criticism from the 1940s to the 1970s*, Weimann.

Adelman, Janet. *Suffocating Mothers: Fantasies of Maternal Origin in Shakespeare's Plays, "Hamlet" to "The Tempest."* Chicago, 1992.

Alexander, Catherine M. S., and Stanley Wells, eds. *Shakespeare and Race*. Cambridge, Eng., 2000.

Auden, W. H. *Lectures on Shakespeare*, ed. Arthur Kirsch. Princeton, 2000.

Bamber, Linda. *Comic Women, Tragic Men: A Study of Gender and Genre in Shakespeare*. Stanford, 1982.

Barber, C. L. *The Whole Journey: Shakespeare's Power of Development*. Berkeley, 1986.

Bate, Jonathan. *The Genius of Shakespeare*. Oxford, 1997.

Belsey, Catherine. *Shakespeare and the Loss of Eden: The Construction of Family Values in Early Modern Culture*. New Brunswick, N.J., 1999.

Berger, Harry, Jr. *Making Trifles of Terrors: Redistributing Complicities in Shakespeare*. ed. Peter Erickson. Stanford, 1997.

Bergeron, David, ed. *Pageantry in the Shakespearean Theater*. Athens, Ga., 1985.

Bevington, David. *Shakespeare*. Oxford, 2002.

Boose, Lynda E. "The Father and the Bride in Shakespeare," *PMLA* 97 (1982), 325–47.

Bristol, Michael. *Shakespeare's America, America's Shakespeare*. London and New York, 1990.

Bulman, James C., ed. *Shakespeare, Theory, and Performance*. London and New York, 1996.

Calderwood, James. *Shakespeare and the Denial of Death*. Amherst, Mass., 1987.

Callaghan, Dympna C. *Shakespeare Without Women: Representing Gender and Race on the Renaissance Stage*. London and New York, 2000.

———, ed. *A Feminist Companion to Shakespeare*. Oxford, 2000.

Callaghan, Dympna, Lorraine Helms, and Jyotsna Singh. *The Weyward Sisters: Shakespeare and Feminist Politics*. Cambridge, Eng., 1994.

Carey, John, ed. *English Renaissance Studies*. Oxford, 1980.

Cartelli, Thomas. *Repositioning Shakespeare: National Formations, Postcolonial Appropriations*. London and New York, 1999.

Cavell, Stanley. *Disowning Knowledge in Six Plays of Shakespeare*. Cambridge, Eng., 1987.

Charnes, Linda. *Notorious Identity: Materializing the Subject in Shakespeare*. Cambridge, Mass., 1993.

Cook, Ann Jennalie. *Making a Match: Courtship in Shakespeare and His Society*. Princeton, 1991.

Cox, John D. *Shakespeare and the Dramaturgy of Power*. Princeton, 1989.

Daileder, Celia R. *Eroticism on the Renaissance Stage: Transcendence, Desire, and the Limits of the Visible*. Cambridge, Eng., 1998.

Danson, Lawrence. *Shakespeare's Dramatic Genres*. Oxford, 2000.

Dawson, Anthony B. *Indirections: Shakespeare and the Art of Illusion*. Toronto, 1984.

De Grazia, Margreta, Maureen Quilligan, and Peter Stallybrass, eds. *Subject and Object in Renaissance Culture*. Cambridge, Eng., 1996.

Desmet, Christy. *Reading Shakespeare's Characters: Rhetoric, Ethics, and Identity*. Amherst, Mass., 1992.

Desmet, Christy, and Robert Sawyer, eds. *Shakespeare and Appropriation*. London and New York, 1999.

Dobson, Michael. *The Making of the National Poet: Shakespeare, Adaptation, and Authorship, 1660–1769*. Oxford, 1992.

Dolan, Frances E. *Dangerous Familiars: Representations of Domestic Crime in England, 1550–1700*. Ithaca, N.Y., 1994.

Dollimore, Jonathan. *Radical Tragedy: Religion, Ideology and Power in the Drama of Shakespeare and His Contemporaries*. Chicago, 1984; New York, 1989.

Dollimore, Jonathan, and Alan Sinfield. *Political Shakespeare: New Essays in Cultural Materialism*. Manchester, Eng., 1985.

Drakakis, John, ed. *Alternative Shakespeares*. London, 1985.

Dubrow, Heather, and Richard Strier, eds. *The Historical Renaissance: New Essays on Tudor and Stuart Literature and Culture*. Chicago, 1988.

Eagleton, Terence. *William Shakespeare*. Oxford, 1986.

Edwards, Philip, et al., eds. *Shakespeare's Styles*. Cambridge, Eng., 1980.

Engle, Lars. *Shakespearean Pragmatism: Market of His Time*. Chicago, 1993.

Erickson, Peter. *Patriarchal Structures in Shakespeare's Drama*. Berkeley, 1985.

Erickson, Peter, and Coppélia Kahn, eds. *Shakespeare's Rough Magic: Essays in Honor of C. L. Barber*. Newark, Del., 1985.

French, Marilyn. *Shakespeare's Division of Experience*. New York, 1981.

Frye, Northrop. *Northrop Frye on Shakespeare*, ed. Robert Sandler. New Haven, 1986.

Fumerton, Patricia, and Simon Hunt, eds. *Renaissance Culture and the Everyday*. Philadelphia, 1999.

Garber, Marjorie. *Coming of Age in Shakespeare*. London, 1981.

———. *Shakespeare's Ghost Writers: Literature as Uncanny Causality*. London and New York, 1987.

———, ed. *Cannibals, Witches, and Divorce: Estranging the Renaissance*. Baltimore, 1987.

Gibbons, Brian. *Shakespeare and Multiplicity*. Cambridge, Eng., 1993.

Gillies, John. *Shakespeare and the Geography of Difference*. Cambridge, Eng., 1994.

Goldberg, Jonathan. *James I and the Politics of Literature: Jonson, Shakespeare, Donne, and Their Contemporaries*. Baltimore, 1983.

———. *Sodometries: Renaissance Texts, Modern Sexualities*. Stanford, 1992.

Grady, Hugh, ed. *Shakespeare and Modernity: Early Modern to Millennium*. London and New York, 2000.

Greenblatt, Stephen. *Learning to Curse: Essays in Early Modern Culture*. London and New York, 1990.

———. *Marvelous Possessions: The Wonder of the New World*. Chicago, 1991.

———. *Renaissance Self-Fashioning: From More to Shakespeare*. Chicago, 1980.

———. *Shakespearean Negotiations: The Circulation of Social Energy in Renaissance England*. Berkeley, 1988.

Habib, Imtiaz. *Shakespeare and Race: Postcolonial Praxis in the Early Modern Period*. Lanham and Oxford, 2000.

Hall, Kim F. *Things of Darkness: Economies of Race and Gender in Early Modern England*. Ithaca, N.Y., 1994.

Hamilton, Donna B. *Shakespeare and the Politics of Protestant England*. Lexington, Ky., 1992.

Hamlin, William M. *The Image of America in Montaigne, Spenser, and Shakespeare: Renaissance Ethnography and Literary Tradition*. New York, 1995.

Hawkes, Terence. *Meaning by Shakespeare*. London and New York, 1992.

———, ed. *Alternative Shakespeares*. Vol. 2. London and New York, 1996.

Holland, Norman, et al., eds. *Shakespeare's Personality*. Berkeley, 1989.

Howard, Jean E. *Shakespeare's Art of Orchestration: Stage Technique and Audience Response*. Urbana, Ill., 1984.

———. *The Stage and Social Struggle in Early Modern England*. London, 1994.

———, and Marion F. O'Connor, eds. *Shakespeare Reproduced: The Text in History and Ideology*. London and New York, 1987.

———, and Scott Cutler Shershow, eds. *Marxist Shakespeares*. London and New York, 2000.

James, Heather. *Shakespeare's Troy: Drama, Politics, and the Translation of Empire*. Cambridge, Eng., 1997.

Jardine, Lisa. *Reading Shakespeare Historically*. London and New York, 1996.

———. *Still Harping on Daughters: Women and Drama in the Age of Shakespeare*. Sussex and Totowa, N.J., 1983; New York, 1989.

Kahn, Coppélia. *Man's Estate: Masculine Identity in Shakespeare*. Berkeley, 1981.

———. *Roman Shakespeare: Warriors, Wounds, and Women*. London and New York, 1997.

Kamps, Ivo, ed. *Materialist Shakespeare: A History*. London, 1995.

———, ed. *Shakespeare Left and Right*. New York and London, 1991.

Kastan, David Scott. *Shakespeare After Theory*. London, 1999.

———. *Shakespeare and the Book*. Cambridge, Eng., 2001.

———. *Shakespeare and the Shapes of Time*. Hanover, N.H., 1982.

———, ed. *A Companion to Shakespeare*. Oxford, 1999.

Kernan, Alvin. *Shakespeare, the King's Playwright: Theater in the Stuart Court, 1603–1613*. New Haven, 1995.

Kerrigan, William. *Shakespeare's Promises*. Baltimore, 1999.

Kirsch, Arthur. *Shakespeare and the Experience of Love*. Cambridge, Eng., 1981.

Knapp, Robert S. *Shakespeare—The Theater and the Book*. Princeton, 1989.

Knowles, Richard, ed. *Shakespeare and Carnival: After Bakhtin*. London and New York, 1998.

Lenz, Carolyn, et al., eds. *The Woman's Part: Feminist Criticism of Shakespeare*. Urbana, Ill., 1980.

Little, Arthur L., Jr. *Shakespeare Jungle Fever: National-Imperial Re-Visions of Race, Rape, and Sacrifice*. Stanford, 2000.

Loomba, Ania. *Gender, Race, Renaissance Drama*. Manchester, Eng., 1989.

Loomba, Ania, and Martin Orkin, eds. *Postcolonial Shakespeares*. London and New York, 1998.

Mahon, John W., and Thomas A. Pendleton, eds. *"Fanned and Winnowed Opinion": Shakespearean Essays Presented to Harold Jenkins*. London, 1987.

Mallin, Eric. *Inscribing the Time: Shakespeare and the End of Elizabethan England.* Berkeley, 1995.

Marcus, Leah. *Puzzling Shakespeare: Local Reading and its Discontents.* Berkeley, 1988.

Mazzio, Carla, and Douglas Trevor, eds. *Historicism, Psychoanalysis, and Early Modern Culture.* London and New York, 2000.

McDonald, Russ, ed. *Shakespeare Reread: The Texts in New Contexts.* Ithaca, N.Y., 1994.

McMullan, Gordon, and Jonathan Hope, eds. *The Politics of Tragicomedy: Shakespeare and After.* London and New York, 1992.

Melchiori, Giorgio. *Shakespeare's Garter Plays: "Edward III" to "Merry Wives of Windsor."* Newark, Del., 1994.

Miola, Robert S. *Shakespeare's Reading.* Oxford and New York, 2000.

——. *Shakespeare's Rome.* Cambridge, Eng., 1983.

Montrose, Louis. *The Purpose of Playing: Shakespeare and Cultural Politics of the Elizabethan Theatre.* Chicago, 1996.

Mullaney, Steven. *The Place of the Stage: License, Play, and Power in Renaissance England.* Chicago, 1988.

Neely, Carol Thomas. *Broken Nuptials in Shakespeare's Plays.* New Haven, 1985.

Newman, Karen. *Fashioning Femininity and the English Renaissance Drama.* Chicago, 1991.

Novy, Marianne. *Love's Argument: Gender Relations in Shakespeare.* Chapel Hill, N.C., 1984.

——, ed. *Women's Re-Visions of Shakespeare.* Urbana, Ill., 1990.

Nuttall, A. D. *A New Mimesis: Shakespeare and the Representation of Reality.* London, 1983.

Orgel, Stephen. *The Authentic Shakespeare and Other Problems of the Early Modern Stage.* London and New York, 2002.

Orgel, Stephen, and Sean Keilen, eds. *Shakespeare and History; Post-modern Shakespeare; Shakespeare and the Interpretive Tradition; Shakespeare and the Literary Tradition; Shakespeare and Gender; Political Shakespeare.* In separate volumes, New York, 1999.

Parker, Patricia. *Shakespeare from the Margins: Language, Culture, Context.* Chicago, 1996.

——, and Geoffrey Hartman, eds. *Shakespeare and the Question of Theory.* London, 1985.

Paster, Gail Kern. *The Body Embarrassed: Drama and the Disciplines of Shame in Early Modern England.* Ithaca, N.Y., 1993.

Patterson, Annabel. *Shakespeare and the Popular Voice.* Oxford, 1989.

Rabkin, Norman. *Shakespeare and the Problem of Meaning.* Chicago, 1981.

Salingar, Leo. *Dramatic Form in Shakespeare and the Jacobeans.* Cambridge, Eng., 1986.

Schwartz, Murray, and Coppélia Kahn, eds. *Representing Shakespeare: New Psychoanalytic Essays.* Baltimore, 1980.

Siemon, James R. *Shakespearean Iconoclasm.* Berkeley, 1985.

Sinfield, Alan. *Faultlines: Cultural Materialism and the Politics of Dissident Reading.* Berkeley, 1992.

Skura, Meredith Anne. *The Literary Use of the Psychoanalytic Process.* New Haven, 1981.

——. *Shakespeare the Actor and the Purposes of Playing.* Chicago, 1993.

Smith, Bruce R. *Homosexual Desire in Shakespeare's England.* Chicago, 1991.

——. *Shakespeare and Masculinity.* Oxford, 2000.

Stockholder, Kay. *Dream Works: Lovers and Families in Shakespeare's Plays.* Toronto, 1987.

Taylor, Gary. *Reinventing Shakespeare: A Cultural History from the Restoration to the Present.* New York, 1989.

Traub, Valerie. *Desire and Anxiety: Circulations of Sexuality in Shakespearean Drama.* London, 1992.

Vickers, Brian. *Appropriating Shakespeare: Contemporary Critical Quarrels.* New Haven, 1993.

Watson, Robert N. *The Rest is Silence: Death as Annihilation in the English Renaissance.* Berkeley, 1994.

——. *Shakespeare and the Hazards of Ambition.* Cambridge, Mass., 1984.

Wayne, Valerie, ed. *The Matter of Difference: Materialist Feminist Criticism of Shakespeare.* Ithaca, N.Y., 1991.

Weimann, Robert. *Author's Pen and Actor's Voice: Playing and Writing in Shakespeare's Theatre.* Cambridge, Eng., 2000.

Wells, Robin Headlam. *Shakespeare on Masculinity.* Cambridge, Eng., 2000.

——. *Shakespeare, Politics, and the State.* London, 1986.

Wheeler, Richard P. *Shakespeare's Development and the Problem Comedies: Turn and Counter-Turn.* Berkeley, 1981.

White, Paul Whitfield, and Suzanne R. Westfall, eds. *Shakespeare and Theatrical Patronage in Early Modern England.* Cambridge, Eng., 2002.

Williams, Gordon. *Shakespeare, Sex, and the Print Revolution.* London and Atlantic Highlands, N.J., 1996.

Woodbridge, Linda. *The Scythe of Saturn: Shakespeare's Magical Thinking.* Urbana, Ill., 1994.

Woodbridge, Linda, and Edward Berry, eds. *True Rites and Maimed Rites: Ritual and Anti-Ritual in Shakespeare and His Age.* Urbana, Ill., 1992.

Ziegler, Georgianna, ed. *Shakespeare's Unruly Women.* Washington, D.C., 1997.

Shakespeare in Performance; Dramaturgy

See also, under *Shakespeare Criticism from the 1940s to the 1970s,* Goldman and Granville-Barker.

Bartholomeusz, Dennis. *Macbeth and the Players.* Cambridge, Eng., 1969.

Barton, John. *Playing Shakespeare.* London, 1984.

Bevington, David. *Action is Eloquence: Shakespeare's Language of Gesture.* Cambridge, Mass., 1984.

Brockbank, Philip, ed. *Players of Shakespeare.* Cambridge, Eng., 1985.

Brown, Ivor. *Shakespeare and the Actors.* London, 1970.

Brown, John Russell. *Shakespeare's Plays in Performance.* London, 1966.

——. *Shakespeare's Dramatic Style.* London, 1970.

Bulman, J. C., and H. R. Coursen, eds. *Shakespeare on Television.* Hanover, N.H., 1988.

Carlisle, Carol Jones. *Shakespeare from the Greenroom: Actors' Criticisms of Four Major Tragedies.* Chapel Hill, N.C., 1969.

Cohn, Ruby. *Modern Shakespeare Offshoots.* Princeton, 1976.

Cook, Judith. *Shakespeare's Players.* London, 1983.

Davies, Anthony, and Stanley Wells, eds. *Shakespeare and the Moving Image: The Plays on Film and Television.* Cambridge, Eng., 1994.

Dessen, Alan C. *Recovering Shakespeare's Theatrical Vocabulary.* Cambridge, Eng., 1995.

——. *Rescripting Shakespeare: The Text, the Director, and Modern Productions.* Cambridge, Eng., 2002.

——, and Leslie Thomson. *A Dictionary of Stage Directions in English Drama, 1580–1642.* Cambridge, Eng., 1999.

Donohue, Joseph W., Jr. *Dramatic Character in the English Romantic Age.* Princeton, 1970.

Downer, Alan S. *The Eminent Tragedian, William Charles Macready.* Cambridge, Mass., 1966.

Edelman, Charles. *Brawl Ridiculous: Swordfighting in Shakespeare's Plays.* Manchester, Eng., 1992.

Hodgdon, Barbara. *The Shakespeare Trade: Performances and Appropriations.* Philadelphia, 1998.

Hogan, Charles B. *Shakespeare in the Theatre, 1701–1800.* 2 vols. Oxford, 1952–1957.

Jackson, Russell, and Robert Smallwood, eds. *Players of Shakespeare 2.* Cambridge, Eng., 1988. Followed by Vols. 3 (1993); and 4, ed. Smallwood (1998).

Jones, Emrys. *Scenic Form in Shakespeare.* Oxford, 1971.

Jorgens, Jack L. *Shakespeare on Film.* Bloomington, Ind., 1977.

Manvell, Roger. *Shakespeare and the Film.* London and New York, 1971.

McGuire, Philip C. *Speechless Dialect: Shakespeare's Open Silences.* Berkeley, 1985.

McGuire, Philip C., and David A. Samuelson. *Shakespeare: The Theatrical Dimension.* New York, 1979.

Odell, George C. D. *Shakespeare from Betterton to Irving.* 2 vols. New York, 1920, 1966.

Poel, William. *Shakespeare in the Theatre.* London, 1913, 1968.

Price, Joseph G., ed. *The Triple Bond: Plays, Mainly Shakespearean, in Performance.* University Park, Pa., 1975.

Rutter, Carol Chillington, ed. *Documents of the Rose Playhouse.* Manchester, Eng., 1999.

Rutter, Carol, et al. *Clamorous Voices: Shakespeare's Women Today.* New York, 1989.

Shapiro, Michael. *Gender in Play on the Shakespearean Stage: Boy Heroines and Female Pages.* Ann Arbor, Mich., 1994.

Shattuck, Charles H. *The Shakespeare Promptbooks: A Descriptive Catalogue.* Urbana, Ill., 1965.

——. *Shakespeare on the American Stage from the Hallams to Edwin Booth.* Washington, D.C., 1976; *from Booth and Barrett to Sothern and Marlowe,* Washington, D.C., 1987.

Slater, Ann Pasternak. *Shakespeare the Director.* Brighton, Sussex, and Totowa, N.J., 1982.

Speaight, Robert. *William Poel and the Elizabethan Revival.* London, 1954.

Sprague, Arthur Colby. *Shakespeare and the Actors*. Cambridge, Mass., 1944.

———. *Shakespearian Players and Performances*. Cambridge, Mass., 1953.

Styan, J. L. *Shakespeare's Stagecraft*. Cambridge, Eng., 1967.

Wells, Stanley. *Royal Shakespeare: Four Major Productions at Stratford-upon-Avon*. Manchester, Eng., 1977.

The Romances

See also, under *Shakespeare Criticism Since 1980*, McMullan and Hope.

Bergeron, David M. *Shakespeare's Romances and the Royal Family*. Lawrence, Kans., 1985.

Brown, John Russell, and Bernard Harris, eds. *Later Shakespeare*. Stratford-upon-Avon Studies 8. London, 1966.

Danby, John F. *Poets on Fortune's Hill*. London, 1952. Reprinted as *Elizabethan and Jacobean Poets*. London, 1964.

Edwards, Philip. "Shakespeare's Romances: 1900–1957," *ShS* 11 (1958), 1–18. See also other articles in this issue.

Fawkner, H. W. *Shakespeare's Miracle Plays: "Pericles," "Cymbeline," and "The Winter's Tale."* Rutherford, N.J., 1992.

Felperin, Howard. *Shakespearean Romance*. Princeton, 1972.

Foakes, R. A. *Shakespeare: From the Dark Comedies to the Last Plays*. London and Charlottesville, Va., 1971.

Frye, Northrop. *Anatomy of Criticism*. Princeton, 1957.

———. *A Natural Perspective: The Development of Shakespearean Comedy and Romance*. New York, 1965.

———. *The Secular Scripture: A Study of the Structure of Romance*. Cambridge, Mass., 1976.

Gesner, Carol. *Shakespeare and the Greek Romance: A Study of Origins*. Lexington, Ky., 1970.

Hartwig, Joan. *Shakespeare's Tragicomic Vision*. Baton Rouge, La., 1972.

Hunter, Robert Grams. *Shakespeare and the Comedy of Forgiveness*. New York, 1965.

James, D. G. "The Failure of the Ballad-Makers," *Scepticism and Poetry*. London, 1937.

Jordan, Constance. *Shakespeare's Monarchies: Ruler and Subject in the Romances*. Ithaca, N.Y., 1997.

Kermode, Frank. *William Shakespeare: The Final Plays*. London, 1963.

Knight, G. Wilson. *The Crown of Life*. London, 1947, 1966.

———. *The Shakespearian Tempest*. London, 1932, 1953.

Leavis, F. R. "A Criticism of Shakespeare's Last Plays," *Scrutiny* 10 (1942), 339–45. Rpt. in *The Common Pursuit*. London, 1952.

Marsh, D. R. C. *The Recurring Miracle: A Study of "Cymbeline" and the Last Plays*. Pietermaritzburg, Natal, 1962, 1964.

Marshall, Cynthia. *Last Things and Last Plays: Shakespearean Eschatology*. Carbondale, Ill., 1991.

Mincoff, Marco. *Things Supernatural and Causeless: Shakespearean Romance*. Newark, Del., 1992.

Mowat, Barbara A. *The Dramaturgy of Shakespeare's Romances*. Athens, Ga., 1976.

Nevo, Ruth. *Shakespeare's Other Language*. New York and London, 1987.

Palfrey, Simon. *Late Shakespeare: A New World of Words*. Oxford, 1997.

Peterson, Douglas L. *Time, Tide, and Tempest: A Study of Shakespeare's Romances*. San Marino, Calif., 1973.

Pettet, E. C. *Shakespeare and the Romance Tradition*. London, 1949.

Platt, Peter G. *Reason Diminished: Shakespeare and the Marvelous*. Lincoln, Neb., 1997.

Richards, Jennifer, and James Knowles, eds. *Shakespeare's Late Plays: New Readings*. Edinburgh, 1999.

Ryan, Kiernan, ed. *Shakespeare: The Late Plays*. New York, 1999.

Smith, Hallett. *Shakespeare's Romances*. San Marino, Calif., 1972.

Strachey, Lytton. "Shakespeare's Final Period," *Books and Characters*. London, 1922.

Traversi, Derek. *Shakespeare: The Last Phase*. New York, 1954.

Yates, Frances A. *Shakespeare's Last Plays: A New Approach*. London, 1975.

Young, David. *The Heart's Forest: A Study of Shakespeare's Pastoral Plays*. New Haven and London, 1972.

Pericles

See also, under *The Romances*, Bergeron, Brown and Harris (essay by Francis Berry), Danby, Felperin, Frye *(Natural Perspective)*, Kermode, Knight *(Crown of Life)*, Nevo, and Peterson; and under *Shakespeare Criticism Since 1980*, Edwards et al. (essay by Ewbank) and Mullaney (Chapter 6).

Barber, C. L. "'Thou That Beget'st Him That Did Thee Beget': Transformation in *Pericles* and *The Winter's Tale*," *ShS* 22 (1969), 59–67.

Bishop, T. G. *Shakespeare and the Theatre of Wonder*. Cambridge, Eng., 1996.

Brockbank, J. Philip. "*Pericles* and the Dream of Immortality," *ShS* 24 (1971), 105–16.

Dunbar, Mary Judith. "'To the Judgement of Your Eye': Iconography and the Theatrical Art of *Pericles*," *Shakespeare, Man of the Theatre*, ed. Kenneth Muir et al., pp. 86–97. Newark, Del., 1983.

Edwards, Philip. "An Approach to the Problem of *Pericles*," *ShS* 5 (1952), 25–49.

Eliot, T. S. "Marina," *The Complete Poems and Plays, 1909–1950*. New York, 1952.

Helms, Lorraine. "The Saint in the Brothel: Or, Eloquence Rewarded," *SQ* 41 (1990), 319–32.

Hoeniger, F. David. "Gower and Shakespeare in *Pericles*," *SQ* 33 (1982), 461–79.

Lewis, Anthony J. "'I feed on mother's flesh': Incest and Eating in *Pericles*," *Essays in Literature* 15 (1988), 147–63.

Pitcher, John. "The Poet and Taboo: The Riddle of Shakespeare's *Pericles*," *English Association Essays and Studies* (1982), 14–29.

Skeele, David. *Thwarting the Wayward Seas: A Critical and Theatrical History of Shakespeare's "Pericles" in the Nineteenth and Twentieth Centuries*. Newark, Del., 1998.

Cymbeline

See also, under *The Romances*, Bergeron, Brown and Harris (essay by Harris), Felperin, Frye *(Natural Perspective)*, Hartwig, Hunter, Kermode, Marsh, Mowat, and Richards and Knowles (essays by Maley and Thorne); under *Shakespeare Criticism to the 1930s*, Shaw; under *Shakespeare Criticism from the 1940s to the 1970s*, Granville-Barker; under *Shakespeare Criticism Since 1980*, Adelman, Bergeron (essay by Wall), Dubrow and Strier (essay by Marcus), Hamilton (Chapter 7), James, Kahn, Kastan, Kirsch, Marcus (Chapter 3), Miola, and Schwartz and Kahn (essay by Skura); and under *The Greek and Roman Tragedies*, Miola.

Belsey, Catherine. "Marriage: Imogen's Bedchamber," *Shakespeare and the Loss of Eden*. New Brunswick, N.J., 1999.

Freer, Coburn, *"Cymbeline," The Poetics of Jacobean Drama*, Chapter 4. Baltimore, 1981.

Gillies, John. "The Problem of Style in *Cymbeline*," *Southern Review* (University of Adelaide and Macquarie University) 15:3 (1982), 269–90.

Hoeniger, F. D. "Irony and Romance in *Cymbeline*," *Studies in English Literature 2* (1962), 219–28.

Kirsch, Arthur C. "*Cymbeline* and Coterie Dramaturgy," *ELH* 34 (1967), 285–306.

Lewis, Cynthia. "'With Simular Proof Enough': Modes of Misperception in *Cymbeline*," *Studies in English Literature* 31 (1991), 343–63.

Marcus, Leah. "*Cymbeline* and the Unease of Topicality," *The Historical Renaissance*, eds. Heather Dubrow and Richard Strier. Chicago, 1988.

Mikalachki, Jodi. "*Cymbeline* and the Masculine Romance of Roman Britain," *The Legacy of Boadicea*. London, 1998.

Olsen, Thomas G. "Iachimo's 'drug-damn'd Italy' and the Problem of British National Character in *Cymbeline*," *Shakespeare Yearbook* 10 (1999), 269–96.

Parker, Patricia. "Romance and Empire: Anachronistic *Cymbeline*," *Unfolded Tales: Essays on Renaissance Romance*, eds. Gordon Teskey and George M. Logan. Ithaca, N.Y., 1989.

Redmond, Michael J. "Rome, Italy, and the (Re) Construction of British National Identity," *Shakespeare Yearbook* 10 (1999), 297–316.

Simonds, Peggy Muñoz. *Myth, Emblem, and Music in Shakespeare's "Cymbeline."* Newark, Del., 1992.

Swander, Homer D. "*Cymbeline* and the 'Blameless Hero'," *ELH* 31 (1964), 259–70.

Warren, Roger. "Theatrical Virtuosity and Poetic Complexity in *Cymbeline*," *ShS* 29 (1976), 41–50.

Woodbridge, Linda. "Palisading the Elizabethan Body Politic," *Texas Studies in Literature and Language* 33 (1991), 327–54.

The Winter's Tale

See also, under *The Romances*, Felperin, Foakes, Hartwig, Hunter, Knight *(Crown of Life)*, Mowat, and Young; and under *Shakespeare Criticism Since 1980*, Cavell

(Chapter 6), Erickson, Neely, and Parker and Hartman (essay by Felperin).

Alpers, Paul. *What Is Pastoral?* Chicago, 1996.

Barber, C. L. "'Thou That Beget'st Him That Did Thee Beget': Transformation in *Pericles* and *The Winter's Tale*," *ShS 22* (1969), 59–67.

Bartholomeusz, Dennis. *"The Winter's Tale" in Performance in England and America, 1611–1976*. Cambridge, Eng., 1982.

Bethell, S. L. *The Winter's Tale: A Study*. London, 1947.

Bishop, T. G. *Shakespeare and the Theatre of Wonder*. Cambridge, Eng., 1996.

Coghill, Nevill. "Six Points of Stage-Craft in *The Winter's Tale*," *ShS 11* (1958), 31–41.

Draper, R. P. *"The Winter's Tale": Text and Performance*. London, 1985.

Ewbank, Inga-Stina. "The Triumph of Time in *The Winter's Tale*," *Review of English Literature* 5:2 (1964), 83–100.

Frey, Charles. *Shakespeare's Vast Romance: A Study of "The Winter's Tale."* Columbia, Mo., 1980.

Frye, Northrop. "Recognition in *The Winter's Tale*," *Essays on Shakespeare and Elizabethan Drama in Honor of Hardin Craig*, ed. R. Hosley, pp. 235–46. Columbia, Mo., 1962.

Kaplan, Lindsay M., and Katherine Eggert. "'Good queen, my lord, good queen': Sexual Slanders and the Trials of Female Authority in *The Winter's Tale*," *Renaissance Drama* n.s. 25 (1994), 89–118.

Lindenbaum, Peter. "Time, Sexual Love, and the Uses of Pastoral in *The Winter's Tale*," *Modern Language Quarterly* 33 (1972), 3–22.

Matchett, William H. "Some Dramatic Techniques in *The Winter's Tale*," *ShS 22* (1969), 93–107.

Siemon, James Edward. " 'But It Appears She Lives': Iteration in *The Winter's Tale*," *PMLA* 89 (1974), 10–16.

Snyder, Susan. "Mamillius and Gender Polarization in *The Winter's Tale*," *SQ* 50 (1999), 1–8.

Sokol, B. J. *Art and Illusion in "The Winter's Tale."* Manchester, Eng., 1994.

Tayler, Edward W. *Nature and Art in Renaissance Literature*. New York, 1964.

Wickham, Glynne. "Romance and Emblem: A Study in the Dramatic Structure of *The Winter's Tale*," *The Elizabethan Theatre III*, ed. David Galloway. Hamden, Conn., 1973.

Williams, John Anthony. *The Natural Work of Art: The Experience of Romance in Shakespeare's "Winter's Tale."* Cambridge, Mass., 1967.

The Tempest

See also, under *The Romances*, Brown and Harris (essay by Brockbank), Felperin, Frye (*Natural Perspective*), Hartwig, Kermode, Mowat, Peterson, and Young; under *Shakespeare's Predecessors and Contemporaries*, Bevington and Holbrook (essay by Bevington); under *Shakespeare Criticism to the 1930s*, Coleridge (*Coleridge's Writings*); under *Shakespeare Criticism from the 1940s to the 1970s*, Fiedler, Kernan (*Playwright as Magician*, Chapter 6), and Kott; and under *Shakespeare Criticism*

Since 1980, Dollimore and Sinfield (essay by Brown), Drakakis (essay by Barker and Hulme), Garber (*Cannibals*, essay by Orgel), Greenblatt (*Shakespearean Negotiations*, Chapter 5), Hamlin, Howard and O'Connor (essay by Cartelli), Lenz et al. (essay by Leininger), Loomba and Orkin (essay by Brotton), McMullan and Hope (essay by Norbrook), and Schwartz and Kahn (essay by Sundelson).

Auden, W. H. "The Sea and the Mirror: A Commentary on Shakespeare's *The Tempest*," *The Collected Poetry*. New York, 1945.

Berger, Harry, Jr. "Miraculous Harp: A Reading of Shakespeare's *Tempest*," *ShakS 5* (1969), 253–83.

Demaray, John G. *Shakespeare and the Spectacles of Strangeness: "The Tempest" and the Transformation of Renaissance Theatrical Forms*. Pittsburgh, Pa., 1998.

Frey, Charles. "*The Tempest* and the New World," *SQ* 30 (1979), 29–41.

Hamilton, Donna. *Virgil and "The Tempest": The Politics of Imitation*. Columbus, Ohio, 1990.

Hulme, Peter, and William H. Sherman, eds. *"The Tempest" and Its Travels*. Philadelphia, 2000.

James, D. G. *The Dream of Prospero*. Oxford, 1967.

James, Henry. "Introduction to *The Tempest*." Rpt. in *Henry James: Selected Literary Criticism*, ed. Morris Shapiro. London, 1963.

Mebane, John S. *Renaissance Magic and the Return of the Golden Age: The Occult Tradition and Marlowe, Jonson, and Shakespeare*. Lincoln, Neb., 1989.

Mowat, Barbara A. "Prospero's Book," *SQ* 52 (2001), 1–33.

Orgel, Stephen. "New Uses of Adversity: Tragic Experience in *The Tempest*," *In Defense of Reading*, ed. Reuben A. Brower and Richard Poirier. New York, 1962.

———. "Prospero's Wife," *Representations* 8 (1984), 1–13. Rpt. in Orgel, under *Shakespeare Criticism Since 1980*.

Skura, Meredith Anne. "Discourse and the Individual: The Case of Colonialism in *The Tempest*," *SQ* 40 (1989), 42–69.

Strier, Richard. " 'I am Power': Normal and Magical Politics in *The Tempest*," in *Writing and Political Engagement in Seventeenth-Century England*, ed. Derek Hirst and Richard Strier. Cambridge, Eng., 1999.

Thompson, Ann. " 'Miranda, where's your sister?': Reading Shakespeare's *The Tempest*," *Feminist Criticism: Theory and Practice*, ed. Susan Sellers. New York, 1991.

Vaughan, Alden T. "Shakespeare's Indian: The Americanization of Caliban," *SQ* 39 (1988), 137–53.

Vaughan, Alden T., and Virginia Mason Vaughan. *Shakespeare's Caliban: A Cultural History*. Cambridge, Eng., 1991.

Vaughan, Virginia Mason, and Alden T. Vaughan, eds. *Critical Essays on Shakespeare's "The Tempest."* New York and London, 1998.

William, David. "*The Tempest* on the Stage," *Jacobean Theatre*, eds. John Russell Brown and Bernard Harris, pp. 133–57. Stratford-upon-Avon Studies 1. London, 1960.

The Two Noble Kinsmen

See also, under *The Romances*, Hartwig and Mowat; under *Textual Criticism and Bibliography*, Masten; and under *Shakespeare Criticism Since 1980*, Smith.

Abrams, Richard. "Gender Confusion and Sexual Politics in *The Two Noble Kinsmen*," *Themes in Drama 7: Drama, Sex and Politics*, ed. J. Redmond. Cambridge, Eng., 1985.

Berggren, Paula. " 'For what we lack, / We laugh': Incompletion and *The Two Noble Kinsmen*," *Modern Language Studies* 14 (1984), 3–17.

Bruster, Douglas. "The Jailer's Daughter and the Politics of Madwomen's Language," *SQ* 46 (1995), 277–300.

Edwards, Philip. "On the Design of *The Two Noble Kinsmen*," *A Review of English Literature* 5 (1964), 89–105.

Frey, Charles H., ed. *Shakespeare, Fletcher, and The Two Noble Kinsmen*. Columbia, Mo., 1989.

Hoy, Cyrus. "The Language of Fletcherian Tragicomedy," *Mirror up to Shakespeare*, ed. J. C. Gray, pp. 99–113. Toronto, 1984.

Lief, Madelon, and Nicholas F. Radel. "Linguistic Subversion and the Artifice of Rhetoric In *The Two Noble Kinsmen*," *SQ* 38 (1987), 405–25.

Mallette, Richard. "Same-Sex Friendship in *The Two Noble Kinsmen*," *Renaissance Drama* n.s. 26 (1995), 29–52.

McMullan, Gordon. "A Rose for Emilia: Collaborative Relations in *The Two Noble Kinsmen*," *Renaissance Configurations: Voices/Bodies/Spaces, 1580–1690*, ed. Gordon McMullan. Basingstoke and New York, 1998.

Potter, Lois. "Topicality or Politics? *The Two Noble Kinsmen, 1613–34*," *The Politics of Tragicomedy: Shakespeare and After*, eds. Gordon McMullan and Jonathan Hope. London, 1992.

Shannon, Laurie J. "Emilia's Argument: Friendship and 'Human Title' in *The Two Noble Kinsmen*," *ELH* 64 (1997), 657–82.

Waith, Eugene. "Shakespeare and Fletcher on Love and Friendship," *ShakS 18* (1986), 235–49.

The Poems

Dubrow, Heather. *Captive Victors: Shakespeare's Narrative Poems and Sonnets*. Ithaca, N.Y., 1987.

Hulse, Clarke. *Metamorphic Verse: The Elizabethan Minor Epic*. Princeton, 1981.

Shakespeare Survey 15 (1962). Devoted chiefly to the poems and music, including the sonnets.

Venus and Adonis

See also, under *The Poems*, Dubrow, and Hulse (pp. 143–75); under *Shakespeare Criticism from the 1940s to the 1970s*, Rabkin; and under *Shakespeare Criticism Since 1980*, Kahn (Chapter 2).

Allen, Michael J. B. "The Chase: The Development of a Renaissance Theme,"

Comparative Literature 20 (1968), 301–12. (Includes discussion of *Venus and Adonis*.)

Asals, Heather. "*Venus and Adonis:* The Education of a Goddess," *Studies in English Literature* 13 (1973), 31–51.

Beauregard, David N. "*Venus and Adonis:* Shakespeare's Representation of the Passions," *ShakS* 8 (1975), 83–98.

Belsey, Catherine. "Love as Trompe-l'oeil: Taxonomies of Desire in *Venus and Adonis,*" *SQ* 46 (1995), 257–76.

Hamilton, A. C. "*Venus and Adonis,*" *Studies in English Literature* 1:1 (1961), 1–15.

Jahn, J. D. "The Lamb of Lust: The Role of Adonis in Shakespeare's *Venus and Adonis,*" *ShakS* 6 (1970), 11–25.

Keach, William. "*Venus and Adonis,*" *Elizabethan Erotic Narratives: Irony and Pathos in the Ovidian Poetry of Shakespeare, Marlowe, and Their Contemporaries.* New Brunswick, N.J., 1977.

Mortimer, Anthony. *Variable Passions: A Reading of Shakespeare's "Venus and Adonis."* New York, 2000.

The Rape of Lucrece

See also, under *Shakespeare's Language,* Lanham; and under *Shakespeare Criticism Since 1980,* Callaghan (*A Feminist Companion,* essay by Hendricks), Kahn, Little, Parker and Hartman (essay by Vickers), and Siemon (Chapter 2).

Belsey, Catherine. "Tarquin Dispossessed: Expropriation and Consent in *The Rape of Lucrece,*" *SQ* 52 (2001), 315–35.

Donaldson, Ian. 'A Theme for Disputation': Shakespeare's Lucrece," *The Rapes of Lucretia: A Myth and Its Transformations.* Oxford, 1982.

Dubrow, Heather. " 'Full of forged lies': *The Rape of Lucrece," Captive Victors: Shakespeare's Narrative Poems and Sonnets.* Ithaca, N.Y., 1987.

Fineman, Joel. "Shakespeare's *Will*: The Temporality of Rape," *Representations* 20 (1987), 25–76.

Hulse, Clark. "*A Skilful Painting of Lucrece," Metamorphic Verse: The Elizabethan Minor Epic.* Princeton, 1981.

Kahn, Coppélia. "The Rape in Shakespeare's Lucrece," *ShakS* 9 (1976), 45–72.

MacDonald, Joyce Green. "Speech, Silence, and History in *The Rape of Lucrece," ShakS* 22 (1994), 77–103.

Maus, Katharine Eisaman. "Taking Tropes Seriously: Language and Violence in Shakespeare's *The Rape of Lucrece," SQ* 37 (1986), 66–82.

Newman, Jane O. " 'And Let Mild Women to Him Lose Their Mildness': Philomela, Female Violence, and Shakespeare's *The Rape of Lucrece," SQ* 45 (1994), 304–26.

Scholz, Susanne. "Textualizing the Body Politic: National Identity and the Female Body in *The Rape of Lucrece," Shakespeare Jahrbuch* 132 (1996), 103–13.

Williams, Carolyn D. "'Silence, like a Lucrece knife': Shakespeare and the Meaning of Rape," *Yearbook of English Studies* 23 (1993), 93–110.

Wilson, R. Rawdon. "Shakespearean Narrative: *The Rape of Lucrece* Reconsidered," *Studies in English Literature* 28 (1988), 39–59.

The Phoenix and Turtle

See also, under *Shakespeare Criticism Since 1980,* Carey (essay by Buxton, pp. 44–55).

Alvarez, A. "William Shakespeare: *The Phoenix and the Turtle," Interpretations,* ed. John Wain. London, 1955.

Arthos, John. *Shakespeare's Use of Dream and Vision,* Chapter 1. London and Totowa, N.J., 1977.

Ellrodt, Robert. "An Anatomy of *The Phoenix and the Turtle," ShS* 15 (1962), 99–110.

Empson, William. "*The Phoenix and the Turtle,*" *Essays in Criticism* 16 (1966), 147–53.

Garber, Marjorie. "Two Birds with One Stone: Lapidary Re-inscription in *The Phoenix and Turtle," The Upstart Crow* 5 (1984), 5–19.

Honigmann, E. A. J. "*The Phoenix and the Turtle," Shakespeare: The "Lost" Years,* pp. 90–113. Totowa, N.J., 1985.

Knight, G. Wilson. *The Mutual Flame: On Shakespeare's Sonnets and "The Phoenix and the Turtle."* London, 1955.

Matchett, William H. "*The Phoenix and the Turtle*": *Shakespeare's Poem and Chester's "Loues Martyr."* The Hague, 1965.

A Lover's Complaint

Jackson, MacD. P. *Shakespeare's "A Lover's Complaint": Its Date and Authenticity.* Auckland, N.Z., 1965.

Muir, Kenneth. "*A Lover's Complaint:* A Reconsideration." *Shakespeare 1564–1964,* ed. E. A. Bloom, pp. 154–66. Providence, 1964.

Underwood, Richard Allan. *Shakespeare on Love: The Poems and the Plays. Prolegomena to a Variorum Edition of "A Lover's Complaint."* Salzburg, 1985.

Warren, Roger. " 'A Lover's Complaint,' *All's Well*, and the Sonnets," *Notes and Queries* n.s. 17 (1970), 130–2.

Sonnets

See also, under. *The Poems,* Dubrow; under *Shakespeare's Predecessors and Contemporaries,* Rasmussen (essay by Alpers); under *Shakespeare Criticism from the 1940s to the 1970s,* Colie, and Kernan (*Playwright as Magician,* Chapter 2); and under *Shakespeare Criticism Since 1980,* Loomba and Orkin (essay by Hall), McDonald (essay by Vendler), Parker and Hartman (essay by Greene), and Wheeler (pp. 179–90).

Allen, Michael J. B. "Shakespeare's Man Descending a Staircase: Sonnets 126 to 154," *ShS* 31 (1978), 127–38.

Booth, Stephen. *An Essay on Shakespeare's Sonnets.* New Haven, 1969.

———. ed. *Shakespeare's Sonnets, Edited with Analytic Commentary.* New Haven, 1977.

Bradley, A. C. *Oxford Lectures on Poetry.* London, 1909, 1961.

Cheney, Patrick. "'O, let my books be . . . dumb presagers': Poetry and Theater in Shakespeare's Sonnets," *SQ* 52 (2001), 222–54.

Clark, S. H. *Sordid Images: The Poetry of Masculine Desire.* London and New York, 1994.

Cousins, A. D. *Shakespeare's Sonnets and Narrative Poems.* Harlow, Eng., 2000.

De Grazia, Margreta. "The Scandal of Shakespeare's Sonnets," *ShS* 46 (1994), 35–49.

Dubrow, Heather. *Echoes of Desire: English Petrarchism and Its Counterdiscourses.* Ithaca, N.Y., 1995.

Fineman, Joel. *Shakespeare's Perjured Eye: The Invention of Poetic Subjectivity in the Sonnets.* Berkeley, 1986.

Giroux, Robert. *The Book Known as Q: A Consideration of Shakespeare's Sonnets.* New York, 1982.

Hubler, Edward, Northrop Frye, Leslie A. Fiedler, Stephen Spender, and R. P. Blackmur. *The Riddle of Shakespeare's Sonnets.* New York, 1962.

Ingram, W. G., and Theodore Redpath, eds. *Shakespeare's Sonnets.* London, 1964.

Innes, Paul. *Shakespeare and the English Renaissance Sonnet: Verses of Feigning Love.* Basingstoke and New York, 1997.

Knight, G. Wilson. *The Mutual Flame: On Shakespeare's Sonnets and "The Phoenix and the Turtle."* London, 1955.

Krieger, Murray. *A Window to Criticism: Shakespeare's Sonnets and Modern Poetics.* Princeton, 1964.

Landry, Hilton. *Interpretations in Shakespeare's Sonnets.* Berkeley, 1963.

———. ed. *New Essays on Shakespeare's Sonnets.* New York, 1976.

Leishman, J. B. *Themes and Variations in Shakespeare's Sonnets.* London, 1961.

Lever, J. W. *The Elizabethan Love Sonnet.* London, 1956.

Melchiori, Giorgio. *Shakespeare's Dramatic Meditations: An Experiment in Criticism.* Oxford, 1976.

Muir, Kenneth. *Shakespeare's Sonnets.* London, 1979.

Pequigney, Joseph. *Such is My Love: A Study of Shakespeare's Sonnets.* Chicago, 1985.

Ramsay, Paul. *The Fickle Glass: A Study of Shakespeare's Sonnets.* New York, 1979.

Ransom, John Crowe. *The World's Body.* New York and London, 1938, 1968.

Schiffer, James, ed. *Shakespeare's Sonnets: Critical Essays.* New York, 1999.

Vendler, Helen. *The Art of Shakespeare's Sonnets.* Cambridge, Mass., 1997.

Textual Notes

These textual notes do not offer an historical collation, either of the early quartos and folios or of more recent editions; they are simply a record of departures in this edition from the copy text. For most plays the notes give the adopted reading of this edition in bold face, followed by the rejected reading in the relevant copy text. Where two substantive early texts are involved, or where a reading from some other earlier edition has been adopted, the notes provide information on the source of the reading in square brackets. In a few texts, adopted readings of editions more recent than the First Folio are indicated by [eds.]. Alterations in lineation are not indicated, nor are some minor and obvious typographical errors; changes in punctuation are indicated when the resulting change in meaning is substantive.

Abbreviations used:

F The First Folio
Q Quarto
O Octavo
s.d. stage direction
s.p. speech prefix

Pericles

Copy text: the First Quarto of 1609. Act and scene divisions, missing in the Quarto, are derived from subsequent editorial tradition.

1.0. 1 GOWER [not in Q; also in subsequent choruses throughout, except at 4.4, 5.2, and Epilogue] **6 holy-ales** Holydayes **11 these** those **39 a** of

1.1. 8 For th' For **18 razed** racte **23 the** th' **25 boundless** bondlesse **57 ANTIOCHUS** [not in Q; also at line 170] **63 advice** advise **100–1 clear . . . them. The** cleare: . . . them, the **106 know; . . . fit,** know, . . . fit; **112 our** your **114 cancel** counsell **128 you're** you **137 'schew** shew **160.1 Enter a Messenger** [after "done" in line 160 in Q]

1.2. 3 Be my By me **5 quiet?** quiet, **16 me: the** me the **20 honor him** honour **25 th'ostent** the stint **30 am** once **41 blast** sparke **69–70 me . . . thyself.** me: . . . thy selfe, **72 Where, as** Whereas **80 seem** seemes **84 Bethought me** Bethought **85 fears** feare **87 doubt—as . . . he doth** doo't, as no doubt he doth **93 call't** call **122 word for faith,** word, for faith **123 will sure** will **124 we'll** will **126.1 Exeunt** Exit

1.3. 1 THALIARD [not in Q] **27 ears it** seas **please** please: **28 seas** Sea **30 HELICANUS** [not in Q] **34 betaken** betake **39.1 Exeunt** Exit

1.4. 5 aspire aspire? **13, 14 do** to **13 deep** deepe: **14 lungs** toungs **17 helps** helpers **36 they** thy **39 two summers** too sauers **44 loved.** lou'de, **58 thou** thee **67 Hath** That **these** the **69 men** mee **74 him 's** himnes **77 fear?** leaue **78 lowest,** lowest? **97 ALL** Omnes **106 ne'er** neare

2.0. 11 Tarsus Tharstill **12 speken** spoken **22 Sends word** Sau'd one **24 intent** in Tent **murder** murdred [some corrected copies of Q have "had . . . murder"]

2.1. 6 left me left my **12 ho** to **Pilch** pelch **31–2 devours** deuowre **39 THIRD FISHERMAN** 1 **48 finny** fenny **53 that?** that, **55 it.** it? **78 quotha** ke-tha **82 holidays** all day **83 moreo'er** more; or **91 your** you **100 is** I **122 pray** pary **123 yet** yeat **all thy** all **130 it.** it **131 thee from !—may 't** thee, Fame may **148 d' ye** di'e [Q uncorr.] do'e [Q corr.] **157 rapture** rupture **160 delightful** delight **167 equal** a Goale

2.2. 1 [and elsewhere] SIMONIDES King **4 daughter** daughter heere **27 Più . . . forza** Pue Per doleera kee per forsa **28 what's** with **29 chivalry** Chiually **30 pompae** Pompey **33 Quod** Qui

2.3. 3 To I **13 yours** your **39 Yon** You **40 tells me** tels **45 son's** sonne **52 stored** stur'd **53 you do** do you **109 s.d. They dance** [after "unclaspe" in Q] **113 to be** be **115 SIMONIDES** [not in Q]

2.4. 22 welcome. Happy welcome happy **34 death's** death **40 ALL** Omnes

2.5. 74 s.d. Aside [after line 75 in Q] **76 you, not** you not, **78 s.d. Aside** [after line 79 in Q] **92 BOTH** Ambo

3.0. 2 the house about about the house **6 'fore** from **7 crickets** Cricket **10 Where, by** Whereby **13 eche** each **17 coigns** Crignes **21 stead** steed **quest. At last from Tyre,** quest at last from Tyre: **29 appease** oppresse **35 Yravishèd** Iranyshed **46 Fortune's mood** fortune mou'd **57 not . . . told.** not? . . . told, **58 hold** hold:

3.1. 1 Thou The **7 Thou stormest** then storme **8 spit** speat **11 midwife** my wife **14 s.d. Enter Lychorida** [after "Lychorida" in Q] [Wilkins; not in Q] **38 MASTER 1. Sayl** [also in lines 43 and 47] **45 SAILOR 2. Sayl** **51 MASTER 1** **52 custom** easterne **53 for . . . straight** [printed in Q as part of the next line, after "As you think meet," the line assigned to Pericles] **60 in the ooze** in oare **62 And aye-** The ayre **65 paper** Taper **70 SAILOR** 2 **73 MASTER** 2 [also in line 76] **81 s.d. Exeunt** Exit

3.2. 6 ne'er neare **19 quit** quite **51 [and elsewhere] FIRST SERVANT** Seru. **58 bitumed** bottomed **61–2 open. / Soft!** open soft; **68–9 too! / Apollo** to Apollo, **79 even** euer **87 lain** lien **95 breathes** breath

A-34

3.3. 0.1 *at Tarsus Artharsus*   **6 haunt** hant   **31 Unscissored** vnsisterd **hair** heyre   **32 ill** will   **37 CLEON** *Cler.*   **41 [and elsewhere] Lychorida** *Lycherida*

3.4. 0.1. *Thaisa Tharsa*   **4 THAISA** *Thar.*   **5 eaning** learning   **9 vestal** vastall   **11 CERIMON** *Cler.*   **17.1** *Exeunt* Exit

4.0. 8 music, letters Musicks letters   **10 high** hie   **14 Seeks** Seeke **15 hath our Cleon** our *Cleon* hath   **16 wench full grown** full growne wench   **17 ripe** right   **rite** sight   **21 she** they   **25 to th'** too'th **26 bird** bed   **29 Dian; still** *Dian* still,   **32 With** [after "might" in Q] **35 given. This** giuen, this   **38 murder** murderer   **47 carry** carried **48 on** one

4.1. 5 inflaming love i'thy in flaming, thy loue   **11 nurse's** Mistresse **25 me.** me?   **27 On . . . margent** ere the sea marre it   **36 here. When** here, when   **40 courses. Go** courses, go   **66 stem** sterne **76–7 killed? / Now** kild now?   **99.1** *Exeunt* Exit   **105 aboard.** if aboord, if

4.2. 4 much much much   **42 FIRST PIRATE** *Sayler*   **73 was like** was **88–9 must stir** stir   **103 i'th'** ethe   **117–18 lovers; seldom but** Louers seldome, but   **124 BAWD** *Mari.*   **150 s.d.** *Exeunt* Exit

4.3. 1 are ere   **6 A** O   **12 fact** face   **14–15 Fates; / To foster is** fates to foster it,   **27 prime** prince   **33 Marina's** *Marianas*   **35 through** thorow

4.4. 3 your our   **7 seem** seemes   **8 i'th'** with   **9 story.** storie   **10 the** thy   **13 along. Behind** along behind,   **14 govern, if** gouerne it, **mind,** mind.   **18 his** this   **19 grow on** grone   **20 gone.** gone **23 See** [Q adds an s.p. here: *Gowr.*]   **24 true-owed** true olde **26 o'er-showered,** ore-showr'd,   **27 embarks. He** imbarques, hee **29 puts** put   **to sea. He bears** to Sea he beares,   **48 scene** Steare

4.5. 9 s.d. *Exeunt* Exit

4.6. 0.1 *three bawds Bawdes* 3   **17 loon** Lowne   **22 may so;** may, so **37 dignifies** dignities   **69 name't** name   **88 aloof** aloft   **130 ways** way   **137 She** He   **154 ways** way   **167 Coistrel** custerell **195 women** woman

5.0. 7 roses: Roses   **8 twin** Twine   **13 lost** left   **20 fervor** [Q corr.] former [Q uncorr.]

5.1. 1 TYRIAN SAILOR 1. *Say*   **7 TYRIAN SAILOR** 2. *Say*   **12 TYRIAN SAILOR** 1. *Say* [Q corr.] Hell [Q uncorr.]   **36 LYSIMACHUS** [not in Q] **37 Behold . . . person** [assigned to Lysimachus in Q]   **38 Till** *Hell.* Till   **night** wight   **43 A LORD** *Lord*   **48 deafened ports** defend parts   **51 with her** her   **is now** now   **60 gods** God   **68 presence** present   **72 I'd** I do   **wed** to wed   **73 one** on   **bounty** beautie **75 feat** fate   **83 Marked** Marke   **91 weighed.** wayde,   **105 You're** your   **countrywoman** Countrey women   **106 Here** heare   **shores . . . shores** shewes . . . shewes   **114 cased** caste   **124 palace** *Pallas* **126 make my** make   **129 say** stay   **134 thought'st** thoughts **143 thou them?** thou   **166 dull** duld   **182 imposter** imposture **185 PERICLES** *Hell.*   **205 me but that,** me, but that   **212 life** like **228–9 music? / Tell** Musicke tell,   **230 doubt** doat   **249 life** like **264 suit** sleight

5.2. 8 Mytilin *Metalin*   **9 King. So** King, so   **14 interim, pray you, all** *Interim* pray, you all   **15 filled** fild   **16 willed** wild

5.3. 6 who whom   **15 nun** mum   **22 one in** one   **29–30 look! / If** looke if **38 Immortal** I, mortall   **51 PERICLES** *Hell.*   **71 I bless** blesse **79 credit, sir,** credit. Sir,   **91 preserved** preferd   **92 Led** Lead **98 deed to** deede,

Cymbeline

Copy text: the First Folio. Act and scene divisions are as in the Folio except as indicated below.

1.1. 2 courtiers' Courtiers: **30 [and elsewhere] Cassibelan** *Cassibulan* **59 swaddling-clothes the other,** swathing cloathes, the other   **70** [F begins "*Scena Secunda*" here]   **98 Philario's** *Filorio's*   **118 cere** seare **160.1 Enter Pisanio** [after *Exit*, line 160, in F] **1.2** [F labels "*Scena Tertia*"]

1.3 [F labels "*Scena Quarta*"]   **9 this** his

1.4 [F labels "*Scena Quinta*"]   **28 Briton** Britaine   **47 offend not** offend **72 Britain.** Brittanie;   **others** others.   **74 but believe** beleeue   **84 purchase** purchases   **128 thousand** thousands   **137 preserve** preseure

1.5 [F labels "*Scena Sexta*"]   **3 s.d.** *Exeunt* Exit   **77 s.d. Exit Pisanio** [at line 76 in F]   **87 s.d.** *Exeunt* Exit

1.6 [F labels "*Scena Septima*"]   **7 desire** desires   **28 takes** take **36 th'unnumbered** the number'd   **61, 67 [and elsewhere] Briton** Britaine   **72 be, will . . . languish** be: will . . . languish: **104 Fixing** Fiering   **109 illustrous** illustrious   **169 men's** men   **170 descended** defended

2.1. 27 Your you   **34 tonight** night   **51.1** *Exeunt* Exit   **61 husband, than** Husband. Then   **62 divorce he'd make!** diuorce, heel'd make **63 honor, keep** Honour. Keepe   **65 s.d.** *Exit Exeunt*

2.2. 1 Helen *La.* [also at line 2]   **49 bare** beare   **51.1** *Exeunt* Exit

2.3. 20 MUSICIAN [not in F]   **29 CLOTEN** [not in F]   **30 vice** voyce **32 amend** amed   **48 solicits** solicity   **130 envy, if** Enuie. If **139 garment** Garments   **147 am** am.   **156 you** your

2.4. 6 hopes hope   **18 legions** Legion   **24 mingled** wing-led **34 through** thorough   **37 PHILARIO** *Post.*   **48 not** note   **58 you** yon **61 leaves** leaue   **63 near** nere   **138 the** her

2.5. [scene not marked in F]   **16 German one** Iarmen on   **27 have a name** name

3.1. 20 rocks Oakes   **53 be. We do say** be, we do. Say

3.2. 2 monster's her accuser Monsters her accuse   **67 score** store **ride** rid   **78 here, nor** heere, not

3.3. 2 Stoop Sleepe   **23 bauble** Babe   **28 know** knowes   **31 known, well** knowne. Well   **34 for** or   **83 wherein they bow,** whereon the Bowe   **86 Polydore** *Paladour*   **106 Morgan** *Mergan*

3.4. 79 afore't a-foot   **90 make** makes   **102 blind first** first   **148 [and elsewhere] haply** happily

3.5. 17.1 *Exeunt* Exit   **32 looks** looke   **40 strokes** stroke;, **42 ATTENDANT** *Mes.*   **44 loud'st** lowd   **55.1** *Exit* [after "days" in F] **141–2 insultment** insulment

3.6. 27 [F begins "*Scena Septima*" here]   **89 Leonatus's** *Leonatus* **3.7** [F labels "*Scena Octaua*"]   **9 commends** commands

4.1. 18 her face thy face

4.2. 50–2 He . . . dieter [assigned in F to Arviragus]   **58 him** them **59 Grow, patience** Grow patient   **124 thanks, ye** thanks the **134 humor** Honor   **172 how** thou   **188 ingenious** ingenuous **207 crare** care   **208 Might** Might'st   **226 ruddock** Raddocke   **293 is** are   **294 IMOGEN (*awakes*)** [as stage direction in F]   **339 are** are heere   **393 wild-wood leaves** wild wood-leaves

4.3. 40 betid betide

4.4 2 find we we finde   **17 the** their   **27 hard** heard

5.1. 1 wished am wisht   **32–3 begin / The fashion:** begin, / The fashion

5.3. 24 harts hearts   **42 stooped** stopt   **43 they** the   **47 before, some** before some

5.4. 1 [and throughout scene] FIRST JAILER *Gao.*   **15 constrained. To** constrain'd, to   **50 deserved** d seru'd   **81 look** looke, looke   **165 Of** Oh, of   **169 sir** Sis   **197 s.d.** *Exeunt* [at line 206 in F]

5.5. 54 fine time   **62 LADIES** *La.*   **65 heard** heare   **71 rased** rac'd **128 saw** see   **136 On,** One   **207 got it** got   **264 from** fro   **277 truth** troth   **315 on 's** one's   **319 leave.** leaue   **338 mere** neere   **339 treason;** Treason   **382 ye** we   **390 brothers** Brother   **391 whither? These,** whether these?   **392 battle,** Battaile?   **395 to chance;** to chance?   **409 so** no   **439 SOOTHSAYER** [not in F]   **473 this yet** yet this

The Winter's Tale

Copy text: the First Folio. Characters' names are groups at the heads of scenes throughout the play. Act and scene divisions are as marked in the Folio.

The Names of the Actors [printed in F at the end of the play] **ARCHIDAMUS** [after *Autoclycus* in F]

1.1. 9 us, we vs: we
1.2. 104 And A   **121 hast** has't   **137–8 be?—/ Affection, thy** be / Affection? thy   **148 What . . . brother** [assigned in F to Leontes]   **151–3 its folly, . . . Its tenderness, . . . bosoms!** it's folly? . . . It's tendernesse? . . . bosomes?   **158 do** do's   **202–3 powerful, think it, . . . south. Be** powrefull: thinke it: . . . South, be   **208 you, they** you   **253 forth. In . . .** forth in . . . (my Lord.)   **275 hobbyhorse** Holy-Horse   **386 How? Caught** How caught   **461 off. Hence!** off, hence:
2.1. 2 [and throughout scene] FIRST LADY *Lady*   **91 fedarie** Federarie
2.2. 32–3 me. / If . . . blister me, / If . . . blister.
2.3. 2 thus, mere weakness. If thus: meere weaknesse, if   **39 What** Who   **61 good, so** good so,
3.2. 10 Silence [printed in F as a s.d.]   **10.1–2 Hermione, as to her trial . . . Ladies** [at start of scene in F, as generally with the s.d. in this play]   **33 Who** Whom   **99 Starred** Star'd   **156 woo** woe
3.3. 64 scar'd scarr'd   **116 made** mad
4.2. 13 thee. Thou , thee, thou
4.3. 1 AUTOLYCUS [not in F]   **7 on** an   **10 With heigh, with heigh** With heigh   **38 currants** Currence
4.4. 12 Digest it Digest   **13 swoon** sworne   **60 a fire** o'fire   **83 bastards. Of** bastards) of   **93 scion** Sien   **98 your** you   **160 out** on't   **218** AUTOLYCUS [not in F]   **244 kilnhole** kill-hole   **297** AUTOLYCUS [in F, appears at line 298]   **299 Whither** Whether [and similarly throughout song]   **310 gentleman** Gent.   **316 cape** Crpe   **339 square** squire   **355 reply, at least** reply at least,   **361 who** whom   **421 acknowledged** acknowledge   **425 who** whom   **430 see** neuer see   **441 hoop** hope   **470 your** my   **473 sight as yet, I fear.** sight, as yet I feare;   **485–6 fancy. If . . . obedient, I** fancie, if . . . obedient: I   **503 our** her   **614 could** would   **filed** fill'd   **off** of   **644 flayed** fled   **708 know not** know   **738 to** at   **833 s.d.** *Exeunt* [at 845 in F]
5.1. 6 Whilst Whilest [also at line 169]   **59 Where . . . appear** (Where we Offendors now appeare)   **61 just** just such   **75 I have done** [assigned in F to Cleomenes]   **84 s.d.** *Gentleman Seruant*   **85** [and through line 110] GENTLEMAN, *Ser.*   **114 s.d.** *Exit* [after "us" in line 115 in F]   **160 his, parting** his parting
5.2. 113 s.d. *Exeunt Exit*
5.3. 18 Lonely Louely   **67 fixture** fixure

The Tempest

Copy text: the First Folio. Characters' names are groups at the heads of scenes throughout. Act and scene divisions are as marked in the Folio.
Names of the Actors [printed in F at the end of the play]
1.1. 8.1 Ferdinand *Ferdinando*   **34 s.d.** *Exeunt Exit*   **36** [and elsewhere] **wi' the** with   **38.1** [at line 37 in F]
1.2. 99 exact, like exact. Like   **166 steaded much.** steeded much,   **174 princes** Princesse   **201 bowsprit** Bore-spritt   **213 me. The** me the   **230 Bermudas** *Bermoothes*   **284 she** he   **288 service. Thou** service, thou   **330 forth at** for that   **377.5, 399.1 Ariel's** Ariel (or Ariell)   **385 s.d. Burden, dispersedly** [before "Hark, hark!" in line 384 in F]   **387** [F provides a speech prefix, *Ar.*]   **400** ARIEL [not in F]
2.1. 38 ANTONIO *Seb.*   **39** SEBASTIAN *Ant.*   **183 mettle** mettal   **232 throes** throwes
2.2. 9 mow moe   **116 spirits** sprights
3.1. 2 sets set
3.2. 51–2 isle; / From me he Isle / From me, he   **123 scout** cout
3.3. 15 travel trauaile   **17.1–2 Solemn . . . invisible** [after "they are fresh" in F, and followed by the s.d. at line 19, *Enter . . . depart*]   **28 me** me?   **29 islanders?** Islands;   **33 human** humaine   **65 plume** plumbe
4.1. 9 off of   **13 gift** guest   **25 love as 'tis now, the** loue, as 'tis now the   **61 vetches** Fetches   **68 poll-clipped** pole-clipt   **74 Her** here   **110** CERES [not in F]   **124.1–2** [after line 127 in F]   **163.1 Exeunt** *Exit*   **193 s.d. Enter Ariel . . . etc.** [after "on this line" in F, and followed by *Enter* Caliban . . . *all wet*]   **193 them on** on them   **232 Let't** let's

5.1. 60 boiled boile   **72 Didst** Did   **75 entertained** entertaine   **82 lies** ly   **88** ARIEL [not in F]   **111 Whe'er** Where   **236 horrible,** horrible.   **238 her** our   **249 business. At** businesse, at   **250 Which . . . single** (Which shall be shortly single)   **260 coraggio** Corasio

The Two Noble Kinsmen

Copy text: the Quarto of 1634. Act and scene divisions follow Q except at 2.1.48, where Q indicates "Scaena 2." Subsequently, "Scaena 3" and the first "Scaena 4" in the Q text of Act 2 are renumbered in this edition as scenes 2 and 3; the second "Scaena 4" in Q corresponds to scene 4 in this edition, perhaps suggesting that the earlier Q markings at "Scaena 3" and the first "Scaena 4" are in error. Act 3 scenes 5 and 6 are misnumbered "6" and "7" in Q, skipping "5" in error.
Prologue. 1 PROLOGUE [not in Q]   **26 tack** *take*   **29 travail** *travell*
1.1. 0.1 Music [after the s.d. in Q, together with indication of "The Song"]   **0.7 Pirithous** Theseus   **1** BOY [not in Q]   **6 thyme** *Time*   **7 firstborn child** *firstborne, child*   **13–14 children sweet / Lie** *children:sweete- / Ly*   **16 angel** *angle*   **20 chough hoar** *Clough hee*   **41 talons** Tallents   **59 Capaneus was your lord; the** *Capaneus,* was your Lord the   **68 Nemean** Nenuan   **90 thy** the   **104 willing way** willing, way   **112 pebbles** peobles   **glassy** glasse   **113 'em. Lady, lady, alack!** 'em (Lady, Lady, alacke)   **123 grief, indeed** greefe indeed   **132 longer** long   **138 move** mooves   **ospreys** Asprayes   **142 drams, precipitance** drams precipitance   **156 Rinsing** Wrinching   **159 Artesius** *Artesuis*   **178 twinning** twyning   **211 soldier. [To Artesius] As before, hence** Soldier (as before) hence   **212 Aulis** Anly   **218.1 [The marriage . . . temple** *Exeunt towards the Temple*   **225.1 Exeunt** [*in procession*] [no s.d. in Q; see textual note at 218.1]
1.2. 41 are here were are, here were   **42 be, mere** be meere   **55 canon** Cannon   **65 power there's nothing; almost** power: there's nothing, almost   **70 glory; one** glory on; [Q corr.], glory on [Q uncorr.]
1.3. 31 one ore   **54 eleven** a eleven   **Flavina** *Flauia*   **58–64** [Q, in left margin, prints: "2. Hearses rea- / dy with Pala- / mon: and Arci- / te: the 3. / Queenes: / Theseus: and / his Lordes / ready."]   **65 not, condemned**—not condemd   **73 happily her careless wear—I** happely, her careles, were, I   **75 one** on   **76 musical** misicall   **79 seely innocence** fury-innocent   **82 dividual** iudividuall   **out** ont
1.4. 13 s.d. [after 13 in Q]   **18 smeared** [Q corr.; succard, Q uncorr.]   **22 Wi'** We   **26** [Q prints s.d. in margin: "3. Hearses rea- / dy."]   **39 do—for** doe for   **40 friends' behests** friends, beheastes   **41 Love's provocations** Loves, provocations   **45 O'er-wrestling** Or wrastling   **49 'fore** for
1.5. 10 We convent . . . woes *We convent, &C.*
2.1. 16.1 Enter . . . Daughter [after "her?" in line 14 in Q]   **20 that now. So** that. / Now, so   **31 grece** greise   **51.1 Enter . . . above** [after "the night" in line 50 in Q]
2.2. 0 [Q reads: "Scaena 2. Enter Palamon, and Arcite in prison."]   **3 war; yet we** warre yet, we   **20 us. Our** us, our   **21 wore** were   **22 Ravished** Bravishd   **64 twinned** twyn'd   **118 This . . . in 't** [printed as the continuation of Arcite's speech in Q]   **129 will't** wilt   **132 was I** I was   **192 your blood** you blood   **223.1 Jailer** *Keeper* [also in s.p. and s.d. at lines 227, 228, 230, 231 s.d., 249.1, and 251 to end of scene]   **243 apricot** Apricocke   **275 you** yon
2.3. 6 sins [Q corr.; fins, Q uncorr.]   **25** FIRST COUNTRYMAN 1 [and so throughout scene]   **44 ye** yet   **59 says** sees   **87 Well I** Well, I
2.4. 34 night; ere night, ere
2.5. [Q marks as "Scaena 4"]   **0.1 [A] This** [s.d. is in margin in Q]   **28 For** Fo
2.6. 3 him. To him to   **12–13 it; / I** it / I   **15–16 dirge, / And** Dirge. / And
3.1. 2 laund land   **11 presence; in** presence, in   **13 thought! Thrice** thought, thrice   **36 looked, the** lookd the   **void'st** voydes   **36–7 honor / That** honour. That   **38 kin! Call'st** kin, call'st   **42 Not** Nor   **96.1 off. Cornets** *of Cornets* [s.d. is placed after line 95 in Q]   **97 muset** Musicke   **107 not** nor   **108 s.d. Wind horns** [after line 106 in Q]   **112 'Tis** If

3.2. 1 mistook the brake mistooke; the Beake   **7 reck** wreake   **19 fed** feed   **25 dozens** dussons   **28 brine** bine
3.3. 3.1 [after line 1 in Q]   **12 sir!** &c.   **24 them** then   **53 Sirrah—** Sir ha:
3.4. 9 Open Vpon   **10 tack** take   **19 a foot** afoote   **20 e'e** eie   **22 He s' buy** He's buy
3.5. [Q marks as "Scaena 6"]   **0.1 six** 4   **0.2 babion** and Baum   *five* 2. or 3   **8 jean** jave   **21 figure, trace and** figure trace, and   **33 babion** Bavian   **60 From** [on previous line in Q; Q prints *"Daughter"* in margin]   **64–5** [Q prints "Chaire and / stooles out" in margin]   **65–6** [printed on one line in Q; also lines 70–1]   **66 I come** come   **68 he said** sed   **94 s.d.** Wind horns [opposite line 92 in Q]   **96 s.d.** Exeunt . . . Schoolmaster [after "Away, boys!" in line 94 in Q]   **101 THESEUS** Per.   **134 beest-eating** beast eating   **135 Babion** Bavian   **139 SCHOOLMASTER** [not in Q]   **139.1** *Music* [Q prints *"Musicke Dance"* after line 138]   **139.2–3** *Enter . . . a morris* [Q prints "Knocke for / Schoole.Enter / The Dance." in margin at lines 139–41]   **141 ye** thee   **144 thee** three   **153 you** yon   **159.1** *Wind horns* [after "made" in line 160 in Q]   **160 deaeque** Deaeq;
3.6. Scaena 7.   **16 s.d.** Enter . . . swords [after "morrow" in line 16 in Q]   **armor** Armors   **39 spared. Your** spard, your   **86 strait** streight   **93 s.d. They . . . stand** [printed in margin at lines 93–5 in Q, keyed to an asterisk after "love" in line 93 in Q]   **112 die in. Gentle cousin,** dye in, gentle Cosen: **145 thine** this   **174–5 us; / As . . . valiant, for** us, / As . . . valiant; for   **228 it. If** it, if   **236 fail** fall   **240 name, opinion.** name; Opinion,   **242 prune** proyne   **272 must** muff   **279 PALAMON AND ARCITE** Both [also in line 280]   **285–6 excellent. / For** excellent / For
4.1. 11 oath o'th   **46 'Tis** [Q repeats s.p. here, *"Woo."*]   **63 sung** song   **84 wreath** wreake   **120 Far** For   **134 JAILER'S BROTHER** Daugh.   **141 SECOND FRIEND** 1. Fr.   **148 cheerly all.** cheerely. / All. [as s.p.]   **150 bowline** Bowling   **158 Tack** take
4.2. 16 Jove afire Love a fire   **25 such** sueh   **27 swart** swarth   **40 'em?** 'em   **49–50 Palamon. / Stand** Palamon, / Stand   **54.1** *Enter a Gentleman* Enter Emil. and Gent: **55 How** Emil. How   **70.1** *Enter a Messenger* Enter Messengers. Curtis [after line 69 in Q]   **76 first** fitst   **81 fire** faire   **104 ivy-tods** Ivy tops   **109 court** corect   **152 stay,** stay.
4.3. 1–39 [lined as verse in Q]   **8.1** *Enter . . . Daughter* [placed in Q after "business" in line 8]   **22 spirits are—there's** spirits, as the'rs   **32 i'th'other** i'th / Thother   **39 enough.** enough. Exit   **45 truth** troth   **punishment** [Q corr.; punishuent, Q uncorr.]   **49–50 engrafted** engraffed   **53 were** [Q corr.; weare, Q uncorr.]   **54 th'other** another   **55 behind** [Q corr.; behold, Q uncorr.]   **69 same** [Q corr.; Sawe, Q uncorr.]   **85 sweet flowers** [Q corr.; sweet, flowers, Q uncorr.]   **90 carve** crave   **96 falsehoods** fashoods
5.1. 0.1 *Flourish* [before *"Exeunt"* at 4.3.104 in Q]   **7.1** *Flourish of cornets* [after line 5 in Q]   **17.1** *Exeunt* Exit   **33.1** *Exeunt . . . knights* [after "coz." in line 33 in Q]   **37 father of** farther off   **46 cistern** Cestron   **51 Whose . . . prewarn** Comets prewarne, whose havocke in vaste Feild   **54 armipotent** armenypotent   **68 design march** designe; march   **boldly.** boldly, [Q corr.; boldly, Q uncorr.]   **76 Her** [Q corr.; His, Q corr.]   **91 than his; the** then his the   **118 Brief, I** briefe I   **119 done, no companion;** done; no Companion   **120 not, a defier;** not; a defyer   **121 cannot, a rejoicer.** cannot; a Rejoycer,   **130 O thou** Pal. O thou   **136 s.d.** They . . . bow [at line 134 in Q]   **is** his   **151 maiden-hearted. A** mayden harted, a   **154 election. Of** election of
5.2. 3 kept hept   **37 Yes** Yet   **40.1** [*mad*] Maide   **41 humor** honour   **55 tune** turne   **85 two coarse** too coarse
5.3. 0.1 *Flourish* [placed before *Exeunt* at 5.2.113 in Q]   **0.2** *attendants* Attendants, T. Tucke: Curtis   **3 decision. Ev'ry blow** decision ev'ry; blow   **16 prize** price   **54 him** them   **66 s.d.** Cornets . . . Palamon! [after line 64 in Q]   *Enter Servant* [after line 66 in Q]   **75 in't else; chance** in't; else chance   **77 s.d.** Another . . . cornets [after line 75 in Q]   **89 s.d.** Cornets. . . . Arcite!" [after line 88 in Q]   **92 s.d.** Cornets. . . . Victory!" [after line 91 in Q]   **121 all I** all; I   **136 lose** loose   **139 your** you   **146.1** *Flourish* [after "deliver" in line 138 in Q]
5.4. 0.2 etc. &c. Gard.   **1 PALAMON** [not in Q]   **10 unwappered, not halting** unwapper'd not, halting   **35 quit** quight   **38 s.d.** *lays* Lies

39 SECOND AND THIRD KNIGHTS 1.2.K.   **47 rarely** early   **69 manège** mannadge   **79 victor's** [victors, Q corr.; victoros, Q uncorr.]   **87 mighty, Arcite. If** mightie *Arcite*, if   **104 arrose** arowze   **107 Hath** Hast   **133–4 sorry, still, / Are** sorry still, / Are
Epilogue 1 EPILOGUE [not in Q]

Venus and Adonis
Copy text: the Quarto of 1593.
185 Souring So wring   **208 Speak, fair,** Speake fair   **304 whe'er** where   **457 marketh.** marketh,   **458 raineth,** raineth: **570 woos** woes   **621 shine when . . . fret;** shine, when . . . fret   **680 overshoot** ouer-shut   **748 th'** the th'   **873 twine** twin'd   **1013 stories** stories,   **1027 falcon** Faulcons   **1031 as** are   **1054 was** had

The Rape of Lucrece
Copy text: the corrected Quarto of 1594 [Q corr.]. A number of corrected readings are however rejected as sophistications; see text notes below at lines 31, 50, 125, 126.
24 morning's [Q corr., mornings] morning [Q uncorr.]   **31 apology** [Q uncorr.] Apologies [Q corr.]   **50 Collatium** [Q uncorr., Colatium] Colatia [Q corr.]   **57 beauty, in . . . entitulèd** Beautie in . . . entituled,   **58 doves, doth . . . field.** doues doth . . . field, [Q uncorr.] themselues betake [Q corr.]   **125 himself betakes** [Q uncorr.] themselues betake [Q corr.]   **126 wakes** [Q uncorr.] wake [Q corr.]   **550 blows** blow   **555 panteth** pateth   **560 wear** were   **650 sovereign, with . . . haste** soueraigne with . . . hast,   **688 lose** loose [also at lines 979 and 1158]   **922 inclination** inclination   **1126 Relish** Ralish   **1129 hair** heare   **1229 eyne, enforced** eien inforst,   **1249 remain** remaine.   **1251 peep** peepe,   **1263–4 ensue / By . . . wrong.** insue. / By . . . wrong,   **1312 schedule** Cedule   **1350 this pattern of the** the patterne of this [in four copies of Q; it is uncertain which is the corrected state]   **1386 far-off** farre of   **1475 Thine** Thy   **1543 travail** trauaile   **1544 too** to   **1580 Losing** Loosing   **1648 forbade** forbod   **1652 robbed** rob'd   **1660 here** heare   **1662 wreathèd** wretched   **1680 one woe** on woe   **1713 in it** it in   **1768 faltering** foultring

A Lover's Complaint
Copy text: the Sonnet Quarto of 1609 [Q].
7 sorrow's sorrowes,   **14 lattice** lettice   **37 beaded** bedded   **51 'gan** gaue   **95 wear** were   **103 breathe** breath   **112 manage** mannad'g   **118 Came** Can   **131 Consents** Consent's   **164 forbade** forbod   **182 woo** vovv   **198 pallid** palyd   **204 hair** heir   **205 metal** mettle   **228 Hallowed** Hollowed   **251 immured** enur'd   **252 procured** procure   **260 nun** Sunne   **293 Oh** Or   **303 strange** straing

The Sonnets
Copy text: the Quarto of 1609 [Q].
2.4 tattered totter'd [also at 26.11]   **2.14 cold** could   **6.4 beauty's** beautits   **8.10 Strikes** Strike [in some copies]   **12.4 all** or   **13.7 Yourself** You selfe   **15.8 wear** were   **17.12 meter** miter   **17.14 twice, in it and** twice in it, and   **18.10** [and elsewhere] lose   loose   **19.3 jaws** yawes   **20.2 Hast** Haste   **22.3 furrows** forrwes   **23.6 rite** right   **23.14 with** wit   **wit** wiht   **24.1 stelled** steeld   **25.9 fight** worth   **26.12 thy** their [also at 27.10, 35.8 (twice), 37.7, 43.11, 45.12, 46.3, 46.8, 46.13, 46.14, 69.5, 70.6, 85.3, 128.11, 128.14]   **27.2 travel** trauaill   **28.12 gild'st** guil'st   **28.14 strength** length   **31.8 thee** there   **34.2 travel** trauaile   **34.12 cross** losse   **34.13 sheds** sheds   **38.2 pour'st** poor'st   **38.3 too** to   **39.12 doth** dost   **41.7 woos** woes   **42.10 losing** loosing   **44.12 attend time's** attend, times   **44.13 naught** naughts   **45.9 life's** liues   **46.9 'cide** side   **46.12 the** he [in some copies]   **47.2 other.** other,   **47.4 smother,** smother;   **47.11 no** nor   **50.6 dully** duly   **51.10 perfect'st** perfects

55.1 monuments monument   **56.3 [and elsewhere] today** too daie
58.7 patience-tame to suffrance, patience tame, to sufferance
59.6 hundred hundreth   **59.11 whe'er** where   **61.14 off** of   **too** to
62.10 chapped chopt   **63.5 traveled** trauaild   **65.12 of** or
67.6 seeming seeing   **69.3 due** end   **69.14 soil** sole   **71.13 Lest**
Least [also at 72.1, 72.9, and elsewhere]   **73.4 ruined** rn'wd   **choirs**
quiers   **76.7 tell** fel   **77.1 wear** were   **77.10 blanks** blacks
82.8 these the   **83.7 too** to   **88.8 losing** loosing   **90.11 shall** stall
91.9 better bitter   **93.5 there** their   **98.11 were** weare   **99.4 dwells**
dwells?   **99.9 One** Our   **99.13 ate** eate   **102.8 her** his   **106.12 skill**
still   **111.1 with** wish   **112.14 are** y'are   **113.6 latch** lack
113.13 more, replete with more repleat, with   **113.14 mine eye**
mine   **116** [numbered 119 in Q]   **117.10 surmise accumulate;**
surmise, accumilate   **118.5 ne'er-cloying** nere cloying   **118.10 were**
not, grew were, not grew   **119.4 losing** loosing   **121.11 bevel.** beuel
125.6 rent, rent   **125.7 sweet forgoing** sweet; Forgoing   **126.2 sickle**
hour; sickle, hower: **126.8 minutes** mynuit   **127.2 were** weare
127.10 brows eyes   **129.9 Mad** Made   **129.10 quest to have,** quest,
to haue   **129.11 proved, a** proud and   **132.6 the east** th' East
132.9 mourning morning   **138.12 to have** t' haue   **140.5 were** weare
144.6 side [adopted from *The Passionate Pilgrim*] sight   **144.9 fiend**
[adopted from *The Passionate Pilgrim*] finde   **146.2 Thrall to** My
sinfull earth   **147.7 approve** approoue.   **153.14 eyes** eye

Glossary

Shakespearean Words and Meanings of Frequent Occurrence

A

'A: he (unaccented form).

Abate: lessen, diminish; blunt, reduce; deprive; bar, leave out of account, except; depreciate; humble.

Abuse (N): insult, error, misdeed, offense, crime; imposture, deception; also the modern sense.

Abuse (V): deceive, misapply, put to a bad use; maltreat; frequently the modern sense.

Addition: something added to one's name to denote rank; mark of distinction; title.

Admiration: wonder; object of wonder.

Admire: wonder at.

Advantage (N): profit, convenience, benefit; opportunity, favorable opportunity; pecuniary profit; often shades toward the modern sense.

Advantage (V): profit, be of benefit to, benefit; augment.

Advice: reflection, consideration, deliberation, consultation.

Affect: aim at, aspire to, incline toward; be fond of, be inclined; love; act upon contagiously (as a disease). (PAST PART.) **Affected**: disposed, inclined, in love, loved.

Affection: passion, love; emotion, feeling, mental tendency, disposition; wish, inclination; affectation.

Alarum: signal calling soldiers to arms (in stage directions).

An: if; but; **an if:** if, though, even if.

Anon: at once, soon; presently, by and by.

Answer: return, requite; atone for; render an account of, account for; obey, agree with; also the modern sense.

Apparent: evident, plain; seeming.

Argument: subject, theme, reason, cause; story; excuse.

As: according as; as far as; namely; as if; in the capacity of; that; so that; that is, that they.

Assay: try, attempt; accost, address; challenge.

Atone: reconcile; set at one.

Attach: arrest, seize.

Aweful, awful: commanding reverential fear or respect; profoundly respectful or reverential.

B

Band: bond, fetters, manacle (leash for a dog). **Band** and **bond** are etymologically the same word; **band** was formerly used in both senses.

Basilisk: fabulous reptile said to kill by its look. The basilisk of popular superstition was a creature with legs, wings, a serpentine and winding tail, and a crest or comb somewhat like a cock. It was the offspring of a cock's egg hatched under a toad or serpent.

Bate: blunt, abate, reduce; deduct, except.

Battle: army; division of an army.

Beshrew: curse, blame; used as a mild curse, "Bad or ill luck to."

Bias: tendency, bent, inclination, swaying influence; term in bowling applied to the form of the bowl, the oblique line in which it runs, and the kind of impetus given to cause it to run obliquely.

Blood: nature, vigor; supposed source of emotion; passion; spirit, animation; one of the four humors (see **humor**).

Boot (N): advantage, profit; something given in addition to the bargain; booty, plunder.

Boot (V): profit, avail.

Brave (ADJ.): fine, gallant; splendid, finely arrayed, showy; ostentatiously defiant.

Brave (V): challenge, defy; make splendid.

Brook: tolerate, endure.

C

Can: can do; know; be skilled; sometimes used for *did*.

Capable: comprehensive; sensible, impressible, susceptible; capable of; gifted, intelligent.

Careful: anxious, full of care; provident; attentive.

Carry: manage, execute; be successful, win; conquer; sustain; endure.

Censure (N): judgment, opinion; critical opinion, unfavorable opinion.

Censure (V): judge, estimate; pass sentence or judgment.

Character (N): writing, printing, record; handwriting; cipher; face, features (bespeaking inward qualities).

Character (V): write, engrave, inscribe.

Check (N): reproof; restraint.

Check (V): reprove, restrain, keep from; control.

Circumstance: condition, state of affairs, particulars; adjunct details; detailed narration, argument, or discourse; formality, ceremony.

Clip: embrace; surround.

Close: secret, private; concealed; uncommunicative; enclosed.

Cog: cheat.

Coil: noise, disturbance, turmoil; fuss, to-do, bustle.

Color: appearance; pretext, pretense; excuse.

Companion: fellow (used contemptuously).

Complete: accomplished, fully endowed; perfect, perfect in quality; also frequently the modern sense.

Complexion: external appearance; temperament, disposition; the four complexions—sanguine, choleric, phlegmatic, and melancholy—corresponding to the four humors (see **humor**); also the modern sense.

Composition: compact, agreement, constitution.

Compound: settle, agree.

Conceit: conception, idea, thought; mental faculty, wit; fancy, imagination; opinion, estimate; device, invention, design.

Condition: temperament, disposition; characteristic, property, quality; social or official position, rank or status; covenant, treaty, contract.

Confound: waste, spend, invalidate, destroy; undo, ruin; mingle indistinguishably, mix, blend.

Confusion: destruction, overthrow, ruin; mental agitation.

Continent: that which contains or encloses; earth, globe; sum, summary.

Contrive: plot; plan; spend or pass (time).

Conversation: conduct, deportment; social intercourse, association.

Converse: hold intercourse; associate with, have to do with.

Cope: encounter, meet; have to do with.

Copy: model, pattern; example; minutes or memoranda.

Cousin: any relative not belonging to one's immediate family.

Cry you mercy: beg your pardon.

Cuckold: husband whose wife is unfaithful.

Curious: careful, fastidious; anxious, concerned; made with care, skillfully, intricately, or daintily wrought; particular.

Cursed, curst: shrewish, perverse, spiteful.

D

Dainty: minute; scrupulous, particular; particular about (with **of**); refined, elegant; also the modern sense.

Date: duration, termination, term of existence; limit or end of a term or period, term.

Dear: precious; best; costly; important; affectionate; hearty; grievous, dire; also the modern sense.

Debate: discuss; fight.

Decay (N): downfall, ruin; cause of ruin.

Decay (V): perish, be destroyed; destroy.

Defeat (N): destruction, ruin.

Defeat (V): destroy, disfigure, ruin.

Defy: challenge, challenge to a fight; reject; despise.

Demand (N): inquiry; request.

Demand (V): inquire, question; request.

Deny: refuse (to do something); refuse permission; refuse to accept; refuse admittance; disown.

Depart (N): departure.

Depart (V): part; go away from, leave, quit; take leave (of one another); **depart with, withal:** part with, give up.

Derive: gain, obtain; draw upon, direct (to); descend; pass by descent, be descended or inherited; trace the origin of.

Difference: diversity of opinion, disagreement, dissension, dispute; characteristic or distinguishing feature; alteration or addition to a coat of arms to distinguish a younger or lateral branch of a family.

Digest: arrange, perfect; assimilate, amalgamate; disperse, dissipate; comprehend, understand; put up with (FIG. from the physical sense of digesting food).

Discourse (N): reasoning, reflection; talk, act of conversing, conversation; faculty of conversing; familiar intercourse; relating (as by speech).

Discourse (V): speak, talk, converse; pass (the time) in talk; say, utter, tell, give forth; narrate, relate.

Discover: uncover, expose to view; divulge, reveal, make known; spy out, reconnoiter; betray; distinguish, discern; also the modern sense.

Dispose (N): disposal; temperament, bent of mind, disposition; external manner.

Dispose (V): distribute, manage, make use of; deposit, put or stow away; regulate, order, direct; come to terms. (PAST PART.) **Disposed:** in a good frame of mind; inclined to be merry.

Dispute: discuss, reason; strive against, resist.

Distemper (V): disturb; (N): disorder, ill humor; illness.

Doit: old Dutch coin, one-half an English farthing.

Doubt (N): suspicion, apprehension; fear, danger, risk; also the modern sense.

Doubt (V): suspect, apprehend; fear; also the modern sense.

Doubtful: inclined to suspect, suspicious, apprehensive; not to be relied on; almost certain.

Duty: reverence, respect, expression of respect; submission to authority, obedience; due.

E

Earnest: money paid as an installment to secure a bargain; partial payment; often used with *quibble* in the modern sense.

Ease: comfort, assistance, leisure; idleness, sloth, inactivity; also the modern sense.

Ecstasy: frenzy, madness, state of being beside oneself, excitement, bewilderment; swoon; rapture.

Element: used to refer to the simple substances of which all material bodies were thought to be composed; specifically earth, air, fire, and water, corresponding to the four humors (see **humor**); atmosphere, sky; atmospheric agencies or powers; that one of the four elements which is the natural abode of a creature; hence, natural surroundings, sphere.

Engage: pledge, pawn, mortgage; bind by a promise, swear to; entangle, involve; enlist; embark on an enterprise.

Engine: mechanical contrivance; artifice, device, plot.

Enlarge: give free scope to; set at liberty, release.

Entertain: keep up, maintain, accept; take into one's service; treat; engage (someone's) attention or thought; occupy, while or pass away pleasurably; engage (as an enemy); receive.

Envious: malicious, spiteful, malignant.

Envy: ill-will, malice; hate; also the modern sense.

Even: uniform; direct, straightforward; exact, precise; equable, smooth, comfortable; equal, equally balanced.

Event: outcome; affair, business; also frequently the modern sense.

Exclaim: protest, rail; accuse, blame (with **on**), reproach.

Excursion: stage battle or skirmish (in stage directions).

Excuse: seek to extenuate (a fault); maintain the innocence of; clear oneself, justify or vindicate oneself; decline.

F

Fact: deed, act; crime.

Faction: party, class, group, set (of persons); party strife, dissension; factious quarrel, intrigue.

Fail: die, die out; err, be at fault; omit, leave undone.

Fair (N): fair thing; one of the fair sex; someone beloved; beauty (the abstract concept).

Fair (ADJ.): just; clear, distinct; beautiful; of light complexion or color of hair.

Fair (ADV): fairly.

Fairly: beautifully, handsomely; courteously, civilly; properly, honorably, honestly; becomingly, appropriately; favorably, fortunately; softly, gently, kindly.

Fall: let fall, drop; happen, come to pass; befall; shades frequently toward the modern senses.

Falsely: wrongly; treacherously; improperly.

Fame: report; rumor; reputation.

Familiar (N): intimate friend; familiar or attendant spirit, demon associated with, and obedient to, a person.

Familiar (ADJ.): intimate, friendly; belonging to household or family, domestic; well-known; habitual, ordinary, trivial; plain, easily understood.

Fancy: fantasticalness; imaginative conception, flight of imagination; amorous inclination or passion, love; liking, taste.

Fantasy: fancy, imagination; caprice, whim.

Favor: countenance, face; complexion; aspect, appearance; leave, permission, pardon; attraction, charm, good will; **in favor:** benevolently.

Fear (N): dread, apprehension; dreadfulness; object of dread or fear.

Fear (V): be apprehensive or concerned about, mistrust, doubt; frighten, make afraid.

Fearful: exciting or inspiring fear, terrible, dreadful; timorous, apprehensive, full of fear.

Feature: shape or form of body, figure; shapeliness, comeliness.

Fellow: companion; partaker, sharer (of); equal, match; customary form of address to a servant or an inferior (sometimes used contemptuously or condescendingly).

Fine (N): end, conclusion; **in fine:** finally.

Fine (ADJ.): highly accomplished or skillful; exquisitely fashioned, delicate; refined, subtle; frequently the modern sense.

Flaw: fragment; crack, fissure; tempest, squall, gust of wind; outburst of passion.

Flesh (V): reward a hawk or hound with a piece of flesh of the game killed to excite its eagerness of the chase; hence, to inflame by a foretaste of success; initiate or inure to bloodshed (used for a first time in battle); harden, train.

Flourish: fanfare of trumpets (in stage directions).

Fond: foolish, doting; **fond of:** eager for; also the modern sense.

Fool: term of endearment and pity; frequently the modern sense.

For that, for why: because.

Forfend: forbid, avert.

Free: generous, magnanimous; candid, open; guiltless, innocent.

Front: forehead, face; foremost line of battle; beginning.

Furnish: equip, fit out (furnish forth); endow; dress, decorate, embellish.

G

Gear: apparel, dress; stuff, substance, thing, article; discourse, talk; matter, business, affair.

Get: beget.

Gloss: specious fair appearance; lustrous surface.

Go to: expression of remonstrance, impatience, disapprobation, or derision.

Grace (N): kindness, favor, charm, divine favor; fortune, luck; beneficent virtue; sense of duty or propriety; mercy, pardon; embellish; **do grace:** reflect credit on, do honor to, do a favor for.

Grace (V): gratify, delight; honor, favor.

Groat: coin equal to four pence.

H

Habit: dress, garb, costume; bearing, demeanor, manner; occasionally in the modern sense.

Happily: haply, perchance, perhaps; fortunately.

Hardly: with difficulty.

Have at: I shall come at (you) (i.e., listen to me), I shall attack (a person or thing); let me at.

Have with: I shall go along with; let me go along with; come along.

Having: possession, property, wealth, estate; endowments, accomplishments.

Head: armed force.

Hind: servant, slave; rustic, boor, clown.

His: its. **His** was historically the possessive form of both the masculine and neuter pronouns. **Its,** although not common in Shakespeare's time, occurs in the plays occasionally.

Holp: helped (archaic past tense).

Home: fully, satisfactorily, thoroughly, plainly, effectually; to the quick.

Honest: holding an honorable position, honorable, respectable; decent, kind, seemly, befitting, proper; chaste; genuine; loosely used as an epithet of approbation.

Humor: mood, temper, cast of mind, temperament, disposition; vagary, fancy, whim; moisture (the literal sense); a physiological and, by transference, a psychological term applied to the four chief fluids of the human body—phlegm, blood, bile or choler, and black bile or melancholy. A person's disposition and temporary state of mind were determined according to the relative proportions of these fluids in the body; consequently, a person was said to be phlegmatic, sanguine, choleric, or melancholy.

I

Image: likeness; visible form; representation; embodiment, type; mental picture, creation of the imagination.

Influence: supposed flowing from the stars or heavens of an ethereal fluid, acting upon the characters and destinies of men (used metaphorically).

Inform: take shape, give form to, imbue, inspire; instruct, teach; charge (against).

Instance: evidence, proof, sign, confirmation; motive, cause.

Invention: power of mental creation, the creative faculty; work of the imagination, artistic creation, premeditated design; device, plan, scheme.

J

Jar (N): discord in music; quarrel, discord.

Jar (V): be out of tune; be discordant, quarrel.

Jump: agree, tally, coincide, fit exactly; risk, hazard.

K

Keep: continue, carry on; dwell, lodge, guard, defend, care for, employ, be with; restrain, control; confine in prison.

Kind (N): nature, established order of things; manner, fashion, respect; race, class, kindred, family; **by kind:** naturally.

Kind (ADJ.): natural; favorable; affectionate.

Kindly (ADJ.): natural, appropriate; agreeable; innate; benign.

Kindly (ADV): naturally; gently, courteously.

L

Large: liberal, bounteous, lavish; free, unrestrained; **at large:** at length, in full; in full detail, as a whole, in general.

Late: lately.

Learn: teach; inform (someone of something); also the modern sense.

Let: hinder.

Level: aim; also shades toward the modern sense.

Liberal: possessed of the characteristics and qualities of wellborn persons; genteel, becoming, refined; free in speech; unrestrained by prudence or decorum; licentious.

Lie: be in bed; be still; be confined, be kept in prison; dwell, sojourn, reside, lodge.

Like: please, feel affection; liken, compare.

List (N): strip of cloth, selvedge; limit, boundary; desire.

List (V): choose, desire, please; listen to.

Liver: the seat of love and of violent passions generally (see also **spleen**).

'Long of: owing to, on account of.

Look: power to see; take care, see to it; expect; seek, search for.

M

Make: do; have to do (with); consider; go; be effective, make up, complete; also the modern sense.

Manage: management, conduct, administration; action and paces to which a horse is trained; short gallop at full speed.

Marry: mild interjection equivalent to "Indeed!" Originally, an oath by the Virgin Mary.

May: can; also frequently the modern sense to denote probability; **might** has corresponding meanings and uses.

Mean, means (N): instrument, agency, method; effort; opportunity (for doing something); something interposed or intervening; money, wealth (frequently in the plural form); middle position, medium; tenor or alto part in singing (usually in the singular form).

Mean (ADJ.): average, moderate, middle; of low degree, station, or position; undignified, base.

Measure (N): grave or stately dance, graceful motion; tune, melody, musical accompaniment; treatment meted out; moderation, proportion; limit; distance, reach.

Measure (V): judge, estimate; traverse.

Mere: absolute, sheer; pure, unmixed; downright, sincere.

Mew (up): coop up (as used of a hawk), shut up, imprison, confine.

Mind (N): thoughts, judgment, opinion; message; purpose, intention, desire; disposition; also the modern sense of the mental faculty.

Mind (V): remind; perceive, notice, attend; intend.

Minion: saucy woman, hussy; follower; favorite, favored person, darling (often used contemptuously).

Misdoubt (N): suspicion.

Misdoubt (V): mistrust, suspect.

Model: pattern, replica, likeness.

Modern: ordinary, commonplace, everyday.

Modest: moderate, marked by moderation, becoming; characterized by decency and propriety; chaste.

Moiety: half; share; small part, lesser share; portion, part of.

Mortal: fatal; deadly, of or for death; belonging to mankind; human, pertaining to human affairs.

Motion: power of movement; suggestion, proposal; movement of the soul; impulse, prompting; also the modern sense.

Move: make angry; urge, incite, instigate, arouse, prompt; propose, make a proposal to, apply to, appeal to, suggest; also the modern sense.

Muse: wonder, marvel; grumble, complain.

N

Napkin: handkerchief.

Natural: related by blood; having natural or kindly feeling; also the modern sense.

Naught: useless, worthless; wicked, naughty.

Naughty: wicked; good for nothing, worthless.

Nerves: sinews.

Nice: delicate; fastidious, dainty, particular, scrupulous; minute, subtle; shy, coy; reluctant, unwilling; unimportant, insignificant, trivial; accurate, precise; wanton, lascivious.

Nothing (ADJ.): not at all.

O

Of: from, away from; during; on; by; as regards; instead of; **out of:** compelled by; made from.

Offer: make an attack; menace; venture, dare, presume.

Opinion: censure; reputation or credit; favorable estimate of oneself; self-conceit, arrogance; self-confidence; public opinion, reputation; also the modern sense.

Or: before; also used conjunctively where no alternative is implied; **or . . . or:** either . . . or; whether . . . or.

Out (ADV): without, outside; abroad; fully, quite; at an end, finished; at variance, aligned the wrong way.

Out (INTERJ.): an expression of reproach, impatience, indignation, or anger.

Owe: own; also the modern sense.

P

Pack (V): load; depart, begone; conspire.

Pageant: show, spectacle, spectacular entertainment; device on a moving carriage.

Pain: punishment, penalty; labor, trouble, effort; also frequently the modern sense.

Painted: specious, unreal, counterfeit.

Parle (N): parley, conference, talk; bugle call for parley.

Part (v): depart, part from; divide.

Particular (N): detail; personal interest or concern; details of a private nature; single person.

Party: faction, side, part, cause; partner, ally.

Pass (v): pass through, traverse; exceed; surpass; pledge.

Passing (ADJ. and ADV.): surpassing, surpassingly, exceedingly.

Passion (N): powerful or violent feeling, violent sorrow or grief; painful affection or disorder of the body; sorrow; feelings or desires of love; passionate speech or outburst.

Passion (v): sorrow, grieve.

Peevish: silly, senseless, childish; perverse, obstinate, stubborn; sullen.

Perforce: by violence or compulsion; forcibly; necessarily.

Phoenix: mythical Arabian bird believed to be the only one of its kind; it lived five or six hundred years, after which it burned itself to ashes and reemerged to live through another cycle.

Physic: medical faculty; healing art, medical treatment; remedy, medicine, healing property.

Pitch: height; specifically, the height to which a falcon soars before swooping on its prey (often used figuratively); tarlike substance.

Policy: conduct of affairs (especially public affairs); prudent management; stratagem, trick; contrivance; craft, cunning.

Port: bearing, demeanor; state, style of living, social station; gate.

Possess: have or give possession or command (of something); inform, acquaint; also the modern sense.

Post (N): courier, messenger; post-horse; haste.

Post (v): convey swiftly; hasten, ignore through haste (with **over** or **off**).

Practice (N): execution; exercise (especially for instruction); stratagem, intrigue; conspiracy, plot, treachery.

Practice (v): perform, take part in; use stratagem, craft, or artifice; scheme, plot; play a joke on.

Pregnant: resourceful; disposed, inclined; clear, obvious.

Present (ADJ.): ready, immediate, prompt, instant.

Present (v): represent.

Presently: immediately, at once.

Prevent: forestall, anticipate, foresee; also the modern sense.

Process: drift, tenor, gist; narrative, story; formal command, mandate.

Proof: test, trial, experiment; experience; issue, result; proved or tested strength of armor or arms; also the modern sense.

Proper: (one's or its) own; peculiar, exclusive; excellent; honest, respectable; handsome, elegant, fine, good-looking.

Proportion: symmetry; size; form, carriage, appearance, shape; portion, allotment; rhythm.

Prove: make trial of; put to test; show or find out by experience.

Purchase (N): acquisition; spoil, booty.

Purchase (v): acquire, gain, obtain; strive, exert oneself; redeem, exempt.

Q

Quaint: skilled, clever; pretty, fine, dainty; handsome, elegant; carefully or ingeniously wrought or elaborated.

Quality: that which constitutes (something); essential being; good natural gifts; accomplishment, attainment, property; art, skill; rank, position; profession, occupation, business; party, side; manner, style; cause, occasion.

Quick: living (used substantively to mean "living flesh"); alive; lively, sharp, piercing; hasty, impatient; with child.

Quillets: verbal niceties, subtle distinctions.

Quit: requite, reward; set at liberty; acquit, remit; pay for, clear off.

R

Rack (v): stretch or strain beyond normal extent or capacity to endure; strain oneself; distort.

Rage (N): madness, insanity; vehement pain; angry disposition; violent passion or appetite; poetic enthusiasm; warlike ardor or fury.

Rage (v): behave wantonly or riotously; act with fury or violence; enrage; pursue furiously.

Range: extend or lie in the same plane (with); occupy a position; rove, roam; be inconstant; traverse.

Rank (ADJ.): coarsely luxuriant; puffed up, swollen, fat, abundant; full, copious; rancid; lustful; corrupt, foul.

Rate (N): estimate; value or worth; estimation, consideration; standard, style.

Rate (v): allot; calculate, estimate, compute; reckon, consider; be of equal value (with); chide, scold, berate; drive away by chiding or scolding.

Recreant (N): traitor, coward, cowardly wretch (also as ADJ.).

Remorse: pity, compassion; also the modern sense.

Remove: removal, absence; period of absence; change.

Require: ask, inquire of, request.

Resolve: dissolve, melt, dissipate; answer; free from doubt or uncertainty, convince; inform; decide; also the modern sense.

Respect (N): consideration, reflection, act of seeing, view; attention, notice; decency, modest deportment; also the modern sense.

Respect (v): esteem, value, prize; regard, consider; heed, pay attention to; also the modern sense.

Round: spherical; plain, direct, brusque; fair; honest.

Roundly: plainly, unceremoniously.

Rub: obstacle (a term in the game of bowls); unevenness; inequality.

S

Sack: generic term for Spanish and Canary wines; sweet white wine.

Sad: grave, serious; also the modern sense.

Sadness: seriousness; also the modern sense.

Sans: without (French preposition).

Scope: object, aim, limit; freedom, license; free play.

Seal: bring to completion or conclusion; conclude, confirm, ratify, stamp; also the modern sense.

Sennet: a series of notes sounded on a trumpet to herald the approach or departure of a procession (used in stage directions).

Sense: mental faculty, mind; mental perception, import, rational meaning; physical perception; sensual nature; **common sense:** ordinary or untutored perception, observation or knowledge.

Sensible: capable of physical feeling or perception, sensitive; capable of or exhibiting emotion; rational; capable of being perceived.

Serve: be sufficient; be favorable; succeed; satisfy the need for; serve a turn; answer the purpose.

Several: separate, distinct, different; particular, private; various.

Shadow: shade, shelter; reflection; likeness, image; ghost; representation, picture of the imagination, phantom; also the modern sense.

Shift: change; stratagem, strategy, trick, contrivance, device to serve a purpose; **make shift:** manage.

Shrewd: malicious, mischievous, ill-natured; shrewish; bad, of evil import, grievous; severe.

Sirrah: ordinary or customary form of address to inferiors or servants; disrespectful form of address.

Sith: since.

Smock: woman's undergarment; used typically for "a woman."

Something: somewhat.

Sometime: sometimes, from time to time; once, formerly; at times, at one time.

Speed (N): fortune, success; protecting and assisting power; also the modern sense.

Speed (v): fare (well or ill); succeed; be successful; assist, guard, favor.

Spleen: the seat of emotions and passions; violent passion; fiery temper; malice; anger, rage; impulse, fit of passion; caprice; impetuosity (see also **liver**).

Spoil: destruction, ruin; plunder; slaughter, massacre.

Starve: die of cold or hunger; be benumbed with cold; paralyze, disable; allow or cause to die.

State: degree, rank; social position, station; pomp, splendor, outward display, clothes; court, household of a great person; shades into the modern sense.

Stay: wait, wait for; sustain; stand; withhold, withstand; stop.

Stead: assist; be of use to, benefit, help.

Still: always, ever, continuously or continually, constant or constantly; silent, mute; also modern senses.

Stomach: appetite, inclination, disposition; resentment; angry temper, resentful feeling; proud spirit, courage.

Straight: immediately.

Strange: belonging to another country or person, foreign, unfriendly; new, fresh; ignorant; estranged.

Success: issue, outcome (good or bad); sequel, succession, descent (as from father to son).

Suggest: tempt; prompt; seduce.

Suggestion: temptation.

T

Table: memorandum, tablet; surface on which something is written or drawn.

Take: strike; bewitch; charm; infect; destroy; repair to for refuge; modern senses.

Tall: goodly, fine; strong in fight, valiant.

Target: shield.

Tax: censure, blame, accuse.

Tell: count; relate.

Thorough: through.

Throughly: thoroughly.

Toward: in preparation; forthcoming, about to take place; modern senses.

Toy: trifle, idle fancy; folly.

Train: lure, entice, allure, attract.

Trencher: wooden dish or plate.

Trow: think, suppose, believe; know.

U

Undergo: undertake, perform; modern sense.

Undo: ruin.

Unfold: disclose, tell, make known, reveal; communicate.

Unhappy: evil, mischievous; fatal, ill-fated; miserable.

Unjust: untrue, dishonest; unjustified, groundless; faithless, false.

Unkind: unnatural, cruel, faulty; compare **kind.**

Use (N): custom, habit; interest paid.

Use (v): make practice of; be accustomed; put out at interest.

V

Vail: lower, let fall.

Vantage: advantage; opportunity; benefit, profit; superiority.

Virtue: general excellence; valor, bravery; merit, goodness, honor; good accomplishment, excellence in culture; power; essence, essential part.

W

Want: lack; be in need of; be without.

Watch: be awake, lie awake, sit up at night, lose sleep; keep from sleep (TRANS.).

Weed: garment, clothes.

Welkin: sky, heavens.

Wink: close the eyes; close the eyes in sleep; have the eyes closed; seem not to see.

Withal: with; with it, this, or these; together with this; at the same time.

Wot: know.

Index

Page ranges in **bold** indicate the page range for the entire play. Page references followed by *n* indicate a footnote. *See* and *See also* cross-references indicate entries throughout the four-volume set.